Quantitative Risk Management

Quantitative Risk Management: Concepts, Techniques and Tools
IS A PART OF THE
PRINCETON SERIES IN FINANCE

Finance as a discipline has been growing rapidly. The numbers of researchers in academy and industry, of students, of methods and models have all proliferated in the past decade or so. This growth and diversity manifests itself in the emerging cross-disciplinary as well as cross-national mix of scholarship now driving the field of finance forward. The intellectual roots of modern finance, as well as the branches, will be represented in the Princeton Series in Finance.

Titles in this series will be scholarly and professional books, intended to be read by a mixed audience of economists, mathematicians, operations research scientists, financial engineers, and other investment professionals. The goal is to provide the finest cross-disciplinary work in all areas of finance by widely recognized researchers in the prime of their creative careers.

OTHER BOOKS IN THIS SERIES

Financial Econometrics: Problems, Models, and Methods by Christian Gourieroux and Joann Jasiak

Credit Risk: Pricing, Measurement, and Management by Darrell Duffie and Kenneth J. Singleton

Microfoundations of Financial Economics: An Introduction to General Equilibrium Asset Pricing by Yvan Lengwiler

Credit Risk Modeling: Theory and Applications by David Lando

Quantitative Risk Management

Concepts, Techniques and Tools

Alexander J. McNeil

Rüdiger Frey

Paul Embrechts

Princeton University Press
Princeton and Oxford

Published by Princeton University Press,
41 William Street, Princeton, New Jersey 08540

In the United Kingdom: Princeton University Press,
3 Market Place, Woodstock, Oxfordshire OX20 1SY

Library of Congress Cataloguing-in-Publication Data

McNeil, Alexander J., 1967–
Quantitative risk management : concepts, techniques, and tools / Alexander J. McNeil, Rüdiger Frey, Paul Embrechts
p.cm.—(Princeton series in finance)
Includes bibliographical references and index.
ISBN 0-691-12255-5 (cloth : alk. paper)
1. Risk management—Mathematical models. 2. Finance—Mathematical models. 3. Insurance—Mathematical models. 4. Mathematical statistics. I. Frey, Rüdiger. II. Embrechts, Paul. III. Title. IV. Series.

HD61.M395 2005
658.15′5′0151—pcc22   2005049603

British Library Cataloguing-in-Publication Data

A catalogue record for this book is available from the British Library

This book has been composed in Times and typeset by T&T Productions Ltd, London
Printed on acid-free paper ∞
www.pup.princeton.edu

Printed in the United States of America

10 9 8 7 6 5 4 3 2

ISBN-13: 978-0-691-12255-7
ISBN-10: 0-691-12255-5

To Janine, Alexander and Calliope
Alexander

Für Catharina und Sebastian
Rüdiger

Voor Gerda, Rita en Guy
Paul

Contents

Preface

Why have we written this book? In recent decades the field of financial risk management has undergone explosive development. This book is devoted specifically to *quantitative* modelling issues arising in this field. As a result of our own discussions and joint projects with industry professionals and regulators over a number of years, we felt there was a need for a textbook treatment of quantitative risk management (QRM) at a technical yet accessible level, aimed at both industry participants and students seeking an entrance to the area.

We have tried to bring together a body of methodology that we consider to be core material for any course on the subject. This material and its mode of presentation represent the blending of our own views, which come from the perspectives of financial mathematics, insurance mathematics and statistics. We feel that a book combining these viewpoints fills a gap in the existing literature and partly anticipates the future need for quantitative risk managers in banks, insurance companies and beyond with broad, interdisciplinary skills.

Who was this book written for? This book is primarily a textbook for courses on QRM aimed at advanced undergraduate or graduate students and professionals from the financial industry. *A knowledge of probability and statistics at least at the level of a first university course in a quantitative discipline and familiarity with undergraduate calculus and linear algebra are fundamental prerequisites.* Though not absolutely necessary, some prior exposure to finance, economics or insurance will be beneficial for a better understanding of some sections.

The book has a secondary function as a reference text for risk professionals interested in a clear and concise treatment of concepts and techniques used in practice. As such, we hope it will facilitate communication between regulators, end-users and academics.

A third audience for the book is the growing community of researchers working in the area. Most chapters take the reader to the frontier of current, practically relevant research and contain extensive, annotated references that guide the reader through the burgeoning literature.

Ways to use this book. Based on our experience of teaching university courses on QRM at ETH Zurich, the Universities of Zurich and Leipzig and the London School of Economics, a two-semester course of 3–4 hours a week can be based on material in Chapters 2–8 and parts of Chapter 10; Chapter 1 is typically given as background reading material. Chapter 9 is a more technically demanding chapter that has been included because of the current interest in quantitative methods for pricing and hedging credit derivatives; it is primarily intended for more advanced, specialized courses on credit risk (see below).

A course on market risk can be based on a fairly complete treatment of Chapters 2–4, with excursions into material in Chapters 5, 6 and 7 (normal mixture copulas, coherent risk measures, extreme value methods for threshold exceedances) as time permits.

A course on credit risk can be based on Chapters 8 and 9 but requires a preliminary treatment of some topics in earlier chapters. Sections 2.1 and 2.2 give the necessary grounding in basic concepts; Sections 3.1, 3.2, 3.4, 5.1 and 5.4 are necessary for an understanding of multivariate models of portfolio credit risk; and Sections 6.1 and 6.3 are required to understand how capital is allocated to credit risks.

A short course or seminar on operational risk could be based on Chapter 10, but would also benefit from some supplementary material from other chapters; Sections 2.1 and 2.2 and Chapters 6 and 7 are particularly relevant.

It is also possible to devise more specialized courses, such as a course on risk-measurement and aggregation concepts based on Chapters 2, 5 and 6, or a course on risk-management techniques for financial econometricians based on Chapters 2–4 and 7. Material from various chapters could be used as interesting examples to enliven statistics courses on subjects like multivariate analysis, time series analysis and generalized linear modelling.

What we have not covered. We have not been able to address all topics that a reader might expect to find under the heading of QRM. Perhaps the most obvious omission is the lack of a section on the risk management of derivatives by hedging. We felt here that the relevant techniques, and the financial mathematics required to understand them, are already well covered in a number of excellent textbooks. Other omissions include RAROC (risk-adjusted return on capital) and performance-measurement issues. Besides these larger areas, many smaller issues have been neglected for reasons of space, but are mentioned with suggestions for further reading in the "Notes and Comments" sections, which should be considered as integral parts of the text.

Acknowledgements. The origins of this book date back to 1996, when A.M. and R.F. began postdoctoral studies in the group of P.E. at the Federal Institute of Technology (ETH) in Zurich. All three authors are grateful to ETH for providing the environment in which the project flourished. A.M. and R.F. thank Swiss Re and UBS, respectively, for providing the financial support for their postdoctoral positions. R.F. has subsequently held positions at the Swiss Banking Institute of the University of Zurich and at the University of Leipzig and is grateful to both institutions for their support.

The Forschungsinstitut für Mathematik (FIM) of the ETH Zurich provided financial support at various stages of the project. At a crucial juncture in early 2004 the Mathematisches Foschungsinstitut Oberwolfach was the venue for a memorable week of progress. P.E. recalls fondly his time as Centennial Professor of Finance at the London School of Economics; numerous discussions with colleagues from the Department of Accounting and Finance helped in shaping his view of the importance of QRM. We also acknowledge the invaluable contribution of RiskLab Zurich to the enterprise: the agenda for the book was strongly influenced by joint projects and discussions with the RiskLab sponsors UBS, Credit Suisse and Swiss Re. We have also benefited greatly from the NCCR FINRISK research program in Switzerland, which funded doctoral and postdoctoral research on topics in the book.

We are indebted to numerous proof-readers who have commented on various parts of the manuscript, and to colleagues in Zurich, Leipzig and beyond who have helped us in our understanding of QRM and the mathematics underlying it. These include Stefan Altner, Philippe Artzner, Jochen Backhaus, Guus Balkema, Uta Beckmann, Reto Baumgartner, Wolfgang Breymann, Reto Bucher, Hans Bühlmann, Peter Bühlmann, Valérie Chavez-Demoulin, Dominik Colangelo, Freddy Delbaen, Rosario Dell'Aquila, Stefan Denzler, Alexandra Dias, Stefano Demarta, Damir Filipovic, Gabriel Frahm, Hansjörg Furrer, Rajna Gibson, Kay Giesecke, Enrico De Giorgi, Bernhard Hodler, Andrea Höing, Christoph Hummel, Alessandro Juri, Roger Kaufmann, Philipp Keller, Hans Rudolf Künsch, Filip Lindskog, Hans-Jakob Lüthi, Natalia Markovich, Benoît Metayer, Johanna Nešlehová, Monika Popp, Giovanni Puccetti, Hanspeter Schmidli, Sylvia Schmidt, Thorsten Schmidt, Uwe Schmock, Philipp Schönbucher, Martin Schweizer, Torsten Steiger, Daniel Straumann, Dirk Tasche, Eduardo Vilela, Marcel Visser and Jonathan Wendin. For her help in preparing the manuscript we thank Gabriele Baltes.

We thank Richard Baggaley and the team at Princeton University Press for all their help in the production of this book. We are also grateful to our anonymous referees who provided us with exemplary feedback, which has shaped this book for the better. Special thanks go to Sam Clark at T&T Productions Ltd, who took our uneven LaTeX code and turned it into a more polished book with remarkable speed and efficiency.

To our wives, Janine, Catharina and Gerda, and our families our sincerest debt of gratitude is due. Though driven to distraction no doubt by our long contemplation of risk, without obvious reward, their support was constant.

Further resources. Readers are encouraged to visit the book's homepage at

www.pupress.princeton.edu/titles/8056.html

to find supplementary resources for this book. Our intention is to make available the computer code (mostly S-PLUS) used to generate the examples in this book, and to list errata.

Special abbreviations. A number of abbreviations for common terms in probability are used throughout the book; these include "rv" for random variable, "df" for distribution function, "iid" for independent and identically distributed and "se" for standard error.

1
Risk in Perspective

In this chapter we provide a non-mathematical discussion of various issues that form the background to the rest of the book. In Section 1.1 we begin with the *nature of risk* itself and how risk relates to *randomness*; in the financial context (which includes insurance) we summarize the main kinds of risks encountered and explain what it means to *measure* and *manage* such risks.

A brief *history* of financial risk management, or at least some of the main ideas that are used in modern practice, is given in Section 1.2, including a summary of the process leading to the Basel Accords. Section 1.3 gives an idea of the new *regulatory framework* that is emerging in the financial and insurance industries.

In Section 1.4 we take a step back and attempt to address the fundamental question of why we might want to measure and manage risk at all. Finally, in Section 1.5, we turn explicitly to quantitative risk management (QRM) and set out our own views concerning the *nature of this discipline* and the challenge it poses. This section in particular should give more insight into why we have chosen to address the particular methodological topics in this book.

1.1 Risk

The Concise Oxford English Dictionary defines risk as "hazard, a chance of bad consequences, loss or exposure to mischance". In a discussion with students taking a course on financial risk management, ingredients which typically enter are events, decisions, consequences and uncertainty. Mostly only the downside of risk is mentioned, rarely a possible upside, i.e. the potential for a gain. For financial risks, the subject of this book, we might arrive at a definition such as "any event or action that may adversely affect an organization's ability to achieve its objectives and execute its strategies" or, alternatively, "the quantifiable likelihood of loss or less-than-expected returns". But while these capture some of the elements of risk, no single one-sentence definition is entirely satisfactory in all contexts.

1.1.1 Risk and Randomness

Independently of any context, risk relates strongly to uncertainty, and hence to the notion of randomness. Randomness has eluded a clear, workable definition for many centuries; it was not until 1933 that the Russian mathematician A. N. Kolmogorov gave an axiomatic definition of randomness and probability (see Kolmogorov 1933). This definition and its accompanying theory, though not without their controversial aspects, now provide the lingua franca for discourses on risk and uncertainty, such as this book.

In Kolmogorov's language a probabilistic model is described by a triplet $(\Omega, \mathcal{F}, P)$. An element ω of Ω represents a realization of an experiment, in economics often referred to as a state of nature. The statement "the probability that an event A occurs" is denoted (and in Kolmogorov's axiomatic system defined) as $P(A)$, where A is an element of $\mathcal{F}$, the set of all events. P denotes the probability measure. For the less mathematically trained reader it suffices to accept that Kolmogorov's system translates our intuition about randomness into a concise, axiomatic language and clear rules.

Consider the following examples: an investor who holds stock in a particular company; an insurance company that has sold an insurance policy; an individual who decides to convert a fixed-rate mortgage into a variable one. All of these situations have something important in common: the investor holds today an asset with an uncertain future value. This is very clear in the case of the stock. For the insurance company, the policy sold may or may not be triggered by the underlying event covered. In the case of a mortgage, our decision today to enter into this refinancing agreement will change (for better or for worse) the future repayments. So randomness plays a crucial role in the valuation of current products held by the investor, the insurance company or the home owner.

To model these situations a mathematician would now define a one-period risky position (or simply risk) X to be a function on the probability space $(\Omega, \mathcal{F}, P)$; this function is called a *random variable*. We leave for the moment the range of X (i.e. its possible values) unspecified. Most of the modelling of a risky position X concerns its *distribution function* $F_X(x) = P(X \leqslant x)$, the probability that by the end of the period under consideration, the value of the risk X is less than or equal to a given number x. Several risky positions would then be denoted by a random vector $(X_1, \dots, X_d)$, also written in bold face as $\boldsymbol{X}$; time can be introduced, leading to the notion of random (or so-called stochastic) processes, usually written $(\boldsymbol{X}_t)$. Throughout this book we will encounter many such processes, which serve as essential building blocks in the mathematical description of risk.

We therefore expect the reader to be at ease with basic notation, terminology and results from elementary *probability and statistics*, the branch of mathematics dealing with *stochastic* models and their application to the real world. The word "stochastic" is derived from the Greek "Stochazesthai", the art of guessing, or "Stochastikos", meaning skilled at aiming, "stochos" being a target. In discussing stochastic methods for risk management we hope to emphasize the skill aspect rather than the guesswork.

1.1.2 Financial Risk

In this book we discuss risk in the context of finance and insurance (although many of the tools introduced are applicable well beyond this context). We start by giving a brief overview of the main risk types encountered in the financial industry.

In banking, the best known type of risk is probably *market risk*, the risk of a change in the value of a financial position due to changes in the value of the underlying components on which that position depends, such as stock and bond prices, exchange rates, commodity prices, etc. The next important category is *credit risk*, the risk of not receiving promised repayments on outstanding investments such as loans and bonds, because of the "default" of the borrower. A further risk category that has received a lot of recent attention is *operational risk*, the risk of losses resulting from inadequate or failed internal processes, people and systems, or from external events.

The boundaries of these three risk categories are not always clearly defined, nor do they form an exhaustive list of the full range of possible risks affecting a financial institution. There are notions of risk which surface in nearly all categories such as *liquidity* and *model risk*. The latter is the risk associated with using a misspecified (inappropriate) model for measuring risk. Think, for instance, of using the Black–Scholes model for pricing an exotic option in circumstances where the basic Black–Scholes model assumptions on the underlying securities (such as the assumption of normally distributed returns) are violated. It may be argued that model risk is always present to some degree. Liquidity risk could be roughly defined as the risk stemming from the lack of marketability of an investment that cannot be bought or sold quickly enough to prevent or minimize a loss. Liquidity can be thought of as "oxygen for a healthy market"; we need it to survive but most of the time we are not aware of its presence. Its absence, however, is mostly recognized immediately, with often disastrous consequences.

The concepts, techniques and tools we will introduce in the following chapters mainly apply to the three basic categories of market, credit and operational risk. We should stress that the only viable way forward for a successful handling of financial risk consists of a *holistic* approach, i.e. an integrated approach taking all types of risk and their interactions into account. Whereas this is a clear goal, current models do not yet allow for a fully satisfactory platform.

As well as banks, the insurance industry has a long-standing relationship with risk. It is no coincidence that the Institute of Actuaries and the Faculty of Actuaries use the following definition of the actuarial profession.

> Actuaries are respected professionals whose innovative approach to making business successful is matched by a responsibility to the public interest. Actuaries identify solutions to financial problems. They manage assets and liabilities by analysing past events, assessing the present risk involved and modelling what could happen in the future.

An additional risk category entering through insurance is *underwriting risk*, the risk inherent in insurance policies sold. Examples of risk factors that play a role here are changing patterns of natural catastrophes, changes in demographic tables underlying (long-dated) life products, or changing customer behaviour (such as prepayment patterns).

1.1.3 Measurement and Management

Much of this book is concerned with techniques for the measurement of risk, an activity which is part of the process of managing risk, as we attempt to clarify in this section.

Risk measurement. Suppose we hold a portfolio consisting of d underlying investments with respective weights $w_1, \dots, w_d$ so that the change in value of the portfolio over a given holding period (the so-called P&L, or profit and loss) can be written as $X = \sum_{i=1}^{d} w_i X_i$, where X_i denotes the change in value of the ith investment. Measuring the risk of this portfolio essentially consists of determining its distribution function $F_X(x) = P(X \leqslant x)$, or functionals describing this distribution function such as its mean, variance or 99th percentile.

In order to achieve this, we need a properly calibrated *joint* model for the underlying random vector of investments $(X_1, \dots, X_d)$. We will consider this problem in more detail in Chapter 2. At this point it suffices to understand that risk measurement is essentially a statistical issue; based on historical observations and given a specific model, a statistical estimate of the distribution of the change in value of a position, or one of its functionals, is calculated. As we shall see later, and this is indeed a main theme throughout the book, this is by no means an easy task with a unique solution.

It should be clear from the outset that good risk measurement is a must. Increasingly, banking clients demand objective and detailed information on products bought and banks can face legal action when this information is found wanting. For any product sold, a proper quantification of the underlying risks needs to be explicitly made, allowing the client to decide whether or not the product on offer corresponds to his or her risk appetite.

Risk management. In a very general answer to the question of what risk management is about, Kloman (1990) writes that:

> To many analysts, politicians, and academics it is the management of environmental and nuclear risks, those technology-generated macro-risks that appear to threaten our existence. To bankers and financial officers it is the sophisticated use of such techniques as currency hedging and interest-rate swaps. To insurance buyers or sellers it is coordination of insurable risks and the reduction of insurance costs. To hospital administrators it may mean "quality assurance". To safety professionals it is reducing accidents and injuries. In summary, risk management is *a discipline for living with the possibility that future events may cause adverse effects.*

The last phrase in particular (the italics are ours) captures the general essence of risk management, although for a financial institution one can perhaps go further. A bank's attitude to risk is not passive and defensive; a bank actively and willingly takes on risk, because it seeks a return and this does not come without risk. Indeed risk management can be seen as the core competence of an insurance company or a bank. By using its expertise, market position and capital structure, a financial institution can manage risks by repackaging them and transferring them to markets in customized ways.

Managing the risk is thus related to preserving the flow of profit and to techniques like *asset liability management* (ALM), which might be defined as managing a financial institution so as to earn an adequate return on funds invested, and to maintain a comfortable surplus of assets beyond liabilities. In Section 1.4 we discuss these corporate finance issues in more depth from a shareholder's point of view.

1.2 A Brief History of Risk Management

In this section we treat the historical development of risk management by sketching some of the innovations and some of the events that have shaped modern risk management for the financial industry. We also describe the more recent development of regulation in that industry, which has to some extent been prompted by a number of recent disasters.

1.2.1 From Babylon to Wall Street

Although risk management has been described as "one of the most important innovations of the 20th century" by Steinherr (1998) and most of the story we tell is relatively modern, some concepts that are used in modern risk management, in particular derivatives, have been around for longer. In our discussion we stress the example of financial derivatives, as these brought the need for increased banking regulation very much to the fore.

The ancient world to the twentieth century. A derivative is a financial instrument derived from an underlying asset, such as an option, future or swap. For example, a European call option with strike K and maturity T gives the holder the right, but not the obligation, to obtain from the seller at maturity the underlying security for a price of K; a European put option gives the holder the right to dispose of the underlying at a price K.

Dunbar (2000) interprets a passage in the Code of Hammurabi from Babylon of 1800 BC as being early evidence of the use of the option concept to provide financial cover in the event of crop failure. A very explicit mention of options appears in Amsterdam towards the end of the seventeenth century and is beautifully narrated by Joseph de la Vega in his 1688 *Confusión de Confusiones*, a discussion between a lawyer, a trader and a philosopher observing the activity on the Beurs of Amsterdam. Their discussion contains what we now recognize as European call and put options, and a description of their use for investment as well as for risk management, and even the notion of short selling. In an excellent recent translation (de la Vega 1966) we read:

> If I may explain "opsies" [further, I would say that] through the payment of the premiums, one hands over values in order to safeguard one's stock or to obtain a profit. One uses them as sails for a happy voyage during a beneficent conjuncture and as an anchor of security in a storm.

After this, de la Vega continues with some explicit examples that would not be out of place in any modern finance course on the topic.

Financial derivatives in general, and options in particular, are not so new. Moreover, they appear here as instruments to manage risk, "anchors of security in a storm", rather than the inventions of the capitalist devil, the "wild beasts of finance" (Steinherr 1998), that many now believe them to be.

Academic innovation in the twentieth century. While the use of risk-management ideas such as derivatives can be traced further back, it was not until the late twentieth century that a theory of valuation for derivatives was developed. This can be seen as perhaps the most important milestone in an age of academic developments in the general area of quantifying and managing financial risk.

Before the 1950s the desirability of an investment was mainly equated to its return. In his ground-breaking publication of 1952, Harry Markowitz laid the foundation of the theory of portfolio selection by mapping the desirability of an investment onto a risk–return diagram, where risk was measured using standard deviation (see Markowitz 1952, 1959). Through the notion of an *efficient frontier* the portfolio manager could optimize the return for a given risk level. The following decades saw an explosive growth in risk-management methodology, including such ideas as the Sharpe ratio, the Capital Asset Pricing Model (CAPM) and Arbitrage Pricing Theory (APT). Numerous extensions and refinements followed, which are now taught in any MBA course on finance.

The famous Black–Scholes–Merton formula for the price of a European call option appeared in 1973 (see Black and Scholes 1973). The importance of this formula was underscored in 1997, when the Bank of Sweden Prize in Economic Sciences in Memory of Alfred Nobel was awarded to Robert Merton and Myron Scholes (Fisher Black had died some years earlier) "for a new method to determine the value of derivatives".

Growth of markets in the twentieth century. The methodology developed for the rational pricing and hedging of financial derivatives changed finance. The *Wizards of Wall Street* (i.e. the mathematical specialists conversant in the new methodology) have had a significant impact on the development of financial markets over the last few decades. Not only did the new option-pricing formula work, it transformed the market. When the Chicago Options Exchange first opened in 1973, less than a thousand options were traded on the first day. By 1995, over a million options were changing hands each day with current nominal values outstanding in the derivatives markets in the tens of trillions. So great was the role played by the Black–Scholes–Merton formula in the growth of the new options market that, when the American stock-market crashed in 1978, the influential business magazine *Forbes* put the blame squarely onto that one formula. Scholes himself has said that it was not so much the formula that was to blame, but rather that market traders had not become sufficiently sophisticated in using it.

Along with academic innovation, technological developments (mainly on the information–technology (IT) side) also laid the foundations for an explosive growth in the volume of new risk-management and investment products. This development was further aided by worldwide deregulation in the 1980s. Important additional factors contributing to an increased demand for risk-management skills and products were the oil crises of the 1970s and the 1970 abolition of the Bretton–Woods system of fixed exchange rates. Both energy prices and foreign exchange risk became highly volatile risk factors and customers required products to hedge them. The

1933 Glass–Steagall Act—passed in the US in the aftermath of the 1929 Depression to prohibit commercial banks from underwriting insurance and most kinds of securities—indirectly paved the way for the emergence of investment banks, hungry for new business. Glass–Steagall was replaced in 1999 by the Financial Services Act, which repealed many of the former's key provisions. Today many more companies are able to trade and use modern risk-management products.

Disasters of the 1990s. In January 1992, the president of the New York Federal Reserve, E. Gerald Corrigan, speaking at the Annual Mid-Winter Meeting of the New York State Bankers Association, said:

> You had all better take a very, very hard look at off-balance-sheet activities. The growth and complexity of [these] activities and the nature of the credit settlement risk they entail should give us cause for concern. ... I hope this sounds like a warning, because it is. Off-balance-sheet activities [i.e. derivatives] have a role, but they must be managed and controlled carefully and they must be understood by top management as well as by traders and rocket scientists.

Corrigan was referring to the growing volume of derivatives on banking books and the way they were accounted for.

Many of us recall the headline "Barings forced to cease trading" in the Financial Times on 26 February 1995. A loss of £700 million ruined the oldest merchant banking group in the UK (established in 1761). Besides numerous operational errors (violating every qualitative guideline in the risk-management handbook), the final straw leading to the downfall of Barings was a so-called straddle position on the Nikkei held by the bank's Singapore-based trader Nick Leeson. A straddle is a short position in a call and a put with the same strike—such a position allows for a gain if the underlying (in this case the Nikkei index) does not move too far up or down. There is, however, considerable loss potential if the index moves down (or up) by a large amount, and this is precisely what happened when the Kobe earthquake occurred.

About three years later, on 17 September 1998, *The Observer* newspaper, referring to the downfall of Long-Term Capital Management (LTCM), summarized the mood of the times when it wrote:

> last week, free market economy died. Twenty five years of intellectual bullying by the University of Chicago has come to a close.

The article continued:

> the derivatives markets are a rarefied world. They are peopled with individuals with an extraordinary grasp of mathematics—"a strange collection of Greeks, misfits and rocket scientists" as one observer put it last week.

And referring to the Black–Scholes formula, the article asked:

> is this really the key to future wealth? Win big, lose bigger.

There were other important cases which led to a widespread discussion of the need for increased regulation: the Herstatt Bank case in 1974, Metallgesellschaft in 1993 or Orange County in 1994. See Notes and Comments below for further reading on the above.

The main reason for the general public's mistrust of these modern tools of finance is their perceived triggering effect for crashes and bubbles. Derivatives have without doubt played a role in some spectacular cases and as a consequence are looked upon with a much more careful regulatory eye. However, they are by now so much part of Wall Street (or any financial institution) that serious risk management without these tools would be unthinkable.

Thus it is imperative that mathematicians take a serious interest in derivatives and the risks they generate. Who has not yet considered a prepayment option on a mortgage or a change from a fixed-interest-rate agreement to a variable one, or vice versa (a so-called swap)? Moreover, many life insurance products now have options embedded.

1.2.2 The Road to Regulation

There is no doubt that regulation goes back a long way, at least to the time of the Venetian banks and the early insurance enterprises sprouting in London's coffee shops in the eighteenth century. In those days one would rely to a large extent on self-regulation or local regulation, but rules were there. However, key developments leading to the present regulatory risk-management framework are very much a twentieth century story.

Much of the regulatory drive originated from the Basel Committee of Banking Supervision. This committee was established by the Central-Bank Governors of the Group of Ten (G-10) at the end of 1974. The Group of Ten is made up (oddly) of eleven industrial countries which consult and cooperate on economic, monetary and financial matters. The Basel Committee does not possess any formal supranational supervising authority, and hence its conclusions do not have legal force. Rather, it formulates broad supervisory standards and guidelines and recommends statements of best practice in the expectation that individual authorities will take steps to implement them through detailed arrangements—statutory or otherwise—which are best suited to their own national system. The summary below is brief. Interested readers can consult, for example, Crouhy, Galai and Mark (2001) for further details, and should also see Notes and Comments below.

The first Basel Accord. The first Basel Accord of 1988 on Banking Supervision (Basel I) took an important step towards an international minimum capital standard. Its main emphasis was on credit risk, by then clearly the most important source of risk in the banking industry. In hindsight, however, the first Basel Accord took an approach which was fairly coarse and measured risk in an insufficiently differentiated way. Also the treatment of derivatives was considered unsatisfactory.

The birth of VaR. In 1993 the G-30 (an influential international body consisting of senior representatives of the private and public sectors and academia) published a seminal report addressing for the first time so-called off-balance-sheet products, like derivatives, in a systematic way. Around the same time, the banking industry clearly saw the need for a proper risk management of these new products. At JPMorgan, for instance, the famous Weatherstone 4.15 report asked for a one-day, one-page summary of the bank's market risk to be delivered to the chief executive officer (CEO) in the late afternoon (hence the "4.15"). Value-at-Risk (VaR) as a market risk measure was born and RiskMetrics set an industry-wide standard.

In a highly dynamic world with round-the-clock market activity, the need for instant market valuation of trading positions (known as *marking-to-market*) became a necessity. Moreover, in markets where so many positions (both long and short) were written on the same underlyings, managing risks based on simple aggregation of nominal positions became unsatisfactory. Banks pushed to be allowed to consider *netting* effects, i.e. the compensation of long versus short positions on the same underlying.

In 1996 the important Amendment to Basel I prescribed a so-called *standardized* model for market risk, but at the same time allowed the bigger (more sophisticated) banks to opt for an *internal*, VaR-based model (i.e. a model developed in house). Legal implementation was to be achieved by the year 2000. The coarseness problem for credit risk remained unresolved and banks continued to claim that they were not given enough incentives to diversify credit portfolios and that the regulatory capital rules currently in place were far too risk insensitive. Because of overcharging on the regulatory capital side of certain credit positions, banks started shifting business away from certain market segments that they perceived as offering a less attractive risk–return profile.

The second Basel Accord. By 2001 a consultative process for a new Basel Accord (Basel II) had been initiated; this process is being concluded as this book goes to press. The main theme is credit risk, where the aim is that banks can use a finer, more risk-sensitive approach to assessing the risk of their credit portfolios. Banks opting for a more advanced, so-called *internal-ratings-based* approach are allowed to use internal and/or external credit-rating systems wherever appropriate. The second important theme of Basel II is the consideration of operational risk as a new risk class.

Current discussions imply an implementation date of 2007, but there remains an ongoing debate on specific details. Industry is participating in several Quantitative Impact Studies in order to gauge the risk-capital consequences of the new accord. In Section 1.3.1 we will come back to some issues concerning this accord.

Parallel developments in insurance regulation. It should be stressed that most of the above regulatory changes concern the banking world. We are also witnessing increasing regulatory pressure on the insurance side, coupled with a drive to combine the two regulatory frameworks, either institutionally or methodologically. As an example, the Joint Forum on Financial Conglomerates (Joint Forum) was established in early 1996 under the aegis of the Basel Committee on Banking Supervision, the International Organization of Securities Commissions (IOSCO) and the

International Association of Insurance Supervisors (IAIS) to take forward the work of the so-called Tripartite Group, whose report was released in July 1995. The Joint Forum is comprised of an equal number of senior bank, insurance and securities supervisors representing each supervisory constituency.

The process is underway in many countries. For instance, in the UK the Financial Services Authority (FSA) is stepping up its supervision across a wide range of financial and insurance businesses. The same is happening in the US under the guidance of the Securities and Exchange Commission (SEC) and the Fed. In Switzerland, discussions are underway between the Bundesamt für Privatversicherungen (BPV) and the Eidgenössische Bankenkommission (EBK) concerning a joint supervisory office. In Section 1.3.2 we will discuss some of the current, insurance-related solvency issues.

1.3 The New Regulatory Framework

This section is intended to describe in more detail the framework that has emerged from the Basel II discussions and the parallel developments in the insurance world.

1.3.1 Basel II

On 26 June 2004 the G-10 central-bank governors and heads of supervision endorsed the publication of the revised capital framework. The following statement is taken from this release.

> The Basel II Framework sets out the details for adopting more risk-sensitive minimum capital requirements [Pillar 1] for banking organizations. The new framework reinforces these risk-sensitive requirements by laying out principles for banks to assess the adequacy of their capital and for supervisors to review such assessments to ensure banks have adequate capital to support their risks [Pillar 2]. It also seeks to strengthen market discipline by enhancing transparency in banks' financial reporting [Pillar 3]. The text that has been released today reflects the results of extensive consultations with supervisors and bankers worldwide. It will serve as the basis for national rule-making and approval processes to continue and for banking organizations to complete their preparations for the new Framework's implementation.

The three-pillar concept. As is apparent from the above quote, a key conceptual change within the Basel II framework is the introduction of the *three-pillar concept*. Through this concept, the Basel Committee aims to achieve a more holistic approach to risk management that focuses on the interaction between the different risk categories; at the same time the three-pillar concept clearly signals the existing difference between quantifiable and non-quantifiable risks.

Under *Pillar 1* banks are required to calculate a *minimum capital charge*, referred to as regulatory capital, with the aim of bringing the quantification of this minimal capital more in line with the banks' economic loss potential. Under the Basel II framework there will be a capital charge for credit risk, market risk and, for the first time, operational risk. Whereas the treatment of market risk is unchanged relative to the 1996 Amendment of the Basel I Capital Accord, the capital charge for credit risk has been revised substantially. In computing the capital charge for credit risk and operational risk banks may choose between three approaches of increasing risk sensitivity and complexity; some details are discussed below.

It is further recognized that any quantitative approach to risk management should be embedded in a well-functioning corporate governance structure. Thus best-practice risk management imposes clear constraints on the organization of the institution, i.e. the board of directors, management, employees, internal and external audit processes. In particular, the board of directors assumes the ultimate responsibility for oversight of the risk landscape and the formulation of the company's risk appetite. This is where *Pillar 2* enters. Through this important pillar, also referred to as the *supervisory review process*, local regulators review the various checks and balances put into place. This pillar recognizes the necessity of an effective overview of the banks' internal assessments of their overall risk and ensures that management is exercising sound judgement and has set aside adequate capital for the various risks.

Finally, in order to fulfil its promise that increased regulation will also diminish systemic risk, clear reporting guidelines on risks carried by financial institutions are called for. *Pillar 3* seeks to establish *market discipline* through a better public disclosure of risk measures and other information relevant to risk management. In particular, banks will have to offer greater insight into the adequacy of their capitalization.

The capital charge for market risk. As discussed in Section 1.2.2, in the aftermath of the Basel I proposals in the early 1990s, there was a general interest in improving the measurement of market risk, particularly where derivative products were concerned. This was addressed in detail in the 1996 Amendment to Basel I, which prescribed standardized market risk models but also allowed more sophisticated banks to opt for *internal* VaR models. In Chapter 2 we shall give a detailed discussion of the calculation of VaR. For the moment it suffices to know that, for instance, a 10-day VaR at 99% of \$20 million means that our market portfolio will incur a loss of \$20 million *or more* with probability 1% by the end of a 10-day holding period, if the composition remains fixed over this period. The choice of the holding period (10 days) and the confidence level (99%) lies in the hands of the regulators when VaR is used for the calculation of regulatory capital. As a consequence of these regulations, we have witnessed a quantum leap in the prominence of quantitative risk modelling throughout all echelons of financial institutions.

Credit risk from Basel I to II. In a banking context, by far the oldest risk type to be regulated is credit risk. As mentioned in Section 1.2.2, Basel I handled this type of risk in a rather coarse way. Under Basel I and II the credit risk of a portfolio is assessed as the sum of *risk-weighted assets*, that is the sum of notional exposures weighted by a coefficient reflecting the creditworthiness of the counterparty (the risk weight). In Basel I, creditworthiness is split into three crude categories: governments, regulated banks and others. For instance, under Basel I, the risk-capital charge for a loan to a corporate borrower is five times higher than for a loan to an OECD bank. Also, the risk weight for all corporate borrowers is identical, independent of their credit-rating category.

Due to its coarseness, the implementation of Basel I is extremely simple. But with the establishment of more detailed credit risk databases, the improvement of analytic models, and the rapid growth in the market for credit derivatives, banks have pressed regulators to come up with more risk-specific capital-adequacy guidelines. This is the main content of the new Basel II proposals, where banks will be allowed to choose between *standardized* approaches or more advanced *internal-ratings-based* (IRB) approaches for handling credit risk. The final choice will, however, also depend on the size and complexity of the bank, with the larger, international banks having to go for the more advanced models.

Already the banks opting for the standardized approach can differentiate better among the various credit risks in their portfolio, since under the Basel II framework the risk sensitivity of the available risk weights has been increased substantially. Under the more advanced IRB approach, a bank's *internal* assessment of the riskiness of a credit exposure is used as an input to the risk-capital calculation. The overall capital charge is then computed by aggregating the internal inputs using formulas specified by the Basel Committee. While this allows for increased risk sensitivity in the IRB capital charge compared with the standardized approach, portfolio and diversification effects are not taken into account; this would require the use of fully internal models as in the market risk case. This issue is currently being debated in the risk community, and it is widely expected that in the longer term a revised version of the Basel II Capital Accord allowing for the use of fully internal models will come into effect. In Chapter 8, certain aspects of the regulatory treatment of credit risk will be discussed in more detail.

Opening the door to operational risk. A basic premise for Basel II was that, whereas the new regulatory framework would enable banks to reduce their credit risk capital charge through internal credit risk models, the overall size of regulatory capital throughout the industry should stay unchanged under the new rules. This opened the door for the new risk category of operational risk, which we discuss in more depth in Section 10.1. Recall that Basel II defines operational risk as the risk of losses resulting from inadequate or failed internal processes, people and systems or from external events. The introduction of this new risk class has led to heated discussions among the various stakeholders. Whereas everyone agrees that risks like human risk (e.g. incompetence, fraud), process risk (e.g. model, transaction and operational control risk) and technology risk (e.g. system failure, programming error) are important, much disagreement exists on how far one should (or can) go towards quantifying such risks. This becomes particularly difficult when the financially more important risks like fraud and litigation are taken into account. Nobody doubts the importance of operational risk for the financial and insurance sector, but much less agreement exists on how to measure this risk.

The Cooke ratio. A crude measure of capitalization is the well-known *Cooke ratio*, which specifies that capital should be at least 8% of the risk-weighted assets of a company. The precise definition of risk capital is rather complex, involving various tiers of differing liquidity and legal character, and is very much related to existing accounting standards. For more detail see, for example, Crouhy, Galai and Mark (2001).

Some criticism. The benefits arising from the regulation of financial services are not generally in doubt. Customer-protection acts, basic corporate governance, clear guidelines on fair and comparable accounting rules, the ongoing pressure for transparent customer and shareholder information on solvency, capital- and risk-management issues are all positive developments. Despite these positive points, the specific proposals of Basel II have also elicited criticism; issues that have been raised include the following.

- The *cost factor* of setting up a well-functioning risk-management system compliant with the present regulatory framework is significant, especially (in relative terms) for smaller institutions.
- So-called *risk-management herding* can take place, whereby institutions following similar (perhaps VaR-based) rules may all be running for the same exit in times of crises, consequently destabilizing an already precarious situation even further. This herding phenomenon has been suggested in connection with the 1987 crash and the events surrounding the 1998 LTCM crisis. On a related note, the *procyclical* effects of financial regulation, whereby capital requirements may rise in times of recession and fall in times of expansion, may contribute negatively to the availability of liquidity in moments where the latter is most needed.
- Regulation could lead to *overconfidence* in the quality of statistical risk measures and tools.

Several critical discussions have taken place questioning to what extent the crocodile of regulatory risk management is eating its own tail. In an article of 12 June 1999, the *Economist* wrote that "attempts to measure and put a price on risk in financial markets may actually be making them riskier"; on the first page of the article, entitled "The price of uncertainty", the proverbial crocodile appeared. The reader should be aware that there are several aspects to the overall regulatory side of risk management which warrant further discussion. As so often, "the truth" of what constitutes good and proper supervision will no doubt be somewhere between the more extreme views. The Basel process has the very laudable aspect that constructive criticism is taken seriously.

1.3.2 Solvency 2

In this section we take a brief look at regulatory developments regarding risk management in the insurance sector. We concentrate on the current solvency discussion, also referred to as *Solvency 2*. The following statement, made by the EU Insurance

Solvency Sub-Committee (2001), focuses on the differences between the Basel II and Solvency 2 frameworks.

> The difference between the two prudential regimes goes further in that their actual objectives differ. The prudential objective of the Basel Accord is to reinforce the soundness and stability of the international banking system. To that end, the initial Basel Accord and the draft New Accord are directed primarily at banks that are internationally active. The draft New Accord attaches particular importance to the self-regulating mechanisms of a market where practitioners are dependent on one another. In the insurance sector, the purpose of prudential supervision is to protect policyholders against the risk of (isolated) bankruptcy facing every insurance company. The systematic risk, assuming that it exists in the insurance sector, has not been deemed to be of sufficient concern to warrant minimum harmonisation of prudential supervisory regimes at international level; nor has it been the driving force behind European harmonisation in this field.

More so than in the case of banking regulation, the regulatory framework for insurance companies has a strong local flavour where many local statutory rules prevail. The various solvency committees in EU member countries and beyond are trying to come up with some global principles which would be binding on a larger geographical scale. We discuss some of the more recent developments below.

From Solvency 1 to 2. The first EU non-life and life directives on solvency margins appeared around 1970. The latter was defined as an extra capital buffer against unforeseen events such as higher than expected claims levels or unfavourable investment results. In 1997, the Müller report appeared under the heading "Solvency of insurance undertakings"—this led to a review of the solvency rules and initiated the Solvency 1 project, which was completed in 2002 and came into force in 2004. Meanwhile, Solvency 2 was initiated in 2001 with the publication of the influential Sharma report—the detailed technical rules of Solvency 2 are currently being worked out.

Solvency 1 was a rather coarse framework calling for a minimum guarantee fund (minimal capital required) of €3 million, and a solvency margin consisting of 16–18% of non-life premiums together with 4% of the technical provisions for life. This led to a single, robust system which is easy to understand and inexpensive to monitor. However, on the negative side, it is mainly volume based and not explicitly risk based; issues like guarantees, embedded options and proper matching of assets and liabilities were largely neglected in many countries. These and further shortcomings will be addressed in Solvency 2.

At the heart of Solvency 2 lies a risk-oriented assessment of overall solvency, honouring the three-pillar concept from Basel II (see the previous section). Insurers are encouraged to measure and manage their risks based on internal models. Consistency between Solvency 2 (Insurance) and Basel II (Banking) is adhered to as much as possible. The new framework should allow for an efficient supervision of insurance groups (holdings) and financial conglomerates (bank-assurance). From the start, an increased harmonization of supervisory methodology between the different legislative entities was envisaged, based on a wide international cooperation with actuarial, financial and accounting bodies.

Without entering into the specifics of the framework, the following points related to Pillar 1 should be mentioned. In principle, *all* risks are to be analysed including underwriting, credit, market, operational (corresponding to internal operational risk under Basel II), liquidity and event risk (corresponding to external operational risk under Basel II). Strong emphasis is put on the modelling of interdependencies and a detailed analysis of stress tests. The system should be as much as possible *principle based* rather than *rules based* and should lead to *prudent regulation* which focuses on the total balance sheet, handling assets and liabilities in a single common framework.

The final decision on solvency is based on a two-tier procedure. This involves setting a first safety barrier at the level of the so-called *target capital* based on risk-sensitive, market-consistent valuation; breaches of this early-warning level would trigger regulatory intervention. The second and final tier is the *minimal capital level* calculated with the old Solvency 1 rules. It is interesting to note that in the definition of target capital, the *expected shortfall* for a holding period is used as a risk measure rather than Value-at-Risk, reflecting actuaries' experience with skewed and heavy-tailed pay-off functions; this alternative risk measure will be defined in Section 2.2.4. The reader interested in finding out more about the ongoing developments in insurance regulation will find relevant references in Notes and Comments.

1.4 Why Manage Financial Risk?

An important issue that we have barely dealt with concerns the reasons why we should invest in QRM in the first place. This question can be posed from various perspectives, including those of the customer of a financial institution, its shareholders, management, board of directors, regulators, politicians, or the public at large. Each of these stakeholders may have a different answer, and, at the end of the day, an equilibrium between the various interests will have to be found. In this section, we will focus on some of the players involved and give a selective account of some of the issues. It is not our aim, nor do we have the competence, to give a full treatment of this important subject.

1.4.1 A Societal View

Modern society relies on the smooth functioning of banking and insurance systems and has a collective interest in the stability of such systems. The regulatory process culminating in Basel II has been strongly motivated by the fear of systemic risk, i.e. the danger that problems in a single financial institution may spill over and, in extreme situations, disrupt the normal functioning of the entire financial system. Consider the following remarks made by Alan Greenspan before the Council on Foreign Relations in Washington, DC, on 19 November 2002 (Greenspan 2002).

> Today, I would like to share with you some of the evolving international financial issues that have so engaged us at the Federal Reserve over the

> past year. I, particularly, have been focusing on innovations in the management of risk and some of the implications of those innovations for our global economic and financial system. . . . The development of our paradigms for containing risk has emphasized dispersion of risk to those willing, and presumably able, to bear it. If risk is properly dispersed, shocks to the overall economic systems will be better absorbed and less likely to create cascading failures that could threaten financial stability.

In the face of such spillover scenarios, society views risk management positively and entrusts regulators with the task of forging the framework that will safeguard its interests. Consider the debate surrounding the use and misuse of derivatives. Regulation serves to reduce the risk of the misuse of these products, but at the same time recognizes their societal value in the global financial system. Perhaps contrary to the popular view, derivatives should be seen as instruments that serve to enhance stability of the system rather than undermine it, as argued by Greenspan in the same address.

> Financial derivatives, more generally, have grown at a phenomenal pace over the past fifteen years. Conceptual advances in pricing options and other complex financial products, along with improvements in computer and telecommunications technologies, have significantly lowered the costs of, and expanded the opportunities for, hedging risks that were not readily deflected in earlier decades. Moreover, the counterparty credit risk associated with the use of derivative instruments has been mitigated by legally enforceable netting and through the growing use of collateral agreements. These increasingly complex financial instruments have especially contributed, particularly over the past couple of stressful years, to the development of a far more flexible, efficient, and resilient financial system than existed just a quarter-century ago.

1.4.2 The Shareholder's View

It is widely believed that proper financial risk management can increase the value of a corporation and hence shareholder value. In fact, this is the main reason why corporations which are not subject to regulation by financial supervisory authorities engage in risk-management activities. Understanding the relationship between shareholder value and financial risk management also has important implications for the design of risk-management (RM) systems. Questions to be answered include the following.

- When does RM increase the value of a firm, and which risks should be managed?
- How should RM concerns factor into investment policy and capital budgeting?

There is a rather extensive corporate finance literature on the issue of "corporate risk management and shareholder value". We briefly discuss some of the main arguments. In this way we hope to alert the reader to the fact that there is more to RM than the mainly technical questions related to the implementation of RM strategies dealt with in the core of this book.

The first thing to note is that from a corporate-finance perspective it is by no means obvious that in a world with perfect capital markets RM enhances shareholder value: while *individual* investors are typically risk averse and should therefore manage the risk in their portfolios, it is not clear that RM or risk reduction at the *corporate level*, such as hedging a foreign-currency exposure or holding a certain amount of risk capital, increases the value of a corporation. The rationale for this—at first surprising—observation is simple: if investors have access to perfect capital markets, they can do the RM transactions they deem necessary via their own trading and diversification. The following statement from the chief investment officer of an insurance company exemplifies this line of reasoning: "If our shareholders believe that our investment portfolio is too risky, they should short futures on major stock market indices".

The potential irrelevance of corporate RM for the value of a corporation is an immediate consequence of the famous *Modigliani–Miller Theorem* (Modigliani and Miller 1958). This result, which marks the beginning of modern corporate finance theory, states that, in an ideal world without taxes, bankruptcy costs and informational asymmetries, and with frictionless and arbitrage-free capital markets, the financial structure of a firm—and hence also its RM decisions—are irrelevant for the firm's value. Hence, in order to find reasons for corporate RM, one has to "turn the Modigliani–Miller Theorem upside down" and identify situations where RM enhances the value of a firm by deviating from the unrealistically strong assumptions of the theorem. This leads to the following rationales for RM.

- RM can reduce *tax costs*. Under a typical tax regime the amount of tax to be paid by a corporation is a *convex* function of its profits; by reducing the variability in a firm's cash flow, RM can therefore lead to a higher expected after-tax profit.
- RM can be beneficial, since a company may (and usually will) have better access to capital markets than individual investors.
- RM can increase the firm value in the presence of *bankruptcy costs*, as it makes bankruptcy less likely.
- RM can reduce the impact of *costly external financing* on the firm value, as it facilitates the achievement of optimal investment.

The last two points merit a more detailed discussion. Bankruptcy costs consist of direct bankruptcy costs, such as the cost of lawsuits, and the more important indirect bankruptcy costs. The latter may include liquidation costs, which can be substantial in the case of intangibles like research and development (R&D) and know-how. This is why high R&D spending appears to be positively related to the use of RM techniques. Moreover, increased likelihood of bankruptcy often has a negative effect on key employees, management and customer relations, in particular in areas where a client wants a long-term business relationship. For instance, few customers would want to enter into a life insurance contract with an insurance company which is known to be close to bankruptcy. On a related note, banks which are close to bankruptcy might be faced with the unpalatable prospect of a bank run, where depositors try to withdraw their money simultaneously. A further discussion of these issues is given in Altman (1993).

It is a "stylized fact of corporate finance" that for a corporation external funds are more costly to obtain than internal funds, an observation which is usually attributed to problems of asymmetric information between the management of a corporation and bond and equity investors. For instance, raising external capital from outsiders by issuing new shares might be costly if the new investors, who have incomplete information about the economic prospects of a firm, interpret the share issue as a sign that the firm is overvalued. This can generate a rationale for RM for the following reason: without RM the increased variability of a company's cash flow will be translated either into an increased variability of the funds which need to be raised externally or to an increased variability in the amount of investment. With increasing marginal costs of raising external capital and decreasing marginal profits from new investment, this leads to a decrease in (expected) profits. Hence proper RM, which amounts to a smoothing of the cash flow generated by a corporation, can be beneficial. For references to the literature see Notes and Comments.

1.4.3 Economic Capital

As we have just seen, a corporation typically has strong incentives to strictly limit the probability of bankruptcy in order to avoid the associated bankruptcy costs. This is directly linked to the notion of economic capital. In a narrow sense, economic capital is the capital that shareholders should invest in the company in order to limit the probability of default to a given confidence level over a given time horizon. More broadly, economic capital offers a firm-wide language for discussing and pricing risk that is related directly to the principal concerns of management and other key stakeholders, namely institutional solvency and profitability (see Matten 2000). In this broader sense, economic capital represents the emerging best practice for measuring and reporting all kinds of risk across a financial organization.

Economic capital is so called because it measures risk in terms of *economic* realities rather than potentially misleading regulatory or accounting rules; moreover, part of the measurement process involves converting a risk distribution into the amount of *capital* that is required to support the risk, in line with the institution's target financial strength (e.g. credit rating). Hence the calculation of economic capital is a process that begins with the quantification of the risks that any given company faces over a given time period. These risks include those that are well defined from a regulatory point of view, such as credit, market and operational risks, and also includes other categories like insurance, liquidity, reputational and strategic or business risk. When modelled in detail and aggregated one obtains a value distribution in line with the Merton model for firm valuation as discussed in Chapter 8.

Given such a value distribution, the next step involves the determination of the probability of default (solvency standard) that is acceptable to the institution. The mapping from risk (solvency standard) to capital often uses standard external benchmarks for credit risk. For instance, a firm that capitalizes to Moody's Aa standard over a one-year horizon determines its economic capital as the "cushion" required to keep the firm solvent over a one-year period with 99.97% probability; firms rated Aa by Moody's have historically defaulted with a 0.03% frequency over a one-year horizon (see, for example, Duffie and Singleton 2003, Table 4.2). The choice of horizon must relate to natural capital planning or business cycles, which might mean one year for a bank but typically longer for an insurance company. In the ideal RM set-up, it is economic capital that is used for setting risk limits. Or, as stated in (Drzik, Nakada and Schuermann 1998), economic capital can serve as a common currency for risk limits. That paper also discusses the way in which economic capital (capital you need) can be compared with physical capital (capital you have) and how corporate-finance decisions can be based on this comparison.

We hope that our brief discussion of the economic issues surrounding modern RM has convinced the reader that there is more to RM than the mere statistical computation of risk measures, important though the latter may be. The Notes and Comments provide some references for readers who want to learn more about the economic foundations of RM.

1.5 Quantitative Risk Management

In this first chapter we have tried to place QRM in a larger historical, institutional, and even societal framework, since a study of QRM without a discussion of its proper setting and motivation makes little sense. In the remainder of the book we adopt a somewhat narrower view and treat QRM as a quantitative science using the language of mathematics in general, and probability and statistics in particular.

In this section we describe the challenge that we have attempted to meet in this book and discuss where QRM may lead in the future.

1.5.1 The Nature of the Challenge

We set ourselves the task of defining a new discipline of QRM and our approach to this task has two main strands. On the one hand, we have attempted to put current practice onto a firmer mathematical footing where, for example, concepts like profit-and-loss distributions, risk factors, risk measures, capital allocation and risk aggregation are given formal definitions and a consistent notation. In doing this we have been guided by the consideration of what topics should form the core of a course on QRM for a wide audience of students interested in RM issues; nonetheless, the list is far from complete and will continue to evolve as the discipline matures. On the other hand, the second strand of our endeavour has been to put together material on techniques and tools which go beyond current practice and address some of the deficiencies that have been raised repeatedly by critics. In the following paragraphs we elaborate on some of these issues.

Extremes matter. A very important challenge in QRM, and one that makes it particularly interesting as a field for probability and statistics, is the need to address unexpected, abnormal or extreme outcomes, rather than the expected, normal or average outcomes that are the focus of many classical applications. This is in tune with the regulatory view expressed by Alan Greenspan:

> From the point of view of the risk manager, inappropriate use of the normal distribution can lead to an understatement of risk, which must be balanced against the significant advantage of simplification. From the central bank's corner, the consequences are even more serious because we often need to concentrate on the left tail of the distribution in formulating lender-of-last-resort policies. Improving the characterization of the distribution of extreme values is of paramount importance.
>
> Joint Central Bank Research Conference, 1995

The need for a response to this challenge became very clear in the wake of the LTCM case in 1998. John Meriwether, the founder of the hedge fund, clearly learned from this experience of extreme financial turbulence; he is quoted as saying:

> With globalisation increasing, you'll see more crises. Our whole focus is on the extremes now—what's the worst that can happen to you in any situation—because we never want to go through that again.
>
> *The Wall Street Journal*, 21 August 2000

Much space is devoted in our book to models for financial risk factors that go beyond the normal (or Gaussian) model and attempt to capture the related phenomena of heavy tails, volatility and extreme values.

The interdependence and concentration of risks. A further important challenge is presented by the multivariate nature of risk. Whether we look at market risk or credit risk, or overall enterprise-wide risk, we are generally interested in some form of aggregate risk that depends on high-dimensional vectors of underlying risk factors such as individual asset values in market risk, or credit spreads and counterparty default indicators in credit risk.

A particular concern in our multivariate modelling is the phenomenon of dependence between extreme outcomes, when many risk factors move against us simultaneously. Again in connection with the LTCM case we find the following quote in *Business Week*, September 1998.

> Extreme, synchronized rises and falls in financial markets occur infrequently but they do occur. The problem with the models is that they did not assign a high enough chance of occurrence to the scenario in which many things go wrong at the same time—the "perfect storm" scenario.

In a perfect storm scenario the risk manager discovers that the diversification he thought he had is illusory; practitioners describe this also as a concentration of risk.

Myron Scholes, a prominent figure in the development of RM, alludes to this in Scholes (2000), where he argues against the regulatory overemphasis of VaR in the face of the more important issue of co-movements in times of market stress:

> Over the last number of years, regulators have encouraged financial entities to use portfolio theory to produce dynamic measures of risk. VaR, the product of portfolio theory, is used for short-run, day-to-day profit-and-loss exposures. Now is the time to encourage the BIS and other regulatory bodies to support studies on stress test and concentration methodologies. Planning for crises is more important than VaR analysis. And such new methodologies are the correct response to recent crises in the financial industry.

The problem of scale. A further challenge in QRM is the typical scale of the portfolios under consideration; in the most general case a portfolio may represent the entire position in risky assets of a financial institution. Calibration of detailed multivariate models for all risk factors is a well-nigh impossible task and hence any sensible strategy involves dimension reduction, that is to say the identification of key risk drivers and a concentration on modelling the main features of the overall risk landscape.

In short we are forced to adopt a fairly "broad-brush" approach. Where we use econometric tools, such as models for financial return series, we are content with relatively simple descriptions of individual series which capture the main phenomenon of volatility, and which can be used in a parsimonious multivariate factor model. Similarly, in the context of portfolio credit risk, we are more concerned with finding suitable models for the default dependence of counterparties than with accurately describing the mechanism for the default of an individual, since it is our belief that the former is at least as important as the latter in determining the risk of a large diversified portfolio.

Interdisciplinarity. Another aspect of the challenge of QRM is the fact that ideas and techniques from several existing quantitative disciplines are drawn together. When one considers the ideal education for a quantitative risk manager of the future, then no doubt a combined quantitative skillset should include concepts, techniques and tools from such fields as mathematical finance, statistics, financial econometrics, financial economics and actuarial mathematics. Our choice of topics is strongly guided by a firm belief that the inclusion of modern statistical and econometric techniques and a well-chosen subset of actuarial methodology are essential for the establishment of best-practice QRM. Certainly QRM is not just about financial mathematics and derivative pricing, important though these may be.

Of course, the quantitative risk manager operates in an environment where additional non-quantitative skills are equally important. Communication is certainly the most important skill of all, as a risk professional by definition of his/her duties will have to interact with colleagues with diverse training and background at all levels of the organization. Moreover, a quantitative risk manager has to familiarize him or herself quickly with all-important market practice and institutional details. Finally, a certain degree of humility will also be required to recognize the role of *quantitative* risk management in a much larger picture.

1.5.2 QRM for the Future

It cannot be denied that the use of QRM in the insurance and banking industry has had an overall positive impact on the development of those industries. However, RM technology is not restricted to the financial-services industry and similar developments are taking place in other sectors of industry. Some of the earliest applications of QRM are to be found in the manufacturing industry, where similar concepts and tools exist under names like reliability or total quality control. Industrial companies have long recognized the risks associated with bringing faulty products to the market. The car manufacturing industry in Japan in particular has been an early driving force in this respect.

More recently, QRM techniques have been adopted in the transport and energy industries, to name but two. In the case of energy there are obvious similarities with financial markets: electrical power is traded on energy exchanges; derivatives contracts are used to hedge future price uncertainty; companies optimize investment portfolios combining energy products with financial products; a current debate in the industry concerns the extent to which existing Basel II methodology can be transferred to the energy sector. However, there are also important dissimilarities due to the specific nature of the industry; most importantly there is the issue of the cost of storage and transport of electricity as an underlying commodity and the necessity of modelling physical networks including the constraints imposed by the existence of national boundaries and quasi-monopolies.

A further exciting area concerns the establishment of markets for environmental emission allowances. For example, the Chicago Climate Futures Exchange (CCFE) currently offers futures contracts on sulphur dioxide emissions. These are traded by industrial companies producing the pollutant in their manufacturing process and force such companies to consider the cost of pollution as a further risk in their risk landscape.

A natural consequence of the evolution of QRM thinking in different industries is an interest in the transfer of risks between industries; this process is known as ART (alternative risk transfer). To date the best examples are of risk transfer between the insurance and banking industries, as illustrated by the establishment in 1992 of catastrophe futures by the Chicago Board of Trade. These came about in the wake of Hurricane Andrew, which caused $20 billion of insured losses on the East Coast of the US. While this was a considerable event for the insurance industry in relation to overall reinsurance capacity, it represented only a drop in the ocean compared with the daily volumes traded worldwide on financial exchanges. This led to the recognition that losses could be covered in future by the issuance of appropriately structured bonds with coupon streams and principal repayments dependent on the occurrence or non-occurrence of well-defined natural catastrophe events, such as storms and earthquakes.

A speculative view of where these developments may lead is given by Shiller (2003), who argues that the proliferation of RM thinking coupled with the technological sophistication of the twenty-first century will allow any agent in society, from a company to a country to an individual, to apply QRM methodology to the risks they face. In the case of an individual this may be the risk of unemployment, depreciation in the housing market or the investment in the education of children.

Notes and Comments

The language of probability and statistics plays a fundamental role throughout the book and readers are expected to have a good knowledge of these subjects. At the elementary level, Rice (1995) gives a good first introduction to both of these. More advanced texts in probability and stochastic processes are Williams (1991), Resnick (1992) and Rogers and Williams (1994); the full depth of these texts is certainly not required for the understanding of this book, though they provide excellent reading material for the mathematically more sophisticated reader who also has an interest in mathematical finance. Further recommended texts on statistical inference include Casella and Berger (2002), Bickel and Doksum (2001), Davison (2003) and Lindsey (1996).

An excellent text on the history of risk and probability with financial applications in mind is Bernstein (1998). Additional useful material on the history of the subject is to be found in Field (2003).

For the mathematical reader looking to acquire more knowledge of relevant economics we recommend Mas-Colell, Whinston and Green (1995) for microeconomics; Campbell, Lo and MacKinlay (1997) or Gourieroux and Jasak (2001) for econometrics; and Brealey and Myers (2000) for corporate finance. From the vast literature on options, an entry-level text for the general reader is Hull (1997). At a more mathematical level we like Bingham and Kiesel (1998) and Musiela and Rutkowski (1997). One of the most readable texts on the basic notion of options is Cox and Rubinstein (1985). For a rather extensive list of the kind of animals to be found in the zoological garden of derivatives, see, for example, Haug (1998).

There are several texts on the spectacular losses due to speculative trading and careless use of derivatives. The LTCM case is well documented in Dunbar (2000), Lowenstein (2000) and Jorion (2000), the latter particularly for the technical risk-measurement issues involved. Boyle and Boyle (2001) give a very readable account of the Orange County, Barings and LTCM stories. A useful website on RM, containing a growing collection of industry case studies, is www.erisk.com.

An overview of options embedded in life insurance products is given in Dillmann (2002), guarantees are discussed in detail in Hardy (2003), and Briys and de Varenne (2001) contains an excellent account of RM issues facing the (life) insurance industry.

The historical development of banking regulation is well described in Crouhy, Galai and Mark (2001) and Steinherr (1998). For details of the current rules and regulations coming from the Basel Committee, see its website at www.bis.org/bcbs.

Besides copies of the various accords, one also finds useful working papers, publications and comments written by stakeholders on the various consultative packages. For Solvency 2, many documents are being prepared, and the Web is the best place to start looking; a forthcoming text is Sandström (2005). The complexity of RM methodology in the wake of Basel II is critically addressed by Hawke (2003), in his capacity as US Comptroller of the Currency.

For a very detailed overview of relevant practical issues underlying RM we again strongly recommend Crouhy, Galai and Mark (2001). A text stressing the use of VaR as a risk measure and containing several worked examples is Jorion (2001), who also has a useful teaching manual on the same subject (Jorion 2002a). Insurance-related issues in RM are well presented in Doherty (2000).

For a comprehensive discussion of the management of bank capital given regulatory constraints see Matten (2000). Graham and Rogers (2002) contains a discussion of RM and tax incentives. A formal account of the Modigliani–Miller Theorem and its implication can be found in many textbooks on corporate finance: a standard reference is Brealey and Myers (2000); de Matos (2001) gives a more theoretical account from the perspective of modern financial economics. Both texts also discuss the implications of informational asymmetries between the various stakeholders in a corporation. Formal models looking at RM from a corporate finance angle are to be found in Froot and Stein (1998), Froot, Scharfstein and Stein (1993) and Stulz (1996, 2002). For a specific discussion on corporate finance issues in insurance see Froot (2005) and Hancock, Huber and Koch (2001).

There are several studies on the use of RM techniques for non-financial firms (see, for example, Bodnar, Hyat and Marston 1999; Geman 2005). Two references in the area of reliability of industrial processes are Bedford and Cooke (2001) and Does, Roes and Trip (1999). An interesting edited volume on alternative risk transfer (ARTs) is Shimpi (1999); a detailed study of model risk in the ART context is Schmock (1999). An area we have not mentioned so far in our discussion of QRM in the future is that of real options. A real option is the right, but not the obligation, to take an action (e.g. deferring, expanding, contracting or abandoning) at a predetermined cost called the exercise price for a predetermined period of time—the life of the option. This definition is taken from Copeland and Antikarov (2001). Examples of real options discussed in the latter are the valuation of an internet project and of a pharmaceutical research and development project. A further useful reference is Brennan and Trigeorgis (2000).

2

Basic Concepts in Risk Management

In this chapter we discuss essential concepts in quantitative risk management. We begin by introducing a probabilistic framework for modelling financial risk and we give formal definitions for notions such as risk, profit and loss, risk factors and mapping. Moreover, we discuss a number of examples from the areas of market and credit risk, illustrating how typical risk-management problems fit into the general framework.

A central issue in modern risk management is the *measurement of risk*. As explained in Chapter 1, the need to quantify risk arises in many different contexts. For instance, a regulator measures the risk exposure of a financial institution in order to determine the amount of capital that institution has to hold as a buffer against unexpected losses. Similarly, the clearing house of an exchange needs to set margin requirements for investors trading on that exchange. In Section 2.2 we give an overview of the existing approaches to measuring risk and discuss their strengths and weaknesses. Particular attention will be given to *Value-at-Risk* and the related notion of *expected shortfall*.

In Section 2.3 we present some *standard methods* used in the financial industry for measuring market risk over a short horizon, such as the variance–covariance method, the historical-simulation method and methods based on Monte Carlo simulation. We consider the use of scaling rules for transforming one-period risk-measure estimates into estimates for longer time horizons and give a short discussion of back-testing approaches for monitoring the performance of risk-measurement systems. We conclude with an example of the application of standard methodology.

2.1 Risk Factors and Loss Distributions

2.1.1 General Definitions

We represent the uncertainty about future states of the world by a probability space $(\Omega, \mathcal{F}, P)$, which is the domain of all random variables (rvs) we introduce below. Consider a given portfolio such as a collection of stocks or bonds, a book of derivatives, a collection of risky loans or even a financial institution's overall position in risky assets. We denote the *value* of this portfolio at time s by $V(s)$ and assume that the rv $V(s)$ is observable at time s. For a given time horizon Δ, such as 1 or 10 days, the *loss* of the portfolio over the period $[s, s+\Delta]$ is given by

$$L_{[s,s+\Delta]} := -(V(s+\Delta) - V(s)).$$

While $L_{[s,s+\Delta]}$ is assumed to be observable at time $s+\Delta$, it is typically random from the viewpoint of time s. The distribution of $L_{[s,s+\Delta]}$ is termed the *loss distribution*.

We distinguish between the *conditional* loss distribution, i.e. the distribution of $L_{[s,s+\Delta]}$ given all available information up to and including time s, and the *unconditional* loss distribution; this issue is taken up in more detail below.

Remark 2.1. Practitioners in risk management are often concerned with the so-called profit-and-loss (P&L) distribution. This is the distribution of the change in value $V(s+\Delta) - V(s)$, i.e. of the rv $-L_{[s,s+\Delta]}$. However, in risk management we are mainly concerned with the probability of large losses and hence with the upper tail of the loss distribution. Hence we often drop the P from P&L, both in notation and language. It is a standard convention in statistics to present results on tail estimation for the upper tail of distributions. Moreover, actuarial risk theory is a theory of positive rvs. Hence our focus on loss distributions facilitates the application of techniques from these fields.

In most parts of the book we consider a fixed horizon Δ. In that case it will be convenient to measure time in units of Δ and to introduce a time series notation, where we move from a generic process $Y(s)$ to the time series $(Y_t)_{t\in\mathbb{N}}$ with $Y_t := Y(t\Delta)$. Using this notation the loss is written as

$$L_{t+1} := L_{[t\Delta,(t+1)\Delta]} = -(V_{t+1} - V_t). \tag{2.1}$$

For instance, in market risk management we often work with financial models where the calendar time s is measured in years and interest rates and volatilities are quoted on an annualized basis. If we are interested in daily losses we set $\Delta = 1/365$ or $\Delta \approx 1/250$; the latter convention is mainly used in markets for equity derivatives since there are approximately 250 trading days per year. The rvs V_t and V_{t+1} then represent the portfolio value on days t and $t+1$, respectively, and L_{t+1} is the loss from day t to day $t+1$.

Following standard risk-management practice the value V_t is modelled as a function of time and a d-dimensional random vector $\boldsymbol{Z}_t = (Z_{t,1}, \dots, Z_{t,d})'$ of *risk factors*, i.e. we have the representation

$$V_t = f(t, \boldsymbol{Z}_t) \tag{2.2}$$

for some measurable function $f : \mathbb{R}_+ \times \mathbb{R}^d \to \mathbb{R}$. Risk factors are usually assumed to be observable so that $\boldsymbol{Z}_t$ is known at time t. The choice of the risk factors and of f is of course a modelling issue and depends on the portfolio at hand and on the desired level of precision. Frequently used risk factors are logarithmic prices of financial assets, yields and logarithmic exchange rates. A representation of the portfolio value in the form (2.2) is termed a *mapping* of risks. Some examples of the mapping of standard portfolios are provided below.

It will be convenient to define the series of *risk-factor changes* $(\boldsymbol{X}_t)_{t\in\mathbb{N}}$ by $\boldsymbol{X}_t := \boldsymbol{Z}_t - \boldsymbol{Z}_{t-1}$; they are the objects of interest in most statistical studies of financial time series. Using the mapping (2.2) the portfolio loss can be written as

$$L_{t+1} = -(f(t+1, \boldsymbol{Z}_t + \boldsymbol{X}_{t+1}) - f(t, \boldsymbol{Z}_t)). \tag{2.3}$$

Since $\mathbf{Z}_t$ is known at time t, the loss distribution is determined by the distribution of the risk-factor change $\mathbf{X}_{t+1}$. We therefore introduce another piece of notation, namely the *loss operator* $l_{[t]} : \mathbb{R}^d \to \mathbb{R}$, which maps risk-factor changes into losses. It is defined by

$$l_{[t]}(\mathbf{x}) := -(f(t+1, \mathbf{Z}_t + \mathbf{x}) - f(t, \mathbf{Z}_t)), \quad \mathbf{x} \in \mathbb{R}^d, \tag{2.4}$$

and we obviously have $L_{t+1} = l_{[t]}(\mathbf{X}_{t+1})$.

If f is differentiable, we consider a first-order approximation L^{Δ}_{t+1} of the loss in (2.3) of the form

$$L^{\Delta}_{t+1} := -\left(f_t(t, \mathbf{Z}_t) + \sum_{i=1}^{d} f_{z_i}(t, \mathbf{Z}_t) X_{t+1,i} \right), \tag{2.5}$$

where the subscripts to f denote partial derivatives. The notation L^{Δ} stems from the standard *delta* terminology in the hedging of derivatives (see Example 2.5 below). The linearized loss operator corresponding to (2.5) is given by

$$l^{\Delta}_{[t]}(\mathbf{x}) := -\left(f_t(t, \mathbf{Z}_t) + \sum_{i=1}^{d} f_{z_i}(t, \mathbf{Z}_t) x_i \right). \tag{2.6}$$

The first-order approximation is convenient as it allows us to represent the loss as a *linear* function of the risk-factor changes. The quality of the approximation (2.5) is obviously best if the risk-factor changes are likely to be small (i.e. if we are measuring risk over a short horizon) and if the portfolio value is almost linear in the risk factors (i.e. if the function f has small second derivatives).

Remark 2.2. In developing formulas (2.2)–(2.6) we have assumed that time is measured in units of the horizon Δ. In order to be in line with market convention in our examples it will sometimes be convenient to consider mappings of the form $g(s, \mathbf{Z})$, where time s is measured in years; in that case, equations (2.2) and (2.3) become, respectively, $V_t = f(t, \mathbf{Z}_t) = g(t\Delta, \mathbf{Z}_t)$ and

$$L_{t+1} = -(g((t+1)\Delta, \mathbf{Z}_t + \mathbf{X}_{t+1}) - g(t\Delta, \mathbf{Z}_t)),$$

where Δ gives the length of the risk-management horizon in years. Care must be taken with the linearized version of the loss in (2.5), which becomes

$$L^{\Delta}_{t+1} := -\left(g_s(t\Delta, \mathbf{Z}_t)\Delta + \sum_{i=1}^{d} g_{z_i}(t\Delta, \mathbf{Z}_t) X_{t+1,i} \right). \tag{2.7}$$

Note that, when working with a short time horizon Δ, the term $g_s(t\Delta, \mathbf{Z}_t)\Delta$ in (2.7) is very small and is therefore often dropped in practice.

Remark 2.3. Note that our definition of the portfolio loss implicitly assumes that the composition of the portfolio remains unchanged over the time horizon Δ. While unproblematic for daily losses this assumption becomes increasingly unrealistic for longer time horizons. This is a problem for non-financial corporations like insurance companies; such companies may prefer to measure the risk of their financial portfolio over a one-year horizon, which is the appropriate horizon for dealing with their usual business risks. We note also that in the context of the Basel Accords, discussed in Chapter 1, it is formally required that calculations for banks be made under the assumption that the portfolio composition remains unchanged over a holding period Δ (10 days in the case of market risk).

2.1.2 Conditional and Unconditional Loss Distribution

As mentioned earlier, in risk management we often have to decide if we are interested in the conditional or the unconditional distribution of losses. Both are relevant for risk-management purposes, but it is important to be aware of the distinction between the two concepts.

The differences between conditional and unconditional loss distributions are strongly related to time series properties of the series of risk-factor changes $(X_t)_{t\in\mathbb{N}}$. Suppose that the risk-factor changes form a stationary time series with *stationary distribution* F_X on $\mathbb{R}^d$. Essentially, this means that the distribution of $(X_t)_{t\in\mathbb{N}}$ is invariant under shifts of time (see Chapter 4 for details) and most time series models used in practice for the modelling of risk-factor changes satisfy this property. Now fix a point in time t (current time), and denote by $\mathcal{F}_t$ the sigma field representing the publicly available information at time t. Typically, $\mathcal{F}_t = \sigma(\{X_s : s \leqslant t\})$, the sigma field generated by past and present risk-factor changes, often called the *history*, up to and including time t. Denote by $F_{X_{t+1}|\mathcal{F}_t}$ the conditional distribution of X_{t+1} given current information $\mathcal{F}_t$. In most stationary time series models relevant for risk management, $F_{X_{t+1}|\mathcal{F}_t}$ is *not* equal to the stationary distribution F_X. An important example is provided by the popular models from the GARCH family (see Section 4.3). In this class of model the variance of the conditional distribution of X_{t+1} is a function of past risk-factor changes and possibly of its own lagged values. On the other hand, if $(X_t)_{t\in\mathbb{N}}$ is an independent and identically distributed (iid) series, we obviously have $F_{X_{t+1}|\mathcal{F}_t} = F_X$.

Fix the loss operator $l_{[t]}$ corresponding to the portfolio currently under consideration. The *conditional loss distribution* $F_{L_{t+1}|\mathcal{F}_t}$ is defined as the distribution of the loss operator $l_{[t]}(\cdot)$ under $F_{X_{t+1}|\mathcal{F}_t}$. Formally we have, for $l \in \mathbb{R}$,

$$F_{L_{t+1}|\mathcal{F}_t}(l) = P(l_{[t]}(X_{t+1}) \leqslant l \mid \mathcal{F}_t) = P(L_{t+1} \leqslant l \mid \mathcal{F}_t),$$

i.e. the conditional loss distribution gives the conditional distribution of the loss L_{t+1} in the next time period given current information $\mathcal{F}_t$. Conditional distributions are particularly relevant in market risk management.

The *unconditional loss-distribution* $F_{L_{t+1}}$ on the other hand is defined as the distribution of $l_{[t]}(\cdot)$ under the stationary distribution F_X of risk-factor changes. It gives the distribution of the portfolio loss if we consider a generic risk-factor change X with the same distribution as $X_1, \dots, X_t$. The unconditional loss distribution is of particular interest if the time horizon over which we want to measure our losses is relatively large, as is frequently the case in credit risk management and insurance.

To define conditional and unconditional distributions of linearized losses we simply replace $l_{[t]}$ by $l_{[t]}^{\Delta}$. Of course, if the risk-factor changes form an iid sequence, conditional and unconditional loss distributions coincide.

Risk-management techniques based on the conditional loss distribution are often termed *conditional* or *dynamic* risk management; techniques based on the unconditional loss distribution are often referred to as *static* risk management. In Section 2.3.6 we illustrate the difference between the two approaches.

2.1.3 *Mapping of Risks: Some Examples*

We now consider a number of examples from the area of market and credit risk, illustrating how typical risk-management problems fit into the framework of the previous section. Altogether there are five examples in this section. While we strongly encourage the reader to study at least two or three of them to develop intuition for the mapping of risks, it is possible to skip some of the examples at first reading.

Example 2.4 (stock portfolio). Consider a fixed portfolio of d stocks and denote by λ_i the number of shares of stock i in the portfolio at time t. The price process of stock i is denoted by $(S_{t,i})_{t\in\mathbb{N}}$. Following standard practice in finance and risk management we use logarithmic prices as risk factors, i.e. we take $Z_{t,i} := \ln S_{t,i}$, $1 \leqslant i \leqslant d$. The risk-factor changes $X_{t+1,i} = \ln S_{t+1,i} - \ln S_{t,i}$ then correspond to the log-returns of the stocks in the portfolio. We get $V_t = \sum_{i=1}^{d} \lambda_i \exp(Z_{t,i})$ and hence

$$L_{t+1} = -(V_{t+1} - V_t) = -\sum_{i=1}^{d} \lambda_i S_{t,i}(\exp(X_{t+1,i}) - 1).$$

The linearized loss L_{t+1}^{Δ} is then given by

$$L_{t+1}^{\Delta} = -\sum_{i=1}^{d} \lambda_i S_{t,i} X_{t+1,i} = -V_t \sum_{i=1}^{d} w_{t,i} X_{t+1,i}, \tag{2.8}$$

where the weight $w_{t,i} := (\lambda_i S_{t,i})/V_t$ gives the proportion of the portfolio value invested in stock i at time t. The corresponding linearized loss operator is given by $l_{[t]}^{\Delta}(\boldsymbol{x}) = -V_t \boldsymbol{w}_t'\boldsymbol{x} := -V_t \sum_{i=1}^{d} w_{t,i} x_i$. Given the mean vector and covariance matrix of the distribution of the risk-factor changes it is very easy to compute the first two moments of the distribution of the linearized loss L^{Δ}. Suppose that the random vector $\boldsymbol{X}$ follows a distribution with mean vector $\boldsymbol{\mu}$ and covariance matrix Σ. Using general rules for the mean and variance of linear combinations of a random vector (see also equations (3.7) and (3.8)) we immediately get

$$E(l_{[t]}^{\Delta}(\boldsymbol{X})) = -V_t \boldsymbol{w}'\boldsymbol{\mu} \quad \text{and} \quad \operatorname{var}(l_{[t]}^{\Delta}(\boldsymbol{X})) = V_t^2 \boldsymbol{w}'\Sigma\boldsymbol{w}. \tag{2.9}$$

Applied to the mean vector $\boldsymbol{\mu}_t$ and the covariance matrix Σ_t of the conditional distribution $F_{X_{t+1}|\mathcal{F}_t}$ of the risk-factor changes, (2.9) yields the first two moments of the conditional loss distribution; applied to the mean vector $\boldsymbol{\mu}$ and the covariance matrix Σ of the unconditional distribution F_X of the risk-factor changes, (2.9) yields the first two moments of the unconditional loss distribution.

Example 2.5 (European call option). We now consider a simple example of a portfolio of derivative securities, namely a standard European call on a non-dividend-paying stock S with maturity date T and exercise price K. We use the *Black–Scholes* *option-pricing formula* for the valuation of our portfolio. Define the function C^{BS} by

$$C^{\text{BS}}(s, S; r, \sigma, K, T) := S\Phi(d_1) - K\mathrm{e}^{-r(T-s)}\Phi(d_2), \tag{2.10}$$

where Φ denotes the standard normal distribution function (df), r represents the continuously compounded risk-free interest rate, σ denotes the annualized volatility of the underlying stock, and where

$$d_1 = \frac{\ln(S/K) + (r + \frac{1}{2}\sigma^2)(T-s)}{\sigma\sqrt{T-s}} \quad \text{and} \quad d_2 = d_1 - \sigma\sqrt{T-s}. \tag{2.11}$$

Following market convention, time in (2.10) is measured in years so that Remark 2.2 applies. We are interested in daily losses and set $\Delta = 1/250$.

An obvious risk factor to choose for this portfolio is the log-price of the underlying stock. While in the Black–Scholes option-pricing model the interest rate and volatility are assumed to be constant, in real markets interest rates change constantly as do the *implied volatilities* that practitioners tend to use as inputs for the volatility parameter. Hence we take $\boldsymbol{Z}_t = (\ln S_t, r_t, \sigma_t)'$ as the vector of risk factors. According to the Black–Scholes formula the value of the call option on day t equals $V_t = C^{\text{BS}}(t\Delta, S_t; r_t, \sigma_t, K, T)$. The risk-factor changes are given by

$$\boldsymbol{X}_{t+1} = (\ln S_{t+1} - \ln S_t, r_{t+1} - r_t, \sigma_{t+1} - \sigma_t),$$

so that the linearized loss is given by

$$L^{\Delta}_{t+1} = -(C^{\text{BS}}_s \Delta + C^{\text{BS}}_S S_t X_{t+1,1} + C^{\text{BS}}_r X_{t+1,2} + C^{\text{BS}}_\sigma X_{t+1,3}),$$

where the subscripts denote partial derivatives. Note that we have omitted the arguments of C^{BS} to simplify the notation. The derivatives of the Black–Scholes option-pricing function are often referred to as the *Greeks*: C^{BS}_S (the partial derivative with respect to the stock price S) is called the *delta* of the option; C^{BS}_s (the partial derivative with respect to calendar time s) is called the *theta* of the option; C^{BS}_r (the partial derivative with respect to the interest rate r) is called the *rho* of the option; in a slight abuse of the Greek language, C^{BS}_σ (the partial derivative with respect to volatility σ) is called the *vega* of the option. The Greeks play an important role in the risk management of derivative portfolios.

The reader should keep in mind that for portfolios with derivatives the linearized loss can be a rather poor approximation of the true loss, since the portfolio value is often a highly nonlinear function of the risk factors. This has led to the development of higher-order approximations such as the *delta–gamma approximation*, where first- and second-order derivatives are used. (The second derivative C^{BS}_{SS} is called the *gamma* of an option.) In Notes and Comments we provide a number of further references dealing with this issue.

Example 2.6 (bond portfolio). Next we consider a portfolio of d default-free zero-coupon bonds with maturity T_i and price $p(s, T_i)$, $1 \leqslant i \leqslant d$ (again time is measured in years, so Remark 2.2 applies). By λ_i we denote the number of bonds with maturity

T_i in the portfolio. While zero-coupon bonds of longer maturities are relatively rare in practice, our example is relevant, since many fixed-income instruments such as coupon bonds or standard swaps can be viewed as portfolios of zero-coupon bonds.

We follow a standard convention in modern interest-rate theory and normalize the face value $p(T, T)$ of the bond to one. Recall that the *continuously compounded yield* of a zero-coupon bond is defined as $y(s, T) := -(1/(T - s)) \ln p(s, T)$, i.e. we have

$$p(s, T) = \exp(-(T - s)y(s, T)).$$

The mapping $T \to y(s, T)$ is referred to as the continuously compounded *yield curve* at time s. In a detailed analysis of the change in value of a bond portfolio one takes all yields $y(s, T_i)$, $1 \leqslant i \leqslant d$, as risk factors. The value of the portfolio at time s is then given by $V(s) = \sum_{i=1}^{d} \lambda_i p(s, T_i)$, and in our mapping notation (2.2) we have

$$V_t = \sum_{i=1}^{d} \lambda_i p(t\Delta, T_i) = \sum_{i=1}^{d} \lambda_i \exp(-(T_i - t\Delta)y(t\Delta, T_i)). \tag{2.12}$$

From this formula the loss L_{t+1} is easily computed. Taking derivatives and using the definition of the linearized loss L_{t+1}^{Δ} in (2.5) we also get

$$L_{t+1}^{\Delta} = -\sum_{i=1}^{d} \lambda_i p(t\Delta, T_i)(y(t\Delta, T_i)\Delta - (T_i - t\Delta)X_{t+1,i}), \tag{2.13}$$

where the risk-factor changes are $X_{t+1,i} = y((t+1)\Delta, T_i) - y(t\Delta, T_i)$.

This formula is closely related to the classical concept of *duration*. Suppose that the yield curve is flat, i.e. $y(s, T) = y(s)$ independently of T and that the only possible changes in interest rates are parallel shifts of the yield curve so that $y(s + \Delta, T) = y(s) + \delta$ for all T. These assumptions are clearly unrealistic but frequently made in practice. Then L_{t+1}^{Δ} can be written as

$$L_{t+1}^{\Delta} = -V_t\left(y_t\Delta - \sum_{i=1}^{d} \frac{\lambda_i p(t\Delta, T_i)}{V_t}(T_i - t\Delta)\delta\right) = -V_t(y_t\Delta - D\delta),$$

where

$$D := \sum_{i=1}^{d} \frac{\lambda_i p(t\Delta, T_i)}{V_t}(T_i - t\Delta)$$

is a weighted sum of the times to maturity of the different cash flows in the portfolio, the weights being proportional to the discounted value of the cash flows. D is usually called the *duration* of a bond portfolio. The duration is an important tool in traditional bond-portfolio or asset-liability management. The standard duration-based strategy to manage the interest risk of a bond portfolio is called *immunization*. Under this strategy an asset manager, who has a certain amount of funds to invest in various bonds and who needs to make certain known payments in the future, allocates these funds to various bonds in such a way that the duration of the overall portfolio consisting of bond investment and liabilities is equal to zero. As we have just seen, duration measures the sensitivity of the portfolio value with respect to parallel shifts of the yield curve. Hence a zero duration means that the position has been immunized against these type of yield-curve changes. However, the portfolio is still exposed to other types of yield-curve changes.

If we consider large portfolios of fixed-income instruments, such as the overall fixed-income position of a major bank, choosing the yield of every bond in the portfolio as a risk factor becomes impractical: one ends up with too many risk factors, which renders the estimation of the distribution of the risk-factor changes impossible. To overcome this problem one therefore picks a few benchmark yields per country and uses a more-or-less ad hoc procedure to map cash flows at days between benchmark points to the two nearest benchmark points. We refer to Section 6.2 of the RiskMetrics technical document (JPMorgan 1996) for details.

Example 2.7 (currency forwards). We now consider the mapping of a long position in a currency forward. A currency or foreign exchange (FX) forward is an agreement between two parties to buy/sell a pre-specified amount $\bar{V}$ of foreign currency at a future time point $T > s$ at a pre-specified exchange rate $\bar{e}$. The future buyer is said to hold a long position, the other party is said to hold a short position in the contract.

To map this position we use the fact that a long position in the forward is equivalent to a long position in a foreign and a short position in a domestic zero-coupon bond. For illustration think of a euro investor holding a long position of size $\bar{V}$ in a currency forward on the USD/euro exchange rate. Denote by $p^{\mathrm{f}}(s, T)$ the USD price of an American (foreign) zero-coupon bond and by $p^{\mathrm{d}}(s, T)$ the corresponding euro (domestic) zero-coupon bond; the USD/euro spot exchange rate is denoted by $e(s)$. Then the value in euro at time T of a portfolio consisting of $\lambda_1 := \bar{V}$ foreign and $\lambda_2 := -\bar{e}\bar{V}$ domestic zero-coupon bonds equals $V_T = \bar{V}(e_T - \bar{e})$, which is obviously equal to the pay-off of the long position in the forward.

The short position in the domestic zero-coupon bond can be dealt with as in Example 2.6. Hence it remains to consider the position in the American zero-coupon bond. Obvious risk factors to choose are the logarithmic exchange rate and the yield of the US zero-coupon bond, i.e. $\boldsymbol{Z}_t = (\ln e_t, y^{\mathrm{f}}(t\Delta, T))'$. The value of the position in the foreign bond then equals

$$V_t = \bar{V} \exp(Z_{t,1} - (T - t\Delta)Z_{t,2}),$$

and we get

$$L_{t+1}^{\Delta} = -V_t(Z_{t,2}\Delta + X_{t+1,1} - (T - t\Delta)X_{t+1,2}),$$

where as usual $\boldsymbol{X}_{t+1}$ represents the risk-factor changes.

Example 2.8 (stylized portfolio of risky loans). In our final example, which comes from the area of credit risk management, we show how losses from a portfolio of loans fit into our general framework; a detailed discussion of models for loan portfolios will be presented in Chapter 8. A loan portfolio is subject to many risks. The most important ones are default risk, i.e. the risk that some counterparties cannot repay their loans; interest-rate risk, i.e. the risk that the present value of the future cash flows from the portfolio is diminished due to rising interest rates; and, finally, the risk of losses caused by rising credit spreads.

We consider a portfolio of loans to m different counterparties; the size of the exposure to counterparty i is denoted by e_i. Following standard practice in credit risk management, our risk-management horizon Δ is taken to be one year so that there is no need to distinguish between the two timescales (i.e. t and s). For simplicity we assume that all loans are repaid at the same date $T > t$ and that there are no payments prior to T. We introduce an rv $Y_{t,i}$ that represents the default state of counterparty i at t; we set $Y_{t,i} = 1$ if counterparty i defaults in the time period $[0, t]$ and $Y_{t,i} = 0$ otherwise. Again for simplicity we assume a recovery rate of zero, i.e. we assume that upon default of obligor i the whole exposure e_i is lost.

In valuing a risky loan we have to take the possibility of default into account. Typically, this is done by discounting the cash flow e_i at a higher rate than the yield $y(t, T)$ of a default-free zero-coupon bond. More precisely, we model the value at time t of such a loan as

$$\exp(-(T - t)(y(t, T) + c_i(t, T)))e_i;$$

$c_i(t, T)$ is then referred to as the *credit spread* of company i corresponding to the maturity T. Credit spreads are often determined from the prices of traded corporate bonds issued by companies with a similar credit quality to the counterparty under consideration. Alternatively, a formal pricing model using, for instance, the market value of the counterparty's stock as main input can be used (see Chapter 8, in particular Section 8.2, for more information). Again for simplicity we ignore variations in credit quality and assume that $c_i(t, T) = c(t, T)$ for all i. Under all these simplifying assumptions the value at time t of our loan portfolio equals

$$V_t = \sum_{i=1}^{m} (1 - Y_{t,i}) \exp(-(T - t)(y(t, T) + c(t, T)))e_i. \tag{2.14}$$

This suggests the following $(m + 2)$-dimensional random vector of risk factors

$$\mathbf{Z}_t = (Y_{t,1}, \dots, Y_{t,m}, y(t, T), c(t, T))'. \tag{2.15}$$

L_{t+1} and $l_{[t]}$ are now easy to compute using (2.14). Due to the discrete nature of the default indicators and the long time horizon, linearized losses are of little importance in credit risk management. It is apparent from (2.14) and (2.15) that the main difficulty in modelling the loss distribution of loan portfolios is in finding and calibrating a good model for the joint distribution of the default indicators $Y_{t+1,i}$, $1 \leqslant i \leqslant m$; this issue is taken up in Chapter 8.

Notes and Comments

The framework introduced in this section is a stylized version of the model introduced by the RiskMetrics Group. A summary of the earlier work of the RiskMetrics Group is the RiskMetrics Technical Document (JPMorgan 1996); an excellent updated summary, which also discusses some recent developments on the academic side, is Mina and Xiao (2001). The mapping of positions is also discussed in Jorion

(2001) and Dowd (1998). The differences between conditional and unconditional risk management are highlighted in McNeil and Frey (2000).

While not very satisfactory from a theoretical point of view, duration-based hedging remains popular with practitioners. For a detailed discussion of duration and its use in the management of interest-rate risk we refer the reader to standard finance textbooks such as Jarrow and Turnbull (1999) or Hull (1997).

The mapping of derivative portfolios using first- and second-order approximations to the portfolio value (the so-called delta–gamma approximation) is discussed in Duffie and Pan (1997) and Rouvinez (1997) (see also Duffie and Pan 2001).

2.2 Risk Measurement

In this section we give an overview of existing approaches to measuring risk in financial institutions. In discussing strengths and weaknesses of these approaches we focus on practical aspects and postpone a proper discussion of the theoretical properties of the risk measures (issues such as subadditivity and coherence) until Chapter 6.

In practice risk measures are used for a variety of purposes. Among the most important are the following.

Determination of risk capital and capital adequacy. As discussed in Chapter 1, one of the principal functions of risk management in the financial sector is to determine the amount of capital a financial institution needs to hold as a buffer against unexpected future losses on its portfolio in order to satisfy a regulator, who is concerned with the solvency of the institution. A related problem is the determination of appropriate margin requirements for investors trading at an organized exchange, which is typically done by the clearing house of the exchange.

Management tool. Risk measures are often used by management as a tool for limiting the amount of risk a unit within a firm may take. For instance, traders in a bank are often constrained by the rule that the daily 95% Value-at-Risk of their position should not exceed a given bound.

Insurance premiums. Insurance premiums compensate an insurance company for bearing the risk of the insured claims. The size of this compensation can be viewed as a measure of the risk of these claims.

2.2.1 Approaches to Risk Measurement

Existing approaches to measuring the risk of a financial position can be grouped into four different categories: the notional-amount approach; factor-sensitivity measures; risk measures based on the loss distribution; risk measures based on scenarios.

Notional-amount approach. This is the oldest approach to quantifying the risk of a portfolio of risky assets. In the notional-amount approach the risk of a portfolio is defined as the sum of the notional values of the individual securities in the portfolio, where each notional value may be weighted by a factor representing an assessment of the riskiness of the broad asset class to which the security belongs. Variants of this approach are still in use in the *standardized approach* of the Basel Committee rules on banking regulation; see, for example, Section 10.1.2 for operational risk, or Chapter 2 of Crouhy, Galai and Mark (2001).

The advantage of the notional-amount approach is its apparent simplicity. However, as we recall from Chapter 1, from an economic viewpoint the approach is flawed for a number of reasons. To begin with, the approach does not differentiate between long and short positions and there is no netting. For instance, the risk of a long position in foreign currency hedged by an offsetting short position in a currency forward would be counted as twice the risk of the unhedged currency position. Moreover, the approach does not reflect the benefits of diversification on the overall risk of the portfolio. For example, if we use the notional-amount approach, it appears that a well-diversified credit portfolio consisting of loans to m companies that default more or less independently has the same risk as a portfolio where the whole amount is lent to a single company. Finally, the notional-amount approach has problems in dealing with portfolios of derivatives, where the notional amount of the underlying and the economic value of the derivative position can differ widely.

Factor-sensitivity measures. Factor-sensitivity measures give the change in portfolio value for a given predetermined change in one of the underlying risk factors; typically they take the form of a derivative (in the calculus sense). Important factor-sensitivity measures are the duration for bond portfolios and the Greeks for portfolios of derivatives. While these measures provide useful information about the robustness of the portfolio value with respect to certain well-defined events, they cannot measure the overall riskiness of a position. Moreover, factor-sensitivity measures create problems in the aggregation of risks.

- For a given portfolio it is not possible to aggregate the sensitivity with respect to changes in different risk factors. For instance, it makes no sense to simply add the delta and the vega of a portfolio of options.
- Factor-sensitivity measures cannot be aggregated across markets to create a picture of the overall riskiness of the portfolio of a financial institution.

Hence these measures are not very useful for capital-adequacy decisions; used in conjunction with other measures they can be useful for setting position limits.

Risk measures based on loss distributions. Most modern measures of the risk in a portfolio are statistical quantities describing the conditional or unconditional loss distribution of the portfolio over some predetermined horizon Δ. Examples include the variance, the Value-at-Risk and the expected shortfall, which we discuss in more detail in Sections 2.2.2–2.2.4. It is of course problematic to rely on any one particular statistic to summarize the risk contained in a distribution. However, the view that the loss distribution as a whole gives an accurate picture of the risk in a portfolio has much to commend it:

- losses are the central object of interest in risk management and so it is natural to base a measure of risk on their distribution;

- the concept of a loss distribution makes sense on all levels of aggregation from a portfolio consisting of a single instrument to the overall position of a financial institution;
- if estimated properly, the loss distribution reflects netting and diversification effects; and, finally,
- loss distributions can be compared across portfolios.

For instance, it makes perfect sense to compare the loss distribution of a book of fixed-income instruments and of a portfolio of equity derivatives, at least if the time horizon Δ is the same in both cases.

There are two major problems when working with loss distributions. First, any estimate of the loss distribution is based on past data. If the laws governing financial markets change, these past data are of limited use in predicting future risk. The second, related problem is practical. Even in a stationary environment it is difficult to estimate the loss distribution accurately, particularly for large portfolios, and many seemingly sophisticated risk-management systems are based on relatively crude statistical models for the loss distribution (incorporating, for example, untenable assumptions of normality).

However, this is not an argument against using loss distributions. Rather, it calls for improvements in the way loss distributions are estimated and, of course, for prudence in the practical application of risk-management models based on estimated loss distributions. In particular, risk measures based on the loss distribution should be complemented by information from hypothetical scenarios. Moreover, forward-looking information reflecting the expectations of market participants, such as implied volatilities, should be used in conjunction with statistical estimates (which are necessarily based on past information) in calibrating models of the loss distribution.

Scenario-based risk measures. In the scenario-based approach to measuring the risk of a portfolio one considers a number of possible future risk-factor changes (scenarios): such as a 10% rise in key exchange rates or a simultaneous 20% drop in major stock market indices or a simultaneous rise of key interest rates around the globe. The risk of the portfolio is then measured as the maximum loss of the portfolio under all scenarios, where certain extreme scenarios can be downweighted to mitigate their effect on the result.

We now give a formal description. Fix a set $\mathcal{X} = \{\boldsymbol{x}_1, \dots, \boldsymbol{x}_n\}$ of risk-factor changes (the scenarios) and a vector $\boldsymbol{w} = (w_1, \dots, w_n)' \in [0, 1]^n$ of weights. Consider a portfolio of risky securities and denote by $l_{[t]}$ the corresponding loss operator. The risk of this portfolio is then measured as

$$\psi_{[\mathcal{X},\boldsymbol{w}]} := \max\{w_1 l_{[t]}(\boldsymbol{x}_1), \dots, w_n l_{[t]}(\boldsymbol{x}_n)\}. \tag{2.16}$$

Many risk measures used in practice are of the form (2.16). For instance, the Chicago Mercantile Exchange (CME) uses a scenario-based approach to determine margin requirements. To compute the initial margin for a simple portfolio consisting of a position in a futures contract and call and put options on this contract, the CME considers sixteen different scenarios. The first fourteen consist of an up move or a down move of volatility combined with no move, an up move or a down move of the futures price by 1/3, 2/3 or 3/3 units of a specified range. The weights w_i, $i = 1, \dots, 14$, of these scenarios are equal to one. In addition there are two extreme scenarios with weights $w_{15} = w_{16} = 0.35$. The amount of capital required by the exchange as margin for a portfolio is then computed according to (2.16).

Remark 2.9. We can give a slightly different mathematical interpretation to formula (2.16), which will be useful in Section 6.1. Assume for the moment that $l_{[t]}(\mathbf{0}) = 0$, i.e. that the value of the position is unchanged if all risk factors stay the same. This is reasonable, at least for a short risk-management horizon Δ. In that case the expression $w_i l_{[t]}(\boldsymbol{x}_i)$ can be viewed as the expected value of $l_{[t]}$ under a probability measure on the space of risk-factor changes; this measure associates a mass of $w_i \in [0, 1]$ to the point $\boldsymbol{x}_i$ and a mass of $1 - w_i$ to the point $\mathbf{0}$. Denote by $\delta_{\boldsymbol{x}}$ the probability measure associating a mass of one to the point $\boldsymbol{x} \in \mathbb{R}^d$ and by $\mathcal{P}_{[\mathcal{X},\boldsymbol{w}]}$ the following set of probability measures on $\mathbb{R}^d$:

$$\mathcal{P}_{[\mathcal{X},\boldsymbol{w}]} = \{w_1\delta_{\boldsymbol{x}_1} + (1 - w_1)\delta_{\mathbf{0}}, \dots, w_n\delta_{\boldsymbol{x}_n} + (1 - w_n)\delta_{\mathbf{0}}\}.$$

Then $\psi_{[\mathcal{X},\boldsymbol{w}]}$ can be written as

$$\psi_{[\mathcal{X},\boldsymbol{w}]} = \max\{E^P(l_{[t]}(\boldsymbol{X})) : P \in \mathcal{P}_{[\mathcal{X},\boldsymbol{w}]}\}. \tag{2.17}$$

A risk measure of the form (2.17), where $\mathcal{P}_{[\mathcal{X},\boldsymbol{w}]}$ is replaced by some arbitrary subset $\mathcal{P}$ of the set of all probability measures on the space of risk-factor changes, is termed a *generalized scenario*. Generalized scenarios play an important role in the theory of coherent risk measures (see Section 6.1).

Scenario-based risk measures are a very useful risk-management tool for portfolios exposed to a relatively small set of risk factors as in the CME example. Moreover, they provide useful complementary information to measures based on statistics of the loss distribution. The main problem is of course to determine an appropriate set of scenarios and weighting factors. Moreover, comparison across portfolios which are affected by different risk factors is difficult.

2.2.2 *Value-at-Risk*

Value-at-Risk (VaR) is probably the most widely used risk measure in financial institutions and has also made its way into the Basel II capital-adequacy framework—hence it merits an extensive discussion. In this chapter we introduce VaR and discuss practical issues surrounding its use; in Section 6.1 we examine VaR from the viewpoint of *coherent* risk measures and highlight certain theoretical deficiencies.

Consider some portfolio of risky assets and a fixed time horizon Δ, and denote by $F_L(l) = P(L \leqslant l)$ the df of the corresponding loss distribution. We do not distinguish between L and L^Δ or between conditional and unconditional loss distributions; rather we assume that the choice has been made at the outset of the analysis and that F_L represents the distribution of interest. We want to define a statistic based on F_L which measures the severity of the risk of holding our portfolio over the time period Δ. An obvious candidate is the maximum possible loss, given by $\inf\{l \in \mathbb{R} : F_L(l) = 1\}$, a risk measure important in reinsurance. However, in most models of interest the support of F_L is unbounded so that the maximum loss is simply infinity. Moreover, by using the maximum loss we neglect any probability information in F_L. Value-at-Risk is a straightforward extension of maximum loss, which takes these criticisms into account. The idea is simply to replace "maximum loss" by "maximum loss which is not exceeded with a given high probability", the so-called confidence level.

Definition 2.10 (Value-at-Risk). Given some confidence level $\alpha \in (0, 1)$. The VaR of our portfolio at the confidence level α is given by the smallest number l such that the probability that the loss L exceeds l is no larger than $(1 - \alpha)$. Formally,

$$\mathrm{VaR}_\alpha = \inf\{l \in \mathbb{R} : P(L > l) \leqslant 1 - \alpha\} = \inf\{l \in \mathbb{R} : F_L(l) \geqslant \alpha\}. \tag{2.18}$$

In probabilistic terms, VaR is thus simply a *quantile* of the loss distribution. Typical values for α are $\alpha = 0.95$ or $\alpha = 0.99$; in market risk management the time horizon Δ is usually 1 or 10 days, in credit risk management and operational risk management Δ is usually one year. Note that by its very definition the VaR at confidence level α does not give any information about the severity of losses which occur with a probability less than $1 - \alpha$. This is clearly a drawback of VaR as a risk measure. For a small case study that illustrates this problem numerically we refer to Example 2.21 below.

Figure 2.1 illustrates the notion of VaR. The probability density function of a loss distribution is shown with a vertical line at the value of the 95% VaR. Note that the mean loss is negative ($E(L) = -2.6$), indicating that we expect to make a profit, but the right tail of the loss distribution is quite long in comparison with the left tail. The 95% VaR value is approximately 2.2, indicating that there is a 5% chance that we lose at least this amount.

Remark 2.11 (mean-VaR). Denote by μ the mean of the loss distribution. Sometimes the statistic $\mathrm{VaR}_\alpha^{\mathrm{mean}} := \mathrm{VaR}_\alpha - \mu$ is used for capital-adequacy purposes instead of ordinary VaR. If the time horizon Δ equals one day, $\mathrm{VaR}_\alpha^{\mathrm{mean}}$ is sometimes referred to as *daily earnings at risk*. The distinction between ordinary VaR and $\mathrm{VaR}_\alpha^{\mathrm{mean}}$ is of little relevance in market risk management, where the time horizon is short and μ is close to zero. It becomes relevant in credit where the risk-management horizon is longer. In particular, in loan pricing one uses $\mathrm{VaR}^{\mathrm{mean}}$ to determine the *economic capital* needed as a buffer against unexpected losses in a loan portfolio (see Section 9.3.4 for details). Taking the expectation of the P&L distribution into account is also important in the growing field of asset-management risk.

Since quantiles play an important role in risk management we recall the precise definition.

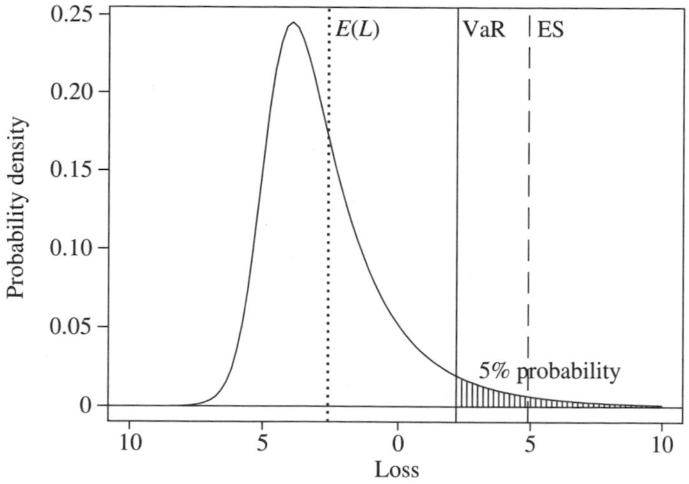

Figure 2.1. An example of a loss distribution with the 95% VaR marked as a vertical line; the mean loss is shown with a dotted line and an alternative risk measure known as the 95% expected shortfall (see Section 2.2.4 and Definition 2.15) is marked with a dashed line.

Definition 2.12 (generalized inverse and quantile function).

(i) Given some increasing function $T : \mathbb{R} \to \mathbb{R}$, the *generalized inverse* of T is defined by $T^{\leftarrow}(y) := \inf\{x \in \mathbb{R} : T(x) \geqslant y\}$, where we use the convention that the infimum of an empty set is ∞.

(ii) Given some df F, the generalized inverse $F^{\leftarrow}$ is called the *quantile function* of F. For $\alpha \in (0, 1)$ the α-quantile of F is given by

$$q_\alpha(F) := F^{\leftarrow}(\alpha) = \inf\{x \in \mathbb{R} : F(x) \geqslant \alpha\}.$$

For an rv X with df F we often use the alternative notation $q_\alpha(X) := q_\alpha(F)$. If F is continuous and strictly increasing, we simply have $q_\alpha(F) = F^{-1}(\alpha)$, where F^{-1} is the ordinary inverse of F. To compute quantiles in more general cases we may use the following simple criterion.

Lemma 2.13. *A point $x_0 \in \mathbb{R}$ is the α-quantile of some df F if and only if the following two conditions are satisfied: $F(x_0) \geqslant \alpha$; $F(x) < \alpha$ for all $x < x_0$.*

The lemma follows immediately from the definition of the generalized inverse and the right-continuity of F. Examples for the computation of quantiles in certain tricky cases and further properties of generalized inverses are given in Section A.1.2.

Example 2.14 (VaR for normal and *t* loss distributions). Suppose that the loss distribution F_L is normal with mean μ and variance σ^2. Fix $\alpha \in (0, 1)$. Then

$$\mathrm{VaR}_\alpha = \mu + \sigma\Phi^{-1}(\alpha) \quad \text{and} \quad \mathrm{VaR}_\alpha^{\mathrm{mean}} = \sigma\Phi^{-1}(\alpha), \tag{2.19}$$

where Φ denotes the standard normal df and $\Phi^{-1}(\alpha)$ is the α-quantile of Φ. The proof is easy: since F_L is strictly increasing, by Lemma 2.13 we only have to show that $F_L(\mathrm{VaR}_\alpha) = \alpha$. Now

$$P(L \leqslant \mathrm{VaR}_\alpha) = P\left(\frac{L-\mu}{\sigma} \leqslant \Phi^{-1}(\alpha)\right) = \Phi(\Phi^{-1}(\alpha)) = \alpha.$$

This result is routinely used in the *variance–covariance* approach (also known as the delta-normal approach) to computing risk measures, which we describe in Section 2.3.1 below; if we work with linearized losses, and assume that our risk-factor changes are multivariate normal, then the resulting loss distribution is normal, and we can compute VaR using (2.19).

Of course a similar result is obtained for any location-scale family and another useful example is the Student t loss distribution. Suppose our loss L is such that $(L-\mu)/\sigma$ has a standard t distribution with ν degrees of freedom; we denote this loss model by $L \sim t(\nu, \mu, \sigma^2)$ and note that the moments are given by $E(L) = \mu$ and $\mathrm{var}(L) = \nu\sigma^2/(\nu-2)$ when $\nu > 2$, so that σ is not the standard deviation of the distribution. We get

$$\mathrm{VaR}_\alpha = \mu + \sigma t_\nu^{-1}(\alpha), \tag{2.20}$$

where t_ν denotes the df of standard t, which is available in most statistical computer packages along with its inverse.

2.2.3 Further Comments on VaR

Non-subadditivity. VaR has been fundamentally criticized as a risk measure on the grounds that is has poor aggregation properties. This critique has its origins in the work of Artzner et al. (1997, 1999), who showed that VaR is not a *coherent* risk measure, since it violates the property of subadditivity that they believe reasonable risk measures should have.

We devote Section 6.1 to an in-depth discussion of this subject. At this point we merely remark that non-subadditivity means that if we have two loss distributions F_{L_1} and F_{L_2} for two portfolios and we denote the overall loss distribution of the merged portfolio $L = L_1 + L_2$ by F_L, we do not necessarily have that $q_\alpha(F_L) \leqslant q_\alpha(F_{L_1}) + q_\alpha(F_{L_2})$, so that the VaR of the merged portfolio is not necessarily bounded above by the sum of the VaRs of the individual portfolios. This contradicts our notion that there should be a diversification benefit associated with merging the portfolios; it also means that a decentralization of risk management using VaR is difficult since we cannot be sure that by aggregating VaR numbers for different portfolios or business units we will obtain a bound for the overall risk of the enterprise.

Model risk and market liquidity. In practice VaR numbers are often given a very literal interpretation, which is misleading and even dangerous; the statement that the daily VaR at confidence level $\alpha = 99\%$ of a particular portfolio is equal to l is understood as "with a probability of 99% the loss on this position will be smaller than l".

This interpretation is misleading for two reasons. To begin with, our estimate of the loss distribution is subject to estimation error and the problem of *model risk*.

Model risk can be defined as the risk that a financial institution incurs losses because its risk-management models are misspecified or because some of the assumptions underlying these models are not met in practice. For instance, we might work with a normal distribution to model losses whereas the real distribution is heavy-tailed, or we might fail to recognize the presence of volatility clustering or tail dependence (see Section 4.1.1) in modelling the distribution of the risk-factor changes. Since "any financial model is by definition a simplified and thus imperfect representation of the economic world and the ways in which economic agents perform investment, trading or financing decisions" (from the introduction of Gibson (2000)), it is fair to say that any risk-management model is subject to model risk to some extent. Of course, these problems are most pronounced if we try to estimate VaR at very high confidence levels such as $\alpha = 99.97\%$, as we might be required to do in the determination of economic capital (see Section 1.4.3).

Moreover, the above interpretation of VaR neglects any problems related to *market liquidity*. Loosely speaking, a market for a security is termed liquid if investors can buy or sell large amounts of the security in a short time without affecting its price very much. Conversely, a market in which an attempt to trade has a large impact on price, or where trading is impossible since there is no counterparty willing to take the other side of the trade, is termed illiquid. The problem this poses for the interpretation of VaR numbers was brought to the attention of professional risk managers by Lawrence and Robinson (1995). To quote from their paper:

> If we ask the question: "Can we be 98% confident that no more than an amount l [the VaR estimate at $\alpha = 0.98$] would be lost in liquidating the position?" the answer must be "no". To see why, consider what this measure of VaR implies about the risk management process and the nature of financial markets. In the liquidation scenario we are considering the following sequence of events is implied: at time t it is decided to liquidate the position; during the next 24 hours nothing is done . . . ; after 24 hours of inaction the position is liquidated at prices which are drawn from a [pre-specified] distribution unaffected by the process of liquidation. This scenario is hardly credible. . . . In particular, the act of liquidating itself would have the effect of moving the price against the trader disposing of a long position or closing out a short position. For large positions and illiquid instruments the costs of liquidation can be significant, in particular if speed is required.

They conclude that "any useful measures of VaR must take into account the costs of liquidation on the prospective loss". The events surrounding the near-bankruptcy of the hedge fund LTCM in Summer 1998 clearly showed that these concerns are more than justified. In fact, illiquidity of markets is nowadays regarded by many risk managers as the most important source of model risk.

Ideally we should try to factor the effects of market illiquidity into formal models, although this is difficult for a number of reasons. First, the price impact of trading a particular amount of a security at a given point in time is hard to measure; it depends on such elusive factors as market mood or the distribution of economic information among investors. Moreover, in illiquid markets traders are forced to close their position gradually over time to minimize the price impact of their transactions. Obviously, this liquidation has to be done on a different timescale depending on the size of the position to be liquidated relative to the market. This in turn would lead to different time horizons Δ for different positions, rendering the aggregation of risk measures across portfolios impossible. In many practical situations the risk manager can therefore do no better than ignore the effect of market liquidity in computing VaR numbers or related risk measures and be aware of the ensuing problems in interpreting the results. See Notes and Comments for pointers to further theoretical and empirical studies of these issues.

Choice of VaR parameters. Whenever we work with risk measures based on the loss distribution we have to choose an appropriate horizon Δ; in the case of VaR we also have to decide on the confidence level α. There is of course no single optimal value for these parameters, but there are some considerations which might influence our choice.

The risk-management horizon Δ should reflect the time period over which a financial institution is committed to hold its portfolio. This period is affected by contractual and legal constraints, and by liquidity considerations. It will typically vary across markets; in choosing a horizon for enterprise-wide risk management, a financial institution or corporation has little choice but to use the horizon appropriate for the market in which its core business activities lie. For instance, insurance companies are typically bound to hold their portfolio of claims for one year, say; in this time they can neither alter the portfolio by a substantial amount nor renegotiate the premiums they receive. Hence, in firm-wide risk management, one year is also the appropriate horizon for measuring the market risk of the investment portfolios of such companies.

As mentioned earlier, even in the absence of contractual constraints, a financial institution can be forced to hold a loss-making position in a risky asset if the market for that asset is not very liquid. For such positions a relatively long horizon may be appropriate. Again, liquidity does vary across markets, and for overall risk management an institution has to choose a horizon which best reflects its main exposures.

There are other, more practical considerations which suggest that Δ should be relatively small: the use of the linearized loss operator, which simplifies many computations, is justified only if the risk-factor changes are relatively small, which is more likely for small Δ. Similarly, the assumption that the composition of the portfolio remains unchanged is tenable only for a small holding period. Moreover, the calibration and testing of statistical models for the risk-factor changes $(X_t)_{t\in\mathbb{N}}$ are easier if Δ is small, since this typically means that we have more data at our disposal.

Concerning the choice of the confidence level α it is again difficult to give a clear-cut recommendation, since different values of α are appropriate for different purposes. Fortunately, once we have an estimate for the loss distribution, it is easy to compute quantiles at different confidence levels simultaneously. For capital-adequacy purposes a high confidence level is certainly called for in order to have a sufficient safety margin. For instance, the Basel Committee proposes the use of VaR at the 99% level and Δ equal to 10 days for market risk. In order to set limits for traders, a bank would typically take 95% and Δ equal to one day. The backtesting of models producing VaR figures should also be carried out at lower confidence levels in order to have more observations where the realized loss is higher than the predicted VaR.

Transforming VaR into regulatory capital. For banks using the *internal model (IM) approach* for market risk (MR), the following risk-capital formula results:

$$\mathrm{RC}^t_{\mathrm{IM}}(\mathrm{MR}) = \max\left\{\mathrm{VaR}^{t,10}_{0.99},\ \frac{k}{60}\sum_{i=1}^{60}\mathrm{VaR}^{t-i+1,10}_{0.99}\right\} + C_{\mathrm{SR}}, \tag{2.21}$$

where $\mathrm{VaR}^{j,10}_{0.99}$ stands for a 10-day VaR at the 99% confidence level, calculated on day j, and t represents today. The *stress factor* $3 \leqslant k \leqslant 4$ is determined as a function of the overall quality of the bank's internal model. The component C_{SR} stands for *specific risk*, i.e. the risk that is due to issuer-specific price movements after accounting for general market factors. A specific risk component should be added to all VaR numbers (see, for example, Crouhy, Galai and Mark 2001, Section 2.2).

A comment on VaR terminology. In practice the term "VaR" is used in various ways. In its most narrow sense the term Value-at-Risk refers to a quantile of the loss distribution as defined in Definition 2.10. Often risk managers refer to "VaR procedures" such as "delta-normal VaR" (see Section 2.3.1 below). A VaR procedure refers to a statistical approach to estimating a model for the loss distribution. Clearly, a VaR procedure could also be used to estimate some other risk measure based on the loss distribution. Finally, the term "VaR approach to risk management" is frequently used and usually refers to the way VaR figures are used in steering a company. In this book we use the term VaR only in the first sense.

2.2.4 *Other Risk Measures Based on Loss Distributions*

The purpose of this section is to discuss a few other statistical summaries of the loss distribution which are frequently used as risk measures in finance, insurance and risk management. As in the previous two sections we assume that a certain loss distribution F_L has been fixed at the outset of the analysis.

Variance. Historically the variance of the P&L distribution has been the dominating risk measure in finance. To a large extent this is due to the huge impact that the portfolio theory of Markowitz, which uses variance as a measure of risk, has had on theory and practice in finance (see, for example, Markowitz 1952). Variance is a well-understood concept which is easy to use analytically. However, as a risk measure it has two drawbacks. On the technical side, if we want to work with variance, we have to assume that the second moment of the loss distribution exists. While unproblematic for most return distributions in finance this can cause problems in certain areas of non-life insurance or for the analysis of operational losses (see Section 10.1.4). On the conceptual side, since it makes no distinction between positive and negative deviations from the mean, variance is a good measure of risk only for distributions which are (approximately) symmetric around the mean, such as the normal distribution or a (finite-variance) Student t distribution. However, in many areas of risk management, such as in credit and operational risk management, we deal with loss distributions which are highly skewed.

Lower and upper partial moments. Partial moments are measures of risk based on the lower or upper part of a distribution. In most of the literature on risk management the main concern is with the risk inherent in the lower tail of a P&L distribution and lower partial moments are used to measure this risk. Under our sign convention we are concerned with the risk inherent in the upper tail of a loss distribution and we focus on upper partial moments. Given an exponent $k \geqslant 0$ and a reference point q the upper partial moment $\mathrm{UPM}(k, q)$ is defined as

$$\mathrm{UPM}(k, q) = \int_q^\infty (l - q)^k \,\mathrm{d}F_L(l) \in [0, \infty]. \tag{2.22}$$

Some combinations of k and q have a special interpretation: for $k = 0$ we obtain $P(L \geqslant q)$; for $k = 1$ we obtain $E((L - q)I_{\{L \geqslant q\}})$; for $k = 2$ and $q = E(L)$ we obtain the *upper semivariance* of L. Of course, the higher the value we choose for k, the more conservative our risk measure becomes since we give more and more weight to large deviations from the reference point q.

Expected shortfall. Expected shortfall is closely related to VaR. It is now preferred to VaR by many risk managers in practice and will be seen in Section 6.1 to overcome the conceptual deficiencies of the latter (related to subadditivity).

Definition 2.15 (expected shortfall). For a loss L with $E(|L|) < \infty$ and df F_L the expected shortfall at confidence level $\alpha \in (0, 1)$ is defined as

$$\mathrm{ES}_\alpha = \frac{1}{1-\alpha} \int_\alpha^1 q_u(F_L) \,\mathrm{d}u, \tag{2.23}$$

where $q_u(F_L) = F_L^{\leftarrow}(u)$ is the quantile function of F_L.

Expected shortfall is thus related to VaR by

$$\mathrm{ES}_\alpha = \frac{1}{1-\alpha} \int_\alpha^1 \mathrm{VaR}_u(L) \,\mathrm{d}u.$$

Instead of fixing a particular confidence level α we average VaR over all levels $u \geqslant \alpha$ and thus "look further into the tail" of the loss distribution. Obviously ES_α depends only on the distribution of L and obviously $\mathrm{ES}_\alpha \geqslant \mathrm{VaR}_\alpha$. See Figure 2.1 for a simple illustration of an expected shortfall value and its relationship to VaR. The 95% expected shortfall value of 4.9 is at least double the 95% VaR value of 2.2 in this case.

For continuous loss distributions an even more intuitive expression can be derived which shows that expected shortfall can be interpreted as the expected loss that is incurred in the event that VaR is exceeded.

Lemma 2.16. *For an integrable loss L with continuous df F_L and any $\alpha \in (0,1)$ we have*

$$\mathrm{ES}_\alpha = \frac{E(L; L \geqslant q_\alpha(L))}{1-\alpha} = E(L \mid L \geqslant \mathrm{VaR}_\alpha), \tag{2.24}$$

where we have used the notation $E(X; A) := E(X I_A)$ for a generic integrable rv X and a generic set $A \in \mathcal{F}$.

Proof. Denote by U an rv with uniform distribution on the interval $[0,1]$. It is a well-known fact from elementary probability theory that the rv $F_L^{\leftarrow}(U)$ has df F_L (see Proposition 5.2 for a proof). We have to show that $E(L; L \geqslant q_\alpha(L)) = \int_\alpha^1 F_L^{\leftarrow}(u)\,\mathrm{d}u$. Now

$$E(L; L \geqslant q_\alpha(L)) = E(F_L^{\leftarrow}(U); F_L^{\leftarrow}(U) \geqslant F_L^{\leftarrow}(\alpha)) = E(F_L^{\leftarrow}(U); U \geqslant \alpha);$$

in the last equality we used the fact that $F_L^{\leftarrow}$ is strictly increasing since F_L is continuous (see Proposition A.3(iii)). Thus we get $E(F_L^{\leftarrow}(U); U \geqslant \alpha) = \int_\alpha^1 F_L^{\leftarrow}(u)\,\mathrm{d}u$. The second representation follows since for a continuous loss distribution F_L we have $P(L \geqslant q_\alpha(L)) = 1 - \alpha$. □

Remark 2.17. For a discontinuous loss df F_L, formula (2.24) does not hold for all α; instead we have the more complicated expression

$$\mathrm{ES}_\alpha = \frac{1}{1-\alpha}(E(L; L \geqslant q_\alpha) + q_\alpha(1 - \alpha - P(L \geqslant q_\alpha))). \tag{2.25}$$

For a proof see Proposition 3.2 of Acerbi and Tasche (2002).

We use Lemma 2.16 to calculate the expected shortfall for two common continuous distributions.

Example 2.18 (expected shortfall for Gaussian loss distribution). Suppose that the loss distribution F_L is normal with mean μ and variance σ^2. Fix $\alpha \in (0,1)$. Then

$$\mathrm{ES}_\alpha = \mu + \sigma \frac{\phi(\Phi^{-1}(\alpha))}{1-\alpha}, \tag{2.26}$$

where ϕ is the density of the standard normal distribution. The proof is elementary. First note that

$$\mathrm{ES}_\alpha = \mu + \sigma E\left(\frac{L-\mu}{\sigma} \;\middle|\; \frac{L-\mu}{\sigma} \geqslant q_\alpha\left(\frac{L-\mu}{\sigma}\right)\right);$$

hence it suffices to compute the expected shortfall for the standard normal rv $\tilde{L} := (L-\mu)/\sigma$. Here we get

$$\mathrm{ES}_\alpha(\tilde{L}) = \frac{1}{1-\alpha}\int_{\Phi^{-1}(\alpha)}^{\infty} l\phi(l)\,\mathrm{d}l = \frac{1}{1-\alpha}[-\phi(l)]_{\Phi^{-1}(\alpha)}^{\infty} = \frac{\phi(\Phi^{-1}(\alpha))}{1-\alpha}.$$

Example 2.19 (expected shortfall for Student *t* loss distribution). Suppose the loss L is such that $\tilde{L} = (L-\mu)/\sigma$ has a standard t distribution with ν degrees of freedom, as in Example 2.14. Suppose further that $\nu > 1$. By the reasoning of Example 2.18, which applies to any location-scale family, we have $\mathrm{ES}_\alpha = \mu + \sigma\,\mathrm{ES}_\alpha(\tilde{L})$.

The expected shortfall of the standard t distribution is easily calculated by direct integration to be

$$\mathrm{ES}_\alpha(\tilde{L}) = \frac{g_\nu(t_\nu^{-1}(\alpha))}{1-\alpha}\left(\frac{\nu + (t_\nu^{-1}(\alpha))^2}{\nu - 1}\right), \tag{2.27}$$

where t_ν denotes the df and g_ν the density of standard t.

The following lemma gives a kind of law of large numbers for expected shortfall in terms of order statistics.

Lemma 2.20. *For a sequence $(L_i)_{i\in\mathbb{N}}$ of iid rvs with df F_L we have*

$$\lim_{n\to\infty} \frac{\sum_{i=1}^{[n(1-\alpha)]} L_{i,n}}{[n(1-\alpha)]} = \mathrm{ES}_\alpha \quad \text{a.s.}, \tag{2.28}$$

where $L_{1,n} \geqslant \cdots \geqslant L_{n,n}$ are the order statistics of $L_1, \dots, L_n$ and where $[n(1-\alpha)]$ denotes the largest integer not exceeding $n(1-\alpha)$.

In other words, expected shortfall at confidence level α can be thought of as the limiting average of the $[n(1-\alpha)]$ upper order statistics from a sample of size n from the loss distribution. This representation suggests an obvious way of estimating expected shortfall in the situation when we have large samples and $[n(1-\alpha)]$ is a relatively large number. This is generally not the case in practice, except perhaps when the Monte Carlo approach to risk estimation is used (see Section 2.3.3). A proof of Lemma 2.20 may be found in Proposition 4.1 of Acerbi and Tasche (2002).

Since ES_α can be thought of as an average over all losses that are greater than or equal to VaR_α, it is sensitive to the severity of losses exceeding VaR_α. This advantage of expected shortfall is illustrated in the following example.

Example 2.21 (VaR and ES for stock returns). We consider daily losses on a position in a particular stock; the current value of the position equals $V_t = 10\,000$. Recall from Example 2.4 that the loss for this portfolio is given by $L_{t+1}^{\Delta} = -V_t X_{t+1}$, where X_{t+1} represents daily log-returns of the stock. We assume that X_{t+1} has mean zero and standard deviation $\sigma = 0.2/\sqrt{250}$, i.e. we assume that the stock has an annualized volatility of 20%. We compare two different models for the distribution, namely (i) a normal distribution and (ii) a t distribution with $\nu = 4$ degrees of freedom scaled to have standard deviation σ. The t distribution is a symmetric distribution with heavy tails, so that large absolute values are much more probable than in the normal model; it is also a distribution that has been shown to fit well in many empirical studies (see Example 3.15). In Table 2.1 we present VaR_α and ES_α for both models and various values of α. In case (i) these values have been computed using (2.26); the expected shortfall for the t model has been computed using (2.27).

Most risk managers would argue that the t model is riskier than the normal model, since under the t distribution large losses are more likely. However, if we use VaR at the 95% or 97.5% confidence level to measure risk, the normal distribution appears to be at least as risky as the t model; only above a confidence level of 99% does the higher risk in the tails of the t model become apparent. On the other hand, if

Table 2.1. VaR_α and ES_α in normal and t model for different values of α.

α	0.90	0.95	0.975	0.99	0.995
VaR_α (normal model)	162.1	208.1	247.9	294.3	325.8
VaR_α (t model)	137.1	190.7	248.3	335.1	411.8
ES_α (normal model)	222.0	260.9	295.7	337.2	365.8
ES_α (t model)	223.4	286.3	356.7	465.8	563.5

we use expected shortfall, the risk in the tails of the t model is reflected in our risk measurement for lower values of α. Of course, simply going to a 99% confidence level in quoting VaR numbers does not help to overcome this deficiency of VaR, as there are other examples where the higher risk becomes apparent only for confidence levels beyond 99%.

Remark 2.22. It is possible to derive results on the asymptotics of the *shortfall-to-quantile ratio* $\mathrm{ES}_\alpha / \mathrm{VaR}_\alpha$ for $\alpha \to 1$. For the normal distribution we have $\lim_{\alpha\to 1} \mathrm{ES}_\alpha / \mathrm{VaR}_\alpha = 1$; for the t distribution with $\nu > 1$ degrees of freedom we have $\lim_{\alpha\to 1} \mathrm{ES}_\alpha / \mathrm{VaR}_\alpha = \nu/(\nu - 1) > 1$. This shows that for a heavy-tailed distribution the difference between ES and VaR is more pronounced than for the normal distribution. We will take up this issue in more detail in Section 7.2.3.

Notes and Comments

An extensive discussion of different approaches to risk quantification is given in Crouhy, Galai and Mark (2001). Value-at-Risk was introduced by JPMorgan in the first version of its RiskMetrics system and was quickly accepted by risk managers and regulators as industry standard. Expected shortfall was made popular by Artzner et al. (1997, 1999). In the latter paper an important axiomatic approach to risk measures was developed; we will discuss their work in Section 6.1. There are a number of variants on the expected shortfall risk measure with a variety of names, such as tail conditional expectation (TCE), worst conditional expectation (WCE) and conditional VaR (CVaR); all coincide for continuous loss distributions. Acerbi and Tasche (2002) discuss the relationships between the various notions. Risk measures based on loss distributions also appear in the literature under the (somewhat unfortunate) heading of *law-invariant* risk measures.

A class of risk measures very much in use throughout the hedge fund industry is based on the peak-to-bottom loss over a given period of time in the performance curve of an investment. These measures are typically referred to as (maximal) *drawdown* risk measures (see, for example, Chekhlov, Uryasev and Zabarankin 2005; Jaeger 2005).

The measurement of financial risk and the computation of actuarial premiums are at least conceptually closely related problems, so that the actuarial literature on premium principles is of relevance in financial risk management. We refer to Chapter 3 of Rolski et al. (1999) for an overview; Goovaerts, De Vylder and Haezendonck (1984) provide a specialist account.

Model risk has become a central issue in modern risk management. The essays collected in Gibson (2000) give a good overview of the academic research on this issue. The problems faced by the hedge fund LTCM in 1998 provide a prime example of model risk in VaR-based risk-management systems. While LTCM had a seemingly sophisticated VaR system in place, errors in parameter estimation, unexpectedly large market moves (heavy tails) and in particular vanishing market liquidity drove the hedge fund into near-bankruptcy, causing major financial turbulence around the globe. Jorion (2000) contains an excellent discussion of the LTCM case, in particular comparing a Gaussian-based VaR model with a t-based approach. At a more general level, Jorion (2002b) discusses the various fallacies surrounding VaR-based market risk management systems.

Most of the academic literature on liquidity focuses on the determinants of bid–ask spreads and/or transaction cost (see, for example, the survey by Stoll (2000)). Risk-management and hedging issues in illiquid markets have received relatively little attention: optimal strategies for unwinding a position in an illiquid market are discussed in Almgren and Chriss (2001); the hedging of derivatives in illiquid markets has been studied by Jarrow (1994), Frey (1998, 2000), Schönbucher and Wilmott (2000) and Bank and Baum (2004), among others.

2.3 Standard Methods for Market Risks

In the following sections we discuss some standard methods used in the financial industry for measuring market risk over short time intervals, such as a day or a fortnight. In the formal framework of Section 2.1.1 this amounts to the problem of estimating risk measures for the loss distribution of a loss $L_{t+1} = l_{[t]}(\boldsymbol{X}_{t+1})$, where $\boldsymbol{X}_{t+1}$ is the vector of risk-factor changes from time t to time $t+1$ and $l_{[t]}$ is the loss operator based on the portfolio at time t; the risk measures on which we concentrate are VaR (Definition 2.10) and expected shortfall (Definition 2.15). We recall from Section 2.1.2 that the issue of whether we base our risk measurement on the unconditional loss distribution of L_{t+1} or the conditional loss distribution based on information denoted by $\mathcal{F}_t$ is relevant. In presenting the standard methods we clarify which of these approaches is generally adopted.

2.3.1 Variance–Covariance Method

We present a generic version of this method which may be turned into an unconditional or conditional method by varying the procedure that is used to estimate certain key inputs. The risk-factor changes $\boldsymbol{X}_{t+1}$ are assumed to have a multivariate normal distribution (either unconditionally or conditionally) denoted by $\boldsymbol{X}_{t+1} \sim N_d(\boldsymbol{\mu}, \Sigma)$, where $\boldsymbol{\mu}$ is the mean vector and Σ the covariance (or variance–covariance) matrix of the distribution. The properties of the multivariate normal distribution are discussed in detail in Section 3.1.3.

We assume that the linearized loss in terms of the risk factors is a sufficiently accurate approximation of the actual loss and simplify the problem by considering the distribution of $L^{\Delta}_{t+1} = l^{\Delta}_{[t]}(\boldsymbol{X}_{t+1})$ with $l^{\Delta}_{[t]}$ defined in (2.6). The linearized loss operator will be a function with general structure

$$l^{\Delta}_{[t]}(\boldsymbol{x}) = -(c_t + \boldsymbol{b}_t'\boldsymbol{x}) \tag{2.29}$$

for some constant c_t and constant vector $\boldsymbol{b}_t$, which are known to us at time t. For a concrete example, consider the stock portfolio of Example 2.4 where the loss operator takes the form $l^{\Delta}_{[t]}(\boldsymbol{x}) = -V_t\boldsymbol{w}_t'\boldsymbol{x}$ and $\boldsymbol{w}_t$ is the vector of portfolio weights at time t.

An important property of the multivariate normal is that a linear function (2.29) of $\boldsymbol{X}_{t+1}$ must have a univariate normal distribution. From general rules on the mean and variance of linear combinations of a random vector we obtain that

$$L^{\Delta}_{t+1} = l^{\Delta}_{[t]}(\boldsymbol{X}_{t+1}) \sim N(-c_t - \boldsymbol{b}_t'\boldsymbol{\mu}, \boldsymbol{b}_t'\Sigma\boldsymbol{b}_t). \tag{2.30}$$

Value-at-Risk may be easily calculated for this loss distribution using (2.19) in Example 2.14. Expected shortfall may be calculated using (2.26) in Example 2.18.

To turn this into a practical procedure we require estimates of $\boldsymbol{\mu}$ and Σ based on historical risk-factor change data $\boldsymbol{X}_{t-n+1}, \dots, \boldsymbol{X}_t$. If we simply estimate $\boldsymbol{\mu}$ and Σ by calculating the sample mean vector and sample covariance matrix, then this amounts to an analysis of the *unconditional* loss distribution under the tacit assumption that the risk-factor change data come from a stationary process. The standard sample estimates of mean and covariance are reviewed in Section 3.1.2.

To obtain a *conditional* version of this method we treat the data as a realization of a multivariate time series and assume that $\boldsymbol{X}_{t+1} \mid \mathcal{F}_t \sim N_d(\boldsymbol{\mu}_{t+1}, \Sigma_{t+1})$, where $\boldsymbol{\mu}_{t+1}$ and Σ_{t+1} now denote the conditional mean and covariance matrix given information to time t. We obtain estimates of these moments for substitution in (2.30) by forecasting. This might involve the formal estimation of a time series model, such as a multivariate GARCH model, and the use of model-based prediction methods. Alternatively, a more informal forecasting technique, such as the *exponentially weighted moving-average* (EWMA) procedure popularized in JPMorgan's RiskMetrics, might be used. The use of these techniques is discussed in greater detail in Chapter 4.

Weaknesses of the method. The variance–covariance method offers a simple analytical solution to the risk-measurement problem but this convenience is achieved at the cost of two crude simplifying assumptions. First, linearization may not always offer a good approximation of the relationship between the true loss distribution and the risk-factor changes, as discussed at the end of Section 2.1.1. Second, the assumption of normality is unlikely to be realistic for the distribution of the risk-factor changes, certainly for daily data and probably also for weekly and even monthly data. A stylized fact of empirical finance suggests that the distribution of financial risk factor returns is leptokurtic and heavier-tailed than the Gaussian distribution. Later, in Example 3.3, we present evidence for this observation in an analysis of daily, weekly, monthly and quarterly stock returns. The implication is that an assumption of Gaussian risk factors will tend to underestimate the tail of the loss distribution and measures of risk, like VaR and expected shortfall, that are based on this tail.

This criticism also applies to the conditional version of the variance–covariance method. Even when we attempt an explicit time series modelling of the return data, analyses mostly suggest that the conditional distribution of risk-factor changes for the next time period, given information up to the present, is not multivariate Gaussian, but rather a distribution whose margins have heavier tails. Another way of putting this is to say that the *innovation distribution* of the time series model is generally heavier-tailed than normal (see Example 4.24).

Extensions of the method. The convenience of the method relies on the fact that a linear combination of a multivariate Gaussian vector has a univariate Gaussian distribution. However, there are other multivariate distribution families that are *closed under linear operations*, and variance-covariance methods can also be developed for these. Examples include multivariate t distributions and multivariate *generalized hyperbolic* distributions, which we describe in detail in Chapter 3.

For example, suppose we model risk-factor changes (either unconditionally or conditionally) with a multivariate t distribution denoted $\boldsymbol{X}_{t+1} \sim t_d(\nu, \boldsymbol{\mu}, \Sigma)$, where this notation is explained in Example 3.7 and Section 3.4. Then the analogous expression to (2.30) is

$$L^{\Delta}_{t+1} = l^{\Delta}_{[t]}(\boldsymbol{X}_{t+1}) \sim t(\nu, -c_t - \boldsymbol{b}_t'\boldsymbol{\mu}, \boldsymbol{b}_t'\tilde{\Sigma}\boldsymbol{b}_t), \qquad (2.31)$$

and risk measures can be calculated using (2.20) and (2.27).

2.3.2 Historical Simulation

Instead of estimating the distribution of $L = l_{[t]}(\boldsymbol{X}_{t+1})$ under some explicit parametric model for $\boldsymbol{X}_{t+1}$, the historical-simulation method can be thought of as estimating the distribution of the loss operator under the *empirical distribution* of data $\boldsymbol{X}_{t-n+1}, \dots, \boldsymbol{X}_t$. The method can be concisely described using the loss-operator notation; we construct a univariate dataset by applying the operator to each of our historical observations of the risk-factor change vector to get a set of historically simulated losses:

$$\{\tilde{L}_s = l_{[t]}(\boldsymbol{X}_s) : s = t - n + 1, \dots, t\}. \qquad (2.32)$$

The values $\tilde{L}_s$ show what would happen to the current portfolio if the risk-factor changes on day s were to recur. We make inference about the loss distribution and risk measures using these historically simulated loss data.

This is an unconditional method. If we assume that the process of risk-factor changes is stationary with df $F_{\boldsymbol{X}}$, then (subject to further technical conditions) the empirical df of the data is a consistent estimator of $F_{\boldsymbol{X}}$. Hence the empirical df of the data $\tilde{L}_{t-n+1}, \dots, \tilde{L}_t$ is a consistent estimator of the df of $l_{[t]}(\boldsymbol{X})$ under $F_{\boldsymbol{X}}$. More formally, an appropriate version of the strong law of large numbers for time series can be used to show that, as $n \to \infty$,

$$F_n(l) := \frac{1}{n} \sum_{s=t-n+1}^{t} I_{\{\tilde{L}_s \leqslant l\}} = \frac{1}{n} \sum_{s=t-n+1}^{t} I_{\{l_{[t]}(\boldsymbol{X}_s) \leqslant l\}}$$
$$\to P(l_{[t]}(\boldsymbol{X}) \leqslant l) = F_L(l),$$

where X is a generic vector of risk-factor changes with distribution F_X and $L := l_{[t]}(X)$.

In practice there are various ways we can use the historically simulated loss data. It is common to estimate VaR using the method of *empirical quantile estimation*, whereby theoretical quantiles of the loss distribution are estimated by sample quantiles of the data. If we denote the ordered values of the data in (2.32) by $\tilde{L}_{n,n} \leqslant \cdots \leqslant \tilde{L}_{1,n}$, one possible estimator of $\mathrm{VaR}_\alpha(L)$ is $\tilde{L}_{[n(1-\alpha)],n}$, where $[n(1-\alpha)]$ denotes the largest integer not exceeding $n(1-\alpha)$. For example, if $n = 1000$ and $\alpha = 0.99$, we would estimate the VaR by taking the 10th largest value. To estimate the associated expected shortfall an obvious empirical estimator following from the representation (2.28) would be the average of the 10 largest losses. As an alternative, particularly in situations where n is relatively modest in size, we could fit a parametric univariate distribution to the data (2.32) and calculate risk measures analytically from this distribution.

Strengths and weaknesses of the method. The historical-simulation method has obvious attractions: it is easy to implement and reduces the risk-measure estimation problem to a one-dimensional problem; no statistical estimation of the multivariate distribution of X is necessary, and no assumptions about the dependence structure of risk-factor changes are made.

However, the success of the approach is highly dependent on our ability to collect sufficient quantities of relevant, synchronized data for all risk factors. Whenever there are gaps in the risk-factor history, or whenever new risk factors are introduced into the modelling, there may be problems filling the gaps and completing the historical record. These problems will tend to reduce the effective value of n and mean that empirical estimates of VaR and expected shortfall have very poor accuracy. Ideally we want n to be fairly large since the method is an unconditional method and we want a number of extreme scenarios in the historical record to provide more informative estimates of the tail of the loss distribution. Indeed the method has been referred to as "driving a car while looking through the rear view mirror"; this obvious deficiency, which is shared by all purely statistical procedures, could be compensated for by adding historical extreme events to the available database or by formulating relevant extreme scenarios.

The fact that the method is an unconditional method could be seen as a further weakness; we have remarked in Section 2.1.2 that the conditional approach is generally considered to be the more relevant for day-to-day market risk management.

Extensions of the method. Simple empirical estimates of the VaR and especially the expected shortfall are likely to be inaccurate, particularly in situations where n is of modest size (say only a few years of daily data). Moreover, the approach of fitting parametric univariate distributions to the historically simulated losses may not result in models that provide a particularly good fit in the tail area where our risk-measure estimates are calculated. A possible solution to this problem is to use the techniques of *extreme value theory* (EVT) to provide estimates of the tail of the loss distribution that are as faithful as possible to the most extreme data and that use parametric forms that are supported by theory. In Chapter 7 we describe a standard EVT method based on the generalized Pareto distribution that is useful in this context.

It is possible to develop conditional approaches based on the basic template of historical simulation. One simple approach might be to model the historically simulated data in (2.32) with a univariate time series and to use this model to calculate conditional estimates for the loss $L_{t+1} = l_{[t]}(\boldsymbol{X}_{t+1})$. Formally speaking, this is not quite the conditional approach as we have previously defined it: we do not consider the conditional distribution of L_{t+1} conditional on $\mathcal{F}_t$, the sigma field generated by $(\boldsymbol{X}_s)_{s\leqslant t}$, but rather conditional on, say, $\mathcal{G}_t$, the sigma field generated by $(l_{[t]}(\boldsymbol{X}_s))_{s\leqslant t}$, which is a less rich information set. In practice, however, this simple method may often work well. See Notes and Comments for references to another conditional version of historical simulation.

2.3.3 *Monte Carlo*

The Monte Carlo method is a rather general name for any approach to risk measurement that involves the simulation of an explicit parametric model for risk-factor changes. As such, the method can be either conditional or unconditional depending on whether the model adopted is a dynamic time series model for risk-factor changes or a static distributional model.

The first step of the method is the choice of the model and the calibration of this model to historical risk-factor change data $\boldsymbol{X}_{t-n+1}, \dots, \boldsymbol{X}_t$. Obviously it should be a model from which we can readily simulate, since in the second stage we generate m independent realizations of risk-factor changes for the next time period, which we denote by $\tilde{\boldsymbol{X}}_{t+1}^{(1)}, \dots, \tilde{\boldsymbol{X}}_{t+1}^{(m)}$.

In a similar fashion to the historical-simulation method, we apply the loss operator to these simulated vectors to obtain simulated realizations $\{\tilde{L}_{t+1}^{(i)} = l_{[t]}(\tilde{\boldsymbol{X}}_{t+1}^{(i)}) : i = 1, \dots, m\}$ from the loss distribution. These simulated loss data are used to estimate risk measures; very often this is done by simple empirical quantile and shortfall estimation, as described above, but it would again be possible to base the inference on fitted univariate distributions or to use an extreme value model to model the tail of the simulated losses. Note that the use of Monte Carlo means that we are free to choose the number of replications m ourselves, within the obvious constraints of computation time. Generally m can be chosen to be much larger than n so that we obtain more accuracy in empirical VaR and expected shortfall estimates than is possible in the case of historical simulation.

Weaknesses of the method. The method does not solve the problem of finding a multivariate model for $\boldsymbol{X}_{t+1}$ and any results that are obtained will only be as good as the model that is used. In a market risk context a dynamic model seems desirable and some kind of GARCH structure with a heavy-tailed multivariate conditional distribution, such as multivariate t, might be considered. The models we describe in Section 4.6 provide possible candidates.

For large portfolios the computational cost of the Monte Carlo approach can be considerable, as every simulation requires the revaluation of the portfolio. This is particularly problematic if the portfolio contains many derivatives which cannot be priced in closed form. Variance-reduction techniques such as importance sampling can be of help here. We discuss the application of importance sampling in models for credit risk management in Section 8.5; further references on variance-reduction techniques are given in Notes and Comments.

2.3.4 Losses over Several Periods and Scaling

So far we have considered one-period loss distributions and associated risk measures. It is often the case that we would like to infer risk measures for the loss distribution over several periods from a model for single-period losses. For example, suppose that we work with a model for daily risk-factor changes which is set up to allow calculations of a daily VaR and expected shortfall. We might want to also obtain estimates of VaR and expected shortfall for the one-week or one-month loss distribution assuming that the portfolio is held constant throughout that time.

An obvious approach is to aggregate daily risk-factor change data in order to obtain risk-factor change data at a *lower frequency* and to make a one-period estimation using these data. Clearly, this results in a reduction in the number of data and necessitates a new analysis of the aggregated data. The former problem can be avoided by the formation of overlapping risk-factor returns (a construction that is described in Section 4.1) but this is not really recommended as it introduces new serial dependencies into the data that greatly complicate statistical modelling.

Scaling. It would be far more attractive if we had simple rules for transforming one-period risk measures into h-period risk measures for $h > 1$. Suppose we denote the loss from time t over the next h periods by $L^{(h)}_{t+h}$. Arguing as in (2.1) and (2.3) we have

$$\begin{aligned} L^{(h)}_{t+h} = -(V_{t+h} - V_t) &= -(f(t+h, \boldsymbol{Z}_{t+h}) - f(t, \boldsymbol{Z}_t)) \\ &= -(f(t+h, \boldsymbol{Z}_t + \boldsymbol{X}_{t+1} + \cdots + \boldsymbol{X}_{t+h}) - f(t, \boldsymbol{Z}_t)) \\ &=: l^{(h)}_{[t]}\biggl(\sum_{i=1}^{h} \boldsymbol{X}_{t+i}\biggr), \end{aligned}$$

where $l^{(h)}_{[t]}$ represents a loss operator at time t for the h-period loss. The general question of interest is how risk measures applied to the distribution of $L^{(h)}_{t+h}$ scale with h, and this has no simple answer except in special cases.

Note that the h-period loss operator differs from the one-period loss operator in situations where the mapping depends explicitly on time (such as derivative portfolios). For simplicity let us consider the case in which the mapping does not depend on calendar time, so that $l^{(h)}_{[t]}(\boldsymbol{x}) = l_{[t]}(\boldsymbol{x})$. The linearized form of this operator will be $l^{\Delta}_{[t]}(\boldsymbol{x}) = \boldsymbol{b}_t'\boldsymbol{x}$ for some vector $\boldsymbol{b}_t$ which is known at time t. We look at the simpler problem of scaling for risk measures applied to the linearized loss distribution:

$$L^{(h)\Delta}_{t+h} = l^{\Delta}_{[t]}\biggl(\sum_{i=1}^{h} \boldsymbol{X}_{t+i}\biggr) = \sum_{i=1}^{h} \boldsymbol{b}_t'\boldsymbol{X}_{t+i}. \tag{2.33}$$

The following example shows a special case where we do have a very simple scaling, known as the *square-root-of-time* rule.

Example 2.23 (square-root-of-time scaling). Suppose the risk-factor change vectors are iid with distribution $N_d(\mathbf{0}, \Sigma)$. Then $\sum_{i=1}^{h} \boldsymbol{X}_{t+i} \sim N_d(\mathbf{0}, h\Sigma)$ and the distribution of $L_{t+h}^{(h)\Delta}$ in (2.33) satisfies (both conditionally and unconditionally) $L_{t+h}^{(h)\Delta} \sim N(0, h\boldsymbol{b}_t' \Sigma \boldsymbol{b}_t)$. It then follows easily from (2.19) and (2.26) that both quantiles and expected shortfalls for this distribution scale according to the square root of time ($\sqrt{h}$). For example, writing $\mathrm{ES}_\alpha^{(h)}$ for the expected shortfall, we have

$$\mathrm{ES}_\alpha^{(h)} = \sqrt{h}\sigma \frac{\phi(\Phi^{-1}(\alpha))}{1-\alpha},$$

where $\sigma^2 = \boldsymbol{b}_t' \Sigma \boldsymbol{b}_t$. Clearly, $\mathrm{ES}_\alpha^{(h)} = \sqrt{h}\,\mathrm{ES}_\alpha^{(1)}$ and, with similar notation, $\mathrm{VaR}_\alpha^{(h)} = \sqrt{h}\,\mathrm{VaR}_\alpha^{(1)}$.

This scaling rule is quite commonly used in practice and is easily implemented in the context of the variance–covariance method. However, empirical risk-factor change data generally support neither a Gaussian distributional assumption nor an iid assumption. It is a stylized fact of empirical finance that, although financial risk-factor changes possess low serial correlation, they show patterns of changing volatility that are not consistent with an iid model (see Section 4.1). To obtain reasonable models for risk-factor change data we require dynamic time series models, such as models from the GARCH family. However, relatively little is known about the scaling of risk measures under such models. When considering the distribution of the h-period loss $L_{t+h}^{(h)}$ (or its linearized form) we have to be aware that the scaling of risk measures applied to this distribution will also depend on whether we consider the unconditional distribution or the conditional distribution given $\mathcal{F}_t$. Very little theory exists for either question but empirical studies suggest that the true scaling can be very different from square-root-of-time scaling (see Notes and Comments for more on this).

Monte Carlo approach. It is possible to use a Monte Carlo approach to the problem of determining risk measures for the h-period loss distribution. Suppose we have a model for risk-factor changes, either distributional or dynamic, depending on whether we are performing an unconditional or conditional analysis.

In the dynamic case we simulate future paths of the process $\tilde{\boldsymbol{X}}_{t+1}^{(j)}, \dots, \tilde{\boldsymbol{X}}_{t+h}^{(j)}$ for $j = 1, \dots, m$, where m is a predetermined large number of replications. (In the unconditional case we would simply simulate realizations from a multivariate distribution.) We then apply the h-period loss operator to these simulated data to obtain Monte Carlo simulated losses:

$$\{\tilde{L}_{t+h}^{(h)(i)} = l_{[t]}^{(h)}(\tilde{\boldsymbol{X}}_{t+1}^{(i)} + \cdots + \tilde{\boldsymbol{X}}_{t+h}^{(i)}) : i = 1, \dots, m\}.$$

These are used to make statistical inference about the loss distribution and associated risk measures, as described in Section 2.3.3.

2.3.5 Backtesting

In the preceding sections we have considered standard methods for estimating risk measures at a time t for the distribution of losses in the next period. When this procedure is continually implemented over time we have the opportunity to monitor the performance of methods and compare their relative performance. This process of monitoring is known as *backtesting*.

Suppose that at time t we make estimates of both VaR and expected shortfall for one period and h periods. We denote the true one-period risk measures by VaR_α^t and ES_α^t and the true h-period measures by $\mathrm{VaR}_\alpha^{t,h}$ and $\mathrm{ES}_\alpha^{t,h}$. These may be unconditional or conditional risk measures, but for the purposes of this section we leave this unspecified. At time $t+1$ we have the opportunity to compare our one-period estimates with what actually happened; at time $t+h$ we have the opportunity to do the same for the h-period estimates.

By definition of VaR (and assuming a continuous loss distribution) we have that $P(L_{t+h} > \mathrm{VaR}_\alpha^{t,h}) = 1-\alpha$ so that the probability of a so-called *violation* of VaR is $1-\alpha$. In practice the risk measures have to be estimated from data and we introduce an indicator notation for violations of the VaR estimates:

$$\hat{I}_{t+1} := I_{\{L_{t+1} > \widehat{\mathrm{VaR}}_\alpha^t\}}, \qquad \hat{I}_{t+h}^{(h)} := I_{\{L_{t+h}^{(h)} > \widehat{\mathrm{VaR}}_\alpha^{t,h}\}}. \tag{2.34}$$

We expect that if our estimation method is reasonable then these indicators should behave like Bernoulli random variables with success (i.e. violation) probability close to $(1-\alpha)$. If we conduct multiple comparisons of VaR predictions and corresponding realized losses, then we expect the proportion of occasions on which VaR is violated to be about $1-\alpha$.

In more specific situations we can say more. For example, if we form one-step-ahead estimates of a conditional one-period VaR using a dynamic approach, then we expect that the violation indicators $\hat{I}_t$ in (2.34) should behave like *iid* Bernoulli rvs with expectation $(1-\alpha)$; the number of violations over m time periods should be binomial with expected value $m(1-\alpha)$. This will be discussed in more detail in Section 4.4.3.

We would also like to be able to backtest the success of our expected shortfall estimation. Considering, for simplicity, the one-period expected shortfall estimate, it follows from Lemma 2.16 that for a continuous loss distribution the identity

$$E((L_{t+1} - \mathrm{ES}_\alpha^t) I_{\{L_{t+1} > \mathrm{VaR}_\alpha^t\}}) = 0$$

is satisfied. This suggests we look at the discrepancy $L_{t+1} - \widehat{\mathrm{ES}}_\alpha^t$ on days when the estimated VaR is violated. These should come from a distribution with mean zero. Under further modelling assumptions we look at this idea in more detail in Section 4.4.3.

2.3.6 An Illustrative Example

We conclude the chapter by giving an example that illustrates some of the ideas we have mentioned and which sets the scene for material presented in Chapters 3

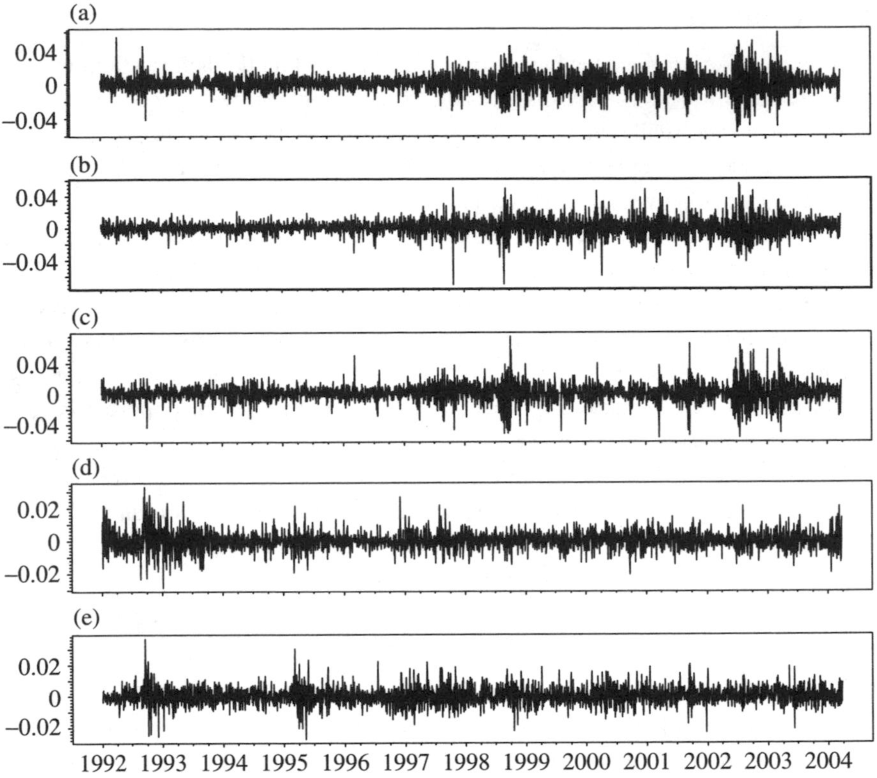

Figure 2.2. Time series of risk-factor changes. These are log-returns on (a) the FTSE 100, (b) the S&P 500 and (c) the SMI indexes, as well as log-returns for (d) the GBP/USD and (e) the GBP/CHF exchange rates for the period 1992–2003.

and 4. We consider the application of methods belonging to the general categories of variance–covariance and historical-simulation methods to the portfolio of an investor in international equity indexes. The investor is assumed to have domestic currency sterling (GBP) and to invest in the Financial Times 100 Shares Index (FTSE 100), the Standard & Poor's 500 (S&P 500) and the Swiss Market Index (SMI). The investor thus has currency exposure to US dollars (USD) and Swiss francs (CHF) and the value of the portfolio is influenced by five risk factors (three log index values and two log exchange rates). The corresponding risk-factor return time series for the period 1992–2003 are shown in Figure 2.2.

On any day t we standardize the total portfolio value V_t in sterling to be one and consider that the portfolio weights (the proportions of this total value invested in each of the indexes FTSE 100, S&P 500, SMI) are 30%, 40% and 30%, respectively. Using similar reasoning to that in Example 2.4, it may be verified that the loss operator is

$$l_{[t]}(\boldsymbol{x}) = 1 - (0.3\mathrm{e}^{x_1} + 0.4\mathrm{e}^{x_2+x_4} + 0.3\mathrm{e}^{x_3+x_5}),$$

and its linearized version is

$$l^{\Delta}_{[t]}(\boldsymbol{x}) = -(0.3x_1 + 0.4(x_2 + x_4) + 0.3(x_3 + x_5)),$$

where x_1, x_2 and x_3 represent log-returns on the three indexes and x_4 and x_5 are log-returns on the GBP/USD and GBP/CHF exchange rates.

Our objective is to calculate VaR estimates at the 95% and 99% levels for all trading days in the period 1996–2003. Where local public holidays take place in individual markets (e.g. the Fourth of July in the US) we record artificial zero returns for the market in question, thus preserving around 260 days of risk-factor return data in each year. We use the last 1000 days of historical data $\boldsymbol{X}_{t-999}, \dots, \boldsymbol{X}_t$ to make all VaR estimates for day $t+1$ with the following methods.

VC. The standard unconditional variance–covariance method assuming multivariate Gaussian risk-factor changes as described in Section 2.3.1.

HS. The standard unconditional historical simulation method as described in Section 2.3.2.

VC-*t*. An unconditional variance–covariance method in which a multivariate t distribution is fitted to the risk-factor change data (see Chapter 3, and Sections 3.2.4 and 3.2.5 in particular).

HS-GARCH. A conditional version of the historical simulation method in which GARCH(1, 1) models with a constant conditional mean term and Gaussian innovations are fitted to the historically simulated losses to estimate the volatility of the next day's loss (see Chapter 4, and Section 4.4.2 in particular).

VC-MGARCH. A conditional version of the variance–covariance method in which a multivariate GARCH model (a first-order constant conditional correlation model) with multivariate normal innovations is used to estimate the conditional covariance matrix of the next day's risk-factor changes (see Chapter 4, and Section 4.6 in particular).

HS-EWMA. A conditional method, similar to HS-GARCH, in which the EWMA method rather than a GARCH model is used to estimate volatility (see Sections 4.4.1 and 4.4.2).

VC-EWMA. A similar method to VC-MGARCH but a multivariate version of the EWMA method is used to estimate the conditional covariance matrix of the next day's risk-factor changes (see Section 4.6.6).

HS-GARCH-*t*. A similar method to HS-GARCH but Student t innovations are assumed in the GARCH model.

VC-MGARCH-*t*. A similar method to VC-MGARCH but multivariate t innovations are used in the MGARCH model.

HS-CONDEVT. A conditional method using a combination of GARCH modelling and EVT (extreme value theory) (see Section 7.2.6).

This collection of methods is of course far from complete and is merely meant as an indication of the kinds of strategies that are possible. In particular, we have confined our interest to rather simple GARCH models and not added, for example, asymmetric innovation distributions or leverage effects (see Section 4.3.3), which can often further improve the performance of such methods.

Table 2.2. Numbers of violations of the 95% and 99% VaR estimate calculated using various methods, as described in Section 2.3.6. The error column shows for each method the average absolute discrepancy per year between observed and expected numbers of violations.

Year	1996	1997	1998	1999	2000	2001	2002	2003	
Trading days	261	260	259	260	259	260	260	260	error
Results for 95% VaR									
Expected no. of violations	13	13	13	13	13	13	13	13	
VC	13	30	29	15	13	20	27	6	7.88
HS	14	30	31	16	14	20	26	8	8.12
VC-t	14	32	35	19	16	23	29	8	10.25
HS-GARCH	15	17	15	15	14	21	19	11	3.38
VC-MGARCH	16	19	19	15	15	21	21	12	4.50
HS-EWMA	16	14	15	15	17	23	18	11	3.62
VC-EWMA	15	13	15	14	18	22	17	9	3.38
HS-GARCH-t	16	18	16	15	15	21	19	12	3.75
VC-MGARCH-t	18	19	19	17	16	23	21	11	5.50
HS-CONDEVT	14	16	15	15	14	18	18	10	2.75
Results for 99% VaR									
Expected no. of violations	2.6	2.6	2.6	2.6	2.6	2.6	2.6	2.6	
VC	5	11	20	5	2	6	12	2	5.58
HS	3	10	13	3	2	3	7	1	3.20
VC-t	3	11	15	4	2	4	9	1	4.08
HS-GARCH	10	7	7	6	5	4	5	3	3.27
VC-MGARCH	8	8	7	6	3	5	7	4	3.40
HS-EWMA	9	5	6	6	6	6	3	2	2.92
VC-EWMA	9	5	6	6	5	5	3	3	2.65
HS-GARCH-t	7	5	5	5	4	3	4	2	1.93
VC-MGARCH-t	7	5	6	4	2	1	4	1	2.10
HS-CONDEVT	5	4	5	5	2	2	3	2	1.35

From the results collected in Table 2.2 we conclude that the three unconditional methods (VC, HS and VC-t) are generally outperformed by the conditional methods. In particular, the years 1997, 1998 and 2002 are handled poorly by the unconditional methods and give rise to too many violations of the 95% and 99% VaR estimates. Historical simulation is preferred to variance–covariance at the 99% level but gives a poor performance compared with variance–covariance at the 95% level. Basing the unconditional variance–covariance method on a multivariate t distribution gives an improvement at the 99% level but actually makes things worse at the 95% level.

The simple univariate GARCH procedures using the historically simulated data work quite well; t innovations are preferred to Gaussian innovations at the 99% level. The simpler method of volatility estimation using EWMA competes well with

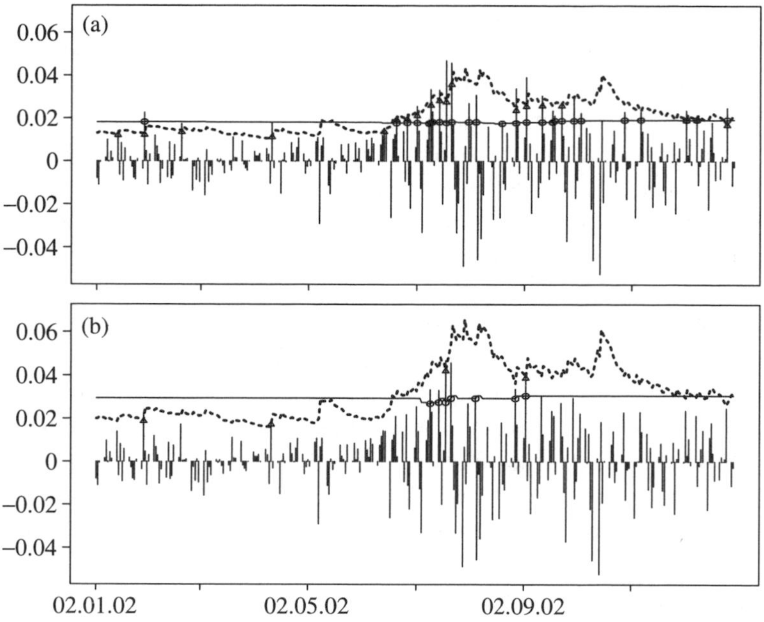

Figure 2.3. Daily losses for 2002 together with risk-measure estimates ((a) 95% VaR estimates, (b) 99% VaR estimates) and violations for the HS and HS-GARCH-t methods. The HS VaR estimates are indicated by a solid line and violations are indicated by circles; the HS-GARCH-t estimates are given by a dotted line with triangles for violations. For more information see Section 2.3.6.

the full GARCH estimation. The best method of all is HS-CONDEVT, combining extreme value theory with GARCH modelling. The multivariate GARCH procedures do not offer any improvement on the univariate procedures in this particular example.

In Figure 2.3 we have singled out the year 2002 and shown actual losses together with risk-measure estimates and violations for two of the methods: HS and HS-GARCH-t. In this volatile year, the standard historical-simulation method did not perform well: there are 26 violations of the 95% VaR estimate and 7 violations of the 99% VaR estimate, or about twice as many as would be expected. The HS-GARCH-t method, being a conditional method, is able to respond to the changes in volatility throughout 2002 and consequently gives 19 and 4 violations; this is still a few more than expected at the 95% level but is a good performance at the 99% level.

Notes and Comments

Standard methods for market risk are described in detail in Jorion (2001) and Crouhy, Galai and Mark (2001). For the variance–covariance approach, particularly in a dynamic form using EWMA, see Mina and Xiao (2001).

Another conditional version of historical simulation is used by Hull and White (1998) and Barone-Adesi, Bourgoin and Giannopoulos (1998). To describe this method succinctly we anticipate some of the notation used in Section 4.6. Suppose that we consider a simple model of risk-factor changes of the form $\boldsymbol{X}_t = \Delta_t \boldsymbol{Z}_t$, where Δ_t is a diagonal matrix containing so-called volatilities and the $\boldsymbol{Z}_t$ are iid vectors of innovations. We would like to apply historical simulation to the innovations but these are unobserved. Univariate time series models (typically GARCH models) are applied to each time series of risk-factor changes; this effectively gives us estimates of the volatility matrices $\{\hat{\Delta}_s : s = t - n + 1, \dots, t\}$ and allows us to make a prediction $\hat{\Delta}_{t+1}$ of the volatility matrix in the next time period. We then construct *residuals* $\{\hat{\boldsymbol{Z}}_s = \hat{\Delta}_s^{-1} \boldsymbol{X}_s : s = t - n + 1, \dots, t\}$, which are treated like observations of the unobserved innovations. To make statistical inference about the distribution of $L_{t+1} = l_{[t]}(\boldsymbol{X}_{t+1}) = l_{[t]}(\Delta_{t+1} \boldsymbol{Z}_{t+1})$ given $\mathcal{F}_t$ we use the historical-simulation data $\{l_{[t]}(\hat{\Delta}_{t+1} \hat{\boldsymbol{Z}}_s) : s = t - n + 1, \dots, t\}$.

The book by Glasserman (2003a) is an excellent general introduction to simulation techniques in finance. Glasserman, Heidelberger and Shahabuddin (1999) present efficient numerical techniques (based on delta–gamma approximations and advanced simulation techniques) for computing VaR for derivative portfolios in the presence of heavy-tailed risk factors.

A useful summary of scaling results for market risk measures may be found in Kaufmann (2004) (see also Brummelhuis and Kaufmann 2004; Embrechts, Kaufmann and Patie 2005). In these papers the message emerges that, for unconditional VaR scaling over longer time horizons, the square-root-of-time rule often works well. On the other hand, for conditional VaR scaling over short time horizons, McNeil and Frey (2000) present evidence against square-root-of-time scaling. For further comments on these and further scaling issues, see Diebold et al. (1998) and Daníelsson and de Vries (1997c). Literature on backtesting is given in the Notes and Comments section of Section 4.4.

3
Multivariate Models

Financial risk models, whether for market or credit risks, are inherently multivariate. The value change of a portfolio of traded instruments over a fixed time horizon depends on a random vector of risk-factor changes or returns. The loss incurred by a credit portfolio depends on a random vector of losses for the individual counterparties in the portfolio. In this chapter we consider some models for random vectors that are particularly useful for financial data. We do this from a *static*, distributional point of view without considering time series aspects, which are introduced later in Chapter 4.

A stochastic model for a random vector can be thought of as simultaneously providing probabilistic descriptions of the behaviour of the components of the random vector and of their *dependence or correlation structure*. The issue of modelling dependent risk factors is by no means straightforward, particularly when we move away from the multivariate normal distribution and simple generalizations thereof. We provide a more in-depth discussion of some of the subtler issues surrounding dependence in Chapter 5, where we introduce the subject of copulas.

The first section of this chapter reviews basic ideas in multivariate statistics and discusses the multivariate normal (or Gaussian) distribution and its deficiencies as a model for empirical return data.

In Section 3.2 we consider a generalization of the multivariate normal distribution known as a *multivariate normal mixture* distribution, which shares much of the structure of the multivariate normal and retains many of its properties. We treat both variance mixtures, which belong to the wider class of elliptical distributions, and mean-variance mixtures, which allow asymmetry. Concrete examples include t distributions and generalized hyperbolic distributions and we show in empirical examples that these models provide a better fit than a Gaussian distribution to asset return data. In some cases multivariate return data are not strongly asymmetric and models from the class of *elliptical distributions* are good enough; in Section 3.3 we review the elegant properties of these distributions.

In the final section we discuss the important issue of dimension reduction techniques for reducing large sets of risk factors to smaller subsets of essential risk drivers. The key idea here is that of a *factor model*, and we also review the *principal components* method of constructing factors.

3.1 Basics of Multivariate Modelling

This first section reviews important basic material from multivariate statistics, which will be known to many readers. The main topic of the section is the multivariate normal distribution and its properties; this distribution is central to much of classical multivariate analysis and was the starting point for attempts to model market risk (the variance–covariance method of Section 2.3.1).

3.1.1 Random Vectors and Their Distributions

Joint and marginal distributions. Consider a general d-dimensional random vector of risk-factor changes (or so-called returns) $\boldsymbol{X} = (X_1, \dots, X_d)'$. The distribution of $\boldsymbol{X}$ is completely described by the joint distribution function (df)

$$F_{\boldsymbol{X}}(\boldsymbol{x}) = F_{\boldsymbol{X}}(x_1, \dots, x_d) = P(\boldsymbol{X} \leqslant \boldsymbol{x}) = P(X_1 \leqslant x_1, \dots, X_d \leqslant x_d).$$

Where no ambiguity arises we simply write F, omitting the subscript.

The *marginal* distribution function of X_i, written F_{X_i} or often simply F_i, is the df of that risk factor considered individually and is easily calculated from the joint df. For all i we have

$$F_i(x_i) = P(X_i \leqslant x_i) = F(\infty, \dots, \infty, x_i, \infty, \dots, \infty). \tag{3.1}$$

If the marginal df $F_i(x)$ is absolutely continuous, then we refer to its derivative $f_i(x)$ as the marginal density of X_i. It is also possible to define k-dimensional marginal distributions of $\boldsymbol{X}$ for $2 \leqslant k \leqslant d-1$. Suppose we partition $\boldsymbol{X}$ into $(\boldsymbol{X}_1', \boldsymbol{X}_2')'$, where $\boldsymbol{X}_1 = (X_1, \dots, X_k)'$ and $\boldsymbol{X}_2 = (X_{k+1}, \dots, X_d)'$, then the marginal distribution function of $\boldsymbol{X}_1$ is

$$F_{\boldsymbol{X}_1}(\boldsymbol{x}_1) = P(\boldsymbol{X}_1 \leqslant \boldsymbol{x}_1) = F(x_1, \dots, x_k, \infty, \dots, \infty).$$

For bivariate and other low-dimensional margins it is convenient to have a simpler alternative notation in which, for example, $F_{ij}(x_i, x_j)$ stands for the marginal distribution of the components X_i and X_j.

The df of a random vector $\boldsymbol{X}$ is said to be absolutely continuous if

$$F(x_1, \dots, x_d) = \int_{-\infty}^{x_1} \cdots \int_{-\infty}^{x_d} f(u_1, \dots, u_d)\, \mathrm{d}u_1 \cdots \mathrm{d}u_d$$

for some non-negative function f, which is then known as the *joint density* of $\boldsymbol{X}$. Note that the existence of a joint density implies the existence of marginal densities for all k-dimensional marginals. However, the existence of a joint density is not necessarily implied by the existence of marginal densities (counterexamples can be found in Chapter 5 on copulas).

In some situations it is convenient to work with the *survival function* of $\boldsymbol{X}$ defined by

$$\bar{F}_{\boldsymbol{X}}(\boldsymbol{x}) = \bar{F}_{\boldsymbol{X}}(x_1, \dots, x_d) = P(\boldsymbol{X} > \boldsymbol{x}) = P(X_1 > x_1, \dots, X_d > x_d),$$

and written simply as $\bar{F}$ when no ambiguity arises. The marginal survival function of X_i, written $\bar{F}_{X_i}$ or often simply $\bar{F}_i$, is given by

$$\bar{F}_i(x_i) = P(X_i > x_i) = \bar{F}(-\infty, \dots, -\infty, x_i, -\infty, \dots, -\infty).$$

Conditional distributions and independence. If we have a multivariate model for risks in the form of a joint df, survival function or density, then we have implicitly described their *dependence structure*. We can make conditional probability statements about the probability that certain components take certain values given that other components take other values. For example, consider again our partition of $\boldsymbol{X}$ into $(\boldsymbol{X}_1', \boldsymbol{X}_2')'$ and assume absolute continuity of the df of $\boldsymbol{X}$. Let $f_{\boldsymbol{X}_1}$ denote the joint density of the k-dimensional marginal distribution $F_{\boldsymbol{X}_1}$. Then the conditional distribution of $\boldsymbol{X}_2$ given $\boldsymbol{X}_1 = \boldsymbol{x}_1$ has density

$$f_{\boldsymbol{X}_2|\boldsymbol{X}_1}(\boldsymbol{x}_2 \mid \boldsymbol{x}_1) = \frac{f(\boldsymbol{x}_1, \boldsymbol{x}_2)}{f_{\boldsymbol{X}_1}(\boldsymbol{x}_1)}, \tag{3.2}$$

and the corresponding df is

$$F_{\boldsymbol{X}_2|\boldsymbol{X}_1}(\boldsymbol{x}_2 \mid \boldsymbol{x}_1) = \int_{u_{k+1}=-\infty}^{x_{k+1}} \cdots \int_{u_d=-\infty}^{x_d} \frac{f(x_1, \dots, x_k, u_{k+1}, \dots, u_d)}{f_{\boldsymbol{X}_1}(\boldsymbol{x}_1)} \, du_{k+1} \cdots du_d.$$

If the joint density of $\boldsymbol{X}$ factorizes into $f(\boldsymbol{x}) = f_{\boldsymbol{X}_1}(\boldsymbol{x}_1) f_{\boldsymbol{X}_2}(\boldsymbol{x}_2)$, then the conditional distribution and density of $\boldsymbol{X}_2$ given $\boldsymbol{X}_1 = \boldsymbol{x}_1$ are identical to the marginal distribution and density of $\boldsymbol{X}_2$: in other words, $\boldsymbol{X}_1$ and $\boldsymbol{X}_2$ are independent. We recall that $\boldsymbol{X}_1$ and $\boldsymbol{X}_2$ are independent if and only if

$$F(\boldsymbol{x}) = F_{\boldsymbol{X}_1}(\boldsymbol{x}_1) F_{\boldsymbol{X}_2}(\boldsymbol{x}_2), \quad \forall \boldsymbol{x},$$

or, in the case where $\boldsymbol{X}$ possesses a joint density, $f(\boldsymbol{x}) = f_{\boldsymbol{X}_1}(\boldsymbol{x}_1) f_{\boldsymbol{X}_2}(\boldsymbol{x}_2)$.

The components of $\boldsymbol{X}$ are *mutually* independent if and only if $F(\boldsymbol{x}) = \prod_{i=1}^d F_i(x_i)$ for all $\boldsymbol{x} \in \mathbb{R}^d$ or, in the case where $\boldsymbol{X}$ possesses a density, $f(\boldsymbol{x}) = \prod_{i=1}^d f_i(x_i)$.

Moments and characteristic function. The *mean vector* of $\boldsymbol{X}$, when it exists, is given by

$$E(\boldsymbol{X}) := (E(X_1), \dots, E(X_d))'.$$

The *covariance matrix*, when it exists, is the matrix $\operatorname{cov}(\boldsymbol{X})$ defined by

$$\operatorname{cov}(\boldsymbol{X}) := E((\boldsymbol{X} - E(\boldsymbol{X}))(\boldsymbol{X} - E(\boldsymbol{X}))'),$$

where the expectation operator acts componentwise on matrices. If we write Σ for $\operatorname{cov}(\boldsymbol{X})$, then the (i, j)th element of this matrix is

$$\sigma_{ij} = \operatorname{cov}(X_i, X_j) = E(X_i X_j) - E(X_i)E(X_j),$$

the ordinary pairwise covariance between X_i and X_j. The diagonal elements $\sigma_{11}, \dots, \sigma_{dd}$ are the variances of the components of $\boldsymbol{X}$.

The *correlation matrix* of $\boldsymbol{X}$, denoted by $\rho(\boldsymbol{X})$, can be defined by introducing a standardized vector $\boldsymbol{Y}$ such that $Y_i = X_i / \sqrt{\operatorname{var}(X_i)}$ for all i and taking $\rho(\boldsymbol{X}) := \operatorname{cov}(\boldsymbol{Y})$. If we write P for $\rho(\boldsymbol{X})$, then the (i, j)th element of this matrix is

$$\rho_{ij} = \rho(X_i, X_j) = \frac{\operatorname{cov}(X_i, X_j)}{\sqrt{\operatorname{var}(X_i) \operatorname{var}(X_j)}}, \tag{3.3}$$

the ordinary pairwise linear correlation of X_i and X_j. To express the relationship between correlation and covariance matrices in matrix form it is useful to introduce operators on a covariance matrix Σ as follows:

$$\Delta(\Sigma) := \text{diag}(\sqrt{\sigma_{11}}, \dots, \sqrt{\sigma_{dd}}), \tag{3.4}$$

$$\wp(\Sigma) := (\Delta(\Sigma))^{-1}\Sigma(\Delta(\Sigma))^{-1}. \tag{3.5}$$

Thus $\Delta(\Sigma)$ extracts from Σ a diagonal matrix of standard deviations, and $\wp(\Sigma)$ extracts a correlation matrix. The covariance and correlation matrices Σ and P of $\boldsymbol{X}$ are related by

$$P = \wp(\Sigma). \tag{3.6}$$

Mean vectors and covariance matrices are manipulated extremely easily under linear operations on the vector $\boldsymbol{X}$. For any matrix $B \in \mathbb{R}^{k\times d}$ and vector $\boldsymbol{b} \in \mathbb{R}^k$ we have

$$E(B\boldsymbol{X} + \boldsymbol{b}) = BE(\boldsymbol{X}) + \boldsymbol{b}, \tag{3.7}$$

$$\text{cov}(B\boldsymbol{X} + \boldsymbol{b}) = B\,\text{cov}(\boldsymbol{X})B'. \tag{3.8}$$

Covariance matrices (and hence correlation matrices) are therefore *positive semi-definite*; writing Σ for $\text{cov}(\boldsymbol{X})$ we see that (3.8) implies that $\text{var}(\boldsymbol{a}'\boldsymbol{X}) = \boldsymbol{a}'\Sigma\boldsymbol{a} \geqslant 0$ for any $\boldsymbol{a} \in \mathbb{R}^d$. If we have that $\boldsymbol{a}'\Sigma\boldsymbol{a} > 0$ for any $\boldsymbol{a} \in \mathbb{R}^d \setminus \{\boldsymbol{0}\}$, we say that Σ is *positive definite*; in this case the matrix is invertible. We will make use of the well-known *Cholesky factorization* of positive-definite covariance matrices at many points; it is well known that such a matrix can be written as $\Sigma = AA'$ for a lower triangular matrix A with positive diagonal elements. The matrix A is known as the Cholesky factor. It will be convenient to denote this factor by $\Sigma^{1/2}$ and its inverse by $\Sigma^{-1/2}$. Note that there are other ways of defining the "square root" of a symmetric, positive-definite matrix (such as the symmetric decomposition) but we will always use $\Sigma^{1/2}$ to denote the Cholesky factor.

In this chapter many properties of the multivariate distribution of a vector $\boldsymbol{X}$ are demonstrated using the characteristic function, which is given by

$$\phi_{\boldsymbol{X}}(\boldsymbol{t}) = E(\exp(\mathrm{i}\boldsymbol{t}'\boldsymbol{X})) = E(\mathrm{e}^{\mathrm{i}\boldsymbol{t}'\boldsymbol{X}}), \quad \boldsymbol{t} \in \mathbb{R}^d.$$

3.1.2 Standard Estimators of Covariance and Correlation

Suppose we have n observations of a d-dimensional risk-factor return vector denoted $\boldsymbol{X}_1, \dots, \boldsymbol{X}_n$. Typically, these would be daily, weekly, monthly or yearly observations forming a multivariate time series. We will assume throughout this chapter that the observations are *identically distributed* in the window of observation and either independent or at least serially *uncorrelated* (also known as a multivariate white noise). As we discuss in Chapter 4, the assumption of independence may be roughly tenable for longer time intervals such as months or years. For shorter time intervals independence may be a less appropriate assumption (due to a phenomenon known as volatility clustering, discussed in Chapter 4) but serial correlation of returns is often quite weak.

We assume that the observations $\boldsymbol{X}_1, \dots, \boldsymbol{X}_n$ come from a distribution with mean vector $\boldsymbol{\mu}$, finite covariance matrix Σ and correlation matrix P. We now briefly review the standard estimators of these vector and matrix parameters.

Standard method-of-moments estimators of $\boldsymbol{\mu}$ and Σ are given by the *sample mean vector* $\bar{\boldsymbol{X}}$ and the *sample covariance matrix* S. These are defined by

$$\bar{\boldsymbol{X}} := \frac{1}{n}\sum_{i=1}^{n} \boldsymbol{X}_i, \qquad S := \frac{1}{n}\sum_{i=1}^{n}(\boldsymbol{X}_i - \bar{\boldsymbol{X}})(\boldsymbol{X}_i - \bar{\boldsymbol{X}})', \tag{3.9}$$

where arithmetic operations on vectors and matrices are performed componentwise. $\bar{\boldsymbol{X}}$ is an unbiased estimator but S is biased; an unbiased version may be obtained by taking $S_u := nS/(n-1)$, as may be seen by calculating

$$\begin{aligned} nE(S) &= E\bigg(\sum_{i=1}^{n}(\boldsymbol{X}_i - \boldsymbol{\mu})(\boldsymbol{X}_i - \boldsymbol{\mu})' - n(\bar{\boldsymbol{X}} - \boldsymbol{\mu})(\bar{\boldsymbol{X}} - \boldsymbol{\mu})'\bigg) \\ &= \sum_{i=1}^{n}\operatorname{cov}(\boldsymbol{X}_i) - n\operatorname{cov}(\bar{\boldsymbol{X}}) = n\Sigma - \Sigma, \end{aligned}$$

since $\operatorname{cov}(\bar{\boldsymbol{X}}) = n^{-1}\Sigma$ when the data vectors are iid, or identically distributed and uncorrelated.

The *sample correlation matrix* R may be easily calculated from the sample covariance matrix; its (j, k)th element is given by $r_{jk} = s_{jk}/\sqrt{s_{jj}s_{kk}}$, where s_{jk} denotes the (j, k)th element of S. Or, using the notation introduced in (3.5), we have

$$R = \wp(S),$$

which is the analogous equation to (3.6) for estimators.

Further properties of the estimators $\bar{\boldsymbol{X}}$, S and R will depend very much on the *true multivariate distribution* of the observations. These quantities are not necessarily the best estimators of the corresponding theoretical quantities in all situations. This point is often forgotten in financial risk management, where sample covariance and correlation matrices are routinely calculated and interpreted with little critical consideration of underlying models.

If our data $\boldsymbol{X}_1, \dots, \boldsymbol{X}_n$ are iid multivariate normal, then $\bar{\boldsymbol{X}}$ and S are the *maximum likelihood estimators* (MLEs) of the mean vector $\boldsymbol{\mu}$ and covariance matrix Σ. Their behaviour as estimators is well understood and statistical inference for the model parameters is described in all standard texts on multivariate analysis.

However, the multivariate normal is certainly not a good description of financial risk factor returns over short time intervals, such as daily data, and is often not good over longer time intervals either. Under these circumstances the behaviour of the standard estimators in (3.9) is often less well understood and other estimators of the true mean vector $\boldsymbol{\mu}$ and covariance matrix Σ may perform better in terms of *efficiency* and *robustness*. Roughly speaking, by a more efficient estimator we mean an estimator with a smaller expected estimation error; by a more robust estimator we mean an estimator whose performance is not so susceptible to the presence of outlying data values.

3.1.3 The Multivariate Normal Distribution

Definition 3.1. $X = (X_1, \dots, X_d)'$ has a multivariate normal or *Gaussian* distribution if

$$X \stackrel{\mathrm{d}}{=} \boldsymbol{\mu} + A\boldsymbol{Z},$$

where $\boldsymbol{Z} = (Z_1, \dots, Z_k)'$ is a vector of iid univariate *standard* normal rvs (mean zero and variance one), and $A \in \mathbb{R}^{d \times k}$ and $\boldsymbol{\mu} \in \mathbb{R}^d$ are a matrix and a vector of constants, respectively.

It is easy to verify, using (3.7) and (3.8), that the mean vector of this distribution is $E(\boldsymbol{X}) = \boldsymbol{\mu}$ and the covariance matrix is $\operatorname{cov}(\boldsymbol{X}) = \Sigma$, where $\Sigma = AA'$ is a positive semidefinite matrix. Moreover, using the fact that the characteristic function of a standard univariate normal variate Z is $\phi_Z(t) = \exp(-\frac{1}{2}t^2)$, the characteristic function of $\boldsymbol{X}$ may be calculated to be

$$\phi_X(\boldsymbol{t}) = E(\exp(\mathrm{i}\boldsymbol{t}'\boldsymbol{X})) = \exp(\mathrm{i}\boldsymbol{t}'\boldsymbol{\mu} - \tfrac{1}{2}\boldsymbol{t}'\Sigma\boldsymbol{t}), \quad \boldsymbol{t} \in \mathbb{R}^d. \tag{3.10}$$

Clearly, the distribution is characterized by its mean vector and covariance matrix, and hence a standard notation is $\boldsymbol{X} \sim N_d(\boldsymbol{\mu}, \Sigma)$. Note that the components of $\boldsymbol{X}$ are mutually independent if and only if Σ is diagonal. For example, $\boldsymbol{X} \sim N_d(\boldsymbol{0}, I_d)$ if and only if $X_1, \dots, X_d$ are iid $N(0, 1)$, the standard univariate normal distribution.

We concentrate on the *non-singular case* of the multivariate normal when $\operatorname{rank}(A) = d \leqslant k$. In this case the covariance matrix Σ has full rank d and is therefore invertible (non-singular) and positive definite. Moreover, $\boldsymbol{X}$ has an absolutely continuous distribution function with joint density given by

$$f(\boldsymbol{x}) = \frac{1}{(2\pi)^{d/2}|\Sigma|^{1/2}} \exp\{-\tfrac{1}{2}(\boldsymbol{x} - \boldsymbol{\mu})'\Sigma^{-1}(\boldsymbol{x} - \boldsymbol{\mu})\}, \quad \boldsymbol{x} \in \mathbb{R}^d, \tag{3.11}$$

where $|\Sigma|$ denotes the determinant of Σ.

The form of the density clearly shows that points with equal density lie on *ellipsoids* determined by equations of the form $(\boldsymbol{x} - \boldsymbol{\mu})'\Sigma^{-1}(\boldsymbol{x} - \boldsymbol{\mu}) = c$, for constants $c > 0$. In two dimensions the contours of equal density are ellipses, as illustrated in Figure 3.1. Whenever a multivariate density $f(\boldsymbol{x})$ depends on $\boldsymbol{x}$ only through the quadratic form $(\boldsymbol{x} - \boldsymbol{\mu})'\Sigma^{-1}(\boldsymbol{x} - \boldsymbol{\mu})$, it is the density of a so-called elliptical distribution, as discussed in more detail in Section 3.3.

Definition 3.1 is essentially a simulation recipe for the multivariate normal distribution. To be explicit, if we wished to generate a vector $\boldsymbol{X}$ with distribution $N_d(\boldsymbol{\mu}, \Sigma)$, where Σ is positive definite, we would use the following algorithm.

Algorithm 3.2 (simulation of multivariate normal distribution).

(1) Perform a Cholesky decomposition of Σ (see, for example, Press et al. 1992) to obtain the Cholesky factor $\Sigma^{1/2}$.

(2) Generate a vector $\boldsymbol{Z} = (Z_1, \dots, Z_d)'$ of independent standard normal variates.

(3) Set $\boldsymbol{X} = \boldsymbol{\mu} + \Sigma^{1/2}\boldsymbol{Z}$.

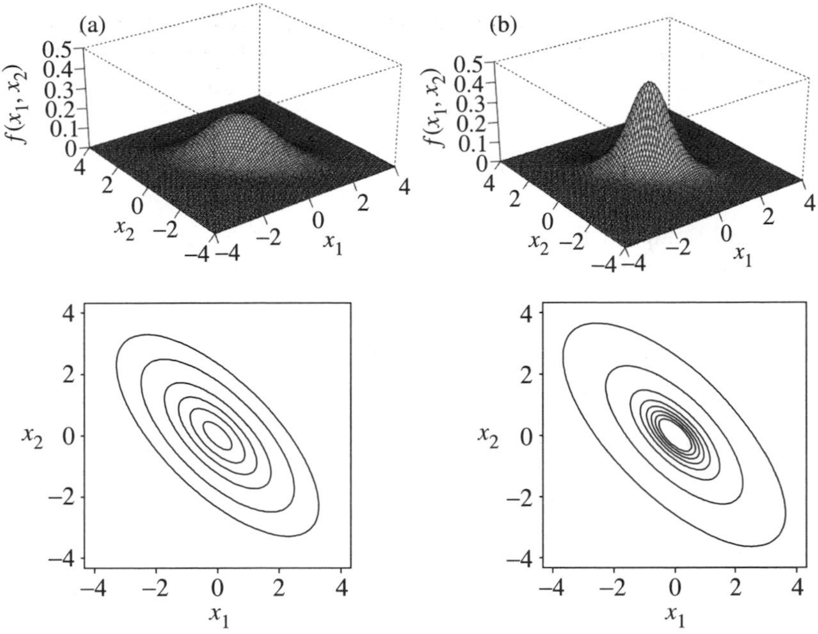

Figure 3.1. (a) Perspective and contour plots for the density of a bivariate normal distribution with standard normal margins and correlation −70%. (b) Corresponding plots for a bivariate t density with four degrees of freedom (see Example 3.7 for details) and the *same mean vector and covariance matrix* as the normal distribution. Contour lines are plotted at the same heights for both densities.

We now summarize further useful properties of the multivariate normal. These properties underline the attractiveness of the multivariate normal for computational work in risk management. Note, however, that many of them are in fact shared by the broader classes of normal mixture distributions and elliptical distributions (see Section 3.3.3 for properties of the latter).

Linear combinations. If we take linear combinations of multivariate normal random vectors, then these remain multivariate normal. Let $\boldsymbol{X} \sim N_d(\boldsymbol{\mu}, \Sigma)$ and take any $B \in \mathbb{R}^{k \times d}$ and $\boldsymbol{b} \in \mathbb{R}^k$. Then it is easily shown, for example using the characteristic function (3.10), that

$$B\boldsymbol{X} + \boldsymbol{b} \sim N_k(B\boldsymbol{\mu} + b, B\Sigma B'). \tag{3.12}$$

As a special case, if $\boldsymbol{a} \in \mathbb{R}^d$, then

$$\boldsymbol{a}'\boldsymbol{X} \sim N(\boldsymbol{a}'\boldsymbol{\mu}, \boldsymbol{a}'\Sigma\boldsymbol{a}), \tag{3.13}$$

and this fact is used routinely in the variance–covariance approach to risk management, as discussed in Section 2.3.1.

In this context it is interesting to note the following elegant characterization of multivariate normality. It is easily shown using characteristic functions that $\boldsymbol{X}$ is multivariate normal *if and only if* $\boldsymbol{a}'\boldsymbol{X}$ is univariate normal for all vectors $\boldsymbol{a} \in \mathbb{R}^d \setminus \{\boldsymbol{0}\}$.

Marginal distributions. It is clear from (3.13) that the univariate marginal distributions of $\boldsymbol{X}$ must be univariate normal. More generally, using the $\boldsymbol{X} = (\boldsymbol{X}_1', \boldsymbol{X}_2')'$ notation from Section 3.1.1 and extending this notation naturally to $\boldsymbol{\mu}$ and Σ,

$$\boldsymbol{\mu} = \begin{pmatrix} \boldsymbol{\mu}_1 \\ \boldsymbol{\mu}_2 \end{pmatrix}, \qquad \Sigma = \begin{pmatrix} \Sigma_{11} & \Sigma_{12} \\ \Sigma_{21} & \Sigma_{22} \end{pmatrix},$$

property (3.12) implies that the marginal distributions of $\boldsymbol{X}_1$ and $\boldsymbol{X}_2$ are also multivariate normal and are given by $\boldsymbol{X}_1 \sim N_k(\boldsymbol{\mu}_1, \Sigma_{11})$ and $\boldsymbol{X}_2 \sim N_{d-k}(\boldsymbol{\mu}_2, \Sigma_{22})$.

Conditional distributions. Assuming that Σ is positive definite, the conditional distributions of $\boldsymbol{X}_2$ given $\boldsymbol{X}_1$ and of $\boldsymbol{X}_1$ given $\boldsymbol{X}_2$ may also be shown to be multivariate normal. For example, $\boldsymbol{X}_2 \mid \boldsymbol{X}_1 = \boldsymbol{x}_1 \sim N_{d-k}(\boldsymbol{\mu}_{2.1}, \Sigma_{22.1})$, where

$$\boldsymbol{\mu}_{2.1} = \boldsymbol{\mu}_2 + \Sigma_{21}\Sigma_{11}^{-1}(\boldsymbol{x}_1 - \boldsymbol{\mu}_1) \quad \text{and} \quad \Sigma_{22.1} = \Sigma_{22} - \Sigma_{21}\Sigma_{11}^{-1}\Sigma_{12}$$

are the conditional mean vector and covariance matrix.

Quadratic forms. If $\boldsymbol{X} \sim N_d(\boldsymbol{\mu}, \Sigma)$ with Σ positive definite, then

$$(\boldsymbol{X} - \boldsymbol{\mu})'\Sigma^{-1}(\boldsymbol{X} - \boldsymbol{\mu}) \sim \chi_d^2, \tag{3.14}$$

a chi-squared distribution with d degrees of freedom. This is seen by observing that $\boldsymbol{Z} = \Sigma^{-1/2}(\boldsymbol{X} - \boldsymbol{\mu}) \sim N_d(\boldsymbol{0}, I_d)$ and $(\boldsymbol{X} - \boldsymbol{\mu})'\Sigma^{-1}(\boldsymbol{X} - \boldsymbol{\mu}) = \boldsymbol{Z}'\boldsymbol{Z} \sim \chi_d^2$. This property (3.14) is useful for checking multivariate normality (see Section 3.1.4).

Convolutions. If $\boldsymbol{X}$ and $\boldsymbol{Y}$ are independent d-dimensional random vectors satisfying $\boldsymbol{X} \sim N_d(\boldsymbol{\mu}, \Sigma)$ and $\boldsymbol{Y} \sim N_d(\tilde{\boldsymbol{\mu}}, \tilde{\Sigma})$, then we may take the product of characteristic functions to show that $\boldsymbol{X} + \boldsymbol{Y} \sim N_d(\boldsymbol{\mu} + \tilde{\boldsymbol{\mu}}, \Sigma + \tilde{\Sigma})$.

3.1.4 Testing Normality and Multivariate Normality

We now consider the issue of testing whether the data $\boldsymbol{X}_1, \dots, \boldsymbol{X}_n$ are observations from a multivariate normal distribution.

Univariate tests. If $\boldsymbol{X}_1, \dots, \boldsymbol{X}_n$ are iid multivariate normal, then for $1 \leqslant j \leqslant d$ the univariate sample $X_{1,j}, \dots, X_{n,j}$ consisting of the observations of the jth component must be iid univariate normal; in fact any univariate sample constructed from a linear combination of the data of the form $\boldsymbol{a}'\boldsymbol{X}_1, \dots, \boldsymbol{a}'\boldsymbol{X}_n$ must be iid univariate normal. This can be assessed graphically with a QQplot against a standard normal reference distribution or tested formally using one of the countless numerical tests of normality. A QQplot (quantile–quantile plot) is a standard visual tool for showing the relationship between empirical quantiles of the data and theoretical quantiles of a reference distribution, with a lack of linearity showing evidence against the hypothesized reference distribution. In Figure 3.2 we show a QQplot of daily returns of the Disney share price from 1993 to 2000 against a normal reference distribution; the inverted "S-shaped" curve of the points suggests that the empirical quantiles of the data tend to be larger than the corresponding quantiles of a normal distribution, indicating that the normal distribution is a poor model for these returns.

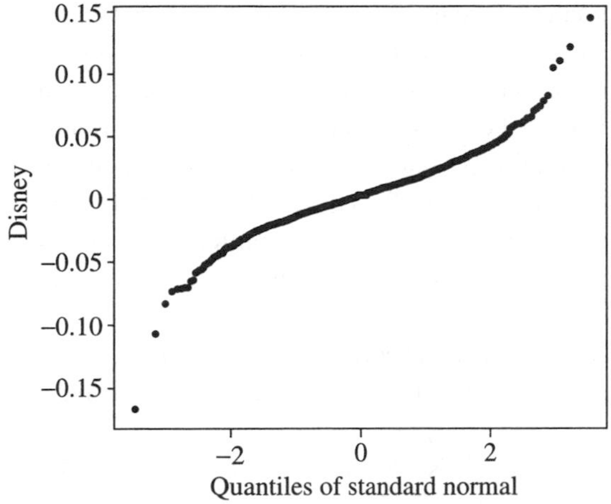

Figure 3.2. QQplot of daily returns of the Disney share price from 1993 to 2000 against a normal reference distribution (see also Example 3.3).

Particularly useful numerical tests include those of Jarque and Bera, Anderson and Darling, Shapiro and Wilk, and D'Agostino. The Jarque–Bera test belongs to the class of omnibus moment tests, i.e. tests which assess simultaneously whether the *skewness* and *kurtosis* of the data are consistent with a Gaussian model. The sample skewness and kurtosis coefficients of a univariate sample $Z_1, \dots, Z_n$ are defined by

$$\sqrt{b} = \frac{(1/n)\sum_{i=1}^n (Z_i - \bar{Z})^3}{((1/n)\sum_{i=1}^n (Z_i - \bar{Z})^2)^{3/2}}, \qquad k = \frac{(1/n)\sum_{i=1}^n (Z_i - \bar{Z})^4}{((1/n)\sum_{i=1}^n (Z_i - \bar{Z})^2)^2}. \tag{3.15}$$

These are designed to estimate the theoretical skewness and kurtosis, which are defined, respectively, by $\sqrt{\beta} = E(Z-\mu)^3/\sigma^3$ and $\kappa = E(Z-\mu)^4/\sigma^4$, where $\mu = E(Z)$ and $\sigma^2 = \text{var}(Z)$ denote mean and variance; $\sqrt{\beta}$ and κ take the values zero and three for a normal variate Z. The Jarque–Bera test statistic is

$$T = \tfrac{1}{6}n(b + \tfrac{1}{4}(k-3)^2)$$

and has an asymptotic chi-squared distribution with two degrees of freedom under the null hypothesis of normality; sample kurtosis values differing widely from three and skewness values differing widely from zero may lead to rejection of normality.

Multivariate tests. To test for multivariate normality it is not sufficient to test that the univariate margins of the distribution are normal. We will see in Chapter 5 that it is possible to have multivariate distributions with normal margins that are not themselves multivariate normal distributions. Thus we also need to be able to test *joint normality* and a simple way of doing this is to exploit the fact that the quadratic form in (3.14) has a chi-squared distribution. Suppose we estimate $\boldsymbol{\mu}$ and Σ using the standard estimators in (3.9) and construct the data

$$\{D_i^2 = (\boldsymbol{X}_i - \bar{\boldsymbol{X}})' S^{-1} (\boldsymbol{X}_i - \bar{\boldsymbol{X}}) : i = 1, \dots, n\}. \tag{3.16}$$

Because the estimates of the mean vector and the covariance matrix are used in the construction of each D_i^2, these data are not independent, even if the original $\boldsymbol{X}_i$ data were. Moreover, the marginal distribution of D_i^2 under the null hypothesis is not exactly chi-squared; we have in fact that $n(n-1)^{-2}D_i^2 \sim \text{Beta}(\frac{1}{2}d, \frac{1}{2}(n-d-1))$, so that the true distribution is a scaled beta distribution, although it turns out to be very close to chi-squared for large n. We expect $D_1^2, \dots, D_n^2$ to behave roughly like an iid sample from a χ_d^2 distribution and for simplicity we construct QQplots against this distribution. (It is also possible to make QQplots against the beta reference distribution and these look very similar.)

Numerical tests of multivariate normality based on multivariate measures of skewness and kurtosis are also possible. Suppose we define, in analogy to (3.15),

$$b_d = \frac{1}{n^2}\sum_{i=1}^{n}\sum_{j=1}^{n} D_{ij}^3, \qquad k_d = \frac{1}{n}\sum_{i=1}^{n} D_i^4, \tag{3.17}$$

where D_i is given in (3.16) and is known as the *Mahalanobis distance* between $\boldsymbol{X}_i$ and $\bar{\boldsymbol{X}}$, and $D_{ij} = (\boldsymbol{X}_i - \bar{\boldsymbol{X}})S^{-1}(\boldsymbol{X}_j - \bar{\boldsymbol{X}})$ is known as the *Mahalanobis angle* between $\boldsymbol{X}_i - \bar{\boldsymbol{X}}$ and $\boldsymbol{X}_j - \bar{\boldsymbol{X}}$. These measures in fact reduce to the univariate measures b and k in the case $d = 1$. Under the null hypothesis of multivariate normality the asymptotic distributions of these statistics as $n \to \infty$ are

$$\tfrac{1}{6}nb_d \sim \chi^2_{d(d+1)(d+2)/6}, \qquad \frac{k_d - d(d+2)}{\sqrt{8d(d+2)/n}} \sim N(0,1). \tag{3.18}$$

Mardia's test of multinormality involves comparing the skewness and kurtosis statistics with the above theoretical reference distributions. Since large values of the statistics cast doubt on the multivariate normal model, one-sided tests are generally performed. Usually the tests of kurtosis and skewness are performed separately, although there are also a number of joint (or so-called omnibus) tests (see Notes and Comments).

Example 3.3 (on the normality of returns on Dow Jones 30 stocks). We applied tests of normality to an arbitrary subgroup of 10 of the stocks comprising the Dow Jones index (see Table 3.1 for the stock codes and Table 4.1 for names). We took eight years of data spanning the period 1993–2000 and formed daily, weekly, monthly and quarterly logarithmic returns. For each stock we calculated sample skewness and kurtosis and applied the Jarque–Bera test to the univariate time series. The daily and weekly return data fail all tests; in particular, it is notable that there are some large values for the sample kurtosis. For the monthly data, the null hypothesis of normality is not formally rejected (p-value greater than 0.05) for four of the stocks; for quarterly data it is not rejected for five of the stocks, although here the sample size is small.

We applied Mardia's tests of multinormality based on both multivariate skewness and kurtosis to the multivariate data for all 10 stocks. The results are shown in Table 3.2. We also compared the D_i^2 data (3.16) to a χ_{10}^2-distribution using a QQplot (see Figure 3.3).

Table 3.1. Sample skewness ($\sqrt{b}$) and kurtosis (k) coefficients as well as p-values for Jarque–Bera tests of normality for an arbitrary set of 10 of the Dow Jones 30 stocks (see Example 3.3 for details).

Stock	$\sqrt{b}$	k	p-value	$\sqrt{b}$	k	p-value
	Daily returns, $n = 2020$			Weekly returns, $n = 416$		
AXP	0.05	5.09	0.00	−0.01	3.91	0.00
EK	−1.93	31.20	0.00	−1.13	14.40	0.00
BA	−0.34	10.89	0.00	−0.26	7.54	0.00
C	0.21	5.93	0.00	0.44	5.42	0.00
KO	−0.02	6.36	0.00	−0.21	4.37	0.00
MSFT	−0.22	8.04	0.00	−0.14	5.25	0.00
HWP	−0.23	6.69	0.00	−0.26	4.66	0.00
INTC	−0.56	8.29	0.00	−0.65	5.20	0.00
JPM	0.14	5.25	0.00	−0.20	4.93	0.00
DIS	−0.01	9.39	0.00	0.08	4.48	0.00
	Monthly returns, $n = 96$			Quarterly returns, $n = 32$		
AXP	−1.22	5.99	0.00	−1.04	4.88	0.01
EK	−1.52	10.37	0.00	−0.63	4.49	0.08
BA	−0.50	4.15	0.01	−0.15	6.23	0.00
C	−1.10	7.38	0.00	−1.61	7.13	0.00
KO	−0.49	3.68	0.06	−1.45	5.21	0.00
MSFT	−0.40	3.90	0.06	−0.56	2.90	0.43
HWP	−0.33	3.47	0.27	−0.38	3.64	0.52
INTC	−1.04	6.50	0.00	−0.42	3.10	0.62
JPM	−0.51	5.40	0.00	−0.78	7.26	0.00
DIS	0.04	3.26	0.87	−0.49	4.32	0.16

Table 3.2. Mardia's tests of multivariate normality based on the multivariate measures of skewness and kurtosis in (3.17) and the asymptotic distributions in (3.18) (see Example 3.3 for details).

n	Daily 2020	Weekly 416	Monthly 96	Quarterly 32
b_{10}	9.31	9.91	21.10	50.10
p-value	0.00	0.00	0.00	0.02
k_{10}	242.45	177.04	142.65	120.83
p-value	0.00	0.00	0.00	0.44

The daily, weekly and monthly return data fail the multivariate tests of normality. For quarterly return data the multivariate kurtosis test does not reject the null hypothesis, but the skewness test does; the QQplot in Figure 3.3(d) looks slightly more linear. Thus there is some evidence that returns over a quarter year are close to being normally distributed, which might indicate a central limit theorem effect taking

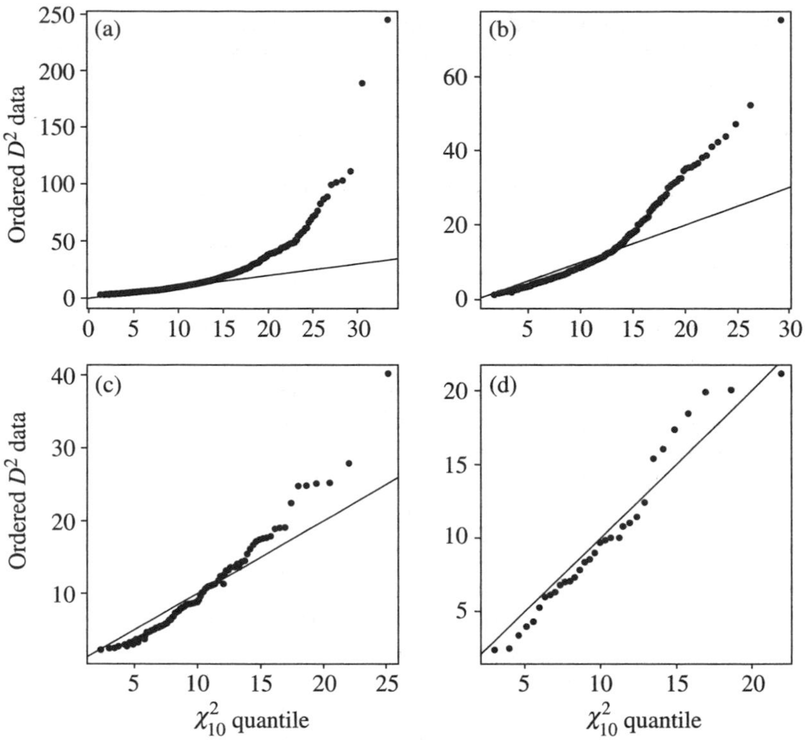

Figure 3.3. QQplot of the D_i^2 data in (3.16) against a χ^2_{10} distribution for the datasets of Example 3.3: (a) daily analysis; (b) weekly analysis; (c) monthly analysis; and (d) quarterly analysis. Under the null hypothesis of *multivariate* normality these should be roughly linear.

place, although the sample size is too small to reach any more reliable conclusion. The evidence against the multivariate normal distribution is certainly overwhelming for daily, weekly and monthly data.

The results in Example 3.3 are fairly typical for financial return data. This suggests that in many risk-management applications the multivariate normal distribution is not a good description of reality. It has three main defects that we will discuss at various points in this book.

(1) The tails of its univariate marginal distributions are too thin; they do not assign enough weight to *extreme* events.

(2) The joint tails of the distribution do not assign enough weight to *joint extreme* outcomes.

(3) The distribution has a strong form of symmetry, known as elliptical symmetry.

In the next section we look at models that address some of these defects. We consider normal variance mixture models, which share the elliptical symmetry of the multivariate normal, but have the flexibility to address (1) and (2) above; we also look at normal mean-variance mixture models, which introduce some asymmetry and thus address (3).

Notes and Comments

Much of the material covered briefly in Section 3.1 can be found in greater detail in standard texts on multivariate statistical analysis such as Mardia, Kent and Bibby (1979), Seber (1984), Giri (1996) or Johnson and Wichern (2002).

There are countless possible tests of univariate normality and a good starting point is the entry on "departures from normality, tests for" in volume 2 of the Encyclopedia of Statistics (Kotz, Johnson and Read 1985). For an introduction to QQplots see Rice (1995, pp. 353–357); for the widely applied Jarque–Bera test based on the sample skewness and kurtosis, see Jarque and Bera (1987).

The true distribution of $D_i^2 = (\boldsymbol{X}_i - \bar{\boldsymbol{X}})S^{-1}(\boldsymbol{X}_i - \bar{\boldsymbol{X}})$ for iid Gaussian data was shown by Gnanadesikan and Kettenring (1972) to be a scaled beta distribution (see also Gnanadesikan 1997). The implications of this fact for the construction of QQplots in small samples are considered by Small (1978). References for multivariate measures of skewness and kurtosis and Mardia's test of multinormality are Mardia (1970, 1974, 1975). See also Mardia, Kent and Bibby (1979), the entry on "multivariate normality, testing for" in volume 6 of the Encyclopedia of Statistics (Kotz, Johnson and Read 1985), and the entry on "Mardia's test of multinormality" in volume 5 of the same publication.

3.2 Normal Mixture Distributions

In this section we generalize the multivariate normal to obtain multivariate normal mixture distributions. The crucial idea is the introduction of randomness into first the covariance matrix and then the mean vector of a multivariate normal distribution via a positive mixing variable, which will be known throughout as W.

3.2.1 Normal Variance Mixtures

Definition 3.4. The random vector $\boldsymbol{X}$ is said to have a (multivariate) normal variance mixture distribution if

$$\boldsymbol{X} \stackrel{\mathrm{d}}{=} \boldsymbol{\mu} + \sqrt{W} A \boldsymbol{Z}, \tag{3.19}$$

where

(i) $\boldsymbol{Z} \sim N_k(\boldsymbol{0}, I_k)$;

(ii) $W \geqslant 0$ is a non-negative, scalar-valued rv which is independent of $\boldsymbol{Z}$, and

(iii) $A \in \mathbb{R}^{d \times k}$ and $\boldsymbol{\mu} \in \mathbb{R}^d$ are a matrix and vector of constants, respectively.

Such distributions are known as variance mixtures, since if we condition on the rv W we observe that $\boldsymbol{X} \mid W = w \sim N_d(\boldsymbol{\mu}, w\Sigma)$, where $\Sigma = AA'$. The distribution of $\boldsymbol{X}$ can be thought of as a composite distribution constructed by taking a set of multivariate normal distributions with the same mean vector and with the same covariance matrix up to a multiplicative constant w. The mixture distribution is constructed by drawing randomly from this set of component multivariate normals according to a set of "weights" determined by the distribution of W; the resulting mixture is not itself a multivariate normal distribution. In the context of modelling risk-factor returns, the mixing variable W could be interpreted as a *shock* that arises from new information and impacts the volatilities of all stocks.

As for the multivariate normal, we are most interested in the case where $\operatorname{rank}(A) = d \leqslant k$ and Σ is a full-rank, positive-definite matrix; this will give us a non-singular normal variance mixture.

Provided that W has a finite expectation, we may easily calculate that

$$E(\boldsymbol{X}) = E(\boldsymbol{\mu} + \sqrt{W}A\boldsymbol{Z}) = \boldsymbol{\mu} + E(\sqrt{W})AE(\boldsymbol{Z}) = \boldsymbol{\mu}$$

and that

$$\operatorname{cov}(\boldsymbol{X}) = E((\sqrt{W}A\boldsymbol{Z})(\sqrt{W}A\boldsymbol{Z})') = E(W)AE(\boldsymbol{Z}\boldsymbol{Z}')A' = E(W)\Sigma. \quad (3.20)$$

We refer to $\boldsymbol{\mu}$ and Σ in general as the *location vector* and the *dispersion matrix* of the distribution. Note that Σ (the covariance matrix of $A\boldsymbol{Z}$) is only the covariance matrix of $\boldsymbol{X}$ if $E(W) = 1$ and that $\boldsymbol{\mu}$ is only the mean vector when $E(\boldsymbol{X})$ is defined, which requires $E(W^{1/2}) < \infty$. The correlation matrices of $\boldsymbol{X}$ and $\boldsymbol{Z}$ are the same when $E(W) < \infty$. Note also that these distributions provide good examples of models where a lack of correlation does not necessarily imply independence of the components of $\boldsymbol{X}$; indeed we have the following simple result.

Lemma 3.5. *Let (X_1, X_2) have a normal mixture distribution with $A = I_2$ and $E(W) < \infty$ so that $\operatorname{cov}(X_1, X_2) = 0$. Then X_1 and X_2 are independent if and only if W is almost surely constant, i.e. (X_1, X_2) are normally distributed.*

Proof. We calculate that

$$\begin{aligned} E(|X_1||X_2|) &= E(W|Z_1||Z_2|) = E(W)E(|Z_1|)E(|Z_2|) \\ &\geqslant (E(\sqrt{W}))^2 E(|Z_1|)E(|Z_2|) = E(|X_1|)E(|X_2|), \end{aligned}$$

with equality throughout only when W is a constant. □

Using (3.10), we can calculate that the characteristic function of a normal variance mixture is given by

$$\begin{aligned} \phi_{\boldsymbol{X}}(\boldsymbol{t}) = E(E(\exp(\mathrm{i}\boldsymbol{t}'\boldsymbol{X}) \mid W)) &= E(\exp(\mathrm{i}\boldsymbol{t}'\boldsymbol{\mu} - \tfrac{1}{2}W\boldsymbol{t}'\Sigma\boldsymbol{t})) \\ &= \exp(\mathrm{i}\boldsymbol{t}'\boldsymbol{\mu})\hat{H}(\tfrac{1}{2}\boldsymbol{t}'\Sigma\boldsymbol{t}). \end{aligned} \quad (3.21)$$

where $\hat{H}(\theta) = \int_0^\infty \mathrm{e}^{-\theta v}\,\mathrm{d}H(v)$ is the Laplace–Stieltjes transform of the df H of W. Based on (3.21) we use the notation $\boldsymbol{X} \sim M_d(\boldsymbol{\mu}, \Sigma, \hat{H})$ for normal variance mixtures.

Assuming that Σ is positive definite and that the distribution of W has no point mass at zero, we may derive the joint density of a normal variance mixture distribution. Writing $f_{\boldsymbol{X}|W}$ for the (Gaussian) conditional density of $\boldsymbol{X}$ given W, the density of $\boldsymbol{X}$ is given by

$$\begin{aligned} f(\boldsymbol{x}) &= \int f_{\boldsymbol{X}|W}(\boldsymbol{x} \mid w)\,\mathrm{d}H(w) \\ &= \int \frac{w^{-d/2}}{(2\pi)^{d/2}|\Sigma|^{1/2}} \exp\left\{-\frac{(\boldsymbol{x}-\boldsymbol{\mu})'\Sigma^{-1}(\boldsymbol{x}-\boldsymbol{\mu})}{2w}\right\}\mathrm{d}H(w), \end{aligned} \quad (3.22)$$

in terms of the Lebesgue–Stieltjes integral; when H has density h we simply mean the Riemann integral $\int_0^\infty f_{X|W}(\boldsymbol{x} \mid w)h(w)\,dw$. All such densities will depend on $\boldsymbol{x}$ only through the quadratic form $(\boldsymbol{x}-\boldsymbol{\mu})'\Sigma^{-1}(\boldsymbol{x}-\boldsymbol{\mu})$ and this means they are the densities of elliptical distributions, as will be discussed in Section 3.3.

Example 3.6 (multivariate two-point normal mixture distribution). Simple examples of normal mixtures are obtained when W is a discrete rv. For example, the two-point normal mixture model is obtained by taking W in (3.19) to be a discrete rv which assumes the distinct positive values k_1 and k_2 with probabilities p and $1-p$, respectively. By setting k_2 large relative to k_1 and choosing p large, this distribution might be used to define two regimes: an *ordinary* regime that holds most of the time and a *stress* regime that occurs with small probability $1-p$. Obviously this idea extends to k-point mixture models.

Example 3.7 (multivariate *t* distribution). If we take W in (3.19) to be an rv with an inverse gamma distribution $W \sim \mathrm{Ig}(\frac{1}{2}\nu, \frac{1}{2}\nu)$ (which is equivalent to saying that $\nu/W \sim \chi^2_\nu$), then $\boldsymbol{X}$ has a multivariate t distribution with ν degrees of freedom (see Section A.2.6 for more details concerning the inverse gamma distribution). Our notation for the multivariate t is $\boldsymbol{X} \sim t_d(\nu, \boldsymbol{\mu}, \Sigma)$ and we note that Σ is not the covariance matrix of $\boldsymbol{X}$ in this definition of the multivariate t. Since $E(W) = \nu/(\nu-2)$ we have $\mathrm{cov}(\boldsymbol{X}) = (\nu/(\nu-2))\Sigma$ and the covariance matrix (and correlation matrix) of this distribution are only defined if $\nu > 2$.

Using (3.22), the density can be calculated to be

$$f(\boldsymbol{x}) = \frac{\Gamma(\frac{1}{2}(\nu+d))}{\Gamma(\frac{1}{2}\nu)(\pi\nu)^{d/2}|\Sigma|^{1/2}}\left(1+\frac{(\boldsymbol{x}-\boldsymbol{\mu})'\Sigma^{-1}(\boldsymbol{x}-\boldsymbol{\mu})}{\nu}\right)^{-(\nu+d)/2}. \qquad (3.23)$$

Clearly, the locus of points with equal density is again an ellipsoid with equation $(\boldsymbol{x}-\boldsymbol{\mu})'\Sigma^{-1}(\boldsymbol{x}-\boldsymbol{\mu}) = c$, for some $c > 0$. A bivariate example with four degrees of freedom is given in Figure 3.1. In comparison with the multivariate normal the contours of equal density rise more quickly in the centre of the distribution and decay more gradually on the "lower slopes" of the distribution. We will see later that, in comparison with the multivariate normal, the multivariate t has heavier marginal tails (Chapter 7) and a more pronounced tendency to generate simultaneous extreme values (Section 5.3.1).

Example 3.8 (symmetric generalized hyperbolic distribution). A flexible family of normal variance mixtures is obtained by taking W in (3.19) to have a generalized inverse Gaussian (GIG) distribution, $W \sim N^-(\lambda, \chi, \psi)$ (see Section A.2.5). Using (3.22), it can be shown that a normal variance mixture constructed with this mixing density has the joint density

$$f(\boldsymbol{x}) = \frac{(\sqrt{\chi\psi})^{-\lambda}\psi^{d/2}}{(2\pi)^{d/2}|\Sigma|^{1/2}K_\lambda(\sqrt{\chi\psi})}\,\frac{K_{\lambda-(d/2)}(\sqrt{(\chi+(\boldsymbol{x}-\boldsymbol{\mu})'\Sigma^{-1}(\boldsymbol{x}-\boldsymbol{\mu}))\psi})}{(\sqrt{(\chi+(\boldsymbol{x}-\boldsymbol{\mu})'\Sigma^{-1}(\boldsymbol{x}-\boldsymbol{\mu}))\psi})^{(d/2)-\lambda}}, \qquad (3.24)$$

where K_λ denotes a modified Bessel function of the third kind (see Section A.2.5 for more details). This distribution is a special case of the more general family of multivariate generalized hyperbolic distributions, which we will discuss in greater detail in Section 3.2.2. The more general family can be obtained as *mean-variance* mixtures of normals, which are not necessarily elliptical distributions.

The GIG mixing distribution is very flexible and contains the gamma and inverse gamma distributions as special boundary cases (corresponding, respectively, to $\lambda > 0$, $\chi = 0$ and to $\lambda < 0$, $\psi = 0$). In these cases the density in (3.24) should be interpreted as a limit as $\chi \to 0$ or as $\psi \to 0$. (Information on the limits of Bessel functions is found in Section A.2.5.) The gamma mixing distribution yields Laplace distributions or so-called symmetric variance-gamma models and the inverse gamma yields the t as in Example 3.7; to be precise the t corresponds to the case when $\lambda = -\nu/2$ and $\chi = \nu$. The special cases $\lambda = -0.5$ and $\lambda = 1$ have also had attention in financial modelling. The former gives rise to the symmetric normal inverse Gaussian (NIG) distribution; the latter gives rise to a symmetric multivariate distribution whose one-dimensional margins are known simply as hyperbolic distributions.

To calculate the covariance matrix of distributions in the symmetric generalized hyperbolic family, we require the mean of the GIG distribution, which is given in (A.9) for the case $\chi > 0$ and $\psi > 0$. The covariance matrix of the multivariate distribution in (3.24) follows from (3.20).

Normal variance mixture distributions are easy to work with under linear operations, as shown in the following simple proposition.

Proposition 3.9. *If* $\boldsymbol{X} \sim M_d(\boldsymbol{\mu}, \Sigma, \hat{H})$ *and* $\boldsymbol{Y} = B\boldsymbol{X} + \boldsymbol{b}$, *where* $B \in \mathbb{R}^{k\times d}$ *and* $\boldsymbol{b} \in \mathbb{R}^k$, *then* $\boldsymbol{Y} \sim M_k(B\boldsymbol{\mu} + \boldsymbol{b}, B\Sigma B', \hat{H})$.

Proof. The characteristic function in (3.21) may be used to show that

$$\phi_{\boldsymbol{Y}}(\boldsymbol{t}) = E(\mathrm{e}^{\mathrm{i}\boldsymbol{t}'(B\boldsymbol{X}+\boldsymbol{b})}) = \mathrm{e}^{\mathrm{i}\boldsymbol{t}'\boldsymbol{b}}\phi_{\boldsymbol{X}}(B'\boldsymbol{t}) = \mathrm{e}^{\mathrm{i}\boldsymbol{t}'(B\boldsymbol{\mu}+\boldsymbol{b})}\hat{H}(\tfrac{1}{2}\boldsymbol{t}'B\Sigma B'\boldsymbol{t}).$$

□

Thus the subclass of mixture distributions specified by $\hat{H}$ is closed under linear transformations. For example, if $\boldsymbol{X}$ has a multivariate t distribution with ν degrees of freedom, then so does any linear transformation of $\boldsymbol{X}$; the linear combination $\boldsymbol{a}'\boldsymbol{X}$ would have a univariate t distribution with ν degrees of freedom (more precisely, the distribution $\boldsymbol{a}'\boldsymbol{X} \sim t_1(\nu, \boldsymbol{a}'\boldsymbol{\mu}, \boldsymbol{a}'\Sigma\boldsymbol{a})$).

Normal variance mixture distributions (and the mean-variance mixtures considered later in Section 3.2.2) are easily simulated, the method being obvious from Definition 3.4. To generate a variate $\boldsymbol{X} \sim M_d(\boldsymbol{\mu}, \Sigma, \hat{H})$ with Σ positive definite we use the following algorithm.

Algorithm 3.10 (simulation of normal variance mixtures).

(1) Generate $\boldsymbol{Z} \sim N_d(\boldsymbol{0}, \Sigma)$ using Algorithm 3.2.

(2) Generate independently a positive mixing variable W with df H (corresponding to the Laplace–Stieltjes transform $\hat{H}$).

(3) Set $\boldsymbol{X} = \boldsymbol{\mu} + \sqrt{W}\boldsymbol{Z}$.

To generate $\boldsymbol{X} \sim t_d(\nu, \boldsymbol{\mu}, \Sigma)$, the mixing variable W should have an $\text{Ig}(\frac{1}{2}\nu, \frac{1}{2}\nu)$ distribution; it is helpful to note that in this case $\nu/W \sim \chi^2_\nu$, a chi-squared distribution on ν degrees of freedom. Sampling from a generalized hyperbolic distribution with density (3.24) requires us to generate $W \sim N^-(\lambda, \chi, \psi)$. Sampling from the GIG distribution can be accomplished using a rejection algorithm proposed by Atkinson (1982).

3.2.2 Normal Mean-Variance Mixtures

All of the multivariate distributions we have considered so far have elliptical symmetry and this may well be an oversimplified model for real risk-factor return data. Among other things, elliptical symmetry implies that all one-dimensional marginal distributions are rigidly symmetric, which contradicts the frequent observation for stock returns that negative returns (losses) have heavier tails than positive returns (gains). The models we now introduce attempt to add some asymmetry to the class of normal mixtures by mixing normal distributions with different means as well as different variances; this yields the class of multivariate normal mean-variance mixtures.

Definition 3.11. The random vector $\boldsymbol{X}$ is said to have a (multivariate) normal mean-variance mixture distribution if

$$\boldsymbol{X} \stackrel{\text{d}}{=} \boldsymbol{m}(W) + \sqrt{W} A \boldsymbol{Z}, \tag{3.25}$$

where

(i) $\boldsymbol{Z} \sim N_k(\boldsymbol{0}, I_k)$;

(ii) $W \geqslant 0$ is a non-negative, scalar-valued rv which is independent of $\boldsymbol{Z}$;

(iii) $A \in \mathbb{R}^{d \times k}$ is a matrix; and

(iv) $\boldsymbol{m} : [0, \infty) \to \mathbb{R}^d$ is a measurable function.

In this case we have that

$$\boldsymbol{X} \mid W = w \sim N_d(\boldsymbol{m}(w), w\Sigma), \tag{3.26}$$

where $\Sigma = AA'$ and it is clear why such distributions are known as mean-variance mixtures of normals. In general, such distributions are not elliptical.

A possible concrete specification for the function $\boldsymbol{m}(W)$ in (3.26) is

$$\boldsymbol{m}(W) = \boldsymbol{\mu} + W\boldsymbol{\gamma}, \tag{3.27}$$

where $\boldsymbol{\mu}$ and $\boldsymbol{\gamma}$ are parameter vectors in $\mathbb{R}^d$. Since $E(\boldsymbol{X} \mid W) = \boldsymbol{\mu} + W\boldsymbol{\gamma}$ and $\text{cov}(\boldsymbol{X} \mid W) = W\Sigma$, it follows in this case by simple calculations that

$$E(\boldsymbol{X}) = E(E(\boldsymbol{X} \mid W)) = \boldsymbol{\mu} + E(W)\boldsymbol{\gamma}, \tag{3.28}$$

$$\begin{aligned} \text{cov}(\boldsymbol{X}) &= E(\text{cov}(\boldsymbol{X} \mid W)) + \text{cov}(E(\boldsymbol{X} \mid W)) \\ &= E(W)\Sigma + \text{var}(W)\boldsymbol{\gamma}\boldsymbol{\gamma}', \end{aligned} \tag{3.29}$$

when the mixing variable W has finite variance. We observe from (3.28) and (3.29) that the parameters $\boldsymbol{\mu}$ and Σ are not, in general, the mean vector and covariance matrix of $\boldsymbol{X}$ (or a multiple thereof). This is only the case when $\boldsymbol{\gamma} = \mathbf{0}$, so that the distribution is a normal variance mixture and the simpler moment formulas given in (3.20) apply.

3.2.3 Generalized Hyperbolic Distributions

In Example 3.8 we looked at the special subclass of the generalized hyperbolic distributions consisting of the elliptically symmetric normal variance mixture distributions. The full generalized hyperbolic family is obtained using the mean-variance mixture construction (3.25) and the conditional mean specification (3.27). For the mixing distribution we assume that $W \sim N^-(\lambda, \chi, \psi)$, a GIG distribution with density (A.8).

Remark 3.12. This class of distributions has received a lot of attention in the financial-modelling literature, particularly in the univariate case. An important reason for this attention is their link to Lévy processes, i.e. processes with independent and stationary increments (like Brownian motion) that are used to model price processes in continuous time. For every generalized hyperbolic distribution it is possible to construct a Lévy process so that the value of the increment of the process over a fixed time interval has that distribution; this is only possible because the generalized hyperbolic law is a so-called infinitely divisible distribution, a property that it inherits from the GIG mixing distribution of W.

The joint density in the non-singular case (Σ has rank d) is

$$f(\boldsymbol{x}) = \int_0^\infty \frac{\mathrm{e}^{(\boldsymbol{x}-\boldsymbol{\mu})'\Sigma^{-1}\boldsymbol{\gamma}}}{(2\pi)^{d/2}|\Sigma|^{1/2}w^{d/2}} \times \exp\left\{-\frac{(\boldsymbol{x}-\boldsymbol{\mu})'\Sigma^{-1}(\boldsymbol{x}-\boldsymbol{\mu})}{2w} - \frac{\boldsymbol{\gamma}'\Sigma^{-1}\boldsymbol{\gamma}}{2/w}\right\} h(w)\,\mathrm{d}w,$$

where $h(w)$ is the density of W. Evaluation of this integral gives the generalized hyperbolic density

$$f(\boldsymbol{x}) = c\frac{K_{\lambda-(d/2)}\left(\sqrt{(\chi + (\boldsymbol{x}-\boldsymbol{\mu})'\Sigma^{-1}(\boldsymbol{x}-\boldsymbol{\mu}))(\psi + \boldsymbol{\gamma}'\Sigma^{-1}\boldsymbol{\gamma})}\right)\mathrm{e}^{(\boldsymbol{x}-\boldsymbol{\mu})'\Sigma^{-1}\boldsymbol{\gamma}}}{\left(\sqrt{(\chi + (\boldsymbol{x}-\boldsymbol{\mu})'\Sigma^{-1}(\boldsymbol{x}-\boldsymbol{\mu}))(\psi + \boldsymbol{\gamma}'\Sigma^{-1}\boldsymbol{\gamma})}\right)^{(d/2)-\lambda}}, \tag{3.30}$$

where the normalizing constant is

$$c = \frac{(\sqrt{\chi\psi})^{-\lambda}\psi^{\lambda}(\psi + \boldsymbol{\gamma}'\Sigma^{-1}\boldsymbol{\gamma})^{(d/2)-\lambda}}{(2\pi)^{d/2}|\Sigma|^{1/2}K_\lambda(\sqrt{\chi\psi})}.$$

Clearly, if $\boldsymbol{\gamma} = \mathbf{0}$, the distribution reduces to the symmetric generalized hyperbolic special case of Example 3.8. In general we have a non-elliptical distribution with asymmetric margins. The mean vector and covariance matrix of the distribution are easily calculated from (3.28) and (3.29) using the information on the GIG and its moments given in Section A.2.5. The characteristic function of the generalized hyperbolic distribution may be calculated using the same approach as in (3.21) to yield

$$\phi_X(t) = E(e^{it'X}) = e^{it'\mu}\hat{H}(\tfrac{1}{2}t'\Sigma t - it'\gamma), \tag{3.31}$$

where $\hat{H}$ is the Laplace–Stieltjes transform of the GIG distribution.

We adopt the notation $X \sim \mathrm{GH}_d(\lambda, \chi, \psi, \mu, \Sigma, \gamma)$. Note that the distributions $\mathrm{GH}_d(\lambda, \chi/k, k\psi, \mu, k\Sigma, k\gamma)$ and $\mathrm{GH}_d(\lambda, \chi, \psi, \mu, \Sigma, \gamma)$ are identical for any $k > 0$, which causes an *identifiability problem* when we attempt to estimate the parameters in practice. This can be solved by constraining the determinant $|\Sigma|$ to be a particular value (such as one) when fitting. Note that, while such a constraint will have an effect on the values of χ and ψ that we estimate, it will not have an effect on the value of $\chi\psi$, so this product is a useful summary parameter for the GH distribution.

Linear combinations. The generalized hyperbolic class is closed under linear operations.

Proposition 3.13. *If $X \sim GH_d(\lambda, \chi, \psi, \mu, \Sigma, \gamma)$ and $Y = BX + b$, where $B \in \mathbb{R}^{k\times d}$ and $b \in \mathbb{R}^k$, then $Y \sim GH_k(\lambda, \chi, \psi, B\mu + b, B\Sigma B', B\gamma)$.*

Proof. We calculate, using (3.31) and a similar method to Proposition 3.9, that

$$\phi_Y(t) = e^{it'(B\mu+b)}\hat{H}(\tfrac{1}{2}t'B\Sigma B't - it'B\gamma).$$

□

Thus the parameters inherited from the GIG mixing distribution remain unchanged under linear operations. This means, for example, that margins of X are easy to calculate; we have that $X_i \sim \mathrm{GH}_1(\lambda, \chi, \psi, \mu_i, \Sigma_{ii}, \gamma_i)$. It also means that it would be relatively easy to base a version of the variance-covariance method on a generalized hyperbolic model for risk factors.

Parametrizations. There is a bewildering array of alternative parametrizations for the generalized hyperbolic distribution in the literature and it is more common to meet this distribution in a reparametrized form. In one common version the dispersion matrix we call Σ is renamed Δ and the constraint is imposed that $|\Delta| = 1$; this addresses the identifiability problem mentioned above. The skewness parameters γ are replaced by parameters β and the non-negative parameters χ and ψ are replaced by the non-negative parameters δ and α according to

$$\beta = \Delta^{-1}\gamma, \qquad \delta = \sqrt{\chi}, \qquad \alpha = \sqrt{\psi + \gamma'\Delta^{-1}\gamma}.$$

These parameters must satisfy the constraints $\delta \geqslant 0$, $\alpha^2 > \beta'\Delta\beta$ if $\lambda > 0$; $\delta > 0$, $\alpha^2 > \beta'\Delta\beta$ if $\lambda = 0$; and $\delta > 0$, $\alpha^2 \geqslant \beta'\Delta\beta$ if $\lambda < 0$. Blæsild (1981) uses this parametrization to show that generalized hyperbolic distributions form a closed class of distributions under linear operations and conditioning. However, the parametrization does have the problem that the important parameters α and δ are not generally invariant under either of these operations.

It is useful to be able to move easily between our χ–ψ–Σ–$\boldsymbol{\gamma}$ parametrization, as in (3.30), and the α–δ–Δ–$\boldsymbol{\beta}$ parametrization; λ and $\boldsymbol{\mu}$ are common to both parametrizations. If the χ–ψ–Σ–$\boldsymbol{\gamma}$ parametrization is used, then the formulas for obtaining the other parametrization are

$$\Delta = |\Sigma|^{-1/d}\Sigma, \quad \boldsymbol{\beta} = \Sigma^{-1}\boldsymbol{\gamma},$$
$$\delta = \sqrt{\chi|\Sigma|^{1/d}}, \qquad \alpha = \sqrt{|\Sigma|^{-1/d}(\psi + \boldsymbol{\gamma}'\Sigma^{-1}\boldsymbol{\gamma})}.$$

If the α–δ–Δ–$\boldsymbol{\beta}$ form is used, then we can obtain our parametrization by setting

$$\Sigma = \Delta, \qquad \gamma = \Delta\boldsymbol{\beta}, \qquad \chi = \delta^2, \qquad \psi = (\alpha^2 - \boldsymbol{\beta}'\Delta\boldsymbol{\beta}).$$

Special cases. The multivariate generalized hyperbolic family is extremely flexible and, as we have mentioned, contains many special cases known by alternative names.

- If $\lambda = \frac{1}{2}(d+1)$ we drop the word "generalized" and refer to the distribution as a d-dimensional hyperbolic distribution. Note that the univariate margins of this distribution also have $\lambda = \frac{1}{2}(d+1)$ and are not one-dimensional hyperbolic distributions.

- If $\lambda = 1$ we get a multivariate distribution whose univariate margins are one-dimensional hyperbolic distributions. The one-dimensional hyperbolic distribution has been widely used in univariate analyses of financial return data (see Notes and Comments).

- If $\lambda = -\frac{1}{2}$ then the distribution is known as an NIG distribution. In the univariate case, this model has also been used in analyses of return data; its functional form is similar to the hyperbolic with a slightly heavier tail. (Note that the NIG and the GIG are different distributions!)

- If $\lambda > 0$ and $\chi = 0$ we get a limiting case of the distribution known variously as a generalized Laplace, Bessel function or variance-gamma distribution.

- If $\lambda = -\frac{1}{2}\nu$, $\chi = \nu$ and $\psi = 0$ we get another limiting case which seems to have been less well studied, but which could be called an asymmetric or skewed t distribution. Evaluating the limit of (3.30) as $\psi \to 0$ yields the multivariate density

$$f(\boldsymbol{x}) = c\frac{K_{(\nu+d)/2}(\sqrt{(\nu + Q(\boldsymbol{x}))\boldsymbol{\gamma}'\Sigma^{-1}\boldsymbol{\gamma}})\exp((\boldsymbol{x}-\boldsymbol{\mu})'\Sigma^{-1}\boldsymbol{\gamma})}{(\sqrt{(\nu + Q(\boldsymbol{x}))\boldsymbol{\gamma}'\Sigma^{-1}\boldsymbol{\gamma}})^{-(\nu+d)/2}(1 + (Q(\boldsymbol{x})/\nu))^{(\nu+d)/2}}, \tag{3.32}$$

where $Q(\boldsymbol{x}) = (\boldsymbol{x}-\boldsymbol{\mu})'\Sigma^{-1}(\boldsymbol{x}-\boldsymbol{\mu})$ and the normalizing constant is

$$c = \frac{2^{1-(\nu+d)/2}}{\Gamma(\frac{1}{2}\nu)(\pi\nu)^{d/2}|\Sigma|^{1/2}}.$$

This density reduces to the standard multivariate t density in (3.23) as $\boldsymbol{\gamma} \to \boldsymbol{0}$.

3.2.4 Fitting Generalized Hyperbolic Distributions to Data

While univariate generalized hyperbolic models have been fitted to return data in many empirical studies, there has been relatively little applied work with the multivariate distributions. However, normal mixture distributions of the kind we have described may be fitted with algorithms of the EM (expectation–maximization) type. In this section we present an algorithm for that purpose and sketch the ideas behind it. Similar methods have been developed independently by other authors and references may be found in Notes and Comments. Readers who are not particularly interested in getting an idea of how the estimation works may skip this section, while noting the existence of Algorithm 3.14.

Assume we have iid data $\boldsymbol{X}_1, \dots, \boldsymbol{X}_n$ and wish to fit the multivariate generalized hyperbolic, or one of its special cases. Summarizing the parameters by $\boldsymbol{\theta} = (\lambda, \chi, \psi, \boldsymbol{\mu}, \Sigma, \boldsymbol{\gamma})'$, the problem is to maximize

$$\ln L(\boldsymbol{\theta}; \boldsymbol{X}_1, \dots, \boldsymbol{X}_n) = \sum_{i=1}^{n} \ln f_{\boldsymbol{X}}(\boldsymbol{X}_i; \boldsymbol{\theta}), \tag{3.33}$$

where $f_{\boldsymbol{X}}(\boldsymbol{x}; \boldsymbol{\theta})$ denotes the generalized hyperbolic density in (3.30).

This problem is not particularly easy at first sight due to the number of parameters and the necessity of maximizing over covariance matrices Σ. However, if we were able to "observe" the latent mixing variables $W_1, \dots, W_n$ coming from the mixture representation in (3.25), it would be much easier. Since the joint density of any pair $\boldsymbol{X}_i$ and W_i is given by

$$f_{\boldsymbol{X},W}(\boldsymbol{x}, w; \boldsymbol{\theta}) = f_{\boldsymbol{X}|W}(\boldsymbol{x} \mid w; \boldsymbol{\mu}, \Sigma, \boldsymbol{\gamma}) h_W(w; \lambda, \chi, \psi), \tag{3.34}$$

we could construct the likelihood

$$\begin{aligned} &\ln \tilde{L}(\boldsymbol{\theta}; \boldsymbol{X}_1, \dots, \boldsymbol{X}_n, W_1, \dots, W_n) \\ &\quad = \sum_{i=1}^{n} \ln f_{\boldsymbol{X}|W}(\boldsymbol{X}_i \mid W_i; \boldsymbol{\mu}, \Sigma, \boldsymbol{\gamma}) + \sum_{i=1}^{n} \ln h_W(W_i; \lambda, \chi, \psi), \end{aligned} \tag{3.35}$$

where the two terms could be maximized separately with respect to the parameters they involve. The apparently more problematic parameters of Σ and $\boldsymbol{\gamma}$ are in the first term of the likelihood and estimates are relatively easy to derive due to the Gaussian form of this term.

To overcome the latency of the W_i data the EM algorithm is used. This is an iterative procedure consisting of an E-step, or expectation step (where essentially W_i is replaced by an estimate given the observed data and current parameter estimates), and an M-step, or maximization step (where the parameter estimates are updated). Suppose at the beginning of step k we have parameter estimates $\boldsymbol{\theta}^{[k]}$. We proceed as follows.

E-step. We calculate the conditional expectation of the so-called augmented likelihood (3.35) given the data $\boldsymbol{X}_1, \dots, \boldsymbol{X}_n$ using the parameter values $\boldsymbol{\theta}^{[k]}$. This results in the objective function

$$Q(\boldsymbol{\theta}; \boldsymbol{\theta}^{[k]}) = E(\ln \tilde{L}(\boldsymbol{\theta}; \boldsymbol{X}_1, \dots, \boldsymbol{X}_n, W_1, \dots, W_n) \mid \boldsymbol{X}_1, \dots, \boldsymbol{X}_n; \boldsymbol{\theta}^{[k]}).$$

M-step. We maximize the objective function with respect to $\boldsymbol{\theta}$ to obtain the next set of estimates $\boldsymbol{\theta}^{[k+1]}$.

Alternating between these steps, the EM algorithm produces improved parameter estimates at each step (in the sense that the value of the original likelihood (3.33) is continually increased) and we converge to the maximum likelihood (ML) estimates.

In practice, performing the E-step amounts to replacing any functions $g(W_i)$ of the latent mixing variables which arise in (3.35) by the quantities $E(g(W_i) \mid \boldsymbol{X}_i; \boldsymbol{\theta}^{[k]})$. To calculate these quantities we can observe that the conditional density of W_i given $\boldsymbol{X}_i$ satisfies $f_{W|\boldsymbol{X}}(w \mid \boldsymbol{x}; \boldsymbol{\theta}) \propto f_{W,\boldsymbol{X}}(w, \boldsymbol{x}; \boldsymbol{\theta})$, up to some constant of proportionality. Thus it may be deduced from (3.34) that

$$W_i \mid \boldsymbol{X}_i \sim N^-(\lambda - \tfrac{1}{2}d, (\boldsymbol{X}_i - \boldsymbol{\mu})'\tilde{\Sigma}^{-1}(\boldsymbol{X}_i - \boldsymbol{\mu}) + \chi, \psi + \boldsymbol{\gamma}'\Sigma^{-1}\boldsymbol{\gamma}). \quad (3.36)$$

If we write out the likelihood (3.35) using (3.26) for the first term and the GIG density (A.8) for the second term, we find that the functions $g(W_i)$ arising in (3.35) are $g_1(w) = w$, $g_2(w) = 1/w$ and $g_3(w) = \ln(w)$. The conditional expectation of these functions in model (3.36) may be evaluated using information about the GIG distribution in Section A.2.5; note that $E(\ln(W_i) \mid \boldsymbol{X}_i; \boldsymbol{\theta}^{[k]})$ involves derivatives of a Bessel function with respect to order and must be approximated numerically. We will introduce the notation

$$\delta_i^{[\cdot]} = E(W_i^{-1} \mid \boldsymbol{X}_i; \boldsymbol{\theta}^{[\cdot]}), \quad \eta_i^{[\cdot]} = E(W_i \mid \boldsymbol{X}_i; \boldsymbol{\theta}^{[\cdot]}), \quad \xi_i^{[\cdot]} = E(\ln(W_i) \mid \boldsymbol{X}_i; \boldsymbol{\theta}^{[\cdot]}), \quad (3.37)$$

which allows us to describe the basic EM scheme as well as a variant below.

In the M-step there are two terms to maximize, coming from the two terms in (3.35); we write these as $Q_1(\boldsymbol{\mu}, \Sigma, \boldsymbol{\gamma}; \boldsymbol{\theta}^{[k]})$ and $Q_2(\lambda, \chi, \psi; \boldsymbol{\theta}^{[k]})$. To address the identifiability issue mentioned in Section 3.2.3 we constrain the determinant of Σ to be some fixed value (in practice we take the determinant of the sample covariance matrix S) in the maximization of Q_1. The maximizing values of $\boldsymbol{\mu}$, Σ and $\boldsymbol{\gamma}$ may then be derived analytically by calculating partial derivatives and setting these equal to zero; the resulting formulas are embedded in Algorithm 3.14 below (see steps (3) and (4)). The maximization of $Q_2(\lambda, \chi, \psi; \boldsymbol{\theta}^{[k]})$ with respect to the parameters of the mixing distribution is performed numerically; the function $Q_2(\lambda, \chi, \psi; \boldsymbol{\theta}^{[\cdot]})$ is

$$(\lambda - 1)\sum_{i=1}^{n}\xi_i^{[\cdot]} - \tfrac{1}{2}\chi\sum_{i=1}^{n}\delta_i^{[\cdot]} - \tfrac{1}{2}\psi\sum_{i=1}^{n}\eta_i^{[\cdot]}$$
$$- \tfrac{1}{2}n\lambda\ln(\chi) + \tfrac{1}{2}n\lambda\ln(\psi) - n\ln(2K_\lambda(\sqrt{\chi\psi})). \quad (3.38)$$

This would complete one iteration of a standard EM algorithm. However, there are a couple of variants on the basic scheme; both involve modification of the final step described above, namely the maximization of Q_2.

Assuming the parameters $\boldsymbol{\mu}$, Σ and $\boldsymbol{\gamma}$ have been updated first in iteration k, we define

$$\boldsymbol{\theta}^{[k,2]} = (\lambda^{[k]}, \chi^{[k]}, \psi^{[k]}, \boldsymbol{\mu}^{[k+1]}, \Sigma^{[k+1]}, \boldsymbol{\gamma}^{[k+1]})',$$

recalculate the weights $\delta_i^{[k,2]}$, $\eta_i^{[k,2]}$ and $\xi_i^{[k,2]}$ in (3.37), and then maximize the function $Q_2(\lambda, \eta, \xi; \boldsymbol{\theta}^{[k,2]})$ in (3.38). This results in a so-called MCECM algorithm (multi-cycle, expectation, conditional maximization), which is the one we present below.

Alternatively, instead of maximizing Q_2 we may maximize the original likelihood (3.33) with respect to λ, χ and ψ with the other parameters held fixed at the values $\boldsymbol{\mu}^{[k]}$, $\Sigma^{[k]}$ and $\boldsymbol{\gamma}^{[k]}$; this results in an ECME algorithm.

Algorithm 3.14 (EM estimation of generalized hyperbolic distribution).

(1) Set iteration count $k = 1$ and select starting values for $\boldsymbol{\theta}^{[1]}$. In particular, reasonable starting values for $\boldsymbol{\mu}$, $\boldsymbol{\gamma}$ and Σ, respectively, are the sample mean, the zero vector and the sample covariance matrix S.

(2) Calculate weights $\delta_i^{[k]}$ and $\eta_i^{[k]}$ using (3.37), (3.36) and (A.9). Average the weights to get

$$\bar{\delta}^{[k]} = n^{-1} \sum_{i=1}^{n} \delta_i^{[k]} \quad \text{and} \quad \bar{\eta}^{[k]} = n^{-1} \sum_{i=1}^{n} \eta_i^{[k]}.$$

(3) For a symmetric model set $\boldsymbol{\gamma}^{[k+1]} = \mathbf{0}$. Otherwise set

$$\boldsymbol{\gamma}^{[k+1]} = \frac{n^{-1} \sum_{i=1}^{n} \delta_i^{[k]} (\bar{\boldsymbol{X}} - \boldsymbol{X}_i)}{\bar{\delta}^{[k]} \bar{\eta}^{[k]} - 1}.$$

(4) Update estimates of the location vector and dispersion matrix by

$$\boldsymbol{\mu}^{[k+1]} = \frac{n^{-1} \sum_{i=1}^{n} \delta_i^{[k]} \boldsymbol{X}_i - \boldsymbol{\gamma}^{[k+1]}}{\bar{\delta}^{[k]}},$$

$$\Psi = \frac{1}{n} \sum_{i=1}^{n} \delta_i^{[k]} (\boldsymbol{X}_i - \boldsymbol{\mu}^{[k+1]})(\boldsymbol{X}_i - \boldsymbol{\mu}^{[k+1]})' - \bar{\eta}^{[k]} \boldsymbol{\gamma}^{[k+1]} \boldsymbol{\gamma}^{[k+1]\prime},$$

$$\Sigma^{[k+1]} = \frac{|S|^{1/d} \Psi}{|\Psi|^{1/d}}.$$

(5) Set

$$\boldsymbol{\theta}^{[k,2]} = (\lambda^{[k]}, \chi^{[k]}, \psi^{[k]}, \boldsymbol{\mu}^{[k+1]}, \Sigma^{[k+1]}, \boldsymbol{\gamma}^{[k+1]})'.$$

Calculate weights $\delta_i^{[k,2]}$, $\eta_i^{[k,2]}$ and $\xi_i^{[k,2]}$ using (3.37), (3.36) and information in Section A.2.5.

(6) Maximize $Q_2(\lambda, \chi, \psi; \boldsymbol{\theta}^{[k,2]})$ in (3.38) with respect to λ, χ and ψ to complete the calculation of $\boldsymbol{\theta}^{[k,2]}$. Increment iteration count $k \to k+1$ and go to step (2).

This algorithm may be easily adapted to fit special cases of the generalized hyperbolic distribution. This involves holding certain parameters fixed throughout and maximizing with respect to the remaining parameters: for the hyperbolic distribution we set $\lambda = 1$; for the NIG distribution $\lambda = -\frac{1}{2}$; for the t distribution $\psi = 0$; for the VG distribution $\chi = 0$. In the case of t and VG in step (6) we have to work with the function Q_2 that results from assuming an inverse gamma or gamma density for h_W.

3.2.5 *Empirical Examples*

In this section we fit the multivariate generalized hyperbolic (GH) distribution to real data and examine which of the subclasses—such as t, hyperbolic or NIG—are most useful; we also explore whether the general mean-variance mixture models can be replaced by (elliptically symmetric) variance mixtures. Our first example prepares the ground for multivariate examples by looking briefly at univariate models.

Example 3.15 (univariate stock returns). In the literature the NIG, hyperbolic and t models have been particularly popular special cases. We fit symmetric and asymmetric cases of these distributions to the data used in Example 3.3, restricting attention to daily and weekly returns, where the data are more plentiful ($n = 2020$ and $n = 468$, respectively). Models are fitted using maximum likelihood under the simplifying assumption that returns form iid samples; a simple quasi-Newton method provides a viable alternative to the EM algorithm in the univariate case.

In the upper two panels of Table 3.3 we show results for symmetric models. The t, NIG and hyperbolic models may be compared directly using the log-likelihood at the maximum, since all have the same number of parameters: for daily data we find that eight out of 10 stocks prefer the t distribution to the hyperbolic and NIG distributions; for weekly returns the t distribution is favoured in six out of 10 cases. Overall, the second best model appears to be the NIG distribution. The mixture models fit much better than the Gaussian model in all cases, and it may be verified easily using the Akaike information criterion (AIC) that they are preferred to the Gaussian model in a formal comparison (see Section A.3.6 for more on the AIC).

For the asymmetric models, we only show cases where at least one of the asymmetric t, NIG or hyperbolic models offered a significant improvement ($p < 0.05$) on the corresponding symmetric model according to a likelihood ratio test. This occurred for weekly returns on Citigroup (C) and Intel (INTC) but for no daily returns. For Citigroup the p-values of the tests were, respectively, 0.06, 0.04 and 0.04 for the t, NIG and hyperbolic cases; for Intel the p-values were 0.01 in all cases, indicating quite strong asymmetry.

In the case of Intel we have superimposed the densities of various fitted asymmetric distributions on a histogram of the data in Figure 3.4. A plot of the log densities shown alongside reveals the differences between the distributions in the tail area. The left tail (corresponding to losses) appears to be heavier for these data and the best-fitting distribution according to the likelihood comparison is the asymmetric t distribution.

Example 3.16 (multivariate stock returns). We fitted multivariate models to the full 10-dimensional dataset of log-returns used in the previous example. The resulting values of the maximized log-likelihood are shown in Table 3.4 along with p-values for a likelihood ratio test of all special cases against the (asymmetric) generalized hyperbolic (GH) model. The number of parameters in each model is also given; note that the general d-dimensional GH model has $\frac{1}{2}d(d+1)$ dispersion parameters, d location parameters, d skewness parameters and three parameters coming

Table 3.3. Comparison of univariate models in the generalized hyperbolic family, showing estimates of selected parameters and the value of the log-likelihood at the maximum; bold numbers indicate the models that give the largest values of the log-likelihood. See Example 3.15 for commentary.

	Gauss	t model		NIG model		Hyperbolic model	
Stock	$\ln L$	ν	$\ln L$	$\sqrt{\chi\psi}$	$\ln L$	$\sqrt{\chi\psi}$	$\ln L$
Daily returns: symmetric models							
AXP	4945.7	5.8	5001.8	1.6	**5002.4**	1.3	5002.1
EK	5112.9	3.8	**5396.2**	0.8	5382.5	0.6	5366.0
BA	5054.9	3.8	**5233.5**	0.8	5229.1	0.5	5221.2
C	4746.6	6.3	**4809.5**	1.9	4806.8	1.7	4805.0
KO	5319.6	5.1	**5411.0**	1.4	5407.3	1.3	5403.3
MSFT	4724.3	5.8	**4814.6**	1.6	4809.5	1.5	4806.4
HWP	4480.1	4.5	**4588.8**	1.1	4587.2	0.9	4583.4
INTC	4392.3	5.4	**4492.2**	1.5	4486.7	1.4	4482.4
JPM	4898.3	5.1	4967.8	1.3	4969.5	0.9	**4969.7**
DIS	5047.2	4.4	**5188.3**	1	5183.8	0.8	5177.6
Weekly returns: symmetric models							
AXP	719.9	8.8	724.2	3.0	**724.3**	2.8	724.3
EK	718.7	3.6	**765.6**	0.7	764.0	0.5	761.3
BA	732.4	4.4	**759.2**	1.0	758.3	0.8	757.2
C	656.0	5.7	**669.6**	1.6	669.3	1.3	669
KO	757.1	6.0	765.7	1.7	766.2	1.3	**766.3**
MSFT	671.5	6.3	**683.9**	1.9	683.2	1.8	682.9
HWP	627.1	6.0	637.3	1.8	**637.3**	1.5	637.1
INTC	595.8	5.2	**611.0**	1.5	610.6	1.3	610
JPM	681.7	5.9	**693.0**	1.7	692.9	1.5	692.6
DIS	734.1	6.4	742.7	1.9	**742.8**	1.7	742.7
Weekly returns: asymmetric models							
C	NA	6.1	**671.4**	1.7	671.3	1.3	671.2
INTC	NA	6.3	**614.2**	1.8	613.9	1.7	613.3

from the GIG mixing distribution, but is subject to one identifiability constraint; this gives $\frac{1}{2}(d(d+5)+4)$ free parameters.

For the daily data the best of the special cases is the skewed t distribution, which gives a value for the maximized likelihood that cannot be discernibly improved by the more general model with its additional parameter. All other non-elliptically symmetric submodels are rejected in a likelihood ratio test. Note, however, that the elliptically symmetric t distribution cannot be rejected when compared with the most general model, so that this seems to offer a simple parsimonious model for these data (the estimated degree of freedom is 6.0).

For the weekly data the best special case is the NIG distribution, followed closely by the skewed t; the hyperbolic and variance gamma are rejected. The best elliptically symmetric special case seems to be the t distribution (the estimated degree of freedom being, this time, 6.2).

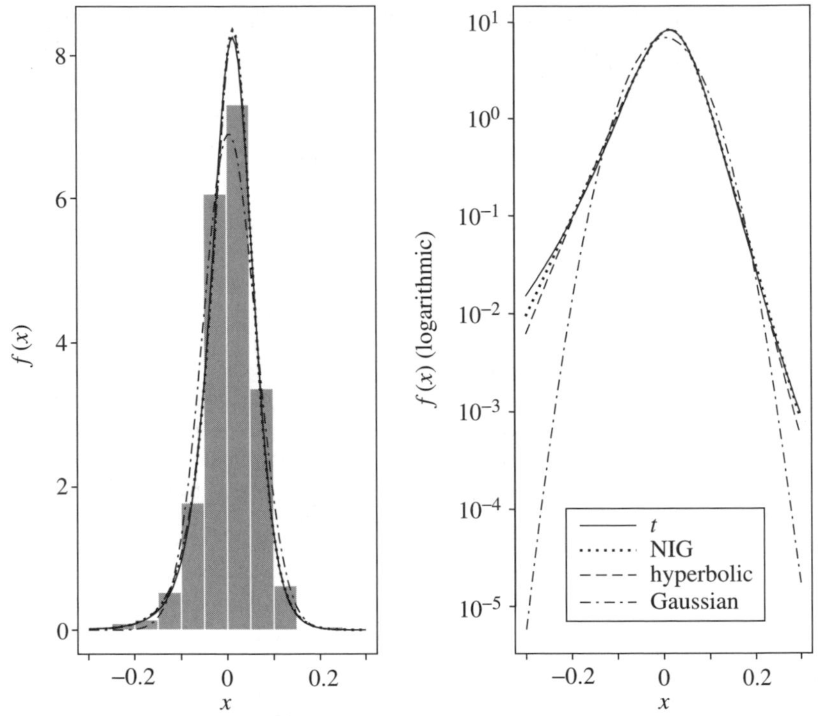

Figure 3.4. Models for weekly returns on Intel (INTC).

Example 3.17 (multivariate exchange-rate returns). We fitted the same multivariate models to a four-dimensional dataset of exchange-rate log-returns, these being GB pound, euro, Japanese yen and Swiss franc against the US dollar for the period January 2000 to the end of March 2004 (1067 daily returns and 222 weekly returns). The resulting values of the maximized log-likelihood are shown in Table 3.5.

For the daily data the best of the special cases (in general and also if we restrict ourselves to symmetric models) is the NIG distribution, followed by the hyperbolic, t and variance-gamma (VG) distributions in that order. In a likelihood ratio test of the special cases against the general GH distribution only the VG model is rejected at the 5% level; the skewed t model is rejected at the 10% level. When tested against the full model, certain elliptical models could not be rejected, the best of these being the NIG.

For the weekly data the best special case is the t distribution, followed by the NIG, hyperbolic and variance gamma; none of the special cases can be rejected in a test at the 5% level although the VG model is rejected at the 10% level. Among the elliptically symmetric distributions the Gauss distribution is clearly rejected, and the VG is again rejected at the 10% level, but otherwise the elliptical special cases are accepted; the best of these seems to be the t distribution, which has an estimated degrees-of-freedom parameter of 5.99.

Table 3.4. A comparison of models in the GH family for 10-dimensional stock-return data. For each model, the table shows the value of the log-likelihood at the maximum ($\ln L$), the numbers of parameters (# par.) and the p-value for a likelihood ratio test against the general GH model. The log-likelihood values for the general model, the best special case and the best elliptically symmetric special case are in bold type. See Example 3.16 for details.

	GH	NIG	Hyperbolic	t	VG	Gauss
Daily returns: asymmetric models						
$\ln L$	**52 174.62**	52 141.45	52 111.65	**52 174.62**	52 063.44	
# par.	77	76	76	76	76	
p-value		0.00	0.00	1.00	0.00	
Daily returns: symmetric models						
$\ln L$	52 170.14	52 136.55	52 106.34	**52 170.14**	52 057.38	50 805.28
# par.	67	66	66	66	66	65
p-value	0.54	0.00	0.00	0.63	0.00	0.00
Weekly returns: asymmetric models						
$\ln L$	**7 639.32**	**7 638.59**	7 636.49	7 638.56	7 631.33	
p-value		0.23	0.02	0.22	0.00	
Weekly returns: symmetric models						
$\ln L$	7 633.65	7 632.68	7 630.44	**7 633.11**	7 625.4	7 433.77
p-value	0.33	0.27	0.09	0.33	0.00	0.00

Table 3.5. A comparison of models in the GH family for four-dimensional exchange-rate return data. For each model, the table shows the value of the log-likelihood at the maximum ($\ln L$), the numbers of parameters (# par.) and the p-value for a likelihood ratio test against the general GH model. The log-likelihood values for the general model, the best special case and the best elliptically symmetric special case are in bold type. See Example 3.17 for details.

	GH	NIG	Hyperbolic	t	VG	Gauss
Daily returns: asymmetric models						
$\ln L$	**17 306.44**	**17 306.43**	17 305.61	17 304.97	17 302.5	
# par.	20	19	19	19	19	
p-value		0.85	0.20	0.09	0.00	
Daily returns: symmetric models						
$\ln L$	17 303.10	**17 303.06**	17 302.15	17 301.85	17 299.15	17 144.38
# par.	16	15	15	15	15	14
p-value	0.15	0.24	0.13	0.10	0.01	0.00
Weekly returns: asymmetric models						
$\ln L$	**2 890.65**	2 889.90	2 889.65	**2 890.65**	2 888.98	
p-value		0.22	0.16	1.00	0.07	
Weekly returns: symmetric models						
$\ln L$	2 887.52	2 886.74	2 886.48	**2 887.52**	2 885.86	2 872.36
p-value	0.18	0.17	0.14	0.28	0.09	0.00

Notes and Comments

Important early papers on multivariate normal mixtures are Kelker (1970) and Cambanis, Huang and Simons (1981). See also Bingham and Kiesel (2002), which contains an overview of the connections between normal mixture, elliptical and hyperbolic models, and discusses their role in financial modelling. Fang, Kotz and Ng (1987) discuss the symmetric normal mixture models as special cases in their account of the more general family of spherical and elliptical distributions.

The generalized hyperbolic distributions (univariate and multivariate) were introduced in Barndorff-Nielsen (1978) and further explored in Barndorff-Nielsen and Blæsild (1981). Useful references on the multivariate distribution are Blæsild (1981) and Blæsild and Jensen (1981). Generalized hyperbolic distributions (particularly in the univariate case) have been popularized as models for financial returns in recent papers by Eberlein and Keller (1995) and Eberlein, Keller and Prause (1998) (see also Bibby and Sørensen 2003). The PhD thesis of Prause (1999) is also a compendium of useful information in this context.

The reasons for their popularity in financial applications are both empirical and theoretical: they appear to provide a good fit to financial return data (again mostly in univariate investigations); they are consistent with continuous-time models, where logarithmic asset prices follow univariate or multivariate Lévy processes (thus generalizing the Black–Scholes model, where logarithmic prices follow Brownian motion) (see Eberlein and Keller 1995).

For the NIG special case see Barndorff-Nielsen (1997), who discusses both univariate and multivariate cases and argues that the NIG is slightly superior to the hyperbolic as a univariate model for return data, a claim that our analyses support for stock-return data. Kotz, Kozubowski and Podgórski (2001) is a useful reference for the variance-gamma special case; the distribution appears here under the name generalized Laplace distribution and a (univariate or multivariate) Lévy process with variance-gamma-distributed increments is called a Laplace motion. The univariate Laplace motion is essentially the model proposed by Madan and Seneta (1990), who derived it as a Brownian motion under a stochastic time change and referred to it as the variance-gamma model (see also Madan, Carr and Chang 1998). The multivariate t distribution is discussed in Kotz and Nadarajah (2004); the asymmetric or skewed t distribution presented in this chapter is also discussed in Bibby and Sørensen (2003). For alternative skewed extensions of the multivariate t, see Kotz and Nadarajah (2004) and Genton (2004).

EM algorithms for the multivariate generalized hyperbolic distribution have been independently proposed by Protassov (2004) and Barndorff-Nielsen and Shephard (2005). Our approach is based on EM-type algorithms for fitting the multivariate t distribution with unknown degrees of freedom. A good starter reference on this subject is Liu and Rubin (1995), where the use of the MCECM algorithm of Meng and Rubin (1993) and the ECME algorithm proposed in Liu and Rubin (1994) is discussed. Further refinements of these algorithms are discussed in Liu (1997) and Meng and van Dyk (1997).

3.3 Spherical and Elliptical Distributions

In the previous section we observed that elliptical distributions—in particular the multivariate t and symmetric multivariate NIG—provided far superior models to the multivariate normal for daily and weekly US stock-return data. The more general asymmetric versions of these distributions did not seem to offer much of an improvement on the symmetric models. While this was a single example, other investigations suggest that multivariate return data for groups of returns of a similar type often look roughly elliptical.

In this section we look more closely at the theory of elliptical distributions. To do this we begin with the special case of spherical distributions.

3.3.1 Spherical Distributions

The spherical family constitutes a large class of distributions for random vectors with *uncorrelated* components and identical, symmetric marginal distributions. It is important to note that within this class, $N_d(\mathbf{0}, I_d)$ is the only model for a vector of mutually independent components. Many of the properties of elliptical distributions can best be understood by beginning with spherical distributions.

Definition 3.18. A random vector $\boldsymbol{X} = (X_1, \dots, X_d)'$ has a spherical distribution if, for every orthogonal map $U \in \mathbb{R}^{d\times d}$ (i.e. maps satisfying $UU' = U'U = I_d$),

$$U\boldsymbol{X} \overset{\mathrm{d}}{=} \boldsymbol{X}.$$

Thus spherical random vectors are distributionally invariant under rotations. There are a number of different ways of defining distributions with this property, as we demonstrate below.

Theorem 3.19. *The following are equivalent.*

(1) *$\boldsymbol{X}$ is spherical.*

(2) *There exists a function ψ of a scalar variable such that, for all $\boldsymbol{t} \in \mathbb{R}^d$,*

$$\phi_{\boldsymbol{X}}(\boldsymbol{t}) = E(\mathrm{e}^{\mathrm{i}\boldsymbol{t}'\boldsymbol{X}}) = \psi(\boldsymbol{t}'\boldsymbol{t}) = \psi(t_1^2 + \cdots + t_d^2). \tag{3.39}$$

(3) *For every $\boldsymbol{a} \in \mathbb{R}^d$,*

$$\boldsymbol{a}'\boldsymbol{X} \overset{\mathrm{d}}{=} \|\boldsymbol{a}\| X_1, \tag{3.40}$$

where $\|\boldsymbol{a}\|^2 = \boldsymbol{a}'\boldsymbol{a} = a_1^2 + \cdots + a_d^2$.

Proof. (1) $\Rightarrow$ (2). If $\boldsymbol{X}$ is spherical, then for any orthogonal matrix U we have

$$\phi_{\boldsymbol{X}}(\boldsymbol{t}) = \phi_{U\boldsymbol{X}}(\boldsymbol{t}) = E(\mathrm{e}^{\mathrm{i}\boldsymbol{t}'U\boldsymbol{X}}) = \phi_{\boldsymbol{X}}(U'\boldsymbol{t}).$$

This can only be true if $\phi_{\boldsymbol{X}}(\boldsymbol{t})$ only depends on the length of $\boldsymbol{t}$, i.e. if $\phi_{\boldsymbol{X}}(\boldsymbol{t}) = \psi(\boldsymbol{t}'\boldsymbol{t})$ for some function ψ of a non-negative scalar variable.

(2) $\Rightarrow$ (3). First observe that $\phi_{X_1}(t) = E(\mathrm{e}^{\mathrm{i}tX_1}) = \phi_X(t\boldsymbol{e}_1) = \psi(t^2)$, where $\boldsymbol{e}_1$ denotes the first unit vector in $\mathbb{R}^d$. It follows that for any $\boldsymbol{a} \in \mathbb{R}^d$,

$$\phi_{\boldsymbol{a}'X}(t) = \phi_X(t\boldsymbol{a}) = \psi(t^2\boldsymbol{a}'\boldsymbol{a}) = \psi(t^2\|\boldsymbol{a}\|^2) = \phi_{X_1}(t\|\boldsymbol{a}\|) = \phi_{\|\boldsymbol{a}\|X_1}(t).$$

(3) $\Rightarrow$ (1). For any orthogonal matrix U we have

$$\phi_{UX}(\boldsymbol{t}) = E(\mathrm{e}^{\mathrm{i}(U'\boldsymbol{t})'X}) = E(\mathrm{e}^{\mathrm{i}\|U'\boldsymbol{t}\|X_1}) = E(\mathrm{e}^{\mathrm{i}\|\boldsymbol{t}\|X_1}) = E(\mathrm{e}^{\mathrm{i}\boldsymbol{t}'X}) = \phi_X(\boldsymbol{t}).$$

□

Part (2) of Theorem 3.19 shows that the characteristic function of a spherically distributed random vector is fully described by a function ψ of a scalar variable. For this reason ψ is known as the *characteristic generator* of the spherical distribution and the notation $X \sim S_d(\psi)$ is used. Part (3) of Theorem 3.19 shows that linear combinations of spherical random vectors always have a distribution of the same *type*, so that they have the same distribution up to changes of location and scale (see Section A.1.1). This important property will be used in Chapter 6 to prove the subadditivity of Value-at-Risk for linear portfolios of elliptically distributed risk factors. We now give examples of spherical distributions.

Example 3.20 (multivariate normal). A random vector X with the standard uncorrelated normal distribution $N_d(\boldsymbol{0}, I_d)$ is clearly spherical. The characteristic function is

$$\phi_X(\boldsymbol{t}) = E(\exp(\mathrm{i}\boldsymbol{t}'X)) = \exp(-\tfrac{1}{2}\boldsymbol{t}'\boldsymbol{t}),$$

so that, using part (2) of Theorem 3.19, $X \sim S_d(\psi)$ with characteristic generator $\psi(t) = \exp(-\frac{1}{2}t)$.

Example 3.21 (normal variance mixtures). A random vector X with a standardized, uncorrelated normal variance mixture distribution $M_d(\boldsymbol{0}, I_d, \hat{H})$ also has a spherical distribution. Using (3.21), we see that $\phi_X(\boldsymbol{t}) = \hat{H}(\frac{1}{2}\boldsymbol{t}'\boldsymbol{t})$, which obviously satisfies (3.39), and the characteristic generator of the spherical distribution is related to the Laplace–Stieltjes transform of the mixture distribution function of W by $\psi(t) = \hat{H}(\frac{1}{2}t)$. Thus $X \sim M_d(\boldsymbol{0}, I_d, \hat{H}(\cdot))$ and $X \sim S_d(\hat{H}(\frac{1}{2}\cdot))$ are two ways of writing the same mixture distribution.

A further, extremely important way of characterizing spherical distributions is given by the following result.

Theorem 3.22. *X has a spherical distribution if and only if it has the stochastic representation*

$$X \overset{\mathrm{d}}{=} RS, \tag{3.41}$$

where S is uniformly distributed on the unit sphere $\mathcal{S}^{d-1} = \{\boldsymbol{s} \in \mathbb{R}^d : \boldsymbol{s}'\boldsymbol{s} = 1\}$ and $R \geqslant 0$ is a radial rv, independent of S.

Proof. First we prove that if $\boldsymbol{S}$ is uniformly distributed on the unit sphere and $R \geqslant 0$ is an independent scalar variable, then $R\boldsymbol{S}$ has a spherical distribution. This is seen by considering the characteristic function

$$\phi_{R\boldsymbol{S}}(\boldsymbol{t}) = E(\mathrm{e}^{\mathrm{i}R\boldsymbol{t}'\boldsymbol{S}}) = E(E(\mathrm{e}^{\mathrm{i}R\boldsymbol{t}'\boldsymbol{S}} \mid R)).$$

Since $\boldsymbol{S}$ is itself spherically distributed, its characteristic function has a characteristic generator, which is usually given the special notation Ω_d. Thus, by Theorem 3.19 (2), we have that

$$\phi_{R\boldsymbol{S}}(\boldsymbol{t}) = E(\Omega_d(R^2\boldsymbol{t}'\boldsymbol{t})) = \int \Omega_d(r^2\boldsymbol{t}'\boldsymbol{t})\,\mathrm{d}F(r), \tag{3.42}$$

where F is the df of R. Since this is a function of $\boldsymbol{t}'\boldsymbol{t}$, it follows, again from Theorem 3.19 (2), that $R\boldsymbol{S}$ has a spherical distribution.

We now prove that if the random vector $\boldsymbol{X}$ is spherical, then it has the representation (3.41). For any arbitrary $\boldsymbol{s} \in \mathcal{S}^{d-1}$ the characteristic generator ψ of $\boldsymbol{X}$ must satisfy $\psi(\boldsymbol{t}'\boldsymbol{t}) = \phi_{\boldsymbol{X}}(\boldsymbol{t}) = \phi_{\boldsymbol{X}}(\|\boldsymbol{t}\|\boldsymbol{s})$. It follows that, if we introduce a random vector $\boldsymbol{S}$ that is uniformly distributed on the sphere $\mathcal{S}^{d-1}$, we can write

$$\psi(\boldsymbol{t}'\boldsymbol{t}) = \int_{\mathcal{S}^{d-1}} \phi_{\boldsymbol{X}}(\|\boldsymbol{t}\|\boldsymbol{s})\,\mathrm{d}F_{\boldsymbol{S}}(\boldsymbol{s}) = \int_{\mathcal{S}^{d-1}} E(\mathrm{e}^{\mathrm{i}\|\boldsymbol{t}\|\boldsymbol{s}'\boldsymbol{X}})\,\mathrm{d}F_{\boldsymbol{S}}(\boldsymbol{s}).$$

Interchanging the order of integration and using the Ω_d notation for the characteristic generator of $\boldsymbol{S}$ we have

$$\psi(\boldsymbol{t}'\boldsymbol{t}) = E(\Omega_d(\|\boldsymbol{t}\|^2\|\boldsymbol{X}\|^2)) = \int \Omega_d(\boldsymbol{t}'\boldsymbol{t}r^2)\,\mathrm{d}F_{\|\boldsymbol{X}\|}(r), \tag{3.43}$$

where $F_{\|X\|}$ is the df of $\|X\|$. By comparison with (3.42) we see that (3.43) is the characteristic function of $R\boldsymbol{S}$, where R is an rv with df $F_{\|X\|}$ that is independent of $\boldsymbol{S}$. □

We often exclude from consideration distributions which place point mass at the origin; that is we consider spherical rvs $\boldsymbol{X}$ in the subclass $S_d^+(\psi)$ for which $P(\boldsymbol{X} = \boldsymbol{0}) = 0$. A particularly useful corollary of Theorem 3.22 is then the following result, which is used in Section 3.3.5 to devise tests for spherical and elliptical symmetry.

Corollary 3.23. *Suppose* $\boldsymbol{X} \stackrel{\mathrm{d}}{=} R\boldsymbol{S} \sim S_d^+(\psi)$. *Then*

$$\left(\|\boldsymbol{X}\|, \frac{\boldsymbol{X}}{\|\boldsymbol{X}\|}\right) \stackrel{\mathrm{d}}{=} (R, \boldsymbol{S}). \tag{3.44}$$

Proof. Let $f_1(\boldsymbol{x}) = \|\boldsymbol{x}\|$ and $f_2(\boldsymbol{x}) = \boldsymbol{x}/\|\boldsymbol{x}\|$. It follows from (3.41) that

$$\left(\|\boldsymbol{X}\|, \frac{\boldsymbol{X}}{\|\boldsymbol{X}\|}\right) = (f_1(\boldsymbol{X}), f_2(\boldsymbol{X})) \stackrel{\mathrm{d}}{=} (f_1(R\boldsymbol{S}), f_2(R\boldsymbol{S})) = (R, \boldsymbol{S}).$$

□

Example 3.24 (working with $\boldsymbol{R}$ and $\boldsymbol{S}$). Suppose $\boldsymbol{X} \sim N_d(\boldsymbol{0}, I_d)$. Since $\boldsymbol{X}'\boldsymbol{X} \sim \chi_d^2$, a chi-squared distribution with d degrees of freedom, it follows from (3.44) that $R^2 \sim \chi_d^2$.

We can use this fact to calculate $E(\boldsymbol{S})$ and $\operatorname{cov}(\boldsymbol{S})$, the first two moments of a uniform distribution on the unit sphere. We have that

$$\begin{aligned} \boldsymbol{0} = E(\boldsymbol{X}) &= E(R)E(\boldsymbol{S}) \Rightarrow E(\boldsymbol{S}) = \boldsymbol{0}, \\ I_d = \operatorname{cov}(\boldsymbol{X}) &= E(R^2)\operatorname{cov}(\boldsymbol{S}) \Rightarrow \operatorname{cov}(\boldsymbol{S}) = I_d/d, \end{aligned} \tag{3.45}$$

since $E(R^2) = d$ when $R^2 \sim \chi_d^2$.

Now suppose that $\boldsymbol{X}$ has a spherical normal variance mixture distribution $\boldsymbol{X} \sim M_d(\boldsymbol{0}, I_d, \hat{H})$ and we wish to calculate the distribution of $R^2 \stackrel{\mathrm{d}}{=} \boldsymbol{X}'\boldsymbol{X}$ in this case. Since $\boldsymbol{X} \stackrel{\mathrm{d}}{=} \sqrt{W}\boldsymbol{Y}$, where $\boldsymbol{Y} \sim N_d(\boldsymbol{0}, I_d)$ and W is independent of $\boldsymbol{Y}$, it follows that $R^2 \stackrel{\mathrm{d}}{=} W\tilde{R}^2$, where $\tilde{R}^2 \sim \chi_d^2$ and W and $\tilde{R}$ are independent. If we can calculate the distribution of the product of W and an independent chi-squared variate, then we have the distribution of R^2.

For a concrete example suppose that $\boldsymbol{X} \sim t_d(\nu, \boldsymbol{0}, I_d)$. For a multivariate t distribution we know from Example 3.7 that $W \sim \operatorname{Ig}(\frac{1}{2}\nu, \frac{1}{2}\nu)$, which means that $\nu/W \sim \chi_\nu^2$. Using the fact that the ratio of independent chi-squared distributions divided by their degrees of freedom is F-distributed, it may be calculated that $R^2/d \sim F(d, \nu)$, the F distribution on d and ν degrees of freedom (see Section A.2.3). Since an $F(d, \nu)$ distribution has mean $\nu/(\nu - 2)$, it follows from (3.45) that

$$\operatorname{cov}(\boldsymbol{X}) = E(\operatorname{cov}(R\boldsymbol{S} \mid R)) = E(R^2 I_d/d) = (\nu/(\nu-2))I_d.$$

The normal mixtures with $\boldsymbol{\mu} = \boldsymbol{0}$ and $\Sigma = I_d$ represent an easily understood subgroup of the spherical distributions. There are other spherical distributions which cannot be represented as normal variance mixtures; an example is the distribution of the uniform vector $\boldsymbol{S}$ on $\mathcal{S}^{d-1}$ itself. However, the normal mixtures have a special role in the spherical world, as summarized by the following theorem.

Theorem 3.25. *Denote by Ψ_∞ the set of characteristic generators that generate a d-dimensional spherical distribution for arbitrary $d \geqslant 1$. Then $\boldsymbol{X} \sim S_d(\psi)$ with $\psi \in \Psi_\infty$ if and only if $\boldsymbol{X} \stackrel{\mathrm{d}}{=} \sqrt{W}\boldsymbol{Z}$, where $\boldsymbol{Z} \sim N_d(\boldsymbol{0}, I_d)$ is independent of $W \geqslant 0$.*

Proof. This is proved in Fang, Kotz and Ng (1987, pp. 48–51). □

Thus, the characteristic generators of normal mixtures generate spherical distributions in arbitrary dimensions, while other spherical generators may only be used in certain dimensions. A concrete example is given by the uniform distribution on the unit sphere. Let Ω_d denote the characteristic generator of the uniform vector $\boldsymbol{S} = (S_1, \dots, S_d)'$ on $\mathcal{S}_{d-1}$. It can be shown that $\Omega_d((t_1, \dots, t_{d+1})'(t_1, \dots, t_{d+1}))$ is not the characteristic function of a spherical distribution in $\mathbb{R}^{d+1}$ (for more details see Fang, Kotz and Ng (1987, pp. 70–72)).

If a spherical distribution has a density f, then, by using the inversion formula

$$f(\boldsymbol{x}) = \frac{1}{(2\pi)^d}\int_{-\infty}^{\infty}\cdots\int_{-\infty}^{\infty} \mathrm{e}^{-\mathrm{i}\boldsymbol{t}'\boldsymbol{x}}\phi_{\boldsymbol{X}}(\boldsymbol{t})\,\mathrm{d}t_1\cdots\mathrm{d}t_d,$$

it is easily inferred from Theorem 3.19 that $f(\boldsymbol{x}) = f(U\boldsymbol{x})$ for any orthogonal matrix U, so that the density must be of the form

$$f(\boldsymbol{x}) = g(\boldsymbol{x}'\boldsymbol{x}) = g(x_1^2 + \cdots + x_d^2) \tag{3.46}$$

for some function g of a scalar variable, which is referred to as the *density generator*. Clearly, the joint density is constant on hyperspheres $\{\boldsymbol{x} : x_1^2 + \cdots + x_d^2 = c\}$ in $\mathbb{R}^d$. To give a single example, the density generator of the multivariate t (i.e. the model $\boldsymbol{X} \sim t_d(\nu, \boldsymbol{0}, I_d)$ of Example 3.7) is

$$g(x) = \frac{\Gamma(\frac{1}{2}(\nu+d))}{\Gamma(\frac{1}{2}\nu)(\pi\nu)^{d/2}}\left(1 + \frac{x}{\nu}\right)^{-(\nu+d)/2}.$$

3.3.2 Elliptical Distributions

Definition 3.26. $\boldsymbol{X}$ has an elliptical distribution if

$$\boldsymbol{X} \stackrel{\mathrm{d}}{=} \boldsymbol{\mu} + A\boldsymbol{Y},$$

where $\boldsymbol{Y} \sim S_k(\psi)$ and $A \in \mathbb{R}^{d\times k}$ and $\boldsymbol{\mu} \in \mathbb{R}^d$ are a matrix and vector of constants, respectively.

In other words, elliptical distributions are obtained by multivariate *affine* transformations of spherical distributions. Since the characteristic function is

$$\phi_{\boldsymbol{X}}(\boldsymbol{t}) = E(\mathrm{e}^{\mathrm{i}\boldsymbol{t}'\boldsymbol{X}}) = E(\mathrm{e}^{\mathrm{i}\boldsymbol{t}'(\boldsymbol{\mu}+A\boldsymbol{Y})}) = \mathrm{e}^{\mathrm{i}\boldsymbol{t}'\boldsymbol{\mu}}E(\mathrm{e}^{\mathrm{i}(A'\boldsymbol{t})'\boldsymbol{Y}}) = \mathrm{e}^{\mathrm{i}\boldsymbol{t}'\boldsymbol{\mu}}\psi(\boldsymbol{t}'\Sigma\boldsymbol{t}),$$

where $\Sigma = AA'$, we denote the elliptical distributions by

$$\boldsymbol{X} \sim E_d(\boldsymbol{\mu}, \Sigma, \psi),$$

and refer to $\boldsymbol{\mu}$ as the location vector, Σ as the dispersion matrix and ψ as the characteristic generator of the distribution.

Remark 3.27. Knowledge of $\boldsymbol{X}$ does not uniquely determine its elliptical representation $E_d(\boldsymbol{\mu}, \Sigma, \psi)$. Although $\boldsymbol{\mu}$ is uniquely determined, Σ and ψ are only determined up to a positive constant. For example, the multivariate normal distribution $N_d(\boldsymbol{\mu}, \Sigma)$ can be written as $E_d(\boldsymbol{\mu}, \Sigma, \psi(\cdot))$ or $E_d(\boldsymbol{\mu}, c\Sigma, \psi(\cdot/c))$ for $\psi(u) = \exp(-\frac{1}{2}u)$ and any $c > 0$. Provided that variances are finite, then an elliptical distribution is fully specified by its mean vector, covariance matrix and characteristic generator and it is possible to find an elliptical representation $E_d(\boldsymbol{\mu}, \Sigma, \psi)$ such that Σ is the covariance matrix of $\boldsymbol{X}$, although this is not always the standard representation of the distribution.

We now give an alternative stochastic representation for the elliptical distributions that follows directly from Definition 3.26 and Theorem 3.22.

Proposition 3.28. *$X \sim E_d(\mu, \Sigma, \psi)$ if and only if there exist S, R and A satisfying*

$$X \overset{d}{=} \mu + RAS, \tag{3.47}$$

with

(i) *S uniformly distributed on the unit sphere $\mathcal{S}^{k-1} = \{s \in \mathbb{R}^k : s's = 1\}$;*

(ii) *$R \geqslant 0$, a radial rv, independent of S, and*

(iii) *$A \in \mathbb{R}^{d \times k}$ with $AA' = \Sigma$.*

For practical examples we are most interested in the case where Σ is positive definite. The relation between the elliptical and spherical cases is then clearly

$$X \sim E_d(\mu, \Sigma, \psi) \iff \Sigma^{-1/2}(X - \mu) \sim S_d(\psi). \tag{3.48}$$

In this case, if the spherical vector Y has density generator g, then $X = \mu + \Sigma^{1/2} Y$ has density

$$f(x) = \frac{1}{|\Sigma|^{1/2}} g((x - \mu)' \Sigma^{-1} (x - \mu)).$$

The joint density is always constant on sets of the form $\{x : (x - \mu)' \Sigma^{-1} (x - \mu) = c\}$, which are ellipsoids in $\mathbb{R}^d$. Clearly, the full family of multivariate normal variance mixtures with general location and dispersion parameters μ and Σ are elliptical, since they are obtained by affine transformations of the spherical special cases considered in the previous section.

It follows from (3.44) and (3.48) that for a non-singular elliptical variate $X \sim E_d(\mu, \Sigma, \psi)$ with no point mass at μ we have

$$\left(\sqrt{(X - \mu)' \Sigma^{-1} (X - \mu)}, \frac{\Sigma^{-1/2}(X - \mu)}{\sqrt{(X - \mu)' \Sigma^{-1} (X - \mu)}} \right) \overset{d}{=} (R, S), \tag{3.49}$$

where S is uniformly distributed on $\mathcal{S}^{d-1}$ and R is an independent scalar rv. This forms the basis of a test of elliptical symmetry described in Section 3.3.5.

The following proposition shows that a particular conditional distribution of an elliptically distributed random vector X has the same correlation matrix as X and can also be used to test for elliptical symmetry.

Proposition 3.29. *Let $X \sim E_d(\mu, \Sigma, \psi)$ and assume Σ is positive definite and $\operatorname{cov}(X)$ is finite. For any $c \geqslant 0$ such that $P((X - \mu)' \Sigma^{-1} (X - \mu) \geqslant c) > 0$ we have*

$$\rho(X \mid (X - \mu)' \Sigma^{-1} (X - \mu) \geqslant c) = \rho(X). \tag{3.50}$$

Proof. It follows easily from (3.49) that

$$X \mid (X - \mu)' \Sigma^{-1} (X - \mu) \geqslant c \overset{d}{=} \mu + R \Sigma^{1/2} S \mid R^2 \geqslant c,$$

where $R \overset{d}{=} \sqrt{(X - \mu)' \Sigma^{-1} (X - \mu)}$ and S is independent of R and uniformly distributed on $\mathcal{S}^{d-1}$. Thus we have

$$X \mid (X - \mu)' \Sigma^{-1} (X - \mu) \geqslant c \overset{d}{=} \mu + \tilde{R} \Sigma^{1/2} S,$$

where $\tilde{R} \overset{d}{=} R \mid R^2 \geqslant c$. It follows from Proposition 3.28 that the conditional distribution remains elliptical with dispersion matrix Σ and (3.50) holds. □

3.3.3 Properties of Elliptical Distributions

We now summarize some of the properties of elliptical distributions in a format that allows their comparison with the properties of multivariate normal distributions in Section 3.1.3. Many properties carry over directly and others need only be slightly modified. These parallels emphasize that it would be fairly easy to base many standard procedures in risk management on an assumption that risk-factor changes have an approximately elliptical distribution, rather than the patently false assumption that they are multivariate normal.

Linear combinations. If we take linear combinations of elliptical random vectors, then these remain elliptical with the same characteristic generator ψ. Let $\boldsymbol{X} \sim E_d(\boldsymbol{\mu}, \Sigma, \psi)$ and take any $B \in \mathbb{R}^{k \times d}$ and $\boldsymbol{b} \in \mathbb{R}^d$. Then it is easily shown, using a similar argument to that in Proposition 3.9, that

$$B\boldsymbol{X} + \boldsymbol{b} \sim E_k(B\boldsymbol{\mu} + b, B\Sigma B', \psi). \tag{3.51}$$

As a special case, if $\boldsymbol{a} \in \mathbb{R}^d$, then

$$\boldsymbol{a}'\boldsymbol{X} \sim E_1(\boldsymbol{a}'\boldsymbol{\mu}, \boldsymbol{a}'\Sigma\boldsymbol{a}, \psi). \tag{3.52}$$

Marginal distributions. It follows from (3.52) that marginal distributions of $\boldsymbol{X}$ must be elliptical distributions with the same characteristic generator. Using the $\boldsymbol{X} = (\boldsymbol{X}_1, \boldsymbol{X}_2)'$ notation from Section 3.1.1 and again extending this notation naturally to $\boldsymbol{\mu}$ and Σ:

$$\boldsymbol{\mu} = \begin{pmatrix} \boldsymbol{\mu}_1 \\ \boldsymbol{\mu}_2 \end{pmatrix}, \qquad \Sigma = \begin{pmatrix} \Sigma_{11} & \Sigma_{12} \\ \Sigma_{21} & \Sigma_{22} \end{pmatrix},$$

we have that $\boldsymbol{X}_1 \sim E_k(\boldsymbol{\mu}_1, \Sigma_{11}, \psi)$ and $\boldsymbol{X}_2 \sim E_{d-k}(\boldsymbol{\mu}_2, \Sigma_{22}, \psi)$.

Conditional distributions. The conditional distribution of $\boldsymbol{X}_2$ given $\boldsymbol{X}_1$ may also be shown to be elliptical, although in general with a *different* characteristic generator $\tilde{\psi}$. For details of how the generator changes see Fang, Kotz and Ng (1987, pp. 45, 46). In the special case of multivariate normality the generator remains the same.

Quadratic forms. If $\boldsymbol{X} \sim E_d(\boldsymbol{\mu}, \Sigma, \psi)$ with Σ non-singular, then we observed in (3.49) that

$$Q := (\boldsymbol{X} - \boldsymbol{\mu})'\Sigma^{-1}(\boldsymbol{X} - \boldsymbol{\mu}) \stackrel{\mathrm{d}}{=} R^2, \tag{3.53}$$

where R is the radial rv in the stochastic representation (3.41). As we have seen in Example 3.24, for some particular cases the distribution of R^2 is well known: if $\boldsymbol{X} \sim N_d(\boldsymbol{\mu}, \Sigma)$, then $R^2 \sim \chi^2_d$; if $\boldsymbol{X} \sim t_d(\nu, \boldsymbol{\mu}, \Sigma)$, then $R^2/d \sim F(d, \nu)$. For all elliptical distributions Q must be independent of $\Sigma^{-1/2}(\boldsymbol{X} - \boldsymbol{\mu})/\sqrt{Q}$.

Convolutions. The convolution of two independent elliptical vectors with the *same dispersion matrix* Σ is also elliptical. If $\boldsymbol{X}$ and $\boldsymbol{Y}$ are independent d-dimensional random vectors satisfying $\boldsymbol{X} \sim E_d(\boldsymbol{\mu}, \Sigma, \psi)$ and $\boldsymbol{Y} \sim E_d(\tilde{\boldsymbol{\mu}}, \Sigma, \tilde{\psi})$, then we may take the product of characteristic functions to show that

$$\boldsymbol{X} + \boldsymbol{Y} \sim E_d(\boldsymbol{\mu} + \tilde{\boldsymbol{\mu}}, \Sigma, \bar{\psi}), \tag{3.54}$$

where $\bar{\psi}(u) = \psi(u)\tilde{\psi}(u)$.

If the dispersion matrices of $\boldsymbol{X}$ and $\boldsymbol{Y}$ differ by more than a constant factor, then the convolution will not necessarily remain elliptical, even when the two generators ψ and $\tilde{\psi}$ are identical.

3.3.4 Estimating Dispersion and Correlation

Suppose we have risk-factor return data $\boldsymbol{X}_1, \dots, \boldsymbol{X}_n$ that we believe come from some elliptical distribution $E_d(\boldsymbol{\mu}, \Sigma, \psi)$ with heavier tails than the multivariate normal. We recall from Remark 3.27 that the dispersion matrix Σ is not uniquely determined, but rather is only fixed up to a constant of proportionality; when covariances are finite the covariance matrix is proportional to Σ.

In this section we consider briefly the problem of estimating the location parameter $\boldsymbol{\mu}$, a dispersion matrix Σ and the correlation matrix P, assuming finiteness of second moments. We could use the standard estimators of Section 3.1.2. Under an assumption of iid or uncorrelated vector observations we observed that $\bar{\boldsymbol{X}}$ and S in (3.9) are unbiased estimators of the mean vector and covariance matrix, respectively. They will also be consistent under quite weak assumptions. However, this does not necessarily mean they are the best estimators of location and dispersion for any given finite sample of elliptical data. There are many alternative estimators that may be more efficient for heavy-tailed data and may enjoy better robustness properties for contaminated data.

One strategy would be to fit a number of normal variance mixture models, such as the t and normal inverse Gaussian, using the approach of Section 3.2.5. From the best-fitting model we would obtain an estimate of the mean vector and could easily calculate the implied estimates of the covariance and correlation matrices. In this section we give simpler, alternative methods that do not require a full fitting of a multivariate distribution; consult Notes and Comments for further references to robust dispersion estimation.

M-estimators. Maronna's M-estimators (Maronna 1976) of location and dispersion are a relatively old idea in robust statistics, but they have the virtue of being particularly simple to implement. Let $\hat{\boldsymbol{\mu}}$ and $\hat{\Sigma}$ denote estimates of the mean vector and dispersion matrix. Suppose for every observation $\boldsymbol{X}_i$ we calculate $D_i^2 = (\boldsymbol{X}_i - \hat{\boldsymbol{\mu}})'\hat{\Sigma}^{-1}(\boldsymbol{X}_i - \hat{\boldsymbol{\mu}})$. If we wanted to calculate improved estimates of location and dispersion, particularly for heavy-tailed data, it might be expected that this could be achieved by reducing the influence of observations for which D_i is large, since these are the observations that might tend to distort the parameter estimates most. M-estimation uses decreasing weight functions $w_j : \mathbb{R}^+ \to \mathbb{R}^+$, $j = 1, 2$, to downweight observations with large D_i values. This can be turned into an iterative procedure that converges to so-called M-estimates of location and dispersion; the dispersion matrix estimate is in general a biased estimate of the true covariance matrix.

Algorithm 3.30 (M-estimators of location and dispersion).

(1) As starting estimates take $\hat{\boldsymbol{\mu}}^{[1]} = \bar{\boldsymbol{X}}$ and $\hat{\Sigma}^{[1]} = S$, the standard estimators in (3.9). Set iteration count $k = 1$.

(2) For $i = 1, \dots, n$ set $D_i^2 = (\boldsymbol{X}_i - \hat{\boldsymbol{\mu}}^{[k]})' \hat{\Sigma}^{[k]-1} (\boldsymbol{X}_i - \hat{\boldsymbol{\mu}}^{[k]})$.

(3) Update the location estimate using

$$\hat{\boldsymbol{\mu}}^{[k+1]} = \frac{\sum_{i=1}^n w_1(D_i)\boldsymbol{X}_i}{\sum_{i=1}^n w_1(D_i)},$$

where w_1 is a weight function, as discussed below.

(4) Update the dispersion matrix estimate using

$$\hat{\Sigma}^{[k+1]} = \frac{1}{n} \sum_{i=1}^n w_2(D_i^2)(\boldsymbol{X}_i - \hat{\boldsymbol{\mu}}^{[k]})(\boldsymbol{X}_i - \hat{\boldsymbol{\mu}}^{[k]})',$$

where w_2 is a weight function.

(5) Set $k = k + 1$ and repeat steps (2)–(4) until estimates converge.

Popular choices for the weight functions w_1 and w_2 are the decreasing functions $w_1(x) = (d + \nu)/(x^2 + \nu) = w_2(x^2)$, for some positive constant ν. Interestingly, use of these weight functions in Algorithm 3.30 corresponds exactly to fitting a multivariate $t_d(\nu, \boldsymbol{\mu}, \Sigma)$ distribution with known degrees of freedom ν using the EM algorithm (see, for example, Meng and van Dyk 1997).

There are many other possibilities for the weight functions. For example, the observations in the central part of the distribution could be given full weight and only the more outlying observations downweighted. This can be achieved by setting $w_1(x) = 1$ for $x \leqslant a$, $w_1(x) = a/x$ for $x > a$, for some value a, and $w_2(x^2) = (w_1(x))^2$.

Correlation estimates via Kendall's tau. A method for estimating correlation that is particularly easy to carry out is based on Kendall's rank correlation coefficient and will turn out to be related to a method for estimating the parameters of certain copulas in Chapter 5. The theoretical version of Kendall's rank correlation (also known as Kendall's tau) for two rvs X_1 and X_2 is denoted $\rho_\tau(X_1, X_2)$ and is defined formally in Section 5.2.2; it is shown in Proposition 5.37 that if $(X_1, X_2) \sim E_2(\boldsymbol{\mu}, \Sigma, \psi)$, then

$$\rho_\tau(X_1, X_2) = \frac{2}{\pi} \arcsin(\rho), \tag{3.55}$$

where $\rho = \sigma_{12}/(\sigma_{11}\sigma_{22})^{1/2}$ is the *pseudo-correlation coefficient* of the elliptical distribution, which is always defined (even when correlation coefficients are undefined because variances are infinite). This relationship can be inverted to provide a method for estimating ρ from data; we simply replace the left-hand side of (3.55) by the standard textbook estimator of Kendall's tau, which is given in (5.50), to get an estimating equation that is solved for $\hat{\rho}$. This method estimates correlation by exploiting the geometry of an elliptical distribution and does not require us to estimate variances and covariances.

The method can be used to estimate a correlation matrix of a higher-dimensional elliptical distribution, by applying the technique to each bivariate margin. This does, however, result in a matrix of pairwise correlation estimates that is not necessarily positive definite; this problem does not always arise and if it does, a matrix

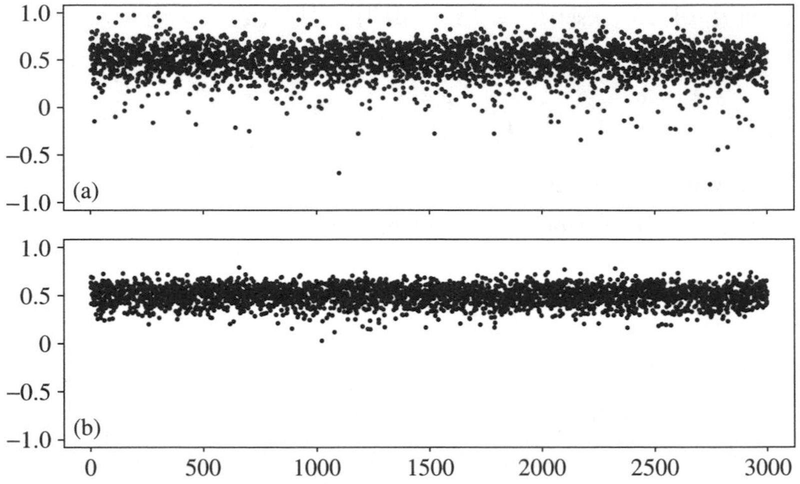

Figure 3.5. For 3000 independent samples of size 90 from a bivariate t distribution with three degrees of freedom and linear correlation 0.5: (a) the standard (Pearson) estimator of correlation; (b) the Kendall's tau transform estimator. See Example 3.31 for commentary.

adjustment method can be used, such as the eigenvalue method of Rousseeuw and Molenberghs (1993), which is given in Algorithm 5.55.

Note that, to turn an estimate of a bivariate correlation matrix into a robust estimate of a dispersion matrix we could estimate the ratio of standard deviations $\lambda = (\sigma_{22}/\sigma_{11})^{1/2}$, for example by using a ratio of *trimmed* sample standard deviations; in other words, we leave out an equal number of outliers from each of the univariate datasets $X_{1,i}, \dots, X_{n,i}$ for $i = 1, 2$ and calculate the sample standard deviations with the remaining observations. This would give us the estimate

$$\hat{\Sigma} = \begin{pmatrix} 1 & \hat{\lambda}\hat{\rho} \\ \hat{\lambda}\hat{\rho} & \hat{\lambda}^2 \end{pmatrix}. \tag{3.56}$$

Example 3.31 (efficient correlation estimation for heavy-tailed data). Suppose we calculate correlations of asset or risk-factor returns based on 90 days (somewhat more than three trading months) of data; it would seem that this ought to be enough data to allow us to accurately estimate the "true" underlying correlation under an assumption that we have identically distributed data for that period.

Figure 3.5 displays the results of a simulation experiment where we have generated 3000 bivariate samples of iid data from a t distribution with three degrees of freedom and correlation $\rho = 0.5$; this is a heavy-tailed elliptical distribution. The distribution of the values of the standard correlation coefficient (also known as the Pearson correlation coefficient) is not particularly closely concentrated around the true value and produces some very poor estimates for a number of samples. On the other hand the Kendall's tau transform method produces estimates that are in general much closer to the true value, and thus provides a more efficient way of estimating ρ.

3.3.5 *Testing for Elliptical Symmetry*

The general problem of this section is to test whether a sample of identically distributed data vectors $\boldsymbol{X}_1, \dots, \boldsymbol{X}_n$ has an elliptical distribution $E_d(\boldsymbol{\mu}, \Sigma, \psi)$ for some $\boldsymbol{\mu}$, Σ and generator ψ. In all of the methods we require estimates of $\boldsymbol{\mu}$ and Σ and these can be obtained using approaches discussed in Section 3.3.4, such as fitting t distributions, calculating M-estimates or perhaps using (3.56) in the bivariate case. We denote the estimates simply by $\hat{\boldsymbol{\mu}}$ and $\hat{\Sigma}$.

Generally in finance we cannot assume that the observations are of iid random vectors, but we assume that they at least have an identical distribution. Note that, even if the data were independent, the fact that we generally estimate $\boldsymbol{\mu}$ and Σ from the whole dataset would introduce dependence in the procedures that we describe below.

Stable correlation estimates: an exploratory method. An easy exploratory graphical method can be based on Proposition 3.29. We could attempt to estimate

$$\rho(\boldsymbol{X} \mid h(\boldsymbol{X}) \geqslant c), \qquad h(\boldsymbol{x}) = (\boldsymbol{x} - \hat{\boldsymbol{\mu}})'\hat{\Sigma}^{-1}(\boldsymbol{x} - \hat{\boldsymbol{\mu}})$$

for various values of $c \geqslant 0$. We expect that for elliptically distributed data the estimates will remain roughly stable over a range of different c values. Of course the estimates of this correlation should again be calculated using some method that is more efficient than the standard correlation estimator for heavy-tailed data. The method is most natural as a bivariate method and in this case the correlation of $\boldsymbol{X} \mid h(\boldsymbol{X}) \geqslant c$ can be estimated by applying the Kendall's tau transform method to those data points $\boldsymbol{X}_i$ which lie outside the ellipse defined by $h(\boldsymbol{x}) = c$. In Figure 3.6 we give an example with both simulated and real data, neither of which show any marked departure from the assumption of stable correlations. The method is of course exploratory and does not allow us to come to any formal conclusion.

QQplots. The remaining methods that we describe rely on the link (3.48) between non-singular elliptical and spherical distributions. If $\boldsymbol{\mu}$ and Σ were known, then we would test for elliptical symmetry by testing the data $\{\Sigma^{-1/2}(\boldsymbol{X}_i - \boldsymbol{\mu}) : i = 1, \dots, n\}$ for spherical symmetry. Replacing these parameters by estimates as above we consider whether the data

$$\{\boldsymbol{Y}_i = \hat{\Sigma}^{-1/2}(\boldsymbol{X}_i - \hat{\boldsymbol{\mu}}) : i = 1, \dots, n\} \tag{3.57}$$

are consistent with a spherical distribution, while ignoring the effect of estimation error.

Some graphical methods based on QQplots have been suggested by Li, Fang and Zhu (1997) and these are particularly useful for large d. These rely essentially on the following result.

Lemma 3.32. *Suppose that $T(\boldsymbol{Y})$ is a statistic such that, almost surely,*

$$T(a\boldsymbol{Y}) = T(\boldsymbol{Y}) \quad \text{for every } a > 0. \tag{3.58}$$

Then $T(\boldsymbol{Y})$ has the same distribution for every spherical vector $\boldsymbol{Y} \sim S_d^+(\psi)$.

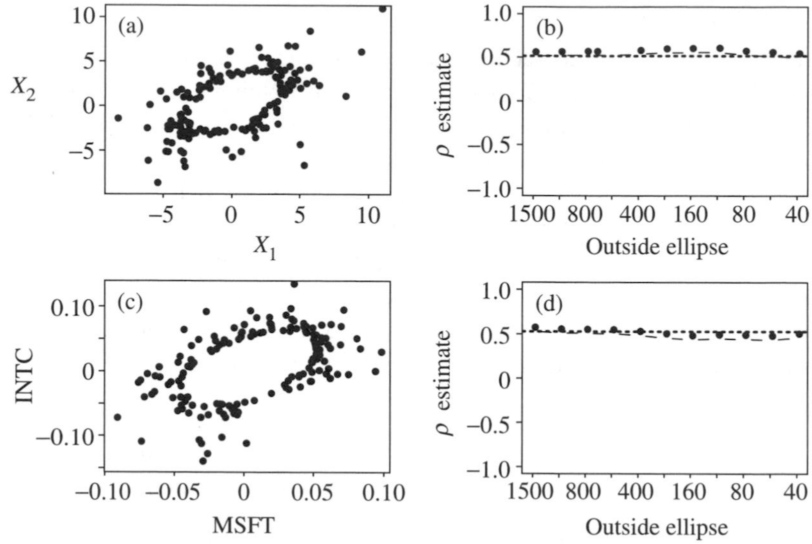

Figure 3.6. Correlations are estimated using the Kendall's tau method for points lying outside ellipses of progressively larger size (as shown in (a) and (c)). (a), (b) Two thousand t-distributed data with four degrees of freedom and $\rho = 0.5$. (c), (d) Two thousand daily log-returns on Microsoft and Intel. Dashed lines and points show estimates for an ellipse that is allowed to grow until there are only 40 points outside; dotted lines show estimates of correlation for all data.

Proof. From Theorem 3.22 we have $T(\boldsymbol{Y}) \stackrel{\mathrm{d}}{=} T(R\boldsymbol{S})$ and $T(R\boldsymbol{S}) \stackrel{\text{a.s.}}{=} T(\boldsymbol{S})$ follows from (3.58). Since the distribution of $T(\boldsymbol{Y})$ only depends on $\boldsymbol{S}$ and not R it must be the same for all $\boldsymbol{Y} \sim S_d^+(\psi)$. □

We exploit this result by looking for statistics $T(\boldsymbol{Y})$ with the property (3.58) whose distribution we know when $\boldsymbol{Y} \sim N_d(\boldsymbol{0}, I_d)$. Two examples are

$$\left.\begin{aligned} T_1(\boldsymbol{Y}) &= \frac{d^{1/2}\bar{Y}}{\sqrt{(1/(d-1))\sum_{i=1}^{d}(Y_i - \bar{Y})^2}}, \qquad \bar{Y} = \frac{1}{d}\sum_{i=1}^{d} Y_i, \\ T_2(\boldsymbol{Y}) &= \frac{\sum_{i=1}^{k} Y_i^2}{\sum_{i=1}^{d} Y_i^2}. \end{aligned}\right\} \tag{3.59}$$

For $\boldsymbol{Y} \sim N_d(\boldsymbol{0}, I_d)$, and hence for $\boldsymbol{Y} \sim S_d^+(\psi)$, we have $T_1(\boldsymbol{Y}) \sim t_{d-1}$ and $T_2(\boldsymbol{Y}) \sim \mathrm{Beta}(\frac{1}{2}k, \frac{1}{2}(d-k))$.

Our experience suggests that the beta-plot is the more revealing of the resulting QQplots. Li, Fang and Zhu (1997) suggest choosing k such that it is roughly equal to $d - k$. In Figure 3.7 we show examples of the QQplots obtained for 2000 simulated data from a 10-dimensional t distribution with four degrees of freedom and for the daily, weekly and monthly return data on 10 Dow Jones 30 stocks analysed in Example 3.3 and Section 3.2.5. The curvature in the plots for daily and weekly returns seems to be evidence against the elliptical hypothesis.

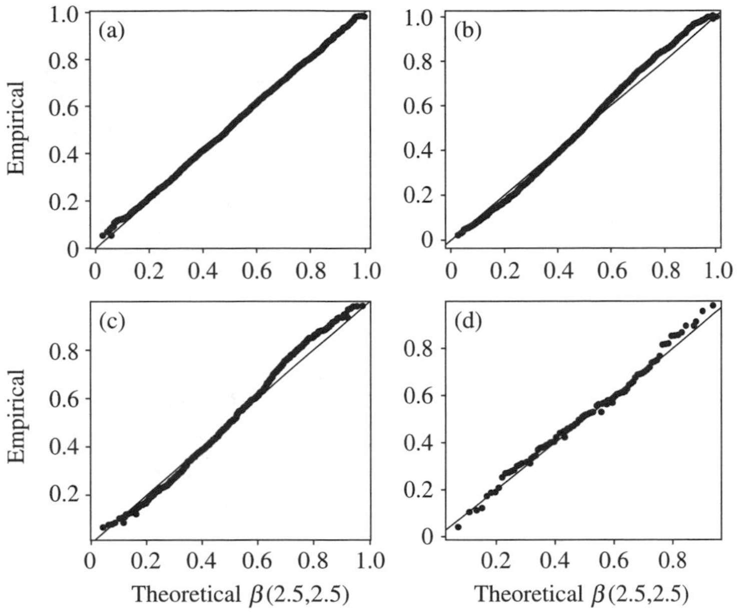

Figure 3.7. QQplots of the beta-statistic (3.59) for four datasets with dimension $d = 10$; we have set $k = 5$. (a) Two thousand simulated observations from t distribution with four degrees of freedom. (b) Daily, (c) weekly and (d) monthly returns on Dow Jones stocks as analysed in Example 3.3 and Section 3.2.5. Daily and weekly returns show evidence against elliptical symmetry.

Numerical tests. We restrict ourselves to simple ideas for bivariate tests; references to more general test ideas are found in Notes and Comments. If we neglect the error involved in estimating location and dispersion, testing for elliptical symmetry amounts to testing the $\boldsymbol{Y}_i$ data in (3.57) for spherical symmetry. For $i = 1, \dots, n$, if we set $R_i = \|\boldsymbol{Y}_i\|$ and $\boldsymbol{S}_i = \boldsymbol{Y}_i / \|\boldsymbol{Y}_i\|$, then under the null hypothesis the $\boldsymbol{S}_i$ data should be uniformly distributed on the unit sphere $\mathcal{S}^{d-1}$, and the paired data $(R_i, \boldsymbol{S}_i)$ should form realizations of independent pairs.

In the bivariate case, testing for uniformity on the unit circle $\mathcal{S}^1$ amounts to a univariate test of uniformity on $[0, 2\pi]$ for the angles Θ_i described by the points $\boldsymbol{S}_i = (\cos \Theta_i, \sin \Theta_i)'$ on the perimeter of the circle; equivalently, we may test the data $\{U_i := \Theta_i / (2\pi) : i = 1, \dots, n\}$ for uniformity on $[0, 1]$. Neglecting issues of serial dependence in the data, this may be done, for instance, by a standard chi-squared goodness-of-fit test (see Rice 1995, p. 241) or a Kolmogorov–Smirnov test (see Conover 1999). Again neglecting issues of serial dependence, the independence of the components of the pairs $\{(R_i, U_i) : i = 1, \dots, n\}$ could be examined by performing a test of association with Spearman's rank correlation coefficient (see, for example, Conover 1999, pp. 312–328).

We have performed these tests for the two datasets used in Figure 3.6, these being 2000 simulated bivariate t data with four degrees of freedom and 2000 daily log-returns for Intel and Microsoft. In Figure 3.8 the transformed data on the unit circle $\boldsymbol{S}_i$ and the implied angles U_i on the $[0, 1]$ scale are shown; the dispersion matrices

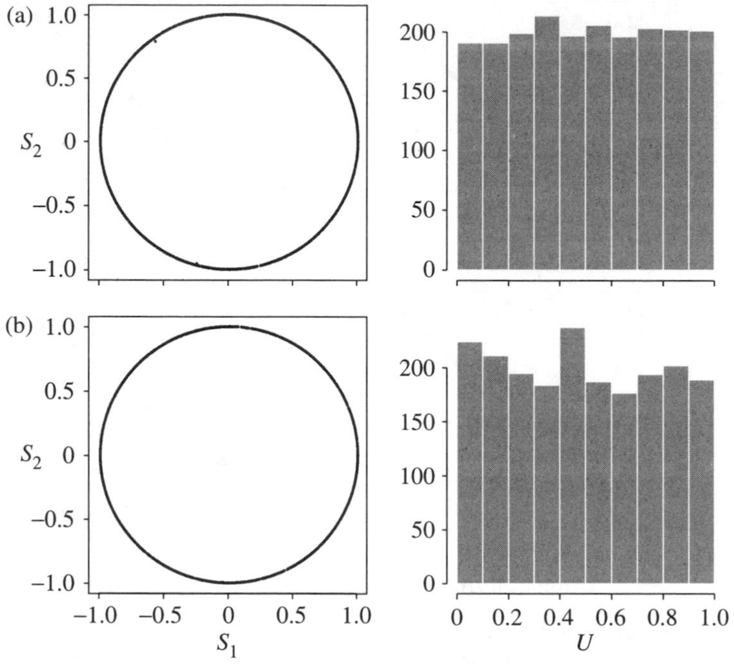

Figure 3.8. Illustration of the transformation of bivariate data to points on the unit circle $\mathcal{S}^1$ using the transformation $S_i = Y_i/\|Y_i\|$, where the Y_i data are defined in (3.57); the angles of these points are then transformed on to the [0, 1] scale, where they can be tested for uniformity. (a) Two thousand simulated t data with four degrees of freedom. (b) Two thousand Intel and Microsoft log-returns. Neither show strong evidence against elliptical symmetry.

have been estimated using the construction (3.56) based on Kendall's tau. Neither of these datasets shows significant evidence against the elliptical hypothesis. For the bivariate t data the p-values for the chi-squared and Kolmogorov–Smirnov tests of uniformity and the Spearman's rank test of association are, respectively, 0.99, 0.90 and 0.10. For the stock-return data they are 0.08, 0.12 and 0.19. Note that simulated data from lightly skewed members of the generalized hyperbolic family often do fail these tests.

Notes and Comments

A comprehensive reference for spherical and elliptical distributions is Fang, Kotz and Ng (1987); we have based our brief presentation of the theory on this account. Other references for the theory are Kelker (1970), Cambanis, Huang and Simons (1981) and Bingham and Kiesel (2002), the latter in the context of financial modelling. The original reference for Theorem 3.22 is Schoenberg (1938). Frahm (2004) suggests a generalization of the elliptical class to allow asymmetric models while preserving many of the attractive properties of the elliptical distributions.

There is a vast literature on alternative estimators of dispersion and correlation matrices, particularly with regard to better robustness properties. Textbooks with relevant sections include Huber (1981), Hampel et al. (1986), Marazzi (1993), Wilcox

(1997) and Dell'Aquila and Ronchetti (2005); the latter book is recommended in general for applications of robust statistics in econometrics and finance.

We have concentrated on M-estimation of dispersion matrices, since this is related to the maximum likelihood estimation of alternative elliptical models. M-estimators have a relatively long history and are known to have good local robustness properties (insensitivity to small data perturbations); they do, however, have relatively low breakdown points in high dimensions, so their performance can be poor under larger contaminations of the data. A small selection of papers on M-estimation includes Maronna (1976), Devlin, Gnanadesikan and Kettenring (1975, 1981) and Tyler (1983, 1987); see also Frahm (2004), in which an interesting alternative derivation of a Tyler estimator is given. The method based on Kendall's tau was suggested in Lindskog, McNeil and Schmock (2003).

The QQplots for testing spherical symmetry were suggested by Li, Fang and Zhu (1997). There is a large literature on tests of spherical symmetry, including Smith (1977), Kariya and Eaton (1977), Beran (1979) and Baringhaus (1991). This work is also related to tests of uniformity for directional data: see Mardia (1972), Giné (1975) and Prentice (1978).

3.4 Dimension Reduction Techniques

The techniques of dimension reduction, such as factor modelling and principal components, are central to multivariate statistical analysis and are widely used in econometric model building. In the high-dimensional world of financial risk management they are essential tools. For this reason, and also because we will build on the techniques in some of the multivariate time series models described in Chapter 4, we include a concise summary of the more important information. For further reading and more detail it will be necessary to consult references listed in Notes and Comments.

3.4.1 Factor Models

By using a factor model we attempt to explain the randomness in the components of a d-dimensional vector $\boldsymbol{X}$ in terms of a smaller set of *common factors*. If the components of $\boldsymbol{X}$ represent, for example, equity returns, it is clear that a large part of their variation can be explained in terms of the variation of a smaller set of market index returns. Formally we define a factor model as follows.

Definition 3.33 (linear factor model). The random vector $\boldsymbol{X}$ is said to follow a p-factor model if it can be decomposed as

$$\boldsymbol{X} = \boldsymbol{a} + B\boldsymbol{F} + \boldsymbol{\varepsilon}, \tag{3.60}$$

where

(i) $\boldsymbol{F} = (F_1, \dots, F_p)'$ is a random vector of *common factors* with $p < d$ and a covariance matrix that is positive definite;

(ii) $\boldsymbol{\varepsilon} = (\varepsilon_1, \dots, \varepsilon_d)'$ is a random vector of *idiosyncratic error terms*, which are uncorrelated and have mean zero;

(iii) $B \in \mathbb{R}^{d\times p}$ is a matrix of constant *factor loadings* and $\boldsymbol{a} \in \mathbb{R}^d$ is a vector of constants; and

(iv) $\operatorname{cov}(\boldsymbol{F}, \boldsymbol{\varepsilon}) = E((\boldsymbol{F} - E(\boldsymbol{F}))\boldsymbol{\varepsilon}') = 0$.

The assumptions that the errors are uncorrelated with each other (ii) and also with the common factors (iv) are an important part of this definition. We do not in general require independence, only uncorrelatedness. However, if the vector $\boldsymbol{X}$ is multivariate normally distributed and follows the factor model in (3.60), then it is possible to find a version of the factor model where $\boldsymbol{F}$ and $\boldsymbol{\varepsilon}$ are Gaussian and the errors can be assumed to be mutually independent and independent of the common factors. We elaborate on this assertion in Example 3.34 below.

It follows from the basic assumptions that factor models imply a special structure for the covariance matrix Σ of $\boldsymbol{X}$. If we denote the covariance matrix of $\boldsymbol{F}$ by Ω and that of $\boldsymbol{\varepsilon}$ by the diagonal matrix Υ, it follows that

$$\Sigma = \operatorname{cov}(\boldsymbol{X}) = B\Omega B' + \Upsilon. \tag{3.61}$$

If the factor model holds, the common factors can always be transformed so that they are mean zero and orthogonal. By setting $\boldsymbol{F}^* = \Omega^{-1/2}(\boldsymbol{F} - E(\boldsymbol{F}))$ and $B^* = B\Omega^{1/2}$, we have a representation of the factor model of the form $\boldsymbol{X} = \boldsymbol{\mu} + B^*\boldsymbol{F}^* + \boldsymbol{\varepsilon}$, where $\boldsymbol{\mu} = E(\boldsymbol{X})$ as usual and $\Sigma = B^*(B^*)' + \Upsilon$.

Conversely, it can be shown that whenever a random vector $\boldsymbol{X}$ has a covariance matrix which satisfies

$$\Sigma = BB' + \Upsilon \tag{3.62}$$

for some $B \in \mathbb{R}^{d\times p}$ with $\operatorname{rank}(B) = p < d$ and diagonal matrix Υ, then $\boldsymbol{X}$ has a factor-model representation for some p-dimensional factor vector $\boldsymbol{F}$ and d-dimensional error vector $\boldsymbol{\varepsilon}$.

Example 3.34 (the equicorrelation model). Suppose $\boldsymbol{X}$ is a random vector with standardized margins (zero mean and unit variance) and an *equicorrelation matrix*; in other words, the correlation between each pair of components is equal to $\rho > 0$. This means that the covariance matrix Σ can be written as $\Sigma = \rho J_d + (1-\rho)I_d$, where J_d is the d-dimensional square matrix of ones and I_d is the identity matrix, so that Σ is obviously of the form (3.62) for the d-vector $B = \sqrt{\rho}\mathbf{1}$.

To find a factor decomposition of $\boldsymbol{X}$ take *any* zero-mean, unit-variance rv Y that is *independent* of $\boldsymbol{X}$ and define a single common factor F and errors $\boldsymbol{\varepsilon}$ by

$$F = \frac{\sqrt{\rho}}{1+\rho(d-1)}\sum_{j=1}^{d} X_j + \sqrt{\frac{1-\rho}{1+\rho(d-1)}}\,Y, \qquad \varepsilon_j = X_j - \sqrt{\rho}F,$$

where we note that in this construction F also has mean zero and unit variance. Thus we have the factor decomposition $\boldsymbol{X} = BF + \boldsymbol{\varepsilon}$ and it may be verified by calculation that $\operatorname{cov}(F, \varepsilon_j) = 0$ for all j and $\operatorname{cov}(\varepsilon_j, \varepsilon_k) = 0$ when $j \neq k$, so that the requirements of Definition 3.33 are satisfied. A random vector with an equicorrelation matrix can be thought of as following a factor model with a single common factor.

Since we can take any Y, the factors and errors in this decomposition are non-unique. Consider the case where the vector $\boldsymbol{X}$ is Gaussian; it is most convenient to take Y to also be Gaussian, since in that case the common factor is normally distributed, the error vector is multivariate normally distributed, Y is independent of ε_j, for all j, and ε_j and ε_k are independent for $j \neq k$. Since $\text{var}(\varepsilon_j) = 1 - \rho$, it is most convenient to write the factor model implied by the equicorrelation model as

$$X_j = \sqrt{\rho}F + \sqrt{1-\rho}Z_j, \quad j = 1, \dots, d, \tag{3.63}$$

where $F, Z_1, \dots, Z_d$ are mutually independent standard Gaussian rvs. This model will be used in Section 8.3.5 in the context of modelling homogeneous credit portfolios. For the more general construction on which this example is based see Mardia, Kent and Bibby (1979, Exercise 9.2.2).

3.4.2 *Statistical Calibration Strategies*

Now assume that we have data $\boldsymbol{X}_1, \dots, \boldsymbol{X}_n \in \mathbb{R}^d$ representing risk-factor returns. Each vector observation $\boldsymbol{X}_t$ recorded at a time t is assumed to be generated by the factor model (3.60) for some common-factor vector $\boldsymbol{F}_t$ and some error vector $\boldsymbol{\varepsilon}_t$.

There are a number of different approaches to the practical calibration of a factor model, depending on the situation and, in particular, on whether or not the factor is also *observable* or considered to be *unobservable or latent*.

In an *observable factor model* we assume that appropriate factors for the return series in question have been identified in advance and data on these factors have been collected. A simple example would be a one-factor model where $F_1, \dots, F_n$ are observations of the return on a market index and $\boldsymbol{X}_1, \dots, \boldsymbol{X}_n$ are individual equity returns to be explained in terms of the market return (a model known in econometrics as Sharpe's single-index model). Fitting of the model (estimation of B and $\boldsymbol{a}$) is accomplished by regression techniques, and is described in Section 3.4.3.

In a *latent factor model* appropriate factors are themselves estimated from the data $\boldsymbol{X}_1, \dots, \boldsymbol{X}_n$. Here we envisage a situation where the $\boldsymbol{X}_t$ represent returns for a set of disparate risk factors and it is not clear *a priori* what the best set of factors might be. There are two general strategies for finding factors. The first strategy, which is quite common in finance, is to use the method of *principal components* to construct factors. We note that the factors we obtain, while being explanatory in a statistical sense, may not have any obvious interpretation.

In the second approach, *classical statistical factor analysis*, it is assumed that the data are identically distributed with a distribution whose covariance matrix has the factor structure (3.62). Various techniques are used to estimate B and Υ and then these estimates are used in turn to construct factor data. We will not go into the details of this method further—they are found in standard texts on multivariate statistical analysis (see Notes and Comments).

In the context of risk management, the goal of all approaches to factor models is to obtain factor data $\boldsymbol{F}_t$ and loading matrices B (and the constant vector $\boldsymbol{a}$ where relevant). If this is achieved, we can then concentrate on modelling the distribution or dynamics of $\boldsymbol{F}_1, \dots, \boldsymbol{F}_n$, which is a lower-dimensional problem than modelling

$\boldsymbol{X}_1, \dots, \boldsymbol{X}_n$. The unobserved errors $\boldsymbol{\varepsilon}_1, \dots, \boldsymbol{\varepsilon}_n$ are of secondary importance. In situations where we have many risk factors the risk embodied in the errors is partly mitigated by a diversification effect, whereas the risk embodied in the common factors remains. The following simple example gives an idea why this is the case.

Example 3.35. We continue our analysis of the one-factor model in Example 3.34. Suppose the random vector $\boldsymbol{X}$ in that example represents the return on d different companies so that the rv $Z_{(d)} = (1/d)\sum_{j=1}^{d} X_j$ can be thought of as the portfolio return for an equal investment in each of the companies. We calculate that

$$Z_{(d)} = \frac{1}{d}\mathbf{1}'BF + \frac{1}{d}\mathbf{1}'\boldsymbol{\varepsilon} = \sqrt{\rho}F + \frac{1}{d}\sum_{j=1}^{d}\varepsilon_j.$$

The risk in the first term is not affected by increasing the size of the portfolio d, whereas the risk in the second term can be reduced. Suppose we measure risk by simply calculating variances; we get

$$\operatorname{var}(Z_{(d)}) = \rho + \frac{1-\rho}{d} \to \rho, \quad d \to \infty,$$

so that the systematic factor is the main contributor to the risk in a large-portfolio situation.

We now discuss in a little more detail the fitting of observable factor models by regression. The approach to factor models based on principal components is described in Section 3.4.4. Principal component analysis is covered there in some detail, since it is an important technique in its own right.

3.4.3 Regression Analysis of Factor Models

Two equivalent approaches may be used to estimate the model parameters. We write the model as

$$\boldsymbol{X}_t = \boldsymbol{a} + B\boldsymbol{F}_t + \boldsymbol{\varepsilon}_t, \quad t = 1, \dots, n, \tag{3.64}$$

where $\boldsymbol{X}_t$ and $\boldsymbol{F}_t$ are vectors of individual returns and factors (for example, index returns) at time t, and $\boldsymbol{a}$ and B are parameters to be estimated. In the first approach we perform d univariate regression analyses, one for each component of the individual return series. In the second approach we estimate all parameters in a single multivariate regression.

Univariate regression. Writing $X_{t,j}$ for the observation at time t of instrument j we consider the univariate regression model

$$X_{t,j} = a_j + \boldsymbol{b}_j'\boldsymbol{F}_t + \varepsilon_{t,j}, \quad t = 1, \dots, n.$$

This is known as a time series regression, since the responses $X_{1,j}, \dots, X_{n,j}$ form a univariate time series and the factors $\boldsymbol{F}_1, \dots, \boldsymbol{F}_n$ form a possibly multivariate time series. Without going into technical details or anticipating any of the time series material in Chapter 4 we simply remark that the parameters a_j and $\boldsymbol{b}_j$ are estimated using the standard ordinary least-squares (OLS) method found in all textbooks on linear regression. To justify the use of the method and to derive statistical properties of the method it is usually assumed that, conditional on the factors, the errors $\varepsilon_{1,j}, \dots, \varepsilon_{n,j}$ are identically distributed and serially uncorrelated. (This means they form what will be referred to in Chapter 4 as white noise.)

The estimate $\hat{a}_j$ obviously estimates the jth component of $\boldsymbol{a}$, while $\hat{\boldsymbol{b}}_j$ is an estimate of the jth row of the matrix B. By performing a regression for each of the univariate time series $X_{1,j}, \dots, X_{n,j}$ for $j = 1, \dots, d$, we complete the estimation of the parameters $\boldsymbol{a}$ and B.

Multivariate regression. To set the problem up as a multivariate linear-regression problem, we construct a number of large matrices:

$$X = \underbrace{\begin{pmatrix} \boldsymbol{X}_1' \\ \vdots \\ \boldsymbol{X}_n' \end{pmatrix}}_{n \times d}, \qquad F = \underbrace{\begin{pmatrix} 1 & \boldsymbol{F}_1' \\ \vdots & \vdots \\ 1 & \boldsymbol{F}_n' \end{pmatrix}}_{n \times (p+1)}, \qquad B_2 = \underbrace{\begin{pmatrix} \boldsymbol{a}' \\ B' \end{pmatrix}}_{(p+1) \times d}, \qquad E = \underbrace{\begin{pmatrix} \boldsymbol{\varepsilon}_1' \\ \vdots \\ \boldsymbol{\varepsilon}_n' \end{pmatrix}}_{n \times d}.$$

Each row of the data X corresponds to a vector observation at a fixed time point t, and each column corresponds to a univariate time series for one of the individual returns. The model (3.64) can then be expressed by the matrix equation

$$X = F B_2 + E, \tag{3.65}$$

where B_2 is the matrix of regression parameters to be estimated.

If we assume that the unobserved error vectors $\boldsymbol{\varepsilon}_1, \dots, \boldsymbol{\varepsilon}_n$ comprising the rows of E are identically distributed and serially uncorrelated, conditional on $\boldsymbol{F}_1, \dots, \boldsymbol{F}_n$, then the equation (3.65) defines a standard multivariate linear regression (see, for example, Mardia, Kent and Bibby (1979) for the standard assumptions). An estimate of B_2 is obtained by multivariate OLS according to the formula

$$\hat{B}_2 = (F'F)^{-1} F'X. \tag{3.66}$$

The factor model is now essentially calibrated, since we have estimates for $\boldsymbol{a}$ and B. The model can now be critically examined with respect to the original conditions of Definition 3.33. Do the errors vectors $\boldsymbol{\varepsilon}_t$ come from a distribution with diagonal covariance matrix, and are they uncorrelated with the factors?

To learn something about the errors, we can form the model residual matrix $\hat{E} = X - F\hat{B}_2$. Each row of this matrix contains an inferred value of an error vector $\hat{\boldsymbol{\varepsilon}}_t$ at a fixed point in time. Examination of the sample correlation matrix of these inferred error vectors will hopefully show that there is little remaining correlation in the errors (or at least much less than in the original data vectors $\boldsymbol{X}_t$). If this is the case, then the diagonal elements of the sample covariance matrix of the $\hat{\boldsymbol{\varepsilon}}_t$ could be taken as an estimator $\hat{\Upsilon}$ for Υ. It is sometimes of interest to form the covariance matrix implied by the factor model and compare this with the original sample covariance matrix S of the data. The implied covariance matrix is

$$\hat{\Sigma}^{(\mathrm{F})} = \hat{B}\hat{\Omega}\hat{B}' + \hat{\Upsilon}, \quad \text{where } \hat{\Omega} = \frac{1}{n-1}\sum_{t=1}^{n}(\boldsymbol{F}_t - \bar{\boldsymbol{F}})(\boldsymbol{F}_t - \bar{\boldsymbol{F}})'.$$

Table 3.6. The first line gives estimates of B for a multivariate regression model fitted to 10 Dow Jones 30 stocks where the observed common factor is the return on the Dow Jones 30 index itself. The second row gives r^2 values for a univariate regression model for each individual time series. The next 10 lines of the table give the sample correlation matrix of the data R, while the middle 10 lines give the correlation matrix implied by the factor model. The final 10 lines show the estimated correlation matrix of the residuals from the regression model, with entries less than 0.1 in absolute value being omitted. See Example 3.36 for full details.

	MO	KO	EK	HWP	INTC	MSFT	IBM	MCD	WMT	DIS
$\hat{B}$	0.87	1.01	0.77	1.12	1.12	1.11	1.07	0.86	1.02	1.03
r^2	0.17	0.33	0.14	0.18	0.17	0.21	0.22	0.23	0.24	0.26
MO	1.00	0.27	0.14	0.17	0.16	0.25	0.18	0.22	0.16	0.22
KO	0.27	1.00	0.17	0.22	0.21	0.25	0.18	0.36	0.33	0.32
EK	0.14	0.17	1.00	0.17	0.17	0.18	0.15	0.14	0.17	0.16
HWP	0.17	0.22	0.17	1.00	0.42	0.38	0.36	0.20	0.22	0.23
INTC	0.16	0.21	0.17	0.42	1.00	0.53	0.36	0.19	0.22	0.21
MSFT	0.25	0.25	0.18	0.38	0.53	1.00	0.33	0.22	0.28	0.26
IBM	0.18	0.18	0.15	0.36	0.36	0.33	1.00	0.20	0.20	0.20
MCD	0.22	0.36	0.14	0.20	0.19	0.22	0.20	1.00	0.26	0.26
WMT	0.16	0.33	0.17	0.22	0.22	0.28	0.20	0.26	1.00	0.28
DIS	0.22	0.32	0.16	0.23	0.21	0.26	0.20	0.26	0.28	1.00
MO	1.00	0.24	0.16	0.18	0.17	0.19	0.20	0.20	0.20	0.21
KO	0.24	1.00	0.22	0.24	0.23	0.26	0.27	0.28	0.28	0.29
EK	0.16	0.22	1.00	0.16	0.15	0.17	0.18	0.18	0.18	0.19
HWP	0.18	0.24	0.16	1.00	0.17	0.19	0.20	0.20	0.21	0.22
INTC	0.17	0.23	0.15	0.17	1.00	0.19	0.19	0.19	0.20	0.21
MSFT	0.19	0.26	0.17	0.19	0.19	1.00	0.22	0.22	0.22	0.23
IBM	0.20	0.27	0.18	0.20	0.19	0.22	1.00	0.23	0.23	0.24
MCD	0.20	0.28	0.18	0.20	0.19	0.22	0.23	1.00	0.23	0.24
WMT	0.20	0.28	0.18	0.21	0.20	0.22	0.23	0.23	1.00	0.25
DIS	0.21	0.29	0.19	0.22	0.21	0.23	0.24	0.24	0.25	1.00
MO	1.00									
KO		1.00					−0.12	0.12		
EK			1.00							
HWP				1.00	0.30	0.24	0.20			
INTC				0.30	1.00	0.43	0.20			
MSFT				0.24	0.43	1.00	0.14			
IBM		−0.12		0.20	0.20	0.14	1.00			
MCD		0.12						1.00		
WMT										
DIS										1.00

We would hope that $\hat{\Sigma}^{(F)}$ captured much of the structure of S and that the correlation matrix $R^{(F)} := \wp(\hat{\Sigma}^{(F)})$ captured much of the structure of the sample correlation matrix $R = \wp(S)$.

Example 3.36 (single-index model for Dow Jones 30 returns). As a simple example of the regression approach to fitting factor models we have fitted a single factor model to a set of 10 Dow Jones 30 daily stock-return series from 1992 to 1998. Note that these are different returns to those analysed in previous sections of this chapter. They have been chosen to be of two types: technology-related titles like Hewlett-Packard, Intel, Microsoft and IBM; and food- and consumer-related titles like Philip Morris, Coca-Cola, Eastman Kodak, McDonald's, Wal-Mart and Disney. The factor chosen is the corresponding return on the Dow Jones 30 index itself.

The estimate of B implied by formula (3.66) is shown in the first line of Table 3.6. The highest values of B correspond to so-called *high beta* stocks; since a one-factor model implies the relationship $E(X_j) = a_j + B_j E(F)$, these stocks potentially offer high expected returns relative to the market (but are often riskier titles); in this case the four technology-related stocks have the highest beta values. In the second row, values of r^2, the so-called coefficient of determination, are given for each of the univariate regression models. This number measures the strength of the regression relationship between X_j and F and can be interpreted as the proportion of the variation of the stock return that is explained by variation in the market return; the highest r^2 corresponds to Coca-Cola (33%) and in general it seems that about 20% of individual stock-return variation is explained by market-return variation.

The next 10 lines of the table give the sample correlation matrix of the data R, while the middle 10 lines give the correlation matrix implied by the factor model (corresponding to $\hat{\Sigma}^{(\mathrm{F})}$). The latter matrix picks up much, but not all, of the structure of the former matrix. The final 10 lines show the estimated correlation matrix of the residuals from the regression model, but only those elements which exceed 0.1 in absolute value. The residuals are indeed much less correlated than the original data, but a few larger entries indicate imperfections in the factor-model representation of the data, particularly for the technology stocks. The index return for the broader market is clearly an important common factor but further systematic effects appear to be present in these data that are not captured by the index.

3.4.4 *Principal Component Analysis*

The aim of principal component analysis (PCA) is to reduce the dimensionality of highly correlated data by finding a small number of uncorrelated linear combinations that *account for most of the variability of the original data*, in some appropriately defined sense. PCA is not itself a model, but rather a data-rotation technique. However, it can be used as a way of constructing appropriate factors for a factor model, and this is the main application we consider in this section.

The key mathematical result behind the technique is the *spectral decomposition theorem* of linear algebra, which says that any symmetric matrix $A \in \mathbb{R}^{d\times d}$ can be written as

$$A = \Gamma \Lambda \Gamma', \tag{3.67}$$

where

(i) $\Lambda = \operatorname{diag}(\lambda_1, \dots, \lambda_d)$ is the diagonal matrix of *eigenvalues of* A which, without loss of generality, are ordered so that $\lambda_1 \geqslant \lambda_2 \geqslant \cdots \geqslant \lambda_d$, and

(ii) Γ is an orthogonal matrix satisfying $\Gamma\Gamma' = \Gamma'\Gamma = I_d$ whose columns are standardized *eigenvectors of* A (i.e. eigenvectors with length 1).

Theoretical principal components. Obviously we can apply this decomposition to any covariance matrix Σ, and in this case the positive semidefiniteness of Σ ensures that $\lambda_j \geqslant 0$ for all j. Suppose the random vector $\boldsymbol{X}$ has mean vector $\boldsymbol{\mu}$ and covariance matrix Σ and we make the decomposition $\Sigma = \Gamma\Lambda\Gamma'$ as in (3.67). Then the principal components transform of $\boldsymbol{X}$ is defined to be

$$\boldsymbol{Y} = \Gamma'(\boldsymbol{X} - \boldsymbol{\mu}), \tag{3.68}$$

and can be thought of as a *rotation* and a *recentring* of $\boldsymbol{X}$. The jth component of the rotated vector $\boldsymbol{Y}$ is known as the *jth principal component* of $\boldsymbol{X}$ and is given by

$$Y_j = \boldsymbol{\gamma}_j'(\boldsymbol{X} - \boldsymbol{\mu}), \tag{3.69}$$

where $\boldsymbol{\gamma}_j$ is the eigenvector of Σ corresponding to the jth ordered eigenvalue; this vector is also known as the jth vector of *loadings*.

Simple calculations reveal that

$$E(\boldsymbol{Y}) = \boldsymbol{0} \quad \text{and} \quad \operatorname{cov}(\boldsymbol{Y}) = \Gamma'\Sigma\Gamma = \Gamma'\Gamma\Lambda\Gamma'\Gamma = \Lambda,$$

so that the principal components of $\boldsymbol{Y}$ are uncorrelated and have variances $\operatorname{var}(Y_j) = \lambda_j, \forall j$. The components are thus ordered by variance, from largest to smallest. Moreover, the first principal component can be shown to be the standardized linear combination of $\boldsymbol{X}$ which has maximal variance among all such combinations; in other words,

$$\operatorname{var}(\boldsymbol{\gamma}_1'\boldsymbol{X}) = \max\{\operatorname{var}(\boldsymbol{a}'\boldsymbol{X}) : \boldsymbol{a}'\boldsymbol{a} = 1\}.$$

For $j = 2, \dots, d$, the jth principal component can be shown to be the standardized linear combination of $\boldsymbol{X}$ with maximal variance among all such linear combinations that are *orthogonal* to (and hence *uncorrelated* with) the first $j - 1$ linear combinations. The final dth principal component has minimum variance among standardized linear combinations of $\boldsymbol{X}$.

To measure the ability of the first few principal components to *explain the variability* in $\boldsymbol{X}$ we observe that

$$\sum_{j=1}^{d} \operatorname{var}(Y_j) = \sum_{j=1}^{d} \lambda_j = \operatorname{trace}(\Sigma) = \sum_{j=1}^{d} \operatorname{var}(X_j).$$

If we interpret $\operatorname{trace}(\Sigma) = \sum_{j=1}^{d} \operatorname{var}(X_j)$ as a measure of the *total variability* in $\boldsymbol{X}$, then, for $k \leqslant d$, the ratio $\sum_{j=1}^{k} \lambda_j / \sum_{j=1}^{d} \lambda_j$ represents the amount of this variability explained by the first k principal components.

Sample principal components. Assume that we have multivariate data observations $\boldsymbol{X}_1, \dots, \boldsymbol{X}_n$ with identical distribution and unknown covariance matrix Σ, which we estimate by the sample covariance matrix

$$S_x = \frac{1}{n} \sum_{t=1}^{n} (\boldsymbol{X}_t - \bar{\boldsymbol{X}})(\boldsymbol{X}_t - \bar{\boldsymbol{X}})'.$$

We apply the spectral decomposition (3.67) to the symmetric, positive semidefinite matrix S_x to get

$$S_x = GLG',$$

where G is the eigenvector matrix, $L = \operatorname{diag}(l_1, \dots, l_d)$ is the diagonal matrix consisting of ordered eigenvalues, and we switch to roman letters to emphasize that these are now calculated from an empirical covariance matrix.

The eigenvectors, or loading vectors, $\boldsymbol{g}_j$ making up the columns of G define the empirical principal components transform and, by analogy with (3.69), the value $Y_{t,j}$ given by

$$Y_{t,j} = \boldsymbol{g}_j'(\boldsymbol{X}_t - \bar{\boldsymbol{X}})$$

can be considered to be an observation of the jth sample principal component at time t. The vectors $\boldsymbol{Y}_t = (Y_{t,1}, \dots, Y_{t,d})' = G'(\boldsymbol{X}_t - \bar{\boldsymbol{X}})$ constitute rotations of the original data vectors $\boldsymbol{X}_t$. The rotated data vectors $\boldsymbol{Y}_1, \dots, \boldsymbol{Y}_n$ have the property that their sample covariance matrix is $L = \operatorname{diag}(l_1, \dots, l_d)$, the diagonal matrix of eigenvalues of S_x, as is easily verified:

$$\begin{aligned} S_y &= \frac{1}{n}\sum_{t=1}^{n}(\boldsymbol{Y}_t - \bar{\boldsymbol{Y}})(\boldsymbol{Y}_t - \bar{\boldsymbol{Y}})' = \frac{1}{n}\sum_{t=1}^{n}\boldsymbol{Y}_t\boldsymbol{Y}_t' \\ &= \frac{1}{n}\sum_{t=1}^{n} G'(\boldsymbol{X}_t - \bar{\boldsymbol{X}})(\boldsymbol{X}_t - \bar{\boldsymbol{X}})'G = G'S_xG = L. \end{aligned}$$

Thus the rotated vectors show no correlation between components and the components are ordered by their sample variances, from largest to smallest.

Remark 3.37. In a situation where the different components of the data vectors $\boldsymbol{X}_1, \dots, \boldsymbol{X}_n$ have very different sample variances (particularly if they are measured on very different scales), it is to be expected that the component (or components) with largest variance will dominate the first loading vector $\boldsymbol{g}_1$ and dominate the first principal component. In these situations the data are often transformed to have identical variances, which effectively means that principal components analysis is applied to the sample correlation matrix R_x. Note also that we could derive sample principal components from a robust estimate of the correlation matrix or a multivariate dispersion matrix.

Principal components as factors. The principal components transform in (3.68) is invertible, giving us $\boldsymbol{X} = \boldsymbol{\mu} + \Gamma\boldsymbol{Y}$, where the random vector $\boldsymbol{Y}$ contains the principal components ordered from top to bottom by their variance. Let us suppose that we believe that the first k components explain the most important portion of the total variability of $\boldsymbol{X}$. We could partition $\boldsymbol{Y}$ according to $(\boldsymbol{Y}_1', \boldsymbol{Y}_2')'$, where $\boldsymbol{Y}_1 \in \mathbb{R}^k$ and $\boldsymbol{Y}_2 \in \mathbb{R}^{d-k}$; similarly, we could partition Γ according to (Γ_1, Γ_2), where $\Gamma_1 \in \mathbb{R}^{d\times k}$ and $\Gamma_2 \in \mathbb{R}^{d\times(d-k)}$. This yields the representation

$$\boldsymbol{X} = \boldsymbol{\mu} + \Gamma_1\boldsymbol{Y}_1 + \Gamma_2\boldsymbol{Y}_2 = \boldsymbol{\mu} + \Gamma_1\boldsymbol{Y}_1 + \boldsymbol{\varepsilon}, \tag{3.70}$$

where $\Gamma_2\boldsymbol{Y}_2$ can be regarded as an error since its covariance matrix contains very small entries in comparison with the covariance matrix of $\Gamma_1\boldsymbol{Y}_1$.

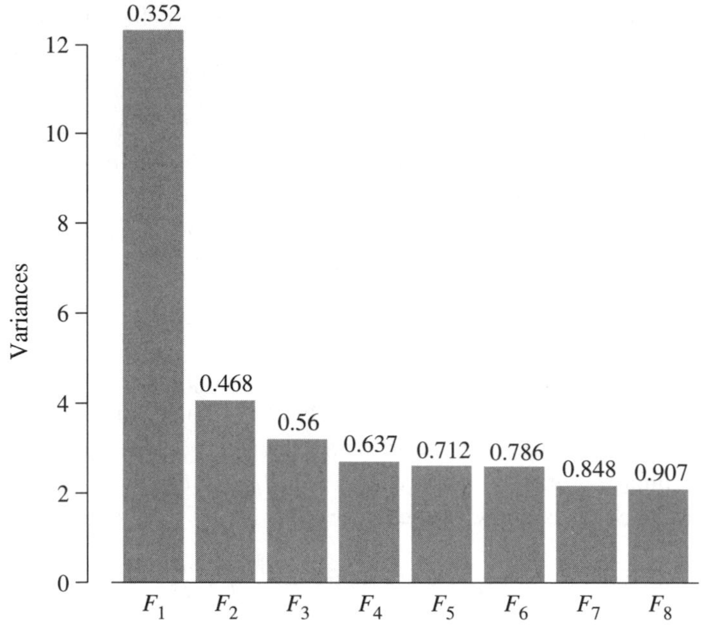

Figure 3.9. Barplot of the sample variances l_j of the first eight principal components; above each bar the cumulative proportion of the total variance explained by the components is given $(\sum_{j=1}^{k} l_j / \sum_{j=1}^{10} l_j,\ k = 1, \dots, 8)$.

Equation (3.70) is reminiscent of the factor model (3.60), except that the errors do not have a diagonal covariance matrix. Nevertheless, the principal components approach to constructing a factor model is generally to equate the first k principal components $\boldsymbol{Y}_1$ with the factors $\boldsymbol{F}$, to equate the matrix Γ_1 containing the first k eigenvectors with the factor loading matrix B, and to ignore the errors entirely. The factors are thus given by $\boldsymbol{F}_t = (\boldsymbol{\gamma}_1'\boldsymbol{X}, \dots, \boldsymbol{\gamma}_k'\boldsymbol{X})'$.

Example 3.38 (PCA-based factor model for Dow Jones 30 returns). We consider the data in Example 3.36 again. Principal components analysis is applied to the sample covariance matrix of the return data and the results are summarized in Figures 3.9 and 3.10. In the former we see a barplot of the sample variances of the first eight principal components l_j; above each bar the cumulative proportion of the total variance explained by the components is given; the first two components explain almost 50% of the variation. In the latter plot the first two loading vectors $\boldsymbol{g}_1$ and $\boldsymbol{g}_2$ are summarized.

The first vector of loadings is positively weighted for all stocks and can be thought of as describing a kind of index portfolio; of course the weights in the loading vector do not sum to one, but they can be scaled to do so and this gives a so-called principal-component-mimicking portfolio. The second vector has positive weights for the consumer titles and negative weights for the technology titles; as a portfolio it can be thought of as prescribing a programme of short-selling of technology to buy the consumer titles. These first two sample principal components loadings vectors are used to define factors.

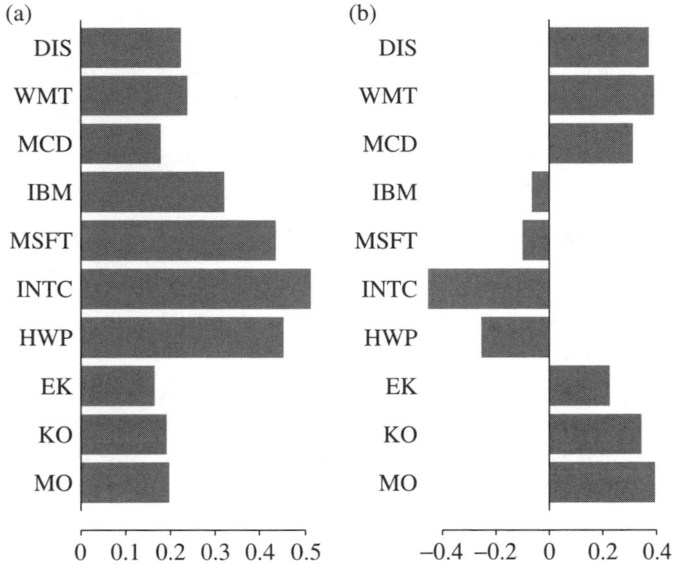

Figure 3.10. Barplot summarizing the loadings vectors $\boldsymbol{g}_1$ and $\boldsymbol{g}_2$ defining the first two principal components: (a) factor 1 loadings; and (b) factor 2 loadings.

In Table 3.7 the transpose of the matrix $\hat{B}$ (containing the loadings estimates in the factor model) is shown; the rows are merely the first two loadings vectors from the principal components analysis. In the third row, values of r^2, the so-called coefficient of determination, are given for each of the univariate regression models and these indicate that more of the variation in the data is explained by the two PCA-based factors than was explained by the observed factor in Example 3.36; Intel returns seem to be best explained by the model.

The next 10 lines give the correlation matrix implied by the factor model (corresponding to $\hat{\Sigma}^{(\mathrm{F})}$). Compared with the true sample correlation matrix in Example 3.36 this seems to pick up more of the structure than did the correlation matrix implied by the observed factor model.

The final 10 lines show the estimated correlation matrix of the residuals from the regression model, but only those elements which exceed 0.1 in absolute value. The residuals are again less correlated than the original data, but there are quite a number of larger entries, indicating imperfections in the factor-model representation of the data. In particular, we have introduced a number of larger negative correlations into the residuals; in practice, we seldom expect to find a factor model where the residuals have a covariance matrix that appears perfectly diagonal.

Notes and Comments

We have based our discussion of factor models, multivariate regression, statistical factor models and principal components on Mardia, Kent and Bibby (1979). Statistical approaches to factor models are also treated in Seber (1984) and Johnson and Wichern (2002).

Table 3.7. The first two lines give estimates of the transpose of B for a factor model fitted to 10 Dow Jones 30 stocks, where the factors are constructed from the first two sample principal components. The third row gives r^2 values for the univariate regression model for each individual time series. The next 10 lines give the correlation matrix implied by the factor model. The final 10 lines show the estimated correlation matrix of the residuals from the regression model, with entries less than 0.1 in absolute value omitted. See Example 3.38 for full details.

	MO	KO	EK	HWP	INTC	MSFT	IBM	MCD	WMT	DIS
$\hat{B}'$	0.20	0.19	0.16	0.45	0.51	0.44	0.32	0.18	0.24	0.22
	0.39	0.34	0.23	−0.26	−0.45	−0.10	−0.07	0.31	0.39	0.37
r^2	0.35	0.42	0.18	0.55	0.75	0.56	0.35	0.34	0.42	0.41
MO	1.00	0.39	0.25	0.17	0.13	0.25	0.20	0.35	0.38	0.38
KO	0.39	1.00	0.28	0.21	0.17	0.29	0.23	0.38	0.42	0.42
EK	0.25	0.28	1.00	0.18	0.15	0.22	0.18	0.25	0.28	0.27
HWP	0.17	0.21	0.18	1.00	0.64	0.55	0.43	0.20	0.23	0.23
INTC	0.13	0.17	0.15	0.64	1.00	0.61	0.48	0.16	0.19	0.18
MSFT	0.25	0.29	0.22	0.55	0.61	1.00	0.44	0.27	0.31	0.30
IBM	0.20	0.23	0.18	0.43	0.48	0.44	1.00	0.21	0.25	0.24
MCD	0.35	0.38	0.25	0.20	0.16	0.27	0.21	1.00	0.38	0.37
WMT	0.38	0.42	0.28	0.23	0.19	0.31	0.25	0.38	1.00	0.41
DIS	0.38	0.42	0.27	0.23	0.18	0.30	0.24	0.37	0.41	1.00
MO	1.00	−0.19	−0.15					−0.19	−0.37	−0.26
KO	−0.19	1.00	−0.15		0.11				−0.16	−0.17
EK	−0.15	−0.15	1.00					−0.15	−0.16	−0.16
HWP				1.00	−0.63	−0.37	−0.14			
INTC		0.11		−0.63	1.00	−0.24	−0.31			
MSFT				−0.37	−0.24	1.00	−0.22			
IBM				−0.14	−0.31	−0.22	1.00			
MCD	−0.19		−0.15					1.00	−0.19	−0.19
WMT	−0.37	−0.16	−0.16					−0.19	1.00	−0.23
DIS	−0.26	−0.17	−0.16					−0.19	−0.23	1.00

We have simply spoken of observed and unobserved or latent factor models, but in the econometrics literature a classification of factor models into three types is more common; these are *macroeconomic* factor models, *fundamental* factor models and *statistical* factor models. In this categorization our observable factor model would be a macroeconomic factor model; index returns, along with other observables such as interest rates or inflation, are the kind of macroeconomic variables that are typically used as explanatory factors in such models. On the other hand, both approaches to calibrating a latent factor model (classical factor analysis and principal components) would fall under the heading of statistical factor models.

The fundamental factor models, which are not described in this book, relate to the situation where factors are unobserved, but the loading matrix B is assumed to be known. More precisely we consider a situation where we have clear ideas of how to group returns by geographical or industrial sector, firm size or other important characteristics. For example, the return of a European technology company might be expected to be explained by an unobserved factor representing the performance of such companies, or perhaps by two unobserved factors representing European and technology companies. Using data for many companies and regression methods it is then possible to estimate the unobserved factors using the known classification information.

For a more detailed discussion of factor models see the paper by Connor (1995), which provides a comparison of the three types of model, and the book of Campbell, Lo and MacKinlay (1997). An excellent practical introduction to these models with examples in S-Plus is Zivot and Wang (2003). Other accounts of factor models and PCA in finance are found in Alexander (2001) and Tsay (2002).

4
Financial Time Series

In this chapter we consider time series models for financial risk-factor change data, in particular differenced logarithmic price and exchange-rate series. We begin by looking more systematically at the *empirical properties* of such data in a discussion of so-called stylized facts.

In Section 4.2 we review essential concepts in the analysis of time series, such as stationarity, autocorrelations and their estimation, white noise processes, and ARMA (autoregressive moving-average) processes. We then devote Section 4.3 to univariate ARCH and GARCH (generalized autoregressive conditionally heteroscedastic) processes for capturing the important phenomenon of *volatility*, before showing how such models are used in the context of quantitative risk management in Section 4.4. A short introduction to concepts in the analysis of multivariate time series, such as cross-correlation and multivariate white noise, is found in Section 4.5, while the final section presents *multivariate GARCH-type models* for multivariate risk-factor change series.

Our focus on the GARCH paradigm in this chapter requires comment. As this book goes to press these models have been with us for around two decades, and modern econometrics and finance have continued to develop other kinds of model for financial return series. We think here of discrete-time stochastic volatility models, long-memory GARCH models, continuous-time models fitted to discrete data, and models based on realized volatility calculated from high-frequency data; none of these new developments are handled in this book.

Our emphasis on GARCH has two main motivations, the first of these being practical. We recall that in risk management we are typically dealing with very large numbers of risk factors and our philosophy, expounded in Section 1.5, is that broad-brush techniques that capture the main risk features of many time series are more important than very detailed analyses of single series. The relatively simple GARCH model lends itself to this approach and proves very easy to fit. There are also some multivariate extensions which build in fairly simple ways on the univariate models and may be calibrated to a multivariate series in stages. This ease of use contrasts with other models where even the fitting of a single series presents a challenging computational problem (e.g. estimation of a stochastic volatility model via filtering or Gibbs sampling), and multivariate extensions have not been widely considered. Related to this is the likelihood that an average financial enterprise will collect, at best, daily data on its complete set of risk factors for the purposes of risk management, and this will rule out some more sophisticated models that require higher-frequency data.

Our second reason for concentrating on ARCH and GARCH models is didactic. These models for volatile return series have a status akin to ARMA models in classical time series; they belong, in our opinion, to the body of standard methodology to which a student of the subject should be exposed. A quantitative risk manager who understands GARCH has a good basis for understanding more complex models and a good framework for talking about volatility in a rational way. He/she may also appreciate more clearly the role of more ad hoc volatility estimation methods such as the *exponentially weighted moving-average* (EWMA) procedure.

4.1 Empirical Analyses of Financial Time Series

4.1.1 *Stylized Facts*

The *stylized facts* of financial time series are a collection of empirical observations, and inferences drawn from these observations, that seem to apply to the majority of *daily series* of risk-factor changes, such as log-returns on equities, indexes, exchange rates and commodity prices; these observations are now so entrenched in econometric experience that they have been elevated to the status of facts. They often continue to hold when we go to longer time intervals, such as weekly or monthly returns, or to shorter time intervals, such as intra-daily returns. A version of the stylized facts is as follows.

(1) Return series are not iid although they show little serial correlation.

(2) Series of absolute or squared returns show profound serial correlation.

(3) Conditional expected returns are close to zero.

(4) Volatility appears to vary over time.

(5) Return series are leptokurtic or heavy-tailed.

(6) Extreme returns appear in clusters.

In the following consider a sample of daily return data $X_1, \dots, X_n$ and assume that these have been formed by logarithmic differencing of a price, index or exchange-rate series $(S_t)_{t=0,1,\dots,n}$, so that $X_t = \ln(S_t/S_{t-1})$, $t = 1, \dots, n$.

Volatility clustering. Evidence for the first two stylized facts is collected in Figures 4.1 and 4.2. Figure 4.1(a) shows 2608 daily log-returns for the DAX index spanning a decade from 2 January 1985 to 30 December 1994, a period including both the stock-market crash of 1987 and the reunification of Germany. Parts (b) and (c) show series of simulated iid data from a normal and Student t model, respectively; in both cases the model parameters have been set by fitting the model to the real return data using the method of maximum likelihood under the iid assumption. In the normal case this means that we simply simulate iid data with distribution $N(\mu, \sigma^2)$, where $\mu = \bar{X} = n^{-1}\sum_{i=1}^{n} X_i$ and $\sigma^2 = n^{-1}\sum_{i=1}^{n}(X_i - \bar{X})^2$. In the t case the likelihood has been maximized numerically and the estimated degrees of freedom parameter is $\nu = 3.8$.

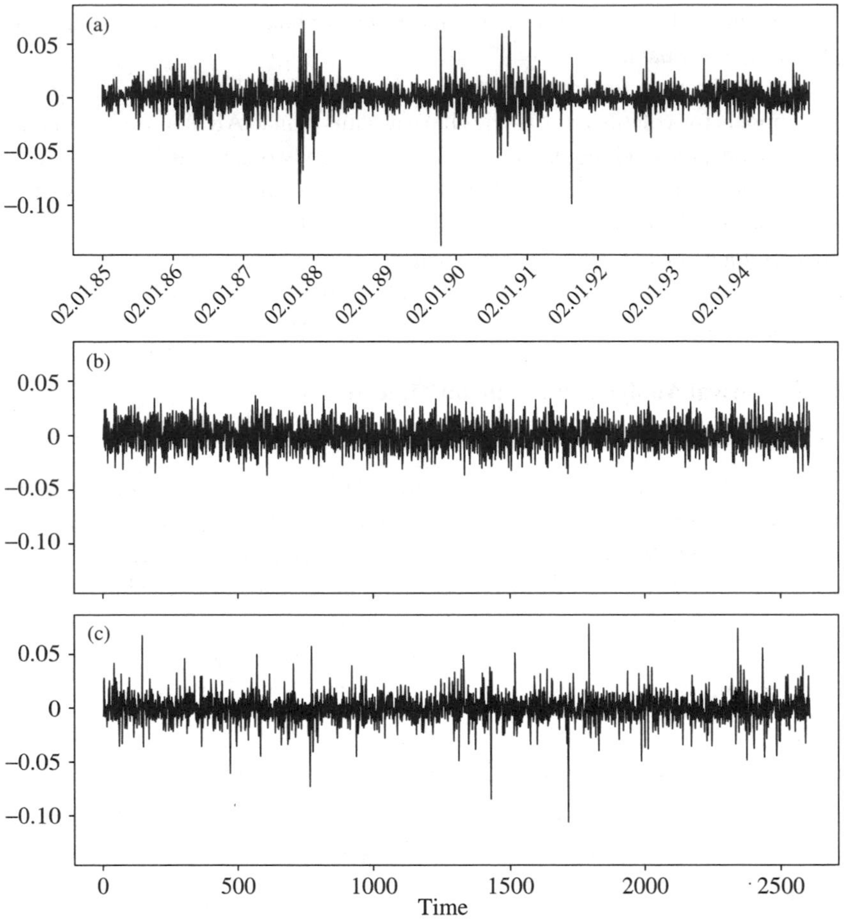

Figure 4.1. (a) Log-returns for the DAX index from 2 January 1985 to 30 December 1994 compared with simulated iid data from (b) a normal and (c) a t distribution, where the parameters have been determined by fitting the models to the DAX data.

The simulated normal data are clearly very different from the DAX return data and do not show the same range of extreme values, which does not surprise us given our observations on the inadequacy of the Gaussian model in Chapter 3. While the Student t model can generate comparable extreme values to the real data, more careful observation reveals that the DAX returns exhibit a phenomenon known as *volatility clustering*, which is not present in the simulated series. Volatility clustering is the tendency for extreme returns to be followed by other extreme returns, although not necessarily with the same sign. In the DAX data we see periods such as the stock-market crash of October 1987 or the political uncertainty in the period between late 1989 and German reunification in 1990 which are marked by large positive and negative moves.

In Figure 4.2 the *correlograms* of the raw data and the absolute data for all three datasets are shown. The correlogram is a graphical display for estimates of serial

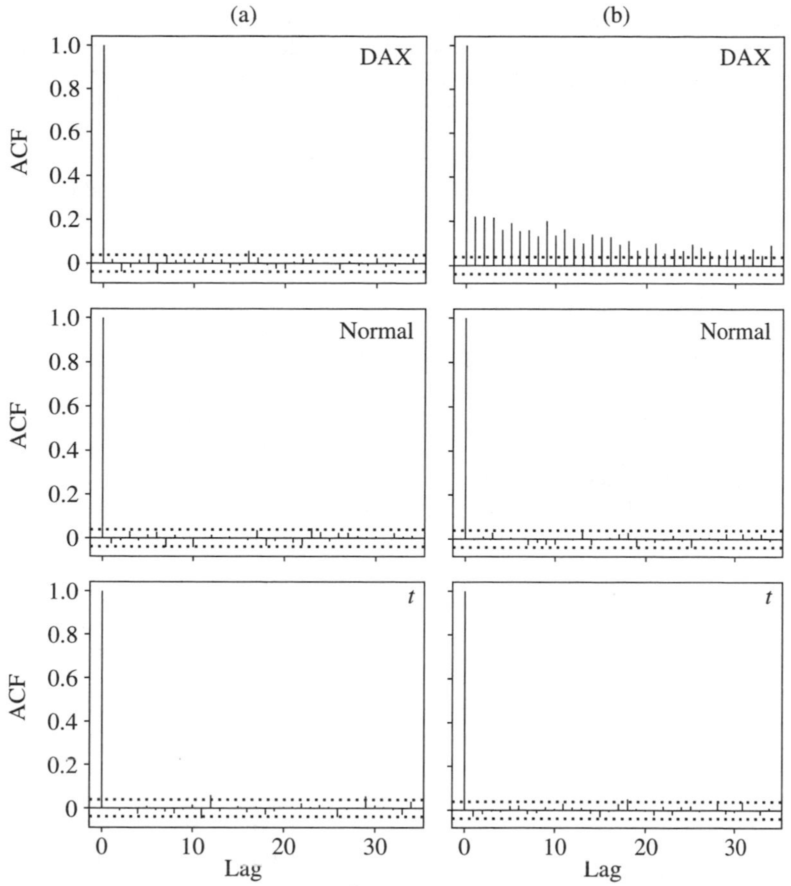

Figure 4.2. Correlograms for (a) the three datasets in Figure 4.1 and (b) the absolute values of these data. Dashed lines mark the standard 95% confidence intervals for the autocorrelations of a process of iid finite-variance rvs.

correlation, and its construction and interpretation are discussed in Section 4.2.3. While there is very little evidence of serial correlation in the raw data for all datasets, the absolute values of the real financial data appear to show evidence of serial dependence. Clearly, more than 5% of the estimated correlations lie outside the dashed lines, which are the 95% confidence intervals for a process of iid finite-variance rvs. This serial dependence in the absolute returns would be equally apparent in squared return values, and seems to confirm the presence of volatility clustering. We conclude that, although there is no evidence against the iid hypothesis for the genuinely iid data, there is strong evidence against the iid hypothesis for the DAX return data.

Table 4.1 contains more evidence against the iid hypothesis for daily stock-return data. The Ljung–Box test of randomness (described in Section 4.2.3) has been performed for the stocks comprising the Dow Jones 30 index in the period 1993–2000. In the two columns for daily returns the test is applied, respectively, to the raw return data (LBraw) and their absolute values (LBabs), and p-values are tabulated;

Table 4.1. Tests of randomness for returns of 30 Dow Jones stocks in the eight-year period 1993–2000. The columns LBraw and LBabs show p-values for Ljung–Box tests applied to the raw and absolute values, respectively.

		Daily		Monthly	
Name	Symbol	LBraw	LBabs	LBraw	LBabs
Alcoa	AA	0.00	0.00	0.23	0.02
American Express	AXP	0.02	0.00	0.55	0.07
AT&T	T	0.11	0.00	0.70	0.02
Boeing	BA	0.03	0.00	0.90	0.17
Caterpillar	CAT	0.28	0.00	0.73	0.07
Citigroup	C	0.09	0.00	0.91	0.48
Coco-Cola	KO	0.00	0.00	0.50	0.03
DuPont	DD	0.03	0.00	0.75	0.00
Eastman Kodak	EK	0.15	0.00	0.61	0.54
Exxon Mobil	XOM	0.00	0.00	0.32	0.22
General Electric	GE	0.00	0.00	0.25	0.09
General Motors	GM	0.65	0.00	0.81	0.27
Hewlett-Packard	HWP	0.09	0.00	0.21	0.02
Home Depot	HD	0.00	0.00	0.00	0.41
Honeywell	HON	0.44	0.00	0.07	0.30
Intel	INTC	0.23	0.00	0.79	0.62
IBM	IBM	0.18	0.00	0.67	0.28
International Paper	IP	0.15	0.00	0.01	0.09
JPMorgan	JPM	0.52	0.00	0.43	0.12
Johnson & Johnson	JNJ	0.00	0.00	0.11	0.91
McDonald's	MCD	0.28	0.00	0.72	0.68
Merck	MRK	0.05	0.00	0.53	0.65
Microsoft	MSFT	0.28	0.00	0.19	0.13
3M	MMM	0.00	0.00	0.57	0.33
Philip Morris	MO	0.01	0.00	0.68	0.82
Proctor & Gamble	PG	0.02	0.00	0.99	0.74
SBC	SBC	0.05	0.00	0.13	0.00
United Technologies	UTX	0.00	0.00	0.12	0.01
Wal-Mart	WMT	0.00	0.00	0.41	0.64
Disney	DIS	0.44	0.00	0.01	0.51

these show strong evidence (particularly when applied to absolute values) against the iid hypothesis. If financial log-returns are not iid, then this contradicts the popular *random-walk* hypothesis for the discrete-time development of log-prices (or, in this case, index values). If log-returns are neither iid nor normal, then this contradicts the *geometric Brownian motion* hypothesis for the continuous-time development of prices on which the Black–Scholes–Merton pricing theory is based.

Moreover, if there is serial dependence in financial return data, then the question arises: to what extent can this dependence be used to make *predictions* about the future? This is the subject of the third and fourth stylized facts. It is very difficult to predict the return in the next time period based on historical data alone. This can be explained to some extent by the lack of serial correlation in the raw return series data. For some series we do see evidence of correlations at the first lag (or first few lags); for example, a small positive correlation at the first lag might suggest that there is some discernible tendency for a return with a particular sign (positive or negative) to be followed in the next period by a return with the same sign. However, this is not apparent in the DAX data, which suggests that our best guess for tomorrow's return based on our observations up to today is zero. This idea is expressed in the assertion of the third stylized fact, that conditional expected returns are close to zero.

Volatility is often formally modelled as the *conditional standard deviation* of financial returns given historical information and, although the conditional expected returns are consistently close to zero, the presence of volatility clustering suggests that conditional standard deviations are continually changing in a partly predictable manner. If we know that returns have been large in the last few days, due to market excitement, then there is reason to believe that the distribution from which tomorrow's return is "drawn" should have a large variance. It is this idea that lies behind the time series models for changing volatility that we will examine in Section 4.3.

Tails and extremal behaviour. We have already observed in Chapter 3 that the normal distribution is a poor model for daily and longer-interval returns (whether univariate or multivariate). The Jarque–Bera test, which is based on empirical skewness and kurtosis measures given in (3.15), clearly rejects the normal hypothesis (see Example 3.3). In particular, daily financial return data appear to have a much higher kurtosis than is consistent with the normal distribution; their distribution is said to be *leptokurtic*, meaning that it is more narrow in the centre but has longer and heavier tails than the normal distribution.

Further empirical analysis often suggests that the distribution of daily or other short-interval financial return data has tails that decay slowly according to a power law, rather than the faster, exponential-type decay of the tails of a normal distribution. This means that we tend to see rather more extreme values than might be expected in such return data; we discuss this phenomenon further in Chapter 7, which is devoted to extreme value theory (EVT).

A further observation about extremes is, however, pertinent to our discussion of serial dependence in financial return data. In the discussion of Figure 4.1 we remarked that there is a tendency for the extreme values in return series to occur in close succession in volatility clusters; further evidence for this phenomenon is given in Figure 4.3, where the time series of the 100 largest daily losses for the DAX returns and the 100 largest values for the simulated t data are plotted. In Section 7.4.1 of Chapter 7 we summarize theory which suggests that the very largest values in iid data will occur like events in a Poisson process, separated by waiting times that are iid with an exponential distribution. Parts (b) and (d) of Figure 4.3 show QQplots of these waiting times against an exponential reference distribution. While the hypothesis of the Poisson occurrence of extreme values for the iid data is supported, there are too

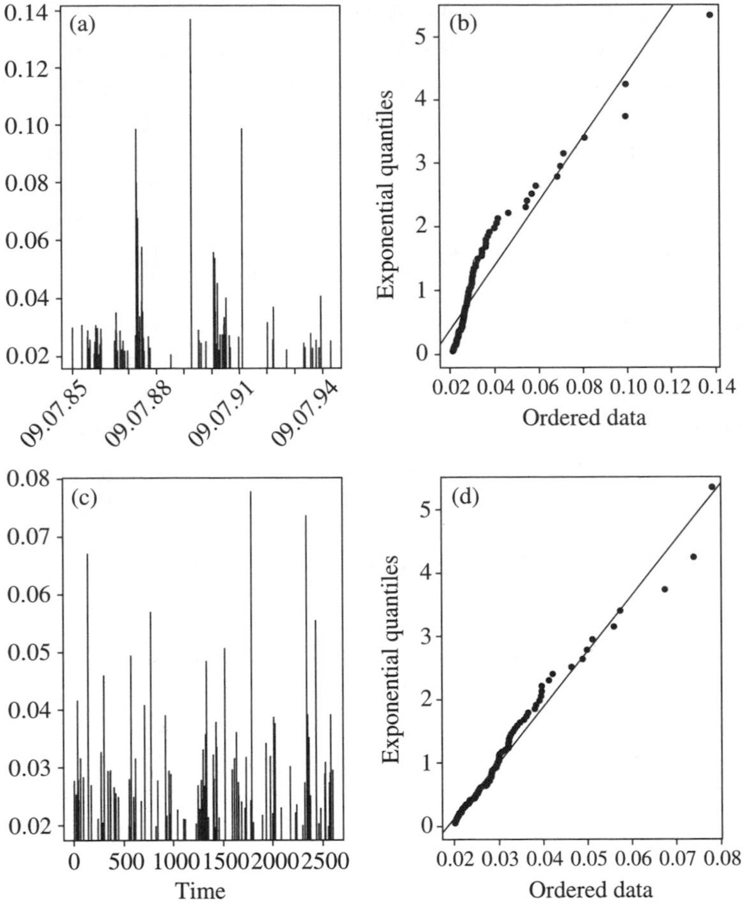

Figure 4.3. Time series plots of the 100 largest negative values for (a) the DAX returns and (c) the simulated t data as well as (b), (d) QQplots of the waiting times between these extreme values against an exponential reference distribution.

many short waiting times caused by the clustering of extreme values in the DAX data to support the exponential hypothesis; this constitutes further evidence against the iid hypothesis for return data.

Longer-interval return series. As we progressively increase the interval of the returns by moving from daily to weekly, monthly, quarterly and yearly data, the phenomena we have identified tend to become less pronounced. Volatility clustering decreases and returns begin to look both more iid and less heavy-tailed.

Suppose we begin with a sample of n returns measured at some time interval (say daily or weekly) and aggregate these to form longer-interval log-returns. The h-period log-return at time t is given by

$$X_t^{(h)} = \ln\left(\frac{S_t}{S_{t-h}}\right) = \ln\left(\frac{S_t}{S_{t-1}} \cdots \frac{S_{t-h+1}}{S_{t-h}}\right) = \sum_{j=0}^{h-1} X_{t-j}, \tag{4.1}$$

and from our original sample we can form a sample of *non-overlapping* h-period returns $\{X_t^{(h)} : t = h, 2h, \dots, [n/h]h\}$, where $[\cdot]$ denotes the integer part. Due to the sum structure of the h-period returns, it is to be expected that some central limit effect takes place, whereby their distribution becomes less leptokurtic and more normal as h is increased. Note that, although we have cast doubt on the iid model for daily data, a central limit theorem applies to many stationary time series processes, including the GARCH models that are a focus of this chapter.

In Table 4.1 the Ljung–Box tests of randomness have also been applied to non-overlapping monthly return data. For 20 out of 30 stocks the null hypothesis of iid data is not rejected at the 5% level in Ljung–Box tests applied to both the raw and absolute returns. Thus it is harder to find evidence of serial dependence in such monthly returns.

Aggregating data to form non-overlapping h-period returns reduces the sample size from n to n/h, and for longer-period returns (such as quarterly or yearly returns) this may be a very serious reduction in the amount of data. An alternative in this case is to form overlapping returns. For $1 \leqslant k \leqslant h$, a general recipe for forming aggregated h-period returns (overlapping or non-overlapping) is to form

$$\left\{X_t^{(h)} = \sum_{j=0}^{h-1} X_{t-j} : t = h, h+k, h+2k, \dots, h + [(n-h)/k]k\right\}; \tag{4.2}$$

this would give $(1 + [(n-h)/k])$ values that overlap by an amount $(h-k)$. In forming overlapping returns we can preserve a large number of data, but we do build additional serial dependence into the data. Even if the original data were iid, overlapping data would be dependent.

4.1.2 Multivariate Stylized Facts

In risk management we are seldom interested in single financial time series, but rather with multiple series of financial risk-factor changes. The stylized facts identified in Section 4.1.1 may be augmented by a number of stylized facts of a multivariate nature.

We now consider multivariate return data $\boldsymbol{X}_1, \dots, \boldsymbol{X}_n$. Each *component series* $X_{1,j}, \dots, X_{n,j}$ for $j = 1, \dots, d$ is a series formed by logarithmic differencing of a daily price, index or exchange-rate series as before. We consider the following set of multivariate stylized facts.

(M1) Multivariate return series show little evidence of cross-correlation, except for contemporaneous returns.

(M2) Multivariate series of absolute returns show profound evidence of cross-correlation.

(M3) Correlations between series (i.e. between contemporaneous returns) vary over time.

(M4) Extreme returns in one series often coincide with extreme returns in several other series.

The first two observations are fairly obvious extensions of univariate stylized facts (1) and (2) from Section 4.1.1. Just as the stock returns for, say, General Motors on days t and $t + h$ (for $h > 0$) show very little serial correlation, so we generally detect very little correlation between the General Motors return on day t and, say, the Coca-Cola return on day $t + h$. Of course, stock returns on the same day may show non-negligible correlation, due to factors that affect the whole market on that day. When we look at absolute returns we should bear in mind that periods of high or low volatility are generally common to more than one stock. Thus returns of large magnitude in one stock may tend to be followed on subsequent days by further returns of large magnitude for both that stock and other stocks, which would explain (M2). The issue of cross-correlation and its estimation will be addressed with an example in Section 4.5.

Stylized fact (M3) is a multivariate counterpart to univariate observation (4): that volatility appears to vary with time. While the latter appears "obvious" to the naked eye from illustrations such as Figure 4.1, the multivariate observation is less straightforward to demonstrate. In fact, although it is widely believed that correlations change, there are various ways of interpreting this stylized fact in terms of underlying models. We may believe that correlations are constant within regimes but that there is evidence of relatively frequent regime changes. Or we may believe that correlation changes continually and dynamically like volatility. Just as volatility is often formally modelled as the conditional standard deviation of returns given historical information, we can also devise models that feature a *conditional correlation* that is allowed to change dynamically. We consider some models of this kind in Section 4.6.

The only way to collect evidence for (M3) and to decide in what way correlation changes is to fit different models for changing correlation and then to make formal statistical comparisons of the models. More ad hoc attempts to demonstrate (M3) should generally be avoided. For example, it is not sufficient to calculate correlations between two daily series for monthly samples and to observe that these values may vary greatly from month to month; there is considerable error in estimating correlations from small samples, particularly when the underlying distribution is something more like a heavy-tailed multivariate t distribution than a Gaussian distribution (see also Example 3.31 in this context).

Stylized fact (M4) is encountered in other forms; one often hears the view that "correlations go to one in times of market stress". The idea this observation attempts to express is that in volatile periods the level of dependence between, for example, various stock returns appears to be higher. Consider, for example, Figure 4.4, which shows the BMW and Siemens log-return series the same 1985–1994 time period as in Figure 4.1. In both the time series plots and the scatterplot three days on which large negative returns occurred for both stocks have been marked with a number; all of these days occurred during periods of volatility on the German market. They are, respectively, 19 October 1987, Black Monday on Wall Street; 16 October 1989, when over 100 000 Germans protested against the East German regime in Leipzig during the chain of events that led to the fall of the Berlin Wall and German reunification; and

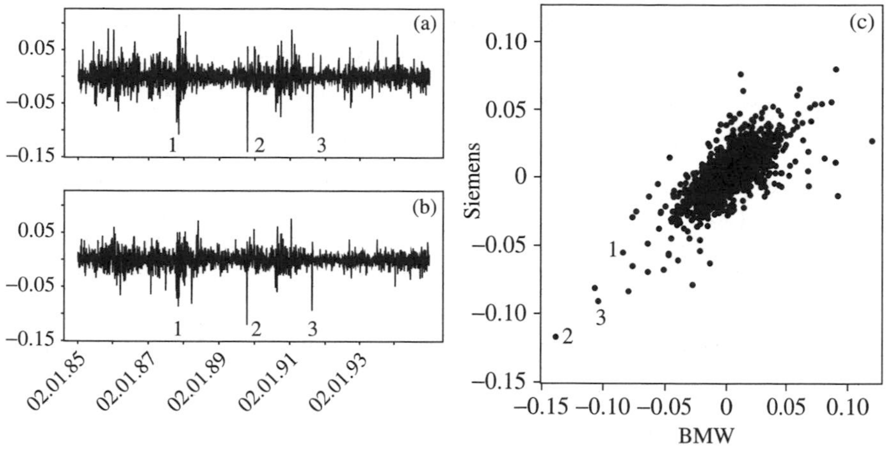

Figure 4.4. Three extreme days on which German stock returns (in this case (a) BMW and (b) Siemens) showed large negative returns. The dates are 19 October 1987, 16 October 1989 and 19 August 1991; see text for historical commentary.

19 August 1991, the day of the coup by communist hardliners during the reforming era of Gorbachev in the USSR. Clearly, the returns on these extreme days are lined up on the diagonal of the scatterplot in the lower-left-hand corner and it is easy to see why one might describe these as occasions on which correlations tend to one.

While it may be partly true that useful multivariate time series models for returns should have the property that conditional correlations tend to become large when volatilities are large, the phenomenon of simultaneous extreme values can also be addressed by choosing distributions in multivariate models that allow so-called *tail or extremal dependence*; a mathematical definition of this notion and a discussion of its importance may be found in Section 5.2.3 of the chapter on copulas.

Notes and Comments

A number of texts contain extensive empirical analyses of financial return series and discussions of their properties. We mention in particular Taylor (1986), Alexander (2001), Tsay (2002) and Zivot and Wang (2003). For more discussion of the random-walk hypothesis for stock returns and its shortcomings see Lo and MacKinlay (1999).

4.2 Fundamentals of Time Series Analysis

This section provides a short summary of the essentials of classical univariate time series analysis with a focus on that which is relevant for modelling risk-factor return series. We have based the presentation on Brockwell and Davis (1991, 2002), so these texts may be used as supplementary reading.

4.2.1 Basic Definitions

A time series model for a single risk factor is a stochastic process $(X_t)_{t\in\mathbb{Z}}$, i.e. a family of rvs, indexed by the integers and defined on some probability space $(\Omega, \mathcal{F}, P)$.

Moments of a time series. Assuming they exist, we define the *mean function* $\mu(t)$ and *autocovariance function* $\gamma(t, s)$ of $(X_t)_{t\in\mathbb{Z}}$ by

$$\mu(t) = E(X_t), \qquad t \in \mathbb{Z},$$
$$\gamma(t, s) = E((X_t - \mu(t))(X_s - \mu(s))), \quad t, s \in \mathbb{Z}.$$

It follows that the autocovariance function satisfies $\gamma(t, s) = \gamma(s, t)$ for all t, s, and $\gamma(t, t) = \operatorname{var}(X_t)$.

Stationarity. Generally, the processes we consider will be stationary in one or both of the following two senses.

Definition 4.1 (strict stationarity). The time series $(X_t)_{t\in\mathbb{Z}}$ is *strictly* stationary if

$$(X_{t_1}, \dots, X_{t_n}) \stackrel{\mathrm{d}}{=} (X_{t_1+k}, \dots, X_{t_n+k}),$$

for all $t_1, \dots, t_n, k \in \mathbb{Z}$ and for all $n \in \mathbb{N}$.

Definition 4.2 (covariance stationarity). The time series $(X_t)_{t\in\mathbb{Z}}$ is *covariance* stationary (or *weakly* or *second-order* stationary) if the first two moments exist and satisfy

$$\mu(t) = \mu, \qquad t \in \mathbb{Z},$$
$$\gamma(t, s) = \gamma(t + k, s + k), \quad t, s, k \in \mathbb{Z}.$$

Both these definitions attempt to formalize the notion that the behaviour of a time series is similar in any epoch in which we might observe it. Systematic changes in mean, variance or the covariances between equally spaced observations are inconsistent with stationarity.

It may be easily verified that a strictly stationary time series with finite variance is covariance stationary, but it is important to note that we may define infinite-variance processes (including certain ARCH and GARCH processes) which are strictly stationary but not covariance stationary.

Autocorrelation in stationary time series. The definition of covariance stationarity implies that for all s, t we have $\gamma(t - s, 0) = \gamma(t, s) = \gamma(s, t) = \gamma(s - t, 0)$, so that the covariance between X_t and X_s only depends on their temporal separation $|s - t|$, which is known as the *lag*. Thus, for a covariance-stationary process we write the autocovariance function as a function of one variable:

$$\gamma(h) := \gamma(h, 0), \quad \forall h \in \mathbb{Z}.$$

Noting that $\gamma(0) = \operatorname{var}(X_t)$, $\forall t$, we can now define the autocorrelation function of a covariance-stationary process.

Definition 4.3 (autocorrelation function). The *autocorrelation function* (ACF) $\rho(h)$ of a covariance-stationary process $(X_t)_{t\in\mathbb{Z}}$ is

$$\rho(h) = \rho(X_h, X_0) = \gamma(h)/\gamma(0), \quad \forall h \in \mathbb{Z}.$$

We speak of the autocorrelation or *serial correlation* $\rho(h)$ at lag h. In classical time series analysis the set of serial correlations and their empirical analogues estimated from data are the objects of principal interest. The study of autocorrelations is known as *analysis in the time domain*.

White noise processes. The basic building blocks for creating useful time series models are stationary processes without serial correlation, known as *white noise* processes and defined as follows.

Definition 4.4 (white noise). $(X_t)_{t\in\mathbb{Z}}$ is a white noise process if it is covariance stationary with autocorrelation function

$$\rho(h) = \begin{cases} 1, & h = 0, \\ 0, & h \neq 0. \end{cases}$$

A white noise process centred to have mean zero with variance $\sigma^2 = \text{var}(X_t)$ will be denoted $\text{WN}(0, \sigma^2)$. A simple example of a white noise process is a series of iid rvs with finite variance, and this is known as a *strict white noise* process.

Definition 4.5 (strict white noise). $(X_t)_{t\in\mathbb{Z}}$ is a strict white noise process if it is a series of iid, finite-variance rvs.

A strict white noise (SWN) process centred to have mean zero and variance σ^2 will be denoted $\text{SWN}(0, \sigma^2)$. Although SWN is the easiest kind of noise process to understand, it is not the only noise that we will use. We will later see that covariance-stationary ARCH and GARCH processes are in fact white noise processes.

Martingale difference. One further noise concept that we use, particularly when we come to discuss volatility and GARCH processes, is that of a *martingale-difference sequence*. To discuss this concept we further assume that the time series $(X_t)_{t\in\mathbb{Z}}$ is adapted to some *filtration* $(\mathcal{F}_t)_{t\in\mathbb{Z}}$ which represents the *accrual of information* over time. The sigma algebra $\mathcal{F}_t$ represents the available information at time t and typically this will be the information contained in past and present values of the time series itself $(X_s)_{s\leqslant t}$, which we refer to as the *history* up to time t and denote by $\mathcal{F}_t = \sigma(\{X_s : s \leqslant t\})$; the corresponding filtration is known as the *natural filtration*.

In a martingale-difference sequence the expectation of the next value, given current information, is always zero, and we have observed in Section 4.1.1 that this property may be appropriate for financial return data. A martingale difference is often said to model our winnings in consecutive rounds of a *fair game*.

Definition 4.6 (martingale difference). The time series $(X_t)_{t\in\mathbb{Z}}$ is known as a martingale-difference sequence with respect to the filtration $(\mathcal{F}_t)_{t\in\mathbb{Z}}$ if $E|X_t| < \infty$, X_t is $\mathcal{F}_t$-measurable (*adapted*) and

$$E(X_t \mid \mathcal{F}_{t-1}) = 0, \quad \forall t \in \mathbb{Z}.$$

Obviously the unconditional mean of such a process is also zero:

$$E(X_t) = E(E(X_t \mid \mathcal{F}_{t-1})) = 0, \quad \forall t \in \mathbb{Z}.$$

Moreover, if $E(X_t^2) < \infty$ for all t, then autocovariances satisfy

$$\begin{aligned} \gamma(t, s) &= E(X_t X_s) \\ &= \begin{cases} E(E(X_t X_s \mid \mathcal{F}_{s-1})) = E(X_t E(X_s \mid \mathcal{F}_{s-1})) = 0, & t < s, \\ E(E(X_t X_s \mid \mathcal{F}_{t-1})) = E(X_s E(X_t \mid \mathcal{F}_{t-1})) = 0, & t > s. \end{cases} \end{aligned}$$

Thus a finite-variance martingale-difference sequence has zero mean and zero covariance. If the variance is constant for all t, it is a white noise process.

4.2.2 ARMA Processes

The family of classical ARMA processes are widely used in many traditional applications of time series analysis. They are covariance-stationary processes that are constructed using white noise as a basic building block. As a general notational convention in this section and the remainder of the chapter we will denote white noise by $(\varepsilon_t)_{t\in\mathbb{Z}}$ and *strict* white noise by $(Z_t)_{t\in\mathbb{Z}}$.

Definition 4.7 (ARMA process). Let $(\varepsilon_t)_{t\in\mathbb{Z}}$ be $\text{WN}(0, \sigma_\varepsilon^2)$. The process $(X_t)_{t\in\mathbb{Z}}$ is a zero-mean ARMA(p, q) process if it is a covariance-stationary process satisfying difference equations of the form

$$X_t - \phi_1 X_{t-1} - \cdots - \phi_p X_{t-p} = \varepsilon_t + \theta_1 \varepsilon_{t-1} + \cdots + \theta_q \varepsilon_{t-q}, \quad \forall t \in \mathbb{Z}. \tag{4.3}$$

(X_t) is an ARMA process with mean μ if the centred series $(X_t - \mu)_{t\in\mathbb{Z}}$ is a zero-mean ARMA(p, q) process.

Note that, according to our definition, there is no such thing as a non-covariance-stationary ARMA process. Whether the process is strictly stationary or not will depend on the exact nature of the driving white noise, also known as the process of *innovations*. If the innovations are iid, or themselves form a strictly stationary process, then the ARMA process will also be strictly stationary.

For all practical purposes we can restrict our study of ARMA processes to *causal* ARMA processes. By this we mean processes satisfying the equations (4.3) which have a representation of the form

$$X_t = \sum_{i=0}^{\infty} \psi_i \varepsilon_{t-i}, \tag{4.4}$$

where the ψ_i are coefficients which must satisfy

$$\sum_{i=0}^{\infty} |\psi_i| < \infty. \tag{4.5}$$

Remark 4.8. The so-called absolute summability condition (4.5) is a technical condition which ensures that $E|X_t| < \infty$. This guarantees that the infinite sum in (4.4) converges absolutely, almost surely, meaning that both $\sum_{i=0}^{\infty} |\psi_i||\varepsilon_{t-i}|$ and $\sum_{i=0}^{\infty} \psi_i \varepsilon_{t-i}$ are finite with probability one (see Brockwell and Davis 1991, Proposition 3.1.1).

We now verify by direct calculation that causal ARMA processes are indeed covariance stationary and calculate the form of their autocorrelation function before going on to look at some simple standard examples.

Proposition 4.9. *Any process satisfying (4.4) and (4.5) is covariance stationary with an autocorrelation function given by*

$$\rho(h) = \frac{\sum_{i=0}^{\infty} \psi_i \psi_{i+|h|}}{\sum_{i=0}^{\infty} \psi_i^2}, \quad h \in \mathbb{Z}. \tag{4.6}$$

Proof. Obviously, for all t we have $E(X_t) = 0$ and $\operatorname{var}(X_t) = \sigma_\varepsilon^2 \sum_{i=0}^{\infty} \psi_i^2 < \infty$, due to (4.5). Moreover, the autocovariances are given by

$$\operatorname{cov}(X_t, X_{t+h}) = E(X_t X_{t+h}) = E\biggl(\sum_{i=0}^{\infty} \psi_i \varepsilon_{t-i} \sum_{j=0}^{\infty} \psi_j \varepsilon_{t+h-j}\biggr).$$

Since (ε_t) is white noise, it follows that $E(\varepsilon_{t-i}\varepsilon_{t+h-j}) \neq 0 \iff j = i + h$, and hence that

$$\gamma(h) = \operatorname{cov}(X_t, X_{t+h}) = \sigma_\varepsilon^2 \sum_{i=0}^{\infty} \psi_i \psi_{i+|h|}, \quad h \in \mathbb{Z}, \tag{4.7}$$

which depends only on the lag h and not on t. The autocorrelation function follows easily. □

Example 4.10 (MA(q) process). It is clear that a pure moving-average process

$$X_t = \sum_{i=1}^{q} \theta_i \varepsilon_{t-i} + \varepsilon_t \tag{4.8}$$

forms a simple example of a causal process of the form (4.4). It is easily inferred from (4.6) that the autocorrelation function is given by

$$\rho(h) = \frac{\sum_{i=0}^{q-|h|} \theta_i \theta_{i+|h|}}{\sum_{i=0}^{q} \theta_i^2}, \quad |h| \in \{0, 1, \dots, q\},$$

where $\theta_0 = 1$. For $|h| > q$ we have $\rho(h) = 0$ and the autocorrelation function is said to *cut off* at lag q. If this feature is observed in the estimated autocorrelations of empirical data, it is often taken as an indicator of moving-average behaviour. A realization of an MA(4) process together with the theoretical form of its ACF is shown in Figure 4.5.

Example 4.11 (AR(1) process). The first-order AR process satisfies the set of difference equations

$$X_t = \phi X_{t-1} + \varepsilon_t, \quad \forall t. \tag{4.9}$$

This process is causal if and only if $|\phi| < 1$, and this may be understood intuitively by iterating the equation (4.9) to get

$$\begin{aligned} X_t &= \phi(\phi X_{t-2} + \varepsilon_{t-1}) + \varepsilon_{t-2} \\ &= \phi^{k+1} X_{t-k-1} + \sum_{i=0}^{k} \phi^i \varepsilon_{t-i}. \end{aligned}$$

Using more careful probabilistic arguments it may be shown that the condition $|\phi| < 1$ ensures that the first term disappears as $k \to \infty$ and the second term converges. The process

$$X_t = \sum_{i=0}^{\infty} \phi^i \varepsilon_{t-i} \tag{4.10}$$

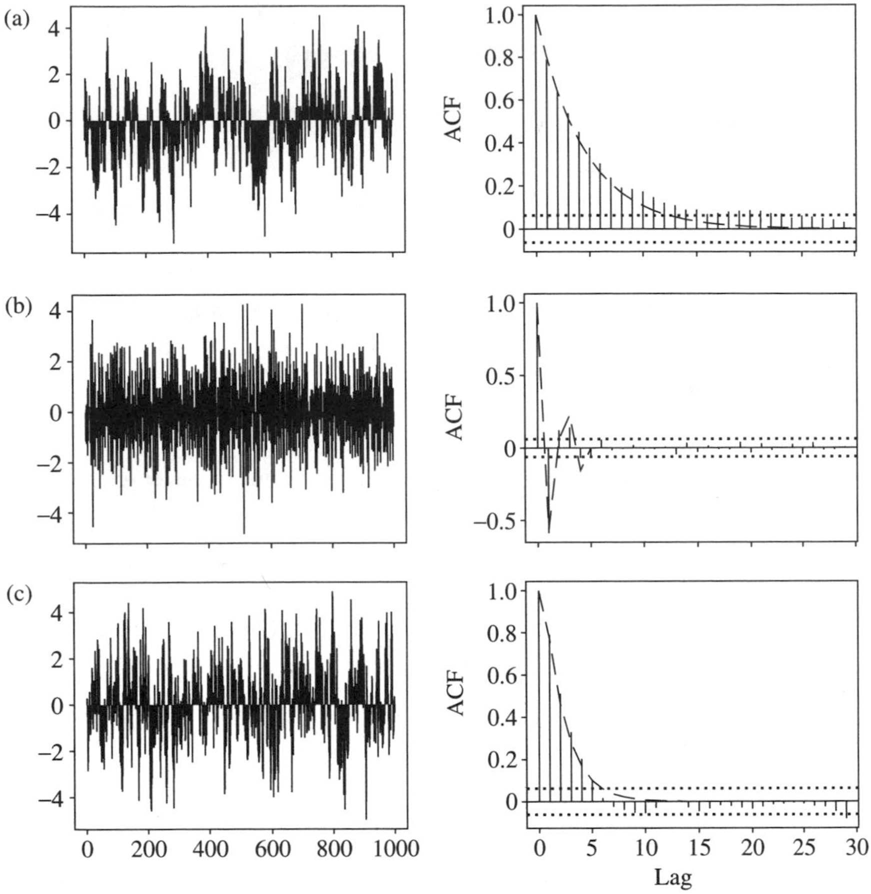

Figure 4.5. A number of simulated ARMA processes with their autocorrelation functions (dashed) and correlograms. Innovations are Gaussian. (a) AR(1), $\phi = 0.8$. (b) MA(4), $\theta = -0.8, 0.4, 0.2, -0.3$. (c) ARMA(1, 1), $\phi = 0.6$, $\theta = 0.5$.

turns out to be the unique solution of the defining equations (4.9). It may be easily verified that this is a process of the form (4.4) and that $\sum_{i=0}^{\infty} |\phi|^i = (1 - |\phi|)^{-1}$ so that (4.5) is satisfied. Looking at the form of the solution (4.10), we see that the AR(1) process can be represented as an MA(∞) process: an infinite-order moving-average process.

The autocovariance and autocorrelation functions of the process may be calculated from (4.7) and (4.6) to be

$$\gamma(h) = \frac{\phi^{|h|}\sigma_\varepsilon^2}{1 - \phi^2}, \quad \rho(h) = \phi^{|h|}, \quad h \in \mathbb{Z}.$$

Thus the ACF is exponentially decaying with possibly alternating sign. A realization of an AR(1) process together with the theoretical form of its ACF is shown in Figure 4.5.

Remarks on general ARMA theory. In the case of the general ARMA process of Definition 4.7, the issue of whether this process has a causal representation of the form (4.4) is resolved by the study of two polynomials in the complex plane, which are given in terms of the ARMA model parameters by

$$\tilde{\phi}(z) = 1 - \phi_1 z - \cdots - \phi_p z^p,$$
$$\tilde{\theta}(z) = 1 + \theta_1 z + \cdots + \theta_q z^q.$$

Provided that $\tilde{\phi}(z)$ and $\tilde{\theta}(z)$ have no common roots, then the ARMA process is a causal process satisfying (4.4) and (4.5) if and only if $\tilde{\phi}(z)$ has no roots in the unit circle $|z| \leqslant 1$. The coefficients ψ_i in the representation (4.4) are determined by the equation

$$\sum_{i=0}^{\infty} \psi_i z^i = \frac{\tilde{\theta}(z)}{\tilde{\phi}(z)}, \qquad |z| < 1.$$

Example 4.12 (ARMA(1, 1) process). For the process given by

$$X_t - \phi X_{t-1} = \varepsilon_t + \theta \varepsilon_{t-1}, \quad \forall t \in \mathbb{Z},$$

the complex polynomials are $\tilde{\phi}(z) = 1 - \phi z$ and $\tilde{\theta}(z) = 1 + \theta z$ and these have no common roots provided $\phi + \theta \neq 0$. The solution of $\tilde{\phi}(z) = 0$ is $z = 1/\phi$ and this is outside the unit circle provided $|\phi| < 1$, so that this is the condition for causality (as in the AR(1) model of Example 4.11).

The representation (4.4) can be obtained by considering

$$\sum_{i=0}^{\infty} \psi_i z^i = \frac{1 + \theta z}{1 - \phi z} = (1 + \theta z)(1 + \phi z + \phi^2 z^2 + \cdots), \qquad |z| < 1,$$

and is easily calculated to be

$$X_t = \varepsilon_t + (\phi + \theta) \sum_{i=1}^{\infty} \phi^{i-1} \varepsilon_{t-i}. \tag{4.11}$$

Using (4.6) we may calculate that for $h \neq 0$ the ACF is

$$\rho(h) = \frac{\phi^{|h|-1}(\phi + \theta)(1 + \phi\theta)}{1 + \theta^2 + 2\phi\theta}.$$

A realization of an ARMA(1, 1) process together with the theoretical form of its ACF is shown in Figure 4.5.

Invertibility. Equation (4.11) shows how the ARMA(1, 1) process may be thought of as an MA(∞) process. In fact, if we impose the condition $|\theta| < 1$, we can also express (X_t) as the AR(∞) process given by

$$X_t = \varepsilon_t + (\phi + \theta) \sum_{i=1}^{\infty} (-\theta)^{i-1} X_{t-i}. \tag{4.12}$$

If we rearrange this to be an equation for ε_t, then we see that we can, in a sense, "reconstruct" the latest innovation ε_t from the entire history of the process $(X_s)_{s \leqslant t}$.

The condition $|\theta| < 1$ is known as an *invertibility* condition, and for the general ARMA(p, q) process the invertibility condition is that $\tilde{\theta}(z)$ should have no roots in the unit circle $|z| \leqslant 1$. In practice, the models we fit to real data will be both invertible and causal solutions of the ARMA-defining equations.

Models for the conditional mean. Consider a general invertible ARMA model with non-zero mean. For what comes later it will be useful to observe that we can write such models as

$$X_t = \mu_t + \varepsilon_t, \qquad \mu_t = \mu + \sum_{i=1}^{p} \phi_i (X_{t-i} - \mu) + \sum_{j=1}^{q} \theta_j \varepsilon_{t-j}. \tag{4.13}$$

Since we have assumed invertibility, the terms ε_{t-j}, and hence μ_t, can be written in terms of the infinite past of the process up to time $t-1$; μ_t is said to be *measurable* with respect to $\mathcal{F}_{t-1} = \sigma(\{X_s : s \leqslant t-1\})$.

If we make the assumption that the white noise $(\varepsilon_t)_{t\in\mathbb{Z}}$ is a martingale-difference sequence (see Definition 4.6) with respect to $(\mathcal{F}_t)_{t\in\mathbb{Z}}$, then $E(X_t \mid \mathcal{F}_{t-1}) = \mu_t$. In other words, such an ARMA process can be thought of as putting a particular structure on the conditional mean μ_t of the process. ARCH and GARCH processes will later be seen to put structure on the conditional variance $\operatorname{var}(X_t \mid \mathcal{F}_{t-1})$.

ARIMA models. In traditional time series analysis we often consider an even larger class of model known as ARIMA, or autoregressive *integrated* moving-average models. Let ∇ denote the *difference operator*, so that for a time series process $(Y_t)_{t\in\mathbb{Z}}$ we have $\nabla Y_t = Y_t - Y_{t-1}$. Denote repeated differencing by ∇^d, where

$$\nabla^d Y_t = \begin{cases} \nabla Y_t, & d = 1, \\ \nabla^{d-1}(\nabla Y_t) = \nabla^{d-1}(Y_t - Y_{t-1}), & d > 1. \end{cases} \tag{4.14}$$

The time series (Y_t) is said to be an ARIMA(p, d, q) process if the differenced series (X_t) given by $X_t = \nabla^d Y_t$ is an ARMA(p, q) process. For $d > 1$ ARIMA processes are non-stationary processes. They are popular in practice because the operation of differencing (once or more than once) can turn a dataset that is obviously "non-stationary" into a dataset that might plausibly be modelled by a stationary ARMA process. For example, if we use an ARMA(p, q) process to model daily log-returns of some price series (S_t), then we are really saying that the original logarithmic price series $(\ln S_t)$ follows an ARIMA$(p, 1, q)$ model.

When the word *integrated* is used in the context of time series it generally implies that we are looking at a non-stationary process that might be made stationary by differencing; see also the discussion of IGARCH models in Section 4.3.2.

4.2.3 Analysis in the Time Domain

We now assume that we have a random sample $X_1, \dots, X_n$ from a covariance-stationary time series model $(X_t)_{t\in\mathbb{Z}}$. Analysis in the time domain involves calculating empirical estimates of autocovariances and autocorrelations from this random sample and using these estimates to make inference about the serial dependence structure of the underlying process.

Correlogram. The sample autocovariances are calculated according to

$$\hat{\gamma}(h) = \frac{1}{n}\sum_{t=1}^{n-h}(X_{t+h} - \bar{X})(X_t - \bar{X}), \quad 0 \leqslant h < n,$$

where $\bar{X} = \sum_{t=1}^{n} X_t/n$ is the sample mean, which estimates μ, the mean of the time series. From these we calculate the sample ACF:

$$\hat{\rho}(h) = \hat{\gamma}(h)/\hat{\gamma}(0), \quad 0 \leqslant h < n.$$

The *correlogram* is the plot $\{(h, \hat{\rho}(h)) : h = 0, 1, 2, \dots\}$, which is designed to facilitate the interpretation of the sample ACF. Correlograms for various simulated ARMA processes are shown in Figure 4.5; note that the estimated correlations correspond reasonably closely to the theoretical ACF for these particular realizations.

To interpret such estimators of serial correlation, we need to know something about their behaviour for particular time series. The following general result is for *causal linear processes*, which are processes of the form (4.4) driven by *strict white noise*.

Theorem 4.13. *Let* $(X_t)_{t\in\mathbb{Z}}$ *be the linear process*

$$X_t - \mu = \sum_{i=0}^{\infty} \psi_i Z_{t-i}, \quad \text{where} \sum_{i=0}^{\infty} |\psi_i| < \infty, \ (Z_t)_{t\in\mathbb{Z}} \sim \text{SWN}(0, \sigma_Z^2).$$

Suppose that either $E(Z_t^4) < \infty$ *or* $\sum_{i=0}^{\infty} i\psi_i^2 < \infty$. *Then, for* $h \in \{1, 2, \dots\}$, *we have*

$$\sqrt{n}(\hat{\boldsymbol{\rho}}(h) - \boldsymbol{\rho}(h)) \xrightarrow{\text{d}} N_h(\mathbf{0}, W),$$

where

$$\hat{\boldsymbol{\rho}}(h) = (\hat{\rho}(1), \dots, \hat{\rho}(h))',$$
$$\boldsymbol{\rho}(h) = (\rho(1), \dots, \rho(h))',$$

and W *has elements*

$$W_{ij} = \sum_{k=1}^{\infty}(\rho(k+i) + \rho(k-i) - 2\rho(i)\rho(k))(\rho(k+j) + \rho(k-j) - 2\rho(j)\rho(k)).$$

Proof. This follows as a special case of a result in Brockwell and Davis (1991, pp. 221–223). □

The condition $\sum_{i=0}^{\infty} i\psi_i^2 < \infty$ holds for ARMA processes, so ARMA processes driven by SWN fall under the scope of this theorem (regardless of whether fourth moments exist for the innovations or not).

Trivially, the theorem also applies to SWN itself. For SWN we have

$$\sqrt{n}\hat{\boldsymbol{\rho}}(h) \xrightarrow{\text{d}} N_h(\mathbf{0}, I_h),$$

so for sufficiently large n the sample autocorrelations of data from an SWN process will behave like iid normal observations with mean zero and variance

$1/n$. Ninety-five per cent of the estimated correlations should lie in the interval $(-1.96/\sqrt{n}, 1.96/\sqrt{n})$, and it is for this reason that correlograms are drawn with confidence bands at these values. If more than 5% of estimated correlations lie outside these bounds, then this is considered as evidence against the null hypothesis that the data are strict white noise.

Remark 4.14. In light of the discussion of the asymptotic behaviour of sample autocorrelations for SWN it might be asked how these estimators behave for white noise. However, this is an extremely general question because white noise encompasses a variety of possible underlying processes (including the standard ARCH and GARCH processes we later address) which only share second-order properties (finiteness of variance and lack of serial correlation). In some cases the standard Gaussian confidence bands apply; in some cases they do not. For a GARCH process the critical issue turns out to be the heaviness of the tail of the stationary distribution (see Mikosch and Stărică 2000, for more details).

Portmanteau tests. It is often useful to combine the visual analysis of the correlogram with a formal numerical test of the strict white noise hypothesis, and a popular test is that of Ljung and Box, as applied in Section 4.1.1. Under the null hypothesis of SWN, the statistic

$$Q_{\mathrm{LB}} = n(n+2)\sum_{j=1}^{h}\frac{\hat{\rho}(j)^2}{n-j}$$

has an asymptotic chi-squared distribution with h degrees of freedom. This statistic is generally preferred to the simpler Box–Pierce statistic $Q_{\mathrm{BP}} = n\sum_{j=1}^{h}\hat{\rho}(j)^2$, which also has an asymptotic χ_h^2 distribution under the null hypothesis, although the chi-squared approximation may not be so good in smaller samples. These tests are the most commonly applied portmanteau tests.

If a series of rvs forms an SWN process, then the series of absolute or squared variables must also be iid. It is a good idea to also apply the correlogram and Ljung–Box tests to absolute values as a further test of the SWN hypothesis. We prefer to perform tests of the SWN hypothesis on the absolute values rather than the squared values because the squared series is only an SWN (according to the definition we use) when the underlying series has a finite fourth moment. Daily log-return data often point to models with an infinite fourth moment

4.2.4 Statistical Analysis of Time Series

In practice, the statistical analysis of time series data $X_1, \dots, X_n$ follows a programme consisting of the following stages.

Preliminary analysis. The data are plotted and the plausibility of a single stationary model is considered. Since we concentrate here on differenced logarithmic value series, we will assume that at most minor preliminary manipulation of our data is required. Classical time series analysis has many techniques for removing *trends and seasonalities* from "non-stationary" data; these techniques are discussed in all standard texts including Brockwell and Davis (2002) and Chatfield (1996). While certain kinds of financial time series certainly do show seasonal patterns, such as earnings time series, we will assume that such effects are relatively minor in the kinds of daily or weekly return series that are the basis of risk-management methods. If we were to base our risk management on high-frequency data, preliminary cleaning would be more of an issue, since these show clear diurnal cycles and other deterministic features (see Dacorogna et al. 2001).

Obviously the assumption of stationarity becomes more questionable if we take long data windows, or if we choose windows in which well-known economic policy shifts have taken place. Although the markets change constantly there will always be a tension between our desire to use the most up-to-date data and our need to include enough data to have precision in statistical estimation. Whether half a year of data, one year, five years or 10 years are appropriate will depend on the situation. It is certainly a good idea to perform a number of analyses with different data windows and to investigate the sensitivity of statistical inference to the amount of data.

Analysis in the time domain. Having settled on the data, the techniques of Section 4.2.3 come into play. By applying correlograms and portmanteau tests such as Ljung–Box to both the raw data and their absolute values, the SWN hypothesis is evaluated. If it cannot be rejected for the data in question, then the formal time series analysis is over and simple distributional fitting could be used instead of dynamic modelling.

For daily risk-factor return series we expect to quickly reject the SWN hypothesis. Despite the fact that correlograms of the raw data may show little evidence of serial correlation, correlograms of the absolute data are likely to show evidence of strong serial dependence. In other words the data may support a white noise model but not a strict white noise. In this case ARMA modelling is not required, but the volatility models of Section 4.3 may be useful.

If the correlogram does provide evidence of the kind of serial correlation patterns produced by ARMA processes, then we can attempt to fit ARMA processes to data.

Model fitting. A traditional approach to model fitting first attempts to *identify the order* of a suitable ARMA process using the correlogram and a further tool known as the partial correlogram (not described in this book but found in all standard texts). For example, the presence of a *cut-off* at lag q in the correlogram (see Example 4.10) is taken as a diagnostic for pure moving-average behaviour of order q (and similar behaviour in a partial correlogram indicates pure AR behaviour). With modern computing power it is now quite easy to simply fit a variety of MA, AR and ARMA models and to use a model-selection criterion like that of Akaike (described in Section A.3.6) to choose the "best" model. There are also automated model choice procedures such as the method of Tsay and Tiao (1984).

Sometimes there are *a priori* reasons for expecting certain kinds of model to be most appropriate. For example, suppose we analyse longer-period returns that overlap, as in Equation 4.2. Consider the case where the raw data are daily returns and we build weekly returns. In (4.2) we set $h = 5$ (to get weekly returns) and $k = 1$ (to get as much data as possible). Assuming that the underlying data are genuinely from a white noise process $(X_t)_{t\in\mathbb{Z}} \sim \mathrm{WN}(0, \sigma^2)$, the weekly aggregated returns at times t and $t + l$ satisfy

$$\operatorname{cov}(X_t^{(5)}, X_{t+l}^{(5)}) = \operatorname{cov}\left(\sum_{i=0}^{4} X_{t-i}, \sum_{j=0}^{4} X_{t+l-j}\right) = \begin{cases} (5-l)\sigma^2, & l = 0, \dots, 4 \\ 0, & l \geqslant 5, \end{cases}$$

so that the overlapping returns have the correlation structure of an MA(4) process, and this would be a natural choice of time series model for them.

Having chosen the model to fit, there are a number of possible fitting methods, including specialized methods for AR processes, such as Yule–Walker, that make minimal assumptions concerning the distribution of the white noise innovations; we refer to the standard time series literature for more details. In Section 4.3.4 we discuss the method of (conditional) maximum likelihood, which may be used to fit ARMA models with (or without) GARCH errors to data.

Residual analysis and model comparison. Recall the representation of a causal and invertible ARMA process in (4.13) and suppose we have fitted such a process and estimated the parameters ϕ_i and θ_j. The residuals are inferred values $\hat{\varepsilon}_t$ for the unobserved innovations ε_t and they are calculated recursively from the data and fitted model by

$$\hat{\varepsilon}_t = X_t - \hat{\mu}_t, \qquad \hat{\mu}_t = \hat{\mu} + \sum_{i=1}^{p} \hat{\phi}_i (X_{t-i} - \hat{\mu}) + \sum_{j=1}^{q} \hat{\theta}_j \hat{\varepsilon}_{t-j}, \tag{4.15}$$

where the values $\hat{\mu}_t$ are sometimes known as the *fitted values*. Obviously, we have a problem calculating the first few values of $\hat{\varepsilon}_t$ due to the finiteness of our data sample and the infinite nature of the recursions (4.15). One of many possible solutions might be to set $\hat{\varepsilon}_{-q+1} = \hat{\varepsilon}_{-q+2} = \cdots = \hat{\varepsilon}_0 = 0$ and $X_{-p+1} = X_{-p+2} = \cdots = X_0 = \bar{X}$ and then to use (4.15) for $t = 1, \dots, n$. Since the first few values will be influenced by these starting values, they might be ignored in later analyses.

The residuals $(\hat{\varepsilon}_t)$ should behave like a realization of a white noise process, since this is our model assumption for the innovations, and this can be assessed by constructing their correlogram. If there is still evidence of serial correlation in the correlogram, then this suggests that a good ARMA model has not yet been found. Moreover, we can use portmanteau tests to test formally that the residuals behave like a realization of a strict white noise process. If the residuals behave like SWN, then no further time series modelling is required; if they behave like WN but not SWN, then the volatility models of Section 4.3 may be required.

It is usually possible to find more than one reasonable ARMA model for the data, and formal model-comparison techniques may be required to decide on an overall best model or models. The Akaike model-selection criterion described in Section A.3.6 might be used, or one of a number of variants on this criterion which are often preferred for time series (see Brockwell and Davis 2002, Section 5.5.2).

4.2.5 Prediction

There are many approaches to the forecasting or prediction of time series and we summarize two which extend easily to the case of GARCH models. The first strategy makes use of fitted ARMA (or ARIMA) models and is sometimes called the Box–Jenkins approach (Box and Jenkins 1970). The second strategy is a model-free approach to forecasting known as *exponential smoothing*, which is related to the exponentially weighted moving-average technique for predicting volatility.

Prediction using ARMA models. Consider the invertible ARMA model and its representation in (4.13). Let $\mathcal{F}_t$ denote the history of the process up to and including time t as before and assume that the innovations $(\varepsilon_t)_{t\in\mathbb{Z}}$ have the martingale-difference property with respect to $(\mathcal{F}_t)_{t\in\mathbb{Z}}$.

For the prediction problem it will be convenient to denote our sample of n data by $X_{t-n+1}, \dots, X_t$. We assume these are realizations of rvs following a particular ARMA model. Our aim is to predict X_{t+1} or more generally X_{t+h}, and we denote our prediction by $P_t X_{t+h}$. The method we describe assumes that we have access to the infinite history of the process up to time t and derives a formula that is then approximated for our finite sample.

As a predictor of X_{t+h} we use the conditional expectation $E(X_{t+h} \mid \mathcal{F}_t)$. Among all predictions $P_t X_{t+h}$ based on the infinite history of the process up to time t, this predictor minimizes the mean squared prediction error $E((X_{t+h} - P_t X_{t+h})^2)$.

The basic idea is that, for $h \geqslant 1$, the prediction $E(X_{t+h} \mid \mathcal{F}_t)$ is recursively evaluated in terms of $E(X_{t+h-1} \mid \mathcal{F}_t)$. We use the fact that $E(\varepsilon_{t+h} \mid \mathcal{F}_t) = 0$ (the martingale-difference property of innovations) and that the rvs $(X_s)_{s\leqslant t}$ and $(\varepsilon_s)_{s\leqslant t}$ are "known" at time t. The assumption of invertibility (4.12) ensures that the innovation ε_t can be written as a function of the infinite history of the process $(X_s)_{s\leqslant t}$. To illustrate the approach it will suffice to consider an ARMA(1, 1) model, the generalization to ARMA(p, q) models following easily.

Example 4.15 (prediction for the ARMA(1, 1) model). Suppose an ARMA(1, 1) model of the form (4.13) has been fitted to the data and its parameters μ, ϕ and θ have been determined. Our one-step prediction for X_{t+1} is

$$E(X_{t+1} \mid \mathcal{F}_t) = \mu_{t+1} = \mu + \phi(X_t - \mu) + \theta\varepsilon_t,$$

since $E(\varepsilon_{t+1} \mid \mathcal{F}_t) = 0$. For a two-step prediction we get

$$\begin{aligned} E(X_{t+2} \mid \mathcal{F}_t) = E(\mu_{t+2} \mid \mathcal{F}_t) &= \mu + \phi(E(X_{t+1} \mid \mathcal{F}_t) - \mu) \\ &= \mu + \phi^2(X_t - \mu) + \phi\theta\varepsilon_t, \end{aligned}$$

and in general we have

$$E(X_{t+h} \mid \mathcal{F}_t) = \mu + \phi^h(X_t - \mu) + \phi^{h-1}\theta\varepsilon_t.$$

Without knowing all historical values of $(X_s)_{s\leqslant t}$ this predictor cannot be evaluated exactly, but it can be accurately approximated if n is reasonably large. The easiest way of doing this is to substitute the model residual $\hat{\varepsilon}_t$ calculated from (4.15) for ε_t. Note that $\lim_{h\to\infty} E(X_{t+h} \mid \mathcal{F}_t) = \mu$, almost surely, so that the prediction converges to the estimate of the unconditional mean of the process for longer time horizons.

Exponential smoothing. This is a popular technique which is used for both prediction of time series and trend estimation. Here we do not necessarily assume that the data come from a stationary model, although we do assume that there is no deterministic seasonal component in the model. In general the method is less well suited to return series with frequently changing signs and is better suited to undifferenced price or value series. It forms the basis of a very common method of volatility prediction (see Section 4.4.1).

Suppose our data represent realizations of rvs $Y_{t-n+1}, \dots, Y_t$, considered without reference to any concrete parametric model. As a forecast for Y_{t+1} we use a prediction of the form

$$P_t Y_{t+1} = \sum_{i=0}^{n-1} \alpha(1-\alpha)^i Y_{t-i}, \quad \text{where } 0 < \alpha < 1.$$

Thus we weight the data from most recent to most distant with a sequence of exponentially decreasing weights that sum to almost one. It is easily calculated that

$$\begin{aligned} P_t Y_{t+1} = \sum_{i=0}^{n-1} \alpha(1-\alpha)^i Y_{t-i} &= \alpha Y_t + (1-\alpha) \sum_{j=0}^{n-2} \alpha(1-\alpha)^j Y_{t-1-j} \\ &= \alpha Y_t + (1-\alpha) P_{t-1} Y_t, \end{aligned} \tag{4.16}$$

so that the prediction at time t is obtained from the prediction at time $t-1$ by a simple recursive scheme. The choice of α is subjective; the larger the value the more weight is put on the most recent observation. Empirical validation studies with different datasets can be used to determine a value of α that gives good results.

Note that, although the method is commonly seen as a model-free forecasting technique, it can be shown to be the natural prediction method based on conditional expectation for a non-stationary ARIMA(0, 1, 1) model.

Notes and Comments

There are many texts covering the subject of classical time series analysis including Box and Jenkins (1970), Priestley (1981), Abraham and Ledolter (1983), Brockwell and Davis (1991, 2002), Hamilton (1994) and Chatfield (1996). Our account of basic concepts, ARMA models and analysis in the time domain closely follows Brockwell and Davis (1991), which should be consulted for the rigorous background to ideas we can only summarize. We have not discussed analysis of time series in the frequency domain, which is less common for financial time series; for this subject see, again, Brockwell and Davis (1991) or Priestley (1981).

For more on tests of the strict white noise hypothesis (that is tests of randomness), see Brockwell and Davis (2002). Original references for the Box–Pierce and Ljung–Box tests are Box and Pierce (1970) and Ljung and Box (1978).

There is a vast literature on forecasting and prediction in linear models. A good non-mathematical introduction is found in Chatfield (1996). The approach we describe based on the infinite history of the time series is discussed in greater detail in Hamilton (1994). Brockwell and Davis (2002) concentrate on exact linear prediction methods for finite samples. A general review of exponential smoothing is found in Gardner (1985).

4.3 GARCH Models for Changing Volatility

The most important models for daily risk-factor return series are addressed in this section. We give definitions of ARCH (autoregressive conditionally heteroscedastic) and GARCH (generalized ARCH) models and discuss some of their mathematical properties before going on to talk about their use in practice.

4.3.1 ARCH Processes

Definition 4.16. Let $(Z_t)_{t\in\mathbb{Z}}$ be SWN(0, 1). The process $(X_t)_{t\in\mathbb{Z}}$ is an ARCH(p) process if it is strictly stationary and if it satisfies, for all $t \in \mathbb{Z}$ and some strictly positive-valued process $(\sigma_t)_{t\in\mathbb{Z}}$, the equations

$$X_t = \sigma_t Z_t, \tag{4.17}$$

$$\sigma_t^2 = \alpha_0 + \sum_{i=1}^{p} \alpha_i X_{t-i}^2, \tag{4.18}$$

where $\alpha_0 > 0$ and $\alpha_i \geqslant 0$, $i = 1, \dots, p$.

Let $\mathcal{F}_t = \sigma(\{X_s : s \leqslant t\})$ again denote the sigma algebra representing the history of the process up to time t so that $(\mathcal{F}_t)_{t\in\mathbb{Z}}$ is the natural filtration. Clearly, the construction (4.18) ensures that σ_t is *measurable* with respect to $\mathcal{F}_{t-1}$. This allows us to calculate that, provided $E(|X_t|) < \infty$,

$$E(X_t \mid \mathcal{F}_{t-1}) = E(\sigma_t Z_t \mid \mathcal{F}_{t-1}) = \sigma_t E(Z_t \mid \mathcal{F}_{t-1}) = \sigma_t E(Z_t) = 0, \tag{4.19}$$

so that the ARCH process has the martingale-difference property with respect to $(\mathcal{F}_t)_{t\in\mathbb{Z}}$. If the process is covariance stationary, it is simply a white noise, as discussed in Section 4.2.1.

Remark 4.17. Note that the independence of Z_t and $\mathcal{F}_{t-1}$ that we have assumed above follows from the fact that an ARCH process must be causal, i.e. the equations (4.17) and (4.18) must have a solution of the form $X_t = f(Z_t, Z_{t-1}, \dots)$ for some f so that Z_t is independent of previous values of the process. This contrasts with ARMA models where the equations can have non-causal solutions (see Brockwell and Davis 1991, Example 3.1.2).

If we simply assume that the process is a covariance-stationary white noise (for which we will give a condition in Proposition 4.18), then $E(X_t^2) < \infty$ and

$$\operatorname{var}(X_t \mid \mathcal{F}_{t-1}) = E(\sigma_t^2 Z_t^2 \mid \mathcal{F}_{t-1}) = \sigma_t^2 \operatorname{var}(Z_t) = \sigma_t^2.$$

Thus the model has the interesting property that its conditional standard deviation σ_t, or *volatility*, is a continually changing function of the previous squared values of the process. If one or more of $|X_{t-1}|, \dots, |X_{t-p}|$ are particularly *large*, then X_t is effectively drawn from a distribution with large variance, and may itself be large; in

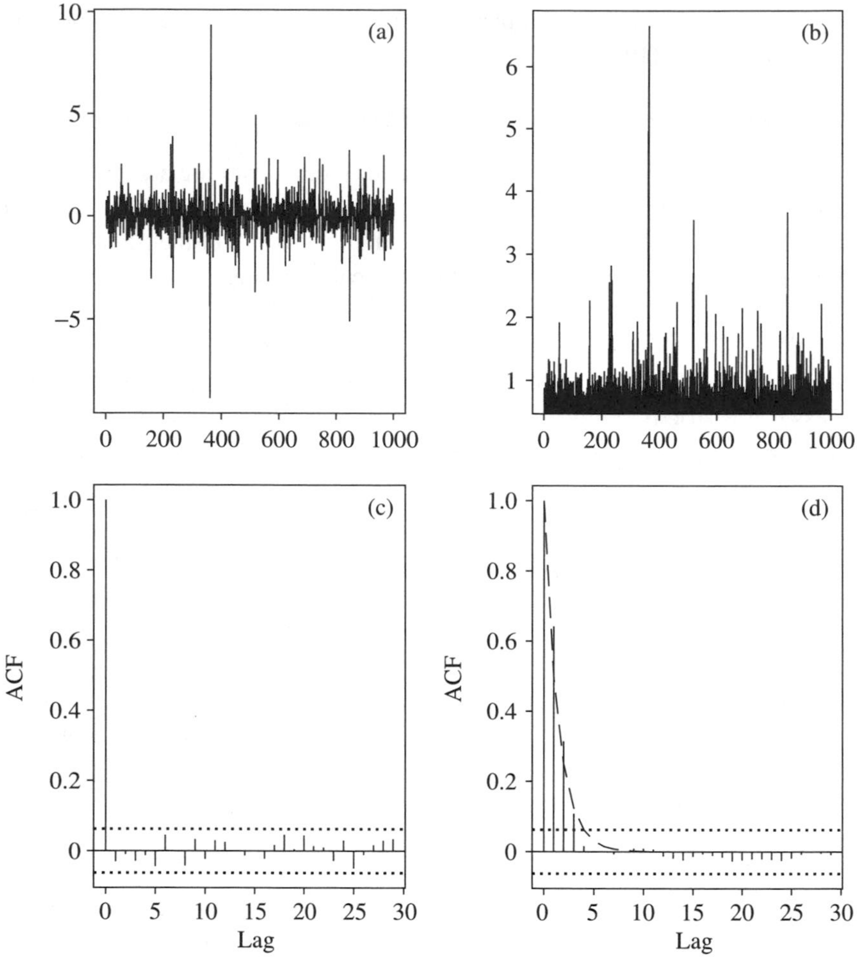

Figure 4.6. A simulated ARCH(1) process with Gaussian innovations and parameters $\alpha_0 = \alpha_1 = 0.5$: (a) the realization of the process; (b) the realization of the volatility; and correlograms of (c) the raw and (d) the squared values. The process is covariance stationary with unit variance and a finite fourth moment (since $\alpha_1 < 1/\sqrt{3}$) and the squared values follow an AR(1) process. The true form of the ACF of the squared values is represented by the dashed line in the correlogram.

this way the model generates volatility clusters. The name ARCH refers to this structure: the model is autoregressive, since X_t clearly depends on previous X_{t-i}, and conditionally heteroscedastic, since the conditional variance changes continually.

The distribution of the innovations $(Z_t)_{t\in\mathbb{Z}}$ can in principle be any zero-mean, unit-variance distribution. For statistical fitting purposes we may or may not choose to actually specify the distribution, depending on whether we implement a maximum likelihood (ML), quasi-maximum likelihood (QML) or non-parametric fitting method (see Section 4.3.4). For ML the most common choices are standard normal innovations or scaled t innovations. By the latter we mean that $Z_t \sim t_1(\nu, 0, (\nu - 2)/\nu)$ in the notation of Example 3.7, so that the variance of the distribution is one. We keep these choices in mind when discussing further theoretical properties of ARCH and GARCH models.

The ARCH(1) model. In the rest of this section we analyse some of the properties of the ARCH(1) model. These properties extend to the whole class of ARCH and GARCH models, but are most easily introduced in the simplest case. A simulated realization of an ARCH(1) process with Gaussian innovations and the corresponding realization of the volatility process are shown in Figure 4.6.

Using $X_t^2 = \sigma_t^2 Z_t^2$ and (4.18) in the case $p = 1$, we deduce that the squared ARCH(1) process satisfies

$$X_t^2 = \alpha_0 Z_t^2 + \alpha_1 Z_t^2 X_{t-1}^2. \tag{4.20}$$

A detailed mathematical analysis of the ARCH(1) model involves the study of equation (4.20), which is a *stochastic recurrence equation* (SRE). Much as for the AR(1) model in Example 4.11, we would like to know when this equation has stationary solutions expressed in terms of the infinite history of the innovations, i.e. solutions of the form $X_t^2 = f(Z_t, Z_{t-1}, \dots)$.

For ARCH models we have to distinguish carefully between solutions that are covariance stationary and solutions that are only strictly stationary. It is possible to have ARCH(1) models with infinite variance, which obviously cannot be covariance stationary.

Stochastic recurrence relations. The detailed theory required to analyse stochastic recurrence relations of the form (4.20) is outside the scope of this book, and we give only brief notes to indicate the ideas involved. Our treatment is based on Brandt (1986) and Mikosch (2003); see Notes and Comments at the end of this section for further references.

Equation (4.20) is a particular example of a class of recurrence equations of the form

$$Y_t = A_t Y_{t-1} + B_t, \tag{4.21}$$

where $(A_t)_{t\in\mathbb{Z}}$ and $(B_t)_{t\in\mathbb{Z}}$ are sequences of iid rvs. Sufficient conditions for a solution are that

$$E(\max\{0, \ln|B_t|\}) < \infty \quad \text{and} \quad E(\ln|A_t|) < 0, \tag{4.22}$$

where $\ln^+ x = \max(0, \ln x)$. The unique solution is given by

$$Y_t = B_t + \sum_{i=1}^{\infty} B_{t-i} \prod_{j=0}^{i-1} A_{t-j}, \tag{4.23}$$

where the sum converges absolutely, almost surely.

We can develop some intuition for the conditions (4.22) and the form of the solution (4.23) by iterating equation (4.21) k times to obtain

$$\begin{aligned} Y_t &= A_t(A_{t-1}Y_{t-2} + B_{t-1}) + B_t \\ &= B_t + \sum_{i=1}^{k} B_{t-i} \prod_{j=0}^{i-1} A_{t-j} + Y_{t-k-1} \prod_{i=0}^{k} A_{t-i}. \end{aligned}$$

The conditions (4.22) ensure that the middle term on the right-hand side converges absolutely and the final term disappears. In particular, note that

$$\frac{1}{k+1}\sum_{i=0}^{k} \ln|A_{t-i}| \xrightarrow{\text{a.s.}} E(\ln|A_t|) < 0$$

by the strong law of large numbers. So

$$\prod_{i=0}^{k} |A_{t-i}| = \exp\left(\sum_{i=0}^{k} \ln|A_{t-i}|\right) \xrightarrow{\text{a.s.}} 0,$$

which shows the importance of the $E(\ln|A_t|) < 0$ condition. The solution (4.23) to the SRE is a strictly stationary process (being a function of iid variables $(A_s, B_s)_{s\leqslant t}$), and the $E(\ln|A_t|) < 0$ condition turns out to be the key to the strict stationarity of ARCH and GARCH models.

Stationarity of ARCH(1). The squared ARCH(1) model (4.20) is an SRE of the form (4.21) with $A_t = \alpha_1 Z_t^2$ and $B_t = \alpha_0 Z_t^2$. Thus the conditions in (4.22) translate into the requirements that $E(\ln^+|\alpha_0 Z_t^2|) < \infty$, which is automatically true for the ARCH(1) process as we have defined it, and $E(\ln(\alpha_1 Z_t^2)) < 0$. This is the condition for a strictly stationary solution of the ARCH(1) equations and it can be shown that it is in fact a necessary and sufficient condition for strict stationarity (see Bougerol and Picard 1992). From (4.23), the solution of equation (4.20) takes the form

$$X_t^2 = \alpha_0 \sum_{i=0}^{\infty} \alpha_1^i \prod_{j=0}^{i} Z_{t-j}^2. \tag{4.24}$$

If the (Z_t) are standard normal innovations, then the condition for a strictly stationary solution is approximately $\alpha_1 < 3.562$; perhaps somewhat surprisingly, if the (Z_t) are scaled t innovations with four degrees of freedom and variance 1, the condition is $\alpha_1 < 5.437$. Strict stationarity depends on the distribution of the innovations but covariance stationarity does not; the necessary and sufficient condition for covariance stationarity is always $\alpha_1 < 1$, as we now prove.

Proposition 4.18. *The* ARCH(1) *process is a covariance-stationary white noise process if and only if* $\alpha_1 < 1$. *The variance of the covariance-stationary process is given by* $\alpha_0/(1-\alpha_1)$.

Proof. Assuming covariance stationarity it follows from (4.20) and $E(Z_t^2) = 1$ that

$$\sigma_x^2 = E(X_t^2) = \alpha_0 + \alpha_1 E(X_{t-1}^2) = \alpha_0 + \alpha_1\sigma_x^2.$$

Clearly, $\sigma_x^2 = \alpha_0/(1-\alpha_1)$ and we must have $\alpha_1 < 1$.

Conversely, if $\alpha_1 < 1$, then, by Jensen's inequality,

$$E(\ln(\alpha_1 Z_t^2)) \leqslant \ln(E(\alpha_1 Z_t^2)) = \ln(\alpha_1) < 0,$$

and we can use (4.24) to calculate that

$$E(X_t^2) = \alpha_0 \sum_{i=0}^{\infty} \alpha_1^i = \frac{\alpha_0}{1-\alpha_1}.$$

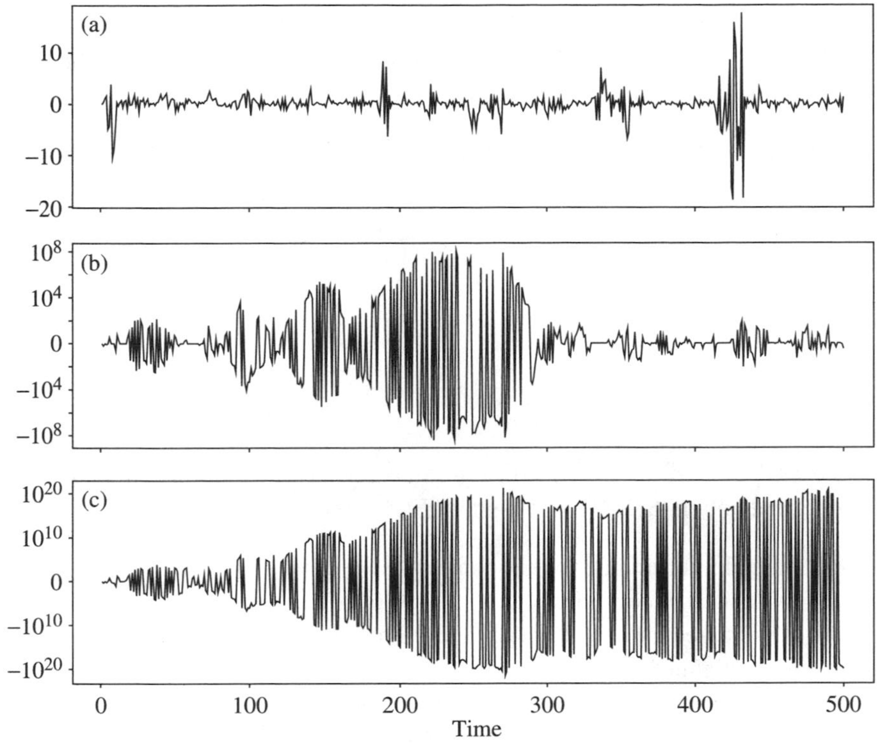

Figure 4.7. (a), (b) Strictly stationary ARCH(1) models with Gaussian innovations which are not covariance stationary ($\alpha_1 = 1.2$ and $\alpha_1 = 3$, respectively). (c) A non-stationary (explosive) process generated by the ARCH(1) equations with $\alpha_1 = 4$. Note that (b) and (c) use a special double-logarithmic y-axis where all values less than one in modulus are plotted at zero.

The process $(X_t)_{t \in \mathbb{Z}}$ is a martingale difference with a finite, non-time-dependent second moment. Hence it is a white noise process. □

See Figure 4.7 for examples of non-covariance-stationary ARCH(1) models as well as an example of a non-stationary (explosive) process generated by the ARCH(1) equations. The process in Figure 4.6 is covariance stationary.

On the stationary distribution of X_t. It is clear from (4.24) that the distribution of the (X_t) in an ARCH(1) model bears a complicated relationship to the distribution of the innovations (Z_t). Even if the innovations are Gaussian, the stationary distribution of the time series is not Gaussian, but rather a leptokurtic distribution with more slowly decaying tails.

Moreover, from (4.17) we see that the distribution of X_t is a normal mixture distribution of the kind discussed in Section 3.2. Its distribution depends on the distribution of σ_t, which has no simple form.

Proposition 4.19. *For $m \geqslant 1$, the strictly stationary* ARCH(1) *process has finite moments of order $2m$ if and only if $E(Z_t^{2m}) < \infty$ and $\alpha_1 < (E(Z_t^{2m}))^{-1/m}$.*

Proof. We rewrite (4.24) in the form $X_t^2 = Z_t^2 \sum_{i=0}^{\infty} Y_{t,i}$ for positive rvs $Y_{t,i} = \alpha_0 \alpha_1^i \prod_{j=1}^{i} Z_{t-j}^2$, $i \geqslant 1$, and $Y_{t,0} = \alpha_0$. For $m \geqslant 1$ the following inequalities hold (the latter being Minkowski's inequality):

$$E(Y_{t,1}^m) + E(Y_{t,2}^m) \leqslant E((Y_{t,1} + Y_{t,2})^m) \leqslant ((E(Y_{t,1}^m))^{1/m} + (E(Y_{t,2}^m))^{1/m})^m.$$

Since

$$E(X_t^{2m}) = E(Z_t^{2m}) E\biggl(\biggl(\sum_{i=0}^{\infty} Y_{t,i}\biggr)^m\biggr),$$

it follows that

$$E(Z_t^{2m}) \sum_{i=0}^{\infty} E(Y_{t,i}^m) \leqslant E(X_t^{2m}) \leqslant E(Z_t^{2m}) \biggl(\sum_{i=0}^{\infty} (E(Y_{t,i}^m))^{1/m}\biggr)^m.$$

Since $E(Y_{t,i}^m) = \alpha_0^m \alpha_1^{im} (E(Z_t^{2m}))^i$, it may be deduced that all three quantities are finite if and only if $E(Z_t^{2m}) < \infty$ and $\alpha_1^m E(Z_t^{2m}) < 1$. □

For example, for a finite fourth moment ($m = 2$) we require $\alpha_1 < 1/\sqrt{3}$ in the case of Gaussian innovations and $\alpha_1 < 1/\sqrt{6}$ in the case of t innovations with six degrees of freedom; for t innovations with four degrees of freedom the fourth moment is undefined.

Assuming the existence of a finite fourth moment, it is easy to calculate its value, and also that of the kurtosis of the process. We square both sides of (4.20), take expectations of both sides and then solve for $E(X_t^4)$ to obtain

$$E(X_t^4) = \frac{\alpha_0^2 E(Z_t^4)(1 - \alpha_1^2)}{(1 - \alpha_1)^2 (1 - \alpha_1^2 E(Z_t^4))}.$$

The kurtosis of the stationary distribution κ_X can then calculated to be

$$\kappa_X = \frac{E(X_t^4)}{E(X_t^2)^2} = \frac{\kappa_Z (1 - \alpha_1^2)}{(1 - \alpha_1^2 \kappa_Z)},$$

where $\kappa_Z = E(Z_t^4)$ denotes the kurtosis of the innovations. Clearly, when $\kappa_Z > 1$, the kurtosis of the stationary distribution is inflated in comparison with that of the innovation distribution; for Gaussian or t innovations $\kappa_X > 3$, so the stationary distribution is leptokurtic. The kurtosis of the process in Figure 4.6 is 9.

Parallels with the AR(1) process. We now turn our attention to the serial dependence structure of the squared series in the case of covariance stationarity ($\alpha_1 < 1$). We write the squared process as

$$X_t^2 = \sigma_t^2 Z_t^2 = \sigma_t^2 + \sigma_t^2 (Z_t^2 - 1). \tag{4.25}$$

Setting $V_t = \sigma_t^2 (Z_t^2 - 1)$ we note that $(V_t)_{t \in \mathbb{Z}}$ forms a martingale difference series, since $E|V_t| < \infty$ and $E(V_t \mid \mathcal{F}_{t-1}) = \sigma_t^2 E(Z_t^2 - 1) = 0$. Now we rewrite (4.25) as $X_t^2 = \alpha_0 + \alpha_1 X_{t-1}^2 + V_t$, and observe that this closely resembles an AR(1) process for X_t^2, except that V_t is not necessarily a white noise process. If we restrict our attention to processes where $E(X_t^4)$ is finite, then V_t has a finite and constant second moment and is a white noise process. Under this assumption, X_t^2 is an AR(1) according to Definition 4.7 of the form

$$\left(X_t^2 - \frac{\alpha_0}{1-\alpha_1}\right) = \alpha_1\left(X_{t-1}^2 - \frac{\alpha_0}{1-\alpha_1}\right) + V_t.$$

It has mean $\alpha_0/(1-\alpha_1)$ and we can use Example 4.11 to conclude that the autocorrelation function is $\rho(h) = \alpha_1^{|h|}$, $h \in \mathbb{Z}$. Figure 4.6 shows an example of an ARCH(1) process with finite fourth moment whose squared values follow an AR(1) process.

4.3.2 GARCH Processes

Definition 4.20. Let $(Z_t)_{t\in\mathbb{Z}}$ be SWN(0, 1). The process $(X_t)_{t\in\mathbb{Z}}$ is a GARCH(p, q) process if it is strictly stationary and if it satisfies, for all $t \in \mathbb{Z}$ and some strictly positive-valued process $(\sigma_t)_{t\in\mathbb{Z}}$, the equations

$$X_t = \sigma_t Z_t, \qquad \sigma_t^2 = \alpha_0 + \sum_{i=1}^{p} \alpha_i X_{t-i}^2 + \sum_{j=1}^{q} \beta_j \sigma_{t-j}^2, \tag{4.26}$$

where $\alpha_0 > 0$, $\alpha_i \geqslant 0$, $i = 1, \dots, p$, and $\beta_j \geqslant 0$, $j = 1, \dots, q$.

The GARCH processes are *generalized* ARCH processes in the sense that the squared volatility σ_t^2 is allowed to depend on previous squared volatilities, as well as previous squared values of the process.

The GARCH(1, 1) *model.* In practice, low-order GARCH models are most widely used and we will concentrate on the GARCH(1, 1) model. In this model periods of high volatility tend to be *persistent*, since $|X_t|$ has a chance of being large if *either* $|X_{t-1}|$ is large *or* σ_{t-1} is large; the same effect can be achieved in ARCH models of high order, but lower-order GARCH models achieve this effect more parsimoniously. A simulated realization of a GARCH(1, 1) process with Gaussian innovations and its volatility are shown in Figure 4.8; in comparison with the ARCH(1) model of Figure 4.6 it is clear that the volatility persists longer at higher levels before decaying to lower levels.

Stationarity. It follows from (4.26) that for a GARCH(1, 1) model we have

$$\sigma_t^2 = \alpha_0 + (\alpha_1 Z_{t-1}^2 + \beta)\sigma_{t-1}^2, \tag{4.27}$$

which is again an SRE of the form $Y_t = A_t Y_{t-1} + B_t$, as in (4.21). This time it is an SRE for $Y_t = \sigma_t^2$ rather than X_t^2, but its analysis follows easily from the ARCH(1) case.

The condition $E(\ln|A_t|) < 0$ for a strictly stationary solution of (4.21) translates to the condition $E(\ln(\alpha_1 Z_t^2 + \beta)) < 0$ for (4.27) and the general solution (4.23) becomes

$$\sigma_t^2 = \alpha_0 + \alpha_0 \sum_{i=1}^{\infty} \prod_{j=1}^{i} (\alpha_1 Z_{t-j}^2 + \beta). \tag{4.28}$$

If $(\sigma_t^2)_{t\in\mathbb{Z}}$ is a strictly stationary process, then so is $(X_t)_{t\in\mathbb{Z}}$, since $X_t = \sigma_t Z_t$ and $(Z_t)_{t\in\mathbb{Z}}$ is simply strict white noise. The solution of the GARCH(1, 1) defining equations is then

$$X_t = Z_t \sqrt{\alpha_0\left(1 + \sum_{i=1}^{\infty}\prod_{j=1}^{i}(\alpha_1 Z_{t-j}^2 + \beta)\right)}, \tag{4.29}$$

and we can use this to derive the condition for covariance stationarity.

Proposition 4.21. *The* GARCH(1, 1) *process is a covariance-stationary white noise process if and only if* $\alpha_1 + \beta < 1$. *The variance of the covariance-stationary process is given by* $\alpha_0/(1 - \alpha_1 - \beta)$.

Proof. We use a similar argument to Proposition 4.18 and make use of (4.29). □

Fourth moments and kurtosis. Using a similar approach to Proposition 4.19 we can use (4.29) to derive conditions for the existence of higher moments of a covariance-stationary GARCH(1, 1) process. For the existence of a fourth moment, a necessary and sufficient condition is that $E((\alpha_1 Z_t^2 + \beta)^2) < 1$, or alternatively that

$$(\alpha_1 + \beta)^2 < 1 - (\kappa_Z - 1)\alpha_1^2.$$

Assuming this to be true we calculate the fourth moment and kurtosis of X_t. We square both sides of (4.27) and take expectations to obtain

$$E(\sigma_t^4) = \alpha_0^2 + (\alpha_1^2\kappa_Z + \beta^2 + 2\alpha_1\beta)E(\sigma_t^4) + 2\alpha_0(\alpha_1 + \beta)E(\sigma_t^2).$$

Solving for $E(\sigma_t^4)$, recalling that $E(\sigma_t^2) = E(X_t^2) = \alpha_0/(1 - \alpha_1 - \beta)$, and setting $E(X_t^4) = \kappa_Z E(\sigma_t^4)$ we obtain

$$E(X_t^4) = \frac{\alpha_0^2\kappa_Z(1 - (\alpha_1 + \beta)^2)}{(1 - \alpha_1 - \beta)^2(1 - \alpha_1^2\kappa_Z - \beta^2 - 2\alpha_1\beta)},$$

from which it follows that

$$\kappa_X = \frac{\kappa_Z(1 - (\alpha_1 + \beta)^2)}{(1 - (\alpha_1 + \beta)^2 - (\kappa_Z - 1)\alpha_1^2)}.$$

Again it is clear that the kurtosis of X_t is greater than that of Z_t whenever $\kappa_Z > 1$, such as for Gaussian and scaled t innovations. The kurtosis of the GARCH(1, 1) model in Figure 4.8 is 3.77.

Parallels with the ARMA(1, 1) *process.* Using the same representation as in equation (4.25), the covariance-stationary GARCH(1, 1) process may be written as

$$X_t^2 = \alpha_0 + \alpha_1 X_{t-1}^2 + \beta\sigma_{t-1}^2 + V_t,$$

where V_t is a martingale difference, given by $V_t = \sigma_t^2(Z_t^2 - 1)$. Since $\sigma_{t-1}^2 = X_{t-1}^2 - V_{t-1}$, we may write

$$X_t^2 = \alpha_0 + (\alpha_1 + \beta)X_{t-1}^2 - \beta V_{t-1} + V_t, \tag{4.30}$$

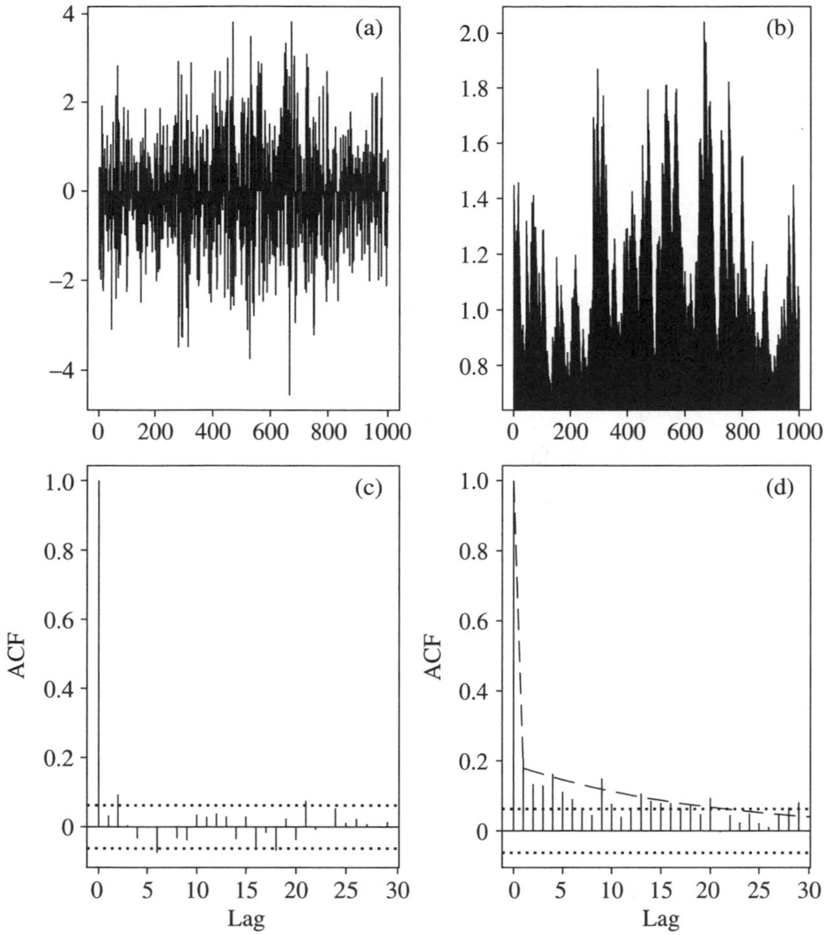

Figure 4.8. A GARCH(1, 1) process with Gaussian innovations and parameters $\alpha_0 = 0.5$, $\alpha_1 = 0.1$, $\beta = 0.85$: (a) the realization of the process; (b) the realization of the volatility; and correlograms of (c) the raw and (d) the squared values. The process is covariance stationary with unit variance and a finite fourth moment and the squared values follow an ARMA(1, 1) process. The true form of the ACF of the squared values is shown by a dashed line in the correlogram.

which begins to resemble an ARMA(1, 1) process for X_t^2. If we further assume that $E(X_t^4) < \infty$, then, recalling that $\alpha_1 + \beta < 1$, we have formally that

$$\left(X_t^2 - \frac{\alpha_0}{1-\alpha_1-\beta}\right) = (\alpha_1+\beta)\left(X_{t-1}^2 - \frac{\alpha_0}{1-\alpha_1-\beta}\right) - \beta V_{t-1} + V_t$$

is an ARMA(1, 1) process. Figure 4.8 shows an example of a GARCH(1, 1) process with finite fourth moment whose squared values follow an ARMA(1, 1) process.

The GARCH(p, q) model. Higher-order ARCH and GARCH models have the same general behaviour as ARCH(1) and GARCH(1, 1), but their mathematical analysis becomes more tedious. The condition for a strictly stationary solution of the defining SRE has been derived by Bougerol and Picard (1992), but is complicated. The necessary and sufficient condition that this solution is covariance stationary is $\sum_{i=1}^{p} \alpha_i + \sum_{j=1}^{q} \beta_j < 1$.

A squared GARCH(p, q) process has the structure

$$X_t^2 = \alpha_0 + \sum_{i=1}^{\max(p,q)} (\alpha_i + \beta_i) X_{t-i}^2 - \sum_{j=1}^{q} \beta_j V_{t-j} + V_t,$$

where $\alpha_i = 0$ for $i = p+1, \dots, q$ if $q > p$, or $\beta_j = 0$ for $j = q+1, \dots, p$ if $p > q$. This resembles the ARMA$(\max(p, q), q)$ process and is formally such a process provided $EX_t^4 < \infty$.

Integrated GARCH. The study of integrated GARCH (or IGARCH) processes has been motivated by the fact that, in some applications of GARCH modelling to daily or higher-frequency risk-factor return series, the estimated ARCH and GARCH coefficients $(\alpha_1, \dots, \alpha_p, \beta_1, \dots, \beta_q)$ are observed to sum to a number very close to one, and sometimes even slightly larger than one. In a model where $\sum_{i=1}^{p} \alpha_i + \sum_{j=1}^{q} \beta_j \geqslant 1$, the process has *infinite variance* and is thus non-covariance-stationary. The special case where $\sum_{i=1}^{p} \alpha_i + \sum_{j=1}^{q} \beta_j = 1$ is known as IGARCH and has received some attention.

For simplicity consider the IGARCH(1, 1) model. We use (4.30) to conclude that the squared process must satisfy

$$\nabla X_t^2 = X_t^2 - X_{t-1}^2 = \alpha_0 - (1 - \alpha_1) V_{t-1} + V_t,$$

where V_t is a noise sequence defined by $V_t = \sigma_t^2 (Z_t^2 - 1)$ and $\sigma_t^2 = \alpha_0 + \alpha_1 X_{t-1}^2 + (1 - \alpha_1) \sigma_{t-1}^2$. This equation is reminiscent of an ARIMA(0, 1, 1) model (see (4.14)) for X_t^2, although the noise V_t is not white noise, nor is it strictly speaking a martingale difference according to Definition 4.6. $E(V_t \mid \mathcal{F}_{t-1})$ is undefined since $E(\sigma_t^2) = E(X_t^2) = \infty$, and therefore $E|V_t|$ is undefined.

4.3.3 Simple Extensions of the GARCH Model

Many variants on and extensions of the basic GARCH model have been proposed. We mention only a few (see Notes and Comments for further reading).

ARMA models with GARCH errors. We have seen that ARMA processes are driven by a white noise $(\varepsilon_t)_{t \in \mathbb{Z}}$ and that a covariance-stationary GARCH process is an example of a white noise. In this section we put the ARMA and GARCH models together by setting the ARMA error ε_t equal to $\sigma_t Z_t$, where σ_t follows a GARCH volatility specification in terms of historical values of ε_t. This gives us a flexible family of ARMA models with GARCH errors that combines the features of both model classes.

Definition 4.22. Let $(Z_t)_{t \in \mathbb{Z}}$ be SWN(0, 1). The process $(X_t)_{t \in \mathbb{Z}}$ is said to be an ARMA(p_1, q_1) process with GARCH(p_2, q_2) errors if it is covariance stationary and satisfies difference equations of the form

$$X_t = \mu_t + \sigma_t Z_t,$$

$$\mu_t = \mu + \sum_{i=1}^{p_1} \phi_i (X_{t-i} - \mu) + \sum_{j=1}^{q_1} \theta_j (X_{t-j} - \mu_{t-j}),$$

$$\sigma_t^2 = \alpha_0 + \sum_{i=1}^{p_2} \alpha_i (X_{t-i} - \mu_{t-i})^2 + \sum_{j=1}^{q_2} \beta_j \sigma_{t-j}^2,$$

where $\alpha_0 > 0$, $\alpha_i \geqslant 0$, $i = 1, \dots, p_2$, $\beta_j \geqslant 0$, $j = 1, \dots, q_2$, and $\sum_{i=1}^{p_2} \alpha_i + \sum_{j=1}^{q_2} \beta_j < 1$.

To be consistent with the previous definition of an ARMA process we build the covariance-stationarity condition for the GARCH errors into the definition. For the ARMA process to be a causal and invertible linear process, as before, the polynomials $\tilde{\phi}(z) = 1 - \phi_1 z - \cdots - \phi_{p_1} z^{p_1}$ and $\tilde{\theta}(z) = 1 + \theta_1 z + \cdots + \theta_{q_1} z^{q_1}$ should have no common roots and no roots inside the unit circle.

Let $(\mathcal{F}_t)_{t \in \mathbb{Z}}$ denote the natural filtration of $(X_t)_{t \in \mathbb{Z}}$ and assume that the ARMA model is invertible. The invertibility of the ARMA process ensures that μ_t is $\mathcal{F}_{t-1}$-measurable as in (4.13). Moreover, since σ_t depends on the infinite history $(X_s - \mu_s)_{s \leqslant t-1}$, the ARMA invertibility also ensures that σ_t is $\mathcal{F}_{t-1}$-measurable. Simple calculations show that $\mu_t = E(X_t \mid \mathcal{F}_{t-1})$ and $\sigma_t^2 = \operatorname{var}(X_t \mid \mathcal{F}_{t-1})$, so that μ_t and σ_t^2 are the conditional mean and variance of the new process.

GARCH with leverage. One of the main criticisms of the standard ARCH and GARCH models is the rigidly symmetric way in which the volatility reacts to recent returns, regardless of their sign. Economic theory suggests that market information should have an asymmetric effect on volatility, whereby bad news leading to a fall in the equity value of a company tends to increase the volatility. This phenomenon has been called a *leverage effect*, because a fall in equity value causes an increase in the debt-to-equity ratio or so-called leverage of a company and should consequently make the stock more volatile. At a less theoretical level it seems reasonable that falling stock values might lead to a higher level of investor nervousness than rises in value of the same magnitude.

One method of adding a leverage effect to a GARCH(1, 1) model is by introducing an additional parameter into the volatility equation (4.26) to get

$$\sigma_t^2 = \alpha_0 + \alpha_1 (X_{t-1} + \delta |X_{t-1}|)^2 + \beta \sigma_{t-1}^2. \tag{4.31}$$

We assume that $\delta \in [-1, 1]$ and $\alpha_1 \geqslant 0$ as in the GARCH(1, 1) model. Observe that (4.31) may be written as

$$\sigma_t^2 = \begin{cases} \alpha_0 + \alpha_1 (1+\delta)^2 X_{t-1}^2 + \beta \sigma_{t-1}^2, & X_{t-1} \geqslant 0, \\ \alpha_0 + \alpha_1 (1-\delta)^2 X_{t-1}^2 + \beta \sigma_{t-1}^2, & X_{t-1} < 0, \end{cases}$$

and hence that

$$\frac{\partial \sigma_t^2}{\partial X_{t-1}^2} = \begin{cases} \alpha_1 (1+\delta)^2 \sigma_{t-1}^2, & X_{t-1} \geqslant 0, \\ \alpha_1 (1-\delta)^2 \sigma_{t-1}^2, & X_{t-1} < 0. \end{cases}$$

The response of volatility to the magnitude of the most recent return depends on the sign of that return, and we generally expect $\delta < 0$, so bad news has the greater effect.

Threshold GARCH. Observe that (4.31) may easily be rewritten in the form

$$\sigma_t^2 = \alpha_0 + \tilde{\alpha}_1 X_{t-1}^2 + \tilde{\delta}_1 I_{\{X_{t-1}<0\}} X_{t-1}^2 + \beta \sigma_{t-1}^2, \tag{4.32}$$

where $\tilde{\alpha}_1 = \alpha_1(1+\delta)^2$ and $\tilde{\delta} = -4\delta\alpha_1$. Equation (4.32) gives the most common version of a threshold GARCH (or TGARCH) model. In effect, a threshold has been set at level zero, and at time t the dynamics depend on whether the previous value of the process X_{t-1} (or innovation Z_{t-1}) was below or above this threshold. However, it is also possible to set non-zero thresholds in TGARCH models, so this represents a more general class of model than GARCH with leverage.

In a less common version of threshold GARCH the coefficients of the GARCH effects depend on the signs of previous values of the process; this gives a first-order process of the form

$$\sigma_t^2 = \alpha_0 + \alpha_1 X_{t-1}^2 + \beta \sigma_{t-1}^2 + \delta \mathbf{1}_{\{X_{t-1}<0\}} \sigma_{t-1}^2. \tag{4.33}$$

Remark 4.23. Note, also, that a further way to introduce asymmetry into a GARCH model is to explicitly use an asymmetric innovation distribution (albeit normalized to have mean zero and variance one). Candidate distributions could come from the generalized hyperbolic family of Section 3.2.3.

4.3.4 Fitting GARCH Models to Data

Building the likelihood. In practice, the most widely used approach to fitting GARCH models to data is maximum likelihood. We consider in turn the fitting of the ARCH(1) and GARCH(1, 1) models, from which the fitting of general ARCH(p) and GARCH(p, q) models easily follows.

For the ARCH(1) and GARCH(1, 1) models suppose we have a total of $n+1$ data values $X_0, X_1, \dots, X_n$. It is useful to recall that we can write the joint density of the corresponding rvs as

$$f_{X_0,\dots,X_n}(x_0,\dots,x_n) = f_{X_0}(x_0) \prod_{t=1}^{n} f_{X_t|X_{t-1},\dots,X_0}(x_t \mid x_{t-1},\dots,x_0). \tag{4.34}$$

For the pure ARCH(1) process, which is first-order Markovian, the conditional densities $f_{X_t|X_{t-1},\dots,X_0}$ in (4.34) depend on the past only through the value of σ_t or, equivalently, X_{t-1}. The conditional density is easily calculated to be

$$f_{X_t|X_{t-1},\dots,X_0}(x_t \mid x_{t-1},\dots,x_0) = f_{X_t|X_{t-1}}(x_t \mid x_{t-1}) = \frac{1}{\sigma_t} g\left(\frac{x_t}{\sigma_t}\right), \tag{4.35}$$

where $\sigma_t = (\alpha_0 + \alpha_1 x_{t-1}^2)^{1/2}$ and $g(z)$ denotes the density of the innovations $(Z_t)_{t\in\mathbb{Z}}$. We recall that this must have mean zero and variance one and typical choices would be the standard normal density or the density of a t distribution scaled to have unit variance.

However, the marginal density f_{X_0} in (4.34) is not known in a tractable closed form for ARCH and GARCH models and this poses a problem for basing a likelihood on (4.34). The solution employed in practice is to construct the *conditional likelihood* given X_0, which is calculated from

$$f_{X_1,\dots,X_n|X_0}(x_1,\dots,x_n \mid x_0) = \prod_{t=1}^{n} f_{X_t|X_{t-1},\dots,X_0}(x_t \mid x_{t-1},\dots,x_0). \tag{4.36}$$

For the ARCH(1) model this follows from (4.35) and is

$$L(\alpha_0,\alpha_1;\boldsymbol{X}) = f_{X_1,\dots,X_n|X_0}(X_1,\dots,X_n \mid X_0) = \prod_{t=1}^{n} \frac{1}{\sigma_t} g\left(\frac{X_t}{\sigma_t}\right),$$

with $\sigma_t = (\alpha_0 + \alpha_1 X_{t-1}^2)^{1/2}$. For an ARCH($p$) model we would use analogous arguments to write down a likelihood conditional on the first p values.

In the GARCH(1, 1) model σ_t is recursively defined in terms of σ_{t-1}, and here, instead of using (4.36), we construct the joint density of $X_1,\dots,X_n$ conditional on realized values of both X_0 and σ_0, which is

$$f_{X_1,\dots,X_n|X_0,\sigma_0}(x_1,\dots,x_n \mid x_0,\sigma_0) = \prod_{t=1}^{n} f_{X_t|X_{t-1},\dots,X_0,\sigma_0}(x_t \mid x_{t-1},\dots,x_0,\sigma_0).$$

The conditional densities $f_{X_t|X_{t-1},\dots,X_0,\sigma_0}$ depend on the past only through the value of σ_t, which is given recursively from $\sigma_0, X_0,\dots,X_{t-1}$ using $\sigma_t^2 = \alpha_0 + \alpha_1 X_{t-1}^2 + \beta\sigma_{t-1}^2$. This gives us the conditional likelihood

$$L(\alpha_0,\alpha_1,\beta;\boldsymbol{X}) = \prod_{t=1}^{n} \frac{1}{\sigma_t} g\left(\frac{X_t}{\sigma_t}\right), \qquad \sigma_t = \sqrt{\alpha_0 + \alpha_1 X_{t-1}^2 + \beta\sigma_{t-1}^2}.$$

The problem remains that the value of σ_0^2 is not actually observed, and this is usually solved by choosing a starting value, such as the sample variance of $X_1,\dots,X_n$, or even simply zero.

For a GARCH(p, q) model we would assume that we had $n + p$ data values labelled $X_{-p+1},\dots,X_0,X_1,\dots,X_n$. We would evaluate the likelihood conditional on the (observed) values of $X_{-p+1},\dots,X_0$ as well as the (unobserved) values of $\sigma_{-q+1},\dots,\sigma_0$, for which starting values would be used as above. For example, if $p = 1$ and $q = 3$, we require starting values for σ_0, σ_{-1} and σ_{-2}.

A similar approach can be used to develop a likelihood for an ARMA model with GARCH errors. In this case we would end up with a conditional likelihood of the form

$$L(\boldsymbol{\theta};\boldsymbol{X}) = \prod_{t=1}^{n} \frac{1}{\sigma_t} g\left(\frac{X_t - \mu_t}{\sigma_t}\right),$$

where σ_t follows a GARCH specification and μ_t follows an ARMA specification as in Definition 4.22, and all unknown parameters (possibly including unknown parameters of the innovation distribution) have been collected in the vector $\boldsymbol{\theta}$. We could of course also consider models with leverage or threshold effects.

Deriving parameter estimates. Consider, then, a log-likelihood of the form

$$\ln L(\boldsymbol{\theta}; \boldsymbol{X}) = \sum_{t=1}^{n} l_t(\boldsymbol{\theta}), \tag{4.37}$$

where l_t denotes the log-likelihood contribution arising from the tth observation. The maximum likelihood estimate $\hat{\boldsymbol{\theta}}$ maximizes the (conditional) log-likelihood in (4.37) and, being in general a local maximum, solves the likelihood equations

$$\frac{\partial}{\partial \boldsymbol{\theta}} \ln L(\boldsymbol{\theta}; \boldsymbol{X}) = \sum_{t=1}^{n} \frac{\partial l_t(\boldsymbol{\theta})}{\partial \boldsymbol{\theta}} = \mathbf{0}, \tag{4.38}$$

where the left-hand side is also known as the *score vector* of the conditional likelihood. The equations (4.38) are usually solved numerically using so-called modified Newton–Raphson procedures. A particular method which is widely used for GARCH models is the BHHH method of Berndt, Hall, Hall and Hausmann.

In describing the behaviour of parameter estimates in the following paragraphs, we distinguish two situations. In the first situation we assume that the model that has been fitted has been *correctly specified*, so that the data are truly generated by a time series model with both the assumed dynamic form and innovation distribution. We describe the asymptotic behaviour of the maximum likelihood estimates (MLEs) under this idealization.

In the second situation we assume that the correct dynamic form is fitted but that the innovations are erroneously assumed to be Gaussian. Under this misspecification the model fitting procedure is known as *quasi-maximum likelihood* (QML) and the estimates obtained are QMLEs. Essentially, the Gaussian likelihood is treated as an objective function to be maximized rather than a proper likelihood; our intuition suggests that this may still give reasonable parameter estimates and this turns out to be the case under appropriate assumptions about the true innovation distribution.

Properties of MLEs. It helps to recall at this point the asymptotic distribution theory for MLEs in the classical iid case, which is summarized in Section A.3. The asymptotic results we give for GARCH models have a similar form to the results in the iid case, but it is important to realize that this is not simply an application of these results. The asymptotics have been separately and laboriously derived in a series of papers for which starting references are given in Notes and Comments. We will give results for pure GARCH models without ARMA components or additional leverage structure, which have been studied rigorously, but the form of the results will apply more generally.

For a pure GARCH(p, q) model with Gaussian innovations it can be shown that (assuming the model has been correctly specified)

$$\sqrt{n}(\hat{\boldsymbol{\theta}}_n - \boldsymbol{\theta}) \xrightarrow{\text{d}} N_{p+q+1}(\mathbf{0}, I(\boldsymbol{\theta})^{-1}),$$

where

$$I(\boldsymbol{\theta}) = E\left(\frac{\partial l_t(\boldsymbol{\theta})}{\partial \boldsymbol{\theta}} \frac{\partial l_t(\boldsymbol{\theta})}{\partial \boldsymbol{\theta}'}\right) = -E\left(\frac{\partial^2 l_t(\boldsymbol{\theta})}{\partial \boldsymbol{\theta} \partial \boldsymbol{\theta}'}\right) \tag{4.39}$$

is the Fisher information matrix arising from any single observation. Thus we have consistent and asymptotically normal estimates of the GARCH parameters. In practice, the *expected* information matrix $I(\boldsymbol{\theta})$ is approximated by an *observed* information matrix, and here we could take the observed information matrix coming from either of the equivalent forms for the expected information matrix in (4.39). That is, we could use

$$\bar{I}(\boldsymbol{\theta}) = \frac{1}{n}\sum_{t=1}^{n}\left(\frac{\partial l_t(\boldsymbol{\theta})}{\partial \boldsymbol{\theta}}\frac{\partial l_t(\boldsymbol{\theta})}{\partial \boldsymbol{\theta}'}\right) \quad \text{or} \quad \bar{J}(\boldsymbol{\theta}) = -\frac{1}{n}\sum_{t=1}^{n}\frac{\partial^2 l_t(\boldsymbol{\theta})}{\partial \boldsymbol{\theta}\,\partial \boldsymbol{\theta}'}, \tag{4.40}$$

where the first matrix is said to have *outer-product* form and the second is said to have *Hessian* form. These matrices are estimated by evaluating them at the MLEs to get $\bar{I}(\hat{\boldsymbol{\theta}})$ or $\bar{J}(\hat{\boldsymbol{\theta}})$. In practice, this is done by numerical first and second differencing of the log-likelihood at the MLE and the necessary matrices are obtained as byproducts of the BHHH procedure for deriving the parameter estimates.

If the model is correctly specified, the estimates $\bar{I}(\hat{\boldsymbol{\theta}})$ and $\bar{J}(\hat{\boldsymbol{\theta}})$ should be broadly similar, being estimators based on two different expressions for the same Fisher information matrix. In practice, we could also estimate $I(\boldsymbol{\theta})$ by $\bar{J}(\hat{\boldsymbol{\theta}})\bar{I}(\hat{\boldsymbol{\theta}})^{-1}\bar{J}(\hat{\boldsymbol{\theta}})$, and this anticipates the so-called *sandwich estimator* that is used in the QML procedure.

Properties of QMLEs. In this approach we assume that the true data-generating mechanism is a GARCH(p, q) model with non-Gaussian innovations, but we attempt to estimate the parameters of the process by maximizing the likelihood for a GARCH(p, q) model with Gaussian innovations. We still obtain consistent estimators of the model parameters and, if the true innovation distribution has a finite fourth moment, we again get asymptotic normality; however, the form of the asymptotic covariance matrix changes.

We now distinguish between matrices $I(\boldsymbol{\theta})$ and $J(\boldsymbol{\theta})$, given by

$$I(\boldsymbol{\theta}) = E\left(\frac{\partial l_t(\boldsymbol{\theta})}{\partial \boldsymbol{\theta}}\frac{\partial l_t(\boldsymbol{\theta})}{\partial \boldsymbol{\theta}'}\right), \qquad J(\boldsymbol{\theta}) = -E\left(\frac{\partial^2 l_t(\boldsymbol{\theta})}{\partial \boldsymbol{\theta}\,\partial \boldsymbol{\theta}'}\right),$$

where the expectation is now taken with respect to the true model (not the misspecified Gaussian model). The matrices $I(\boldsymbol{\theta})$ and $J(\boldsymbol{\theta})$ differ in general (unless the Gaussian model is correct). It may be shown that

$$\sqrt{n}(\hat{\boldsymbol{\theta}}_n - \boldsymbol{\theta}) \xrightarrow{\text{d}} N_{p+q+1}(\mathbf{0}, J(\boldsymbol{\theta})^{-1}I(\boldsymbol{\theta})J(\boldsymbol{\theta})^{-1}), \tag{4.41}$$

and the asymptotic covariance matrix is said to be of sandwich form; it can be estimated by $\bar{J}(\hat{\boldsymbol{\theta}})^{-1}\bar{I}(\hat{\boldsymbol{\theta}})\bar{J}(\hat{\boldsymbol{\theta}})^{-1}$, where $\bar{I}(\boldsymbol{\theta})$ and $\bar{J}(\boldsymbol{\theta})$ are defined in (4.40). If the model-checking procedures described below suggest that the dynamics have been adequately described by the GARCH model, but the Gaussian assumption seems doubtful, then standard errors for parameter estimates should be based on this covariance matrix estimate.

Model checking. As with ARMA models it is usual to check fitted GARCH models using residuals. We consider a general ARMA–GARCH model of the form $X_t - \mu_t = \varepsilon_t = \sigma_t Z_t$, with μ_t and σ_t as in Definition 4.22. In this model we distinguish between *unstandardized* and *standardized* residuals. The former are the residuals $\hat{\varepsilon}_1, \dots, \hat{\varepsilon}_n$ from the ARMA part of the model; they are calculated using the approach in (4.15), and under the hypothesized model they should behave like a realization of a pure GARCH process. The latter are reconstructed realizations of the SWN that is assumed to drive the GARCH part of the model, and they are calculated from the former by

$$\hat{Z}_t = \hat{\varepsilon}_t / \hat{\sigma}_t, \qquad \hat{\sigma}_t^2 = \hat{\alpha}_0 + \sum_{i=1}^{p_2} \hat{\alpha}_i \hat{\varepsilon}_{t-i}^2 + \sum_{j=1}^{q_2} \hat{\beta}_j \hat{\sigma}_{t-j}^2. \tag{4.42}$$

To use (4.42) we need some initial values, and one solution is to set required starting values of $\hat{\varepsilon}_t$ equal to zero and required starting values of the volatility $\hat{\sigma}_t$ equal to either the sample variance or zero. Because the first few values will be influenced by these starting values, as well as the starting values required to calculate the unstandardized residuals, they may be ignored in later analyses.

The standardized residuals should behave like an SWN and this can be investigated by constructing correlograms of raw and absolute values and applying portmanteau tests of strict white noise, as described in Section 4.2.3.

Assuming that the SWN hypothesis is not rejected, so that the dynamics have been satisfactorily captured, the validity of the distribution used in the ML fitting can also be investigated using QQplots and goodness-of-fit tests for the normal or scaled t distributions. If the Gaussian likelihood does a reasonable job of estimating dynamics, but the residuals do not behave like iid standard normal observations, then the QML fitting philosophy can be adopted and standard errors can be estimated using the sandwich estimator implied by (4.41) above.

This opens up the possibility of *two-stage analyses* where first the dynamics are estimated by QML methods and then the innovation distribution is modelled using the residuals from the dynamic model as data. The first stage is sometimes called *pre-whitening* of the data. In the second stage we might consider using heavier-tailed models than the Gaussian that also allow some asymmetry in the innovations.

A disadvantage of the two-stage approach is that the error from the time series modelling propagates through to the distributional fitting in the second stage and the overall error is hard to quantify, but the procedure does lead to more transparency in model building and allows us to separate the tasks of volatility modelling and modelling the shocks that drive the process. In higher-dimensional risk-factor modelling it may be a useful pragmatic approach.

Example 4.24 (GARCH model for Microsoft log-returns). We consider the Microsoft daily log-returns for the period 1997–2000 (1009 values), as shown in Figure 4.9. Although the raw returns show no evidence of serial correlation (see Figure 4.10), their absolute values do show serial correlation and they fail a Ljung–Box test (based on the first 10 estimated correlations) at the 5% level.

For these data, models with Student t innovations are clearly preferred to models with Gaussian innovations, so we adopt an ML approach to fitting models with t innovations. We compare the standard GARCH(1, 1) model (with a constant mean term)

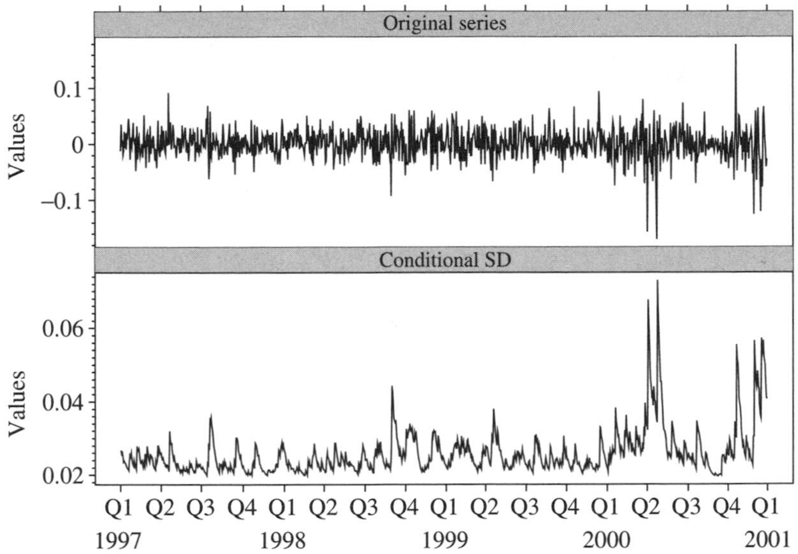

Figure 4.9. Microsoft log-returns 1997–2000; data and estimate of volatility from a GARCH(1, 1) model with a leverage term.

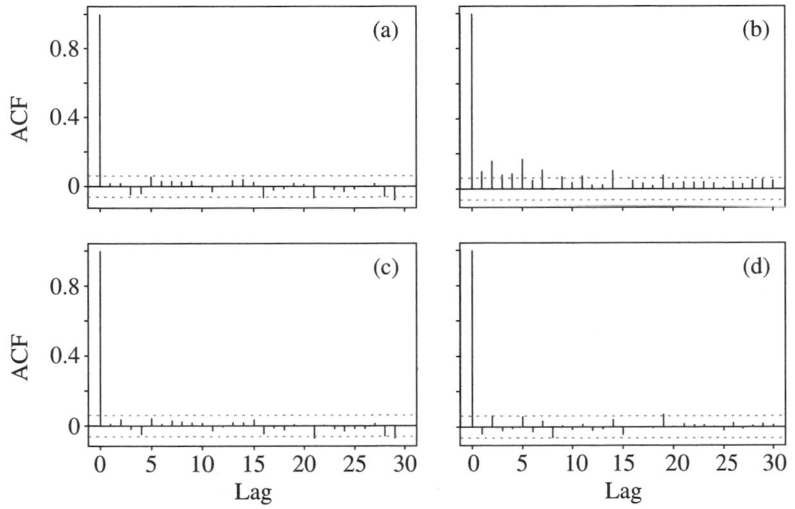

Figure 4.10. Microsoft log-returns 1997–2000; correlograms of data ((a) raw and (b) absolute values) and residuals ((c) raw and (d) absolute values) from a GARCH(1, 1) model.

with models that incorporate ARMA structure (AR(1), MA(1) and ARMA(1, 1)) for the conditional mean; the ARMA structure seems to offer little improvement in the model and the basic GARCH(1, 1) model is favoured in an Akaike comparison. However, a model with a leverage term as in (4.31) does seem to offer an improvement. Both the raw and absolute standardized residuals obtained from this model show no visual evidence of serial correlation (see again Figure 4.10) and they do not fail Ljung–Box tests. The estimated degrees-of-freedom parameter of the (scaled)

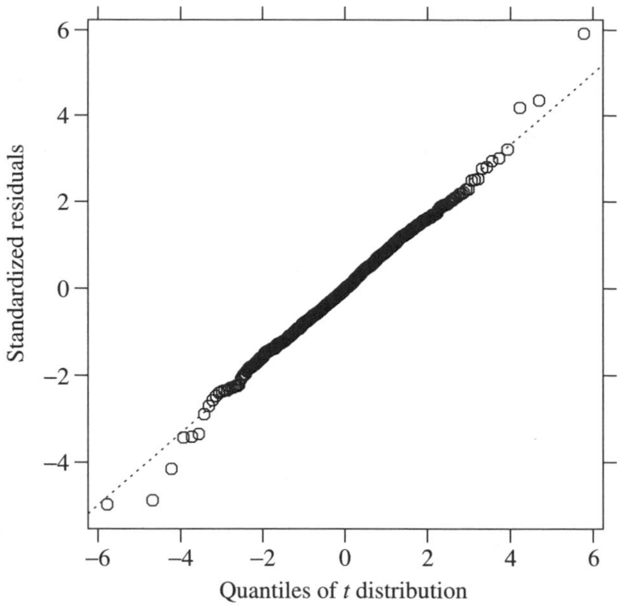

Figure 4.11. Microsoft log-returns 1997–2000; QQplot of residuals from a GARCH(1, 1) model with leverage against a Student t distribution with 6.30 degrees of freedom.

Table 4.2. Analysis of Microsoft log-returns for the period 1997–2000; ML estimates of parameters and standard errors for a GARCH(1, 1) model with a leverage term under the assumption of t innovations.

Parameter	Estimate	Standard error	Ratio
μ	9.35×10^{-4}	7.21×10^{-4}	1.30
α_0	7.79×10^{-5}	3.07×10^{-5}	2.54
α_1	0.108	0.0369	2.91
β	0.778	0.0673	11.57
δ	−0.178	0.123	−1.45

t distribution is 6.30 (the standard error is 1.07) and a QQplot of the residuals against this reference distribution reveals a satisfactory correspondence (see Figure 4.11). The estimates of the remaining parameters (with standard errors) in this model are given in Table 4.2.

Notes and Comments

The ARCH process was originally proposed by Engle (1982), and the GARCH process by Bollerslev (1986), who gave the condition for covariance stationarity. Overview texts on GARCH models include the book by Gourieroux (1997) and a number of useful review articles including Bollerslev, Chou and Kroner (1992), Bollerslev, Engle and Nelson (1994) and Shephard (1996). There are also substantial sections on GARCH models in the books by Alexander (2001), Tsay (2002) and

Zivot and Wang (2003). The IGARCH model was first discussed by Engle and Bollerslev (1986).

The condition for strict stationarity of GARCH models was derived by Nelson (1990) in the case of the GARCH(1, 1) model and Bougerol and Picard (1992) for GARCH(p, q). The necessary theory involves the study of stochastic recurrence relations and goes back to Kesten (1973); Brandt (1986) is also a useful reference. Readable accounts of this theory may be found in Embrechts, Klüppelberg and Mikosch (1997), Mikosch and Stărică (2000) and Mikosch (2003).

For more on the derivation of conditional likelihood functions for ARCH and GARCH models see Hamilton (1994) and Tsay (2002). The BHHH algorithm (Berndt et al. 1974) is the most commonly used approach to numerically maximizing the likelihood. For an informative general discussion of numerical optimization procedures in the context of maximum likelihood see Hamilton (1994, pp. 133–142). Standard general references on the QML approach are White (1981) and Gourieroux, Montfort and Trognon (1984).

The essential asymptotic properties of MLEs and QMLEs in GARCH models are described in many publications, but the detailed mathematical proof has often lagged behind the assertions. Early papers appealed to regularity conditions for conditionally specified models such as those of Crowder (1976), which are essentially unverifiable. Lee and Hansen (1994) and Lumsdaine (1996) proved consistency and asymptotic normality of QMLEs in the GARCH(1, 1) model. More recently, Berkes, Horváth and Kokoszka (2003) have extended this to the GARCH(p, q) model under minimal assumptions, and Mikosch and Straumann (2005) and Straumann (2003) have given similar results for a wide variety of first-order models.

From a more practical point-of-view, it is not easy to estimate GARCH model parameters to a high degree of accuracy because of the flatness of the typical likelihoods and the non-negligible influence of starting values in finite samples. Readers who write their own code may wish to compare their estimates with benchmark studies by McCullough and Renfro (1999) and Brooks, Burke and Persand (2001).

Alternative innovation distributions to the Gaussian and scaled t distributions that have been considered include the generalized error distribution (GED) in Nelson (1991) and the normal inverse Gaussian (NIG) in Venter and de Jongh (2001); the latter authors present extensive evidence that the NIG is a good choice of innovation distribution for practical work and that GARCH inference based on the NIG is relatively robust to misspecification of the distribution.

A great many extensions to the GARCH class have been proposed and thorough surveys may be found in Bollerslev, Engle and Nelson (1994) and Shephard (1996). Leverage effects in the GARCH model and the more general PGARCH (power GARCH) model are examined in Ding, Granger and Engle (1993). Various threshold GARCH models have been suggested; the model (4.32) is of the type suggested by Glosten, Jagannathan and Runkle (1993), while (4.33) is the switching-volatility GARCH (SV-GARCH) model of Fornari and Mele (1997). There have been proposals for non-parametric ARCH and GARCH modelling, including the multiplicative ARCH(p)-model of Yang, Härdle and Nielsen (1999) and the non-parametric GARCH procedure of Bühlmann and McNeil (2002).

4.4 Volatility Models and Risk Estimation

In this section we elaborate on some issues raised in the discussion of standard methods for market risks in Section 2.3. At that point the discussion of dynamic risk estimation procedures was kept relatively vague, but now, armed with more knowledge of time series models in general and GARCH in particular, we can give some more detail. The main issues are the estimation of conditional risk measures like VaR and expected shortfall and the backtesting of such estimates. Estimating VaR for a future time period requires us to be able to forecast volatility and we start with this topic.

4.4.1 Volatility Forecasting

As in our earlier discussion of time series prediction in Section 4.2.5, we describe a model-based strategy using a GARCH-type model, before presenting the more ad hoc technique of exponentially weighted moving-average (EWMA) prediction.

GARCH-based volatility prediction. Suppose that the return data $X_{t-n+1}, \dots, X_t$ follow a particular model in the GARCH family. We want to forecast future volatility, i.e. to predict the value of σ_{t+h} for $h \geqslant 1$. This is closely related to the problem of predicting X_{t+h}^2 and uses an analogous method to that used for prediction in ARMA models in Section 4.2.5. We again assume that we have access to the infinite history of the process up to time t, represented by $\mathcal{F}_t = \sigma(\{X_s : s \leqslant t\})$, and then adapt our prediction formula to take account of the finiteness of the sample.

Assume that the GARCH model has been fitted and its parameters estimated; we will suppress estimator notation for the parameters in the remainder of the section. We make calculations for simple models, from which the general procedure for more complex models should be clear.

Example 4.25 (prediction in the GARCH(1, 1) model). Suppose that we use a pure GARCH(1, 1) model conforming to Definition 4.20. Assume the model is covariance stationary so that $E(X_t^2) = E(\sigma_t^2) < \infty$. Since $(X_t)_{t \in \mathbb{Z}}$ is a martingale difference, optimal predictions of X_{t+h} are zero. A natural prediction of X_{t+1}^2 based on $\mathcal{F}_t$ is its conditional mean σ_{t+1}^2 given by

$$E(X_{t+1}^2 \mid \mathcal{F}_t) = \sigma_{t+1}^2 = \alpha_0 + \alpha_1 X_t^2 + \beta \sigma_t^2,$$

and if $E(X_t^4) < \infty$, then this is the optimal squared error prediction. Note that the prediction of the random variable X_{t+1}^2 based on the information $\mathcal{F}_t$ is the value of σ_{t+1}^2, which is *known* at time t, being a function of the infinite history of the process. (The process $(\sigma_t)_{t \in \mathbb{Z}}$ is said to be previsible.)

In practice we have to make an approximation based on this formula because the infinite series of past values that would allow us to calculate σ_t^2 is not available to us. A natural approach in applications is to approximate σ_t^2 by an estimate of squared volatility $\hat{\sigma}_t^2$ calculated from the residual equations (4.42). Our approximate forecast of X_{t+1}^2 also functions as an estimate of the squared volatility at time $t+1$ and is given by

$$\hat{\sigma}_{t+1}^2 = \hat{E}(X_{t+1}^2 \mid \mathcal{F}_t) = \alpha_0 + \alpha_1 X_n^2 + \beta \hat{\sigma}_t^2. \tag{4.43}$$

Thus equation (4.43) can be thought of as a recursive scheme for estimating volatility one step ahead.

When we look $h > 1$ steps ahead given the information at time t, both X_{t+h}^2 and σ_{t+h}^2 are rvs. Their predictions coincide and are

$$\begin{aligned} E(X_{t+h}^2 \mid \mathcal{F}_t) &= E(\sigma_{t+h}^2 \mid \mathcal{F}_t) \\ &= \alpha_0 + \alpha_1 E(X_{t+h-1}^2 \mid \mathcal{F}_t) + \beta E(\sigma_{t+h-1}^2 \mid \mathcal{F}_t) \\ &= \alpha_0 + (\alpha_1 + \beta) E(X_{t+h-1}^2 \mid \mathcal{F}_t), \end{aligned}$$

so that a general formula is

$$E(X_{t+h}^2 \mid \mathcal{F}_t) = \alpha_0 \sum_{i=0}^{h-1} (\alpha_1 + \beta)^i + (\alpha_1 + \beta)^{h-1} (\alpha_1 X_t^2 + \beta \sigma_t^2),$$

and we obtain a practical formula by substituting an estimate of squared volatility $\hat{\sigma}_t^2$ as before. As $h \to \infty$ we observe that $E(\sigma_{t+h}^2 \mid \mathcal{F}_t) \to \alpha_0/(1 - \alpha_1 - \beta_1)$, almost surely, so that the prediction of squared volatility converges to the unconditional variance of the process. A concrete example of volatility prediction in a GARCH(1, 1) model is given in Figure 4.12 for the Microsoft data analysed in Example 4.24.

We now consider a second example, which combines what we know about prediction in ARMA and GARCH models.

Example 4.26 (prediction in an ARMA(1, 1)–GARCH(1, 1) model). Consider a process of the form $X_t - \mu_t = \varepsilon_t = \sigma_t Z_t$, where μ_t and σ_t are $\mathcal{F}_{t-1}$-measurable rvs describing, respectively, an ARMA(1, 1) model and a GARCH(1, 1) model as in Definition 4.22. Prediction formulas for this model follow easily from Examples 4.15 and 4.25. We calculate that

$$E(X_{t+h} \mid \mathcal{F}_t) = \mu + \phi^h (X_t - \mu) + \phi^{h-1} \theta \varepsilon_t, \tag{4.44}$$

$$\operatorname{var}(X_{t+h} \mid \mathcal{F}_t) = \alpha_0 \sum_{i=0}^{h-1} (\alpha_1 + \beta)^i + (\alpha_1 + \beta)^{h-1} (\alpha_1 \varepsilon_t^2 + \beta \sigma_t^2), \tag{4.45}$$

and these are approximated by substituting inferred values for ε_t and σ_t obtained from the residual equations (4.42). Equation (4.44) yields predictions of μ_{t+h} or X_{t+h}, and equation (4.45) yields predictions of ε_{t+h}^2 or σ_{t+h}^2.

Exponential smoothing for volatility. Suppose we believe our return data follow some kind of underlying time series model in which a volatility (conditional standard deviation) is defined, but that we do not wish to specify the exact parametric model.

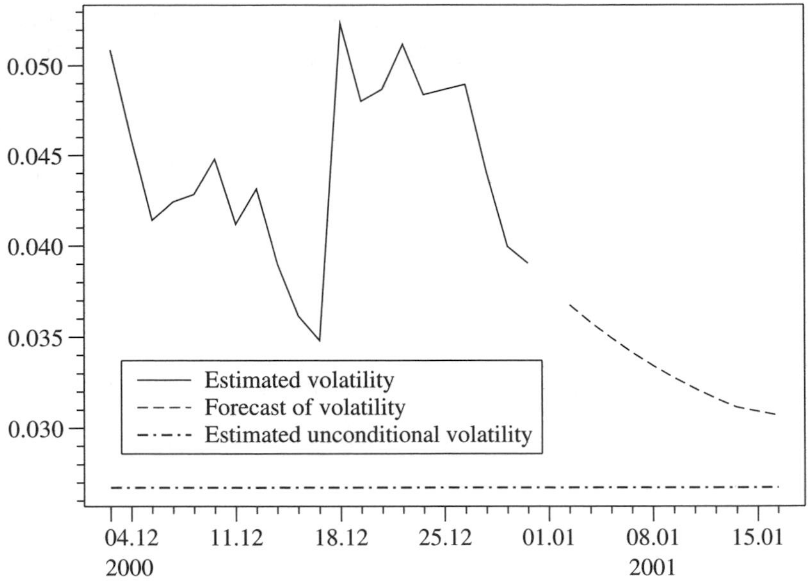

Figure 4.12. Estimate of volatility for the final days of the year 2000 and predictions of volatility for the first 10 days of 2001 based on a GARCH(1, 1) model (without leverage) fitted to the Microsoft return data in Example 4.24.

We can apply exponential smoothing as in (4.16) to the squared observations to get a procedure that follows the updating scheme

$$P_t X_{t+1}^2 = \alpha X_t^2 + (1-\alpha) P_{t-1} X_t^2, \tag{4.46}$$

for some value of α.

Since the expectations of X_{t+1}^2 and σ_{t+1}^2 coincide, we could alternatively regard (4.46) as an exponential smoothing scheme for the unobserved squared volatility. We could define a recursive scheme for one-step-ahead volatility forecasting by

$$\hat{\sigma}_{t+1}^2 = \alpha X_t^2 + (1-\alpha)\hat{\sigma}_t^2. \tag{4.47}$$

This is the essential idea of the EWMA approach to volatility forecasting.

If we compare (4.47) with the one-step-ahead volatility estimation scheme defined by a GARCH(1, 1) model in (4.43), it is tempting to say that EWMA corresponds to estimating volatility using a conditional-expectation-based technique in an IGARCH model where the parameter α_0 equals zero, although this analogy should be used with care. GARCH and IGARCH models with $\alpha_0 = 0$ are not well defined and the solution of the stochastic recurrence relation in (4.29) vanishes. Moreover, IGARCH is not covariance stationary. It is better to regard EWMA as a sensible model-free approach to volatility forecasting based on the classical technique of exponential smoothing.

4.4.2 Conditional Risk Measurement

We now return to the conditional risk-measurement problem discussed in Chapter 2 and consider the situation where we wish to measure risk for an investment in a single stock, index or currency. On day t the value of the position is V_t and the log-return for the next day is X_{t+1}, so the (linearized) loss over the next day is $L_{t+1} = l^{\Delta}_{[t]}(X_{t+1}) = -V_t X_{t+1}$. We require risk-measure estimates, such as VaR and ES, for the conditional distribution $F_{L_{t+1}|\mathcal{F}_t}$, where $\mathcal{F}_t = \sigma(\{X_s : s \leqslant t\})$. We set $V_t = 1$ for all t and write $L_t = -X_t$, so (L_t) is the process of negative log-returns.

Remark 4.27. Although we consider a simple univariate situation, the methodology of this section can be applied to portfolio losses in the context of historical simulation. Suppose we have constructed historical-simulation data $(\tilde{L}_t)$ using the approach described in Section 2.3.2. Writing $L_{t+1} = l_{[t]}(\boldsymbol{X}_{t+1})$ for our loss over the next day, where $l_{[t]}$ is the loss operator and $\boldsymbol{X}_{t+1}$ the vector of risk-factor changes, we wish to calculate risk-measure estimates for the conditional distribution $F_{L_{t+1}|\mathcal{G}_t}$, where $\mathcal{G}_t = \sigma(\{\tilde{L}_s : s \leqslant t\})$. We simply apply the methodology of this section to the time series $(\tilde{L}_t)$; this strategy was used in Section 2.3.6.

To calculate conditional risk measures we make the following assumption.

Assumption 4.28. *The process of losses $(L_t)_{t\in\mathbb{Z}}$ is adapted to the filtration $(\mathcal{F}_t)_{t\in\mathbb{Z}}$ and follows a stationary model of the form $L_t = \mu_t + \sigma_t Z_t$, where μ_t and σ_t are $\mathcal{F}_{t-1}$-measurable and the (Z_t) are* SWN(0, 1) *innovations.*

A concrete example of a model satisfying Assumption 4.28 would be an (invertible) ARMA process with GARCH errors of the kind analysed in this chapter. Under the assumption, if we write G for the df of (Z_t), we can easily calculate that

$$F_{L_{t+1}|\mathcal{F}_t}(l) = P(\mu_{t+1} + \sigma_{t+1} Z_{t+1} \leqslant l \mid \mathcal{F}_t) = G((l - \mu_{t+1})/\sigma_{t+1}). \tag{4.48}$$

Thus calculation of risk measures for the conditional one-period loss distribution amounts to calculating risk measures for the innovation distribution G. Using the approach of Examples 2.14 and 2.18 we easily obtain

$$\mathrm{VaR}^t_\alpha = \mu_{t+1} + \sigma_{t+1} q_\alpha(Z), \tag{4.49}$$

$$\mathrm{ES}^t_\alpha = \mu_{t+1} + \sigma_{t+1}\,\mathrm{ES}_\alpha(Z), \tag{4.50}$$

where Z is a generic rv with df G. In general, to estimate the risk measures (4.49) and (4.50), we require estimates of μ_{t+1} and σ_{t+1}, the conditional mean and volatility of the loss process. We also require the quantile and expected shortfall of the innovation df G. In a model with Gaussian innovations the latter are $q_\alpha(Z) = \Phi^{-1}(\alpha)$ and $\mathrm{ES}_\alpha(Z) = \phi(\Phi^{-1}(\alpha))/(1-\alpha)$. In a model with non-Gaussian innovations, $q_\alpha(Z)$ and $\mathrm{ES}_\alpha(Z)$ depend on any further parameters of the innovation distribution. For example, we might assume (scaled) t innovations; in this case the quantile and expected shortfall of a standard univariate t distribution (the latter given in (2.27)) would have to be scaled by the factor $\sqrt{(\nu-2)/\nu}$ to take account of the fact that the innovation distribution is scaled to have variance one.

Concrete estimation strategies we might adopt, in order of decreasing sophistication, include the following.

(1) Fit an ARMA–GARCH model with an appropriate innovation distribution to the data $L_{t-n+1}, \dots, L_t$ by ML and use the prediction methodology discussed in Section 4.4.1 to estimate σ_{t+1} and μ_{t+1}. Any further parameters of the innovation distribution would be estimated simultaneously in the model fitting.

(2) Fit an ARMA–GARCH model by QML and use prediction methodology as in strategy (1) to estimate σ_{t+1} and μ_{t+1}. In a separate second step we use the model residuals to find an appropriate innovation distribution and estimate its parameters.

(3) Use EWMA to estimate σ_{t+1} and set μ_{t+1} to zero (as it is less important). In conjunction with an assumption of Gaussian innovations this is essentially the RiskMetrics method. Instead of making the Gaussian assumption, we could standardize each of the losses $L_{t-n+1}, \dots, L_t$ by dividing by volatility estimates $\hat{\sigma}_{t-n+1}, \dots, \hat{\sigma}_t$ calculated using EWMA. This would yield a set of residuals, from which the innovation distribution could be estimated as in strategy (2).

4.4.3 Backtesting

Backtesting VaR. Using the notation of the previous section, we first observe that if we define indicator variables $I_{t+1} = I_{\{L_{t+1} > \mathrm{VaR}_\alpha^t\}}$, indicating violations of the quantiles of the conditional loss distribution, then the process $(I_t)_{t \in \mathbb{Z}}$ is a process of iid Bernoulli variables with success (i.e. violation) probability $1 - \alpha$. This property is certainly true under Assumption 4.28, since it follows from (4.49) that $I_{t+1} = I_{\{L_{t+1} > \mathrm{VaR}_\alpha^t\}} = I_{\{Z_{t+1} > q_\alpha(Z)\}}$ and the innovations (Z_t) are themselves iid. However, it is also more generally true, as the following lemma shows.

Lemma 4.29. *Let $(Y_t)_{t \in \mathbb{Z}}$ be a sequence of Bernoulli indicator variables adapted to a filtration $(\mathcal{F}_t)_{t \in \mathbb{Z}}$ and satisfying $E(Y_t \mid \mathcal{F}_{t-1}) = p > 0$ for all t. Then (Y_t) is a process of iid Bernoulli variables.*

Proof. The process $(Y_t - p)_{t \in \mathbb{Z}}$ has the martingale-difference property (see Definition 4.6). Moreover, $\mathrm{var}(Y_t - p) = E(E((Y_t - p)^2 \mid \mathcal{F}_{t-1})) = p(1 - p)$ for all t. Therefore $(Y_t - p)$ and hence (Y_t) are white noise processes of uncorrelated variables. It is easily shown that identically distributed uncorrelated Bernoulli variables are iid. □

In practice, we make one-step-ahead conditional VaR estimates $\widehat{\mathrm{VaR}}_\alpha^t$ and consider the violation indicators

$$\hat{I}_{t+1} := I_{\{L_{t+1} > \widehat{\mathrm{VaR}}_\alpha^t\}}. \tag{4.51}$$

If we are successful in estimating conditional quantiles, we would expect that the empirical violation indicators would behave like realizations of iid Bernoulli trials with success probability $(1 - \alpha)$.

Checking for iid Bernoulli violations of the one-step-ahead VaR has two aspects: checking that the number of violations is correct on average; checking that the pattern of violations is consistent with iid behaviour. Certainly, if we calculate VaR estimates for times $t = 1, \dots, m$, we expect that $\sum_{t=1}^{m} \hat{I}_t \sim B(m, 1-\alpha)$, and this is easily addressed with a standard two-sided binomial test (see, for example, Casella and Berger 2002, pp. 493–495). Departures from the null hypothesis would suggest either systematic underestimation or overestimation of VaR.

To check for independence of the Bernoulli indicators one possibility is to perform a *runs test* of the kind described by David (1947), which involves counting runs of successive zeros or ones in the realizations of the indicator variables and comparing the realized number of runs with the known sampling distribution of the number of runs in iid Bernoulli data (see also Notes and Comments).

The backtesting of conditional VaR estimates for the h-period loss distribution is more complicated. To use the kind of ideas above we would have to base our backtests on non-overlapping periods. For example, if we calculated two-week VaRs, we could make a comparison of the VaR estimate and the realized loss every two weeks, which would clearly lead to a relatively small amount of violation data with which to monitor the performance of the model. If we used overlapping periods, for example by recording the violation indicator value every day for the loss incurred over the previous two weeks, we would create a series of dependent Bernoulli trials for which formal inference would be difficult.

Backtesting expected shortfall. We begin by observing that if ES_α^t is the expected shortfall of the (continuous) conditional loss distribution $F_{L_{t+1}|\mathcal{F}_t}$ and we define $S_{t+1} = (L_{t+1} - \mathrm{ES}_\alpha^t)I_{t+1}$, then for an arbitrary loss process $(L_t)_{t\in\mathbb{Z}}$ the process $(S_t)_{t\in\mathbb{Z}}$ forms a martingale difference series satisfying $E(S_{t+1} \mid \mathcal{F}_t) = 0$. Moreover, under Assumption 4.28 and using (4.49) and (4.50), we have

$$S_{t+1} = \sigma_{t+1}(Z_{t+1} - \mathrm{ES}_\alpha(Z))I_{\{Z_{t+1} > q_\alpha(Z)\}},$$

which takes the form of a volatility times a zero-mean iid sequence of innovation variables $((Z_{t+1} - \mathrm{ES}_\alpha(Z))I_{\{Z_{t+1} > q_\alpha(Z)\}})$. This suggests that, in practice, when the risk measures and volatility are estimated, we could form *violation residuals* of the form

$$\hat{R}_{t+1} := \hat{S}_{t+1}/\hat{\sigma}_{t+1}, \qquad \hat{S}_{t+1} := (L_{t+1} - \widehat{\mathrm{ES}}_\alpha^t)\hat{I}_{t+1}, \tag{4.52}$$

where $\hat{I}_{t+1}$ is the violation indicator defined in (4.51). We expect these to behave like realizations of iid variables from a distribution with mean zero and an atom of probability mass of size α at zero. To test for mean-zero behaviour we could perform a bootstrap test on the non-zero violation residuals that makes no assumption about their distribution. See Efron and Tibshirani (1994, p. 224) for a description of such a test.

Backtesting the predictive distribution. As well as backtesting VaR and expected shortfall we can also devise tests that assess the overall quality of the estimated conditional loss distributions from which the risk-measure estimates are derived. Of course, our primary interest focuses on the measures of tail risk, but it is still useful to backtest our estimates of the whole predictive distribution to obtain additional confirmation of the risk-measure estimation procedure.

Suppose we define the process $(U_t)_{t\in\mathbb{Z}}$ by setting $U_{t+1} := F_{L_{t+1}|\mathcal{F}_t}(L_{t+1})$. Under Assumption 4.28 it follows easily from (4.48) that $U_{t+1} = G_Z(Z_{t+1})$, so (U_t) is a strict white noise process. Moreover, if G_Z is continuous, then the stationary or unconditional distribution of (U_t) must be standard uniform (see, for example, Proposition 5.2).

In actual applications we estimate $F_{L_{t+1}|\mathcal{F}_t}$ from data up to time t and we back-test our estimates by forming $\hat{U}_{t+1} := \hat{F}_{L_{t+1}|\mathcal{F}_t}(L_{t+1})$ on day $t+1$. Suppose we estimate the predictive distribution on days $t = 0, \dots, m-1$ and form backtesting data $\hat{U}_1, \dots, \hat{U}_m$; we expect these to behave like a sample of iid uniform data. The distributional assumption can be assessed by standard goodness-of-fit tests like the chi-squared test or Kolmogorov–Smirnov test (see Section 3.3.5 for references). It is also possible to form the data $\Phi^{-1}(\hat{U}_1), \dots, \Phi^{-1}(\hat{U}_m)$, where Φ is the standard normal df; these should behave like iid standard normal data (see again Proposition 5.2) and this can be tested as in Section 3.1.4. The strict white noise assumption can be tested using the approach described in Section 4.2.3.

Notes and Comments

The backtesting material is mainly taken from McNeil and Frey (2000), where examples of the binomial test for violation counts and the test of expected shortfall using exceedance residuals can be found. Use of the runs test for testing the randomness of VaR violations is suggested by Christoffersen, Diebold and Schuermann (1998). This test is shown to be uniformly most powerful against Markovian alternatives by Lehmann (1986). Christoffersen, Diebold and Schuermann also suggest the use of a further test for randomness based on the non-trivial eigenvalue of the transition matrix in a Markov chain model for the violation indicator variables.

The idea of testing the estimate of the predictive distribution may be found in Berkowitz (2001, 2002). See also Berkowitz and O'Brien (2002) for a more general article on testing the accuracy of the VaR models of commercial banks.

4.5 Fundamentals of Multivariate Time Series

The presentation of the basic concepts of multivariate time series in this section closely parallels the presentation of the corresponding ideas for univariate time series in Section 4.2. Again the approach is similar to that of Brockwell and Davis (1991, 2002).

4.5.1 Basic Definitions

A multivariate time series model for multiple risk factors is a stochastic process $(\boldsymbol{X}_t)_{t\in\mathbb{Z}}$, i.e. a family of random vectors, indexed by the integers and defined on some probability space $(\Omega, \mathcal{F}, P)$.

Moments of a multivariate time series. Assuming they exist, we define the *mean function* $\boldsymbol{\mu}(t)$ and the *covariance matrix function* $\Gamma(t,s)$ of $(\boldsymbol{X}_t)_{t\in\mathbb{Z}}$ by

$$\begin{aligned} \boldsymbol{\mu}(t) &= E(\boldsymbol{X}_t), & t &\in \mathbb{Z}, \\ \Gamma(t,s) &= E((\boldsymbol{X}_t - \boldsymbol{\mu}(t))(\boldsymbol{X}_s - \boldsymbol{\mu}(s))'), & t, s &\in \mathbb{Z}. \end{aligned}$$

Analogously to the univariate case, we have $\Gamma(t,t) = \mathrm{cov}(\boldsymbol{X}_t)$. By observing that the elements $\gamma_{ij}(t,s)$ of $\Gamma(t,s)$ satisfy

$$\gamma_{ij}(t,s) = \mathrm{cov}(X_{t,i}, X_{s,j}) = \mathrm{cov}(X_{s,j}, X_{t,i}) = \gamma_{ji}(s,t), \tag{4.53}$$

it is clear that $\Gamma(t,s) = \Gamma(s,t)'$ for all t, s. However, the matrix Γ need not be symmetric, so in general $\Gamma(t,s) \neq \Gamma(s,t)$, which is in contrast to the univariate case. Lagged values of one of the component series can be more strongly correlated with future values of another component series than vice versa. This property, when observed in empirical data, is known as a *lead-lag* effect and is discussed in more detail in Example 4.36.

Stationarity. Again the concrete multivariate models we consider will be stationary in one or both of the following senses.

Definition 4.30 (strict stationarity). The multivariate time series $(\boldsymbol{X}_t)_{t\in\mathbb{Z}}$ is *strictly* stationary if

$$(\boldsymbol{X}_{t_1}', \dots, \boldsymbol{X}_{t_n}') \stackrel{\mathrm{d}}{=} (\boldsymbol{X}_{t_1+k}', \dots, \boldsymbol{X}_{t_n+k}'),$$

for all $t_1, \dots, t_n, k \in \mathbb{Z}$ and for all $n \in \mathbb{N}$.

Definition 4.31 (covariance stationarity). The multivariate time series $(\boldsymbol{X}_t)_{t\in\mathbb{Z}}$ is *covariance* stationary (or *weakly* or *second-order* stationary) if the first two moments exist and satisfy

$$\begin{aligned} \boldsymbol{\mu}(t) &= \boldsymbol{\mu}, & t &\in \mathbb{Z}, \\ \Gamma(t,s) &= \Gamma(t+k, s+k), & t, s, k &\in \mathbb{Z}. \end{aligned}$$

A strictly stationary multivariate time series with finite covariance matrix is covariance stationary, but we again note that it is possible to define infinite-variance processes (including certain multivariate ARCH and GARCH processes) that are strictly stationary but not covariance stationary.

Serial and cross-correlation in stationary multivariate time series. The definition of covariance stationarity implies that for all s, t we have $\Gamma(t-s, 0) = \Gamma(t,s)$, so that the covariance between X_t and X_s only depends on their temporal separation $t - s$, which is known as the *lag*. In contrast to the univariate case, the sign of the lag is important. For a covariance-stationary multivariate process we write the covariance matrix function as a function of one variable: $\Gamma(h) := \Gamma(h, 0)$, $\forall h \in \mathbb{Z}$. Noting that $\Gamma(0) = \mathrm{cov}(\boldsymbol{X}_t)$, $\forall t$, we can now define the correlation matrix function of a covariance-stationary process.

Definition 4.32 (correlation matrix function). Writing $\Delta := \Delta(\Gamma(0))$, where $\Delta(\cdot)$ is the operator defined in (3.4), the correlation matrix function $P(h)$ of a covariance-stationary multivariate time series $(\boldsymbol{X}_t)_{t\in\mathbb{Z}}$ is

$$P(h) := \Delta^{-1}\Gamma(h)\Delta^{-1}, \quad \forall h \in \mathbb{Z}. \tag{4.54}$$

The diagonal entries $\rho_{ii}(h)$ of this matrix-valued function give the autocorrelation function of the ith component series $(X_{t,i})_{t\in\mathbb{Z}}$. The off-diagonal entries give so-called cross-correlations between different component series at different times. It follows from (4.53) that $P(h) = P(-h)'$, but $P(h)$ need not be symmetric, and in general $P(h) \neq P(-h)$.

White noise processes. As in the univariate case, *multivariate white noise* processes are building blocks for more interesting classes of time series model.

Definition 4.33 (multivariate white noise). $(\boldsymbol{X}_t)_{t\in\mathbb{Z}}$ is multivariate white noise if it is covariance stationary with correlation matrix function given by

$$P(h) = \begin{cases} P, & h = 0, \\ 0, & h \neq 0, \end{cases}$$

for some positive-definite correlation matrix P.

A multivariate white noise process with mean zero and covariance matrix $\Sigma = \operatorname{cov}(\boldsymbol{X}_t)$ will be denoted $\mathrm{WN}(\boldsymbol{0}, \Sigma)$. Such a process has no cross-correlation between component series, except for contemporaneous cross-correlation at lag zero. A simple example is a series of iid random vectors with finite covariance matrix, and this is known as a *multivariate strict white noise*.

Definition 4.34 (multivariate strict white noise). $(\boldsymbol{X}_t)_{t\in\mathbb{Z}}$ is multivariate strict white noise if it is a series of iid random vectors with finite covariance matrix.

A strict white noise process with mean zero and covariance matrix Σ will be denoted $\mathrm{SWN}(\boldsymbol{0}, \Sigma)$.

The martingale-difference noise concept may also be extended to higher dimensions. As before we assume that the time series $(\boldsymbol{X}_t)_{t\in\mathbb{Z}}$ is adapted to some *filtration* $(\mathcal{F}_t)$, typically the natural filtration $(\sigma(\{\boldsymbol{X}_s : s \leqslant t\}))$, which represents the information available at time t.

Definition 4.35 (multivariate martingale difference). $(\boldsymbol{X}_t)_{t\in\mathbb{Z}}$ has the multivariate martingale-difference property with respect to the filtration $(\mathcal{F}_t)$ if $E|\boldsymbol{X}_t| < \infty$ and

$$E(\boldsymbol{X}_t \mid \mathcal{F}_{t-1}) = \boldsymbol{0}, \quad \forall t \in \mathbb{Z}.$$

The unconditional mean of such a process is obviously also zero and, if $\operatorname{cov}(\boldsymbol{X}_t) < \infty$ for all t, the covariance matrix function satisfies $\Gamma(t, s) = 0$ for $t \neq s$. If the covariance matrix is also constant for all t, then a process with the multivariate martingale-difference property is also a multivariate white noise process.

4.5.2 Analysis in the Time Domain

We now assume that we have a random sample $\boldsymbol{X}_1, \dots, \boldsymbol{X}_n$ from a covariance-stationary multivariate time series model $(\boldsymbol{X}_t)_{t\in\mathbb{Z}}$. In the time domain we construct empirical estimators of the covariance matrix function and the correlation matrix function from this random sample.

The *sample covariance matrix function* is calculated according to

$$\hat{\Gamma}(h) = \frac{1}{n}\sum_{t=1}^{n-h}(X_{t+h} - \bar{X})(X_t - \bar{X})', \quad 0 \leqslant h < n,$$

where $\bar{X} = \sum_{t=1}^{n} X_t/n$ is the sample mean, which estimates $\boldsymbol{\mu}$, the mean of the time series. Writing $\hat{\Delta} := \Delta(\hat{\Gamma}(0))$, where $\Delta(\cdot)$ is the operator defined in (3.4), the *sample correlation matrix function* is

$$\hat{P}(h) = \hat{\Delta}^{-1}\hat{\Gamma}(h)\hat{\Delta}^{-1}, \quad 0 \leqslant h < n.$$

The information contained in the elements $\hat{\rho}_{ij}(h)$ of the sample correlation matrix function is generally displayed in the *cross-correlogram*, which is a $d \times d$ matrix of plots (see Figure 4.13 for an example). The ith diagonal plot in this graphic display is the correlogram of the ith component series, given by $\{(h, \hat{\rho}_{ii}(h)) : h = 0, 1, 2, \dots\}$. For the off-diagonal plots containing the estimates of *cross-correlation* there are various possible presentations and we will consider the following convention: for $i < j$ we plot $\{(h, \hat{\rho}_{ij}(h)) : h = 0, 1, 2, \dots\}$; for $i > j$ we plot $\{(-h, \hat{\rho}_{ij}(h)) : h = 0, 1, 2, \dots\}$. An interpretation of the meaning of the off-diagonal pictures is given in Example 4.36.

It can be shown that for causal processes driven by multivariate strict white noise innovations (see Section 4.5.3) the estimates that comprise the components of the sample correlation matrix function $\hat{P}(h)$ are consistent estimates of the underlying theoretical quantities. For example, if the data themselves are from an SWN, then the cross-correlation estimators $\hat{\rho}_{ij}(h)$ for $h \neq 0$ converge to zero as the sample size is increased. However, results concerning the asymptotic distribution of cross-correlation estimates are, in general, more complicated than the univariate result for autocorrelation estimates given in Theorem 4.13. Some relevant theory is found in Chapter 11 of Brockwell and Davis (1991) and Chapter 7 of Brockwell and Davis (2002). It is standard to plot the off-diagonal pictures with Gaussian confidence bands at $(-1.96\sqrt{n}, 1.96\sqrt{n})$, but these bands should be used as rough guidance for the eye and not relied upon too heavily to draw conclusions.

Example 4.36 (cross-correlogram of trivariate index returns). In Figure 4.13 the cross-correlogram of daily log-returns is shown for the Dow Jones, Nikkei and Swiss Market indices for 26 July 1996 to 25 July 2001. Although every vector observation in this trivariate time series relates to the same trading day, the returns are of course not properly synchronized due to time zones; nonetheless, this picture shows interpretable lead-lag effects which help us to understand the off-diagonal pictures in the cross-correlogram.

Part (b) of the figure shows estimated correlations between the Dow Jones index return on day $t + h$ and the Nikkei index return on day t, for $h \geqslant 0$; clearly these estimates are small and lie mainly within the confidence band, with the obvious exception of the correlation estimate for returns on the same trading day $\hat{P}_{12}(0) \approx 0.14$. Part (d) shows estimated correlations between the Dow Jones index return on day $t + h$ and the Nikkei index return on day t, for $h \leqslant 0$; the estimate corresponding to

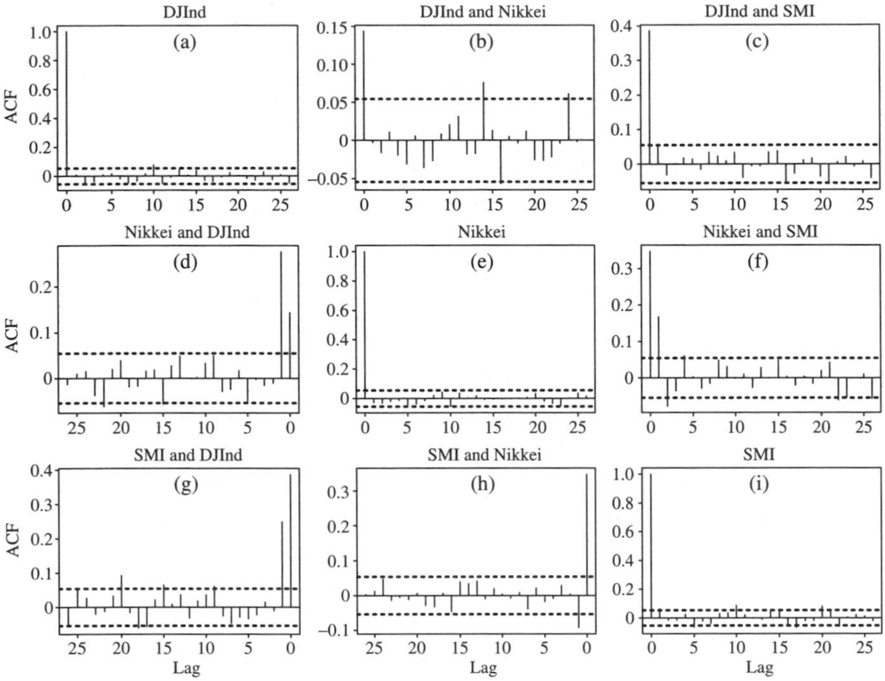

Figure 4.13. Cross-correlogram of daily log-returns of Dow Jones, Nikkei and Swiss Market indices for 26 July 1996 to 25 July 2001 (see Example 4.36 for commentary).

$h = -1$ is approximately 0.28 and can be interpreted as showing how the American market leads the Japanese market. Comparing parts (c) and (g) we see, unsurprisingly, that the American market also leads the Swiss market, so that returns on day $t-1$ in the former are quite strongly correlated with returns on day t in the latter.

4.5.3 Multivariate ARMA Processes

We provide a brief excursion into multivariate ARMA models to indicate how the ideas of Section 4.2.2 generalize to higher dimensions. For daily data, capturing multivariate ARMA effects is much less important than capturing multivariate volatility effects (and dynamic correlation effects) through multivariate GARCH modelling, but, for longer-period returns, the more traditional ARMA processes become increasingly useful. In the econometrics literature they are more commonly known as vector ARMA (or VARMA) processes.

Definition 4.37 (VARMA process). Let $(\boldsymbol{\varepsilon}_t)_{t\in\mathbb{Z}}$ be $\mathrm{WN}(\mathbf{0}, \Sigma_\varepsilon)$. The process $(\boldsymbol{X}_t)_{t\in\mathbb{Z}}$ is a zero-mean VARMA(p,q) process if it is a covariance-stationary process satisfying difference equations of the form

$$\boldsymbol{X}_t - \Phi_1 \boldsymbol{X}_{t-1} - \cdots - \Phi_p \boldsymbol{X}_{t-p} = \boldsymbol{\varepsilon}_t + \Theta_1 \boldsymbol{\varepsilon}_{t-1} + \cdots + \Theta_q \boldsymbol{\varepsilon}_{t-q}, \quad \forall t \in \mathbb{Z}$$

for parameter matrices Φ_i and Θ_j in $\mathbb{R}^{d\times d}$. $(\boldsymbol{X}_t)$ is a VARMA process with mean $\boldsymbol{\mu}$ if the centred series $(\boldsymbol{X}_t - \boldsymbol{\mu})_{t\in\mathbb{Z}}$ is a zero-mean VARMA(p,q) process.

For practical applications we again consider only causal VARMA processes, which are processes where the solution of the defining equations has a representation of the form

$$X_t = \sum_{i=0}^{\infty} \Psi_i \varepsilon_{t-i}, \qquad (4.55)$$

where $(\Psi_i)_{i \in \mathbb{N}_0}$ is a sequence of matrices in $\mathbb{R}^{d \times d}$ with absolutely summable components, meaning that, for any j and k,

$$\sum_{i=0}^{\infty} |\psi_{i,jk}| < \infty. \qquad (4.56)$$

As in the univariate case (see Proposition 4.9), it can be verified by direct calculation that such linear processes are covariance stationary. Obviously, for all t, we have $E(X_t) = \mu$. For $h \geqslant 0$ the covariance matrix function is given by

$$\Gamma(t+h, t) = \operatorname{cov}(X_t + h, X_t) = E\biggl(\sum_{i=0}^{\infty} \Psi_i \varepsilon_{t+h-i} \sum_{j=0}^{\infty} \varepsilon'_{t-j} \Psi'_j\biggr).$$

Arguing much as in the univariate case it is easily shown that this depends only on h and not on t and that it is given by

$$\Gamma(h) = \sum_{i=0}^{\infty} \Psi_{i+h} \Sigma_\varepsilon \Psi'_i, \quad h = 0, 1, 2, \dots. \qquad (4.57)$$

The correlation matrix function is easily derived from (4.57) and (4.54).

The requirement that a VARMA process be causal imposes conditions on the values that the parameter matrices Φ_i (in particular) and Θ_j may take. The theory is remarkably similar to univariate ARMA theory. We will give a single useful example from the VARMA class; this is the first-order vector autoregressive (or VAR(1)) model.

Example 4.38 (VAR(1) process). The first-order VAR process satisfies the set of vector difference equations

$$X_t = \Phi X_{t-1} + \varepsilon_t, \quad \forall t. \qquad (4.58)$$

It is possible to find a causal process satisfying (4.55) and (4.56) that is a solution of (4.58) if and only if all eigenvalues of the matrix Φ are less than one in absolute value. The causal process

$$X_t = \sum_{i=0}^{\infty} \Phi^i \varepsilon_{t-i} \qquad (4.59)$$

is then the unique solution. This solution can be thought of as an infinite-order vector moving-average process, a so-called VMA(∞) process. The covariance matrix function of this process follows from (4.55) and (4.57) and is

$$\Gamma(h) = \sum_{i=0}^{\infty} \Phi^{i+h} \Sigma_\varepsilon \Phi^{i\prime} = \Phi^h \Gamma(0), \quad h = 0, 1, 2, \dots.$$

In practice, full VARMA models are less common than models from the VAR and VMA subfamilies, one reason being that identifiability problems arise when estimating parameters. For example, we can have situations where the first-order VARMA(1, 1) model $X_t - \Phi X_{t-1} = \varepsilon_t + \Theta \varepsilon_{t-1}$ can be rewritten as $X_t - \Phi^* X_{t-1} = \varepsilon_t + \Theta^* \varepsilon_{t-1}$ for completely different parameter matrices Φ^* and Θ^* (see Tsay (2002, p. 323) for an example). Of the two subfamilies, VAR models are easier to estimate. Fitting options for VAR models range from multivariate least-squares estimation without strong assumptions concerning the distribution of the driving white noise, to full maximum likelihood estimation; models combining VAR and multivariate GARCH features can be estimated using a conditional ML approach in a very similar manner to that described for univariate models in Section 4.3.4.

Notes and Comments

Many standard texts on time series also handle the multivariate theory (see, for example, Brockwell and Davis (1991, 2002) or Hamilton (1994)). A key reference aimed at an econometrics audience is Lütkepohl (1993). For examples, in the area of finance see Tsay (2002) and Zivot and Wang (2003).

4.6 Multivariate GARCH Processes

4.6.1 General Structure of Models

Definition 4.39. Let $(Z_t)_{t\in\mathbb{Z}}$ be SWN$(\mathbf{0}, I_d)$. The process $(X_t)_{t\in\mathbb{Z}}$ is said to be a multivariate GARCH process if it is strictly stationary and satisfies equations of the form

$$X_t = \Sigma_t^{1/2} Z_t, \quad t \in \mathbb{Z}, \tag{4.60}$$

where $\Sigma_t^{1/2} \in \mathbb{R}^{d\times d}$ is the Cholesky factor of a positive-definite matrix Σ_t which is measurable with respect to $\mathcal{F}_{t-1} = \sigma(\{X_s : s \leqslant t-1\})$, the history of the process up to time $t-1$.

Conditional moments. It is easily calculated that a covariance-stationary process of this type has the multivariate martingale-difference property

$$E(X_t \mid \mathcal{F}_{t-1}) = E(\Sigma_t^{1/2} Z_t \mid \mathcal{F}_{t-1}) = \Sigma_t^{1/2} E(Z_t) = \mathbf{0},$$

and must therefore be a multivariate white noise process, as argued in Section 4.5. Moreover, Σ_t will be the *conditional covariance matrix* since

$$\operatorname{cov}(X_t \mid \mathcal{F}_{t-1}) = E(X_t X_t' \mid \mathcal{F}_{t-1}) = \Sigma_t^{1/2} E(Z_t Z_t')(\Sigma_t^{1/2})' = \Sigma_t^{1/2}(\Sigma_t^{1/2})' = \Sigma_t. \tag{4.61}$$

The conditional covariance matrix Σ_t in a multivariate GARCH model corresponds to the squared volatility σ_t^2 in a univariate GARCH model. The use of the Cholesky factor of Σ_t to describe the relationship to the driving noise in (4.60) is not important, and in fact any type of "square root" of Σ_t could be used (such as the root derived from a symmetric decomposition). (The only implication is the way we construct residuals when fitting the model in practice.) We denote the elements of Σ_t by $\sigma_{t,ij}$

and also use the notation $\sigma_{t,i} = \sqrt{\sigma_{t,ii}}$ to denote the conditional standard deviation (or volatility) of the ith component series $(X_{t,i})_{t\in\mathbb{Z}}$.

We recall that we can write $\Sigma_t = \Delta_t P_t \Delta_t$, where

$$\Delta_t = \Delta(\Sigma_t) = \operatorname{diag}(\sigma_{t,1}, \dots, \sigma_{t,d}), \quad P_t = \wp(\Sigma_t), \tag{4.62}$$

using the operator notation defined in (3.5). The diagonal matrix Δ_t will be known as the *volatility matrix* and P_t is known as the *conditional correlation matrix*. The art of building multivariate GARCH models is to specify the dependence of Σ_t (or of Δ_t and P_t) on the past in such a way that Σ_t always remains symmetric and positive definite. A covariance matrix must of course be symmetric and positive semidefinite, and in practice we restrict our attention to the positive-definite case (which facilitates fitting, since the conditional distribution of $X_t \mid \mathcal{F}_{t-1}$ never has a singular covariance matrix).

Unconditional moments. The *unconditional covariance matrix* Σ of a process of this type is given by

$$\Sigma = \operatorname{cov}(X_t) = E(\operatorname{cov}(X_t \mid \mathcal{F}_{t-1})) + \operatorname{cov}(E(X_t \mid \mathcal{F}_{t-1})) = E(\Sigma_t),$$

from which it can be calculated that the *unconditional correlation matrix* P has elements

$$\rho_{ij} = \frac{E(\sigma_{t,ij})}{\sqrt{E(\sigma_{t,ii})E(\sigma_{t,jj})}} = \frac{E(\rho_{t,ij}\sigma_{t,i}\sigma_{t,j})}{\sqrt{E(\sigma_{t,i}^2)E(\sigma_{t,j}^2)}}, \tag{4.63}$$

which is in general difficult to evaluate and is usually not simply the expectation of the conditional correlation matrix.

Innovations. In practical work the innovations are generally taken to be from either a multivariate Gaussian distribution ($Z_t \sim N_d(\mathbf{0}, I_d)$) or, more realistically for daily returns, an appropriately scaled spherical multivariate t distribution ($Z_t \sim t_d(\nu, \mathbf{0}, (\nu - 2)I_d/\nu)$). Any distribution with mean zero and covariance matrix I_d is permissible, and appropriate members of the normal mixture family of Section 3.2 or the spherical family of Section 3.3.1 may be considered.

Presentation of models. In the following sections we present some of the more important multivariate GARCH specifications. In doing this we concentrate on the following aspects of the models.

- The form of the dynamic equations, with economic arguments and criticisms where appropriate.
- The conditions required to guarantee that the conditional covariance matrix Σ_t remains positive definite. Other mathematical properties of these models, such as conditions for covariance stationarity, are difficult to derive with full mathematical rigour; references in Notes and Comments contain further information.

- The parsimoniousness of the parametrization. A major problem with most multivariate GARCH specifications is that the number of parameters tends to explode with the dimension of the model, making them unsuitable for analyses of many risk factors.
- Simple intuitive fitting methods where available. All models can be fitted by a general global-maximization approach described in Section 4.6.4 but certain models lend themselves to estimation in stages, particularly the models of Section 4.6.2.

4.6.2 *Models for Conditional Correlation*

In this section we present models which focus on specifying the conditional correlation matrix P_t while allowing volatilities to be described by univariate GARCH models; we begin with a popular and relatively parsimonious model where P_t is assumed to be constant for all t.

Constant conditional correlation (CCC).

Definition 4.40. The process $(\boldsymbol{X}_t)_{t\in\mathbb{Z}}$ is a CCC-GARCH process if it is a process with the general structure given in Definition 4.39 such that the conditional covariance matrix is of the form $\Sigma_t = \Delta_t P_{\mathrm{c}} \Delta_t$, where

(i) P_{c} is a constant, positive-definite correlation matrix; and

(ii) Δ_t is a diagonal volatility matrix with elements $\sigma_{t,k}$ satisfying

$$\sigma_{t,k}^2 = \alpha_{k0} + \sum_{i=1}^{p_k} \alpha_{ki} X_{t-i,k}^2 + \sum_{j=1}^{q_k} \beta_{kj} \sigma_{t-j,k}^2, \quad k = 1, \dots, d, \tag{4.64}$$

where $\alpha_{k0} > 0$, $\alpha_{ki} \geqslant 0$, $i = 1, \dots, p_k$, $\beta_{kj} \geqslant 0$, $j = 1, \dots, q_k$.

The CCC-GARCH specification represents a simple way of combining univariate GARCH processes. This can be seen by observing that in a CCC-GARCH model observations and innovations are connected by equations $\boldsymbol{X}_t = \Delta_t P_{\mathrm{c}}^{1/2} \boldsymbol{Z}_t$, which may be rewritten as $\boldsymbol{X}_t = \Delta_t \tilde{\boldsymbol{Z}}_t$ for an SWN$(\boldsymbol{0}, P_{\mathrm{c}})$ process $(\tilde{\boldsymbol{Z}}_t)_{t\in\mathbb{Z}}$. Clearly, the component processes are univariate GARCH.

Proposition 4.41. *The CCC-GARCH model is well defined in the sense that Σ_t is almost surely positive definite for all t. Moreover, it is covariance stationary if and only if $\sum_{i=1}^{p_k} \alpha_{ki} + \sum_{j=1}^{q_k} \beta_{kj} < 1$ for $k = 1, \dots, d$.*

Proof. For a vector $\boldsymbol{v} \neq \boldsymbol{0}$ in $\mathbb{R}^d$ we have

$$\boldsymbol{v}' \Sigma_t \boldsymbol{v} = (\Delta_t \boldsymbol{v})' P_{\mathrm{c}} (\Delta_t \boldsymbol{v}) > 0,$$

since P_{c} is positive definite and the strict positivity of the individual volatility processes ensures that $\Delta_t \boldsymbol{v} \neq \boldsymbol{0}$ for all t.

If $(\boldsymbol{X}_t)_{t\in\mathbb{Z}}$ is covariance stationary, then each component series $(X_{t,k})_{t\in\mathbb{Z}}$ is a covariance-stationary GARCH process for which a necessary and sufficient condition is $\sum_{i=1}^{p_k} \alpha_{ki} + \sum_{j=1}^{q_k} \beta_{kj} < 1$ by Proposition 4.21. Conversely, if the component series are covariance stationary, then for all i and j the Cauchy–Schwarz inequality implies

$$\sigma_{ij} = E(\sigma_{t,ij}) = \rho_{ij} E(\sigma_{t,i}\sigma_{t,j}) \leqslant \rho_{ij}\sqrt{E(\sigma_{t,i}^2)}\sqrt{E(\sigma_{t,j}^2)} < \infty.$$

Since $(\boldsymbol{X}_t)_{t\in\mathbb{Z}}$ is a multivariate martingale difference with finite, non-time-dependent second moments σ_{ij}, it is a covariance-stationary white noise. □

The CCC model is often a useful starting point from which to proceed to more complex models. In some empirical settings it gives an adequate performance, but it is generally considered that the constancy of conditional correlation in this model is an unrealistic feature and that the impact of news on financial markets requires models that allow a dynamic evolution of conditional correlation as well as a dynamic evolution of volatilities. A further criticism of the model (which applies in fact to the majority of MGARCH specifications) is the fact that the individual volatility dynamics (4.64) do not allow for the possibility that large returns in one component series at a particular point in time can contribute to increased volatility of another component time series at future points in time.

To describe a simple method of fitting the CCC model we introduce the notion of a *devolatized* process. For any multivariate time series process $\boldsymbol{X}_t$, the devolatized process is the process $\boldsymbol{Y}_t = \Delta_t^{-1}\boldsymbol{X}_t$, where Δ_t is, as usual, the diagonal matrix of volatilities. In the case of a CCC model it is easily seen that the devolatized process $(\boldsymbol{Y}_t)_{t\in\mathbb{Z}}$ is an SWN$(\boldsymbol{0}, P_{\mathrm{c}})$ process.

This structure suggests a simple two-stage fitting method in which we first estimate the individual volatility processes for the component series by fitting univariate GARCH processes; note that, although we have specified in Definition 4.40 that the individual volatilities should follow standard GARCH models, we could of course extend the model to allow any of the univariate models in Section 4.3.3, such as GARCH with leverage or threshold GARCH. In a second stage we construct an estimate of the devolatized process by taking $\hat{\boldsymbol{Y}}_t = \hat{\Delta}_t^{-1}\boldsymbol{X}_t$, where $\hat{\Delta}_t^{-1}$ is the estimate of Δ_t; in other words, we collect the standardized residuals from the univariate GARCH models. If the CCC-GARCH model is adequate, then the $\hat{\boldsymbol{Y}}_t$ data should behave like a realization from an SWN$(\boldsymbol{0}, P_{\mathrm{c}})$ process and this can be investigated with the correlogram and cross-correlogram applied to raw and absolute values. Assuming the adequacy of the model, the conditional correlation matrix P_{c} can then be estimated from the standardized residuals using methods from Chapter 3.

A special case of CCC-GARCH which we call a pure diagonal model occurs when $P_{\mathrm{c}} = I_d$. A covariance-stationary model of this kind is a multivariate white noise where the contemporaneous components $X_{t,i}$ and $X_{t,j}$ are also uncorrelated for $i \neq j$. Whether they are independent or not depends on further assumptions about the driving SWN$(\boldsymbol{0}, I_d)$ process: if the innovations have independent components, as would be the case if they were multivariate Gaussian, then the component series are independent; however, if, for example, $\boldsymbol{Z}_t \sim t_d(\nu, \boldsymbol{0}, ((\nu-2)/\nu)I_d)$, the component processes are dependent.

Dynamic conditional correlation (DCC). This model generalizes the CCC model to allow conditional correlations to evolve dynamically according to a relatively parsimonious scheme, but is constructed in a way that still allows estimation in stages using univariate GARCH models. Its formal analysis as a stochastic process is difficult due to the use of the correlation matrix extraction operator $\wp$ in its definition.

Definition 4.42. The process $(\boldsymbol{X}_t)_{t\in\mathbb{Z}}$ is a DCC-GARCH process if it is a process with the general structure given in Definition 4.39, where the volatilities comprising Δ_t follow univariate GARCH specifications as in (4.64) and the conditional correlation matrices P_t satisfy, for $t \in \mathbb{Z}$, the equations

$$P_t = \wp\left(\left(1 - \sum_{i=1}^{p}\alpha_i - \sum_{j=1}^{q}\beta_j\right)P_{\mathrm{c}} + \sum_{i=1}^{p}\alpha_i \boldsymbol{Y}_{t-i}\boldsymbol{Y}_{t-i}' + \sum_{j=1}^{q}\beta_j P_{t-j}\right), \quad (4.65)$$

where P_{c} is a positive-definite correlation matrix, $\wp$ is the operator in (3.5), $\boldsymbol{Y}_t = \Delta_t^{-1}\boldsymbol{X}_t$ denotes the devolatized process, and the coefficients satisfy $\alpha_i \geqslant 0$, $\beta_j \geqslant 0$ and $\sum_{i=1}^{p}\alpha_i - \sum_{j=1}^{q}\beta_j < 1$.

Observe first that if all the α_i and β_j coefficients in (4.65) are zero, then the model reduces to the CCC model. If one makes an analogy with a covariance-stationary univariate GARCH model with unconditional variance σ^2, for which the volatility equation can be written

$$\sigma_t^2 = \left(1 - \sum_{i=1}^{p}\alpha_i - \sum_{j=1}^{q}\beta_j\right)\sigma^2 + \sum_{i=1}^{p}\alpha_i X_{t-i} + \sum_{j=1}^{q}\beta_j\sigma_{t-j}^2,$$

then the correlation matrix P_{c} in (4.65) can be thought of as representing the long-run correlation structure. Although this matrix could be estimated by fitting the DCC model to data by ML estimation in one step, it is quite common to estimate it using an empirical correlation matrix calculated from the devolatized data, as in the estimation of the CCC model.

Observe also that the dynamic equation (4.65) preserves the positive definiteness of P_t. If we define

$$Q_t := \left(1 - \sum_{i=1}^{p}\alpha_i - \sum_{j=1}^{q}\beta_j\right)P_{\mathrm{c}} + \sum_{i=1}^{p}\alpha_i \boldsymbol{Y}_{t-i}\boldsymbol{Y}_{t-i}' + \sum_{j=1}^{q}\beta_j P_{t-j},$$

and assume that $P_{t-q}, \dots, P_{t-1}$ are positive definite, then it follows that, for a vector $\boldsymbol{v} \neq \boldsymbol{0}$ in $\mathbb{R}^d$, we have

$$\boldsymbol{v}'Q_t\boldsymbol{v} = \left(1 - \sum_{i=1}^{p}\alpha_i - \sum_{j=1}^{q}\beta_j\right)\boldsymbol{v}'P_{\mathrm{c}}\boldsymbol{v} + \sum_{i=1}^{p}\alpha_i \boldsymbol{v}'\boldsymbol{Y}_{t-i}\boldsymbol{Y}_{t-i}'\boldsymbol{v} + \sum_{j=1}^{q}\beta_j \boldsymbol{v}'P_{t-j}\boldsymbol{v} > 0,$$

since the first term is strictly positive and the second and third terms are non-negative. If Q_t is positive definite, then so is P_t.

The usual estimation method for the DCC model is as follows.

(1) Fit univariate GARCH-type models to the component series to estimate the volatility matrix Δ_t. Form an estimated realization of the devolatized process by taking $\hat{Y}_t = \hat{\Delta}_t X_t$.

(2) Estimate P_c by taking the sample correlation matrix of the devolatized data (or better still some robust estimator of correlation).

(3) Estimate the remaining parameters α_i and β_j in equation (4.65) by fitting a model with structure $Y_t = P_t^{1/2} Z_t$ to the devolatized data. We leave this step vague for the time being and note that this will be a simple application of the methodology for fitting general multivariate GARCH models in Section 4.6.4; in a first-order model ($p = q = 1$), there will only be two remaining parameters to estimate.

4.6.3 Models for Conditional Covariance

The models of this section specify explicitly a dynamic structure for the conditional covariance matrix Σ_t. These models are not designed for multiple-stage estimation based on univariate GARCH estimation procedures.

Vector GARCH Models (VEC and DVEC). The most general vector GARCH model—the VEC model—has too many parameters for practical purposes and our task will be to simplify the model by imposing various restrictions on parameter matrices.

Definition 4.43 (VEC model). The process $(X_t)_{t\in\mathbb{Z}}$ is a VEC process if it has the general structure given in Definition 4.39, and the dynamics of the conditional covariance matrix Σ_t are given by the equations

$$\operatorname{vech}(\Sigma_t) = a_0 + \sum_{i=1}^{p} \bar{A}_i \operatorname{vech}(X_{t-i}X'_{t-i}) + \sum_{j=1}^{q} \bar{B}_j \operatorname{vech}(\Sigma_{t-j}), \tag{4.66}$$

for a vector $a_0 \in \mathbb{R}^{d(d+1)/2}$ and matrices $\bar{A}_i$ and $\bar{B}_j$ in $R^{(d(d+1)/2)\times(d(d+1)/2)}$.

In this definition "vech" denotes the *vector half* operator, which stacks the columns of the lower triangle of a symmetric matrix in a single column vector of length $d(d+1)/2$. Thus (4.66) should be understood as specifying the dynamics for the lower-triangular portion of the conditional covariance matrix, and the remaining elements of the matrix are determined by symmetry.

In this very general form the model has $(1 + (p+q)d(d+1)/2)d(d+1)/2$ parameters; this number grows rapidly with dimension so that even a trivariate model has 78 parameters. The most common simplification has been to restrict attention to cases when $\bar{A}_i$ and $\bar{B}_j$ are diagonal matrices, which gives us the diagonal VEC or DVEC model. This special case can be written very elegantly in terms of a different kind of matrix product, namely the *Hadamard product*, denoted "$\circ$", which signifies element-by-element multiplication of two matrices of the same size. We obtain the representation

$$\Sigma_t = A_0 + \sum_{i=1}^{p} A_i \circ (\boldsymbol{X}_{t-i}\boldsymbol{X}'_{t-i}) + \sum_{j=1}^{q} B_j \circ \Sigma_{t-j}, \tag{4.67}$$

where A_0 and the A_i and B_j must all be symmetric matrices in $\mathbb{R}^{d\times d}$ such that A_0 has positive diagonal elements and all other matrices have non-negative diagonal elements (standard univariate GARCH assumptions). This representation emphasizes structural similarities with the univariate GARCH model of Definition 4.20.

To understand better the dynamic implications of (4.67), consider a bivariate model of order (1, 1) and write $a_{0,ij}$, $a_{1,ij}$ and b_{ij} for the elements of A_0, A_1 and B, respectively. The model amounts to the three simple equations

$$\left.\begin{aligned} \sigma_{t,1}^2 &= a_{0,11} + a_{1,11}X_{t-1,1}^2 + b_{11}\sigma_{t-1,1}^2, \\ \sigma_{t,12} &= a_{0,12} + a_{1,12}X_{t-1,1}X_{t-1,2} + b_{12}\sigma_{t-1,12}, \\ \sigma_{t,2}^2 &= a_{0,22} + a_{1,22}X_{t-1,2}^2 + b_{22}\sigma_{t-1,2}^2. \end{aligned}\right\} \tag{4.68}$$

The volatilities of the two component series ($\sigma_{t,1}$ and $\sigma_{t,2}$) follow univariate GARCH updating patterns, and the conditional covariance $\sigma_{t,12}$ has a similar structure driven by the products of the lagged values $X_{t-1,1}X_{t-1,2}$. As for the CCC and DCC models, the volatility of a single component series is only driven by large lagged values of that series and cannot be directly affected by large lagged values in another series; the more general but overparametrized VEC model would allow this feature.

The requirement that Σ_t in (4.67) should be a proper positive-definite covariance matrix does impose conditions on the A_0, A_i and B_j matrices that we have not yet discussed. In practice, in some software implementations of this model, formal conditions are not imposed, other than that the matrices should be symmetric with non-negative diagonal elements; the positive definiteness of the resulting estimates of the conditional covariance matrices can be checked after model fitting.

However, a sufficient condition for Σ_t to be almost surely positive definite is that A_0 should be positive definite and the matrices $A_1, \dots, A_p$, $B_1, \dots, B_q$ should all be positive semidefinite (see Notes and Comments) and this condition is easy to impose. We can constrain all parameter matrices to have a form based on a Cholesky decomposition; that is we can parametrize the model in terms of lower-triangular Cholesky factor matrices $A_0^{1/2}$, $A_i^{1/2}$ and $B_j^{1/2}$ satisfying

$$A_0 = A_0^{1/2}(A_0^{1/2})', \qquad A_i = A_i^{1/2}(A_i^{1/2})', \qquad B_j = B_j^{1/2}(B_j^{1/2})'. \tag{4.69}$$

Because the sufficient condition only prescribes that $A_1, \dots, A_p$ and $B_1, \dots, B_q$ should be positive semidefinite, we can in fact also consider much simpler parametrizations, such as

$$A_0 = A_0^{1/2}(A_0^{1/2})', \qquad A_i = \boldsymbol{a}_i\boldsymbol{a}_i', \qquad B_j = \boldsymbol{b}_j\boldsymbol{b}_j', \tag{4.70}$$

where $\boldsymbol{a}_i$ and $\boldsymbol{b}_j$ are vectors in $\mathbb{R}^d$. An even cruder model, satisfying the requirement of positive definiteness of Σ_t, would be

$$A_0 = A_0^{1/2}(A_0^{1/2})', \qquad A_i = a_i I_d, \qquad B_j = b_j I_d, \tag{4.71}$$

where a_i and b_j are simply positive constants. In fact the specifications of the multivariate ARCH and GARCH effects in (4.69)–(4.71) can be mixed and matched in obvious ways.

The BEKK model of Baba, Engle, Kroner and Kraft. The next family of models have the great advantage that their construction ensures the positive definiteness of Σ_t without the need for further conditions.

Definition 4.44. The process $(\boldsymbol{X}_t)_{t\in\mathbb{Z}}$ is a BEKK process if it has the general structure given in Definition 4.39, and if the conditional covariance matrix Σ_t satisfies, for all $t \in \mathbb{Z}$,

$$\Sigma_t = A_0 + \sum_{i=1}^{p} A_i' \boldsymbol{X}_{t-i} \boldsymbol{X}_{t-i}' A_i + \sum_{j=1}^{q} B_j' \Sigma_{t-j} B_j, \tag{4.72}$$

where all coefficient matrices are in $\mathbb{R}^{d\times d}$ and A_0 is symmetric and positive definite.

Proposition 4.45. *In the BEKK model (4.72), the conditional covariance matrix Σ_t is almost surely positive definite for all t.*

Proof. Consider a first-order model for simplicity. For a vector $\boldsymbol{v} \neq \boldsymbol{0}$ in $\mathbb{R}^d$ we have

$$\boldsymbol{v}'\Sigma_t\boldsymbol{v} = \boldsymbol{v}'A_0\boldsymbol{v} + (\boldsymbol{v}'A_1'\boldsymbol{X}_{t-1})^2 + (B_1\boldsymbol{v})'\Sigma_{t-1}(B_1\boldsymbol{v}) > 0,$$

since the first term is strictly positive and the second and third terms are non-negative. □

To gain an understanding of the BEKK model it is again useful to consider the bivariate special case of order (1, 1) and to consider the dynamics that are implied while comparing these with equations (4.68):

$$\begin{aligned}
\sigma_{t,1}^2 &= a_{0,11} + a_{1,11}^2 X_{t-1,1}^2 + 2a_{1,11}a_{1,12}X_{t-1,1}X_{t-1,2} + a_{1,12}^2 X_{t-1,2}^2 \\
&\quad + b_{11}^2\sigma_{t-1,1}^2 + 2b_{11}b_{12}\sigma_{t-1,12} + b_{12}^2\sigma_{t-1,2}^2; \qquad (4.73)\\
\sigma_{t,12} &= a_{0,12} + (a_{1,11}a_{1,22} + a_{1,12}a_{1,21})X_{t-1,1}X_{t-1,2} \\
&\quad + a_{1,11}a_{1,21}X_{t-1,1}^2 + a_{1,22}a_{1,12}X_{t-1,2}^2 \\
&\quad + (b_{11}b_{22} + b_{12}b_{21})\sigma_{t-1,12} + b_{11}b_{21}\sigma_{t-1,1}^2 + b_{22}b_{12}\sigma_{t-1,2}^2; \qquad (4.74)\\
\sigma_{t,2}^2 &= a_{0,22} + a_{1,22}^2 X_{t-1,2}^2 + 2a_{1,22}a_{1,21}X_{t-1,1}X_{t-1,2} + a_{1,21}^2 X_{t-1,1}^2 \\
&\quad + b_{22}^2\sigma_{t-1,2}^2 + 2b_{22}b_{21}\sigma_{t-1,21} + b_{21}^2\sigma_{t-1,1}^2. \qquad (4.75)
\end{aligned}$$

From (4.73) it follows that we now have a model where a large lagged value of the second component $X_{t-1,2}$ can influence the volatility of the first series $\sigma_{t,1}$. The BEKK model has more parameters than the DVEC model and appears to have much richer dynamics. Note, however, that the DVEC model cannot be obtained as a special case of the BEKK model as we have defined it. To eliminate all crossover effects in the conditional variance equations of the BEKK model in (4.73) and (4.75) we would have to set the diagonal terms $a_{1,12}$, $a_{1,21}$, b_{12} and b_{21} to be zero and the

Table 4.3. Summary of numbers of parameters in various multivariate GARCH models: in CCC it is assumed that the numbers of ARCH and GARCH terms for all volatility equations are, respectively, p and q; in DCC it is assumed that the conditional correlation equation has $p+q$ parameters. The second column gives the general formula; the final columns give the numbers for models of dimensions 2, 5 and 10 when $p=q=1$. Additional parameters in the innovation distribution are not considered.

Model	Parameter count	2	5	10
VEC	$d(d+1)(1+(p+q)d(d+1)/2)/2$	21	465	6105
BEKK	$d(d+1)/2+d^2(p+q)$	11	65	255
DVEC as in (4.69)	$d(d+1)(1+p+q)/2$	9	45	165
DCC	$d(d+1)/2+(d+1)(p+q)$	9	27	77
CCC	$d(d+1)/2+d(p+q)$	7	25	75
DVEC as in (4.70)	$d(d+1)/2+d(p+q)$	7	25	75
DVEC as in (4.71)	$d(d+1)/2+(p+q)$	5	17	57

parameters governing the individual volatilities would also govern the conditional covariance $\sigma_{t,12}$ in (4.74).

Remark 4.46. A broader definition of the BEKK class, which does subsume all DVEC models, was originally given by Engle and Kroner (1995). In this definition we have

$$\Sigma_t = A_0A_0' + \sum_{k=1}^{K}\sum_{i=1}^{p} A_{k,i}'X_{t-i}X_{t-i}'A_{k,i} + \sum_{k=1}^{K}\sum_{j=1}^{q} B_{k,j}'\Sigma_{t-j}B_{k,j},$$

where $\frac{1}{2}d(d+1) > K \geqslant 1$ and the choice of K determines the richness of the model. This model class is of largely theoretical interest and tends to be too complex for practical applications; even the case $K=1$ is difficult to fit in higher dimensions.

In Table 4.3 we have summarized the numbers of parameters in these models. Broad conclusions concerning the practical implications are as follows: the general VEC model is of purely theoretical interest; the BEKK and general DVEC models are for very low-dimensional use; the remaining models are the most practically useful.

4.6.4 Fitting Multivariate GARCH Models

Model fitting. We have already given notes on fitting some models in stages and it should be stressed that in the high-dimensional applications of risk management this may in fact be the only feasible strategy. Where interest centres on a multivariate risk-factor return series of more modest dimension (perhaps less than 10), we can attempt to fit multivariate GARCH models by maximizing an appropriate likelihood with respect to all parameters in a single step. The procedure follows from the method for univariate time series described in Section 4.3.4.

The method of building a likelihood for a generic multivariate GARCH model $X_t = \Sigma_t^{1/2}Z_t$ is completely analogous to the univariate case; consider again a first-order model ($p=q=1$) for simplicity and assume that our data are labelled

$\boldsymbol{X}_0, \boldsymbol{X}_1, \dots, \boldsymbol{X}_n$. A conditional likelihood is based on the conditional joint density of $\boldsymbol{X}_1, \dots, \boldsymbol{X}_n$, given $\boldsymbol{X}_0$ and an initial value Σ_0 for the conditional covariance matrix. This conditional joint density is

$$f_{\boldsymbol{X}_1,\dots,\boldsymbol{X}_n \mid \boldsymbol{X}_0,\Sigma_0}(\boldsymbol{x}_1, \dots, \boldsymbol{x}_n \mid \boldsymbol{x}_0, \Sigma_0) = \prod_{t=1}^{n} f_{\boldsymbol{X}_t \mid \boldsymbol{X}_{t-1},\dots,\boldsymbol{X}_0,\Sigma_0}(\boldsymbol{x}_t \mid \boldsymbol{x}_{t-1}, \dots, \boldsymbol{x}_0, \Sigma_0).$$

If we denote the multivariate innovation density of $\boldsymbol{Z}_t$ by $g(\boldsymbol{z})$, then we have

$$f_{\boldsymbol{X}_t \mid \boldsymbol{X}_{t-1},\dots,\boldsymbol{X}_0,\Sigma_0}(\boldsymbol{x}_t \mid \boldsymbol{x}_{t-1}, \dots, \boldsymbol{x}_0, \Sigma_0) = |\Sigma_t|^{-1/2} g(\Sigma_t^{-1/2}\boldsymbol{x}_t),$$

where Σ_t is a matrix-valued function of $\boldsymbol{x}_{t-1}, \dots, \boldsymbol{x}_0$ and Σ_0. Most common choices of $g(\boldsymbol{z})$ are in the spherical family so that by (3.46) we have $g(\boldsymbol{z}) = h(\boldsymbol{z}'\boldsymbol{z})$ for some function h of a scalar variable (known as a density generator), yielding a conditional likelihood of the form

$$L(\boldsymbol{\theta}; \boldsymbol{X}_1, \dots, \boldsymbol{X}_n) = \prod_{t=1}^{n} |\Sigma_t|^{-1/2} h(\boldsymbol{X}_t' \Sigma_t^{-1} \boldsymbol{X}_t),$$

where all parameters appearing in the volatility equation and the innovation distribution are collected in $\boldsymbol{\theta}$. It would of course be possible to add a constant mean term or a conditional mean term with, say, vector autoregressive structure to the model and to adapt the likelihood accordingly.

Evaluation of the likelihood requires us to input a value for Σ_0. Maximization can again be performed in practice using a modified Newton–Raphson procedure, such as that of Berndt et al. (1974). References concerning properties of estimators are given in Notes and Comments, although the literature for multivariate GARCH is small.

Model checking and comparison. Residuals are calculated according to $\hat{\boldsymbol{Z}}_t = \hat{\Sigma}_t^{-1/2}\boldsymbol{X}_t$ and should behave like a realization of an SWN$(\boldsymbol{0}, I_d)$ process. The usual univariate procedures (correlograms, correlograms of absolute values and portmanteau tests such as Ljung–Box) can be applied to the component series of the residuals. Also, there should not be any evidence of cross-correlations at any lags for either the raw or the absolute residuals in the cross-correlogram.

Model selection is usually performed by a standard comparison of Akaike AIC numbers, although it should be stressed that there is not yet much literature on theoretical aspects of the use of Akaike in a univariate GARCH context, let alone a multivariate one.

4.6.5 Dimension Reduction in MGARCH

It is still true that attempting to model all financial risk factors with general multivariate GARCH models is not recommended. Rather, these models have to be combined with factor-model strategies to reduce the overall dimension of the time series modelling problem. This is a large subject with many possible approaches and model structures and we give brief notes on some general strategies.

As discussed in Section 3.4.1, a fundamental consideration is whether factors are identified *a priori* and treated as observable exogenous variables, or whether they are treated as latent and are manufactured from the observed data.

Observed factors. Suppose we adopted the former approach and identified a small number of common factors $\boldsymbol{F}_t$ to explain the variation in many risk factors $\boldsymbol{X}_t$; we might, for example, use stock index returns to explain the variation in individual equity returns. These common factors could be modelled with relatively detailed multivariate GARCH models. The dependence of the individual returns on the factor returns could then be modelled by calibrating a factor model of the type

$$\boldsymbol{X}_t = \boldsymbol{a} + B\boldsymbol{F}_t + \boldsymbol{\varepsilon}_t, \quad t = 1, \dots, n.$$

In Section 3.4.3 we showed how this may be done in a static way using regression techniques. We now assume that, conditional on the factors $\boldsymbol{F}_t$, the errors $\boldsymbol{\varepsilon}_t$ form a multivariate white noise process with GARCH volatility structure.

In an ideal factor model these errors would have a diagonal covariance matrix, because they would be attributable to idiosyncratic effects alone. In GARCH terms they might follow a pure diagonal model, i.e. a CCC model where the constant conditional correlation matrix is the identity matrix. A pure diagonal model can be fitted in two ways, which correspond to the two ways of estimating a static regression model.

(1) Fit univariate models to the component series $X_{1,k}, \dots, X_{n,k}$, $k = 1, \dots, d$. For each k assume that

$$X_{t,k} = \mu_{t,k} + \varepsilon_{t,k}, \quad \mu_{t,k} = a_k + \boldsymbol{b}_k'\boldsymbol{F}_t, \quad t = 1, \dots, n,$$

where the errors $\varepsilon_{t,k}$ follow some univariate GARCH specification.

(2) Fit in one step the multivariate model

$$\boldsymbol{X}_t = \boldsymbol{\mu}_t + \boldsymbol{\varepsilon}_t, \quad \boldsymbol{\mu}_t = \boldsymbol{a} + B\boldsymbol{F}_t, \quad t = 1, \dots, n,$$

where the errors $\boldsymbol{\varepsilon}_t$ follow a pure diagonal CCC model and the SWN$(\boldsymbol{0}, I_d)$ process driving the GARCH model is some non-Gaussian spherical distribution, such as an appropriate scaled t distribution. (If the SWN is Gaussian, approaches (1) and (2) give the same results.)

In practice, it is never possible to find the "right" common factors such that the idiosyncratic errors have a diagonal covariance structure. The pure diagonal assumption can be examined by looking at the errors from the GARCH modelling, estimating their correlation matrix and assessing its closeness to the identity matrix. In the case where correlation structure remains, the formal concept of the factor model can be loosened by allowing errors with a CCC-GARCH structure, which could be calibrated by two-stage estimation.

Principal components GARCH. As an alternative approach we could attempt to extend the idea of principal components to the time series context. A way of doing this is suggested by the following formally defined model.

Definition 4.47. The process $(\boldsymbol{X}_t)_{t\in\mathbb{Z}}$ follows a PC-GARCH (or orthogonal GARCH) model if there exists some orthogonal matrix $\Gamma \in \mathbb{R}^{d\times d}$ satisfying $\Gamma\Gamma' = \Gamma'\Gamma = I_d$ such that $(\Gamma'\boldsymbol{X}_t)_{t\in\mathbb{Z}}$ follows a pure diagonal GARCH model.

If $(\boldsymbol{X}_t)_{t\in\mathbb{Z}}$ follows a PC-GARCH process for some matrix Γ, then we can introduce the process $(\boldsymbol{Y}_t)_{t\in\mathbb{Z}}$ defined by $\boldsymbol{Y}_t = \Gamma'\boldsymbol{X}_t$, which satisfies $\boldsymbol{Y}_t = \Delta_t \boldsymbol{Z}_t$, where $(\boldsymbol{Z}_t)_{t\in\mathbb{Z}}$ is $\mathrm{SWN}(\boldsymbol{0}, I_d)$ and Δ_t is a (diagonal) volatility matrix with elements that are updated according to univariate GARCH schemes and past values of the components of $\boldsymbol{Y}_t$. Since $\boldsymbol{X}_t = \Gamma\Delta_t\boldsymbol{Z}_t$, the conditional and unconditional covariance matrices have the structure

$$\Sigma_t = \Gamma\Delta_t^2\Gamma', \qquad \Sigma = \Gamma E(\Delta_t^2)\Gamma', \tag{4.76}$$

and are obviously symmetric and positive definite.

Comparing with (3.67) we see that the PC-GARCH model implies a spectral decomposition of the conditional and unconditional covariance matrices. The *eigenvalues* of the conditional covariance matrix, which are the elements of the diagonal matrix Δ_t^2, are given a GARCH updating structure. The *eigenvectors* form the columns of Γ and are used to construct the time series $(\boldsymbol{Y}_t)_{t\in\mathbb{Z}}$, the principal component transform of $(\boldsymbol{X}_t)_{t\in\mathbb{Z}}$. It should be noted that despite the simple structure of (4.76), the conditional correlation matrix of $\boldsymbol{X}_t$ is not constant in this model.

This is again a model whose structure permits estimation in stages; in the first step we calculate the spectral decomposition of the sample covariance matrix of the data S as in Section 3.4.4; this gives us an estimator G of Γ. We then rotate the original data to obtain sample principal components $\{G'\boldsymbol{X}_t : t = 1, \dots, n\}$. These should be consistent with a pure diagonal model if the PC-GARCH is appropriate for the original data; there should be no cross-correlation between the series at any lag. In a second stage we fit univariate GARCH models to each time series of principal components in turn; the residuals from these GARCH models should behave like $\mathrm{SWN}(\boldsymbol{0}, I_d)$.

The main motivation for using principal components is to reduce dimensionality. We expect that a subset of the principal components can explain the majority of variability in both the conditional and unconditional covariance matrices. We use the idea embodied in equation (3.70), that the first k loading vectors in the matrix Γ specify the most important principal components, and we write these columns in the submatrix $\Gamma_1 \in \mathbb{R}^{d\times k}$ and use them to define factors $\boldsymbol{F}_t = (F_{t,1}, \dots, F_{t,k})' := \Gamma_1'\boldsymbol{X}_t$. These factors satisfy $\boldsymbol{F}_t = \tilde{\Delta}_t\tilde{\boldsymbol{Z}}_t$, where $\tilde{\Delta}_t$ contains the upper $k \times k$ submatrix of Δ_t and $\tilde{\boldsymbol{Z}}_t \sim \mathrm{SWN}(\boldsymbol{0}, I_k)$. In other words, the factors follow a pure diagonal model of dimension $k < d$.

Following the idea in (3.70), the PC-GARCH model can then be thought of as a factor model of the form $\boldsymbol{X}_t = \Gamma_1\boldsymbol{F}_t + \boldsymbol{\varepsilon}_t$, where the error term is usually ignored in practice. The conditional covariance matrix is effectively approximated by

$\Sigma_t \approx \Gamma_1 \tilde{\Delta}_t^2 \Gamma_1'$. In practical terms, calibrating the model simply means that we only need to fit GARCH models to the first k time series of sample principal components.

4.6.6 MGARCH and Conditional Risk Measurement

Suppose we calibrate an MGARCH model (possibly with VARMA conditional mean structure) having the general structure $X_t = \mu_t + \Sigma_t^{1/2} Z_t$ to historical risk-factor return data $X_{t-n+1}, \dots, X_t$. We are interested in the loss distribution of $L_{t+1} = l_{[t]}(X_{t+1})$ conditional on $\mathcal{F}_t = \sigma(\{X_s : s \leqslant t\})$, as described in Sections 2.1.1 and 2.1.2. (We may also be interested in longer-period losses as in Section 2.3.4.)

A general method that could be applied is the Monte Carlo method of Section 2.3.3: we could simulate many times the next value X_{t+1} (and subsequent values if needed) of the stochastic process $(X_t)_{t\in\mathbb{Z}}$ using estimates of μ_{t+1} and Σ_{t+1}.

Alternatively, a variance–covariance calculation as in Section 2.3.1 could be made. Considering a linearized loss operator with the general form $l_{[t]}^{\Delta}(x) = -(c_t + b_t' x)$, the moments of the conditional loss distribution would be

$$E(L_{t+1}^{\Delta} \mid \mathcal{F}_t) = -c_t - b_t' \mu_{t+1}, \qquad \operatorname{cov}(L_{t+1}^{\Delta} \mid \mathcal{F}_t) = b_t' \Sigma_{t+1} b_t.$$

Under an assumption of Gaussian innovations, $L_{t+1}^{\Delta} \mid \mathcal{F}_t$ would be univariate Gaussian as in (2.30). Under an assumption of (scaled) t innovations, it would be univariate t. Again we would need estimates of Σ_{t+1} and μ_{t+1} from our time series model, as in Section 4.4.2, and VaR and ES estimates would then follow easily for these distributions from calculations in Examples 2.14, 2.18 and 2.19.

Example 4.48. Consider again the simple stock portfolio in Example 2.4 and suppose our time series model is a first-order DVEC model with a constant mean term. The model takes the form

$$X_t - \mu = \Sigma_t^{1/2} Z_t, \qquad \Sigma_t = A_0 + A_1 \circ ((X_{t-1} - \mu)(X_{t-1}' - \mu')) + B \circ \Sigma_{t-1}. \tag{4.77}$$

Suppose we assume that the innovations are multivariate Student t. The standard risk measures applied to the linearized loss distribution would take the form

$$\mathrm{VaR}_\alpha^t = -V_t w_t' \mu + V_t \sqrt{\frac{w_t' \Sigma_{t+1} w_t (\nu - 2)}{\nu}}\, t_\nu^{-1}(\alpha),$$

$$\mathrm{ES}_\alpha^t = -V_t w_t' \mu + V_t \sqrt{\frac{w_t' \Sigma_{t+1} w_t (\nu - 2)}{\nu}}\, \frac{g_\nu(t_\nu^{-1}(\alpha))}{1-\alpha} \left(\frac{\nu + (t_\nu^{-1}(\alpha))^2}{\nu - 1} \right),$$

where the notation is as in Example 2.19. Estimates of the risk measures are obtained by replacing μ, ν and Σ_{t+1} by estimates. The latter can be calculated iteratively from (4.77) using estimates of A_0, A_1 and B and a starting value for Σ_0.

Multivariate EWMA. In Section 4.4.1 we saw how the EWMA or exponential smoothing procedure could be used as a simple alternative to GARCH volatility prediction. We note that there is a multivariate extension that may be used to make one-step forecasts of conditional covariance matrices and that this can be thought of as a simple alternative to using the updating scheme in (4.77).

We recall the univariate EWMA updating equation (4.47) and note that the multivariate analogue is

$$\hat{\Sigma}_{t+1} = \alpha \boldsymbol{X}_t \boldsymbol{X}_t' + (1-\alpha)\hat{\Sigma}_t, \tag{4.78}$$

where α is some small positive number (typically of the order $\alpha \approx 0.04$). This method of updating is consistent with the idea of estimating Σ_{t+1} by a weighted sum of past values of the matrices $\boldsymbol{X}_t \boldsymbol{X}_t$, where the weights decay exponentially:

$$\hat{\Sigma}_{t+1} = \alpha \sum_{i=0}^{n-1} (1-\alpha)^i \boldsymbol{X}_{t-i} \boldsymbol{X}_{t-i}.$$

Notes and Comments

The CCC-GARCH model was suggested by Bollerslev (1990), who used it to model European exchange-rate data before and after the introduction of the European Monetary System (EMS) and came to the expected conclusion that conditional correlations after the introduction of the EMS were higher. The idea of the DCC model is explored by Engle (2002), Engle and Sheppard (2001) and Tse and Tsui (2002). Fitting in stages is promoted in the formulation of Engle and Sheppard (2001) and asymptotic statistical theory for this procedure is given. Hafner and Franses (2003) suggest that the dynamics of CCC are too simple for collections of many asset returns and give a generalization.

The DVEC model was proposed by Bollerslev, Engle and Wooldridge (1988). The more general (but overparametrized) VEC model is discussed in Engle and Kroner (1995) alongside the BEKK model, named after these two authors as well as Baba and Kraft, who co-authored an earlier unpublished manuscript. The condition for the positive definiteness of Σ_t in (4.67), which suggests the parametrizations (4.69)–(4.71), is described in Attanasio (1991).

There is limited work on statistical properties of QMLEs in multivariate models: Jeantheau (1998) shows consistency for a general formulation and Comte and Lieberman (2003) show asymptotic normality for the BEKK formulation.

The principal components GARCH (PC-GARCH) model was first described by Ding (1994) in a PhD thesis; under the name of orthogonal GARCH it has been extensively investigated by Alexander (2001). The latter shows how PC-GARCH can be used as a dimension reduction tool for expressing the conditional covariances of a number of asset return series in terms of a much smaller number of principal component return series.

Survey articles by Bollerslev, Engle and Nelson (1994) and Bauwens, Laurent and Rombouts (2005) are useful sources of additional information and references for all of these multivariate models.

5
Copulas and Dependence

In this chapter we look more closely at the issue of modelling the dependence among components of a random vector of financial risk factors using the concept of a copula. All readers are encouraged to read Section 5.1 in order to grasp the basic idea of a copula and to see examples. Thereafter the choice of material in this chapter may be based on the applied interests of the reader.

Section 5.2 goes further into the issue of what it means to *measure dependence*. The limitations of *linear correlation* as a dependence measure are highlighted, particularly when we leave the multivariate normal and elliptical distributions of Chapter 3 behind. Alternative dependence measures derived from copulas, such as *rank correlations* and *coefficients of tail dependence*, are discussed. Rank correlations are mainly of interest to readers who want to go on to calibrate copulas to data, while tail dependence is an important concept for all readers, since it addresses the phenomenon of *joint extreme values* in several risk factors, which is one of the major concerns in financial risk management (see also Section 4.1.2).

In Section 5.3 we look in more detail at the *copulas of normal mixture distributions*; these are the copulas that are used implicitly when normal mixture distributions are fitted to multivariate risk-factor change data, as in Chapter 3. In Section 5.4 we consider *Archimedean copulas*, which are widely used as dependence models in low-dimensional applications and which have also found an important niche in portfolio credit risk modelling, as will be seen in Chapters 8 and 9. The chapter ends with a section on fitting copulas to data.

5.1 Copulas

In a sense, every joint distribution function for a random vector of risk factors implicitly contains both a description of the marginal behaviour of individual risk factors and a description of their *dependence structure*; the copula approach provides a way of isolating the description of the dependence structure. It is of course only one way of treating dependence in multivariate risk models and is perhaps most natural in a static distributional context rather than a dynamic time series one. Nonetheless, we view copulas as an extremely useful concept and see several advantages in introducing and studying them.

First, copulas help in the understanding of dependence at a deeper level. They allow us to see the potential pitfalls of approaches to dependence that focus only on correlation and show us how to define a number of useful alternative dependence measures. Copulas express dependence on a *quantile scale*, which is useful for describing the dependence of extreme outcomes and is natural in a risk-management context, where VaR has led us to think of risk in terms of quantiles of loss distributions.

Moreover, copulas facilitate a *bottom-up approach to multivariate model building*. This is particularly useful in risk management, where we very often have a much better idea about the marginal behaviour of individual risk factors than we do about their dependence structure. An example is furnished by credit risk, where the individual default risk of an obligor, while in itself difficult to estimate, is at least something we can get a better handle on than the dependence among default risks for several obligors. The copula approach allows us to combine our more developed marginal models with a variety of possible dependence models and to investigate the sensitivity of risk to the dependence specification. Since the copulas we present are easily simulated, they lend themselves in particular to Monte Carlo studies of risk.

5.1.1 Basic Properties

Definition 5.1 (copula). A d-dimensional copula is a distribution function on $[0, 1]^d$ with standard uniform marginal distributions.

We reserve the notation $C(\boldsymbol{u}) = C(u_1, \dots, u_d)$ for the multivariate dfs that are copulas. Hence C is a mapping of the form $C : [0, 1]^d \to [0, 1]$, i.e. a mapping of the unit hypercube into the unit interval. The following three properties must hold.

(1) $C(u_1, \dots, u_d)$ is increasing in each component u_i.

(2) $C(1, \dots, 1, u_i, 1, \dots, 1) = u_i$ for all $i \in \{1, \dots, d\}$, $u_i \in [0, 1]$.

(3) For all $(a_1, \dots, a_d), (b_1, \dots, b_d) \in [0, 1]^d$ with $a_i \leqslant b_i$ we have

$$\sum_{i_1=1}^{2} \cdots \sum_{i_d=1}^{2} (-1)^{i_1+\cdots+i_d} C(u_{1i_1}, \dots, u_{di_d}) \geqslant 0, \tag{5.1}$$

where $u_{j1} = a_j$ and $u_{j2} = b_j$ for all $j \in \{1, \dots, d\}$.

The first property is clearly required of any multivariate df and the second property is the requirement of uniform marginal distributions. The third property is less obvious, but the so-called rectangle inequality in (5.1) ensures that if the random vector $(U_1, \dots, U_d)'$ has df C, then $P(a_1 \leqslant U_1 \leqslant b_1, \dots, a_d \leqslant U_d \leqslant b_d)$ is non-negative. These three properties characterize a copula; if a function C fulfills them, then it is a copula. Note also that, for $2 \leqslant k < d$, the k-dimensional margins of a d-dimensional copula are themselves copulas.

Some preliminaries. In working with copulas we must be familiar with the operations of *probability* and *quantile transformation*, as well as the properties of generalized inverses, which are summarized in Section A.1.2. The following elementary proposition is found in many probability texts.

Proposition 5.2. *Let G be a distribution function and let $G^{\leftarrow}$ denote its generalized inverse, i.e. the function $G^{\leftarrow}(y) = \inf\{x : G(x) \geqslant y\}$.*

(1) Quantile transformation. *If $U \sim U(0,1)$ has a standard uniform distribution, then $P(G^{\leftarrow}(U) \leqslant x) = G(x)$.*

(2) Probability transformation. *If Y has df G, where G is a continuous univariate df, then $G(Y) \sim U(0,1)$.*

Proof. Let $y \in \mathbb{R}$ and $u \in (0,1)$. For the first part use the fact that

$$G(y) \geqslant u \iff G^{\leftarrow}(u) \leqslant y$$

(see Proposition A.3(iv) in Section A.1.2), from which it follows that

$$P(G^{\leftarrow}(U) \leqslant y) = P(U \leqslant G(y)) = G(y).$$

For the second part we infer that

$$P(G(Y) \leqslant u) = P(G^{\leftarrow} \circ G(Y) \leqslant G^{\leftarrow}(u)) = P(Y \leqslant G^{\leftarrow}(u)) = G \circ G^{\leftarrow}(u) = u,$$

where the first inequality follows from the fact that $G^{\leftarrow}$ is strictly increasing (Proposition A.3(ii)), the second follows from Proposition A.4, and the final equality is Proposition A.3(viii). □

Proposition 5.2(1) is the key to stochastic simulation. If we can generate a uniform variate U and compute the inverse of a df G, then we can sample from that df. Both parts of the proposition taken together imply that we can transform risks with a particular continuous df to have any other continuous distribution. For example, if Y has a standard normal distribution, then $\Phi(Y)$ is uniform by Proposition 5.2(1), and, since the quantile function of a standard exponential df G is $G^{\leftarrow}(y) = -\ln(1-y)$, the transformed variable $Z := -\ln(1-\Phi(Y))$ has a unit exponential distribution by Proposition 5.2(2).

Sklar's Theorem. The importance of copulas in the study of multivariate distribution functions is summarized by the following elegant theorem, which shows, firstly, that all multivariate dfs contain copulas and, secondly, that copulas may be used in conjunction with univariate dfs to construct multivariate dfs.

Theorem 5.3 (Sklar 1959). *Let F be a joint distribution function with margins $F_1, \dots, F_d$. Then there exists a copula $C : [0,1]^d \to [0,1]$ such that, for all $x_1, \dots, x_d$ in $\bar{\mathbb{R}} = [-\infty, \infty]$,*

$$F(x_1, \dots, x_d) = C(F_1(x_1), \dots, F_d(x_d)). \tag{5.2}$$

If the margins are continuous, then C is unique; otherwise C is uniquely determined on $\operatorname{Ran} F_1 \times \operatorname{Ran} F_2 \times \cdots \times \operatorname{Ran} F_d$, where $\operatorname{Ran} F_i = F_i(\bar{\mathbb{R}})$ denotes the range of F_i. Conversely, if C is a copula and $F_1, \dots, F_d$ are univariate distribution functions, then the function F defined in (5.2) is a joint distribution function with margins $F_1, \dots, F_d$.

Proof. We prove the existence and uniqueness of a copula in the case when $F_1, \dots, F_d$ are continuous and the converse statement in its general form. For a full proof see Schweizer and Sklar (1983) or Nelsen (1999, p. 18).

For any $x_1, \dots, x_d$ in $\bar{\mathbb{R}} = [-\infty, \infty]$ we may use similar reasoning to that used in Lemma A.2(ii) to infer that if $\boldsymbol{X}$ has df F, then

$$F(x_1, \dots, x_d) = P(F_1(X_1) \leqslant F_1(x_1), \dots, F_d(X_d) \leqslant F_d(x_d)).$$

Since $F_1, \dots, F_d$ are continuous, Proposition 5.2(2) and Definition 5.1 imply that the df of $(F_1(X_1), \dots, F_d(X_d))$ is a copula, which we denote by C, and thus we obtain the identity (5.2).

If we evaluate (5.2) at the arguments $x_i = F_i^{\leftarrow}(u_i)$, $0 \leqslant u_i \leqslant 1$, $i = 1, \dots, d$, and use Proposition A.3(viii), we obtain

$$C(u_1, \dots, u_d) = F(F_1^{\leftarrow}(u_1), \dots, F_d^{\leftarrow}(u_d)), \tag{5.3}$$

which gives an explicit representation of C in terms of F and its margins, and thus shows uniqueness.

For the converse statement assume that C is a copula and that $F_1, \dots, F_d$ are univariate dfs. We construct a random vector with df (5.2) by taking $\boldsymbol{U}$ to be a random vector with df C and setting $\boldsymbol{X} := (F_1^{\leftarrow}(U_1), \dots, F_d^{\leftarrow}(U_d))$. We then verify, using Proposition A.3(iv), that

$$\begin{aligned} P(X_1 \leqslant x_1, \dots, X_d \leqslant x_d) &= P(F_1^{\leftarrow}(U_1) \leqslant x_1, \dots, F_d^{\leftarrow}(U_d) \leqslant x_d) \\ &= P(U_1 \leqslant F_1(x_1), \dots, U_d \leqslant F(x_d)) \\ &= C(F_1(x_1), \dots, F_d(x_d)). \end{aligned}$$

□

Formulas (5.2) and (5.3) are fundamental in dealing with copulas. The former shows how joint distributions F are formed by *coupling together* marginal distributions with copulas C; the latter shows how copulas are *extracted* from multivariate dfs with continuous margins. Moreover, (5.3) shows how copulas express dependence on a quantile scale, since the value $C(u_1, \dots, u_d)$ is the joint probability that X_1 lies below its u_1-quantile, X_2 lies below its u_2-quantile, and so on. Sklar's Theorem also suggests that, in the case of continuous margins, it is natural to define the notion of the copula of a distribution.

Definition 5.4 (copula of F). If the random vector $\boldsymbol{X}$ has joint df F with continuous marginal distributions $F_1, \dots, F_d$, then the copula of F (or $\boldsymbol{X}$) is the df C of $(F_1(X_1), \dots, F_d(X_d))$.

Discrete distributions. The copula concept is slightly less natural for multivariate discrete distributions. This is because there is more than one copula that can be used to join the margins to form the joint df, as the following example shows.

Example 5.5 (copulas of bivariate Bernoulli). Let (X_1, X_2) have a bivariate Bernoulli distribution satisfying

$$P(X_1 = 0, X_2 = 0) = \tfrac{1}{8}, \quad P(X_1 = 1, X_2 = 1) = \tfrac{3}{8}$$
$$P(X_1 = 0, X_2 = 1) = \tfrac{2}{8}, \quad P(X_1 = 1, X_2 = 0) = \tfrac{2}{8}.$$

Clearly, $P(X_1 = 0) = P(X_2 = 0) = \frac{3}{8}$ and the marginal distributions F_1 and F_2 of X_1 and X_2 are the same. From Sklar's Theorem we know that

$$P(X_1 \leqslant x_1, X_2 \leqslant x_2) = C(P(X_1 \leqslant x_1), P(X_2 \leqslant x_2))$$

for all x_1, x_2 and some copula C. Since $\operatorname{Ran} F_1 = \operatorname{Ran} F_2 = \{0, \frac{3}{8}, 1\}$, clearly the only constraint on C is that $C(\frac{3}{8}, \frac{3}{8}) = \frac{1}{8}$. Any copula fulfilling this constraint is a copula of (X_1, X_2), and there are infinitely many such copulas.

Invariance. A useful property of the copula of a distribution is its invariance under *strictly increasing* transformations of the marginals. In view of Sklar's Theorem and this invariance property, we interpret the copula of a distribution as a very natural way of representing the dependence structure of that distribution, certainly in the case of continuous margins.

Proposition 5.6. *Let $(X_1, \dots, X_d)$ be a random vector with continuous margins and copula C and let $T_1, \dots, T_d$ be strictly increasing functions. Then $(T_1(X_1), \dots, T_d(X_d))$ also has copula C.*

Proof. First we show that the transformed variable $T_i(X_i)$ has continuous df $\tilde{F}_i(y) := F_i \circ T_i^{\leftarrow}(y)$. To see this, observe that Proposition A.3(vii) implies

$$\tilde{F}_i(y) = P(X_i \leqslant T_i^{\leftarrow}(y)) = P(T_i^{\leftarrow} \circ T_i(X_i) \leqslant T_i^{\leftarrow}(y)).$$

Since $T_i^{\leftarrow}$ is an increasing (but not strictly increasing) transformation, we may use Lemma A.2(ii) to deduce

$$\tilde{F}_i(y) = P(T_i(X_i) \leqslant y) + P(X_i = T_i^{\leftarrow}(y), T(X_i) > y),$$

but the second probability on the right-hand side is zero, since F_i is continuous.

Since C is the copula of $\boldsymbol{X}$, we can now calculate that

$$\begin{aligned} C(u_1, \dots, u_n) &= P(F_1(X_1) \leqslant u_1, \dots, F_d(X_d) \leqslant u_d) \\ &= P(\tilde{F}_1(T_1(X_1)) \leqslant u_1, \dots, \tilde{F}_d(T_d(X_d)) \leqslant u_d), \end{aligned}$$

because $\tilde{F}_i \circ T_i(x) = F_i \circ T_i^{\leftarrow} \circ T_i(x) = F_i(x)$ by Proposition A.3(vii). It follows from Definition 5.4 that C is also the copula of $(T_1(X_1), \dots, T_d(X_d))$. □

Fréchet bounds. We close this section by establishing the important *Fréchet bounds* for copulas, which turn out to have important dependence interpretations that are discussed further in Sections 5.1.2 and 5.1.6.

Theorem 5.7. *For every copula $C(u_1, \dots, u_d)$ we have the bounds*

$$\max\left\{\sum_{i=1}^{d} u_i + 1 - d, 0\right\} \leqslant C(\boldsymbol{u}) \leqslant \min\{u_1, \dots, u_d\}. \tag{5.4}$$

Proof. The second inequality follows from the fact that, for all i,

$$\bigcap_{1\leqslant j\leqslant d}\{U_j \leqslant u_j\} \subset \{U_i \leqslant u_i\}.$$

For the first inequality observe that

$$C(\boldsymbol{u}) = P\bigg(\bigcap_{1\leqslant i\leqslant d}\{U_i \leqslant u_i\}\bigg) = 1 - P\bigg(\bigcup_{1\leqslant i\leqslant d}\{U_i > u_i\}\bigg)$$
$$\geqslant 1 - \sum_{i=1}^{d} P(U_i > u_i) = 1 - d + \sum_{i=1}^{d} u_i.$$

□

The lower and upper bounds will be given the notation $W(u_1, \dots, u_d)$ and $M(u_1, \dots, u_d)$, respectively.

Remark 5.8. Although we give Fréchet bounds for a copula, Fréchet bounds may be given for any multivariate df. For a multivariate df F with margins $F_1, \dots, F_d$ we establish by similar reasoning that

$$\max\bigg\{\sum_{i=1}^{d} F_i(x_i) + 1 - d, 0\bigg\} \leqslant F(\boldsymbol{x}) \leqslant \min\{F(x_1), \dots, F(x_d)\}, \tag{5.5}$$

so we have bounds for F in terms of its own marginal distributions.

5.1.2 Examples of Copulas

We provide a number of examples of copulas in this section and these are subdivided into three categories: *fundamental* copulas represent a number of important special dependence structures; *implicit* copulas are extracted from well-known multivariate distributions using Sklar's Theorem, but do not necessarily possess simple closed-form expressions; *explicit* copulas have simple closed-form expressions and follow general mathematical constructions known to yield copulas.

Fundamental copulas. The *independence copula* is

$$\Pi(u_1, \dots, u_d) = \prod_{i=1}^{d} u_i. \tag{5.6}$$

It is clear from Sklar's Theorem, and equation (5.2) in particular, that rvs with continuous distributions are independent if and only if their dependence structure is given by (5.6).

The *comonotonicity copula* is the Fréchet upper bound copula from (5.4):

$$M(u_1, \dots, u_d) = \min\{u_1, \dots, u_d\}. \tag{5.7}$$

Observe that this special copula is the joint df of the random vector $(U, \dots, U)$, where $U \sim U(0, 1)$. Suppose that the rvs $X_1, \dots, X_d$ have continuous dfs and

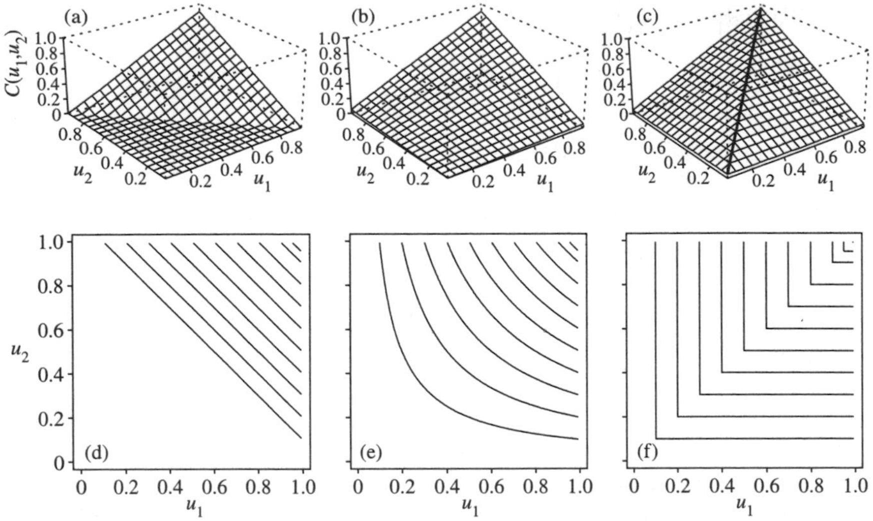

Figure 5.1. (a)–(c) Perspective plots and (d)–(f) contour plots of the three fundamental copulas: (a), (d) countermonotonicity, (b), (e) independence and (c), (f) comonotonicity. Note that these are plots of distribution functions.

are *perfectly positively dependent* in the sense that they are almost surely strictly increasing functions of each other so that $X_i = T_i(X_1)$ almost surely for $i = 2, \dots, d$. As we have shown in the proof of Proposition 5.6, the df of X_i, $i \geqslant 2$, is given by $F_i = F_1 \circ T_i^{\leftarrow}$, and by Definition 5.4 the copula of $(X_1, \dots, X_d)$ is the df of

$$(F_1(X_1), F_1 \circ T_2^{\leftarrow} \circ T_2(X_1), \dots, F_1 \circ T_d^{\leftarrow} \circ T_d(X_1)).$$

Writing $U = F_1(X_1)$ and using Proposition A.3(vii), we see that this is the df of $(U, \dots, U)$, i.e. the copula (5.7). The comonotonicity copula thus represents perfect dependence and we discuss this concept further in Section 5.1.6.

The *countermonotonicity copula* is the two-dimensional Fréchet lower bound copula from (5.4) given by

$$W(u_1, u_2) = \max\{u_1 + u_2 - 1, 0\}. \tag{5.8}$$

This copula is the joint df of the random vector $(U, 1 - U)$, where $U \sim U(0, 1)$. If X_1 and X_2 have continuous dfs and are *perfectly negatively dependent* in the sense that X_2 is almost surely a strictly decreasing function of X_1, then (5.8) is their copula. We discuss perfect negative dependence in more detail in Section 5.1.6, where we see that an extension of the countermonotonicity concept to dimensions higher than two is not possible.

Perspective pictures and contour plots for the three fundamental copulas are given in Figure 5.1. The Fréchet bounds (5.4) imply that all bivariate copulas lie between the surfaces in (a) and (c).

Implicit copulas. If $\boldsymbol{Y} \sim N_d(\boldsymbol{\mu}, \Sigma)$ is a Gaussian random vector, then its copula is a so-called *Gauss copula*. Since the operation of standardizing the margins amounts to applying a series of strictly increasing transformations, Proposition 5.6 implies that the copula of $\boldsymbol{Y}$ is exactly the same as the copula of $\boldsymbol{X} \sim N_d(\mathbf{0}, P)$, where $P = \wp(\Sigma)$ is the correlation matrix of $\boldsymbol{Y}$. By Definition 5.4 this copula is given by

$$\begin{aligned} C_P^{\mathrm{Ga}}(\boldsymbol{u}) &= P(\Phi(X_1) \leqslant u_1, \dots, \Phi(X_d) \leqslant u_d) \\ &= \boldsymbol{\Phi}_P(\Phi^{-1}(u_1), \dots, \Phi^{-1}(u_d)), \end{aligned} \tag{5.9}$$

where Φ denotes the standard univariate normal df and $\boldsymbol{\Phi}_P$ denotes the joint df of $\boldsymbol{X}$. The notation C_P^{Ga} emphasizes that the copula is parametrized by the $\frac{1}{2}d(d-1)$ parameters of the correlation matrix; in two dimensions we write C_ρ^{Ga}, where $\rho = \rho(X_1, X_2)$.

The Gauss copula does not have a simple closed form, but can be expressed as an integral over the density of $\boldsymbol{X}$; in two dimensions for $|\rho| < 1$ we have, using (5.9), that

$$C_\rho^{\mathrm{Ga}}(u_1, u_2) = \int_{-\infty}^{\Phi^{-1}(u_1)} \int_{-\infty}^{\Phi^{-1}(u_2)} \frac{1}{2\pi(1-\rho^2)^{1/2}} \exp\left\{\frac{-(s_1^2 - 2\rho s_1 s_2 + s_2^2)}{2(1-\rho^2)}\right\} \mathrm{d}s_1\, \mathrm{d}s_2.$$

Note that both the independence and comonotonicity copulas are special cases of the Gauss copula. If $P = I_d$, we obtain the independence copula (5.6); if $P = J_d$, the $d \times d$ matrix consisting entirely of ones, then we obtain comonotonicity (5.7). Also, for $d = 2$ and $\rho = -1$ the Gauss copula is equal to the countermonotonicity copula (5.8). Thus in two dimensions the Gauss copula can be thought of as a dependence structure that interpolates between perfect positive and negative dependence, where the parameter ρ represents the strength of dependence.

Perspective plots and contour lines of the bivariate Gauss copula with $\rho = 0.7$ are shown in Figure 5.2(a),(c); these may be compared with the contour lines of the independence and perfect dependence copulas in Figure 5.1. Note that these pictures show contour lines of distribution functions and not densities; a picture of the Gauss copula density is given in Figure 5.5.

In the same way that we can extract a copula from the multivariate normal distribution, we can extract an implicit copula from any other distribution with continuous marginal dfs. For example, the d-dimensional *t copula* takes the form

$$C_{\nu,P}^{t}(\boldsymbol{u}) = \boldsymbol{t}_{\nu,P}(t_\nu^{-1}(u_1), \dots, t_\nu^{-1}(u_d)), \tag{5.10}$$

where t_ν is the df of a standard univariate t distribution, $\boldsymbol{t}_{\nu,P}$ is the joint df of the vector $\boldsymbol{X} \sim t_d(\nu, \mathbf{0}, P)$ and P is a correlation matrix. As in the case of the Gauss copula, if $P = J_d$ then we obtain comonotonicity (5.8). However, in contrast to the Gauss copula, if $P = I_d$ we do not obtain the independence copula (assuming $\nu < \infty$) since uncorrelated multivariate t-distributed rvs are not independent (see Lemma 3.5).

Explicit copulas. While the Gaussian and t copulas are copulas implied by well-known multivariate dfs and do not themselves have simple closed forms, we can

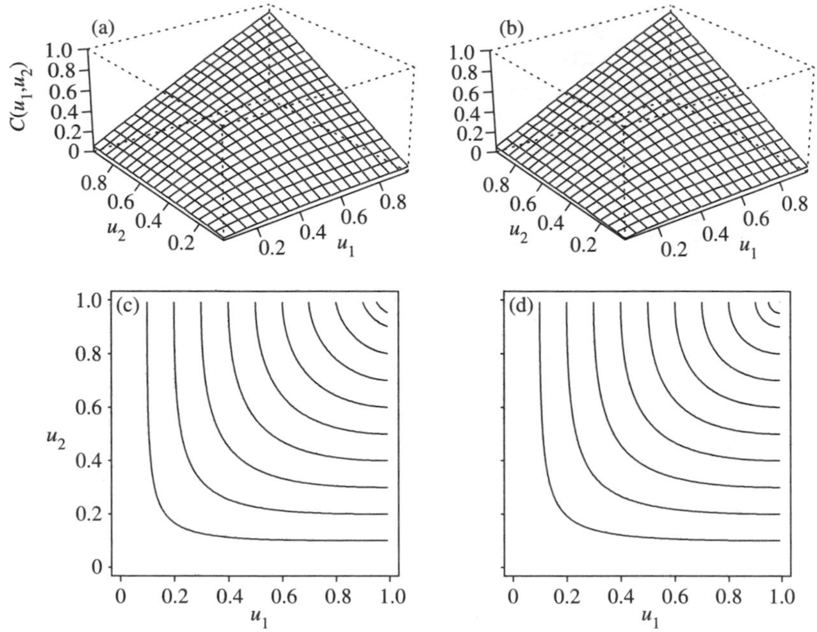

Figure 5.2. (a), (b) Perspective plots and (c), (d) contour plots of the Gaussian and Gumbel copulas, with parameters $\rho = 0.7$ and $\theta = 2$, respectively. Note that these are plots of distribution functions; a picture of the Gauss copula density is given in Figure 5.5.

write down a number of copulas which do have simple closed forms. An example is the bivariate *Gumbel copula*:

$$C_\theta^{\mathrm{Gu}}(u_1, u_2) = \exp\{-((-\ln u_1)^\theta + (-\ln u_2)^\theta)^{1/\theta}\}, \quad 1 \leqslant \theta < \infty. \tag{5.11}$$

If $\theta = 1$ we obtain the independence copula as a special case, and the limit of C_θ^{Gu} as $\theta \to \infty$ is the two-dimensional comonotonicity copula. Thus the Gumbel copula interpolates between independence and perfect dependence and the parameter θ represents the strength of dependence. Perspective plot and contour lines for the Gumbel copula with parameter $\theta = 2$ are shown in Figure 5.2(b),(d). They appear to be very similar to the picture for the Gauss copula, but Example 5.11 will show that the Gaussian and Gumbel dependence structures are quite different.

A further example is the bivariate *Clayton copula*:

$$C_\theta^{\mathrm{Cl}}(u_1, u_2) = (u_1^{-\theta} + u_2^{-\theta} - 1)^{-1/\theta}, \quad 0 < \theta < \infty. \tag{5.12}$$

In the limit as $\theta \to 0$ we approach the independence copula, and as $\theta \to \infty$ we approach the two-dimensional comonotonicity copula.

The Gumbel and Clayton copulas belong to the *Archimedean* copula family and we provide more discussion of this family, including the issue of higher-dimensional extensions, in Section 5.4.

5.1.3 Meta Distributions

The converse statement of Sklar's Theorem provides a very powerful technique for constructing multivariate distributions with arbitrary margins and copulas; we know that if we start with a copula C and margins $F_1, \dots, F_d$, then $F(\boldsymbol{x}) := C(F_1(x_1), \dots, F_d(x_d))$ defines a multivariate df with margins $F_1, \dots, F_d$.

Consider, for example, building a distribution with the Gauss copula C_P^{Ga} but arbitrary margins; such a model is known as a *meta-Gaussian* distribution. In the area of credit risk modelling an example is Li's model (see Example 8.7), where the Gauss copula is used to join together exponential margins to obtain a model for the default times of companies when these default times are considered to be dependent.

We extend the meta terminology to other distributions, so, for example, a *meta-t_ν* distribution has the copula $C_{\nu,P}^t$ and arbitrary margins, and a *meta-Clayton* distribution has the Clayton copula and arbitrary margins.

5.1.4 Simulation of Copulas and Meta Distributions

It should be apparent from the way the implicit copulas in Section 5.1.2 were extracted from well-known distributions that it is particularly easy to sample from these copulas, provided we can sample from the distribution from which they are extracted. If we can generate a vector $\boldsymbol{X}$ with the df F, we can transform each component with its own marginal df to obtain a vector $\boldsymbol{U} = (U_1, \dots, U_d)' = (F_1(X_1), \dots, F_d(X_d))'$ with df C, the copula of F. Particular examples are given in the following algorithms.

Algorithm 5.9 (simulation of Gauss copula).

(1) Generate $\boldsymbol{Z} \sim N_d(\boldsymbol{0}, P)$ using Algorithm 3.2.

(2) Return $\boldsymbol{U} = (\Phi(Z_1), \dots, \Phi(Z_d))'$, where Φ is the standard normal df. The random vector $\boldsymbol{U}$ has df C_P^{Ga}.

Algorithm 5.10 (simulation of *t* copula).

(1) Generate $\boldsymbol{X} \sim t_d(\nu, \boldsymbol{0}, P)$ using Algorithm 3.10.

(2) Return $\boldsymbol{U} = (t_\nu(X_1), \dots, t_\nu(X_d))'$, where t_ν denotes the df of a standard univariate t distribution. The random vector $\boldsymbol{U}$ has df $C_{\nu,P}^t$.

The Clayton and Gumbel copulas present slightly more challenging simulation problems and we give algorithms in Section 5.4 after looking at the structure of these copulas in more detail. These algorithms will, however, be used in Example 5.11 below.

Assume that the problem of generating realizations $\boldsymbol{U}$ from a particular copula has been solved. The converse of Sklar's Theorem shows us how we can sample from interesting meta distributions that combine this copula with an arbitrary choice of marginal distribution. If $\boldsymbol{U}$ has df C, then we use quantile transformation to obtain $\boldsymbol{X} := (F_1^{\leftarrow}(U_1), \dots, F_d^{\leftarrow}(U_d))'$, which is a random vector with margins $F_1, \dots, F_d$ and multivariate df $C(F_1(x_1), \dots, F_d(x_d))$. This technique is extremely useful in Monte Carlo studies of risk and will be discussed further in the context of Example 5.56.

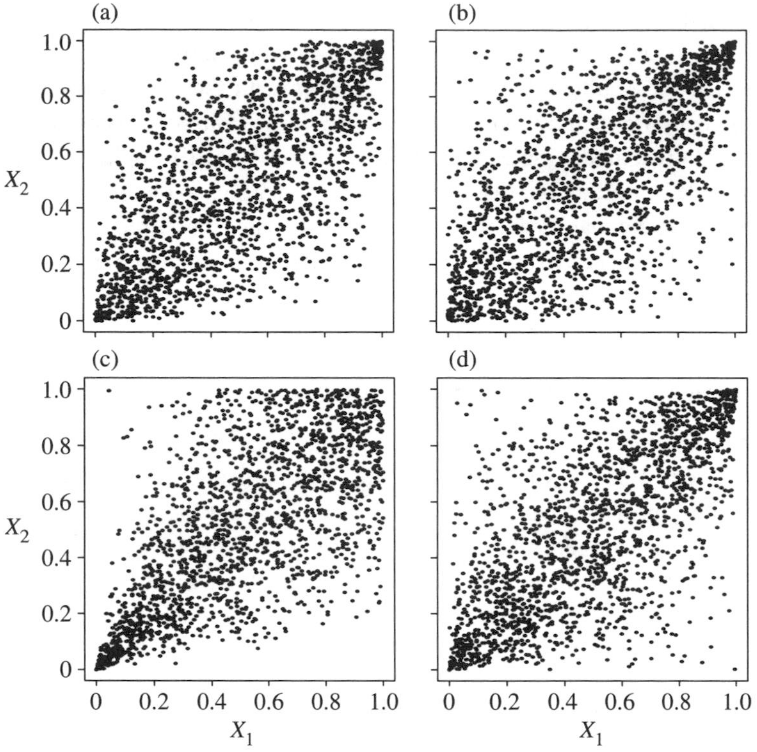

Figure 5.3. Two thousand simulated points from the (a) Gaussian, (b) Gumbel, (c) Clayton and (d) t copulas. See Example 5.11 for parameter choices and interpretation.

Example 5.11 (various copulas compared). In Figure 5.3 we show 2000 simulated points from four copulas: the Gauss copula (5.9) with parameter $\rho = 0.7$; the Gumbel copula (5.11) with parameter $\theta = 2$; the Clayton copula (5.12) with parameter $\theta = 2.2$; the t copula (5.10) with parameters $\nu = 4$ and $\rho = 0.71$.

In Figure 5.4 we transform these points componentwise using the quantile function of the standard normal distribution to get realizations from four different meta distributions with standard normal margins. The Gaussian picture shows data generated from a standard bivariate normal distribution with correlation 70%. The other pictures show data generated from unusual distributions that have been created using the converse of Sklar's Theorem; the parameters of the copulas have been chosen so that all of these distributions have a linear correlation that is roughly 70%.

Considering the Gumbel picture, these are bivariate data with a meta-Gumbel distribution with df $C_\theta^{\text{Gu}}(\Phi(x_1), \Phi(x_2))$, where $\theta = 2$. The Gumbel copula causes this distribution to have *upper tail dependence*, a concept defined formally in Section 5.2.3. Roughly speaking, there is much more of a tendency for X_2 to be extreme when X_1 is extreme, and vice versa, a phenomenon which would obviously be worrying when X_1 and X_2 are interpreted as potential financial losses. The Clayton copula turns out to have *lower tail dependence*, and the t copula to have both lower

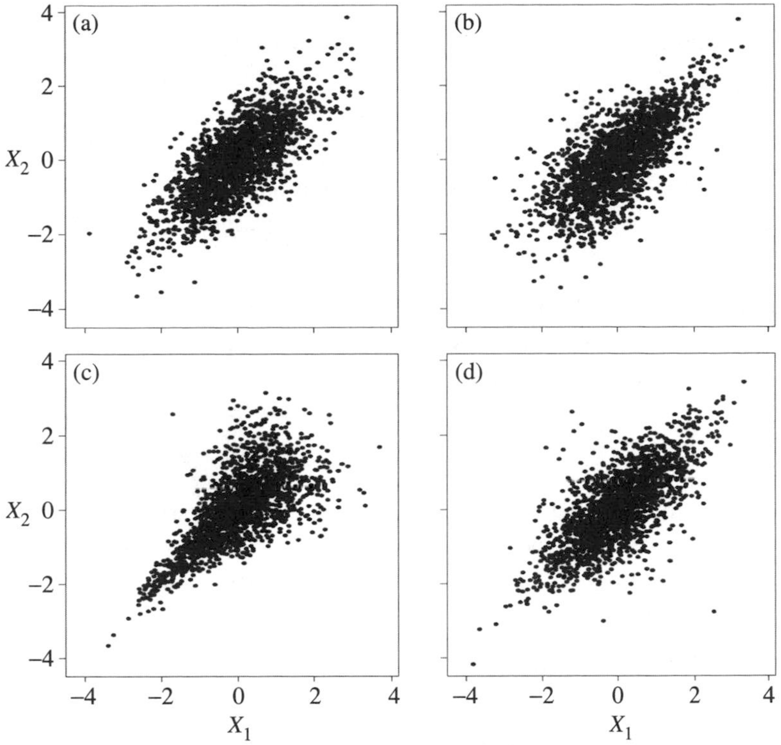

Figure 5.4. Two thousand simulated points from four distributions with standard normal margins, constructed using the copula data from Figure 5.3 ((a) Gaussian, (b) Gumbel, (c) Clayton and (d) t). The Gaussian picture shows points from a standard bivariate normal with correlation 70%; other pictures show distributions with non-Gauss copulas constructed to have a linear correlation of roughly 70%. See Example 5.11 for parameter choices and interpretation.

and upper tail dependence; in contrast, the Gauss copula does not have tail dependence and this can also be glimpsed in Figure 5.2. In the upper-right-hand corner the contours of the Gauss copula are more like those of the independence copula of Figure 5.1 than the perfect dependence copula.

Note that the qualitative differences between the distributions are explained by the copula alone; we can construct similar pictures where the marginal distributions are exponential or Student t, or any other univariate distribution.

5.1.5 Further Properties of Copulas

Survival copulas. A version of Sklar's identity (5.2) also applies to multivariate survival functions of distributions. Let $\boldsymbol{X}$ be a random vector with multivariate survival function $\bar{F}$, marginal dfs $F_1, \dots, F_d$ and marginal survival functions $\bar{F}_1, \dots, \bar{F}_d$, i.e. $\bar{F}_i = 1 - F_i$. We have the identity

$$\bar{F}(x_1, \dots, x_d) = \hat{C}(\bar{F}_1(x_1), \dots, \bar{F}_d(x_d)) \tag{5.13}$$

for a copula $\hat{C}$, which is known as a survival copula. In the case when $F_1, \dots, F_d$ are continuous this identity is easily established by noting that

$$\begin{aligned}\bar{F}(x_1, \dots, x_d) &= P(X_1 > x_1, \dots, X_d > x_d) \\ &= P(1 - F_1(X_1) \leqslant \bar{F}_1(x_1), \dots, 1 - F_d(X_d) \leqslant \bar{F}_d(x_d)),\end{aligned}$$

so (5.13) follows by writing $\hat{C}$ for the distribution function of $\mathbf{1} - \boldsymbol{U}$, where $\boldsymbol{U} := (F_1(X_1), \dots, F_d(X_d))$. In general, the term *survival copula of a copula C* will be used to denote the df of $\mathbf{1} - \boldsymbol{U}$ when $\boldsymbol{U}$ has df C.

Example 5.12 (survival copula of a bivariate Pareto distribution). A well-known generalization of the important univariate Pareto distribution is the bivariate Pareto distribution with survivor function given by

$$\bar{F}(x_1, x_2) = \left(\frac{x_1 + \kappa_1}{\kappa_1} + \frac{x_2 + \kappa_2}{\kappa_2} - 1\right)^{-\alpha}, \quad x_1, x_2 \geqslant 0, \ \alpha, \kappa_1, \kappa_2 > 0.$$

It is easily confirmed that the marginal survivor functions are given by $\bar{F}_i(x) = (\kappa_i/(\kappa_i + x))^\alpha$, $i = 1, 2$, and we then infer from (5.13) that the survival copula is given by $\hat{C}(u_1, u_2) = (u_1^{-1/\alpha} + u_2^{-1/\alpha} - 1)^{-\alpha}$. Comparison with (5.12) reveals that this is the Clayton copula.

The useful concept of *radial symmetry* can be expressed in terms of copulas and survival copulas.

Definition 5.13 (radial symmetry). A random vector $\boldsymbol{X}$ (or its df) is radially symmetric about $\boldsymbol{a}$ if $\boldsymbol{X} - \boldsymbol{a} \stackrel{\mathrm{d}}{=} \boldsymbol{a} - \boldsymbol{X}$.

An elliptical random vector $\boldsymbol{X} \sim E_d(\boldsymbol{\mu}, \Sigma, \psi)$ is obviously radially symmetric about $\boldsymbol{\mu}$. If $\boldsymbol{U}$ has df C, where C is a copula, then the only possible centre of symmetry is $(0.5, \dots, 0.5)$, so C is radially symmetric if

$$(U_1 - 0.5, \dots, U_d - 0.5) \stackrel{\mathrm{d}}{=} (0.5 - U_1, \dots, 0.5 - U_d) \iff \boldsymbol{U} \stackrel{\mathrm{d}}{=} \mathbf{1} - \boldsymbol{U}.$$

Thus if a copula C is radially symmetric and $\hat{C}$ is its survival copula, we have $\hat{C} = C$. It is easily seen that the copulas of elliptical distributions are radially symmetric but the Gumbel and Clayton copulas are not.

Survival copulas should not be confused with the *survival functions* of copulas, which are not themselves copulas. Since copulas are simply multivariate dfs, they have survival or tail functions, which we denote by $\bar{C}$. If $\boldsymbol{U}$ has df C and the survival copula of C is $\hat{C}$, then

$$\begin{aligned}\bar{C}(u_1, \dots, u_d) &= P(U_1 > u_1, \dots, U_d > u_d) \\ &= P(1 - U_1 \leqslant 1 - u_1, \dots, 1 - U_d \leqslant 1 - u_d) \\ &= \hat{C}(1 - u_1, \dots, 1 - u_d).\end{aligned}$$

A useful relationship between a copula and its survival copula in the bivariate case is that

$$\hat{C}(1 - u_1, 1 - u_2) = 1 - u_1 - u_2 + C(u_1, u_2). \tag{5.14}$$

Conditional distributions of copulas. It is often of interest to look at conditional distributions of copulas. We concentrate on two dimensions and suppose that (U_1, U_2) has df C. Since a copula is an increasing continuous function in each argument,

$$C_{U_2|U_1}(u_2 \mid u_1) = P(U_2 \leqslant u_2 \mid U_1 = u_1) = \lim_{\delta \to 0} \frac{C(u_1 + \delta, u_2) - C(u_1, u_2)}{\delta} = \frac{\partial}{\partial u_1} C(u_1, u_2), \tag{5.15}$$

where this partial derivative exists almost everywhere (see Nelsen (1999) for precise details). The conditional distribution is a distribution on the interval [0, 1] which is only a uniform distribution in the case where C is the independence copula. A risk-management interpretation of the conditional distribution is the following. Suppose continuous risks (X_1, X_2) have the (unique) copula C. Then $1 - C_{U_2|U_1}(q \mid p)$ is the probability that X_2 exceeds its qth quantile given that X_1 attains its pth quantile.

Copula densities. Copulas do not always have joint densities; the comonotonicity and countermonotonicity copulas are examples of copulas that are not absolutely continuous. However, the parametric copulas that we have met so far do have densities given by

$$c(u_1, \dots, u_d) = \frac{\partial C(u_1, \dots, u_d)}{\partial u_1 \cdots \partial u_d}, \tag{5.16}$$

and we are sometimes required to calculate them, for example if we wish to fit copulas to data by maximum likelihood.

It is useful to note that, for the implicit copula of an absolutely continuous joint df F with strictly increasing, continuous marginal dfs $F_1, \dots, F_d$, we may differentiate $C(u_1, \dots, u_d) = F(F_1^{\leftarrow}(u_1), \dots, F_d^{\leftarrow}(u_d))$ to see that the copula density is given by

$$c(u_1, \dots, u_d) = \frac{f(F_1^{-1}(u_1), \dots, F_d^{-1}(u_d))}{f_1(F_1^{-1}(u_1)) \cdots f_d(F_d^{-1}(u_d))}, \tag{5.17}$$

where f is the joint density of F, $f_1, \dots, f_d$ are the marginal densities, and $F_1^{-1}, \dots, F_d^{-1}$ are the ordinary inverses of the marginal dfs.

Using this technique we can calculate the densities of the Gaussian and t copulas as shown in Figures 5.5 and 5.6, respectively. Observe that the t copula assigns much more probability mass to the corners of the unit square; this may be explained by the tail dependence of the t copula, as discussed in Section 5.2.3.

Exchangeability.

Definition 5.14 (exchangeability). A random vector $\boldsymbol{X}$ is exchangeable if

$$(X_1, \dots, X_d) \stackrel{\mathrm{d}}{=} (X_{\Pi(1)}, \dots, X_{\Pi(d)})$$

for any permutation $(\Pi(1), \dots, \Pi(d))$ of $(1, \dots, d)$.

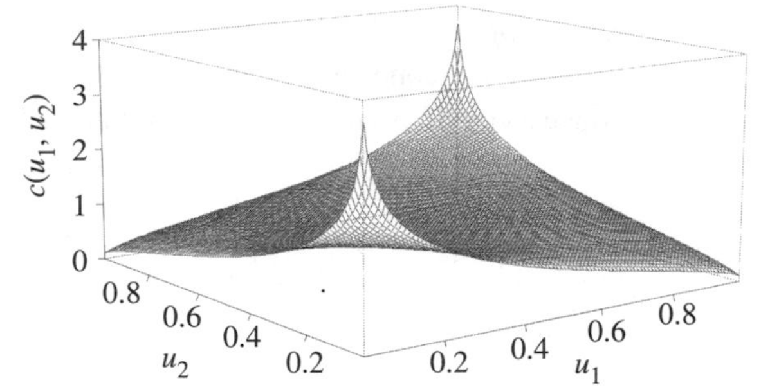

Figure 5.5. Perspective plot of the density of the bivariate Gauss copula with parameter $\rho = 0.3$.

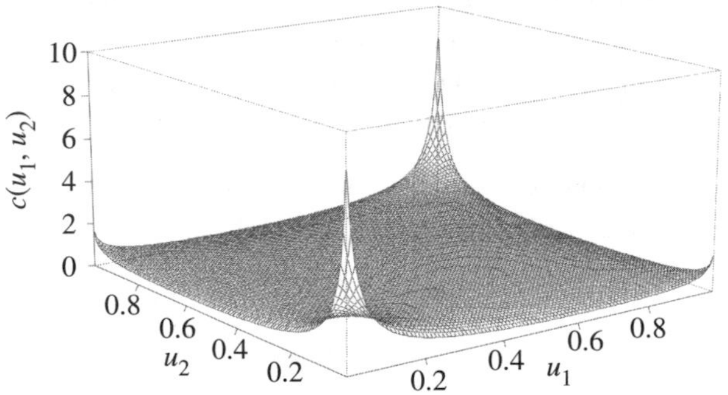

Figure 5.6. Perspective plot of the density of the bivariate t copula with parameters $\nu = 4$ and $\rho = 0.3$.

We will refer to a copula as an *exchangeable* copula if it is the df of an exchangeable random vector of uniform variates $\boldsymbol{U}$. Clearly, for such a copula we must have

$$C(u_1, \dots, u_d) = C(u_{\Pi(1)}, \dots, u_{\Pi(d)}) \tag{5.18}$$

for all possible permutations of the arguments of C. Such copulas will prove useful in modelling the default dependence for homogeneous groups of companies in the context of credit risk.

Examples of exchangeable copulas include both the Gumbel and Clayton copulas as well as the Gaussian and t copulas, C_P^{Ga} and $C_{\nu,P}^t$, in the case that P is an *equicorrelation matrix*, i.e. a matrix of the form $P = \rho J_d + (1 - \rho) I_d$, where J_d is the square matrix consisting entirely of ones and $\rho \geqslant -1/(d-1)$.

It follows from (5.18) and (5.15) that if the df of the vector (U_1, U_2) is an exchangeable bivariate copula, then

$$P(U_2 \leqslant u_2 \mid U_1 = u_1) = P(U_1 \leqslant u_2 \mid U_2 = u_1), \tag{5.19}$$

which implies quite strong symmetry. If a random vector (X_1, X_2) has such a copula, then the probability that X_2 exceeds its u_2-quantile given that X_1 attains its u_1-quantile is exactly the same as the probability that X_1 exceeds its u_2-quantile given that X_2 attains its u_1-quantile. Not all bivariate copulas must satisfy (5.19). For an example of a non-exchangeable bivariate copula see Section 5.4.3 and Figure 5.13.

5.1.6 Perfect Dependence

There are many equivalent ways of defining the concept of comonotonicity. We saw in Section 5.1.2 that continuously distributed rvs which are almost surely strictly increasing functions of one another have as copula the Fréchet upper bound. We will in fact use this copula to give a general definition of comonotonicity for *any* random vector (continuous margins or otherwise), and then look at an equivalent condition.

Definition 5.15 (comonotonicity). The rvs $X_1, \dots, X_d$ are said to be comonotonic if they admit as copula the Fréchet upper bound $M(u_1, \dots, u_d) = \min\{u_1, \dots, u_d\}$.

More insight into this definition is afforded by the following result, which essentially shows that comonotonic rvs are really only functions of a single rv.

Proposition 5.16. *$X_1, \dots, X_d$ are comonotonic if and only if*

$$(X_1, \dots, X_d) \stackrel{\mathrm{d}}{=} (v_1(Z), \dots, v_d(Z)) \tag{5.20}$$

for some rv Z and increasing functions $v_1, \dots, v_d$.

Proof. Assume that $X_1, \dots, X_d$ are comonotonic according to Definition 5.15. Let U be any uniform rv and write $F, F_1, \dots, F_d$ for the joint df and marginal dfs of $X_1, \dots, X_d$, respectively. From (5.2) we have

$$\begin{aligned} F(x_1, \dots, x_d) &= \min\{F_1(x_1), \dots, F_d(x_d)\} \\ &= P(U \leqslant \min\{F_1(x_1), \dots, F_d(x_d)\}) \\ &= P(U \leqslant F_1(x_1), \dots, U \leqslant F_d(x_d)) \\ &= P(F_1^{\leftarrow}(U) \leqslant x_1, \dots, F_d^{\leftarrow}(U) \leqslant x_d) \end{aligned}$$

for any $U \sim U(0, 1)$, where we use Proposition A.3(iv) in the last equality. It follows that

$$(X_1, \dots, X_d) \stackrel{\mathrm{d}}{=} (F_1^{\leftarrow}(U), \dots, F_d^{\leftarrow}(U)), \tag{5.21}$$

which is of the form (5.20). Conversely, if (5.20) holds, then

$$F(x_1, \dots, x_d) = P(v_1(Z) \leqslant x_1, \dots, v_d(Z) \leqslant x_d) = P(Z \in A_1, \dots, Z \in A_d),$$

where each A_i is an interval of the form $(-\infty, k_i]$ or $(-\infty, k_i)$, so one interval A_i is a subset of all other intervals. Therefore,

$$F(x_1, \dots, x_d) = \min\{P(Z \in A_1), \dots, P(Z \in A_d)\} = \min\{F_1(x_1), \dots, F_d(x_d)\},$$

which proves comonotonicity. □

In the case of rvs with continuous marginal distributions we have a simpler and stronger result.

Corollary 5.17. *Let $X_1, \dots, X_d$ be rvs with continuous dfs. They are comonotonic if and only if for every pair (i, j) we have $X_j = T_{ji}(X_i)$ almost surely for some increasing transformation T_{ji}.*

Proof. The result follows from the proof of Proposition 5.16 by noting that the rv U may be taken to be $F_i(X_i)$ for any i. Without loss of generality set $d = 2$ and $i = 1$ and use (5.21) and Proposition A.4 to obtain

$$(X_1, X_2) \stackrel{\mathrm{d}}{=} (F_1^{\leftarrow} \circ F_1(X_1), F_2^{\leftarrow} \circ F_1(X_1)) \stackrel{\mathrm{d}}{=} (X_1, F_2^{\leftarrow} \circ F_1(X_1)).$$

□

An important property of comonotonic risks is that their quantiles are additive and this is demonstrated in Proposition 6.15.

In an analogous way to comonotonicity, we define countermonotonicity as a copula concept, albeit restricted to the case $d = 2$.

Definition 5.18 (countermonotonicity). The rvs X_1 and X_2 are countermonotonic if they have as copula the Fréchet lower bound $W(u_1, u_2) = \max\{u_1 + u_2 - 1, 0\}$.

Proposition 5.19. *X_1 and X_2 are countermonotonic if and only if*

$$(X_1, X_2) \stackrel{\mathrm{d}}{=} (v_1(Z), v_2(Z))$$

for some rv Z with v_1 increasing and v_2 decreasing, or vice versa.

Proof. The proof is similar to that of Proposition 5.16 and is given in Embrechts, McNeil and Straumann (2002). □

Remark 5.20. In the case where X_1 and X_2 are continuous we have the simpler result that countermonotonicity is equivalent to $X_2 = T(X_1)$ almost surely for some decreasing function T.

The concept of countermonotonicity does not generalize to higher dimensions. The Fréchet lower bound $W(u_1, \dots, u_d)$ is not itself a copula for $d > 2$ since it is not a proper distribution function and does not satisfy (5.1), as the following example taken from Nelsen (1999, Exercise 2.35) shows.

Example 5.21 (the Fréchet lower bound is not a copula for $d > 2$). Consider the d-cube $[1/2, 1]^d \subset [0, 1]^d$. If the Fréchet lower bound for copulas were a df on $[0, 1]^d$, then (5.1) implies that the probability mass $P(d)$ of this cube would be given by

$$\begin{aligned} P(d) &= \max(1 + \cdots + 1 - d + 1, 0) - d\max(\tfrac{1}{2} + 1 + \cdots + 1 - d + 1, 0) \\ &\quad + \binom{d}{2}\max(\tfrac{1}{2} + \tfrac{1}{2} + \cdots + 1 - d + 1, 0) - \cdots \\ &\quad + \max(\tfrac{1}{2} + \cdots + \tfrac{1}{2} - d + 1, 0) \\ &= 1 - \tfrac{1}{2}d. \end{aligned}$$

Hence the Fréchet lower bound cannot be a copula for $d > 2$.

Some additional insight into the impossibility of countermonotonicity for dimensions higher than two is given by the following simple example.

Example 5.22. Let X_1 be a positive-valued rv and take $X_2 = 1/X_1$ and $X_3 = \exp(-X_1)$. Clearly, (X_1, X_2) and (X_1, X_3) are countermonotonic random vectors. However, (X_2, X_3) is comonotonic and the copula of the vector (X_1, X_2, X_3) is the df of the vector $(U, 1-U, 1-U)$ which may be calculated to be

$$C(u_1, u_2, u_3) = \max\{\min\{u_2, u_3\} + u_1 - 1, 0\}.$$

Notes and Comments

Sklar's Theorem is first found in Sklar (1959); see also Schweizer and Sklar (1983) for a proof of the result. A systematic development of the theory of copulas, particularly bivariate ones, with many examples is found in Nelsen (1999). Pitfalls related to discontinuity of marginal distributions are presented in Marshall (1996). For extensive lists of parametric copula families see Hutchinson and Lai (1990), Joe (1997) and Nelsen (1999). A recent reference on copula methods in finance is Cherubini, Luciano and Vecchiato (2004).

The concept of comonotonicity or perfect positive dependence is discussed by many authors, including Schmeidler (1986) and Yaari (1987). See also Wang and Dhaene (1998), whose proof we use in Proposition 5.16, and the entry in the *Encyclopedia of Actuarial Science* by Vyncke (2004).

5.2 Dependence Measures

In this section we focus on three kinds of dependence measure: the usual Pearson linear correlation; rank correlation; and the coefficients of tail dependence. All of these dependence measures yield a *scalar measurement* for a pair of rvs (X_1, X_2), although the nature and properties of the measure are different in each case.

Correlation plays a central role in financial theory, but it is important to realize that the concept is only really a natural one in the context of multivariate normal or, more generally, elliptical models. As we have seen, elliptical distributions are fully described by a mean vector, a covariance matrix and a characteristic generator function. Since means and variances are features of marginal distributions, the copulas of elliptical distributions can be thought of as depending only on the correlation matrix and characteristic generator; the correlation matrix thus has a natural parametric role in these models, which it does not have in more general multivariate models. Our discussion of correlation will focus on the shortcomings of correlation and the subtle pitfalls that the naive user of correlation may encounter when moving away from elliptical models. The concept of copulas will help us to illustrate these pitfalls.

The other two kinds of dependence measure—rank correlations and tail-dependence coefficients—are *copula-based* dependence measures. In contrast to ordinary correlation, these measures are functions of the copula only and can thus be used in the parametrization of copulas, as will be seen.

5.2.1 Linear Correlation

The correlation $\rho(X_1, X_2)$ between rvs X_1 and X_2 was defined in (3.3). It is a measure of *linear* dependence and takes values in $[-1, 1]$. If X_1 and X_2 are independent, then $\rho(X_1, X_2) = 0$, but it should be well known to all users of correlation that the converse is false: the uncorrelatedness of X_1 and X_2 does not in general imply their independence. Examples are provided by the class of uncorrelated normal mixture distributions (see Lemma 3.5) and the class of spherical distributions (with the single exception of the multivariate normal).

If $|\rho(X_1, X_2)| = 1$, then this is equivalent to saying that X_2 and X_1 are *perfectly linearly dependent*, meaning that $X_2 = \alpha + \beta X_1$ almost surely for some $\alpha \in \mathbb{R}$ and $\beta \neq 0$, with $\beta > 0$ for positive linear dependence and $\beta < 0$ for negative linear dependence. Moreover, for $\beta_1, \beta_2 > 0$,

$$\rho(\alpha_1 + \beta_1 X_1, \alpha_2 + \beta_2 X_2) = \rho(X_1, X_2),$$

so correlation is invariant under strictly increasing *linear* transformations. However, correlation is *not* invariant under nonlinear strictly increasing transformations $T : \mathbb{R} \to \mathbb{R}$. For two real-valued rvs we have, in general, $\rho(T(X_1), T(X_2)) \neq \rho(X_1, X_2)$.

Another obvious, but important, remark is that correlation is only defined when the variances of X_1 and X_2 are finite. This restriction to finite-variance models is not ideal for a dependence measure and can cause problems when we work with heavy-tailed distributions. For example, actuaries who model losses in different business lines with infinite-variance distributions may not describe the dependence of their risks using correlation. We will encounter similar examples in Section 10.1.4 on operational risk.

Correlation fallacies. We now discuss two further pitfalls in the use of correlation, which we present in the form of fallacies. We believe these fallacies are worth highlighting because they illustrate the dangers of attempting to construct multivariate risk models starting from marginal distributions, and ideas about the correlation between risks. Both of the statements we make are true if we restrict our attention to elliptically distributed risk factors, but are false in general. A third fallacy concerning correlation and VaR is presented later, in Section 6.2.2. For background to these fallacies, alternative examples and a discussion of the relevance to multivariate Monte Carlo simulation, see Embrechts, McNeil and Straumann (2002).

Fallacy 1. The marginal distributions and pairwise correlations of a random vector determine its joint distribution.

It should already be clear to readers of this chapter that this is not true. Figure 5.4 shows the key to constructing counterexamples. Suppose the rvs X_1 and X_2 have continuous marginal distributions F_1 and F_2 and joint df $C(F_1(x_1), F_2(x_2))$ for some copula C and suppose their linear correlation is $\rho(X_1, X_2) = \rho$. It will generally be possible to find an alternative copula $C_2 \neq C$ and to construct a random vector (Y_1, Y_2) with df $C_2(F_1(x_1), F_2(x_2))$ such that $\rho(Y_1, Y_2) = \rho$. The following example illustrates this idea in a case where $\rho = 0$.

Example 5.23. Consider two rvs representing profits and losses on two portfolios. Suppose we are given the information that both risks have standard normal distributions and that their correlation is zero. We construct two random vectors that are consistent with this information.

Model 1 is the standard bivariate normal $\boldsymbol{X} \sim N_2(\mathbf{0}, I_2)$. Model 2 is constructed by taking V to be an independent discrete rv such that $P(V = 1) = P(V = -1) = 0.5$ and setting $(Y_1, Y_2) = (X_1, VX_1)$ with X_1 as in model 1. This model obviously also has normal margins and correlation zero; its copula is given by

$$C(u_1, u_2) = 0.5 \max\{u_1 + u_2 - 1, 0\} + 0.5 \min\{u_1, u_2\},$$

which is a mixture of the two-dimensional Fréchet-bound copulas. This could be roughly interpreted as representing two equiprobable states of the world: in one state financial outcomes in the two portfolios are comonotonic and we are certain to make money in both or lose money in both; in the other state they are countermonotonic and we will make money in one and lose money in the other.

We can calculate analytically the distribution of the total losses $X_1 + X_1$ and $Y_1 + Y_2$; the latter sum does not itself have a univariate normal distribution. For $k \geqslant 0$ we get that

$$P(X_1 + X_2 > k) = \bar{\Phi}(k/\sqrt{2}), \qquad P(Y_1 + Y_2 > k) = \tfrac{1}{2}\bar{\Phi}(\tfrac{1}{2}k),$$

from which it follows that, for $\alpha > 0.75$,

$$F^{\leftarrow}_{X_1+X_2}(\alpha) = \sqrt{2}\Phi^{-1}(\alpha), \qquad F^{\leftarrow}_{Y_1+Y_2}(\alpha) = 2\Phi^{-1}(2\alpha - 1).$$

In Figure 5.7 we see that the quantile of $Y_1 + Y_2$ dominates that of $X_1 + X_2$ for probability levels above 93%. This example also illustrates that the VaR of a sum of risks is clearly not determined by marginal distributions and pairwise correlations. In Section 6.2 we will look at the problem of discovering how "bad" the quantile of the sum of two risks can be when the marginal distributions are known.

The correlation of two risks does not only depend on their copula—if it did, then correlation would be invariant under strictly increasing transformations. Correlation is also inextricably linked to the marginal distributions of the risks and this imposes certain constraints on the values that correlation can take. This is the subject of the second fallacy.

Fallacy 2. For given univariate distributions F_1 and F_2 and any correlation value ρ in $[-1, 1]$ it is always possible to construct a joint distribution F with margins F_1 and F_2 and correlation ρ.

Again, this statement is true if F_1 and F_2 are the margins of an elliptical distribution, but is in general false. The so-called *attainable* correlations can form a strict subset of the interval $[-1, 1]$, as is shown in the next theorem. In the proof of the theorem we require the formula of Höffding, which is given in the next lemma.

Lemma 5.24. *If (X_1, X_2) has joint df F and marginal dfs F_1 and F_2, then the covariance of X_1 and X_2, when finite, is given by*

$$\operatorname{cov}(X_1, X_2) = \int_{-\infty}^{\infty} \int_{-\infty}^{\infty} (F(x_1, x_2) - F_1(x_1)F_2(x_2))\, \mathrm{d}x_1\, \mathrm{d}x_2. \tag{5.22}$$

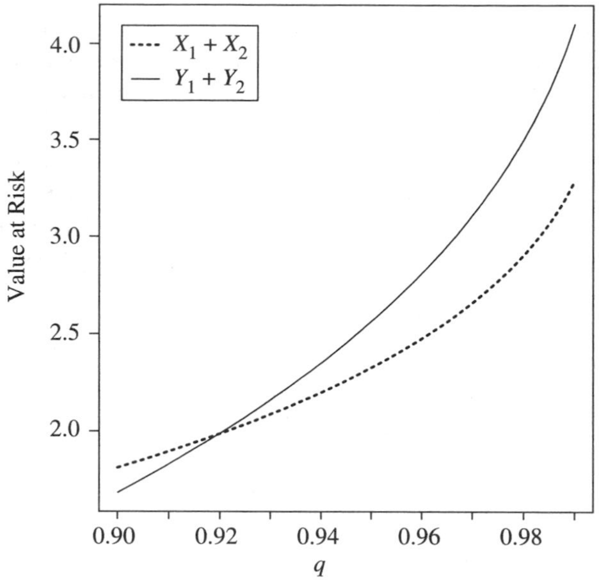

Figure 5.7. VaR for the risks X_1+X_2 and Y_1+Y_2 as described in Example 5.23. Both these pairs have standard normal margins and a correlation of zero; X_1 and X_2 are independent, whereas Y_1 and Y_2 are dependent.

Proof. Let (X_1, X_2) have df F and let $(\tilde{X}_1, \tilde{X}_2)$ be an *independent copy* (i.e. a second pair with df F independent of (X_1, X_2)). We have

$$2\operatorname{cov}(X_1, X_2) = E((X_1 - \tilde{X}_1)(X_2 - \tilde{X}_2)).$$

We now use a useful identity which says that, for any $a \in \mathbb{R}$ and $b \in \mathbb{R}$, we can always write $(a-b) = \int_{-\infty}^{\infty}(I_{\{b\leqslant x\}} - I_{\{a\leqslant x\}})\,\mathrm{d}x$ and apply this to the random pairs $(X_1 - \tilde{X}_1)$ and $(X_2 - \tilde{X}_2)$. We obtain

$$\begin{aligned}
&2\operatorname{cov}(X_1, X_2)\\
&\quad = E\biggl(\int_{-\infty}^{\infty}\int_{-\infty}^{\infty}(I_{\{\tilde{X}_1\leqslant x_1\}} - I_{\{X_1\leqslant x_1\}})(I_{\{\tilde{X}_2\leqslant x_2\}} - I_{\{X_2\leqslant x_2\}})\,\mathrm{d}x_1\,\mathrm{d}x_2\biggr)\\
&\quad = 2\int_{-\infty}^{\infty}\int_{-\infty}^{\infty}(P(X_1\leqslant x_1, X_2\leqslant x_2) - P(X_1\leqslant x_1)P(X_2\leqslant x_2))\,\mathrm{d}x_1\,\mathrm{d}x_2.
\end{aligned}$$

□

Theorem 5.25 (attainable correlations). *Let (X_1, X_2) be a random vector with finite-variance marginal dfs F_1 and F_2 and an unspecified joint df; assume also that* $\operatorname{var}(X_1) > 0$ *and* $\operatorname{var}(X_2) > 0$*. The following statements hold.*

(1) *The attainable correlations form a closed interval $[\rho_{\min}, \rho_{\max}]$ with $\rho_{\min} < 0 < \rho_{\max}$.*

(2) *The minimum correlation $\rho = \rho_{\min}$ is attained if and only if X_1 and X_2 are countermonotonic. The maximum correlation $\rho = \rho_{\max}$ is attained if and only if X_1 and X_2 are comonotonic.*

(3) $\rho_{\min} = -1$ *if and only if* X_1 *and* $-X_2$ *are of the same type (see Section A.1.1), and* $\rho_{\max} = 1$ *if and only if* X_1 *and* X_2 *are of the same type.*

Proof. We begin with (2) and use the identity (5.22). We also recall the two-dimensional Fréchet bounds for a general df in (5.5):

$$\max\{F_1(x_1) + F_2(x_2) - 1, 0\} \leqslant F(x_1, x_2) \leqslant \min\{F_1(x_1), F_2(x_2)\}.$$

Clearly, when F_1 and F_2 are fixed, the integrand in (5.22) is maximized pointwise when X_1 and X_2 have the Fréchet upper bound copula $C(u_1, u_2) = \min\{u_1, u_2\}$, i.e. when they are comonotonic. Similarly, the integrand is minimized when X_1 and X_2 are countermonotonic.

To complete the proof of (1), note that clearly $\rho_{\max} \geqslant 0$. However, $\rho_{\max} = 0$ can be ruled out since this would imply that $\min\{F_1(x_1), F_2(x_2)\} = F_1(x_1)F_2(x_2)$ for all x_1, x_2. This can only occur if F_1 or F_2 is a degenerate distribution consisting of point mass at a single point, but this is excluded by the assumption that variances are non-zero. By a similar argument we have that $\rho_{\min} < 0$. If $W(F_1, F_2)$ and $M(F_1, F_2)$ denote the Fréchet lower and upper bounds, respectively, then the mixture $\lambda W(F_1, F_2) + (1-\lambda)M(F_1, F_2)$, $0 \leqslant \lambda \leqslant 1$, has correlation $\lambda\rho_{\min} + (1-\lambda)\rho_{\max}$. Thus for any $\rho \in [\rho_{\min}, \rho_{\max}]$ we can set $\lambda = (\rho_{\max} - \rho)/(\rho_{\max} - \rho_{\min})$ to construct a joint df that attains the correlation value ρ.

Part (3) is clear since $\rho_{\min} = -1$ or $\rho_{\max} = 1$ if and only if there is an almost sure linear relationship between X_1 and X_2. □

Example 5.26 (attainable correlations for lognormal rvs). An example where the maximal and minimal correlations can be easily calculated occurs when $\ln X_1 \sim N(0, 1)$ and $\ln X_2 \sim N(0, \sigma^2)$. For $\sigma \neq 1$ the lognormally distributed rvs X_1 and X_2 are not of the same type (although $\ln X_1$ and $\ln X_2$ are) so that, by part (3) of Theorem 5.25, we have $\rho_{\max} < 1$. The rvs X_1 and $-X_2$ are also not of the same type, so $\rho_{\min} > -1$.

To calculate the actual boundaries of the attainable interval let $Z \sim N(0, 1)$ and observe that if X_1 and X_2 are comonotonic, then $(X_1, X_2) \stackrel{\mathrm{d}}{=} (\mathrm{e}^Z, \mathrm{e}^{\sigma Z})$. Clearly, $\rho_{\max} = \rho(\mathrm{e}^Z, \mathrm{e}^{\sigma Z})$ and, by a similar argument, $\rho_{\min} = \rho(\mathrm{e}^Z, \mathrm{e}^{-\sigma Z})$. The analytical calculation now follows easily and yields

$$\rho_{\min} = \frac{\mathrm{e}^{-\sigma} - 1}{\sqrt{(\mathrm{e}-1)(\mathrm{e}^{\sigma^2} - 1)}}, \qquad \rho_{\max} = \frac{\mathrm{e}^{\sigma} - 1}{\sqrt{(\mathrm{e}-1)(\mathrm{e}^{\sigma^2} - 1)}}.$$

See Figure 5.8 for an illustration of the attainable correlation interval for different values of σ and note how the boundaries of the interval both tend rapidly to zero as σ is increased. This shows, for example, that we can have situations where comonotonic rvs have very small correlation values. Since comonotonicity is the strongest form of positive dependence, this provides a correction to the widely held view that small correlations imply weak dependence.

A common message can be extracted from both the fallacies of this section: namely that the concept of correlation is meaningless unless applied in the context of a well-defined joint model. Any interpretation of correlation values in the absence of such a model should be avoided.

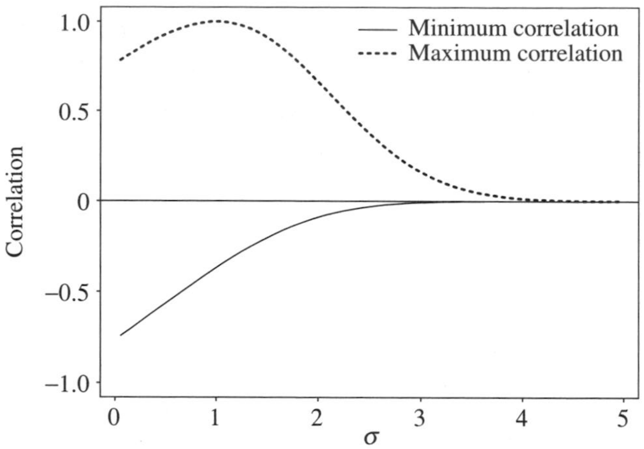

Figure 5.8. Maximum and minimum attainable correlations for lognormal rvs X_1 and X_2, where $\ln(X_1)$ is standard normal and $\ln(X_2)$ is normal with mean zero and variance σ^2.

5.2.2 *Rank Correlation*

Rank correlations are simple scalar measures of dependence that depend only on the copula of a bivariate distribution and not on the marginal distributions, unlike linear correlation, which depends on both. The standard empirical estimators of rank correlation may be calculated by looking at the *ranks* of the data alone, hence the name. In other words, we only need to know the ordering of the sample for each variable of interest and not the actual numerical values.

The main practical reason for looking at rank correlations is that they can be used to calibrate copulas to empirical data. At a theoretical level, being direct functionals of the copula, rank correlations have more appealing properties than linear correlations, as is discussed below. There are two main varieties of rank correlation, Kendall's and Spearman's, which we discuss in turn.

Kendall's tau. Kendall's rank correlations can be understood as a measure of concordance for bivariate random vectors. Two points in $\mathbb{R}^2$, denoted by (x_1, x_2) and $(\tilde{x}_1, \tilde{x}_2)$, are said to be *concordant* if $(x_1 - \tilde{x}_1)(x_2 - \tilde{x}_2) > 0$ and to be *discordant* if $(x_1 - \tilde{x}_1)(x_2 - \tilde{x}_2) < 0$. Now consider a random vector (X_1, X_2) and an independent copy $(\tilde{X}_1, \tilde{X}_2)$ (i.e. a second vector with the same distribution, but independent of the first). If X_2 tends to increase with X_1, then we expect the probability of concordance to be high relative to the probability of discordance; if X_2 tends to decrease with increasing X_1, then we expect the opposite. This motivates Kendall's rank correlation, which is simply the probability of concordance minus the probability of discordance for these pairs:

$$\rho_\tau(X_1, X_2) = P((X_1 - \tilde{X}_1)(X_2 - \tilde{X}_2) > 0) - P((X_1 - \tilde{X}_1)(X_2 - \tilde{X}_2) < 0). \quad (5.23)$$

It is easily seen that there is a more compact way of writing this as an expectation, which also leads to an obvious estimator in Section 5.5.1.

Definition 5.27. For rvs X_1 and X_2 Kendall's tau is given by

$$\rho_\tau(X_1, X_2) = E(\text{sign}((X_1 - \tilde{X}_1)(X_2 - \tilde{X}_2))),$$

where $(\tilde{X}_1, \tilde{X}_2)$ is an independent copy of (X_1, X_2).

In higher dimensions the Kendall's tau matrix of a random vector may be written as $\rho_\tau(\boldsymbol{X}) = \text{cov}(\text{sign}(\boldsymbol{X} - \tilde{\boldsymbol{X}}))$, where $\tilde{\boldsymbol{X}}$ is an independent copy of $\boldsymbol{X}$; since it can be expressed as a covariance matrix, $\rho_\tau(\boldsymbol{X})$ is obviously positive semidefinite.

Spearman's rho. This measure can also be defined in terms of concordance and discordance for random pairs (see Kruskal 1958, p. 824) but the most intuitive definition for our purposes involves copulas.

Definition 5.28. For rvs X_1 and X_2 with marginal dfs F_1 and F_2 Spearman's rho is given by $\rho_S(X_1, X_2) = \rho(F_1(X_1), F_2(X_2))$.

In other words, Spearman's rho is simply the linear correlation of the probability-transformed rvs, which for continuous rvs is the linear correlation of their unique copula. The Spearman's rho matrix for the general multivariate random vector $\boldsymbol{X}$ is given by $\rho_S(\boldsymbol{X}) = \rho(F_1(X_1), \dots, F_d(X_d))$ and must again be positive semidefinite.

Properties of rank correlation. Kendall's tau and Spearman's rho have many properties in common. They are both symmetric dependence measures taking values in the interval $[-1, 1]$. They give the value zero for independent rvs, although a rank correlation of 0 does not necessarily imply independence. It can be shown that they take the value 1 when X_1 and X_2 are comonotonic (see Embrechts, McNeil and Straumann 2002) and the value -1 when they are countermonotonic (which contrasts with the behaviour of linear correlation observed in Theorem 5.25). Now we will show that, for continuous marginal distributions, both rank correlations depend only on the unique copula of the risks and thus inherit its property of invariance under strictly increasing transformations.

Proposition 5.29. *Suppose X_1 and X_2 have continuous marginal distributions and unique copula C. Then the rank correlations are given by*

$$\rho_\tau(X_1, X_2) = 4\int_0^1\int_0^1 C(u_1, u_2)\,\mathrm{d}C(u_1, u_2) - 1, \tag{5.24}$$

$$\rho_S(X_1, X_2) = 12\int_0^1\int_0^1 (C(u_1, u_2) - u_1u_2)\,\mathrm{d}u_1\,\mathrm{d}u_2. \tag{5.25}$$

Proof. It follows easily from (5.23) that we can also write

$$\rho_\tau(X_1, X_2) = 2P((X_1 - \tilde{X}_1)(X_2 - \tilde{X}_2) > 0) - 1,$$

and from the interchangeability of the pairs (X_1, X_2) and $(\tilde{X}_1, \tilde{X}_2)$ we have

$$\begin{aligned}\rho_\tau(X_1, X_2) &= 4P(X_1 < \tilde{X}_1, X_2 < \tilde{X}_2) - 1\\ &= 4E(P(X_1 < \tilde{X}_1, X_2 < \tilde{X}_2 \mid \tilde{X}_1, \tilde{X}_2)) - 1\\ &= 4\int_{-\infty}^{\infty}\int_{-\infty}^{\infty} P(X_1 < x_1, X_2 < x_2)\,\mathrm{d}F(x_1, x_2) - 1. \end{aligned} \tag{5.26}$$

Since X_1 and X_2 have continuous margins, we infer that

$$\rho_\tau(X_1, X_2) = \int_{-\infty}^{\infty}\int_{-\infty}^{\infty} C(F_1(x_1), F_2(x_2))\,\mathrm{d}C(F_1(x_1), F_2(x_2)) - 1,$$

from which (5.24) follows upon substituting $u_1 := F_1(x_1)$ and $u_2 := F_2(x_2)$. For Spearman's rho observe that $\rho_S(X_1, X_2) = 12\operatorname{cov}(F_1(X_1), F_2(X_2))$, since $F_i(X_i)$ has a uniform distribution with variance $\frac{1}{12}$. Formula (5.25) follows upon applying Höffding's formula (5.22). □

To what extent do the two fallacies of linear correlation identified in Section 5.2.1 carry over to rank correlation? Clearly, Fallacy 1 remains relevant: marginal distributions and pairwise rank correlations do not fully determine the joint distribution of a vector of risks. However, Fallacy 2 is essentially taken out of play when we consider rank correlations: for any choice of continuous marginal distributions it is possible to specify a bivariate distribution that has any desired rank correlation value in $[-1, 1]$. One way of doing this is to take a convex combination of the form

$$F(x_1, x_2) = \lambda W(F_1(x_1), F_2(x_2)) + (1 - \lambda)M(F_1(x_1), F_2(x_2)),$$

where W and M are the countermonotonicity and comonotonicity copulas, respectively. A random pair (X_1, X_2) with this df has rank correlation

$$\rho_\tau(X_1, X_2) = \rho_S(X_1, X_2) = (1 - 2\lambda),$$

which yields any desired value in $[-1, 1]$ for an appropriate choice of λ in $[0, 1]$. But this is only one of many possible constructions; a model with the Gauss copula of the form $F(x_1, x_2) = C_\rho^{\mathrm{Ga}}(F_1(x_1), F_2(x_2))$ can also be parametrized by an appropriate choice of $\rho \in [-1, 1]$ to have any rank correlation in $[-1, 1]$. In Section 5.3.2 we will explicitly calculate Spearman's rank correlation coefficients for the Gauss copula, and Kendall's tau values for the Gauss copula and other copulas of normal variance mixture distributions.

5.2.3 Coefficients of Tail Dependence

Like the rank correlations, the coefficients of tail dependence are measures of pairwise dependence that depend only on the copula of a pair of rvs X_1 and X_2 with continuous marginal dfs. The motivation for looking at these coefficients is that they provide measures of *extremal dependence* or, in other words, measures of the strength of dependence in the tails of a bivariate distribution. The coefficients we describe are defined in terms of limiting conditional probabilities of *quantile exceedances*. We note that there are a number of other definitions of tail-dependence measures in the literature (see Notes and Comments).

In the case of upper tail dependence we look at the probability that X_2 exceeds its q-quantile, given that X_1 exceeds its q-quantile, and then consider the limit as q goes to infinity. Obviously the roles of X_1 and X_2 are interchangeable. Formally we have the following.

Definition 5.30. Let X_1 and X_2 be rvs with dfs F_1 and F_2. The coefficient of upper tail dependence of X_1 and X_2 is

$$\lambda_u := \lambda_u(X_1, X_2) = \lim_{q \to 1^-} P(X_2 > F_2^{\leftarrow}(q) \mid X_1 > F_1^{\leftarrow}(q)),$$

provided a limit $\lambda_u \in [0, 1]$ exists. If $\lambda_u \in (0, 1]$, then X_1 and X_2 are said to show upper tail dependence or extremal dependence in the upper tail; if $\lambda_u = 0$, they are *asymptotically independent* in the upper tail. Analogously, the coefficient of lower tail dependence is

$$\lambda_l := \lambda_l(X_1, X_2) = \lim_{q \to 0^+} P(X_2 \leqslant F_2^{\leftarrow}(q) \mid X_1 \leqslant F_1^{\leftarrow}(q)),$$

provided a limit $\lambda_l \in [0, 1]$ exists.

If F_1 and F_2 are continuous dfs, then we get simple expressions for λ_l and λ_u in terms of the unique copula C of the bivariate distribution. Using elementary conditional probability and (5.3) we have

$$\begin{aligned} \lambda_l &= \lim_{q \to 0^+} \frac{P(X_2 \leqslant F_2^{\leftarrow}(q), X_1 \leqslant F_1^{\leftarrow}(q))}{P(X_1 \leqslant F_1^{\leftarrow}(q))} \\ &= \lim_{q \to 0^+} \frac{C(q, q)}{q}. \end{aligned} \tag{5.27}$$

For upper tail dependence we use (5.13) to obtain

$$\lambda_u = \lim_{q \to 1^-} \frac{\hat{C}(1-q, 1-q)}{1-q} = \lim_{q \to 0^+} \frac{\hat{C}(q, q)}{q}, \tag{5.28}$$

where $\hat{C}$ is the survival copula of C (see (5.14)). For radially symmetric copulas we must have $\lambda_l = \lambda_u$, since $C = \hat{C}$ for such copulas.

Calculation of these coefficients is straightforward if the copula in question has a simple closed form, as is the case for the Gumbel copula in (5.11) and the Clayton copula in (5.12). In Section 5.3.1 we will use a slightly more involved method to calculate tail-dependence coefficients for copulas of normal variance mixture distributions, such as the Gaussian and t copulas.

Example 5.31 (Gumbel and Clayton copulas). Writing $\hat{C}_\theta^{\mathrm{Gu}}$ for the Gumbel survival copula we first use (5.14) to infer that

$$\lambda_u = \lim_{q \to 1^-} \frac{\hat{C}_\theta^{\mathrm{Gu}}(1-q, 1-q)}{1-q} = 2 - \lim_{q \to 1^-} \frac{C_\theta^{\mathrm{Gu}}(q, q) - 1}{q - 1}.$$

We now use L'Hôpital's rule and the fact that $C_\theta^{\mathrm{Gu}}(u, u) = u^{2^{1/\theta}}$ to infer that

$$\lambda_u = 2 - \lim_{q \to 1^-} \frac{\mathrm{d}C_\theta^{\mathrm{Gu}}(q, q)}{\mathrm{d}q} = 2 - 2^{1/\theta}.$$

Provided that $\theta > 1$, the Gumbel copula has upper tail dependence. The strength of this tail dependence tends to 1 as $\theta \to \infty$, which is to be expected since the Gumbel copula tends to the comonotonicity copula as $\theta \to \infty$. Using a similar technique the coefficient of lower tail dependence for the Clayton copula may be shown to be $\lambda_l = 2^{-1/\theta}$ for $\theta > 0$.

The consequences of the lower tail dependence of the Clayton copula and the upper tail dependence of the Gumbel copula can be seen in Figures 5.3 and 5.4, where there is obviously an increased tendency for these copulas to generate joint extreme values in the respective corners. In Section 5.3.1 we will see that the Gauss copula is asymptotically independent in both tails, while the t copula has both upper and lower tail dependence of the same magnitude (due to its radial symmetry).

Notes and Comments

The discussion of correlation fallacies is based on Embrechts, McNeil and Straumann (2002), which contains a number of other examples illustrating these pitfalls. For Höffding's formula and its use in proving the bounds on attainable correlations see Höffding (1940), Fréchet (1951) and Shea (1983).

Useful references for rank correlations are Kruskal (1958) and Joag-Dev (1984). The relationship between rank correlation and copulas is discussed in Schweizer and Wolff (1981) and Nelsen (1999). The definition of tail dependence that we use stems from Joe (1993, 1997). There are a number of alternative definitions of tail-dependence measures, as discussed, for example, in Coles, Heffernan and Tawn (1999).

5.3 Normal Mixture Copulas

A unique copula is contained in every multivariate distribution with continuous marginal distributions, and a useful class of parametric copulas are those contained in the multivariate normal mixture distributions of Section 3.2. We view these copulas as particularly important in market risk applications; indeed, in most cases, these copulas are used implicitly, without the user necessarily recognizing the fact. Whenever normal mixture distributions are fitted to multivariate return data or used as innovation distributions in multivariate time series models, normal mixture copulas are used. They are also found in a number of credit risk models, both implicitly and explicitly; an example is Li's model in Example 8.7.

In this section we first focus on normal variance mixture copulas; in Section 5.3.1 we examine their tail-dependence properties; and in Section 5.3.2 we calculate rank correlation coefficients, which are useful for calibrating these copulas to data. Then, in Sections 5.3.3 and 5.3.4, we look at more exotic examples of copulas arising from multivariate normal mixture constructions.

5.3.1 Tail Dependence

Coefficients of tail dependence. Consider a pair of uniform rvs (U_1, U_2) whose distribution $C(u_1, u_2)$ is a normal variance mixture copula. Due to the radial symmetry of C (see Section 5.1.5), it suffices to consider the formula for the lower tail-dependence coefficient in (5.27) to calculate the coefficient of tail dependence λ of C. By applying L'Hôpital's rule and using (5.15) we obtain

$$\lambda = \lim_{q \to 0^+} \frac{\mathrm{d}C(q,q)}{\mathrm{d}q} = \lim_{q \to 0^+} P(U_2 \leqslant q \mid U_1 = q) + \lim_{q \to 0^+} P(U_1 \leqslant q \mid U_2 = q).$$

Since C is *exchangeable* we have from (5.19) that

$$\lambda = 2 \lim_{q \to 0+} P(U_2 \leqslant q \mid U_1 = q). \tag{5.29}$$

We now show the interesting contrast between the Gaussian and t copulas that we alluded to in Example 5.11, namely that the t copula has tail dependence, whereas the Gauss copula is asymptotically independent in the tail.

Example 5.32 (asymptotic independence of the Gauss copula). To evaluate the tail-dependence coefficient for the Gauss copula C_{ρ}^{Ga}, let $(X_1, X_2) := (\Phi^{-1}(U_1), \Phi^{-1}(U_2))$, so that (X_1, X_2) has a bivariate normal distribution with standard margins and correlation ρ. It follows from (5.29) that

$$\begin{aligned}\lambda &= 2 \lim_{q \to 0+} P(\Phi^{-1}(U_2) \leqslant \Phi^{-1}(q) \mid \Phi^{-1}(U_1) = \Phi^{-1}(q)) \\ &= 2 \lim_{x \to -\infty} P(X_2 \leqslant x \mid X_1 = x).\end{aligned}$$

Using the fact that $X_2 \mid X_1 = x \sim N(\rho x, 1 - \rho^2)$, it can be calculated that

$$\lambda = 2 \lim_{x \to -\infty} \Phi(x\sqrt{1-\rho}/\sqrt{1+\rho}) = 0,$$

provided $\rho < 1$. Hence, the Gauss copula is asymptotically independent in both tails. Regardless of how high a correlation we choose, if we go far enough into the tail, extreme events appear to occur independently in each margin.

Example 5.33 (asymptotic dependence of the t copula). To evaluate the tail-dependence coefficient for the t copula $C_{\nu,\rho}^{t}$, let $(X_1, X_2) := (t_{\nu}^{-1}(U_1), t_{\nu}^{-1}(U_2))$, where t_ν denotes the df of a univariate t distribution with ν degrees of freedom. Thus $(X_1, X_2) \sim t_2(\nu, \mathbf{0}, P)$, where P is a correlation matrix with off-diagonal element ρ. By calculating the conditional density from the joint and marginal densities of a bivariate t distribution, it may be verified that, conditional on $X_1 = x$,

$$\left(\frac{\nu+1}{\nu+x^2}\right)^{1/2} \frac{X_2 - \rho x}{\sqrt{1-\rho^2}} \sim t_{\nu+1}. \tag{5.30}$$

Using an argument similar to Example 5.32 we find that

$$\lambda = 2t_{\nu+1}\left(-\sqrt{\frac{(\nu+1)(1-\rho)}{1+\rho}}\right). \tag{5.31}$$

Provided that $\rho > -1$, the copula of the bivariate t distribution is asymptotically dependent in both the upper and lower tail.

In Table 5.1 we tabulate the coefficient of tail dependence for various values of ν and ρ. For fixed ρ the strength of the tail dependence increases as ν decreases and for fixed ν tail dependence increases as ρ increases. Even for zero or negative correlation values there is some tail dependence. This is not too surprising and can be grasped intuitively by recalling from Section 3.2.1 that the t distribution is a normal mixture distribution with a mixing variable W whose distribution is inverse gamma (which is a heavy-tailed distribution): if $|X_1|$ is large, there is a good chance that this is because W is large, increasing the probability of $|X_2|$ being large.

Table 5.1. Values of λ, the coefficient of upper and lower tail dependence, for the t copula $C^t_{\nu,\rho}$ for various values of ν, the degrees of freedom, and ρ, the correlation. The last row represents the Gauss copula.

	ρ				
ν	−0.5	0	0.5	0.9	1
2	0.06	0.18	0.39	0.72	1
4	0.01	0.08	0.25	0.63	1
10	0.00	0.01	0.08	0.46	1
∞	0	0	0	0	1

We could use the same method used in the previous examples to calculate tail-dependence coefficients for other copulas of normal variance mixtures. In doing so we would find that most examples, such as copulas of symmetric hyperbolic or NIG distributions, fell into the same category as the Gauss copula and were asymptotically independent in the tails. The essential determinant of whether the copula of a normal variance mixture has tail dependence or not is the tail of the distribution of the mixing variable W in Definition 3.4. If W has a distribution with a power tail, then we get tail dependence, otherwise we get asymptotic independence. This is a consequence of a general result for elliptical distributions given in Section 7.3.3.

Joint quantile exceedance probabilities. Coefficients of tail dependence are of course asymptotic quantities, and in the remainder of this section we look at joint exceedances of *finite high quantiles* for the Gauss and t copulas in order to learn more about the practical consequences of the differences between the extremal behaviours of these two models.

As motivation we consider Figure 5.9, where 5000 simulated points from four different distributions are displayed. The distributions in (a) and (b) are meta-Gaussian distributions (see Section 5.1.3); they share the same copula C^{Ga}_{ρ}. The distributions in (c) and (d) are meta-t distributions; they share the same copula $C^t_{\nu,\rho}$. The values of ν and ρ in all parts are 4 and 0.5, respectively. The distributions in (a) and (c) share the same margins, namely standard normal margins. The distributions in (b) and (d) both have Student t margins with four degrees of freedom. The distributions in (a) and (d) are, of course, elliptical, being a standard bivariate normal and a bivariate t distribution with four degrees of freedom; they both have linear correlation $\rho = 0.5$. The other distributions are not elliptical and do not necessarily have linear correlation 50%, since altering the margins alters the linear correlation. All four distributions have identical Kendall's tau values (see Proposition 5.37). The meta-Gaussian distributions have the same Spearman's rho value, as do the meta-t distributions, although the two values are not identical (see Section 5.3.2).

The vertical and horizontal lines mark the true theoretical 0.005 and 0.995 quantiles for all distributions. Note that for the meta-t distributions the number of points that lie below both 0.005 quantiles or exceed both 0.995 quantiles is clearly greater

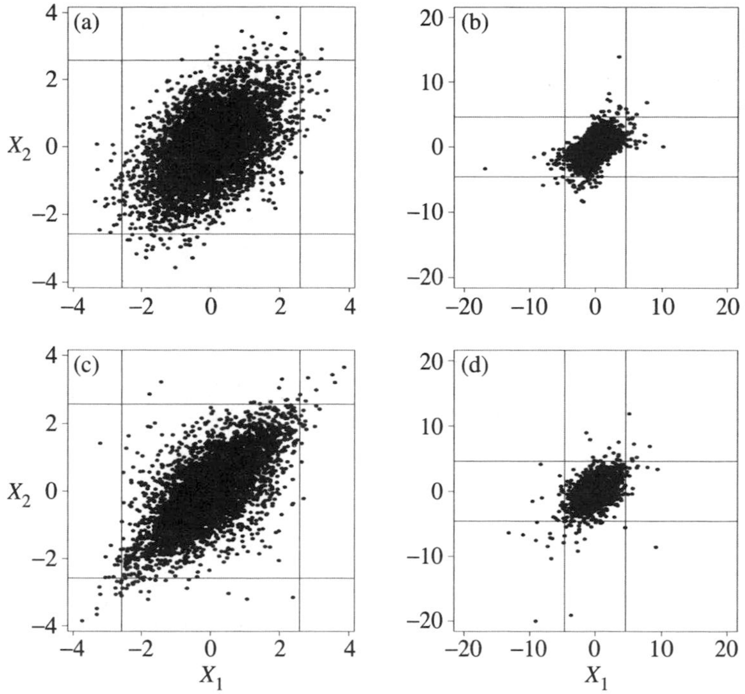

Figure 5.9. Five thousand simulated points from four distributions. (a) Standard bivariate normal with correlation parameter $\rho = 0.5$. (b) Meta-Gaussian distribution with copula C_ρ^{Ga} and Student t margins with four degrees of freedom. (c) Meta-t distribution with copula $C_{4,\rho}^t$ and standard normal margins. (d) Standard bivariate t distribution with four degrees of freedom and correlation parameter $\rho = 0.5$. Horizontal and vertical lines mark the 0.005 and 0.995 quantiles. See Section 5.3.1 for a commentary.

than for the meta-Gaussian distributions, and this can be explained by the tail dependence of the t copula. The true theoretical ratio by which the number of these joint exceedances in the meta-t models should exceed the number in the meta-Gaussian models is 2.79, as may be read from Table 5.2, whose interpretation we now discuss.

In Table 5.2 we have calculated values of $C_\rho^{\mathrm{Ga}}(u, u)/C_{\nu,\rho}^t(u, u)$ for various ρ and ν and $u = 0.05, 0.01, 0.005, 0.001$. The rows marked Gauss contain values of $C_\rho^{\mathrm{Ga}}(u, u)$, which is the probability that two rvs with this copula are below their u-quantiles; we term this event a joint quantile exceedance (thinking of exceedance in the downwards direction). Obviously it is identical to the probability that both rvs are larger than their $(1 - u)$-quantiles. The remaining rows give the values of the ratio and thus express the amount by which the joint quantile exceedance probabilities must be inflated when we move from models with a Gauss copula to models with a t copula.

In Table 5.3 we extend Table 5.2 to higher dimensions. We now focus only on joint exceedances of the 1% (or 99%) quantile(s). We tabulate values of the ratio $C_P^{\mathrm{Ga}}(u, \dots, u)/C_{\nu,P}^t(u, \dots, u)$, where P is an equicorrelation matrix with all correlations equal to ρ. It is noticeable that not only do these values grow as the corre-

Table 5.2. Joint quantile exceedance probabilities for bivariate Gauss and t copulas with correlation parameter values of 0.5 and 0.7. For Gauss copulas the probability of joint quantile exceedance is given; for the t copulas the factors by which the Gaussian probability must be multiplied are given.

			Quantile			
ρ	Copula	ν	0.05	0.01	0.005	0.001
0.5	Gauss		1.21×10^{-2}	1.29×10^{-3}	4.96×10^{-4}	5.42×10^{-5}
0.5	t	8	1.20	1.65	1.94	3.01
0.5	t	4	1.39	2.22	2.79	4.86
0.5	t	3	1.50	2.55	3.26	5.83
0.7	Gauss		1.95×10^{-2}	2.67×10^{-3}	1.14×10^{-3}	1.60×10^{-4}
0.7	t	8	1.11	1.33	1.46	1.86
0.7	t	4	1.21	1.60	1.82	2.52
0.7	t	3	1.27	1.74	2.01	2.83

Table 5.3. Joint 1% quantile exceedance probabilities for multivariate Gaussian and t equicorrelation copulas with correlation parameter values of 0.5 and 0.7. For Gauss copulas the probability of joint quantile exceedance is given; for the t copulas the factors by which the Gaussian probability must be multiplied are given.

			Dimension d			
ρ	Copula	ν	2	3	4	5
0.5	Gauss		1.29×10^{-3}	3.66×10^{-4}	1.49×10^{-4}	7.48×10^{-5}
0.5	t	8	1.65	2.36	3.09	3.82
0.5	t	4	2.22	3.82	5.66	7.68
0.5	t	3	2.55	4.72	7.35	10.34
0.7	Gauss		2.67×10^{-3}	1.28×10^{-3}	7.77×10^{-4}	5.35×10^{-4}
0.7	t	8	1.33	1.58	1.78	1.95
0.7	t	4	1.60	2.10	2.53	2.91
0.7	t	3	1.74	2.39	2.97	3.45

lation parameter or number of degrees of freedom falls, but they also grow with the dimension of the copula. The next example gives an interpretation of one of these numbers.

Example 5.34 (joint quantile exceedances: an interpretation). Consider daily returns on five stocks. Suppose we are unsure about the best multivariate elliptical model for these data returns, but we believe that the correlation between any two returns on the same day is 50%. If returns follow a multivariate Gaussian distribution, then the probability that on any day all returns are below the 1% quantiles of their respective distributions is 7.48×10^{-5}. In the long run such an event will happen once every 13 369 trading days on average, that is roughly once every 51.4 years (assuming 260 trading days in a year). On the other hand, if returns follow a multivariate t distribution with four degrees of freedom, then such an event will happen

7.68 times more often, that is roughly once every 6.7 years. In the life of a risk manager, 50-year events and 7-year events have a very different significance.

5.3.2 Rank Correlations

To calculate rank correlations for normal variance mixture copulas we use the following preliminary result for elliptical distributions.

Proposition 5.35. *Let $X \sim E_2(\mathbf{0}, \Sigma, \psi)$ and $\rho = \wp(\Sigma)_{12}$, where $\wp$ denotes the correlation operator in (3.5). Assume $P(X = \mathbf{0}) = 0$. Then*

$$P(X_1 > 0, X_2 > 0) = \tfrac{1}{4} + \frac{\arcsin \rho}{2\pi}.$$

Proof. First we make a standardization of the variables and observe that if $Y \sim E_2(0, P, \psi)$ and $P = \wp(\Sigma)$, then $P(X_1 > 0, X_2 > 0) = P(Y_1 > 0, Y_2 > 0)$. Now introduce a pair of spherical variates $Z \sim S_2(\psi)$; it follows that

$$\begin{aligned}(Y_1, Y_2) &\stackrel{\mathrm{d}}{=} (Z_1, \rho Z_1 + \sqrt{1-\rho^2} Z_2) \\ &\stackrel{\mathrm{d}}{=} R(\cos\Theta, \rho\cos\Theta + \sqrt{1-\rho^2}\sin\Theta),\end{aligned}$$

where R is a positive radial rv and Θ is an independent, uniformly distributed angle on $[-\pi, \pi)$ (see Section 3.3.1 and Theorem 3.22). Let $\phi = \arcsin \rho$ and observe that $\sin\phi = \rho$ and $\cos\phi = \sqrt{1-\rho^2}$. Since $P(R = 0) = P(X = \mathbf{0}) = 0$ we conclude that

$$\begin{aligned}P(X_1 > 0, X_2 > 0) &= P(\cos\Theta > 0, \sin\phi\cos\Theta + \cos\phi\sin\Theta > 0) \\ &= P(\cos\Theta > 0, \sin(\Theta + \phi) > 0).\end{aligned}$$

The angle Θ must jointly satisfy $\Theta \in (-\frac{1}{2}\pi, \frac{1}{2}\pi)$ and $\Theta + \phi \in (0, \pi)$ and it is easily seen that for any value of ϕ this has probability $(\frac{1}{2}\pi + \phi)/(2\pi)$, which gives the result. □

Theorem 5.36 (rank correlations for Gauss copula). *Let X have a bivariate meta-Gaussian distribution with copula C_ρ^{Ga} and continuous margins. Then the rank correlations are*

$$\rho_\tau(X_1, X_2) = \frac{2}{\pi}\arcsin\rho, \tag{5.32}$$

$$\rho_S(X_1, X_2) = \frac{6}{\pi}\arcsin\tfrac{1}{2}\rho. \tag{5.33}$$

Proof. Since rank correlation is a copula property we can of course simply assume that $X \sim N_2(\mathbf{0}, P)$, where P is a correlation matrix with off-diagonal element ρ; the calculations are then easy. For Kendall's tau, formula (5.26) implies

$$\rho_\tau(X_1, X_2) = 4P(Y_1 > 0, Y_2 > 0) - 1,$$

where $Y = \tilde{X} - X$ and $\tilde{X}$ is an independent copy of X. Since $Y \sim N_2(\mathbf{0}, 2P)$, by the convolution property of multivariate normal in Section 3.1.3, we have that

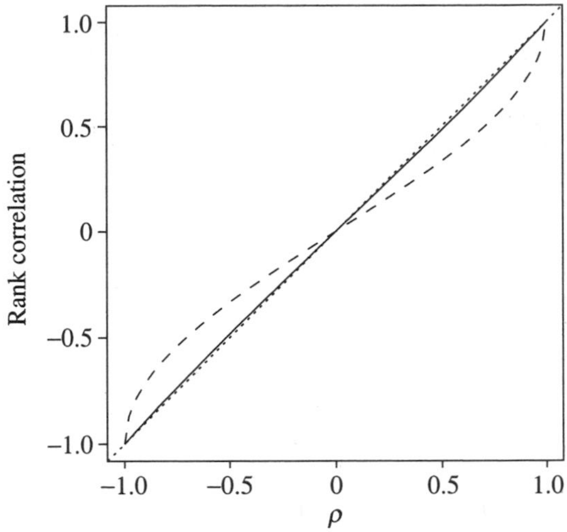

Figure 5.10. The solid line shows the relationship between Spearman's rho and the correlation parameter ρ of the Gauss copula C_ρ^{Ga} for meta-Gaussian rvs with continuous dfs; this is very close to the line $y = x$, which is just visible as a dotted line. The dashed line shows the relationship between Kendall's tau and ρ; this relationship holds for the copulas of other normal variance mixture distributions with correlation parameter ρ, such as the t copula $C_{\nu,\rho}^t$.

$\rho(Y_1, Y_2) = \rho$ and formula (5.32) follows from Proposition 5.35. For Spearman's rho we observe that (5.25) implies

$$\begin{aligned}\rho_S(X_1, X_2) &= 12 \int_0^1 \int_0^1 P(\Phi(X_1) \leqslant u_1, \Phi(X_2) \leqslant u_2)\,\mathrm{d}u_1\,\mathrm{d}u_2 - 3 \\ &= 3\biggl(4 \int_0^1 \int_0^1 P(X_1 \leqslant \Phi^{-1}(u_1), X_2 \leqslant \Phi^{-1}(u_2))\,\mathrm{d}u_1\,\mathrm{d}u_2 - 1\biggr) \\ &= 3\biggl(4 \int_{-\infty}^{\infty} \int_{-\infty}^{\infty} P(X_1 \leqslant x_1, X_2 \leqslant x_1)\phi(x_1)\phi(x_2)\,\mathrm{d}x_1\,\mathrm{d}x_2 - 1\biggr),\end{aligned}$$

where $x_i := \Phi^{-1}(u_i)$ and ϕ is the standard normal density. Now let Z_1 and Z_2 denote two standard normal variates, independent of $\boldsymbol{X}$ and of each other. We see that

$$\begin{aligned}\rho_S(X_1, X_2) &= 3(4E(P(X_1 < Z_1, X_2 < Z_2 \mid Z_1, Z_2)) - 1) \\ &= 3(4P(X_1 < Z_1, X_2 < Z_2) - 1) \\ &= 3(4P(Y_1 > 0, Y_2 > 0) - 1),\end{aligned}$$

where $\boldsymbol{Y} = \boldsymbol{Z} - \boldsymbol{X}$. Since $\boldsymbol{Y} \sim N_2(\boldsymbol{0}, (P + I_2))$, the formula (5.33) follows from Proposition 5.35. □

These relationships between the rank correlations and ρ are illustrated in Figure 5.10. Note that the right-hand side of (5.33) may be approximated by the value ρ itself. This approximation turns out to be very accurate, as shown in the figure; the error bounds are $|6 \arcsin(\rho/2)/\pi - \rho| \leqslant (\pi - 3)|\rho|/\pi \leqslant 0.0181$.

The relationship between Kendall's tau and the correlation parameter of the Gauss copula C^{Ga}_{ρ} expressed by (5.32) holds more generally for the copulas of essentially all normal variance mixture distributions, such as the t copula $C^t_{\nu,\rho}$. This is implied by the following general result for elliptical distributions, which was used to derive an alternative correlation estimator for bivariate distributions in Section 3.3.4.

Proposition 5.37. *Let* $X \sim E_2(\mathbf{0}, P, \psi)$ *for a correlation matrix* P *with off-diagonal element* ρ, *and assume that* $P(X = \mathbf{0}) = 0$. *Then the relationship* $\rho_\tau(X_1, X_2) = (2/\pi)\arcsin\rho$ *holds.*

Proof. The result relies on the convolution property of elliptical distributions in (3.54). Setting $Y = \tilde{X} - X$, where $\tilde{X}$ is an independent copy of X, we note that $Y \sim E_2(\mathbf{0}, P, \tilde{\psi})$ for some characteristic generator $\tilde{\psi}$. We need to evaluate $\rho_\tau(X_1, X_2) = 4P(Y_1 > 0, Y_2 > 0) - 1$ as in the proof of Theorem 5.36, but Proposition 5.35 shows that $P(Y_1 > 0, Y_2 > 0)$ takes the same value whenever Y is elliptical. □

Remark 5.38. The relationship (5.33) between Spearman's rho and linear correlation does not hold for all elliptical distributions. A counterexample is found in Hult and Lindskog (2002). Simple formulas for elliptical distributions other than the Gaussian, such as the multivariate t, are not known to us.

5.3.3 Skewed Normal Mixture Copulas

A skewed normal mixture copula is the copula of any normal mixture distribution that is not elliptically symmetric. An example is provided by the *skewed t copula*, which is the copula of the distribution whose density is given in (3.32).

A random vector X with a skewed t distribution and ν degrees of freedom is denoted $X \sim \mathrm{GH}_d(-\frac{1}{2}\nu, \nu, 0, \boldsymbol{\mu}, \Sigma, \boldsymbol{\gamma})$ in the notation of Section 3.2.3. Its marginal distributions satisfy $X_i \sim \mathrm{GH}_1(-\frac{1}{2}\nu, \nu, 0, \mu_i, \Sigma_{ii}, \gamma_i)$ (from Proposition 3.13) and its copula depends on ν, $P = \wp(\Sigma)$ and $\boldsymbol{\gamma}$ and will be denoted by $C^t_{\nu,P,\boldsymbol{\gamma}}$ or, in the bivariate case, $C^t_{\nu,\rho,\gamma_1,\gamma_2}$. Random sampling from the skewed t copula follows the same approach as for the t copula in Algorithm 5.10.

Algorithm 5.39 (simulation of skewed t copula).

(1) Generate $X \sim \mathrm{GH}_d(-\frac{1}{2}\nu, \nu, 0, \mathbf{0}, P, \boldsymbol{\gamma})$ using Algorithm 3.10.

(2) Return $U = (F_1(X_1), \dots, F_d(X_d))'$, where F_i is the distribution function of a $\mathrm{GH}_1(-\frac{1}{2}\nu, \nu, 0, 0, 1, \gamma_i)$ distribution. The random vector U has df $C^t_{\nu,P,\boldsymbol{\gamma}}$.

Note that the evaluation of F_i requires the numerical integration of the density of a skewed univariate t density.

To appreciate the flexibility of the skewed t copula it suffices to consider the bivariate case for different values of the skewness parameters γ_1 and γ_2. In Figure 5.11 we have plotted simulated points from nine different examples of this copula. Part (e) corresponds to the case when $\gamma_1 = \gamma_2 = 0$ and is thus the ordinary t copula. All other pictures show copulas which are non-radially symmetric (see

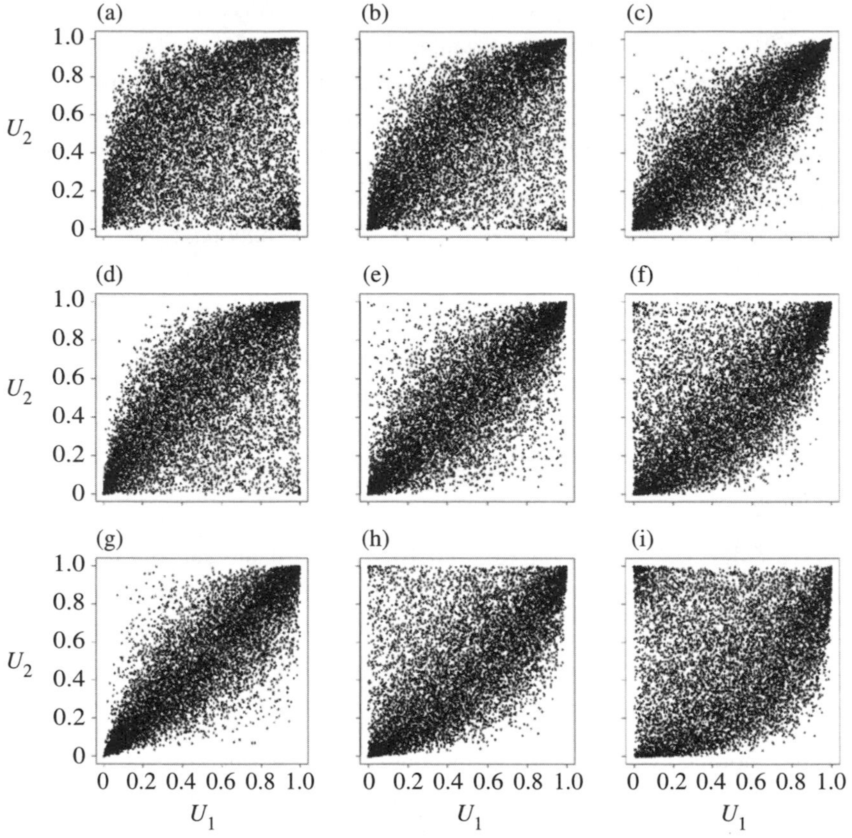

Figure 5.11. Ten thousand simulated points from bivariate skewed t copula $C^t_{\nu,\rho,\gamma_1,\gamma_2}$ for $\nu = 5$, $\rho = 0.8$ and various values of the parameters (γ_1, γ_2): (a) $\gamma = (0.8, -0.8)$; (b) $\gamma = (0.8, 0)$; (c) $\gamma = (0.8, 0.8)$; (d) $\gamma = (0, -0.8)$; (e) $\gamma = (0, 0)$; (f) $\gamma = (0, 0.8)$; (g) $\gamma = (-0.8, -0.8)$; (h) $\gamma = (-0.8, 0)$; and (i) $\gamma = (-0.8, 0.8)$.

Section 5.1.5), as is obvious by rotating each picture 180° about the point $(\frac{1}{2}, \frac{1}{2})$; (c), (e) and (g) show exchangeable copulas satisfying (5.18), while the remaining six are non-exchangeable.

Obviously the main advantage of the skewed t copula over the ordinary t copula is that its asymmetry allows us to have different levels of tail dependence in "opposite corners" of the distribution. In the context of market risk it is often claimed that joint negative returns on stocks show more tail dependence than joint positive returns.

5.3.4 Grouped Normal Mixture Copulas

Technically speaking, a grouped normal mixture copula is not itself the copula of a normal mixture distribution, but rather a way of attaching together a set of normal mixture copulas. We will illustrate the idea by considering the *grouped t copula*. Here, the basic idea is to construct a copula for a random vector $\boldsymbol{X}$ such that certain subvectors of $\boldsymbol{X}$ have t copulas but quite different levels of tail dependence.

We create a distribution using a generalization of the variance-mixing construction $X = \sqrt{W}Z$ in (3.19). Rather than multiplying all components of a correlated Gaussian vector Z with the root of a single inverse-gamma-distributed variate W, as in Example 3.7, we instead multiply different subgroups with different variates W_j, where $W_j \sim \text{Ig}(\frac{1}{2}\nu_j, \frac{1}{2}\nu_j)$ and the W_j are themselves comonotonic (see Section 5.1.6). Thus we create subgroups whose dependence properties are described by t copulas with different ν_j parameters.

Like the t copula, the skewed t copula and anything based on a mixture of multivariate normals, a grouped t copula is easy to simulate and thus to use in Monte Carlo risk studies—this has been a major motivation for its development. We formally define the grouped t copula by explaining in more detail how to generate a random vector U with that distribution.

Algorithm 5.40 (simulation of grouped t copula).

(1) Generate independently $Z \sim N_d(\mathbf{0}, P)$ and $U \sim U(0, 1)$.

(2) Partition $\{1, \dots, d\}$ into m subsets of sizes $s_1, \dots, s_m$, and for $k = 1, \dots, m$ let ν_k be the degrees-of-freedom parameter associated with group k.

(3) Set $W_k = G_{\nu_k}^{-1}(U)$, where G_ν is the df of the univariate $\text{Ig}(\frac{1}{2}\nu, \frac{1}{2}\nu)$ distribution, so that $W_1, \dots, W_m$ are comonotonic and inverse-gamma-distributed variates.

(4) Construct vectors X and U by

$$X = (\sqrt{W_1}Z_1, \dots, \sqrt{W_1}Z_{s_1}, \sqrt{W_2}Z_{s_1+1}, \dots, \sqrt{W_2}Z_{s_1+s_2}, \dots, \sqrt{W_m}Z_d)',$$
$$U = (t_{\nu_1}(X_1), \dots, t_{\nu_1}(X_{s_1}), t_{\nu_2}(X_{s_1+1}), \dots, t_{\nu_2}(X_{s_1+s_2}), \dots, t_{\nu_m}(X_d))'.$$

The former has a grouped t distribution and the latter is distributed according to a grouped t copula.

If we have an *a priori* idea of the desired group structure, we can calibrate the grouped t copula to data using a method based on Kendall's tau rank correlations. The use of this method for the ordinary t copula is described later in Section 5.5.1 and Example 5.54.

Notes and Comments

The coefficient of tail dependence for the t copula was first derived in Embrechts, McNeil and Straumann (2002). A more general result for the copulas of elliptical distributions is given in Hult and Lindskog (2002) and will be discussed in Section 7.3.3. The formula for Kendall's tau for elliptical distributions can be found in Lindskog, McNeil and Schmock (2003) and Fang and Fang (2002).

The skewed t copula was introduced in Demarta and McNeil (2005), which also describes the grouped t copula. The grouped t copula and a method for its calibration was first proposed in Daul et al. (2003).

Table 5.4. Table summarizing the generators, permissible parameter values and limiting special cases for four selected Archimedean copulas. The case $\theta = 0$ should be taken to mean the limit $\lim_{\theta\to 0}\phi_\theta(t)$. For the Clayton and Frank copulas this limit is $-\ln t$, which is the generator of the independence copula.

Copula	Generator $\phi(t)$	Parameter range	Strict	Lower	Upper
C_θ^{Gu}	$(-\ln t)^\theta$	$\theta \geqslant 1$	Yes	Π	M
C_θ^{Cl}	$\frac{1}{\theta}(t^{-\theta}-1)$	$\theta \geqslant -1$	$\theta \geqslant 0$	W	M
C_θ^{Fr}	$-\ln\left(\frac{\mathrm{e}^{-\theta t}-1}{\mathrm{e}^{-\theta}-1}\right)$	$\theta \in \mathbb{R}$	Yes	W	M
$C_{\theta,\delta}^{\mathrm{GC}}$	$\theta^{-\delta}(t^{-\theta}-1)^\delta$	$\theta \geqslant 0, \delta \geqslant 1$	Yes	N/A	N/A

5.4 Archimedean Copulas

The Gumbel copula (5.11) and the Clayton copula (5.12) belong to the family of so-called Archimedean copulas, which has been very extensively studied. This family has proved useful for modelling portfolio credit risk, as will be seen in Example 8.9. In this section we look at the simple structure of these copulas and establish some of the properties that we will need.

5.4.1 Bivariate Archimedean Copulas

As well as the Gumbel and Clayton copulas, two further examples we consider are the *Frank copula*

$$C_\theta^{\mathrm{Fr}}(u_1,u_2) = -\frac{1}{\theta}\ln\left(1+\frac{(\exp(-\theta u_1)-1)(\exp(-\theta u_2)-1)}{\exp(-\theta)-1}\right), \quad \theta \in \mathbb{R},$$

and a two-parameter copula that we refer to as a *generalized Clayton copula*:

$$C_{\theta,\delta}^{\mathrm{GC}}(u_1,u_2) = \{((u_1^{-\theta}-1)^\delta + (u_2^{-\theta}-1)^\delta)^{1/\delta}+1\}^{-1/\theta}, \quad \theta \geqslant 0,\ \delta \geqslant 1.$$

It may be verified that, provided the parameter θ lies in the ranges we have specified in the copula definitions, all four examples that we have met have the form

$$C(u_1,u_2) = \phi^{-1}(\phi(u_1)+\phi(u_2)), \tag{5.34}$$

where ϕ is a decreasing function from $[0,1]$ to $[0,\infty]$, satisfying $\phi(0)=\infty$, $\phi(1)=0$, known as the *generator* of the copula, and ϕ^{-1} is its inverse. For example, for the Gumbel copula $\phi(t) = (-\ln t)^\theta$ for $\theta \geqslant 1$, and for the other copulas the generators $\phi(t)$ are given in Table 5.4.

When we introduced the Clayton copula in (5.12) we insisted that its parameter should be positive. Note that it is in fact possible to have a Clayton copula with $-1 \leqslant \theta < 0$, although in this case the construction (5.34) must be generalized slightly. Suppose, for example, that $\theta = -\frac{1}{2}$; the Clayton copula generator $\phi(t) = \theta^{-1}(t^{-\theta}-1)$ is then a strictly decreasing function mapping $[0,1]$ into $[0,2]$. If we attempt to evaluate (5.34) in, say, the point $u_1 = u_2 = 0.16$, we have a problem since $\phi(u_1)+\phi(u_2) = 2.4$ and $\phi^{-1}(2.4)$ is undefined.

To obtain a copula in a case when $\phi(0) < \infty$ we introduce a so-called pseudo-inverse of the generator and give a theorem that explains exactly when a construction resembling (5.34) yields a copula.

Definition 5.41 (pseudo-inverse). Suppose $\phi : [0, 1] \to [0, \infty]$ is continuous and strictly decreasing with $\phi(1) = 0$ and $\phi(0) \leqslant \infty$. We define a pseudo-inverse of ϕ with domain $[0, \infty]$ by

$$\phi^{[-1]}(t) = \begin{cases} \phi^{-1}(t), & 0 \leqslant t \leqslant \phi(0), \\ 0, & \phi(0) < t \leqslant \infty. \end{cases} \tag{5.35}$$

Theorem 5.42 (bivariate Archimedean copula). *Let $\phi : [0, 1] \to [0, \infty]$ be continuous and strictly decreasing with $\phi(1) = 0$ and $\phi^{[-1]}(t)$ as in (5.35). Then*

$$C(u_1, u_2) = \phi^{[-1]}(\phi(u_1) + \phi(u_2)) \tag{5.36}$$

is a copula if and only if ϕ is convex.

Proof. See Nelsen (1999, pp. 91, 92). □

All copulas constructed according to (5.36) are called bivariate Archimedean copulas. If $\phi(0) = \infty$ the generator is said to be *strict* and we may replace the pseudo-inverse $\phi^{[-1]}$ by the ordinary functional inverse ϕ^{-1} as in (5.34). In summary we have the following.

Definition 5.43 (Archimedean copula generator). A continuous, strictly decreasing, convex function $\phi : [0, 1] \to [0, \infty]$ satisfying $\phi(1) = 0$ is known as an Archimedean copula generator. It is known as a strict generator if $\phi(0) = \infty$.

In Table 5.4 we indicate when the generators of the four Archimedean copulas are strict and give the lower and upper limits of the families as the parameter θ goes to the boundaries of the parameter space. Both the Frank and Clayton copulas are known as *comprehensive* copulas, since they interpolate between a lower limit of countermonotonicity and an upper limit of comonotonicity. For a more extensive table of Archimedean copulas see Nelsen (1999).

Remark 5.44. Consider again the Clayton copula with $\theta = -\frac{1}{2}$ and non-strict generator $\phi(t) = -2(\sqrt{t} - 1)$. The copula may be written as $C(u_1, u_2) = \max\{(u_1^{0.5} + u_2^{0.5} - 1)^2, 0\}$ and this "maximum-with-zero" notation is the common way of writing Archimedean copulas with non-strict generators. The countermonotonicity copula is a further example; it is an Archimedean copula with non-strict generator $\phi(t) = 1 - t$.

Kendall's rank correlations can be calculated for Archimedean copulas directly from the generator using Proposition 5.45 below. The formula obtained can be used to calibrate Archimedean copulas to empirical data using the sample version of Kendall's tau, as we discuss in Section 5.5.

Table 5.5. Kendall's rank correlations and coefficients of tail dependence for the copulas of Table 5.4. $D_1(\theta)$ is the Debye function $D_1(\theta) = \theta^{-1} \int_0^\theta t/(\exp(t) - 1)\,\mathrm{d}t$.

Copula	ρ_τ	λ_u	λ_l
C_θ^{Gu}	$1 - 1/\theta$	$2 - 2^{1/\theta}$	0
C_θ^{Cl}	$\theta/(\theta + 2)$	0	$\begin{cases} 2^{-1/\theta}, & \theta > 0, \\ 0, & \theta \leqslant 0, \end{cases}$
C_θ^{Fr}	$1 - 4\theta^{-1}(1 - D_1(\theta))$	0	0
$C_{\theta,\delta}^{\mathrm{GC}}$	$\dfrac{(2+\theta)\delta - 2}{(2+\theta)\delta}$	$2 - 2^{1/\delta}$	$2^{-1/(\theta\delta)}$

Proposition 5.45. *Let X_1 and X_2 be continuous rvs with unique Archimedean copula C generated by ϕ. Then*

$$\rho_\tau(X_1, X_2) = 1 + 4 \int_0^1 \frac{\phi(t)}{\phi'(t)}\,\mathrm{d}t. \tag{5.37}$$

Proof. See Nelsen (1999, p. 130). □

For the closed-form copulas of the Archimedean class, coefficients of tail dependence are easily calculated using methods of the kind used in Example 5.31. Values for Kendall's tau and the coefficients of tail dependence for the copulas of Table 5.4 are given in Table 5.5. It is interesting to note that the generalized Clayton copula $C_{\theta,\delta}^{\mathrm{GC}}$ subsumes, in a sense, both Gumbel's family and the strict part of Clayton's family, and thus succeeds in having tail dependence in both tails.

5.4.2 *Multivariate Archimedean Copulas*

It seems natural to attempt to construct a higher-dimensional Archimedean copula according to $C(u_1, \dots, u_d) = \phi^{[-1]}(\phi(u_1) + \cdots + \phi(u_d))$. However, this construction may fail to define a proper distribution function for arbitrary dimension d. An example where this occurs is obtained if we take the generator $\phi(t) = 1 - t$, which is not strict. In this case we obtain the Fréchet lower bound for copulas, which is not itself a copula for $d > 2$.

A necessary condition for the d-dimensional construction to succeed in all dimensions is that ϕ should be a strict Archimedean copula generator, although this is not sufficient. It was shown by Kimberling (1974) that if $\phi : [0, 1] \to [0, \infty]$ is a strict Archimedean copula generator, then

$$C(u_1, \dots, u_d) = \phi^{-1}(\phi(u_1) + \cdots + \phi(u_d)) \tag{5.38}$$

gives a copula in any dimension d if and only if the generator inverse $\phi^{-1} : [0, \infty] \to [0, 1]$ is *completely monotonic*. A decreasing function $f(t)$ is completely monotonic on an interval $[a, b]$ if it satisfies

$$(-1)^k \frac{\mathrm{d}^k}{\mathrm{d}t^k} f(t) \geqslant 0, \quad k \in \mathbb{N},\ t \in (a, b). \tag{5.39}$$

All of the generators in Table 5.4 have inverses which are completely monotonic on $[0, \infty]$ (if we restrict to $\theta \geqslant 0$ for the Clayton copula) and all extend to arbitrary dimensions using the construction (5.38). For example, a d-dimensional Clayton copula is

$$C^{\mathrm{Cl}}_{\theta,\delta}(\boldsymbol{u}) = (u_1^{-\theta} + \cdots + u_d^{-\theta} - d + 1)^{-1/\theta}, \quad \theta \geqslant 0, \tag{5.40}$$

where the limiting case $\theta = 0$ should be interpreted as the d-dimensional independence copula.

Another way of describing these Archimedean copulas which extend to arbitrary dimensions is in terms of Laplace–Stieltjes transforms of dfs on $\mathbb{R}^+$, since every completely monotonic function mapping from $[0, \infty]$ to $[0, 1]$ can be expressed in terms of such transforms. Let G be a df on $\mathbb{R}^+$ satisfying $G(0) = 0$ with Laplace–Stieltjes transform

$$\hat{G}(t) = \int_0^\infty \mathrm{e}^{-tx} \, \mathrm{d}G(x), \quad t \geqslant 0. \tag{5.41}$$

If we define $\hat{G}(\infty) := 0$, it is not difficult to verify that $\hat{G} : [0, \infty] \to [0, 1]$ is a continuous, strictly decreasing, function with the property of complete monotonicity (5.39). It therefore provides a candidate for an Archimedean generator inverse.

In the following result we show how Laplace–Stieltjes transforms are used to construct random vectors whose distributions are multivariate Archimedean copulas. In so doing, we also reveal how such copulas may be simulated.

Proposition 5.46. *Let G be a df on $\mathbb{R}^+$ satisfying $G(0) = 0$ with Laplace–Stieltjes transform $\hat{G}$ as in (5.41) and set $\hat{G}(\infty) := 0$. Let V be an rv with df G and let $U_1, \dots, U_d$ be a sequence of rvs that are conditionally independent given V with conditional distribution function given by $F_{U_i \mid V}(u \mid v) = \exp(-v\hat{G}^{-1}(u))$ for $u \in [0, 1]$. Then*

$$P(U_1 \leqslant u_1, \dots, U_d \leqslant u_d) = \hat{G}(\hat{G}^{-1}(u_1) + \cdots + \hat{G}^{-1}(u_d)), \tag{5.42}$$

so that the df of $\boldsymbol{U} = (U_1, \dots, U_d)'$ is an Archimedean copula with generator $\phi = \hat{G}^{-1}$.

Proof. We have

$$\begin{aligned} P(U_1 \leqslant u_1, \dots, U_d \leqslant u_d) &= \int_0^\infty P(U_1 \leqslant u_1, \dots, U_d \leqslant u_d \mid V = v) \, \mathrm{d}G(v) \\ &= \int_0^\infty \prod_{i=1}^d F_{U_i \mid V}(u_i \mid v) \, \mathrm{d}G(v) \\ &= \int_0^\infty \exp(-x(\hat{G}^{-1}(u_1) + \cdots + \hat{G}^{-1}(u_d))) \, \mathrm{d}G(v) \\ &= \hat{G}(\hat{G}^{-1}(u_1) + \cdots + \hat{G}^{-1}(u_d)). \end{aligned}$$

□

Because of the importance of such copulas, particularly in the field of credit risk, we will call these copulas LT-Archimedean (LT stands for "Laplace transform") and make the following definition.

Definition 5.47 (LT-Archimedean copula). An LT-Archimedean copula is a copula of the form (5.38), where ϕ is the inverse of the Laplace–Stieltjes transform of a df G on $\mathbb{R}^+$ satisfying $G(0) = 0$.

In the following algorithm we explain how to sample from such copulas using Proposition 5.46 and give explicit instructions for the Clayton, Gumbel and Frank copulas.

Algorithm 5.48 (simulation of LT-Archimedean copulas).

(1) Generate a variate V with df G such that $\hat{G}$, the Laplace–Stieltjes transform of G, is the inverse of the generator ϕ of the required copula.

(2) Generate independent uniform variates $X_1, \dots, X_d$.

(3) Return $\boldsymbol{U} = (\hat{G}(-\ln(X_1)/V), \dots, \hat{G}(-\ln(X_d)/V))'$.

(a) For the special case of the Clayton copula we generate a gamma variate $V \sim \text{Ga}(1/\theta, 1)$ with $\theta > 0$ (see Section A.2.4). The df of V has Laplace transform $\hat{G}(t) = (1 + t)^{-1/\theta}$. Note that the inverse $\hat{G}^{-1}(t) = t^{-\theta} - 1$ differs from the generator in Table 5.4 by a constant factor that is unimportant.

(b) For the special case of the Gumbel copula we generate a positive stable variate $V \sim \text{St}(1/\theta, 1, \gamma, 0)$, where $\gamma = (\cos(\pi/(2\theta)))^{\theta}$ and $\theta > 1$ (see Section A.2.9 for more details and a reference to a simulation algorithm). This df has Laplace transform $\hat{G}(t) = \exp(-t^{1/\theta})$ as desired.

(c) For the special case of the Frank copula we generate a discrete rv V with probability mass function $p(k) = P(V = k) = (1 - \exp(-\theta))^k/(k\theta)$ for $k = 1, 2, \dots$ and $\theta > 0$. This can be achieved by standard simulation methods for discrete distributions (see Ripley 1987, p. 71).

See Figure 5.12 for an example of data simulated from a four-dimensional Gumbel copula using this algorithm. Note the upper tail dependence in each bivariate margin of this copula.

5.4.3 *Non-exchangeable Archimedean Copulas*

A copula obtained from construction (5.38) is obviously an *exchangeable* copula conforming to (5.18). While exchangeable bivariate Archimedean copulas are widely used in modelling applications, their exchangeable multivariate extensions represent a very specialized form of dependence structure and have more limited applications. An exception to this is in the area of credit risk, as will be seen in Chapter 8, although even here more general models with group structures are also needed. It is certainly natural to enquire whether there are extensions to the Archimedean class that are not rigidly exchangeable, and we devote this section to a short discussion of some possible extensions.

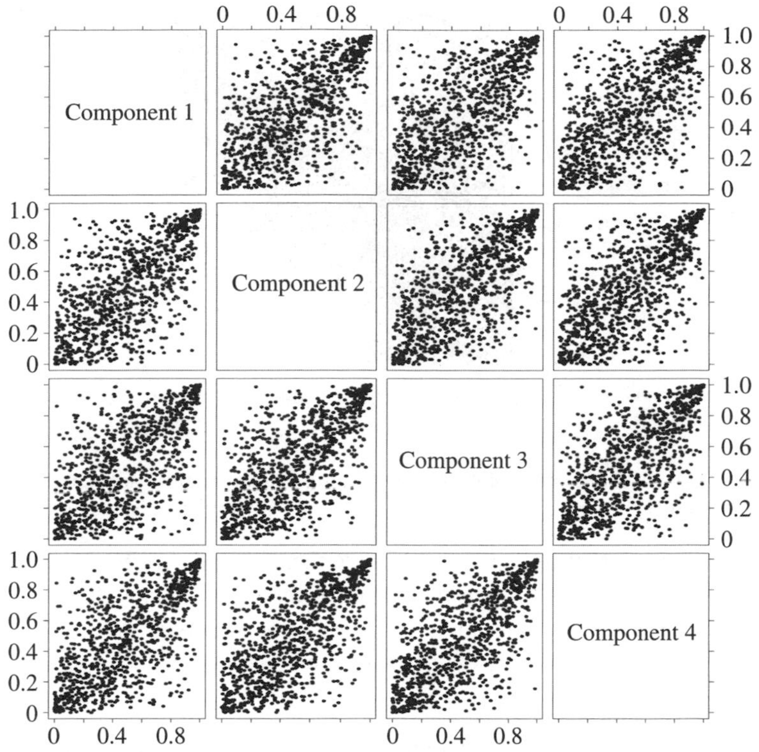

Figure 5.12. Pairwise scatterplots of 1000 simulated points from a four-dimensional exchangeable Gumbel copula with $\theta = 2$. Data are simulated using Algorithm 5.48.

Asymmetric bivariate copulas. Let C_θ be any exchangeable bivariate copula. Then a parametric family of asymmetric copulas $C_{\theta,\alpha,\beta}$ is obtained by setting

$$C_{\theta,\alpha,\beta}(u_1, u_2) = u_1^{1-\alpha} u_2^{1-\beta} C_\theta(u_1^\alpha, u_2^\beta), \quad 0 \leqslant u_1, u_2 \leqslant 1, \tag{5.43}$$

where $0 \leqslant \alpha, \beta \leqslant 1$. Only in the special case $\alpha = \beta$ is the copula (5.43) exchangeable. Note also that when both parameters are zero, $C_{\theta,0,0}$ is the independence copula, and when both parameters are one, $C_{\theta,1,1}$ is simply C_θ. When C_θ is an Archimedean copula, we refer to copulas constructed by (5.43) as asymmetric bivariate Archimedean copulas.

We check that (5.43) defines a copula by constructing a random vector with this df and observing that its margins are standard uniform. Since the construction of a random vector amounts to a simulation recipe, we present it as such.

Algorithm 5.49 (asymmetric bivariate Archimedean copula).

(1) Generate a random pair (V_1, V_2) with df C_θ.

(2) Generate, independently of V_1, V_2, two independent standard uniform variates $\tilde{U}_1$ and $\tilde{U}_2$.

(3) Return $U_1 = \max\{V_1^{1/\alpha}, \tilde{U}_1^{1/(1-\alpha)}\}$ and $U_2 = \max\{V_2^{1/\beta}, \tilde{U}_2^{1/(1-\beta)}\}$.

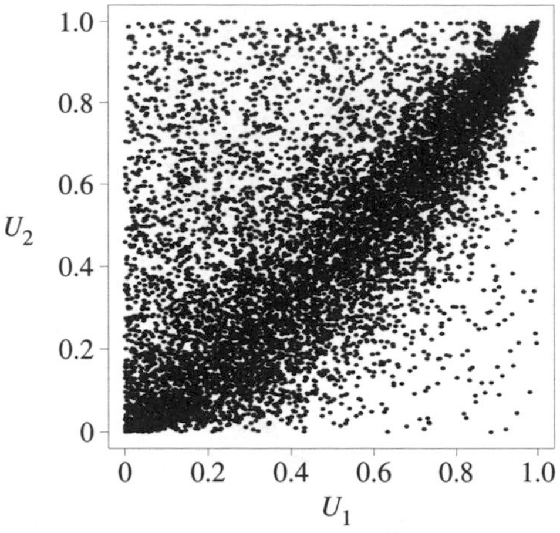

Figure 5.13. Pairwise scatterplots of 10 000 simulated points from an extension of the Gumbel copula C_4^{Gu} given by $C_{4,0.95,0.7}$ in (5.43). This is simulated using Algorithm 5.49.

It may be easily verified that (U_1, U_2) have the df (5.43). See Figure 5.13 for an example of simulated data from an asymmetric copula based on Gumbel's copula. Note that an alternative copula may be constructed by taking (V_1, V_2) in Algorithm 5.49 to be distributed according to some copula other than the independence copula.

Non-exchangeable, higher-dimensional Archimedean copulas. Non-exchangeable, higher-dimensional Archimedean copulas with exchangeable bivariate margins can be constructed by recursive application of Archimedean generators and their inverses, and we will give examples in this section. The biggest problem with these constructions lies in checking that they lead to valid multivariate distributions satisfying (5.1). The necessary theory is complicated and we will simply indicate the nature of the conditions that are necessary without providing justification; a comprehensive reference is Joe (1997). It turns out that with some care we can construct situations of *partial exchangeability*. We give three- and four-dimensional examples which indicate the pattern of construction.

Example 5.50 (three-dimensional non-exchangeable Archimedean copulas). Suppose that ϕ_1 and ϕ_2 are two strict Archimedean generators and consider

$$C(u_1, u_2, u_3) = \phi_2^{-1}(\phi_2 \circ \phi_1^{-1}(\phi_1(u_1) + \phi_1(u_2)) + \phi_2(u_3)). \tag{5.44}$$

Conditions that ensure that this is a copula are that the generator inverses ϕ_1^{-1} and ϕ_2^{-1} are completely monotonic decreasing functions, as in (5.39), and the composition $\phi_2 \circ \phi_1^{-1} : [0, \infty] \to [0, \infty]$ is a completely monotonic increasing function, i.e. a function g satisfying

$$(-1)^{k-1} \frac{\mathrm{d}^k}{\mathrm{d}t^k} g(t) \geqslant 0, \quad k \in \mathbb{N}.$$

Observe that when $\phi_2 = \phi_1 = \phi$ we are back in the situation of full exchangeability, as in (5.38). Otherwise, if $\phi_1 \neq \phi_2$ and (U_1, U_2, U_3) is a random vector with df given by (5.44), then only U_1 and U_2 are exchangeable, i.e. $(U_1, U_2, U_3) \stackrel{\mathrm{d}}{=} (U_2, U_1, U_3)$, but no other swapping of subscripts is possible. All bivariate margins of (5.44) are themselves Archimedean copulas. The margins C_{13} and C_{23} have generator ϕ_2 and C_{12} has generator ϕ_1.

Example 5.51 (four-dimensional non-exchangeable Archimedean copulas). A possible four-dimensional construction is

$$C(u_1, u_2, u_3, u_4) = \phi_3^{-1}(\phi_3 \circ \phi_1^{-1}(\phi_1(u_1) + \phi_1(u_2)) + \phi_3 \circ \phi_2^{-1}(\phi_2(u_3) + \phi_2(u_4))), \tag{5.45}$$

where ϕ_1, ϕ_2 and ϕ_3 are three distinct, strict Archimedean generators and we assume that their inverses and the composite functions $\phi_3 \circ \phi_1^{-1}$ and $\phi_3 \circ \phi_2^{-1}$ are completely monotonic to obtain a proper distribution function. This is not the only possible four-dimensional construction (Joe 1997), but it is a useful construction because it gives two exchangeable groups. If (U_1, U_2, U_3, U_4) has the df (5.45), then U_1 and U_2 are exchangeable, as are U_3 and U_4.

The same kinds of construction can be extended to higher dimensions, subject again to complete monotonicity conditions on the compositions of generators and generator inverses.

LT-Archimedean copulas with p-factor structure. Recall from Definition 5.47 the family of LT-Archimedean copulas. It follows easily from (5.42) that these have the form

$$C(u_1, \dots, u_d) = E\biggl(\exp\biggl(-V \sum_{i=1}^{d} \hat{G}^{-1}(u_i)\biggr)\biggr) \tag{5.46}$$

for strictly positive rvs V with Laplace–Stieltjes transform $\hat{G}$. It is possible to generalize the construction (5.46) to obtain a larger family of non-exchangeable copulas, which will be useful in the context of dynamic credit risk models (see Section 9.7). An LT-Archimedean copula with p-factor structure is constructed from a p-dimensional random vector $\boldsymbol{V} = (V_1, \dots, V_p)'$ with independent, strictly positive components and a matrix $A \in \mathbb{R}^{d \times p}$ with elements $a_{ij} > 0$ as follows:

$$C(u_1, \dots, u_d) = E\biggl(\exp\biggl(-\sum_{i=1}^{d} \boldsymbol{a}_i' \boldsymbol{V} \hat{G}_i^{-1}(u_i)\biggr)\biggr), \tag{5.47}$$

where $\boldsymbol{a}_i$ is the ith row of A and $\hat{G}_i^{-1}$ is the Laplace–Stieltjes transform of the strictly positive rv $\boldsymbol{a}_i' \boldsymbol{V}$.

We can write (5.47) in a different way, which facilitates the computation of $C(u_1, \dots, u_d)$. Note that

$$\sum_{i=1}^{d} \boldsymbol{a}_i' \boldsymbol{V} \hat{G}_i^{-1}(u_i) = \sum_{j=1}^{p} V_j \sum_{i=1}^{d} a_{ij} \hat{G}_i^{-1}(u_i).$$

It follows from the independence of the V_j that

$$C(u_1, \dots, u_d) = \prod_{j=1}^{p} E\biggl(\exp\biggl(-V_j \sum_{i=1}^{d} a_{ij}\hat{G}_i^{-1}(u_i)\biggr)\biggr)$$
$$= \prod_{j=1}^{p} \hat{G}_{V_j}\biggl(\sum_{i=1}^{d} a_{ij}\hat{G}_i^{-1}(u_i)\biggr). \tag{5.48}$$

Note that (5.48) is easy to evaluate when $\hat{G}_{V_j}$, the Laplace–Stieltjes transform of the V_j, is available in closed form, because $\hat{G}_i(t) = \prod_{j=1}^{p} \hat{G}_{V_j}(a_{ij}t)$ by the independence of the V_j.

Notes and Comments

The name *Archimedean* relates to an algebraic property of the copulas which resembles the Archimedean axiom for real numbers (see Nelsen 1999, p. 98). Clayton's copula was introduced in Clayton (1978), although it has also been called the Cook and Johnson copula (see Genest and MacKay 1986) and the Pareto copula (see Hutchinson and Lai 1990). For Frank's copula see Frank (1979); this copula has radial symmetry and is the only such Archimedean copula.

Theorem 5.42 is a result of Alsina, Frank and Schweizer (2005). The formula for Kendall's tau in the Archimedean family is due to Genest and MacKay (1986). The link between completely monotonic functions and generators which give Archimedean copulas of the form (5.38) is found in Kimberling (1974). See also Feller (1971) for more on the concept of complete monotonicity. For more on the important connection between Archimedean generators and Laplace transforms, see Joe (1997). For a single reference containing most of the main theory for bivariate Archimedean copulas and some of the results on higher-dimensional exchangeable Archimedean copulas consult Nelsen (1999).

Proposition 5.46 and Algorithm 5.48 are due to Marshall and Olkin (1988). See Frees and Valdez (1997), Schönbucher (2002), Frey and McNeil (2003) and Chapters 8 and 9 of this book for further discussion of this technique.

For more details on the asymmetric bivariate copulas obtained from construction (5.43) and ideas for more general asymmetric copulas see Genest, Ghoudi and Rivest (1998). These copula classes were introduced in the PhD thesis of Khoudraji (1995). For additional theory concerning partially exchangeable higher-dimensional Archimedean copulas with exchangeable bivariate margins, see Joe (1997). LT-Archimedean copulas with p-factor structure have been proposed by Rogge and Schönbucher (2003) with applications in credit risk in mind.

Other copula families we have not considered include the Marshall–Olkin copulas (Marshall and Olkin 1967a,b) and the extremal copulas in Tiit (1996).

5.5 Fitting Copulas to Data

We assume that we have data vectors $\boldsymbol{X}_1, \dots, \boldsymbol{X}_n$ with identical distribution function F, describing financial losses or financial risk factor returns; we write

$\boldsymbol{X}_t = (X_{t,1}, \dots, X_{t,d})'$ for an individual data vector and $\boldsymbol{X} = (X_1, \dots, X_d)'$ for a generic random vector with df F. We assume further that this df F has continuous margins $F_1, \dots, F_d$ and thus, by Sklar's Theorem, a unique representation $F(x) = C(F_1(x_1), \dots, F_d(x_d))$.

It is often very difficult, particularly in higher dimensions and in situations where we are dealing with skewed loss distributions or heterogeneous risk factors, to find a good multivariate model that describes both marginal behaviour and dependence structure effectively. For multivariate risk-factor return data of a similar kind, such as stock returns or exchange-rate returns, we have discussed useful overall models such as the generalized hyperbolic family of Section 3.2.3, but even in these situations there can be value in separating the marginal-modelling and dependence-modelling issues and looking at each in more detail. The copula approach to multivariate models facilitates this approach and allows us to consider, for example, the issue of whether tail dependence appears to be present in our data.

This section is thus devoted to the problem of estimating the parameters $\boldsymbol{\theta}$ of a parametric copula $C_{\boldsymbol{\theta}}$. The main method we consider is maximum likelihood in Section 5.5.3. First we outline a simpler method-of-moments procedure using sample rank correlation estimates. This method has the advantage that marginal distributions do not need to be estimated, and consequently inference about the copula is in a sense "margin-free".

5.5.1 Method-of-Moments using Rank Correlation

Depending on which particular copula we want to fit, it may be easier to use empirical estimates of either Spearman's or Kendall's rank correlation to infer an estimate for the copula parameter. We begin by discussing the standard estimators of both of these rank correlations.

Definition 5.28 suggests that we could estimate $\rho_S(X_i, X_j)$ by calculating the usual correlation coefficient for the *pseudo-observations*: $\{(F_{i,n}(X_{t,i}), F_{j,n}(X_{t,j})) : t = 1, \dots, n\}$, where $F_{i,n}$ denotes the standard empirical df for the ith margin. Equivalently, if we use $\mathrm{rank}(X_{t,i})$ to denote the rank of $X_{t,i}$ in $X_{1,i}, \dots, X_{n,i}$ (i.e. its position in the ordered sample), we can calculate the correlation coefficient for the rank data $\{(\mathrm{rank}(X_{t,i}), \mathrm{rank}(X_{t,j}))\}$, and this gives us the Spearman's rank correlation coefficient:

$$\frac{12}{n(n^2-1)} \sum_{t=1}^{n} (\mathrm{rank}(X_{t,i}) - \tfrac{1}{2}(n+1))(\mathrm{rank}(X_{t,j}) - \tfrac{1}{2}(n+1)). \tag{5.49}$$

We will denote by R^{S} the matrix of pairwise Spearman's rank correlation coefficients; since this is the sample correlation matrix of the vectors of ranks it is clearly a positive semidefinite matrix.

The standard estimator of Kendall's tau $\rho_\tau(X_i, X_j)$ is Kendall's rank correlation coefficient:

$$\binom{n}{2}^{-1} \sum_{1 \leqslant t < s \leqslant n} \mathrm{sign}((X_{t,i} - X_{s,i})(X_{t,j} - X_{s,j})). \tag{5.50}$$

This is clearly the empirical analogue of the theoretical Kendall's tau in Definition 5.27. Note that the actual evaluation of this estimator for large n is time-consuming (in comparison with Spearman's rank) because every pair of observations must be considered. Again we can collect pairwise Kendall's rank correlation coefficients in a matrix R^τ; by observing that this matrix may be written as

$$R^\tau = \binom{n}{2}^{-1} \sum_{1\leqslant t<s\leqslant n} \operatorname{sign}(\boldsymbol{X}_t - \boldsymbol{X}_s)\operatorname{sign}(\boldsymbol{X}_t - \boldsymbol{X}_s)',$$

it is again apparent that this gives a positive semidefinite matrix.

In a series of examples we show how these sample rank correlations can be used to calibrate (or partially calibrate) various copulas. Obviously we assume that there are *a priori* grounds for considering the chosen copula to be an appropriate model, such as symmetry or the lack of it and the presence or absence of tail dependence. The general method will always be similar: we look for a theoretical relationship between one of the rank correlations and the parameters of the copula and substitute empirical values of the rank correlation into this relationship to get estimates of some or all of the copula parameters.

Example 5.52 (bivariate Archimedean copulas with a single parameter). Suppose our assumed model is of the form $F(x_1, x_2) = C_\theta(F_1(x_1), F_2(x_2))$, where θ is a single parameter to be estimated. For many such copulas a simple functional relationship exists between either Kendall's tau and θ or Spearman's rho and θ. For specific examples consider the Gumbel, Clayton and Frank copulas of Section 5.4; in these cases we have simple relationships of the form $\rho_\tau(X_1, X_2) = f(\theta)$, as shown in Table 5.5. This suggests we can calibrate these copulas by first calculating a sample value r^τ for Kendall's tau and then solving the equation $r^\tau = f(\hat{\theta})$ for $\hat{\theta}$, assuming that $\hat{\theta}$ is a valid value in the parameter space of the copula. For example, Gumbel's copula is calibrated by taking $\hat{\theta} = (1 - r^\tau)^{-1}$, provided that $r^\tau \geqslant 0$. Clayton's copula interpolates between perfect negative and perfect positive dependence and can be calibrated to any sample Kendall's tau value in $(-1, 1)$.

Example 5.53 (calibrating Gauss copulas using Spearman's rho). Suppose we assume a meta-Gaussian model for $\boldsymbol{X}$ with copula C_P^{Ga} and we wish to estimate the correlation matrix P. It follows from Theorem 5.36 that

$$\rho_{\mathrm{S}}(X_i, X_j) = (6/\pi)\arcsin \tfrac{1}{2}\rho_{ij} \approx \rho_{ij},$$

where the final approximation is very accurate (see Figure 5.10). This suggests we estimate P by the matrix of pairwise Spearman's rank correlation coefficients R^{S}.

The method of Example 5.53 could be used to estimate P in a t copula model $C_{\nu,P}^t(F_1(x_1), \dots, F_d(x_d))$, although the calibration would not be as accurate as in the Gaussian case. The value of $\rho_{\mathrm{S}}(X_i, X_j)$ in terms of ρ_{ij} is not known in closed form but simulation studies suggest that the error $|\rho_{\mathrm{S}}(X_i, X_j) - \rho_{ij}|$, while still modest, is larger than in the Gaussian case. Instead we propose a method based on Kendall's tau in the next example, which is based on Proposition 5.37 and could be applied to all elliptical copulas.

Example 5.54 (calibrating t copulas using Kendall's tau). Suppose we assume a meta-t model for $\boldsymbol{X}$ with copula $C^t_{\nu,P}$ and we wish to estimate the correlation matrix P. It follows from Proposition 5.37 that

$$\rho_\tau(X_i, X_j) = (2/\pi)\arcsin \rho_{ij},$$

so that a possible estimator of P is the matrix R^* with components given by $r^*_{ij} = \sin(\frac{1}{2}\pi r^\tau_{ij})$. However, there is no guarantee that this componentwise transformation of the matrix of Kendall's rank correlation coefficients will remain positive definite (although in our experience it very often does). In this case R^* can be transformed by the eigenvalue method given in Algorithm 5.55 to obtain a positive-definite matrix that is close to R^*. The remaining parameter ν of the copula could then be estimated by maximum likelihood, as discussed in Section 5.5.3.

Algorithm 5.55 (eigenvalue method). Let R^* be a so-called *pseudo*-correlation matrix, i.e. a symmetric matrix of pairwise correlation estimates with unit diagonal entries and off-diagonal entries in $[-1, 1]$ that is not positive semidefinite.

(1) Calculate the spectral decomposition $R^* = GLG'$ as in (3.67), where L is the matrix of eigenvalues and G is an orthogonal matrix whose columns are eigenvectors of R^*.

(2) Replace all negative eigenvalues in L by small values $\delta > 0$ to obtain $\tilde{L}$.

(3) Calculate $Q = G\tilde{L}G'$, which will be symmetric and positive definite but not a correlation matrix, since its diagonal elements will not necessarily equal one.

(4) Return the correlation matrix $R = \wp(Q)$, where $\wp$ denotes the correlation matrix operator defined in (3.5).

In Examples 5.53 and 5.54 we saw that it is relatively easy to calibrate the Gauss copula and the correlation parameter matrix P of the t copula to sample rank correlations. This technique is particularly useful when we have limited multivariate data and formal estimation of a full multivariate model is unrealistic. Consider the following hypothetical example.

Example 5.56 (fictitious risk integration situation). Suppose a company is divided into a number of business units that function semiautonomously. The company management would like to calculate an enterprise-wide P&L distribution for a one-month period. They have historical data on monthly results for each of the business units for the last two years only, i.e. 24 observations. However, each business unit believes that through detailed knowledge of their own business going back over a longer period they can specify their own P&L fairly accurately. Rather than attempting to fit a multivariate distribution to 24 observations, the risk-management team decides to combine the individual marginal models provided by each of the business units using a matrix of rank correlations estimated from the 24 data points.

In this situation we can build multivariate models by combining the known marginal distributions using any copula that can be calibrated to the estimated rank correlations. The Gaussian and t copulas lend themselves to this purpose and can be used to build meta-Gaussian and meta-t models that are consistent with the available information.

Typically, these models could then be used in a Monte Carlo risk analysis; we have seen in Section 5.1.4 that meta-Gaussian and meta-t models are particularly easy to simulate. Because the approach is obviously prone to model risk (24 observations provide very meagre multivariate data) it should be seen as a form of sensitivity analysis performed using detailed marginal information and only vague dependence information; we might choose to compare a meta-Gaussian model with no tail dependence and a meta-t model with, say, three degrees of freedom and very strong tail dependence.

5.5.2 Forming a Pseudo-Sample from the Copula

We now turn to the estimation of parametric copulas by maximum likelihood (ML). In practical situations we are seldom interested in the copula alone, but also require estimates of the margins to form a full multivariate model; even when the copula is of central interest, as it is for us in this chapter, we are forced to estimate margins in order to estimate the copula, since copula data are almost never observed directly.

While we may attempt to estimate margins and copula in one single optimization, splitting the modelling into two steps can yield more insight and allow a more detailed analysis of the different model components. In this section we describe briefly some general approaches to the first step of estimating margins and constructing a *pseudo-sample* of observations from the copula. In the following section we describe how the copula parameters are estimated by ML from the pseudo-sample.

Let $\hat{F}_1, \dots, \hat{F}_d$ denote estimates of the marginal dfs (possible methods are discussed below). The pseudo-sample from the copula consists of the vectors $\hat{\boldsymbol{U}}_1, \dots, \hat{\boldsymbol{U}}_n$, where

$$\hat{\boldsymbol{U}}_t = (U_{t,1}, \dots, U_{t,d})' = (\hat{F}_1(X_{t,1}), \dots, \hat{F}_d(X_{t,d}))'. \tag{5.51}$$

Observe that, even if the original data vectors $\boldsymbol{X}_1, \dots, \boldsymbol{X}_n$ are iid, the pseudo-sample data are generally dependent, because the marginal estimates $\hat{F}_i$ will in most cases be constructed from all of the original data vectors through the univariate samples $X_{1,i}, \dots, X_{n,i}$. Possible methods for obtaining the marginal estimate $\hat{F}_i$ include the following.

(1) Parametric estimation. We choose an appropriate parametric model for the data in question and fit it by ML: for financial risk factor return data we might consider the generalized hyperbolic distribution, or one of its special cases such as Student t or normal inverse Gaussian (NIG); for insurance or operational loss data we might consider a standard actuarial loss distribution such as Pareto or lognormal.

(2) Non-parametric estimation with variant of empirical df. We could estimate F_j using

$$F^*_{i,n}(x) = \frac{1}{n+1}\sum_{t=1}^{n} I_{\{X_{t,i} \leqslant x\}}, \tag{5.52}$$

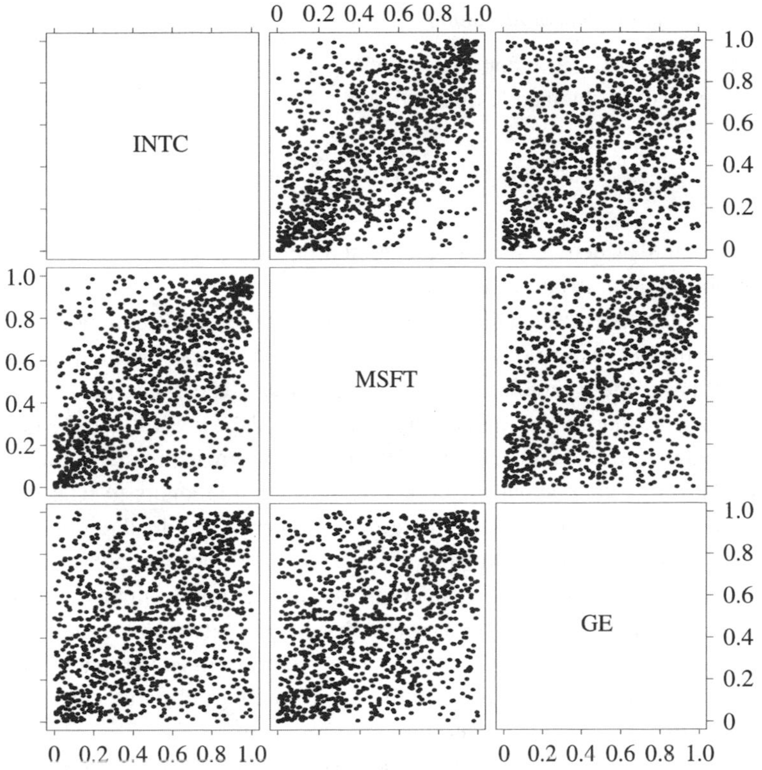

Figure 5.14. Pairwise scatterplots of pseudo-sample from copula for trivariate Intel, Microsoft and General Electric log-returns (see Example 5.57).

which differs from the usual empirical df by the use of the denominator $n+1$ rather than n. This guarantees that the pseudo-copula data in (5.51) lie strictly in the interior of the unit cube; to implement ML we must be able to evaluate the copula density at each $\hat{\boldsymbol{U}}_i$, and in many cases this density is infinite on the boundary of the cube.

(3) **Extreme value theory for the tails.** Empirical distribution functions are known to be poor estimators of the underlying distribution in the tails. An alternative is to use a technique from extreme value theory, described in Section 7.2.6, whereby the tails are modelled semiparametrically using a generalized Pareto distribution (GPD); the body of the distribution may be modelled empirically.

Example 5.57. We analyse five years of daily log-return data (1996–2000) for Intel, Microsoft and General Electric stocks. The marginal distributions are estimated empirically (method (2)) and the pseudo-sample from the copula is shown in Figure 5.14. Essentially, the points are plotted at the coordinates $(\text{rank}(X_{t,i})/(n+1), \text{rank}(X_{t,j})/(n+1))$, where $\text{rank}(X_{t,i})$ denotes the rank of $X_{t,i}$ in the sample $X_{1,i}, \dots, X_{n,i}$.

5.5.3 *Maximum Likelihood Estimation*

Let $C_{\boldsymbol{\theta}}$ denote a parametric copula, where $\boldsymbol{\theta}$ is the vector of parameters to be estimated. The MLE is obtained by maximizing

$$\ln L(\boldsymbol{\theta}; \hat{\boldsymbol{U}}_1, \dots, \hat{\boldsymbol{U}}_n) = \sum_{t=1}^{n} \ln c_{\boldsymbol{\theta}}(\hat{\boldsymbol{U}}_t) \tag{5.53}$$

with respect to $\boldsymbol{\theta}$, where $c_{\boldsymbol{\theta}}$ denotes the copula density as in (5.16) and $\hat{\boldsymbol{U}}_t$ denotes a pseudo-observation from the copula.

Obviously the statistical quality of the estimates of the copula parameters depends very much on the quality of the estimates of the marginal distributions used in the formation of the pseudo-sample from the copula. The properties of estimates derived using the marginal estimation methods (1) and (2) in Section 5.5.2 have both been studied in more theoretical detail. When margins are estimated parametrically (method (1)), inference about the copula using (5.53) amounts to what has been termed the inference-functions for margins (IFM) approach by Joe (1997). When margins are estimated non-parametrically (method (2)), the estimates of the copula parameters may be regarded as semiparametric and the approach has been labelled pseudo-maximum likelihood by Genest and Rivest (1993) (see Notes and Comments for more references). One could envisage using the two-stage method to decide on the most appropriate copula family and then estimating all parameters (marginal and copula) in a final fully parametric round of estimation.

In practice, to implement the ML method we need to derive the copula density. This is straightforward, if tedious, for the exchangeable Archimedean copulas of Section 5.4, and these have been popular models in bivariate and trivariate applications to insurance loss data. For implicit copulas like the Gaussian and t copulas we use (5.17). The MLE is generally found by numerical maximization of the resulting log-likelihood (5.53).

Example 5.58 (fitting the Gauss copula). In the case of a Gauss copula we use (5.17) to see that the log-likelihood (5.53) becomes

$$\begin{aligned}
&\ln L(P; \hat{\boldsymbol{U}}_1, \dots, \hat{\boldsymbol{U}}_n) \\
&\quad = \sum_{t=1}^{n} \ln f_P(\Phi^{-1}(\hat{U}_{t,1}), \dots, \Phi^{-1}(\hat{U}_{t,d})) - \sum_{t=1}^{n}\sum_{j=1}^{d} \ln \phi(\Phi^{-1}(\hat{U}_{t,j})),
\end{aligned}$$

where f_Σ will be used to denote the joint density of a random vector with $N_d(\mathbf{0}, \Sigma)$ distribution. It is clear that the second term is not relevant in the maximization with respect to P, and the MLE is given by

$$\hat{P} = \arg\max_{\Sigma \in \mathcal{P}} \sum_{t=1}^{n} \ln f_\Sigma(\boldsymbol{Y}_t), \tag{5.54}$$

where $Y_{t,j} = \Phi^{-1}(\hat{U}_{t,j})$ for $j = 1, \dots, d$ and $\mathcal{P}$ denotes the set of all possible linear correlation matrices. To perform this maximization in practice, note that the set $\mathcal{P}$ can be constructed as

$$\mathcal{P} = \{P = \wp(Q) : Q = AA', \ A \text{ lower triangular with ones on the diagonal}\},$$

where $\wp$ is defined in (3.5). In other words, we can search over the set of unrestricted lower-triangular matrices with ones on the diagonal. This search is feasible in low dimensions but very slow in high dimensions, since the number of parameters is $O(d^2)$.

An approximate solution to the maximization may be obtained easily as follows. Suppose that instead of maximizing over $\mathcal{P}$ as in (5.54) we maximize over the set of all covariance matrices. This maximization problem has the analytical solution $\hat{\Sigma} = (1/n)\sum_{t=1}^{n} \boldsymbol{Y}_t \boldsymbol{Y}_t'$, which is the MLE of the covariance matrix Σ for iid normal data with $N_d(\boldsymbol{0}, \Sigma)$ distribution. In practice, $\hat{\Sigma}$ is likely to be *close* to being a correlation matrix. As an approximate solution to the original problem we could take the correlation matrix $\tilde{P} = \wp(\hat{\Sigma})$.

When a Gauss copula is fitted to the trivariate data in Example 5.57 by full ML, the estimated correlation matrix has entries 0.58 (INTC-MSFT), 0.34 (INTC-GE) and 0.40 (MSFT-GE); the value of the log-likelihood at the maximum is 376.65. Using the alternative method gives estimates that are identical to two significant figures and that yield a log-likelihood value of 376.62.

A further alternative would be to use the estimation procedure in Example 5.53, based on Spearman's rank correlations. Using the Spearman method we get, respectively, 0.57, 0.34 and 0.40 for the parameter estimates; the value of the log-likelihood at this value of P is 376.50, which is also not so far from the maximum.

Example 5.59 (fitting the *t* copula). In the case of the t copula, (5.17) implies that the log-likelihood (5.53) is

$$\ln L(\nu, P; \hat{\boldsymbol{U}}_1, \dots, \hat{\boldsymbol{U}}_n)$$
$$= \sum_{t=1}^{n} \ln g_{\nu,P}(t_\nu^{-1}(\hat{U}_{t,1}), \dots, t_\nu^{-1}(\hat{U}_{t,d})) - \sum_{t=1}^{n}\sum_{j=1}^{d} \ln g_\nu(t_\nu^{-1}(\hat{U}_{t,j})),$$

where $g_{\nu,P}$ denotes the joint density of a random vector with $t_d(\nu, \boldsymbol{0}, P)$ distribution, P is a linear correlation matrix, g_ν is the density of a univariate $t_1(\nu, 0, 1)$ distribution, and t_ν^{-1} is the corresponding quantile function.

Again, in relatively low dimensions, we could search over the set of correlation matrices P and degrees of freedom parameter ν for a global maximum. For higher-dimensional work it would be easier to estimate P using Kendall's tau estimates, as in Example 5.54, and to estimate the single parameter ν by maximum likelihood.

When a t copula is fitted to the trivariate data in Example 5.57 by full ML the estimated matrix P has entries 0.59 (INTC-MSFT), 0.36 (INTC-GE) and 0.42 (MSFT-GE); the estimate of ν is 6.5 and the value of the log-likelihood at the maximum is 420.39. Using the simpler method based on Kendall's tau gives identical parameter estimates to two significant figures and a log-likelihood value of 420.32. Clearly, the t model fits much better than a Gauss copula model; the log-likelihood is increased by over 40. This would be massively significant in a likelihood ratio test (although, strictly speaking, such a test introduces a technical difficulty, since the Gauss copula represents a boundary case of the t copula model ($\nu = \infty$), which violates standard regularity conditions (see Notes and Comments)).

Notes and Comments

The copula estimation procedure based on empirical values of Kendall's tau is discussed in detail for bivariate Archimedean copulas by Genest and Rivest (1993); they explain why the procedure may be considered to be a method-of-moments technique and show how confidence intervals for the copula parameter (in the case of single-parameter copulas) may be derived.

The method of calibrating the Gauss copula with Spearman's rank correlation in Example 5.53 is essentially due to Iman and Conover (1982). The use of this calibration method to build meta-Gaussian models with prescribed margins and the Monte Carlo simulation of data from these models is implemented in the @RISK software (Palisade 1997), which is widely used in insurance. Our Example 5.54 is intended to show that this approach can be extended to meta-t models, which may well be more interesting due to their tail dependence.

The eigenvalue method for correcting the positive definiteness of correlation matrices given in Algorithm 5.55 is described by Rousseeuw and Molenberghs (1993). An empirical comparison of the eigenvalue method with different approaches to this problem, including so-called shrinkage methods, is found in Lindskog (2000).

The inference-functions for margins (IFM) approach to the estimation of copulas (method (1) of Section 5.5.2 followed by maximization of (5.53)) is described by Joe (1997), who gives asymptotic theory; the name of the approach (IFM) follows terminology of McLeish and Small (1988).

The pseudo-likelihood approach to copula estimation (method (2) of Section 5.5.2 followed by maximization of (5.53)) is described in Genest and Rivest (1993), and the consistency and asymptotic normality of the resulting parameter estimates are demonstrated. In Monte Carlo simulations it is found that this method outperforms the Kendall's tau method for a bivariate Clayton copula (see also Genest, Ghoudi and Rivest 1995).

Frees and Valdez (1997) discuss the relevance of copulas in actuarial applications and give an example where copulas are fitted to data using the Kendall's tau method and the IFM method. Also in an insurance context, Klugman and Parsa (1999) discuss ML inference for copulas and bivariate goodness-of-fit tests while Chen and Fan (2005) describe a likelihood-ratio test for semiparametric copula selection.

The fitting of the t copula to data and statistical aspects of testing this copula against the Gauss copula are discussed at length in Mashal and Zeevi (2002); the technical problem that the Gauss copula is a boundary case of the t copula is addressed in this paper and a correction is suggested. The authors provide a number of financial examples suggesting that extremal dependence is a feature of financial data. Breymann, Dias and Embrechts (2003) fit various bivariate copulas to high-frequency financial return data at different timescales and provide extensive comparisons with respect to goodness-of-fit.

Papers developing dynamic time series models for financial return data using copulas include Chen and Fan (2005), Patton (2004, 2005) and Fortin and Kuzmics (2002).

6
Aggregate Risk

This chapter is devoted to a number of theoretical concepts in quantitative risk management that fall under the broad heading of aggregate risk. We understand aggregate risk as the risk of a portfolio, which could even be the entire position in risky assets of a financial enterprise. The material builds on general ideas in risk measurement discussed in Section 2.2 and also uses in certain places the copula theory of Chapter 5 and some facts about elliptical distributions from Section 3.3.

In Section 6.1 we treat the issue of *measuring* aggregate risk. We discuss properties that a good measure of risk should have with particular emphasis on aggregation properties. This leads us to study the class of *coherent* risk measures. In Section 6.2 we consider the problem of *bounding* an aggregate risk if we know something about the individual risks that contribute to the whole but have only limited information about their dependence. We discuss specific difficulties that arise when risk is measured with a non-subadditive risk measure like VaR. Finally, in Section 6.3, we treat the subject of *allocating* risk capital, i.e. of distributing the risk capital for a portfolio to the individual risks in the portfolio. This issue is relevant for purposes of performance measurement, loan pricing and capital budgeting.

6.1 Coherent Measures of Risk

The premise of this section is the idea of approaching risk measurement by first writing down a list of properties that a good risk measure should have. Such a list was proposed for applications in financial risk management in the seminal paper by Artzner et al. (1999). Using economic reasoning, they specified a number of axioms that any so-called *coherent* risk measure should satisfy. Moreover, they studied the coherence properties of widely used risk measures such as VaR or expected shortfall and gave a characterization of all coherent risk measures in terms of generalized scenarios. Our development of the subject will follow their approach. It should be mentioned that the idea of axiomatic systems for risk measures bears some relationship to similar systems for premium principles in the actuarial literature, which have a long and independent history (see, for example, Goovaerts et al. (2003) and further references in Notes and Comments).

6.1.1 The Axioms of Coherence

In order to introduce the axioms of coherence we have to give a formal definition of risk measures. Fix some probability space $(\Omega, \mathcal{F}, P)$ and a time horizon Δ.

Denote by $L^0(\Omega, \mathcal{F}, P)$ the set of all rvs on $(\Omega, \mathcal{F})$, which are almost surely finite. Financial risks are represented by a set $\mathcal{M} \subset L^0(\Omega, \mathcal{F}, P)$ of rvs, which we interpret as portfolio losses over some time horizon Δ. The time horizon is left unspecified and will only enter when specific problems are considered. We often assume that $\mathcal{M}$ is a *convex cone*, i.e. that $L_1 \in \mathcal{M}$ and $L_2 \in \mathcal{M}$ implies that $L_1 + L_2 \in \mathcal{M}$ and $\lambda L_1 \in \mathcal{M}$ for every $\lambda > 0$. Risk measures are real-valued functions $\varrho : \mathcal{M} \to \mathbb{R}$ defined on such cones of rvs, satisfying certain properties.

We interpret $\varrho(L)$ as the amount of capital that should be added to a position with loss given by L, so that the position becomes acceptable to an external or internal risk controller. Positions with $\varrho(L) \leqslant 0$ are acceptable without injection of capital; if $\varrho(L) < 0$, capital may even be withdrawn. Note that our interpretation of L differs from that in Artzner et al. (1999), where an rv $L \in \mathcal{M}$ is interpreted as the future value (instead of the loss) of a position currently held. This leads to some sign changes in the discussion of the axioms of coherence compared with other presentations in the literature. Also note that in order to simplify the presentation we set interest rates equal to zero so that there is no discounting.

Now we can introduce the axioms that a risk measure $\varrho : \mathcal{M} \to \mathbb{R}$ on a convex cone $\mathcal{M}$ should satisfy in order to be called coherent.

Axiom 6.1 (translation invariance). For all $L \in \mathcal{M}$ and every $l \in \mathbb{R}$ we have $\varrho(L + l) = \varrho(L) + l$.

Axiom 6.1 states that by adding or subtracting a deterministic quantity l to a position leading to the loss L we alter our capital requirements by exactly that amount. The axiom is in fact necessary for the risk-capital interpretation of ϱ to make sense. Consider a position with loss L and $\varrho(L) > 0$. Adding the amount of capital $\varrho(L)$ to the position leads to the adjusted loss $\tilde{L} = L - \varrho(L)$, with $\varrho(\tilde{L}) = \varrho(L) - \varrho(L) = 0$, so that the position $\tilde{L}$ is acceptable without further injection of capital.

Axiom 6.2 (subadditivity). For all $L_1, L_2 \in \mathcal{M}$ we have $\varrho(L_1 + L_2) \leqslant \varrho(L_1) + \varrho(L_2)$.

The rationale behind Axiom 6.2 is summarized by Arztner et al. in the statement that "a merger does not create extra risk" (ignoring of course any problematic practical aspects of a merger!). Axiom 6.2 is the most debated of the four axioms characterizing coherent risk measures, probably because it rules out VaR as a risk measure in certain situations. We provide some arguments explaining why subadditivity is indeed a reasonable requirement.

- Subadditivity reflects the idea that risk can be reduced by diversification, a time-honoured principle in finance and economics. In particular, we will see in Section 6.1.5 that the use of non-subadditive risk measures in a Markowitz-type portfolio optimization problem may lead to optimal portfolios that are very concentrated and that would be deemed quite risky by normal economic standards.

- If a regulator uses a non-subadditive risk measure in determining the regulatory capital for a financial institution, that institution has an incentive to legally break up into various subsidiaries in order to reduce its regulatory capital requirements. Similarly, if the risk measure used by an organized exchange in determining the margin requirements of investors is non-subadditive, an investor could reduce the margin he has to pay by opening a different account for every position in his portfolio.
- Subadditivity makes decentralization of risk-management systems possible. Consider as an example two trading desks with positions leading to losses L_1 and L_2. Imagine that a risk manager wants to ensure that $\varrho(L)$, the risk of the overall loss $L = L_1 + L_2$, is smaller than some number M. If he uses a risk measure ϱ, which is subadditive, he may simply choose bounds M_1 and M_2 such that $M_1 + M_2 \leqslant M$ and impose on each of the desks the constraint that $\varrho(L_i) \leqslant M_i$; subadditivity of ϱ then ensures automatically that $\varrho(L) \leqslant M_1 + M_2 \leqslant M$.

Axiom 6.3 (positive homogeneity). For all $L \in \mathcal{M}$ and every $\lambda > 0$ we have $\varrho(\lambda L) = \lambda \varrho(L)$.

Axiom 6.3 is easily justified if we assume that Axiom 6.2 holds. Subadditivity implies that, for $n \in \mathbb{N}$,

$$\varrho(nL) = \varrho(L + \cdots + L) \leqslant n\varrho(L). \tag{6.1}$$

Since there is no netting or diversification between the losses in this portfolio, it is natural to require that equality should hold in (6.1), which leads to positive homogeneity. Note that subadditivity and positive homogeneity imply that the risk measure ϱ is *convex* on $\mathcal{M}$.

Axiom 6.4 (monotonicity). For $L_1, L_2 \in \mathcal{M}$ such that $L_1 \leqslant L_2$ almost surely we have $\varrho(L_1) \leqslant \varrho(L_2)$.

From an economic viewpoint this axiom is obvious: positions that lead to higher losses in every state of the world require more risk capital.

For a risk measure satisfying Axioms 6.2 and 6.3, the monotonicity axiom is equivalent to the requirement that $\varrho(L) \leqslant 0$ for all $L \leqslant 0$. To see this, observe that Axiom 6.4 implies that if $L \leqslant 0$, then $\varrho(L) \leqslant \varrho(0) = 0$; the latter equality follows from Axiom 6.3 since $\varrho(0) = \varrho(\lambda 0) = \lambda\varrho(0)$ for all $\lambda > 0$. Conversely, if $L_1 \leqslant L_2$ and we assume that $\varrho(L_1 - L_2) \leqslant 0$, then $\varrho(L_1) = \varrho(L_1 - L_2 + L_2) \leqslant \varrho(L_1 - L_2) + \varrho(L_2)$ by Axiom 6.2, which implies that $\varrho(L_1) \leqslant \varrho(L_2)$.

Definition 6.5 (coherent risk measure). A risk measure ϱ whose domain includes the convex cone $\mathcal{M}$ is called *coherent* (on $\mathcal{M}$) if it satisfies Axioms 6.1–6.4.

Note that the domain is an integral part of the definition of a coherent risk measure. We will often encounter functionals on $L^0(\Omega, \mathcal{F}, P)$, which are coherent only if restricted to a sufficiently small convex cone $\mathcal{M}$.

Remark 6.6 (convex measures of risk). Axiom 6.3 (positive homogeneity) has been criticized and, in particular, it has been suggested that for large values of the multiplier λ we should have $\varrho(\lambda L) > \lambda\varrho(L)$ to penalize a concentration of risk and the ensuing liquidity problems. As shown in (6.1), this is impossible for a subadditive risk measure. This problem has led to the study of the larger class of *convex risk measures*. In this class the conditions of subadditivity and positive homogeneity have been relaxed; instead one requires only the weaker property of convexity, i.e. for all $L_1, L_2 \in \mathcal{M}$:

$$\varrho(\lambda L_1 + (1-\lambda)L_2) \leqslant \lambda\varrho(L_1) + (1-\lambda)\varrho(L_2), \quad \lambda \in [0, 1]. \tag{6.2}$$

The economic justification of (6.2) is again the idea that diversification reduces risk. Within the class of convex risk measures it is possible to find risk measures penalizing concentration of risk in the sense that $\varrho(\lambda L) \geqslant \varrho(L)$ for $\lambda > 1$. Convex risk measures have recently attracted a lot of attention: some references are provided in Notes and Comments.

In the following sections we study the coherence properties of several popular risk measures.

6.1.2 Value-at-Risk

It is immediately seen from the representation of VaR as a quantile of the loss distribution in Section 2.2.2 that VaR is translation invariant, positive homogeneous and monotone on $L^0(\Omega, \mathcal{F}, P)$. However, as the following example shows, the subadditivity property (Axiom 6.2) fails to hold for VaR in general, so VaR is not a coherent risk measure.

Example 6.7 (VaR for a portfolio of defaultable bonds). Consider a portfolio of $d = 100$ defaultable corporate bonds. We assume that defaults of different bonds are independent; the default probability is identical for all bonds and is equal to 2%. The current price of the bonds is 100. If there is no default, a bond pays in $t+1$ (one year from now, say) an amount of 105; otherwise there is no repayment. Hence L_i, the loss of bond i, is equal to 100 when the bond defaults and to -5 otherwise. Denote by Y_i the default indicator of firm i, i.e. Y_i is equal to one if bond i defaults in $[t, t+1]$ and equal to zero otherwise. We get $L_i = 100Y_i - 5(1-Y_i) = 105Y_i - 5$. Hence the L_i form a sequence of iid rvs with $P(L_i = -5) = 0.98$ and $P(L_i = 100) = 0.02$.

We compare two portfolios, both with current value equal to 10 000. Portfolio A is fully concentrated and consists of 100 units of bond one. Portfolio B is completely diversified: it consists of one unit of each of the bonds. Economic intuition suggests that portfolio B is less risky than portfolio A and hence should have a lower VaR. Let us compute VaR at a confidence level of 95% for both portfolios.

For portfolio A the portfolio loss is given by $L_A = 100L_1$, so $\mathrm{VaR}_{0.95}(L_A) = 100\,\mathrm{VaR}_{0.95}(L_1)$. Now $P(L_1 \leqslant -5) = 0.98 \geqslant 0.95$ and $P(L_1 \leqslant l) = 0 < 0.95$ for $l < -5$. Hence $\mathrm{VaR}_{0.95}(L_1) = -5$, and therefore $\mathrm{VaR}_{0.95}(L_A) = -500$. This means that even after a *withdrawal* of a risk capital of 500 the portfolio is still acceptable to a risk controller working with VaR at the 95% level.

For portfolio B we have

$$L_B = \sum_{i=1}^{100} L_i = 105 \sum_{i=1}^{100} Y_i - 500,$$

and hence $\mathrm{VaR}_\alpha(L_B) = 105 q_\alpha(\sum_{i=1}^{100} Y_i) - 500$. The sum $M := \sum_{i=1}^{100} Y_i$ has a binomial distribution $M \sim B(100, 0.02)$. We get by inspection that $P(M \leqslant 5) \approx 0.984 \geqslant 0.95$ and $P(M \leqslant 4) \approx 0.949 < 0.95$, so $q_{0.95}(M) = 5$. Hence $\mathrm{VaR}_{0.95}(L_B) = 525 - 500 = 25$. In this case a bank would need an *additional* risk capital of 25 to satisfy a regulator working with VaR at the 95% level. Clearly, the risk capital required for portfolio B is higher than for portfolio A.

This illustrates that measuring risk with VaR can lead to nonsensical results. Moreover, our example shows that VaR is not subadditive in general. In fact, for any coherent risk measure ϱ, which depends only on the distribution of L, we get

$$\varrho\left(\sum_{i=1}^{100} L_i\right) \leqslant \sum_{i=1}^{100} \varrho(L_i) = 100\varrho(L_1) = \varrho(100 L_1).$$

Hence *any* coherent risk measure, which depends only on the loss distribution, will lead to a higher risk-capital requirement for portfolio A than for portfolio B.

In Example 6.7 the non-subbaditivity of VaR is caused by the fact that the assets making up the portfolio have very skewed loss distributions; such a situation can clearly occur if we have defaultable bonds or options in our portfolio. Note, however, that the assets in this example have an innocuous dependence structure because they are independent. We will see in Example 6.22 in Section 6.2 that non-subadditivity can also occur when the loss distributions of the individual assets are smooth and symmetric, but their dependence structure or copula is of a special, highly asymmetric form. Finally, non-subadditivity of VaR also occurs when the underlying rvs are independent but very heavy-tailed; see Example 7 in Embrechts, McNeil and Straumann (2002) and Example 5.2.7 in Denuit and Charpentier (2004), which both use infinite-mean Pareto risks.

VaR is, however, subadditive in the idealized situation where all portfolios can be represented as linear combinations of the same set of underlying elliptically distributed risk factors. In this case both the marginal loss distributions of the risk factors and the copula possess strong symmetry. We have seen in Chapter 3 that an elliptical model may be a reasonable approximate model for various kinds of risk-factor data, such as stock or exchange-rate returns.

Theorem 6.8 (subadditivity of VaR for elliptical risk factors). *Suppose that* $\boldsymbol{X} \sim E_d(\boldsymbol{\mu}, \Sigma, \psi)$ *and define the set* $\mathcal{M}$ *of linearized portfolio losses of the form*

$$\mathcal{M} = \left\{ L : L = \lambda_0 + \sum_{i=1}^{d} \lambda_i X_i,\ \lambda_i \in \mathbb{R} \right\}.$$

Then for any two losses $L_1, L_2 \in \mathcal{M}$ *and* $0.5 \leqslant \alpha < 1$,

$$\mathrm{VaR}_\alpha(L_1 + L_2) \leqslant \mathrm{VaR}_\alpha(L_1) + \mathrm{VaR}_\alpha(L_2).$$

Proof. Without any loss of generality we assume that $\lambda_0 = 0$. For any $L \in \mathcal{M}$ it follows from Definition 3.26 that we can write $L = \boldsymbol{\lambda}'\boldsymbol{X} \overset{\mathrm{d}}{=} \boldsymbol{\lambda}'A\boldsymbol{Y} + \boldsymbol{\lambda}'\boldsymbol{\mu}$ for a spherical random vector $\boldsymbol{Y} \sim S_k(\psi)$, a matrix $A \in \mathbb{R}^{d\times k}$ and a constant vector $\boldsymbol{\mu} \in \mathbb{R}^d$. By part (3) of Theorem 3.19 we have

$$L \overset{\mathrm{d}}{=} \|\boldsymbol{\lambda}'A\| Y_1 + \boldsymbol{\lambda}'\boldsymbol{\mu}, \tag{6.3}$$

showing that every $L \in \mathcal{M}$ is an rv of the same type. Moreover, the translation invariance and homogeneity of VaR imply that, for $L = \boldsymbol{\lambda}'\boldsymbol{X}$,

$$\mathrm{VaR}_\alpha(L) = \|\boldsymbol{\lambda}'A\|\, \mathrm{VaR}_\alpha(Y_1) + \boldsymbol{\lambda}'\boldsymbol{\mu}. \tag{6.4}$$

Now set $L_1 = \boldsymbol{\lambda}_1'\boldsymbol{X}$ and $L_2 = \boldsymbol{\lambda}_2'\boldsymbol{X}$. Since $\|(\boldsymbol{\lambda}_1 + \boldsymbol{\lambda}_2)'A\| \leqslant \|\boldsymbol{\lambda}_1'A\| + \|\boldsymbol{\lambda}_2'A\|$ and since $\mathrm{VaR}_\alpha(Y_1) \geqslant 0$ for $\alpha \geqslant 0.5$, the result follows. □

6.1.3 Coherent Risk Measures Based on Loss Distributions

We give two examples of coherent risk measures that are based on loss distributions.

Expected shortfall. A proof of the coherence of expected shortfall, defined in Definition 2.15, can be based on Lemma 2.20, which gives a representation of expected shortfall as the limit of the averages of upper order statistics.

Proposition 6.9. *Expected shortfall is a coherent risk measure.*

Proof. The translation invariance, positive homogeneity and monotonicity properties follow easily from the representation $\mathrm{ES}_\alpha = (1/(1-\alpha)) \int_\alpha^1 \mathrm{VaR}_u(L)\,\mathrm{d}u$ and the corresponding properties for quantiles. It remains to show subadditivity.

Consider a generic sequence of rvs $L_1, \dots, L_n$ with associated order statistics $L_{1,n} \geqslant \cdots \geqslant L_{n,n}$ and note that for arbitrary m satisfying $1 \leqslant m \leqslant n$ we have

$$\sum_{i=1}^m L_{i,n} = \sup\{L_{i_1} + \cdots L_{i_m} : 1 \leqslant i_1 < \cdots < i_m \leqslant m\}.$$

Now consider two rvs L and $\tilde{L}$ with joint df F and a sequence of iid bivariate random vectors $(L_1, \tilde{L}_1), \dots, (L_n, \tilde{L}_n)$ with the same df F. Writing $(L + \tilde{L})_i := L_i + \tilde{L}_i$ and $(L + \tilde{L})_{i,n}$ for an order statistic of $(L+\tilde{L})_1, \dots, (L+\tilde{L})_n$, we observe that we must have

$$\begin{aligned}\sum_{i=1}^m (L+\tilde{L})_{i,n} &= \sup\{(L+\tilde{L})_{i_1} + \cdots + (L+\tilde{L})_{i_m} : 1 \leqslant i_1 < \cdots < i_m \leqslant m\} \\ &\leqslant \sup\{L_{i_1} + \cdots + L_{i_m} : 1 \leqslant i_1 < \cdots < i_m \leqslant m\} \\ &\qquad + \sup\{\tilde{L}_{i_1} + \cdots + \tilde{L}_{i_m} : 1 \leqslant i_1 < \cdots < i_m \leqslant m\} \\ &= \sum_{i=1}^m L_{i,n} + \sum_{i=1}^m \tilde{L}_{i,n}.\end{aligned}$$

By setting $m = [n(1-\alpha)]$ and letting $n \to \infty$, we infer from Lemma 2.20 that $\mathrm{ES}_\alpha(L + \tilde{L}) \leqslant \mathrm{ES}_\alpha(L) + \mathrm{ES}_\alpha(\tilde{L})$. □

A coherent premium principle. In Fischer (2003), a class of coherent risk measures closely resembling certain actuarial premium principles is proposed. These risk measures could be useful for an insurance company that wants to compute premiums on a coherent basis without deviating too far from standard actuarial practice.

Given constants $p > 1$ and $\alpha \in [0, 1)$, this coherent premium principle $\varrho_{[\alpha,p]}$ is defined as follows. Let $\mathcal{M} := L^p(\Omega, \mathcal{F}, P)$, the space of all L with $\|L\|_p := E(|L|^p)^{1/p} < \infty$, and define, for $L \in \mathcal{M}$,

$$\varrho_{[\alpha,p]}(L) = E(L) + \alpha\|(L - E(L))^+\|_p. \tag{6.5}$$

Under (6.5) the risk of a loss L is measured by the sum of $E(L)$, the actuarial value of a loss, and a *risk loading* given by a fraction α of the L^p-norm of the positive part of the centred loss $L - E(L)$. This loading can be written more explicitly as $(\int_{E(L)}^{\infty}(l - E(L))^p \, \mathrm{d}F_L(l))^{1/p}$. The higher the values of α and p, the more conservative the risk measure $\varrho_{[\alpha,p]}$ becomes.

The coherence of $\varrho_{[\alpha,p]}$ is easy to check. Translation invariance and positive homogeneity are immediate. To prove subadditivity observe that for any two rvs X and Y we have $(X + Y)^+ \leqslant X^+ + Y^+$. Hence we get from Minkowski's inequality (the triangle inequality for the L^p-norm) for any two $L_1, L_2 \in \mathcal{M}$:

$$\begin{aligned}\|(L_1 - E(L_1) + L_2 - E(L_2))^+\|_p &\leqslant \|(L_1 - E(L_1))^+ + (L_2 - E(L_2))^+\|_p \\ &\leqslant \|(L_1 - E(L_1))^+\|_p + \|(L_2 - E(L_2))^+\|_p,\end{aligned}$$

which shows that $\varrho_{[\alpha,p]}$ is subadditive. To verify monotonicity assume that $L \leqslant 0$ almost surely; in that case we have $(L - E(L))^+ \leqslant -E(L)$ almost surely, and hence $\|(L - E(L))^+\|_p \leqslant -E(L)$, so $\varrho_{[\alpha,p]} \leqslant 0$ since $\alpha < 1$.

6.1.4 Coherent Risk Measures as Generalized Scenarios

In this section we present a general class of coherent risk measures based on the idea of generalized scenarios; recall from Remark 2.9 that scenario-based risk measures are used in practice at the Chicago Mercantile Exchange. We show that if we restrict our attention to discrete probability spaces, then in fact all coherent risk measures belong to this class. It is possible to extend the idea to general (infinite) probability spaces but the results become somewhat more technical (see Notes and Comments for further references).

Definition 6.10. Denote by $\mathcal{P}$ a set of probability measures on our underlying measurable space $(\Omega, \mathcal{F})$, and set $\mathcal{M}_{\mathcal{P}} := \{L : E^Q(|L|) < \infty \text{ for all } Q \in \mathcal{P}\}$. Then the risk measure induced by the set of generalized scenarios $\mathcal{P}$ is the mapping $\varrho_{\mathcal{P}} : \mathcal{M}_{\mathcal{P}} \to \mathbb{R}$ such that $\varrho_{\mathcal{P}}(L) := \sup\{E^Q(L) : Q \in \mathcal{P}\}$.

Proposition 6.11.

(i) *For any set $\mathcal{P}$ of probability measures on $(\Omega, \mathcal{F})$ the risk measure $\varrho_{\mathcal{P}}$ is coherent on $\mathcal{M}_{\mathcal{P}}$.*

(ii) *Suppose that Ω is a finite set $\{\omega_1, \dots, \omega_d\}$ and let $\mathcal{M} = \{L : \Omega \to \mathbb{R}\}$. Then, for any coherent risk measure ϱ on $\mathcal{M}$, there is a set $\mathcal{P}$ of probability measures on Ω such that $\varrho = \varrho_{\mathcal{P}}$.*

Proof. The proof of (i) is straightforward. The properties of translation invariance, positive homogeneity and monotonicity follow easily from Definition 6.10. For subadditivity observe that

$$\begin{aligned}\sup\{E^Q(L_1+L_1) : Q \in \mathcal{P}\} &= \sup\{E^Q(L_1)+E^Q(L_2) : Q \in \mathcal{P}\}\\ &\leqslant \sup\{E^Q(L_1) : Q \in \mathcal{P}\} + \sup\{E^Q(L_2) : Q \in \mathcal{P}\}.\end{aligned}$$

The proof of (ii) is more technical and can be skipped by a reader interested mainly in applications. Essentially, the argument is an application of the separating hyperplane theorem for convex sets.

We start with some notation. For $\boldsymbol{l} \in \mathbb{R}^d$ we write $\boldsymbol{l} \geqslant \mathbf{0}$ if $l_i \geqslant 0$ for all $1 \leqslant i \leqslant d$; by $\mathbf{1} \in \mathbb{R}^d$ we denote the vector $(1, \dots, 1)'$. Since Ω is finite, we may identify $\mathcal{M}$ with $\mathbb{R}^d$ by associating an rv L with the vector $\boldsymbol{l} \in \mathbb{R}^d$ with $l_i = L(\omega_i)$, $1 \leqslant i \leqslant d$. Similarly, a linear functional λ on $\mathbb{R}^d$ with $\lambda(\boldsymbol{l}) \geqslant 0$ for all $\boldsymbol{l} \geqslant \mathbf{0}$ and $\lambda(\mathbf{1}) = 1$ can be identified with a probability measure P_λ on Ω via $P_\lambda(\omega_i) = \lambda(\boldsymbol{e}_i)$, $\boldsymbol{e}_i$ the ith unit vector. Below we will use these identifications freely.

We have proved claim (ii) if we can show that for every rv $L_0 \in \mathcal{M}$ there is a probability measure $Q = Q(L_0)$ such that

$$E^Q(L) \leqslant \varrho(L) \quad \text{for all } L \in \mathcal{M} \text{ and } E^Q(L_0) = \varrho(L_0). \tag{6.6}$$

In fact, in that case we may take $\mathcal{P} = \{Q(L_0) : L_0 \in \mathcal{M}\}$.

Now we turn to the proof of (6.6). If this relation holds for some L_0 and some Q, it holds simultaneously for Q and all rvs of the form $aL_0 + b$, $a \in \mathbb{R}^+$, $b \in \mathbb{R}$ (by translation invariance and positive homogeneity). We may therefore assume that $\varrho(L_0) = 1$. Define $\tilde{\mathcal{U}} := \{L \in \mathcal{M} : \varrho(L) < 1\}$. As explained above we can identify $\tilde{\mathcal{U}}$ with a subset $\mathcal{U} \subset \mathbb{R}^d$. The set $\mathcal{U}$ is open (as ϱ is continuous) and convex (as ϱ is coherent and hence a convex functional on $\mathcal{M}$); moreover, $\boldsymbol{l}_0$ (the vector corresponding to the rv L_0) does not belong to $\mathcal{U}$. Using the separating hyperplane theorem (see, for example, Rockafellar (1970) or Appendix B of Duffie (2001)) we conclude that there is a linear functional λ on $\mathbb{R}^d$ such that

$$\lambda(\boldsymbol{l}) < \lambda(\boldsymbol{l}_0) \quad \text{for all } \boldsymbol{l} \in \mathcal{U}. \tag{6.7}$$

Since $\mathbf{0} \in \mathcal{U}$, it follows that $0 = \lambda(\mathbf{0}) < \lambda(\boldsymbol{l}_0)$, and we may normalize $\lambda(\boldsymbol{l}_0)$ to one. We now check that λ induces a probability measure, i.e. that (a) $\lambda(\boldsymbol{l}) \geqslant 0$ for all $\boldsymbol{l} \geqslant \mathbf{0}$ and (b) $\lambda(\mathbf{1}) = 1$. Note that we may write (6.7) as

$$\lambda(\boldsymbol{l}) < 1 \quad \text{for all } L \text{ such that } \varrho(L) < 1. \tag{6.8}$$

To prove (a) we use that for $L < 0$ we have $\varrho(L) < 0$ and hence $\lambda(\boldsymbol{l}) < 1$. This implies that for $L \geqslant 0$ and $a > 0$ we get, using the linearity of λ, $a\lambda(\boldsymbol{l}) = -\lambda(-a\boldsymbol{l}) > -1$, and hence $\lambda(\boldsymbol{l}) > -1/a$. Letting a tend to ∞ yields (a).

To prove (b) we first note that for any constant $a < 1$ we have $\varrho(a) = a < 1$, and hence by (6.8) we have $\lambda(a\mathbf{1}) < 1$, so $\lambda(\mathbf{1}) \leqslant 1$. On the other hand, we get for $a > 1$ that $\varrho(2L_0 - a) = 2\varrho(L_0) - a = 2 - a < 1$, hence $1 > \lambda(2\boldsymbol{l}_0 - a) = 2 - a\lambda(\mathbf{1})$, and therefore $a\lambda(\mathbf{1}) > 1$; this implies that $\lambda(\mathbf{1}) \geqslant 1$, and hence (b).

We now show that $Q := P_\lambda$ is the desired probability measure. For this we need to verify (6.6), i.e. we have to show that $E_\lambda(L) \leqslant \varrho(L)$ for all $L \in \mathcal{M}$. This is equivalent to the implication $\varrho(L) < b \Rightarrow \lambda(\boldsymbol{l}) < b$ for all $L \in \mathcal{M}$, $b \in \mathbb{R}$. Now, by translation invariance, $\varrho(L) < b \Longleftrightarrow \varrho(L-(b-1)) = \varrho(L)+1-b < 1$. Hence we get from (6.8) that $1 > E_\lambda(L-(b-1)) = E_\lambda(L)-b+1$, and therefore $E_\lambda(L) < b$, as required. □

6.1.5 Mean-VaR Portfolio Optimization

In this section we show what can happen if investors optimize the expected return on their portfolios under some constraint on VaR in a situation where VaR is not coherent—the portfolios resulting from such an optimization procedure exploit the conceptual weaknesses of VaR and lead to highly risky, non-diversified allocations. This is illustrated in the simplistic Example 6.12 below but we stress that the same phenomenon can be observed in more realistic situations (see Notes and Comments). At the end of this section we discuss again the idealized situation of linear portfolios of elliptical risk factors, where VaR is coherent and where mean variance portfolio optimization turns out to be equivalent to the standard Markowitz approach.

Example 6.12. Consider in the context of Example 6.7 a portfolio manager who has an amount of capital V which can be invested in the $d = 100$ defaultable bonds with current price 100. For simplicity we assume that it is not possible to borrow additional money or to take short positions in the defaultable bonds. Denote by $\Lambda_V := \{\boldsymbol{\lambda} \in \mathbb{R}^d : \boldsymbol{\lambda} \geqslant \mathbf{0},\ \sum_{i=1}^d 100\lambda_i = V\}$ the set of all admissible portfolios with value V at time t. The loss of some portfolio $\boldsymbol{\lambda} \in \Lambda_V$ will be denoted by $L(\boldsymbol{\lambda})$; the expected profit of a portfolio is thus given by $E(-L(\boldsymbol{\lambda}))$. We assume that the portfolio manager determines the portfolio using a mean-VaR optimality criterion, as follows. Given some risk-aversion coefficient $\beta > 0$, a portfolio $\boldsymbol{\lambda}^*$ is chosen in order to maximize

$$E(-L(\boldsymbol{\lambda})) - \beta\,\mathrm{VaR}_\alpha(L(\boldsymbol{\lambda})) \tag{6.9}$$

over all $\boldsymbol{\lambda} \in \Lambda_V$. Portfolio optimization problems of the form (6.9) are frequently considered in practice. Moreover, optimization problems closely related to (6.9) do arise implicitly in the context of *risk-adjusted performance measurement*; often the performance of trading desks within a financial institution is measured by the ratio of profits earned by the desk and risk capital needed as a backup against losses from its operations. If this risk capital is determined using VaR, traders have similar incentives in choosing their portfolios as if operating directly under the simple criterion (6.9).

Next we determine the optimal portfolio $\boldsymbol{\lambda}^*$. Since the L_i are identically distributed, every admissible portfolio $\boldsymbol{\lambda} \in \Lambda_V$ has the same expected loss. Hence, maximizing (6.9) over all admissible portfolios amounts to minimizing $\mathrm{VaR}_\alpha(L)$ over Λ_V. Consider the case where $\alpha = 0.95$. In order to minimize $\mathrm{VaR}_\alpha(L)$ we should invest all funds into one bond (for example the first), as was shown in Example 6.7.

In our symmetric situation economic intuition suggests that the optimal portfolio should be given by a mixture of an investment in the riskless asset and a portfolio consisting of an equal amount of each of the risky bonds. It can be shown that this is indeed the case, if we replace VaR by a coherent risk measure which depends only on the distribution of losses such as generalized expected shortfall (see Frey and McNeil (2002) for details).

Portfolio optimization for elliptical risk factors. In the elliptical world, the use of any positive-homogeneous, translation-invariant measure of risk to rank risks or to determine the optimal risk-minimizing portfolio under the condition that a certain *return* is attained is equivalent to the Markowitz approach, where the variance is used as the risk measure. Alternative risk measures, such as VaR or expected shortfall, give different numerical values, but have no effect on the management of risk. We make these assertions more precise in the next proposition.

Proposition 6.13. *Suppose that* $\boldsymbol{X} \sim E_d(\boldsymbol{\mu}, \Sigma, \psi)$, *with* $\operatorname{var}(X_i) < \infty$ *for all* i. *Denote by* $\mathcal{W} = \{\boldsymbol{w} \in \mathbb{R}^d : \sum_{i=1}^d w_i = 1\}$ *the set of portfolio weights. Assume that the current value of the portfolio is* V *and let* $L(\boldsymbol{w}) = V \sum_{i=1}^d w_i X_i$ *be the (linearized) portfolio loss. Let* ϱ *be a real-valued risk measure depending only on the distribution of a risk. Suppose* ϱ *is positive homogeneous and translation invariant. Let* $\mathcal{E} = \{\boldsymbol{w} \in \mathcal{W} : -\boldsymbol{w}'\boldsymbol{\mu} = m\}$ *be the subset of portfolios giving expected return* m. *Then* $\operatorname{argmin}_{\boldsymbol{w}\in\mathcal{E}} \varrho(L(\boldsymbol{w})) = \operatorname{argmin}_{\boldsymbol{w}\in\mathcal{E}} \operatorname{var}(L(\boldsymbol{w}))$.

Proof. Recall from the proof of Theorem 6.8 that for every $\boldsymbol{w} \in \mathcal{E}$ the loss $L = L(\boldsymbol{w})$ is an rv of the same type, so $\varrho((L + mV)/\sqrt{\operatorname{var}(L)}) = k$ for some constant k. From positive homogeneity and translation invariance it follows that $\varrho(L) = k\sqrt{\operatorname{var}(L)} - mV$, from which it is clear that the Markowitz portfolio also minimizes ϱ. □

Notes and Comments

The basic paper on coherent risk measures is Artzner et al. (1999); a non-technical introduction by the same authors is Artzner et al. (1997). Technical extensions such as the characterization of coherent risk measures on infinite probability spaces are given in Delbaen (2000, 2002). Example 6.7 is due to Albanese (1997) and Artzner et al. (1999). Different existing notions of expected shortfall are discussed in the very readable paper by Acerbi and Tasche (2002). Expected shortfall has been independently studied by Rockafellar and Uryasev (2000, 2002) under the name *conditional Value-at-Risk*; in particular, these papers show that expected shortfall can be obtained as the value of a convex optimization problem.

The study of convex risk measures in the context of risk management and mathematical finance began with Föllmer and Schied (2002) (see also Frittelli and Rosazza 2002). A good treatment at advanced textbook level is given in Chapter 4 of Föllmer and Schied (2004). Cont (2005) provides an interesting link between convex risk measures and model risk in the pricing of derivatives.

Our exposition in Section 6.1.5 follows Frey and McNeil (2002) closely. Related portfolio optimization problems have been studied in Basak and Shapiro (2001), Krokhmal, Palmquist and Uryasev (2002) and Emmer, Klüppelberg and Korn

(2001). Risk-adjusted performance measures are widely used in industry in the context of capital budgeting and performance measurement. A good overview of current practice is given in Chapter 14 of Crouhy, Galai and Mark (2001); an analysis of risk management and capital budgeting for financial institutions from an economic viewpoint is Froot and Stein (1998).

There is an extensive body of economic theory related to the use of elliptical distributions in finance. The papers by Owen and Rabinovitch (1983), Chamberlain (1983) and Berk (1997) provide an entry to the area. Landsman and Valdez (2003) discuss the explicit calculation of the quantity $E(L \mid L > q_\alpha(L))$ for portfolios of elliptically distributed risks. This coincides with expected shortfall for continuous loss distributions (see Proposition 2.16).

There has been recent interest in the subject of multiperiod risk measures, which take into account the evolution of the final value of a position over several time periods and consider the effect of intermediate information and actions. Important papers in this area include Artzner et al. (2005), Riedel (2004) and Weber (2004).

6.2 Bounds for Aggregate Risks

In this section we consider the general problem of finding bounds for functionals of aggregate risks when marginal information about the individual risks is available. From a mathematical viewpoint this turns out to be a so-called Fréchet problem. We begin by presenting the general problem before concentrating on the problem of bounding the VaR of an aggregate risk.

6.2.1 *The General Fréchet Problem*

Consider a random vector $\boldsymbol{L} = (L_1, \dots, L_d)'$, representing losses associated with various individual investments or risks, and a measurable function $\Psi : \mathbb{R}^d \to \mathbb{R}$, representing the operation of aggregation. The rv $\Psi(\boldsymbol{L})$ is interpreted as an aggregate financial position and typical examples are

- the total loss $S_d = \sum_{k=1}^d L_k$;
- the maximum loss $M_d = \max(L_1, \dots, L_d)$;
- the excess-of-loss treaty $\sum_{k=1}^d (L_i - k_i)^+$ for thresholds $k_i \in \mathbb{R}^+$;
- the stop-loss treaty $(\sum_{i=1}^d L_i - k)^+$ for a threshold $k \in \mathbb{R}^+$; and
- a combined position $M_d I_{\{S_d > q_\alpha\}}$.

All of these examples have an immediate interpretation in insurance and finance. For instance, in the context of credit risk, the last example might correspond to a basket position paying out the largest loss M_d, but only if the total loss S_d exceeds its α-quantile $q_\alpha(S_d)$ for α close to one.

Consider also a real-valued functional ϱ depending on the distribution of $\Psi(\boldsymbol{L})$; ϱ can be interpreted as a risk measure, premium principle or pricing function. Ideally we would like to calculate $\varrho(\Psi(\boldsymbol{L}))$, but, in order to do so, we need the df of $\Psi(\boldsymbol{L})$ and hence the joint distribution of the random vector $\boldsymbol{L}$. Often we are required to work with much less information. Throughout Section 6.2 we assume that we know the marginal dfs of the risks $L_1, \dots, L_d$; we formalize this as Assumption (A1).

(A1) The *marginal dfs* F_i of L_i, $i = 1, \dots, d$, are given.

Of course, in practice, this really means that we have sufficient information concerning the marginal loss distributions that we can treat them as known. In the absence of additional information concerning the dependence of $L_1, \dots, L_d$ we cannot calculate $\varrho(\Psi(\boldsymbol{L}))$, but we can look for numerical bounds on the risk subject to (A1).

For a particular Ψ and ϱ the problem thus consists of finding lower and upper bounds $\varrho_{\min}$ and $\varrho_{\max}$ such that, under (A1),

$$\varrho_{\min} \leqslant \varrho(\Psi(\boldsymbol{L})) \leqslant \varrho_{\max}. \tag{6.10}$$

We would like these bounds to be sharp, meaning that narrower bounds would be violated by some random vector $\boldsymbol{L}$ whose distribution is consistent with (A1). When $\Psi(\boldsymbol{L})$ represents the aggregate loss of a financial position and ϱ represents a risk measure, the analysis of this problem can be thought of as a *stress-testing* exercise for risk measures with respect to the dependence structure of the individual risks involved. The value $\varrho_{\max}$ represents the worst possible "riskiness" of the position.

The problem has a very rich history in the field of probability, where it typically appears under the name *Fréchet problem*. Indeed, its mathematics is intimately related to the Fréchet bounds given in Theorem 5.7 and Remark 5.8. We shall sketch a solution to the problem, give some examples and, in Notes and Comments, guide the interested reader to the existing literature for more details.

The problem of finding the bounds in (6.10) assuming (A1) only can be reformulated as a pair of optimization problems. We are required to calculate

$$\left.\begin{aligned} &\inf\{\varrho(\Psi(\boldsymbol{L})) : L_i \sim F_i,\ i = 1, \dots, d\} \\ &\sup\{\varrho(\Psi(\boldsymbol{L})) : L_i \sim F_i,\ i = 1, \dots, d\} \end{aligned}\right\} \tag{6.11}$$

where $F_1, \dots, F_d$ are given dfs and $L_i \sim F_i$ means that L_i has df F_i. The solutions can be found analytically in some cases, but there also exist various numerical techniques to solve the problems in general.

We have already encountered problems of the form (6.11) in our analysis of attainable correlations (see Höffding's Theorem (Theorem 5.25)), and we revisit this problem briefly.

Example 6.14 (attainable correlations). Assume without loss of generality that we have two risks which are standardized to have mean zero and variance one. The problem of finding maximum and minimum correlations for fixed margins can be formulated as a Fréchet problem in two dimensions, where $\Psi(L_1, L_2) = L_1 L_2$ and $\varrho(\Psi(L_1, L_2)) = E(\Psi(L_1, L_2)) = \rho(L_1, L_2)$, the linear correlation coefficient between L_1 and L_2.

Theorem 5.25 shows that the possible range of the correlations between L_1 and L_2 over all possible bivariate models for the vector (L_1, L_2) is a closed interval

$[\rho_{\min}, \rho_{\max}] \subset [-1, 1]$, where possibly $\rho_{\min} > -1$ and/or $\rho_{\max} < 1$. An example where the margins were taken to be lognormal and for which $\rho_{\min} > -1$ and $\rho_{\max} < 1$ was given in Example 5.26. Furthermore, we showed that the boundary cases $\rho_{\min}$ and $\rho_{\max}$ are attained for countermonotonic and comonotonic risks, respectively; this result is crucial for our discussion below. The case $\rho_{\max} = 1$ can only occur when L_1 and L_2 are rvs of the same type, and the case $\rho_{\min} = -1$ can only occur when L_1 and $-L_2$ are rvs of the same type (see Definition A.1).

Because of Sklar's Theorem (Theorem 5.3), the inf and sup in (6.11) can be interpreted as being taken over all copulas C on $[0, 1]^d$. In some situations we may have some information concerning the dependence structure of $\boldsymbol{L}$, and it is natural to translate this dependence information into constraints on C; for instance, we might take inf and sup over all copulas $C \geqslant C_0$, for some fixed copula C_0. We discuss specific examples below.

6.2.2 The Case of VaR

In this section we show the type of results that are obtained in the case when $\varrho = \mathrm{VaR}_\alpha$. We want to find (sharp) bounds for $\mathrm{VaR}_\alpha(\Psi(\boldsymbol{L}))$ given the marginal dfs F_i of L_i, $i = 1, \dots, d$, and partial information on the dependence of the L_i variables, in particular when Ψ is the sum operator. For the interpretation of the results it will be useful to first consider the behaviour of the VaR risk measure for comonotonic risks as defined in Section 5.1.6.

Additivity of VaR for comonotonic risks. The following result summarizes additivity of VaR.

Proposition 6.15. *Let $0 < \alpha < 1$ and $L_1, \dots, L_d$ be comonotonic rvs with dfs $F_1, \dots, F_d$ which are continuous and strictly increasing. Then*

$$\mathrm{VaR}_\alpha(L_1 + \cdots + L_d) = \mathrm{VaR}_\alpha(L_1) + \cdots + \mathrm{VaR}_\alpha(L_d). \tag{6.12}$$

Proof. For ease of notation take $d = 2$. From Proposition 5.16 we have that $(L_1, L_2) \stackrel{\mathrm{d}}{=} (F_1^{\leftarrow}(U), F_2^{\leftarrow}(U))$ for some $U \sim U(0, 1)$. It follows that

$$\mathrm{VaR}_\alpha(L_1 + L_2) = \mathrm{VaR}_\alpha(F_1^{\leftarrow}(U) + F_2^{\leftarrow}(U)) = F_{T(U)}^{\leftarrow}(\alpha),$$

where T is the strictly increasing continuous function given by $T(x) = F_1^{\leftarrow}(x) + F_2^{\leftarrow}(x)$. Now $P(T(U) \leqslant T(\alpha)) = P(U \leqslant \alpha) = \alpha$, so the result follows by observing that

$$F_{T(U)}^{\leftarrow}(\alpha) = T(\alpha) = F_1^{\leftarrow}(\alpha) + F_2^{\leftarrow}(\alpha) = \mathrm{VaR}_\alpha(L_1) + \mathrm{VaR}_\alpha(L_2).$$

□

Remark 6.16 (extensions). A more general form of the above result can be found in Embrechts, Höing and Juri (2003) and is as follows. Let $\Psi : \mathbb{R}^d \to \mathbb{R}$ be increasing and left-continuous in each argument, $0 < \alpha < 1$, and let $L_1, \dots, L_d$ be comonotonic rvs (not necessarily with continuous, strictly increasing dfs). Then

$$\mathrm{VaR}_\alpha(\Psi(L_1, \dots, L_d)) = \Psi(\mathrm{VaR}_\alpha(L_1), \dots, \mathrm{VaR}_\alpha(L_d)).$$

A third correlation fallacy. Based on the above result we can highlight a third important fallacy concerning correlation to add to the two in Section 5.2.1.

Fallacy 3. VaR for the sum of two risks is at its worst when these two risks have maximal correlation, i.e. are comonotonic.

Any superadditive VaR example yields a correction to this statement; one such case was shown in Example 6.7 and a further one is given below in Example 6.22. In a superadditive VaR situation we have $\text{VaR}_\alpha(L_1 + L_2) > \text{VaR}_\alpha(L_1) + \text{VaR}_\alpha(L_2)$ for two risks L_1 and L_2 and some confidence level α. By Proposition 6.15 and Remark 6.16 the right-hand side $\text{VaR}_\alpha(L_1) + \text{VaR}_\alpha(L_2)$ corresponds to the VaR of $L_1 + L_2$ when L_1 and L_2 are comonotonic. Moreover, Theorem 5.25 and Example 6.14 imply that the correlation of L_1 and L_2 is maximal in the comonotonic case. Hence the superadditive portfolio case must correspond to a smaller correlation. The remainder of Section 6.2 is devoted to the issue of finding the worst case.

Remark 6.17. For expected shortfall the expression $\varrho(L_1 + L_2)$ is maximized for comonotonic losses. To see this, note that Proposition 6.15 together with (2.23) imply that expected shortfall also has the comonotonic additivity property. Since expected shortfall is coherent, we have $\varrho(L_1 + L_2) \leqslant \varrho(L_1) + \varrho(L_2)$, so that comonotonicity is in fact the worst possible case. There exists a whole class of coherent risk measures, known as *spectral risk measures*, which share this property (see Notes and Comments). Note, also, that if we work with VaR but restrict our attention to elliptical distributions for the vector $\boldsymbol{L}$, then VaR is a coherent risk measure (Theorem 6.8). Fallacy 3 is taken out of play and comonotonicity does correspond to the worst case.

Restrictions on dependence using copulas. Before discussing bounds on VaR we need to formalize the restrictions we make on the dependence structure of the df F of $\boldsymbol{L}$. Recall that in the case of continuous marginal dfs F_i, there is a unique copula C such that $F = C(F_1, \dots, F_d)$, and one possibility is to impose dependence restrictions on $L_1, \dots, L_d$ through conditions on C. Recall from Theorem 5.7 that $W \leqslant C \leqslant M$, where W and M denote the Fréchet lower and upper bounds, respectively.

We introduce dependence restrictions of the following type.

(A2) $C \geqslant C_0$ for a copula C_0.

When $d = 2$ the case of unconstrained optimization can be treated as a special case of restriction (A2) by setting $C_0 = W$, since W is a proper copula in this case; however, for $d > 2$ unconstrained optimization is not a special case of restriction (A2). The case where $C_0 = \Pi$, the independence copula in (5.6), corresponds to so-called *positive lower orthant dependence* (PLOD) (see Müller and Stoyan 2002, Definition 3.10.1). In Theorem 3.10.4 of Müller and Stoyan (2002), it is shown that, if $\text{cov}(f(\boldsymbol{L}), g(\boldsymbol{L})) \geqslant 0$ for all increasing functions $f, g : \mathbb{R}^d \to \mathbb{R}$, then $\boldsymbol{L}$ is PLOD.

Note that the relation "$\geqslant$" in (A2) is not a *complete ordering* on the space of all copulas, meaning that for any two copulas C_1 and C_2 it is not necessarily true that either $C_1 \geqslant C_2$ or $C_2 \geqslant C_1$. As a consequence, a constraint of the type (A2) may only give a restrictive view on dependence alternatives.

Notation for the optimization problem. In order to formulate some of the key results for the optimization problem (6.11), we need some extra notation. Given a vector $\boldsymbol{x} = (x_1, \dots, x_d)' \in \mathbb{R}^d$, we write $\boldsymbol{x}_{-i} = (x_1, \dots, x_{i-1}, x_{i+1}, \dots, x_d)'$. Also, for $\boldsymbol{x}_{-d} \in \mathbb{R}^{d-1}$ fixed, we define $\Psi^{\wedge}_{\boldsymbol{x}_{-d}}(s) := \sup\{x_d \in \mathbb{R} : \Psi(\boldsymbol{x}_{-d}, x_d) < s\}$ for $s \in \mathbb{R}$. In our set-up, it is convenient to identify the df F of $\boldsymbol{L}$ given fixed margins with the copula C that combines the margins to give the df $C(F_1, \dots, F_d)$. Denote by μ_C the corresponding probability measure on $\mathbb{R}^d$ and define, for $s \in \mathbb{R}$,

$$\begin{aligned} \sigma_{C,\Psi}(F_1, \dots, F_d)(s) &:= \mu_C(\Psi(\boldsymbol{L}) < s), \\ \tau_{C,\Psi}(F_1, \dots, F_d)(s) &:= \sup_{x_1,\dots,x_{d-1} \in \mathbb{R}} C(F_1(x_1), \dots, F_{d-1}(x_{d-1}), F_d^-(\Psi^{\wedge}_{\boldsymbol{x}_{-d}}(s))), \end{aligned}$$

where $F_d^-(x)$ stands for the left limit of F_d in x. It follows that

$$\begin{aligned} m_\Psi(s) &:= \inf\{P(\Psi(\boldsymbol{L}) < s) : L_i \sim F_i,\ i = 1, \dots, d\} \\ &= \inf\{\sigma_{C,\Psi}(F_1, \dots, F_d)(s) : C \in \mathfrak{C}_d\}, \end{aligned}$$

where $\mathfrak{C}_d$ denotes the set of all d-dimensional copulas.

Remark 6.18. The strict inequality "$<$" in the definition of $m_\Psi(s)$ is essential (see Embrechts and Puccetti 2005, Remark 3.1(ii)).

Optimization subject to proper copula constraints. It turns out that a *proper* lower copula constraint as in (A2) allows for an easier analysis. Recall that the unconstrained case $C \geqslant W$ is a special case of (A2) only if $d = 2$.

Theorem 6.19 (lower bound with partial information). *Let $\boldsymbol{L}$ be a random vector in $\mathbb{R}^d$ ($d \geqslant 2$) having margins $F_1, \dots, F_d$ and copula C. Assume that there exists a copula C_0 such that $C \geqslant C_0$ (i.e. Assumption (A2) holds). If $\Psi : \mathbb{R}^d \to \mathbb{R}$ is increasing, then, for $s \in \mathbb{R}$,*

$$\sigma_{C,\Psi}(F_1, \dots, F_d)(s) \geqslant \tau_{C_0,\Psi}(F_1, \dots, F_d)(s). \tag{6.13}$$

If, moreover, Ψ is right-continuous in its last argument, then the copula

$$C_t(\boldsymbol{u}) := \begin{cases} \max(t, C_0(\boldsymbol{u})), & \boldsymbol{u} \in [t, 1]^d, \\ \min\{u_1, \dots, u_d\}, & \textit{otherwise}, \end{cases}$$

where $t = \tau_{C_0,\Psi}(F_1, \dots, F_d)(s)$ attains the bound in (6.13).

Proof. See Theorems 3.1 and 3.2 in Embrechts and Puccetti (2005). □

Translated into the language of VaR and using the notation $\mathrm{VaR}_{\alpha,\max} := \tau_{C_0,\Psi}(F_1, \dots, F_d)^{\leftarrow}(\alpha)$ for the inverse of the τ function in (6.13), Theorem 6.19 becomes

$$\mathrm{VaR}_\alpha(\Psi(\boldsymbol{L})) \leqslant \mathrm{VaR}_{\alpha,\max}, \tag{6.14}$$

for $0 < \alpha < 1$, which gives an upper bound of the kind in (6.10). If Ψ is given by the sum operator, abbreviated to $\Psi = +$, this bound is

$$\mathrm{VaR}_{\alpha,\max} = \inf_{\boldsymbol{u}\in[0,1]^d, C_0(\boldsymbol{u})=\alpha} (F_1^{\leftarrow}(u_1) + \cdots + F_d^{\leftarrow}(u_d)). \tag{6.15}$$

The unconstrained case. The unconstrained case for $d > 2$ is more difficult. First of all, the standard bound (6.13) evaluated at $C_0 = W$ still holds but may fail to be sharp. For $\Psi = +$ and $F_1 = \cdots = F_d = F$ with F a continuous df on $\mathbb{R}^+$, it reduces to

$$\tau_{W,+}(F, \dots, F)(s) = (dF(s/d) - d + 1)^+ \tag{6.16}$$

for large enough s (see Embrechts and Puccetti (2005) for details). The next result yields a better bound.

Theorem 6.20 (a better bound in the unconstrained case). *Let F be a continuous df on $\mathbb{R}^+$ and let $F_1 = \cdots = F_d = F$. Then, for all $s \geqslant 0$ and $\bar{F} = 1 - F$,*

$$m_+(s) \geqslant 1 - d \inf_{r\in[0,s/d]} \frac{\int_r^{s-(d-1)r} \bar{F}(x)\,\mathrm{d}x}{s - dr}. \tag{6.17}$$

Proof. See Theorem 4.2 in Embrechts and Puccetti (2005). □

Remark 6.21. The value of $m_+(s)$ can be closely approximated by solving two linear programmes (see Embrechts and Puccetti 2005; Embrechts, Höing and Juri 2003).

Examples. In a first example we consider the special, though important, case when $F_1 = F_2 = \Phi$, the standard normal df. The second example considers higher-dimensional portfolios with Pareto margins.

Example 6.22 (worst VaR for a portfolio with normal margins). For $i = 1, 2$ let $F_i = \Phi$. In Figure 6.1 we have plotted the worst $\mathrm{VaR}_\alpha(L_1 + L_2)$ calculated using (6.16) as a function of α together with the curve corresponding to the comonotonic case calculated using Proposition 6.15. The fact that the former lies above the latter implies the existence of portfolios with normal margins for which VaR is not subadditive. For example, for $\alpha = 0.95$, the upper bound is 3.92, whereas $\mathrm{VaR}_\alpha(L_i) = 1.645$, so, for the worst VaR portfolio, $\mathrm{VaR}_{0.95}(L_1 + L_2) = 3.92 > 3.29 = \mathrm{VaR}_{0.95}(L_1) + \mathrm{VaR}_{0.95}(L_2)$. The worst-case copula is shown in Figure 6.2 (see Embrechts, Höing and Puccetti (2005) for further details).

As explained in Theorem 6.20, the case $d \geqslant 3$ is more subtle, as the standard bound (6.15) fails to be sharp. The strictly lower bound (6.17) in the case of identical distributions can be computed easily. In Section 10.1.4 we will show that operational risk losses can be modelled reasonably well by heavy-tailed Pareto distributions with infinite variance. In the case of operational risk one faces the calculation of VaRs at the 99% (or even higher) level across numerous (up to 56) classes of risk. The dependence between the loss rvs for these classes is mostly unknown, so we face the above unconstrained optimization problem for $\mathrm{VaR}_\alpha(L_1 + \cdots + L_d)$. The next example contains some calculations for Pareto portfolios.

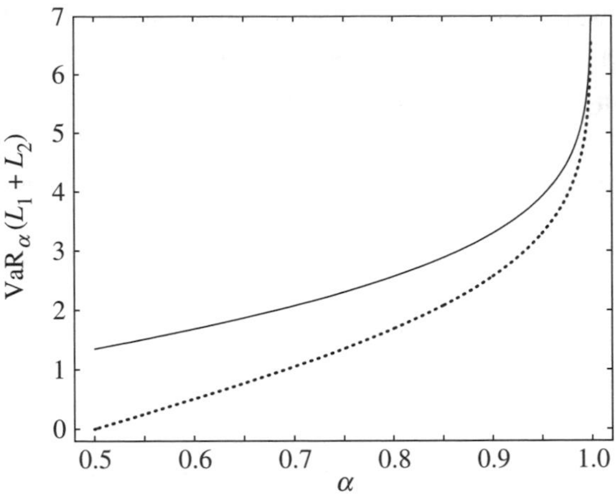

Figure 6.1. The worst-case VaR_α (solid line) plotted against α for two standard normal risks; the case of comonotonic risks (dotted line) is shown as a comparison.

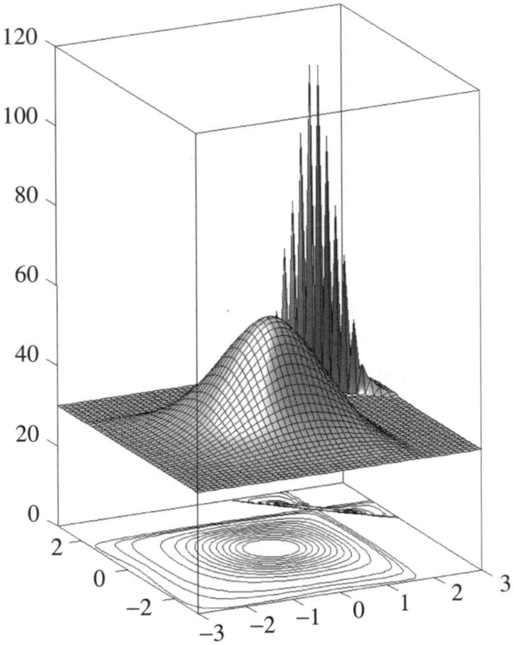

Figure 6.2. Contour and perspective plots of the density function of the distribution of (L_1, L_2) leading to the worst-case VaR for $L_1 + L_2$ at the $\alpha = 0.95$ level when the L_i are standard normal.

Example 6.23 (VaR bounds for Pareto portfolios). Suppose that $L_i \sim \mathrm{Pa}(1.5, 1)$ for $i = 1, \dots, d$ so that $E(L_i) = 2$ and $\mathrm{VaR}(L_i) = \infty$. In the unconstrained case, Table 6.1 contains the bounds obtained from Theorem 6.20 (which, for reasons we will not discuss, are known as dual bounds). The portfolio sizes 8 and 56 have been chosen with the operational risk problem in mind, as explained above, whereas 100

Table 6.1. Bounds for $\mathrm{VaR}_\alpha(\sum_{i=1}^d L_i)$ for portfolios of Pa(1.5, 1)-distributed risks are given in columns marked "dual"; columns marked "com" give values in the comonotonic case. Numbers are expressed in thousands.

	$\mathrm{VaR}_\alpha(\sum_{i=1}^{8} L_i)$		$\mathrm{VaR}_\alpha(\sum_{i=1}^{56} L_i)$		$\mathrm{VaR}_\alpha(\sum_{i=1}^{100} L_i)$		$\mathrm{VaR}_\alpha(\sum_{i=1}^{1000} L_i)$	
α	com	dual	com	dual	com	dual	com	dual
0.90	0.03	0.08	0.20	0.67	0.36	1.23	3.64	12.73
0.95	0.05	0.14	0.36	1.10	0.64	2.00	6.37	20.77
0.99	0.16	0.41	1.15	3.32	2.05	6.05	20.54	62.66
0.999	0.79	1.93	5.54	15.63	9.90	28.43	99.00	294.47

and 1000 could represent the sizes of typical credit portfolios. The assumption of a single common Pareto distribution for all individual losses is of course a simplification for computational purposes.

Notes and Comments

There is a large literature on Fréchet problems. Our discussion is mainly based on Embrechts, Höing and Juri (2003), Embrechts, Höing and Puccetti (2005) and Embrechts and Puccetti (2005). These papers also contain the most important references to the existing literature. Historically, the question of bounding the df of a sum of rvs with given marginals goes back to Kolmogorov and was answered by Makarov (1981) for $d = 2$. Frank, Nelsen and Schweizer (1987) restated Makarov's result using the notion of a copula. Independently, Rüschendorf (1982) gave a very elegant proof of the same result using duality. Williamson and Downs (1990) introduced the use of dependence information.

Fallacy 3 originally appeared in Embrechts, McNeil and Straumann (2002); it ceases to be a fallacy if we replace VaR by expected shortfall or a spectral risk measure. For spectral risk measures see Kusuoka (2001), Acerbi (2002) and Tasche (2002). A closely related class of risk measures mainly used in insurance applications is referred to as *distortion* or *Wang* measures (see Wang 1996). A nice discussion is to be found in Denuit and Charpentier (2004).

Embrechts, Höing and Juri (2003) gave the most general theorem for general d and Ψ; their main result on the sharpness of the bounds for $d \geqslant 3$ and no constraints, however, contains an error: this was corrected in Embrechts and Puccetti (2005). For the construction of the copula(s) leading to the worst VaR, see Embrechts, Höing and Puccetti (2005). Numerous other authors (especially in analysis and actuarial mathematics) have contributed to this area and we refer to the above papers for references. Besides the comprehensive book by Müller and Stoyan (2002), several other texts in actuarial mathematics contain interesting contributions on dependence modelling (see, for example, Chapter 10 in Kaas et al. (2001) for a start). A rich set of optimization problems within an actuarial context are to be found in De Vylder (1996): see especially "Part II: Optimization Theory", where the author "shows how to obtain best upper and lower bounds on functionals $T(F)$ of the df F of a risk, under moment or other integral constraints". An excellent account is to be found in Denuit and Charpentier (2004). The definitive account from an actuarial point of view is Denuit et al. (2005).

Rosenberg and Schuermann (2004) give some idea of the applicability of aggregation ideas used in this chapter. They construct the joint risk distribution for a typical, large, internationally active bank using the method of copulas and aggregate risk measures across the categories of market, credit and operational risk.

6.3 Capital Allocation

6.3.1 *The Allocation Problem*

Consider an investor who can invest in a fixed set of d different investment possibilities with losses represented by the rvs $L_1, \dots, L_d$. We have the following economic interpretations depending on the area of application.

Performance measurement. Here the investor is a financial institution and the L_i represent the (negative of the) P&L of d different lines of business.

Loan pricing. Here the investor is a loan book manager responsible for a portfolio of d loans.

General investment. Here we consider either an individual or institutional investor and the standard interpretation that the L_i are (negative) P&Ls corresponding to a set of investments in various assets.

The performance of the different business units or investments is usually measured using some sort of RORAC (return on risk-adjusted capital) approach, i.e. by considering a ratio of the form

$$\text{expected profit/risk capital}, \tag{6.18}$$

where we leave the precise definition of the terms vague. In many applications risk capital might correspond to economic capital: the capital derived by considering the fluctuation of the loss around the expected loss (the unexpected loss), rather than the absolute loss. Similarly, in a modern approach to loan pricing, the spread of a loan contains a risk premium component, which is computed by applying a target interest rate to the risk capital needed to sustain an individual loan (see Section 9.3.4 for details).

Obviously the general approach embodied in (6.18) raises the question of what the appropriate risk capital for an individual investment opportunity might be. Thus the question of performance of the investment is intimately connected with the subject of risk measurement as addressed in Sections 2.2 and 6.1. A two-step procedure is used in practice.

(1) Compute the overall risk capital $\varrho(L)$, where $L = \sum_{i=1}^{d} L_i$ and ϱ is a particular risk measure such as VaR or ES; note that at this stage we are not stipulating that ϱ must be coherent.

(2) Allocate the capital $\varrho(L)$ to the individual investment possibilities according to some mathematical *capital allocation principle* such that, if AC_i denotes the capital allocated to the investment with potential loss L_i, the sum of the allocated amounts corresponds to the overall risk capital $\varrho(L)$.

In this section we are interested in step (2) of the procedure; loosely speaking we require a mapping that takes as input the individual losses $L_1, \dots, L_d$ and the risk measure ϱ and yields as output the vector $(\mathrm{AC}_1, \dots, \mathrm{AC}_d)$ such that

$$\varrho(L) = \sum_{i=1}^{d} \mathrm{AC}_i, \tag{6.19}$$

and such a mapping will be called a capital allocation principle. The relation (6.19) is sometimes called the *full allocation property* since all of the overall risk capital $\varrho(L)$ (not more, not less) is allocated to the investment possibilities; we consider this property to be an integral part of the definition of an allocation principle. Of course, there are other properties of a capital allocation principle that are desirable from an economic viewpoint; we first make some formal definitions and give examples of allocation properties before discussing further properties.

The formal set-up. Let $L_1, \dots, L_d$ be rvs on a common probability space $(\Omega, \mathcal{F}, P)$ representing losses (or profits) for d investment possibilities. For our discussion it will be useful to consider portfolios where the weights of the individual investment opportunities are varied with respect to our basic portfolio $(L_1, \dots, L_d)$, which is regarded as a fixed random vector. That is, we consider an open set $\Lambda \subset \mathbb{R}^d \setminus \{\mathbf{0}\}$ of portfolio weights and define for $\boldsymbol{\lambda} \in \Lambda$ the loss $L(\boldsymbol{\lambda}) = \sum_{i=1}^{d} \lambda_i L_i$; the loss of our actual portfolio is of course $L(\mathbf{1})$. Let ϱ be some risk measure defined on a set $\mathcal{M}$ which contains the rvs $\{L(\boldsymbol{\lambda}) : \boldsymbol{\lambda} \in \Lambda\}$. We then define the associated *risk-measure function* $r_\varrho : \Lambda \to \mathbb{R}$ by $r_\varrho(\boldsymbol{\lambda}) = \varrho(L(\boldsymbol{\lambda}))$. Thus $r_\varrho(\boldsymbol{\lambda})$ is the required risk capital for a position $\boldsymbol{\lambda}$ in the set of investment possibilities.

Definition 6.24. Let r_ϱ be a risk-measure function on some set $\Lambda \subset \mathbb{R}^d \setminus \{\mathbf{0}\}$ such that $\mathbf{1} \in \Lambda$. A mapping $\pi^{r_\varrho} : \Lambda \to \mathbb{R}^d$ is called a per-unit *capital allocation principle* associated with r_ϱ if, for all $\boldsymbol{\lambda} \in \Lambda$, we have

$$\sum_{i=1}^{d} \lambda_i \pi_i^{r_\varrho}(\boldsymbol{\lambda}) = r_\varrho(\boldsymbol{\lambda}). \tag{6.20}$$

The interpretation of this definition is that $\pi_i^{r_\varrho}$ gives the amount of capital allocated to one unit of L_i, when the overall position has loss $L(\boldsymbol{\lambda})$. The amount of capital allocated to the position $\lambda_i L_i$ is thus $\lambda_i \pi_i^{r_\varrho}$ and the equality (6.20) simply means that the overall risk capital $r_\varrho(\boldsymbol{\lambda})$ is fully allocated to the individual portfolio positions.

6.3.2 The Euler Principle and Examples

From now on we restrict our attention to risk measures that are positive homogeneous (satisfying Axiom 6.3 in Section 6.1.1), such as a coherent risk measure, but also the standard deviation risk measure or VaR. Obviously the associated risk-measure function must satisfy $r_\varrho(t\boldsymbol{\lambda}) = tr_\varrho(\boldsymbol{\lambda})$ for all $t > 0$, $\boldsymbol{\lambda} \in \Lambda$, so $r_\varrho : \Lambda \to \mathbb{R}$ is a positive-homogeneous function of a vector argument. Recall Euler's well-known rule that states that if r_ϱ is positive homogeneous and differentiable at $\boldsymbol{\lambda} \in \Lambda$, we have

$$r_\varrho(\boldsymbol{\lambda}) = \sum_{i=1}^{d} \lambda_i \frac{\partial r_\varrho}{\partial \lambda_i}(\boldsymbol{\lambda}). \tag{6.21}$$

Comparison of (6.21) with (6.20) suggests the following definition.

Definition 6.25 (Euler capital allocation principle). If r_ϱ is a positive-homogeneous risk-measure function, which is differentiable on the set Λ, then the per-unit Euler capital allocation principle associated with r_ϱ is the mapping

$$\pi^{r_\varrho} : \Lambda \to \mathbb{R}^d, \qquad \pi_i^{r_\varrho}(\boldsymbol{\lambda}) = \frac{\partial r_\varrho}{\partial \lambda_i}(\boldsymbol{\lambda}). \tag{6.22}$$

The Euler principle is sometimes called *allocation by the gradient*, since $\pi^{r_\varrho}(\boldsymbol{\lambda}) = \nabla r_\varrho(\boldsymbol{\lambda})$. Obviously the Euler principle gives a full allocation of the risk capital. We now look at a number of concrete examples of Euler allocations corresponding to different choices of risk measure ϱ.

Standard deviation and the covariance principle. Consider the risk measure function $r_{\mathrm{SD}}(\boldsymbol{\lambda}) = \sqrt{\mathrm{var}(L(\boldsymbol{\lambda}))}$ and write Σ for the covariance matrix of $(L_1, \dots, L_d)$. Then we have $r_{\mathrm{SD}}(\boldsymbol{\lambda}) = (\boldsymbol{\lambda}'\Sigma\boldsymbol{\lambda})^{1/2}$, from which it follows that

$$\pi_i^{r_{\mathrm{SD}}}(\boldsymbol{\lambda}) = \frac{\partial r_{\mathrm{SD}}}{\partial \lambda_i}(\boldsymbol{\lambda}) = \frac{(\Sigma\boldsymbol{\lambda})_i}{r_{\mathrm{SD}}(\boldsymbol{\lambda})} = \frac{\sum_{j=1}^{d} \mathrm{cov}(L_i, L_j)\lambda_j}{r_{\mathrm{SD}}(\boldsymbol{\lambda})} = \frac{\mathrm{cov}(L_i, L(\boldsymbol{\lambda}))}{\sqrt{\mathrm{var}(L(\boldsymbol{\lambda}))}}.$$

In particular, for the original portfolio of investment possibilities corresponding to $\boldsymbol{\lambda} = \mathbf{1}$, the capital allocated to the ith investment possibility is

$$\mathrm{AC}_i = \pi_i^{r_{\mathrm{SD}}}(\mathbf{1}) = \frac{\mathrm{cov}(L_i, L)}{\sqrt{\mathrm{var}(L)}}, \qquad L := L(\mathbf{1}). \tag{6.23}$$

This formula is known as the *covariance principle.*

VaR and VaR contributions. Suppose that $r_{\mathrm{VaR}}^{\alpha}(\boldsymbol{\lambda}) = q_\alpha(L(\boldsymbol{\lambda}))$. In this case it can be shown that, subject to technical conditions,

$$\pi_i^{r_{\mathrm{VaR}}^{\alpha}}(\boldsymbol{\lambda}) = \frac{\partial r_{\mathrm{VaR}}^{\alpha}}{\partial \lambda_i}(\boldsymbol{\lambda}) = E(L_i \mid L(\boldsymbol{\lambda}) = q_\alpha(L(\boldsymbol{\lambda}))), \quad 1 \leqslant i \leqslant d. \tag{6.24}$$

The derivation of (6.24) is more involved than that of the covariance principle and we give a justification following Tasche (2000) under the simplifying assumption that the loss distribution of $(L_1, \dots, L_d)$ has a joint density. In the following lemma we denote by $\phi(u, l_2, \dots, l_d) = f_{L_1|L_2,\dots,L_d}(u \mid l_2, \dots, l_d)$ the conditional density of L_1.

Lemma 6.26. *Assume that $d \geqslant 2$ and that $(L_1, \dots, L_d)$ has a joint density. Then, for any vector $(\lambda_1, \dots, \lambda_d)$ of portfolio weights such that $\lambda_1 \neq 0$, we find that*

(i) *$L(\boldsymbol{\lambda})$ has density*

$$f_{L(\boldsymbol{\lambda})}(t) = |\lambda_1|^{-1} E\biggl(\phi\biggl(\lambda_1^{-1}\biggl(t - \sum_{j=2}^{d} \lambda_j L_j\biggr), L_2, \dots, L_d\biggr)\biggr);$$

and

(ii) *for $i = 2, \dots, d$,*

$$E(L_i \mid L(\boldsymbol{\lambda}) = t) = \frac{E(L_i \phi(\lambda_1^{-1}(t - \sum_{j=2}^{d} \lambda_j L_j), L_2, \dots, L_d))}{E(\phi(\lambda_1^{-1}(t - \sum_{j=2}^{d} \lambda_j L_j), L_2, \dots, L_d))}, \quad \text{a.s.}$$

Proof. For (i) consider the case $\lambda_1 > 0$ and observe that we can write

$$\begin{aligned} P(L(\boldsymbol{\lambda}) \leqslant t) &= E(P(L(\boldsymbol{\lambda}) \leqslant t \mid L_2, \dots, L_d)) \\ &= E\biggl(P\biggl(L_1 \leqslant \lambda_1^{-1}\biggl(t - \sum_{j=2}^{d} \lambda_j L_j\biggr) \biggm| L_2, \dots, L_d\biggr)\biggr) \\ &= E\biggl(\int_{-\infty}^{\lambda_1^{-1}(t - \sum_{j=2}^{d} \lambda_j L_j)} \phi(u, L_2, \dots, L_d)\, \mathrm{d}u\biggr). \end{aligned}$$

The assertion follows on differentiating under the expectation.

For (ii) observe that we can write

$$E(L_i \mid L(\boldsymbol{\lambda}) = t) = \lim_{\delta \to 0} \frac{\delta^{-1} E(L_i I_{\{t < L(\boldsymbol{\lambda}) \leqslant t + \delta\}})}{\delta^{-1} P(t < L(\boldsymbol{\lambda}) \leqslant t + \delta)} = \frac{(\partial/\partial t) E(L_i I_{\{L(\boldsymbol{\lambda}) \leqslant t\}})}{f_{L(\boldsymbol{\lambda})}(t)},$$

provided $f_{L(\boldsymbol{\lambda})}(t) \neq 0$. The result follows on applying a similar conditioning technique to the ones used in the proof of (i) to the numerator. □

We now explain why (6.24) follows from Lemma 6.26. Since the rv $L(\boldsymbol{\lambda})$ has a density, we have $P(L(\boldsymbol{\lambda}) \leqslant q_\alpha(L(\boldsymbol{\lambda}))) = \alpha$. Writing $k(t) = \lambda_1^{-1}(t - \sum_{j=2}^{d} \lambda_j L_j)$ we have

$$\alpha = P(L(\boldsymbol{\lambda}) \leqslant r_{\mathrm{VaR}}^{\alpha}(\boldsymbol{\lambda})) = E\biggl(\int_{-\infty}^{k(r_{\mathrm{VaR}}^{\alpha}(\boldsymbol{\lambda}))} \phi(u, L_2, \dots, L_d)\, \mathrm{d}u\biggr). \tag{6.25}$$

We take derivatives of (6.25) with respect to λ_i for $i = 2, \dots, d$ to get

$$0 = \lambda_1^{-1} E\biggl(\biggl(\frac{\partial r_{\mathrm{VaR}}^{\alpha}(\boldsymbol{\lambda})}{\partial \lambda_i} - L_i\biggr) \phi(k(r_{\mathrm{VaR}}^{\alpha}(\boldsymbol{\lambda})), L_2, \dots, L_d)\biggr).$$

Solving this expression for $\partial r_{\mathrm{VaR}}^{\alpha}(\boldsymbol{\lambda})/\partial \lambda_i$ and using part (ii) of Lemma 6.26 yields (6.24), as desired. Analogous calculations can be done for $i = 1$ and $\lambda_1 < 0$. Tasche (2000) makes the derivations mathematically rigorous by using the implicit function theorem and giving all necessary conditions. In summary, the capital allocation takes the form $\mathrm{AC}_i = E(L_i \mid L = \mathrm{VaR}_\alpha(L))$, $L := L(\mathbf{1})$.

Expected shortfall and shortfall contributions. Now consider using the risk-measure function $r_{\mathrm{ES}}^{\alpha}(\boldsymbol{\lambda}) = E(L \mid L \geqslant q_\alpha(L(\boldsymbol{\lambda})))$ corresponding to expected shortfall. It follows from Definition 2.15 that we can write

$$r_{\mathrm{ES}}^{\alpha}(\boldsymbol{\lambda}) = \frac{1}{1-\alpha}\int_\alpha^1 r_{\mathrm{VaR}}^{u}(\boldsymbol{\lambda})\,\mathrm{d}u,$$

where we make use of the notation $r_{\mathrm{VaR}}^{\alpha}(\boldsymbol{\lambda}) = q_\alpha(L(\boldsymbol{\lambda}))$ as above. We apply the Euler principle by again computing the derivative with respect to λ_i. Assuming the differentiability of $r_{\mathrm{VaR}}^{u}(\boldsymbol{\lambda})$, we have

$$\frac{\partial r_{\mathrm{ES}}^{\alpha}}{\partial \lambda_i}(\boldsymbol{\lambda}) = \frac{1}{1-\alpha}\int_\alpha^1 \frac{\partial r_{\mathrm{VaR}}^{u}}{\partial \lambda_i}(\boldsymbol{\lambda})\,\mathrm{d}u = \frac{1}{1-\alpha}\int_\alpha^1 E(L_i \mid L(\boldsymbol{\lambda}) = q_u(L(\boldsymbol{\lambda})))\,\mathrm{d}u.$$

Now we assume that $f_{L(\boldsymbol{\lambda})}$ is strictly positive so that the df of $L(\boldsymbol{\lambda})$ has a differentiable inverse and we can make the change of variables $v = q_u(L(\boldsymbol{\lambda})) = F_{L(\boldsymbol{\lambda})}^{\leftarrow}(u)$. Since $\mathrm{d}v/\mathrm{d}u = (f_{L(\boldsymbol{\lambda})}(v))^{-1}$, we get

$$\begin{aligned}\frac{\partial r_{\mathrm{ES}}^{\alpha}}{\partial \lambda_i}(\boldsymbol{\lambda}) &= \frac{1}{1-\alpha}\int_{q_\alpha(L(\boldsymbol{\lambda}))}^{\infty} E(L_i \mid L(\boldsymbol{\lambda}) = v) f_{L(\boldsymbol{\lambda})}(v)\,\mathrm{d}v \\ &= \frac{1}{1-\alpha}E(L_i; L(\boldsymbol{\lambda}) \geqslant q_\alpha(L(\boldsymbol{\lambda}))).\end{aligned}$$

This gives a capital allocation of the form

$$\mathrm{AC}_i = E(L_i \mid L \geqslant \mathrm{VaR}_\alpha(L)), \quad L := L(\mathbf{1}), \tag{6.26}$$

where AC_i is known as the *expected shortfall contribution* of investment possibility (or line of business) i. This is a popular allocation principle in practice, and is generally considered to be preferable to the covariance principle and the principle based on VaR contributions. See Notes and Comments for literature on its use in practice in the context of credit portfolios.

Euler allocation for elliptical loss distributions. In the following corollary to Theorem 6.8 we consider the special case of an elliptical loss distribution for the vector of investment opportunities $(L_1, \dots, L_d)$. We consider this distribution to be centred at zero so that it really represents fluctuations of the loss around the expected loss. We find that the relative amounts of capital allocated to each investment opportunity are always the same, regardless of whether we base an Euler allocation on the standard deviation, VaR or expected shortfall risk measures, or indeed any positive-homogeneous risk measure. Thus allocation is very simple in this case: depending on our choice of risk measure we calculate the total risk capital to be allocated and then use a simple partitioning formula given in (6.27) below.

Corollary 6.27. *Assume that $r_\varrho : \Lambda \to \mathbb{R}$ is the risk-measure function of a positive-homogeneous risk measure ϱ depending only on the distribution of the loss. Let $\boldsymbol{L} \sim E_d(\mathbf{0}, \Sigma, \psi)$. Then, under an Euler allocation, the relative capital allocation is given by*

$$\frac{\mathrm{AC}_i}{\mathrm{AC}_j} = \frac{\pi_i^{r_\varrho}(\mathbf{1})}{\pi_j^{r_\varrho}(\mathbf{1})} = \frac{\sum_{k=1}^d \Sigma_{ik}}{\sum_{k=1}^d \Sigma_{jk}}, \quad 1 \leqslant i, j \leqslant d. \tag{6.27}$$

Proof. From the proof of Theorem 6.8 we deduce that, by the positive homogeneity of the risk measure, we have

$$r_\varrho(\boldsymbol{\lambda}) = \varrho(L(\boldsymbol{\lambda})) = \varrho\biggl(\sum_{i=1}^{d} \lambda_i L_i\biggr) = \sqrt{\boldsymbol{\lambda}' \Sigma \boldsymbol{\lambda}}\, \varrho(Y_1),$$

where Y_1 is the first component of a spherical random vector with characteristic generator ψ. For the allocation we get

$$\pi^{r_\varrho}(\boldsymbol{\lambda}) = \nabla r_\varrho(\boldsymbol{\lambda}) = \frac{\Sigma\boldsymbol{\lambda}}{\sqrt{\boldsymbol{\lambda}'\Sigma\boldsymbol{\lambda}}}\varrho(Y_1),$$

from which the result follows. □

6.3.3 Economic Justification of the Euler Principle

Signals for performance measurement. A first economic justification for capital allocation based on the Euler principle was given by Tasche (1999), who addressed the issue of whether it gave "the right signals for investment decisions". He formalized the idea as follows.

Definition 6.28. Let r_ϱ be a risk-measure function which is differentiable on Λ and π^{r_ϱ} an associated per-unit capital allocation principle. Then π^{r_ϱ} is *suitable for performance measurement* if, for all $\boldsymbol{\lambda} \in \Lambda$, we have

$$\frac{\partial}{\partial \lambda_i}\biggl(\frac{-E(L(\boldsymbol{\lambda}))}{r_\varrho(\boldsymbol{\lambda})}\biggr) \begin{cases} > 0, & \text{if } \dfrac{-E(L_i)}{\pi_i^{r_\varrho}(\boldsymbol{\lambda})} > \dfrac{-E(L(\boldsymbol{\lambda}))}{r_\varrho(\boldsymbol{\lambda})}, \\ < 0, & \text{if } \dfrac{-E(L_i)}{\pi_i^{r_\varrho}(\boldsymbol{\lambda})} < \dfrac{-E(L(\boldsymbol{\lambda}))}{r_\varrho(\boldsymbol{\lambda})}. \end{cases}$$

In words, this says that if the performance of investment opportunity i as measured by its per-unit return divided by per-unit risk capital $\pi_i^{r_\varrho}$ is better (respectively, worse) than the performance of the overall portfolio, then increasing (respectively, decreasing) the weight λ_i of that investment opportunity by a small amount improves the overall performance of the portfolio. Tasche then proves the following result, for the proof of which we refer to the original paper.

Proposition 6.29. *Under the assumptions of Definition 6.28, the only per-unit capital allocation principle suitable for performance measurement is the Euler principle.*

Fairness considerations. Another justification for the Euler principle was given by Denault (2001). His approach uses cooperative game theory and is based on the notion of "fairness". Assume that the risk-measure function r_ϱ derives from a coherent risk measure ϱ. In that case, since $\varrho(L) \leqslant \sum_{i=1}^{d} \varrho(L_i)$, the overall risk capital required for the portfolio is smaller than the sum of the risk capital required for the business units on a stand-alone basis. Fairness now means that each business unit profits from this diversification benefit, in the sense that $\mathrm{AC}_i \leqslant \varrho(L_i)$. In the next definition we slightly extend this intuitive notion of fairness.

Definition 6.30. Given a coherent risk measure ϱ with associated risk-measure function r_ϱ, a per-unit capital allocation principle π^{r_ϱ} is said to be *fair* if, for all $\boldsymbol{\lambda} \in \Lambda$ and all $\boldsymbol{\gamma} \in [0, 1]^d$, the following inequality holds:

$$\sum_{i=1}^{d} \gamma_i \lambda_i \pi_i^{r_\varrho}(\boldsymbol{\lambda}) \leqslant r_\varrho(\gamma_1 \lambda_1, \dots, \gamma_d \lambda_d). \tag{6.28}$$

Note that, by the definition of a per-unit capital allocation principle in (6.20), we have equality in (6.28) if we take $\boldsymbol{\gamma} = \mathbf{1}$. The economic interpretation of (6.28) is straightforward for a vector $\boldsymbol{\gamma} \in \{0, 1\}^d$ satisfying $\gamma_i = I_{\{i \in N\}}$, where $N \subset \{1, \dots, d\}$ is a subset of the investment opportunities. In that case the left-hand side of (6.28) gives the combined capital that is allocated to the investment opportunities in the set N given that the overall portfolio is represented by the vector $\boldsymbol{\lambda}$ with loss $L(\boldsymbol{\lambda}) = \sum_{i=1}^d \lambda_i L_i$. The right-hand side is the combined capital allocated to the opportunities in the set N on a stand-alone basis, i.e. in a portfolio with no investments in the opportunities $N^c := \{1, \dots, d\} \setminus N$ and loss given by $\sum_{i \in N} \lambda_i L_i$.

Since ϱ is coherent and, in particular, subadditive, we have

$$\varrho\left(\sum_{i=1}^{d} \lambda_i L_i\right) \leqslant \varrho\left(\sum_{i \in N} \lambda_i L_i\right) + \varrho\left(\sum_{i \in N^c} \lambda_i L_i\right),$$

which essentially says that the investments in N enjoy a diversification benefit by being part of the overall portfolio represented by $\boldsymbol{\lambda}$. Fairness suggests that they should profit from this benefit by being allocated a smaller amount of capital than they would have on a stand-alone basis; this is exactly the content of (6.28).

The interpretation of (6.28) for general $\gamma \in (0, 1]^d$ is more involved, but perhaps easiest if we use the interpretation that the L_i represent losses for different lines of business. We introduce the portfolio $\tilde{\boldsymbol{\lambda}} = (\gamma_1 \lambda_1, \dots, \gamma_d \lambda_d)'$ and note that it represents a *scaling back* of activity across the firm with respect to the original portfolio $\boldsymbol{\lambda}$. We can rewrite (6.28) as

$$\sum_{i=1}^{d} \tilde{\lambda}_i \pi_i^{r_\varrho}(\boldsymbol{\lambda}) \leqslant \sum_{i=1}^{d} \tilde{\lambda}_i \pi_i^{r_\varrho}(\tilde{\boldsymbol{\lambda}}).$$

The left-hand side represents the overall capital allocated to the scaled-back portfolio considered as part of the original portfolio. The right-hand side represents the overall capital allocated to the scaled-back portfolio considered as a stand-alone entity. If the inequality were the other way round, there would be a systematic incentive for business units to scale back their activities.

Translating a game-theoretical result of Aubin (1979) into the context of capital allocation with a coherent risk measure, Denault (2001) shows that for a differentiable risk-measure function r_ϱ that is derived from a coherent risk measure ϱ, the only fair allocation principle is the Euler principle. Obviously, this gives additional support for using the Euler principle if one works in the realm of coherent risk measures.

From a practical point of view, the use of expected shortfall and expected shortfall contributions might be a reasonable choice in many application areas, particularly for credit risk management and loan pricing (see Notes and Comments, where this issue is discussed further).

Notes and Comments

A broad, non-technical discussion of capital allocation and performance measurement is to be found in Matten (2000). The term "Euler principle" seems to have been first used in Patrik, Bernegger and Rüegg (1999). The result (6.24) is found in Gourieroux and Scaillet (2000) and Tasche (2000); the former paper assumes that the losses have a joint density and the latter gives a slightly more general result as well as technical details concerning the differentiability of the VaR and ES risk measures with respect to the portfolio composition. Differentiability of the coherent premium principle of Section 6.1.3 is discussed in Fischer (2003). The derivation of allocation principles from properties of risk measures is also to be found in Goovaerts, Dhaene and Kaas (2003) and Goovaerts, van den Boor and Laeven (2005).

For the arguments concerning suitability of risk measures for performance measurement, see Tasche (1999). The game-theoretic approach to allocation is found in Denault (2001); see also Kalkbrener (2005) for similar arguments. For an early contribution on game theory applied to cost allocation in an insurance context, see Lemaire (1984).

Applications to credit risk are found in Kalkbrener, Lotter and Overbeck (2004) and Merino and Nyfeler (2003); these make strong arguments in favour of the use of expected shortfall contributions. However, Pfeifer (2004) contains some compelling examples to show that expected shortfall as a risk measure and expected shortfall contributions as an allocation method may have some serious deficiencies when used in non-life insurance. The existence of rare, extreme events may lead to absurd capital allocations when based on expected shortfall. The reader is therefore urged to reflect carefully before settling on a specific risk measure and allocation principle. It may also be questionable to base a "coherent" risk-sensitive capital allocation on formal criteria only; for further details on this see Koryciorz (2004).

7 Extreme Value Theory

Much of this chapter is based on the presentation of extreme value theory (EVT) in Embrechts, Klüppelberg and Mikosch (1997) (henceforth EKM) and whenever theoretical detail is missing the reader should consult that text. Our intention here is to provide more information about *the statistical methods of EVT* than is given in EKM, while briefly summarizing the theoretical ideas on which the statistical methods are based.

Broadly speaking, there are two main kinds of model for extreme values. The most traditional models are the *block maxima* models described in Section 7.1: these are models for the largest observations collected from large samples of identically distributed observations.

A more modern and powerful group of models are those for *threshold exceedances*, described in Section 7.2. These are models for all large observations that exceed some high level, and are generally considered to be the most useful for practical applications, due to their more efficient use of the (often limited) data on extreme outcomes.

Section 7.3 is a shorter, theoretical section providing more information about the *tails of some of the distributions* and models that are prominent in this book, including the tails of normal variance mixture models and strictly stationary GARCH models.

Sections 7.5 and 7.6 provide a concise summary of the more important ideas in multivariate extreme value theory; they deal, respectively, with *multivariate maxima* and *multivariate threshold exceedances*. The novelty of these sections is that the ideas are presented as far as possible using the copula methodology of Chapter 5. The style is similar to Sections 7.1 and 7.2, with the main results being mostly stated without proof and an emphasis being given to examples relevant for applications.

7.1 Maxima

To begin with we consider a sequence of iid rvs $(X_i)_{i\in\mathbb{N}}$ representing financial losses. These may have a variety of interpretations, such as operational losses, insurance losses and losses on a credit portfolio over fixed time intervals. Later we relax the assumption of independence and consider that the rvs form a strictly stationary time series of dependent losses; they might be (negative) returns on an investment in a single stock, an index, or a portfolio of investments.

7.1.1 Generalized Extreme Value Distribution

Convergence of sums. The role of the generalized extreme value (GEV) distribution in the theory of extremes is analogous to that of the normal distribution (and more generally the stable laws) in the central limit theory for sums of rvs. Assuming that the underlying rvs $X_1, X_2, \dots$ are iid with a finite variance and writing $S_n = X_1 + \cdots + X_n$ for the sum of the first n rvs, the standard version of the central limit theorem (CLT) says that appropriately normalized sums $(S_n - a_n)/b_n$ converge in distribution to the standard normal distribution as n goes to infinity. The appropriate normalization uses sequences of normalizing constants (a_n) and (b_n) defined by $a_n = nE(X_1)$ and $b_n = \sqrt{\mathrm{var}(X_1)}$. In mathematical notation we have

$$\lim_{n\to\infty} P\left(\frac{S_n - a_n}{b_n} \leqslant x\right) = \Phi(x), \quad x \in \mathbb{R}.$$

Convergence of maxima. Classical EVT is concerned with limiting distributions for normalized maxima $M_n = \max(X_1, \dots, X_n)$ of iid rvs; we refer to these as block maxima. The only possible non-degenerate limiting distributions for normalized block maxima are in the GEV family.

Definition 7.1 (the generalized extreme value (GEV) distribution). The df of the (standard) GEV distribution is given by

$$H_\xi(x) = \begin{cases} \exp(-(1+\xi x)^{-1/\xi}), & \xi \neq 0, \\ \exp(-\mathrm{e}^{-x}), & \xi = 0, \end{cases}$$

where $1 + \xi x > 0$. A three-parameter family is obtained by defining $H_{\xi,\mu,\sigma}(x) := H_\xi((x - \mu)/\sigma)$ for a location parameter $\mu \in \mathbb{R}$ and a scale parameter $\sigma > 0$.

The parameter ξ is known as the *shape* parameter of the GEV distribution and H_ξ defines a *type* of distribution, meaning a family of distributions specified up to location and scaling (see Section A.1.1 for a formal definition). The extreme value distribution in Definition 7.1 is generalized in the sense that the parametric form subsumes three types of distribution which are known by other names according to the value of ξ: when $\xi > 0$ the distribution is a Fréchet distribution; when $\xi = 0$ it is a Gumbel distribution; when $\xi < 0$ it is a Weibull distribution. We also note that for fixed x we have $\lim_{\xi\to 0} H_\xi(x) = H_0(x)$ (from either side) so that the parametrization in Definition 7.1 is *continuous* in ξ, which facilitates the use of this distribution in statistical modelling.

The df and density of the GEV distribution are shown in Figure 7.1 for the three cases $\xi = 0.5$, $\xi = 0$ and $\xi = -0.5$, corresponding to Fréchet, Gumbel and Weibull types, respectively. Observe that the Weibull distribution is a short-tailed distribution with a so-called finite *right endpoint*. The right endpoint of a distribution will be denoted by $x_F = \sup\{x \in \mathbb{R} : F(x) < 1\}$. The Gumbel and Fréchet distributions have infinite right endpoints, but the decay of the tail of the Fréchet distribution is much slower than that of the Gumbel distribution.

Suppose that block maxima M_n of iid rvs converge in distribution under an appropriate normalization. Recalling that $P(M_n \leqslant x) = F^n(x)$, we observe that this

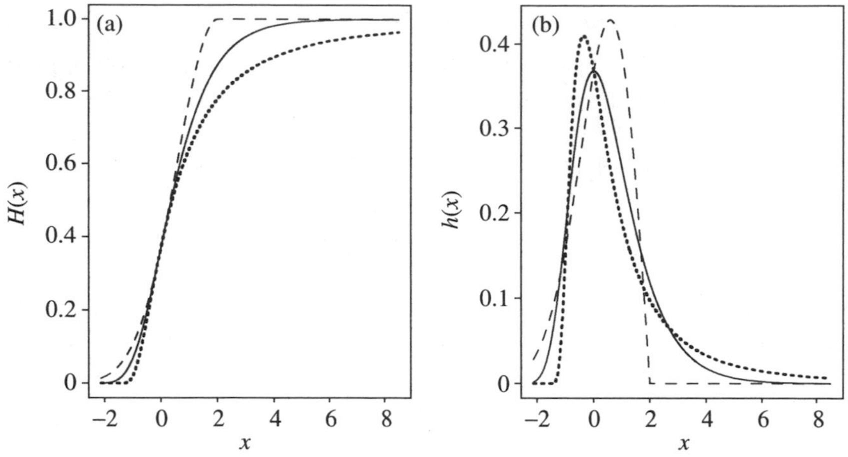

Figure 7.1. (a) The df of a standard GEV distribution in three cases: the solid line corresponds to $\xi = 0$ (Gumbel); the dotted line is $\xi = 0.5$ (Fréchet); and the dashed line is $\xi = -0.5$ (Weibull). (b) Corresponding densities. In all cases $\mu = 0$ and $\sigma = 1$.

convergence means that there exist sequences of real constants (d_n) and (c_n), where $c_n > 0$ for all n, such that

$$\lim_{n\to\infty} P((M_n - d_n)/c_n \leqslant x) = \lim_{n\to\infty} F^n(c_n x + d_n) = H(x) \tag{7.1}$$

for some non-degenerate df $H(x)$. The role of the GEV distribution in the study of maxima is formalized by the following definition and theorem.

Definition 7.2 (maximum domain of attraction). If (7.1) holds for some non-degenerate df H, then F is said to be in the maximum domain of attraction of H, written $F \in \mathrm{MDA}(H)$.

Theorem 7.3 (Fisher–Tippett, Gnedenko). *If $F \in \mathrm{MDA}(H)$ for some non-degenerate df H then H must be a distribution of type H_ξ, i.e. a GEV distribution.*

Remarks 7.4.

(1) If convergence of normalized maxima takes place, the type of the limiting distribution (as specified by ξ) is uniquely determined, although the location and scaling of the limit law (μ and σ) depend on the exact normalizing sequences chosen; this is guaranteed by the so-called "convergence to types theorem" (EKM, p. 554). It is always possible to choose these sequences such that the limit appears in the standard form H_ξ.

(2) By non-degenerate df we mean a limiting distribution which is not concentrated on a single point.

Examples. We calculate two examples to show how the GEV limit emerges for two well-known underlying distributions and appropriately chosen normalizing sequences. To discover how normalizing sequences may be constructed in general we refer to Section 3.3 of EKM.

Example 7.5 (exponential distribution). If the underlying distribution is an exponential distribution with df $F(x) = 1 - \exp(-\beta x)$ for $\beta > 0$ and $x \geqslant 0$, then by choosing normalizing sequences $c_n = 1/\beta$ and $d_n = \ln n/\beta$ we can directly calculate the limiting distribution of maxima using (7.1). We get

$$F^n(c_n x + d_n) = \left(1 - \frac{1}{n}\exp(-x)\right)^n, \quad x \geqslant -\ln n,$$

$$\lim_{n\to\infty} F^n(c_n x + d_n) = \exp(-\mathrm{e}^{-x}), \quad x \in \mathbb{R},$$

from which we conclude that $F \in \mathrm{MDA}(H_0)$.

Example 7.6 (Pareto distribution). If the underlying distribution is a Pareto distribution ($\mathrm{Pa}(\alpha, \kappa)$) with df $F(x) = 1 - (\kappa/(\kappa + x))^{\alpha}$ for $\alpha > 0$, $\kappa > 0$ and $x \geqslant 0$, we can take normalizing sequences $c_n = \kappa n^{1/\alpha}/\alpha$ and $d_n = \kappa n^{1/\alpha} - \kappa$. Using (7.1) we get

$$F^n(c_n x + d_n) = \left(1 - \frac{1}{n}\left(1 + \frac{x}{\alpha}\right)^{-\alpha}\right)^n, \quad 1 + \frac{x}{\alpha} \geqslant n^{-1/\alpha},$$

$$\lim_{n\to\infty} F^n(c_n x + d_n) = \exp\left(-\left(1 + \frac{x}{\alpha}\right)^{-\alpha}\right), \quad 1 + \frac{x}{\alpha} > 0,$$

from which we conclude that $F \in \mathrm{MDA}(H_{1/\alpha})$.

Convergence of minima. The limiting theory for convergence of maxima encompasses the limiting behaviour of minima using the identity

$$\min(X_1, \dots, X_n) = -\max(-X_1, \dots, -X_n). \tag{7.2}$$

It is not difficult to see that normalized minima of iid samples with df F will convergence in distribution if the df $\tilde{F}(x) = 1 - F(-x)$, which is the df of the rvs $-X_1, \dots, -X_n$, is in the maximum domain of attraction of an extreme value distribution. Writing $M_n^* = \max(-X_1, \dots, -X_n)$ and assuming that $\tilde{F} \in \mathrm{MDA}(H_\xi)$ we have

$$\lim_{n\to\infty} P\left(\frac{M_n^* - d_n}{c_n} \leqslant x\right) = H_\xi(x),$$

from which it follows easily, using (7.2), that

$$\lim_{n\to\infty} P\left(\frac{\min(X_1, \dots, X_n) + d_n}{c_n} \leqslant x\right) = 1 - H_\xi(-x).$$

Thus appropriate limits for minima are distributions of type $1 - H_\xi(-x)$. For a symmetric distribution F we have $\tilde{F}(x) = F(x)$, so that if H_ξ is the limiting type of distribution for maxima for a particular value of ξ, then $1 - H_\xi(-x)$ is the limiting type of distribution for minima.

7.1.2 Maximum Domains of Attraction

For most applications it is sufficient to note that essentially all the common continuous distributions of statistics or actuarial science are in $\mathrm{MDA}(H_\xi)$ for some value of ξ. In this section we consider the issue of which underlying distributions lead to which limits for maxima.

The Fréchet case. The distributions that lead to the Fréchet limit $H_\xi(x)$ for $\xi > 0$ have a particularly elegant characterization involving *slowly varying* or *regularly varying* functions.

Definition 7.7 (slowly varying and regularly varying functions).

(i) A positive, Lebesgue-measurable function L on $(0, \infty)$ is slowly varying at ∞ if

$$\lim_{x\to\infty} \frac{L(tx)}{L(x)} = 1, \quad t > 0.$$

(ii) A positive, Lebesgue-measurable function h on $(0, \infty)$ is regularly varying at ∞ with index $\rho \in \mathbb{R}$ if

$$\lim_{x\to\infty} \frac{h(tx)}{h(x)} = t^\rho, \quad t > 0.$$

Slowly varying functions are functions which, in comparison with power functions, change relatively slowly for large x, an example being the logarithm $L(x) = \ln(x)$. Regularly varying functions are functions which can be represented by power functions multiplied by slowly varying functions, i.e. $h(x) = x^\rho L(x)$.

Theorem 7.8 (Fréchet MDA, Gnedenko). *For $\xi > 0$,*

$$F \in \mathrm{MDA}(H_\xi) \iff \bar{F}(x) = x^{-1/\xi} L(x) \tag{7.3}$$

for some function L slowly varying at ∞.

This means that distributions giving rise to the Fréchet case are distributions with tails that are regularly varying functions with a negative index of variation. Their tails decay essentially like a power function and the rate of decay $\alpha = 1/\xi$ is often referred to as the *tail index* of the distribution.

These distributions are the most studied distributions in EVT and they are of particular interest in financial applications because they are heavy-tailed distributions with infinite higher moments. If X is a non-negative rv whose df F is an element of $\mathrm{MDA}(H_\xi)$ for $\xi > 0$, then it may be shown that $E(X^k) = \infty$ for $k > 1/\xi$ (EKM, p. 568). If, for some small $\varepsilon > 0$, the distribution is in $\mathrm{MDA}(H_{(1/2)+\varepsilon})$, it is an infinite-variance distribution, and if the distribution is in $\mathrm{MDA}(H_{(1/4)+\varepsilon})$, it is a distribution with infinite fourth moment.

Example 7.9 (Pareto distribution). In Example 7.6 we verified by direct calculation that normalized maxima of iid Pareto variates converge to a Fréchet distribution. Observe that the tail of the Pareto df in (A.13) may be written $\bar{F}(x) = x^{-\alpha} L(x)$, where it may be easily checked that $L(x) = (\kappa^{-1} + x^{-1})^{-\alpha}$ is a slowly varying function; indeed, as $x \to \infty$, $L(x)$ converges to the constant κ^α. Thus we verify that the Pareto df has the form (7.3).

Further examples of distributions giving rise to the Fréchet limit for maxima include the Fréchet distribution itself, inverse gamma, Student t, loggamma, F and Burr distributions. We will provide further demonstrations for some of these distributions in Section 7.3.1.

The Gumbel case. The characterization of distributions in this class is more complicated than in the Fréchet class. We have seen in Example 7.5 that the exponential distribution is in the Gumbel class and, more generally, it could be said that the distributions in this class have tails that have an essentially exponential decay. A positive-valued rv with a df in $\text{MDA}(H_0)$ has finite moments of any positive order, i.e. $E(X^k) < \infty$ for every $k > 0$ (EKM, p. 148).

However, there is a great deal of variety in the tails of distributions in this class, so, for example, both the normal and the lognormal distributions belong to the Gumbel class (EKM, pp. 145–147). The normal distribution, as discussed in Section 3.1.4, is thin tailed, but the lognormal distribution has much heavier tails and we would need to collect a lot of data from the lognormal distribution before we could distinguish its tail behaviour from that of a distribution in the Fréchet class.

In financial modelling it is often erroneously assumed that the only interesting models for financial returns are the power-tailed distributions of the Fréchet class. The Gumbel class is also interesting because it contains many distributions with much heavier tails than the normal, even if these are not regularly varying power tails. Examples are hyperbolic and generalized hyperbolic distributions (with the exception of the special boundary case that is Student t).

Other distributions in $\text{MDA}(H_0)$ include the gamma, chi-squared, standard Weibull (to be distinguished from the Weibull special case of the GEV distribution) and Benktander type I and II distributions (which are popular actuarial loss distributions) and the Gumbel itself. We provide demonstrations for some of these examples in Section 7.3.2.

The Weibull case. This is perhaps the least important case for financial modelling, at least in the area of market risk, since the distributions in this class all have finite *right endpoints*. Although all potential financial and insurance losses are, in practice, bounded, we will still tend to favour models that have infinite support for loss modelling. An exception may be in the area of credit risk modelling, where we will see in Chapter 8 that probability distributions on the unit interval [0, 1] are very useful. A characterization of the Weibull class is as follows.

Theorem 7.10 (Weibull MDA, Gnedenko). *For* $\xi < 0$,

$$F \in \text{MDA}(H_{1/\xi}) \iff x_F < \infty \text{ and } \bar{F}(x_F - x^{-1}) = x^{1/\xi} L(x)$$

for some function L slowly varying at ∞.

It can be shown (EKM, p. 137) that a beta distribution with density $f_{\alpha,\beta}$ as given in (A.4) is in $\text{MDA}(H_{-1/\beta})$. This includes the special case of the uniform distribution for $\beta = \alpha = 1$.

7.1.3 Maxima of Strictly Stationary Time Series

The standard theory of the previous sections concerns maxima of iid sequences. With financial time series in mind, we now look briefly at the theory for maxima of strictly stationary time series and find that the same types of limiting distribution apply.

In this section let $(X_i)_{i \in \mathbb{Z}}$ denote a strictly stationary time series with stationary distribution F and let $(\tilde{X}_i)_{i \in \mathbb{N}}$ denote the *associated iid process*, i.e. a strict white noise process with the same df F. Let $M_n = \max(X_1, \dots, X_n)$ and $\tilde{M}_n = \max(\tilde{X}_1, \dots, \tilde{X}_n)$ denote block maxima of the original series and the iid series, respectively.

For many processes $(X_i)_{i \in \mathbb{N}}$, it may be shown that there exists a real number θ in $(0, 1]$ such that

$$\lim_{n \to \infty} P\{(\tilde{M}_n - d_n)/c_n \leqslant x\} = H(x) \tag{7.4}$$

for a non-degenerate limit $H(x)$ if and only if

$$\lim_{n \to \infty} P\{(M_n - d_n)/c_n \leqslant x\} = H^{\theta}(x). \tag{7.5}$$

For such processes this value θ is known as the *extremal index* of the process (not to be confused with the tail index of distributions in the Fréchet class). A formal definition is more technical (see Notes and Comments) but the basic ideas behind (7.4) and (7.5) are easily explained.

For processes with an extremal index, normalized block maxima converge in distribution provided that maxima of the associated iid process converge in distribution: that is, provided the underlying distribution F is in $\mathrm{MDA}(H_\xi)$ for some ξ. Moreover, since $H_\xi^{\theta}(x)$ can be easily verified to be a distribution of the same type as $H_\xi(x)$, the limiting distribution of the normalized block maxima of the dependent series is a GEV distribution with exactly the same ξ parameter as the limit for the associated iid data; only the location and scaling of the distribution may change.

Writing $u = c_n x + d_n$ we observe that, for large enough n, (7.4) and (7.5) imply that

$$P(M_n \leqslant u) \approx P^{\theta}(\tilde{M}_n \leqslant u) = F^{n\theta}(u), \tag{7.6}$$

so that for u large the probability distribution of the maximum of n observations from the time series with extremal index θ can be approximated by the distribution of the maximum of $n\theta < n$ observations from the associated iid series. In a sense, $n\theta$ can be thought of as counting the number of roughly independent *clusters* of observations in n observations, and θ is often interpreted as the reciprocal of the mean cluster size.

Not every strictly stationary process has an extremal index (see EKM, p. 418, for a counterexample) but, for the kinds of time series processes that interest us in financial modelling, an extremal index generally exists. Essentially, we only have to distinguish between the cases when $\theta = 1$ and the cases when $\theta < 1$: for the former there is no tendency to cluster at high levels and large sample maxima from the time series behave exactly like maxima from similarly sized iid samples; for the latter we must be aware of a tendency for extreme values to cluster.

Table 7.1. Approximate values of the extremal index as a function of the parameter α_1 for the ARCH(1) process in (4.24).

α_1	0.1	0.3	0.5	0.7	0.9
θ	0.999	0.939	0.835	0.721	0.612

- Strict white noise processes (iid rvs) have extremal index $\theta = 1$.
- ARMA processes with Gaussian strict white noise innovations have $\theta = 1$ (EKM, pp. 216–218). However, if the innovation distribution is in MDA(H_ξ) for $\xi > 0$, then $\theta < 1$ (EKM, pp. 415, 416).
- ARCH and GARCH processes have $\theta < 1$ (EKM, pp. 476–480).

The final fact is particularly relevant to our financial applications, since we saw in Chapter 4 that ARCH and GARCH processes provide good models for many financial return series.

Example 7.11 (the extremal index of the ARCH(1) process). In Table 7.1 we reproduce some results from de Haan et al. (1989), who calculate approximate values for the extremal index of the ARCH(1) process (see Definition 4.16) using a Monte Carlo simulation approach. Clearly, the stronger the ARCH effect (that is, the magnitude of the parameter α_1), the greater the tendency of the process to cluster. For a process with parameter 0.9 the extremal index value $\theta = 0.612$ is interpreted as suggesting that the average cluster size is $1/\theta = 1.64$.

7.1.4 The Block Maxima Method

Fitting the GEV distribution. Suppose we have data from an unknown underlying distribution F, which we suppose lies in the domain of attraction of an extreme value distribution H_ξ for some ξ. If the data are realizations of iid variables, or variables from a process with an extremal index such as GARCH, the implication of the theory is that the true distribution of the n-block maximum M_n can be approximated for large enough n by a three-parameter GEV distribution $H_{\xi,\mu,\sigma}$.

We make use of this idea by fitting the GEV distribution $H_{\xi,\mu,\sigma}$ to data on the n-block maximum. Obviously we need repeated observations of an n-block maximum and we assume that the data can be divided into m blocks of size n. This makes most sense when there are natural ways of blocking the data. The method has its origins in hydrology, where, for example, daily measurements of water levels might be divided into yearly blocks and the yearly maxima collected. Analogously, we will consider financial applications where daily return data (recorded on trading days) are divided into yearly (or semesterly or quarterly) blocks and the maximum daily falls within these blocks are analysed.

We denote the block maximum of the jth block by M_{nj}, so our data are $M_{n1}, \dots, M_{nm}$. The GEV distribution can be fitted using various methods, including maximum likelihood. An alternative is the method of probability-weighted moments (see Notes and Comments). In implementing maximum likelihood it will be assumed that the block size n is quite large so that, regardless of whether the underlying data are dependent or not, the block maxima observations can be taken to be independent.

In this case, writing $h_{\xi,\mu,\sigma}$ for the density of the GEV distribution, the log-likelihood is easily calculated to be

$$
\begin{aligned}
l(\xi, \mu, \sigma; M_{n1}, \dots, M_{nm}) \\
&= \sum_{i=1}^{m} \ln h_{\xi,\mu,\sigma}(M_{ni}) \\
&= -m \ln \sigma - \left(1 + \frac{1}{\xi}\right) \sum_{i=1}^{m} \ln \left(1 + \xi \frac{M_{ni} - \mu}{\sigma}\right) - \sum_{i=1}^{m} \left(1 + \xi \frac{M_{ni} - \mu}{\sigma}\right)^{-1/\xi},
\end{aligned}
$$

which must be maximized subject to the parameter constraints that $\sigma > 0$ and $1 + \xi(M_{ni} - \mu)/\sigma > 0$ for all i. While this represents an irregular likelihood problem, due to the dependence of the parameter space on the values of the data, the consistency and asymptotic efficiency of the resulting MLEs can be established for the case when $\xi > -\frac{1}{2}$ using results in Smith (1985).

In determining the number and size of the blocks (m and n, respectively), a trade-off necessarily takes place: roughly speaking, a large value of n leads to a more accurate approximation of the block maxima distribution by a GEV distribution and a low bias in the parameter estimates; a large value of m gives more block maxima data for the ML estimation and leads to a low variance in the parameter estimates. Note also that, in the case of dependent data, somewhat larger block sizes than are used in the iid case may be advisable; dependence generally has the effect that convergence to the GEV distribution is slower, since the effective sample size is $n\theta$, which is smaller than n.

Example 7.12 (block maxima analysis of S&P return data). Suppose we turn the clock back and imagine it is the early evening of Friday 16 October 1987. An unusually turbulent week in the equity markets has seen the S&P 500 index fall by 9.21%. On that Friday alone the index is down 5.25% on the previous day, the largest one-day fall since 1962.

We fit the GEV distribution to annual maximum daily percentage falls in value for the S&P index. Using data going back to 1960, shown in Figure 7.2, gives us 28 observations of the annual maximum fall (including the latest observation from the incomplete year 1987). The estimated parameter values are $\hat{\xi} = 0.27$, $\hat{\mu} = 2.04$ and $\hat{\sigma} = 0.72$ with standard errors 0.21, 0.16 and 0.14, respectively. Thus the fitted distribution is a heavy-tailed Fréchet distribution with an infinite fourth moment, suggesting that the underlying distribution is heavy-tailed. Note that the standard errors imply considerable uncertainty in our analysis, as might be expected with only 28 observations of maxima. In fact, in a likelihood ratio test of the null hypothesis that a Gumbel model fits the data ($H_0 : \xi = 0$), the null hypothesis cannot be rejected.

To increase the number of blocks we also fit a GEV model to 56 semesterly maxima and obtain the parameter estimates $\hat{\xi} = 0.36$, $\hat{\mu} = 1.65$ and $\hat{\sigma} = 0.54$ with standard errors 0.15, 0.09 and 0.08. This model has an even heavier tail, and the null hypothesis that a Gumbel model is adequate is now rejected.

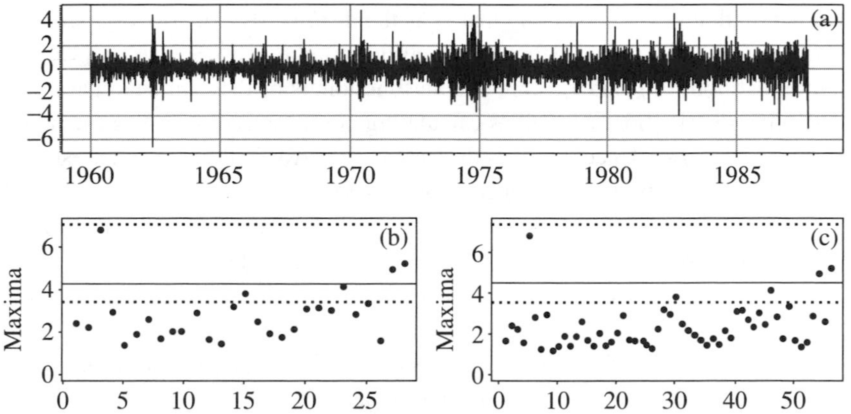

Figure 7.2. (a) S&P percentage returns for the period 1960 to 16 October 1987. (b) Annual maxima of daily falls in the index; superimposed is an estimate of the 10-year return level with associated 95% confidence interval (dotted lines). (c) Semesterly maxima of daily falls in the index; superimposed is an estimate of the 20-semester return level with associated 95% confidence interval. See Examples 7.12 and 7.15 for full details.

Return levels and stress losses. The fitted GEV model can be used to analyse stress losses and we focus here on two possibilities: in the first approach we define the frequency of occurrence of the stress event and estimate its magnitude, this being known as the *return-level* estimation problem; in the second approach we define the size of the stress event and estimate the frequency of its occurrence, this being the *return-period* problem.

Definition 7.13 (return level). Let H denote the df of the true distribution of the n-block maximum. The k n-block return level is $r_{n,k} = q_{1-1/k}(H)$, i.e. the $(1 - 1/k)$-quantile of H.

The k n-block return level can be roughly interpreted as that level which is exceeded in one out of every k n-blocks on average. For example, the 10-trading-year return level $r_{260,10}$ is that level which is exceeded in one out of every 10 years on average. (In the notation we assume that every year has 260 trading days, although this is only an average and there will be slight differences from year to year.) Using our fitted model we would estimate a return level by

$$\hat{r}_{n,k} = H^{-1}_{\hat{\xi},\hat{\mu},\hat{\sigma}}\left(1 - \frac{1}{k}\right) = \hat{\mu} + \frac{\hat{\sigma}}{\hat{\xi}}\left(\left(-\ln\left(1 - \frac{1}{k}\right)\right)^{-\hat{\xi}} - 1\right). \tag{7.7}$$

Definition 7.14 (return period). Let H denote the df of the true distribution of the n-block maximum. The return period of the event $\{M_n > u\}$ is given by $k_{n,u} = 1/\bar{H}(u)$.

Observe that the return period $k_{n,u}$ is defined in such a way that the $k_{n,u}$ n-block return level is u. In other words, in $k_{n,u}$ n-blocks we would expect to observe a single block in which the level u was exceeded. If there was a strong tendency for the extreme values to cluster, we might expect to see multiple exceedances of the level within that block. Assuming that H is the df of a GEV distribution and using our fitted model, we would estimate the return period by $\hat{k}_{n,u} = 1/\bar{H}_{\hat{\xi},\hat{\mu},\hat{\sigma}}(u)$.

Note that both $\hat{r}_{n,k}$ and $\hat{k}_{n,u}$ are simple functionals of the estimated parameters of the GEV distribution. As well as calculating point estimates for these quantities we should give confidence intervals that reflect the error in the parameter estimates of the GEV distribution. A good method is to base such confidence intervals on the likelihood ratio statistic, as described in Section A.3.5. To do this we reparametrize the GEV distribution in terms of the quantity of interest. For example, in the case of return level, let $\phi = H^{-1}_{\xi,\mu,\sigma}(1 - (1/k))$ and parametrize the GEV distribution by $\boldsymbol{\theta} = (\phi, \xi, \sigma)'$ rather than $\boldsymbol{\theta} = (\xi, \mu, \sigma)'$. The maximum likelihood estimate of ϕ is the estimate (7.7) and a confidence interval can be constructed according to the method in Section A.3.5 (see (A.22) in particular).

Example 7.15 (stress losses for S&P return data). We continue Example 7.12 by estimating the 10-year return level and the 20-semester return level based on data up to 16 October 1987, using (7.7) for the point estimate and the likelihood ratio method as described above to get confidence intervals. The point estimator of the 10-year return level is 4.3% with a 95% confidence interval of (3.4, 7.1); the point estimator of the 20-semester return level is 4.5% with a 95% confidence interval of (3.5, 7.4). Clearly, there is some uncertainty about the size of events of this frequency even with 28 years or 56 semesters of data.

The day after the end of our dataset, 19 October 1987, was Black Monday. The index fell by the unprecedented amount of 20.5% in one day. This event is well outside our confidence interval for a 10-year loss. If we were to estimate a 50-year return level (an event beyond our experience if we have 28 years of data), then our point estimate would be 7.0 with a confidence interval of (4.7, 22.2), so the 1987 crash lies close to the upper boundary of our confidence interval for a much rarer event. But the 28 maxima are really too few to get a reliable estimate for an event as rare as the 50-year event.

If we turn the problem around and attempt to estimate the return period of a 20.5% loss, the point estimate is 2100 years (i.e. a 2 millennium event) but the 95% confidence interval encompasses everything from 45 years to essentially never! The analysis of semesterly maxima gives only moderately more informative results: the point estimate is 1400 semesters; the confidence interval runs from 100 semesters to 1.6×10^6 semesters. In summary, on 16 October 1987 we simply did not have the data to say anything meaningful about an event of this magnitude. This illustrates the inherent difficulties of attempting to quantify events beyond our empirical experience.

Notes and Comments

The main source for this chapter is Embrechts, Klüppelberg and Mikosch (1997) (EKM). Further important texts on EVT include Gumbel (1958), Leadbetter, Lindgren and Rootzén (1983), Galambos (1987), Resnick (1987), Falk, Hüsler and Reiss (1994), Reiss and Thomas (1997), Coles (2001) and Beirlant et al. (2004).

The forms of the limit law for maxima were first studied by Fisher and Tippett (1928). The subject was brought to full mathematical fruition in the fundamental papers of Gnedenko (1941, 1943). The concept of the extremal index, which appears in the theory of maxima of stationary series, has a long history. The first mathematically precise definition seems to have been given by Leadbetter (1983). See also Leadbetter, Lindgren and Rootzén (1983) and Smith and Weissman (1994) for more details. The theory required to calculate the extremal index of an ARCH(1) process (as in Table 7.1) is found in de Haan et al. (1989) and also in EKM, pp. 473–480. For the GARCH(1, 1) process consult Mikosch and Stărică (2000).

A further difficult task is the statistical estimation of the extremal index from time series data under the assumption that these data do indeed come from a process with an extremal index. Two general methods known as the *blocks* and *runs* methods are described in EKM, Section 8.1.3; these methods go back to work of Hsing (1991) and Smith and Weissman (1994). Although the estimators have been used in real-world data analyses (see, for example, Davison and Smith 1990)), it remains true that the extremal index is a very difficult parameter to estimate accurately.

The maximum likelihood fitting of the GEV distribution is described by Hosking (1985) and Hosking, Wallis and Wood (1985). Consistency and asymptotic normality can be demonstrated for the case $\xi > -0.5$ using results in Smith (1985). An alternative method known as probability-weighted moments (PWM) has been proposed by Hosking, Wallis and Wood (1985) (see also EKM, pp. 321–323). The analysis of block maxima in Examples 7.12 and 7.15 is based on McNeil (1998). Analyses of financial data using the block maxima method may also be found in Longin (1996), one of the earliest papers to apply EVT methodology to financial data.

7.2 Threshold Exceedances

The block maxima method discussed in Section 7.1.4 has the major defect that it is very wasteful of data; to perform our analyses we retain only the maximum losses in large blocks. For this reason it has been largely superseded in practice by methods based on threshold exceedances, where we use all data that are extreme in the sense that they exceed a particular designated high level.

7.2.1 Generalized Pareto Distribution

The main distributional model for exceedances over thresholds is the generalized Pareto distribution (GPD).

Definition 7.16 (GPD). The df of the GPD is given by

$$G_{\xi,\beta}(x) = \begin{cases} 1 - (1 + \xi x/\beta)^{-1/\xi}, & \xi \neq 0, \\ 1 - \exp(-x/\beta), & \xi = 0, \end{cases} \tag{7.8}$$

where $\beta > 0$, and $x \geqslant 0$ when $\xi \geqslant 0$ and $0 \leqslant x \leqslant -\beta/\xi$ when $\xi < 0$. The parameters ξ and β are referred to, respectively, as the *shape* and *scale* parameters.

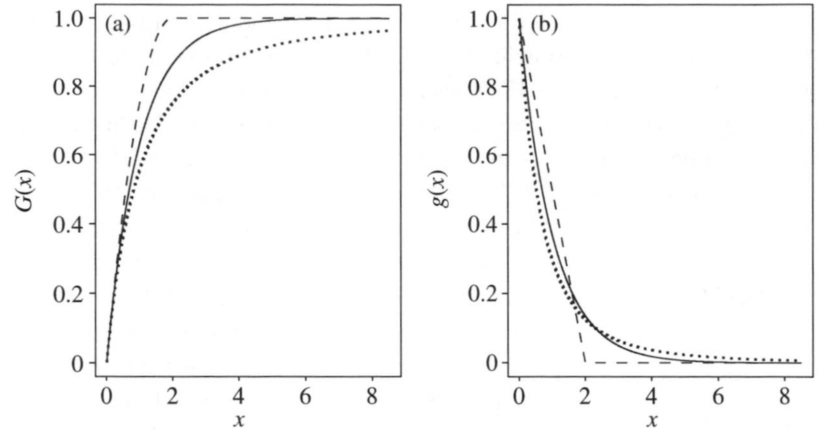

Figure 7.3. (a) Distribution function of GPD in three cases: the solid line corresponds to $\xi = 0$ (exponential); the dotted line to $\xi = 0.5$ (a Pareto distribution); and the dashed line to $\xi = -0.5$ (Pareto type II). The scale parameter β is equal to 1 in all cases. (b) Corresponding densities.

Like the GEV distribution in Definition 7.1, the GPD is generalized in the sense that it contains a number of special cases: when $\xi > 0$ the df $G_{\xi,\beta}$ is that of an ordinary Pareto distribution with $\alpha = 1/\xi$ and $\kappa = \beta/\xi$ (see Section A.2.8); when $\xi = 0$ we have an exponential distribution; when $\xi < 0$ we have a short-tailed, Pareto type II distribution. Moreover, as in the case of the GEV distribution, for fixed x the parametric form is continuous in ξ, so $\lim_{\xi \to 0} G_{\xi,\beta}(x) = G_{0,\beta}(x)$. The df and density of the GPD for various values of ξ and $\beta = 1$ are shown in Figure 7.3.

In terms of domains of attraction we have that $G_{\xi,\beta} \in \mathrm{MDA}(H_\xi)$ for all $\xi \in \mathbb{R}$. Note that, for $\xi > 0$ and $\xi < 0$, this assertion follows easily from the characterizations in Theorems 7.8 and 7.10. In the heavy-tailed case, $\xi > 0$, it may be easily verified that $E(X^k) = \infty$ for $k \geqslant 1/\xi$. The mean of the GPD is defined provided $\xi < 1$ and is

$$E(X) = \beta/(1 - \xi). \tag{7.9}$$

The role of the GPD in EVT is as a natural model for the *excess distribution* over a high threshold. We define this concept along with the *mean excess function*, which will also play an important role in the theory.

Definition 7.17 (excess distribution over threshold u). Let X be an rv with df F. The excess distribution over the threshold u has df

$$F_u(x) = P(X - u \leqslant x \mid X > u) = \frac{F(x + u) - F(u)}{1 - F(u)} \tag{7.10}$$

for $0 \leqslant x < x_F - u$, where $x_F \leqslant \infty$ is the right endpoint of F.

Definition 7.18 (mean excess function). The mean excess function of an rv X with finite mean is given by

$$e(u) = E(X - u \mid X > u). \tag{7.11}$$

The excess df F_u describes the distribution of the excess loss over the threshold u, given that u is exceeded. The mean excess function $e(u)$ expresses the mean of F_u as a function of u. In survival analysis the excess df is more commonly known as the residual life df—it expresses the probability that, say, an electrical component which has functioned for u units of time fails in the time period $(u, u + x]$. The mean excess function is known as the mean residual life function and gives the expected residual lifetime for components with different ages. For the special case of the GPD, the excess df and mean excess function are easily calculated.

Example 7.19 (excess distribution of exponential and GPD). If F is the df of an exponential rv, then it is easily verified that $F_u(x) = F(x)$ for all x, which is the famous *lack-of-memory* property of the exponential distribution—the residual lifetime of the aforementioned electrical component would be independent of the amount of time that component has already survived. More generally, if X has df $F = G_{\xi,\beta}$, then, using (7.10), the excess df is easily calculated to be

$$F_u(x) = G_{\xi,\beta(u)}(x), \quad \beta(u) = \beta + \xi u, \tag{7.12}$$

where $0 \leqslant x < \infty$ if $\xi \geqslant 0$ and $0 \leqslant x \leqslant -(\beta/\xi) - u$ if $\xi < 0$. The excess distribution remains a GPD with the same shape parameter ξ but with a scaling that grows linearly with the threshold u. The mean excess function of the GPD is easily calculated from (7.12) and (7.9) to be

$$e(u) = \frac{\beta(u)}{1-\xi} = \frac{\beta + \xi u}{1-\xi}, \tag{7.13}$$

where $0 \leqslant u < \infty$ if $0 \leqslant \xi < 1$ and $0 \leqslant u \leqslant -\beta/\xi$ if $\xi < 0$. It may be observed that the mean excess function is *linear in the threshold* u, which is a characterizing property of the GPD.

Example 7.19 shows that the GPD has a kind of stability property under the operation of calculating excess distributions. We now give a mathematical result that shows that the GPD is, in fact, a natural limiting excess distribution for many underlying loss distributions. The result can also be viewed as a characterization theorem for the domain of attraction of the GEV distribution. In Section 7.1.2 we looked separately at characterizations for each of the three cases $\xi > 0$, $\xi = 0$ and $\xi < 0$; the following result offers a global characterization of $\mathrm{MDA}(H_\xi)$ for all ξ in terms of the limiting behaviour of excess distributions over thresholds.

Theorem 7.20 (Pickands–Balkema–de Haan). *We can find a (positive-measurable function) $\beta(u)$ such that*

$$\lim_{u \to x_F} \sup_{0 \leqslant x < x_F - u} |F_u(x) - G_{\xi,\beta(u)}(x)| = 0,$$

if and only if $F \in \mathrm{MDA}(H_\xi)$, $\xi \in \mathbb{R}$.

Thus the distributions for which normalized maxima converge to a GEV distribution constitute a set of distributions for which the excess distribution converges to the GPD as the threshold is raised; moreover, the shape parameter of the limiting

GPD for the excesses is the same as the shape parameter of the limiting GEV distribution for the maxima. We have already stated in Section 7.1.2 that essentially all the commonly used continuous distributions of statistics are in $\mathrm{MDA}(H_\xi)$ for some ξ, so Theorem 7.20 proves to be a very widely applicable result that essentially says that the GPD is *the canonical distribution* for modelling excess losses over high thresholds.

7.2.2 Modelling Excess Losses

We exploit Theorem 7.20 by assuming that we are dealing with a loss distribution $F \in \mathrm{MDA}(H_\xi)$ so that, for some suitably chosen high threshold u, we can model F_u by a generalized Pareto distribution. We formalize this with the following assumption.

Assumption 7.21. *Let F be a loss distribution with right endpoint x_F and assume that for some high threshold u we have $F_u(x) = G_{\xi,\beta}(x)$ for $0 \leqslant x < x_F - u$ and some $\xi \in \mathbb{R}$ and $\beta > 0$.*

This is clearly an idealization, since in practice the excess distribution will generally not be *exactly* GPD, but we use Assumption 7.21 to make a number of calculations in the following sections.

The method. Given loss data $X_1, \dots, X_n$ from F, a random number N_u will exceed our threshold u; it will be convenient to relabel these data $\tilde{X}_1, \dots, \tilde{X}_{N_u}$. For each of these exceedances we calculate the amount $Y_j = \tilde{X}_j - u$ of the excess loss. We wish to estimate the parameters of a GPD model by fitting this distribution to the N_u excess losses. There are various ways of fitting the GPD including maximum likelihood (ML) and probability-weighted moments (PWM). The former method is more commonly used and is easy to implement if the excess data can be assumed to be realizations of independent rvs, since the joint density will then be a product of marginal GPD densities.

Writing $g_{\xi,\beta}$ for the density of the GPD, the log-likelihood may be easily calculated to be

$$\begin{aligned} \ln L(\xi, \beta; Y_1, \dots, Y_{N_u}) &= \sum_{j=1}^{N_u} \ln g_{\xi,\beta}(Y_j) \\ &= -N_u \ln \beta - \left(1 + \frac{1}{\xi}\right) \sum_{j=1}^{N_u} \ln\left(1 + \xi \frac{Y_j}{\beta}\right), \end{aligned} \tag{7.14}$$

which must be maximized subject to the parameter constraints that $\beta > 0$ and $1 + \xi Y_j/\beta > 0$ for all j. Solving the maximization problem yields a GPD model $G_{\hat{\xi},\hat{\beta}}$ for the excess distribution F_u.

Non-iid data. For insurance or operational risk data the iid assumption is often unproblematic, but this is clearly not true for time series of financial returns. If the data are serially dependent but show no tendency to give clusters of extreme values, then this might suggest that the underlying process has extremal index $\theta = 1$. In this case, asymptotic theory that we summarize in Section 7.4 suggests a limiting model for high-level threshold exceedances, in which exceedances occur according to a Poisson process and the excess loss amounts are iid generalized Pareto distributed. If extremal clustering is present, suggesting an extremal index $\theta < 1$ (as would be consistent with an underlying GARCH process), the assumption of independent excess losses is less satisfactory. The easiest approach is to neglect this problem and to consider the ML method to be a quasi-maximum likelihood (QML) method, where the likelihood is misspecified with respect to the serial dependence structure of the data; we follow this course in this section. The point estimates should still be reasonable, although standard errors may be too small. In Section 7.4 we discuss threshold exceedances in non-iid data in more detail.

Excesses over higher thresholds. From the model we have fitted to the excess distribution over u we can easily infer a model for the excess distribution over any higher threshold. We have the following lemma.

Lemma 7.22. *Under Assumption 7.21 it follows that $F_v(x) = G_{\xi,\beta+\xi(v-u)}(x)$ for any higher threshold $v \geqslant u$.*

Proof. We use (7.10) and the df of the GPD in (7.8) to infer that

$$\begin{aligned}\bar{F}_v(x) &= \frac{\bar{F}(v+x)}{\bar{F}(v)} = \frac{\bar{F}(u+(x+v-u))}{\bar{F}(u)} \frac{\bar{F}(u)}{\bar{F}(u+(v-u))} \\ &= \frac{\bar{F}_u(x+v-u)}{\bar{F}_u(v-u)} = \frac{\bar{G}_{\xi,\beta}(x+v-u)}{\bar{G}_{\xi,\beta}(v-u)} \\ &= \bar{G}_{\xi,\beta+\xi(v-u)}(x).\end{aligned}$$

□

Thus the excess distribution over higher thresholds remains a GPD with the same ξ parameter but a scaling that grows linearly with the threshold v. Provided that $\xi < 1$, the mean excess function is given by

$$e(v) = \frac{\beta+\xi(v-u)}{1-\xi} = \frac{\xi v}{1-\xi} + \frac{\beta-\xi u}{1-\xi}, \tag{7.15}$$

where $u \leqslant v < \infty$ if $0 \leqslant \xi < 1$ and $u \leqslant v \leqslant u - \beta/\xi$ if $\xi < 0$.

The linearity of the mean excess function (7.15) in v is commonly used as a diagnostic for data admitting a GPD model for the excess distribution. It forms the basis for the following simple graphical method for choosing an appropriate threshold.

Sample mean excess plot. For positive-valued loss data $X_1, \dots, X_n$ we define the *sample mean excess function* to be an empirical estimator of the mean excess function in Definition 7.18. The estimator is given by

$$e_n(v) = \frac{\sum_{i=1}^n (X_i - v) I_{\{X_i > v\}}}{\sum_{i=1}^n I_{\{X_i > v\}}}. \tag{7.16}$$

To study this function we generally construct the mean excess plot $\{(X_{i,n}, e_n(X_{i,n})) : 2 \leqslant i \leqslant n\}$, where $X_{i,n}$ denotes the ith order statistic. If the data support a GPD model over a high threshold, then (7.15) suggests that this plot should become increasingly "linear" for higher values of v. A linear upward trend indicates a GPD model with positive shape parameter ξ; a plot tending towards the horizontal indicates a GPD with approximately zero shape parameter, or, in other words, an exponential excess distribution; a linear downward trend indicates a GPD with negative shape parameter.

These are the ideal situations but in practice some experience is required to read mean excess plots. Even for data that are genuinely generalized Pareto distributed, the sample mean excess plot is seldom perfectly linear, particularly towards the right-hand end, where we are averaging a small number of large excesses. In fact we often omit the final few points from consideration, as they can severely distort the picture. If we do see visual evidence that the mean excess plot becomes linear, then we might select as our threshold u a value towards the beginning of the linear section of the plot (see, in particular, Example 7.24).

Example 7.23 (Danish fire loss data). The Danish fire insurance data are a well-studied set of financial losses that neatly illustrate the basic ideas behind modelling observations that seem consistent with an iid model. The dataset consists of 2156 fire insurance losses over 1 000 000 Danish kroner from 1980 to 1990 inclusive. The loss figure represents a combined loss for a building and its contents, as well as in some cases a loss of business earnings; the losses are inflation adjusted to reflect 1985 values and are shown in Figure 7.4(a).

The mean excess plot in Figure 7.4(b) is in fact fairly "linear" over the entire range of the losses and its upward slope leads us to expect that a GPD with positive shape parameter ξ could be fitted to the entire dataset. However, there is some evidence of a "kink" in the plot below the value 10 and a "straightening out" of the plot above this value, so we have chosen to set our threshold at $u = 10$ and fit a GPD to excess losses above this threshold, in the hope of obtaining a model that is a good fit to the largest of the losses. The ML parameter estimates are $\hat{\xi} = 0.50$ and $\hat{\beta} = 7.0$ with standard errors 0.14 and 1.1, respectively. Thus the model we have fitted is essentially a very heavy-tailed, infinite-variance model. A picture of the fitted GPD model for the excess distribution $\hat{F}_u(x - u)$ is also given in Figure 7.4(c), superimposed on points plotted at empirical estimates of the excess probabilities for each loss; note the good correspondence between the empirical estimates and the GPD curve.

In insurance we might use the model to estimate the expected size of the insurance loss, given that it enters a given insurance *layer*. Thus we can estimate the expected loss size given exceedance of the threshold of 10 000 000 kroner or of any other higher threshold by using (7.15) with the appropriate parameter estimates.

Example 7.24 (AT&T weekly loss data). Suppose we have an investment in AT&T stock and want to model weekly losses in value using an unconditional approach. If

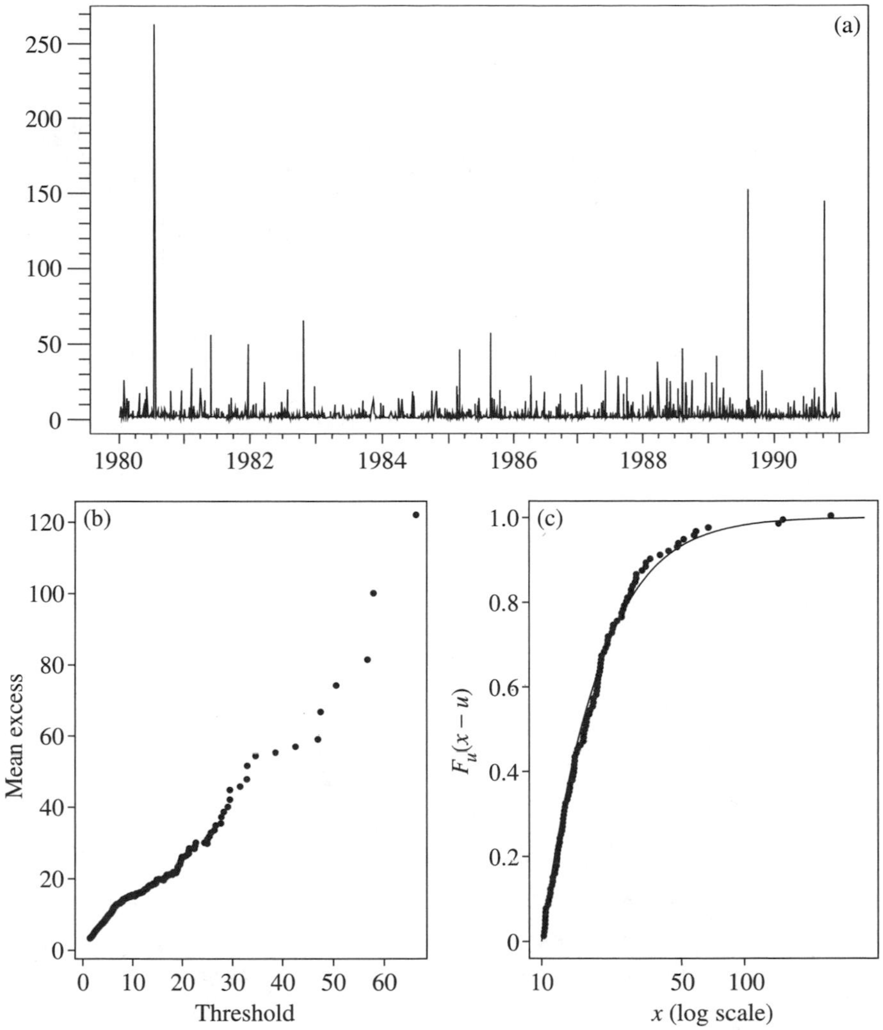

Figure 7.4. (a) Time series plot of the Danish data. (b) Sample mean excess plot. (c) Empirical distribution of excesses and fitted GPD. See Example 7.23 for full details.

X_t denotes the weekly log-return, then the percentage loss in value of our position over a week is given by $L_t = 100(1 - \exp(X_t))$ and data on this loss for the 521 complete weeks in the period 1991–2000 are shown in Figure 7.5(a).

A sample mean excess plot of the positive loss values is shown in Figure 7.5(b) and this suggests that a threshold can be found above which a GPD approximation to the excess distribution should be possible. We have chosen to position the threshold at a loss value of 2.75%, which is marked by a vertical line on the plot and gives 102 exceedances.

We observed in Section 4.1 that monthly AT&T return data over the period 1993–2000 do not appear consistent with a strict white noise hypothesis, so the issue of whether excess losses can be modelled as independent is relevant. This issue is taken

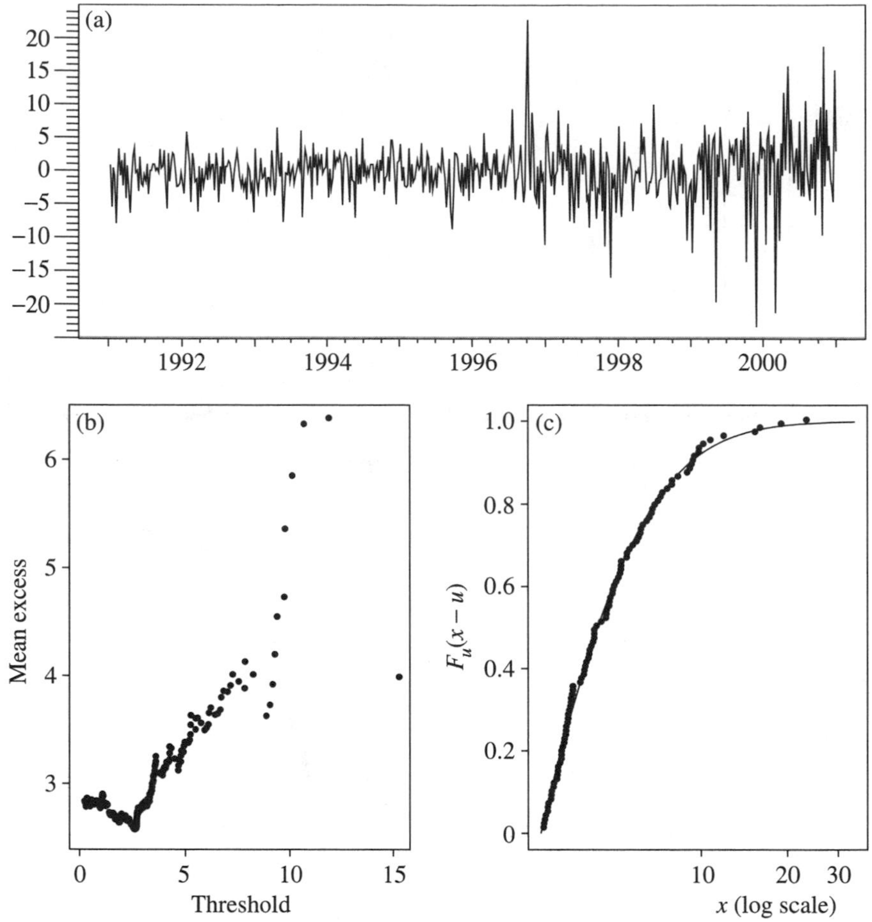

Figure 7.5. (a) Time series plot of AT&T weekly percentage loss data. (b) Sample mean excess plot. (c) Empirical distribution of excesses and fitted GPD. See Example 7.24 for full details.

up in Section 7.4 but for the time being we ignore it and implement a standard ML approach to estimating the parameters of a GPD model for the excess distribution; we obtain the estimates $\hat{\xi} = 0.22$ and $\hat{\beta} = 2.1$ with standard errors 0.13 and 0.34, respectively. Thus the model we have fitted is a model that is close to having an infinite fourth moment. A picture of the fitted GPD model for the excess distribution $\hat{F}_u(x - u)$ is also given in Figure 7.5(c), superimposed on points plotted at empirical estimates of the excess probabilities for each loss.

7.2.3 Modelling Tails and Measures of Tail Risk

In this section we describe how the GPD model for the excess losses is used to estimate the tail of the underlying loss distribution F and associated risk measures. To make the necessary theoretical calculations we again make Assumption 7.21.

Tail probabilities and risk measures. We observe firstly that under Assumption 7.21 we have, for $x \geqslant u$,

$$\begin{aligned}\bar{F}(x) &= P(X > u)P(X > x \mid X > u)\\ &= \bar{F}(u)P(X - u > x - u \mid X > u)\\ &= \bar{F}(u)\bar{F}_u(x-u)\\ &= \bar{F}(u)\left(1 + \xi\frac{x-u}{\beta}\right)^{-1/\xi},\end{aligned} \tag{7.17}$$

which, if we know $F(u)$, gives us a formula for tail probabilities. This formula may be inverted to obtain a high quantile of the underlying distribution, which we interpret as a VaR. For $\alpha \geqslant F(u)$ we have that VaR is equal to

$$\mathrm{VaR}_\alpha = q_\alpha(F) = u + \frac{\beta}{\xi}\left(\left(\frac{1-\alpha}{\bar{F}(u)}\right)^{-\xi} - 1\right). \tag{7.18}$$

Assuming that $\xi < 1$ the associated expected shortfall can be calculated easily from (2.23) and (7.18). We obtain

$$\mathrm{ES}_\alpha = \frac{1}{1-\alpha}\int_\alpha^1 q_x(F)\,\mathrm{d}x = \frac{\mathrm{VaR}_\alpha}{1-\xi} + \frac{\beta - \xi u}{1-\xi}. \tag{7.19}$$

Note that Assumption 7.21 and Lemma 7.22 imply that excess losses above VaR_α have a GPD distribution satisfying $F_{\mathrm{VaR}_\alpha} = G_{\xi,\beta+\xi(\mathrm{VaR}_\alpha - u)}$. The expected shortfall estimator in (7.19) can also be obtained by adding the mean of this distribution to VaR_α, i.e. $\mathrm{ES}_\alpha = \mathrm{VaR}_\alpha + e(\mathrm{VaR}_\alpha)$, where $e(\mathrm{VaR}_\alpha)$ is given in (7.15). It is interesting to look at how the *ratio* of the two risk measures behaves for large values of the quantile probability α. It is easily calculated from (7.18) and (7.19) that

$$\lim_{\alpha\to 1}\frac{\mathrm{ES}_\alpha}{\mathrm{VaR}_\alpha} = \begin{cases}(1-\xi)^{-1}, & \xi \geqslant 0,\\ 1, & \xi < 0,\end{cases} \tag{7.20}$$

so the shape parameter ξ of the GPD effectively determines the ratio when we go far enough out into the tail.

Estimation in practice. We note that, under Assumption 7.21, tail probabilities, VaRs and expected shortfalls are all given by formulas of the form $g(\xi, \beta, \bar{F}(u))$. Assuming that we have fitted a GPD to excess losses over a threshold u, as described in Section 7.2.2, we estimate these quantities by first replacing ξ and β in formulas (7.17)–(7.19) by their estimates. Of course, we also require an estimate of $\bar{F}(u)$ and here we take the simple empirical estimator N_u/n. In doing this, we are implicitly assuming that there is a sufficient proportion of sample values above the threshold u to estimate $\bar{F}(u)$ reliably. However, we hope to gain over the empirical method by using a kind of extrapolation based on the GPD for more extreme tail probabilities and risk measures. For tail probabilities we obtain an estimator, first proposed by Smith (1987), of the form

$$\hat{\bar{F}}(x) = \frac{N_u}{n}\left(1 + \hat{\xi}\frac{x-u}{\hat{\beta}}\right)^{-1/\hat{\xi}}, \tag{7.21}$$

which we stress is only valid for $x \geqslant u$. For $\alpha \geqslant 1 - N_u/n$ we obtain analogous point estimators of VaR_α and ES_α from (7.18) and (7.19).

Of course we would also like to obtain confidence intervals. If we have taken the likelihood approach to estimating ξ and β, then it is quite easy to give confidence intervals for $g(\hat{\xi}, \hat{\beta}, N_u/n)$ that take into account the uncertainty in $\hat{\xi}$ and $\hat{\beta}$, but neglect the uncertainty in N_u/n as an estimator of $\bar{F}(u)$. We use the approach described at the end of Section 7.1.4 for return levels, whereby the GPD model is reparametrized in terms of $\phi = g(\xi, \beta, N_u/n)$ and a confidence interval for $\hat{\phi}$ is constructed based on the likelihood ratio test as in Section A.3.5.

Example 7.25 (risk measures for AT&T loss data). Suppose we have fitted a GPD model to excess weekly losses above the threshold $u = 2.75\%$ as in Example 7.24. We use this model to obtain estimates of the 99% VaR and expected shortfall of the underlying weekly loss distribution. The essence of the method is displayed in Figure 7.6; this is a plot of estimated tail probabilities on logarithmic axes, with various dotted lines superimposed to indicate the estimation of risk measures and associated confidence intervals. The points on the graph are the 102 threshold exceedances and are plotted at y-values corresponding to the tail of the empirical distribution function; the smooth curve running through the points is the tail estimator (7.21).

Estimation of the 99% quantile amounts to determining the point of intersection of the tail estimation curve and the horizontal line $\bar{F}(x) = 0.01$ (not marked on graph); the first vertical dotted line shows the quantile estimate. The horizontal dotted line aids in the visualization of a 95% confidence interval for the VaR estimate; the degree of confidence is shown on the alternative y-axis to the right of the plot. The boundaries of a 95% confidence interval are obtained by determining the two points of intersection of this horizontal line with the dotted curve, which is a profile likelihood curve for the VaR as a parameter of the GPD model and is constructed using likelihood ratio test arguments as in Section A.3.5. Dropping the horizontal line to the 99% mark would correspond to constructing a 99% confidence interval for the estimate of the 99% VaR. The point estimate and 95% confidence interval for the 99% quantile are estimated to be 11.7% and (9.6, 16.1).

The second vertical line on the plot shows the point estimate of the 99% expected shortfall. A 95% confidence interval is determined from the dotted horizontal line and its points of intersection with the second dotted curve. The point estimate and 95% confidence interval are 17.0% and (12.7, 33.6). Note that if we divide the point estimates of the shortfall and the VaR we get $17/11.7 \approx 1.45$, which is larger than the asymptotic ratio $(1 - \hat{\xi})^{-1} = 1.29$ suggested by (7.20); this is generally the case at finite levels and is explained by the second term in (7.19) being a non-negligible positive quantity.

Before leaving the topic of GPD tail modelling it is clearly important to see how sensitive our risk-measure estimates are to the choice of the threshold. Hitherto we have considered single choices of threshold u and looked at a series of incremental calculations that always build on the same GPD model for excesses over that threshold. We would hope that there is some robustness to our inference for different choices of threshold.

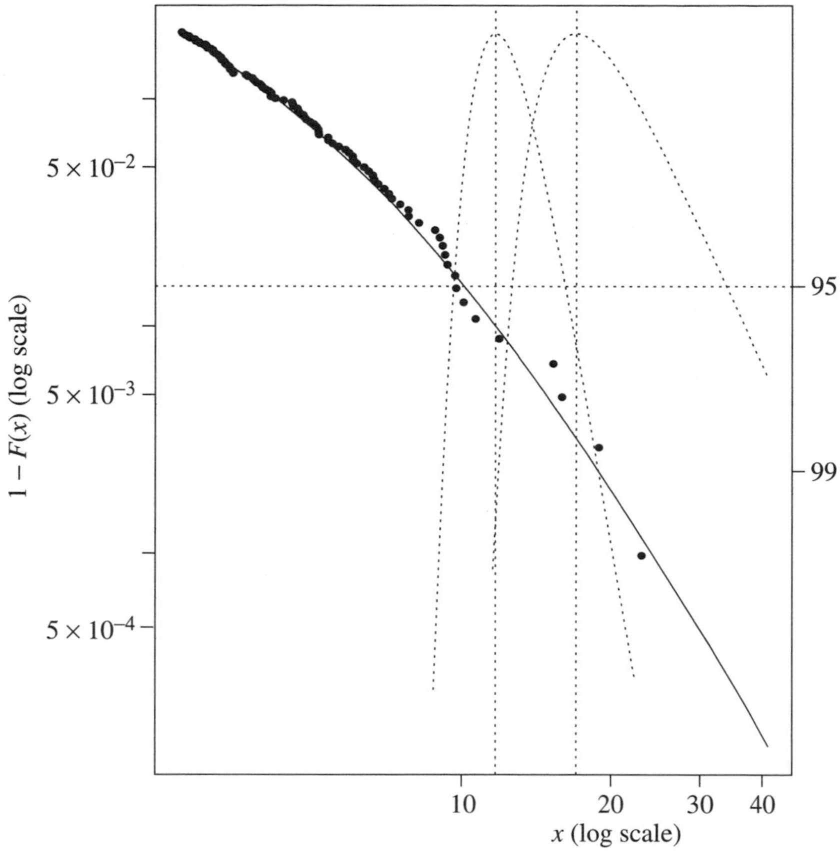

Figure 7.6. The smooth curve through the points shows the estimated tail of the AT&T weekly percentage loss data using the estimator (7.21). Points are plotted at empirical tail probabilities calculated from empirical df. The vertical dotted lines show estimates of 99% VaR and expected shortfall. The other curves are used in the construction of confidence intervals. See Example 7.25 for full details.

Example 7.26 (varying the threshold). In the case of the AT&T weekly loss data the influence of different thresholds is investigated in Figure 7.7. Given the importance of the ξ parameter in determining the weight of the tail and the relationship between quantiles and expected shortfalls, we first show how estimates of ξ vary as we consider a series of thresholds that give us between 20 and 150 exceedances. In fact, the estimates remain fairly constant around a value of approximately 0.2; a symmetric 95% confidence interval constructed from the standard error estimate is also shown, and indicates how the uncertainty about the parameter value decreases as the threshold is lowered or the number of threshold exceedances is increased.

Point estimates of the 99% VaR and expected shortfall estimates are also shown. The former remain remarkably constant around 12%, while the latter show modest variability that essentially tracks the variability of the ξ estimate. These pictures provide some reassurance that different thresholds do not lead to drastically different conclusions. We return to the issue of threshold choice again in Section 7.2.5.

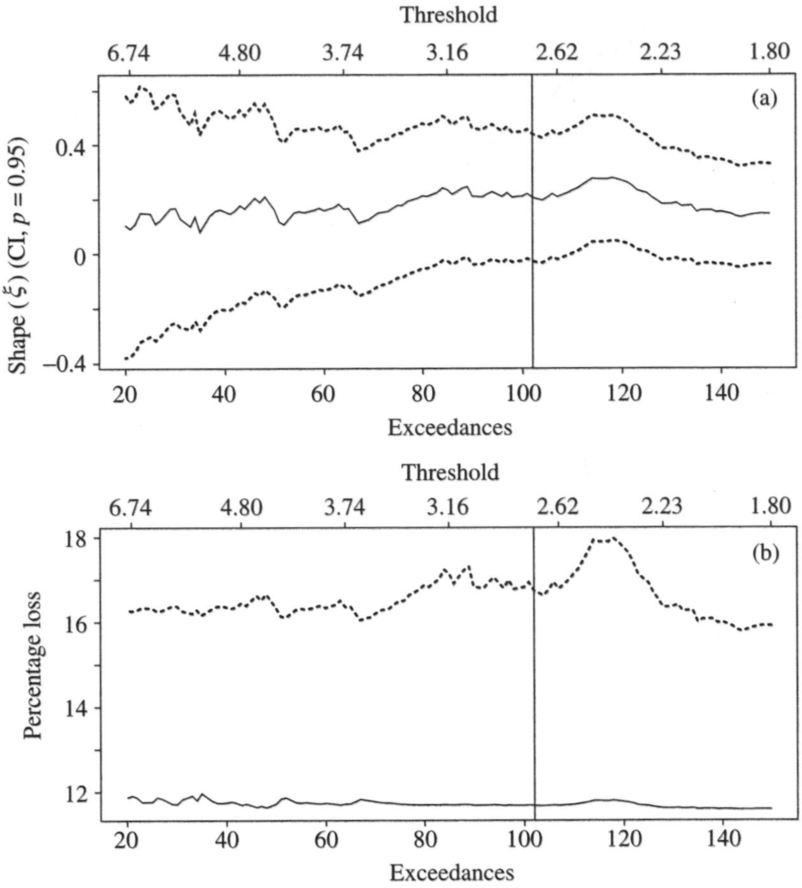

Figure 7.7. (a) Estimate of ξ for different thresholds u and numbers of exceedances N_u, together with a 95% confidence interval based on the standard error. (b) Associated point estimates of the 99% VaR (solid line) and expected shortfall (dotted line). See Example 7.26 for commentary.

7.2.4 *The Hill Method*

The GPD method is not the only way to estimate the tail of a distribution and, as an alternative, we describe in this section the well-known Hill approach to modelling the tails of heavy-tailed distributions.

Estimating the tail index. For this method we assume that the underlying loss distribution is in the maximum domain of attraction of the Fréchet distribution so that, by Theorem 7.8, it has a tail of the form

$$\bar{F}(x) = L(x)x^{-\alpha}, \tag{7.22}$$

for a slowly varying function L (see Definition 7.7) and a positive parameter α. Traditionally, in the Hill approach, interest centres on the *tail index* α, rather than its reciprocal ξ, which appears in (7.3). The goal is to find an estimator of α based on identically distributed data $X_1, \dots, X_n$.

The Hill estimator can be derived in various ways (see EKM, pp. 330–336). Perhaps the most elegant is to consider the mean excess function of the generic logarithmic loss $\ln X$, where X is an rv with df (7.22). Writing e^* for the mean excess function of $\ln X$ and using integration by parts we find that

$$\begin{aligned} e^*(\ln u) &= E(\ln X - \ln u \mid \ln X > \ln u) \\ &= \frac{1}{\bar{F}(u)} \int_u^\infty (\ln x - \ln u)\,\mathrm{d}F(x) \\ &= \frac{1}{\bar{F}(u)} \int_u^\infty \frac{\bar{F}(x)}{x}\,\mathrm{d}x \\ &= \frac{1}{\bar{F}(u)} \int_u^\infty L(x) x^{-(\alpha+1)}\,\mathrm{d}x. \end{aligned}$$

For u sufficiently large, the slowly varying function $L(x)$ for $x \geqslant u$ can essentially be treated as a constant and taken outside the integral. More formally, using Karamata's Theorem (see Section A.1.3), we get, for $u \to \infty$,

$$e^*(\ln u) \sim \frac{L(u)u^{-\alpha}\alpha^{-1}}{\bar{F}(u)} = \alpha^{-1},$$

so $\lim_{u\to\infty} \alpha e^*(\ln u) = 1$. We expect to see similar tail behaviour in the sample mean excess function e_n^* (see (7.16)) constructed from the log observations. That is, we expect that $e_n^*(\ln X_{k,n}) \approx \alpha^{-1}$ for n large and k sufficiently small, where $X_{n,n} \leqslant \cdots \leqslant X_{1,n}$ are the order statistics as usual. Evaluating $e_n^*(\ln X_{k,n})$ gives us the estimator $\hat{\alpha}^{-1} = ((k-1)^{-1} \sum_{j=1}^{k-1} \ln X_{j,n} - \ln X_{k,n})$. The standard form of the Hill estimator is obtained by a minor modification:

$$\hat{\alpha}_{k,n}^{(\mathrm{H})} = \left(\frac{1}{k}\sum_{j=1}^{k} \ln X_{j,n} - \ln X_{k,n}\right)^{-1}, \quad 2 \leqslant k \leqslant n. \tag{7.23}$$

The Hill estimator is one of the best-studied estimators in the EVT literature. The asymptotic properties (consistency, asymptotic normality) of this estimator (as sample size $n \to \infty$, number of extremes $k \to \infty$ and the so-called tail-fraction $k/n \to 0$) have been extensively investigated under various assumed models for the data, including ARCH and GARCH (see Notes and Comments). We concentrate on the use of the estimator in practice and, in particular, on its performance relative to the GPD estimation approach.

When the data are from a distribution with a tail that is close to a perfect power function, the Hill estimator is often a good estimator of α, or its reciprocal ξ. In practice, the general strategy is to plot Hill estimates for various values of k. This gives the Hill plot $\{(k, \hat{\alpha}_{k,n}^{(\mathrm{H})}) : k = 2, \dots, n\}$. We hope to find a stable region in the Hill plot where estimates constructed from different numbers of order statistics are quite similar.

Example 7.27 (Hill plots). We construct Hill plots for the Danish fire data of Example 7.23 and the weekly percentage loss data (positive values only) of Example 7.24 (shown in Figure 7.8).

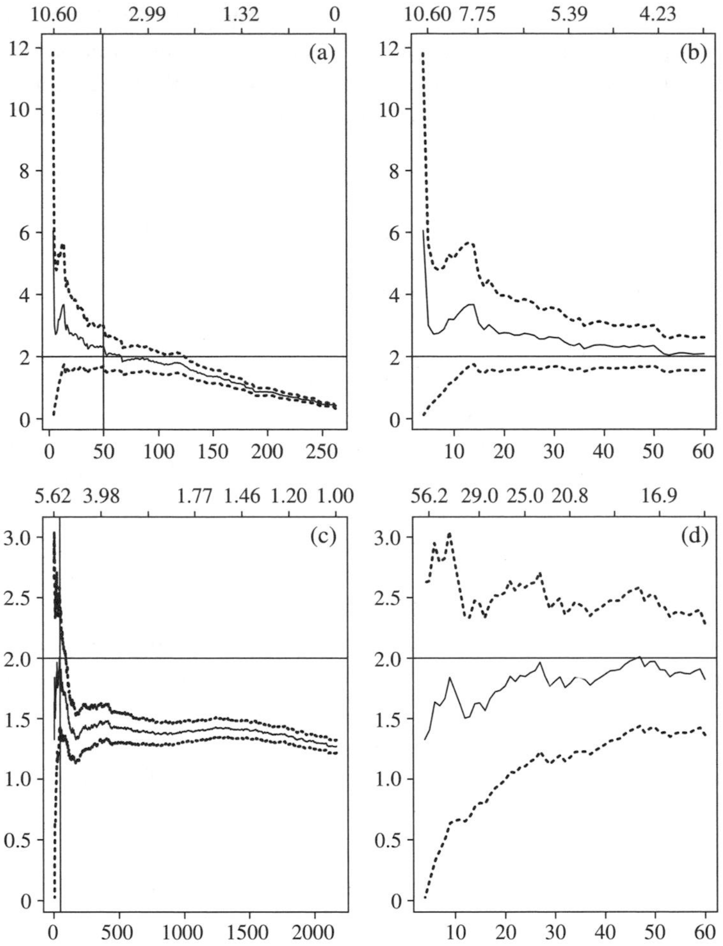

Figure 7.8. Hill plots showing estimates of the tail index $\alpha = 1/\xi$ for (a), (b) the AT&T weekly percentages losses and (c), (d) the Danish fire loss data. Parts (b) and (d) are expanded versions of sections of (a) and (c) showing Hill estimates based on up to 60 order statistics.

It is very easy to construct the Hill plot for all possible values of k, but it can be misleading to do so; practical experience (see Example 7.28) suggests that the best choices of k are relatively small—say 10–50 order statistics in a sample of size 1000. For this reason we have enlarged sections of the Hill plots showing the estimates obtained for values of k less than 60.

For the Danish data the estimates of α obtained are between 1.5 and 2, suggesting ξ estimates between 0.5 and 0.67, all of which correspond to infinite-variance models for these data. Recall that the estimate derived from our GPD model in Example 7.23 was $\hat{\xi} = 0.50$. For the AT&T data there is no particularly stable region in the plot. The α estimates based on $k = 2, \dots, 60$ order statistics mostly range from 2 to 4, suggesting a ξ value in the range 0.25–0.5, which is larger than the values estimated in Example 7.26 with a GPD model.

Example 7.27 shows that the interpretation of Hill plots can be difficult. In practice, various deviations from the ideal situation can occur. If the data do not come from a distribution with a regularly varying tail, the Hill method is really not appropriate and Hill plots can be very misleading. Serial dependence in the data can also spoil the performance of the estimator, although this is also true for the GPD estimator. EKM contains a number of Hill "horror plots" based on simulated data illustrating the issues that arise (see Notes and Comments).

Hill-based tail estimates. For the risk-management applications of this book we are less concerned with estimating the tail index of heavy-tailed data and more concerned with tail and risk-measure estimates. We give a heuristic argument for a standard tail estimator based on the Hill approach. We assume a tail model of the form $\bar{F}(x) = Cx^{-\alpha}$, $x \geqslant u > 0$, for some high threshold u; in other words, we replace the slowly varying function by a constant for sufficiently large x. For an appropriate value of k the tail index α is estimated by $\hat{\alpha}^{(\mathrm{H})}_{k,n}$ and the threshold u is replaced by $X_{k,n}$ (or $X_{(k+1),n}$ in some versions); it remains to estimate C. Since C can be written as $C = u^{\alpha}\bar{F}(u)$, this is equivalent to estimating $\bar{F}(u)$, and the obvious empirical estimator is k/n (or $(k-1)/n$ in some versions). Putting these ideas together gives us the Hill tail estimator in its standard form:

$$\hat{\bar{F}}(x) = \frac{k}{n}\left(\frac{x}{X_{k,n}}\right)^{-\hat{\alpha}^{(\mathrm{H})}_{k,n}}. \tag{7.24}$$

Writing the estimator in this way emphasizes the way it is treated mathematically. For any pair k and n, both the Hill estimator and the associated tail estimator are treated as functions of the k upper order statistics from the sample of size n. Obviously it is possible to invert this estimator to get a quantile estimator and it is also possible to devise an estimator of expected shortfall using arguments about regularly varying tails.

The GPD-based tail estimator (7.21) is usually treated as a function of a random number N_u of upper order statistics for a fixed threshold u. The different presentation of these estimators in the literature is a matter of convention and we can easily recast both estimators in a similar form. Suppose we rewrite (7.24) in the notation of (7.21) by substituting $\hat{\xi}^{(\mathrm{H})}$, u and N_u for $1/\hat{\alpha}^{(\mathrm{H})}_{k,n}$, $X_{k,n}$ and k, respectively. We get

$$\hat{\bar{F}}(x) = \frac{N_u}{n}\left(1 + \hat{\xi}^{(\mathrm{H})}\frac{x-u}{\hat{\xi}^{(\mathrm{H})}u}\right)^{-1/\hat{\xi}^{(\mathrm{H})}}.$$

This estimator lacks the additional scaling parameter β in (7.21) and tends not to perform as well, as is shown in simulated examples in the next section.

7.2.5 Simulation Study of EVT Quantile Estimators

First we consider estimation of ξ and then estimation of the high quantile VaR_{α}. In both cases estimators are compared using mean squared errors (MSEs); we recall that the MSE of an estimator $\hat{\theta}$ of a parameter θ is given by $\mathrm{MSE}(\hat{\theta}) = E(\hat{\theta}-\theta)^2 = (E(\hat{\theta}-\theta))^2 + \mathrm{var}(\hat{\theta})$, and thus has the well-known decomposition into *squared*

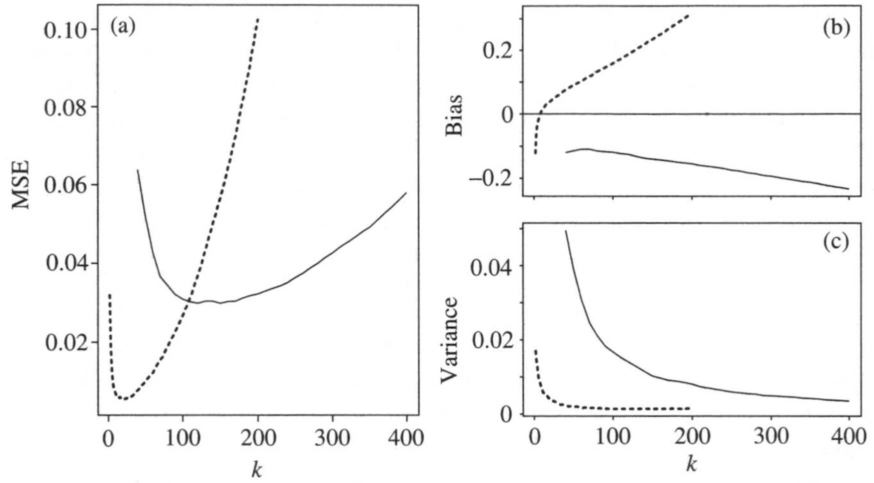

Figure 7.9. Comparison of (a) estimated MSE, (b) bias and (c) variance for the Hill (dotted line) and GPD (solid line) estimators of ξ, the reciprocal of the tail index, as a function of k (or N_u), the number of upper order statistics from a sample of 1000 t-distributed data with four degrees of freedom. See Example 7.28 for details.

bias plus *variance*. A good estimator should keep both the bias term $E(\hat{\theta} - \theta)$ and the variance term $\text{var}(\hat{\theta})$ small.

Since analytical evaluation of bias and variance is not possible, we calculate Monte Carlo estimates by simulating 1000 datasets in each experiment. The parameters of the GPD are determined in all cases by ML; PWM, the main alternative, gives slightly different results, but the conclusions are similar.

We calculate estimates using the Hill method and the GPD method based on different numbers of upper order statistics (or differing thresholds) and try to determine the choice of k (or N_u) that is most appropriate for a sample of size n. In the case of estimating VaR we also compare the EVT estimators with the simple empirical quantile estimator.

Example 7.28 (Monte Carlo experiment). We assume that we have a sample of 1000 iid data from a t distribution with four degrees of freedom and want to estimate ξ, the reciprocal of the tail index, which in this case has the true value 0.25. (This is demonstrated in Example 7.29 at the end of this chapter.) The Hill estimate is constructed for k values in the range $\{2, \dots, 200\}$ and the GPD estimate is constructed for k (or N_u) values in $\{30, 40, 50, \dots, 400\}$. The results are shown in Figure 7.9.

The t distribution has a well-behaved regularly varying tail and the Hill estimator gives better estimates of ξ than the GPD method, with an optimal value of k around 20–30. The variance plot shows where the Hill method gains over the GPD method; the variance of the GPD-based estimator is much higher than that of the Hill estimator for small numbers of order statistics. The magnitudes of the biases are closer together, with the Hill method tending to overestimate ξ and the GPD

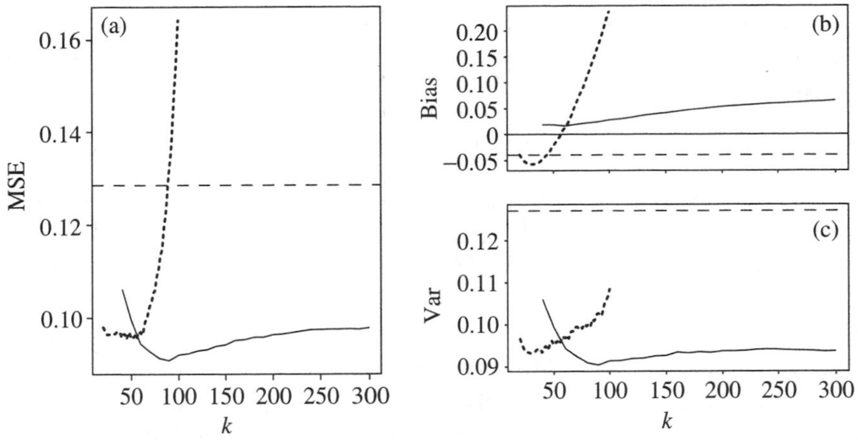

Figure 7.10. Comparison of (a) estimated MSE, (b) bias and (c) variance for the Hill (dotted line) and GPD (solid line) estimators of $\mathrm{VaR}_{0.99}$, as a function of k (or N_u), the number of upper order statistics from a sample of 1000 t-distributed data with four degrees of freedom. Dashed line also shows results for the (threshold-independent) empirical quantile estimator. See Example 7.28 for details.

method tending to underestimate it. If we were to use the GPD method, the optimal choice of threshold would be one giving 100–150 exceedances.

The conclusions change when we attempt to estimate the 99% VaR; the results are shown in Figure 7.10. The Hill method has a negative bias for low values of k but a rapidly growing positive bias for larger values of k; the GPD estimator has a positive bias that grows much more slowly; the empirical method has a negative bias. The GPD attains its lowest MSE value for a value of k around 100, but, more importantly, the MSE is very robust to the choice of k because of the slow growth of the bias. The Hill method performs well for $20 \leqslant k \leqslant 75$ (we only use k values that lead to a quantile estimate beyond the effective threshold $X_{k,n}$) but then deteriorates rapidly. Both EVT methods obviously outperform the empirical quantile estimator. Given the relative robustness of the GPD-based tail estimator to changes in k, the issue of threshold choice for this estimator seems less critical than for the Hill method.

7.2.6 Conditional EVT for Financial Time Series

The GPD method when applied to threshold exceedances in a financial return series (as in Examples 7.24 and 7.25) is essentially an unconditional method for estimating the tail of the P&L distribution and associated risk measures. In Chapter 2 we argued that a conditional risk-measurement approach may be more appropriate for short time horizons, and in Section 2.3.6 we observed that this generally led to better backtesting results. We now consider a simple adaptation of the GPD method to obtain conditional risk-measure estimates in a time series context. This adaptation uses the GARCH model and related ideas in Chapter 4.

We assume in particular that we are in the framework of Section 4.4.2 so that $L_{t-n+1}, \dots, L_t$ are negative log-returns generated by a strictly stationary time series process (L_t). This process is assumed to be of the form $L_t = \mu_t + \sigma_t Z_t$, where μ_t

and σ_t are $\mathcal{F}_{t-1}$-measurable and (Z_t) are iid innovations with some unknown df G; an example would be an ARMA model with GARCH errors. To obtain estimates of the risk measures

$$\mathrm{VaR}_\alpha^t = \mu_{t+1} + \sigma_{t+1} q_\alpha(Z), \qquad \mathrm{ES}_\alpha^t = \mu_{t+1} + \sigma_{t+1}\, \mathrm{ES}_\alpha(Z),$$

we first fit a GARCH model by the QML procedure of Section 4.3.4 (since we do not assume a particular innovation distribution) and use this to estimate μ_{t+1} and σ_{t+1}. As an alternative we could use EWMA volatility forecasting instead. To estimate $q_\alpha(Z)$ and $\mathrm{ES}_\alpha(Z)$ we essentially apply the GPD tail estimation procedure to the innovation distribution G. To get round the problem that we do not observe data directly from the innovation distribution, we treat the residuals from the GARCH analysis as our data and apply the GPD tail estimation method of Section 7.2.3 to the residuals. In particular, we estimate $q_\alpha(Z)$ and $\mathrm{ES}_\alpha(Z)$ using the VaR and expected shortfall formulas in (7.18) and (7.19).

In Section 2.3.6 it was shown that this method gives good VaR estimates; in that example the sample size was taken to be $n = 1000$ and the threshold was always set so that there were 100 exceedances. In fact, the method also gives very good conditional expected shortfall estimates, as is shown in the original paper of McNeil and Frey (2000).

Notes and Comments

The ideas behind the important Theorem 7.20, which underlies GPD modelling, may be found in Pickands (1975) and Balkema and de Haan (1974). Important papers developing the technique in the statistical literature are Davison (1984) and Davison and Smith (1990). The estimation of the parameters of the GPD, both by ML and by the method of probability-weighted moments, is discussed in Hosking and Wallis (1987). The tail estimation formula (7.21) was suggested by Smith (1987) and the theoretical properties of this estimator for iid data in the domain of attraction of an extreme value distribution are extensively investigated in this paper. The Danish fire loss example is taken from McNeil (1997).

The Hill estimator goes back to Hill (1975) (see also Hall 1982). The theoretical properties for dependent data, including linear processes with heavy-tailed innovations and ARCH and GARCH processes, were investigated by Resnick and Stărică (1995, 1996). The idea of smoothing the estimator is examined in Resnick and Stărică (1997) and Resnick (1997). For Hill "horror plots", showing situations when the Hill estimator delivers particularly poor estimates of the tail index, see EKM, pp. 194, 270 and 343.

Alternative estimators based on order statistics include the estimator of Pickands (1975), which is also discussed in Dekkers and de Haan (1989), and the DEdH estimator of Dekkers, Einmahl and de Haan (1989). This latter estimator is used as the basis of a quantile estimator in de Haan and Rootzén (1993). Both the Pickands and DEdH estimators are designed to estimate general ξ in the extreme value limit (in contrast to the Hill estimator, which is designed for positive ξ); in empirical studies the DEdH estimator seems to work better than the Pickands estimator. The issue of the optimal number of order statistics in such estimators is taken up in a series of papers by Dekkers and de Haan (1993) and Daníelsson et al. (2001). A method is proposed which is essentially based on the bootstrap approach to estimating mean squared error discussed in Hall (1990). A review paper relevant for applications to insurance and finance is Matthys and Beirlant (2000).

Analyses of the tails of financial data using methods based on the Hill estimator can be found in Koedijk, Schafgans and de Vries (1990), Lux (1996) and various papers by Daníelsson and de Vries (1997a,b,c). The conditional EVT method was developed in McNeil and Frey (2000); a Monte Carlo method using the GPD model to estimate risk measures for the h-day loss distribution is also described. See also Gençay, Selçuk and Ulugülyağci (2003) and Gençay and Selçuk (2004) for interesting applications of EVT methodology to VaR estimation.

7.3 Tails of Specific Models

In this short section we survey the tails of some of the more important distributions and models that we have encountered in this book.

7.3.1 Domain of Attraction of Fréchet Distribution

As stated in Section 7.1.2, the domain of attraction of the Fréchet distribution consists of distributions with regularly varying tails of the form $\bar{F}(x) = x^{-\alpha}L(x)$ for $\alpha > 0$, where α is known as the tail index. These are heavy-tailed models where higher-order moments cease to exist. Normalized maxima of random samples from such distributions converge to a Fréchet distribution with shape parameter $\xi = 1/\alpha$, and excesses over sufficiently high thresholds converge to a generalized Pareto distribution with shape parameter $\xi = 1/\alpha$.

We now show that the Student t distribution and the inverse gamma distribution are in this class; we analyse the former because of its general importance in financial modelling and the latter because it appears as the mixing distribution that yields the Student t in the class of normal variance mixture models (see Example 3.7). In Section 7.3.3 we will see that the mixing distribution in a normal variance mixture model essentially determines the tail of that model.

Both the t and inverse gamma distributions are presented in terms of their density, and the analysis of their tails proves to be a simple application of a useful result known as Karamata's Theorem, which is given in Section A.1.3.

Example 7.29 (Student t distribution). It is easily verified that the standard univariate t distribution with $\nu \geqslant 1$ has a density of the form $f_\nu(x) = x^{-(\nu+1)}L(x)$. Hence Karamata's Theorem (see Theorem A.5) allows us to calculate the form of the tail $\bar{F}_\nu(x) = \int_x^\infty f_\nu(y)\,\mathrm{d}y$ by essentially treating the slowly varying function as a constant and taking it out of the integral. We get

$$\bar{F}_\nu(x) = \int_x^\infty y^{-(\nu+1)}L(y)\,\mathrm{d}y \sim \nu^{-1}x^{-\nu}L(x), \quad x \to \infty,$$

from which we conclude that the df F_ν of a t distribution has tail index ν and $F_\nu \in \mathrm{MDA}(H_{1/\nu})$ by Theorem 7.8.

Example 7.30 (inverse gamma distribution). The density of the inverse gamma distribution is given in (A.11). It is of the form $f_{\alpha,\beta}(x) = x^{-(\alpha+1)}L(x)$, since $\exp(-\beta/x) \to 1$ as $x \to \infty$. Using the same technique as in Example 7.29, we deduce that this distribution has tail index α, so $F_{\alpha,\beta} \in \text{MDA}(H_{1/\alpha})$.

7.3.2 *Domain of Attraction of Gumbel Distribution*

A mathematical characterization of the Gumbel class is that it consists of the so-called *von Mises* distribution functions and any other distributions which are *tail equivalent* to von Mises distributions (see EKM, pp. 138–150). We give the definitions of both of these concepts below. Note that distributions in this class can have both infinite and finite right endpoints; again we write $x_F = \sup\{x \in \mathbb{R} : F(x) < 1\} \leqslant \infty$ for the right endpoint of F.

Definition 7.31 (von Mises distribution function). Suppose there exists some $z < x_F$ such that F has the representation

$$\bar{F}(x) = c\exp\left\{-\int_z^x \frac{1}{a(t)}\,\mathrm{d}t\right\}, \qquad z < x < x_F,$$

where c is some positive constant, $a(t)$ is a positive and absolutely continuous function with density a', and $\lim_{x\to x_F} a'(x) = 0$. Then F is called a von Mises distribution function.

Definition 7.32 (tail equivalence). Two dfs F and G are called *tail equivalent* if they have the same right endpoints (i.e. $x_F = x_G$) and $\lim_{x\to x_F} \bar{F}(x)/\bar{G}(x) = c$ for some constant $0 < c < \infty$.

To decide whether a particular df F is a von Mises df, the following condition is extremely useful. Assume there exists some $z < x_F$ such that F is twice differentiable on (z, x_F) with density $f = F'$ and $F'' < 0$ in (z, x_F). Then F is a von Mises df if and only if

$$\lim_{x\to x_F} \frac{\bar{F}(x)F''(x)}{f^2(x)} = -1. \tag{7.25}$$

We now use this condition to show that the gamma df is a von Mises df.

Example 7.33 (gamma distribution). The density $f = f_{\alpha,\beta}$ of the gamma distribution is given in (A.7), and a straightforward calculation yields $F''(x) = f'(x) = -f(x)(\beta + (1-\alpha)/x) < 0$, provided $x > \max((\alpha-1)/\beta, 0)$. Clearly, $\lim_{x\to\infty} F''(x)/f(x) = -\beta$. Moreover, using L'Hôpital's rule we get $\lim_{x\to\infty} \bar{F}(x)/f(x) = \lim_{x\to\infty} -f(x)/f'(x) = \beta^{-1}$. Combining these two limits establishes (7.25).

Example 7.34 (GIG distribution). The density of an rv $X \sim N^-(\lambda, \chi, \psi)$ with the GIG distribution is given in (A.8). Let $F_{\lambda,\chi,\psi}(x)$ denote the df and consider the case where $\psi > 0$. If $\psi = 0$, then the GIG is an inverse gamma distribution, which was shown in Example 7.30 to be in the Fréchet class. If $\psi > 0$, then $\lambda \geqslant 0$, and a similar technique to Example 7.33 could be used to establish that the GIG is a von Mises df. In the case where $\lambda > 0$ it is easier to demonstrate tail equivalence with a gamma distribution, which is the special case when $\chi = 0$. We observe that

$$\lim_{x\to\infty} \frac{\bar{F}_{\lambda,\chi,\psi}(x)}{\bar{F}_{\lambda,0,\psi}(x)} = \lim_{x\to\infty} \frac{f_{\lambda,\chi,\psi}(x)}{f_{\lambda,0,\psi}(x)} = c_{\lambda,\chi,\psi}$$

for some constant $c_{\lambda,\chi,\psi}$. It follows that $F_{\lambda,\chi,\psi} \in \mathrm{MDA}(H_0)$.

7.3.3 Mixture Models

In this book we have considered a number of models for financial risk-factor changes that arise as mixtures of rvs. In Chapter 3 we introduced multivariate normal variance mixture models including the Student t, and (symmetric) generalized hyperbolic distributions, which have the general structure given in (3.19). A one-dimensional normal variance mixture (or the marginal distribution of a d-dimensional normal variance mixture) is of the same type (see Section A.1.1) as an rv X satisfying

$$X \stackrel{\mathrm{d}}{=} \sqrt{W} Z, \tag{7.26}$$

where $Z \sim N(0, 1)$ and W is an independent, positive-valued scalar rv. We would like to know more about the tails of distributions satisfying (7.26).

More generally, to understand the tails of the marginal distributions of elliptical distributions it suffices to consider spherical distributions, which have the stochastic representation

$$\boldsymbol{X} \stackrel{\mathrm{d}}{=} R\boldsymbol{S} \tag{7.27}$$

for a random vector $\boldsymbol{S}$ that is uniformly distributed on the unit sphere $\mathcal{S}^{d-1} = \{\boldsymbol{s} \in \mathbb{R}^d : \boldsymbol{s}'\boldsymbol{s} = 1\}$, and an independent radial variate R (see Section 3.3.1 and Theorem 3.22 in particular). Again we would like to know more about the tails of the marginal distributions of the vector $\boldsymbol{X}$ in (7.27).

In Section 4.3 of Chapter 4 we considered strictly stationary stochastic processes (X_t), such as GARCH processes satisfying equations of the form

$$X_t = \sigma_t Z_t, \tag{7.28}$$

where (Z_t) are strict white noise innovations, typically with a Gaussian or (more realistically) a scaled Student t distribution, and σ_t is a $\mathcal{F}_{t-1}$-measurable rv representing volatility. These models can also be seen as mixture models and we would like to know something about the tail of the stationary distribution of (X_t).

A useful result for analysing the tails of mixtures is the following theorem due to Breiman (1965), which we immediately apply to spherical distributions.

Theorem 7.35 (tails of mixture distributions). *Let X be given by $X = YZ$ for independent, non-negative rvs Y and Z such that*

(1) *Y has a regularly varying tail with tail index α;*

(2) *$E(Z^{\alpha+\varepsilon}) < \infty$ for some $\varepsilon > 0$.*

Then X has a regularly varying tail with tail index α and

$$P(X > x) \sim E(Z^{\alpha}) P(Y > x), \quad x \to \infty.$$

Proposition 7.36 (tails of spherical distributions). *Let $X \stackrel{d}{=} RS \sim S_d(\psi)$ have a spherical distribution. If R has a regularly varying tail with tail index α, then so does $|X_i|$ for $i = 1, \dots, d$. If $E(R^k) < \infty$ for all $k > 0$, then $|X_i|$ does not have a regularly varying tail.*

Proof. Suppose that R has a regularly varying tail with tail index α and consider RS_i. Since $|S_i|$ is a non-negative rv with finite support $[0, 1]$ and finite moments, it follows from Theorem 7.35 that $R|S_i|$, and hence $|X_i|$, are regularly varying with tail index α. If $E(R^k) < \infty$ for all $k > 0$, then $E|X_i|^k < \infty$ for all $k > 0$, so that $|X_i|$ cannot have a regularly varying tail. □

Example 7.37 (tails of normal variance mixtures). Suppose that $X \stackrel{d}{=} \sqrt{W} Z$ with $Z \sim N_d(\mathbf{0}, I_d)$ and W an independent scalar rv, so that both Z and X have spherical distributions and X has a normal variance mixture distribution. The vector Z has the spherical representation $Z \stackrel{d}{=} \tilde{R} S$, where $\tilde{R}^2 \sim \chi^2_d$ (see Example 3.24). The vector X has the spherical representation $X \stackrel{d}{=} RS$, where $R \stackrel{d}{=} \sqrt{W} \tilde{R}$.

Now, the chi-squared distribution (being a gamma distribution) is in the domain of attraction of the Gumbel distribution, so $E(\tilde{R}^k) = E((\tilde{R}^2)^{k/2}) < \infty$ for all $k > 0$. We first consider the case when W has a regularly varying tail with tail index α so that $\bar{F}_W(w) = L(w)w^{-\alpha}$. It follows that $P(\sqrt{W} > x) = P(W > x^2) = L_2(x)x^{-2\alpha}$, where $L_2(x) := L(x^2)$ is also slowly varying, so that $\sqrt{W}$ has a regularly varying tail with tail index 2α. By Theorem 7.35, $R \stackrel{d}{=} \sqrt{W}\tilde{R}$ also has a regularly varying tail with tail index 2α and, by Proposition 7.36, so do the components of $|X|$.

To consider a particular case, suppose that $W \sim \mathrm{Ig}(\frac{1}{2}\nu, \frac{1}{2}\nu)$, so that, by Example 7.30, W is regularly varying with tail index $\frac{1}{2}\nu$. Then $\sqrt{W}$ has a regularly varying tail with tail index ν and so does $|X_i|$; this is hardly surprising because $X \sim t_d(\nu, \mathbf{0}, I_d)$, implying that X_i has a univariate Student t distribution with ν degrees of freedom, and we already know from Example 7.29 that this has tail index ν.

On the other hand, if $F_W \in \mathrm{MDA}(H_0)$, then $E(R^k) < \infty$ for all $k > 0$ and $|X_i|$ cannot have a regularly varying tail by Proposition 7.36. This means, for example, that univariate generalized hyperbolic distributions do not have power tails (except for the special boundary case corresponding to Student t) because the GIG is in the maximum domain of attraction of the Gumbel distribution, as was shown in Example 7.34.

Analysis of the tails of the stationary distribution of GARCH-type models is more challenging. In view of Theorem 7.35 and the foregoing examples, it is clear that when the innovations (Z_t) are Gaussian, then the law of the process (X_t) in (7.28) will have a regularly varying tail if the volatility σ_t has a regularly varying tail. Mikosch and Stărică (2000) analyse the GARCH(1, 1) model (see Definition 4.20), where the squared volatility satisfies $\sigma_t^2 = \alpha_0 + \alpha_1 X_{t-1}^2 + \beta\sigma_{t-1}^2$. They show that under relatively weak conditions on the innovation distribution of (Z_t), the volatility σ_t has a regularly varying tail with tail index κ given by the solution of the equation

$$E((\alpha_1 Z_t^2 + \beta)^{\kappa/2}) = 1. \tag{7.29}$$

Table 7.2. Approximate theoretical values of the tail index κ solving (7.29) for various GARCH(1, 1) processes with Gaussian and Student t innovation distributions.

		t distribution	
Parameters	Gauss	$\nu = 8$	$\nu = 4$
$\alpha_1 = 0.2,\ \beta = 0.75$	4.4	3.5	2.7
$\alpha_1 = 0.1,\ \beta = 0.85$	9.1	5.8	3.4
$\alpha_1 = 0.05,\ \beta = 0.95$	21.1	7.9	3.9

In Table 7.2 we have calculated approximate values of κ for various innovation distributions and parameter values using numerical integration and root-finding procedures. By Theorem 7.35 these are the values of the tail index for the stationary distribution of the GARCH(1, 1) model itself.

Two main findings are obvious: for any fixed set of parameter values, the tail index gets smaller and the tail of the GARCH model gets heavier as we move to heavier-tailed innovation distributions; for any fixed innovation distribution, the tail of the GARCH model gets lighter as we decrease the ARCH effect (α_1) and increase the GARCH effect (β).

Tail dependence in elliptical distributions. We close this section by giving a result that reveals an interesting connection between tail dependence in elliptical distributions and regular variation of the radial rv R in the representation $\boldsymbol{X} \overset{\mathrm{d}}{=} \boldsymbol{\mu} + RA\boldsymbol{S}$ of an elliptically symmetric distribution given in Proposition 3.28.

Theorem 7.38. *Let $\boldsymbol{X} \overset{\mathrm{d}}{=} \boldsymbol{\mu} + RA\boldsymbol{S} \sim E_d(\boldsymbol{\mu}, \Sigma, \psi)$, where $\boldsymbol{\mu}$, R, A and $\boldsymbol{S}$ are as in Proposition 3.28 and we assume that $\sigma_{ii} > 0$ for all $i = 1, \dots, d$. If R has a regularly varying tail with tail index $\alpha > 0$, then the coefficient of upper and lower tail dependence between X_i and X_j is given by*

$$\lambda(X_i, X_j) = \frac{\int_{(\pi/2 - \arcsin \rho_{ij})}^{\pi/2} \cos^{\alpha}(t)\,\mathrm{d}t}{\int_0^{\pi/2} \cos^{\alpha}(t)\,\mathrm{d}t}, \tag{7.30}$$

where ρ_{ij} is the (i, j)th element of $P = \wp(\Sigma)$ and $\wp$ is the correlation operator defined in (3.5).

An example where R has a regularly varying tail occurs in the case of the multivariate t distribution $\boldsymbol{X} \sim t_d(\nu, \boldsymbol{\mu}, \Sigma)$. It is obvious from the arguments used in Example 7.37 that the tail of the df of R is regularly varying with tail index $\alpha = \nu$. Thus (7.30) with α replaced by ν gives an alternative expression to (5.31) for calculating tail-dependence coefficients for the t copula $C^t_{\nu,P}$.

Arguably, the original expression (5.31) is easier to work with, since the df of a univariate t distribution is available in statistical software packages. Moreover, the equivalence of the two formulas allows us to conclude that we can use (5.31) to evaluate tail-dependence coefficients for any bivariate elliptical distribution with correlation parameter ρ when the distribution of the radial rv R has a regularly varying tail with tail index ν.

Notes and Comments

Section 7.3 has been a highly selective account tailored to the study of a number of very specific models, and all of the theoretical subjects touched upon—regular variation, von Mises distributions, tails of products, tails of stochastic recurrence equations—can be studied in much greater detail.

For more about regular variation, slow variation and Karamata's Theorem see Bingham, Goldie and Teugels (1987) and Seneta (1976). A summary of the more important ideas with regard to the study of extremes is found in Resnick (1987). Section 7.3.2, with the exception of the examples, is taken from EKM, and detailed references to results on von Mises distributions and the maximum domain of attraction of the Gumbel distribution are found therein.

Theorem 7.35 follows from results of Breiman (1965). Related results on distributions of products are found in Embrechts and Goldie (1980). The discussion of tails of GARCH models is based on Mikosch and Stărică (2000); the theory involves the study of stochastic recurrence relations and is essentially due to Kesten (1973). See also Mikosch (2003) for an excellent introduction to these ideas.

The formula for tail-dependence coefficients in elliptical distributions when the radial rv has a regularly varying tail is taken from Hult and Lindskog (2002). Similar results were derived independently by Schmidt (2002); see also Frahm, Junker and Szimayer (2003) for a discussion of the applicability of such results to financial returns.

7.4 Point Process Models

In our discussion of threshold models in Section 7.2 we considered only the magnitude of excess losses over high thresholds. In this section we consider exceedances of thresholds as events in time and use a point process approach to model the occurrence of these events. We begin by looking at the case of regularly spaced iid data and discuss the well-known peaks-over-threshold (POT) model for the occurrence of extremes in such data; this model elegantly subsumes the models for maxima and the GPD models for excess losses that we have so far described.

However, the assumptions of the standard POT model are typically violated by financial return series, because of the kind of serial dependence that volatility clustering generates in such data. Our ultimate aim is to find more general point process models to describe the occurrence of extreme values in financial time series, and we find suitable candidates in the class of self-exciting point processes. These models are of a dynamic nature and can be used to estimate conditional VaRs; they offer an interesting alternative to the conditional EVT approach of Section 7.2.6 with the advantage that no prewhitening of data with GARCH processes is required.

The following section gives an idea of the theory behind the POT model, but may be skipped by readers who are content to go directly to a description of the standard POT model in Section 7.4.2.

7.4.1 Threshold Exceedances for Strict White Noise

Consider a strict white noise process $(X_i)_{i\in\mathbb{N}}$ representing financial losses. While we discuss the theory for iid variables for simplicity, the results we describe also hold for dependent processes with extremal index $\theta = 1$, i.e. processes where extreme values show no tendency to cluster (see Section 7.1.3 for examples of such processes).

Throughout this section we assume that the common loss distribution is in the maximum domain of attraction of an extreme value distribution (MDA(H_ξ)) so that (7.1) holds for the non-degenerate limiting distribution H_ξ and normalizing sequences c_n and d_n. From (7.1) it follows, by taking logarithms and using $\ln(1-y) \sim -y$ as $y \to 0$, that for any fixed x we have

$$\left.\begin{aligned} \lim_{n\to\infty} n\ln(1-\bar{F}(c_n x + d_n)) &= \ln H_\xi(x), \\ \lim_{n\to\infty} n\bar{F}(c_n x + d_n) &= -\ln H_\xi(x). \end{aligned}\right\} \tag{7.31}$$

Throughout this section we also consider a sequence of thresholds $(u_n(x))$ defined by $u_n(x) := c_n x + d_n$ for some fixed value of x. Clearly, (7.31) implies that we have $n\bar{F}(u_n(x)) \to -\ln H_\xi(x)$ as $n \to \infty$ for this sequence of thresholds.

The number of losses in the sample $X_1, \dots, X_n$ exceeding the threshold $u_n(x)$ is a binomial rv, $N_{u_n(x)} \sim B(n, \bar{F}(u_n(x)))$, with expectation $n\bar{F}(u_n(x))$. Since (7.31) holds, the standard Poisson limit result implies that, as $n \to \infty$, the number of exceedances $N_{u_n(x)}$ converges to a Poisson rv with mean $\lambda(x) = -\ln H_\xi(x)$, depending on the particular x chosen.

The theory goes further. Not only is the number of exceedances asymptotically Poisson, these exceedances occur according to a Poisson point process. To state the result it is useful to give a brief summary of some ideas concerning point processes.

On point processes. Suppose we have a sequence of rvs or vectors $Y_1, \dots, Y_n$ taking values in some *state space* $\mathcal{X}$ (for example, $\mathbb{R}$ or $\mathbb{R}^2$) and we define, for any set $A \subset \mathcal{X}$, the rv

$$N(A) = \sum_{i=1}^{n} I_{\{Y_i \in A\}}, \tag{7.32}$$

which counts the random number of Y_i in the set A. Under some technical conditions (see EKM, pp. 220–223), (7.32) is said to define a point process $N(\cdot)$. An example of a point process is the Poisson point process.

Definition 7.39 (Poisson point process). The point process $N(\cdot)$ is called a Poisson point process (or Poisson random measure) on $\mathcal{X}$ with intensity measure Λ if the following two conditions are satisfied.

(a) For $A \subset \mathcal{X}$ and $k \geqslant 0$,

$$P(N(A) = k) = \begin{cases} \mathrm{e}^{-\Lambda(A)}\dfrac{\Lambda(A)^k}{k!}, & \Lambda(A) < \infty, \\ 0, & \Lambda(A) = \infty. \end{cases}$$

(b) For any $m \geqslant 1$, if $A_1, \dots, A_m$ are mutually disjoint subsets of $\mathcal{X}$, then the rvs $N(A_1), \dots, N(A_m)$ are independent.

The intensity measure $\Lambda(\cdot)$ of $N(\cdot)$ is also known as the mean measure because $E(N(A)) = \Lambda(A)$. We also speak of the intensity function (or simply intensity) of the process, which is the derivative $\lambda(\boldsymbol{x})$ of the measure satisfying $\Lambda(A) = \int_A \lambda(\boldsymbol{x})\, \mathrm{d}\boldsymbol{x}$.

Asymptotic behaviour of the point process of exceedances. Consider again the strict white noise $(X_i)_{i\in\mathbb{N}}$ and sequence of thresholds $u_n(x) = c_n x + d_n$ for some fixed x. For $n \in \mathbb{N}$ and $1 \leqslant i \leqslant n$ let $Y_{i,n} = (i/n) I_{\{X_i > u_n(x)\}}$ and observe that $Y_{i,n}$ can be thought of as returning either the normalized "time" i/n of an exceedance, or zero. The point process of exceedances of the threshold u_n is the process $N_n(\cdot)$ with state space $\mathcal{X} = (0, 1]$ given by

$$N_n(A) = \sum_{i=1}^{n} I_{\{Y_{i,n} \in A\}} \tag{7.33}$$

for $A \subset \mathcal{X}$. As the notation indicates, we consider this process to be an element in a sequence of point processes indexed by n. The point process (7.33) counts the exceedances with time of occurrence in the set A and we are interested in the behaviour of this process as $n \to \infty$.

It may be shown (see Theorem 5.3.2 in EKM) that $N_n(\cdot)$ converges in distribution on $\mathcal{X}$ to a Poisson process $N(\cdot)$ with intensity measure $\Lambda(\cdot)$ satisfying $\Lambda(A) = (t_2 - t_1)\lambda(x)$ for $A = (t_1, t_2) \subset \mathcal{X}$, where $\lambda(x) = -\ln H_\xi(x)$ as before. This implies, in particular, that $E(N_n(A)) \to E(N(A)) = \Lambda(A) = (t_2 - t_1)\lambda(x)$. Clearly, the intensity does not depend on time and takes the constant value $\lambda := \lambda(x)$; we refer to the limiting process as a *homogeneous Poisson process* with intensity or rate λ.

Application of the result in practice. We give a heuristic argument explaining how this limiting result is used in practice. We consider a fixed large sample size n and a fixed high threshold u, which we assume satisfies $u = c_n y + d_n$ for some value y. We expect that the number of threshold exceedances can be approximated by a Poisson rv and that the point process of exceedances of u can be approximated by a homogeneous Poisson process with rate $\lambda = -\ln H_\xi(y) = -\ln H_\xi((u - d_n)/c_n)$. If we replace the normalizing constants c_n and d_n by $\sigma > 0$ and μ, we have a Poisson process with rate $-\ln H_{\xi,\mu,\sigma}(u)$. Clearly, we could repeat the same argument with any high threshold so that, for example, we would expect it to be approximately true that exceedances of the level $x \geqslant u$ occur according to a Poisson process with rate $-\ln H_{\xi,\mu,\sigma}(x)$.

We thus have an intimate relationship between the GEV model for block maxima and a Poisson model for the occurrence in time of exceedances of a high threshold. The arguments of this section thus provide theoretical support for the observation in Figure 4.3: that exceedances for simulated iid t data are separated by waiting times that behave like iid exponential observations.

7.4.2 The POT Model

The theory of the previous section combined with the theory of Section 7.2 suggests an asymptotic model for threshold exceedances in regularly spaced iid data (or data from a process with extremal index $\theta = 1$). The so-called POT model makes the following assumptions.

- Exceedances occur according to a homogeneous Poisson process in time.
- Excess amounts above the threshold are iid and independent of exceedance times.
- The distribution of excess amounts is generalized Pareto.

There are various alternative ways of describing this model. It might also be called a *marked Poisson* point process, where the exceedance times constitute the points and the GPD-distributed excesses are the marks. It can also be described as a (non-homogeneous) *two-dimensional Poisson* point process, where points (t, x) in two-dimensional space record times and magnitudes of exceedances. The latter representation is particularly powerful, as we now discuss.

Two-dimensional Poisson formulation of POT model. Assume that we have regularly spaced random losses $X_1, \dots, X_n$ and that we set a high threshold u. We *assume* that, on the state space $\mathcal{X} = (0, 1] \times (u, \infty)$, the point process defined by $N(A) = \sum_{i=1}^{n} I_{\{(i/n, X_i) \in A\}}$ is a Poisson process with intensity at a point (t, x) given by

$$\lambda(t, x) = \frac{1}{\sigma}\left(1 + \xi \frac{x - \mu}{\sigma}\right)^{-1/\xi - 1}, \tag{7.34}$$

provided $(1 + \xi(x - \mu)/\sigma) > 0$, and by $\lambda(t, x) = 0$ otherwise. Note that this intensity does not depend on t but does depend on x, and hence the two-dimensional Poisson process is non-homogeneous; we simplify the notation to $\lambda(x) := \lambda(t, x)$. For a set of the form $A = (t_1, t_2) \times (x, \infty) \subset \mathcal{X}$, the intensity measure is

$$\Lambda(A) = \int_{t_1}^{t_2} \int_{x}^{\infty} \lambda(y)\, \mathrm{d}y\, \mathrm{d}t = -(t_2 - t_1) \ln H_{\xi,\mu,\sigma}(x). \tag{7.35}$$

It follows from (7.35) that for any $x \geqslant u$ the implied one-dimensional process of exceedances of the level x is a homogeneous Poisson process with rate $\tau(x) := -\ln H_{\xi,\mu,\sigma}(x)$. Now consider the excess amounts over the threshold u. The tail of the excess df over the threshold u, denoted $\bar{F}_u(x)$ before, can be calculated as the ratio of the rates of exceeding the levels $u + x$ and u. We obtain

$$\bar{F}_u(x) = \frac{\tau(u + x)}{\tau(u)} = \left(1 + \frac{\xi x}{\sigma + \xi(u - \mu)}\right)^{-1/\xi} = \bar{G}_{\xi,\beta}(x)$$

for a positive scaling parameter $\beta = \sigma + \xi(u - \mu)$. This is precisely the tail of the GPD model for excesses over the threshold u used in Section 7.2.2. Thus this seemingly complicated model is indeed the POT model described informally at the beginning of this section.

Note also that the model implies the GEV distributional model for maxima. To see this, consider the event that $\{M_n \leqslant x\}$ for some value $x \geqslant u$. This may be expressed in point process language as the event that there are no points in the set $A = (0, 1] \times (x, \infty)$. The probability of this event is calculated to be $P(M_n \leqslant x) = P(N(A) = 0) = \exp(-\Lambda(A)) = H_{\xi,\mu,\sigma}(x)$, $x \geqslant u$, which is precisely the GEV model for maxima of n-blocks used in Section 7.1.4.

Statistical estimation of the POT model. The most elegant way of fitting the POT model to data is to fit the point process with intensity (7.34) to the exceedance data in one step. Given the exceedance data $\{\tilde{X}_j : j = 1, \dots, N_u\}$, the likelihood can be written as

$$L(\xi, \sigma, \mu; \tilde{X}_1, \dots, \tilde{X}_{N_u}) = \exp(-\tau(u)) \prod_{j=1}^{N_u} \lambda(\tilde{X}_j). \tag{7.36}$$

Parameter estimates of ξ, σ and μ are obtained by maximizing this expression, which is easily accomplished by numerical means. For literature on the derivation of this likelihood, see Notes and Comments.

There are, however, simpler ways of getting the same parameter estimates. Suppose we reparametrize the POT model in terms of $\tau := \tau(u) = -\ln H_{\xi,\mu,\sigma}(u)$, the rate of the one-dimensional Poisson process of exceedances of the level u, and $\beta = \sigma + \xi(u - \mu)$, the scaling parameter of the implied GPD for the excess losses over u. Then the intensity in (7.34) can be rewritten as

$$\lambda(x) = \lambda(t, x) = \frac{\tau}{\beta}\left(1 + \xi\frac{x - u}{\beta}\right)^{-1/\xi-1}, \tag{7.37}$$

where $\xi \in \mathbb{R}$ and $\tau, \beta > 0$. Using this parametrization it is easily verified that the log of the likelihood in (7.36) becomes

$$\ln L(\xi, \sigma, \mu; \tilde{X}_1, \dots, \tilde{X}_{N_u}) = \ln L_1(\xi, \beta; \tilde{X}_1 - u, \dots, \tilde{X}_{N_u} - u) + \ln L_2(\tau; N_u),$$

where L_1 is precisely the likelihood for fitting a GPD to excess losses given in (7.14) and $\ln L_2(\tau; N_u) = -\tau + N_u \ln \tau$, which is the log-likelihood for a one-dimensional homogeneous Poisson process with rate τ. Such a partition of a log-likelihood into a sum of two terms involving two different sets of parameters means that we can make separate inferences about the two sets of parameters; we can estimate ξ and β in a GPD analysis and then estimate τ by its MLE N_u and use these to infer estimates of μ and σ.

Advantages of the POT model formulation. One might ask what the advantages of approaching the modelling of extremes through the two-dimensional Poisson point process model described by the intensity (7.34) could be? One advantage is the fact that the parameters ξ, μ and σ in the Poisson point process model do not have any theoretical dependence on the threshold chosen, unlike the parameter β in the GPD model, which appears in the theory as a function of the threshold u. In practice, we would expect the estimated parameters of the Poisson model to be roughly stable over a range of high thresholds, whereas the estimated β parameter varies with threshold choice.

For this reason the intensity (7.34) is a framework that is often used to introduce covariate effects into extreme value modelling. One method of doing this is to replace the parameters μ and σ in (7.34) by parameters that vary over time as a function of deterministic covariates. For example, we might have $\mu(t) = \alpha + \boldsymbol{\gamma}'\boldsymbol{y}(t)$, where $\boldsymbol{y}(t)$ represents a vector of covariate values at time t. This would give us Poisson processes that are also non-homogeneous in time.

Applicability of the POT model to return series data. We now turn to the use of the POT model with financial return data. An initial comment is that returns do not really form genuine point events in time, in contrast to recorded water levels or wind speeds, for example. Returns are discrete-time measurements that describe changes in value taking place over the course of, say, a day or a week. Nonetheless, we assume that if we take a longer-term perspective, such data can be approximated by point events in time.

In Section 4.1.1 and in Figure 4.3 in particular, we saw evidence that, in contrast to iid data, exceedances of a high threshold for daily financial return series do not necessarily occur according to a homogeneous Poisson process. They tend instead to form clusters corresponding to episodes of high volatility. Thus the standard POT model is not directly applicable to financial return data.

Theory suggests that for stochastic processes with extremal index $\theta < 1$, such as GARCH processes, the extremal clusters themselves should occur according to a homogeneous Poisson process in time, so that the individual exceedances occur according to a *Poisson cluster process* (see, for example, Leadbetter 1991). Thus a suitable model for the occurrence and magnitude of exceedances in a financial return series might be some form of marked Poisson cluster process.

Rather than attempting to specify the mechanics of cluster formation, it is quite common to try to circumvent the problem by *declustering* financial return data: we attempt to formally identify clusters of exceedances and then we apply the POT model to cluster maxima only. This method is obviously somewhat ad hoc, as there is usually no clear way of deciding where one cluster ends and another begins. A possible declustering algorithm is given by the *runs method*. In this method a run size r is fixed and two successive exceedances are said to belong to two different clusters if they are separated by a run of at least r values below the threshold (see EKM, pp. 422–424). In Figure 7.11 the DAX daily negative returns of Figure 4.3 have been declustered with a run length of 10 trading days; this reduces the 100 exceedances to 42 cluster maxima.

However, it is not clear that applying the POT model to declustered data gives us a particularly useful model. We can estimate the rate of occurrence of clusters of extremes and say something about average cluster size; we can also derive a GPD model for excess losses over thresholds for cluster maxima (where standard errors for parameters may be more realistic than if we fitted the GPD to the dependent sample of all threshold exceedances). However, by neglecting the modelling of cluster formation, we cannot make more dynamic statements about the intensity of occurrence of threshold exceedances at any point in time. In the next section we will describe point process models that attempt to do just that.

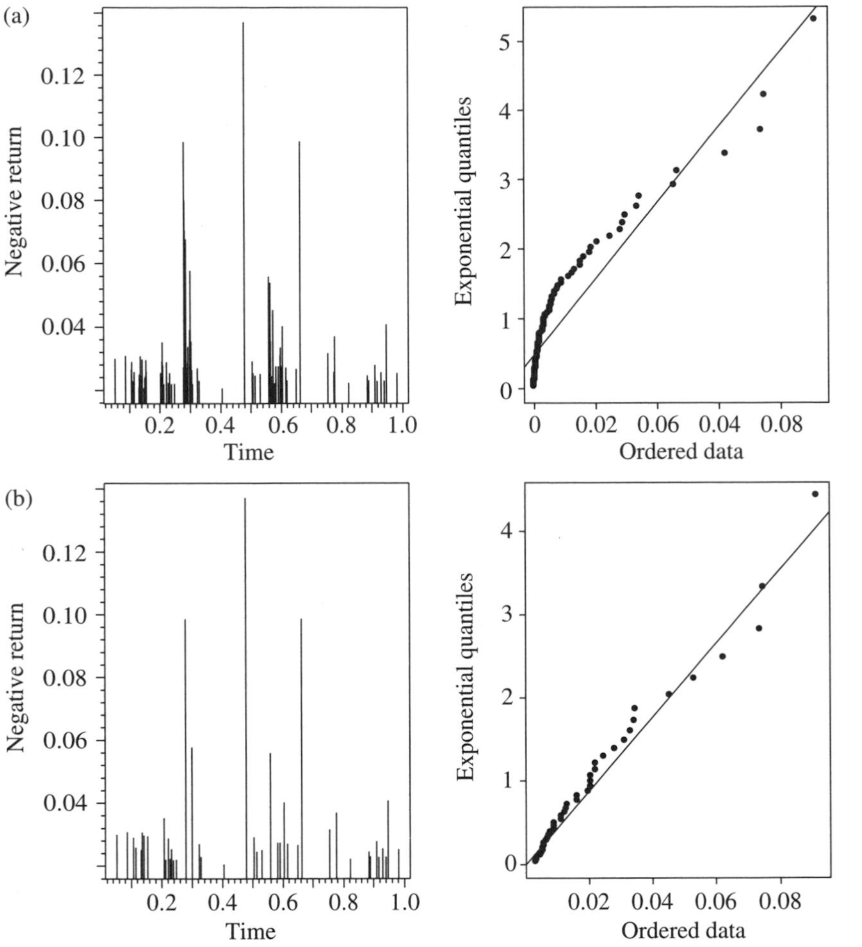

Figure 7.11. (a) DAX daily negative returns and a QQplot of their spacings as in Figure 4.3. (b) Data have been declustered with the runs method using a run length of 10 trading days. The spacings of the 42 cluster maxima are more consistent with a Poisson model.

Example 7.40 (POT analysis of AT&T weekly losses). We close this section with an example of a standard POT model applied to extremes in financial return data. To mitigate the clustering phenomenon discussed above we use weekly return data, as previously analysed in Examples 7.24 and 7.25. Recall that these yield 102 weekly percentage losses for the AT&T stock price exceeding a threshold of 2.75%. The data are shown in Figure 7.12, where we observe that the inter-exceedance times seem to have a roughly exponential distribution, although the discrete nature of the times and the relatively low value of n means that there are some tied values for the spacings, which makes the plot look a little granular. Another noticeable feature is that the exceedances of the threshold appear to become more frequent over time, which might be taken as evidence against the homogeneous Poisson assumption for threshold exceedances and against the implicit assumption that the underlying data form a realization from a stationary time series. It would be possible to consider a

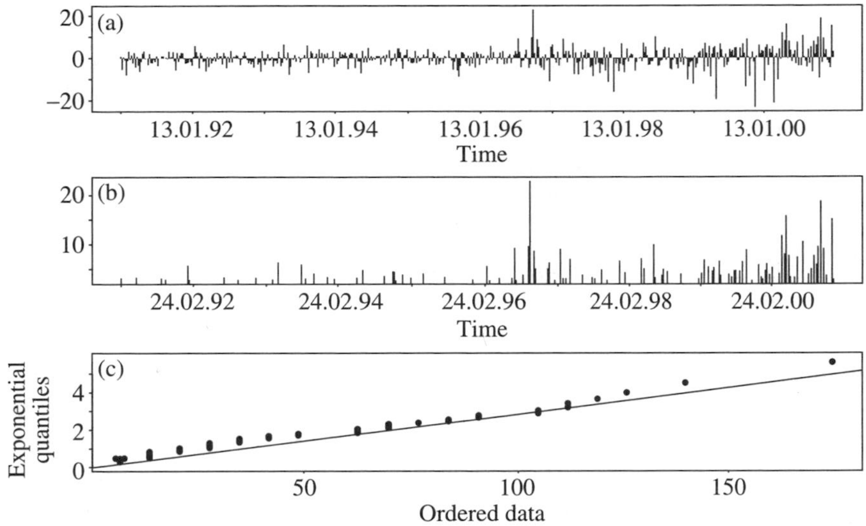

Figure 7.12. (a) Time series of AT&T weekly percentage losses from 1991 to 2000. (b) Corresponding realization of the marked point process of exceedances of the threshold 2.75%. (c) QQplot of inter-exceedance times against an exponential reference distribution. See Example 7.40 for details.

POT model incorporating a trend of increasingly frequent exceedances, but we will not go this far.

We fit the standard two-dimensional Poisson model to the 102 exceedances of the threshold 2.75% using the likelihood in (7.36) and obtain parameter estimates $\hat{\xi} = 0.22$, $\hat{\mu} = 19.9$ and $\hat{\sigma} = 5.95$. The implied GPD shape parameter for the distribution of excess losses over the threshold u is $\hat{\beta} = \hat{\sigma} + \hat{\xi}(u - \hat{\mu}) = 2.1$, so we have exactly the same estimates of ξ and β as in Example 7.24.

The estimated exceedance rate for the threshold $u = 2.75$ is given by $\hat{\tau}(u) = -\ln H_{\hat{\xi},\hat{\mu},\hat{\sigma}}(u) = 102$, which is precisely the number of exceedances of that threshold, as theory suggests. It is of more interest to look at estimated exceedance rates for higher thresholds. For example, we get $\hat{\tau}(15) = 2.50$, which implies that losses exceeding 15% occur as a Poisson process with rate 2.5 losses per 10-year period, so that such a loss is, roughly speaking, a four-year event. Thus the Poisson model gives us an alternative method of defining the return period of a stress event and a more powerful way of calculating such a risk measure. Similarly we can invert the problem to estimate return levels: suppose we define the 10-year return level as that level which is exceeded according to a Poisson process with rate one loss per 10 years, then we can easily estimate the level in our model by calculating

$$H^{-1}_{\hat{\xi},\hat{\mu},\hat{\sigma}}(\exp(-1)) = 19.9,$$

so the 10-year event is a weekly loss of roughly 20%. Using the profile likelihood method in Section A.3.5 we could also give confidence intervals for such estimates.

7.4.3 Self-Exciting Processes

In this section we move away from homogeneous Poisson models for the occurrence times of exceedance of high thresholds and consider self-exciting point processes, or so-called Hawkes processes. In these models a series of recent threshold exceedances causes the instantaneous risk of a threshold exceedance at the present point in time to be higher. The main area of application of these models has traditionally been in the modelling of earthquakes and their aftershocks; however, their structure also seems appropriate for modelling market shocks and the tremors that follow these.

Given data $X_1, \dots, X_n$ and a threshold u, we will assume as usual that there are N_u exceedances, comprising the data $\{(i, X_i) : 1 \leqslant i \leqslant n,\ X_i > u\}$. Note that from now on we will express the time of an exceedance on the natural timescale of the time series, so if, for example, the data are daily observations, then our times are expressed in days. It will also be useful to have the alternative notation $\{(T_j, \tilde{X}_j) : j = 1, \dots, N_u\}$, which enumerates exceedances consecutively.

We first consider a model for exceedance times only. In point process notation we let $Y_i = i I_{\{X_i > u\}}$, so Y_i returns an exceedance time, in the event that one takes place at time i, and returns zero otherwise. The point process of exceedances is the process $N(\cdot)$ with state space $\mathcal{X} = (0, n]$ given by $N(A) = \sum_{i=1}^{n} I_{\{Y_i \in A\}}$ for $A \subset \mathcal{X}$.

We assume that the point process $N(\cdot)$ is a self-exciting process with *conditional intensity*

$$\lambda^*(t) = \tau + \psi \sum_{j:0<T_j<t} h(t - T_j, \tilde{X}_j - u), \tag{7.38}$$

where $\tau > 0$, $\psi \geqslant 0$ and h is some positive-valued function. Each previous exceedance $(T_j, \tilde{X}_j)$ contributes to the conditional intensity and the amount that it contributes can depend on both the elapsed time $(t - T_j)$ since that exceedance and the amount of the excess loss $(\tilde{X}_j - u)$ over the threshold. Informally, we understand the conditional intensity as expressing the instantaneous chance of a new exceedance of the threshold at time t, like the rate or intensity of an ordinary Poisson process. However, in the self-exciting model, the conditional intensity is itself a stochastic process which depends on ω, the state of nature, through the history of threshold exceedances up to (but not including) time t.

Possible parametric specifications of the h function are

- $h(s, x) = \exp(\delta x - \gamma s)$, where $\delta, \gamma > 0$; or
- $h(s, x) = \exp(\delta x)(s + \gamma)^{-(\rho+1)}$, where $\delta, \gamma, \rho > 0$.

Collecting all parameters in $\boldsymbol{\theta}$, the likelihood takes the form

$$L(\boldsymbol{\theta}; \text{data}) = \exp\left(- \int_0^n \lambda^*(s)\, \mathrm{d}s \right) \prod_{i=1}^{N_u} \lambda^*(T_i),$$

and may be maximized numerically to obtain parameter estimates.

Example 7.41 (S&P daily percentage losses 1996–2003). We apply the self-exciting process methodology to all daily percentage losses incurred by the Standard

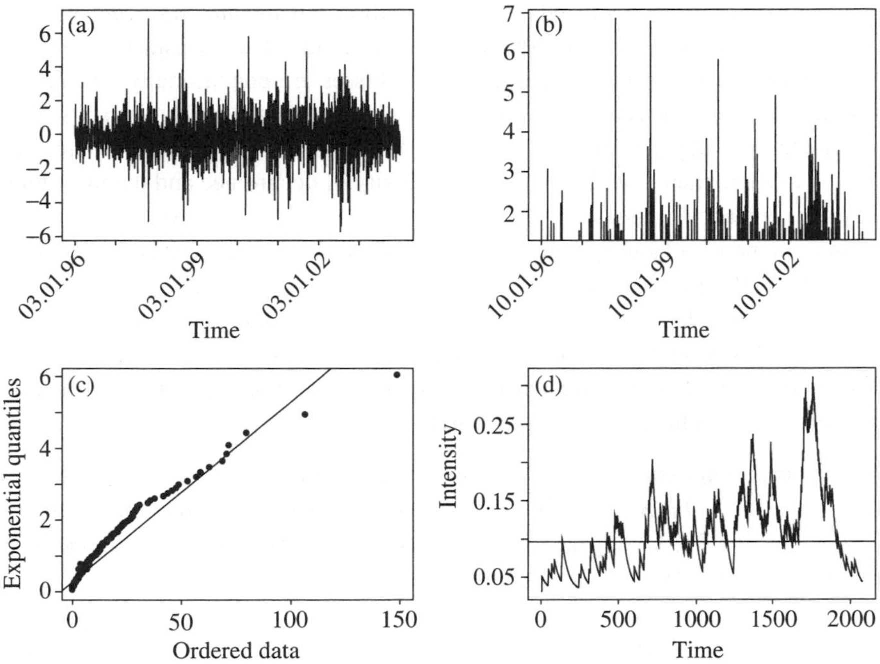

Figure 7.13. (a) S&P daily percentage loss data. (b) Two hundred largest losses. (c) A QQplot of inter-exceedance times against an exponential reference distribution. (d) The estimated intensity of exceeding the threshold in a self-exciting model. See Example 7.41 for details.

& Poor's index in the eight-year period 1996–2003 (2078 values). In Figure 7.13 the loss data are shown as well as the point process of the 200 largest daily losses exceeding a threshold of 1.50%. Clearly, there is clustering in the pattern of exceedance data and the QQplot shows that the inter-exceedance times are not exponential.

We fit the simpler self-exciting model with $h(s, x) = \exp(\delta x - \gamma s)$. The parameter estimates (and standard errors) are $\hat{\tau} = 0.032(0.011)$, $\hat{\psi} = 0.016(0.0069)$, $\hat{\gamma} = 0.026(0.011)$, $\hat{\delta} = 0.13(0.27)$, suggesting that all parameters except δ are significant. The log-likelihood for the fitted model is -648.2, whereas the log-likelihood for a homogeneous Poisson model is -668.2; thus the Poisson special case can clearly be rejected. The final picture shows the estimated intensity $\lambda^*(t)$ of crossing the threshold throughout the data observation period, which seems to reflect the pattern of exceedances observed.

Note that a simple refinement of this model (and those of the following section) would be to consider a self-exciting structure where both extreme negative and extreme positive returns contributed to the conditional intensity; this would involve setting upper and lower thresholds and considering exceedances of both.

7.4.4 A Self-Exciting POT Model

We now consider how the POT model of Section 7.4.2 might be generalized to incorporate a self-exciting component. We first develop a marked self-exciting model where marks have a generalized Pareto distribution, but are *unpredictable*, meaning that the excess losses are iid GPD. In the second model we consider the case of *predictable* marks. In this model the excess losses are conditionally generalized Pareto, given the exceedance history up to the time of the mark, with a scaling parameter that depends on that history. In this way we get a model where, in a period of excitement, both the temporal intensity of occurrence and the magnitude of the exceedances increase.

In point process language our models are processes $N(\cdot)$ on a state space of the form $\mathcal{X} = (0, n] \times (u, \infty)$ such that $N(A) = \sum_{i=1}^{n} I_{\{(i,X_i)\in A\}}$ for sets $A \subset \mathcal{X}$. To build these models we start with the intensity of the reparametrized version of the standard POT model given in (7.37). We recall that this model simply says that exceedances of the threshold u occur as a homogeneous Poisson process with rate τ and that excesses have a generalized Pareto distribution with df $G_{\xi,\beta}$.

Model with unpredictable marks. We first introduce the notation $v^*(t) = \sum_{j:0<T_j<t} h(t - T_j, \tilde{X}_j - u)$ for the *self-excitement function*, where the function h is as in Section 7.4.3. We generalize (7.37) and consider a self-exciting model with conditional intensity

$$\lambda^*(t, x) = \frac{\tau + \psi v^*(t)}{\beta}\left(1 + \xi\frac{x - u}{\beta}\right)^{-1/\xi-1} \tag{7.39}$$

on a state space $\mathcal{X} = (0, n] \times (u, \infty)$, where $\tau > 0$ and $\psi \geqslant 0$. Effectively, we have combined the one-dimensional intensity in (7.38) with a GPD density. When $\psi = 0$ we have an ordinary POT model with no self-exciting structure.

It is easy to calculate that the conditional rate of crossing the threshold $x \geqslant u$ at time t, given information up to that time, is

$$\tau^*(t, x) = \int_x^\infty \lambda^*(t, y)\,\mathrm{d}y = (\tau + \psi v^*(t))\left(1 + \xi\frac{x - u}{\beta}\right)^{-1/\xi}, \tag{7.40}$$

which, for fixed x, is simply a one-dimensional self-exciting process of the form (7.38). The implied distribution of the excess losses when an exceedance takes place is generalized Pareto, because

$$\frac{\tau^*(t, u + x)}{\tau^*(t, u)} = \left(1 + \frac{\xi x}{\beta}\right)^{-1/\xi} = \bar{G}_{\xi,\beta}(x), \tag{7.41}$$

independently of t. Statistical fitting of this model is performed by maximizing a likelihood of the form

$$L(\boldsymbol{\theta}; \text{data}) = \exp\left(-n\tau - \psi\int_0^n v^*(s)\,\mathrm{d}s\right)\prod_{j=1}^{N_u}\lambda^*(T_j, \tilde{X}_j). \tag{7.42}$$

A model with predictable marks. A model with predictable marks can be obtained by generalizing (7.39) to get

$$\lambda^*(t, x) = \frac{\tau + \psi v^*(t)}{\beta + \alpha v^*(t)}\left(1 + \xi\frac{x - u}{\beta + \alpha v^*(t)}\right)^{-1/\xi-1}, \tag{7.43}$$

where $\beta > 0$ and $\alpha \geqslant 0$. For simplicity we have assumed that the GPD scaling is also linear in the self-excitement function $v^*(t)$. The properties of this model follow immediately from the model with unpredictable marks. The conditional crossing rate of the threshold $x \geqslant u$ at time t is as in (7.40) with the parameter β replaced by the time-dependent self-exciting function $\beta + \alpha v^*(t)$. By repeating the calculation in (7.41) we find that the distribution of the excess loss over the threshold, given that an exceedance takes place at time t and given the history of exceedances up to time t, is generalized Pareto with df $G_{\xi,\beta+\alpha v^*(t)}$. The likelihood for fitting the model is again (7.42), where the function $\lambda^*(t,x)$ is now given by (7.43). Note that by comparing a model with $\alpha = 0$ and a model with $\alpha > 0$ we can formally test the hypothesis that the marks are unpredictable using a likelihood ratio test

Example 7.42 (self-exciting POT model for S&P daily loss data). We continue the analysis of the data of Example 7.41 by fitting self-exciting POT models with both unpredictable and predictable marks to the 200 exceedances of the threshold $u = 1.5\%$. The former is equivalent to fitting a self-exciting model to the exceedance times as in Example 7.41 and then fitting a GPD to the excess losses over the threshold; thus the estimated intensity of crossing the threshold is identical to the one shown in Figure 7.13. The log-likelihood for this model is -783.4, whereas a model with predictable marks gives a value of -779.3 for one extra parameter α; in a likelihood ratio test the p-value is 0.004, showing a significant improvement.

In Figure 7.14 we show the exceedance data as well as the estimated intensity $\tau^*(t,u)$ of exceeding the threshold in the model with predictable marks. We also show the estimated mean of the GPD for the conditional distribution of the excess loss above the threshold, given that an exceedance takes place at time t. The GPD mean $(\beta + \alpha v^*(t))/(1-\xi)$ and the intensity $\tau^*(t,u)$ are both affine functions of the self-excitement function $v^*(t)$ and obviously follow its path.

Calculating conditional risk measures. Finally, we note that self-exciting POT models can be used to estimate a kind of analogue of a conditional VaR and also a conditional expected shortfall. If we have analysed n daily data ending on day t and want to calculate, say, a 99% VaR, then we treat the problem as a (conditional) return-level problem; we look for the level at which the conditional exceedance intensity at a time point just after t (denoted by $t+$) is 0.01. In general, to calculate a conditional estimate of VaR_α^t (for α sufficiently large) we would attempt to solve the equation $\tau^*(t+,x) = (1-\alpha)$ for some value of x satisfying $x \geqslant u$. In the model with predictable marks this is possible if $\tau + \psi v^*(t+) > 1-\alpha$ and gives the formula

$$\mathrm{VaR}_\alpha^t = u + \frac{\beta + \alpha v^*(t+)}{\xi}\left(\left(\frac{1-\alpha}{\tau + \psi v^*(t+)}\right)^{-\xi} - 1\right).$$

The associated conditional expected shortfall could then be calculated by observing that the conditional distribution of excess losses above VaR_α^t given information up to time t is GPD with shape parameter ξ and scaling parameter given by $\beta + \alpha v^*(t+) + \xi(\mathrm{VaR}_\alpha^t - u)$.

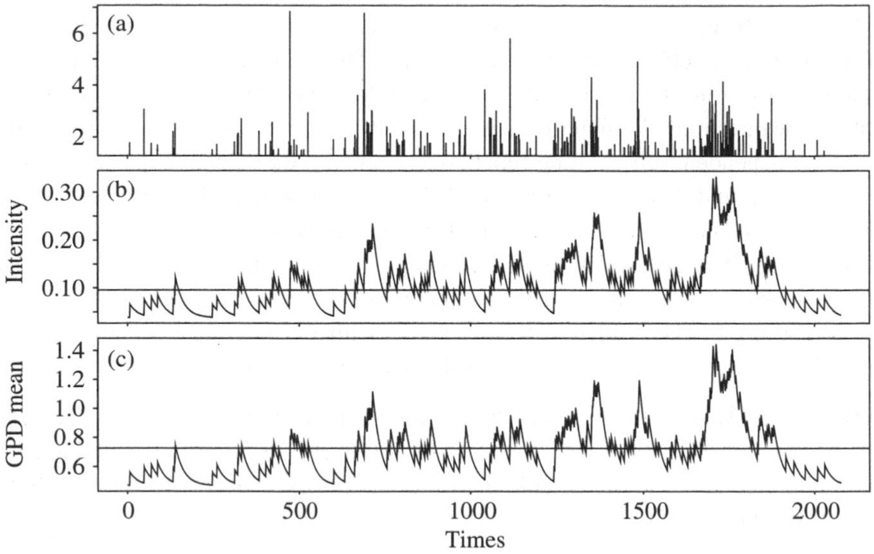

Figure 7.14. (a) Exceedance pattern for 200 largest daily losses in S&P data. (b) Estimated intensity of exceeding the threshold in a self-exciting POT model with predictable marks. (c) Mean of the conditional generalized Pareto distribution of the excess loss above the threshold. See Example 7.42 for details.

Notes and Comments

For more information about point processes consult EKM, Cox and Isham (1980), Kallenberg (1983) and Resnick (1987). The point process approach to extremes dates back to Pickands (1971) and is also discussed in Leadbetter, Lindgren and Rootzén (1983), Leadbetter (1991) and Falk, Hüsler and Reiss (1994).

The two-dimensional Poisson point process model was first used in practice by Smith (1989) and may also be found in Smith and Shively (1995); both these papers discuss the adaptation of the point process model to incorporate covariates or time trends in the context of environmental data. An insurance application is treated in Smith and Goodman (2000), which also treats the point process model from a Bayesian perspective. An interesting application to wind storm losses is Rootzén and Tajvidi (1997). A further application of the bivariate point process framework to model insurance loss data showing trends in both intensity and severity of occurrence is found in McNeil and Saladin (2000). For further applications to insurance and finance, see Chavez-Demoulin and Embrechts (2004). An excellent overview of statistical approaches to the GPD and point process models is found in Coles (2001).

The derivation of likelihoods for point process is beyond the scope of this book and we have simply recorded the likelihoods to be maximized without further justification. See Daley and Vere-Jones (2003, Chapter 7) for more details on this subject; see also Coles (2001, p. 127) for a good intuitive account in the Poisson case.

The original reference to the Hawkes self-exciting process is Hawkes (1971). There is a large literature on the application of such processes to earthquake modelling; a starter reference is Ogata (1988). The application to financial data was suggested in Chavez-Demoulin, Davison and McNeil (2005). The idea of a POT model with self-exciting structure explored in Section 7.4.4 is new.

7.5 Multivariate Maxima

In this section we give a brief overview of the theory of multivariate maxima, stating the main results in terms of copulas. A class of copulas known as extreme value copulas emerges as the class of natural limiting dependence structures for multivariate maxima. These provide useful dependence structures for modelling the joint tail behaviour of risk factors that appear to show tail dependence. The main reference is Galambos (1987), which is one of the few texts to treat the theory of multivariate maxima as a copula theory (although Galambos does not use the word, referring to copulas simply as dependence functions).

7.5.1 *Multivariate Extreme Value Copulas*

Let $\boldsymbol{X}_1, \dots, \boldsymbol{X}_n$ be iid random vectors in $\mathbb{R}^d$ with joint df F and marginal dfs $F_1, \dots, F_d$. We label the components of these vectors $\boldsymbol{X}_i = (X_{i,1}, \dots, X_{i,d})'$ and interpret them as losses of d different types. We define the maximum of the jth component to be $M_{n,j} = \max(X_{1,j}, \dots, X_{n,j})$, $j = 1, \dots, d$. In classical multivariate EVT the object of interest is the vector of *componentwise block maxima*: $\boldsymbol{M}_n = (M_{n,1}, \dots, M_{n,d})'$. In particular, we are interested in the possible multivariate limiting distributions for $\boldsymbol{M}_n$ under appropriate normalizations, much as in the univariate case. It should, however, be observed that the vector $\boldsymbol{M}_n$ will in general not correspond to any of the vector observations $\boldsymbol{X}_i$.

We seek limit laws for

$$\frac{\boldsymbol{M}_n - \boldsymbol{d}_n}{\boldsymbol{c}_n} = \left(\frac{M_{n,1} - d_{n,1}}{c_{n,1}}, \dots, \frac{M_{n,d} - d_{n,d}}{c_{n,d}}\right)',$$

as $n \to \infty$, where $\boldsymbol{c}_n = (c_{n,1}, \dots, c_{n,d})'$ and $\boldsymbol{d}_n = (d_{n,1}, \dots, d_{n,d})'$ are vectors of normalizing constants, the former satisfying $\boldsymbol{c}_n > \boldsymbol{0}$. Note that in this and other statements in this section, arithmetic operations on vectors of equal length are understood as componentwise operations. Supposing that $(\boldsymbol{M}_n - \boldsymbol{d}_n)/\boldsymbol{c}_n$ converges in distribution to a random vector with joint df H, we have

$$\lim_{n\to\infty} P\left(\frac{\boldsymbol{M}_n - \boldsymbol{d}_n}{\boldsymbol{c}_n} \leqslant \boldsymbol{x}\right) = \lim_{n\to\infty} F^n(\boldsymbol{c}_n\boldsymbol{x} + \boldsymbol{d}_n) = H(\boldsymbol{x}). \qquad (7.44)$$

Definition 7.43 (MEV distribution and domain of attraction). If (7.44) holds for some F and some H, we say that F is in the maximum domain of attraction of H, written $F \in \mathrm{MDA}(H)$, and we refer to H as a multivariate extreme value distribution (MEV distribution).

The convergence issue for multivariate maxima is already partly solved by the univariate theory. If H has non-degenerate margins, then these must be univariate extreme value distributions of Fréchet, Gumbel or Weibull type. Since these are continuous, Sklar's Theorem tells us that H must have a unique copula. The following theorem asserts that this copula C must have a particular kind of scaling behaviour.

Theorem 7.44 (EV copula). *If (7.44) holds for some F and some H with GEV margins, then the unique copula C of H satisfies*

$$C(\boldsymbol{u}^t) = C^t(\boldsymbol{u}), \quad \forall t > 0. \tag{7.45}$$

Any copula with the property (7.45) is known as an *extreme value copula* (EV copula) and can be the copula of an MEV distribution. The independence and comonotonicity copulas are EV copulas and the Gumbel copula provides an example of a parametric EV copula family. The bivariate version in (5.11) obviously has property (7.45), as does the exchangeable higher-dimensional Gumbel copula based on (5.38) as well as the non-exchangeable versions based on (5.43)–(5.45).

There are a number of mathematical results characterizing MEV distributions and EV copulas. One such result is the following.

Theorem 7.45 (Pickands representation). *The copula C is an EV copula if and only if it has the representation*

$$C(\boldsymbol{u}) = \exp\left\{B\left(\frac{\ln u_1}{\sum_{k=1}^d \ln u_k}, \dots, \frac{\ln u_d}{\sum_{k=1}^d \ln u_k}\right)\sum_{i=1}^d \ln u_i\right\}, \tag{7.46}$$

where $B(\boldsymbol{w}) = \int_{S_d} \max(x_1 w_1, \dots, x_d w_d)\, \mathrm{d}H(\boldsymbol{x})$ and H is a finite measure on the d-dimensional simplex, i.e. the set $S_d = \{\boldsymbol{x} : x_i \geqslant 0,\ i = 1, \dots, d,\ \sum_{i=1}^d x_i = 1\}$.

The function $B(\boldsymbol{w})$ is sometimes referred to as the dependence function of the EV copula. In the general case, such functions are difficult to visualize and work with, but in the bivariate case they have a simple form which we discuss in more detail.

In the bivariate case we redefine $B(\boldsymbol{w})$ as a function of a scalar argument by setting $A(w) := B((w, 1-w)')$ with $w \in [0, 1]$. It follows from Theorem 7.45 that a bivariate copula is an EV copula if and only if it takes the form

$$C(u_1, u_2) = \exp\left\{(\ln u_1 + \ln u_2) A\left(\frac{\ln u_1}{\ln u_1 + \ln u_2}\right)\right\}, \tag{7.47}$$

where $A(w) = \int_0^1 \max((1-x)w, x(1-w))\, \mathrm{d}H(x)$ for a measure H on $[0, 1]$. It can be inferred that such bivariate dependence functions must satisfy

$$\max(w, 1-w) \leqslant A(w) \leqslant 1, \quad 0 \leqslant w \leqslant 1, \tag{7.48}$$

and must moreover be convex. Conversely, a differentiable, convex function $A(w)$ satisfying (7.48) can be used to construct an EV copula using (7.47).

The upper and lower bounds in (7.48) have intuitive interpretations. If $A(w) = 1$ for all w, then the copula (7.47) is clearly the independence copula, and if $A(w) = \max(w, 1-w)$, then it is the comonotonicity copula. It is also useful to note, and easy to show, that we can extract the dependence function from the EV copula in (7.47) by setting

$$A(w) = -\ln C(\mathrm{e}^{-w}, \mathrm{e}^{-(1-w)}), \quad w \in [0, 1]. \tag{7.49}$$

Example 7.46 (Gumbel copula). We consider the asymmetric version of the bivariate Gumbel copula defined by (5.11) and construction (5.43), i.e. the copula

$$C^{\mathrm{Gu}}_{\theta,\alpha,\beta}(u_1, u_2) = u_1^{1-\alpha} u_2^{1-\beta} \exp\{-((-\alpha \ln u_1)^\theta + (-\beta \ln u_2)^\theta)^{1/\theta}\}.$$

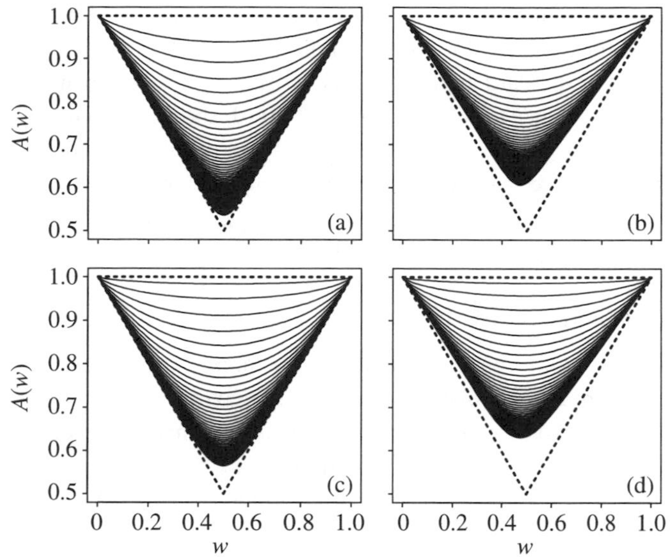

Figure 7.15. Plot of dependence functions for (a) the symmetric Gumbel, (b) the asymmetric Gumbel, (c) the symmetric Galambos and (d) the asymmetric Galambos copulas (asymmetric cases have $\alpha = 0.9$ and $\beta = 0.8$) as described in Examples 7.46 and 7.47. Dashed lines show boundaries of the triangle in which the dependence function must reside; solid lines show dependence functions for a range of parameter values.

As already remarked, this copula has the scaling property (7.45) and is an EV copula. Using (7.49) we calculate that the dependence function is given by

$$A(w) = (1-\alpha)w + (1-\beta)(1-w) + ((\alpha w)^{\theta} + (\beta(1-w))^{\theta})^{1/\theta}.$$

We have plotted this function in Figure 7.15 for a range of θ values running from 1.1 to 10 in steps of size 0.1. Part (a) shows the standard symmetric Gumbel copula with $\alpha = \beta = 1$; the dependence function essentially spans the whole range from independence, represented by the upper edge of the dashed triangle, to comonotonicity, represented by the two lower edges of the dashed triangle which comprise the function $A(w) = \max(w, 1-w)$. Part (b) shows an asymmetric example with $\alpha = 0.9$ and $\beta = 0.8$; in this case we still have independence when $\theta = 1$, but the limit as $\theta \to \infty$ is no longer the comonotonicity model. The Gumbel copula model is also sometimes known as the logistic model.

Example 7.47 (Galambos copula). This time we begin with the dependence function given by

$$A(w) = 1 - ((\alpha w)^{-\theta} + (\beta(1-w))^{-\theta})^{-1/\theta}, \tag{7.50}$$

where $0 \leqslant \alpha, \beta \leqslant 1$ and $0 < \theta < \infty$. It can be verified that this is a convex function satisfying $\max(w, 1-w) \leqslant A(w) \leqslant 1$ for $0 \leqslant w \leqslant 1$, so it can be used to create an EV copula in (7.47). We obtain the copula

$$C^{\text{Gal}}_{\theta,\alpha,\beta}(u_1, u_2) = u_1 u_2 \exp\{((-\alpha \ln u_1)^{-\theta} + (-\beta \ln u_2)^{-\theta})^{-1/\theta}\},$$

which has also been called the negative logistic model. We have plotted this function in Figure 7.15 for a range of θ values running from 0.2 to 5 in steps of size 0.1. Part (c) shows the standard symmetric case with $\alpha = \beta = 1$ spanning the whole range from independence to comonotonicity. Part (d) shows an asymmetric example with $\alpha = 0.9$ and $\beta = 0.8$; in this case we still approach independence as $\theta \to 0$, but the limit as $\theta \to \infty$ is no longer the comonotonicity model.

A number of other bivariate EV copulas have been described in the literature (see Notes and Comments).

7.5.2 Copulas for Multivariate Minima

The structure of limiting copulas for multivariate minima can be easily inferred from the structure of limiting copulas for multivariate maxima; moving from maxima to minima essentially involves the same considerations that we made at the end of Section 7.1.1 and uses identity (7.2) in particular.

Normalized componentwise minima of iid random vectors $\boldsymbol{X}_1, \dots, \boldsymbol{X}_n$ with df F will converge in distribution to a non-degenerate limit if the df $\tilde{F}$ of the random vectors $-\boldsymbol{X}_1, \dots, -\boldsymbol{X}_n$ is in the maximum domain of attraction of an MEV distribution (see Definition 7.43), written $\tilde{F} \in \mathrm{MDA}(H)$. Of course, for a radially symmetric distribution, $\tilde{F}$ coincides with F.

Let $\boldsymbol{M}_n^*$ be the vector of componentwise maxima of $-\boldsymbol{X}_1, \dots, -\boldsymbol{X}_n$ so that $M_{n,j}^* = \max(-X_{1,j}, \dots, -X_{n,j})$. If $\tilde{F} \in \mathrm{MDA}(H)$ for some non-degenerate H, we have

$$\lim_{n\to\infty} P\left(\frac{\boldsymbol{M}_n^* - \boldsymbol{d}_n}{\boldsymbol{c}_n} \leqslant \boldsymbol{x}\right) = \lim_{n\to\infty} \tilde{F}^n(\boldsymbol{c}_n\boldsymbol{x} + \boldsymbol{d}_n) = H(\boldsymbol{x}) \tag{7.51}$$

for appropriate sequences of normalizing vectors $\boldsymbol{c}_n$ and $\boldsymbol{d}_n$, and an MEV distribution H of the form $H(\boldsymbol{x}) = C(H_{\xi_1}(x_1), \dots, H_{\xi_d}(x_d))$, where H_{ξ_j} denotes a GEV distribution with shape parameter ξ_j and C is an EV copula satisfying (7.45).

Defining the vector of componentwise minima by $\boldsymbol{m}_n$ and using (7.2), it follows from (7.51) that

$$\lim_{n\to\infty} P\left(\frac{\boldsymbol{m}_n + \boldsymbol{d}_n}{\boldsymbol{c}_n} \geqslant \boldsymbol{x}\right) = H(-\boldsymbol{x}),$$

so that normalized minima converge in distribution to a limit with survival function $H(-\boldsymbol{x}) = C(H_{\xi_1}(-x_1), \dots, H_{\xi_d}(-x_d))$. It follows that the copula of the limiting distribution of the minima is the survival copula of C (see Section 5.1.5 for discussion of survival copulas). In general, the limiting copulas for minima are *survival copulas of EV copulas* and concrete examples of such copulas are the Gumbel and Galambos survival copulas.

In the special case of a radially symmetric underlying distribution, the limiting copula of the minima is precisely the survival copula of the limiting EV copula of the maxima.

7.5.3 Copula Domains of Attraction

As in the case of univariate maxima we would like to know which underlying multivariate dfs F are attracted to which MEV distributions H. We now give a useful result in terms of copulas which is essentially due to Galambos (see Notes and Comments).

Theorem 7.48. *Let $F(\boldsymbol{x}) = C(F_1(x_1), \dots, F_d(x_d))$ for continuous marginal dfs $F_1, \dots, F_d$ and some copula C. Let $H(\boldsymbol{x}) = C_0(H_1(x_1), \dots, H_d(x_d))$ be an MEV distribution with EV copula C_0. Then $F \in \mathrm{MDA}(H)$ if and only if $F_i \in \mathrm{MDA}(H_i)$ for $1 \leqslant i \leqslant d$ and*

$$\lim_{t\to\infty} C^t(u_1^{1/t}, \dots, u_d^{1/t}) = C_0(u_1, \dots, u_d), \quad \boldsymbol{u} \in [0, 1]^d. \tag{7.52}$$

This result shows that the copula C_0 of the limiting MEV distribution is determined solely by the copula C of the underlying distribution according to (7.52); the marginal distributions of F determine the margins of the MEV limit but are irrelevant to the determination of its dependence structure. This motivates us to introduce the concept of a copula domain of attraction.

Definition 7.49. If (7.52) holds for some C and some EV copula C_0, we say that C is in the copula domain of attraction of C_0, written $C \in \mathrm{CDA}(C_0)$.

There are a number of equivalent ways of writing (7.52). First, by taking logarithms and using the asymptotic identity $\ln(x) \sim x - 1$ as $x \to 1$, we get, for $\boldsymbol{u} \in (0, 1]^d$,

$$\left.\begin{aligned} \lim_{t\to\infty} t(1 - C(u_1^{1/t}, \dots, u_d^{1/t})) &= -\ln C_0(u_1, \dots, u_d), \\ \lim_{s\to 0+} \frac{1 - C(u_1^s, \dots, u_d^s)}{s} &= -\ln C_0(u_1, \dots, u_d). \end{aligned}\right\} \tag{7.53}$$

By inserting $u_i = \exp(-x_i)$ in the latter identity and using $\exp(-sx) \sim 1 - sx$ as $s \to 0$, we get, for $\boldsymbol{x} \in [0, \infty)^d$,

$$\lim_{s\to 0+} \frac{1 - C(1 - sx_1, \dots, 1 - sx_d)}{s} = -\ln C_0(\mathrm{e}^{-x_1}, \dots, \mathrm{e}^{-x_d}). \tag{7.54}$$

Example 7.50 (limiting copula for bivariate Pareto distribution). In Example 5.12 we saw that the bivariate Pareto distribution has univariate Pareto margins $F_i(x) = 1 - (\kappa_i/(\kappa_i + x))^\alpha$ and Clayton survival copula. It follows from Example 7.6 that $F_i \in \mathrm{MDA}(H_{1/\alpha})$, $i = 1, 2$. Using (5.14) the Clayton survival copula is calculated to be $C(u_1, u_2) = u_1 + u_2 - 1 + ((1 - u_1)^{-1/\alpha} + (1 - u_2)^{-1/\alpha} - 1)^{-\alpha}$. Using (7.54) it is easily calculated that $C_0(u_1, u_2) = u_1 u_2 \exp(((-\ln u_1)^{-1/\alpha} + (-\ln u_2)^{-1/\alpha})^{-\alpha})$, which is the standard exchangeable Galambos copula of Example 7.47. Thus the limiting distribution of maxima consists of two Fréchet dfs connected by the Galambos copula.

The coefficients of upper tail dependence play an interesting role in the copula domain of attraction theory. In particular, they can help us to recognize copulas that lie in the copula domain of attraction of the independence copula.

Proposition 7.51. *Let C be a bivariate copula with upper tail-dependence coefficient λ_{u} and assume that C satisfies $C \in \mathrm{MDA}(C_0)$ for some EV copula C_0. Then λ_{u} is also the upper tail-dependence coefficient of C_0 and is related to its dependence function by $\lambda_{\mathrm{u}} = 2(1 - A(\frac{1}{2}))$.*

Proof. We use (5.28) and (5.14) to see that

$$\lambda_u = \lim_{q\to 1^-} \frac{\hat{C}(1-q, 1-q)}{1-q} = 2 - \lim_{q\to 1^-} \frac{1-C(q,q)}{1-q}.$$

By using the asymptotic identity $\ln x \sim x-1$ as $x \to 1$ and the CDA condition (7.53) we can calculate

$$\begin{aligned}\lim_{q\to 1^-} \frac{1-C_0(q,q)}{1-q} = \lim_{q\to 1^-} \frac{\ln C_0(q,q)}{\ln q} &= \lim_{q\to 1^-}\lim_{s\to 0^+} \frac{1-C(q^s,q^s)}{-s\ln q} \\ &= \lim_{q\to 1^-}\lim_{s\to 0^+} \frac{1-C(q^s,q^s)}{-\ln(q^s)} \\ &= \lim_{v\to 1^-} \frac{1-C(v,v)}{1-v},\end{aligned}$$

which shows that C and C_0 share the same coefficient of upper tail dependence. Using the formula $\lambda_u = 2 - \lim_{q\to 1^-} \ln C_0(q,q)/\ln q$ and the representation (7.47) we easily obtain that $\lambda_u = 2(1 - A(\frac{1}{2}))$. □

In the case when $\lambda_u = 0$ we must have $A(\frac{1}{2}) = 1$, and the convexity of dependence functions dictates that $A(w)$ is identically one, so C_0 must be the independence copula. In the higher-dimensional case this is also true: if C is a d-dimensional copula with all upper tail-dependence coefficients equal to zero, then the bivariate margins of the limiting copula C_0 must all be independence copulas, and, in fact, it can be shown that C_0 must therefore be the d-dimensional independence copula (see Notes and Comments).

As an example consider the limiting distribution of multivariate maxima of Gaussian random vectors. Since the pairwise coefficients of tail dependence of Gaussian vectors are zero (see Example 5.32), the limiting distribution is a product of marginal Gumbel distributions. The convergence is extremely slow, but ultimately normalized componentwise maxima are independent in the limit.

Now consider the multivariate t distribution, which has been an important model throughout this book. If $\boldsymbol{X}_1, \dots, \boldsymbol{X}_n$ are iid random vectors with a $t_d(\nu, \boldsymbol{\mu}, \Sigma)$ distribution, we know from Example 7.29 that univariate maxima of the individual components are attracted to univariate Fréchet distributions with parameter $1/\nu$. Moreover, we know from Example 5.33 that tail dependence coefficients for the t copula are strictly positive; the limiting EV copula cannot be the independence copula.

In fact, the limiting EV copula for t-distributed random vectors can be calculated using (7.54), although the calculations are tedious. In the bivariate case it is found that the limiting copula, which we call the t-EV copula, has dependence function

$$A(w) = w t_{\nu+1}\left(\frac{(w/(1-w))^{1/\nu} - \rho}{\sqrt{(1-\rho^2)/(\nu+1)}}\right) + (1-w) t_{\nu+1}\left(\frac{((1-w)/w)^{1/\nu} - \rho}{\sqrt{(1-\rho^2)/(\nu+1)}}\right), \tag{7.55}$$

where ρ is the off-diagonal component of $P = \wp(\Sigma)$. This dependence function is shown in Figure 7.16 for four different values of ν and ρ values ranging from

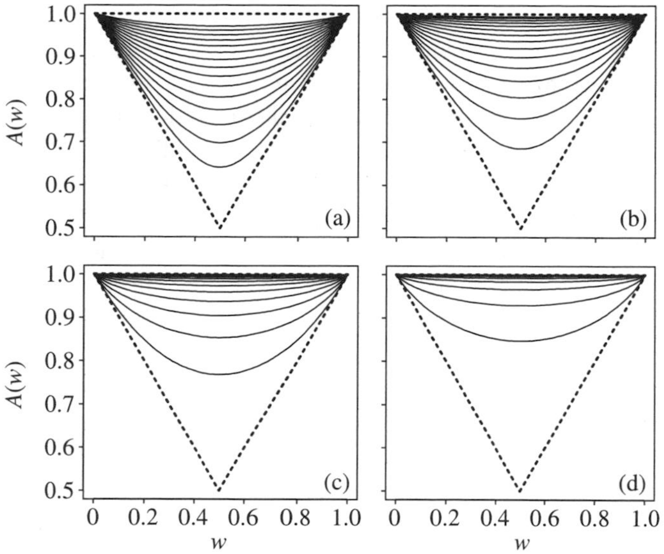

Figure 7.16. Plots of dependence function for the t-EV copula for (a) $\nu = 2$, (b) $\nu = 4$, (c) $\nu = 10$ and (d) $\nu = 20$, and with various values of ρ.

-0.5 to 0.9 with increments of 0.1. As $\rho \to 1$ the t-EV copula converges to the comonotonicity copula; as $\rho \to -1$ or as $\nu \to \infty$ it converges to the independence copula.

7.5.4 Modelling Multivariate Block Maxima

A multivariate block maxima method analogous to the univariate method of Section 7.1.4 could be developed, although similar criticisms apply, namely that the block maxima method is not the most efficient way of making use of extreme data. Also, the kind of inference that this method allows may not be exactly what is desired in the multivariate case, as will be seen.

Suppose we divide our underlying data into blocks as before and we denote the realizations of the block maxima vectors by $\boldsymbol{M}_{n,1}, \dots, \boldsymbol{M}_{n,m}$, where m is the total number of blocks. The distributional model suggested by the univariate and multivariate maxima theory consists of GEV margins connected by an extreme value copula.

In the multivariate theory there is, in a sense, a "correct" EV copula to use, which is the copula C_0 to which the copula C of the underlying distribution of the raw data is attracted. However, the underlying copula C is unknown and so the approach is generally to work with any tractable EV copula that appears appropriate for the task in hand. In a bivariate application, if we restrict to exchangeable copulas, then we have at our disposal the Gumbel, Galambos and t-EV copulas, and a number of other possibilities for which references in Notes and Comments should be consulted. As will be apparent from Figures 7.15 and 7.16, the essential functional form of all these families is really very similar; it makes sense to work with either Gumbel or Galambos as these have simple forms that permit a relatively easy calculation of the copula density (which is needed for likelihood inference). Even if the "true" underlying copula were t, it would not really make sense to use the more complicated t-EV copula, since the dependence function in (7.55) for any ν and ρ can be very accurately approximated by the dependence function of a Gumbel copula.

The Gumbel copula also allows us to explore the possibility of asymmetry by using the general non-exchangeable family described in Example 7.46. For applications in dimensions higher than two, the higher-dimensional extensions of Gumbel discussed in Sections 5.4.2 and 5.4.3 may be useful, although we should stress again that multivariate extreme value models are best suited to low-dimensional applications.

Putting these considerations together, data on multivariate maxima could be modelled using the df $H_{\boldsymbol{\xi},\boldsymbol{\mu},\boldsymbol{\sigma},\boldsymbol{\theta}}(\boldsymbol{x}) = C_{\boldsymbol{\theta}}(H_{\xi_1,\mu_1,\sigma_1}(x_1), \dots, H_{\xi_d,\mu_d,\sigma_d}(x_d))$ for some tractable parametric EV copula $C_{\boldsymbol{\theta}}$. The usual method involves maximum likelihood inference and the maximization can either be performed in one step for all parameters of the margins and copula or broken into two steps, whereby marginal models are estimated first and then a parametric copula is fitted using the ideas in Sections 5.5.2 and 5.5.3. The following bivariate example gives an idea of the kind of inference that can be made with such a model.

Example 7.52. Let $M_{65,1}$ represent the quarterly maximum of daily percentage falls of the US dollar against the euro and let $M_{65,2}$ represent the quarterly maximum of daily percentage falls of the US dollar against the yen. We define a stress event for each of these daily return series: for the dollar against the euro we might be concerned about a 4% fall in any one day; for the dollar against the yen we might be concerned about a 5% fall in any one day. We want to estimate the unconditional probability that one or both of these stress events occurs over any quarter. The probability p of interest is given by $p = 1 - P(M_{65,1} \leqslant 4\%, M_{65,2} \leqslant 5\%)$ and approximated by $1 - H_{\boldsymbol{\xi},\boldsymbol{\mu},\boldsymbol{\sigma},\boldsymbol{\theta}}(0.04, 0.05)$, where the parameters are estimated from the block maxima data. Of course, a more worrying scenario might be that both of these stress events should occur on the *same* day. To calculate the probability of simultaneous extreme events we require a different methodology, which is developed in Section 7.6.

Notes and Comments

Early works on distributions for bivariate extremes include Geffroy (1958), Tiago de Oliveira (1958) and Sibuya (1960). A selection of further important papers in the development of the subject include Galambos (1975), de Haan and Resnick (1977), Balkema and Resnick (1977), Deheuvels (1980) and Pickands (1981). The texts by Galambos (1987) and Resnick (1987) have both been influential; our presentation more closely resembles the former.

Theorem 7.44 is proved in Galambos (1987) (see Theorem 5.2.1 and Lemma 5.4.1 therein (see also Joe 1997, p. 173)). Theorem 7.45 is essentially a result of Pickands (1981). A complete version of the proof is given in Theorem 5.4.5 of Galambos (1987), although it is given in the form of a characterization of MEV distributions with Gumbel margins. This is easily reformulated as a characterization of the EV copulas. In the bivariate case necessary and sufficient conditions for $A(w)$ in (7.47) to define a bivariate EV copula are given in Joe (1997, Theorem 6.4).

The copula of Example 7.47 appears in Galambos (1975). A good summary of other bivariate and multivariate extreme value copulas is found in Kotz and Nadarajah (2000); they are presented as MEV distributions with unit Fréchet margins but the EV copulas are easily inferred from this presentation. See also Joe (1997, Chapters 5 and 6), in which EV copulas and their higher-dimensional extensions are discussed. Many parametric models for extremes have been suggested by Tawn (1988, 1990).

Theorem 7.48 is found in Galambos (1987), where the necessary and sufficient copula convergence criterion is given as $\lim_{n\to\infty} C^n(\boldsymbol{u}^{1/n}) = C_0(\boldsymbol{u})$ for positive integers n; by noting that for any $t > 0$ we have the inequalities

$$C^{[t]+1}(\boldsymbol{u}^{1/[t]}) \leqslant C^t(\boldsymbol{u}^{1/t}) \leqslant C^{[t]}(\boldsymbol{u}^{1/([t]+1)}),$$

it can be inferred that this is equivalent to $\lim_{t\to\infty} C^t(\boldsymbol{u}^{1/t}) = C_0(\boldsymbol{u})$. Further equivalent CDA conditions are found in Takahashi (1994). The idea of a domain of attraction of an EV copula also appears in Abdous, Ghoudi and Khoudraji (1999). Not every copula is in a copula domain of attraction; a counterexample may be found in Schlather and Tawn (2002).

We have shown that pairwise asymptotic independence for the components of random vectors implies pairwise independence of the corresponding components in the limiting MEV distribution of the maxima. Pairwise independence for an MEV distribution in fact implies mutual independence, as recognized and described by a number of authors: see Galambos (1987, Corollary 5.3.1), Resnick (1987, Theorem 5.27), and the earlier work of Geffroy (1958) and Sibuya (1960).

7.6 Multivariate Threshold Exceedances

In this section we describe practically useful models for multivariate extremes (again in low-dimensional applications) that build on the basic idea of modelling excesses over high thresholds with the generalized Pareto distribution (GPD) as in Section 7.2. The idea is to use GPD-based tail models of the kind discussed in Section 7.2.3 together with appropriate copulas to obtain models for multivariate threshold exceedances.

7.6.1 Threshold Models Using EV Copulas

Assume that the vectors $\boldsymbol{X}_1, \dots, \boldsymbol{X}_n$ have unknown joint distribution $F(\boldsymbol{x}) = C(F_1(x_1), \dots, F_d(x_d))$ for some unknown copula C and margins $F_1, \dots, F_d$, and that F is in the domain of attraction of an MEV distribution. Much as in the univariate case we would like to approximate the upper tail of $F(\boldsymbol{x})$ above some vector of high thresholds $\boldsymbol{u} = (u_1, \dots, u_d)'$. The univariate theory of Sections 7.2.2 and 7.2.3 tells us that, for $x_j \geqslant u_j$ and u_j high enough, the tail of the marginal distribution F_j may be approximated by a GPD-based functional form

$$\tilde{F}_j(x_j) = 1 - \lambda_j \left(1 + \xi_j \frac{x_j - u_j}{\beta_j}\right)^{-1/\xi_j}, \tag{7.56}$$

where $\lambda_j = \bar{F}_j(u_j)$. This suggests that for $\boldsymbol{x} \geqslant \boldsymbol{u}$ we use the approximation $F(\boldsymbol{x}) \approx C(\tilde{F}_1(x_1), \dots, \tilde{F}_d(x_d))$. But C is also unknown and must itself be approximated in the tail. The following heuristic argument suggests that we should be able to replace C by its limiting copula C_0.

The CDA condition (7.52) suggests that for any value $\boldsymbol{v} \in (0, 1)^d$ and t sufficiently large we may make the approximation $C(\boldsymbol{v}^{1/t}) \approx C_0^{1/t}(\boldsymbol{v})$. If we now write $\boldsymbol{w} = \boldsymbol{v}^{1/t}$, we have

$$C(\boldsymbol{w}) \approx C_0^{1/t}(\boldsymbol{w}^t) = C_0(\boldsymbol{w}), \tag{7.57}$$

by the scaling property of EV copulas. The approximation (7.57) will be best for large values of $\boldsymbol{w}$, since $\boldsymbol{v}^{1/t} \to \mathbf{1}$ as $t \to \infty$.

We assume then that we can substitute the copula C with its EV limit C_0 in the tail, and this gives us the overall model

$$\tilde{F}(\boldsymbol{x}) = C_0(\tilde{F}_1(x_1), \dots, \tilde{F}_d(x_d)), \quad \boldsymbol{x} \geqslant \boldsymbol{u}. \tag{7.58}$$

We complete the model specification by choosing a flexible and tractable parametric EV copula for C_0. As before, the Gumbel copula family is particularly convenient.

7.6.2 Fitting a Multivariate Tail Model

Assume we have observations $\boldsymbol{X}_1, \dots, \boldsymbol{X}_n$ from a df F with a tail that permits the approximation (7.58). Of these observations, only a minority are likely to be in the joint tail ($\boldsymbol{x} \geqslant \boldsymbol{u}$); other observations may exceed some of the individual thresholds but lie below others. The usual way of making inferences about all the parameters of such a model (the marginal parameters $\xi_j, \beta_j, \lambda_j$, for $j = 1, \dots, d$, and the copula parameter (or parameter vector) θ) is to maximize a likelihood for *censored data*.

Let us suppose that m_i components of the data vector $\boldsymbol{X}_i$ exceed their respective thresholds in the vector $\boldsymbol{u}$. The only relevant information that the remaining components convey is that they lie below their thresholds; such a component $X_{i,j}$ is said to be censored at the value u_j. The contribution to the likelihood of $\boldsymbol{X}_i$ is given by

$$L_i = L_i(\boldsymbol{\xi}, \boldsymbol{\beta}, \boldsymbol{\lambda}, \boldsymbol{\theta}; \boldsymbol{X}_i) = \left. \frac{\partial^{m_i} \tilde{F}(x_1, \dots, x_d)}{\partial x_{j_1} \cdots \partial x_{j_{m_i}}} \right|_{\max(\boldsymbol{X}_i, \boldsymbol{u})},$$

where the indices $j_1, \dots, j_{m_i}$ are those of the components of $\boldsymbol{X}_i$ exceeding their thresholds.

For example, in a bivariate model with Gumbel copula (5.11) the likelihood contribution would be

$$L_i = \begin{cases} C_\theta^{\mathrm{Gu}}(1-\lambda_1, 1-\lambda_2), & X_{i,1} \leqslant u_1, \ X_{i,2} \leqslant u_2, \\ C_{\theta,1}^{\mathrm{Gu}}(\tilde{F}_1(X_{i,1}), 1-\lambda_2)\tilde{f}_1(X_{i,1}), & X_{i,1} > u_1, \ X_{i,2} \leqslant u_2, \\ C_{\theta,2}^{\mathrm{Gu}}(1-\lambda_1, \tilde{F}_2(X_{i,2}))\tilde{f}_2(X_{i,2}), & X_{i,1} \leqslant u_1, \ X_{i,2} > u_2, \\ c_\theta^{\mathrm{Gu}}(\tilde{F}_1(X_{i,1}), \tilde{F}_2(X_{i,2}))\tilde{f}_1(X_{i,1})\tilde{f}_2(X_{i,2}), & X_{i,1} > u_1, \ X_{i,2} > u_2, \end{cases} \tag{7.59}$$

where $\tilde{f}_j$ denotes the density of the univariate tail model $\tilde{F}_j$ in (7.56), $c_\theta^{\mathrm{Gu}}(u_1, u_2)$ denotes the Gumbel copula density and $C_{\theta,j}^{\mathrm{Gu}}(u_1, u_2) := (\partial/\partial u_j)C_\theta^{\mathrm{Gu}}(u_1, u_2)$

Table 7.3. Parameter estimates and standard errors (in brackets) for a bivariate tail model fitted to exchange-rate return data; see Example 7.53 for details.

	\$/€	\$/¥
u	0.75	1.00
N_u	189	126
λ	0.094 (0.0065)	0.063 (0.0054)
ξ	−0.049 (0.066)	0.095 (0.11)
β	0.33 (0.032)	0.38 (0.053)
θ	1.10 (0.030)	

denotes a conditional distribution of the copula, as in (5.15). The overall likelihood is a product of such contributions and is maximized with respect to all parameters of the marginal models and copula.

In a simpler approach, parameters of the marginal GPD models could be estimated as in Section 7.2.3 and only the parameters of the copula obtained from the above likelihood. In fact this is also a sensible way of getting starting values before going on to the global maximization over all parameters.

The model described by the likelihood (7.59) has been studied in some detail by Ledford and Tawn (1996) and a number of related models have been studied in the statistical literature on multivariate EVT (see Notes and Comments for more details).

Example 7.53 (bivariate tail model for exchange-rate return data). We analyse daily percentage falls in the value of the US dollar against the euro and the Japanese yen, taking data for the eight-year period 1996–2003. We have 2008 daily returns and choose to set thresholds at 0.75% and 1.00%, giving 189 and 126 exceedances, respectively. In a full maximization of the likelihood over all parameters, we obtained the estimates and standard errors shown in Table 7.3. The value of the maximized log-likelihood is -1064.7, compared with -1076.4 in a model where independence in the tail is assumed (i.e. a Gumbel copula with $\theta = 1$), showing strong evidence against an independence assumption.

We can now use the fitted model (7.58) to make various calculations about stress events. For example, an estimate of the probability that on any given day the dollar falls by more than 2% against both currencies is given by

$$p_{12} := 1 - \tilde{F}_1(2.00) - \tilde{F}_2(2.00) + C_\theta^{\mathrm{Gu}}(\tilde{F}_1(2.00), \tilde{F}_2(2.00)) = 0.000\,315,$$

with $\tilde{F}_j$ as in (7.56), making this approximately a 13-year event (assuming 250 trading days per year). The marginal probabilities of falls in value of this magnitude are $p_1 := 1 - \tilde{F}_1(2.00) = 0.0014$ and $p_2 := 1 - \tilde{F}_2(2.00) = 0.0061$. We can use this information to calculate so-called spillover probabilities for the conditional occurrence of stress events; for example, the probability that the dollar falls 2% against the yen given that it falls 2% against the euro is estimated to be $p_{12}/p_1 = 0.23$.

7.6.3 Threshold Copulas and Their Limits

Another, more recent, approach to multivariate extremes looks explicitly at the kind of copulas we get when we condition observations to lie above or below extreme thresholds. Just as the GPD is a natural limiting model for univariate threshold exceedances, so we can find classes of copula that are natural limiting models for the dependence structure of multivariate exceedances.

The theory has been studied in most detail in the case of exchangeable bivariate copulas, and we concentrate on this case. Moreover, it proves slightly easier to switch our focus at this stage and first consider the lower-left tail of a probability distribution, before showing how the theory is adapted to the upper-right tail.

Lower threshold copulas and their limits. Consider a random vector (X_1, X_2) with continuous margins F_1 and F_2 and an exchangeable copula C. We consider the distribution of (X_1, X_2) conditional on both being below their v-quantiles, an event we denote by $A_v = \{X_1 \leqslant F_1^{\leftarrow}(v), X_2 \leqslant F_2^{\leftarrow}(v)\}$, $0 < v \leqslant 1$. Assuming $C(v, v) \neq 0$, the probability that X_1 lies below its x_1-quantile and X_2 lies below its x_2-quantile conditional on this event is

$$P(X_1 \leqslant F_1^{\leftarrow}(x_1), X_2 \leqslant F_2^{\leftarrow}(x_2) \mid A_v) = \frac{C(x_1, x_2)}{C(v, v)}, \quad x_1, x_2 \in [0, v].$$

Considered as a function of x_1 and x_2 this defines a bivariate df on $[0, v]^2$, and by Sklar's Theorem we can write

$$\frac{C(x_1, x_2)}{C(v, v)} = C_v^0(F_{(v)}(x_1), F_{(v)}(x_2)), \quad x_1, x_2 \in [0, v], \tag{7.60}$$

for a unique copula C_v^0 and continuous marginal distribution functions

$$F_{(v)}(x) = P(X_1 \leqslant F_1^{\leftarrow}(x) \mid A_v) = \frac{C(x, v)}{C(v, v)}, \quad 0 \leqslant x \leqslant v. \tag{7.61}$$

This unique copula may be written as

$$C_v^0(u_1, u_2) = \frac{C(F_{(v)}^{\leftarrow}(u_1), F_{(v)}^{\leftarrow}(u_2))}{C(v, v)}, \tag{7.62}$$

and will be referred to as the *lower threshold copula* of C at level v. Juri and Wüthrich (2002), who developed the approach we describe in this section, refer to it as a lower tail dependence copula (LTDC). It is of interest to attempt to evaluate limits for this copula as $v \to 0$; such a limit will be known as a *limiting lower threshold copula.*

Much like the GPD in Example 7.19, limiting lower threshold copulas must possess a stability property under the operation of calculating lower threshold copulas in (7.62). A copula C is a limiting lower threshold copula if, for any threshold $0 < v \leqslant 1$, it satisfies

$$C_v^0(u_1, u_2) = C(u_1, u_2). \tag{7.63}$$

Example 7.54 (Clayton copula as limiting lower threshold copula). For the standard bivariate Clayton copula in (5.12) we can easily calculate that $F_{(v)}$ in (7.61) is

$$F_{(v)}(x) = \frac{(x^{-\theta} + v^{-\theta} - 1)^{-1/\theta}}{(2v^{-\theta} - 1)^{-1/\theta}}, \quad 0 \leqslant x \leqslant v,$$

and its inverse is

$$F_{(v)}^{\leftarrow}(u) = u(2v^{-\theta} - 1 + u^{\theta}(1 - v^{-\theta}))^{-1/\theta}, \quad 0 \leqslant u \leqslant 1.$$

Thus the lower threshold copula for the Clayton copula can be calculated from (7.62) and it may be verified that this is again the Clayton copula. In other words, the Clayton copula is a limiting lower threshold copula because (7.63) holds.

Upper threshold copulas. To define upper threshold copulas we consider again a random vector (X_1, X_2) with copula C and margins F_1 and F_2. We now condition on the event $\bar{A}_v = \{X_1 > F_1^{\leftarrow}(v),\ X_2 > F_2^{\leftarrow}(v)\}$ for $0 \leqslant v < 1$. We have the identity

$$P(X_1 > F_1^{\leftarrow}(x_1), X_2 > F_2^{\leftarrow}(x_2) \mid \bar{A}_v) = \frac{\bar{C}(x_1, x_2)}{\bar{C}(v, v)}, \quad x_1, x_2 \in [v, 1].$$

Since $\bar{C}(x_1, x_2)/\bar{C}(v, v)$ defines a bivariate survival function on $[v, 1]^2$, by (5.13) we can write

$$\frac{\bar{C}(x_1, x_2)}{\bar{C}(v, v)} = \hat{C}_v^1(\bar{G}_{(v)}(x_1), \bar{G}_{(v)}(x_2)), \quad x_1, x_2 \in [v, 1], \tag{7.64}$$

for some survival copula $\hat{C}_v^1$ of a copula C_v^1 and marginal survival functions

$$\bar{G}_{(v)}(x) = P(X_1 > F_1^{\leftarrow}(x) \mid \bar{A}_v) = \frac{\bar{C}(x, v)}{\bar{C}(v, v)}, \quad v \leqslant x \leqslant 1. \tag{7.65}$$

The copula C_v^1 is known as the *upper threshold copula* at level v and it is now of interest to find limits as $v \to 1$, which are known as limiting upper threshold copulas. In fact, as the following lemma shows, it suffices to study either lower or upper threshold copulas because results for one follow easily from results for the other.

Lemma 7.55. *The survival copula of the upper threshold copula of C at level v is the lower threshold copula of $\hat{C}$ at level $1 - v$.*

Proof. We use the identity $\bar{C}(u_1, u_2) = \hat{C}(1 - u_1, 1 - u_2)$ and (7.65) to rewrite (7.64) as

$$\frac{\hat{C}(1 - x_1, 1 - x_2)}{\hat{C}(1 - v, 1 - v)} = \hat{C}_v^1\left(\frac{\hat{C}(1 - x_1, 1 - v)}{\hat{C}(1 - v, 1 - v)}, \frac{\hat{C}(1 - v, 1 - x_2)}{\hat{C}(1 - v, 1 - v)}\right).$$

Writing $y_1 = 1 - x_1$, $y_2 = 1 - x_2$ and $w = 1 - v$ we have

$$\frac{\hat{C}(y_1, y_2)}{\hat{C}(w, w)} = \hat{C}_{1-w}^1\left(\frac{\hat{C}(y_1, w)}{\hat{C}(w, w)}, \frac{\hat{C}(w, y_2)}{\hat{C}(w, w)}\right), \quad y_1, y_2 \in [0, w],$$

and comparison with (7.60) and (7.61) shows that $\hat{C}_{1-w}^1$ must be the lower threshold copula of $\hat{C}$ at the level $w = 1 - v$. □

It follows that the survival copulas of limiting lower threshold copulas are limiting upper threshold copulas. The Clayton survival copula is a limiting upper threshold copula.

Relationship between limiting threshold copulas and EV copulas. We give one result which shows how limiting upper threshold copulas may be calculated for underlying exchangeable copulas C that are in the domain of attraction of EV copulas with tail dependence, thus linking the study of threshold copulas to the theory of Section 7.5.3.

Theorem 7.56. *If C is an exchangeable copula with upper tail-dependence coefficient $\lambda_u > 0$ satisfying $C \in \mathrm{CDA}(C_0)$, then C has a limiting upper threshold copula which is the survival copula of the df*

$$G(x_1, x_2) = \frac{(x_1 + x_2)(1 - A(x_1/(x_1 + x_2)))}{\lambda_u}, \tag{7.66}$$

where A is the dependence function of C_0. Also, $\hat{C}$ has a limiting lower threshold copula which is the copula of G.

Example 7.57 (upper threshold copula of Galambos copula). We use this result to calculate the limiting upper threshold copula for the Galambos copula. We recall that this is an EV copula with dependence function given in (7.50) and consider the standard exchangeable case with $\alpha = \beta = 1$. Using the methods of Section 5.2.3 it may easily be calculated that the coefficient of upper tail dependence of this copula is $\lambda_u = 2^{-1/\theta}$. Thus the bivariate distribution $G(x_1, x_2)$ in (7.66) is

$$G(x_1, x_2) = (\tfrac{1}{2}(x_1^{-\theta} + x_2^{-\theta}))^{-1/\theta}, \quad (x_1, x_2) \in (0, 1]^2,$$

the copula of which is the Clayton copula. Thus the limiting upper threshold copula in this case is the Clayton survival copula. Moreover, the limiting lower threshold copula of the Galambos survival copula is the Clayton copula.

The Clayton copula turns out to be an important attractor for a large class of underlying exchangeable copulas. Juri and Wüthrich (2003) have shown that all Archimedean copulas whose generators are regularly varying at 0 with negative parameter (meaning that $\phi(t)$ satisfies $\lim_{t\to 0} \phi(xt)/\phi(t) = x^{-\alpha}$ for all x and some $\alpha > 0$) share the Clayton copula C_α^{Cl} as their limiting lower threshold copula.

It is of interest to calculate limiting lower and upper threshold copulas for the t copula, and this can be done using Theorem 7.56 and the expression for the dependence function in (7.55). However, the resulting limit is not convenient for practical purposes because of the complexity of this dependence function. We have already remarked in Section 7.5.4 that the dependence function of the t-EV copula is indistinguishable for all practical purposes from the dependence functions of other exchangeable EV copulas, such as Gumbel and Galambos. Thus Theorem 7.56 suggests that instead of working with the true limiting upper threshold copula of the t copula we could instead work with the limiting upper threshold copula of, say, the Galambos copula, i.e. the Clayton survival copula. Similarly, we could work with the Clayton copula as an approximation for the true limiting lower threshold copula of the t copula.

Limiting threshold copulas in practice Limiting threshold copulas in dimensions higher than two have not yet been extensively studied, nor have limits for non-exchangeable bivariate copulas or limits when we define two thresholds v_1 and v_2 and let these tend to zero (or one) at different rates. Thus the practical use of these ideas is largely in bivariate applications when thresholds are set at approximately similar quantiles and a symmetric dependence structure is assumed.

Let us consider a situation where we have a bivariate distribution that appears to exhibit tail dependence in both the upper-right and lower-left corners. While true lower and upper limiting threshold copulas may exist for this unknown distribution, we could in practice simply adopt a tractable and flexible parametric limiting threshold copula family. It is particularly easy to use the Clayton copula and its survival copula as lower and upper limits, respectively.

Suppose, for example, that we set high thresholds at $\boldsymbol{u} = (u_1, u_2)'$, so that $P(X_1 > u_1) \approx P(X_2 > u_2)$ and both probabilities are small. For the conditional distribution of (X_1, X_2) over the threshold $\boldsymbol{u}$ we could assume a model of the form

$$P(\boldsymbol{X} \leqslant \boldsymbol{x} \mid \boldsymbol{X} > \boldsymbol{u}) \approx \hat{C}_\theta^{\mathrm{Cl}}(G_{\xi_1,\beta_1}(x_1 - u_1), G_{\xi_2,\beta_2}(x_2 - u_2)), \quad \boldsymbol{x} > \boldsymbol{u},$$

where $\hat{C}_\theta^{\mathrm{Cl}}$ is the Clayton survival copula and G_{ξ_j,β_j} denotes a GPD, as defined in 7.16. Inference about the model parameters $(\theta, \xi_1, \beta_1, \xi_2, \beta_2)$ would be based on the exceedance data above the thresholds and would use the methods discussed in Section 5.5.

Similarly, for a vector of low thresholds $\boldsymbol{u}$ satisfying $P(X_1 \leqslant u_1) \approx P(X_2 \leqslant u_2)$ with both these probabilities small, we could approximate the conditional distribution of (X_1, X_2) below the threshold $\boldsymbol{u}$ by a model of the form

$$P(\boldsymbol{X} \leqslant \boldsymbol{x} \mid \boldsymbol{X} < \boldsymbol{u}) \approx C_\theta^{\mathrm{Cl}}(\bar{G}_{\xi_1,\beta_1}(u_1 - x_1), \bar{G}_{\xi_2,\beta_2}(u_2 - x_2)), \quad \boldsymbol{x} < \boldsymbol{u},$$

where C_θ^{Cl} is the Clayton copula and $\bar{G}_{\xi_j,\beta_j}$ denotes a GPD survival function. Inference about the model parameters would be based on the data below the thresholds and would use the methods of Section 5.5.

Note and Comments

The GPD-based tail model (7.58) and inference for censored data using a likelihood of the form (7.59) have been studied by Ledford and Tawn (1996), although the derivation of the model uses somewhat different asymptotic reasoning based on a characterization of multivariate domains of attraction of MEV distributions with unit Fréchet margins found in Resnick (1987). The authors concentrate on the model with Gumbel (logistic) dependence structure and discuss, in particular, testing for asymptotic independence of extremes. Likelihood inference is non-problematic (the problem being essentially regular) when $\theta > 0$ and $\xi_j > -\frac{1}{2}$, but testing for independence of extremes $\theta = 1$ is not quite so straightforward since this is a boundary point of the parameter space. This case is possibly more interesting in environmental applications than in financial ones, where we tend to expect dependence of extreme values.

A related bivariate GPD model is presented in Smith, Tawn and Coles (1997). In our notation they essentially consider a model of the form

$$\bar{F}(x_1, \dots, x_d) = 1 + \ln C_0(\exp(\tilde{F}(x_1) - 1), \dots, \exp(\tilde{F}(x_d) - 1)), \quad \boldsymbol{x} \geqslant \boldsymbol{k},$$

where C_0 is an extreme value copula. This model is also discussed in Smith (1994) and Ledford and Tawn (1996); it is pointed out that $\bar{F}$ does not reduce to a product of marginal distributions in the case when C_0 is the independence copula, unlike the model in (7.58).

Another style of statistical model for multivariate extremes is based on the point process theory of multivariate extremes developed in de Haan (1985), de Haan and Resnick (1977) and Resnick (1987). Statistical models using this theory are found in Coles and Tawn (1991) and Joe, Smith and Weissman (1992); see also the texts of Joe (1997) and Coles (2001). New approaches to modelling multivariate extremes can be found in Heffernan and Tawn (2004) and Balkema and Embrechts (2004); the latter paper considers applications to stress testing high-dimensional portfolios in finance.

Limiting threshold copulas are studied in Juri and Wüthrich (2002, 2003). In the latter paper it is demonstrated that the Clayton copula is an attractor for the threshold copulas of a wide class of Archimedean copulas; moreover a version of our Theorem 7.57 is proved. Limiting threshold copulas for the t copula are investigated in Demarta and McNeil (2005). The usefulness of Clayton's copula and survival copula for describing the dependence in the tails of bivariate financial return data was confirmed in a large-scale empirical study of high-frequency exchange-rate returns by Breymann, Dias and Embrechts (2003).

8
Credit Risk Management

Credit risk is the risk that the value of a portfolio changes due to unexpected changes in the credit quality of issuers or trading partners. This subsumes both losses due to defaults and losses caused by changes in credit quality, such as the downgrading of a counterparty in an internal or external rating system. Credit risk is omnipresent in the portfolio of a typical financial institution. To begin with, the lending and corporate bond portfolios are obviously affected by credit risk. Perhaps less obviously, credit risk accompanies any OTC (over-the-counter, i.e. non-exchange-guaranteed) derivative transaction such as a swap, because the default of one of the parties involved may substantially affect the actual pay-off of the transaction. Moreover, in recent years a specialized market for credit derivatives has emerged in which financial institutions are active players (see Section 9.1 for details).

This brief list should convince the reader that credit risk is a highly relevant risk category indeed, as it relates to the core activities of most banks. Credit risk is also at the heart of many recent developments on the regulatory side, such as the new Basel II Capital Accord discussed in Chapter 1. We devote two chapters to this important risk category. In the present chapter we focus on *static* models and credit risk management; *dynamic* models and credit derivatives are discussed in Chapter 9.

8.1 Introduction to Credit Risk Modelling

In this section we provide a brief overview of the various model types that are used in credit risk before discussing some of the main challenges that are encountered in credit risk management.

8.1.1 Credit Risk Models

The development of the market for credit derivatives and the Basel II process has generated a lot of interest in quantitative credit risk models in industry, academia and among regulators, so that credit risk modelling is at present a very active subfield of quantitative finance and risk management. In this context it is interesting that parts of the new minimum capital requirements for credit risk are closely linked to the structure of existing credit portfolio models, as will be explained in more detail in Section 8.4.5.

There are two main areas of application for quantitative credit risk models: credit risk management and the analysis of credit-risky securities. Credit risk management models are used to determine the loss distribution of a loan or bond portfolio over a fixed time period (typically at least one year), and to compute loss-distribution-based risk measures or to make risk-capital allocations of the kind discussed in Section 6.3. Hence these models are typically static, meaning that the focus is on the loss distribution for the fixed time period rather than a stochastic process describing the evolution of risk in time.

For the analysis of credit-risky securities, on the other hand, dynamic models (generally in continuous time) are needed, because the pay-off of most products depends on the exact timing of default. Moreover, in building a pricing model one often works directly under an equivalent martingale or risk-neutral probability measure (as opposed to the real-world probability measure). Issues related to dynamic credit risk models and risk-neutral and real-world measures will be studied in detail in Chapter 9.

Depending on their formulation, credit risk models can be divided into *structural* or *firm-value models* on the one hand and *reduced-form models* on the other; this division cuts across that of dynamic and static models. The progenitor of all firm-value models is the model of Merton (1974), which postulates a mechanism for the default of a firm in terms of the relationship between its assets and the liabilities that it faces at the end of a given time period. More generally, in firm-value models default occurs whenever a stochastic variable (or in dynamic models a stochastic process) generally representing an asset value falls below a threshold representing liabilities. For this reason static structural models are referred to in this book as *threshold models*, particularly when applied at portfolio level. The general structural model approach is discussed in Section 8.2 (where the emphasis is on modelling the default of a single firm). In Section 8.3 we look at threshold models for portfolios; in particular we show that copulas play an important role in understanding the multivariate nature of these models.

In reduced-form models the precise mechanism leading to default is left unspecified. The default time of a firm is modelled as a non-negative rv, whose distribution typically depends on economic covariables. The *mixture models* that we treat in Section 8.4 can be thought of as static portfolio versions of reduced-form models. More specifically, a mixture model assumes conditional independence of defaults given common underlying stochastic factors.

It is important to realize that mixture models are not a new class of models; on the contrary, the most useful static threshold models all have mixture model representations, as will be shown in Section 8.4.4. In continuous time a similar mapping between firm-value and reduced-form models is also possible if one makes the realistic assumption that assets and/or liabilities are not perfectly observable (see Notes and Comments).

From a practical point of view, mixture models represent perhaps the most useful way of analysing and comparing one-period portfolio credit risk models. For these models, *Monte Carlo techniques* from the area of importance sampling can be used to approximate risk measures for the portfolio loss distribution, and to calculate associated capital allocations, as will be shown in Section 8.5. Moreover, it is possible to devise efficient methods of *statistical inference* for portfolio models using historical default data. These models exploit the connection between mixture models and the well-known class of generalized linear mixed models in statistics; this is the topic of Section 8.6.

8.1.2 The Nature of the Challenge

Credit risk management poses certain specific challenges for quantitative modelling, which are less relevant in the context of market risk.

Lack of public information and data. Publicly available information regarding the credit quality of corporations is typically scarce. This creates problems for corporate lending, as the management of a firm is usually better informed about the true economic prospects of the firm and hence about default risk than are prospective lenders. The implications of this informational asymmetry are widely discussed in the microeconomics literature (see Notes and Comments). The lack of publicly available credit data is also a substantial obstacle to the use of statistical methods in credit risk, a problem that is compounded by the fact that in credit risk the risk-management horizon is usually at least one year. It is fair to say that data problems are the main obstacle to the reliable calibration of credit models.

Skewed loss distributions. Typical credit loss distributions are strongly skewed with a relatively heavy upper tail. Over the years a typical credit portfolio will produce frequent small profits accompanied by occasional large losses. A fairly large amount of risk capital is therefore required to sustain such a portfolio: the economic capital required for a loan portfolio (the risk capital deemed necessary by shareholders and the board of directors of a financial institution, independent of the regulatory environment) is often equated to the 99.97% quantile of the loss distribution (see Section 1.4.3).

The role of dependence modelling. A major cause for concern in managing the credit risk in a given loan or bond portfolio is the occurrence in a particular time period of disproportionately many defaults of different counterparties. This risk is directly linked to the dependence structure of the default events. In fact, default dependence has a crucial impact on the upper tail of a credit loss distribution for a large portfolio. This is illustrated in Figure 8.1, where we compare the loss distribution for a portfolio of 1000 firms that default independently (portfolio 1) with a more realistic portfolio of the same size where defaults are dependent (portfolio 2). In portfolio 2 defaults are weakly dependent, in the sense that the correlation between default events (see Section 8.3.1) is approximately 0.5%. In both cases the default probability is approximately 1% so that on average we expect 10 defaults. As will be seen in Section 8.6, portfolio 2 can be viewed as a realistic model for the loss distribution generated by a homogeneous portfolio of 1000 loans with a Standard & Poor's rating of BB. We clearly see from Figure 8.1 that the loss distribution of portfolio 2 is skewed and that its right tail is substantially heavier than the right tail of the loss distribution of portfolio 1, illustrating the drastic impact of default dependence on credit loss distributions. Typically, more dependence is reflected in the loss distribution by a shift of the mode to the left and a longer right tail. For this

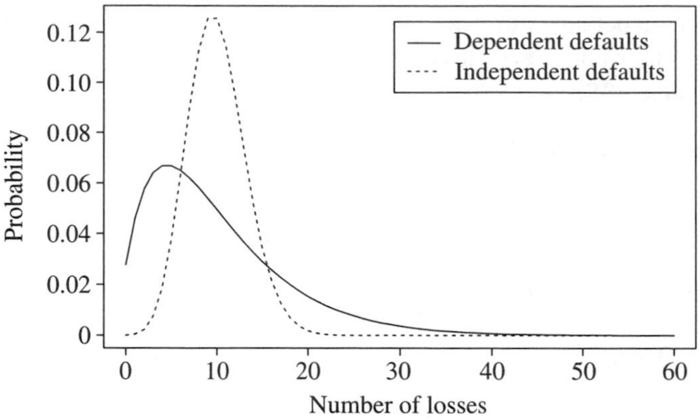

Figure 8.1. Comparison of the loss distribution of two homogeneous portfolios of 1000 loans with a default probability of 1% and different dependence structure. In portfolio 1 defaults are assumed to be independent; in portfolio 2 we assume a default correlation of 0.5%. Portfolio 2 can be considered as representative for BB-rated loans. We clearly see that the default dependence generates a loss distribution with a heavier right tail.

reason we devote a large part of our exposition to the analysis of credit portfolio models and dependent defaults.

There are sound economic reasons for expecting default dependence. To begin with, the financial health of a firm varies with randomly fluctuating macroeconomic factors, such as changes in economic growth. Since different firms are affected by common macroeconomic factors, we have dependence between their defaults. Moreover, default dependence is caused by direct economic links between firms, such as a strong borrower–lender relationship. Given the enormous size of typical loan portfolios it can be argued that, in credit risk management, direct business relations play a less prominent role in explaining default dependence. Dependence due to common factors, on the other hand, is of crucial importance and will be a recurring theme in our analysis. In the pricing of portfolio credit derivatives, the portfolios of interest are smaller, so modelling direct business relationships becomes more relevant (see Section 9.8 for models of this kind).

Notes and Comments

Chapter 2 of Duffie and Singleton (2003) contains a good discussion of the economic principles of credit risk management, elaborating on some of the issues discussed above. For a microeconomic analysis of the functioning of credit markets in the presence of informational asymmetries between borrowers and lenders we refer to the seminal paper by Stiglitz and Weiss (1981).

Duffie and Lando (2001) established a relationship between firm-value models and reduced-form models in continuous time. Essentially, they showed that, from the perspective of investors with *incomplete accounting information* (i.e. incomplete information about assets or liabilities of a firm), a firm-value model becomes a reduced-form model. A less technical discussion of these issues can be found in Jarrow and Protter (2004).

The available empirical evidence for the existence of macroeconomic common factors is surveyed in Section 3.1 of Duffie and Singleton (2003). Without going into details, it seems that a substantial amount of the variation over time in empirical default rates (the proportion of firms with a given credit rating that actually defaulted in a given year) can be explained by fluctuations in GDP growth rates, with empirical default rates going up in recessions and down in periods of economic recovery.

8.2 Structural Models of Default

A model of default is known as a structural or firm-value model when it attempts to explain the mechanism by which default takes place. Because the kind of thinking embodied in these models has been so influential in the development of the study of credit risk and the emergence of industry solutions (like the KMV model discussed in Section 8.2.3), we consider this to be the best starting point for a treatment of credit risk models.

From now on we denote a generic stochastic process in continuous time by (X_t); the value of the process at time $t \geqslant 0$ is given by the rv X_t.

8.2.1 The Merton Model

The model proposed in Merton (1974) is the prototype of all firm-value models. Many extensions of this model have been developed over the years, but Merton's original model remains an influential benchmark and is still popular with practitioners in credit risk analysis.

Consider a firm whose asset value follows some stochastic process (V_t). The firm finances itself by *equity* (i.e. by issuing shares) and by *debt*. In Merton's model debt has a very simple structure: it consists of one single debt obligation or zero-coupon bond with face value B and maturity T. The value at time t of equity and debt is denoted by S_t and B_t and, if we assume that markets are frictionless (no taxes or transaction costs), the value of the firm's assets is simply the sum of these, i.e. $V_t = S_t + B_t$, $0 \leqslant t \leqslant T$. In the Merton model it is assumed that the firm cannot pay out dividends or issue new debt. Default occurs if the firm misses a payment to its debt holders, which in the Merton model can occur only at the maturity T of the bond. At maturity we have to distinguish between two cases.

(i) $V_T > B$: the value of the firm's assets exceeds the liabilities. In that case the debtholders receive B, the shareholders receive the residual value $S_T = V_T - B$, and there is no default.

(ii) $V_T \leqslant B$: the value of the firm's assets is less than its liabilities and the firm cannot meet its financial obligations. In that case shareholders have no interest in providing new equity capital, which would go immediately to the bondholders. Instead they "exercise their limited-liability option" and hand over control of the firm to the bondholders, who liquidate the firm and distribute the proceeds among themselves. Shareholders pay and receive nothing, so that we have $B_T = V_T$, $S_T = 0$.

Summarizing, we have the relations

$$S_T = \max(V_T - B, 0) = (V_T - B)^+, \tag{8.1}$$
$$B_T = \min(V_T, B) = B - (B - V_T)^+. \tag{8.2}$$

Equation (8.1) implies that the value of the firm's equity at time T equals the pay-off of a European call option on V_T, while (8.2) implies that the value of the firm's debt at maturity equals the nominal value of the liabilities minus the pay-off of a European put option on V_T with exercise price equal to B.

The above model is of course a stylized description of default. In reality the structure of a company's debt is much more complex, so that default can occur on many different dates. Moreover, under modern bankruptcy code, default does not automatically imply bankruptcy, i.e. liquidation of a firm. Nonetheless, Merton's model is a useful starting point for modelling credit risk and for pricing securities subject to default.

Remark 8.1. The option interpretation of equity and debt is useful in explaining potential conflicts of interest between shareholders and debtholders of a company. It is well known that the value of an option increases if the volatility of the underlying security is increased, provided of course that the mean is not adversely affected. Hence shareholders have an interest in the firm taking on very risky projects. Bondholders, on the other hand, have a short position in a put option on the firm's assets and would therefore like to see the volatility of the asset value reduced.

In the Merton model it is assumed that under the real-world or physical probability measure P the process (V_t) follows a diffusion model (known as Black–Scholes model or geometric Brownian motion) of the form

$$\mathrm{d}V_t = \mu_V V_t \,\mathrm{d}t + \sigma_V V_t \,\mathrm{d}W_t \tag{8.3}$$

for constants $\mu_V \in \mathbb{R}, \sigma_V > 0$, and a standard Brownian motion (W_t). Equation (8.3) implies that $V_T = V_0 \exp((\mu_V - \frac{1}{2}\sigma_V^2)T + \sigma_V W_T)$, and, in particular, that $\ln V_T \sim N(\ln V_0 + (\mu_V - \frac{1}{2}\sigma_V^2)T, \sigma_V^2 T)$. Under the dynamics (8.3) the default probability of our firm is readily computed. We have

$$P(V_T \leqslant B) = P(\ln V_T \leqslant \ln B) = \Phi\left(\frac{\ln(B/V_0) - (\mu_V - \frac{1}{2}\sigma_V^2)T}{\sigma_V \sqrt{T}}\right). \tag{8.4}$$

It is immediately seen from (8.4) that the default probability is increasing in B, decreasing in V_0 and μ_V and, for $V_0 > B$, increasing in σ_V, which is all perfectly in line with economic intuition.

8.2.2 *Pricing in Merton's Model*

In the context of Merton's model we can price securities whose pay-off depends on the value V_T of the firm's assets at T. Prime examples are the firm's debt (or, equivalently, zero-coupon bonds issued by the firm) and the firm's equity. We briefly explain the main results, since we need them in our treatment of the KMV model in Section 8.2.3. The derivation of pricing formulas uses basic results from financial mathematics. Readers not familiar with these results should simply accept the valuation formulas we present in the remainder of this section as facts and proceed quickly to Section 8.2.3; references to useful texts in financial mathematics are given in Notes and Comments.

We make the following assumptions.

Assumption 8.2.

(i) *We have frictionless markets with continuous trading.*

(ii) *The risk-free interest rate is deterministic and equal to* $r \geqslant 0$.

(iii) *The firm's asset-value process* (V_t) *is independent of the way the firm is financed, and in particular it is independent of the debt level* B. *Moreover,* (V_t) *is a traded security with dynamics given in (8.3).*

Assumption (iii) merits some comment. First, the independence of (V_t) from the financial structure of the firm is questionable, because a very high debt level and hence a high default probability may adversely affect the capability of a firm to generate business and hence affect the value of its assets. This is a special case of the indirect bankruptcy costs discussed in Section 1.4.2. Second, while there are many firms with traded equity, the value of the assets of a firm is usually neither completely observable nor traded. We come back to this issue in Section 8.2.3 below.

General pricing results. Consider a claim on the value of the firm with maturity T and pay-off $h(V_T)$, such as the firm's equity and debt in (8.1) and (8.2), and suppose that Assumption 8.2 holds. Standard derivative pricing theory offers two ways for computing the fair value $f(t, V_t)$ of this claim at time $t \leqslant T$. Under the partial differential equation (PDE) approach the function $f(t, v)$ is computed by solving the PDE (subscripts denote partial derivatives)

$$f_t(t, v) + \tfrac{1}{2}\sigma_V^2 v^2 f_{vv}(t, v) + rvf_v(t, v) = rf(t, v) \quad \text{for } t \in [0, T), \tag{8.5}$$

with terminal condition $f(T, v) = h(v)$ reflecting the exact form of the claim to be priced. Equation (8.5) is the famous *Black–Scholes PDE* for terminal-value claims.

Alternatively, the value $f(t, V_t)$ can be computed as the expectation of the discounted pay-off under the risk-neutral measure Q (the so-called *risk-neutral pricing approach*). Under Q the process (V_t) satisfies the stochastic differential equation (SDE) $\mathrm{d}V_t = rV_t\,\mathrm{d}t + \sigma_V V_t\,\mathrm{d}\tilde{W}_t$ for a standard Q-Brownian motion $\tilde{W}$; in particular, the drift μ_V in (8.3) has been replaced by the risk-free interest rate r. The risk-neutral pricing rule now states that

$$f(t, V_t) = E^Q(\mathrm{e}^{-r(T-t)}h(V_T) \mid \mathcal{F}_t), \tag{8.6}$$

where E^Q denotes expectation with respect to Q. For details we refer to the textbooks on financial mathematics listed in Notes and Comments; the relationship between physical probability measure P and risk-neutral measure Q and the economic foundations of the risk-neutral pricing rule will be discussed in more detail in Section 9.3.

Application to equity and debt. According to (8.1), the firm's equity corresponds to a European call on (V_t) with exercise price B and maturity T. The solution of the PDE (8.5), or the risk-neutral value of equity obtained from (8.6), is simply given by the Black–Scholes price C^{BS} of a European call. This yields

$$\left.\begin{aligned} S_t &= C^{\text{BS}}(t, V_t; r, \sigma_V, B, T) := V_t\Phi(d_{t,1}) - B\mathrm{e}^{-r(T-t)}\Phi(d_{t,2}), \\ d_{t,1} &= \frac{\ln V_t - \ln B + (r + \frac{1}{2}\sigma_V^2)(T-t)}{\sigma_V\sqrt{T-t}} \quad \text{and } d_{t,2} = d_{t,1} - \sigma_V\sqrt{T-t}. \end{aligned}\right\} \tag{8.7}$$

Note that under the risk-neutral measure Q the distribution of the logarithmic asset value at maturity is given by $\ln V_T \sim N(\ln V_0 + (r - \frac{1}{2}\sigma_V^2)T, \sigma_V^2 T)$. Hence we get at time $t = 0$

$$Q(V_T \leqslant B) = Q\biggl(\frac{\ln V_T - (\ln V_0 + (r - \frac{1}{2}\sigma_V^2)T)}{\sigma_V\sqrt{T}} \leqslant -d_{0,2}\biggr) = 1 - \Phi(d_{0,2}),$$

where we have used the fact that $\Phi(d) = 1 - \Phi(-d)$. Hence $1 - \Phi(d_{0,2})$ gives the risk-neutral default probability. Similarly, $1 - \Phi(d_{t,2})$ gives the risk-neutral default probability given information up to time t.

Next we turn to the valuation of the risky debt issued by the firm. Note that by Assumption 8.2(ii) the price at $t \leqslant T$ of a default-free zero coupon bond with maturity T equals $p_0(t, T) = \exp(-r(T - t))$. According to (8.2) we have

$$B_t = Bp_0(t, T) - P^{\text{BS}}(t, V_t; r, \sigma_V, B, T), \tag{8.8}$$

where $P^{\text{BS}}(t, V; r, \sigma_V, B, T)$ denotes the Black–Scholes price of a European put with strike B, maturity T on (V_t) for given interest rate r, and volatility σ_V. It is well known that

$$P^{\text{BS}}(t, V_t; r, \sigma_V, B, T) = B\mathrm{e}^{-r(T-t)}\Phi(-d_{t,2}) - V_t\Phi(-d_{t,1}), \tag{8.9}$$

with $d_{t,1}$ and $d_{t,2}$ as in (8.7). Combining (8.8) and (8.9) we get

$$B_t = p_0(t, T)B\Phi(d_{t,2}) + V_t\Phi(-d_{t,1}). \tag{8.10}$$

Credit spread. We may use (8.10) to infer the credit spread $c(t, T)$ implied by Merton's model. The credit spread measures the difference of the continuously compounded yield to maturity of a default-free zero coupon bond $p_0(t, T)$ and of a defaultable zero coupon bond $p_1(t, T)$ and is defined by

$$c(t, T) = \frac{-1}{T-t}(\ln p_1(t, T) - \ln p_0(T, t)) = \frac{-1}{T-t}\ln\frac{p_1(t, T)}{p_0(t, T)}. \tag{8.11}$$

In Merton's model we obviously have $p_1(t, T) = (1/B)B_t$ and hence

$$c(t, T) = \frac{-1}{T-t}\ln\biggl(\Phi(d_{t,2}) + \frac{V_t}{Bp_0(t, T)}\Phi(-d_{t,1})\biggr). \tag{8.12}$$

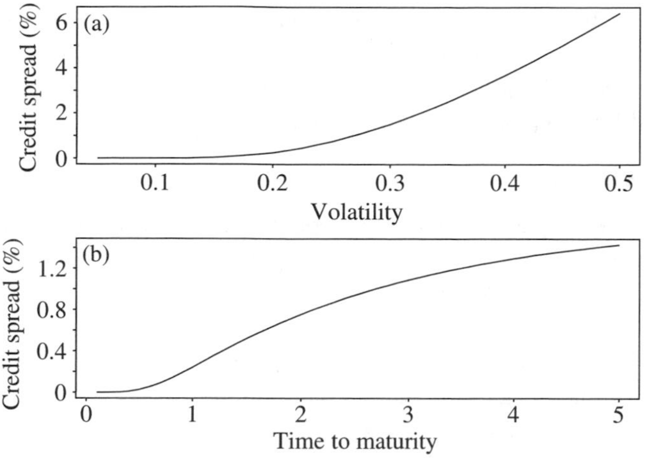

Figure 8.2. Credit spread $c(t, T)$ in per cent as a function of (a) the firm's volatility σ_V and (b) the time to maturity $\tau = T - t$ for fixed leverage measure $d = 0.6$ (in (a) $\tau = 2$ years; in (b) $\sigma_V = 0.25$). Note that, for a time to maturity smaller than approximately three months, the credit spread implied by Merton's model is basically equal to zero. This is not in line with most empirical studies of corporate bond spreads and has given rise to a number of extensions of Merton's model, which are listed in Notes and Comments. We will see in Section 9.4.4 that reduced-form models lead to a more reasonable behaviour of short-term credit spreads.

Since $d_{t,1}$ can be rewritten as

$$d_{t,1} = \frac{-\ln(Bp_0(t, T)/V_t) + \frac{1}{2}\sigma_V^2(T-t)}{\sigma_V\sqrt{T-t}},$$

and similarly for $d_{t,2}$, we conclude that, for a fixed time to maturity $T - t$, the spread $c(t, T)$ depends only on the volatility σ_V and on the ratio $d := Bp_0(t, T)/V_t$, which is the ratio of the present value of the firm's debt to the value of the firm's assets and hence a measure of the relative debt level or *leverage* of the firm. As the price of a European put is increasing in the volatility, it is immediate from (8.8) that $c(t, T)$ is increasing in σ_V. In Figure 8.2 we plot the credit-spread as a function of σ_V and of the time to maturity $\tau = T - t$.

Extensions. Merton's model is quite simplistic. Over the years this has given rise to a rich literature on firm-value models. We briefly comment on the most important research directions (bibliographic references are given in Notes and Comments). To begin with, the observation that, in reality, firms can default at essentially any time (and not only at a deterministic point in time T) has led to the development of so-called *first-passage-time models*. In this class of model default occurs when the asset-value process crosses for the first time a default threshold B, which is usually interpreted as the average value of the liabilities. Formally, the default time τ is defined by $\tau = \inf\{t \geqslant 0 : V_t \leqslant B\}$. Further technical developments include models with stochastic default-free interest rates and models where the asset-value process (V_t) is given by a diffusion with jumps.

Firm-value models with *endogenous default threshold* are an interesting economic extension of Merton's model. Here the default boundary B is determined endogenously by the strategic considerations of the shareholders and not fixed *a priori* by the modeller. Finally, structural models with *incomplete information* on asset value and/or liabilities provide an important link between the structural and the reduced-form approach to credit risk modelling.

8.2.3 The KMV Model

An important example of an industry model that descends from the Merton model is the KMV model, which was developed by KMV (a private company named after its founders Kealhofer, McQuown and Vasicek) in the 1990s and which is now maintained by Moody's KMV. The KMV model is widely used in industry: Berndt et al. (2004) report that 40 out of the world's largest 50 financial institutions are subscribers to the model. The major contribution of KMV is not the theoretical development of the model, which is a relatively straightforward extension of the Merton model, but its empirical testing and implementation using a huge proprietary database. Our presentation of the KMV model follows Crosbie and Bohn (2002) and Crouhy, Galai and Mark (2000). We have omitted certain details of the model, since detailed information about actual implementation and calibration procedures is hard to obtain; indeed, such procedures are likely to change as the model is developed further.

Overview. The key quantity of interest in the KMV model is the so-called *expected default frequency* (EDF); this is simply the probability (under the physical probability measure P) that a given firm will default within one year as estimated using the KMV methodology. Recall that in the classic Merton model the default probability of a given firm is given by the probability that the asset value in one year, V_1 say, lies below the threshold B representing the overall liabilities of the firm. Under Assumption 8.2, the EDF is a function of the current asset value V_0, the asset value's annualized mean μ_V and volatility σ_V and the threshold B; using (8.4) and recalling that $\Phi(d) = 1 - \Phi(-d)$, with $T = 1$, we get

$$\text{EDF}_{\text{Merton}} = 1 - \Phi\left(\frac{\ln V_0 - \ln B + (\mu_V - \frac{1}{2}\sigma_V^2)}{\sigma_V}\right). \tag{8.13}$$

In the KMV model the EDF has a similar structure; however, $1 - \Phi$ is replaced by some decreasing function which is estimated empirically, B is replaced by a new default threshold $\tilde{B}$ representing the structure of the firm's liabilities more closely, and the argument of the normal df in (8.13) is replaced by a slightly simpler expression. Moreover, KMV does not assume that the asset value V_0 of the firm is directly observable. Rather, it uses an iterative technique to infer V_0 from the value of the firm's equity.

Determination of the asset value. Firm-value-based credit risk models usually take the *market value* of the firm's assets as a primitive. The market value reflects investor expectations about the business prospects of the firm and is hence a good measure of the value of its ongoing business. Unfortunately, the market value of a firm is typically not fully observable for a number of reasons. To begin with, market value can differ widely from the value of a company as measured by accountancy rules (the book value) (see, for instance, Section 3.1.1 of Crouhy, Galai and Mark (2000) for an example). Moreover, while the market value of the firm's assets is simply the sum of the market values of the firm's equity and debt, only the equity and parts of the debt, such as bonds issued by the firm, are actively traded, so that we do not know the market value of the entire debt. For these reasons KMV relies on an indirect approach and infers the asset value V_0 from the more easily observed value S_0 of a firm's equity.

We explain the approach in the context of the Merton model. Recall that under Assumption 8.2 we have that

$$S_t = C^{\mathrm{BS}}(t, V_t; r, \sigma_V, B, T). \tag{8.14}$$

Obviously, at a fixed point in time, $t = 0$ say, (8.14) is an equation with two unknowns, V_0 and σ_V. To overcome this difficulty, KMV uses an iterative procedure. In step (1), (8.14) with some initial estimate $\sigma_V^{(0)}$ is used to infer a time series of asset values $(V_t^{(0)})$ from equity values. Then a new volatility estimate $\sigma_V^{(1)}$ is constructed from this time series; a new time series $(V_t^{(1)})$ is then constructed using (8.14) with $\sigma_V^{(1)}$. This procedure is iterated several times (see Crosbie and Bohn (2002) for details).

In the version of the model that is actually implemented, the capital structure of the firm is modelled in a more sophisticated manner than in Merton's model. The equity value is thus no longer given by (8.14), but by some different function $f(t, V_t; r, \sigma_V, d, T, c)$, which has to be computed numerically. Here d represents the leverage ratio of the firm and c is the average coupon paid by the long-term debt. The philosophy of the approach is, however, exactly as described above.

Calculation of EDFs. In the Merton model default, and hence bankruptcy, occurs if the value of a firm's assets falls below the value of its liabilities. With lognormally distributed asset values, as implied for instance by Assumption 8.2, this leads to default probabilities of the form (8.13). This relationship between asset value and default probability may be too simplistic to be an accurate description of actual default probabilities for a number of reasons: asset values are not necessary lognormal but might follow a distribution with heavy tails; our assumptions about the capital structure of the firm are too simplistic; there might be payments due at an intermediate point in time causing default at that date; finally, under modern bankruptcy code, default need not automatically lead to bankruptcy, i.e. to liquidation of the firm.

To account for these factors, KMV introduces as an intermediary step a state variable, the so-called *distance to default* (DD), given by

$$\mathrm{DD} := (V_0 - \tilde{B})/(\sigma_V V_0), \tag{8.15}$$

where $\tilde{B}$ represents the default threshold (often the liabilities payable within one year). Sometimes practitioners call the distance to default the "number of standard deviations a company is away from its default threshold $\tilde{B}$". Note that (8.15) is in

Table 8.1. A summary of the KMV approach. The example is taken from Crosbie and Bohn (2002); it is concerned with the situation of Philip Morris Inc. at the end of April 2001. Financial quantities are in millions of US dollars.

Variable	Value	Notes
Market value of equity S_0	110 688	Share price $\times$ shares outstanding
Overall book liabilities B	64 062	Determined from balance sheet
Market value of assets V_0	170 558	Determined from option-pricing model
Asset volatility σ_V	0.21	(Determined from option-pricing model)
Default threshold $\tilde{B}$	47 499	Liabilities payable within one year
DD	3.5	Given by the ratio $(170 - 47)/(0.21 \times 170)$, using relation (8.15)
EDF (one year)	0.25%	Determined using empirical mapping between distance to default and default frequency

fact an approximation of the argument of (8.13), since μ_V and σ_V^2 are small and since $\ln V_0 - \ln \tilde{B} \approx (V_0 - \tilde{B})/V_0$.

In the KMV model it is assumed that firms with equal DD have equal default probabilities. The functional relationship between DD and EDF is determined empirically. Using a database of historical default events, KMV estimates for every horizon the proportion of firms with DD in a given small range that defaulted within the given horizon. This proportion is the empirically estimated EDF. As one would expect, the empirically estimated EDF is a decreasing function; its precise form is proprietary to Moody's KMV.

In Table 8.1, we illustrate the computation of the EDF using the KMV approach for Philip Morris Inc.

8.2.4 Models Based on Credit Migration

In this section we present models where the default probability of a given firm is determined from an analysis of *credit migration*. The standard industry model in this class is CreditMetrics, developed by JPMorgan and the RiskMetrics Group (see, for instance, RiskMetrics Group 1997). We first describe the basic idea of a credit-migration model and the kind of data that is used to calibrate such a model, before showing how a migration model can be embedded in a firm-value model and thus treated as a structural model.

Credit ratings and migration. In the credit-migration approach each firm is assigned to a credit-rating category at any given time point. There are a finite number of such ratings and they are ordered by credit quality and include the category of default. The probability of moving from one credit rating to another credit rating over the given risk horizon (typically one year) is then specified.

Credit ratings for major companies or sovereigns and rating-transition matrices are provided by rating agencies such as Moody's or Standard & Poor's (S&P); alternatively, proprietary rating systems internal to a financial institution can be used. In the S&P rating system there are seven rating categories (AAA, AA, A,

Table 8.2. Probabilities of migrating from one rating quality to another within one year. Source: Standard & Poor's CreditWeek (15 April 1996).

Initial rating	Rating at year-end (%) AAA	AA	A	BBB	BB	B	CCC	Default
AAA	90.81	8.33	0.68	0.06	0.12	0.00	0.00	0.00
AA	0.70	90.65	7.79	0.64	0.06	0.14	0.02	0.00
A	0.09	2.27	91.05	5.52	0.74	0.26	0.01	0.06
BBB	0.02	0.33	5.95	86.93	5.30	1.17	1.12	0.18
BB	0.03	0.14	0.67	7.73	80.53	8.84	1.00	1.06
B	0.00	0.11	0.24	0.43	6.48	83.46	4.07	5.20
CCC	0.22	0.00	0.22	1.30	2.38	11.24	64.86	19.79

BBB, BB, B, CCC) with AAA being the highest and CCC the lowest rating of companies which have not defaulted; there is also a default state. Moody's uses seven pre-default rating categories labelled Aaa, Aa, A, Baa, Ba, B, C; a finer alpha-numeric system is also in use. Transition probabilities are typically presented in the form of a rating-transition probability matrix; an example from Standard & Poor's is presented in Table 8.2. These transition matrices are determined from historical default data. Approaches for estimating rating-transition matrices are listed in Notes and Comments.

In the credit-migration approach one assumes that the current credit rating completely determines the default probability, so that this probability can be read off from the transition matrix. For instance, if we use the transition matrix presented in Table 8.2, we obtain that the one-year default probability of a company whose current S&P credit rating is A is 0.06%, whereas the default probability of a CCC-rated company is almost 20%. Rating agencies also produce cumulative default probabilities over larger time horizons. In Table 8.3 we present estimates (due to Standard & Poor's) for cumulative default probabilities of companies with a given current credit rating. For instance, according to this table the probability that a company whose current credit rating is BBB defaults within the next four years is 1.27%. These cumulative default probabilities have been estimated directly. Alternatively, we could have used the one-year transition matrix presented in Table 8.2 to estimate these numbers. If we assume that the credit-migration process follows a time-homogeneous *Markov chain*, the n-year transition matrix is simply the n-fold product of the one-year transition matrix, and the n-year default probabilities can be read off from the last column of the n-year transition matrix. Of course, under the Markov assumption, both approaches should produce roughly similar results. In the BBB-case above, the four-year default probability under the Markov assumption becomes 1.41%, whereas the cumulative default probability for a BBB company according to Table 8.3 is 1.27%, which is relatively close. Nonetheless, the hypothesis that rating transitions occur in a Markovian way has been criticized heavily on empirical grounds (see Notes and Comments).

Table 8.3. Average cumulative default rates (%).
Source: Standard & Poor's CreditWeek (15 April 1996).

Initial rating	Term 1	2	3	4	5	7	10	15
AAA	0.00	0.00	0.07	0.15	0.24	0.66	1.40	1.40
AA	0.00	0.02	0.12	0.25	0.43	0.89	1.29	1.48
A	0.06	0.16	0.27	0.44	0.67	1.12	2.17	3.00
BBB	0.18	0.44	0.72	1.27	1.78	2.99	4.34	4.70
BB	1.06	3.48	6.12	8.68	10.97	14.46	17.73	19.91
B	5.20	11.00	15.95	19.40	21.88	25.14	29.02	30.65
CCC	19.79	26.92	31.63	35.97	40.15	42.64	45.10	45.10

Remark 8.3 (accounting for business cycles). As discussed in Section 8.1, empirical default rates tend to vary with the state of the economy, being high during recessions and low during periods of economic expansion. Transition rates as estimated by Standard & Poor's or Moody's on the other hand are historical averages over longer time horizons covering several business cycles. Moreover, rating agencies focus on the average credit quality "through the business cycle" when attributing a credit rating to a particular firm. Hence the default probabilities from the credit-migration approach are estimates for the average default probability, independent of the current economic environment. In situations where we are interested in "point-in-time" estimates of default probabilities reflecting the current macroeconomic environment, such as in the pricing of a short-term loan, adjustments to the long-term average default probabilities from the credit-migration approach have to be made. For instance, we could use equity prices as an additional source of information, as is done in the KMV approach.

The KMV model and credit-migration approaches compared. The KMV approach has the following advantages.

- Rating agencies are typically slow in adjusting their credit ratings, so that the current rating does not always reflect the economic condition of a firm. This is particularly important if the credit quality of a firm deteriorates rapidly, as is typically the case with companies which are close to default. The EDF as estimated by KMV, on the other hand, reacts quickly to changes in the economic prospects of a firm, as these tend to be reflected in the firm's share price and hence in the estimated distance to default. Examples that show that the KMV approach often detects a deterioration in the credit quality of a company prior to a downgrading by the rating agencies are given in Crosbie and Bohn (2002).
- EDFs tend to reflect the current macroeconomic environment. The distance to default is observed to rise in periods of economic expansion (essentially due to higher share prices reflecting better economic conditions) and to decrease in recession periods. The historical rating-transition probabilities provided by

Moody's and Standard & Poor's on the other hand are relatively insensitive to the current macroeconomic environment. Hence KMV's EDFs might be better predictors of default probabilities over short time horizons.

The following points are drawbacks of the KMV methodology and can be viewed as advantages of the credit-migration approach.

- The KMV methodology is quite sensitive to global over- and underreaction of equity markets. In particular, the breaking of a stock market bubble may lead to drastically increased EDFs, even if the economic outlook for a given corporation has not changed very much. This can be problematic if a KMV-type model is widely used to determine the regulatory capital that a bank needs to support its loan book. The breaking of a stock market bubble might lead to a substantial increase in the required regulatory capital. This limits the ability of banks to supply new credit, which might have an adverse impact on the real economy. This is a prime example of the potential negative-feedback effects of risk management and regulation that we discussed in Section 1.3 under the label "the crocodile of risk management is (possibly) eating its own tail".
- Finally, the KMV methodology as presented here applies only to firms with publicly traded stock, whereas a ratings-based approach can be applied to all companies for which some internal rating is available.

Credit-migration models as firm-value models. We now show how credit-migration models such as CreditMetrics can be embedded in a firm-value model of the Merton type. We consider a firm which has been assigned to some rating category at the outset of the time period of interest $[0, T]$ and for which transition probabilities $\bar{p}(j), 0 \leqslant j \leqslant n$, are available on the basis of that rating. These express the probability that the firm belongs to rating class j at the time horizon T and constitute a row of some table similar to Table 8.2. In particular, $\bar{p}(0)$ is the default probability of the firm.

Suppose that the asset-value process (V_t) of the firm follows the model given in (8.3), so that

$$V_T = V_0 \exp((\mu_V - \tfrac{1}{2}\sigma_V^2)T + \sigma_V W_T) \tag{8.16}$$

is lognormally distributed. We can now choose thresholds

$$-\infty = \tilde{d}_0 < \tilde{d}_1 < \cdots < \tilde{d}_n < \tilde{d}_{n+1} = \infty \tag{8.17}$$

such that $P(\tilde{d}_j < V_T \leqslant \tilde{d}_{j+1}) = \bar{p}(j)$ for $j \in \{0, \dots, n\}$. Thus we have translated the transition probabilities into a series of thresholds for an assumed asset-value process. The threshold $\tilde{d}_1$ is the default threshold; in the Merton model of Section 8.2.1, $\tilde{d}_1$ was interpreted as the value of the firm's liabilities. The higher thresholds are the asset-value levels that mark the boundaries of higher rating categories. The firm-value model in which we have embedded the migration model can be summarized by saying that the firm belongs to rating class j at the time horizon T if and only if $\tilde{d}_j < V_T \leqslant \tilde{d}_{j+1}$.

The migration probabilities in the firm-value model obviously remain invariant under simultaneous strictly increasing transformations of V_T and the thresholds $\tilde{d}_j$. If we define

$$X_T := \frac{\ln V_T - \ln V_0 - (\mu_V - \frac{1}{2}\sigma_V^2)T}{\sigma_V\sqrt{T}}, \tag{8.18}$$

$$d_j := \frac{\ln \tilde{d}_j - \ln V_0 - (\mu_V - \frac{1}{2}\sigma_V^2)T}{\sigma_V\sqrt{T}}, \tag{8.19}$$

then we can equivalently say that the firm belongs to rating class j at the time horizon T if and only if $d_j < X_T \leqslant d_{j+1}$. Observe that X_T is a standardized version of the *asset-value log-return* $\ln V_T - \ln V_0$; we can easily verify that $X_T = W_T/\sqrt{T}$ and that it therefore has a standard normal distribution.

8.2.5 Multivariate Firm-Value Models

The firm-value models of this section, such as KMV and CreditMetrics, have been discussed in relation to the default (or credit migration) risk of a single firm. In order to apply these models at portfolio level we require a multivariate version of Merton's model.

Now assume that we have m companies and that the multivariate asset-value process $(\boldsymbol{V}_t)$ with $\boldsymbol{V}_t = (V_{t,1}, \dots, V_{t,m})'$ follows an m-dimensional geometric Brownian motion with drift vector $\boldsymbol{\mu}_V = (\mu_{V1}, \dots, \mu_{Vm})'$, vector of volatilities $\boldsymbol{\sigma}_V = (\sigma_{V1}, \dots, \sigma_{Vm})'$ and instantaneous correlation matrix P.

This implies that for all i the asset value $V_{T,i}$ is of the form (8.16), with $\mu_V = \mu_{Vi}$ and $\sigma_V = \sigma_{Vi}$ and $W_T = W_{T,i}$. Moreover, $\boldsymbol{W}_T := (W_{T,1}, \dots, W_{T,m})'$ is a multivariate normal random vector satisfying $\boldsymbol{W}_T \sim N_m(\boldsymbol{0}, TP)$. The model is completed by setting thresholds as in (8.17) for each firm: in a Merton-style model each firm would have a default threshold corresponding to liabilities, and in a CreditMetrics model the thresholds would be determined by the credit-migration probabilities of the firms. Note that we could again transform asset values and thresholds using transformations of the form (8.18) and (8.19). This would result in variables $X_{T,i} = W_{T,i}/\sqrt{T}$ satisfying $\boldsymbol{X}_T = (X_{T,1}, \dots, X_{T,m})' \sim N_m(\boldsymbol{0}, P)$ and the model would have again been translated onto a standard Gaussian scale. Models of this kind will studied in more detail in Section 8.3.

Notes and Comments

There are many excellent texts, at varying technical levels, in which the basic results on mathematical finance used in Section 8.2.2 can be found. Models in discrete time are discussed in Cox and Rubinstein (1985), Jarrow and Turnbull (1999) and in the more advanced book by Föllmer and Schied (2004). Excellent introductions to continuous-time models include Baxter and Rennie (1996), Duffie (2001), Björk (1998), Bingham and Kiesel (1998) and Lamberton and Lapeyre (1996). More advanced texts are Musiela and Rutkowski (1997) and Karatzas and Shreve (1998); the technical level of the latter two volumes is not needed in this book.

Lando (2004) gives a good overview of the rich literature on firm-value models. First-passage-time models have been considered by, among others, Black and Cox (1976) and, including stochastic interest rates, by Longstaff and Schwartz (1995). The problem of the unrealistically low credit spreads for small maturities $\tau = T - t$, which we pointed out in Figure 8.2, has also led to extensions of Merton's model. Partial remedies within the class of firm-value models include models with jumps in the firm value, as in Zhou (2001), time-varying default thresholds, as in Hull and White (2001), stochastic volatility models for the firm-value process with time-dependent dynamics, as in Overbeck and Schmidt (2003), and incomplete information on firm value or default threshold, as in Duffie and Lando (2001) and Giesecke (2005). Models with endogenous default thresholds have been considered by, among others, Leland (1994), Leland and Toft (1996) and Hilberink and Rogers (2002).

The original documentation for the KMV model is Crosbie and Bohn (2002) (for the modelling of default of a single entity) and Kealhofer and Bohn (2001) (for portfolio aspects of the model). Moreover, Moody's KMV has recently developed a private firm model, which provides EDFs for small-to-medium-size private firms without publicly traded stock (see Nyberg, Sellers and Zhang 2001).

A good discussion of industry models for credit risk is given in Crouhy, Galai and Mark (2000) (see also Chapters 8–10 of Crouhy, Galai and Mark (2001) for a more detailed presentation). Chapter 7 of Crouhy, Galai and Mark (2001) contains useful background information on credit-rating systems. Statistical approaches to the estimation of rating-transition matrices are discussed in Hu, Kiesel and Perraudin (2002) and in Lando and Skodeberg (2002). The latter paper also shows that there is some *momentum* in rating-transition data, which contradicts the assumption that rating transitions form a Markov chain. The literature on statistical properties of rating transitions is surveyed extensively in Chapter 4 of Duffie and Singleton (2003).

8.3 Threshold Models

The models of this section are one-period models for portfolio credit risk inspired by the firm-value models of Section 8.2. Their defining attribute is the idea that default occurs for a company i when some critical rv $X_i := X_{T,i}$ lies below some critical deterministic threshold d_i at the end of the time period $[0, T]$. In Merton's model X_i is a lognormally distributed asset value and d_i represents liabilities; in CreditMetrics X_i is a normally distributed rv, interpreted as a change in logarithmic asset value. Portfolio extensions of firm-value models typically use multivariate lognormal or normal distributions for the vector $\boldsymbol{X} = (X_1, \dots, X_m)'$. The dependence among defaults stems from the dependence among the components of the vector $\boldsymbol{X}$.

The very general set-up of the threshold models of this section will allow both more general interpretations for the critical variable and more general distributional models. For example, in Li's model, discussed in Example 8.7, the critical variables are the "times to default" of the firms, and the critical threshold is the time horizon T itself. The distributions assumed for $\boldsymbol{X}$ can be completely general and indeed a major issue of this section will be the influence of the copula of the multivariate distribution of $\boldsymbol{X}$ on the risk of the portfolio.

8.3.1 Notation for One-Period Portfolio Models

It is convenient to introduce some notation for one-period portfolio models which will be in force throughout the remainder of the chapter. We consider a portfolio of m obligors and fix a time horizon T. For $1 \leqslant i \leqslant m$, we let the rv S_i be a state indicator for obligor i at time T and assume that $S_i := S_{T,i}$ takes integer values in the set $\{0, 1, \dots, n\}$ representing, for example, rating classes; as in the previous section, we interpret the value 0 as default and non-zero values as states of increasing credit quality. At time $t = 0$ obligors are assumed to be in some non-default state.

Mostly we will concentrate on the binary outcomes of default and non-default and ignore the finer categorization of non-defaulted companies. In this case we write $Y_i := Y_{T,i}$ for the default indicator variables so that $Y_i = 1 \iff S_i = 0$ and $Y_i = 0 \iff S_i > 0$. The random vector $\boldsymbol{Y} = (Y_1, \dots, Y_m)'$ is a vector of default indicators for the portfolio and $p(\boldsymbol{y}) = P(Y_1 = y_1, \dots, Y_m = y_m)$, $\boldsymbol{y} \in \{0, 1\}^m$, is its joint probability function; the marginal default probabilities are denoted by $\bar{p}_i = P(Y_i = 1)$, $i = 1, \dots, m$.

The *default or event correlations* will be of particular interest to us; they are defined to be the correlation of the default indicators. Because

$$\operatorname{var}(Y_i) = E(Y_i^2) - \bar{p}_i^2 = E(Y_i) - \bar{p}_i^2 = \bar{p}_i - \bar{p}_i^2,$$

we obtain for firms i and j, with $i \neq j$,

$$\rho(Y_i, Y_j) = \frac{E(Y_i Y_j) - \bar{p}_i \bar{p}_j}{\sqrt{(\bar{p}_i - \bar{p}_i^2)(\bar{p}_j - \bar{p}_j^2)}}. \tag{8.20}$$

We count the number of defaulted obligors at time T with the rv $M := \sum_{i=1}^m Y_i$. The actual loss if company i defaults—termed *loss given default* (LGD) in practice—is modelled by the random quantity $\delta_i e_i$, where e_i represents the overall exposure to company i and $0 \leqslant \delta_i \leqslant 1$ represents a random proportion of the exposure which is lost in the event of default. We will denote the overall loss by $L := \sum_{i=1}^m \delta_i e_i Y_i$ and make further assumptions about the e_i and δ_i variables as and when we need them.

It is possible to set up different credit risk models leading to the same multivariate distribution of $\boldsymbol{S}$ or $\boldsymbol{Y}$. Since this distribution is the main object of interest in the analysis of portfolio credit risk, we call two models with state vectors $\boldsymbol{S}$ and $\tilde{\boldsymbol{S}}$ (or $\boldsymbol{Y}$ and $\tilde{\boldsymbol{Y}}$) *equivalent* if $\boldsymbol{S} \stackrel{\mathrm{d}}{=} \tilde{\boldsymbol{S}}$ (or $\boldsymbol{Y} \stackrel{\mathrm{d}}{=} \tilde{\boldsymbol{Y}}$).

The exchangeable special case. To simplify the analysis we will often assume that the state indicator $\boldsymbol{S}$, and thus the default indicator $\boldsymbol{Y}$, are *exchangeable*. This seems the correct way to mathematically formalize the notion of *homogeneous* groups that is used in practice. Recall that a random vector $\boldsymbol{S}$ is said to be exchangeable if $(S_1, \dots, S_m) \stackrel{\mathrm{d}}{=} (S_{\Pi(1)}, \dots, S_{\Pi(m)})$ for any permutation $(\Pi(1), \dots, \Pi(m))$ of $(1, \dots, m)$. Exchangeability implies in particular that, for any $k \in \{1, \dots, m-1\}$, all of the $\binom{m}{k}$ possible k-dimensional marginal distributions of $\boldsymbol{S}$ are identical. In this situation we introduce a simple notation for default probabilities where

$\pi := P(Y_i = 1), i \in \{1, \dots, m\}$, is the default probability of any firm and

$$\pi_k := P(Y_{i_1} = 1, \dots, Y_{i_k} = 1), \quad \{i_1, \dots, i_k\} \subset \{1, \dots, m\},\ 2 \leqslant k \leqslant m, \tag{8.21}$$

is the joint default probability for k firms. In other words, π_k is the probability that an arbitrarily selected subgroup of k companies defaults in $[0, T]$. When default indicators are exchangeable, we get

$$\begin{aligned} E(Y_i) = E(Y_i^2) &= P(Y_i = 1) = \pi, \quad \forall i, \\ E(Y_i Y_j) &= P(Y_i = 1, Y_j = 1) = \pi_2, \quad \forall i \neq j, \end{aligned}$$

so that $\operatorname{cov}(Y_i, Y_j) = \pi_2 - \pi^2$; this implies that the default correlation in (8.20) is given by

$$\rho_Y := \rho(Y_i, Y_j) = \frac{\pi_2 - \pi^2}{\pi - \pi^2}, \quad i \neq j, \tag{8.22}$$

which is a simple function of the first- and second-order default probabilities.

8.3.2 Threshold Models and Copulas

We start with a general definition of a threshold model before discussing the link to copulas.

Definition 8.4. Let $X = (X_1, \dots, X_m)'$ be an m-dimensional random vector and let $D \in \mathbb{R}^{m \times n}$ be a deterministic matrix with elements d_{ij} such that, for every i, the elements of the ith row form a set of increasing thresholds satisfying $d_{i1} < \cdots < d_{in}$. Augment these thresholds by setting $d_{i0} = -\infty$ and $d_{i(n+1)} = \infty$ for all obligors and then set

$$S_i = j \iff d_{ij} < X_i \leqslant d_{i(j+1)}, \quad j \in \{0, \dots, n\},\ i \in \{1, \dots, m\}.$$

Then (X, D) is said to define a threshold model for the state vector $S = (S_1, \dots, S_m)'$.

We refer to X as the vector of *critical variables* and denote its marginal dfs by $F_i(x) = P(X_i \leqslant x)$. The ith row of D contains the *critical thresholds* for firm i. By definition, default (corresponding to the event $S_i = 0$) occurs if $X_i \leqslant d_{i1}$ so that the default probability of company i is given by $\bar{p}_i = F_i(d_{i1})$.

In the context of such models it is important to distinguish the default correlation $\rho(Y_i, Y_j)$ of two firms $i \neq j$ from the so-called *asset correlation* (the correlation of the critical variables X_i and X_j). For given default probabilities, $\rho(Y_i, Y_j)$ is determined by $E(Y_i Y_j)$ according to (8.20), and in a threshold model $E(Y_i Y_j) = P(X_i \leqslant d_{i1},\ X_j \leqslant d_{j1})$, so default correlation depends on the joint distribution of X_i and X_j. If X is multivariate normal, as in the CreditMetrics/KMV-type models, the correlation of X_i and X_j determines the copula of their joint distribution and hence the default correlation (see Lemma 8.5 below). For general critical variables outside the multivariate normal class, the correlation of the critical variables does not fully determine the default correlation; this can have serious implications for the tail of the distribution of $M = \sum_{i=1}^{m} Y_i$, as will be shown in Section 8.3.5.

We now give a simple criterion for equivalence of two threshold models in terms of the marginal distributions of the state vector $\boldsymbol{S}$ and the copula of $\boldsymbol{X}$. While straightforward from a mathematical viewpoint, the result is useful for studying the structural similarities between various industry models for portfolio credit risk management. For the necessary background information on copulas we refer to Chapter 5.

Lemma 8.5. *Let $(\boldsymbol{X}, D)$ and $(\tilde{\boldsymbol{X}}, \tilde{D})$ be a pair of threshold models with state vectors $\boldsymbol{S} = (S_1, \dots, S_m)'$ and $\tilde{\boldsymbol{S}} = (\tilde{S}_1, \dots, \tilde{S}_m)'$, respectively. The models are equivalent if the following conditions hold.*

(i) *The marginal distributions of the random vectors $\boldsymbol{S}$ and $\tilde{\boldsymbol{S}}$ coincide, i.e.*

$$P(S_i = j) = P(\tilde{S}_i = j), \quad j \in \{1, \dots, n\},\ i \in \{1, \dots, m\}.$$

(ii) *$\boldsymbol{X}$ and $\tilde{\boldsymbol{X}}$ admit the same copula C.*

Proof. According to Definition 8.4, $\boldsymbol{S} \stackrel{\mathrm{d}}{=} \tilde{\boldsymbol{S}}$ if and only if, for all $j_1, \dots, j_m \in \{1, \dots, n\}$,

$$\begin{aligned} &P(d_{1j_1} < X_1 \leqslant d_{1(j_1+1)}, \dots, d_{mj_m} < X_m \leqslant d_{m(j_m+1)}) \\ &\qquad = P(\tilde{d}_{1j_1} < \tilde{X}_1 \leqslant \tilde{d}_{1(j_1+1)}, \dots, \tilde{d}_{mj_m} < \tilde{X}_m \leqslant \tilde{d}_{m(j_m+1)}). \end{aligned}$$

By standard measure-theoretic arguments this holds if, for all $j_1, \dots, j_m \in \{1, \dots, n\}$,

$$P(X_1 \leqslant d_{1j_1}, \dots, X_m \leqslant d_{mj_m}) = P(\tilde{X}_1 \leqslant \tilde{d}_{1j_1}, \dots, \tilde{X}_m \leqslant \tilde{d}_{mj_m}).$$

By Sklar's theorem (Theorem 5.3) this is equivalent to

$$C(F_1(d_{1j_1}), \dots, F_m(d_{mj_m})) = C(\tilde{F}_1(\tilde{d}_{1j_1}), \dots, \tilde{F}_m(\tilde{d}_{mj_m})),$$

where C is the copula of $\boldsymbol{X}$ and $\tilde{\boldsymbol{X}}$ (using condition (ii)). Condition (i) implies that $F_i(d_{ij}) = \tilde{F}_i(\tilde{d}_{ij})$ for all $j \in \{1, \dots, n\}, i \in \{1, \dots, m\}$, and the claim follows. □

The copula in a threshold model determines the link between marginal probabilities of migration for individual firms and joint probabilities of migration for groups of firms. Consider for simplicity a two-state model for default and non-default and a subgroup of k companies $\{i_1, \dots, i_k\} \subset \{1, \dots, m\}$ with individual default probabilities $\bar{p}_{i_1}, \dots, \bar{p}_{i_k}$. Then

$$\begin{aligned} P(Y_{i_1} = 1, \dots, Y_{i_k} = 1) &= P(X_{i_1} \leqslant d_{i_1 1}, \dots, X_{i_k} \leqslant d_{i_k 1}) \\ &= C_{i_1 \cdots i_k}(\bar{p}_{i_1}, \dots, \bar{p}_{i_k}), \end{aligned} \tag{8.23}$$

where $C_{i_1 \cdots i_k}$ denotes the corresponding k-dimensional margin of C. As a special case consider now a model for a single homogeneous group. We assume that $\boldsymbol{X}$ has an exchangeable copula (i.e. a copula of the form (5.18)) and that all individual default probabilities are equal to some constant π so that the default indicator vector $\boldsymbol{Y}$ is exchangeable. The formula (8.23) reduces to the useful formula

$$\pi_k = C_{1 \dots k}(\pi, \dots, \pi), \quad 2 \leqslant k \leqslant m, \tag{8.24}$$

which will be used for the calibration of some copula models later on.

8.3.3 Industry Examples

As we have remarked, a number of popular industry models fit into the general framework of threshold models and we give some more detail in this section.

Example 8.6 (CreditMetrics and KMV models). The portfolio versions of the KMV and CreditMetrics models introduced in Section 8.2.5 use a similar mechanism to model the joint distribution of defaults; they differ only with respect to the approach used for the determination of individual default probabilities.

In both models the vector of critical variables $\boldsymbol{X}$ is assumed to have a multivariate normal distribution and X_i can be interpreted as a change in asset value for obligor i over the time horizon of interest; d_{i1} is chosen so that the probability that $X_i \leqslant d_{i1}$ matches the given default probability $\bar{p}_i$ for company i. Obviously, both the CreditMetrics and KMV models work with a Gauss copula for the critical variables $\boldsymbol{X}$ and are hence structurally similar. In particular, by Proposition 8.5 the two-state versions of the models are equivalent, provided that the individual default probabilities $\bar{p}_1, \dots, \bar{p}_m$ and the correlation matrix P of $\boldsymbol{X}$ are identical.

In both models the covariance matrix of $\boldsymbol{X}$ is calibrated using a factor model of the kind described in Section 3.4.1. Assume that we have transformed the critical variables and thresholds in such a way that the margins of $\boldsymbol{X}$ are standard normal. It is assumed that $\boldsymbol{X}$ can be written as

$$\boldsymbol{X} = B\boldsymbol{F} + \boldsymbol{\varepsilon} \tag{8.25}$$

for a p-dimensional random vector of common factors $\boldsymbol{F} \sim N_p(\boldsymbol{0}, \Omega)$ with $p < m$, a loading matrix $B \in \mathbb{R}^{m\times p}$, and an m-dimensional vector of independent univariate normally distributed errors $\boldsymbol{\varepsilon}$, which are also independent of $\boldsymbol{F}$. Here the random vector $\boldsymbol{F}$ represents country and industry effects. Obviously, the factor structure (8.25) implies that the covariance matrix P of $\boldsymbol{X}$ (which will be a correlation matrix due to our assumptions on the marginal distributions of $\boldsymbol{X}$) is of the form $P = B\Omega B' + \Upsilon$, where Υ is the diagonal covariance matrix of $\boldsymbol{\varepsilon}$.

Writing $\boldsymbol{b}_i = (b_{i1}, \dots, b_{ip})'$ for the ith row of B, the ith critical variable has the structure $X_i = \boldsymbol{b}_i'\boldsymbol{F} + \varepsilon_i$. Recalling that $\operatorname{var}(X_i) = 1$, it follows that

$$\beta_i := \boldsymbol{b}_i'\Omega\boldsymbol{b}_i \tag{8.26}$$

can be viewed as the *systematic risk* of X_i: that is, the part of the variance of X_i which is explained by the common factors $\boldsymbol{F}$. The *idiosyncratic risk* not explained by the common factors is $\operatorname{var}(\varepsilon_i) = 1 - \beta_i$.

In the factor model employed by KMV the factors are assumed to be observable, and a time series of factor returns is constructed by forming appropriate indices of asset values of publicly traded companies. The factor weights comprising B are determined using non-quantitative economic arguments combined with regression techniques; some details can be found in Kealhofer and Bohn (2001).

Example 8.7 (Li's model). This model, proposed in Li (2001), is a simple dynamic model used by practitioners to price basket credit derivatives. The author interprets the critical variable X_i as the default time of company i and assumes that X_i is exponentially distributed with parameter λ_i so that $F_i(t) = 1 - \exp(-\lambda_i t)$. Obviously, company i defaults by time T if and only if $X_i \leqslant T$, so $\bar{p}_i = F_i(T)$. To determine the multivariate distribution of $\boldsymbol{X}$, Li assumes that $\boldsymbol{X}$ has the Gauss copula C_P^{Ga} for some correlation matrix P (see, for example, (5.9) in Section 5.1.2) so that $P(X_1 \leqslant t_1, \dots, X_m \leqslant t_m) = C_P^{\mathrm{Ga}}(F_1(t_1), \dots, F_m(t_m))$. It is immediate from Lemma 8.5 that in Li's model the distribution of the default indicators at some fixed horizon T is equivalent to a model of CreditMetrics/KMV type, provided that individual default probabilities coincide and that the correlation matrix of the asset-value change $\boldsymbol{X}$ in the KMV-type model equals P. This equivalence is often used to calibrate Li's model. We will have a closer look at the model in our analysis of dynamic copula models in Section 9.7.

8.3.4 Models Based on Alternative Copulas

While most threshold models used in industry are based explicitly or implicitly on the Gauss copula, there is no reason why we have to assume a Gauss copula. In fact, simulations presented in Section 8.3.5 show that the choice of copula may be very critical to the tail of the distribution of the number of defaults M. We now look at threshold models based on alternative copulas.

The first class of model attempts to preserve some of the flexibility of models of KMV/CreditMetrics type, which do have the appealing feature that they can accommodate a wide range of different correlation structures for the critical variables. This is clearly an advantage in modelling a portfolio where obligors are exposed to several risk factors and where the exposure to different risk factors differs markedly across obligors, such as a portfolio of loans to companies from different industry sectors or countries.

Example 8.8 (normal mean-variance mixtures). For the distribution of the critical variables we consider the kind of model described in Section 3.2.2. We start with an m-dimensional multivariate normal vector $\boldsymbol{Z} \sim N_m(\boldsymbol{0}, \Sigma)$ and a positive, scalar rv W, which is independent of $\boldsymbol{Z}$. The vector of critical variables $\boldsymbol{X}$ is assumed to have the structure

$$\boldsymbol{X} = \boldsymbol{m}(W) + \sqrt{W}\boldsymbol{Z}, \tag{8.27}$$

where $\boldsymbol{m} : [0, \infty) \to \mathbb{R}^m$ is a measurable function. In the special case where $\boldsymbol{m}(W)$ takes a constant value $\boldsymbol{\mu}$ not depending on W, the distribution is called a normal variance mixture.

An important example of a normal variance mixture is the multivariate t distribution, as discussed in Example 3.7, which is obtained when W has an inverse gamma distribution, $W \sim \mathrm{Ig}(\frac{1}{2}\nu, \frac{1}{2}\nu)$, or equivalently when $\nu/W \sim \chi^2_\nu$. An example of a general mean-variance mixture is the generalized hyperbolic distribution discussed in Section 3.2.3.

In a normal mean-variance mixture model the default condition may be written as

$$X_i \leqslant d_{i1} \iff Z_i \leqslant \frac{d_{i1}}{\sqrt{W}} - \frac{m_i(W)}{\sqrt{W}} =: \tilde{D}_i, \tag{8.28}$$

where $m_i(W)$ is the ith component of $\boldsymbol{m}(W)$. A possible economic interpretation of the model (8.27) is to consider Z_i as the asset value of company i and d_{i1} as an *a priori* estimate of the corresponding default threshold. The actual default threshold is *stochastic* and is represented by $\tilde{D}_i$, which is obtained by applying a multiplicative and an additive shock to the estimate d_{i1}. If we interpret this shock as a stylized representation of global factors such as the overall liquidity and risk appetite in the banking system, it makes sense to assume that the shocks to the default thresholds of different obligors are driven by the same rv W.

Normal variance mixtures, such as the multivariate t, provide the most tractable examples of normal mean-variance mixtures; they admit a similar calibration approach using linear factor models to models based on the Gauss copula. In normal variance mixture models the correlation matrices of $\boldsymbol{X}$ (when defined) and $\boldsymbol{Z}$ coincide. Moreover, if $\boldsymbol{Z}$ follows a linear factor model (8.25), then $\boldsymbol{X}$ inherits the linear factor structure from $\boldsymbol{Z}$. Note however, that the systematic factors $\sqrt{W}\boldsymbol{F}$ and the idiosyncratic factors $\sqrt{W}\boldsymbol{\varepsilon}$ are no longer independent but merely uncorrelated.

A threshold model based on the t copula can be thought of as containing the standard KMV/CreditMetrics model based on the Gauss copula as a limiting case as $\nu \to \infty$. However, the additional parameter ν adds a great deal of flexibility to the model. We will come back to this point in Section 8.3.5.

Another class of parametric copulas that could be used in threshold models is the Archimedean family of Section 5.4.

Example 8.9 (Archimedean copulas). Recall that an Archimedean copula is the distribution function of a uniform random vector of the form

$$C(u_1, \dots, u_m) = \phi^{-1}(\phi(u_1) + \cdots + \phi(u_m)), \tag{8.29}$$

where $\phi : [0, 1] \to [0, \infty]$ is a continuous, strictly decreasing function, known as the copula generator, and ϕ^{-1} is its inverse. We assume that $\phi(0) = \infty, \phi(1) = 0$ and that ϕ^{-1} is completely monotonic (see equation (5.39) and surrounding discussion). As explained in Section 5.4, these conditions ensure that (8.29) defines a copula for any portfolio size m. Our main example in this chapter will be Clayton's copula. Recall from Section 5.4 that the Clayton copula has generator $\phi_\theta(t) = t^{-\theta} - 1$, where $\theta > 0$, leading to the copula

$$C_\theta^{\mathrm{Cl}}(u_1, \dots, u_m) = (u_1^{-\theta} + \cdots + u_m^{-\theta} + 1 - m)^{-1/\theta}. \tag{8.30}$$

As discussed in Section 5.4, exchangeable Archimedean copulas suffer from the deficiency that they are not rich in parameters and can model only exchangeable dependence and not a fully flexible dependence structure for the critical variables. Nonetheless, they yield useful parsimonious models for relatively small homogeneous portfolios, which are easy to calibrate and simulate, as we discuss in more detail in Section 8.4.4.

Suppose that $\boldsymbol{X}$ is a random vector with an Archimedean copula and with marginal distributions F_i, $1 \leqslant i \leqslant m$, so that $(\boldsymbol{X}, D)$ specifies a threshold model with individual default probabilities $F_i(d_{i1})$. As a particular example consider the Clayton copula and assume a homogeneous situation where all individual default probabilities are identical to π. Using relation (8.23), we can calculate that the probability that an arbitrarily selected group of k obligors from a portfolio of m such obligors defaults over the time horizon is given by $\pi_k = (k\pi^{-\theta} - k + 1)^{-1/\theta}$. Essentially, the dependent default mechanism of the homogeneous group is now determined by this equation and the parameters π and θ. We study this Clayton copula model further in Example 8.22.

8.3.5 Model Risk Issues

Recall from Chapter 2 that model risk may be roughly defined as the risk associated with working with misspecified models—in our case, models which are a poor representation of the true mechanism governing defaults and migrations in a credit portfolio. For example, if we intend to use our models to estimate measures of tail risk, like VaR and expected shortfall, then we should be particularly concerned with the possibility that they might underestimate the tail of the portfolio loss distribution.

As we have seen, a threshold model essentially consists of a collection of default (and migration) probabilities for individual firms and a copula that describes the dependence of certain critical variables. In discussing model risk in this context we will concentrate on models for default only and assume that individual default probabilities have been satisfactorily determined. It is much more difficult to determine the copula describing default dependence and we will look at model risk associated with the misspecification of this component of the threshold model.

The impact of the choice of copula. Since most threshold models used in industry use the Gauss copula, we are particularly interested in the sensitivity of the distribution of the number of defaults M with respect to the assumption of Gaussian dependence. Our interest is motivated by the observation made in Section 5.3.1 that, by assuming a Gaussian dependence structure, we may underestimate the probability of joint large movements of risk factors, with potentially drastic implications for the performance of risk-management models.

We compare a model with multivariate normal critical variables and a model where the critical variables are multivariate t. For simplicity we consider a homogeneous group model with factor structure, which we now describe. Given a standard normal rv F, an iid sequence $\varepsilon_1, \dots, \varepsilon_m$ of standard normal variates independent of F and an asset correlation parameter $\rho \in [0, 1]$, we define a random vector $\boldsymbol{Z}$ by $Z_i = \sqrt{\rho}F + \sqrt{1-\rho}\varepsilon_i$. Observe that this vector follows the so-called equicorrelation factor model described in Example 3.34 and equation (3.63).

In the t copula case we define the critical variables $X_i := \sqrt{W}Z_i$, where $W \sim \mathrm{Ig}(\frac{1}{2}\nu, \frac{1}{2}\nu)$ is independent of $\boldsymbol{Z}$, so that $\boldsymbol{X}$ has a multivariate t distribution. In the Gauss copula case we simply set $\boldsymbol{X} := \boldsymbol{Z}$. In both cases we choose thresholds so that $P(Y_i = 1) = \pi$ for all i and for some $\pi \in (0, 1)$. Note that the correlation matrix P of $\boldsymbol{X}$ (the asset correlation matrix) is identical in both models and is given by an equicorrelation matrix with off-diagonal element ρ. However, the copula of $\boldsymbol{X}$ differs, and we expect more joint defaults in the t model due to the higher level of dependence in the joint tail of the t copula.

Table 8.4. Results of simulation study. We tabulate the estimated 95th and 99th percentiles of the distribution of M in an exchangeable model with 10 000 firms. The values for the default probability π and the asset correlation ρ corresponding to the three groups A, B and C are given in the text.

	$q_{0.95}(M)$			$q_{0.99}(M)$		
Group	$\nu = \infty$	$\nu = 50$	$\nu = 10$	$\nu = \infty$	$\nu = 50$	$\nu = 10$
A	14	23	24	21	49	118
B	109	153	239	157	261	589
C	1618	1723	2085	2206	2400	3067

We define three groups of decreasing credit quality, labelled A, B and C. These groups do not correspond exactly to the A, B and C rating categories used by any of the well-known rating agencies, but they are nonetheless realistic values for Gaussian threshold models for real obligors. In group A we set $\pi = 0.06\%$ and $\rho = 2.58\%$; in group B we set $\pi = 0.50\%$ and $\rho = 3.80\%$; in group C we set $\pi = 7.50\%$ and $\rho = 9.21\%$. We consider a portfolio of size $m = 10\,000$. For each group we vary the degrees-of-freedom parameter ν. In order to represent the tail of the number of defaults M, we use simulations to determine (approximately) the 95% and 99% quantiles, $q_{0.95}(M)$ and $q_{0.99}(M)$, and tabulate them in Table 8.4. The actual simulation was performed using a representation of threshold models as Bernoulli mixture models that is discussed later in Section 8.4.4.

Table 8.4 shows that ν clearly has a massive influence on the high quantiles. For the important 99% quantile the impact is most pronounced for group A, where $q_{0.99}(M)$ is increased by a factor of almost six when we go from a Gaussian model to a model with $\nu = 10$.

The impact of changing asset correlation. Here we stick to the assumption that $\boldsymbol{X}$ has a Gauss copula and study the impact of the factor structure of the asset returns on joint default events and hence on the tail of M. More specifically, we increase the systematic risk component of the critical variables for the obligors in our portfolio (see equation (8.26)) and analyse how this affects the tail of M. We use the homogeneous group model introduced above as a vehicle for our analysis. We fix the default probability at $\pi = 0.50\%$ (the value for group B above) and vary the asset correlation ρ, which gives the systematic risk for all obligors in the homogeneous group model, using the values $\rho = 2.58\%$, $\rho = 3.80\%$ and $\rho = 9.21\%$. In Table 8.5 we tabulate $q_{0.95}(M)$ and $q_{0.99}(M)$ for a portfolio with 10 000 counterparties. Clearly, varying ρ also has a sizeable effect on the quantiles of M. However, this effect is less drastic and, in particular, less surprising than the impact of varying the copula in our previous experiment.

Commentary. Both simulation experiments indicate that attempts to calibrate threshold models using estimates of marginal default probabilities and crude estimates of the factor structure of the critical variables obtained from asset return data are prone to substantial model risk. Ideally, historical default data should also be

Table 8.5. Results of simulation study. Estimated 95th and 99th percentiles of the distribution of M in an exchangeable model for varying values of asset correlation ρ.

Quantile	$\rho = 2.58\%$	$\rho = 3.80\%$	$\rho = 9.21\%$
$q_{0.95}(M)$	98	109	148
$q_{0.99}(M)$	133	157	250

used to estimate parameters describing default dependence; indeed, the best strategy might involve combining factor models for asset-value returns with statistical estimation of some of the key parameters (such as the systematic risk parameter β in (8.26)) using historical default data.

Notes and Comments

Our presentation of threshold models is based, to a large extent, on Frey and McNeil (2001, 2003). In those papers we referred to the models as "latent variable" models, because of structural similarities with statistical models of that name (see Joe 1997). However, whereas in statistical latent variable models the critical variables are treated as unobserved, in credit models they are often formally identified, for example, as asset values or asset-value returns.

The first systematic study of model risk for credit portfolio models is Gordy (2000). Our analysis of the impact of the copula of $\boldsymbol{X}$ on the tail of M follows Frey, McNeil and Nyfeler (2001). For an excellent discussion of various aspects of model risk in risk management in general we refer to Gibson (2000).

8.4 The Mixture Model Approach

In a mixture model the default risk of an obligor is assumed to depend on a set of common economic factors, such as macroeconomic variables, which are also modelled stochastically. Given a realization of the factors, defaults of individual firms are assumed to be independent. Dependence between defaults stems from the dependence of individual default probabilities on the set of common factors. We start with general definitions of Bernoulli and Poisson mixture models before going on to specific examples.

Definition 8.10 (Bernoulli mixture model). Given some $p < m$ and a p-dimensional random vector $\boldsymbol{\Psi} = (\Psi_1, \dots, \Psi_p)'$, the random vector $\boldsymbol{Y} = (Y_1, \dots, Y_m)'$ follows a Bernoulli mixture model with factor vector $\boldsymbol{\Psi}$ if there are functions $p_i : \mathbb{R}^p \to [0, 1]$, $1 \leqslant i \leqslant m$, such that conditional on $\boldsymbol{\Psi}$ the components of $\boldsymbol{Y}$ are independent Bernoulli rvs satisfying $P(Y_i = 1 \mid \boldsymbol{\Psi} = \boldsymbol{\psi}) = p_i(\boldsymbol{\psi})$.

For $\boldsymbol{y} = (y_1, \dots, y_m)'$ in $\{0, 1\}^m$ we have that

$$P(\boldsymbol{Y} = \boldsymbol{y} \mid \boldsymbol{\Psi} = \boldsymbol{\psi}) = \prod_{i=1}^{m} p_i(\boldsymbol{\psi})^{y_i}(1 - p_i(\boldsymbol{\psi}))^{1-y_i}, \tag{8.31}$$

and the unconditional distribution of the default indicator vector $\boldsymbol{Y}$ is obtained by integrating over the distribution of the factor vector $\boldsymbol{\Psi}$. In particular, the default probability of company i is given by $\bar{p}_i = P(Y_i = 1) = E(p_i(\boldsymbol{\Psi}))$.

Since default is a rare event, we also explore the idea of approximating Bernoulli rvs with Poisson rvs in Poisson mixture models. Here a company may potentially "default more than once" in the period of interest, albeit with a very low probability; we will use the notation $\tilde{Y}_i \in \{0, 1, 2, \dots\}$ for the counting rv giving the number of "defaults" of company i. The formal definition parallels the definition of a Bernoulli mixture model.

Definition 8.11 (Poisson mixture model). Given p and $\boldsymbol{\Psi}$ as in Definition 8.10, the random vector $\tilde{\boldsymbol{Y}} = (\tilde{Y}_1, \dots, \tilde{Y}_m)'$ follows a Poisson mixture model with factors $\boldsymbol{\Psi}$ if there are functions $\lambda_i : \mathbb{R}^p \to (0, \infty)$, $1 \leqslant i \leqslant m$, such that conditional on $\boldsymbol{\Psi} = \boldsymbol{\psi}$ the random vector $\tilde{\boldsymbol{Y}}$ is a vector of independent Poisson distributed rvs with rate parameter $\lambda_i(\boldsymbol{\psi})$.

CreditRisk+, which is discussed in Section 8.4.2, is an industry example of a Poisson mixture model. Poisson mixture models also play an important role in actuarial mathematics (see Section 10.2.4).

We define the rv $\tilde{M} = \sum_{i=1}^{m} \tilde{Y}_i$ and observe that, for small Poisson parameters λ_i, $\tilde{M}$ is approximately equal to the number of defaulting companies. Given the factors, it is the sum of conditionally independent Poisson variables and therefore its distribution satisfies

$$P(\tilde{M} = k \mid \boldsymbol{\Psi} = \boldsymbol{\psi}) = \exp\biggl(-\sum_{i=1}^{m} \lambda_i(\boldsymbol{\psi})\biggr) \frac{(\sum_{i=1}^{m} \lambda_i(\boldsymbol{\psi}))^k}{k!}. \tag{8.32}$$

If $\tilde{\boldsymbol{Y}}$ follows a Poisson mixture model and we define the indicators $Y_i = I_{\{\tilde{Y}_i \geqslant 1\}}$, then $\boldsymbol{Y}$ follows a Bernoulli mixture model and the mixing variables are related by $p_i(\cdot) = 1 - \exp(-\lambda_i(\cdot))$.

Note that the two-stage hierarchical structure of mixture models facilitates sampling from the models: first we generate the economic factor realizations, and then the pattern of defaults conditional on those realizations. The second step is easy because of the conditional independence assumption.

8.4.1 One-Factor Bernoulli Mixture Models

In many practical situations it is useful to consider a one-factor model. The information may not always be available to calibrate a model with more factors, and one-factor models may be fitted statistically to default data without great difficulty (see Section 8.6). Their behaviour for large portfolios is also particularly easy to understand, as will be shown in Section 8.4.3.

Throughout this section, Ψ is an rv with values in $\mathbb{R}$ and $p_i(\Psi) : \mathbb{R} \to [0, 1]$ are functions such that, conditional on Ψ, the default indicator $\boldsymbol{Y}$ is a vector of independent Bernoulli rvs with $P(Y_i = 1 \mid \Psi = \psi) = p_i(\psi)$. We now consider a variety of special cases.

Exchangeable Bernoulli mixture models. A further simplification occurs if the functions p_i are all identical. In this case the Bernoulli mixture model is termed *exchangeable*, since the random vector $\boldsymbol{Y}$ is exchangeable. It is convenient to introduce the rv $Q := p_1(\Psi)$ and to denote the distribution function of this mixing variable by $G(q)$. Conditional on $Q = q$ the number of defaults M is the sum of m independent Bernoulli variables with parameter q and hence has a binomial distribution with parameters q and m, i.e. $P(M = k \mid Q = q) = \binom{m}{k} q^k (1-q)^{m-k}$. The unconditional distribution of M is obtained by integrating over q. We have

$$P(M = k) = \binom{m}{k} \int_0^1 q^k (1-q)^{m-k} \, \mathrm{d}G(q). \tag{8.33}$$

Using the notation of Section 8.3.1 we can calculate default probabilities and joint default probabilities for the exchangeable group. Simple calculations give $\pi = E(Y_1) = E(E(Y_1 \mid Q)) = E(Q)$ and, more generally,

$$\pi_k = P(Y_1 = 1, \dots, Y_k = 1) = E(E(Y_1 \cdots Y_k \mid Q)) = E(Q^k), \tag{8.34}$$

so that unconditional default probabilities of first and higher order are seen to be moments of the mixing distribution. Moreover, for $i \neq j$, $\mathrm{cov}(Y_i, Y_j) = \pi_2 - \pi^2 = \mathrm{var}(Q) \geqslant 0$, which means that in an exchangeable Bernoulli mixture model the default correlation ρ_Y defined in (8.22) is always non-negative. Any value of ρ_Y in $[0, 1]$ can be obtained by an appropriate choice of the mixing distribution G. In particular, if $\rho_Y = \mathrm{var}(Q) = 0$, the rv Q has a degenerate distribution with all mass concentrated on the point π and the default indicators are independent. The case $\rho_Y = 1$ corresponds to a model where $\pi = \pi_2$ and the distribution of Q is concentrated on the points 0 and 1.

Example 8.12 (beta, probit-normal and logit-normal mixtures). The following mixing distributions are frequently used in Bernoulli mixture models.

Beta mixing distribution. Here we assume that $Q \sim \mathrm{Beta}(a, b)$ for some parameters $a > 0$ and $b > 0$. See Section A.2.1 for more details concerning the beta distribution.

Probit-normal mixing distribution. Here $Q = \Phi(\mu + \sigma\Psi)$ for $\Psi \sim N(0, 1)$, $\mu \in \mathbb{R}$ and $\sigma > 0$, where Φ is the standard normal distribution function. It turns out that this model can be viewed as a one-factor version of the CreditMetrics and KMV-type models; this is a special case of a general result in Section 8.4.4 (see equation (8.45) in particular).

Logit-normal mixing distribution. Here $Q = F(\mu + \sigma\Psi)$ for $\Psi \sim N(0, 1)$, $\mu \in \mathbb{R}$ and $\sigma > 0$, where $F(x) = (1 + \exp(-x))^{-1}$ is the df of a so-called logistic distribution.

In the model with beta mixing distribution, the higher-order default probabilities π_k and the distribution of M can be computed explicitly (see Example 8.13 below). Calculations for the logit-normal, probit-normal and other models generally require numerical evaluation of the integrals in (8.33) and (8.34). If we fix any two of

π, π_2 and ρ_Y in a beta, logit-normal or probit-normal model, then this fixes the parameters a and b or μ and σ of the mixing distribution and higher-order joint default probabilities are automatic.

Example 8.13 (beta mixing distribution). By definition, the density of a beta distribution is given by

$$g(q) = \frac{1}{\beta(a,b)} q^{a-1}(1-q)^{b-1}, \quad a, b > 0,\ 0 < q < 1,$$

where $\beta(a,b)$ denotes the beta function. Below we use the fact that the beta function satisfies the recursion formula $\beta(a+1,b) = (a/(a+b))\beta(a,b)$; this is easily established from the representation of the beta function in terms of the gamma function in Section A.2.1. Using (8.34) we obtain for the higher-order default probabilities

$$\pi_k = \frac{1}{\beta(a,b)} \int_0^1 q^k q^{a-1}(1-q)^{b-1}\,\mathrm{d}q = \frac{\beta(a+k,b)}{\beta(a,b)}, \quad k = 1, 2, \ldots.$$

The recursion formula for the beta function yields $\pi_k = \prod_{j=0}^{k-1}(a+j)/(a+b+j)$; in particular, $\pi = a/(a+b)$, $\pi_2 = \pi(a+1)/(a+b+1)$ and $\rho_Y = (a+b+1)^{-1}$. The rv M has a so-called beta-binomial distribution. We obtain from (8.33) that

$$\begin{aligned} P(M=k) &= \binom{m}{k} \frac{1}{\beta(a,b)} \int_0^1 q^{k+a-1}(1-q)^{m-k+b-1}\,\mathrm{d}q \\ &= \binom{m}{k} \frac{\beta(a+k, b+m-k)}{\beta(a,b)}. \end{aligned} \tag{8.35}$$

One-factor models with covariates. It is quite straightforward to construct Bernoulli mixture models that have a single common mixing variable Ψ but which allow covariates for individual firms to influence the default probability; these covariates might be indicators for group membership, such as rating class or industry sector, or key ratios taken from a company's balance sheet.

Writing $\boldsymbol{x}_i \in \mathbb{R}^k$ for a vector of deterministic covariates, a typical model for the conditional default probabilities $p_i(\Psi)$ in (8.31) would be to assume that

$$p_i(\Psi) = h(\mu + \boldsymbol{\beta}'\boldsymbol{x}_i + \sigma\Psi), \tag{8.36}$$

where $h : \mathbb{R} \to (0,1)$ is a strictly increasing *link function*, such as $h(x) = \Phi(x)$ or $h(x) = (1 + \exp(-x))^{-1}$, the vector $\boldsymbol{\beta} = (\beta_1, \ldots, \beta_k)'$ contains regression parameters, $\mu \in \mathbb{R}$ is an intercept parameter, and $\sigma > 0$ is a scaling parameter. Such a specification is commonly used in the class of generalized linear models in statistics (see Section 8.6.3). We could complete the mixture model by specifying that Ψ is standard normally distributed, which would mean that the mixing distribution for the conditional default probability of each individual firm was of either probit-normal or logit-normal form.

Clearly, if $\boldsymbol{x}_i = \boldsymbol{x}$ for all i, so that all risks have the same covariates, then we are back in the situation of full exchangeability. Note also that, since the function $p_i(\Psi)$ is increasing in Ψ, the conditional default probabilities $(p_1(\Psi), \ldots, p_m(\Psi))$ form a comonotonic random vector; hence, in a state of the world where the default probability is comparatively high for one counterparty, it is high for all counterparties. For a discussion of comonotonicity we refer to Section 5.1.6.

Example 8.14 (model for several exchangeable groups). The regression structure in (8.36) includes partially exchangeable models where we define a number of groups within which risks are exchangeable. These groups might represent rating classes according to some internal or rating-agency classification.

If the covariates $\boldsymbol{x}_i$ are simply k-dimensional unit vectors of the form $\boldsymbol{x}_i = \boldsymbol{e}_{r(i)}$, where $r(i) \in \{1, \dots, k\}$ indicates, say, the rating class of firm i, then the model (8.36) can be written in the form

$$p_i(\Psi) = h(\mu_{r(i)} + \sigma\Psi) \tag{8.37}$$

for parameters $\mu_r := \mu + \beta_r$ for $r = 1, \dots, k$.

Inserting this specification in (8.31) we can find the conditional distribution of the default indicator vector. Suppose there are m_r obligors in rating category r for $r = 1, \dots, k$, and write M_r for the number of defaults. The conditional distribution of the vector $\boldsymbol{M} = (M_1, \dots, M_k)'$ is given by

$$P(\boldsymbol{M} = \boldsymbol{l} \mid \Psi = \psi) = \prod_{r=1}^{k} \binom{m_r}{l_r} (h(\mu_r + \sigma\psi))^{l_r}(1 - h(\mu_r + \sigma\psi))^{m_r - l_r}, \tag{8.38}$$

where $\boldsymbol{l} = (l_1, \dots, l_k)'$. A model of precisely the form (8.38) will be fitted to Standard & Poor's default data in Section 8.6.4. The asymptotic behaviour of such a model (when m is large) is investigated in Example 8.17.

8.4.2 CreditRisk+

CreditRisk+ is an industry model for credit risk that was proposed by Credit Suisse Financial Products in 1997 (see Credit Suisse Financial Products 1997). The model has the structure of a Poisson mixture model, where the factor vector $\boldsymbol{\Psi}$ consists of p independent, gamma-distributed rvs. The distributional assumptions and functional forms imposed in CreditRisk+ make it possible to compute the distribution of M fairly explicitly using techniques for mixture distributions that are well known in actuarial mathematics and which are also discussed in Chapter 10.

The structure of CreditRisk+. CreditRisk+ is a Poisson mixture model in the sense of Definition 8.11. The (stochastic) parameter $\lambda_i(\boldsymbol{\Psi})$ of the conditional Poisson distribution for firm i is given by $\lambda_i(\boldsymbol{\Psi}) = k_i \boldsymbol{w}_i'\boldsymbol{\Psi}$ for a constant $k_i > 0$, non-negative factor weights $\boldsymbol{w}_i = (w_{i1}, \dots, w_{ip})'$ satisfying $\sum_j w_{ij} = 1$, and p independent $\mathrm{Ga}(\alpha_j, \beta_j)$-distributed factors $\Psi_1, \dots, \Psi_p$ with parameters set to be $\alpha_j = \beta_j = \sigma_j^{-2}$ for some $\sigma_j > 0$. This parametrization of the gamma variables ensures that we have $E(\Psi_j) = 1$, $\mathrm{var}(\Psi_j) = \sigma_j^2$ and $E(\lambda_i(\boldsymbol{\Psi})) = k_i E(\boldsymbol{w}_i'\boldsymbol{\Psi}) = k_i$. Observe that in this model the default probability is given by $P(Y_i = 1) = P(\tilde{Y}_i > 0) = E(P(\tilde{Y}_i > 0 \mid \boldsymbol{\Psi}))$. Since $\tilde{Y}_i$ is Poisson given $\boldsymbol{\Psi}$, we have that

$$E(P(\tilde{Y}_i > 0 \mid \boldsymbol{\Psi})) = E(1 - \exp(-k_i \boldsymbol{w}_i'\boldsymbol{\Psi})) \approx k_i E(\boldsymbol{w}_i'\boldsymbol{\Psi}) = k_i, \tag{8.39}$$

where the approximation holds because k_i is typically small. Hence k_i is approximately equal to the default probability for firm i.

Gamma–Poisson mixtures. The distribution of $\tilde{M} = \sum_{i=1}^{m} \tilde{Y}_i$ in CreditRisk+ is conditionally Poisson and satisfies

$$\tilde{M} \mid \boldsymbol{\Psi} = \boldsymbol{\psi} \sim \mathrm{Poi}\left(\sum_{i=1}^{m} k_i \boldsymbol{w}_i' \boldsymbol{\psi}\right). \tag{8.40}$$

To compute the unconditional distribution of $\tilde{M}$ we require a well-known result on mixed Poisson distributions, which appears as Proposition 10.20 in a discussion of relevant actuarial methodology for quantitative risk management in Chapter 10. This result says that if the rv N is conditionally Poisson with a gamma-distributed rate parameter, $\Lambda \sim \mathrm{Ga}(\alpha, \beta)$, then N has a negative binomial distribution, $N \sim \mathrm{Nb}(\alpha, \beta/(\beta + 1))$.

In the case when $p = 1$ we may apply this result directly to (8.40) to deduce that $\tilde{M}$ has a negative binomial distribution (since a constant times a gamma variable remains gamma distributed).

For arbitrary p we now show that $\tilde{M}$ is equal in distribution to a sum of p independent negative binomial rvs. This follows by observing that

$$\sum_{i=1}^{m} k_i \boldsymbol{w}_i' \boldsymbol{\Psi} = \sum_{i=1}^{m} k_i \sum_{j=1}^{p} w_{ij} \Psi_j = \sum_{j=1}^{p} \Psi_j \left(\sum_{i=1}^{m} k_i w_{ij}\right).$$

Now consider rvs $\tilde{M}_1, \dots, \tilde{M}_p$ such that $\tilde{M}_j$ is conditionally Poisson with mean $(\sum_{i=1}^{m} k_i w_{ij})\psi_j$ conditional on $\Psi_j = \psi_j$. The independence of the components $\Psi_1, \dots, \Psi_p$ implies that the $\tilde{M}_j$ are independent, and by construction we have $\tilde{M} \stackrel{\mathrm{d}}{=} \sum_{j=1}^{p} \tilde{M}_j$. Moreover, the rvs $(\sum_{i=1}^{m} k_i w_{ij})\Psi_j$ are gamma distributed, so that each of the $\tilde{M}_j$ has a negative binomial distribution by Proposition 10.20.

This observation is the starting point for the computation of the distribution of $\tilde{M}$ in CreditRisk+. Using Panjer recursion (see Section 10.2.3), it is in fact possible to derive simple recursion formulas for the probabilities $P(\tilde{M} = k)$.

8.4.3 Asymptotics for Large Portfolios

We now provide some asymptotic results for large portfolios in Bernoulli mixture models. These results can be used to approximate the credit loss distribution and associated risk measures in a large portfolio. Moreover, they are useful for identifying the crucial parts of a Bernoulli mixture model. In particular, we will see that in one-factor models the tail of the loss distribution is essentially determined by the tail of the mixing distribution, which has direct consequences for the analysis of model risk in mixture models and for the setting of capital-adequacy rules for loan books.

Since we are interested in asymptotic properties of the overall loss distribution, we also consider exposures and losses given default. Let $(e_i)_{i \in \mathbb{N}}$ be an infinite sequence of positive deterministic exposures, let $(Y_i)_{i \in \mathbb{N}}$ be the corresponding sequence of default indicators, and let $(\delta_i)_{i\in\mathbb{N}}$ be a sequence of rvs with values in $(0, 1]$ representing percentage losses given that default occurs. In this setting the loss for a portfolio of size m is given by $L^{(m)} = \sum_{i=1}^{m} L_i$, where $L_i = e_i \delta_i Y_i$ are the individual losses. We now make some technical assumptions for our model.

(A1) There is a p-dimensional random vector $\boldsymbol{\Psi}$ and functions $\ell_i : \mathbb{R}^p \to [0, 1]$ such that, conditional on $\boldsymbol{\Psi}$, the $(L_i)_{i\in\mathbb{N}}$ form a sequence of independent rvs with mean $\ell_i(\boldsymbol{\psi}) = E(L_i \mid \boldsymbol{\Psi} = \boldsymbol{\psi})$.

In this assumption the conditional independence structure is extended from the default indicators to the losses. Note that it is not assumed that losses given default δ_i and default indicators are independent, an assumption which is made in many standard models. In particular, (A1) allows for the situation where Y_i and δ_i are only conditionally independent given $\boldsymbol{\Psi}$, such that $\ell_i(\boldsymbol{\psi}) = \delta_i(\boldsymbol{\psi}) p_i(\boldsymbol{\psi})$, where $\delta_i(\boldsymbol{\psi})$ gives the expected percentage loss given default, given $\boldsymbol{\Psi} = \boldsymbol{\psi}$. This extension is relevant from an empirical viewpoint since evidence suggests that losses given default tend to depend on the state of the underlying economy (see Notes and Comments).

(A2) There is a function $\bar{\ell} : \mathbb{R}^p \to \mathbb{R}^+$ such that

$$\lim_{m\to\infty} \frac{1}{m} E(L^{(m)} \mid \boldsymbol{\Psi} = \boldsymbol{\psi}) = \lim_{m\to\infty} \frac{1}{m} \sum_{i=1}^{m} \ell_i(\boldsymbol{\psi}) = \bar{\ell}(\boldsymbol{\psi})$$

for all $\boldsymbol{\psi} \in \mathbb{R}^p$. We call $\bar{\ell}(\boldsymbol{\psi})$ the asymptotic conditional loss function.

Assumption (A2) implies that we preserve the essential composition of the portfolio as we allow it to grow (see, for instance, Example 8.17).

(A3) There is some $C < \infty$ such that $\sum_{i=1}^{m} (e_i/i)^2 < C$ for all m.

This assumption prevents exposures from growing systematically with portfolio size.

The following result shows that under these assumptions the average portfolio loss is essentially determined by the asymptotic conditional loss function $\bar{\ell}$ and the realization of the factor random vector $\boldsymbol{\Psi}$. The proof is based on a suitable version of the strong law of large numbers (see Frey and McNeil (2003) for details).

Proposition 8.15. *Consider a sequence $L^{(m)} = \sum_{i=1}^{m} L_i$ satisfying Assumptions (A1)–(A3) above. Denote by $P(\cdot \mid \boldsymbol{\Psi} = \boldsymbol{\psi})$ the conditional distribution of the sequence $(L_i)_{i\in\mathbb{N}}$ given $\boldsymbol{\Psi} = \boldsymbol{\psi}$. Then*

$$\lim_{m\to\infty} \frac{1}{m} L^{(m)} = \bar{\ell}(\boldsymbol{\psi}), \quad P(\cdot \mid \boldsymbol{\Psi} = \boldsymbol{\psi}) \text{ a.s.}$$

Proposition 8.15 obviously applies to the number of defaults $M^{(m)} = \sum_{i=1}^{m} Y_i$ if we set $\delta_i = e_i \equiv 1$. For a given sequence $(Y_i)_{i\in\mathbb{N}}$ following a p-factor Bernoulli mixture model with default probabilities $p_i(\boldsymbol{\psi})$, Assumptions (A1) and (A3) are automatically satisfied and (A2) becomes

$$\lim_{m\to\infty} \frac{1}{m} \sum_{i=1}^{m} p_i(\boldsymbol{\psi}) = \bar{p}(\boldsymbol{\psi}) \quad \text{for some function } \bar{p} : \mathbb{R}^p \to [0, 1]. \tag{8.41}$$

For one-factor Bernoulli mixture models we can obtain a stronger result which links the quantiles of $L^{(m)}$ to quantiles of the mixing distribution. Again we refer to Frey and McNeil (2003) for a proof.

Proposition 8.16. *Consider a sequence $L^{(m)} = \sum_{i=1}^{m} L_i$ satisfying Assumptions (A1)–(A3) with a one-dimensional mixing variable Ψ with df G. Assume that the conditional asymptotic loss function $\bar{\ell}(\psi)$ is strictly increasing and right continuous and that G is strictly increasing at $q_\alpha(\Psi)$, i.e. that $G(q_\alpha(\Psi) + \delta) > \alpha$ for every $\delta > 0$. Then*

$$\lim_{m\to\infty} \frac{1}{m} q_\alpha(L^{(m)}) = \bar{\ell}(q_\alpha(\Psi)). \tag{8.42}$$

Comments. The assumption that $\bar{\ell}$ is strictly increasing makes sense if it is assumed that low values of Ψ correspond to good states of the world with lower conditional default probabilities and lower losses given default than average, and that high values of ψ correspond to bad states with correspondingly higher losses given default.

It follows from Proposition 8.16 that the tail of the credit loss in large one-factor Bernoulli mixture models is essentially driven by the tail of the mixing variable Ψ. Consider in particular two exchangeable Bernoulli mixture models with mixing distributions $G_i(q) = P(Q_i \leqslant q), i = 1, 2$. Suppose that the tail of G_1 is heavier than the tail of G_2, i.e. that we have $G_1(q) < G_2(q)$ for q close to 1. Then Proposition 8.16 implies that for large m the tail of $M^{(m)}$ is heavier in model 1 than in model 2.

Example 8.17. Consider the one-factor Bernoulli mixture model for k exchangeable groups defined by (8.37). In this case equation (8.41) becomes

$$\lim_{m\to\infty} \frac{1}{m} \sum_{r=1}^{k} m_r^{(m)} h(\mu_r + \sigma\psi) = \bar{p}(\psi)$$

for some function $\bar{p}$, which is fulfilled if the proportions of obligors in each group, $m_r^{(m)}/m$, converge to fixed constants λ_r as $m \to \infty$. Assuming unit exposures and 100% losses given default, our asymptotic conditional loss function is $\bar{\ell}(\psi) = \bar{p}(\psi) = \sum_{r=1}^{k} \lambda_r h(\mu_r + \sigma\psi)$. Since Ψ is assumed to have a standard normal distribution, (8.42) implies, for large m, that

$$q_\alpha(L^{(m)}) \approx m \sum_{r=1}^{k} \lambda_r h(\mu_r + \sigma\Phi^{-1}(\alpha)). \tag{8.43}$$

8.4.4 Threshold Models as Mixture Models

Although the mixture models of this section seem, at first glance, to be different in structure to the threshold models of Section 8.3, it is important to realize that the majority of useful threshold models, including all the examples we have given, can be represented as Bernoulli mixture models. This is a very useful insight, because the Bernoulli mixture format has a number of advantages over the threshold format.

- Bernoulli mixture models lend themselves to Monte Carlo risk studies. From the analyses of this section we obtain methods for sampling from many of the models we have discussed, such as the t copula threshold model used in Section 8.3.5.
- Mixture models are arguably more convenient for statistical fitting purposes. We show in Section 8.6.3 that statistical techniques for generalized linear mixed models can be used to fit mixture models to empirical default data gathered over several time periods.
- The large-portfolio behaviour of Bernoulli mixtures can be understood in terms of the behaviour of the distribution of the common economic factors, as was shown in Section 8.4.3.

The following condition ensures that a threshold model can be written as a Bernoulli mixture model.

Definition 8.18. A random vector $\boldsymbol{X}$ has a p-dimensional *conditional independence structure* with conditioning variable $\boldsymbol{\Psi}$ if there is some $p < m$ and a p-dimensional random vector $\boldsymbol{\Psi} = (\Psi_1, \dots, \Psi_p)'$ such that, conditional on $\boldsymbol{\Psi}$, the rvs $X_1, \dots, X_m$ are independent.

Lemma 8.19. *Let $(\boldsymbol{X}, D)$ be a threshold model for an m-dimensional random vector $\boldsymbol{X}$. If $\boldsymbol{X}$ has a p-dimensional conditional independence structure with conditioning variable $\boldsymbol{\Psi}$, then the default indicators $Y_i = I_{\{X_i \leqslant d_{i1}\}}$ follow a Bernoulli mixture model with factor $\boldsymbol{\Psi}$, where the conditional default probabilities are given by $p_i(\boldsymbol{\psi}) = P(X_i \leqslant d_{i1} \mid \boldsymbol{\Psi} = \boldsymbol{\psi})$.*

Proof. For $\boldsymbol{y} \in \{0, 1\}^m$ define the set $B := \{1 \leqslant i \leqslant m : y_i = 1\}$ and let $B^c = \{1, \dots, m\} \backslash B$. We have

$$P(\boldsymbol{Y} = \boldsymbol{y} \mid \boldsymbol{\Psi} = \boldsymbol{\psi}) = P\biggl(\bigcap_{i \in B} \{X_i \leqslant d_{i1}\} \bigcap_{i \in B^c} \{X_i > d_{i1}\} \biggm| \boldsymbol{\Psi} = \boldsymbol{\psi}\biggr)$$

$$= \prod_{i \in B} P(X_i \leqslant d_{i1} \mid \boldsymbol{\Psi} = \boldsymbol{\psi}) \prod_{i \in B^c} (1 - P(X_i \leqslant d_{i1} \mid \boldsymbol{\Psi} = \boldsymbol{\psi})).$$

Hence, conditional on $\boldsymbol{\Psi} = \boldsymbol{\psi}$, the Y_i are independent Bernoulli variables with success probability $p_i(\boldsymbol{\psi}) := P(X_i \leqslant d_{i1} \mid \boldsymbol{\Psi} = \boldsymbol{\psi})$. □

Application to normal mixtures with factor structure. Suppose that the critical variables $\boldsymbol{X} = (X_1, \dots, X_m)'$ have a normal mean-variance mixture distribution as in Example 8.8 so that $\boldsymbol{X} = \boldsymbol{m}(W) + \sqrt{W}\boldsymbol{Z}$ for W independent of $\boldsymbol{Z}$. Suppose also that $\boldsymbol{Z}$ (and hence $\boldsymbol{X}$) follows the linear factor model (8.25), so that $\boldsymbol{Z} = B\boldsymbol{F} + \boldsymbol{\varepsilon}$ for a random vector $\boldsymbol{F} \sim N_p(\boldsymbol{0}, \Omega)$, a loading matrix $B \in \mathbb{R}^{m \times p}$, and independent, normally distributed rvs $\varepsilon_1, \dots, \varepsilon_m$, which are also independent of $\boldsymbol{F}$. Then $\boldsymbol{X}$ has a $(p + 1)$-dimensional conditional independence structure.

To see this, define the random vector $\boldsymbol{\Psi} = (F_1, \dots, F_p, W)'$ and observe that, conditional on $\boldsymbol{\Psi} = \boldsymbol{\psi}$, $\boldsymbol{X}$ is $N_m(\boldsymbol{m}(w) + \sqrt{w}B\boldsymbol{f}, w\Upsilon)$-distributed, where Υ is the (diagonal) covariance matrix of $\boldsymbol{\varepsilon}$. Since the covariance structure is diagonal, the rvs X_i are conditionally independent. For a threshold model $(\boldsymbol{X}, D)$, the equivalent Bernoulli mixture model is now easy to compute. The conditional default probabilities are

$$p_i(\boldsymbol{\psi}) = P(X_i \leqslant d_{i1} \mid \boldsymbol{\Psi} = \boldsymbol{\psi}) = \Phi\left(\frac{d_{i1} - m_i(w) - \sqrt{w}\boldsymbol{b}_i'\boldsymbol{f}}{\sqrt{w\upsilon_i}}\right), \tag{8.44}$$

where $m_i(w)$ is the ith component of $\boldsymbol{m}(w)$, $\boldsymbol{b}_i$ is the ith row of B, and υ_i is the ith diagonal element of Υ.

Example 8.20 (threshold model of KMV/CreditMetrics type). Consider the special case of Gaussian critical variables where $\boldsymbol{X} = \boldsymbol{Z}$ and $\boldsymbol{\Psi} = \boldsymbol{F}$. If we standardize the critical variables $X_1, \dots, X_n$ to have variance one and reparametrize the formula in terms of the individual default probabilities $\bar{p}_i$ and the systematic variance component $\beta_i = \boldsymbol{b}_i'\Omega\boldsymbol{b}_i = 1 - \upsilon_i$ (see Example 8.6), we can infer from (8.44) that

$$p_i(\boldsymbol{\Psi}) = \Phi\left(\frac{\Phi^{-1}(\bar{p}_i) - \boldsymbol{b}_i'\boldsymbol{\Psi}}{\sqrt{1-\beta_i}}\right). \tag{8.45}$$

By comparison with Example 8.12 we see that the individual stochastic default probabilities $p_i(\boldsymbol{\Psi})$ have a probit-normal distribution with parameters μ_i and σ_i given by

$$\mu_i = \Phi^{-1}(\bar{p}_i)/\sqrt{1-\beta_i} \quad \text{and} \quad \sigma_i^2 = \beta_i/(1-\beta_i).$$

Example 8.21 (threshold model with Student t copula). Consider the special case of multivariate t-distributed critical variables where $\boldsymbol{X} = \sqrt{W}\boldsymbol{Z}$ and $W \sim \text{Ig}(\frac{1}{2}\nu, \frac{1}{2}\nu)$. Suppose that the margins of $X_1, \dots, X_m$ have been standardized to be standard univariate t with ν degrees of freedom. Again writing β_i for the proportion of the variance of the critical variable X_i explained by the factors $\boldsymbol{F}$, we infer from (8.44) that

$$p_i(\boldsymbol{\Psi}) = \Phi\left(\frac{t_\nu^{-1}(\bar{p}_i)W^{-1/2} - \boldsymbol{b}_i'\boldsymbol{F}}{\sqrt{1-\beta_i}}\right). \tag{8.46}$$

The formula (8.44) is the key to Monte Carlo simulation for threshold models when the critical variables have a normal mixture distribution, particularly in a large-portfolio context. For example, rather than simulating an m-dimensional t distribution to implement the t model, one only needs to simulate a p-dimensional normal vector $\boldsymbol{F}$ with $p \ll m$ and an independent gamma-distributed variate $V = W^{-1}$. In the second step of the simulation one simply conducts a series of independent Bernoulli experiments with default probabilities $p_i(\boldsymbol{\Psi})$ to decide whether individual companies default.

Application to Archimedean copula models. Another class of threshold models with an equivalent mixture representation is provided by models where the critical variables have an exchangeable LT-Archimedean copula in the sense of Definition 5.47. Consider a threshold model $(\boldsymbol{X}, D)$, where $\boldsymbol{X}$ has an exchangeable LT-Archimedean copula C with generator ϕ such that ϕ^{-1} is the Laplace transform of some df G on $[0, \infty)$ with $G(0) = 0$. Let $\boldsymbol{d} = (d_{11}, \dots, d_{m1})'$ denote the first column of D containing the default thresholds and write $(\boldsymbol{X}, \boldsymbol{d})$ for a threshold model of default with Archimedean copula dependence. Write $\bar{p}_i = P(X_i \leqslant d_{i1})$ as usual and $\bar{\boldsymbol{p}} = (\bar{p}_1, \dots, \bar{p}_m)'$ for the vector of default probabilities.

Consider now a non-negative rv $\Psi \sim G$ and rvs $U_1, \dots, U_m$ that are conditionally independent given Ψ with conditional distribution function $P(U_i \leqslant u \mid \Psi = \psi) = \exp(-\psi\phi(u))$ for $u \in [0, 1]$. Then Proposition 5.46 shows that $\boldsymbol{U}$ has df C. Moreover, by Lemma 8.5, $(\boldsymbol{X}, \boldsymbol{d})$ and $(\boldsymbol{U}, \bar{\boldsymbol{p}})$ are two equivalent threshold models for default. By construction $\boldsymbol{U}$ has a one-dimensional conditional independence structure with conditioning variable Ψ and the conditional default probabilities are given by

$$p_i(\psi) = P(U_i \leqslant \bar{p}_i \mid \Psi = \psi) = \exp(-\psi\phi(\bar{p}_i)). \tag{8.47}$$

In order to simulate from a threshold model based on an LT-Archimedean copula we may therefore use the following efficient and simple approach. In a first step we simulate a realization ψ of Ψ and then we conduct m independent Bernoulli experiments with default probabilities $p_i(\psi)$ as in (8.47) to simulate a realization of defaulting counterparties.

Example 8.22 (the Clayton copula). As an example consider the Clayton copula with generator $\phi(t) = t^{-\theta} - 1$. Suppose we wish to construct an exchangeable Bernoulli mixture model with default probability π and joint default probability π_2 that is equivalent to a threshold model driven by the Clayton copula. As mentioned in Algorithm 5.48, an rv $\Psi \sim \text{Ga}(1/\theta, 1)$ (see Section A.2.4) has Laplace transform equal to the generator inverse $\phi^{-1}(t) = (t + 1)^{-1/\theta}$, so the mixing variable of the equivalent Bernoulli mixture model can be defined by setting $Q = \exp(-\Psi(\pi^{-\theta} - 1))$.

Using (8.23), the required value of θ to give the desired joint default probabilities is the solution to the equation $\pi_2 = C_\theta(\pi, \pi) = (2\pi^{-\theta} - 1)^{-1/\theta}$, $\theta > 0$. It is easily seen that π_2 and, hence, the default correlation in our exchangeable Bernoulli mixture model are increasing in θ; for $\theta \to 0$ we obtain independent defaults and for $\theta \to \infty$ defaults become comonotonic and default correlation tends to one.

8.4.5 Model-Theoretic Aspects of Basel II

In this section we examine how the considerations of Sections 8.4.3 and 8.4.4 have influenced the new Basel II capital-adequacy framework, which was discussed in more general terms in Section 1.3. Under this framework a bank is required to hold 8% of the so-called *risk-weighted assets* (RWA) of its credit portfolio as risk capital. The RWA of a portfolio is given by the sum of the RWA of the individual risks in the portfolio, i.e. $\text{RWA}^{\text{portfolio}} = \sum_{i=1}^m \text{RWA}_i$. The quantity RWA_i reflects exposure size and riskiness of obligor i; it takes the form $\text{RWA}_i = w_i e_i$, where w_i is a risk weight and e_i denotes exposure size.

Banks may choose between two options for determining the risk weight w_i, which must then be implemented for the entire portfolio. Under the simpler *standardized approach*, the risk weight w_i is determined by the type (sovereign, bank or corporation) and the credit rating of counterparty i. For instance, $w_i = 50\%$ for a corporation with a Moody's rating in the range of A+ to A−. Under the more advanced *internal-ratings-based* (IRB) approach, the risk weight takes the form

$$w_i = (0.08)^{-1} c\delta_i \Phi\left(\frac{\Phi^{-1}(\bar{p}_i) + \sqrt{\rho}\Phi^{-1}(0.999)}{\sqrt{1-\rho}}\right). \tag{8.48}$$

Here c is a technical adjustment factor that is of minor interest to us, $\bar{p}_i$ represents the marginal default probability, and δ_i is the percentage loss given default of obligor i. The parameter $\rho \in (0.12, 0.24)$ can be viewed as an asset correlation, as will be explained below. Estimates for $\bar{p}_i$ and (under the so-called advanced IRB approach) for δ_i and e_i are provided by the individual bank; the adjustment factor c and, most importantly, the value of ρ are determined by fixed rules within the Basel II Accord independently of the structure of the specific portfolio under consideration. The risk capital to be held for counterparty i is thus given by

$$\mathrm{RC}_i = 0.08\mathrm{RWA}_i = c\delta_i e_i \Phi\left(\frac{\Phi^{-1}(\bar{p}_i) + \sqrt{\rho}\Phi^{-1}(0.999)}{\sqrt{1-\rho}}\right). \tag{8.49}$$

The interesting part of equation (8.49) is, of course, the expression involving the standard normal df, and we now give a derivation. Consider a one-factor threshold model of KMV/CreditMetrics type with marginal default probabilities $\bar{p}_1, \dots, \bar{p}_m$ and critical variables given by

$$X_i = \sqrt{\rho}F + \sqrt{1-\rho}\varepsilon_i \tag{8.50}$$

for iid standard normal rvs $F, \varepsilon_1, \dots, \varepsilon_m$. It follows from Example 8.20 that an equivalent Bernoulli mixture model can be constructed by setting $\Psi = -F$ (the sign change facilitates the derivation) and conditional default probabilities $p_i(\Psi) = \Phi((\Phi^{-1}(\bar{p}_i) + \sqrt{\rho}\Psi)/\sqrt{1-\rho})$. Assume, moreover, that the loss given default of the firms is deterministic and equal to $\delta_i e_i$ and that exposures are relatively homogeneous. According to Proposition 8.16, under these assumptions the quantiles of the portfolio loss $L = \sum_{i=1}^m \delta_i e_i Y_i$ satisfy, for m large, the asymptotic relation

$$q_\alpha(L) \approx \sum_{i=1}^m \delta_i e_i p_i(q_\alpha(\Psi)) = \sum_{i=1}^m \delta_i e_i \Phi\left(\frac{\Phi^{-1}(\bar{p}_i) + \sqrt{\rho}\Phi^{-1}(\alpha)}{\sqrt{1-\rho}}\right).$$

For $c = 1$, the risk capital RC_i in (8.49) can thus be considered as the asymptotic contribution of risk i to the 99.9% VaR of the overall portfolio in a one-factor Gaussian threshold model with asset correlation ρ.

While formula (8.48) is influenced by portfolio-theoretic considerations, the new Basel II framework falls short of reflecting the true dependence structure of a bank's credit portfolio for a number of reasons: first, in the Basel II framework the correlation parameter ρ is specified ad hoc by regulatory rules irrespective of "true" asset correlations; second, the simple one-factor model (8.50) is typically an oversimplified representation of the factor structure underlying default dependence, particularly for internationally active banks; third, the rule is based on an asymptotic result. Moreover, historical default experience for the portfolio under consideration has no formal role to play in setting capital-adequacy standards. For these reasons

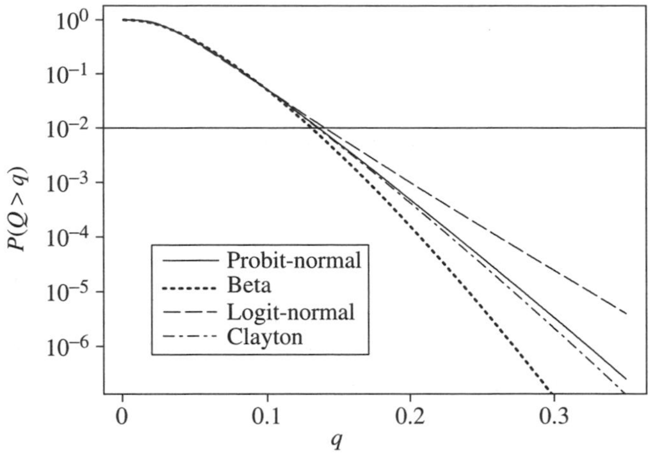

Figure 8.3. Tail of the mixing distribution of Q in four different exchangeable Bernoulli-mixture models: beta; probit-normal (one-factor KMV/CreditMetrics); logit-normal (CreditPortfolioView); Clayton. In all cases the first two moments have the values $\pi = 0.049$ and $\pi_2 = 0.003\,13$, which correspond roughly to Standard & Poor's rating category B; the actual parameter values can be found in Table 8.6. The horizontal line at 10^{-2} shows that the models only really start to differ around the 99th percentile of the mixing distribution.

the IRB approach is heavily debated in the risk-management community, and it is widely expected that, with improved availability of credit loss data, in the long run regulators will permit the use of internal portfolio models for capital-adequacy purposes for credit risk, as was allowed for market risk in the 1996 Amendment of the first Basel Accord (see Section 1.2.2).

8.4.6 Model Risk Issues

In this section, which is complementary to Section 8.3.5, we look briefly at an aspect of model risk for Bernoulli mixture models. We consider an exchangeable Bernoulli mixture model for a homogeneous portfolio and investigate the risk related to the choice of mixing distribution under the constraint that the default probability π and the default correlation ρ_Y (or equivalently π and π_2) are known and fixed.

According to Proposition 8.16, the tail of M is essentially determined by the tail of the mixing variable Q. In Figure 8.3 we plot the tail function of the probit-normal distribution (corresponding to a one-factor KMV/CreditMetrics model), the logit-normal distribution (corresponding to CreditPortfolioView), the beta distribution (close to CreditRisk+) and the mixture distribution (corresponding to the Clayton copula; see Example 8.22). The plots are shown on a logarithmic scale and in all cases the first two moments have the values $\pi = 0.049$ and $\pi_2 = 0.003\,13$, which correspond roughly to Standard & Poor's rating category B; the parameter values for each of the models can be found in Table 8.6.

Inspection of Figure 8.3 shows that the tail functions differ significantly only after the 99% quantile, the logit-normal distribution being the one with the heaviest tail.

Table 8.6. Parameter values for various exchangeable Bernoulli mixture models with identical values of π and π_2 (and ρ_Y). The values of π and π_2 correspond roughly to Standard & Poor's ratings CCC, B and BB (in fact, they have been estimated from 20 years of Standard & Poor's default data using the simple moment estimator in (8.61)). This table is used in the model-risk study of Section 8.4.6 and the simulation study of Section 8.6.2.

Model	Parameter	CCC	B	BB
All models	π	0.188	0.049	0.0112
	π_2	0.042	0.00313	0.000197
	ρ_Y	0.0446	0.0157	0.00643
Beta	a	4.02	3.08	1.73
	b	17.4	59.8	153
Probit-normal	μ	−0.93	−1.71	−2.37
	σ	0.316	0.264	0.272
Logit-normal	μ	−1.56	−3.1	−4.71
	σ	0.553	0.556	0.691
Clayton	π	0.188	0.049	0.0112
	θ	0.0704	0.032	0.0247

From a practical point of view this means that the particular parametric form of the mixing distribution in a Bernoulli mixture model is of minor importance once π and ρ_Y have been fixed. Of course this does not mean that Bernoulli mixtures are immune to model risk; the tail of M is quite sensitive to π and in particular to ρ_Y, and these parameters are not easily estimated (see Section 8.6.4 for a discussion of statistical inference for mixture models).

Systematic recovery risk. Another important source of model risk in credit risk management models is the modelling of loss given default or equivalently of the recovery rates. In standard portfolio risk models it is assumed that the loss given default is independent of the default event. However, one expects the loss given default to depend on the same risk factors as default probabilities; in that case we speak of systematic recovery risk. The presence of systematic recovery risk is confirmed in a number of empirical studies. In particular, Frye (2000) has carried out a formal empirical analysis using recovery data collected by Moody's on rated corporate bonds. He found that recovery rates are substantially lower than average in times of economic recession. To quote from his paper:

> Using that data [the Moody's data] to estimate an appropriate credit model, we can extrapolate that in a severe economic downturn recoveries might decline 20–25 percentage points from the normal-year average. This could cause loss given default to increase by nearly 100% and to have a similar effect on economic capital. Such systematic recovery risk is absent from first-generation credit risk models. Therefore these models may significantly understate the capital required at banking institutions.

Clearly, this calls for the inclusion of systematic recovery risk in standard credit risk models. The challenge is not in building models allowing for systematic recovery risk—this can be accomplished easily in the framework of Section 8.4.3—but in estimating the dependence of the loss given default δ_i on the economic factors. At present there are few empirical studies dealing with recovery risk; a good survey is Schuermann (2003).

Notes and Comments

The logit-normal mixture model can be thought of as a one-factor version of the CreditPortfolioView model of Wilson (1997a,b). Details of this model can be found in Section 5 of Crouhy, Galai and Mark (2000). Further details of the beta binomial distribution can be found in Joe (1997).

The rating agency Moody's uses a so-called binomial expansion technique to model default dependence in a simplistic way. The method, which is very popular with practitioners, is not based on a formal default risk model, but is related to binomial distributions. The basic idea is to approximate a portfolio of m dependent counterparties by a homogeneous portfolio of $d < m$ independent counterparties with adjusted exposures and identical default probabilities; the index d is called the *diversity score* and is chosen according to rules defined by Moody's. For further information we refer to Davis and Lo (2001) and Section 9.2.7 of Lando (2004).

A comprehensive description of CreditRisk+ is given in the original manual for CreditRisk+ (Credit Suisse Financial Products 1997). An excellent discussion of the model structure from a more academic viewpoint is provided in Gordy (2000). Both sources also provide further information on the calibration of the factor variances σ_i and factor weights w_{ij}. The derivation of recursion formulas for the probabilities $P(\tilde{M} = k)$, $k = 0, 1, \dots$, via Panjer recursion is given in Appendix A10 of CreditRisk+ (Credit Suisse Financial Products 1997). In Gordy (2002) an alternative approach to the computation of the loss distribution in CreditRisk+ is proposed—one which uses the saddle-point approximation (see, for instance, Jensen 1995). Further numerical work for CreditRisk+ can be found in papers by Kurth and Tasche (2003), Glasserman (2003b) and Haaf, Reiss and Schoenmakers (2004). Importance-sampling techniques for CreditRisk+ are discussed in Glasserman and Li (2003b). In Frey and McNeil (2002) it is shown that the Bernoulli mixture model corresponding to a one-factor exchangeable version of CreditRisk+ is very close to an exchangeable Bernoulli mixture model with beta mixing distribution.

The results in Section 8.4.3 are taken from Frey and McNeil (2003); related results have been derived by Gordy (2001). The first limit result for large portfolios was obtained in Vasicek (1997) for a probit-normal mixture model equivalent to the KMV model. Asymptotic results for credit portfolios related to the theory of large deviations are discussed in Dembo, Deuschel and Duffie (2004).

The equivalence between threshold models and mixture models has been observed by Koyluoglu and Hickman (1998) and Gordy (2000) for the special case of CreditMetrics and CreditRisk+. Applications of Proposition 5.46 to credit risk modelling are also discussed in Schönbucher (2002). It is of course possible to develop multi-state mixture models to describe credit migrations as well as defaults and to derive equivalence results between multi-state latent threshold models and multi-state mixture models; see, for instance, Section 4.4 of Frey and McNeil (2001) for an application to credit risk and Joe (1997) for mathematical background information. The study of mixture representations for sequences of exchangeable Bernoulli rvs is related to a well-known result of de Finetti, which states that any *infinite* sequence $Y_1, Y_2, \dots$ of exchangeable Bernoulli rvs has a representation as an exchangeable Bernoulli mixture; see, for instance, Theorem 35.10 in Billingsley (1995) for a precise statement. Hence any exchangeable model for $\boldsymbol{Y}$ that can be extended to arbitrary portfolio size m has a representation as an exchangeable Bernoulli mixture model.

For details of the IRB approach, and the Basel II Capital Accord in general, we refer to the website of the Basel Committee: www.bis.org/bcbs. Our discussion in Section 8.4.5 is related to the analysis by Gordy (2001).

8.5 Monte Carlo Methods

In this section we consider a Bernoulli mixture model for a loan portfolio and assume that the overall loss is of the form $L = \sum_{i=1}^{m} L_i$, where the L_i are conditionally independent given some economic factor vector $\boldsymbol{\Psi}$. A possible method for calculating risk measures and related quantities such as capital allocations is to use Monte Carlo (MC) simulation, although the problem of *rare-event simulation* arises. Suppose, for example, that we wish to compute expected shortfall and expected shortfall contributions at the confidence level α for our portfolio. We need to evaluate the conditional expectations

$$E(L \mid L \geqslant q_\alpha(L)) \quad \text{and} \quad E(L_i \mid L \geqslant q_\alpha(L)). \tag{8.51}$$

If $\alpha = 0.99$, say, then only 1% of our standard Monte Carlo draws will lead to a portfolio loss higher than $q_{0.99}(L)$. The standard MC estimator of (8.51), which consists of averaging the simulated values of L or L_i over all draws leading to a simulated portfolio loss $L \geqslant q_\alpha(L)$, will be unstable and subject to high variability, unless the number of simulations is very large. The problem is of course that most simulations are "wasted", in that they lead to a value of L which is smaller than $q_\alpha(L)$. Fortunately, there exists a variance-reduction technique known as *importance sampling* (IS), which is well suited to such problems.

8.5.1 Basics of Importance Sampling

Consider an rv X on some probability space $(\Omega, \mathcal{F}, P)$ and assume that it has an absolutely continuous df with density f. A generalization to general probability spaces is discussed below. The problem we consider is the computation of the expected value

$$\theta = E(h(X)) = \int_{-\infty}^{\infty} h(x) f(x)\, \mathrm{d}x \tag{8.52}$$

for some known function h. To calculate the probability of an event we consider a function of the form $h(x) = I_{\{x \in A\}}$ for some set $A \subset \mathbb{R}$; for expected shortfall computation we consider functions of the form $h(x) = xI_{\{x \geqslant c\}}$ for some $c \in \mathbb{R}$. Where the analytical evaluation of (8.52) is difficult, due to the complexity of the distribution of X, we can resort to an MC approach, for which we only have to be able to simulate variates from the distribution with density f.

Algorithm 8.23 (Monte Carlo integration).

(1) Generate $X_1, \dots, X_n$ independently from density f.

(2) Compute the standard MC estimate $\hat{\theta}_n^{\mathrm{MC}} = (1/n) \sum_{i=1}^n h(X_i)$.

The MC estimator converges to θ by the strong law of large numbers, but the speed of convergence may not be particularly fast, particularly when we are dealing with rare-event simulation.

Importance sampling is based on an alternative representation of the integral in (8.52). Consider a second probability density g (whose support should contain that of f) and define the *likelihood ratio* $r(x)$ by $r(x) := f(x)/g(x)$ whenever $g(x) > 0$, and $r(x) = 0$ otherwise. The integral (8.52) may be written in terms of the likelihood ratio as

$$\theta = \int_{-\infty}^{\infty} h(x)r(x)g(x)\,\mathrm{d}x = E_g(h(X)r(X)), \tag{8.53}$$

where E_g denotes expectation with respect to the density g. Hence we can approximate the integral with the following algorithm.

Algorithm 8.24 (importance sampling).

(1) Generate $X_1, \dots, X_n$ independently from density g.

(2) Compute the IS estimate $\hat{\theta}_n^{\mathrm{IS}} = (1/n) \sum_{i=1}^n h(X_i)\, r(X_i)$.

The density g is often termed the *importance-sampling density*. The art (or science) of importance sampling is in choosing an importance-sampling density such that, for fixed n, the variance of the IS estimator is considerably smaller than that of the standard Monte Carlo estimator. In this way we can hope to obtain a prescribed accuracy in evaluating the integral of interest using far fewer random draws than are required in standard Monte Carlo simulation. The variances of the estimators are given by

$$\begin{aligned} \operatorname{var}_g(\hat{\theta}_n^{\mathrm{IS}}) &= (1/n)(E_g(h(X)^2 r(X)^2) - \theta^2), \\ \operatorname{var}(\hat{\theta}_n^{\mathrm{MC}}) &= (1/n)(E(h(X)^2) - \theta^2), \end{aligned}$$

so that the aim is to make $E_g(h(X)^2 r(X)^2)$ small compared with $E(h(X)^2)$. In theory, the variance of $\hat{\theta}^{\mathrm{IS}}$ can be reduced to zero by choosing an optimal g. To see this, suppose for the moment that h is non-negative and set

$$g^*(x) = f(x)h(x)/E(h(X)). \tag{8.54}$$

With this choice, the likelihood ratio becomes $r(x) = E(h(X))/h(x)$. Hence $\hat{\theta}_1^{\text{IS}} = h(X_1)r(X_1) = E(h(X))$, and the IS estimator gives the correct answer in a single draw. In practice, it is of course impossible to choose an IS density of the form (8.54), as this requires knowledge of the quantity $E(h(X))$ that one wants to compute; nonetheless, (8.54) can provide useful guidance in choosing an IS density, as we will see in the next section.

Consider the case of estimating a rare-event probability corresponding to $h(x) = I_{\{x \geqslant c\}}$ for c significantly larger than the mean of X. Then we have that $E(h(X)^2) = P(X \geqslant c)$ and, using (8.53), that

$$E_g(h(X)^2 r(X)^2) = E_g(r(X)^2; X \geqslant c) = E(r(X); X \geqslant c). \tag{8.55}$$

Clearly, we should try to choose g such that the likelihood ratio $r(x) = f(x)/g(x)$ is small for $x \geqslant c$; in other words, we should make the event $\{X \geqslant c\}$ more likely under the IS density g than it is under the original density f.

Exponential tilting. We now describe a useful way of finding IS densities when X is light tailed. For $t \in \mathbb{R}$ we write $M_X(t) = E(\mathrm{e}^{tX}) = \int_{-\infty}^{\infty} \mathrm{e}^{tx} f(x)\,\mathrm{d}x$ for the moment-generating function of X, which we assume is finite for $t \in \mathbb{R}$. If $M_X(t)$ is finite, we can define an IS density by $g_t(x) := \mathrm{e}^{tx} f(x)/M_X(t)$. The likelihood ratio is $r_t(x) = f(x)/g_t(x) = M_X(t)\mathrm{e}^{-tx}$. Define μ_t to be the mean of X with respect to the density g_t, i.e.

$$\mu_t := E_{g_t}(X) = E(X \exp(tX))/M_X(t). \tag{8.56}$$

How can we choose t optimally for a particular importance-sampling problem? We consider the case of tail probability estimation and recall from (8.55) that the objective is to make

$$E(r(X); X \geqslant c) = E(I_{\{X \geqslant c\}} M_X(t)\mathrm{e}^{-tX}) \tag{8.57}$$

small. Now observe that $\mathrm{e}^{-tx} \leqslant \mathrm{e}^{-tc}$ for $x \geqslant c$ and $t \geqslant 0$, so

$$E(I_{\{X \geqslant c\}} M_X(t)\mathrm{e}^{-tX}) \leqslant M_X(t)\mathrm{e}^{-tc}.$$

Instead of solving the (difficult) problem of minimizing (8.57) over t, we choose t so that this bound becomes minimal. Equivalently, we try to find t minimizing $\ln M_X(t) - tc$. Using (8.56) we obtain that

$$\frac{\mathrm{d}}{\mathrm{d}t} \ln M_X(t) - tc = \frac{E(X \exp(tX))}{M_X(t)} - c = \mu_t - c,$$

which suggests choosing $t = t(c)$ as the solution of the equation $\mu_t = c$, so that the rare event $\{X \geqslant c\}$ becomes a normal event if we compute probabilities using the density $g_{t(c)}$. A unique solution of the equation $\mu_t = c$ exists for all relevant values of c. In the cases that are of interest to us this is immediately obvious from the form of the exponentially tilted distributions, so we omit a formal proof.

Example 8.25 (exponential tilting for normal distribution). We illustrate the concept of exponential tilting in the simple case of a standard normal rv. Suppose that $X \sim N(0, 1)$ with density $\phi(x)$. Using exponential tilting we obtain the new density $g_t(x) = \exp(tx)\phi(x)/M_X(t)$. The moment-generating function of X is known to be $M_X(t) = \exp(\frac{1}{2}t^2)$. Hence

$$g_t(x) = \frac{1}{\sqrt{2\pi}} \exp(tx - \tfrac{1}{2}(t^2 + x^2)) = \frac{1}{\sqrt{2\pi}} \exp(\tfrac{1}{2}(x - t)^2),$$

so that, under the tilted distribution, $X \sim N(t, 1)$. Note that in this case exponential tilting corresponds to changing the mean of X.

An abstract view of importance sampling. To handle the more complex application to portfolio credit risk in the next section it helps to consider importance sampling from a slightly more general viewpoint. Given densities f and g as above, define probability measures P and Q by

$$P(A) = \int_A f(x)\,\mathrm{d}x \quad \text{and} \quad Q(A) = \int_A g(x)\,\mathrm{d}x, \qquad A \subset \mathbb{R}.$$

With this notation, (8.53) becomes $\theta = E^P(h(X)) = E^Q(h(X)r(X))$, so that $r(X)$ equals $\mathrm{d}P/\mathrm{d}Q$, the (measure-theoretic) density of P with respect to Q. Using this more abstract view, exponential tilting can be applied in more general situations: given an rv X on $(\Omega, \mathcal{F}, P)$ such that $M_X(t) = E^P(\exp(tX)) < \infty$, define the measure Q_t on $(\Omega, \mathcal{F})$ by

$$\frac{\mathrm{d}Q_t}{\mathrm{d}P} = \frac{\exp(tX)}{M_X(t)}, \quad \text{i.e. } Q_t(A) = E^P\left(\frac{\exp(tX)}{M_X(t)}; A\right),$$

and note that $(\mathrm{d}Q_t/\mathrm{d}P)^{-1} = M_X(t)\exp(-tX) = r_t(X)$. The IS algorithm remains essentially unchanged: simulate independent realizations X_i under the measure Q_t and set $\hat{\theta}^{\mathrm{IS}} = (1/n)\sum_{i=1}^n X_i r_t(X_i)$ as before.

8.5.2 Application to Bernoulli-Mixture Models

In this section we return to the subject of credit losses and consider a portfolio loss of the form $L = \sum_{i=1}^m e_i Y_i$, where the e_i are deterministic, positive exposures and the Y_i are default indicators with default probabilities $\bar{p}_i$. We assume that $\boldsymbol{Y}$ follows a Bernoulli mixture model in the sense of Definition 8.10 with factor vector $\boldsymbol{\Psi}$ and conditional default probabilities $p_i(\boldsymbol{\Psi})$. We study the problem of estimating exceedance probabilities $\theta = P(L \geqslant c)$ for c substantially larger than $E(L)$ using importance sampling. This is useful for risk-management purposes, as, for $c \approx q_\alpha(L)$, a good importance-sampling distribution for the computation of $P(L \geqslant c)$ also yields a substantial variance reduction for computing expected shortfall or expected shortfall contributions.

We consider first the situation where the default indicators $Y_1, \dots, Y_m$ are independent and discuss subsequently the extension to the case of conditionally independent default indicators. Our exposition is based on Glasserman and Li (2003a).

Independent default indicators. Here we use the more general IS approach outlined at the end of the previous section. Set $\Omega = \{0, 1\}^m$, the state space of $\boldsymbol{Y}$. The probability measure P is given by

$$P(\{\boldsymbol{y}\}) = \prod_{i=1}^{m} \bar{p}_i^{y_i}(1-\bar{p}_i)^{1-y_i}, \quad \boldsymbol{y} \in \{0, 1\}^m.$$

We need to understand how this measure changes under exponential tilting using L. The moment-generating function of L is easily calculated to be

$$M_L(t) = E\biggl(\exp\biggl(t\sum_{i=1}^{m} e_i Y_i\biggr)\biggr) = \prod_{i=1}^{m} E(\mathrm{e}^{te_i Y_i}) = \prod_{i=1}^{m}(\mathrm{e}^{te_i}\bar{p}_i + 1 - \bar{p}_i).$$

The measure Q_t is given by $Q_t(\{\boldsymbol{y}\}) = E^P(\mathrm{e}^{tL}/M_L(t); \boldsymbol{Y} = \boldsymbol{y})$ and hence

$$Q_t(\{\boldsymbol{y}\}) = \frac{\exp(t\sum_{i=1}^{m} e_i y_i)}{M_L(t)} P(\{\boldsymbol{y}\}) = \prod_{i=1}^{m} \frac{\exp(te_i y_i)}{\exp(te_i)\bar{p}_i + 1 - \bar{p}_i} \bar{p}_i^{y_i}(1-\bar{p}_i)^{1-y_i}.$$

Define new default probabilities by $\bar{q}_{t,i} := \exp(te_i)\bar{p}_i/(\exp(te_i)\bar{p}_i + 1 - \bar{p}_i)$. It follows that $Q_t(\{\boldsymbol{y}\}) = \prod_{i=1}^{m} \bar{q}_{t,i}^{y_i}(1-\bar{q}_{t,i})^{1-y_i}$, so that after exponential tilting the default indicators remain independent but with new default probability $\bar{q}_{t,i}$. Note that $\bar{q}_{t,i}$ tends to one for $t \to \infty$ and to zero for $t \to -\infty$, so that we can shift the mean of L to any point in $(0, \sum_{i=1}^{m} e_i)$.

In analogy with our previous discussion, for IS purposes, the optimal value of t is chosen such that $E^{Q_t}(L) = c$, leading to the equation $\sum_{i=1}^{m} e_i \bar{q}_{t,i} = c$.

Conditionally independent default indicators. The first step in the extension of the importance-sampling approach to conditionally independent defaults is obvious: given a realization $\boldsymbol{\psi}$ of the economic factors, the conditional exceedance probability $\theta(\boldsymbol{\psi}) := P(L \geqslant c \mid \boldsymbol{\Psi} = \boldsymbol{\psi})$ is estimated using the approach for independent default indicators described above. We have the following algorithm.

Algorithm 8.26 (IS for conditional loss distribution).

(1) Given $\boldsymbol{\psi}$, calculate the conditional default probabilities $p_i(\boldsymbol{\psi})$ according to the particular model, and solve the equation

$$\sum_{i=1}^{m} e_i \frac{\exp(te_i)p_i(\boldsymbol{\psi})}{\exp(te_i)p_i(\boldsymbol{\psi}) + 1 - p_i(\boldsymbol{\psi})} = c;$$

the solution $t = t(c, \boldsymbol{\psi})$ gives the optimal degree of tilting.

(2) Generate n_1 conditional realizations of the default vector $(Y_1, \dots, Y_m)$. The defaults of the companies are simulated independently, with the default probability of the ith company given by

$$\frac{\exp(t(c, \boldsymbol{\psi})e_i)p_i(\boldsymbol{\psi})}{\exp(t(c, \boldsymbol{\psi})e_i)p_i(\boldsymbol{\psi}) + 1 - p_i(\boldsymbol{\psi})}.$$

(3) Denote by $M_L(t, \psi) := \prod_{i=1}^{m}\{\exp(te_i)p_i(\psi) + 1 - p_i(\psi)\}$ the conditional moment-generating function of L. From the simulated default data construct n_1 conditional realizations of $L = \sum_{i=1}^{m} e_i Y_i$ and label these $L^{(1)}, \dots, L^{(n_1)}$. Determine the IS estimator for the conditional loss distribution:

$$\hat{\theta}_{n_1}^{\mathrm{IS},1}(\psi) = M_L(t(c, \psi), \psi)\frac{1}{n_1}\sum_{j=1}^{n_1} I_{\{L^{(j)} \geqslant c\}} \exp(-t(c, \psi)L^{(j)}).$$

In principle, the approach discussed above also applies in the more general situation where the loss given default is random; all we need to assume is that the L_i are conditionally independent given $\boldsymbol{\Psi}$, as in Assumption (A1) of Section 8.4.3. However, the actual implementation can become quite involved.

IS for the distribution of the factor variables. Suppose we now want to estimate the unconditional probability $\theta = P(L \geqslant c)$. A naive approach would be to generate realizations of the factor vector $\boldsymbol{\Psi}$ and to estimate θ by averaging the IS estimator of Algorithm 8.26 over these realizations. As is shown in Glasserman and Li (2003a), this is not the best solution for large portfolios of dependent credit risks. Intuitively, this is due to the fact that for such portfolios most of the variation in L is caused by fluctuations of the economic factors, and we have not yet applied IS to the distribution of $\boldsymbol{\Psi}$. For this reason we now discuss a full IS algorithm that combines IS for the economic factor variables with Algorithm 8.26.

We consider the important case of a Bernoulli mixture model with multivariate Gaussian factors and conditional default probabilities $p_i(\boldsymbol{\Psi})$ for $\boldsymbol{\Psi} \sim N_p(\mathbf{0}, \Omega)$, such as the probit-normal Bernoulli mixture model described by (8.45). In this context it is natural to choose an importance-sampling density such that $\boldsymbol{\Psi} \sim N_p(\boldsymbol{\mu}, \Omega)$ for a new mean vector $\boldsymbol{\mu} \in \mathbb{R}^p$, i.e. we take g as the density of $N_p(\boldsymbol{\mu}, \Omega)$. For a good choice of $\boldsymbol{\mu}$ we expect to generate realizations of $\boldsymbol{\Psi}$ leading to high conditional default probabilities more frequently. The corresponding likelihood ratio $r_{\boldsymbol{\mu}}(\boldsymbol{\Psi})$ is given by the ratio of the respective multivariate normal densities, so that

$$r_{\boldsymbol{\mu}}(\boldsymbol{\Psi}) = \frac{\exp(-\frac{1}{2}\boldsymbol{\Psi}'\Omega^{-1}\boldsymbol{\Psi})}{\exp(-\frac{1}{2}(\boldsymbol{\Psi} - \boldsymbol{\mu})'\Omega^{-1}(\boldsymbol{\Psi} - \boldsymbol{\mu}))} = \exp(-\boldsymbol{\mu}'\Omega^{-1}\boldsymbol{\Psi} + \tfrac{1}{2}\boldsymbol{\mu}'\Omega^{-1}\boldsymbol{\mu}).$$

Essentially, this is a multivariate analogue of the exponential tilting applied to a univariate normal distribution in Example 8.25.

Now we can describe the algorithm for full IS. At the outset we have to choose the overall number of simulation rounds, n, the number of repetitions of conditional IS per simulation round, n_1, and the mean of the IS distribution for the factors, $\boldsymbol{\mu}$. Whereas the value of n depends on the desired degree of precision and is best determined in a simulation study, n_1 should be taken to be fairly small. An approach to determine a sensible value of $\boldsymbol{\mu}$ is discussed below.

Algorithm 8.27 (full IS for mixture models with Gaussian factors).

(1) Generate $\boldsymbol{\Psi}_1, \dots, \boldsymbol{\Psi}_n \sim N(\boldsymbol{\mu}, I_p)$.

(2) For each $\boldsymbol{\Psi}_i$ calculate $\hat{\theta}_{n_1}^{\mathrm{IS},1}(\boldsymbol{\Psi}_i)$ as in Algorithm 8.26.

(3) Determine the full IS estimator:

$$\hat{\theta}_n^{\mathrm{IS}} = \frac{1}{n}\sum_{i=1}^{n} r_{\boldsymbol{\mu}}(\boldsymbol{\Psi}_i)\hat{\theta}_{n_1}^{\mathrm{IS},1}(\boldsymbol{\Psi}_i).$$

Choosing $\boldsymbol{\mu}$. A key point in the full IS approach is the determination of a good value for $\boldsymbol{\mu}$, which leads to a low variance of the importance-sampling estimator. Here we sketch the solution proposed by Glasserman and Li (2003a). Since $\hat{\theta}_{n_1}^{\mathrm{IS},1}(\boldsymbol{\psi}) \approx P(L \geqslant c \mid \boldsymbol{\Psi} = \boldsymbol{\psi})$, applying IS to the factors essentially amounts to finding a good importance-sampling density for the function $\boldsymbol{\psi} \to P(L \geqslant c \mid \boldsymbol{\Psi} = \boldsymbol{\psi})$. Now recall from our discussion in the previous section that the optimal IS density g^* satisfies

$$g^*(\boldsymbol{\psi}) \propto P(L \geqslant c \mid \boldsymbol{\Psi} = \boldsymbol{\psi}) \exp(-\tfrac{1}{2}\boldsymbol{\psi}'\Omega^{-1}\boldsymbol{\psi}), \tag{8.58}$$

"$\propto$" standing for "proportional to". Sampling from that density is obviously not feasible, as the normalizing constant involves the exceedance probability $P(L \geqslant c)$ that we are interested in. In this situation the authors suggest using a multivariate normal density with the same mode as g^* as an approximation to the optimal IS density. Since a normal density attains its mode at the mean $\boldsymbol{\mu}$, this amounts to choosing $\boldsymbol{\mu}$ as the solution to the optimization problem

$$\max_{\boldsymbol{\psi}} P(L \geqslant c \mid \boldsymbol{\Psi} = \boldsymbol{\psi}) \exp(-\tfrac{1}{2}\boldsymbol{\psi}'\Omega^{-1}\boldsymbol{\psi}). \tag{8.59}$$

An exact (numerical) solution of (8.59) is difficult because the function $P(L \geqslant c \mid \boldsymbol{\Psi} = \boldsymbol{\psi})$ is usually not available in closed form. Glasserman and Li (2003a) discuss several approaches to overcoming this difficulty; see their paper for details.

Notes and Comments

Our discussion of IS for credit portfolios follows Glasserman and Li (2003a) closely. Theoretical results on the asymptotics of the IS estimator for large portfolios and numerical case studies contained in Glasserman and Li (2003a) indicate that full IS is a very useful tool for dealing with large Bernoulli mixture models. Merino and Nyfeler (2003) and Kalkbrener, Lotter and Overbeck (2004) undertook related work—the latter paper gives an interesting alternative solution to finding a reasonable IS mean $\boldsymbol{\mu}$ for the factors.

For a general introduction to importance sampling we refer to the excellent textbook by Glasserman (2003a) (see also Robert and Casella 1999). For applications of importance sampling to heavy-tailed distributions, where exponential families cannot be applied directly, see Asmussen, Binswanger and Højgaard (2000) and Glasserman, Heidelberger and Shahabuddin (1999).

As an alternative to simulation one can try to determine analytic approximations for the loss distributions. Applications of the saddle-point approximation (see Jensen 1995) are discussed in Martin, Thompson and Browne (2001) and Gordy (2002).

8.6 Statistical Inference for Mixture Models

In this section we consider the statistical estimation of model parameters from historical default data for the kind of mixture models described in Section 8.4. This is quite a specific issue in the general area of statistical inference for credit risk models and the reader seeking more general literature should consult Notes and Comments. Before turning to statistical methods we provide a word of motivation for the approach we take in this section.

8.6.1 Motivation

The calibration of portfolio credit risk models used in industry (such as KMV, CreditMetrics or CreditRisk+) has, in general, not relied on the formal statistical estimation of model parameters from historical default and migration data. There are good reasons for this, the main one being that, particularly for higher-rated companies, there are simply not enough relevant data on historical defaults to obtain reliable parameter estimates by formal inference alone.

Industry approaches generally separate the problems of estimating (i) default probabilities and (ii) additional model parameters describing the dependence of defaults. The default probability of an individual company is usually estimated by an appropriate historical default rate for "similar companies", where the similarity metric may be based on a credit-rating system (CreditMetrics) or a proprietary measure like distance-to-default (DD) in the case of KMV.

It is in the determination of other model parameters that current industry models are much less "formally statistical". While most industry models postulate plausible factor-model structures for the mechanism generating default dependence, the parameters of these factor models are very often either simply "assigned" by economic arguments or determined by auxiliary factor analyses of proxy variables. To give an example of the latter, some threshold models that equate the critical variable with a change in asset value (in the style of Merton's model) calibrate the factor model by taking equity returns as a proxy for asset-value changes and fitting a factor model to equity returns.

The ad hoc nature of such approaches raises the question of how much confidence can be placed in the model parameters thus derived, and how much model risk remains? For example, in a model of KMV/CreditMetrics type, how confident are we that we have correctly determined the size of the systematic risk component (8.26) due to the factors? In Section 8.3.5 we showed that there is considerable model risk associated with the size of the specific risk component, particularly when the tail of a credit loss distribution is of central importance.

In this final section of this chapter we describe methods for the pure statistical estimation of all model parameters from default data. Currently, such an approach is perhaps only feasible for lower-grade credit risks where historical databases contain sufficient material to estimate parameters relating to default probability as well as parameters relating to default dependence. This picture may change as data become more plentiful over the years. Moreover, someone who grasps the principles of model fitting in this section will see that current industry approaches could even be combined with the approach of this section to yield a hybrid methodology. More explicitly, components of the factor-model structure could be based on external inputs from industry models, while key parameters, such as parameters governing the overall sensitivity to systematic effects, could be statistically estimated from historical data.

The models we describe are motivated by the format of the data we consider, which can be described as *repeated cross-sectional data*. This kind of data, comprising observations of the default or non-default of groups of monitored companies in a number of time periods, is readily available from rating agencies. Since the group of companies may differ from period to period, as new companies are rated and others default or cease to be rated, we have a cross-section of companies in each period, but the cross-section may change from period to period. A different kind of data that we do not consider would be *panel* data or *repeated-measures* data (particularly panels of ratings) for individual companies that are actively followed over time.

Our examples are relatively simple, but illustrate the main ideas. In Section 8.6.2 we discuss the estimation of default probabilities and default correlations for homogeneous groups, e.g. groups with the same credit rating. In Section 8.6.3 we consider more complicated one-factor models allowing more heterogeneity and make a link to the important class of generalized linear mixed models (GLMMs) used in many statistical applications; an example is given in Section 8.6.4.

8.6.2 Exchangeable Bernoulli-Mixture Models

Suppose that we observe historical default numbers over n periods of time for a homogeneous group; typically these might be yearly data. For $t = 1, \dots, n$, let m_t denote the number of observed companies at the start of period t and let M_t denote the number that defaulted during the period; the former will be treated as fixed at the outset of the period and the latter as an rv. Suppose further that within a time period these defaults are generated by an exchangeable Bernoulli mixture model of the kind described in Section 8.4.1. In other words, assume that, given some mixing variable Q_t taking values in $(0, 1)$ and the cohort size m_t, the number of defaults M_t is conditionally binomially distributed and satisfies $M_t \mid Q_t = q \sim B(m_t, q)$. Further assume that the mixing variables $Q_1, \dots, Q_n$ are identically distributed. We consider two methods for estimating the fundamental parameters of the mixing distribution $\pi = \pi_1$, π_2 and ρ_Y (default correlation); these are the method of moments and the maximum likelihood method.

A simple moment estimator. For $1 \leqslant t \leqslant n$, let $Y_{t,1}, \dots, Y_{t,m_t}$ be default indicators for the m_t companies in the cohort. Suppose we define the rv

$$\binom{M_t}{k} := \sum_{\{i_1,\dots,i_k\}\subset\{1,\dots,m_t\}} Y_{t,i_1} \cdots Y_{t,i_k}; \tag{8.60}$$

this represents the number of possible subgroups of k obligors among the defaulting obligors in period t (and takes the value zero when $k > M_t$). By taking expectations in (8.60) we get

$$E\left(\binom{M_t}{k}\right) = \binom{m_t}{k}\pi_k$$

and hence

$$\pi_k = E\left(\binom{M_t}{k}\right) \Big/ \binom{m_t}{k}.$$

We estimate the unknown theoretical moment π_k by taking a natural empirical average (8.61) constructed from the n years of data:

$$\hat{\pi}_k = \frac{1}{n}\sum_{t=1}^{n}\frac{\binom{M_t}{k}}{\binom{m_t}{k}} = \frac{1}{n}\sum_{t=1}^{n}\frac{M_t(M_t-1)\cdots(M_t-k+1)}{m_t(m_t-1)\cdots(m_t-k+1)}. \tag{8.61}$$

For $k = 1$ we get the standard estimator of default probability

$$\hat{\pi} = \frac{1}{n}\sum_{t=1}^{n}\frac{M_t}{m_t},$$

and ρ_Y can obviously be estimated by taking $\hat{\rho}_Y = (\hat{\pi}_2 - \hat{\pi}^2)/(\hat{\pi} - \hat{\pi}^2)$. The estimator is unbiased for π_k and consistent as $n \to \infty$ (for more details see Frey and McNeil (2001)). Note that, for Q_t random, consistency requires observations for a large number of years; it is not sufficient to observe a large pool in a single year.

Maximum likelihood estimators. To implement a maximum likelihood (ML) procedure we assume a simple parametric form for the density of the Q_t (such as beta, logit-normal or probit-normal). The joint probability function of the default counts $M_1, \dots, M_n$ given the cohort sizes $m_1, \dots, m_n$ can then be calculated using (8.33), under the assumption that the Q_t variables in different years are independent. This expression is then maximized with respect to the natural parameters of the mixing distribution (i.e. a and b in the case of beta and μ and σ for the logit-normal and probit-normal). Of course, independence may be an unrealistic assumption for the mixing variables, due to the phenomenon of economic cycles, but the method could then be regarded as a quasi-maximum likelihood (QML) procedure, which misspecifies the serial dependence structure but correctly specifies the marginal distribution of defaults in each year and still gives reasonable parameter estimates.

In practice, it is easiest to use the beta mixing distribution, since, in this case, given the group size m_t in period t, the rv M_t has a beta-binomial distribution with probability function given in (8.35). The likelihood to be maximized thus takes the form

$$L(a, b; \text{data}) = \prod_{t=1}^{n}\binom{m_t}{M_t}\frac{\beta(a + M_t, b + m_t - M_t)}{\beta(a, b)},$$

and maximization can be performed numerically with respect to a and b. For further information about the ML method consult, as usual, Section A.3. The ML estimates of $\pi = \pi_1, \pi_2$ and ρ_Y are calculated by evaluating moments of the fitted distribution using (8.34); the formulas are given in Example 8.13.

A comparison of moment estimation and ML estimation. To compare these two approaches we conduct a simulation study summarized in Table 8.7. To generate data in the simulation study we consider the beta, probit-normal and logit-normal mixture models of Section 8.4.1. In any single experiment we generate 20 years of data using parameter values that roughly correspond to one of the Standard & Poor's credit ratings CCC, B or BB (see Table 8.6 for the parameter values). The number of firms m_t in each of the years is generated randomly using a binomial-beta model to give a spread of values typical of real data; the defaults are then generated using one of the Bernoulli mixture models and estimates of π, π_2 and ρ_Y are calculated. The experiment is repeated 5000 times and a relative root mean square error (RRMSE) is estimated for each parameter and each method: that is, we take the square root of the estimated MSE and divide by the true parameter value. Methods are compared by calculating the percentage increase of the estimated RRMSE with respect to the better method (i.e. the RRMSE minimizing method) for each parameter.

It may be concluded from Table 8.7 that the ML method is better in all but one experiment. Surprisingly, it is better even in the experiments when it is misspecified and the true mixing distribution is either probit-normal or logit-normal; in fact, in these cases, it offers more of an improvement than in the beta case. This can partly be explained by the fact that when we constrain well-behaved, unimodal mixing distributions with densities to have the same first and second moments, these distributions are very similar (see Figure 8.3). Finally, we observe that the ML method tends to outperform the moment method more as we increase the credit quality, so that defaults become rarer.

8.6.3 Mixture Models as GLMMs

A one-factor Bernoulli mixture model. Recall the simple one-factor model (8.36) generalizing the exchangeable model in Section 8.4.1. Rewriting slightly, this has the form

$$p_i(\Psi) = h(\mu + \boldsymbol{\beta}'\boldsymbol{x}_i + \Psi), \tag{8.62}$$

where h is a link function, the vector $\boldsymbol{x}_i$ contains covariates for the ith firm, such as indicators for group membership or key balance sheet ratios, and $\boldsymbol{\beta}$ and μ are model parameters. Examples of link functions include the standard normal df $\Phi(x)$ and the logistic df $(1 + \exp(-x))^{-1}$. The scale parameter σ has been subsumed in the normally distributed random variable $\Psi \sim N(0, \sigma^2)$, representing a common or systematic factor.

This model can be turned into a multiperiod model for default counts in different periods, by considering that a series of mixing variables $\Psi_1, \dots, \Psi_n$ generate default dependence in each time period $t = 1, \dots, n$. The default indicator $Y_{t,i}$ for the ith company in time period t is assumed to be Bernoulli with default probability $p_{t,i}(\Psi_t)$ depending on Ψ_t according to

$$p_{t,i}(\Psi_t) = h(\mu + \boldsymbol{x}_{t,i}'\boldsymbol{\beta} + \Psi_t), \tag{8.63}$$

Table 8.7. Each part of the table relates to a block of 5000 simulations using a particular exchangeable Bernoulli mixture model with parameter values roughly corresponding to a particular S&P rating class. For each parameter of interest, an estimated RRMSE is tabulated for both estimation methods: moment estimation using (8.61) and ML estimation based on the beta model. Methods can be compared by using Δ, the percentage increase of the estimated RRMSE with respect to the better method (i.e. the RRMSE minimizing method) for each parameter. Thus, for each parameter the better method has $\Delta = 0$. The table clearly shows that MLE is better in all but one case.

			Moment		MLE-beta	
Group	True model	Parameter	RRMSE	Δ	RRMSE	Δ
CCC	Beta	π	0.101	0	0.101	0
CCC	Beta	π_2	0.202	0	0.201	0
CCC	Beta	ρ_Y	0.332	5	0.317	0
CCC	Probit-normal	π	0.100	0	0.100	0
CCC	Probit-normal	π_2	0.205	1	0.204	0
CCC	Probit-normal	ρ_Y	0.347	11	0.314	0
CCC	Logit-normal	π	0.101	0	0.101	0
CCC	Logit-normal	π_2	0.209	1	0.208	0
CCC	Logit-normal	ρ_Y	0.357	11	0.320	0
B	Beta	π	0.130	0	0.130	0
B	Beta	π_2	0.270	0	0.269	0
B	Beta	ρ_Y	0.396	8	0.367	0
B	Probit-normal	π	0.130	0	0.130	0
B	Probit-normal	π_2	0.286	3	0.277	0
B	Probit-normal	ρ_Y	0.434	19	0.364	0
B	Logit-normal	π	0.131	0	0.132	0
B	Logit-normal	π_2	0.308	7	0.289	0
B	Logit-normal	ρ_Y	0.493	26	0.392	0
BB	Beta	π	0.199	0	0.199	0
BB	Beta	π_2	0.435	0	0.438	1
BB	Beta	ρ_Y	0.508	7	0.476	0
BB	Probit-normal	π	0.197	0	0.197	0
BB	Probit-normal	π_2	0.492	10	0.446	0
BB	Probit-normal	ρ_Y	0.607	27	0.480	0
BB	Logit-normal	π	0.196	0	0.196	0
BB	Logit-normal	π_2	0.572	24	0.462	0
BB	Logit-normal	ρ_Y	0.752	45	0.517	0

where $\Psi_t \sim N(0, \sigma^2)$ and $\boldsymbol{x}_{t,i}$ are covariates for the ith company in time period t. Moreover, the default indicators $Y_{t,1}, \dots, Y_{t,m_t}$ in period t are assumed to be conditionally independent given Ψ_t.

To complete the model we need to specify the joint distribution of $\Psi_1, \dots, \Psi_n$, and it is easiest to assume that these are iid mixing variables. To capture possible economic cycle effects causing dependence between numbers of defaults in successive time periods one could either enter covariates at the level of $\boldsymbol{x}_{ti}$ that are known to be good proxies for "state of the economy", such as changes in GDP over the time period, or an index like the Chicago Fed National Activity Index (CFNAI) in the US, or one could consider a serially dependent time series structure for the systematic factors (Ψ_t).

A one-factor Poisson mixture model. When considering higher-grade portfolios of companies with relatively low default risk, there may sometimes be advantages (particularly in the stability of fitting procedures) in formulating Poisson mixture models instead of Bernoulli mixture models. A multiperiod mixture model based on Definition 8.11 can be constructed by assuming that the default count variable $\tilde{Y}_{t,i}$ for the ith company in time period t is conditionally Poisson with rate parameter $\lambda_{t,i}(\Psi_t)$ depending on Ψ_t according to

$$\lambda_{t,i}(\Psi_t) = \exp(\mu + \boldsymbol{x}'_{t,i}\boldsymbol{\beta} + \Psi_t), \tag{8.64}$$

with all other elements of the model as in (8.63). Again the variables $\tilde{Y}_{t,1}, \dots, \tilde{Y}_{t,m_t}$ are assumed to be conditionally independent given Ψ_t.

GLMMs. Both the multiperiod Bernoulli and Poisson mixture models in (8.63) and (8.64) belong to a family of widely used statistical models known as *generalized linear mixed models* (GLMMs). The three basic elements of such a model are as follows.

(1) The vector of *random effects*. In our examples this is the vector $(\Psi_1, \dots, \Psi_n)$ containing the systematic factors for each time period.

(2) A distribution from the *exponential family* for the conditional distribution of the responses ($Y_{t,i}$ or $\tilde{Y}_{t,i}$) given the random effects. Responses are assumed to be conditionally independent given the random effects. The Bernoulli, binomial and Poisson distributions all belong to the exponential family (see, for example, McCullagh and Nelder 1989, p. 28).

(3) A *link function* relating $E(Y_{t,i} \mid \Psi_t)$, the mean response conditional on the random effects, to the so-called *linear predictor*. In our examples the linear predictor for $Y_{t,i}$ is

$$\eta_{t,i}(\Psi_t) = \mu + \boldsymbol{x}'_{t,i}\boldsymbol{\beta} + \Psi_t. \tag{8.65}$$

We have considered the so-called probit and logit link functions in the Bernoulli case and the log-link function in the Poisson case. (Note that it is usual in GLMMs to write the model as $g(E(Y_{t,i} \mid \Psi_t)) = \eta_{t,i}(\Psi_t)$ and to refer to g as the link function; hence the probit link function is the quantile function of standard normal and the link in the Poisson case (8.64) is referred to as "log" rather than "exponential".)

When no random effects are modelled in a GLMM, the model is simply known as a generalized linear model or GLM. The role of the random effects in the GLMM is, in a sense, to capture patterns of variability in the responses that cannot be explained by the observed covariates alone, but which might be explained by additional unobserved factors. In our case, these unobserved factors are bundled into a time-period effect that we loosely describe as the state of the economy in that time period; alternatively, we refer to it as the systematic risk.

The GLMM framework allows models of much greater complexity. We can add further random effects to obtain multi-factor mixture models. For example, we might know the industry sector of each firm and wish to include a random effect for sector nested inside the year effect; in this way we might capture additional variability associated with economic effects in different sectors over and above the global variability associated with the year effect. Such models can be considered in the GLMM framework by allowing the linear predictor in (8.65) to take the form $\eta_{t,i}(\Psi_t) = \mu + x_{t,i}'\boldsymbol{\beta} + z_{t,i}'\boldsymbol{\Psi}_t$ for some vector of random effects $\boldsymbol{\Psi}_t = (\Psi_{t,1}, \dots, \Psi_{t,p})'$; the vector $z_{t,i}$ is a known *design element* of the model that picks out the random effects that are relevant to the response $Y_{t,i}$. We would then have a total of $p \times n$ random effects in the model. We may or may not want to model serial dependence in the time series $\boldsymbol{\Psi}_1, \dots, \boldsymbol{\Psi}_n$.

Inference for GLMMs. Full ML inference for a GLMM is only a viable option for the simplest models. Consider the form of the likelihood for the one-factor models in (8.63) and (8.64). If we write $p_{Y_{t,i}|\Psi_t}(y \mid \psi)$ for the conditional probability mass function of the response $Y_{t,i}$ (or $\tilde{Y}_{t,i}$) given Ψ_t, we have, for data $\{Y_{t,i} : t = 1, \dots, n,\ i = 1, \dots, m_t\}$,

$$L(\boldsymbol{\beta}, \sigma; \text{data}) = \int \cdots \int \biggl(\prod_{t=1}^{n} \prod_{i=1}^{m_t} p_{Y_{t,i}|\Psi_t}(Y_{t,i} \mid \psi_t)\biggr) f(\psi_1, \dots, \psi_n)\, \mathrm{d}\psi_1 \cdots \mathrm{d}\psi_n, \tag{8.66}$$

where f denotes the assumed joint density of the random effects. If we do not assume independent random effects from time period to time period, then we are faced with an n-dimensional integral (or an $(n \times p)$-dimensional integral in multi-factor models). Assuming iid Gaussian random effects with marginal Gaussian density f_Ψ, the likelihood (8.66) becomes

$$L(\boldsymbol{\beta}, \sigma; \text{data}) = \prod_{t=1}^{n} \biggl(\int \prod_{i=1}^{m_t} p_{Y_{t,i}|\Psi_t}(Y_{t,i} \mid \psi_t) f_\Psi(\psi_t)\, \mathrm{d}\psi_t\biggr), \tag{8.67}$$

so that we have a product of one-dimensional integrals and this can be easily evaluated numerically and maximized over the unknown parameters. Alternatively, faster approximate likelihood methods, such as penalized quasi-likelihood (PQL) and marginal quasi-likelihood (MQL), can be used (see Notes and Comments).

Another attractive possibility is to treat inference for these models from a Bayesian point of view and to use Markov Chain Monte Carlo (MCMC) methods to make inference about parameters. We believe that this holds particular promise for two main reasons. First, a Bayesian MCMC approach allows us to work with much more complex models than can be handled in the likelihood framework, such as a model with serially dependent random effects. Second, the Bayesian approach may be ideal for handling the considerable parameter uncertainty that we are currently faced with in portfolio credit risk, particularly in models for higher-rated counterparties where default data are scarce. In the Bayesian approach, *prior* distributions are used to express opinions about parameters before data analysis; these opinions are then updated with the help of the data and Bayes' theorem to arrive at a *posterior* distribution for the parameters. This mechanism could be used to combine the parameter information coming from non-statistical industry models with the evidence in historical data to achieve improved model calibration.

8.6.4 One-Factor Model with Rating Effect

In this section we fit a Bernoulli mixture model to annual default count data from Standard & Poor's for the period 1981–2000; these data may be easily reconstructed from published default rates in Brand and Bahr (2001, Table 13, pp. 18–21). Standard & Poor's uses the ratings AAA, AA, A, BBB, BB, B, CCC, but because the observed one-year default rates for AAA-rated and AA-rated firms are mostly zero, we concentrate on the rating categories A to CCC.

In our model we assume a single yearly random effect representing "state of the economy" and treat rating category as an observed covariate for each firm in each time period. Our model is a particular instance of the single-factor Bernoulli mixture model in (8.63) and a multiperiod extension of the model described in Example 8.14. We assume for simplicity that random effects in each year are iid normal, which allows us to use the likelihood (8.67).

Since we are able to pool companies into groups by year and rating category, we note that it is possible to reformulate the model as a binomial mixture model. Let $r = 1, \dots, 5$ index the five rating categories in our study and write $m_{t,r}$ for the number of followed companies in year t with rating r, and $M_{t,r}$ for the number of these that default. Our model assumption is that, conditional on Ψ_t (and the group sizes), the default counts $M_{t,1}, \dots, M_{t,5}$ are independent and distributed in such a way that $M_{t,r} \mid \Psi_t = \psi \sim B(m_{t,r}, p_r(\psi))$. Using the probit link the conditional default probability of an r-rated company in year t is given by

$$p_r(\Psi_t) = \Phi(\mu_r + \Psi_t). \tag{8.68}$$

The model may be fitted under the assumption of iid random effects in each year by straightforward maximization of the likelihood in (8.67). The parameter estimates and obtained standard errors are given in Table 8.8, together with the estimated default probabilities $\hat{\pi}^{(r)}$ for each rating category and estimated default correlations $\hat{\rho}_Y^{(r_1,r_2)}$ implied by the parameter estimates. Writing Ψ for a generic random effect variable, the default probability for rating category r is given by

$$\hat{\pi}^{(r)} = E(\hat{p}_r(\Psi)) = \int_{-\infty}^{\infty} \Phi(\hat{\mu}_r + \hat{\sigma} z)\phi(z)\,\mathrm{d}z, \quad 1 \leqslant r \leqslant 5,$$

where ϕ is the standard normal density. The default correlation for two firms with ratings r_1 and r_2 in the same year is calculated easily from the joint default probability for these two firms, which is

$$\hat{\pi}_2^{(r_1,r_2)} = E(\hat{p}_{r_1 1}(\Psi)\hat{p}_{r_2}(\Psi)) = \int_{-\infty}^{\infty} \Phi(\hat{\mu}_{r_1} + \hat{\sigma} z)\Phi(\hat{\mu}_{r_2} + \hat{\sigma})\phi(z)\,\mathrm{d}z.$$

Table 8.8. Maximum likelihood parameter estimates and standard errors (se) for a one-factor Bernoulli mixture model fitted to historical Standard & Poor's one-year default data, together with the implied estimates of default probabilities $\hat{\pi}^{(r)}$ and default correlations $\hat{\rho}_Y^{(r_1,r_2)}$. The MLE of the scaling parameter σ is 0.24 with standard error 0.05. Note that we have tabulated default correlation in absolute terms and not in percentage terms.

Parameter	A	BBB	BB	B	CCC	
μ_r	−3.43	−2.92	−2.40	−1.69	−0.84	
se (μ_r)	0.13	0.09	0.07	0.06	0.08	
$\pi^{(r)}$	0.000 4	0.002 3	0.009 7	0.050 3	0.207 8	
$\rho_Y^{(r_1,r_2)}$	0.000 40	0.000 77	0.001 30	0.002 19	0.003 04	A
	0.000 77	0.001 49	0.002 55	0.004 35	0.006 15	BBB
	0.001 30	0.002 55	0.004 40	0.007 63	0.010 81	BB
	0.002 19	0.004 35	0.007 63	0.013 28	0.019 06	B
	0.003 04	0.006 15	0.010 81	0.019 06	0.027 88	CCC

The default correlation is then

$$\hat{\rho}_Y^{(r_1,r_2)} = \frac{\hat{\pi}_2^{(r_1,r_2)} - \hat{\pi}^{(r_1)}\hat{\pi}^{(r_2)}}{\sqrt{(\hat{\pi}^{(r_1)} - (\hat{\pi}^{(r_1)})^2)(\hat{\pi}^{(r_2)} - (\hat{\pi}^{(r_2)})^2)}}.$$

Note that the default correlations are correlations between event indicators for very low probability events and are necessarily very small.

The model in (8.68) assumes that the variance of the systematic factor Ψ_t is the same for all firms in all years. When compared with the very general Bernoulli mixture model corresponding to CreditMetrics/KMV in (8.45), we might be concerned that the simple model considered in this section does not allow for enough heterogeneity in the variance of the systematic risk. A simple extension of the model is to allow the variance to be different for different rating categories, that is to fit a model where $p_r(\Psi_t) = \Phi(\mu_r + \sigma_r \Psi_t)$ and Ψ_t is a standard normally distributed random effect. This increases the number of parameters in the model by four, but is no more difficult to fit than the basic model. The maximized value of the log-likelihood in the model with heterogeneous scaling is −2557.4, and the value in the model with homogeneous scaling is −2557.7; a likelihood ratio test suggests that no significant improvement results from allowing heterogeneous scaling. If rating is the only categorical variable, the simple model seems adequate but, if we had more information on the industrial and geographical sectors to which the companies belonged, it would be natural to introduce further random effects for these sectors and to allow more heterogeneity in the model in this way.

The implied default probability and default correlation estimates in Table 8.8 can be a useful resource for calibrating simple credit models to homogeneous groups defined by rating. For example, to calibrate a Clayton copula to group BB we use the inputs $\pi^{(3)} = 0.0097$ and $\rho_Y^{(3,3)} = 0.004\,40$ to determine the parameter θ of the Clayton copula (see Example 8.22). Note also that we can now immediately use the scaling results of Section 8.4.3 to calculate approximate risk measures for large portfolios of companies that have been rated with the Standard & Poor's system (see Example 8.17).

Notes and Comments

The estimator (8.61) for joint default probabilities is also used in Lucas (1995) and Nagpal and Bahar (2001), although de Servigny and Renault (2002) suggest there may be problems with this estimator for groups with low default rates. A related moment-style estimator has been suggested by Gordy (2000) but it appears to have a similar performance to (8.61) (see Frey and McNeil 2003). A further paper on default correlation estimation is Gordy and Heitfield (2002).

A good overview article on generalized linear mixed models is Clayton (1996). For generalized linear models a standard reference is McCullagh and Nelder (1989) (see also Fahrmeir and Tutz 1994).

The analysis of Section 8.6.4 is very similar to the analysis in Frey and McNeil (2003) (where heterogeneous variances for each rating category were assumed). While the results reported in this book were obtained by full maximization of the likelihood with our own code, we could also have used a number of existing software packages for GLMMs. For example, we have verified that the `glme` function in the S-PLUS *correlated data* library gives very similar results using the default penalized quasi-likelihood method; for more information about penalized quasi-likelihood and the related marginal quasi-likelihood method, see Breslow and Clayton (1993). For a Bayesian approach to fitting the model using Markov chain Monte Carlo techniques, see McNeil and Wendin (2003); this approach allows fairly complicated models to be fitted, including models where the random effects have an autoregressive time series structure.

Although we have only described default models it is also possible to analyse rating migrations in the generalized linear model framework (with or without random effects). A standard model is the ordered probit model, which is used without random effects in Nickell, Perraudin and Varotto (2000) to provide evidence of time variation in default rates attributable to macroeconomic factors; a similar message is found in Bangia et al. (2002). Wendin and McNeil (2004) show how random effects may be included in such models and discuss Bayesian inference.

A further strand of the literature is the modelling of rating-transition data with Markov chain methods. Lando and Skodeberg (2002) estimate Markov chains in continuous time from Standard & Poor's data giving the exact dates of ratings transitions. They find evidence of non-Markovian behaviour in the data and raise the issue of "ratings momentum", whereby information about the previous rating history of a company beyond its current rating is predictive of the risk of downgrading. See also Chapter 4 of Lando (2004) for more information on the Markov chain approach as well as the application of survival analysis methodology to default data.

A number of authors have looked at models with latent structure to capture the dynamics of systematic risk; an example is Crowder, Davis and Giampieri (2005), who use a two-state hidden Markov structure to capture periods of high and low default risk (see also Gagliardini and Gourieroux 2005).

There is a huge amount of literature on the estimation of models for pricing credit-risky securities that uses mainly data on corporate bond prices as input: Chapter 7 of Duffie and Singleton (2003) is a good starting point. Empirical work on the calibration of credit risk models to loan data, on the other hand, is relatively sparse, which is probably related to data problems. An example of the latter type of work is Altman and Suggitt (2000).

9

Dynamic Credit Risk Models and Credit Derivatives

In this chapter we study credit risk models in continuous time and consider the pricing of credit derivatives in the framework of reduced-form models (see Section 8.1 for an overview of model types). Reduced-form models are popular in practice, since they lead to tractable formulas explaining the price of credit-risky securities in terms of economic covariates, which facilitates estimation. Moreover, with reduced-form models it is possible to apply the well-developed pricing machinery for default-free term structure models to the analysis of defaultable securities.

We begin with a brief introduction to credit derivatives in Section 9.1. These products have become indispensable tools for the management of credit risk, and the corresponding markets have seen a massive growth in recent years. We continue with two preparatory sections: Section 9.2 contains *mathematical tools* for reduced-form models; Section 9.3 briefly introduces key concepts from *mathematical finance*, thereby providing the methodological basis for our analysis. Particular attention will be given to the distinction between real-world and risk-neutral default probabilities. Sections 9.4 and 9.5 review standard but indispensable material on the *pricing of defaultable securities* in reduced-form models; in particular, the relationship between pricing problems for defaultable and default-free securities is discussed. Sections 9.6–9.8 are devoted to reduced-form models for credit *portfolios*. We begin with models with *conditionally independent defaults*. In this model class, default times are independent given the realization of some observable economic background process, making these models a straightforward extension of the static Bernoulli mixture models discussed in Chapter 8. More sophisticated models, where there is *interaction between defaults* in the sense that the default of one firm influences the conditional survival probability of the remaining firms in the portfolio, are discussed thereafter.

In this book we have so far concentrated on static or discrete-time models and risk-management issues; continuous-time models and the pricing of derivatives have played only a minor role. In this chapter we make an exception for a number of reasons. First, credit risk management and credit derivatives are intimately linked. In fact, the quest of financial institutions for better tools to manage and diversify the credit risk in their portfolios and the recent developments in the regulation of credit risk are the main drivers of the tremendous growth of the credit derivatives market that we are currently witnessing. Since the pay-off of most credit derivatives depends on the timing of default, dynamic credit risk models are clearly needed to analyse these products. Second, the pricing of portfolio credit derivatives is a key area of application for many of the concepts for modelling dependent risks discussed in this book; in particular, copulas play a prominent role. Third, dynamic models of portfolio credit risk have recently generated a lot of interest in academia and in industry, and we want to offer our readership an introduction to the field.

Credit risk modelling is a large area that cannot be covered in a few chapters, and consequently we have had to omit a lot of interesting and relevant material. Important omissions include advanced firm-value models (other than Merton); continuous-time models for rating transitions; an analysis of credit risk in interest-rate swaps; and forward-rate models of Heath–Jarrow–Morton type for corporate bonds. The main reason for these omissions is our decision to focus on the growing field of dynamic portfolio credit risk models. Much of the material in this area is of recent vintage and to our knowledge has not been discussed extensively at textbook level before.

There are several full textbook treatments of dynamic credit risk models including Bielecki and Rutkowski (2002), Bluhm, Overbeck and Wagner (2002), Duffie and Singleton (2003), Lando (2004) and Schönbucher (2003). Excellent survey articles include Schmidt and Stute (2004) and Giesecke (2004). While each text has a different focus, some overlap with the material treated here is unavoidable and will be indicated, together with suggestions for further reading, in Notes and Comments of the respective sections.

9.1 Credit Derivatives

9.1.1 Overview

We find it convenient to divide the universe of credit-risky securities into three different types: *vulnerable claims*, *single-name credit derivatives*, and *portfolio-related credit derivatives*. Vulnerable claims are securities whose promised pay-off is not linked to credit events, but whose issuer may default. Hence the actual pay-off received by the buyer of the security (for instance, a counterparty in a swap transaction) is adversely affected by the default of the issuer. Important examples include corporate bonds and interest-rate swaps. While the pricing of certain vulnerable claims raises challenging issues, these products are of no concern to us here, as credit risk is not their primary focus; some references can be found in Notes and Comments.

Credit derivatives are securities which are primarily used for the management and trading of credit risk. In the case of a single-name credit derivative the promised pay-off depends on the occurrence of a credit event affecting a single financial entity; otherwise the pay-off is related to credit events in a whole portfolio. Credit derivatives are a fairly young asset class and the market continues to evolve, with new products appearing frequently. Credit derivatives are traded over the counter, so the precise pay-off specification may vary a lot between contracts of similar type. Nonetheless, due to efforts of bodies such as the International Swap Dealers

Association (ISDA), in recent years some standardization has taken place. Credit derivatives have become popular because they help financial firms to manage the credit risk on their books by dispersing parts of it through the wider financial sector, thereby reducing concentration of risk. In fact, the widespread use of these instruments may have enhanced the resilience of the overall financial system. In this context the following remarks made by Alan Greenspan in his speech before the Council on Foreign Relations in November 2002 (see Section 1.4.1) are of interest.

> More recently, instruments ... such as credit default swaps, collateralized debt obligations and credit-linked notes have been developed and their use has grown rapidly in recent years. The result? Improved credit risk management together with more and better risk-management tools appear to have significantly reduced loan concentrations in telecommunications and, indeed, other areas and the associated stress on banks and other financial institutions.
>
> More generally, such instruments appear to have effectively spread losses from defaults by Enron, Global Crossing, Railtrack, WorldCom, Swissair, and sovereign Argentinian credits over the past year to a wider set of banks than might previously have been the case in the past, and from banks, which have largely short-term leverage, to insurance firms, pension funds or others with diffuse long-term liabilities or no liabilities at all. Many sellers of credit risk protection, as one might presume, have experienced large losses, but because of significant capital, they were able to avoid the widespread defaults of earlier periods of stress. It is noteworthy that payouts in the still relatively small but rapidly growing market in credit derivatives have been proceeding smoothly for the most part. Obviously this market is still too new to have been tested in a widespread down-cycle for credit, but, to date, it appears to have functioned well.

Major participants in the market for credit derivatives are banks, insurance companies and investment funds. Banks are typically net buyers of protection against credit events; insurance companies and other investors are net sellers of credit protection.

9.1.2 Single-Name Credit Derivatives

Credit default swaps. Credit default swaps (CDSs) are the workhorse of the credit derivatives market; according to a study by Patel (2002), in 2002 the market share of CDSs in the credit derivatives market was approximately 67%. Hence the market for CDSs written on larger corporations is fairly liquid. Moreover, in contrast to corporate bonds, the profitability of CDSs is barely affected by tax issues. For these reasons CDSs are the natural underlying security for many more complex credit derivatives, and models for pricing portfolio-related credit derivatives are usually calibrated to quoted CDS spreads (see Section 9.3.3 below for details).

The basic structure of a CDS is depicted in Figure 9.1. There are three parties involved in a CDS: the *reference entity*, the *protection buyer* and the *protection*

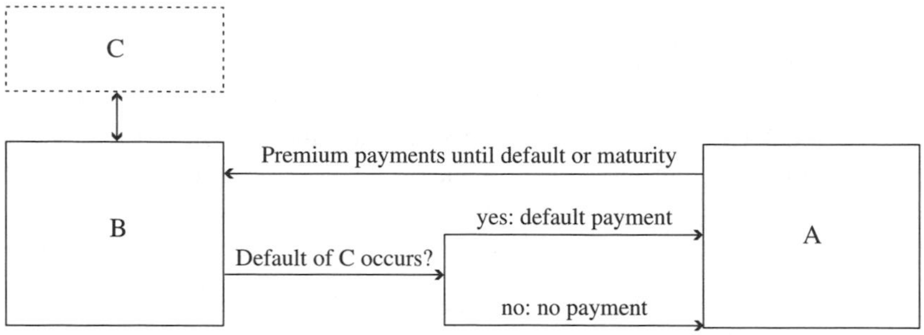

Figure 9.1. The basic structure of a CDS. Firm C is the reference entity, firm A is the protection buyer, and firm B is the protection seller.

seller. If the reference entity experiences a default event before the maturity date T of the contract, the protection seller makes a default payment to the protection buyer, which mimics the loss on a security issued by the reference entity (often a corporate bond) due to the default; this part of a CDS is called the *default payment leg*. In this way the protection buyer has acquired financial protection against the loss on the reference asset he would incur in case of a default; note, however, that the protection buyer is not obliged to hold the reference asset. As a compensation the protection buyer makes a periodic premium payment (typically quarterly or semiannually) to the protection seller (the *premium payment leg*); after the default of the reference entity, premium payments stop. There is no initial payment. The premium payments are quoted in the form of an annualized percentage x^* of the notional value of the reference asset; x^* is termed the (fair or market quoted) *CDS spread*. For a mathematical description of the payments, see Section 9.3.3 below.

There are a number of technical and legal issues in the specification of a CDS. In particular, the parties have to agree on the precise definition of a default event and on a procedure to determine the size of the default payment in case a default event of the reference entity occurs. Note that a CDS is traded over the counter and is not guaranteed by some clearing house. Hence it is possible that the protection seller itself defaults before the maturity of the contract, in which case the default protection acquired by the protection buyer becomes worthless.

Credit-linked notes. A credit-linked note is a combination of a credit derivative and a coupon bond that is sold as a fixed package. The coupon payments (and sometimes also the repayment of the principal) are reduced if a third party (the reference entity) experiences a default event during the lifetime of the contract, so the buyer of a credit-linked note is providing credit protection for the seller. Credit-linked notes are issued essentially for two reasons. First, from a legal point of view, a credit-linked note is treated as a fixed-income investment, so that investors who are unable to enter into a transaction involving credit derivatives directly may nonetheless sell credit protection by buying credit-linked notes. Second, an investor buying a credit-linked note pays the price up front, so that the credit protection sale is *fully collaterized*, i.e. the protection buyer (the issuer of the credit-linked note) is protected against losses caused by the default of the protection seller.

9.1.3 Portfolio Credit Derivatives

Notation. In order to describe the pay-off of portfolio credit derivatives we introduce some notation. We consider a portfolio with m firms. The random vector $Y_t = (Y_{t,1}, \dots, Y_{t,m})'$ describes the state of our portfolio at time $t \geqslant 0$. In keeping with the notation introduced in Chapter 8, $Y_{t,i} = 1$ if firm i has defaulted up to time t, and $Y_{t,i} = 0$ otherwise; $(Y_{t,i})$ is termed the *default indicator process* of firm i. The default time of firm i is denoted by $\tau_i > 0$. Assuming that there are no simultaneous defaults in our portfolio, we may define the *ordered default times* $T_0 < T_1 < \dots < T_m$ recursively by $T_0 = 0$ and, for $1 \leqslant n \leqslant m$, $T_n = \min\{\tau_i : \tau_i > T_{n-1},\ 1 \leqslant i \leqslant m\}$. By $\xi_n \in \{1, \dots, m\}$ we denote the identity of the firm defaulting at time T_n, i.e. $\xi_n = i$ if $\tau_i = T_n$. As in Chapter 8, the exposure to reference entity i is denoted by e_i; the percentage loss given default of firm i is denoted by $\delta_i \in [0, 1]$. The cumulative loss of the portfolio up to time t is thus given by $L_t = \sum_{i=1}^{m} \delta_i e_i Y_{t,i}$.

Basket default swaps. Basket default swaps, or, more technically, kth-to-default swaps, offer protection against the kth default in a portfolio with $m > k$ obligors (the basket). As in the case of an ordinary CDS the premium payments on a kth-to-default swap take the form of a periodic payment stream, which stops at the kth default time T_k. The default payment is triggered if T_k is smaller than the maturity date of the swap; the size of the default payment may depend on the identity ξ_k of the kth defaulting firm. While first-to-default swaps are traded frequently, higher-order default swaps are encountered only occasionally in real markets. We discuss the pricing of first-to-default swaps in Sections 9.6.3 and 9.8.1 below.

Collaterized debt obligations (CDOs). CDOs are, at the time of writing, the most important class of portfolio credit derivatives. A CDO is a financial instrument for the securitization of credit-risky securities related to a pool of reference entities such as bonds, loans or protection-seller positions in single-name CDSs; these securities form the *asset side* of the CDO. While many different types of CDO exist, the basic structure is the same. The assets are sold to a so-called *special-purpose vehicle* (SPV), a company that has been set up with the single purpose of carrying out the securitization deal. To finance the acquisition of the assets, the SPV issues notes belonging to tranches of different seniorities, which form the *liability side* of the structure. This amounts to a repackaging of the assets. The tranches of the liability side are called (in order of increasing seniority) equity, mezzanine and senior (sometimes also super-senior) tranches. In this way most of the losses on the asset side generated by credit events are borne by the equity tranche, so the notes issued by the SPV belonging to the more senior tranches have a credit rating which is substantially higher than the average credit quality of the asset pool. This makes the notes attractive to certain investor classes.

If the asset side consists mainly of bonds and loans, one speaks of asset-based structures; if the underlying asset pool consists mainly of protection-seller positions in single-name CDSs, the structure is termed *synthetic CDO*. The cash-flows of a synthetic CDO are slightly different from those of an asset-based CDO: on the asset

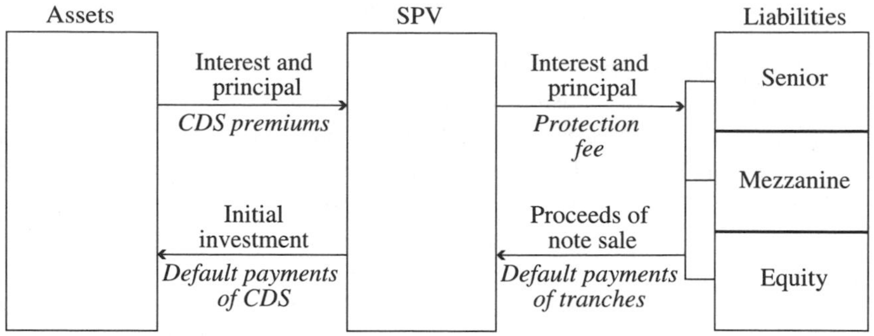

Figure 9.2. Schematic representation of the payments in a CDO structure. Payments corresponding to synthetic CDOs are indicated in italics.

side the SPV receives the premium payments on the CDSs in the asset pool and makes the corresponding default payments; on the liability side the SPV receives default payments from the noteholders, which are triggered by credit events in the asset pool, and makes periodic premium payments as a compensation. The payments associated with a typical CDO are depicted schematically in Figure 9.2.

Asset-based structures where the asset pool consists mainly of bonds are known as collaterized bond obligation (CBO); if the asset side consists mainly of loans, a CDO is termed collaterized loan obligation (CLO). If the underlying asset pool is actively traded with the goal of enhancing its value, a CDO structure is known as an *arbitrage CDO*; if the asset side remains relatively constant during the lifetime of the structure, one speaks of a *balance-sheet CDO*. Necessarily the asset pool of an arbitrage CDO consists of tradable securities such as bonds or CDSs.

There are a number of economic motivations for arranging a CDO transaction.

- The proceeds from the sale of the notes issued by the SPV are often higher than the initial value of the asset side of the structure, as the risk–return profile of the notes is more favourable for investors. Similarly, in a synthetic CDO the present value of the premium payments received by the SPV may exceed the present value of the premium payments the SPV has to make. Arbitrage CDOs are set up with the explicit purpose of exploiting this difference.
- Balance-sheet CDOs are often set up by banks who want to sell some of the credit-risky securities on their balance sheet in order to reduce their regulatory capital requirements; this is the typical motivation for arranging a balance-sheet CLO transaction. In this way a bank can free up regulatory capital.

Stylized CDOs. Existing CDO contracts can be quite complicated. We therefore discuss only stylized CDOs, as this allows us to gain a better understanding of the main qualitative features of these products without getting bogged down in institutional details. We consider a portfolio of m different firms with cumulative loss $L_t = \sum_{i=1}^m \delta_i e_i Y_{t,i}$. We consider a CDO with k tranches, indexed by $\kappa \in \{1, \dots, k\}$, and characterized by *attachment points* $0 = K_0 < K_1 < \cdots < K_k \leqslant \sum_{i=1}^m e_i$. The value of the *notional* corresponding to tranche κ can be described as follows. Initially, the notional is equal to $K_\kappa - K_{\kappa-1}$; it is reduced whenever there is a default event such that the cumulative loss falls in the layer $[K_{\kappa-1}, K_\kappa]$. In mathematical terms, $N_\kappa(t)$, the notional of tranche κ at time t, is given by

$$N_\kappa(t) = f_\kappa(L_t) \quad \text{with } f_\kappa(l) = \begin{cases} K_\kappa - K_{\kappa-1}, & \text{for } l < K_{\kappa-1}, \\ K_\kappa - l, & \text{for } l \in [K_{\kappa-1}, K_\kappa], \\ 0, & \text{for } l > K_\kappa. \end{cases} \tag{9.1}$$

Note that f_κ can be written more succinctly as $f_\kappa(l) = (K_\kappa - l)^+ - (K_{\kappa-1} - l)^+$, i.e. the notional is equal to the sum of a long position in a put option on L_t with strike price K_κ and a short position in a put with strike price $K_{\kappa-1}$. Such positions are sometimes called a *put spread.*

In a stylized CDO with maturity T as considered here, the pay-off of tranche κ is equal to $N_\kappa(T)$. In Figure 9.3 we have graphed the pay-off for a stylized CDO with three tranches (equity, mezzanine, senior) on a homogeneous portfolio of $m = 1000$ firms, each with exposure one unit. The attachment points are $K_1 = 20$, $K_2 = 40$, $K_3 = 60$, corresponding to 2%, 4% and 6% of the overall exposure; tranches with higher attachment points are ignored. Assuming that T equals one year and that we have a homogeneous portfolio with $\delta_i = 0.5$ for all firms, we have plotted two distributions for L_1: first, a loss distribution corresponding to a one-year default probability of 0.5% and a default correlation of 2%; second, a loss distribution with a one-year default probability of 0.5% but with independent defaults. In both cases the expected loss is given by $E(L_1) = 25$. Figure 9.3 illustrates how the value of different CDO-tranches depends on the nature of the dependence between default events.

- For independent defaults, L_1 is typically close to its mean duc to diversification effects within the portfolio. Hence it is quite unlikely that a tranche κ with lower attachment point $K_{\kappa-1}$ substantially larger than $E(L_1)$ (such as the senior tranche in Figure 9.3) suffers a loss, so the value of such a tranche is quite high. On the other hand, since the attachment point K_1 of the equity tranche is typically lower than $E(L_1)$, it is quite unlikely that L_1 is substantially smaller than K_1, and the value of the equity tranche is low.

- If defaults are (strongly) dependent, diversification effects in the portfolio are less pronounced. Realizations with L_1 bigger than the lower attachment point K_2 of the senior tranche are more likely, as are realizations with L_1 smaller than the upper attachment point K_1 of the equity tranche. This reduces the value of tranches with high seniority and increases the value of the equity tranche compared with the case with (almost) independent defaults.

The impact of changing default correlations on mezzanine tranches is unclear and cannot be predicted up front. The relationship between default dependence and the value of CDO tranches carries over to the more complex structures that are actually traded, so dependence modelling is a key issue in any model for pricing CDO tranches.

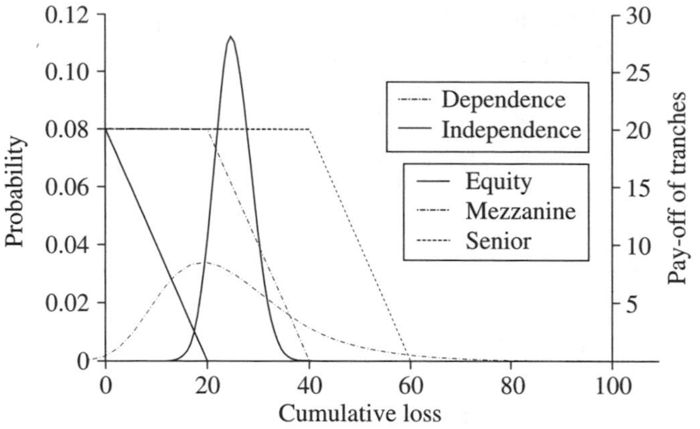

Figure 9.3. Pay-off of a stylized CDO contract and distribution of the one-year loss L_1 for a default probability of 0.5% and different default correlations. Detailed explanations are given in the text.

Notes and Comments

In this brief introduction we have discussed a few essential features of credit derivatives, but have omitted the rather involved regulatory, legal and accounting issues related to these instruments. Reader interested in these topics are referred to the book by Tavakoli (2001) or the recent paper collections edited by Gregory (2003) and Perraudin (2004); the last two references also discuss pricing issues. An excellent treatment of credit derivatives at textbook level is Schönbucher (2003). The pricing of interest swaps in the presence of default risk is discussed, for example, in Chapter 7 of Lando (2004); a good starting point for tackling the rich literature on pricing convertible bonds with credit risk is Chapter 9 of Duffie and Singleton (2003).

The credit derivatives market is evolving rapidly and new publications on these instruments appear on a regular basis. The excellent website www.defaultrisk.com, maintained by Greg Gupton, is a good place to look for new developments.

9.2 Mathematical Tools

In this section we present some mathematical tools for the analysis of reduced-form credit risk models. In particular, we discuss random times (in applications, usually the default time of a firm), hazard rates and martingale intensities. We start with random times with deterministic hazard rates or, alternatively, with a situation where the only observable quantity is the default time itself. This forms the basis for an analysis of a more realistic situation where additional information, generated for instance by economic background processes, is available, so the hazard rate will typically be stochastic. We give a detailed treatment of doubly stochastic random times. Doubly stochastic random times are the simplest example of random times with stochastic hazard rates and are thus frequently used in dynamic credit risk models.

In our analysis we inevitably have to use basic notions from the theory of stochastic processes, such as filtrations, stopping times or basic martingale theory. These issues are covered in many standard textbooks on mathematical finance and probability theory. For our purposes the technical level of Williams (1991) is sufficient.

In this chapter we use the following notational convention. A generic stochastic process in continuous time is denoted by (X_t); the rv X_t gives the value of the process at time $t \geqslant 0$. Deterministic functions of time are denoted $f(t)$ for $t \geqslant 0$. For typographical reasons the notation $X(t)$ is occasionally used for random quantities as well. While this notation differs slightly from the conventions introduced in Chapter 2, no confusion can arise, as we are dealing exclusively with continuous-time processes.

9.2.1 Random Times and Hazard Rates

We consider a probability space $(\Omega, \mathcal{F}, P)$ and a random time τ defined on this space, i.e. an $\mathcal{F}$-measurable rv taking values in $[0, \infty]$, to be interpreted as the default time of some company. By $F(t) = P(\tau \leqslant t)$ we denote the df of τ and by $\bar{F}(t) := 1 - F(t)$ the tail or survival function of τ; we assume that $P(\tau = 0) = F(0) = 0$, and that $\bar{F}(t) > 0$ for all $t < \infty$. We define the jump or default indicator process (Y_t) associated with τ by $Y_t = I_{\{\tau \leqslant t\}}$ for $t \geqslant 0$. Note that (Y_t) is a right-continuous process which jumps from 0 to 1 at the default time τ and that $1 - Y_t = I_{\{\tau > t\}}$.

A *filtration* $(\mathcal{F}_t)$ on $(\Omega, \mathcal{F})$ is an increasing family $\{\mathcal{F}_t : t \geqslant 0\}$ of sub-σ-algebras of $\mathcal{F}$: $\mathcal{F}_t \subset \mathcal{F}_s \subset \mathcal{F}$ for $0 \leqslant t \leqslant s < \infty$. For a generic filtration $(\mathcal{F}_t)$ we set $\mathcal{F}_\infty = \sigma(\bigcup_{t \geqslant 0} \mathcal{F}_t)$. Filtrations are used to model the flow of information in a random system. $\mathcal{F}_t$ represents the state of knowledge of an observer at time t, and $A \in \mathcal{F}_t$ is taken to mean that at time t the observer is able to determine if the event A has occurred. In this section we assume that the only observable quantity is the random time τ or, equivalently, the associated jump indicator process (Y_t). The appropriate filtration is therefore given by $(\mathcal{H}_t)$ with

$$\mathcal{H}_t = \sigma(\{Y_u : u \leqslant t\}), \tag{9.2}$$

the history of the default information up to and including time t. By definition, τ is an $(\mathcal{H}_t)$-stopping time, as $\{\tau \leqslant t\} = \{Y_t = 1\} \in \mathcal{H}_t$ for all $t \geqslant 0$; moreover, $(\mathcal{H}_t)$ is obviously the smallest filtration with this property.

Definition 9.1 (cumulative hazard function and hazard rate). The function $\Gamma(t) := -\ln(\bar{F}(t))$ is called the *cumulative hazard function* of the random time τ. If F is absolutely continuous with density f, the function $\gamma(t) := f(t)/(1 - F(t)) = f(t)/\bar{F}(t)$ is called the *hazard rate* of τ.

By definition we have $F(t) = 1 - \mathrm{e}^{-\Gamma(t)}$ and $\Gamma'(t) = f(t)/\bar{F}(t) = \gamma(t)$, so $\Gamma(t) = \int_0^t \gamma(s)\,\mathrm{d}s$. The hazard rate $\gamma(t)$ can be interpreted as the instantaneous chance of default at t, given survival up to time t. In fact, for $h > 0$ we have $P(\tau \leqslant t + h \mid \tau > t) = (F(t+h) - F(t))/\bar{F}(t)$. Hence we obtain

$$\lim_{h \to 0} \frac{1}{h} P(\tau \leqslant t + h \mid \tau > t) = \frac{1}{\bar{F}(t)} \lim_{h \to 0} \frac{F(t+h) - F(t)}{h} = \gamma(t).$$

Example 9.2. Consider two popular distributions for survival times: the exponential distribution and the Weibull distribution. Recall that the df of the exponential distribution with parameter λ equals $F(t) = 1 - \mathrm{e}^{-\lambda t}$, so that $\gamma(t) = \lambda$ for all $t > 0$. The df of the Weibull distribution is given by $F(t) = 1 - \exp(-\lambda t^{\alpha})$ for parameters $\lambda, \alpha > 0$. This yields $f(t) = \lambda\alpha t^{\alpha-1}\exp(-\lambda t^{\alpha})$ and $\gamma(t) = \lambda\alpha t^{\alpha-1}$, which is decreasing in t if $\alpha < 1$ and increasing if $\alpha > 1$. For $\alpha = 1$ we have the special case of the exponential distribution.

Next we discuss conditional expectations with respect to the σ-algebra $\mathcal{H}_t$. We need the following auxiliary result on the structure of $\mathcal{H}_t$-measurable rvs.

Lemma 9.3. *Every $\mathcal{H}_t$-measurable rv H is of the form $H = h(\tau)I_{\{\tau\leqslant t\}} + cI_{\{\tau>t\}}$ for a measurable function $h : [0, t] \to \mathbb{R}$ and some constant $c \in \mathbb{R}$.*

Proof. Intuitively the result is obvious, since $\mathcal{H}_t$-measurable rvs can be expressed as functions of events related to the default history at t. More formally, we argue as follows. The σ-algebra $\mathcal{H}_t$ is generated by the events $\{Y_u = 1\} = \{\tau \leqslant u\}$, $u < t$, and $\{Y_t = 0\} = \{\tau > t\}$, and hence by the rvs $\min\{\tau, t\} =: (\tau \wedge t)$ and $I_{\{\tau>t\}}$. This implies that any $\mathcal{H}_t$-measurable rv H can be written as $H = g(\tau \wedge t, I_{\{\tau>t\}})$ for some measurable function $g : [0, t] \times \{0, 1\} \to \mathbb{R}$. The claim follows if we define $h(u) := g(u, 0)$, $u \leqslant t$, and $c := g(t, 1)$. □

Lemma 9.4. *Let τ be a random time with jump indicator process $Y_t = I_{\{\tau\leqslant t\}}$ and natural filtration $(\mathcal{H}_t)$. Then, for any integrable rv X and any $t \geqslant 0$, we have*

$$E(I_{\{\tau>t\}}X \mid \mathcal{H}_t) = I_{\{\tau>t\}}\frac{E(X; \tau > t)}{P(\tau > t)}. \tag{9.3}$$

Proof. Since $E(I_{\{\tau>t\}}X \mid \mathcal{H}_t)$ is $\mathcal{H}_t$-measurable and zero on $\{\tau \leqslant t\}$, we obtain from Lemma 9.3 that $E(I_{\{\tau>t\}}X \mid \mathcal{H}_t) = I_{\{\tau>t\}}c$ for some constant c. Taking expectations yields $E(X; \tau > t) = cP(\tau > t)$ and hence $c = E(X; \tau > t)/P(\tau > t)$. □

As an example we compute conditional survival probabilities. Taking $X := I_{\{\tau>s\}}$ for $s > t$ in (9.3), we get

$$P(\tau > s \mid \mathcal{H}_t) = E(X \mid \mathcal{H}_t) = E(I_{\{\tau>t\}}X \mid \mathcal{H}_t) = I_{\{\tau>t\}}\frac{\bar{F}(s)}{\bar{F}(t)}. \tag{9.4}$$

The next proposition contains the first result on the stochastic-process properties of the jump indicator process of a random time τ. Let $(\mathcal{F}_t)$ be a generic filtration. An $(\mathcal{F}_t)$-adapted and integrable process (M_t) is called an *$(\mathcal{F}_t)$-martingale* if $E(M_s \mid \mathcal{F}_t) = M_t$ for all $0 \leqslant t \leqslant s$, i.e. if the current value M_t is the best prediction (in the mean square sense) of the future value M_s.

Proposition 9.5. *Let τ be a random time with absolutely continuous df $F(t)$ and hazard-rate function $\gamma(t)$. Then $M_t := Y_t - \int_0^{t\wedge\tau}\gamma(s)\,\mathrm{d}s$, $t \geqslant 0$, is an (H_t)-martingale.*

Here and below $\tau \wedge t$ is short for $\min\{\tau, t\}$. In Section 9.2.3 we extend this result to doubly stochastic random times and discuss its financial and mathematical relevance.

Proof. Let $s > t$. We have to show that $E(M_s - M_t \mid \mathcal{H}_t) = 0$, i.e. that $E(Y_s - Y_t \mid \mathcal{H}_t) = E(\int_t^s \gamma(u) I_{\{u<\tau\}}\, du \mid \mathcal{H}_t)$. Using (9.4), we get

$$E(Y_s - Y_t \mid \mathcal{H}_t) = I_{\{\tau>t\}} P(\tau \leqslant s \mid \mathcal{H}_t) = I_{\{\tau>t\}}\left(1 - \frac{\bar{F}(s)}{\bar{F}(t)}\right)$$
$$= I_{\{\tau>t\}} \frac{\bar{F}(t) - \bar{F}(s)}{\bar{F}(t)}.$$

Note that $X := \int_t^s \gamma(u) I_{\{u<\tau\}}\, du$ is zero on $\{\tau \leqslant t\}$, so $X = X I_{\{\tau>t\}}$. Hence we obtain from Lemma 9.4, Fubini's Theorem and the identity $\bar{F}'(t) = -f(t) = -\gamma(t)\bar{F}(t)$ that

$$E(X \mid \mathcal{H}_t) = I_{\{\tau>t\}} \frac{E(X)}{\bar{F}(t)} = I_{\{\tau>t\}} \frac{\int_t^s \gamma(u)\bar{F}(u)\, du}{\bar{F}(t)} = I_{\{\tau>t\}} \frac{\bar{F}(t) - \bar{F}(s)}{\bar{F}(t)},$$

and the result follows. □

9.2.2 Modelling Additional Information

We now consider a situation where additional information affecting the distribution of τ is available. In the context of credit risk models this information is typically generated by background processes, often modelled as diffusions or continuous-time Markov chains, representing, for instance, economic activity in a country or in an industry sector, risk-free interest rates or rating transitions between non-default states. Formally, we represent this additional information by some filtration $(\mathcal{F}_t)$ on $(\Omega, \mathcal{F}, P)$.

Definition 9.6 (cumulative hazard and hazard-rate processes). Let τ be a random time on the filtered probability space $(\Omega, \mathcal{F}, (\mathcal{F}_t), P)$ with $P(\tau > 0) = 1$. Let $F_t = P(\tau \leqslant t \mid \mathcal{F}_t)$ and $\bar{F}_t = 1 - F_t$. If $F_t < 1$ for all $t \geqslant 0$, the $(\mathcal{F}_t)$-conditional cumulative hazard process (Γ_t) is defined by $\Gamma_t := -\ln(\bar{F}_t)$. If (Γ_t) is strictly increasing and absolutely continuous, i.e. $\Gamma_t = \int_0^t \gamma_s\, ds$ for some a.s. strictly positive, $(\mathcal{F}_t)$-adapted process (γ_t), then we call (γ_t) the $(\mathcal{F}_t)$-conditional hazard-rate process of τ.

Recall the definition of the filtration $(\mathcal{H}_t)$ in (9.2) and introduce a new filtration $(\mathcal{G}_t)$ by

$$\mathcal{G}_t = \mathcal{F}_t \vee \mathcal{H}_t, \quad t \geqslant 0, \tag{9.5}$$

meaning that $\mathcal{G}_t$ is the smallest σ-algebra that contains $\mathcal{F}_t$ and $\mathcal{H}_t$. Obviously τ is an $(\mathcal{H}_t)$ stopping time and hence also a $(\mathcal{G}_t)$-stopping time. In the context of credit risk models the filtration $(\mathcal{G}_t)$ contains information about the background processes and the occurrence or non-occurrence of default up to time t, and thus typically corresponds to the information available to investors.

Remark 9.7. The notion of an $(\mathcal{F}_t)$-conditional hazard-rate process is most useful for the doubly stochastic random times discussed in Section 9.2.3 below. Note that if we assume that $F_t < 1$ for all $t > 0$ so that (Γ_t) is well defined, τ cannot be an $(\mathcal{F}_t)$-stopping time. Otherwise we would have $F_t = P(\tau \leqslant t \mid \mathcal{F}_t) = I_{\{\tau \leqslant t\}} \in \{0, 1\}$, as $\{\tau \leqslant t\} \in \mathcal{F}_t$ by the definition of a stopping time. An important example of a random time, which does not admit a conditional cumulative hazard process, is provided by the first exit time of Brownian motion from some layer. More precisely, let (W_t) be standard Brownian motion and let $(\mathcal{F}_t)$ be the filtration generated by (W_t). Consider some threshold $a < 0$ and define $\tau_a = \inf\{t \geqslant 0 : W_t \leqslant a\}$. It is well known that τ_a is an $(\mathcal{F}_t)$-stopping time, so the $(\mathcal{F}_t)$-conditional cumulative hazard process is not well defined. A similar argument shows that the default time in a first-passage-time model (see Section 8.2) does not admit a cumulative hazard process (with respect to the filtration generated by the firm-value process); hence the results derived below do not apply to those models.

Conditional expectations. Next we extend the results of Section 9.2.1 and discuss the structure of conditional expectations with respect to the full-information σ-algebra $\mathcal{G}_t$. We need the following auxiliary result on the relationship between the σ-algebras $\mathcal{F}_t$ and $\mathcal{G}_t$.

Lemma 9.8. *For every $\mathcal{G}_t$-measurable rv X there is some $\mathcal{F}_t$-measurable rv $\tilde{X}$ such that $XI_{\{\tau>t\}} = \tilde{X}I_{\{\tau>t\}}$.*

In economic terms this result tells us that before default all information is generated by the background filtration $(\mathcal{F}_t)$; we omit a formal proof. Now we turn to conditional expectations with respect to $\mathcal{G}_t$.

Lemma 9.9. *For every integrable rv X we have*

$$E(I_{\{\tau>t\}}X \mid \mathcal{G}_t) = I_{\{\tau>t\}}\frac{E(I_{\{\tau>t\}}X \mid \mathcal{F}_t)}{P(\tau > t \mid \mathcal{F}_t)}.$$

Note that Lemma 9.9 allows us to replace certain conditional expectations with respect to $\mathcal{G}_t$ by conditional expectations with respect to the background information $\mathcal{F}_t$.

Proof. $E(I_{\{\tau>t\}}X \mid \mathcal{G}_t)$ is $\mathcal{G}_t$-measurable and zero on $\{\tau \leqslant t\}$. By Lemma 9.8 there is therefore an $\mathcal{F}_t$-measurable rv $\tilde{Z}$ such that $E(I_{\{\tau>t\}}X \mid \mathcal{G}_t) = I_{\{\tau>t\}}\tilde{Z}$. Taking conditional expectations with respect to $\mathcal{F}_t$ yields, as $\mathcal{F}_t \subset \mathcal{G}_t$,

$$E(I_{\{\tau>t\}}X \mid \mathcal{F}_t) = P(\tau > t \mid \mathcal{F}_t)\tilde{Z}.$$

Hence $\tilde{Z} = E(I_{\{\tau>t\}}X \mid \mathcal{F}_t)/P(\tau > t \mid \mathcal{F}_t)$, which proves the lemma. □

Corollary 9.10. *Let $s > t$. If $\tilde{X}$ is integrable and $\mathcal{F}_s$-measurable, we have*

$$E(I_{\{\tau>s\}}\tilde{X} \mid \mathcal{G}_t) = I_{\{\tau>t\}}E(\mathrm{e}^{-(\Gamma_s-\Gamma_t)}\tilde{X} \mid \mathcal{F}_t).$$

Proof. Let $X := I_{\{\tau>s\}}\tilde{X}$. Since $X = I_{\{\tau>t\}}X$ (as $s > t$), Lemma 9.9 yields

$$E(I_{\{\tau>s\}}\tilde{X} \mid \mathcal{G}_t) = E(I_{\{\tau>t\}}X \mid \mathcal{G}_t) = I_{\{\tau>t\}}e^{\Gamma_t}E(I_{\{\tau>s\}}\tilde{X} \mid \mathcal{F}_t),$$

where we have used the fact that $P(\tau > t \mid \mathcal{F}_t) = e^{-\Gamma_t}$. Since $\tilde{X}$ is $\mathcal{F}_s$-measurable,

$$E(I_{\{\tau>s\}}\tilde{X} \mid \mathcal{F}_t) = E(\tilde{X}P(\tau > s \mid \mathcal{F}_s) \mid \mathcal{F}_t) = E(\tilde{X}e^{-\Gamma_s} \mid \mathcal{F}_t),$$

and the result follows. □

Corollary 9.10 will be useful in the pricing of corporate bonds. Suppose that the default time τ admits the conditional hazard-rate process (γ_t), that the default-free interest rate (r_t) is adapted to the background filtration $(\mathcal{F}_t)$, and that P represents the probability measure used for pricing (to be explained in Section 9.3). Consider a corporate zero-coupon bond with zero recovery and maturity $T > t$; at maturity its value is given by $I_{\{\tau>T\}}$. Define $\tilde{X} := \exp(-\int_t^T r_s \, ds)$; the price at time t of our bond is hence given by $E(I_{\{\tau>T\}}\tilde{X} \mid \mathcal{G}_t)$. We get, from Corollary 9.10,

$$E(I_{\{\tau>T\}}\tilde{X} \mid \mathcal{G}_t) = I_{\{\tau>t\}}E\biggl(\exp\biggl(-\int_t^T (r_s + \gamma_s) \, ds\biggr) \biggm| \mathcal{F}_t\biggr).$$

Expressions of this type are often easily computed using techniques from standard default-free term structure models (for details we refer to Sections 9.4.3 and 9.5 below).

Corollary 9.10 moreover implies that in the above setting γ_t gives a good approximation of the one-year default probability in the following sense. We have

$$P(\tau > t + 1 \mid \mathcal{G}_t) = I_{\{\tau>t\}}E\biggl(\exp\biggl(-\int_t^{t+1} \gamma_s \, ds\biggr) \biggm| \mathcal{F}_t\biggr). \tag{9.6}$$

Suppose now that the hazard rate remains relatively stable over time so that $P(\gamma_s \approx \gamma_t \text{ for all } s \in [t, t+1])$ is close to one and that $\tau > t$. Under these assumptions, the right-hand side of (9.6) is approximated reasonably well by $\exp(-\gamma_t)$. If γ_t is not too large, we thus get on $\{\tau > t\}$ for the one-year default probability

$$P(\tau < t + 1 \mid \mathcal{G}_t) \approx 1 - \exp(-\gamma_t) \approx \gamma_t. \tag{9.7}$$

9.2.3 Doubly Stochastic Random Times

Doubly stochastic random times—also called *conditional Poisson* or *Cox* random times in the literature—are the main example of random times with a stochastic hazard rate. For our analysis of these random times we use the framework introduced in the previous section. In particular, $(\mathcal{F}_t)$ denotes the background filtration, $(\mathcal{H}_t)$ is the filtration generated by the jump indicator process associated with the random time τ, and the filtration $(\mathcal{G}_t)$ is defined by $\mathcal{G}_t = \mathcal{F}_t \vee \mathcal{H}_t$.

Definition 9.11 (doubly stochastic random time). A random time τ is called doubly stochastic with respect to the background filtration $(\mathcal{F}_t)$ if τ admits the $(\mathcal{F}_t)$-conditional hazard-rate process (γ_t), if $\Gamma_t = \int_0^t \gamma_s \, ds$ is strictly increasing, and if, for all $t > 0$,

$$P(\tau \leqslant t \mid \mathcal{F}_\infty) = P(\tau \leqslant t \mid \mathcal{F}_t). \tag{9.8}$$

Condition (9.8) is most easily interpreted if we assume that the background filtration is generated by some stochastic state variable process $(\boldsymbol{\Psi}_t)$, i.e. if $\mathcal{F}_t = \sigma(\{\boldsymbol{\Psi}_u : u \leqslant t\})$. In that case (9.8) states that, given past values $(\boldsymbol{\Psi}_u)_{u \leqslant t}$ of the state variable, the future $(\boldsymbol{\Psi}_s)_{s>t}$ does not contain any extra information for predicting the probability that τ occurs before time t. Obviously, (9.8) excludes models where the probability that $\tau \leqslant t$ depends on the future evolution $(\boldsymbol{\Psi}_s)_{s>t}$ of the state variable.

Construction and simulation via thresholds. In the next lemma we give an explicit construction of a doubly stochastic random time. This construction is very useful for simulation purposes.

Lemma 9.12. *Let E be a standard exponentially distributed rv on $(\Omega, \mathcal{F}, P)$ independent of $\mathcal{F}_\infty$, i.e. $P(E \leqslant t \mid \mathcal{F}_\infty) = 1 - \mathrm{e}^{-t}$ for all $t \geqslant 0$. Let (γ_t) be a positive $(\mathcal{F}_t)$-adapted process such that $\Gamma_t = \int_0^t \gamma_s \,\mathrm{d}s$ is strictly increasing and finite for every $t > 0$. Define the random time τ by*

$$\tau := \Gamma^{-1}(E) = \inf\{t \geqslant 0 : \Gamma_t \geqslant E\}. \tag{9.9}$$

Then τ is doubly stochastic with $(\mathcal{F}_t)$-conditional hazard-rate process (γ_t).

Proof. We have, by definition,

$$P(\tau \leqslant t \mid \mathcal{F}_\infty) = P(\Gamma_t \geqslant E \mid \mathcal{F}_\infty) = 1 - \exp(-\Gamma_t),$$

since Γ_t is $\mathcal{F}_\infty$-measurable and E is independent of $\mathcal{F}_\infty$. Moreover, since $1 - \exp(-\Gamma_t)$ is $\mathcal{F}_t$-measurable, we get, using iterated conditional expectations,

$$P(\tau \leqslant t \mid \mathcal{F}_t) = E(P(\tau \leqslant t \mid \mathcal{F}_\infty) \mid \mathcal{F}_t) = 1 - \exp(-\Gamma_t),$$

which proves the claim. □

Lemma 9.12 has a converse, which is presented next.

Lemma 9.13. *Let τ be a doubly stochastic random time with $(\mathcal{F}_t)$-conditional hazard-rate process (γ_t). Denote by $\Gamma_t = \int_0^t \gamma_s \,\mathrm{d}s$ the conditional cumulative hazard process of τ and put $E := \Gamma_\tau$. Then the rv E is standard exponentially distributed and independent of $\mathcal{F}_\infty$, and $\tau = \Gamma^{-1}(E)$ almost surely.*

Proof. Since (Γ_t) is strictly increasing by assumption, the relation $\tau = \Gamma^{-1}(E)$ is clear from the definition of E. To prove that E has the correct distribution we argue as follows:

$$P(E \leqslant t \mid \mathcal{F}_\infty) = P(\Gamma_\tau \leqslant t \mid \mathcal{F}_\infty) = P(\tau \leqslant \Gamma^{-1}(t) \mid \mathcal{F}_\infty).$$

Since τ is doubly stochastic, the last expression equals $1 - \exp(-\Gamma(\Gamma^{-1}(t))) = 1 - \mathrm{e}^{-t}$, which shows that E is independent of $\mathcal{F}_\infty$ and that it is standard exponentially distributed. □

Lemma 9.12 forms the basis for the following algorithm for the simulation of doubly stochastic random times.

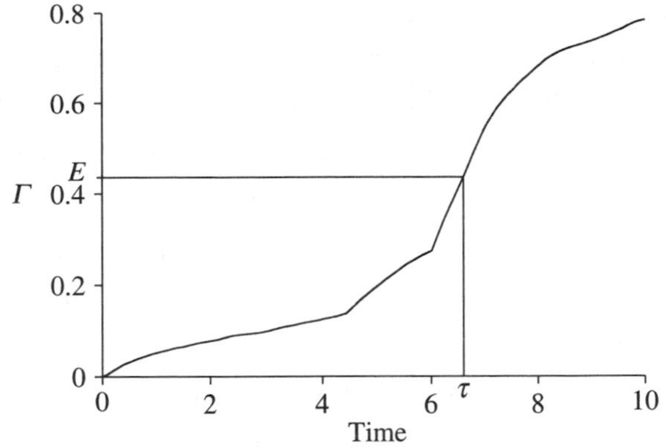

Figure 9.4. A graphical illustration of Algorithm 9.14: $E \approx 0.44$, $\tau \approx 6.59$.

Algorithm 9.14 (univariate threshold simulation).

(1) Generate a trajectory of the hazard-rate process (γ_t). References for suitable simulation approaches are given in Notes and Comments.

(2) Generate a unit exponential rv E independent of (γ_t) (the threshold) and set $\tau = \Gamma^{-1}(E)$; this step is illustrated in Figure 9.4.

Moreover, Lemmas 9.12 and 9.13 provide an interesting interpretation of doubly stochastic random times in terms of *operational time*: for a given $(\mathcal{F}_t)$-adapted hazard-rate process (γ_t), define a new timescale (operational time) by the associated cumulative hazard process $\Gamma_t = \int_0^t \gamma_s \, ds$, so that c units of operational time correspond to $\Gamma^{-1}(c)$ units of real time. Take a standard exponential rv E independent of $\mathcal{F}_\infty$ and measure time in units of operational time. Then the associated calendar time $\tau := \Gamma^{-1}(E)$ is doubly stochastic by Lemma 9.12. Conversely, by Lemma 9.13, if we take a doubly stochastic random time τ, the associated operational time $E := \Gamma_\tau$ is standard exponential, independent of $\mathcal{F}_\infty$. The notion of operational time plays an important role in insurance mathematics (see Section 10.2.7).

Martingale intensity of doubly stochastic random times. We have seen in Proposition 9.5 that the jump indicator process (Y_t) can be turned into an $(\mathcal{H}_t)$-martingale if we subtract the process $\int_0^{t \wedge \tau} \gamma(s) \, ds$. Here we generalize this result to doubly stochastic random times.

Proposition 9.15. *Let τ be a doubly stochastic random time with $(\mathcal{F}_t)$-conditional hazard-rate process (γ_t). Then $M_t := Y_t - \int_0^{t \wedge \tau} \gamma_s \, ds$ is a $(\mathcal{G}_t)$-martingale.*

Proof. Define a new artificial filtration $(\tilde{\mathcal{G}}_t)$ by $\tilde{\mathcal{G}}_t = \mathcal{F}_\infty \vee \mathcal{H}_t$; in particular, $\tilde{\mathcal{G}}_0 = \mathcal{F}_\infty$ and $\mathcal{G}_t \subset \tilde{\mathcal{G}}_t$ for all t. Conditioning on $\tilde{\mathcal{G}}_0$ turns τ into a random time with deterministic hazard rate $\gamma(s)$: we have

$$P(\tau \leqslant t \mid \tilde{\mathcal{G}}_0) = 1 - \exp\left(- \int_0^t \gamma_s \, ds \right),$$

and γ is known given $\tilde{\mathcal{G}}_0$. Hence Proposition 9.5 implies that $M_t := Y_t - \int_0^{t\wedge\tau} \gamma_s \, ds$ is a martingale with respect to $(\tilde{\mathcal{G}}_t)$. Since (M_t) is $(\mathcal{G}_t)$-adapted and $\mathcal{G}_t \subset \tilde{\mathcal{G}}_t$, (M_t) is also a martingale with respect to $(\mathcal{G}_t)$. □

We conclude with a brief discussion on Proposition 9.15 from the viewpoint of stochastic calculus.

Definition 9.16. Given the set-up of Section 9.2.2, a non-negative $(\mathcal{G}_t)$-adapted process (λ_t) is called a $(\mathcal{G}_t)$-*martingale intensity* process of the random time τ if $M_t := Y_t - \int_0^{t\wedge\tau} \lambda_s \, ds$ is a $(\mathcal{G}_t)$-martingale.

In reduced-form credit risk models, (λ_t) is usually called the *default intensity* of the default time τ. It is well known that the martingale intensity (λ_t) is uniquely defined on $\{t < \tau\}$. This is an immediate consequence of general results from stochastic calculus concerning the uniqueness of semimartingale decompositions (see, for example, Chapter 2 of Protter (1992)). Martingale intensities are important tools in the analysis of jump indicators and random times from the viewpoint of stochastic calculus. In credit risk, martingale default intensities and credit spreads of defaultable bonds are closely related, as will be discussed in Section 9.4 below.

Using the terminology of Definition 9.16, we may restate Proposition 9.15 in the form "the $(\mathcal{G}_t)$-martingale intensity of a doubly stochastic random time τ is given by its $(\mathcal{F}_t)$-conditional hazard-rate process (γ_t)". Outside the realm of doubly stochastic random times, the relationship between martingale default intensities and hazard-rate processes becomes more subtle. In fact, in the analysis of reduced-form credit portfolios one naturally encounters random times which admit a martingale intensity process in the sense of Definition 9.16, but whose conditional cumulative hazard process Γ_t is not absolutely continuous, for instance because it has jumps. In that case Proposition 9.15 obviously no longer holds.

Notes and Comments

The material discussed in this section is treated in various sources; our presentation is based on the book by Bielecki and Rutkowski (2002), where many extensions of our results can also be found. In particular, Bielecki and Rutkowski discuss various probabilistic characterizations of doubly stochastic random times. The threshold-simulation approach for doubly stochastic random times requires the simulation of trajectories of the hazard-rate process. An excellent source for simulation techniques for stochastic processes is Glasserman (2003a).

More general reduced-form models where the default time τ is not doubly stochastic are discussed, for example, in Kusuoka (1999), Elliot, Jeanblanc and Yor (2000), Bélanger, Shreve and Wong (2004), Collin-Dufresne, Goldstein and Hugonnier (2004) and in Chapter 7 of Bielecki and Rutkowski (2002).

9.3 Financial and Actuarial Pricing of Credit Risk

Essentially, two approaches are used for the pricing of credit-risky securities: the *financial* or *risk-neutral* pricing approach on the one hand, and the *actuarial* pricing

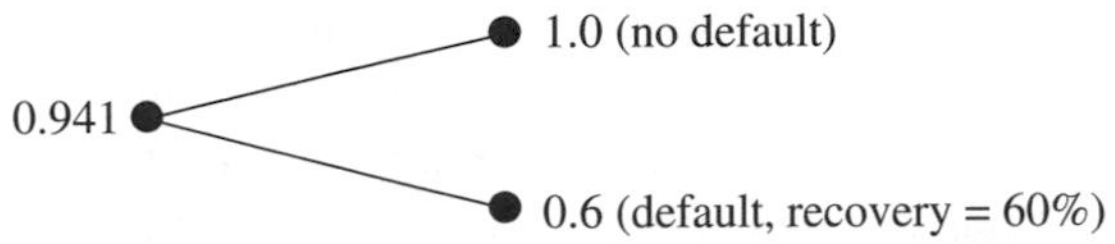

Figure 9.5. Evolution of the price of $p_1(\cdot, 1)$ in Example 9.17.

approach on the other. Under the risk-neutral pricing approach, prices are computed as expected discounted values under some equivalent martingale measure (see below). This approach is based on the notions of absence of arbitrage and dynamic hedging. Nowadays, the risk-neutral pricing approach is standard for pricing non-defaultable securities. In credit risk it is used for pricing traded securities such as corporate bonds and credit default swaps and derivative securities related to these products.

In the actuarial approach, prices are computed as the sum of the expected pay-off under the physical measure and a risk premium. The size of the risk premium is often related to the notion of economic capital. In credit risk, the actuarial approach is applied mainly to the pricing of non-traded loans or structured products related to illiquid securities.

In this section we discuss and compare both approaches with a view towards pricing credit-risky securities. Our discussion provides the methodological basis for the derivation of pricing formulas in subsequent sections.

9.3.1 Physical and Risk-Neutral Probability Measure

We begin with a discussion of the relationship between the *real-world* or *physical* measure, which models the actual probability of default, and an *equivalent martingale measure* or *risk-neutral* measure. We use the following simple example as a vehicle for our analysis.

Example 9.17 (the basic static model). We consider a defaultable zero-coupon bond with maturity T equal to one year. We assume that the recovery rate $1 - \delta$ is deterministic and equal to 60%; that the real-world default probability is equal to $\bar{p} = 1\%$; and that the risk-free simple interest rate equals 5%. Moreover, we assume that the current ($t = 0$) price of the bond equals $p_1(0, 1) = 0.941$; and that the price of the corresponding default-free bond is $p_0(0, 1) = (1.05)^{-1} = 0.952$. The price evolution of the bond is depicted in Figure 9.5.

The expected discounted value of the bond equals $(1.05)^{-1}(0.99 \cdot 1 + 0.01 \cdot 0.6) = 0.949 > p_1(0, 1)$. We see that the price $p_1(0, 1)$ is smaller than the expected discounted value of the claim. This is the typical situation in real markets for corporate bonds, as investors demand a premium for bearing the default risk of the bond. In real markets, the price of corporate bonds is also affected by tax issues (interest income from corporate bonds is often taxed at a higher rate than interest income on treasury bonds) and by liquidity issues; both factors tend to further decrease the price of corporate bonds relative to treasury bonds. An equivalent martingale measure or risk-neutral measure is an artificial measure Q equivalent to the physical probability measure P such that the discounted price process of any security is a

Q-martingale. According to a standard result of mathematical finance (the so-called *first fundamental theorem of asset pricing*), a model for security prices is arbitrage free if and, modulo technicalities, only if it admits at least one equivalent martingale measure Q. In our two-state model, Q is simply given by an artificial default probability $\bar{q}$ such that $p_1(0,1) = (1.05)^{-1}((1-\bar{q}) \cdot 1 + \bar{q} \cdot 0,6)$; $\bar{q}$ is uniquely determined from this equation and is given by $\bar{q} = 0.03$. Note that in our example $\bar{q}$ is bigger than the physical default probability $\bar{p} = 0.01$; again this is typical for real markets and reflects the risk premium demanded by buyers of defaultable bonds.

The risk-neutral default probability $\bar{q}$ is closely related to the credit spread of the defaultable bond (see (8.11)). Since $c(0,1) = -(\ln p_1(0,1) - \ln p_0(0,1))$, we obtain, in our two-state model,

$$c(0,1) = -\ln((1-\bar{q}) \cdot 1 + \bar{q} \cdot 0.6) = -\ln(1 - \bar{q} \cdot 0.4) \approx \bar{q} \cdot 0.4,$$

i.e. the credit spread is approximately equal to the product of default probability and (percentage) loss given default. Similar relationships hold in more general reduced-form credit risk models (see Section 9.4.2 below). Hence spread data for corporate bonds can be used to estimate risk-neutral default probabilities. This observation forms the basis for many empirical studies on the relationship between physical and risk-neutral default probabilities; we discuss the findings of a recent extensive study below.

From physical to risk-neutral default probabilities. How does the structure of credit risk models and hence default probabilities change if we go from the physical measure (labelled P) to a risk-neutral measure (labelled Q)? A concise mathematical answer to this question requires the use of sophisticated tools from stochastic calculus (variants of Girsanov's theorem for diffusions and point processes) and is beyond the scope of this book. We therefore content ourselves with an informal discussion of the transition from physical to risk-neutral probabilities in firm-value and reduced-form models.

In firm-value models such as Merton's model (see Section 8.2.1), when going from P to Q the drift of the asset-value process V is changed from some arbitrary μ to the default-free short rate of interest r. According to (8.4), in Merton's model the physical default probability over the interval $[0, T]$ is given by

$$\bar{p} = P(V_T \leqslant F) = \Phi\left(\frac{\ln F - \ln V_0 - (\mu - \frac{1}{2}\sigma^2)T}{\sigma\sqrt{T}}\right);$$

the risk-neutral default probability over the same horizon is

$$\bar{q} = Q(V_T \leqslant F) = \Phi\left(\frac{\ln F - \ln V_0 - (r - \frac{1}{2}\sigma^2)T}{\sigma\sqrt{T}}\right).$$

We obtain from these equations that

$$\bar{q} = \Phi\left(\Phi^{-1}(\bar{p}) + \frac{\mu - r}{\sigma}\sqrt{T}\right). \tag{9.10}$$

Note that the correction term $(\mu - r)/\sigma$ equals the *Sharpe ratio* of V (a popular measure of the risk premium earned by the firm). The transition formula (9.10) is frequently applied in practice to go from physical to risk-neutral default probabilities. Note, however, that (9.10) is only justified, strictly speaking, in the narrow context of the Merton model.

In standard reduced-form models the default time is modelled as a doubly stochastic random time with hazard rate $\gamma_t^P = h^P(\boldsymbol{\Psi}_t)$ (under the physical measure P) and $\gamma_t^Q = h^Q(\boldsymbol{\Psi}_t)$ (under a risk-neutral measure Q). Here $(\boldsymbol{\Psi}_t)$ is some d-dimensional process representing economic factors, which is adapted to the background filtration $(\mathcal{F}_t)$; h^P and h^Q are functions from $\mathbb{R}^d$ to $\mathbb{R}_+$. In this context arbitrage theory alone gives little guidance on the form of the ratio h^Q/h^P, the only restriction being that h^Q must be chosen so that the model is consistent with observed prices of traded credit-risky securities. Recent research has therefore tried to derive further restrictions on the ratio h^Q/h^P by bringing in economic arguments (see, for example, Jarrow, Lando and Yu 2005).

In practice, one usually postulates that h^P and h^Q belong to a given parametric family of functions from $\mathbb{R}^d$ to $\mathbb{R}_+$. For instance, one might assume that $h^Q = \nu h^P$ for some scaling factor $\nu > 0$. The function h^P can be determined by fitting the model to historical default probabilities; ν is found by fitting the model to observed prices of corporate bonds or credit default swaps. Alternatively, the model is set up directly under Q and one restricts oneself to determining h^Q from observed market prices of corporate bonds or credit default swaps; this is the martingale-modelling approach discussed in Section 9.3.3 below.

Empirical evidence. As discussed above, the risk-neutral default probability of a corporation can be estimated from credit-spread data for bonds issued by that corporation. By comparing these estimates with estimates for the physical default probability—obtained, for instance, from the KMV model introduced in Section 8.2.3—it is possible to gain some empirical evidence on the relationship of physical and risk-neutral default probabilities in real markets. Understanding this relationship is important, as it enables market participants to use information on historical default probabilities in pricing credit-risky securities, and conversely to use prices of defaultable bonds or market quotes for credit default swaps as additional input in determining historical default probabilities.

An extensive empirical study of the relationship between physical and historical default probabilities is Berndt et al. (2004). In this study market quotes for fair CDS spreads (instead of credit spreads of corporate bonds) are used to infer risk-neutral default probabilities. In this way, problems related to the differing taxation of corporate and treasury bonds can be circumvented. The authors ran regression analyses of the observed spreads for five-year CDSs against five-year EDFs for a large pool of firms. The five-year EDF of a firm with publicly traded stock is an annualized estimate of the physical five-year default probability. The computation of EDFs is described in detail in Section 8.2.3, and annualization is a way of expressing EDFs for different time horizons on a common yearly scale. A formal treatment of CDS pricing is given below in Section 9.3.3 (for models where the default time τ has a deterministic risk-neutral hazard rate) and in Section 9.4.3 (for the case of a doubly stochastic default time).

For the interpretation of the regression results, it suffices to know that, in an environment where the default-free interest rate (r_t) and the risk-neutral hazard rate ($\gamma_{t,i}^Q$) of some firm i do not fluctuate too much, we have an approximate relationship between the risk-neutral hazard rate $\gamma_{t,i}^Q$, the fair CDS spread x_i^* observed at time t and the percentage loss given default δ_i (assumed deterministic) of the form

$$\gamma_{t,i}^Q \approx x_i^*/\delta_i \tag{9.11}$$

(see Section 9.3.3 for details). Moreover, it is an immediate consequence of (9.7) that in models with a doubly stochastic default time the risk-neutral hazard rate $\gamma_{t,i}^Q$ is approximately equal to the conditional risk-neutral one-year default probability $\bar{q}_{t,i}$ of firm i at time t.

Berndt et al. (2004) began by estimating the following simple linear model for the relationship between the observed swap spread x_i^* of firm i and the five-year EDF, labelled EDF_i, on the same day, both measured in basis points (one basis point equals 0.01%):

$$x_i^* = 52.26 + 1.627\,\text{EDF}_i + \varepsilon_i. \tag{9.12}$$

The model (9.12) was estimated using a large sample of more than 18 000 CDS–EDF observations from September 2000 to August 2003 for firms from three industry sectors (North American Oil and Gas, North American Healthcare and North American Broadcasting and Entertainment). The authors propose the following interpretation of this regression result. Under the model (9.12) the fair swap spread x_i^* increases by approximately 16 basis points for every 10 basis point increase in the five-year EDF; neglecting the intercept, which is small, we have approximately that $x_i^*/\text{EDF}_i \approx 1.6$. Assuming that the risk-neutral loss given default, δ, equals, say, 0.75, and that risk-neutral and physical default intensities are relatively stable over time, this would imply a ratio of risk-neutral to physical default intensity of

$$\frac{\gamma^Q}{\gamma^P} \approx \frac{x_i^*/\delta}{\text{EDF}_i} = \frac{1}{\delta}\frac{x_i^*}{\text{EDF}_i} \approx \frac{1}{0.75} \cdot 1.6 = 2.13.$$

As explained above, $\gamma^Q/\gamma^P \approx \bar{q}/\bar{p}$, so these numbers also relate to the ratio of risk-neutral and physical default probabilities. A loss given default of $\delta = 0.75$ is a very conservative (high) estimate. If we take a lower value for δ, say $\delta = 0.5$, we obtain a ratio of $\bar{q}/\bar{p} \approx \frac{1}{0.5} \cdot 1.6 = 3.2$, i.e. the ratio of risk-neutral to actual default probability gets even higher.

A careful inspection of the CDS–EDF relationship shows that the simple linear model (9.12) might not be appropriate for a number of reasons. First, the high intercept of 52.26 basis points is implausible, as it would imply that even for a firm with historical default probability $\bar{p}$ close to zero the swap spread is still of the order of 50 basis points. Second, Berndt et al. (2004) found that the ratio x_i^*/EDF_i varies between industry sectors—reflecting different recovery rates for different industries—and over time, as is illustrated in Figure 9.6. Third, there seems to be some concavity in the relationship between swap spreads and EDFs; in particular, the ratio x_i^*/EDF_i is higher for high-quality firms with low EDF values than for

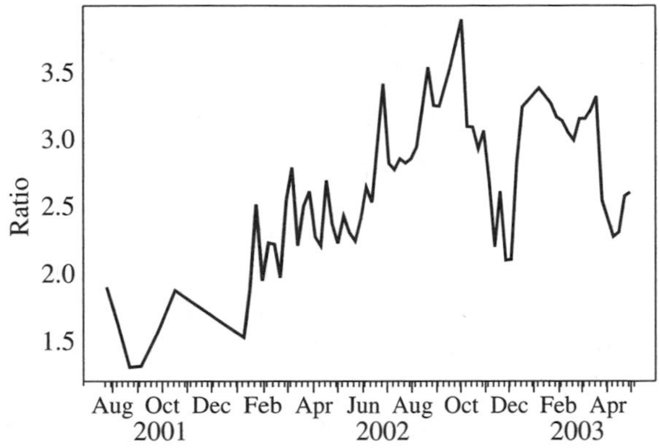

Figure 9.6. Ratio of one-year risk-neutral and historical default probabilities for Vintage Petroleum, as estimated by Berndt et al. (2004).

low-quality firms. For these reasons the authors go on to consider a more refined logarithmic regression model, which fits the data significantly better.

The analysis of Berndt et al. (2004) is corroborated by other empirical work on default risk premiums mentioned in Notes and Comments. This empirical research clearly shows that physical and risk-neutral default probabilities can differ substantially, and care must be taken to distinguish between the two concepts.

9.3.2 Risk-Neutral Pricing and Market Completeness

It is a fundamental insight of modern mathematical finance that in a complete market the price of derivative securities can be computed as the mathematical expectation of the discounted pay-off under a risk-neutral measure. In this section we explain the idea underlying this important result and discuss its applicability to the pricing of credit derivatives. We refrain from a general analysis; instead we use variants of the simple static model introduced in Example 9.17 as a vehicle for our discussion.

Consider, in the context of Example 9.17, an investor, for example an investment bank, who plans to sell credit derivatives on the zero-coupon bond with price $p_1(\cdot, T)$. In particular, consider a *default put option* with maturity date $T = 1$. This contract pays one unit if the bond defaults and zero otherwise; it can be thought of as a simplified version of a CDS. Obviously, the pay-off of the default put is unknown at date $t = 0$ and thus constitutes a risk. Therefore, two questions arise for our investor: how should the option be priced, and how should the risk incurred by selling it be dealt with? The answer given by the modern theory of mathematical finance goes back to the seminal papers of Black and Scholes (1973) and Merton (1973), who showed that it is often possible to replicate the pay-off of a derivative security by (dynamic) trading in the underlying assets. It follows that the risk incurred by the seller can be eliminated; moreover, the fair price of the derivative is given by the initial price of the replicating portfolio.

Let us apply this insight to the default put. We form a portfolio in the defaultable bond and cash, with value at time $t = 1$ equal to the pay-off of the put. At time

$t = 0$ we go short 2.5 units of the bond and hold $\frac{50}{21} \approx 2.38$ units of cash. At time $t = 1$ there are two possibilities for the value V_1 of this portfolio.

- Default occurs: in which case $V_1 = (-2.5) \cdot 0.6 + \frac{50}{21} \cdot 1.05 = 1$.
- No default: in which case $V_1 = (-2.5) \cdot 1 + \frac{50}{21} \cdot 1.05 = 0$.

In either case the value V_1 of the hedge portfolio equals the pay-off of the option. Hence the fair price at $t = 0$ of the option should equal the value of the hedge portfolio at $t = 0$ given by $V_0 = (-2.5) \cdot 0.941 + \frac{50}{21} \approx 0.0285$; otherwise either the buyer or the seller could make some riskless profit. To construct the portfolio in this simple one-period, two-state setting we have to consider two linear equations. Denote by ξ_1 and ξ_2 the units of the defaultable bond and the amount of cash in our portfolio. At time $t = 1$ we must have $\xi_1 \cdot 0.6 + \xi_2 \cdot 1.05 = 1$ (the default case), and $\xi_1 \cdot 1 + \xi_2 \cdot 1.05 = 0$ (the no-default case), which leads to the above values of $\xi_1 = -2.5$ and $\xi_2 = \frac{50}{21}$.

In mathematical finance a derivative security is called *attainable* if there is a (dynamic) portfolio strategy in traded underlying assets that replicates the pay-off of the derivative. The above argument shows that in our simple one-period two-state model every derivative security is attainable. Such models are termed *complete*.

Note that the physical default probability $\bar{p}$ did not enter the pricing argument. It is nonetheless possible to compute the fair price of the default put as the expected value of the discounted pay-off, if the risk-neutral measure Q is used instead of the physical measure P. Recall that the risk-neutral default probability is given by $\bar{q} = 0.03$. The expected discounted pay-off under Q is given by $(1.05)^{-1}(0.97 \cdot 0 + 0.03 \cdot 1) = 0.0285$ and is thus equal to the fair price V_0. This is, of course, not a lucky coincidence. In fact, a basic result from mathematical finance, the so-called *risk-neutral pricing rule*, states that the fair price of any attainable claim can be computed as the expected value of the discounted pay-off under a risk-neutral measure. Armed with this result, one typically first computes the candidate price (the expected value of the discounted pay-off under a risk-neutral measure) and second determines the replicating strategy. For this reason a lot of research focuses on the problem of computing prices. However, one should bear in mind that the main economic justification for computing prices as expected discounted value under a risk-neutral measure stems from the hedging argument, and is therefore strictly speaking only justified for attainable claims. This issue has, to a large extent, been neglected in the literature on the pricing of credit-risky securities. The next example illustrates some of the difficulties arising in *incomplete* markets, where most derivatives are not attainable.

Example 9.18 (a model with random recovery). As there is a substantial amount of randomness in real recovery rates (see Section 8.4.6), it is interesting to study the impact of random recovery rates on the validity of the above pricing arguments. Consider the following variant of Example 9.17 with random recovery: the loss given default may be either 30% or 50%, $p_1(0, 1) = 0.941$, and the riskless interest-rate equals 5%. The price evolution of $p_1(\cdot, 1)$ is illustrated in Figure 9.7. We leave

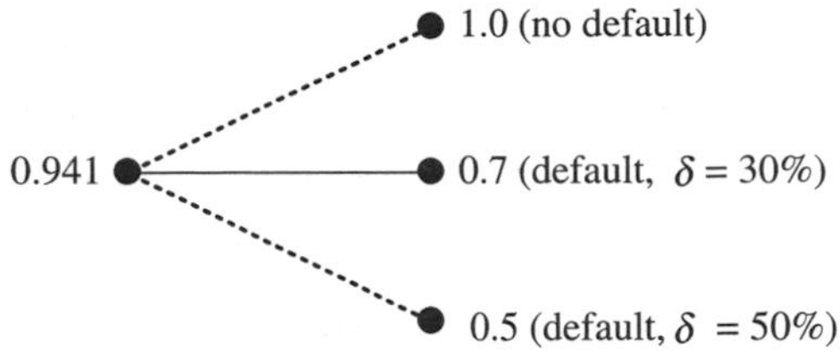

Figure 9.7. Evolution of the price of $p_1(\cdot, 1)$ in Example 9.18.

the physical measure unspecified—we assume only that all three possible outcomes have strictly positive probability.

We begin our analysis of this model by determining the equivalent martingale measures. Put $q_1 := Q(p_1(1,1) = 0.5)$, $q_2 := Q(p_1(1,1) = 0.7)$ and $q_3 := Q(p_1(1,1) = 1)$, so that $q_3 = 1 - q_1 - q_2$. We obtain the following equation for q_1 and q_2,

$$p_1(0,1) = 1.05^{-1}(q_1 \cdot 0.5 + q_2 \cdot 0.7 + (1 - q_1 - q_2) \cdot 1), \tag{9.13}$$

and the restrictions $q_1 > 0$, $q_2 > 0$, $1 - q_1 - q_2 > 0$. Obviously, Q is no longer unique. It is easily seen from (9.13) that the set $\mathcal{Q}$ of equivalent martingale measures is given by

$$\mathcal{Q} = \{\boldsymbol{q} \in \mathbb{R}^3 : q_1 \in (0, 0.024),\ q_2 = \tfrac{10}{3}(1 - 1.05 \cdot p_1(0,1) - 0.5 \cdot q_1),\\ q_3 = 1 - (q_1 + q_2)\}. \tag{9.14}$$

It is interesting to look at the boundary cases. For $q_1 = 0$ we obtain $q_2 = 4\%$, $q_3 = 96\%$; this is the scenario where the risk-neutral default probability $\bar{q} = q_1 + q_2$ is maximized. For $q_1 = 2.4\%$ we obtain $q_2 = 0$, $q_3 = 97.6\%$; this is the scenario where $\bar{q}$ is minimized. Note, however, that the measures $\boldsymbol{q}_0 := (0.024, 0, 0.976)$ and $\boldsymbol{q}_1 := (0, 0.04, 0.96)$ do not belong to $\mathcal{Q}$, as they are not equivalent to the physical measure P.

Consider a derivative security with pay-off H and maturity $T = 1$, such as the default put with $H = 0$ if $p_1(1,1) = 1$ and $H = 1$ otherwise. Every price of the form $H_0 = E^Q(1.05^{-1}H)$ for some $Q \in \mathcal{Q}$ is consistent with no arbitrage and will therefore be called an *admissible value* for the derivative. If $\mathcal{Q}$ contains more than one element, as in our case, there is typically more than one admissible value. For instance, we obtain for the default put option that

$$\inf_{Q \in \mathcal{Q}} E^Q\left(\frac{H}{1.05}\right) \approx 0.023 \quad \text{and} \quad \sup_{Q \in \mathcal{Q}} E^Q\left(\frac{H}{1.05}\right) \approx 0.038; \tag{9.15}$$

obviously, the infimum and supremum in (9.15) correspond to the measures $\boldsymbol{q}_0$ and $\boldsymbol{q}_1$, where $\bar{q}$ is minimized and maximized, respectively. This non-uniqueness of admissible values reflects the fact that in our three-state model the put is no longer attainable. In fact, the hedging portfolio (ξ_1, ξ_2) now has to solve the following three equations:

$$\left.\begin{aligned} \xi_1 \cdot 0.5 + \xi_2 \cdot 1.05 &= 1 \quad \text{(default, low recovery)},\\ \xi_1 \cdot 0.7 + \xi_2 \cdot 1.05 &= 1 \quad \text{(default, high recovery)},\\ \xi_1 \cdot 1 + \xi_2 \cdot 1.05 &= 0 \quad \text{(no default)}. \end{aligned}\right\} \tag{9.16}$$

It is immediately seen that the system (9.16) of three equations and only two unknowns has no solution, so that the default put is not attainable. This illustrates two fundamental results from modern mathematical finance: a claim with bounded pay-off is attainable if and only if the set of admissible values consists of a single number; an arbitrage-free market is complete if and only if there is exactly one equivalent martingale measure Q. The second result is known as the *second fundamental theorem of asset pricing*.

Example 9.18 shows that in an incomplete market conceptual issues arise which are not present in models for complete markets. In particular, it is not obvious how to choose the correct price of a derivative security from the range of admissible values or how to deal with the risk incurred by selling a derivative security. This is unfortunate, as realistic models, which capture the dynamics of financial time series, are typically incomplete. In recent years a number of interesting concepts for the risk management of derivative securities in incomplete markets have been developed. These approaches typically propose mitigating the risk by an appropriate trading strategy and often suggest a pricing formula for the remaining risk. However, the systematic application of these approaches to the pricing and the hedging of credit-risky securities is currently still in its infancy, and we refrain from further discussion. A brief overview of the existing work on incomplete markets is given in Notes and Comments.

9.3.3 Martingale Modelling

Recall that, according to the first fundamental theorem of asset pricing, a model for security prices is arbitrage free if and (essentially) only if it admits at least one equivalent martingale measure Q. Moreover, in a complete market, the only thing that matters for the pricing of derivative securities is the Q-dynamics of the traded underlying assets. When building a model for pricing derivatives it is therefore a natural shortcut to model the objects of interest—such as interest rates, default times and the price processes of traded bonds—directly, under some exogenously specified martingale measure Q. In the literature this approach is termed *martingale modelling*.

Martingale modelling is particularly convenient if the value of the underlying assets at some maturity date T is exogenously given, as in the case of zero-coupon bonds. In that case the price of the underlying asset at time $t < T$ can be computed as the conditional expectation under Q of the discounted value at maturity. Formally, denoting by $B(t) > 0$ the so-called numéraire (often the default-free savings account) and by $\mathcal{G}_t$ the information available to investors at time t, we have the following formula for the price at time t of a security, whose value at T is given by the $\mathcal{F}_T$-measurable rv $H \geqslant 0$:

$$H_t = B(t)E^Q(B(T)^{-1}H \mid \mathcal{G}_t), \quad t \leqslant T. \tag{9.17}$$

Model parameters are then determined using the requirement that at time $t = 0$ the price of traded securities as computed from the model using (9.17) should coincide with the price of these securities as observed in the market; this is known as *calibration* of the model to market data.

Martingale modelling ensures that the resulting model is arbitrage free, which is advantageous if one has to model the prices of many different securities simultaneously. Therefore the approach is frequently adopted in default-free term structure models and in reduced-form models for credit-risky securities. Martingale modelling has two drawbacks. First, historical information is, to a large extent, useless in estimating model parameters, as these may change in the transition from the real-world measure to the equivalent martingale measure. For instance, as explained above, physical and risk-neutral default probabilities and default intensities may differ substantially. Second, as illustrated in Example 9.18, realistic models for pricing credit derivatives are typically incomplete, so that one cannot eliminate all risk by dynamic hedging. In those situations one is interested in the distribution of the remaining risk under the actual risk measure P, so martingale modelling alone is not sufficient. In summary, the martingale-modelling approach is most suitable in situations where the market for underlying securities is relatively liquid. In that case we have sufficient price information to calibrate our models, and issues of market completeness become less relevant.

Martingale modelling with given CDS spreads. We now use the martingale-modelling approach to construct a simple reduced-form pricing model with deterministic hazard rate for credit derivatives on a given reference entity. We assume that market information consists of quotes for fair spreads for CDSs of varying maturities on this entity. This example illustrates the model-building process if martingale modelling is used. Moreover, the example is of practical relevance: since the CDS market is among the most liquid markets for credit-risky securities, the task of building a model using CDS spreads as input is frequently encountered in practice.

Using martingale modelling we model the objects of interest directly under some martingale measure Q. We assume that under Q the default time τ is a random time with deterministic risk-neutral hazard rate $\gamma^Q(t)$. For simplicity we take interest rates and recovery rates (or equivalently loss given default) to be deterministic. The percentage loss given default is denoted by $\delta \in (0, 1)$. The continuously compounded interest rate at time t is denoted by $r(t) \geqslant 0$, so $p_0(0, t) = \exp(-\int_0^t r(s)\,ds)$ is the price of the default-free zero-coupon bond with maturity t. This is the simplest type of model that can be calibrated to a given term structure of default-free interest rates and CDS spreads; generalizations allowing for stochastic interest rates, recovery rates and hazard rates will be discussed in Section 9.4.3 below.

We consider the following CDS. We take the notional to be one, so that percentage loss given default and absolute loss given default are the same. The premium payments are due at N points in time $0 < t_1 < \cdots < t_N$. If $\tau > t_k$, the protection buyer pays in t_k a premium of size $x^*(t_k - t_{k-1})$, where x^* denotes the swap spread. After default, no premium payments are made. If default occurs before the maturity date t_N of the swap, the protection seller makes a default payment of size δ to the buyer at the default time τ. In a standard CDS the protection buyer pays the protection seller at default the part of the premium which has accrued since the last regular premium payment date; here we ignore these accrued premium payments to simplify the exposition.

Given the risk-neutral hazard rate γ^Q and a generic spread x, we now price the payments made by the protection buyer (the so-called premium payment leg of the swap) and the payments made by the protection seller (the default payment leg) separately. The price of the premium payment leg at $t = 0$ (the expected discounted value of the payments) is given by

$$\begin{aligned} V^{\text{prem}}(x;\gamma^Q) &= E^Q\biggl(\sum_{k=1}^{N} \exp\biggl(-\int_0^{t_k} r(u)\,\mathrm{d}u\biggr)x(t_k - t_{k-1})I_{\{t_k<\tau\}}\biggr) \\ &= x\sum_{k=1}^{N} p_0(0,t_k)(t_k - t_{k-1})Q(\tau > t_k), \end{aligned} \tag{9.18}$$

which is easily computed using the fact that $Q(\tau > t_k) = \exp(-\int_0^{t_k}\gamma^Q(s)\,\mathrm{d}s)$. The expected discounted value of the default payment leg equals

$$V^{\text{def}}(\gamma^Q) = E^Q\biggl(\exp\biggl(-\int_0^{\tau} r(u)\,\mathrm{d}u\biggr)\delta I_{\{\tau<t_N\}}\biggr).$$

Since τ has density $f_\tau(t) = \gamma^Q(t)\exp(-\int_0^t \gamma^Q(u)\,\mathrm{d}u)$, defining $R(u) := r(u) + \gamma^Q(u)$, we get

$$\begin{aligned} V^{\text{def}}(\gamma^Q) &= \delta\int_0^{t_N} \exp\biggl(-\int_0^t r(s)\,\mathrm{d}s\biggr)f_\tau(t)\,\mathrm{d}t \\ &= \delta\int_0^{t_N} \gamma^Q(t)\exp\biggl(-\int_0^t R(s)\,\mathrm{d}s\biggr)\,\mathrm{d}t. \end{aligned} \tag{9.19}$$

According to market convention there are no payments when two parties enter into a CDS agreement. This implies that the *fair CDS spread* x^* has to be chosen such that the value of the contract at $t = 0$ is equal to zero. Hence x^* is defined by the relation $V^{\text{prem}}(x^*;\gamma^Q) = V^{\text{def}}(\gamma^Q)$, which is easily solved for x^*. Obviously, x^* depends on the intensity function γ^Q, as V^{prem} and V^{def} depend on γ^Q. Note that in our pricing argument we have neglected the possibility of default for the protection seller. More sophisticated CDS-pricing approaches would take this possibility into account (see Notes and Comments).

Assume now that we observe spreads quoted in the market for one or more CDSs on the same reference entity. Under the martingale-modelling approach we have to calibrate our model to the available market information. In the context of our simple default model we hence have to determine the *implied risk-neutral hazard rate* γ^Q, which ensures that the fair CDS spreads implied by the model equal the spreads which are quoted in the market.

We consider the following simple example: market information consists of the fair spread x^* of one CDS with maturity t_N; the risk-neutral hazard rate γ^Q is constant, i.e. $\gamma^Q(t) = \bar{\gamma}^Q$ for some $\bar{\gamma}^Q > 0$. In this context, by (9.18) and (9.19), the implied risk-neutral hazard rate $\bar{\gamma}^Q$ satisfies the equation

$$x^* \sum_{k=1}^{N} p_0(0, t_k)(t_k - t_{k-1})\mathrm{e}^{-\bar{\gamma}^Q t_k} = \delta\bar{\gamma}^Q \int_0^{t_N} p_0(0, t)\mathrm{e}^{-\bar{\gamma}^Q t}\, \mathrm{d}t. \tag{9.20}$$

Now, the left-hand side of this equation (the value of the premium payments) is decreasing in $\bar{\gamma}^Q$, whereas the right-hand side (the value of the default payments) is increasing in $\bar{\gamma}^Q$. Therefore, in this example there is a unique implied risk-neutral hazard rate, which is easily computed numerically.

If we observe spreads for several CDSs on the same reference entity but with different maturities, a time-independent risk-neutral hazard rate is generally not sufficient to calibrate the model to the observed swap spreads. Instead one typically uses hazard-rate functions $\gamma^Q(t)$ that are piecewise constant or piecewise linear. An exception occurs in the special case where the spread curve is *flat* (i.e. all CDSs on the reference entity have the same spread x^*, independent of the maturity), where the risk-free interest rate is constant and where the time points t_k are equally spaced (i.e. $t_k - t_{k-1} = \Delta t$ for all t). In that case the implied risk-neutral hazard rate $\bar{\gamma}^Q$ is given as the solution to the following equation (equation (9.20) for the case $N = 1$):

$$x^* \Delta t p_0(0, \Delta t)\mathrm{e}^{-\bar{\gamma}^Q \Delta t} = \delta\bar{\gamma}^Q \int_0^{\Delta t} p_0(0, t)\exp(-\bar{\gamma}^Q t)\, \mathrm{d}t. \tag{9.21}$$

For Δt relatively small (quarterly or semiannual spread payments) a good approximation to the solution of (9.21) is given by $\bar{\gamma}^Q \approx x^*/\delta$, i.e. by the ratio of the fair swap spread and the percentage loss given default. This approximation is frequently used in practice.

Remark 9.19. Recall that in reduced-form models historical default information is of no use in determining the form of the risk-neutral hazard rate. For our simple example it follows that the hypothesis of a constant risk-neutral hazard rate cannot be tested by looking at historical default patterns: it is perfectly possible that under the historical measure P default intensities are time dependent, but that under a risk-neutral measure Q they are constant, and vice versa. The only way of testing the assumption that $\gamma^Q(t)$ is a constant or has any other functional form would be to test the implications of this assumption on the dynamics of observable CDS spreads or prices of other traded credit-risky securities.

9.3.4 The Actuarial Approach to Credit Risk Pricing

The actuarial approach is mainly used for the pricing of loans and related products, which are relatively illiquid. Under the actuarial approach the *total spread* a loan should earn (the difference between the interest rate which should be charged for the loan and the interest rate on a default-free bond with similar characteristics) is computed according to the following schematic formula:

$$\text{total spread} = \text{administrative cost} + \text{expected loss} + \text{risk premium}. \tag{9.22}$$

Administrative cost is of no concern to us here. Expected loss refers to expected loss under the physical probability measure and, assuming independence between default and recovery rates, it is given by the product of the annual default probability and the expected percentage loss given default. The determination of an appropriate risk premium is more involved from a methodological viewpoint and is discussed below. Formula (9.22) for the total spread has the same structure as the standard actuarial premium principles, hence the name actuarial approach to pricing credit risk. Of course, in practice a formal loan-pricing rule of the form (9.22) is not applied rigorously across the board; other factors, such as competitive pressure from other lenders or a long-standing business relationship between borrower and lender, play an important role in determining the yield spread for a loan.

Risk premiums and economic capital. In modern loan-pricing systems the risk premium of a loan is computed by applying a target interest rate or *hurdle rate* to the economic capital required as buffer against losses from the deal. Hurdle rates are set by management; they reflect the return on equity aspired to by a financial institution. Under a modern economic capital framework, the economic capital required for a particular loan is determined in two steps. First, the economic capital of the entire credit portfolio is determined. Here the financial industry typically distinguishes between the so-called expected loss, given by the expected value $E(L)$, and the so-called unexpected loss, given by $\mathrm{UL} := L - E(L)$. Usually, the economic capital for the entire loan portfolio is determined by applying a risk measure such as VaR or expected shortfall to UL, whereas the expected loss is charged directly to the borrower according to the general actuarial loan-pricing formula (9.22).

In a second step the total economic capital needs to be allocated to the individual loans in the portfolio, a process called *economic capital allocation*. A fair economic capital allocation has to reflect the contributions of the individual loans to the total risk of the portfolio. For instance, a large loan, which is (almost) independent of the overall portfolio, might contribute less to total risk than a smaller loan, which is likely to default in circumstances where the portfolio produces large losses. Formally, economic capital allocation is done using a capital allocation principle such as standard deviation contributions or expected shortfall contributions (see Section 6.3 for details).

Financial and actuarial pricing compared. We conclude this section with a brief comparison of the two pricing methodologies. The financial-pricing approach is a *relative pricing theory*, which explains prices of credit products in terms of observable prices of other securities. If properly applied, it leads to arbitrage-free prices of credit-risky securities, which are consistent with prices quoted in the market. These features make the financial-pricing approach the method of choice in an environment where credit risk is actively traded and, in particular, for valuing credit instruments when the market for related products is relatively liquid. On the other hand, since financial-pricing models have to be calibrated to prices of traded credit instruments, they are difficult to apply when we lack sufficient market information. Moreover, in such cases prices quoted using an ad hoc choice of some risk-neutral measure are more or less "plucked out of thin air".

The actuarial pricing approach is an *absolute pricing approach*, based on the paradigm of *risk bearing*: a credit product such as a loan is taken on the balance sheet if the spread earned on the loan is deemed by the lender to be a sufficient compensation for the risk contribution of the loan to the total risk of the lending portfolio. Moreover, the approach relies mainly on historical default information. Therefore, the actuarial approach is well suited to situations where the market for related credit instruments is relatively illiquid, such that little or no price information is available; loans to medium or small businesses are a prime case in point. On the other hand, the approach does not necessarily lead to prices that are consistent (in the sense of absence of arbitrage) across products or that are compatible with quoted market prices for credit instruments, so it is less suitable for a trading environment.

As markets for credit products become more and more liquid, the financial-valuation paradigm is gaining in importance. This transition poses a challenge for risk management in financial institutions, since it may well be that a particular credit risk is priced differently by different parts of an institution, such as the loan department and a trading desk for credit derivatives. It is the task of a sound risk-management process to ensure that these inconsistencies are kept to a minimum; a profound understanding of the differences between financial and actuarial valuation is an important prerequisite for that.

Notes and Comments

Theoretical results on the relationship between physical and risk-neutral default probabilities were obtained by Artzner and Delbaen (1995), Jarrow, Lando and Yu (2005), Giesecke and Goldberg (2005) and others. General mathematical results for the behaviour of point processes (such as default indicators) under a change of measure (Girsanov-type theorems) can be found in Brémaud (1981) or Jacod and Shiryaev (1987). Empirical studies on the relationship between actual and risk-neutral default probabilities include Fons (1994), Bohn (2000), Driessen (2005), Huang and Huang (2003) and Berndt et al. (2004). In their paper, Berndt et al. go beyond the regression analysis presented in our text and estimate a full time series model for the joint evolution of risk-neutral and actual default intensities.

The fundamental theorems of asset pricing are discussed in most textbooks on mathematical finance (see, for example, Bingham and Kiesel 1998; Duffie 2001; Shreve 2004). In recent years a number of interesting approaches to the risk management of derivative securities in incomplete markets have been developed. *Quadratic hedging* approaches were first developed by Föllmer and Sondermann (1986) and Föllmer and Schweizer (1991); Schweizer (2001b) is an excellent survey. The theory of *superhedging* is developed in El Karoui and Quenez (1995) and Kramkov (1996); the related idea of quantile hedging is explored in Föllmer and Leukert

(1999). *Utility-based* approaches to pricing and hedging in incomplete markets are discussed in Delbaen et al. (2002) and Becherer (2004); the latter paper explicitly considers applications of utility-based hedging strategies to credit risk models. A discussion of incomplete-market models in discrete time can be found in Föllmer and Schied (2004). Early papers dealing with market incompleteness in credit risk models include Becherer (2004), Becherer and Schweizer (2005) and Bielecki, Jeanblanc and Rutkowski (2004).

The term martingale modelling was coined by Björk (1998) in the context of default-free short-rate models (see also Baxter and Rennie 1996). The pricing of CDSs is discussed in most standard textbooks on credit risk models (see, for example, Bielecki and Rutkowski 2002; Bluhm, Overbeck and Wagner 2002; Duffie and Singleton 2003; Lando 2004; Schönbucher 2003). For results on CDS pricing with possible default of protection seller see, for example, Hull and White (2001).

The relationship between actuarial and financial-pricing approaches is discussed by Jensen and Nielsen (1996), Embrechts (2000), Schweizer (2001a) and Embrechts, Frey and Furrer (2001), among others.

9.4 Pricing with Doubly Stochastic Default Times

The main result of this section concerns the pricing of two types of contingent claims that can be used as building blocks for constructing the pay-off of many important credit-risky securities. We will show that, for a default time which is doubly stochastic, the computation of prices for these claims can be reduced to a pricing problem for a corresponding default-free claim if we adjust the interest rate and replace the default-free interest rate r_t by the sum $R_t = r_t + \gamma_t$ of the default-free interest rate and the hazard rate of the default time.

9.4.1 *Recovery Payments of Corporate Bonds*

To clarify the form of our building blocks we briefly survey different models for the recovery of corporate zero-coupon bonds. As in previous sections, we denote the price at time t of a corporate zero-coupon bond with maturity $T \geqslant t$ by $p_1(t, T)$; $p_0(t, T)$ denotes the price of the corresponding default-free zero-coupon bond. The face value of these bonds is always taken to be one. The following three recovery models are frequently used in the literature.

Recovery of Treasury (RT). The RT model was proposed by Jarrow and Turnbull (1995). Under RT, if default occurs at some point in time $\tau \leqslant T$, the owner of the defaulted bond receives $(1 - \delta_\tau)$ units of the default-free zero-coupon bond $p_0(\cdot, T)$ at time τ, where the rv δ_τ models the loss given default. At maturity T the holder of the defaultable bond therefore receives the payment $p_1(T, T) = I_{\{\tau>T\}} + (1 - \delta_\tau)I_{\{\tau\leqslant T\}}$. In particular, if $\delta_\tau = \delta$ for some constant $\delta \in (0, 1)$, we get $p_1(T, T) = (1 - \delta) + \delta I_{\{\tau>T\}}$, so the price of the corporate bond at time $t < T$ equals the sum of $(1 - \delta)p_0(t, T)$ and δ times the price of the claim $I_{\{\tau>T\}}$.

Recovery of Face Value (RF). Under RF, if default occurs at $\tau \leqslant T$, the holder of the bond receives a (possibly random) recovery payment of size $(1 - \delta_\tau)$ immediately at the default time τ. The value at maturity T is therefore given by

$$p_1(T, T) = I_{\{\tau > T\}} + \frac{1 - \delta_\tau}{p_0(\tau, T)} I_{\{\tau \leqslant T\}}.$$

Even with deterministic loss given default $\delta_\tau \equiv \delta$ and deterministic interest rates, the value at maturity of the recovery payment is random as it depends on the exact timing of default. This makes the pricing of recovery payments under RF more difficult than under RT.

Recovery of Market Value (RM). This recovery assumption has been put forward by Duffie and Singleton (1999a); its main virtue is the fact that it leads to particularly simple pricing formulas for corporate bonds. Under RM it is assumed that the recovery payment at the default-time $\tau \leqslant T$ is given by a fraction $(1 - \delta_\tau)$ of the pre-default value of the bond. Obviously, this is a recursive definition, as the pre-default value depends on the recovery payment. Nonetheless, under some assumptions it is possible to obtain a unique price for corporate bonds, where recovery is modelled using the RM assumption (see Proposition 9.24 below).

In real markets recovery is a complex issue with many legal and institutional features, and all three recovery models are at best a crude approximation of reality. The RF-assumption comes closest to legal practice, as debt with the same seniority is assigned the same (fractional) recovery, independent of the maturity. On the other hand, for "extreme" parameter values (long maturities and high risk-free interest rate), RF may lead to negative credit spreads, as we will see in Section 9.5.3 below. Moreover, the RF model leads to slightly more involved pricing formulas for corporate bonds than the RM and RT models. Empirical evidence on recovery rates for loans and corporate bonds is discussed in Section 8.4.6.

9.4.2 The Model

We consider a firm whose default time is given by a doubly stochastic random time as in Section 9.2.3. The economic background filtration represents the information generated by an arbitrage-free and complete model for non-defaultable security prices. More precisely, let $(\Omega, \mathcal{F}, (\mathcal{F}_t), Q)$ denote a filtered probability space, where Q is already the equivalent martingale measure. Prices of default-free securities such as default-free bonds are $(\mathcal{F}_t)$-adapted processes. By (r_t) we denote the default-free rate of interest; $B_t = \exp(\int_0^t r_s \, \mathrm{d}s)$ models the default-free savings account.

Let τ be the default time of some company under consideration and let $Y_t = I_{\{\tau \leqslant t\}}$ be the associated default indicator process. As in Section 9.2.2 we set $\mathcal{H}_t = \sigma(\{Y_s : s \leqslant t\})$ and $\mathcal{G}_t = \mathcal{F}_t \vee \mathcal{H}_t$; we assume that default is observable and that investors have access to the information contained in the background filtration $(\mathcal{F}_t)$, so that the information available to investors at time t is given by $\mathcal{G}_t$. We consider a market for credit products which is liquid enough that we may use the martingale-modelling approach, and we use Q as the pricing measure for defaultable securities. Finally, we assume that, under Q, the default time τ is a doubly stochastic random time with background filtration $(\mathcal{F}_t)$ and hazard-rate process (γ_t). This latter assumption is crucial for the results that follow.

9.4.3 Pricing Formulas

Definition 9.20. We introduce the following building blocks.

(i) A *vulnerable claim*, i.e. an $\mathcal{F}_T$-measurable promised payment X which is made at time T if there is no default; the actual payment of the vulnerable claim equals $X I_{\{\tau>T\}}$.

(ii) A *recovery payment* at the time of default of the form $Z_\tau I_{\{\tau\leqslant T\}}$, where $Z=(Z_t)_{t\geqslant 0}$ is an $(\mathcal{F}_t)$-adapted stochastic process and where Z_τ is short for $Z_{\tau(\omega)}(\omega)$. T is the maturity of the recovery payment.

Example 9.21 (corporate bonds). The actual payments of a corporate zero-coupon bond can be represented as a combination of a vulnerable claim and a recovery payment. Suppose that the loss given default is given by some $(\mathcal{F}_t)$-adapted process (δ_t) with values in $(0,1)$. Under the RT hypothesis the actual payments are given by the vulnerable claim $I_{\{\tau>T\}}$ and the recovery payment $(1-\delta_\tau)p_0(\tau,T)I_{\{\tau\leqslant T\}}$. In the case where $\delta_\tau=\delta$ for some $\delta\in(0,1)$, the pay-off at maturity simplifies further to the sum of the deterministic payment $(1-\delta)$ and the vulnerable claim $\delta I_{\{\tau>T\}}$.

Under RF the actual payment of the bond consists of the vulnerable claim $I_{\{\tau>T\}}$ and the recovery payment $(1-\delta_\tau)I_{\{\tau\leqslant T\}}$. Obviously, since coupon-paying corporate bonds can be represented as a portfolio of zero-coupon bonds issued by a corporation, coupon-paying bonds can also be constructed from building blocks (i) and (ii). However, see Remark 9.25 for a word of warning on the validity of linear pricing rules in reduced-form models.

Example 9.22 (vulnerable option). Consider a call option with exercise price K and maturity T on some default-free security (S_t), and assume that the writer of the option may default. Assume that in case of default of the writer at time $\tau<T$ the owner of the option receives a fraction $(1-\delta_\tau)$ of the intrinsic value of the option at the time of default. This can be modelled as a combination of the vulnerable claim $(S_T-K)^+I_{\{\tau>T\}}$ and the recovery payment $(1-\delta_\tau)(S_\tau-K)^+I_{\{\tau\leqslant T\}}$.

Credit default swaps can also be viewed as a combination of vulnerable claims and a recovery payment (see Section 9.4.4 below).

According to (9.17), we obtain the following formula for the price at time t of an arbitrary, non-negative, $\mathcal{G}_T$-measurable contingent claim H:

$$H_t = E^Q\biggl(\exp\biggl(-\int_t^T r_s\,\mathrm{d}s\biggr)H \biggm| \mathcal{G}_t\biggr). \tag{9.23}$$

Consider a default-free claim with $\mathcal{F}_T$-measurable pay-off X. Since τ is a doubly stochastic random time, the additional information about the default history contained in $(\mathcal{G}_t)$ is of no use in computing the conditional expectation (9.23), and we have

$$E^Q\biggl(\exp\biggl(-\int_t^T r_s\,\mathrm{d}s\biggr)X \biggm| \mathcal{G}_t\biggr) = E^Q\biggl(\exp\biggl(-\int_t^T r_s\,\mathrm{d}s\biggr)X \biggm| \mathcal{F}_t\biggr). \tag{9.24}$$

A formal proof of this equality can be based on the representation of τ obtained in Lemma 9.13; we omit the details. Relation (9.24) shows that we may write the price of a non-negative default-free claim X as $X_t = E^Q(\exp(-\int_t^T r_s\,\mathrm{d}s)X \mid \mathcal{F}_t)$, which is obviously an $(\mathcal{F}_t)$-adapted process. In particular, it does not matter if we model default-free security prices using $(\mathcal{F}_t)$ or the larger filtration $(\mathcal{G}_t)$. In the following theorem we show that, in a similar vein, the pricing of the building blocks introduced in Definition 9.20 can be reduced to a pricing problem in a default-free security market model with adjusted default-free interest rate.

Theorem 9.23. *Suppose that, under Q, τ is doubly stochastic with background filtration $(\mathcal{F}_t)$ and hazard-rate process (γ_t). Define $R_s := r_s + \gamma_s$. Assume that the rvs $\exp(-\int_t^T r_s\,\mathrm{d}s)|X|$ and $\int_t^T |Z_s\gamma_s| \exp(-\int_t^s R_u\,\mathrm{d}u)\,\mathrm{d}s$ are all integrable with respect to Q. Then the following identities hold:*

$$E^Q\biggl(\exp\biggl(-\int_t^T r_s\,\mathrm{d}s\biggr)I_{\{\tau>T\}}X \biggm| \mathcal{G}_t\biggr) = I_{\{\tau>t\}}E^Q\biggl(\exp\biggl(-\int_t^T R_s\,\mathrm{d}s\biggr)X \biggm| \mathcal{F}_t\biggr), \tag{9.25}$$

$$E^Q\biggl(I_{\{\tau>t\}}\exp\biggl(-\int_t^\tau r_s\,\mathrm{d}s\biggr)Z_\tau I_{\{\tau\leqslant T\}} \biggm| \mathcal{G}_t\biggr) = I_{\{\tau>t\}}E^Q\biggl(\int_t^T Z_s\gamma_s\exp\biggl(-\int_t^s R_u\,\mathrm{d}u\biggr)\mathrm{d}s \biggm| \mathcal{F}_t\biggr). \tag{9.26}$$

Proof. The integrability conditions ensure that all conditional expectations are well defined. We start with the pricing formula (9.25) for the vulnerable claim. Define the $\mathcal{F}_T$-measurable rv $\tilde{X} := \exp(-\int_t^T r_s\,\mathrm{d}s)X$. We obtain, using Corollary 9.10 with $s = T$ and $\Gamma_t = \int_0^t \gamma_s\,\mathrm{d}s$, that

$$E^Q(\tilde{X}I_{\{\tau>T\}} \mid \mathcal{G}_t) = I_{\{\tau>t\}}E^Q(\exp(-(\Gamma_T - \Gamma_t))\tilde{X} \mid \mathcal{F}_t).$$

Using the relation $\Gamma_T - \Gamma_t = \int_t^T \gamma_s\,\mathrm{d}s$ and the definition of $\tilde{X}$, we immediately obtain that the right-hand side equals $I_{\{\tau>t\}}E^Q(\exp(-\int_t^T R_s\,\mathrm{d}s)X \mid \mathcal{F}_t)$. Next we turn to (9.26). We obtain from Lemma 9.9 that

$$E^Q\biggl(I_{\{\tau>t\}}\exp\biggl(-\int_t^\tau r_s\,\mathrm{d}s\biggr)Z_\tau I_{\{\tau\leqslant T\}} \biggm| \mathcal{G}_t\biggr) = I_{\{\tau>t\}}\frac{E^Q(I_{\{\tau>t\}}\exp(-\int_t^\tau r_s\,\mathrm{d}s)Z_\tau I_{\{\tau\leqslant T\}} \mid \mathcal{F}_t)}{P(\tau>t \mid \mathcal{F}_t)}. \tag{9.27}$$

Now note that

$$P(\tau \leqslant t \mid \mathcal{F}_T) = 1 - \exp\biggl(-\int_0^t \gamma_s\,\mathrm{d}s\biggr),$$

so the conditional density of τ given $\mathcal{F}_T$ equals $f_{\tau|\mathcal{F}_T}(t) = \gamma_t \exp(-\int_0^t \gamma_s \, ds)$. Hence

$$E^Q\bigg(I_{\{\tau>t\}} \exp\bigg(-\int_t^\tau r_s \, ds\bigg) Z_\tau I_{\{\tau\leqslant T\}} \,\bigg|\, \mathcal{F}_T\bigg)$$
$$= \int_t^T \exp\bigg(-\int_t^s r_u \, du\bigg) Z_s \gamma_s \exp\bigg(-\int_0^s \gamma_u \, du\bigg) ds$$
$$= \exp\bigg(-\int_0^t \gamma_u \, du\bigg) \int_t^T Z_s \gamma_s \exp\bigg(-\int_t^s R_u \, du\bigg) ds.$$

Hence we obtain, using iterated conditional expectations, that

$$E^Q\bigg(I_{\{\tau>t\}} \exp\bigg(-\int_t^\tau r_s \, ds\bigg) Z_\tau I_{\{\tau\leqslant T\}} \,\bigg|\, \mathcal{F}_t\bigg)$$
$$= \exp\bigg(-\int_0^t \gamma_u \, du\bigg) E^Q\bigg(\int_t^T Z_s \gamma_s \exp\bigg(-\int_t^s R_u \, du\bigg) ds \,\bigg|\, \mathcal{F}_t\bigg);$$

the identity (9.26) follows because of (9.27). □

9.4.4 Applications

Credit default swaps. We extend our analysis of Section 9.3.3 and discuss the pricing of CDSs in the model introduced in Section 9.4.2. This allows us to incorporate stochastic interest rates, recovery rates and hazard rates into our analysis. As in our previous analysis, the premium payments are due at N points in time $0 < t_1 < \cdots < t_N$; at a pre-default date t_k, the protection buyer pays a premium of size $x(t_k - t_{k-1})$, where x denotes the swap spread in percentage points (again we take the nominal of the swap to be one). Moreover, if $\tau \leqslant t_N$, there is an *accrued premium payment* of size $x(\tau - t_{k-1})$, provided that $t_{k-1} < \tau \leqslant t_k$. If $\tau \leqslant t_N$, the protection seller makes the default payment of size δ_τ to the buyer at the default time τ, where the percentage loss given default is now a general $(\mathcal{F}_t)$-adapted process. Using Theorem 9.23, both legs of the swap can be priced. The regular premium payments constitute a sequence of vulnerable claims. Using (9.25), we obtain, for the fair price in $t = 0$,

$$V^{\text{prem},1} = \sum_{k=1}^N E^Q\bigg(\exp\bigg(-\int_0^{t_k} r_u \, du\bigg) x(t_k - t_{k-1}) I_{\{t_k<\tau\}}\bigg)$$
$$= x \sum_{k=1}^N (t_k - t_{k-1}) E^Q\bigg(\exp\bigg(-\int_0^{t_k} R_u \, du\bigg)\bigg).$$

The accrued premium payments constitute a recovery payment, where Z is given by $Z_s = x\sum_{k=1}^N (s - t_{k-1}) I_{\{t_{k-1}<s\leqslant t_k\}}$; by (9.26) the fair price in $t = 0$ is given by

$$V^{\text{prem},2} = x \sum_{k=1}^N E^Q\bigg(\int_{t_{k-1}}^{t_k} (s - t_{k-1}) \gamma_s \exp\bigg(-\int_0^s R_u \, du\bigg) ds\bigg).$$

The default payments also form a recovery payment, this time with $Z_s = \delta_s$ and maturity t_N, so their value is given by $V^{\text{def}} = E^Q(\int_0^{t_N} \delta_s \gamma_s \exp(-\int_0^s R_u \, du) \, ds)$.

Hence we have reduced the pricing of credit default swaps to a pricing problem in the default-free world. Methods for solving this problem will be discussed in the next section.

Recovery of market value. Next we turn to the pricing of credit-risky securities whose recovery payment is described by the RM assumption introduced in Section 9.4.1. More precisely, we consider a claim whose pay-off consists of the vulnerable claim X and a recovery-payment of size $(1-\delta_\tau)V_\tau I_{\{\tau\leqslant T\}}$, where the $(\mathcal{F}_t)$-adapted process $(\delta_t)\in(0,1)$ gives the percentage loss given default of the claim and where the $(\mathcal{F}_t)$-adapted process (V_t) gives the pre-default value of the claim. Note that this is a recursive definition, as the pre-default value at time t also depends on the form of the future recovery payments in the time-period $(t,T]$. Nonetheless, we have the following result.

Proposition 9.24. *Suppose that, under Q, τ is doubly stochastic with hazard-rate process (γ_t), that X is integrable, and that the RM assumption holds. Then the pre-default value process (V_t) is uniquely determined and is given by*

$$V_t = E^Q\biggl(\exp\biggl(-\int_t^T r_s+\delta_s\gamma_s\,\mathrm{d}s\biggr)X \biggm| \mathcal{F}_t\biggr), \quad 0\leqslant t\leqslant T. \tag{9.28}$$

Note that for $\delta_t \equiv 1$ the claim is a standard vulnerable claim; in that case, (9.28) reduces to the formula (9.25). On the other hand, for $\delta_t \equiv 0$ the claim is essentially default free; in that case, (9.28) reduces to the standard pricing formula for the claim X in a default-free security market model. For a formal proof of Proposition 9.24 we refer to the references given in Notes and Comments.

Credit spreads and hazard rates. With doubly stochastic default times the risk-neutral hazard-rate process (γ_t) and the credit spread

$$c(t,T) = -\frac{1}{T-t}(\ln p_1(t,T)-\ln p_0(t,T))$$

of defaultable bonds are closely related. Analytic results are most easily derived for the instantaneous credit spread given by

$$c(t,t) = \lim_{T\to t} c(t,T) = -\frac{\partial}{\partial T}\bigg|_{T=t}(\ln p_1(t,T)-\ln p_0(t,T)). \tag{9.29}$$

Assume that $\tau>t$, so that $p_1(t,t)=p_0(t,t)=1$. Hence we get

$$\frac{\partial}{\partial T}\bigg|_{T=t}\ln p_1(t,T) = \frac{\partial}{\partial T}\bigg|_{T=t} p_1(t,T), \tag{9.30}$$

and similarly for $p_0(t,T)$. To compute the derivative in (9.30) we need to distinguish between the different recovery models. Under RM, we have, from Proposition 9.24, exchanging expectation and differentiation,

$$\begin{aligned}-\frac{\partial}{\partial T}\bigg|_{T=t} p_1(t,T) &= -E^Q\biggl(\frac{\partial}{\partial T}\bigg|_{T=t}\exp\biggl(-\int_t^T r_s+\delta_s\gamma_s\,\mathrm{d}s\biggr) \biggm| \mathcal{F}_t\biggr)\\ &= r_t+\delta_t\gamma_t. \end{aligned}\tag{9.31}$$

Applying (9.31) with $\delta_t \equiv 0$ yields

$$-\frac{\partial}{\partial T}\bigg|_{T=t} p_0(t,T) = r_t,$$

so that $c(t,t) = \delta_t \gamma_t$, i.e. the instantaneous credit spread equals the product of hazard rate and percentage loss given default, which is quite intuitive from an economic point of view. Under RF, $p_1(t,T)$ is given by the sum of the price of the vulnerable claim $I_{\{\tau > T\}}$ and the recovery payment $(1-\delta)_\tau$. Relation (9.31) with $\delta_t \equiv 0$ shows that the derivative with respect to T of the vulnerable claim at $T = t$ is equal to $-(r_t + \gamma_t)$. For the recovery payment we get

$$\frac{\partial}{\partial T}\bigg|_{T=t} E\biggl(\int_t^T \gamma_s(1-\delta_s)\exp\biggl(-\int_t^s R_u \,\mathrm{d}u\biggr)\mathrm{d}s \;\bigg|\; \mathcal{F}_t\biggr) = (1-\delta_t)\gamma_t.$$

Hence

$$-\frac{\partial}{\partial T}\bigg|_{T=t} p_1(t,T) = r_t + \gamma_t - (1-\delta_t)\gamma_t = r_t + \delta_t\gamma_t,$$

so that $c_1(t,t)$ is again equal to $\delta_t\gamma_t$. An analogous computation shows that we also have $c_1(t,t) = \delta_t\gamma_t$ under RT. However, for $T - t > 0$ the credit spread corresponding to the different recovery models differs, as is illustrated in Section 9.5.3 below.

Remark 9.25 (limitations of reduced-form models). The analogy with default-free term structure models makes the reduced-form models with doubly stochastic default times relatively easy to apply. However, in interpreting the results some care is required. In particular, one must bear in mind that in these models the default intensity does not explicitly take into account the structure of a firm's outstanding risky debt. This can lead to nonsensical results, as is illustrated in the following simple example. Consider a firm whose risky debt consists of a single bond with maturity $\bar{T}$. Suppose that the firm raises new funds by issuing another zero-coupon bond with maturity $T < \bar{T}$. In order to value this new debt, in a naive application of the reduced-form approach, one would set up a model with doubly stochastic default time τ and calibrate the risk-neutral hazard rate to the price of the existing debt (the bond with maturity $\bar{T}$). This model would then be used to price the zero-coupon bond with the short maturity. If the face value of the new debt is large relative to the value of the firm, the price obtained in this way is out of line with economic reality. As an extreme case, suppose that the firm uses the funds raised by the bond issue to buy back a some of its own shares. Clearly, this makes the firm riskier and raises the probability that the firm defaults on the new issue. This should be reflected in the default intensity and, in fact, since $T < \bar{T}$, in the price of the existing debt. More generally, these considerations show that the validity of the *linear pricing rules* for corporate debt implied by the reduced-form approach must be interpreted with care. A formal analysis of these issues is best carried out in firm-value models, where the default is explicitly modelled in terms of fundamental economic quantities. An excellent discussion can be found in Chapter 2 of Lando (2004).

Notes and Comments

The results of this section, and in particular Theorem 9.23, are originally due to Lando (1998); related results were obtained by Jarrow and Turnbull (1995) and Jarrow, Lando and Turnbull (1997). An alternative treatment at the textbook level (including a more detailed discussion of the RM recovery model) is given in Chapter 5 of Lando (2004). Proposition 9.24 is due to Duffie and Singleton (1999a); extensions are discussed in Becherer and Schweizer (2005). For a generalization of Theorem 9.23 to reduced-form models where the default time is not doubly stochastic we refer to Duffie, Schroder and Skiadas (1996) and Collin-Dufresne, Goldstein and Hugonnier (2004).

9.5 Affine Models

In order to apply the pricing formulas for doubly stochastic random times obtained in Theorem 9.23 we need effective ways to evaluate the conditional expectations on the right-hand side of equations (9.25) and (9.26). In most models, where default is modelled by a doubly stochastic random time, (r_t) and (γ_t) are modelled as functions of some p-dimensional Markovian state variable process $(\boldsymbol{\Psi}_t)$ with state space given by the domain $D \subset \mathbb{R}^p$, so that $R_t := r_t + \gamma_t$ is of the form $R_t = R(\boldsymbol{\Psi}_t)$ for some function $R : D \subseteq \mathbb{R}^p \to \mathbb{R}_+$, and thus the natural background filtration is given by $(\mathcal{F}_t) = \sigma(\{\boldsymbol{\Psi}_s : s \leqslant t\})$. We hence have to compute conditional expectations of the form $E(\exp(-\int_t^T R(\boldsymbol{\Psi}_s)\,\mathrm{d}s) g(\boldsymbol{\Psi}_T) \mid \mathcal{F}_t)$ for generic $g : D \subset \mathbb{R}^p \to \mathbb{R}_+$. Since $(\boldsymbol{\Psi}_t)$ is a Markov process, this conditional expectation is given by some function $f(t, \boldsymbol{\Psi}_t)$ of time and current value $\boldsymbol{\Psi}_t$ of the state variable process. It is well known that the function f can be characterized in terms of a parabolic PDE—this is the celebrated *Feynman–Kac formula*.

This yields an approach to determine f using analytical or numerical techniques for PDEs. In particular, it is known that in the case where $(\boldsymbol{\Psi}_t)$ belongs to the class of *affine jump diffusions* (see below), where R is an affine function and where $g(\boldsymbol{\psi}) = \exp(\boldsymbol{u}'\boldsymbol{\psi})$ for some $\boldsymbol{u} \in \mathbb{R}^p$, the function f is of the form

$$f(t, \boldsymbol{\psi}) = \exp(\alpha(t, T) + \boldsymbol{\beta}(t, T)'\boldsymbol{\psi}) \tag{9.32}$$

for deterministic functions $\alpha : [0, T] \to \mathbb{R}$ and $\boldsymbol{\beta} : [0, T] \to R^p$; moreover, α and $\boldsymbol{\beta}$ are determined by a $(p + 1)$-dimensional ordinary differential equation (ODE) system that is easily solved numerically. A relationship of the form (9.32) is often termed an *affine term structure*, as it implies that continuously compounded yields of bonds at time t are affine functions of $\boldsymbol{\Psi}_t$. Because of the ease of implementation, most reduced-form models used in practice work with affine jump diffusions as state variable process.

In this section we discuss these results. We concentrate on the case where the state variable process is given by a one-dimensional diffusion; extensions to processes with jumps will be considered briefly at the end.

9.5.1 Basic Results

The PDE characterization of f. We assume that the state variable process (Ψ_t) is the unique solution of the SDE

$$d\Psi_t = \mu(\Psi_t)\,dt + \sigma(\Psi_t)\,dW_t, \quad \Psi_0 = \psi \in D, \tag{9.33}$$

with state space given by the domain $D \subseteq \mathbb{R}$. Here (W_t) is a standard, one-dimensional Brownian motion on some filtered probability space $(\Omega, \mathcal{F}, P, (\mathcal{F}_t))$, and μ and σ are continuous functions from D to $\mathbb{R}$, respectively $\mathbb{R}_+$. Consider functions $R, g : D \to \mathbb{R}_+$. Since (Ψ_t) is Markovian, given the present value Ψ_t, the future evolution $(\Psi_s)_{s \geqslant t}$ of the state variable process is independent of $\mathcal{F}_t$, and we obtain

$$E\bigg(\exp\bigg(-\int_t^T R(\Psi_s)\,ds\bigg)g(\Psi_T)\;\bigg|\;\mathcal{F}_t\bigg) = f(t, \Psi_t) \tag{9.34}$$

for some function $f : [0, T] \times D \to \mathbb{R}_+$. The next lemma gives the characterization of f in terms of a parabolic PDE announced above.

Lemma 9.26 (Feynman–Kac). *If f is once continuously differentiable in t and twice continuously differentiable in ψ, it solves the terminal-value problem*

$$\left.\begin{aligned} f_t + \mu(\psi)f_\psi + \tfrac{1}{2}\sigma^2(\psi)f_{\psi\psi} &= R(\psi)f, \quad (t, \psi) \in [0, T) \times D, \\ f(T, \psi) &= g(\psi), \quad \psi \in D, \end{aligned}\right\} \tag{9.35}$$

where lower indices denote partial derivatives. Conversely, suppose that the function g is bounded, that $R(\psi) \geqslant 0$ for all $\psi \in D$, and that $\tilde{f} : [0, T] \times D \to \mathbb{R}_+$ is a bounded solution of the terminal value problem (9.35). Let (Ψ_t) be a solution of the SDE (9.33). Then $E(\exp(-\int_t^T R(\Psi_s)\,ds)g(\Psi_T) \mid \mathcal{F}_t) = \tilde{f}(t, \Psi_t)$.

The Feynman–Kac formula is a standard result of stochastic calculus and it is discussed in many textbooks on stochastic processes and financial mathematics, so we omit the proof (references are given in Notes and Comments).

Affine term structure. The following assumption ensures that the solution of the PDE (9.35), with terminal condition $g(\psi) = \exp(u\psi)$, $u\psi \leqslant 0$ for $\psi \in D$, is of the form (9.32), so that we have an affine term structure. Note that $g \equiv 1$ for $u = 0$; this is the appropriate terminal condition for pricing zero-coupon bonds.

Assumption 9.27. *R, μ and σ^2 are affine functions of ψ, i.e. there are constants ρ^0, ρ^1, k^0, k^1, h^0 and h^1 such that $R(\psi) = \rho^0 + \rho^1\psi$, $\mu(\psi) = k^0 + k^1\psi$ and $\sigma^2(\psi) = h^0 + h^1\psi$. Moreover, for all $\psi \in D$ we have $h^0 + h^1\psi \geqslant 0$ and $\rho_0 + \rho_1\psi \geqslant 0$.*

Fix some $T > 0$. We try to find a solution of (9.35) of the form $\tilde{f}(t, \psi) = \exp(\alpha(t, T) + \beta(t, T)\psi)$ for continuously differentiable functions $\alpha(\cdot, T)$ and $\beta(\cdot, T)$. As $\tilde{f}(T, \psi) = \exp(u\psi)$, we immediately obtain the terminal condition $\alpha(T, T) = 0$, $\beta(T, T) = u$. Denote by $\alpha'(\cdot, T)$ and $\beta'(\cdot, T)$ the derivative of α and β with respect to t. Using the special form of $\tilde{f}$ we obtain that

$$\tilde{f}_t = (\alpha' + \beta'\psi)\tilde{f}, \quad \tilde{f}_\psi = \beta\tilde{f} \quad \text{and} \quad \tilde{f}_{\psi\psi} = \beta^2\tilde{f}.$$

Hence, under Assumption 9.27 the PDE (9.35) takes the form

$$(\alpha' + \beta'\psi)\tilde{f} + (k^0 + k^1\psi)\beta\tilde{f} + \tfrac{1}{2}(h^0 + h^1\psi)\beta^2\tilde{f} = (\rho^0 + \rho^1\psi)\tilde{f}.$$

Dividing by $\tilde{f}$ and rearranging we obtain

$$\alpha' + k^0\beta + \tfrac{1}{2}h^0\beta^2 - \rho^0 + (\beta' + k^1\beta + \tfrac{1}{2}h^1\beta^2 - \rho^1)\psi = 0.$$

Since this equation must hold for all $\psi \in D$, we obtain the following ODE system:

$$\beta'(t,T) = \rho^1 - k^1\beta(t,T) - \tfrac{1}{2}h^1\beta^2(t,T), \quad \beta(T,T) = u, \tag{9.36}$$

$$\alpha'(t,T) = \rho^0 - k^0\beta(t,T) - \tfrac{1}{2}h^0\beta^2(t,T), \quad \alpha(T,T) = 0. \tag{9.37}$$

The ODE (9.36) for $\beta(\cdot\,,T)$ is a so-called *Ricatti equation*. While explicit solutions exist only in certain special cases, the ODE is easily solved numerically. The ODE (9.37) for $\alpha(\cdot\,,T)$ can be solved by simple (numerical) integration once β has been determined. Summing up, we have the following proposition.

Proposition 9.28. *Suppose that Assumption 9.27 holds, that the ODE system (9.36), (9.37) has a unique solution (α, β) on $[0, T]$ and that there is some C such that $\beta(t,T)\psi \leqslant C$ for all $t \in [0,T]$, $\psi \in D$. Then*

$$E\left(\exp\left(-\int_t^T R(\Psi_s)\,\mathrm{d}s\right)\exp(u\Psi_T) \,\middle|\, \mathcal{F}_t\right) = \exp(\alpha(t,T) + \beta(t,T)\Psi_t).$$

Proof. The result follows immediately from Lemma 9.26, as our assumption on β implies that $\tilde{f}(t,\psi) = \exp(\alpha(t,T) + \beta(t,T)\psi)$ is bounded. □

9.5.2 *The CIR Square-Root Diffusion*

A very popular affine model is the square-root diffusion model proposed by Cox, Ingersoll and Ross (1985) as a model for the short rate of interest. In this model (Ψ_t) is given by the solution of the SDE

$$\mathrm{d}\Psi_t = \kappa(\bar{\theta} - \Psi_t)\,\mathrm{d}t + \sigma\sqrt{\Psi_t}\,\mathrm{d}W_t, \quad \Psi_0 = \psi > 0, \tag{9.38}$$

for parameters $\kappa, \bar{\theta}, \sigma > 0$ and state space $D = [0, \infty)$. Clearly, (9.38) is an affine model in the sense of Assumption 9.27; the parameters are given by $k^0 = \kappa\bar{\theta}$, $k^1 = -\kappa$, $h^0 = 0$ and $h^1 = \sigma^2$.

It is well known that the SDE (9.38) admits a global solution (see Notes and Comments for a reference). This issue is non-trivial since the square-root function is not Lipschitz and since one has to ensure that the solution remains in D for all $t > 0$. Note that (9.38) implies that (Ψ_t) is a *mean reverting process*: if Ψ_t deviates from the mean-reversion level $\bar{\theta}$, the process is pulled back towards $\bar{\theta}$. Moreover, if the mean reversion is sufficiently strong relative to the volatility, trajectories never reach zero. More precisely, let $\tau_0(\Psi) := \inf\{t \geqslant 0 : \Psi_t = 0\}$. It is well known that for $\kappa\bar{\theta} \geqslant \frac{1}{2}\sigma^2$ we have $P(\tau_0(\Psi) < \infty) = 0$, whereas for $\kappa\bar{\theta} < \frac{1}{2}\sigma^2$ we have $P(\tau_0(\Psi) < \infty) = 1$.

In the CIR square-root model the Ricatti equations (9.36) and (9.37) can be solved explicitly. Using Proposition 9.28, one has

$$E\left(\exp\left(-\int_t^T (\rho^0+\rho^1\Psi_s)\,\mathrm{d}s\right) \,\Big|\, \mathcal{F}_t\right) = \exp(\alpha(T-t)+\beta(T-t)\Psi_t),$$

with

$$\beta(\tau) = \frac{-2\rho^1(\mathrm{e}^{\gamma\tau}-1)}{\gamma-\kappa+\mathrm{e}^{\gamma\tau}(\gamma+\kappa)}, \tag{9.39}$$

$$\alpha(\tau) = -\rho^0\tau + 2\frac{\kappa\bar{\theta}}{\sigma^2}\ln\left(\frac{2\gamma\mathrm{e}^{1/2}\tau(\gamma+\kappa)}{\gamma-\kappa+\mathrm{e}^{\gamma\tau}(\gamma+\kappa)}\right), \tag{9.40}$$

and $\tau := T-t$, $\gamma := \sqrt{\kappa^2+2\sigma^2\rho^1}$. These formulas are the key to pricing bonds in models where the risk-free short rate and default intensities are affine functions of independent square-root processes, as is shown in the next example.

Example 9.29 (a three-factor model). We now consider the pricing of zero-coupon bonds in a three-factor model similar to models that are frequently used in the literature. We assume that $\boldsymbol{\Psi}_t = (\Psi_{t,1},\Psi_{t,2},\Psi_{t,3})'$ is a vector of three independent square-root diffusions with dynamics $\mathrm{d}\Psi_{t,i} = \kappa_i(\bar{\theta}_i-\Psi_{t,i})\,\mathrm{d}t + \sigma_i\sqrt{\Psi_{t,i}}\,\mathrm{d}W_{t,i}$ for independent Brownian motions $(W_{t,i})$, $i=1,2,3$. The risk-free short rate of interest is given by $r_t = r_0+\Psi_{t,2}-\Psi_{t,1}$ for a constant $r_0 \geqslant 0$; the hazard rate of the counterparty under consideration is given by $\gamma_t = \gamma_1\Psi_{t,1}+\Psi_{t,3}$ for some constant $\gamma_1 > 0$. This parametrization allows for negative instantaneous correlation between (r_t) and (γ_t), which is in line with empirical evidence. Note, however, that this negative correlation comes at the expense of possibly negative riskless interest rates. In this context the price of a default-free zero-coupon bond is given by

$$\begin{aligned} p_0(t,T) &= E\left(\exp\left(-\int_t^T r_s\,\mathrm{d}s\right)\,\Big|\,\mathcal{F}_t\right) \\ &= \mathrm{e}^{-r_0(T-t)}E\left(\exp\left(-\int_t^T \Psi_{s,2}\,\mathrm{d}s\right)\,\Big|\,\mathcal{F}_t\right)E\left(\exp\left(\int_t^T \Psi_{s,1}\,\mathrm{d}s\right)\,\Big|\,\mathcal{F}_t\right), \end{aligned} \tag{9.41}$$

where we have used the independence of $(\Psi_{t,1})$, $(\Psi_{t,2})$, $(\Psi_{t,3})$. Each of the terms in (9.41) can be evaluated using the above formulas for α and β (equations (9.39) and (9.40)). Assuming that we have recovery of treasury in default (see Section 9.4.1) and a deterministic percentage loss given default δ, we obtain that the price of a defaultable zero-coupon bond is given by

$$p_1(t,T) = (1-\delta)p_0(t,T) + \delta E\left(\exp\left(-\int_t^T (r_s+\gamma_s)\,\mathrm{d}s\right)\,\Big|\,\mathcal{F}_t\right).$$

By definition of r_t and γ_t the last term on the right-hand side equals

$$\delta E\left(\exp\left(-\int_t^T r_0+(\gamma_1-1)\Psi_{s,1}+\Psi_{s,2}+\Psi_{s,3}\,\mathrm{d}s\right)\,\Big|\,\mathcal{F}_t\right),$$

which can be evaluated in a similar way to the evaluation of expression (9.41). In the next section we will show how one deals with more complicated recovery models, such as recovery of face value.

9.5.3 Extensions

A jump-diffusion model for (Ψ_t). We briefly discuss an extension of the basic model (9.33), where the economic factor process (Ψ_t) follows a diffusion with jumps. Adding jumps to the dynamics of (Ψ_t) provides more flexibility for modelling default correlations in models with conditionally independent defaults (see Section 9.6.3 below).

In this section we assume that (Ψ_t) is the unique solution of the SDE

$$\mathrm{d}\Psi_t = \mu(\Psi_t)\,\mathrm{d}t + \sigma(\Psi_t)\,\mathrm{d}W_t + \mathrm{d}Z_t, \quad \Psi_0 = \psi \in D. \tag{9.42}$$

Here (Z_t) is a pure jump process whose jump intensity at time t is equal to $\lambda^Z(\Psi_t)$ for some function $\lambda^Z : D \to \mathbb{R}_+$ and whose jump-size distribution has df ν on $\mathbb{R}$. Intuitively this means that given the trajectory $(\Psi_t(\omega))_{t \geqslant 0}$ of the factor process, (Z_t) jumps at the jump times of an inhomogeneous Poisson process (see Section 10.2.7) with time-varying intensity $\lambda^Z(t, \Psi_t)$; the size of the jumps has df ν.

Suppose now that Assumption 9.27 holds, and that $\lambda^Z(\psi) = l^0 + l^1\psi$ for constants l^0, l^1 such that $\lambda^Z(\psi) > 0$ for all $\psi \in D$. In that case we say that (Ψ_t) follows an *affine jump diffusion*. For $x \in \mathbb{R}$ denote by $\hat{\nu}(x) = \int_{\mathbb{R}} \mathrm{e}^{-xy}\,\mathrm{d}\nu(y) \in (0, \infty]$ the extended Laplace–Stieltjes transform of ν (with domain $\mathbb{R}$ instead of the usual domain $[0, \infty)$). Consider the following extension of the ODE system (9.36), (9.37):

$$\beta'(t, T) = \rho^1 - k^1\beta(t, T) - \tfrac{1}{2}h^1\beta^2(t, T) - l^1(\hat{\nu}(-\beta(t, T)) - 1), \tag{9.43}$$

$$\alpha'(t, T) = \rho^0 - k^0\beta(t, T) - \tfrac{1}{2}h^0\beta^2(t, T) - l^0(\hat{\nu}(-\beta(t, T)) - 1), \tag{9.44}$$

with terminal condition $\beta(T, T) = u$ for some $u \leqslant 0$ and $\alpha(T, T) = 0$. Suppose that the system (9.44), (9.43) has a unique solution α, β and that $\beta(t, T)\psi \leqslant C$ for all $t \in [0, T]$, $\psi \in D$ (for l^0 or $l^1 \neq 0$ this implicitly implies that $\hat{\nu}(-\beta(t, T)) < \infty$ for all t). Define $\tilde{f}(t, \psi) = \exp(\alpha(t, T) + \beta(t, T)\psi)$. Using similar arguments to those above, it can then be shown that the conditional expectation $E(\exp(-\int_t^T R(\Psi_s)\,\mathrm{d}s)\exp(u\Psi_T) \mid \mathcal{F}_t)$ equals $\tilde{f}(t, \Psi_t)$.

Example 9.30 (the model of Duffie and Gârleanu (2001)). The following jump-diffusion model has been used in the literature on CDO pricing. The dynamics of (Ψ_t) are given by

$$\mathrm{d}\Psi_t = \kappa(\bar{\theta} - \Psi_t)\,\mathrm{d}t + \sigma\sqrt{\Psi_t}\,\mathrm{d}W_t + \mathrm{d}Z_t \tag{9.45}$$

for parameters $\kappa, \bar{\theta}, \sigma > 0$ and a jump process (Z_t) with constant jump intensity $l^0 > 0$ and exponentially distributed jump sizes with parameter $1/\mu$. Following Duffie and Gârleanu, we will sometimes call the model (9.45) a *basic affine jump diffusion*. Note that these assumptions imply that the mean of ν is equal to μ and that ν has support $[0, \infty)$, so that (Ψ_t) has only upward jumps. Hence the existence of a solution to (9.45) follows from the existence of solutions in the pure diffusion case. It is relatively easy to show that for $t \to \infty$ we obtain $E(\Psi_t) \to \bar{\theta} + l^0\mu/\kappa$. For illustrative purposes we present the parameter values used in Duffie and Gârleanu

Table 9.1. Parameters used in the model of Duffie and Gârleanu (2001). Recall that l^0 gives the intensity of jump in the factor process, μ gives the average jump size. With these parameters the average waiting time for a jump in the systematic factor process is $1/l^0 = 5$ years.

κ	$\bar{\theta}$	σ	l^0	μ
0.6	0.02	0.14	0.2	0.1

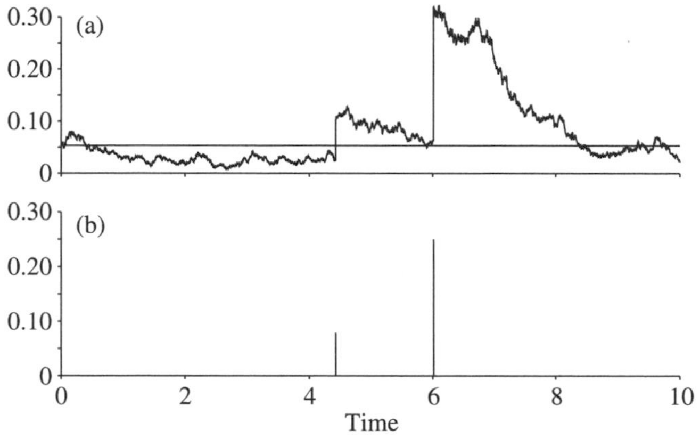

Figure 9.8. (a) A typical trajectory of the basic affine jump diffusion model (9.45) and (b) the corresponding jumps of (Z_t). The parameter values used are given in Table 9.1; the initial value Ψ_0 is equal to the long-run mean $\bar{\theta} + (l^0\mu)/\kappa$ marked by the horizontal line.

(2001) in Table 9.1; a typical trajectory of (Ψ_t) is simulated in Figure 9.8. Next we compute the Laplace–Stieltjes transform $\hat{\nu}$. We obtain for $u > -1/\mu$ that

$$\hat{\nu}(u) = \int_0^\infty \mathrm{e}^{-ux}(1/\mu)\mathrm{e}^{-x/\mu}\,\mathrm{d}x = \frac{1}{1+\mu u};$$

for $u \leqslant -1/\mu$ we get $\hat{\nu}(u) = \infty$. We therefore have all the necessary ingredients to set up the Ricatti equations (9.44) and (9.43). In the case of the model (9.45) it is in fact possible to solve these equations explicitly (see, for example, Chapter 11 of Duffie and Singleton (2003)). However, the explicit solution is given by a very lengthy expression, so we omit the details.

Application to recovery payments. According to Theorem 9.23, in a model with a doubly stochastic default time τ with risk-neutral hazard rate $\gamma(\Psi_t)$, the price in t of a recovery payment of size $(1-\delta)$ at the default time τ equals

$$(1-\delta)E\biggl(\int_t^T \gamma(\Psi_s)\exp\biggl(-\int_t^s R(\Psi_u)\,\mathrm{d}u\biggr)\,\mathrm{d}s \biggm| \mathcal{F}_t\biggr), \tag{9.46}$$

where again $R(\psi) = r(\psi) + \gamma(\psi)$. Using the Fubini Theorem this equals

$$(1-\delta)\int_t^T E\biggl(\gamma(\Psi_s)\exp\biggl(-\int_t^s R(\Psi_u)\,\mathrm{d}u\biggr) \biggm| \mathcal{F}_t\biggr)\,\mathrm{d}s. \tag{9.47}$$

Suppose now that $\gamma(\psi) = \gamma^0 + \gamma^1\psi$, that $R(\psi) = \rho^0 + \rho^1\psi$ and that (Ψ_t) is given by an affine jump diffusion as introduced above. In that case the inner expectation in (9.47) is given by a function $F(t, s, \Psi_t)$. This function can be computed using an extension of the basic affine methodology, so that (9.47) can be computed by one-dimensional numerical integration. Define for $0 \leqslant t \leqslant s$ the function $\tilde{f}(t, s, \psi) = \exp(\alpha(t, s) + \beta(t, s)\psi)$, where $\alpha(\cdot\,, s)$ and $\beta(\cdot\,, s)$ solve the ODEs (9.44), (9.43) with terminal condition $\alpha(s, s) = \beta(s, s) = 0$. Denote by $\hat{\nu}'(x)$ the derivative of the Laplace–Stieltjes transform of ν. Then it is a straightforward application of standard calculus to show that, modulo some integrability conditions, $F(t, s, \psi) = \tilde{f}(t, s, \psi)(A(t, s) + B(t, s)\psi)$, where $A(\cdot\,, s)$ and $B(\cdot\,, s)$ solve the following ODE system:

$$B'(t, s) + k^1 B(t, s) + h^1 \beta B(t, s) - l^1 \hat{\nu}'(-\beta) B(t, s) = 0, \tag{9.48}$$

$$A'(t, s) + k^0 B(t, s) + h^0 \beta B(t, s) - l^0 \hat{\nu}'(-\beta) B(t, s) = 0, \tag{9.49}$$

with terminal condition $A(s, s) = \gamma_0$, $B(s, s) = \gamma_1$. Again, (9.48) and (9.49) are straightforward to evaluate numerically.

Example 9.31 (defaultable zero-coupon bonds and CDS). We now have all the necessary ingredients to compute prices and credit spreads of defaultable zero-coupon bonds and CDS spreads in a model with a doubly stochastic default time with hazard rate $\gamma_t = \Psi_t$ for a one-dimensional affine jump diffusion (Ψ_t). In Figure 9.9 we plot the credit spread for defaultable bonds for the recovery assumptions discussed in Section 9.4.1. Note that, for $T \to t$, i.e. for time to maturity close to zero, the spread tends to $c(t, t) = \delta\Psi_t > 0$, as claimed in Section 9.4.3; in particular, the credit spread does not vanish as $T \to t$. This is in stark contrast to firm-value models, where typically $c(t, t) = 0$, as was shown in Section 8.2.1. Note further that, for $T - t$ large, under the RF assumption we obtain *negative* credit spreads, which is clearly unrealistic. These negative credit spreads are caused by the fact that under RF we obtain a payment of fixed size $1 - \delta$ immediately at default. If the default-free interest rate r is relatively large, it may happen that

$$E^Q\biggl(\exp\biggl(-\int_0^\tau r_s\,\mathrm{d}s\biggr)(1-\delta)I_{\{\tau\leqslant T\}}\biggr) < E^Q\biggl(\exp\biggl(-\int_0^T r_s\,\mathrm{d}s\biggr)I_{\{\tau\leqslant T\}}\biggr),$$

even if $\delta > 0$. This stems from the fact that on the right-hand side discounting is done over the whole period $[0, T]$ (as opposed to $[0, \tau]$), so that discounting has a large impact on the value of the right-hand side, compensating the higher terminal pay-off. In Figure 9.10 we have plotted the fair spreads for CDS with and without accrued payments for varying maturities, assuming that the risk-neutral hazard rate follows a basic affine jump diffusion.

Notes and Comments

The Feynman–Kac formula is discussed, for example, in Section 4.5 of Björk (1998), or, at a slightly more technical level, in Section 5.7 of Karatzas and Shreve (1988).

Important original papers on affine models in term structure modelling are Duffie and Kan (1996) for diffusion models and Duffie, Pan and Singleton (2000) for jump diffusions. The latter paper also contains other applications of affine models, such

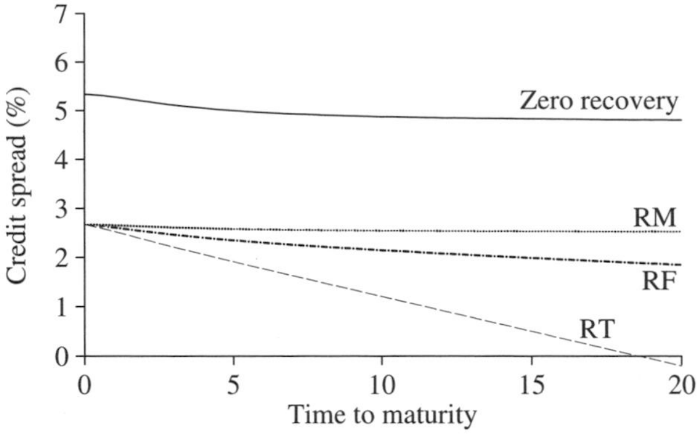

Figure 9.9. Spreads of corporate zero-coupon bonds in the Duffie–Gârleanu model (9.45) for various recovery assumptions. The parameters of (Ψ_t) are given in Table 9.1; the initial value is $\Psi_0 \approx 0.0533$. The risk-free interest rate and the loss given default are deterministic and are given by $r = 6\%$ and $\delta = 0.5$. Note that under the RT recovery model, the spread becomes negative for large times to maturity.

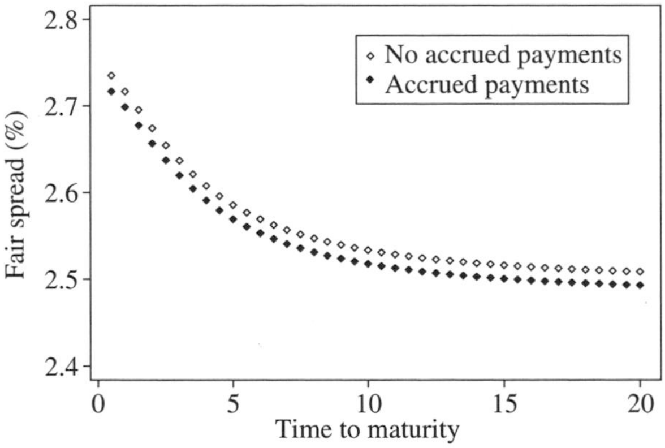

Figure 9.10. Fair CDS spreads in the Duffie–Gârleanu model (9.45) for a CDS contract with semiannual premium payments and varying time to maturity. The parameters of (Ψ_t) are given in Table 9.1; the initial value is $\Psi_0 \approx 0.0533$. The risk-free interest rate and the loss given default are deterministic and are given by $r = 6\%$ and $\delta = 0.5$. Note that, for small time to maturity, the fair swap spread is approximately equal to $\delta\Psi_0 \approx 2.7\%$.

as the pricing of equity options under stochastic volatility and econometric issues related to affine models. It should be mentioned that there is also a converse to Proposition 9.28: if the conditional expectations $E(\exp(-\int_t^T R(\Psi_s)\,\mathrm{d}s)\mathrm{e}^{u\Psi_T} \mid \mathcal{F}_t)$ are all exponentially affine functions of Ψ_t, the process (Ψ_t) is necessarily affine (see Duffie and Kan (1996) and in particular Duffie, Filipovic and Schachermayer (2003) for details).

The mathematical properties of the CIR model are discussed in, for example, Chapter 6.2 of Lamberton and Lapeyre (1996), where the explicit solution (9.39) and (9.40) of the Ricatti equations in the CIR model is also derived. The model studied in Example 9.29 is akin to models proposed by Duffie and Singleton (1999a). Problems related to the modelling of negative correlation between state variable process in an affine setting are discussed in Section 5.8 of Lando (2004). It is possible to compute the conditional expectation (9.46) for the price of a recovery payment as the solution of a parabolic PDE, which stems from the Feynman–Kac formula (see, for example, Lando 1998 for details). Empirical work on affine models for defaultable bonds includes the publications of Duffee (1999) and Driessen (2005).

9.6 Conditionally Independent Defaults

We begin our analysis of reduced-form models for portfolio credit risk with a brief overview of the existing model classes.

9.6.1 Reduced-Form Models for Portfolio Credit Risk

The simplest reduced-form models for portfolio credit risk are models with conditionally independent defaults. In this class default times are independent given the realization of some observable economic background process; hence these models are an extension of the static Bernoulli mixture models of Section 8.4. More sophisticated models for dependent defaults include *copula models* and models with *interacting intensities*. Copula models have become popular in practice and we give an in-depth discussion of this model class in Sections 9.7 and 9.8; models with interacting intensities are discussed in Section 9.8.3.

The common feature of the latter two model classes, as opposed to models with conditionally independent defaults, is the presence of *default contagion* and *counterparty risk*. Loosely speaking, this means that the conditional default probability of a non-defaulted firm jumps (usually upwards) given the additional information that some other firm has defaulted. As a consequence the credit spread of bonds issued by a non-defaulted firm increases given the news that some other firm has defaulted. Mathematically, default contagion is reflected in jumps in the martingale default intensity of non-defaulted firms at the default times of other firms in the portfolio. The impact of the default of some firm on the conditional default probability of other firms can arise via different channels. On the one hand it might be due to direct economic links between firms, such as a close business relationship or a strong borrower–lender relationship. For instance, the default probability of a corporate bank is likely to increase if one of its major borrowers defaults. This direct channel of default interaction is termed counterparty risk. On the other hand, changes in the conditional default probability of non-defaulted firms can be caused by *information effects*: investors might revise their estimate of the financial health of non-defaulted firms in light of the news that a particular firm has defaulted. In that case one speaks of information-based default contagion.

A lot of recent research deals with the modelling of counterparty risk and default contagion for a number of reasons. First, there is substantial empirical evidence for interaction between default events. A recent example is provided by the downfall of the energy giant Enron in autumn 2001: the news that Enron had used illegal accounting practices led to rising credit spreads for many other corporations as bond investors lost confidence in the accounting statements of these corporations—a striking example of default contagion. Moreover, the stock price of major lenders to Enron fell in anticipation of large losses on these loans, reflecting counterparty risk. Formal empirical evidence for interaction between default events is listed in Notes and Comments. A second reason for modelling default contagion is that this might help to explain the clustering of defaults around economic recessions observed in real data. However, this is not to say that models with conditionally independent defaults are of little interest. Yu (2005a) shows that the low default correlations in models with conditionally independent defaults may be related more closely to an unsatisfactory modelling of state variables than to a problem of the approach per se. We will discuss this issue in more detail in Section 9.6.3 below. On a related note, not every default of a major corporation leads to changes in the credit spreads of the remaining firms, so conditional independence is often realistic. Moreover, more sophisticated models of default dependence may be hard to calibrate in practice, particularly for large portfolios. In any case, the discussion of models with conditionally independent defaults will provide a methodological basis for studying more complicated models.

Notation. In keeping with Section 9.1, we use the following notation for our analysis of dynamic portfolio credit risk models. We consider a portfolio of m obligors with default times τ_i and default indicator processes $Y_{t,i} = Y_i(t) = I_{\{\tau_i \leqslant t\}}$, $1 \leqslant i \leqslant m$, on some generic probability space $(\Omega, \mathcal{F}, P)$, where the interpretation of P (physical measure or equivalent martingale measure) will depend on the context. (Note that we switch freely between the notation $X_{t,i}$ and the notation $X_i(t)$ for generic processes defined at the level of individual obligors; generally we favour $X_{t,i}$ for stochastic processes and $X_i(t)$ for deterministic ones, but we also depart from this for reasons of notational elegance in individual formulas.)

In dynamic portfolio credit risk models it is convenient to consider survival functions instead of distribution functions. As usual, $\bar{F}_i(t) = P(\tau_i > t)$ denotes the tail or survival function of obligor i; the joint survival function is denoted by $\bar{F}(t_1, \dots, t_m) = P(\tau_1 > t_1, \dots, \tau_m > t_m)$. Throughout our analysis we restrict ourselves to models without simultaneous defaults. We may therefore denote the *ordered default times* by $T_0 < T_1 < \dots < T_m$, where $T_0 = 0$ and, for $1 \leqslant n \leqslant m$, $T_n = \min\{\tau_i : \tau_i > T_{n-1},\ 1 \leqslant i \leqslant m\}$. By $\xi_n \in \{1, \dots, m\}$ we denote the identity of the firm defaulting at time T_n. Finally,

$$A_n = \{1 \leqslant i \leqslant m : Y_i(T_n) = 0\} = \{1, \dots, m\} \setminus \{\xi_1, \dots, \xi_n\}$$

is the set of non-defaulted firms immediately after time T_n.

As in the previous sections, $(\mathcal{F}_t)$ represents our background filtration, typically generated by some observable process $(\boldsymbol{\Psi}_t)$ representing economic factors. Moreover, we introduce the filtrations $\{\mathcal{H}_t^i\}$, $1 \leqslant i \leqslant m$, $(\mathcal{H}_t)$ and $(\mathcal{G}_t)$ by

$$\mathcal{H}_t^i = \sigma(\{Y_{s,i} : s \leqslant t\}), \quad \mathcal{H}_t = \mathcal{H}_t^i \vee \dots \vee \mathcal{H}_t^m \quad \text{and} \quad \mathcal{G}_t = \mathcal{F}_t \vee \mathcal{H}_t. \tag{9.50}$$

$\{\mathcal{H}_t^i\}$ is the filtration generated by default observation for obligor i alone; $(\mathcal{H}_t)$ is the filtration generated by default observation for all obligors; $(\mathcal{G}_t)$ contains default information for all obligors and observable background information and thus represents the information available to investors at time t. Often $(\mathcal{H}_t)$ is called the *internal filtration* generated by the default times τ_i, $1 \leqslant i \leqslant m$.

9.6.2 Conditionally Independent Default Times

In this section we discuss general mathematical properties of models with conditionally independent defaults; specific examples from the literature are considered in the next section. We start with a formal definition of conditionally independent default times.

Definition 9.32. Given a probability space $(\Omega, \mathcal{F}, P)$ with background filtration $(\mathcal{F}_t)$ and random times $\tau_1, \dots, \tau_m$, the τ_i are conditionally independent doubly stochastic random times if

(i) each of the τ_i is a doubly stochastic random time in the sense of Definition 9.11 with background filtration $(\mathcal{F}_t)$ and $(\mathcal{F}_t)$-conditional hazard-rate process $(\gamma_{t,i})$; and

(ii) the rvs $\tau_1, \dots, \tau_m$ are conditionally independent given $\mathcal{F}_\infty$, i.e. we have, for all $t_1, \dots, t_m > 0$,

$$P(\tau_1 \leqslant t_1, \dots, \tau_m \leqslant t_m \mid \mathcal{F}_\infty) = \prod_{i=1}^{m} P(\tau_i \leqslant t_i \mid \mathcal{F}_\infty). \tag{9.51}$$

Construction and simulation via thresholds. The lemma that follows extends Lemma 9.12.

Lemma 9.33. *Let $(\gamma_{t,1}), \dots, (\gamma_{t,m})$ be positive, $(\mathcal{F}_t)$-adapted processes such that $\Gamma_{t,i} := \int_0^t \gamma_{s,i}\,\mathrm{d}s$ is strictly increasing and finite for any $t > 0$. Let $\boldsymbol{E} = (E_1, \dots, E_m)'$ be a vector of independent, standard exponentially distributed rvs independent of $\mathcal{F}_\infty$. Define τ_i by $\tau_i = \Gamma_i^{-1}(E_i)$. Then $\tau_1, \dots, \tau_m$ are conditionally independent doubly stochastic random times.*

Proof. According to Lemma 9.12, each of the τ_i is a doubly stochastic random time with $(\mathcal{F}_t)$-hazard-rate process $(\gamma_{t,i})$. It remains to verify the conditional independence. Using the fact that $\tau_i \leqslant t \iff E_i \leqslant \Gamma_{t,i}$, we have

$$\begin{aligned} P(\tau_1 \leqslant t_1, \dots, \tau_m \leqslant t_m \mid \mathcal{F}_\infty) &= P(E_1 \leqslant \Gamma_{t_1,1}, \dots, E_m \leqslant \Gamma_{t_m,m} \mid \mathcal{F}_\infty) \\ &= \prod_{i=1}^{m} P(E_i \leqslant \Gamma_{t_i,i} \mid \mathcal{F}_\infty) \\ &= \prod_{i=1}^{m} P(\tau_i \leqslant t_i \mid \mathcal{F}_\infty). \end{aligned} \tag{9.52}$$

Note that (9.52) holds since the rvs $\Gamma_{t_i,i}$ are measurable with respect to $\mathcal{F}_\infty$, whereas the E_i are mutually independent and independent of $\mathcal{F}_\infty$. □

Lemma 9.33 is the basis for the following simulation algorithm.

Algorithm 9.34 (multivariate threshold simulation).

(1) Generate a trajectory of the hazard-rate processes $(\gamma_{t,i})$ for $i = 1, \dots, m$. Here the same techniques as in the univariate case can be used; note, however, that for a high-dimensional factor vector this step can become quite time-consuming.

(2) Generate a vector $\boldsymbol{E}$ of independent standard exponentially distributed rvs (the threshold vector) and set $\tau_i = \Gamma_i^{-1}(E_i)$, $1 \leqslant i \leqslant m$.

As in the univariate case, Lemma 9.33 has a converse, which we state without the simple proof.

Lemma 9.35. *Let $\tau_1, \dots, \tau_m$ be conditionally independent doubly stochastic random times with $(\mathcal{F}_t)$-hazard-rate processes $(\gamma_{t,i})$. Define a random vector $\boldsymbol{E}$ by $E_i = \Gamma_i(\tau_i)$, $1 \leqslant i \leqslant m$. Then $\boldsymbol{E}$ is a vector of independent, standard exponentially distributed rvs that is independent of $\mathcal{F}_\infty$, and $\tau_i = \Gamma_i^{-1}(E_i)$ almost surely.*

Recursive default time simulation. We now describe a second recursive algorithm for simulating conditionally independent default times, which is sometimes more efficient than multivariate threshold simulation. Moreover, the algorithm generalizes naturally to reduced-form models with interacting intensities (see Section 9.8.3). We need the following lemma, which gives properties of the first default time T_1.

Lemma 9.36. *Let $\tau_1, \dots, \tau_m$ be conditionally independent doubly stochastic random times with hazard-rate processes $(\gamma_{t,1}), \dots, (\gamma_{t,m})$. Then T_1 is a doubly stochastic random time with $(\mathcal{F}_t)$-conditional hazard-rate process $\bar{\gamma}_t := \sum_{i=1}^m \gamma_{t,i}$, $t \geqslant 0$.*

Proof. Using the conditional independence of the τ_i we get

$$P(T_1 > t \mid \mathcal{F}_\infty) = P(\tau_1 > t, \dots, \tau_m > t \mid \mathcal{F}_\infty) = \prod_{i=1}^m \exp\biggl(-\int_0^t \gamma_{s,i}\,\mathrm{d}s\biggr),$$

which is obviously equal to $\exp(-\int_0^t \bar{\gamma}_s\,\mathrm{d}s)$. As this expression is $\mathcal{F}_t$-measurable, the result follows. $\square$

Next we compute the conditional probability of the event $\{\xi_1 = i\}$ given the first default time T_1 and full information about the background filtration.

Proposition 9.37. *Under the assumptions of Lemma 9.36 we have*

$$P(\xi_1 = i \mid \mathcal{F}_\infty \vee \sigma(T_1)) = \gamma_i(T_1)/\bar{\gamma}(T_1), \quad i \in \{1, \dots, m\}.$$

Proof. Conditional on $\mathcal{F}_\infty$ the τ_i are independent with deterministic hazard rate $\gamma_i(t)$, so it is enough to prove the proposition for independent random times with deterministic hazard rate. Fix some $t > 0$ and note that the probability of having more than one default in the interval $(t-h, t]$ is of order $o(h)$, as the random vector $(\tau_1, \dots, \tau_m)$ has a joint density. Hence

$$\begin{aligned} P(\{\xi_1 = i\} \cap \{T_1 \in (t-h, t]\}) &= P(\{\tau_i \in (t-h, t]\} \cap \{\tau_j > t,\ j \neq i\}) + o(h) \\ &= P(\tau_i \in (t-h, t]) \prod_{j \neq i} P(\tau_j > t) \end{aligned}$$

by the independence of the τ_i. Since $P(\tau_i > t) = \exp(-\int_0^t \gamma_i(s)\,\mathrm{d}s)$, $1 \leqslant i \leqslant m$, this equals

$$\exp\biggl(-\int_0^{t-h}\gamma_i(s)\,\mathrm{d}s\biggr)\biggl(1-\exp\biggl(-\int_{t-h}^{t}\gamma_i(s)\,\mathrm{d}s\biggr)\biggr) \times \prod_{j\neq i}\exp\biggl(-\int_0^t \gamma_j(s)\,\mathrm{d}s\biggr) + o(h).$$

Hence we get

$$\lim_{h\to 0+} h^{-1}P(\{\xi_1 = i\}\cap\{T_1 \in (t-h,t]\}) = \gamma_i(t)\exp\biggl(-\int_0^t \bar{\gamma}(s)\,\mathrm{d}s\biggr).$$

Moreover, by Lemma 9.36,

$$\lim_{h\to 0+} h^{-1}P(T_1 \in (t-h,t]) = \bar{\gamma}(t)\exp\biggl(-\int_0^t \bar{\gamma}(s)\,\mathrm{d}s\biggr),$$

so the claim follows from the definition of elementary conditional expectation and L'Hôpital's rule. □

Algorithm 9.38 (recursive default time simulation). This algorithm simulates a realization of the sequence (T_n, ξ_n) up to some maturity date T. Recall that for $n \geqslant 1$ the set of non-defaulted firms immediately after T_n is denoted by A_n and set $A_0 := \{1,\dots,m\}$. Define $\bar{\gamma}_t^n := \sum_{i\in A_n}\gamma_{t,i}$, $0 \leqslant n \leqslant m$. Then the algorithm proceeds in the following steps.

(1) Generate a trajectory of the hazard-rate processes $(\gamma_{t,i})$.

(2) Generate T_1 by standard univariate threshold simulation, using the fact that T_1 has hazard rate $(\bar{\gamma}_t^0)$ by Lemma 9.36.

(3) Determine ξ_1 as a realization of an rv ξ with $P(\xi = i) = \gamma_i(T_1)/\bar{\gamma}^0(T_1)$ (using Proposition 9.37).

(4) If $T_1 \geqslant T$ stop. Otherwise note that, for conditionally independent defaults,

$$\begin{aligned} P(T_2 - T_1 > t \mid T_1, \xi_1, \mathcal{F}_\infty) &= \frac{P(\tau_j > T_1 + t,\ j \in A_1, \mid T_1, \xi_1, \mathcal{F}_\infty)}{P(\tau_j > T_1,\ j \in A_1, \mid T_1, \xi_1, \mathcal{F}_\infty)} \\ &= \exp\biggl(-\int_{T_1}^{T_1+t}\bar{\gamma}_s^1\,\mathrm{d}s\biggr). \end{aligned} \tag{9.53}$$

Generate the waiting time $T_2 - T_1$ via univariate threshold simulation using (9.53); determine ξ_2 as before, using the fact that, for $i \in A_1$,

$$P(\xi_2 = i \mid T_1, T_2, \xi_1, \mathcal{F}_\infty) = \gamma_i(T_2)/\bar{\gamma}^1(T_2).$$

(5) Proceed in this way until $T_n \geqslant T$ for some $n \leqslant m$ or until all firms have defaulted.

Recursive default time simulation is particularly efficient if we want to simulate only defaults occurring before some maturity date T and if defaults are rare. In that case, typically $T_n > T$ already for n relatively small, so only a few ordered default times need to be simulated. With multivariate threshold simulation, on the other hand, we need to simulate the default times of all obligors in the portfolio.

Martingale intensities. The following proposition shows that, for conditionally independent defaults, martingale intensities and hazard rates coincide.

Proposition 9.39. *Let $\tau_1, \dots, \tau_m$ be conditionally independent doubly stochastic random times with hazard-rate processes $(\gamma_{t,1}), \dots, (\gamma_{t,m})$. Then the process $M_{t,i} := Y_{t,i} - \int_0^{t\wedge\tau_i} \gamma_{s,i}\,\mathrm{d}s$ is a $(\mathcal{G}_t)$-martingale with $(\mathcal{G}_t)$ as in (9.50).*

Proof. We know from Proposition 9.15 that $(M_{t,i})$ is a martingale with respect to the filtration $\{\mathcal{G}_t^i\}$ with $\mathcal{G}_t^i = \mathcal{F}_t \vee \mathcal{H}_t^i$, i.e. that $E(M_{s,i} \mid \mathcal{G}_t^i) = M_{t,i}$, $s > t$. However, this does not automatically imply that $(M_{t,i})$ is also a $(\mathcal{G}_t)$-martingale, as $\mathcal{G}_t^i \subset \mathcal{G}_t$, and so we could have $E(M_{s,i} \mid \mathcal{G}_t) \neq E(M_{s,i} \mid \mathcal{G}_t^i)$. In fact, this typically happens in copula models (see Section 9.8.1 below). In the present situation the conditional independence of the τ_i permits us to overcome this difficulty. This is quite intuitive: since the τ_i are conditionally independent, default information for obligor $j \neq i$ is of no use in predicting the default of obligor i. A formal argument is as follows. Using Lemma 9.35, we may assume that there is a vector $\boldsymbol{E}$ of independent, standard exponential rvs, independent of $\mathcal{F}_\infty$, such that for all $1 \leqslant j \leqslant m$ we have $\tau_j = \Gamma_j^{-1}(E_j)$. Obviously, τ_i is independent of E_j for $j \neq i$, so

$$E(M_{s,i} \mid \mathcal{G}_t^i \vee \sigma(\{E_j : j \neq i\})) = E(M_{s,i} \mid \mathcal{G}_t^i) = M_{t,i}. \tag{9.54}$$

On the other hand, if we know E_j and the trajectory $(\gamma_{u,j})_{0\leqslant u\leqslant t}$, we can determine $Y_{u,j}$ for $0 \leqslant u \leqslant t$. Hence $\mathcal{G}_t = \mathcal{F}_t \vee \mathcal{H}_t^1 \vee \cdots \vee \mathcal{H}_t^m$ is a subset of $\mathcal{G}_t^i \vee \sigma(\{E_j : j \neq i\})$, so (9.54) implies that $E(M_{s,i} \mid \mathcal{G}_t) = M_{t,i}$, as required. □

Remark 9.40 (pricing of single-name credit products). Suppose that $\tau_1, \dots, \tau_m$ are conditionally independent doubly stochastic random times. Consider a single-name credit product with maturity T whose pay-off H depends only on the default history of firm i and on the evolution of default-free security prices and is thus $\mathcal{G}_T^i$-measurable. A typical example is a vulnerable claim of the form $H = I_{\{\tau_i > T\}} X$ for an $\mathcal{F}_T$-measurable rv X. A similar argument to that in the proof of Proposition 9.39 shows that

$$E^Q\bigg(\exp\bigg(-\int_t^T r_s\,\mathrm{d}s\bigg)H \biggm| \mathcal{G}_t^i\bigg) = E^Q\bigg(\exp\bigg(-\int_t^T r_s\,\mathrm{d}s\bigg)H \biggm| \mathcal{G}_t\bigg), \quad t \leqslant T,$$

where (r_t) is the $\mathcal{F}_t$-adapted default-free short rate. Now, the left-hand side of the above equation gives the price of the claim H in a single-firm model where the information available to investors at time t is given by $\mathcal{G}_t^i$, whereas the right-hand side gives the price of H in the portfolio model where at time t investors have access to the larger information set $\mathcal{G}_t$ containing default information on all firms in the portfolio. Hence pricing formulas for single-name credit products obtained in a single-firm model with a doubly stochastic default time, such as the pricing formulas from Theorem 9.23, remain valid in a portfolio model with conditionally independent default times. If we go beyond conditional independence this is no longer true, as will be discussed in Section 9.8.1.

9.6.3 Examples and Applications

In most models with conditionally independent defaults, hazard rates are modelled as linear combinations of independent affine diffusions, possibly with jumps. A typical model is as follows:

$$\gamma_{t,i} = \gamma_{i0} + \sum_{j=1}^{p} \gamma_{ij} \Psi_{t,j}^{\text{syst}} + \Psi_{t,i}^{\text{id}}, \quad 1 \leqslant i \leqslant m. \tag{9.55}$$

Here $(\Psi_{t,j}^{\text{syst}})$, $1 \leqslant j \leqslant p$, and $(\Psi_{t,i}^{\text{id}})$, $1 \leqslant i \leqslant m$, are independent CIR square-root diffusions or, slightly more generally, basic affine jump diffusions as in (9.45); the factor weights γ_{ij}, $0 \leqslant j \leqslant p$, are non-negative constants. Obviously, $(\boldsymbol{\Psi}_t^{\text{syst}})$ represents the common or systematic factors, whereas $(\Psi_{t,i}^{\text{id}})$ is an idiosyncratic factor process affecting only the hazard rate of obligor i. Note that the weight of the idiosyncratic factor can be incorporated into the parameters of the dynamics of (Ψ_t^{id}), so we do not need an extra factor weight. Throughout this section we assume that the background filtration is generated by $(\boldsymbol{\Psi}_t^{\text{syst}})$ and $(\Psi_{t,i}^{\text{id}})$, $1 \leqslant i \leqslant m$. In practical applications of the model, the current value of these processes is derived from observed prices of defaultable bonds.

We now present a few examples proposed in the literature. Duffee (1999) has estimated a model of the form (9.55) with $p = 2$; in his model all factor processes are assumed to follow CIR square-root diffusions, so that their dynamics are characterized by the parameter triplet $(\kappa, \bar{\theta}, \sigma)$. In Duffee's model, $(\boldsymbol{\Psi}_t^{\text{syst}})$ represents factors driving the default-free short rate; the parameters of these processes are estimated from treasury data. The factor weights γ_{ij} and the parameters of (Ψ_t^{id}), on the other hand, are estimated from corporate bond-price data.

In their influential case study on CDO pricing, Duffie and Gârleanu (2001) use basic affine jump diffusion processes of the form (9.45) to model the factors driving the hazard rates. Jumps in (γ_t) represent shocks which increase the default probability of a firm. They consider a homogeneous model with one systematic factor, i.e. $\gamma_{t,i} = \Psi_t^{\text{syst}} + \Psi_{t,i}^{\text{id}}$, $1 \leqslant i \leqslant m$, and assume that the speed of mean-reversion κ, the volatility σ and the mean jump size μ are identical for (Ψ_t^{syst}) and $(\Psi_{t,i}^{\text{id}})$. It is straightforward to show that this implies that the sum $\gamma_{t,i} = \Psi_t^{\text{syst}} + \Psi_{t,i}^{\text{id}}$ follows a basic affine jump diffusion with parameters κ, $\bar{\theta}^{\text{syst}} + \bar{\theta}^{\text{id}}$, σ, $(l^0)^{\text{syst}} + (l^0)^{\text{id}}$ and μ; the parameters of $(\gamma_{t,i})$ used in Duffie and Gârleanu (2001) can be found in the row labelled "base case" in Table 9.2.

Pricing single-name credit products. As discussed in Remark 9.40, with conditionally independent defaults, pricing formulas obtained in a single-firm model remain valid in the portfolio context. Moreover, with hazard rates as in (9.55) most actual computations can be reduced to a one-dimensional problem involving affine processes, to which the results of Section 9.5 apply. As a simple specific example we

Table 9.2. Parameter sets of the Duffie–Gârleanu model used in Figure 9.11.

Parameter set	κ	$\bar{\theta}$	σ	l^0	μ
Pure diffusion	0.6	0.0505	0.141	0	0
Base case	0.6	0.02	0.141	0.2	0.1
High jump intensity	0.6	0.0018	0.141	0.32	0.1

consider the computation of the conditional survival probability of obligor i. We obtain from Remark 9.40 and Theorem 9.23 that

$$P(\tau_i > T \mid \mathcal{G}_t) = P(\tau_i > T \mid \mathcal{G}_t^i) = I_{\{\tau_i > t\}} E\biggl(\exp\biggl(-\int_t^T \gamma_{s,i}\, \mathrm{d}s \biggr) \biggm| \mathcal{F}_t \biggr).$$

For hazard-rate processes of the form (9.55) this equals

$$I_{\{\tau_i > t\}} \mathrm{e}^{-\gamma_{i0}(T-t)} E\biggl(\exp\biggl(-\int_t^T \Psi_{s,i}^{\mathrm{id}}\, \mathrm{d}s \biggr) \biggm| \mathcal{F}_t \biggr) \times \prod_{j=1}^{p} E\biggl(\exp\biggl(-\int_t^T \Psi_{s,j}^{\mathrm{syst}}\, \mathrm{d}s \biggr) \biggm| \mathcal{F}_t \biggr). \tag{9.56}$$

Each of the conditional expectations in (9.56) can now be computed using the results on one-dimensional affine models from Section 9.5. More general models, where hazard rates are given by a general multivariate affine process (and not simply by a linear combination of independent one-dimensional affine processes) can be dealt with using the general affine-model technology from Duffie, Pan and Singleton (2000).

Static version of the model. It is interesting to look at the implications of conditional independence and the factor structure (9.55) of the hazard rates for the distribution of the default indicators at a given point in time T, as this links our analysis to the static models of Chapter 8. For simplicity we suppose that the idiosyncratic factor $(\Psi_{t,i}^{\mathrm{id}})$ vanishes for all firms. Fix some $T > 0$ and consider the random vector $\boldsymbol{Y}_T = (Y_{T,1}, \dots, Y_{T,m})'$. We get, for $\boldsymbol{y} \in \{0,1\}^m$,

$$\begin{aligned} P(\boldsymbol{Y}_T = \boldsymbol{y}) &= E(P(\boldsymbol{Y}_T = \boldsymbol{y} \mid \mathcal{F}_\infty)) \\ &= E\biggl(\prod_{j:y_j=1} P(\tau_j \leqslant T \mid \mathcal{F}_\infty) \prod_{j:y_j=0} P(\tau_j > T \mid \mathcal{F}_\infty) \biggr). \end{aligned}$$

Now we obviously have, using (9.55),

$$P(\tau_i \leqslant T \mid \mathcal{F}_\infty) = 1 - \exp\biggl(-\gamma_{i0} T - \sum_{j=1}^{p} \gamma_{ij} \int_0^T \Psi_{s,j}^{\mathrm{syst}}\, \mathrm{d}s \biggr). \tag{9.57}$$

This shows that $\boldsymbol{Y}_T$ follows a Bernoulli mixture model with p-factor structure as in Definition 8.10 with factor vector given by

$$\boldsymbol{\Psi} := \biggl(\int_0^T \Psi_{s,1}^{\mathrm{syst}}\, \mathrm{d}s, \dots, \int_0^T \Psi_{s,p}^{\mathrm{syst}}\, \mathrm{d}s \biggr)'$$

and conditional default probabilities $p_i(\boldsymbol{\Psi})$ as in (9.57).

Default correlation. As we have seen in Chapter 8, default correlations (defined as correlation $\rho(Y_{T,i}, Y_{T,j})$, $i \neq j$, of the default indicators) are crucial for the tail of the credit loss distribution. In computing default correlations in models with conditionally independent defaults it is more convenient to work with the *survival indicator* $1 - Y_{T,i}$. By the definition of standard linear correlation we have

$$\begin{aligned}\rho(Y_{T,i}, Y_{T,j}) &= \rho(1 - Y_{T,i}, 1 - Y_{T,j}) \\ &= \frac{P(\tau_i > T, \tau_j > T) - \bar{F}_i(T)\bar{F}_j(T)}{(\bar{F}_i(T)(1 - \bar{F}_i(T)))^{1/2}(\bar{F}_j(T)(1 - \bar{F}_j(T)))^{1/2}}. \end{aligned} \tag{9.58}$$

For models with hazard rates as in (9.55), the computation of the survival probabilities $\bar{F}_i(T)$ using affine-model technology has been discussed above. For the joint survival probability we obtain, using conditional independence,

$$\begin{aligned} P(\tau_i > T, \tau_j > T) &= E(P(\tau_i > T, \tau_j > T \mid \mathcal{F}_\infty)) \\ &= E(P(\tau_i > T \mid \mathcal{F}_\infty) P(\tau_j > T \mid \mathcal{F}_\infty)) \\ &= E\bigg(\exp\bigg(-\int_0^T (\gamma_{s,i} + \gamma_{s,j})\,\mathrm{d}s\bigg)\bigg). \end{aligned} \tag{9.59}$$

For hazard rates of the form (9.55), expression (9.59) can be decomposed in a similar way to the decomposition in (9.56) and can thus be evaluated using our results on one-dimensional affine models.

It is often claimed that the default correlation values that can be attained in models with conditionally independent defaults are too low compared with empirical default correlations (see, for example, Hull and White 2001; Schönbucher and Schubert 2001). Since default correlations do have a significant impact on the loss distribution generated by a model, we discuss this issue further. As a concrete example we use the Duffie–Gârleanu model and assume that (Ψ_t^{id}) vanishes. As discussed above, in that case the default indicator vector $\boldsymbol{Y}_T$ follows an exchangeable Bernoulli mixture model with mixing variable $\tilde{Q}$ given by $1 - \exp(-\int_0^T \Psi_s^{\mathrm{syst}}\,\mathrm{d}s)$.

We have seen in Section 8.4.1 that in exchangeable Bernoulli mixture models every default correlation $\rho \in (0, 1)$ can be obtained by choosing the variance of the mixing variable sufficiently high. It follows that in the Duffie–Gârleanu model high levels of default correlation can be obtained if the variance of the rv $\Gamma_T := \int_0^T \Psi_s^{\mathrm{syst}}\,\mathrm{d}s$ is sufficiently high. A high variance of Γ_T can be obtained by choosing a high value for the volatility σ of the diffusion part of $(\boldsymbol{\Psi}_t^{\mathrm{syst}})$ or by choosing a high value for the mean of the jump-size distribution μ or for the jump intensity l^0. A high value for σ translates into very volatile day-to-day fluctuations of credit spreads, which might contradict the behaviour of real bond-price data. This shows that it might be difficult to generate very high levels of default correlation in models where hazard rates follow pure diffusion processes (see, however, Yu (2005a) for an alternative view).

In the Duffie–Gârleanu model we may alternatively raise the frequency or size of the jumps in the hazard rate by increasing l^0 or μ. This is a very effective

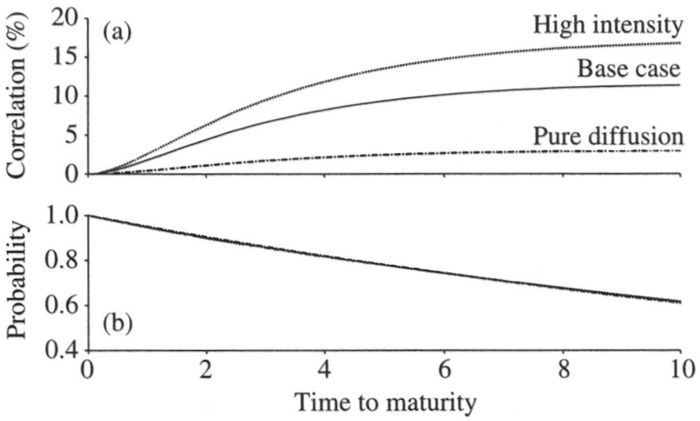

Figure 9.11. (a) Default correlations for varying time to maturity and three different parameter sets in the Duffie–Gârleanu model for $(\Psi_t^{\mathrm{id}}) \equiv 0$ and different parameter sets for (Ψ_t^{syst}). The parameters of (Ψ_t^{syst}) are given in Table 9.2. We see that by increasing the intensity of jumps in (Z_t) the default correlation is increased substantially. (b) The survival probabilities for the three parameter sets are essentially equal, so that the differences in default correlations are solely due to the impact of the dynamics of (Ψ_t^{syst}) on the dependence structure of the default times.

mechanism for generating default correlation, as is shown in Figure 9.11. In fact, this additional flexibility in modelling default correlations is an important motivation for considering affine jump diffusions instead of the simpler CIR diffusion models.

These qualitative findings obviously carry over to other models with conditionally independent defaults. Summing up, we conclude that it is certainly possible to generate high levels of default correlation in models with conditionally independent defaults; however, the required models for the hazard-rate processes may become relatively complex.

First-to-default swaps. As a final application we study the pricing of first-to-default swaps in models with conditionally independent defaults. We consider a portfolio of m firms. Premium payments on the swap are due at N points in time $0 < t_1 < \cdots < t_N =: T$. Provided that $T_1 > t_n$, the premium at time t_n is of the form $x(t_n - t_{n-1})$; at T_1 premium payments stop. For simplicity we neglect accrued premium payments. The default payment occurs at time T_1 provided $T_1 < T$. We assume that the payment depends on the identity ξ_1 of the first defaulting firm (perhaps because of differing exposure sizes) but is otherwise deterministic, i.e. there are constants $l_1, \dots, l_m$ such that the default payment is equal to l_i if $T_1 < T$ and $\xi_1 = i$. As usual, the fair spread x^* of the swap is the value of x such that at $t = 0$ the default payment leg and premium payment leg have the same value.

Since, in practice, first-to-default swaps are always priced relative to traded single-name CDSs, it is natural to adopt the martingale-modelling approach. We assume that under the equivalent martingale measure Q the default times τ_i are conditionally independent doubly stochastic random times with hazard rates of the form (9.55); moreover, the risk-free short rate (r_t) is assumed to be of the form (9.55). In this set-up, for generic swap spread x the value of the premium payment equals

$$V^{\text{prem}} = \sum_{n=1}^{N} E^Q\biggl(\exp\biggl(-\int_0^{t_n} r_s \, \mathrm{d}s\biggr) I_{\{T_1 > t_n\}}\biggr) x(t_n - t_{n-1}). \tag{9.60}$$

Using Theorem 9.23 and Lemma 9.36 we get

$$E^Q\biggl(\exp\biggl(-\int_0^{t_n} r_s \, \mathrm{d}s\biggr) I_{\{T_1 > t_n\}}\biggr) = E^Q\biggl(\exp\biggl(-\int_0^{t_n} (r_s + \sum_{i=1}^{m} \gamma_{s,i}) \, \mathrm{d}s\biggr)\biggr).$$

For hazard rates and a risk-free short rate of the form (9.55) this can be expressed as a product of expectations of the form $E^Q(\exp(-C \int_0^{t_n} \Psi_s \, \mathrm{d}s))$ for a constant C and a one-dimensional affine jump diffusion (Ψ_t), so the premium payments can be computed using the methods developed in Section 9.5. Next we turn to the default payments. We have

$$V^{\text{def}} = \sum_{i=1}^{m} l_i E^Q\biggl(\exp\biggl(-\int_0^{T_1} r_s \, \mathrm{d}s\biggr) I_{\{T_1 \leqslant T\}} I_{\{\xi_1 = i\}}\biggr).$$

We begin by computing

$$E^Q\biggl(\exp\biggl(-\int_0^{T_1} r_s \, \mathrm{d}s\biggr) I_{\{T_1 \leqslant T\}} I_{\{\xi_1 = i\}} \biggm| \mathcal{F}_\infty\biggr).$$

Conditioning on T_1 we obtain that this equals

$$\int_0^T \exp\biggl(-\int_0^t r(s) \, \mathrm{d}s\biggr) Q(\xi_1 = i \mid T_1 = t, \mathcal{F}_\infty) f^Q_{T_1|\mathcal{F}_\infty}(t) \, \mathrm{d}t, \tag{9.61}$$

where $f^Q_{T_1|\mathcal{F}_\infty}(t)$ is the Q-density of T_1 given $\mathcal{F}_\infty$. By Lemma 9.36,

$$f^Q_{T_1|\mathcal{F}_\infty}(t) = \bar{\gamma}(t) \exp\biggl(-\int_0^t \bar{\gamma}(s) \, \mathrm{d}s\biggr).$$

Moreover, by Proposition 9.37,

$$Q(\xi_1 = i \mid T_1 = t, \mathcal{F}_\infty) = \gamma_i(t)/\bar{\gamma}(t).$$

Hence (9.61) equals $\int_0^T \gamma_i(t) \exp(-\int_0^t (r(s) + \bar{\gamma}(s)) \, \mathrm{d}s) \, \mathrm{d}t$. To compute the value of V^{def} we thus have to compute $E^Q(\int_0^T \gamma_{t,i} \exp(-\int_0^t r_s + \bar{\gamma}_s \, \mathrm{d}s) \, \mathrm{d}t)$. For hazard rates of the form (9.55) this can be evaluated using the extended transform discussed in Section 9.5.3; we omit the details. If the default payments l_i are all identical, the first-to-default swap can be priced like a single-name CDS, with the hazard rate of the default time given by $(\bar{\gamma}_t)$; this follows immediately from Lemma 9.36.

In certain special cases higher-order default swaps can be evaluated analytically. However, in most cases that are practically relevant, one has to use Monte Carlo simulation, and the recursive default time simulation algorithm from the previous section comes in handy.

Notes and Comments

The empirical literature on default contagion and counterparty risk has two different strands. On the one hand, there are papers such as Collin-Dufresne, Goldstein and Helwege (2003) or Lang and Stulz (1992) which focus on the impact of defaults or credit-spread widenings of a given firm on the credit spreads or stock returns of other firms and hence on default contagion under a *risk-neutral measure*. For instance, Collin-Dufresne, Goldstein and Helwege (2003) found that, even after controlling for other macroeconomic variables influencing bond returns, the return of large corporate bond indices in months where one or several large firms experienced a significant (above 200 basis points) widening in credit spreads is significantly lower than the return of these indices in other months; this is clear evidence supporting contagion. Das, Duffie and Kapadia (2005) and Jarrow and Yu (2001), on the other hand, look at default contagion under the *physical measure*. Jarrow and Yu provide a lot of anecdotal evidence for counterparty risk in small portfolios. Das, Duffie and Kapadia formally test whether models with conditionally independent defaults driven by observable macroeconomic factors are sufficient to explain the degree of clustering one finds in actual default data for large portfolios (their default database contains approximately 2000 firms). In their words, they "do not find substantial evidence of default clustering beyond that predicted by the doubly stochastic model in their data". These findings are only preliminary, but indicate nonetheless that default contagion is relevant for the pricing and the hedging of portfolio-related credit derivatives; for credit risk management issues, on the other hand, a model with conditionally independent defaults and appropriately specified factors might be sufficient.

The results of Section 9.6.2 are well known; for an alternative treatment at textbook level, see, for example, Chapter 9 of Bielecki and Rutkowski (2002). The simulation of conditionally independent default times is discussed in Duffie and Singleton (1999b) (see also Duffie and Singleton 2003). Further empirical work on affine models for credit portfolios includes that of Duffee (1999) and Driessen (2005). Default correlations in models with conditionally independent defaults are discussed in Yu (2005a).

9.7 Copula Models

Copula models are widely used in practice for the pricing of basket credit derivatives and CDO structures. They are easy to calibrate to a given term structure of defaultable bonds or CDS spreads; moreover, they can be used to model default contagion. In this section we introduce theses models; particular attention will be given to models where the copula has a factor structure, since these models have a convenient representation as mixture models. Dynamic properties of copula models and default contagion are studied in Section 9.8 below.

9.7.1 Definition and General Properties

To motivate our definition of copula models we return briefly to models with conditionally independent defaults. According to Lemma 9.35, if $\tau_1, \dots, \tau_m$ are conditionally independent doubly stochastic random times with $(\mathcal{F}_t)$-adapted hazard-rate processes $(\gamma_{t,1}), \dots, (\gamma_{t,m})$, we can find a random vector $\boldsymbol{E}$ with independent, unit exponentially distributed components, independent of $\mathcal{F}_\infty$, such that $\tau_i = \inf\{t \geqslant 0 : \Gamma_{t,i} \geqslant E_i\}$. We may rewrite this as

$$\tau_i = \inf\{t \geqslant 0 : 1 - \exp(-\Gamma_{t,i}) \geqslant \tilde{U}_i := 1 - \exp(-E_i)\}. \tag{9.62}$$

Note that $\tilde{\boldsymbol{U}} = (\tilde{U}_1, \dots, \tilde{U}_m)'$ is a vector of m independent rvs with uniform margins, so that its joint df is the m-dimensional independence copula (see Section 5.1.2). In the copula models we generalize this construction and replace the independence copula with some other copula; obviously, this allows for a richer dependence structure of the τ_i than in the case of conditionally independent default times. Defining $U_i := 1 - \tilde{U}_i$ we may rewrite (9.62) as $\tau_i = \inf\{t \geqslant 0 : \exp(-\Gamma_{t,i}) \leqslant U_i\}$. To be in line with the literature we work with this description of the τ_i and define copula models in terms of the copula C of $\boldsymbol{U}$ (or equivalently the survival copula $\hat{C}$ of $\tilde{\boldsymbol{U}}$ introduced in Section 5.1.5). We call C the conditional survival copula of the firms; this terminology will be justified below.

Definition 9.41 (copula model for default times). Let $(\gamma_{t,i}), \dots, (\gamma_{t,m})$ be non-negative, $(\mathcal{F}_t)$-adapted processes such that $\Gamma_{t,i} < \infty$ for all $t > 0$, and let C be an m-dimensional copula. Then the random times $\tau_1, \dots, \tau_m$ follow a copula model with *marginal hazard-rate processes* $(\gamma_{t,i})$, $i = 1, \dots, m$, and *conditional survival copula* C, if there is an m-dimensional random vector $\boldsymbol{U} \sim C$, independent of $\mathcal{F}_\infty$, such that

$$\tau_i = \inf\{t \geqslant 0 : \exp(-\Gamma_{t,i}) \leqslant U_i\}, \quad 1 \leqslant i \leqslant m. \tag{9.63}$$

Note that Definition 9.41 provides an obvious way to simulate a copula model of default, provided we know how to simulate the copula C. To simulate a realization of $\tau_1, \dots, \tau_m$ we generate a realization of the hazard-rate processes $(\gamma_{t,1}), \dots, (\gamma_{t,m})$ and, independently, a realization of the random vector $\boldsymbol{U}$; the τ_i are then constructed according to (9.63).

The crucial part in setting up a copula model is the choice of the threshold copula C. Useful copulas and the resulting copula models will be discussed in the next subsection; for the moment we merely recall that we obtain conditionally independent default times if and only if we take C to be the independence copula.

We now collect some elementary consequences of Definition 9.41. Since $E_i := -\ln(1 - U_i) \sim \text{Exp}(1)$, Lemma 9.12, together with (9.63), immediately yields that each of the τ_i is a doubly stochastic random time with $(\mathcal{F}_t)$-conditional hazard-rate process $(\gamma_{t,i})$. Hence $M_{t,i} := Y_{t,i} - \Gamma_i(t \wedge \tau_i)$ is a martingale with respect to the filtration $\{\mathcal{G}_t^i\} := (\mathcal{F}_t) \vee \{\mathcal{H}_t^i\}$. Unless C is the independence copula, it is, however, not true that $M_{t,i}$ is also a martingale with respect to the filtration $(\mathcal{G}_t)$, i.e. given default information for other obligors as well (see Section 9.8.1 for details).

At time $t = 0$ the marginal distribution of the τ_i can be computed as in the single-firm case. We have, using iterated conditional expectations,

$$P(\tau_i \leqslant T) = E(P(\tau_i \leqslant T \mid \mathcal{F}_\infty)) = 1 - E\biggl(\exp\biggl(-\int_0^T \gamma_{s,i}\,\mathrm{d}s\biggr)\biggr). \tag{9.64}$$

In particular, at time $t = 0$ it is possible to calibrate the model to a given term structure of credit or CDS spreads by calibrating each of the marginal hazard-rate processes $(\gamma_{s,i})$ using methods for the single-firm case. This is an important feature of the model in practical applications. Note, however, that for $t > 0$ the conditional distribution of τ_i given the default history of all obligors in the portfolio generally differs from the conditional distribution of τ_i given that $\tau_i > t$, so for $t > 0$ the single-firm and the portfolio versions of the model differ. We discuss this point in more detail in Section 9.8.1 below.

Next we show that the threshold copula C is in fact the survival copula of the τ_i conditional on $\mathcal{F}_\infty$. By definition we have

$$\bar{F}_{\tau_i|\mathcal{F}_\infty}(t) := P(\tau_i > t \mid \mathcal{F}_\infty) = \exp\biggl(-\int_0^t \gamma_{s,i}\,\mathrm{d}s\biggr).$$

Moreover, according to (9.63), $\tau_i > t$ if and only if $U_i < \bar{F}_{\tau_i|\mathcal{F}_\infty}(t)$. Hence we obtain, using the independence of $\boldsymbol{U}$ and $\mathcal{F}_\infty$,

$$\begin{aligned} P(\tau_1 > t_1, \dots, \tau_m > t_m \mid \mathcal{F}_\infty) &= P(U_1 < \bar{F}_{\tau_1|\mathcal{F}_\infty}(t_1), \dots, U_m < \bar{F}_{\tau_m|\mathcal{F}_\infty}(t_m)) \\ &= C(\bar{F}_{\tau_1|\mathcal{F}_\infty}(t_1), \dots, \bar{F}_{\tau_m|\mathcal{F}_\infty}(t_m)). \end{aligned} \tag{9.65}$$

By Sklar's identity for survival functions (see (5.13)), C is thus the conditional survival copula of the τ_i given $\mathcal{F}_\infty$.

Models with deterministic hazard rates. From now on we concentrate on models where the marginal hazard rate $\gamma_i(s)$ is deterministic. Since dependence between the τ_i can be introduced via the threshold copula C, this gives rise to interesting models. In fact, the literature on copula models focuses almost exclusively on models with deterministic marginal hazard rates. Moreover, understanding the properties of models with deterministic hazard rates is an important step in the analysis of more general models with stochastic hazard rates. These models are usually studied first under the artificial filtration $(\tilde{\mathcal{G}}_t)$, with $\tilde{\mathcal{G}}_t = \mathcal{F}_\infty \vee \mathcal{H}_t$, $t \geqslant 0$, for which hazard rates are deterministic; pricing formulas with respect to the smaller filtration $\mathcal{G}_t = \mathcal{F}_t \vee \mathcal{H}_t$, $t \geqslant 0$, are then derived using the theorem of iterated conditional expectations.

With deterministic marginal hazard rates $\gamma_i(t)$, the default times τ_i are independent of the background filtration $(\mathcal{F}_t)$, and we may restrict our attention to the filtration $(\mathcal{H}_t)$, which is generated by the default indicators. Moreover, in that case the conditional survival function with respect to $\mathcal{F}_\infty$ and the unconditional survival functions obviously coincide: we have $\bar{F}_i(t) = \bar{F}_{\tau_i|\mathcal{F}_\infty}(t) = \exp(-\Gamma_i(t))$. Hence relation (9.65) yields

$$\bar{F}_i(t_1, \dots, t_m) = C(\bar{F}_1(t_1), \dots, \bar{F}_m(t_m)) \tag{9.66}$$

$$= C\biggl(\exp\biggl(-\int_0^t \gamma_1(s)\,\mathrm{d}s\biggr), \dots, \exp\biggl(-\int_0^t \gamma_m(s)\,\mathrm{d}s\biggr)\biggr). \tag{9.67}$$

Relation (9.66) shows that with deterministic marginal hazard rates the conditional survival copula C is the survival copula of the default times; (9.67) shows how this copula and the marginal hazard rates determine the joint survival function of the default times. We will use both relations frequently below. From a mathematical point of view it makes no difference whether we specify the copula and marginal hazard rates or the joint survival function $\bar{F}$ directly, because every joint survival function $\bar{F}$ with absolutely continuous marginal distributions has a unique representation of the form (9.67) (put $\gamma_i(t) = -(\partial/\partial t) \ln \bar{F}_i(t)$ and define C using Sklar's identity for survival functions). When deriving mathematical results we will therefore work directly with $\bar{F}$. The representation (9.67) is, however, convenient for the calibration of the model, as will be discussed below.

Finally, a word of warning is in order: for models with stochastic hazard rates, the unconditional survival copula of $(\tau_1, \dots, \tau_m)$ is different from the conditional survival copula given $\mathcal{F}_\infty$; for example, in models with conditionally independent defaults but dependent hazard-rate processes the conditional survival copula given $\mathcal{F}_\infty$ is the independence copula, but $(\tau_1, \dots, \tau_m)$ is obviously not a vector of independent rvs.

Static version. It is interesting to link copula models to the static threshold models considered in Section 8.3. Fix some horizon $T > 0$. Obviously, $Y_{T,i} = 1$ if and only $\tau_i \leqslant T$, so $\boldsymbol{Y}_T$ follows a threshold model in the sense of Definition 8.4 with critical variables $\boldsymbol{X} = (\tau_1, \dots, \tau_m)$ and default threshold T. By (9.66) the survival copula of $(\tau_1, \dots, \tau_m)$ equals C; if C is radially symmetric (see Definition 5.13), C is also the copula of $(\tau_1, \dots, \tau_m)$. This is true, in particular, if C is an elliptical copula such as the Gauss copula or the t copula. The findings of Section 8.3.5 on the implications of the choice of C for the portfolio loss distribution thus carry over to dynamic models. In particular, if C is an elliptical copula, increasing the degree of dependence in the tail of C or choosing higher asset correlations leads to a heavier-tailed distribution for $M_T = \sum_{i=1}^{m} Y_{T,i}$.

On calibration. The calibration of a copula model with deterministic marginal hazard rates for pricing purposes proceeds in two steps. Marginal risk-neutral hazard rates are calibrated to a given term structure of credit spreads from defaultable bonds or CDS spreads, as described in Section 9.3.3. If there is a liquid market for portfolio-related credit derivatives, the parameters of the threshold copula C can be calibrated to the observed prices of these products. While this is a straightforward concept, the technical details of this procedure can be quite involved (see Notes and Comments for references).

Otherwise one typically calibrates the copula to estimates of default correlation over the maturity of the products to be priced; such estimates are either obtained using asset correlations in conjunction with the multivariate version of the Merton model introduced in Section 8.2.4, or via one of the statistical procedures described in Section 8.6. Note that in this approach it is implicitly assumed that risk-neutral and historical default correlations are equal, which is a strong assumption. When we calibrate a copula model under the real-world probability measure, hazard rates are calibrated to estimates of historical default probabilities; parameters of the copula are again calibrated to estimates of historical default correlations.

9.7.2 Factor Copula Models

In this section we consider models where the threshold vector $\boldsymbol{U}$ has a conditional independence structure in the sense of Definition 8.18, i.e. where there is a p-dimensional random vector $\boldsymbol{V}$, $p < m$, such that, conditional on $\boldsymbol{V}$, the U_i are independent. These models are sometimes called *factor copula models*. Under our assumption of deterministic marginal hazard rates $\gamma_i(t)$, we get from (9.63) and the conditional independence of the U_i given $\boldsymbol{V}$ that

$$\begin{aligned}\bar{F}(t_1, \dots, t_m) &= E(P(U_1 \leqslant \bar{F}_1(t_1), \dots, U_m \leqslant \bar{F}_m(t_m) \mid \boldsymbol{V})) \\ &= E\biggl(\prod_{i=1}^{m} P(U_i \leqslant \bar{F}_i(t_i) \mid \boldsymbol{V})\biggr). \end{aligned} \tag{9.68}$$

Denote by $\bar{F}_{\tau_i|\boldsymbol{V}}(t \mid \boldsymbol{v})$ the conditional survival function of τ_i given $\boldsymbol{V} = \boldsymbol{v}$ and note that, by construction, $\bar{F}_{\tau_i|\boldsymbol{V}}(t \mid \boldsymbol{v}) = P(U_i < \bar{F}_i(t) \mid \boldsymbol{V} = \boldsymbol{v})$. Hence

$$\bar{F}(t_1, \dots, t_m) = E\biggl(\prod_{i=1}^{m} \bar{F}_{\tau_i|\boldsymbol{V}}(t_i \mid \boldsymbol{V})\biggr). \tag{9.69}$$

Denoting by $G_{\boldsymbol{V}}$ the df of $\boldsymbol{V}$ and by $g_{\boldsymbol{V}}$ the density (if it exists), we will sometimes write (9.69) more explicitly as

$$\bar{F}(t_1, \dots, t_m) = \int_{\mathbb{R}^p} \prod_{i=1}^{m} \bar{F}_{\tau_i|\boldsymbol{V}}(t_i \mid \boldsymbol{v}) G_{\boldsymbol{V}}(\mathrm{d}\boldsymbol{v}) = \int_{\mathbb{R}^p} \prod_{i=1}^{m} \bar{F}_{\tau_i|\boldsymbol{V}}(t_i \mid \boldsymbol{v}) g_{\boldsymbol{V}}(\boldsymbol{v})\, \mathrm{d}\boldsymbol{v}.$$

Note that the representation (9.69) is analogous to the representation of static one-period threshold models with conditional independence structure as Bernoulli mixture models, obtained in Section 8.4.4. In particular, (9.69) shows that for T fixed the default indicators follow a Bernoulli mixture model with factor vector $\boldsymbol{V}$ and conditional default probabilities $Q_i(\boldsymbol{v}) = 1 - \bar{F}_{\tau_i|\boldsymbol{V}}(t \mid \boldsymbol{v})$. Following standard terminology from survival analysis the unobservable vector $\boldsymbol{V}$ is sometimes termed the *frailty* of the default times. As in the case of static models, the mixture-model representation of a factor copula model is very useful. It leads to a natural interpretation of default contagion in terms of incomplete information (see Section 9.8.2 below for details). Moreover, it can be used for simulation purposes; we sketch the algorithm below.

Algorithm 9.42 (simulation of factor copula models).

(1) Generate a realization of $\boldsymbol{V}$.

(2) Generate independent rvs τ_i with df $1 - \bar{F}_{\tau_i|\boldsymbol{V}}(t \mid \boldsymbol{V})$, $1 \leqslant i \leqslant m$. In order to generate a sequence (T_n, ξ_n), $T_n \leqslant T$, of default times up to some maturity date, one might use recursive generation of default times (Algorithm 9.38).

The importance-sampling techniques discussed in Section 8.5 in the context of static Bernoulli mixture models can be employed to improve the performance of Algorithm 9.42. These techniques are particularly useful if one deals with rare-event simulation, such as in the pricing of CDO tranches with high attachment points.

At first sight, the mathematical structure of factor copula models looks very similar to the structure of models with conditionally independent defaults; in particular, the static versions of both model classes are Bernoulli mixture models. However, the model classes differ with respect to the way information is revealed to investors over time, which leads to completely different dynamic behaviour. In the models with conditionally independent defaults it is assumed that the economic factor process $(\boldsymbol{\Psi}_t)$ is $(\mathcal{F}_t)$-adapted, i.e. that its current value is known to investors at time t. Hence a default event does not convey additional information for predicting the default of other obligors.

In the factor copula models, on the other hand, the threshold $\boldsymbol{U}$ and the frailty $\boldsymbol{V}$ are assumed to be unobservable. Since default probabilities depend on $\boldsymbol{V}$, default information such as the news that a particular obligor j has defaulted at a given point in time t does convey additional information about the distribution of $\boldsymbol{V}$. The survival probabilities of the remaining obligors $i \neq j$ change, as they are computed as the average of the conditional survival function $\bar{F}_{\tau_i|\boldsymbol{V}}(t \mid \boldsymbol{v})$ with respect to the conditional distribution of $\boldsymbol{V}$ given the default history $\mathcal{H}_t$. The updating of the distribution of the unobservable random vector $\boldsymbol{V}$ can lead to default contagion, as will be discussed in more detail in Section 9.8.2 below. This comparison between factor copula models and models with conditionally independent defaults shows that dynamic models do possess a much richer structure than static models.

Below we consider specific examples of factor copula models. Obviously, every continuous multivariate distribution with p-dimensional conditional independence structure can be used to construct a factor copula model. Practically important examples include the Gauss copula C_P^{Ga}, the t copula $C_{\nu,P}^t$ (provided that the correlation matrix P corresponds to a factor model, as explained in Section 3.4.1), and the LT-Archimedean copulas discussed in Section 5.4.2. We consider certain special cases; in particular, we derive the dynamic version of the two most important mixture models from Section 8.4, namely the probit-normal mixture model and CreditRisk+.

Example 9.43 (one-factor Gauss copula). Factor copula models based on a Gauss copula C_P^{Ga} are frequently employed in practice. The static version of these models corresponds to the popular CreditMetrics/KMV-type models discussed in Example 8.6. Here we compute the conditional survival functions for the one-factor case. Let $X_i = \sqrt{\rho_i}V + \sqrt{1-\rho_i}\varepsilon_i$, where $\rho_i \in (0,1)$ and V, $(\varepsilon_i)_{1\leqslant i\leqslant m}$ are iid standard normal rvs, so $\boldsymbol{X} \sim N_m(\boldsymbol{0}, P)$, with (i,j)th element of P given by $\rho_{ij} = \sqrt{\rho_i\rho_j}$. Set $U_i = \Phi(X_i)$, i.e. $\boldsymbol{U} \sim C_P^{\mathrm{Ga}}$. The conditional survival function is easy to compute. With $d_i(t) := \Phi^{-1}(\bar{F}_i(t))$, we have that

$$\bar{F}_{\tau_i|V}(t \mid v) = P(U_i \leqslant \bar{F}_i(t) \mid V = v) = P\biggl(\varepsilon_i \leqslant \frac{d_i(t) - \sqrt{\rho_i}V}{\sqrt{1-\rho_i}} \biggm| V = v\biggr),$$

leading to $\bar{F}_{\tau_i|V}(t \mid v) = \Phi((d_i(t) - \sqrt{\rho_i}v)/(\sqrt{1-\rho_i}))$. Hence

$$\bar{F}(t_1, \dots, t_m) = \frac{1}{\sqrt{2\pi}} \int_{\mathbb{R}} \prod_{i=1}^{m} \Phi\biggl(\frac{d_i(t_i) - \sqrt{\rho_i}v}{\sqrt{1-\rho_i}}\biggr) \mathrm{e}^{-v^2/2}\,\mathrm{d}v, \tag{9.70}$$

which is easily computed using one-dimensional numerical integration. The conditional survival functions for general mean-variance mixture copulas with factor structure such as the t copula can be derived by an analogous computation.

In applications of a one-factor Gauss copula model to the pricing of portfolio credit derivatives it is frequently assumed that $\rho_i = \rho$ for all i. In that case the dependence structure of the model is governed by the single parameter ρ, the copula of $(\tau_1, \dots, \tau_m)$ is exchangeable and $\rho = \operatorname{corr}(X_i, X_j)$, so ρ is readily interpreted in terms of asset correlation. This feature makes the exchangeable version of the one-factor Gauss copula popular with practitioners. In fact, it is common practice on CDO markets to quote prices for tranches of synthetic CDOs in terms of *implied asset correlation*, i.e. to quote the value of ρ which, if plugged into an exchangeable one-factor Gauss copula model with marginal survival probabilities calibrated to the CDS spreads of the asset pool, yields the price of the tranche. References regarding the technical details of this procedure can be found in Notes and Comments. In this way, prices of CDO tranches can be made comparable across attachment points and asset pools, in much the same way that implied volatilities are used as a common yardstick on options markets. This is clearly convenient. Nonetheless, one should bear in mind that the dependence structure of the default times in a portfolio is a complex object which cannot, in general, be characterized by a single number (see, for example, Duffie (2004) for a discussion of this point).

Example 9.44 (LT-Archimedean copulas). Recall from Definition 5.47 in Chapter 5 that an LT-Archimedean copula is defined in terms of a positive rv V with df G_V, Laplace–Stieltjes transform $\hat{G}_V$ and $G_V(0) = 0$ using the relation

$$C(u_1, \dots, u_m) = E\biggl(\exp\biggl(-V\sum_{i=1}^{m}\hat{G}_V^{-1}(u_i)\biggr)\biggr).$$

As usual, denote by $\bar{F}_i(t_i)$ the marginal survival function of τ_i. We thus get the following joint survival function of $(\tau_1, \dots, \tau_m)$:

$$\bar{F}(t_1, \dots, t_m) = E\biggl(\prod_{i=1}^{m}\exp\{-V\hat{G}_V^{-1}(\bar{F}_i(t_i))\}\biggr), \tag{9.71}$$

which is obviously of the general form (9.69). Recall that in the special case of the Clayton copula with parameter θ we have $V \sim \operatorname{Ga}(1/\theta, 1)$; explicit formulas for $\hat{G}_V$ and $\hat{G}_V^{-1}$ for that case are given in Algorithm 5.48 for the simulation of LT-Archimedean copulas. Note that LT-Archimedean copulas are in general not radially symmetric, so the static version of a dynamic LT-Archimedean threshold copula model with survival function (9.71) is *not* a threshold model with Archimedean copula as discussed in Example 8.9. Nonetheless, default correlations in a dynamic LT-Archimedean threshold copula model are easily computed using (9.58) and the relation

$$P(\tau_i > T, \tau_j > T) = \hat{G}_V(\hat{G}_V^{-1}(\bar{F}_i(T)) + \hat{G}_V^{-1}(\bar{F}_j(T))), \quad i \neq j.$$

Example 9.45 (LT-Archimedean copulas with p-factor structure). As explained in detail in Section 5.4.2, an LT-Archimedean copula with p-factor structure is constructed from a p-dimensional random vector $\boldsymbol{V} = (V_1, \dots, V_p)'$ with independent strictly positive components and a matrix $A \in \mathbb{R}^{m \times p}$ with elements $a_{ij} > 0$ as follows:

$$C(u_1, \dots, u_m) = E\left(\prod_{i=1}^{m} \exp(-\boldsymbol{a}_i' \boldsymbol{V} \hat{G}_i^{-1}(u_i))\right), \tag{9.72}$$

where $\boldsymbol{a}_i$ is the ith row of A and $\hat{G}_i^{-1}$ is the Laplace–Stieltjes transform of the strictly positive rv $\boldsymbol{a}_i' \boldsymbol{V}$. The joint survival function $\bar{F}(t_1, \dots, t_m)$ of the τ_i is then obtained from (9.72) by replacing u_i with $\bar{F}_i(t_i)$. Expression (9.72) is fairly easy to evaluate if the Laplace–Stieltjes transform of the V_i is available in closed form (see Section 5.4.3 for details). LT-Archimedean copulas with p-factor structure are useful factor copulas, since they allow for a more flexible dependence structure between the τ_i than the exchangeable standard LT-Archimedean copulas while retaining many of the computational advantages of the latter class.

If the V_i follow a gamma distribution with mean one, the static version of a generalized LT-Archimedean factor copula model is the popular CreditRisk+ model discussed in Section 8.4.2. In fact, for T fixed, the default indicators $Y_{T,i}$, $1 \leqslant i \leqslant m$, are conditionally independent given $\boldsymbol{V}$ with default probability

$$p_i(\boldsymbol{V}) = 1 - \bar{F}_{\tau_i \mid \boldsymbol{V}}(T \mid \boldsymbol{V}) = 1 - \exp(-\boldsymbol{a}_i' \boldsymbol{V} \hat{G}_i^{-1}(\bar{F}_i(T))).$$

This corresponds to the structure of CreditRisk+ as given in (8.39) with

$$w_{ij} := \frac{a_{ij}}{\sum_{j=1}^{p} a_{ij}} \quad \text{and} \quad k_i = \left(\sum_{j=1}^{p} a_{ij}\right) \hat{G}_i^{-1}(\bar{F}_i(T)).$$

Notes and Comments

The first copula model for portfolio credit risk was given by Li (2001); his model is based on the Gauss copula. General copula models were introduced for the first time in Schönbucher and Schubert (2001). Factor copula models for portfolio credit risk have been studied by Laurent and Gregory (2003). Models where the threshold copula is given by an LT-Archimedean copula with p-factor structure have been developed by Rogge and Schönbucher (2003).

We have not said much about the important topic of pricing portfolio-related credit derivatives such as CDOs. This is mainly because, as this book goes to press, the market for these products and the methodology for pricing them is in a state of rapid development. Hence any summary of the current status of this topic is likely to become outdated quickly. Given the practical relevance of the subject, we try to compensate somewhat for this omission by briefly discussing the available literature. For asset-based CDOs pricing is typically done using Monte Carlo simulation. Semianalytic approaches for the pricing of synthetic CDOs in factor copula models have been developed by Laurent and Gregory (2003), Hull and White (2004) and Andersen and Sidenius (2004), among others. Laurent and Gregory exploit the conditional independence structure of factor copula models and develop methods based on Fourier analysis; Andersen and Sidenius and Hull and White propose recursive methods.

The recent introduction of a quoted market for standardized synthetic CDO tranches has made the calibration of copula models to observable market prices an issue of high priority amongst financial engineers working in credit markets. In this context a deficiency of the exchangeable Gauss copula model has become apparent: the value of the implied asset correlation ρ needed to explain observable market quotes varies with the attachment points of the tranches; in particular, ρ is quite high for senior mezzanine and senior tranches. This phenomenon, which is frequently called *base-correlation skew*, bears some similarities to the well-known smile and skew patterns of implied volatility on options markets (see, for example, Dumas, Fleming and Whaley 1998). Base-correlation skews on CDO markets are discussed by McGinty et al. (2004), Andersen and Sidenius (2004) and others; the latter paper develops several extensions of the standard one-factor Gauss copula model that can be used to explain the base-correlation skew. A comparative analysis of copula-based CDO pricing models is done in Burtschell, Gregory and Laurent (2005). As mentioned previously, the methodology for pricing CDOs and related products is developing rapidly. A good place to monitor new developments is www.defaultrisk.com/.

9.8 Default Contagion in Reduced-Form Models

In this section we discuss default contagion in reduced-form models. We begin with a detailed analysis of default contagion in general models for dependent defaults; information-based default contagion in factor copula models is discussed in Section 9.8.2. In Section 9.8.3 we briefly look at models with interacting intensities, where default contagion and counterparty risk are modelled explicitly.

9.8.1 Default Contagion and Default Dependence

Martingale intensities. We start with a general result which characterizes the martingale default intensities of dependent default times. As we have seen before, when discussing the martingale property of stochastic processes we have to be precise about the information available to investors, or, in mathematical terms, the filtration we use. Here we assume that investors only have access to the default history of firms in the portfolio under consideration, i.e. we are interested in martingale properties with respect to the internal filtration $(\mathcal{H}_t)$ introduced in (9.50). Note that $\mathcal{H}_t$ can be described as $\mathcal{H}_t = \sigma(\{(T_n, \xi_n) : T_n \leqslant t\})$, as the sequence (T_n, ξ_n), $T_n \leqslant t$ gives an alternative description of the default history up to time t. By $\mathcal{H}_{T_n}$ we denote the σ-algebra of events observable up to and including the nth default time T_n, i.e. $\mathcal{H}_{T_n} = \sigma(\{(T_j, \xi_j) : 1 \leqslant j \leqslant n\})$. (This coincides with the general abstract definition of the σ-algebra of events observable up to some stopping time.)

Theorem 9.46. *Consider default times $\tau_1, \dots, \tau_m$ and denote by $(\mathcal{H}_t)$ the corresponding internal filtration. Suppose that for every $0 \leqslant n \leqslant m-1$ and every $i \in \{1, \dots, m\}$ there is a random mapping $g_i^{(n)} : \Omega \times \mathbb{R}_+ \to \mathbb{R}_+$, measurable with* *respect to the product σ-algebra $\mathcal{H}_{T_n} \otimes \mathcal{B}(\mathbb{R}_+)$, such that*

$$P(T_{n+1}-T_n \leqslant s,\ \xi_{n+1} = i \mid \mathcal{H}_{T_n})(\omega) = \int_0^s g_i^{(n)}(\omega, u)\,\mathrm{d}u, \quad 1 \leqslant i \leqslant m. \tag{9.73}$$

Then the martingale default intensity of $(Y_{t,i})$ with respect to $(\mathcal{H}_t)$ is given by

$$\lambda_{t,i}(\omega) = \frac{g_i^{(n)}(\omega, t - T_n)}{P(T_{n+1} > t \mid \mathcal{H}_{T_n})(\omega)}, \quad T_n < t \leqslant T_{n+1}. \tag{9.74}$$

The proof of this result is beyond the scope of this text. In Notes and Comments we reference several texts in which a proof of Theorem 9.46 and extensions to copula models with stochastic marginal hazard rates can be found.

Comments. The measurability requirement on the random function $g_i^{(n)}$ simply means that the functional form of $g_i^{(n)}(\omega, \cdot)$ depends only on the default history $\mathcal{H}_{T_n}$. We will see below that (9.73) is always satisfied if the vector $(\tau_1, \dots, \tau_m)$ admits a joint density.

The form (9.74) for the martingale intensity is in fact quite natural. If investors observe only past and present defaults, they obtain significant new information only at the time points $T_1(\omega), \dots, T_m(\omega)$. Hence we expect the martingale default intensity $(\lambda_{t,i})$ of some firm $i \in A_n$ (a surviving firm) to evolve in a deterministic fashion for $t \in (T_n, T_{n+1}]$ and to change with the random arrival of new information at T_{n+1}. Moreover, it is possible to derive a different expression for $(\lambda_{t,i})$ which resembles more closely the common notion of an intensity as "the conditional probability of default in the next instant". Applying the fundamental theorem of calculus and (9.73) we get, for $t \in [T_n, T_{n+1})$ and arbitrary $n < m$,

$$\begin{aligned} g_i^{(n)}(\omega, t - T_n) &= \lim_{h \to 0} \frac{1}{h} \int_{t-T_n}^{t-T_n+h} g_i^{(n)}(\omega, u)\,\mathrm{d}u \\ &= \lim_{h \to 0} \frac{1}{h} P(T_{n+1} \in (t, t+h], \xi_{n+1} = i \mid \mathcal{H}_{T_n})(\omega). \end{aligned}$$

Hence we get, for a surviving firm $i \in A_n$, using (9.74),

$$\lambda_{t,i} = \lim_{h \to 0} \frac{1}{h} P(\tau_i \leqslant t + h \mid \{\tau_j > t \text{ for all } j \in A_n\}, \mathcal{H}_{T_n}). \tag{9.75}$$

Now note that at time $t \in [T_n, T_{n+1})$ default information consists of $\mathcal{H}_{T_n}$ and the atom $B := \{\tau_j > t \text{ for all } j \in A_n\}$. If we denote by $\bar{F}_{\tau_i \mid \mathcal{H}_t}(T) := P(\tau_i > T \mid \mathcal{H}_t)$ the conditional survival probability of firm i given the default history up to time t, we thus get, on $\{\tau_i > t\}$,

$$\lambda_{t,i} = \lim_{h \to 0} \frac{1}{h} P(\tau_i \leqslant t + h \mid \mathcal{H}_t) = -\frac{\partial}{\partial T}\bigg|_{T=t} \bar{F}_{\tau_i \mid \mathcal{H}_t}(T). \tag{9.76}$$

Hence $\lambda_{t,i}$ gives the instantaneous conditional probability that a surviving firm $i \in A_n$ defaults at time t given the default history of all firms in the portfolio up to time t. Below we explain how the conditional survival $\bar{F}_{\tau_i \mid \mathcal{H}_t}$ can be expressed in terms of derivatives of the unconditional survival function of $(\tau_1, \dots, \tau_m)$.

Remark 9.47 (martingale intensities and marginal hazard rates). Consider random times $\tau_1, \dots, \tau_m$ following a threshold copula model with deterministic marginal hazard rates $\gamma_1(t), \dots, \gamma_m(t)$ and a survival copula C admitting a density. In this case the assumptions from Theorem 9.46 are satisfied. However, for $t > 0$ the martingale intensity $\lambda_{t,i}$ is in general different from the marginal hazard rate $\gamma_i(t)$. As explained earlier, this shows that $Y_{t,i} - \int_0^{t\wedge\tau} \gamma_i(s)\,\mathrm{d}s$ is an $(\mathcal{H}_t^i)$-martingale but not a martingale with respect to the full default information $(\mathcal{H}_t)$. To see that in general, for $t > 0$, $\lambda_{t,i} \neq \gamma_i(t)$, recall from Section 9.2.1 that

$$\gamma_i(t) = \lim_{h\to 0} \frac{1}{h} P(\tau_i \leqslant t + h \mid \tau_i > t). \tag{9.77}$$

Hence $\gamma_i(t)$ gives the instantaneous default probability of firm i given $\tau_i > t$, whereas $\lambda_{t,i}$ gives the instantaneous default probability given $\tau_i > t$ *and* the default history of all other firms in the portfolio. With default dependence the two conditional expectations will typically differ; a numeric illustration is given in Example 9.50 below. With (conditionally) independent defaults on the other hand, the additional information about the default history of firms $j \neq i$ in the portfolio is of no use in predicting the default time of firm i, and we have $\lambda_{t,i} = \gamma_i(t)$, as was shown formally in Proposition 9.39.

Conditional survival functions. Let $T_n \leqslant t < T_{n+1}$ for some $0 \leqslant n \leqslant m - 1$. We want to compute the conditional survival function $\bar{F}_{\tau_i \mid \mathcal{H}_t}$ for some firm $i \in A_n$. To simplify the notation we assume from now on that the indices have been permuted in such a way that $A_n^{\mathrm{c}} = \{1, \dots, n\}$ and $A_n = \{n+1, \dots, m\}$, i.e. the defaulted firms correspond to the first n firms in our index set. Put $\boldsymbol{\tau}_1 = (\tau_1, \dots, \tau_n)'$ and $\boldsymbol{\tau}_2 = (\tau_{n+1}, \dots, \tau_m)'$. As an intermediate step we consider $\bar{F}_{\boldsymbol{\tau}_2 \mid \boldsymbol{\tau}_1}(t_1, \dots, t_{m-n} \mid \boldsymbol{\tau}_1)$, the conditional survival function of the last $m - n$ firms given the vector of the default times of the first n firms. We have the following lemma.

Lemma 9.48. *Assume that the vector* $(\tau_1, \dots, \tau_m)$ *has a density. Then*

$$\bar{F}_{\boldsymbol{\tau}_2 \mid \boldsymbol{\tau}_1}(t_1, \dots, t_{m-n} \mid \tau_1, \dots, \tau_n) = \frac{\dfrac{\partial^n}{\partial t_1 \cdots \partial t_n} \bar{F}(\tau_1, \dots, \tau_n, t_1, \dots, t_{m-n})}{\dfrac{\partial^n}{\partial t_1 \cdots \partial t_n} \bar{F}(\tau_1, \dots, \tau_n, 0, \dots, 0)}.$$

Proof. Recall that the joint density of $(\tau_1, \dots, \tau_m)$ is given by

$$(-1)^m \frac{\partial^m \bar{F}}{\partial t_1 \cdots \partial t_m}.$$

Hence the result follows from the conditional density formula (3.2) for the conditional density of $\boldsymbol{\tau}_2$ given $\boldsymbol{\tau}_1$; we omit the details. □

Finally, we turn to the conditional survival function $\bar{F}_{\tau_i \mid \mathcal{H}_t}$. At time t default information consists of the vector $\boldsymbol{\tau}_1$ of the default times of the firms from A_n^{c} and of the atom $B := \{\tau_2 > t\}$. Hence we have, for $i \in \{n+1, \dots, m\}$ and $T \geqslant t$, using the definition of elementary conditional expectation and Lemma 9.48, that

$$\bar{F}_{\tau_i \mid \mathcal{H}_t}(T) = P(\tau_i > T \mid B, \boldsymbol{\tau_1}) = \frac{P(\tau_i > T, \boldsymbol{\tau_2} > t \mid \boldsymbol{\tau_1})}{P(\boldsymbol{\tau_2} > t \mid \boldsymbol{\tau_1})}$$

$$= \frac{\dfrac{\partial^n}{\partial t_1 \cdots \partial t_n} \bar{F}(\tau_1, \dots, \tau_n, t, \dots, T, \dots, t)}{\dfrac{\partial^n}{\partial t_1 \cdots \partial t_n} \bar{F}(\tau_1, \dots, \tau_n, t, \dots, t, \dots, t)}. \tag{9.78}$$

Combining (9.76) and (9.78) we can characterize martingale default intensities in terms of the unconditional survival function of $(\tau_1, \dots, \tau_m)$.

Corollary 9.49. *Suppose that the random vector $(\tau_1, \dots, \tau_m)$ admits a density. Let $T_n < t \leqslant T_{n+1}, 0 \leqslant n < m$, and suppose that $A_n^{\mathrm{c}} = \{1, \dots, n\}$. Then the martingale default intensity of firm $i \in A_n$ with respect to $(\mathcal{H}_t)$ equals*

$$\lambda_{t,i} = -\frac{\dfrac{\partial^{n+1}}{\partial t_1 \cdots \partial t_n \partial t_i} \bar{F}(\tau_1, \dots, \tau_n, t, \dots t)}{\dfrac{\partial^n}{\partial t_1 \cdots \partial t_n} \bar{F}(\tau_1, \dots, \tau_n, t, \dots, t)}.$$

If we have a closed-form expression for the unconditional survival function $\bar{F}$ (or equivalently for the survival copula C) of $(\tau_1, \dots, \tau_m)$, then it is straightforward, in principle, to compute the martingale default intensities. However, Corollary 9.49 conveys little economic intuition, as it expresses martingale intensities and hence default contagion in terms of purely mathematical objects, namely higher-order derivatives of the unconditional survival function. Moreover, it seems difficult to use the corollary in order to build a model where default contagion follows a particular pattern. In Section 9.8.2 we will therefore study conditional survival functions in factor copula models, where default contagion permits a natural economic interpretation in terms of incomplete information.

Applications to credit-risky securities. It is interesting to investigate the implications of our general results for martingale intensities for the pricing of credit-risky securities. Following the literature we use the martingale-modelling approach and assume that under the risk-neutral measure Q used for pricing the default times, $\tau_1, \dots, \tau_m$ follow a copula model with deterministic hazard rates $\gamma_1(t), \dots, \gamma_m(t)$ and survival copula C. Moreover, we assume that the risk-free short rate $r(t) \geqslant 0$ is deterministic; $B(t) = \exp(\int_0^t r(s)\,\mathrm{d}s)$ denotes the default-free savings account. The assumption of deterministic interest rates is routinely made in the literature on pricing portfolio credit derivatives, essentially because the impact of stochastic interest rates on prices is low compared with the impact of the assumptions on default dependence.

We begin with the problem of pricing a first-to-default swap. We consider a similar contract as in Section 9.6.3. Premiums are due at times $0 < t_1 < \cdots < t_N = T$, provided that no default has yet occurred; if $T_1 < T$ and, moreover, $\xi_1 = i$, there is a default payment equal to the constant l_i. In this set-up the value at time $t = 0$ of the default payment leg equals

$$V^{\text{def}} = \sum_{i=1}^{m} l_i E^Q(B(\tau_i)^{-1} I_{\{\tau_i = T_1\}} I_{\{\tau_i \leqslant T\}}).$$

If we condition on τ_i, we get, for a single term of this sum,

$$E^Q(B(\tau_i)^{-1} I_{\{T_1 = \tau_i\}} I_{\{\tau_i \leqslant T\}}) = \int_0^T B(t)^{-1} Q(\tau_i = T_1 \mid \tau_i = t) f_i(t)\,\mathrm{d}t,$$

where $f_i(t)$ is the marginal density of τ_i. Now Lemma 9.48 yields

$$Q(\tau_i = T_1 \mid \tau_i = t) = Q(\tau_j > t \text{ for all } j \neq i \mid \tau_i = t) = -\frac{1}{f_i(t)} \frac{\partial \bar{F}}{\partial t_i}(t, \dots, t),$$

and we obtain

$$V^{\text{def}} = -\sum_{i=1}^{m} l_i \int_0^T B(t)^{-1} \frac{\partial \bar{F}}{\partial t_i}(t, \dots, t)\,\mathrm{d}t.$$

If $\bar{F}$ or, equivalently, the threshold copula C is known in closed form, this is straightforward to compute by one-dimensional (numerical) integration. Note that, by definition, $Q(T_1 > t) = \bar{F}(t_n, \dots, t_n)$; hence the value in $t = 0$ of the premium payments (assuming a generic swap spread x) is given by

$$V^{\text{prem}} = x \sum_{n=1}^{N} B(t_n)^{-1} (t_n - t_{n-1}) \bar{F}(t_n, \dots, t_n).$$

Next we consider the relationship between the instantaneous credit spread and martingale intensities. Denote by $p_{1,i}(t, T)$ the price of a zero-coupon bond with maturity T issued by firm i and assume that the recovery rate of this bond is equal to zero. Hence the price of the bond at time $t < \tau_i$ is given by

$$p_{1,i}(t, T) = \exp\biggl(-\int_t^T r(s)\,\mathrm{d}s\biggr) Q(\tau_i > T \mid \mathcal{H}_t), \tag{9.79}$$

so that the credit spread is given by $c_i(t, T) = -1/(T - t) \ln Q(\tau_i > T \mid \mathcal{H}_t)$. Since $Q(\tau_i > t \mid \mathcal{H}_t) = 1$ on $\{t < \tau_i\}$, by (9.76), the instantaneous credit spread $c_i(t) = \lim_{T \to t} c_i(t, T)$ is given by

$$c_i(t, T) = -\frac{\partial}{\partial T}\bigg|_{T=t} \ln Q(\tau_i > T \mid \mathcal{H}_t) = -\frac{\partial}{\partial T}\bigg|_{T=t} Q(\tau_i > T \mid \mathcal{H}_t) = \lambda_{t,i},$$

i.e. the martingale default intensity of τ_i under the equivalent martingale measure Q is equal to the instantaneous credit spread of a zero-recovery bond issued by firm i.

Finally, we discuss issues related to *dynamic consistency* in the use of copula models. In Section 9.7.1 we showed that at $t = 0$ pricing formulas for single-name products remain valid in a portfolio model; we also mentioned that this is no longer true at $t > 0$. Here we take a closer look at this fact. Consider a corporate zero-coupon bond with zero recovery. According to (9.79), the price of this security at $t > 0$ is given by the discounted conditional survival probability of the firm given the default history of all obligors up to time t. In a single-firm model, on the other hand, we have $p_{1,i}(t, T) = I_{\{\tau_i > t\}} \exp(-\int_t^T r(s)\,ds) Q(\tau_i > T \mid \tau_i > t)$, i.e. the price of the bond equals the discounted conditional survival probability of firm i given only its own default history. As discussed previously, these two conditional survival probabilities generally differ for $t > 0$.

Note, however, that, while correct from a theoretical point of view, (9.79) does not correspond to the way practitioners tend to use a copula model. In deriving (9.79) we fixed in $t_0 = 0$ a model for the joint distribution of $(\tau_1, \dots, \tau_m)$, a model with constant hazard rates and a Clayton survival copula with parameter θ_0, say; at time $t_1 > 0$ we priced the bond using the conditional distribution of this model given the default history $\mathcal{H}_{t_1}$. Practitioners typically proceed in a different way: at time t_1 they calibrate a new model—in our case again a Clayton copula model but with parameter θ_1, which may be different from θ_0—to the market information available in t_1 and use the new model to price the bond. In general, both approaches lead to different distributions for the default times of surviving firms and hence to different prices. Clearly, the second approach is inconsistent over time; however, it leads to prices which are consistent with the available market information at any given point in time—a property that practitioners regard as highly important.

9.8.2 *Information-Based Default Contagion*

Default contagion in factor copula models can be attributed to the fact that information about the default history alters the conditional distribution of the unobservable factor vector $\boldsymbol{V}$. In this section we make this statement precise and compute the conditional distribution of $\boldsymbol{V}$ given the default history up to and including time t. Moreover, we explain how the martingale default intensity at time t can be computed as expectations with respect to the conditional distribution of $\boldsymbol{V}$. We assume throughout that the conditional distribution of τ_j given $\boldsymbol{V}$ admits the density

$$f_{\tau_j \mid \boldsymbol{V}}(t \mid \boldsymbol{V}) = -\frac{\partial}{\partial t} \bar{F}_{\tau_j \mid \boldsymbol{V}}(t \mid \boldsymbol{V}).$$

To simplify the exposition, we further assume that $\boldsymbol{V}$ admits the density $g_{\boldsymbol{V}}(\boldsymbol{v})$. By $g_{\boldsymbol{V} \mid \mathcal{H}_t}(\boldsymbol{v})$ we denote the conditional density of $\boldsymbol{V}$ given $\mathcal{H}_t$.

Computation of $g_{\boldsymbol{V} \mid \mathcal{H}_t}(\boldsymbol{v})$. We begin with the case $t < T_1$. Using the definition of elementary conditional expectation, we obtain for $A \subseteq \mathbb{R}^p$ that

$$P(\boldsymbol{V} \in A \mid T_1 > t) = \frac{1}{\bar{F}(t, \dots, t)} \int_A \prod_{j=1}^{m} \bar{F}_{\tau_j \mid \boldsymbol{V}}(t \mid \boldsymbol{v}) g_{\boldsymbol{V}}(\boldsymbol{v})\,d\boldsymbol{v}.$$

Hence, for $t < T_1$, the conditional density of $\boldsymbol{V}$ given $\mathcal{H}_t$ is given by

$$g_{\boldsymbol{V} \mid \mathcal{H}_t}(\boldsymbol{v}) = \frac{\prod_{j=1}^{m} \bar{F}_{\tau_j \mid \boldsymbol{V}}(t \mid \boldsymbol{v})}{\bar{F}(t, \dots, t)} g_{\boldsymbol{V}}(\boldsymbol{v}), \quad t < T_1. \tag{9.80}$$

Now we turn to the case $t \in [T_1, T_2)$. As an intermediary step we determine the conditional density $g_{V|\tau_j}(v \mid \tau_j)$. The conditional density formula (3.2) gives

$$g_{V|\tau_j}(v \mid \tau_j) = \frac{f_{\tau_j|V}(\tau_j \mid v) g_V(v)}{\int_{\mathbb{R}^p} f_j(\tau_j \mid v) g_V(v)\,\mathrm{d}v} = \frac{f_{\tau_j|V}(\tau_j \mid v)}{f_j(\tau_j)} g_V(v), \tag{9.81}$$

where $f_j(t)$ is the unconditional density of τ_j. To keep the notation simple, we assume, as in the previous subsection, that $\xi_1 = 1$. For $t \in [T_1, T_2)$, default information consists therefore of the default time τ_1 and of the atom $B := \{\tau_j > t,\ 2 \leqslant j \leqslant m\}$. Now we get, for $A \subset \mathbb{R}^p$,

$$\begin{aligned} P(V \in A \mid B, \tau_1) &= \frac{P(\{V \in A\} \cap B \mid \tau_1)}{P(B \mid \tau_1)} \\ &= \int_A \frac{\prod_{j=2}^m \bar{F}_{\tau_j|V}(t \mid v)}{P(B \mid \tau_1)} g_{V|\tau_1}(v \mid \tau_1)\,\mathrm{d}v \end{aligned}$$

and

$$P(B \mid \tau_1) = \int_{\mathbb{R}^p} \bigg(\prod_{j=2}^m \bar{F}_{\tau_j|V}(t \mid v) \bigg) g_{V|\tau_1}(v \mid \tau_1)\,\mathrm{d}v.$$

Hence

$$g_{V|\mathcal{H}_t}(v) = \frac{\prod_{j=2}^n \bar{F}_{\tau_j|V}(t \mid v)}{P(B \mid \tau_1)} \frac{f_{\tau_1|V}(\tau_1 \mid v)}{f_1(\tau_1)} g_V(v), \quad t \in [T_1, T_2). \tag{9.82}$$

For $t \geqslant T_2$, the conditional density $g_{V|\mathcal{H}_t}(v)$ can be determined analogously; we omit the details. For models with Clayton threshold copula, explicit expressions for $g_{V|\mathcal{H}_t}(v)$ can be given (see Example 9.50 below).

Martingale default intensities. In factor copula models we can give an intuitive explanation for the dynamics of martingale default intensities. Suppose for the moment that the factor vector V is observable, so that the information available to investors is given by the artificial filtration $\tilde{\mathcal{H}}_t = \mathcal{H}_t \vee \sigma(V)$, $t \geqslant 0$. Since the τ_i are conditionally independent given V, by Proposition 9.39 the martingale intensity of τ_i with respect to the large filtration $(\tilde{\mathcal{H}}_t)$ is given by $\tilde{\lambda}_i(t \mid V) = f_{\tau_i|V}(t \mid V)/\bar{F}_{\tau_i|V}(t \mid V)$. Now, it is well known that the martingale intensity of τ_i with respect to the internal filtration $(\mathcal{H}_t)$ can be computed by *projection*, i.e. $\lambda_{t,i} = E(\tilde{\lambda}_i(t \mid V) \mid \mathcal{H}_t)$ (see, for example, Theorem 14 in Chapter 2 of Brémaud (1981)). Hence we get

$$\lambda_{t,i} := \int_{\mathbb{R}^p} \frac{f_{\tau_i|V}(t \mid v)}{\bar{F}_{\tau_i|V}(t \mid v)} g_{V|\mathcal{H}_t}(v)\,\mathrm{d}v. \tag{9.83}$$

Example 9.50 (Clayton copula model). For models with a Clayton threshold copula the conditional density $g_{V|\mathcal{H}_t}(v)$ and the martingale default intensities $(\lambda_{t,i})$ can be computed explicitly. Recall that the Clayton copula with parameter $\theta > 0$ is an LT-Archimedean copula model, as introduced in Example 9.44 with $V \sim \mathrm{Ga}(1/\theta, 1)$. Fix $\theta > 0$ and denote by $\hat{G}$ and $\hat{G}^{-1}$ the Laplace Stieltjes transform of the $\mathrm{Ga}(1/\theta, 1)$ distribution and its functional inverse. Recall that for arbitrary $\alpha, \beta > 0$ the density $g(v; \alpha, \beta)$ of the $\mathrm{Ga}(\alpha, \beta)$ distribution satisfies $g(v; \alpha, \beta) \propto v^{\alpha-1} \exp(-\beta v)$, where "$\propto$" denotes "is proportional to". As shown in Example 9.44, in LT-Archimedean threshold copula models the conditional survival function $\bar{F}_{\tau_i | V}(t \mid v)$ equals $\exp(-v\hat{G}^{-1}(\bar{F}_i(t)))$. Hence the density of τ_i given $V = v$ is given by

$$f_{\tau_i|V}(t \mid v) = -\frac{\partial}{\partial t}\bar{F}_{\tau_i|V}(t \mid v) = \frac{-f_i(t)}{\hat{G}'(\hat{G}^{-1}(\bar{F}_i(t)))} v \exp(-v\hat{G}^{-1}(\bar{F}_i(t))).$$

We obtain, for $t < T_1$, using (9.80),

$$g_{V|\mathcal{H}_t}(v) \propto v^{1/\theta-1} \exp\biggl\{ -v\biggl(1 + \sum_{i=1}^{m} \hat{G}^{-1}(\bar{F}_i(t))\biggr)\biggr\}, \quad t < T_1. \tag{9.84}$$

Hence, for $t < T_1$, the conditional distribution of V given $\mathcal{H}_t$ is again a gamma distribution but now with parameters $\alpha = 1/\theta$ and $\beta = 1 + \sum_{i=1}^{m} \hat{G}^{-1}(\bar{F}_i(t))$. Recall that the mean of a $\mathrm{Ga}(\alpha, \beta)$ distributed rv equals α/β. Hence the conditional mean of V given $T_1 > t$ is lower than the unconditional mean of V. This is in line with economic intuition, since the fact that $T_1 > t$ is "good news" for the portfolio.

According to (9.81), the density of V given τ_1 satisfies

$$\begin{aligned} g_{V|\tau_1}(v \mid \tau_1) &\propto v \exp\{-v\hat{G}^{-1}(\bar{F}_1(\tau_1))\} g(v; 1/\theta, 1) \\ &= v^{1/\theta} \exp\{-v(1 + \hat{G}^{-1}(\bar{F}_1(\tau_1)))\}, \end{aligned} \tag{9.85}$$

so, given τ_1, V is gamma distributed with parameters $\alpha = 1 + 1/\theta$ and $\beta = 1 + \hat{G}^{-1}(\bar{F}_1(\tau_1))$. It is instructive to look at the impact of τ_1 on the mean of the conditional distribution of V, given by $(1/\theta + 1)/\hat{G}^{-1}(\bar{F}_1(\tau_1))$. Suppose that τ_1 occurs unusually early, i.e. that $\bar{F}_1(\tau_1)$ is close to one. This implies that $\hat{G}^{-1}(\bar{F}_1(\tau_1))$ is close to zero, and the mean of the conditional distribution is bigger than the unconditional mean $1/\theta$. Since the conditional survival functions $\bar{F}_{\tau_i|V}(t \mid v)$ are decreasing in v, the conditional survival probabilities of the remaining obligors are thus decreased. A similar qualitative reasoning applies if τ_1 occurs late in the sense that $\bar{F}_1(\tau_1)$ is close to zero; obviously, in that case conditional survival probabilities are increased.

Next we turn to the case $t \in [T_1, T_2)$. For notational simplicity again we assume that $\xi_1 = 1$. Using (9.82), it is easily seen that, given $\mathcal{H}_t$, V follows a gamma distribution with parameters $\alpha = 1 + 1/\theta$ and $\beta = 1 + \hat{G}^{-1}(\tau_1) + \sum_{j=2}^{m} \hat{G}^{-1}(\bar{F}_j(t))$. Note that, in T_1, the conditional mean $\mu_{V|\mathcal{H}_t}$ of V jumps upwards: we have

$$\begin{aligned} \lim_{t \overset{<}{\to} T_1} \mu_{V|\mathcal{H}_t} &= \frac{1/\theta}{1 + \sum_{j=1}^{m} \hat{G}^{-1}(\bar{F}_j(T_1))}, \\ \mu_{V|\mathcal{H}_{T_1}} &= \frac{1 + 1/\theta}{1 + \sum_{j=1}^{m} \hat{G}^{-1}(\bar{F}_j(T_1))}. \end{aligned}$$

Finally, we compute the martingale intensity $\lambda_{t,i}$ using (9.83). We obtain

$$\tilde{\lambda}_i(t, V) = \frac{-f_i(t)V}{\hat{G}'(\hat{G}^{-1}(\bar{F}_i(t)))} \quad \text{so} \quad \lambda_{t,i} = \frac{-f_i(t)E(V \mid \mathcal{H}_t)}{\hat{G}'(\hat{G}^{-1}(\bar{F}_i(t)))}.$$

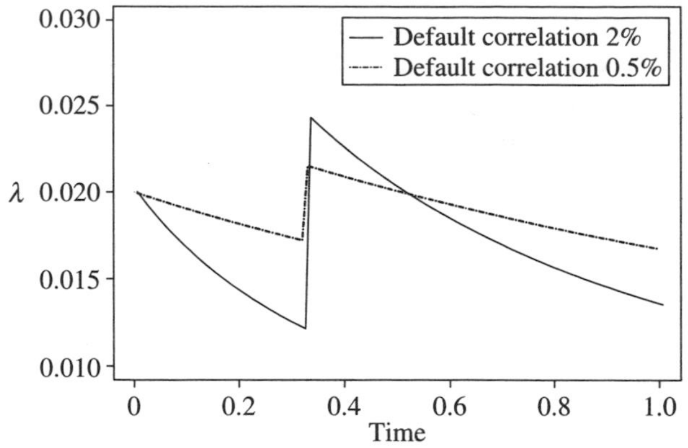

Figure 9.12. Paths of the default intensity (λ_t) in the Clayton copula model, assuming that the first default time T_1 equals four months. The parameters are as follows: portfolio size $m = 100$; marginal default intensity $\gamma = 0.02$; one-year default correlation 2% (alternatively, 0.5%). As one would expect, a higher default correlation implies a stronger contagion effect.

The martingale default intensity is thus proportional to $E(V \mid \mathcal{H}_t)$, the conditional mean of V given $\mathcal{H}_t$. In particular, $\lambda_{t,i}$ jumps upward at each successive default time T_n and decreases gradually between defaults. This is illustrated in Figure 9.12.

9.8.3 *Interacting Intensities*

In copula models the dependence structure of the default times is exogenously specified; the form of the resulting default contagion can then be computed from the model primitives. In models with interacting intensities, on the other hand, the impact of defaults on the default intensities of surviving firms is exogenously specified; the joint distribution of the default times is then endogenously derived. This leads to a very intuitive parametrization of counterparty risk and default dependence. The main drawback of models with interacting intensities is the fact that the marginal distribution of individual default times is typically not available in closed form, so the calibration of the model to defaultable term structure data is more evolved than in copula models.

In models with interacting intensities the martingale default intensity of firm i belonging to a given portfolio is given by an exogenously specified function $\lambda_i(t, \boldsymbol{Y}_t)$ of time and the current state $\boldsymbol{Y}_t$ of the portfolio. The dependence on the current state of the portfolio is the major innovation of the model; in this way, counterparty risk can be modelled explicitly. Suppose, for instance, that firm i is a commercial bank and that firm j is a major borrower from bank i, so that we expect the conditional default probability of firm i to increase given that firm j defaults. This can be modelled by taking $\lambda_i(t, \boldsymbol{y}) = a_{i0}(t) + a_{i1}(t) I_{\{y_j=1\}}(\boldsymbol{y})$ for non-negative and bounded functions $a_{i0}, a_{i1} : [0, \infty) \to \mathbb{R}_+$. It is straightforward to extend the model to stochastic default intensities of the form $\lambda_i(\boldsymbol{\Psi}_t, \boldsymbol{Y}_t)$ for some observable background process $(\boldsymbol{\Psi}_t)$ (references are given in Notes and Comments).

It is convenient to model the default indicator process $(\boldsymbol{Y}_t)$ in a model with interacting intensities as a time-inhomogeneous continuous-time *Markov chain*. In this way the computational tools from the theory of Markov chains can be used for the analysis and simulation of the model. Below we summarize a few essential facts about continuous-time Markov chains; several textbooks on stochastic processes containing a detailed discussion of continuous-time Markov chains are listed in Notes and Comments.

Continuous-time Markov chains. A time-inhomogeneous continuous-time Markov chain $(\boldsymbol{X}_t)$ on a finite state space S is characterized by non-negative and bounded *transition rate functions* $\lambda(t, \boldsymbol{x}, \boldsymbol{y})$, $\boldsymbol{x}, \boldsymbol{y} \in S$, $\boldsymbol{x} \neq \boldsymbol{y}$, $t \geqslant 0$, with the following interpretation. Fix $t \geqslant 0$ and let $T := \inf\{s \geqslant t : \boldsymbol{X}_s \neq \boldsymbol{X}_t\}$, i.e. T gives the time of the first jump of the chain after time t. Define, for $\boldsymbol{x} \in S$,

$$\lambda(t, \boldsymbol{x}, \boldsymbol{x}) := -\sum_{\boldsymbol{y} \in S, \boldsymbol{y} \neq \boldsymbol{x}} \lambda(t, \boldsymbol{x}, \boldsymbol{y}), \quad t \geqslant 0,$$

and denote by $\mathcal{H}_t := \sigma(\{\boldsymbol{X}_s : s \leqslant t\})$ the internal filtration of the chain. Then

$$P(T > s \mid \mathcal{H}_t) = P(T > s \mid \boldsymbol{X}_t) = \exp\left(\int_t^s \lambda(u, \boldsymbol{X}_t, \boldsymbol{X}_t)\,\mathrm{d}u\right), \quad s \geqslant t. \tag{9.86}$$

In the special case of a time-homogeneous Markov chain where the transition rate functions are independent of time, given $\mathcal{H}_t$, the rv $(T - t)$ (the waiting time for the next jump after time t) is thus $\mathrm{Exp}(-\lambda(\boldsymbol{X}_t, \boldsymbol{X}_t))$ distributed. Moreover, we have, for $\boldsymbol{y} \in S$ and T as before,

$$P(\boldsymbol{X}_T = \boldsymbol{y} \mid \mathcal{H}_t, T) = -\lambda(T, \boldsymbol{X}_t, \boldsymbol{y})/\lambda(T, \boldsymbol{X}_t, \boldsymbol{X}_t); \tag{9.87}$$

given that the chain has a jump at time t, the probability of jumping to a particular state $\boldsymbol{y}$ is thus proportional to the transition rate $\lambda(t, \boldsymbol{X}_{t-}, \boldsymbol{y})$, where $\boldsymbol{X}_{t-}$ denotes the state of the chain immediately before the jump. Next we introduce the *generator* $G_{[t]}$, $t \geqslant 0$, of the chain $(\boldsymbol{X}_t)$. For fixed t the operator $G_{[t]}$ associates with every function $f : S \to \mathbb{R}$ a new function $G_{[t]}f : S \to \mathbb{R}$ with

$$G_{[t]}f(\boldsymbol{x}) = \sum_{\boldsymbol{y} \in S,\ \boldsymbol{y} \neq \boldsymbol{x}} \lambda(t, \boldsymbol{x}, \boldsymbol{y})(f(\boldsymbol{y}) - f(\boldsymbol{x})). \tag{9.88}$$

The generator is a very useful mathematical object for a number of reasons. First, it is a well-known result that, for any $f : S \to \mathbb{R}$, the process

$$M_t^f := f(\boldsymbol{X}_t) - \int_0^t G_{[s]}f(\boldsymbol{X}_s)\,\mathrm{d}s, \quad t \geqslant 0, \tag{9.89}$$

is an $(\mathcal{H}_t)$-martingale. Second, as explained below, the generator appears in the Kolmogorov equations, a system of ODEs characterizing the transition probabilities of the chain $(\boldsymbol{X}_t)$.

Construction of interacting intensities via Markov chains. Now we turn to the formal construction of models with interacting intensities. Set $S := \{0, 1\}^m$ and define, for $\boldsymbol{y} \in S$ and $i \in \{1, \dots, m\}$, the state $\boldsymbol{y}^i$ by $y_j^i = y_j$ for $j \in \{1, \dots, m\} \setminus i$ and $y_i^i = 1 - y_i$, i.e. $\boldsymbol{y}^i$ is constructed from $\boldsymbol{y}$ by flipping the ith coordinate. Given, for $1 \leqslant i \leqslant m$, non-negative and bounded functions $\lambda_i : [0, \infty) \times S \to \mathbb{R}_+$ (the candidate martingale default intensities), we define the default indicator process $(\boldsymbol{Y}_t)$ as a time-inhomogeneous continuous-time Markov chain with state space S and transition rates

$$\lambda(t, \boldsymbol{y}, \boldsymbol{x}) = \begin{cases} I_{\{y_i=0\}}\lambda_i(t, \boldsymbol{y}), & \text{if } \boldsymbol{x} = \boldsymbol{y}^i \text{ for some } i \in \{1 \dots, m\}, \\ 0, & \text{otherwise.} \end{cases} \tag{9.90}$$

Relation (9.90) implies that the chain can jump only to those neighbouring states $\boldsymbol{Y}_t^i$ that differ from the current state $\boldsymbol{Y}_t$ by exactly one default; in particular, there are no joint defaults. If $Y_{t,i} = 0$, the probability that firm i defaults in the small time interval $[t, t+h)$, i.e. the probability of jumping to the neighbouring state $\boldsymbol{Y}_t^i$ in $[t, t+h)$, is approximately equal to $h\lambda_i(t, \boldsymbol{Y}_t)$. The generator of $(\boldsymbol{Y}_t)$ is given by

$$G_{[t]}f(\boldsymbol{y}) = \sum_{i=1}^{m} I_{\{y_i=0\}}\lambda_i(t, \boldsymbol{y})(f(t, \boldsymbol{y}^i) - f(t, \boldsymbol{y})), \quad \boldsymbol{y} \in S. \tag{9.91}$$

The definition of $(\boldsymbol{Y}_t)$ suggests that $(\lambda_i(t, \boldsymbol{Y}_t))$ is the martingale default intensity of firm i. Using (9.89), a formal proof is easy. Let $f_i(\boldsymbol{y}) = y_i$, so $Y_{t,i} = f_i(\boldsymbol{Y}_t)$ and $G_{[t]}f_i(\boldsymbol{y}) = I_{\{y_i=0\}}\lambda_i(t, \boldsymbol{y})$. Hence

$$Y_{t,i} - \int_0^{t\wedge\tau_i} \lambda_i(s, \boldsymbol{Y}_s)\,\mathrm{d}s = Y_{t,i} - \int_0^t G_{[s]}f_i(\boldsymbol{Y}_s)\,\mathrm{d}s$$

is a martingale by (9.89).

Transition functions and Kolmogorov equations. The *transition probabilities* of the chain $(\boldsymbol{Y}_t)$ are given by

$$p(t, s, \boldsymbol{x}, \boldsymbol{y}) := P(\boldsymbol{Y}_s = \boldsymbol{y} \mid \boldsymbol{Y}_t = \boldsymbol{x}), \quad \boldsymbol{x}, \boldsymbol{y} \in S,\ 0 \leqslant t \leqslant s < \infty. \tag{9.92}$$

It is well known that the function $p(t, s, \boldsymbol{x}, \boldsymbol{y})$ satisfies the Kolmogorov backward and forward equations. These equations are very useful numerical tools in the analysis of the model. The backward equation is a system of ODEs for the function $(t, \boldsymbol{x}) \to p(t, s, \boldsymbol{x}, \boldsymbol{y})$, $0 \leqslant t \leqslant s$; s and $\boldsymbol{y}$ are considered as parameters. The general form of the equation is $(\partial/\partial t)p(t, s, \boldsymbol{x}, \boldsymbol{y}) + G_{[t]}p(t, s, \boldsymbol{x}, \boldsymbol{y}) = 0$, with terminal condition $p(s, s, \boldsymbol{x}, \boldsymbol{y}) = I_{\{\boldsymbol{y}\}}(\boldsymbol{x})$. In our model this leads to the following system of ODEs:

$$\frac{\partial p(t, s, \boldsymbol{x}, \boldsymbol{y})}{\partial t} + \sum_{i=1}^{m}(1 - x_i)\lambda_i(t, \boldsymbol{x})(p(t, s, \boldsymbol{x}^i, \boldsymbol{y}) - p(t, s, \boldsymbol{x}, \boldsymbol{y})) = 0.$$

The forward equation is an ODE system for the function $(s, \boldsymbol{y}) \to p(t, s, \boldsymbol{x}, \boldsymbol{y})$, $s \geqslant t$, which is governed by the adjoint operator $G^*_{[t]}$ of the generator $G_{[t]}$. The derivation of the precise form of the equation is slightly more involved and we refer to Frey and Backhaus (2004) for details.

For m small, the ODE systems corresponding to the Kolmogorov backward (and forward) equation are easily solved numerically. Note, however, that the cardinality of the state space equals $\#S = 2^m$, so for m large the Kolmogorov equations are no longer useful and one has to resort to simulation. A model with interacting intensities is easily simulated using a variant of Algorithm 9.38 (recursive default time simulation) (see, for example, Appendix C of Lando (2004) for details). Alternatively, one may reduce the size of the state space by considering a model with a homogeneous group structure, as will be explained below.

Models for the default intensities. The functions $\lambda_i(t, \boldsymbol{y})$ are an essential ingredient in any model with interacting intensities. We therefore discuss several specifications proposed in the literature. Jarrow and Yu (2001) study a model with stochastic background process (Ψ_t), but restrict themselves to a special form of interacting intensities called the *primary–secondary framework*. In this framework firms are divided into two classes: primary and secondary. The default intensity of primary firms depends only on (Ψ_t); the default intensity of secondary firms depends on (Ψ_t) and on the default state of the primary firms. This simplifying assumption facilitates the mathematical analysis of the model. Below we present a specific example from their paper. We let $m = 2$ and identify (Ψ_t) with the short rate of interest (r_t). The default intensities are then given by

$$\lambda_1(r_t, \boldsymbol{Y}_t) = a_{10} + a_{11} r_t \quad \text{and} \quad \lambda_2(r_t, \boldsymbol{Y}_t) = a_{20} + a_{21} r_t + a_{22} I_{\{Y_{t,1}=1\}},$$

so company one is a primary firm and company two is a secondary firm. A typical scenario for the primary–secondary framework is as follows: primary firms correspond to large corporations; secondary firms correspond to commercial banks which have a major credit exposure to the primary firms. Note that, under the primary–secondary framework, cyclical default dependence, such as a situation where the default intensity of firm i is affected by the default of firm $j \neq i$, and vice versa, cannot be modelled.

Yu (2005b) analyses a model where the whole portfolio enters an "enhanced risk state" after the first default. Default intensities of the form

$$\lambda_i(t, \boldsymbol{Y}_t) = a_0 + a_1 I_{\{\boldsymbol{Y}_t \neq \boldsymbol{0}\}}, \quad i \in \{1, \dots, m\}, \ a_0, a_1 > 0 \tag{9.93}$$

are used. Hence, at the first default time T_1, the default intensities of the surviving firms jump from a_0 to $a_0 + a_1$. The assumption of identical default intensities for all firms implies that the portfolio is homogeneous, i.e. that the default times $(\tau_1, \dots, \tau_m)$ are exchangeable. Yu suggests that for a portfolio of high-quality credits a reasonable order of magnitude for the model parameters is $a_0 \approx 1\%$ and $a_1 \approx 0.1\%$. Simulation studies reported in his paper indicate that the model might be able to explain certain features of credit spreads in the market for European telecom bonds.

Frey and Backhaus (2004) study a model where the default intensity of a given firm depends on the overall proportion of companies that have defaulted so far. The homogeneous-portfolio version of the model can be described as follows. Denote the proportion of defaulted companies in state $\boldsymbol{y}$ by $\bar{m}(\boldsymbol{y}) := 1/m \sum_{i=1}^{m} y_i$, for $\boldsymbol{y} \in S$. Then

$$\lambda_i(t, \boldsymbol{Y}_t) = h(t, \bar{m}(\boldsymbol{Y}_t)) \tag{9.94}$$

for some bounded function $h : \mathbb{R}_+ \times [0,1] \to \mathbb{R}_+$ that is increasing in its second argument. This type of interaction between default intensities makes immediate sense: to begin with, if a financial institution has incurred an unusually high number of losses in its loan portfolio, it is less likely to extend credit lines if another obligor experiences financial distress. Obviously, this raises the default probability of the remaining obligors. Moreover, an unusually small number of defaults might have a negative impact on the overall business climate. From a mathematical point of view, if we assume that the default times $(\tau_1, \dots, \tau_m)$ are exchangeable, the default intensities are necessarily of the form (9.94). For instance, the default intensities in the homogeneous model (9.93) are of the form (9.94) with $h(t,l) = a_0 + a_1 I_{\{l>0\}}$.

Exchangeable models. We conclude with a few results for the exchangeable case (9.94). For default intensities of the form (9.94), the process $(\bar{M}_t)$ with $\bar{M}_t = \bar{m}(\boldsymbol{Y}_t)$ is itself a Markov chain with state space $\bar{S} = \{0, 1/m, \dots, 1\}$. In fact, at time t the process $\bar{M}_t$ can only jump to the state $\bar{M}_t + 1/m$, which happens with intensity $\sum_{i=1}^m (1 - Y_i(t))\lambda_i(t, \boldsymbol{Y}_t) = m(1 - \bar{M}_t)h(t, \bar{M}_t)$. This shows that $(\bar{M}_t)$ is itself a Markov chain with generator

$$G_{[t]}^{\bar{M}} f(l) = m(1-l)h(t,l)(f(l+1/m) - f(l)). \tag{9.95}$$

Note that the state space $\bar{S}$ of $(\bar{M}_t)$ is of size $m+1$, whereas the state space of $(\boldsymbol{Y}_t)$ is of size 2^m. Hence, under the interaction (9.94), the distribution of $\bar{M}_T$ can be inferred using analytical tools such as the Kolmogorov equations, even for m relatively large. In the exchangeable model (9.94), many quantities of interest can be easily computed from the distribution of M_T. For instance, we obtain for the default probability π of some firm i from our portfolio $\pi = 1/mE(M_T)$, and similar expressions can be obtained for the higher-order default probabilities π_k introduced in Section 8.3.1.

Finally, we present some numerical results from Frey and Backhaus (2004) that illustrate the impact of interacting intensities on default correlations and quantiles of $\bar{M}_T$. We consider a model with a stochastic background process given by a one-dimensional CIR square-root diffusion, as in Section 9.5.2, with parameters $\kappa = 0.03$, $\bar{\theta} = 0.005$, $\sigma = 0.016$ and initial value $\Psi_0 = \bar{\theta}$. These values have been taken from the empirical study by Driessen (2005). The default intensities are given by

$$h(t, \psi, \bar{m}) = [\alpha(0.004 + 5.707\psi) + a_1(\bar{m} - (1 - \mathrm{e}^{-\bar{\lambda}t}))]^+.$$

The interpretation of this model is as follows. The number $1 - \mathrm{e}^{-\bar{\lambda}t}$ measures the expected proportion of defaulted firms at time t. For $a_1 > 0$ the default intensity of non-defaulted companies is increased (decreased) if the proportion of defaulted companies is higher (lower) than the expected proportion $1 - \mathrm{e}^{-\bar{\lambda}t}$ and we have interaction between default events. For $a_1 = 0$, on the other hand, we are in a standard model with conditionally independent defaults, as studied in Section 9.6.3. We take the horizon to be $T = 1$ year. In the simulations, the parameter a_1, which controls the strength of the interaction, is increased from 0 to 3; the parameter α is adjusted in order to ensure that the one-year default probabilities $P(Y_{1,i} = 1)$ remain unchanged as we vary a_1. Simulation results are presented in Table 9.3 for

Table 9.3. Default correlation and quantiles of $\bar{M}_1$ in a homogeneous model with interacting intensities for $m = 500$ firms and varying interaction a_1.

a_1	$P(Y_{1,i} = 1)$	ρ_Y	$q_{0.9}$	$q_{0.95}$	$q_{0.975}$	$q_{0.99}$
0	0.031 99	0.000 415 79	0.044	0.046	0.05	0.054
1	0.031 98	0.005 075 3	0.052	0.058	0.066	0.072
3	0.031 99	0.058 283	0.096	0.128	0.156	0.19

the case $m = 500$. We see that the default correlation $\rho(Y_{1,i}, Y_{1,j})$, $i \neq j$, and the quantiles of the distribution of $\bar{M}_1$ increase substantially as a_1 increases. This makes perfect sense: for $a_1 > 0$ a higher (lower) than usual number of defaults in the portfolio leads to an increase (decrease) in the default intensity of the remaining firms in the portfolio and thus to a further increase (decrease) in the ratio of realized versus expected defaults, so the resulting distribution of $\bar{M}_1$ will have more mass in the tails.

Notes and Comments

Theorem 9.46 is taken from Brémaud but is originally due to Jacod (1975). Both texts are excellent references that study point processes from the viewpoint of stochastic calculus. Dynamic properties of copula models were first studied in Schönbucher and Schubert (2001). The pricing of first-to-default swaps follows Laurent and Gregory (2003).

The techniques used in Section 9.8.2 are popular in survival analysis (see, for example, Chapter 10 of Andersen et al. 1993); in the context of portfolio credit risk, related ideas can be found in Schönbucher (2004). Collin-Dufresne, Goldstein and Helwege (2003) propose a model for information-based default contagion that starts from the mixture representation (9.69) of the survival function. Giesecke and Goldberg (2004) study information-based default contagion in a structural multi-firm model with incomplete information about the default thresholds.

Our presentation of models with interacting intensities is based on Frey and Backhaus (2004). The first model with interacting intensities is due to Jarrow and Yu (2001). Davis and Lo (2001) pointed out the link between models with interacting intensities and finite-state Markov chains. Mathematical aspects of the Jarrow–Yu model are discussed in Kusuoka (1999), Bielecki and Rutkowski (2002) and Collin-Dufresne, Goldstein and Hugonnier (2004). Yu (2005b) provides an alternative construction of the Jarrow–Yu model using the general hazard construction from survival analysis. Moreover, certain features of the model are studied using simulation. The pricing of portfolio credit derivatives in models with interacting intensities is discussed in Frey and Backhaus (2004); this paper also contains an analysis of the asymptotic behaviour of the homogeneous model (9.94) for large portfolios. Credit risk models with explicitly specified interaction between default intensities are conceptually and mathematically close to models for interacting particle systems developed in statistical physics. Föllmer (1994) contains an inspiring discussion of the relevance of ideas from the interacting-particle-systems literature for financial modelling; the link to credit risk is explored by Giesecke and Weber (2004, 2005), Horst (2004) and Focardi and Fabozzi (2004). Egloff, Leippold and Vanini (2004) study credit contagion in a firm-value model. Allen and Gale (2000) discuss financial contagion from a financial economics viewpoint; an interesting analysis of systemic risk in financial networks in general can be found in Eisenberg and Noe (2001).

Many textbooks on stochastic processes contain an introduction to continuous-time Markov chains. Excellent texts are Resnick (1992), Davis (1993) and Norris (1997); a good summary is given in Appendix C of Lando (2004). Continuous-time Markov chains are frequently used to build dynamic models for rating-transitions (see, for example, Jarrow, Lando and Turnbull (1997) or Chapter 6 of Lando (2004)).

10
Operational Risk and Insurance Analytics

We have so far concentrated on the modelling of market and credit risk, which reflects the historical development of quantitative risk management in the banking context. Some of the techniques we have discussed are also relevant in operational risk modelling, in particular the techniques of extreme value theory (EVT) in Chapter 7 and the aggregation methodology of Chapter 6. But we also need other techniques tailored specifically to operational risk, and we believe that *actuarial models* used in non-life insurance are particularly relevant.

In the first half of this chapter (Section 10.1) we examine the Basel II requirements for the quantitative modelling of operational risk, discussing various potential approaches. On the basis of some industry data we highlight the possibilities and limitations of existing tools for the calculation of an operational risk-capital charge.

In Section 10.2 we summarize the techniques from actuarial modelling that are relevant to operational risk, under the heading of *insurance analytics*. Our discussion in that section, though motivated by quantitative modelling of operational risk, has a much wider applicability in quantitative risk management. For example, some techniques have implicitly been used in the credit risk chapters. The Notes and Comments section at the end of the chapter gives an overview of further techniques from insurance mathematics that we feel will become useful in the years to come.

10.1 Operational Risk in Perspective

10.1.1 A New Risk Class

In our overview of Basel II, in Section 1.3.1, we introduced *operational risk* as a new risk class for which financial institutions, bound by the Basel Committee rules (Basel II) and to some extent also by Solvency 2 (Section 1.3.2), are required to put aside regulatory capital. We first recall the Basel II definition as it appears in the final document (Basel Committee on Banking Supervision 2004).

> Operational risk is defined as the risk of loss resulting from inadequate or failed internal processes, people and systems or from external events. This definition includes legal risk, but excludes strategic and reputational risk.

Examples of losses falling within this category are, for instance, fraud (internal as well as external), losses due to IT failures, errors in settlements of transactions, litigation and losses due to external events like flooding, fire, earthquake or terrorism.

Losses due to unfortunate management decisions, such as many of the mergers and acquisitions of the 1990s or the launch of larger-scale bank-assurance projects, are definitely not included.

A case that touched upon almost all aspects of the above definition was that of Barings (see also Section 1.2.2). From insufficient internal checks and balances (processes), to fraud (human risk), to external events (the Kobe earthquake), many operational risk factors contributed to the downfall of this once proud merchant bank. Further examples include the $691 million rogue trading loss at Allfirst Financial, the $484 million settlement due to misleading sales practices at Household Finance, and the estimated $140 million loss for the Bank of New York stemming from the September 11 attacks. All examples offer a clear proof of the fundamental importance of operational risk as a risk class to be monitored. Current estimates for capital allocated to operational risk at large international banks are in the range $2–7 billion (see deFontnouvelle et al. 2003).

An essential difference between operational risk, on the one hand, and market and credit risk, on the other, is that operational risk has no upside for a bank. It comes about through the malfunctioning of parts of daily business and hence is as much a question of quality control as anything else. Clearly, banks try as hard as possible to avoid operational risk but, despite their best efforts, operational losses will continue to occur.

This has prompted the Basel Committee to decide that banks must set aside risk capital under Pillar I of the three-pillar system (see Section 1.3.1). The Pillar II and Pillar III proposals of the new accord imply that a supervisory review process for operational risk must also be put in place and that an appropriate market discipline with respect to public disclosure must be adhered to. The market has not been slow to provide various ways of mitigating the effects of the new risk category, ranging from IT solutions and data warehouses to improve the measurement of operational risk, to insurance-type solutions for banks willing and able to enter into such deals.

Currently, and for the foreseeable future, the lack of operational loss data is a major issue, and this is similar to the problem faced by underwriters of catastrophe insurance. The insurance industry's answer to the problem has involved data-pooling across industry participants and a similar discussion is now taking place in the banking industry. Once representative data sources become available, the implementation of many of the methods discussed in this book (such as EVT in Chapter 7 and the insurance analytics of Section 10.2) will become increasingly feasible. Existing sources of data at present are the databases produced by the Quantitative Impact Studies (QISs) of the Basel Committee and by the Federal Reserve Bank of Boston. Moreover, some private companies are also providing data.

In Section 10.1.3 we discuss the kind of *advanced-measurement* (AM) approach that an analysis of operational loss data allows. Before this we discuss so-called *elementary approaches* to operational risk modelling. In these approaches, aimed at smaller banks without extensive international activities, the detailed modelling of loss distributions for different risk classes and risk types is not required; a fairly simple volume-based capital charge is proposed. We note that, as in the case of credit risk, the approaches proposed by Basel II for the calculation of regulatory capital represent a gradation in complexity. Recall that, for credit risk, banks must implement either the standardized approach or the internal-ratings-based (IRB) approach, as discussed in Section 1.3.1 and Section 8.1.

10.1.2 The Elementary Approaches

There are two elementary approaches to operational risk measurement. Under the *basic-indicator* (BI) approach, banks must hold capital for operational risk equal to the average over the previous three years of a fixed percentage (denoted by α) of positive annual gross income (GI). Figures for any year in which annual gross income is negative or zero should be excluded from both the numerator and denominator when calculating the average. Hence the risk capital under the BI approach for operational risk in year t is given by

$$\mathrm{RC}^t_{\mathrm{BI}}(\mathrm{OR}) = \frac{1}{Z_t}\sum_{i=1}^{3} \alpha \max(\mathrm{GI}^{t-i}, 0), \tag{10.1}$$

where $Z_t = \sum_{i=1}^{3} I_{\{\mathrm{GI}^{t-i}>0\}}$ and GI^{t-i} stands for gross income in year $t-i$. Note that an operational risk-capital charge is calculated on a yearly basis. The BI approach gives a fairly straightforward, volume-based, one-size-fits-all capital charge. Based on the various QISs, the Basel Committee suggests that $\alpha = 15\%$.

Under the *standardized* (S) approach, banks' activities are divided into eight *business lines*: corporate finance; trading & sales; retail banking; commercial banking; payment & settlement; agency services; asset management; and retail brokerage. Precise definitions of these business lines are to be found in the Basel Committee's final document (Basel Committee on Banking Supervision 2004). Within each business line, gross income is a broad indicator that serves as a proxy for the scale of business operations and thus the likely scale of operational risk exposure. The capital charge for each business line is calculated by multiplying gross income by a factor (denoted by β) assigned to that business line. As in (10.1), the total capital charge is calculated as a three-year average over positive GIs, resulting in the following capital charge formula:

$$\mathrm{RC}^t_{\mathrm{S}}(\mathrm{OR}) = \frac{1}{3}\sum_{i=1}^{3} \max\left[\sum_{j=1}^{8} \beta_j \mathrm{GI}_j^{t-i}, 0\right]. \tag{10.2}$$

It is to be noted that in formula (10.2), in any given year $t-i$, negative capital charges (resulting from negative gross income) in some business line j may offset positive capital charges in other business lines (albeit at the discretion of the national supervisor). This kind of "netting" should induce banks to go from the basic indicator to the standardized approach; the word "netting" is of course to be used with care here. Based on the QISs, the Basel Committee has set the beta coefficients as in Table 10.1. Moscadelli (2004) gives a critical analysis of these beta factors, based on the full database of more than 47 000 operational losses of the second QIS of the summer of 2002 (see also Section 10.1.4).

Table 10.1. Beta factors for the standardized approach.

Business line (j)	Beta factors (β_j)
$j = 1$, corporate finance	18%
$j = 2$, trading & sales	18%
$j = 3$, retail banking	12%
$j = 4$, commercial banking	15%
$j = 5$, payment & settlement	18%
$j = 6$, agency services	15%
$j = 7$, asset management	12%
$j = 8$, retail brokerage	12%

In both approaches (BI, S) the Basel Committee expects further guidelines (mainly under Pillars II and III) to be adhered to. Also, at national discretion, supervisors may adopt slight (often more conservative) changes to aspects of the above rules, the latter clearly with a level playing field for the different market participants in mind. Widely adopted risk-management rules should be formulated as much as possible in such a way as to avoid regulatory arbitrage within and across national jurisdictions.

10.1.3 Advanced Measurement Approaches

Under an AM approach, the regulatory capital is determined by a bank's own internal risk-measurement system according to a number of quantitative and qualitative criteria set forth in documentation produced by the Basel Committee (Basel Committee on Banking Supervision 2004). We will not go into all relevant steps of the procedure leading towards the acceptance of an AM approach for an internationally active bank and its subsidiaries; the Basel Committee's documents give a clear and readable account of this. We focus instead on the methodological aspects of a full quantitative approach to operational risk measurement. It should be stated, however, that, as in the case of market and credit risk, the adoption of an AM approach to operational risk is subject to approval and continuing quality checking by the national supervisor.

While the BI and S approaches prescribe the explicit formulas (10.1) and (10.2), the AM approach lays down general guidelines. In the words of the Basel Committee (Basel Committee on Banking Supervision 2004).

> Given the continuing evolution of analytical approaches for operational risk, the Committee is not specifying the approach or distributional assumptions used to generate the operational risk measure for regulatory capital purposes. However, a bank must be able to demonstrate that its approach captures potentially severe "tail" loss events. Whatever approach is used, a bank must demonstrate that its operational risk measure meets a soundness standard comparable to that of the internal ratings-based approach for credit risk (comparable to a one year holding period and the 99.9 percent confidence interval).

In an AM approach, operational losses should be categorized according to the eight business lines mentioned in Section 10.1.2 as well as the following seven *loss-event types*: internal fraud; external fraud; employment practices & workplace safety; clients, products & business practices; damage to physical assets; business disruption & system failures; and execution, delivery & process management. Banks are expected to gather internal data on repetitive, high-frequency losses (three to five years of data), as well as relevant external data on non-repetitive low-frequency losses. Moreover, they must add stress scenarios both at the level of loss severity (parameter shocks to model parameters) and correlation between loss types. In the absence of detailed joint models for different loss types, risk measures for the aggregate loss should be calculated by summing across the different loss categories. In general, both so-called *expected* and *unexpected* losses should be taken into account (i.e. risk-measure estimates cannot be reduced by subtraction of an expected loss amount).

We now describe a skeletal version of a typical AM solution for the calculation of an operational risk charge for year t. We assume that historical loss data from previous years have been collected in a data warehouse with the structure

$$\{X_k^{t-i,b,\ell} : i = 1, \dots, T;\ b = 1, \dots, 8;\ \ell = 1, \dots, 7;\ k = 1, \dots, N^{t-i,b,\ell}\}, \tag{10.3}$$

where $X_k^{t-i,b,\ell}$ stands for the kth loss of type ℓ for business line b in year $t-i$; $N^{t-i,b,\ell}$ is the number of such losses and $T \geqslant 5$ years, say. Note that thresholds may be imposed for each (i, b, ℓ) category and small losses less than the threshold may be neglected; a threshold is typically of the order of €10 000. The total historical loss amount for business line b in year $t-i$ is obviously

$$L^{t-i,b} = \sum_{\ell=1}^{7} \sum_{k=1}^{N^{t-i,b,\ell}} X_k^{t-i,b,\ell}, \tag{10.4}$$

and the total loss amount for year $t-i$ is

$$L^{t-i} = \sum_{b=1}^{8} L^{t-i,b}. \tag{10.5}$$

The problem in the AM approach is to use the loss data to estimate the distribution of L_t for year t and to calculate risk measures such as VaR or expected shortfall (see Section 2.2) for the estimated distribution. Writing ϱ_α for the risk measure at a confidence level α, the regulatory capital is determined by

$$\mathrm{RC}^t_{\mathrm{AM}}(\mathrm{OR}) = \varrho_\alpha(L^t), \tag{10.6}$$

where α would typically take a value in the range 0.99–0.999 imposed by the local regulator. Because the joint distributional structure of the losses in (10.4) and (10.5) for any given year is generally unknown, we would typically resort to simple aggregation of risk measures across loss categories to obtain a formula of the form

$$\mathrm{RC}^t_{\mathrm{AM}}(\mathrm{OR}) = \sum_{b=1}^{8} \varrho_\alpha(L^{t,b}). \tag{10.7}$$

In view of our discussions in Chapter 6, the choice of an additive rule in (10.7) can be understood. Indeed, for any coherent risk measure ϱ_α, the right-hand side of (10.7) yields an upper bound for the total risk $\varrho_\alpha(L^t)$. In the important case of VaR, the right-hand side of (10.7) corresponds to the comonotonic scenario (see Proposition 6.15). The optimization results of Section 6.2 can be used to calculate bounds for $\varrho_\alpha(L^t)$ under different dependence scenarios for the business lines; see, in particular, Example 6.23 and Table 6.1.

Reduced to its most stylized form in the case when $\varrho_\alpha = \text{VaR}_\alpha$ and $\alpha = 0.999$, a capital charge under the AM approach requires the calculation of a quantity of the type

$$\text{VaR}_{0.999}\left(\sum_{k=1}^{N} X_k\right), \tag{10.8}$$

where (X_k) is some sequence of loss *severities* and N is an rv describing the *frequency* with which operational losses occur. Random variables of the type (10.8) are one of the prime examples of the actuarial models that we treat in Section 10.2.2. Before we move on to those models in the next section, we highlight some "stylized facts" of operational loss data.

10.1.4 Operational Loss Data

In order to reliably estimate (10.6), (10.7) or, in a stylized version, a quantity like (10.8), we need extensive data. The data situation for operational risk is much worse than that for credit risk, and is clearly an order of magnitude worse than for market risk, where vast quantities of data are publicly available. Banks have only recently started gathering data and pooling initiatives are in their infancy, so, as far as we know, no reliable *publicly* available data source on operational risk exists. Our discussion below is based on some industry data we have been able to analyse as well as on the findings in Moscadelli (2004) for the QIS database and the results of the 2004 loss-data collection exercise by the Federal Reserve Bank of Boston (see Federal Reserve System 2005). An excellent overview of some of the data characteristics is to be found in the Basel Committee's report (Basel Committee on Banking Supervision 2003). From the latter report we quote:

> Despite this progress, inferences based on the data should still be made with caution. ... In addition, the most recent data collection exercise provides data for only one year and, even under the best of circumstances, a one-year collection window will provide an incomplete picture of the full range of potential operational risk events, especially of rare but significant "tail events".

In Figure 10.1 we have plotted operational loss data obtained from several sources; parts (a)–(c) show losses for three business lines for the period 1992–2001. It is less important for the reader to know the exact loss type—it is sufficient to accept that the data are typical for (b, ℓ) categories in (10.3). In part (d), the data from the three previous figures have been pooled.

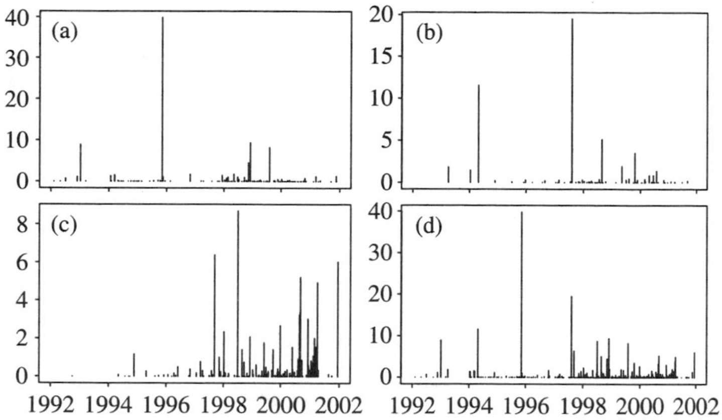

Figure 10.1. Operational risk losses: (a) type 1, $n = 162$; (b) type 2, $n = 80$; (c) type 3, $n = 175$; and (d) pooled losses $n = 417$.

Exploratory data analysis reveals the following stylized facts (confirmed in several other studies):

- loss severities have a heavy-tailed distribution;
- losses occur randomly in time;
- loss frequency may vary substantially over time.

The third observation is partly explained by the fact that banks have only recently started gathering operational risk data prompted by Basel II. There is a considerable amount of *reporting bias* resulting in fewer losses in the first half of the 1990s and more losses afterwards. Moreover, several classes of loss may have a considerable cyclical component and/or may depend on changing economic covariables. For instance, back-office errors may depend on volume traded and fraud may be linked to the overall level of the economy (depressions versus boom cycles). This clear inhomogeneity in the loss frequency makes an immediate application of statistical methodology difficult. However, it may be reasonable to at least assume that the (inflation-adjusted) loss sizes have a common severity distribution, which would allow, for instance, the application of methods from Chapter 7.

In Figure 10.2 we have plotted the sample mean excess functions (7.16) for the data in Figure 10.1. This figure clearly indicates the first stylized fact of heavy-tailed loss severities. The mean excess plots in (a) and (b) are clearly increasing in an approximately linear fashion, pointing to Pareto-type behaviour. This contrasts with (c), where the plot appears to level off from a threshold of one. This hints at a loss distribution with finite upper limit, but this could only be substantiated by more detailed knowledge of the type of loss concerned. Pooling the data in (d) masks the different kinds of behaviour, and perhaps illustrates the dangers of naive statistical analyses that do not consider the data-generating mechanism.

Moscadelli (2004) performed a detailed EVT analysis (including a first attempt to solve the frequency problem) of the full QIS data set of more than 47 000 operational

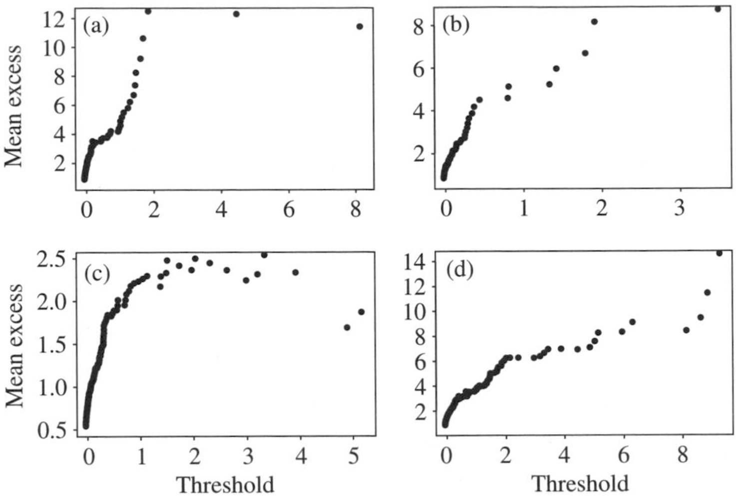

Figure 10.2. Corresponding sample mean excess plots for the data in Figure 10.1: (a) type 1; (b) type 2; (c) type 3; (d) pooled.

losses and concluded that the loss dfs are well fitted by generalized Pareto distributions (GPDs) in the upper-tail area (see Section 7.2.2 for the necessary statistical background). The estimated tail parameters (ξ in (7.14)) for the different business lines range from 0.85 for asset management to 1.39 for commercial banking. Six of the business lines have an estimate of ξ greater than one, corresponding to an *infinite mean model*! Based on these QIS data, the estimated RC/GI ratios (the β in Table 10.1) range from 8.3% for retail banking to 33.3% for payment & settlement, with an overall alpha value (see (10.1)) of 13.3%, slightly below the Basel II value of 15% used in the BI approach. Note the much broader range of values of the β emerging from the analysis of the QIS data compared with the prescribed range of 12–18% for the standardized approach in Table 10.1.

As more data become available, more conclusive analyses may be possible. It is clear, however, from Moscadelli (2004) that the GPD method of Section 7.2 is one of the most useful statistical tools at our disposal and yields a fit that is superior to other loss distributions in the high-tail area; this has been corroborated by several practitioners from the banking and insurance industry. In view of the heavy-tailedness of the data, and the necessity of calculating capital charges corresponding to high quantiles, it seems very natural to use EVT methodology.

Notes and Comments

Several textbooks on operational risk have been published: see, for example, Cruz (2002, 2004), King (2001), the Risk Books publication edited by Risk Books (2003) and chapters in Ong (2004) and Crouhy, Galai and Mark (2001). In particular, Chapter 4 of Cruz (2004), written by Carolyn Currie, gives an excellent overview of the regulatory issues surrounding operational risk.

A practical implementation is discussed in Ebnöther et al. (2003). Frachot, Georges and Roncalli (2001) discuss the loss-distribution approach to operational risk. Döbeli, Leippold and Vanini (2003) elaborate on the way in which a good operational risk framework may lead to an overall improvement in quality of the business operations.

Figure 10.1 is taken from Embrechts, Kaufmann and Samorodnitsky (2004). The latter paper also stresses the important difference between so-called repetitive and non-repetitive losses. For the former (to some extent less important) losses, statistical modelling can be very useful. For non-repetitive, low-probability, high-severity losses, much more care has to be taken before a statistical analysis can be performed (see Pézier 2002a,b).

EVT methods for operational risk quantification have been used by numerous authors (see, for example, Coleman 2002, 2003; Medova 2000a,b). Because of the non-stationarity of operational loss data over several years, more refined EVT models are called for. See, for example, Chavez-Demoulin and Embrechts (2004); Chavez-Demoulin, Embrechts and Nešlehová (2005) for some examples of such models. For a critical article on the use of EVT for the calculation of an operational risk-capital charge, see Embrechts, Furrer and Kaufmann (2003), which contains a simulation study of the number of data needed to come up with a reasonable estimate of a high quantile. The use of statistical methods other than EVT are discussed in the textbooks referred to above. These methods include linear predictive models, Bayesian belief networks and discriminant analysis. Excellent data-analytic papers using published operational risk losses are deFontnouvelle et al. (2003) and Moscadelli (2004). Finally, recall from Notes and Comments of Section 6.2 the paper by Rosenberg and Schuermann (2004), which addresses the aggregation of market, credit and operational risk measures.

10.2 Elements of Insurance Analytics

10.2.1 The Case for Actuarial Methodology

Actuarial tools and techniques for the modelling, pricing and reserving of insurance products in the traditional fields of life, non-life and reinsurance have a long history going back more than a century. More recently, the border between financial and insurance products has become blurred, examples of this process being equity-linked life products and alternative risk-transfer vehicles (see Section 1.5.2 and Notes and Comments of that chapter).

Whereas some of the combined bank-assurance products have not met with the success that was originally hoped for, it remains true that there exists an increasing need for financial and actuarial professionals who can close the methodological gaps between the two fields. In the sections that follow we discuss *insurance analytical* tools that we believe the more traditional finance-oriented risk manager ought to be aware of; the story behind the name insurance analytics can be found in Embrechts (2002).

It is not only the occasional instance of joint product development between the banking and insurance worlds that prompts us to make a case for actuarial methodology in QRM, but also the observation that many of the concepts and techniques of QRM described in the preceding chapters are in fact borrowed from the actuarial literature.

- Risk measures like expected shortfall (Definition 2.15) have been studied in a systematic way in the insurance literature. Expected shortfall is also the standard risk measure to be used under the Solvency 2 guidelines.
- Many of the dependence modelling tools presented in Chapter 5 saw their first applications in the realm of insurance. Moreover, notions like comonotonicity of risk factors have their origins in actuarial questions.
- In Section 6.1 we discussed the axiomatization of financial risk measures and pointed at the parallel development of insurance premium principles (often with very similar goals and results).
- The statistical modelling of extremal events has been a bread-and-butter subject for actuaries since the start of insurance. Hence, many of the tools presented in Chapter 7 are well known to actuaries.
- Within the world of credit risk management, the industry model CreditRisk+ (Section 8.4.2) is known as an actuarial model.
- The actuarial approach to the modelling of operational risk is apparent in the AM approach of Section 10.1.3.

In the sections that follow, we give a brief discussion of relevant actuarial techniques. The material presented should enable the reader to transfer actuarial concepts to QRM in finance more easily. We do not strive for a full treatment of relevant tools as these could fill a separate (voluminous) textbook (see, for example, Denuit and Charpentier (2004), Mikosch (2004) and Partrat and Besson (2004) for excellent accounts of many of the relevant techniques).

10.2.2 The Total Loss Amount

Reconsider formula (10.8), where a random number N of random losses or severities X_k occurring in a given time period are summed. To apply a risk measure like VaR we need to make assumptions about the (X_k) and N, which leads us to one of the fundamental concepts of (non-life) insurance mathematics.

Definition 10.1 (total loss amount and distribution). Denote by $N(t)$ the (random) number of losses over a fixed time period $[0, t]$ and write $X_1, X_2, \dots$ for the individual losses. The *total loss amount* (or *aggregate loss*) is defined as

$$S_{N(t)} = \sum_{k=1}^{N(t)} X_k, \tag{10.9}$$

with df $F_{S_{N(t)}}(x) = P(S_{N(t)} \leqslant x)$, the *total* (or *aggregate*) *loss df*. Whenever t is fixed, $t = 1$ say, we may drop the time index from the notation and simply write S_N and F_{S_N}.

Remark 10.2. The definition of (10.9) as an rv is to be understood as $S_{N(t)}(\omega) = \sum_{k=1}^{N(t)(\omega)} X_k(\omega)$, $\omega \in \Omega$, and is referred to as a random (or randomly indexed) sum.

A prime goal of this section will be the analytical and numerical calculation of F_{S_N}, which requires further assumptions about (X_k) and N.

Assumption 10.3 (independence, compound sums). *We assume that the rvs (X_k) are iid with common df G, $G(0) = 0$. We further assume that the rvs N and (X_k) are independent; in that case we refer to (10.9) as a compound sum. The probability mass function of N is denoted by $p_N(k) = P(N = k)$, $k = 0, 1, 2, \dots$. The rv N is referred to as the compounding rv.*

Proposition 10.4 (compound distribution). *Let S_N be a compound sum and suppose that Assumption 10.3 holds. Then, for all $x \geqslant 0$,*

$$F_{S_N}(x) = P(S_N \leqslant x) = \sum_{k=0}^{\infty} p_N(k) G^{(k)}(x), \tag{10.10}$$

where $G^{(k)}(x) = P(S_k \leqslant x)$, the kth convolution of G. Note that $G^{(0)}(x) = 1$ for $x \geqslant 0$, and $G^{(0)}(x) = 0$ for $x < 0$.

Proof. Suppose $x \geqslant 0$. Then

$$F_{S_N}(x) = \sum_{k=0}^{\infty} P(S_N \leqslant x \mid N = k) P(N = k) = \sum_{k=0}^{\infty} p_N(k) G^{(k)}(x).$$

□

Although formula (10.10) is explicit, its actual calculation in specific cases is difficult because the convolution powers $G^{(k)}$ of a df G are in general not available in closed form. Hence, one resorts to (numerical) approximation methods. A first class of these uses the fact that the Laplace–Stieltjes transform of a convolution is the product of the Laplace–Stieltjes transforms. Using the usual notation $\hat{F}(s) = \int_0^{\infty} \mathrm{e}^{-sx}\, \mathrm{d}F(x)$, where $s \geqslant 0$ for Laplace–Stieltjes transforms, we have that $\widehat{G^{(k)}}(s) = (\hat{G}(s))^k$. It follows from Proposition 10.4 that

$$\hat{F}_{S_N}(s) = \sum_{k=0}^{\infty} p_N(k)\, \hat{G}^k(s) = M_N(\hat{G}(s)), \quad s \geqslant 0, \tag{10.11}$$

where M_N denotes the *moment-generating function* of N.

Example 10.5 (the compound Poisson df). Suppose that N has a Poisson df with intensity parameter $\lambda > 0$, denoted $N \sim \mathrm{Poi}(\lambda)$. In that case, $p_N(k) = \mathrm{e}^{-\lambda}\lambda^k/k!$, $k \geqslant 0$, and, for $s \in \mathbb{R}$,

$$M_N(s) = \sum_{k=0}^{\infty} \mathrm{e}^{-\lambda} \frac{\lambda^k}{k!} s^k = \exp(-\lambda(1-s)).$$

Hence from (10.11) it follows that, for $s \geqslant 0$,

$$\hat{F}_{S_N}(s) = \exp(-\lambda(1 - \hat{G}(s))).$$

In this case, the df of S_N is referred to as the *compound Poisson df* and we write $S_N \sim \mathrm{CPoi}(\lambda, G)$. Formula (10.11) facilitates the calculation of moments of S_N

and lends itself to numerical evaluation through Fourier inversion, known as the fast Fourier transform (FFT) (see Notes and Comments for references on the latter). For the calculation of moments, note that, under the assumption of the existence of sufficiently high moments and hence differentiability of $\hat{G}$ and M_N, we obtain

$$\frac{\mathrm{d}^k}{\mathrm{d}s^k} M_N(s)\bigg|_{s=1} = E(N(N-1)\cdots(N-k+1))$$

and

$$(-1)^k \frac{\mathrm{d}^k}{\mathrm{d}s^k} \hat{G}(s)\bigg|_{s=0} = E(X_1^k) = \mu_k.$$

Example 10.6 (continuation of Example 10.5). In the case of the compound Poisson df, one obtains

$$\begin{aligned}E(S_N) = (-1)\frac{\mathrm{d}}{\mathrm{d}s} \hat{F}_{S_N}(s)\bigg|_{s=0} &= \exp(-\lambda(1-\hat{G}(0)))\lambda(-\hat{G}'(0)) \\ &= \lambda\mu_1 = E(N)E(X_1).\end{aligned}$$

Similar calculations yield $\mathrm{var}(S_N) = E(S_N^2) - (E(S_N))^2 = \lambda\mu_2$.

For the general compound case one obtains the following useful result.

Proposition 10.7 (moments of compound dfs). *Under Assumption 10.3 and assuming that $E(N) < \infty$, $\mu_2 < \infty$, we have that*

$$E(S_N) = E(N)E(X_1) \quad \textit{and} \quad \mathrm{var}(S_N) = \mathrm{var}(N)(E(X_1))^2 + E(N)\,\mathrm{var}(X_1). \tag{10.12}$$

Proof. This follows readily from (10.11), differentiating with respect to s. The following direct proof avoids the use of transforms. Conditioning on N and using Assumption 10.3, one obtains

$$\begin{aligned}E(S_N) = E(E(S_N \mid N)) &= E\bigg(E\bigg(\sum_{k=1}^N X_k \,\bigg|\, N\bigg)\bigg) \\ &= E\bigg(\sum_{k=1}^N E(X_k)\bigg) = E(N)E(X_1)\end{aligned}$$

and, similarly,

$$\begin{aligned}E(S_N^2) = E\bigg(E\bigg(\bigg(\sum_{k=1}^N X_k\bigg)^2 \,\bigg|\, N\bigg)\bigg) &= E\bigg(E\bigg(\sum_{k=1}^N \sum_{\ell=1}^N X_k X_\ell \,\bigg|\, N\bigg)\bigg) \\ &= E(N\mu_2 + N(N-1)\mu_1^2) = E(N)\mu_2 + (E(N^2) - E(N))\mu_1^2 \\ &= E(N)\,\mathrm{var}(X_1) + E(N^2)(E(X_1))^2,\end{aligned}$$

so $\mathrm{var}(S_N) = E(S_N^2) - (E(S_N))^2 = E(N)\,\mathrm{var}(X_1) + \mathrm{var}(N)(E(X_1))^2$. □

Remark 10.8. Formula (10.12) elegantly combines the randomness of the frequency ($\mathrm{var}(N)$) with that of the severity ($\mathrm{var}(X_1)$). In the compound Poisson case it reduces to the formula $\mathrm{var}(S_N) = \lambda E(X_1^2) = \lambda\mu_2$, as in Example 10.6. In the deterministic-sum case, when $P(N = n) = 1$, say, we find the well-known results $E(S_N) = n\mu_1$ and $\mathrm{var}(S_N) = n\,\mathrm{var}(X_1)$; indeed, in this degenerate case, $\mathrm{var}(N) = 0$.

The compound Poisson model is a basic model for aggregate financial or insurance risk losses. The ubiquitousness of the Poisson distribution in insurance can be understood as follows. Consider a time interval $[0, 1]$ and let N denote the total number of losses in that interval. Suppose further that we have a number of potential loss generators (transactions, credit positions, insurance policies, etc.) that can produce, with probability p_n, one loss or, with probability $1 - p_n$, no loss in each small subinterval $((k - 1)/n, k/n]$ for $k = 1, \dots, n$. Moreover, suppose that the occurrence or non-occurrence of a loss in any particular subinterval is not influenced by the occurrence of losses in other intervals. Then the number N_n of losses has a binomial df with parameters n and p_n, so

$$P(N_n = k) = \binom{n}{k} p_n^k (1 - p_n)^{n-k}, \quad k = 0, \dots, n.$$

Combined with a loss-severity distribution this frequency distribution gives rise, in (10.10), to the so-called *binomial loss model*. Next suppose that $n \to \infty$ in such a way that $\lim_{n\to\infty} np_n = \lambda > 0$. It follows from *Poisson's theorem of rare events* (see also Section 7.4.1) that

$$\lim_{n\to\infty} P(N_n = k) = \mathrm{e}^{-\lambda}\frac{\lambda^k}{k!}, \quad k = 0, 1, 2, \dots,$$

i.e. $N_\infty \sim \mathrm{Poi}(\lambda)$, explaining why the Poisson model assumption is very natural as a frequency distribution and the compound Poisson model is a common aggregate loss model. The compound Poisson model has several nice properties, one of which concerns aggregation and is useful in the operational risk context in situations such as (10.5).

Proposition 10.9 (sums of compound Poisson rvs). *Suppose that the compound sums $S_{N_i} \sim \mathrm{CPoi}(\lambda_i, G_i)$, $i = 1, \dots, d$, and that these rvs are independent, then $S_N = \sum_{i=1}^d S_{N_i} \sim \mathrm{CPoi}(\lambda, G)$, where $\lambda = \sum_{i=1}^d \lambda_i$ and $G = \sum_{i=1}^d (\lambda_i/\lambda) G_i$.*

Proof. (For $d = 2$, the general case being similar.) Because of independence and Example 10.5 we have, for the Laplace–Stieltjes transform of S_N,

$$\begin{aligned}\hat{F}_{S_N}(s) &= \hat{F}_{S_{N_1}}(s)\hat{F}_{S_{N_2}}(s) \\ &= \exp\biggl(-(\lambda_1 + \lambda_2)\biggl(1 - \frac{1}{\lambda_1 + \lambda_2}(\lambda_1\hat{G}_1(s) + \lambda_2\hat{G}_2(s))\biggr)\biggr) \\ &= \exp(-\lambda(1 - \hat{G}(s))),\end{aligned}$$

where $\lambda = \lambda_1 + \lambda_2$ and

$$G = \frac{\lambda_1}{\lambda_1 + \lambda_2}G_1 + \frac{\lambda_2}{\lambda_1 + \lambda_2}G_2.$$

The result follows since the Laplace–Stieltjes transform uniquely determines the underlying df. □

Hence the new intensity λ is just the sum of the old ones, whereas the new severity df G is a *discrete mixture* of the loss dfs G_i with weights λ_i/λ, $i = 1, \dots, d$. We can easily simulate losses from such a model through a two-stage procedure: first draw i ($i = 1, \dots, d$) with probability λ_i/λ, and then draw a loss with df G_i.

Beyond the Poisson model. The Poisson model can serve as a stylized representation of the loss-generating mechanism from which more realistic models can be derived. For instance, we may wish to introduce a time parameter in N to capture different occurrence patterns over time (see Section 10.2.6). Also, the intensity parameter λ may be assumed to be random (see Example 10.20). Indeed, a further step is to turn λ into a stochastic process, which gives rise to such models as doubly stochastic (or Cox) processes (see Section 9.2.3) or self-exciting processes, as encountered in Section 7.4.3. Furthermore, various forms of dependence among the X_k rvs or between N and (X_k) could be modelled. Finally, multiline portfolios require multivariate models for vectors of the type $(S_{N_1}, \dots, S_{N_d})$. An ultimate goal of the AM approach to operational risk would be to model such random vectors where where, for instance, d might stand for seven risk types, eight business lines, or in total 56 loss category cells.

10.2.3 Approximations and Panjer Recursion

As mentioned in Section 10.2.2, the analytic calculation of F_{S_N} is not possible for the majority of reasonable models, which has led actuaries to come up with several numerical approximations. Below we review some of these approximations and illustrate their use for several choices of the severity df G. The basic example we look at is the compound Poisson case, $S_N \sim \text{CPoi}(\lambda, G)$, though most of the approximations discussed can be adjusted to deal with other distributions for N. Given λ and G we can easily simulate F_{S_N} and, by repeating this many times, we can get an empirical estimate that is close to the true df. Figure 10.3 contains a simulation of $n = 100\,000$ realizations of $S_N \sim \text{CPoi}(100, \text{Exp}(1))$. Although the histogram exhibits mild skewness (which can easily be shown theoretically (see (10.15))), a clear central limit effect takes place. This is used in the first approximation below.

Normal approximation. As the loss rvs X_i are iid (with finite second moment, say) and S_N is a (random) sum of the X_i variables, one can apply Theorem 2.5.16 in Embrechts, Klüppelberg and Mikosch (1997) and Proposition 10.7 to obtain the following approximation, for general N:

$$F_{S_N}(x) \approx \Phi\left(\frac{x - E(N)E(X_1)}{\sqrt{\operatorname{var}(N)(E(X_1))^2 + E(N)\operatorname{var}(X_1)}}\right). \tag{10.13}$$

Here, and in the approximations below, "$\approx$" has no specific mathematical interpretation beyond "there exists a limit result justifying the right-hand side to be used as approximation of the left-hand side". In particular, for the compound Poisson case

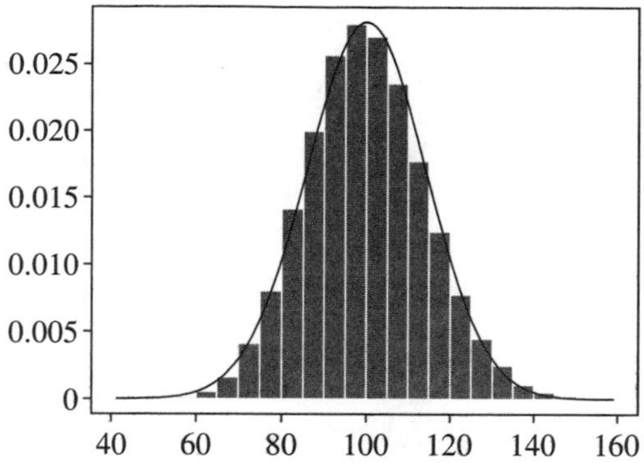

Figure 10.3. Histogram of simulated compound loss data ($n = 100\,000$) for $S_N \sim \text{CPoi}(100, \text{Exp}(1))$ together with normal approximation (10.14).

above, (10.13) reduces to

$$F_{S_N}(x) \approx \Phi\left(\frac{x - 100}{\sqrt{200}}\right), \tag{10.14}$$

where Φ is the standard normal df, as usual. It is this normal approximation that is superimposed on the histogram in Figure 10.3. Clearly, there are conditions underlying the approximation (10.13): for example, claims should not be too heavy-tailed (see Theorem 10.21).

For $\text{CPoi}(\lambda, G)$ it is not difficult to show that the skewness parameter satisfies

$$\frac{E((S_N - E(S_N))^3)}{(\text{var}(S_N))^{3/2}} = \frac{E(X_1^3)}{\sqrt{\lambda(E(X_1^2))^3}} > 0 \tag{10.15}$$

(note that $X_1 \geqslant 0$ almost surely), so an approximation by a df with positive skewness may improve the approximation (10.14), especially in the tail area. This is indeed the case and leads to the next approximation.

Translated-gamma approximation. We approximate S_N by $k + Y$, where k is a translation parameter and $Y \sim \text{Ga}(\alpha, \beta)$ has a gamma distribution (see Section A.2.4). The parameters (k, α, β) are found by matching the mean, the variance and the skewness of $k + Y$ and S_N. It is not difficult to check that the following equations result:

$$k + \frac{\alpha}{\beta} = \lambda E(X_1), \qquad \frac{\alpha}{\beta^2} = \lambda E(X_1^2), \qquad \frac{2}{\sqrt{\alpha}} = \frac{E(X_1^3)}{\sqrt{\lambda(E(X_1^2))^3}}.$$

In our case, where $\lambda = 100$ and X_1 has a standard exponential distribution, these yield the equations $k + \alpha/\beta = 100$, $\alpha/\beta^2 = 200$ and $2/\sqrt{\alpha} = 0.2121$ with solution $\alpha = 88.89$, $\beta = 0.67$, $k = -32.72$.

Commentary on these approximations. Both approximations work reasonably well in the bulk of the data. However, for risk-management purposes, we are mainly interested in upper tail risk; in Figure 10.4 we have therefore plotted both approximations for $x \geqslant 120$ on a log–log scale. This corresponds to the tail area beyond

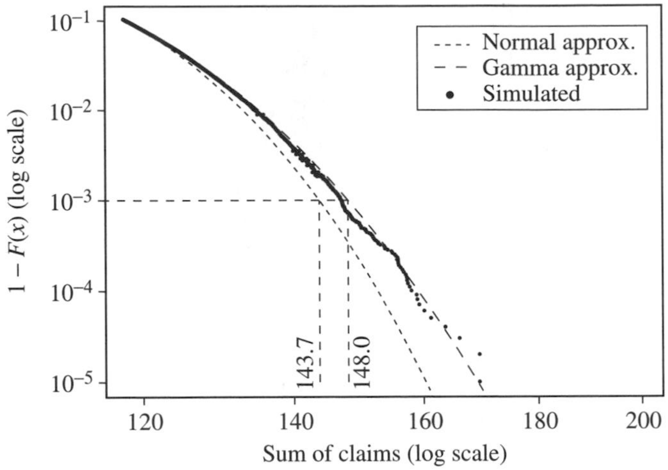

Figure 10.4. Simulated CPoi(100, Exp(1)) data together with normal- and translated-gamma approximations (log–log scale). The 99.9% quantile estimates are also given.

the 90% quantile of F_{S_N}. Similar plots were routinely used in Chapter 7 on EVT (see, for example, Figure 7.6). It becomes clear that, as can be expected, the gamma approximation works better in this upper tail area where the normal approximation underestimates the loss potential.

Of course, for loss data with heavier tails than exponential (lognormal or Pareto, say), even the translated-gamma approximation will be insufficient and other approximations can be devised based on heavier-tailed distributions, such as translated F, inverse gamma or generalized Pareto.

Another approach could be based on Monte Carlo simulation of aggregate losses S_N to which an appropriate heavy-tailed loss distribution could then be fitted. One possible approach would be to model the tail of these simulated compound losses with the GPD using the methodology of Section 7.2.2. This is what has been done in Figures 10.5 and 10.6, where we have plotted various approximations for CPoi(100, $LN(1, 1)$) and CPoi(100, Pa(4, 1)). The former corresponds to a standard industry model for operational risk (see Frachot 2004). The latter corresponds to a class of operational risk models used in Moscadelli (2004). From these figures the message is clear: if the data satisfy the compound Poisson assumption, then the GPD yields a superior fit for high quantiles.

We now turn to an important class of approximations based on recursive methods. In the case where the loss sizes (X_i) are discrete and the distribution function of N satisfies a specific condition (see Definition 10.10 below) a reliable recursive method can be worked out.

Suppose that X_1 has a discrete distribution so that $P(X_1 \in \mathbb{N}_0) = 1$ with $g_k = P(X_1 = k)$, $p_k = P(N = k)$ (for notational convenience we write p_k for $p_N(k)$) and $s_k = P(S_N = k)$. For simplicity assume that $g_0 = 0$ and let $g_k^{(n)} = P(X_1 + \dots + X_n = k)$, the discrete convolution of the probability mass function g_k. Note that, by definition, $g_k^{(n+1)} = \sum_{i=1}^{k-1} g_i^{(n)} g_{k-i}$. We immediately obtain the following

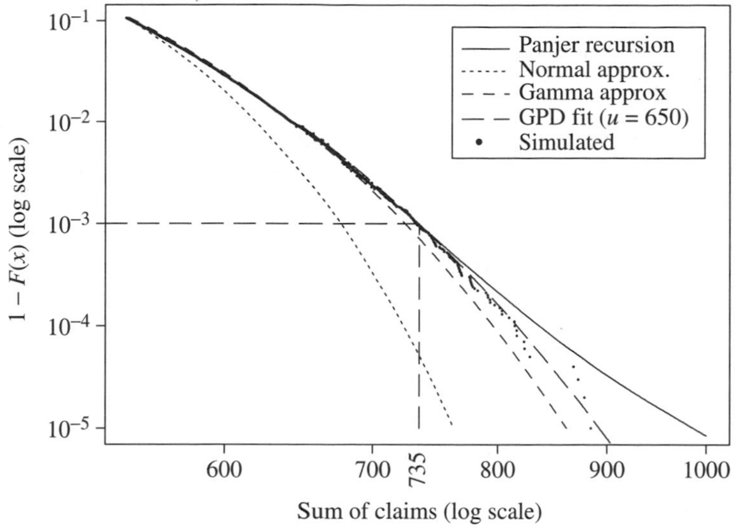

Figure 10.5. Simulated CPoi(100, $LN(1, 1)$) data ($n = 100\,000$) with normal-, translated-gamma, GPD and Panjer recursion (see Example 10.17) approximations (on log–log scale).

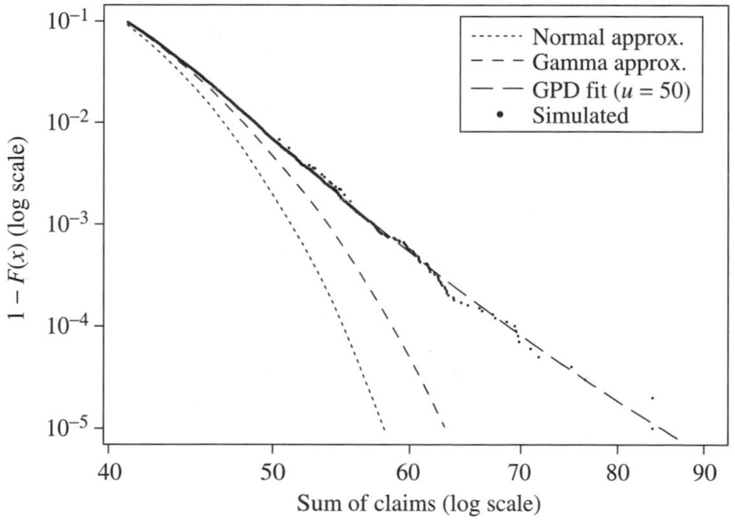

Figure 10.6. Simulated CPoi(100, Pa(4, 1)) data ($n = 100\,000$) with normal-, translated-gamma, and GPD approximations (on log–log scale).

identities:

$$\left.\begin{aligned} s_0 &= P(S_N = 0) = P(N = 0) = p_0, \\ s_n &= P(S_N = n) = \sum_{k=1}^{\infty} p_k g_n^{(k)}, \quad n \geqslant 1, \end{aligned}\right\} \tag{10.16}$$

where the latter formula corresponds to Proposition 10.4 but now in the discrete case. As in Proposition 10.4 we note that (10.16) is difficult to calculate, mainly due to the convolutions $g_n^{(k)}$. However, for an important class of counting variables N, (10.16) can be reduced to a simple recursion. For this, we introduce the so-called *Panjer classes*.

Definition 10.10 (Panjer class). The probability mass function (p_k) of N belongs to the Panjer(a, b) *class* for some $a, b \in \mathbb{R}$ if the following relationship holds for $r \geqslant 1$: $p_r = (a + (b/r))p_{r-1}$.

Example 10.11 (binomial). If $N \sim \mathrm{B}(n, p)$, then its probability mass function is $p_r = \binom{n}{r} p^r (1-p)^{n-r}$ for $0 \leqslant r \leqslant n$ and it can be easily checked that

$$\frac{p_r}{p_{r-1}} = -\frac{p}{1-p} + \frac{(n+1)p}{r(1-p)},$$

showing that N belongs to the Panjer(a, b) class with $a = -p/(1-p)$ and $b = (n+1)p/(1-p)$.

Example 10.12 (Poisson). If $N \sim \mathrm{Poi}(\lambda)$, then its probability mass function $p_r = \mathrm{e}^{-\lambda}\lambda^r/r!$ satisfies $p_r/p_{r-1} = \lambda/r$, so N belongs to the Panjer(a, b) class with $a = 0$ and $b = \lambda$.

Example 10.13 (negative binomial). If N has a negative binomial distribution, denoted $N \sim \mathrm{NB}(\alpha, p)$, then its probability mass function is

$$p_r = \binom{\alpha + r - 1}{r} p^\alpha (1-p)^r, \quad r \geqslant 0,\ \alpha > 0,\ 0 < p < 1$$

(see Section A.2.7 for further details). We can easily check that

$$\frac{p_r}{p_{r-1}} = 1 - p + \frac{(\alpha - 1)(1-p)}{r}.$$

Hence N belongs to the Panjer(a, b) class with $a = 1 - p$ and $b = (\alpha - 1)(1 - p)$. In Proposition 10.20 we will show that the negative binomial model follows very naturally from the Poisson model when one randomizes the intensity parameter of the latter using a gamma distribution.

Remark 10.14. One can show that, neglecting degenerate models for (p_k), the above three examples are the *only* counting distributions satisfying Definition 10.10. This result goes back to Johnson and Kotz (1969) and was formulated explicitly in the actuarial literature in Sundt and Jewell (1982).

Theorem 10.15 (Panjer recursion). *Suppose that N satisfies the* Panjer(a, b) *class condition and $g_0 = P(X_1 = 0) = 0$, then $s_0 = p_0$ and, for $r \geqslant 1$, $s_r = \sum_{i=1}^{r}(a + (bi/r))g_i s_{r-i}$.*

Proof. We already know that $s_0 = p_0$ from (10.16), so suppose that $r \geqslant 1$. Noting that $X_1, \dots, X_n$ are iid, we require the following well-known identity for exchangeable rvs:

$$E\left(X_1 \,\middle|\, \sum_{i=1}^{n} X_i = r\right) = \frac{1}{n}\sum_{j=1}^{n} E\left(X_j \,\middle|\, \sum_{i=1}^{n} X_i = r\right)$$
$$= \frac{1}{n} E\left(\sum_{j=1}^{n} X_j \,\middle|\, \sum_{i=1}^{n} X_i = r\right) = \frac{r}{n}. \tag{10.17}$$

Moreover, using the fact that $g_0^{(n-1)} = 0$ for $n \geqslant 2$, we make the preliminary calculation that

$$p_{n-1}\sum_{i=1}^{r-1}\left(a + \frac{bi}{r}\right) g_i g_{r-i}^{(n-1)} = p_{n-1}\sum_{i=1}^{r}\left(a + \frac{bi}{r}\right) g_i g_{r-i}^{(n-1)}$$
$$= p_{n-1}\sum_{i=1}^{r}\left(a + \frac{bi}{r}\right) P\left(X_1 = i,\ \sum_{j=2}^{n} X_j = r - i\right)$$
$$= p_{n-1}\sum_{i=1}^{r}\left(a + \frac{bi}{r}\right) P\left(X_1 = i,\ \sum_{j=1}^{n} X_j = r\right)$$
$$= p_{n-1}\sum_{i=1}^{r}\left(a + \frac{bi}{r}\right) P\left(X_1 = i \,\middle|\, \sum_{j=1}^{n} X_j = r\right) g_r^{(n)}$$
$$= p_{n-1} E\left(a + \frac{bX_1}{r} \,\middle|\, \sum_{j=1}^{n} X_j = r\right) g_r^{(n)}$$
$$= p_{n-1}\left(a + \frac{b}{n}\right) g_r^{(n)} = p_n g_r^{(n)},$$

where (10.17) is used in the final step. Therefore, the identity (10.16) yields

$$s_r = \sum_{n=1}^{\infty} p_n g_r^{(n)} = p_1 g_r + \sum_{n=2}^{\infty} p_n g_r^{(n)}$$
$$= (a+b) p_0 g_r + \sum_{n=2}^{\infty}\sum_{i=1}^{r-1}\left(a + \frac{bi}{r}\right) g_i p_{n-1} g_{r-i}^{(n-1)}$$
$$= (a+b) s_0 g_r + \sum_{i=1}^{r-1}\left(a + \frac{bi}{r}\right) g_i \sum_{n=2}^{\infty} p_{n-1} g_{r-i}^{(n-1)}$$
$$= (a+b) g_r s_0 + \sum_{i=1}^{r-1}\left(a + \frac{bi}{r}\right) g_i s_{r-i}$$
$$= \sum_{i=1}^{r}\left(a + \frac{bi}{r}\right) g_i s_{r-i}.$$

□

Remark 10.16. In the case of both the FFT method and the Panjer recursion, an initial discretization of the loss df G generally has to be made, which introduces an approximation error. An in-depth discussion of discretization errors for the computation of compound distributions is to be found in Grübel and Hermesmeier (1999, 2000) (see also references therein for a comparison of these approaches). A slight correction to Theorem 10.15 has to be made if $g_0 = P(X_1 = 0) > 0$. One obtains $s_0 = \sum_{k=0}^{\infty} p_k g_0^k$ and, for $r \geqslant 1$, $s_r = (1 - ag_0)^{-1} \sum_{i=1}^{r} (a + bi/r) g_i s_{r-i}$ (see Mikosch 2004, Theorem 3.3.10). In Notes and Comments we give further references.

Example 10.17 (Panjer recursion for the CPoi(100, $LN(1, 1)$) case). In Figure 10.5 we have included the Panjer approximation for the CPoi(100, $LN(1, 1)$) case. In order to apply Theorem 10.15, we first have to discretize the lognormal df. An equispaced discretization of about 0.5 yields the Panjer approximation in Figure 10.5, which is excellent for quantile values around 0.999, relevant for applications. The 99.9% quantile estimate based on the Panjer recursion is 735, a value very close to the GPD estimate. Far out in the tail, beyond 0.999, say, rounding errors become important (the tail drifts off) and one has to be more careful; in Notes and Comments we give some references on how to improve recursive methods far out in the tail.

10.2.4 Poisson Mixtures

Poisson mixture models have been used in both credit and operational risk modelling; for an example in the latter case see Cruz (2002, Section 5.2.2) as well as the book jacket, which features a negative binomial distribution (a particular Poisson mixture model). Poisson mixtures have been used by actuaries for a long time; the negative binomial made its first appearance in the actuarial literature as the distribution of the number of repeated accidents suffered by an individual in a given time span (see Seal 1969).

In Example 10.5 we introduced the compound Poisson model CPoi(λ, G), where $N \sim \text{Poi}(\lambda)$ counts the number of losses and G is the loss severity df. One disadvantage of the Poisson frequency distribution is that $\text{var}(N) = \lambda = E(N)$, whereas count data often exhibit so-called *over-dispersion*, meaning that they indicate a model where $\text{var}(N) > E(N)$. A standard way to achieve this is by mixing the intensity λ over some df $F_\Lambda(\lambda)$, i.e. assume that $\lambda > 0$ is a realization of a positive rv Λ with this df so that, by definition,

$$p_N(k) = P(N = k) = \int_0^\infty P(N = k \mid \Lambda = \lambda) \, \mathrm{d}F_\Lambda(\lambda)$$
$$= \int_0^\infty \mathrm{e}^{-\lambda} \frac{\lambda^k}{k!} \, \mathrm{d}F_\Lambda(\lambda). \qquad (10.18)$$

Definition 10.18 (the mixed Poisson distribution). The rv N with df (10.18) is called a *mixed Poisson* rv with *structure* (or *mixing*) distribution F_Λ.

A consequence of the next result is that mixing leads to over-dispersion.

Proposition 10.19. *Suppose that N is mixed Poisson with structure df F_Λ. Then $E(N) = E(\Lambda)$ and $\mathrm{var}(N) = E(\Lambda) + \mathrm{var}(\Lambda)$, i.e. for Λ non-degenerate, N is over-dispersed.*

Proof. One immediately obtains

$$E(N) = \sum_{k=0}^{\infty} k p_N(k) = \int_0^\infty \sum_{k=0}^{\infty} k \mathrm{e}^{-\lambda} \frac{\lambda^k}{k!} \, \mathrm{d}F_\Lambda(\lambda) = \int_0^\infty \lambda \, \mathrm{d}F_\Lambda(\lambda) = E(\Lambda).$$

And, similarly,

$$E(N^2) = \sum_{k=0}^{\infty} k^2 p_N(k) = E(\Lambda) + E(\Lambda^2),$$

so the result follows. □

We now give a concrete example of a mixed Poisson distribution, which is particularly important in both operational risk and credit risk modelling. Indeed we have already used the following result when describing the industry credit risk model CreditRisk+ in Section 8.4.2.

Proposition 10.20 (negative binomial as Poisson mixture). *Suppose that the rv N has a mixed Poisson distribution with a gamma-distributed mixing variable $\Lambda \sim \mathrm{Ga}(\alpha, \beta)$. Then N has a negative binomial distribution $N \sim \mathrm{NB}(\alpha, \beta/(\beta + 1))$.*

Proof. Using the definition of a gamma distribution in Section A.2.4 we have

$$P(N = k) = \int_0^\infty \frac{\beta^\alpha}{\Gamma(\alpha)} \frac{\lambda^k}{k!} \mathrm{e}^{-\lambda} \lambda^{\alpha-1} \mathrm{e}^{-\beta\lambda} \, \mathrm{d}\lambda = \frac{\beta^\alpha}{k!\Gamma(\alpha)} \int_0^\infty \lambda^{\alpha+k-1} \mathrm{e}^{-(\beta+1)\lambda} \, \mathrm{d}\lambda.$$

Substituting $u = (\beta + 1)\lambda$, the integral can be evaluated to be

$$\int_0^\infty (\beta + 1)^{-(\alpha+k)} u^{\alpha+k-1} \mathrm{e}^{-u} \, \mathrm{d}u = \frac{\Gamma(\alpha + k)}{(\beta + 1)^{\alpha+k}}.$$

This yields

$$P(N = k) = \left(\frac{\beta}{\beta + 1}\right)^\alpha \left(\frac{1}{\beta + 1}\right)^k \frac{\Gamma(\alpha + k)}{k!\Gamma(\alpha)}.$$

Using the relation $\Gamma(\alpha + k) = (\alpha + k - 1) \cdots \alpha\Gamma(\alpha)$, we see that this is equal to the probability mass function of a negative binomial rv with $p := \beta/(\beta + 1)$ (see Section A.2.7). □

Recall the definition of compound sums from Section 10.2.2 (Assumption 10.3 and Proposition 10.4). In the special case of mixed Poisson rvs, compounding leads to so-called *compound mixed Poisson distributions*. There is much literature on dfs of this type (see Notes and Comments).

10.2.5 Tails of Aggregate Loss Distributions

In Section 7.1.2 we defined the class of rvs with regularly varying or power tails. If the (claim size) df G is regularly varying with index $\alpha > 0$, then there exists a slowly varying function L (Definition 7.7) such that $\bar{G}(x) = 1 - G(x) = x^{-\alpha}L(x)$. The next result shows that, for a wide class of counting dfs $(p_N(k))$, the df of the compound sum S_N, F_{S_N}, inherits the power-like behaviour of G.

Theorem 10.21 (power-like behaviour of compound-sum distribution). *Suppose that S_N is a compound sum and that there exists an $\varepsilon > 0$ such that $\sum_{k=0}^{\infty}(1+\varepsilon)^k p_N(k) < \infty$. If $\bar{G}(x) = x^{-\alpha}L(x)$ with $\alpha \geqslant 0$ and L slowly varying, then*

$$\lim_{x\to\infty} \frac{\bar{F}_{S_N}(x)}{\bar{G}(x)} = \lambda,$$

so $\bar{F}_{S_N}$ inherits the power-like behaviour of $\bar{G}$.

Proof. This result holds more generally for *subexponential* dfs; a proof together with further discussions can be found in Embrechts, Klüppelberg and Mikosch (1997, Section 1.3.3). □

Example 10.22 (negative binomial). It is not difficult to show that the negative binomial case satisfies the condition on N in Theorem 10.21. The kind of argument required is to be found in Embrechts, Klüppelberg and Mikosch (1997, Example 1.3.11). Hence, if $\bar{G}(x) = x^{-\alpha}L(x)$, the tail of the compound-sum df behaves like the tail of G, i.e.

$$\bar{F}_{S_N}(x) \sim \frac{\alpha}{\beta}\bar{G}(x), \quad \text{as } x \to \infty.$$

(For details, see Embrechts, Klüppelberg and Mikosch (1997, Section 1.3.3).)

Under the conditions of Theorem 10.21 the asymptotic behaviour of $\bar{F}_{S_N}(x)$ in the case of a Pareto loss df is again Pareto with the same index. This is clearly seen in Figure 10.6 in the linear behaviour of the simulated losses as well as the fitted GPD. In the case of Figure 10.5, one can show that $\bar{F}_{S_N}(x)$ decays like a lognormal tail; see the reference given in the proof of Theorem 10.21 for details. Note that the GPD is able to pick up the features of the tail in both cases.

10.2.6 The Homogeneous Poisson Process

In the previous sections we looked at counting rvs N over a fixed time interval $[0, 1]$, say. Without any additional difficulty, we could have looked at $N(t)$ counting the number of events in $[0, t]$ for $t \geqslant 0$. In the Poisson case this would correspond to $N(t) \sim \text{Poi}(\lambda t)$; hence, for fixed t and on replacing λ by λt, all of the previous results concerning $\text{Poi}(\lambda)$ rvs can be suitably adapted.

In this section we want to integrate the rvs $N(t)$, $t \geqslant 0$, into a stochastic process framework. The less mathematically trained reader should realize that there is a big difference between a family of rvs indexed by time for which we only specify the one-dimensional dfs (which is what we have done so far) and a stochastic process

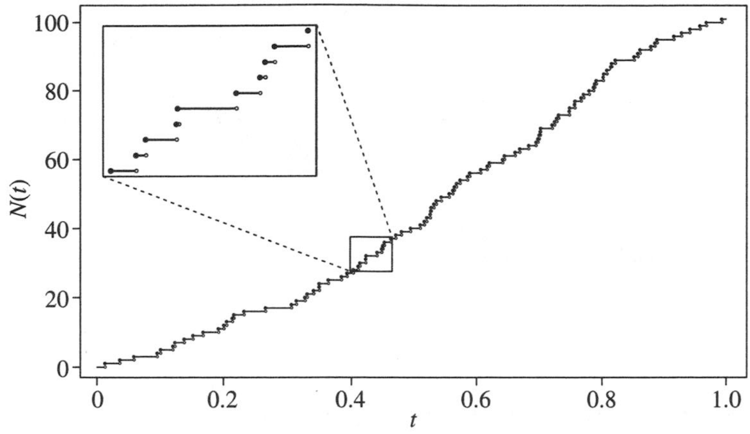

Figure 10.7. Sample path of a counting process.

with a specific structure in which these rvs are embedded. This difference is akin to the difference between marginal and joint distributions, a topic we have highlighted as very important in Chapter 5 through the notion of copulas; of course, in the stochastic process case, there also has to be some probabilistic consistency across time. In a certain sense, the finite-dimensional problem of Chapter 5 becomes an infinite-dimensional problem.

After these words of warning on the difference between rvs and stochastic processes, we now take some methodological shortcuts to arrive at our goal. The interested reader wanting to learn more will have to delve deeper into the mathematical background of stochastic processes in general and counting processes in particular. The Notes and Comments contain some references.

Definition 10.23 (counting processes). A stochastic process $N = (N(t))_{t \geqslant 0}$ is a *counting process* if its sample paths are right continuous with left limits existing, and there exists a sequence of rvs $T_0 = 0, T_1, T_2, \dots$ tending almost surely to ∞ such that $N(t) = \sum_{k=1}^{\infty} I_{\{T_k \leqslant t\}}$.

A typical realization of such a process is given in Figure 10.7. We now define the homogeneous Poisson process as a special counting process.

Definition 10.24 (homogeneous Poisson process). A stochastic process $N = (N(t))_{t \geqslant 0}$ is a *homogeneous Poisson process* with intensity (rate) $\lambda > 0$ if the following properties hold:

(i) N is a counting process;

(ii) $N(0) = 0$, almost surely;

(iii) N has stationary and independent increments; and

(iv) for each $t > 0$, $N(t) \sim \text{Poi}(\lambda t)$.

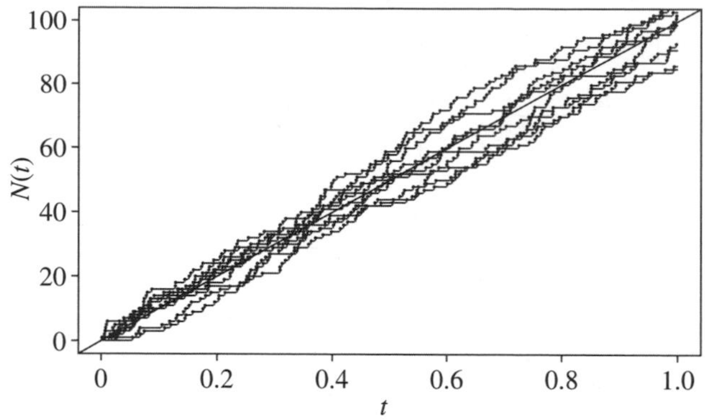

Figure 10.8. Ten realizations of a homogeneous Poisson process with $\lambda = 100$.

Remark 10.25. Note that conditions (iii) and (iv) imply that, for $0 < u < v < t$, the rvs $N(v) - N(u)$ and $N(t) - N(v)$ are independent and that, for $k \geqslant 0$,

$$\begin{aligned} P(N(v) - N(u) = k) &= P(N(v-u) = k) \\ &= \mathrm{e}^{-\lambda(v-u)} \frac{(\lambda(v-u))^k}{k!}. \end{aligned}$$

The rv $N(v) - N(u)$ counts the number of events (claims, losses) in the interval $(u, v]$; by stationarity, it has the same df as $N(v-u)$. In Figure 10.8 we have generated 10 realizations of a homogeneous Poisson process on $[0, 1]$ with $\lambda = 100$. Note the rather narrow band within which the various sample paths fall.

For practical purposes, the following result contains the main properties of the homogeneous Poisson process.

Theorem 10.26 (characterizations of the homogeneous Poisson process). *Suppose that N is a counting process. Then the following statements are equivalent:*

(1) *N is a homogeneous Poisson process with rate $\lambda > 0$;*

(2) *N has stationary and independent increments and*

$$\begin{aligned} P(N(t) = 1) &= \lambda t + o(t), \quad \text{as } t \downarrow 0, \\ P(N(t) \geqslant 2) &= o(t), \quad \text{as } t \downarrow 0; \end{aligned}$$

(3) *the inter-event times $(\Delta_k = T_k - T_{k-1})_{k \geqslant 1}$ are iid with df* $\mathrm{Exp}(\lambda)$*; and*

(4) *for all $t > 0$, $N(t) \sim \mathrm{Poi}(\lambda t)$ and, given that $(N(t) = k)$, the occurrence times $T_1, T_2, \dots, T_k$ have the same distribution as the ordered sample from k independent rvs, uniformly distributed on $[0, t]$; as a consequence, we can write the conditional joint density as*

$$f_{T_1,\dots,T_k \mid N(t)=k}(t_1, \dots, t_k) = \frac{k!}{t^k} I_{\{0 < t_1 < \dots < t_k < t\}}.$$

Proof. Many standard textbooks on stochastic processes contain proofs of this important theorem (see, for example, Mikosch 2004; Resnick 1992). □

Discussion. Statement (2) in Theorem 10.26 implies that λ can indeed be interpreted as a rate or intensity: $\lambda = \lim_{t\downarrow 0}(1/t)P(N(t) = 1)$. Moreover, the same statement implies that a homogeneous Poisson process does not allow for clustering of events: $\lim_{t\downarrow 0} P(N(t) \geqslant 2) = 0$. Statement (3) gives an event-time definition of a homogeneous Poisson process. It follows immediately that the first event-time has an $\text{Exp}(\lambda)$ df: $P(T_1 > t) = P(N(t) = 0) = e^{-\lambda t}$, $t \geqslant 0$. Statement (3), however, goes well beyond this by stating that the inter-event times Δ_k are iid with $\Delta_k \sim \text{Exp}(\lambda)$. This leads to a straightforward way to simulate a stream of loss events from a homogeneous Poisson process with rate λ. Moreover, this equivalent definition immediately yields a generalization by assuming that the Δ_k are still iid but that $\Delta_k \sim F_\Delta$, a general df. The resulting process is a so-called *renewal process* (note that the only Markovian renewal process is the homogeneous Poisson process).

Finally, statement (4) yields an easy algorithm to generate the occurrences of homogeneous Poisson times over the interval $[0, t]$ given that we have in total k events till t—we simply generate k uniform rvs on $[0, t]$ and order them.

Multivariate Poisson processes. In many applications we want to model the frequencies of different loss types with a number of Poisson processes while considering possible dependence between loss frequencies for different loss types. More generally, we might want to construct a number of compound Poisson processes where loss severities for the different business lines were also dependent. A natural approach to modelling this dependence is to assume that all losses can be related to a series of underlying and independent Poisson *shock* processes. In insurance these shocks might be natural catastrophes; in credit risk modelling they might be a variety of economic events, such as local or global recessions; in operational risk modelling they might be the failure of various IT systems. When a shock occurs this may cause losses of several different types; the common shock causes the numbers of losses of each type to be dependent. See Lindskog and McNeil (2003), Pfeifer and Nešlehová (2004) and Chavez-Demoulin, Embrechts and Nešlehová (2005) for models of this kind.

10.2.7 Processes Related to the Poisson Process

Using the fundamental building block of the homogeneous Poisson process, one can construct more general counting processes that are useful for loss-event modelling in finance and insurance. Such generalizations include the following.

Renewal processes (mentioned above). The exponential waiting time distribution is replaced by a general df F_Δ.

Inhomogeneous Poisson processes. The constant intensity λ is replaced by a deterministic function $\lambda(\cdot)$.

Mixed Poisson processes. The deterministic constant intensity λ is replaced by an rv Λ.

Doubly stochastic or Cox processes. λ is replaced by a stochastic process $\{\lambda_t : t \geqslant 0\}$ in accordance with notation used in Chapter 9 (see, for example, Definition 9.16).

Self-exciting or Hawkes processes. λ is replaced by a stochastic process depending only on previous event times. See Section 7.4.3 for a concrete example.

Below, we highlight some features of some of these processes.

Inhomogeneous Poisson process.

Definition 10.27 (inhomogeneous Poisson). A counting process N is an *inhomogeneous Poisson process* if, for some deterministic function $\lambda(s) \geqslant 0$, the following conditions hold:

(i) $N(0) = 0$, almost surely;

(ii) N has independent increments; and

(iii) for all $t \geqslant 0$,

$$\begin{aligned} P(N(t+h) - N(t) = 1) &= \lambda(t)h + o(h), \quad && h \downarrow 0, \\ P(N(t+h) - N(t) \geqslant 2) &= o(h), && h \downarrow 0. \end{aligned}$$

The function $\lambda(\cdot)$ is referred to as the *intensity* or *rate function*. The integral $\Lambda(t) = \int_0^t \lambda(s)\,\mathrm{d}s$ is referred to as the *intensity measure* (or *cumulative intensity function*).

Remark 10.28. A characterization theorem, similar to Theorem 10.26, can be derived. In particular, we find that, for $0 < s < t$, $N(t) - N(s) \sim \mathrm{Poi}(\Lambda(t) - \Lambda(s))$.

The inhomogeneous Poisson process is a useful tool in loss modelling whenever a deterministic trend or seasonality component is to be modelled in the loss frequency. The next example also shows that this process naturally emerges as a counting process for record losses.

Example 10.29 (records). The world of finance and insurance abounds with statements on *record events*: the largest single day drop in the dollar/yen, the most expensive hurricane, the three best fund managers during the last year, the second largest loss due to internal fraud, the biggest one-day change in the credit spread of a particular company, etc. Likewise, the world of records is intimately related to the (general) theory of Poisson processes. In Notes and Comments we shall give several references for this. Below we indicate how an easy example related to a question on records leads to an inhomogeneous Poisson process as a model.

Suppose that the loss rvs $X_i \geqslant 0$ are iid with density function $f(x) > 0$, $x \geqslant 0$. Define the counting process N:

$$N(t) = \sum_{i=1}^{\infty} I_{\{X_i \leqslant t \text{ and } X_i > X_{i-j},\ j=1,\dots,i-1\}}.$$

$N(t)$ counts the number of records in the sequence $(X_i)_{i\geqslant 1}$ of size less than t and $(N(t))$ is referred to as the *record process*. It follows that, for $h, t > 0$,

$$\begin{aligned}
P(N(t+h) - N(t) \geqslant 1) &= \sum_{i=1}^{\infty} P(X_i \in (t, t+h] \text{ and } X_{i-1} \leqslant t, \dots, X_1 \leqslant t) \\
&= \sum_{i=1}^{\infty} (F(t+h) - F(t))(F(t))^{i-1} \\
&= \frac{F(t+h) - F(t)}{1 - F(t)} \\
&= \frac{f(t)}{1 - F(t)} h + o(h), \quad \text{as } h \downarrow 0.
\end{aligned}$$

Moreover, for $h, t > 0$:

$$\begin{aligned}
&P(N(t+h) - N(t) \geqslant 2) \\
&\quad \leqslant \sum_{i<j} P(X_1 \leqslant t, \dots, X_{i-1} \leqslant t,\ X_i \in (t, t+h], \\
&\qquad\qquad X_{i+1} \leqslant t+h, \dots, X_{j-1} \leqslant t+h,\ X_j \in (t, t+h]) \\
&\quad = \left(\int_t^{t+h} f(s)\,\mathrm{d}s \right)^2 \sum_{i<j} (F(t))^{i-1} (F(t))^{j-i-1} \\
&\quad = o(h^2), \quad \text{as } h \downarrow 0.
\end{aligned}$$

From these calculations one deduces that the record process N is inhomogeneous Poisson with rate function $\lambda(t) = f(t)/(1 - F(t))$, the so-called *hazard rate* of F, a notion that we encountered in Section 9.2.1.

Suppose now that, as in most practical cases, $\Lambda(t)$ is strictly increasing, so $\Lambda(\Lambda^{-1}(t)) = \Lambda^{-1}(\Lambda(t)) = t$. We can then always transform an inhomogeneous Poisson process N with integrated intensity Λ into a homogeneous Poisson process with intensity 1 by a *change of time*.

Proposition 10.30 (time change, operational time). *Suppose that N is an inhomogeneous Poisson process with Λ strictly increasing and define, for $t \geqslant 0$, $\tilde{N}(t) = N(\Lambda^{-1}(t))$, then $\tilde{N}$ is homogeneous Poisson with intensity* 1.

Proof. For $t > 0$ fixed and $k \geqslant 0$,

$$P(\tilde{N}(t) = k) = P(N(\Lambda^{-1}(t)) = k) = \mathrm{e}^{-\Lambda(\Lambda^{-1}(t))} \frac{(\Lambda(\Lambda^{-1}(t)))^k}{k!} = \mathrm{e}^{-t} \frac{t^k}{k!},$$

so $\tilde{N}(t) \sim \mathrm{Poi}(t)$. By definition, the increments of $\tilde{N}$ are independent; moreover, for $0 < u < v$ we have that

$$\begin{aligned}
P(\tilde{N}(v) - \tilde{N}(u) = k) &= P(N(\Lambda^{-1}(v)) - N(\Lambda^{-1}(u)) = k) \\
&= \mathrm{e}^{-(\Lambda(\Lambda^{-1}(v)) - \Lambda(\Lambda^{-1}(u)))} \frac{(\Lambda(\Lambda^{-1}(v)) - \Lambda(\Lambda^{-1}(u)))^k}{k!} \\
&= \mathrm{e}^{-(v-u)} \frac{(v-u)^k}{k!},
\end{aligned}$$

from which stationarity follows. □

This is one of the many examples in insurance and finance where a more complicated process (N) can be reduced to a standard (easier) model ($\tilde{N}$) through the careful choice of a new time clock (a so-called *time change construction*) (see also Section 9.2.3 on credit risk). Proposition 10.30 can be formulated more generally for Λ not strictly increasing and the converse also holds. Proposition 10.30 justifies the common simplifying assumption that a loss frequency model is homogeneous (unit rate) Poisson, albeit in many cases only in operational time. The original time-scale of N is slowed down or speeded up in such a way that, on average, $\tilde{N}$ has one claim per time unit, whereas N has, on average, $\Lambda(1)$ claims.

Remark 10.31. A standard way in which an inhomogeneous Poisson process can be obtained from a homogeneous Poisson process is by random sampling. Suppose an intensity function λ satisfies $\lambda(s) \leqslant c < \infty$ for $s \geqslant 0$. Start from a homogeneous Poisson process with rate $c > 0$ and denote its arrival times by $T_0 = 0, T_1, T_2, \dots$. Construct a new process $\tilde{N}$ from $(T_i)_{i \geqslant 0}$ through deletion of each T_i independently of the other T_j with probability $1 - (\lambda(T_i)/c)$. The so-called *thinned* counting process $\tilde{N}$ consists of the remaining (undeleted) points. It can be shown that this process is inhomogeneous Poisson with intensity function $\lambda(\cdot)$.

Mixed Poisson process. The mixed Poisson rvs of Section 10.2.4 can be embedded into a so-called *mixed Poisson process*. A single realization of such a process cannot be distinguished through statistical means from a realization of a homogeneous Poisson process; indeed, to simulate a sample path, one first draws a realization of the random intensity $\lambda = \Lambda(\omega)$ and then draws the sample path of the homogeneous Poisson process with rate λ. (Here Λ denotes an rv and not the intensity measure in the inhomogeneous Poisson case above.) Only by repeating this simulation more frequently does one see the different probabilistic nature of the mixed Poisson process: compare Figure 10.9 with Figure 10.8. In the former we have simulated 10 sample paths from a mixed Poisson process with mixing variable $\Lambda \sim \text{Ga}(100, 1)$ so that $E(\Lambda) = 100$. Note the much greater variability in the paths.

Example 10.32. When counting processes are used in credit risk modelling the times T_k typically correspond to credit events, for instance default or downgradings. More precisely, a credit event can be constructed as the first jump of a counting process N. The df of the time to the credit event can be easily derived by observing that $P(T_1 > t) = P(N(t) = 0)$. This probability can be calculated in a straightforward way for a homogeneous Poisson process with intensity λ; we obtain $P(N(t) = 0) = \mathrm{e}^{-\lambda t}$. When N is a mixed Poisson process with mixing df F_Λ we obtain

$$P(T_1 > t) = P(N(t) = 0) = \int_0^\infty \mathrm{e}^{-t\lambda} \, \mathrm{d}F_\Lambda(\lambda) = \hat{F}_\Lambda(t),$$

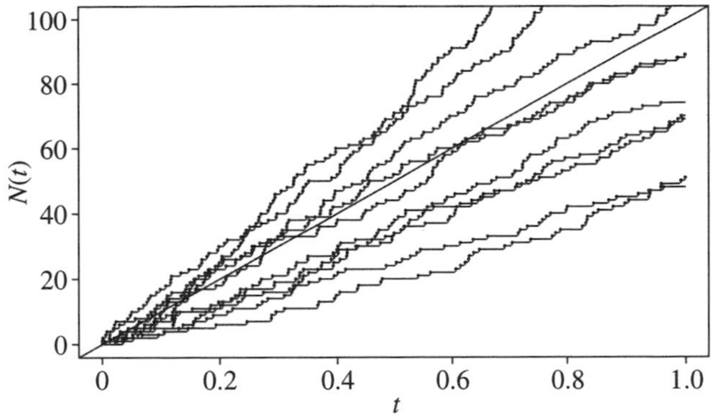

Figure 10.9. Ten realizations of a mixed Poisson process with $\Lambda \sim \text{Ga}(100, 1)$.

the Laplace–Stieltjes transform of F_Λ in t. In the special case when $\Lambda \sim \text{Ga}(\alpha, \beta)$, the negative binomial case treated in Proposition 10.20, one finds that

$$\begin{aligned} P(T_1 > t) &= \int_0^\infty \mathrm{e}^{-t\lambda} \frac{\beta^\alpha}{\Gamma(\alpha)} \lambda^{\alpha-1} \mathrm{e}^{-\beta\lambda} \, \mathrm{d}\lambda \\ &= \frac{\beta^\alpha}{\Gamma(\alpha)} (t+\beta)^{-\alpha} \int_0^\infty \mathrm{e}^{-s} s^{\alpha-1} \, \mathrm{d}s \\ &= \beta^\alpha (t+\beta)^{-\alpha}, \quad t \geqslant 0, \end{aligned}$$

so that T_1 has a Pareto distribution $T_1 \sim \text{Pa}(\alpha, \beta)$ (see Section A.2.8).

Processes with stochastic intensity. A further important class of models is obtained when λ in the homogeneous Poisson case is replaced by a general stochastic process (λ_t), yielding a two-tier stochastic model or so-called *doubly stochastic* process.

For example, one could take λ_t to be a diffusion or, alternatively, a finite-state Markov chain. The latter case gives rise to a *regime-switching* model: in each state of the Markov chain the intensity has a different constant level and the process remains in that state for an exponential length of time, before jumping to another state. In Figure 10.10 we have simulated the sample path of such a process randomly switching between $\lambda = 10$ and $\lambda = 100$. In Section 9.2.3 we looked at doubly stochastic random times, which correspond to the first jump of a doubly stochastic Poisson process.

Notes and Comments

The story behind the name *insurance analytics* is told in Embrechts (2002). A good place to start a search for actuarial literature is the website of the International Actuarial Association: www.actuaries.org. Several interesting books can be found on the website of the Society of Actuaries, www.soa.org (whose postal address is, coincidentally, 475 North *Martingale* Rd #600, Schaumburg, Illinois). A standard Society of Actuaries textbook on actuarial mathematics is Bowers et al. (1986); financial economics for actuaries is to be found in Panjer et al. (1998). For our purposes excellent texts are Mikosch (2004) and Partrat and Besson (2004). Rolski et al. (1999)

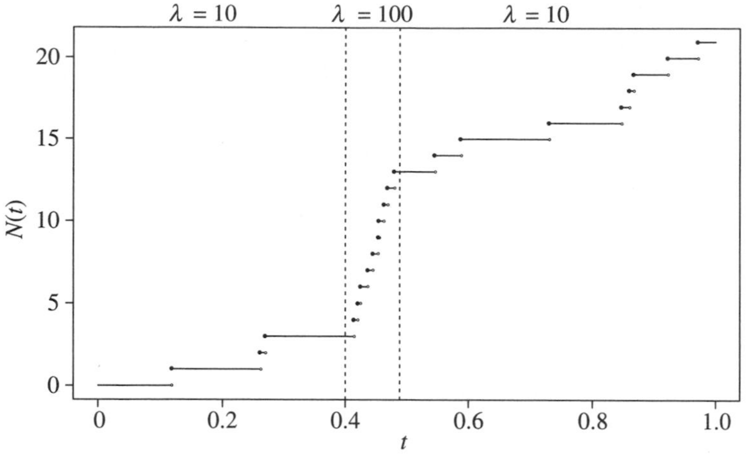

Figure 10.10. Realization of a counting process with a regime switch from $\lambda = 10$ to $\lambda = 100$.

gives a broad, more technical overview of the relevant stochastic process models. In Chapter 6 we have given several references to actuarial tools relevant for the study of risk measures; key words there were premium principles (Section 6.1), comonotonicity (Sections 5.1.6 and 6.2.2) and Fréchet bounds (Sections 5.1.6 and 6.2). Finally, an overview of the state of the art of actuarial modelling is to be found in Teugels and Sundt (2004).

Actuarial textbooks dealing in particular with the modelling of loss distributions in insurance are Hogg and Klugman (1984) and Klugman, Panjer and Willmot (1998). Besides the general references above, an early textbook discussion of the use of numerical methods for the calculation of the df of total loss amount rvs is Feilmeier and Bertram (1987); Bühlmann (1984) contains a first comparison between the FFT method and Panjer recursion. More extensive comparisons, taking rounding and discretization errors into account, are found in Grübel and Hermesmeier (1999, 2000). A discussion of the use of the FFT in insurance is given in Embrechts, Grübel and Pitts (1993). Algorithms for the FFT are freely available on the Web, as a search will quickly reveal. The original paper by Panjer (1981) also contains a density version of Theorem 10.15. For an application of Panjer recursion to credit risk measurement within the CreditRisk+ framework, see Credit Suisse Financial Products (1997). Based on Giese (2003), Haaf, Reiss and Schoenmakers (2004) propose an alternative recursive method. For more recent work on Panjer recursion, especially in the multivariate case, see, for example, Hesselager (1996) and Sundt (1999, 2000).

Asymptotic approximation methods going beyond the normal approximation (10.13) are known in statistics under the names Berry–Esséen, Edgeworth and *saddle-point*. The former two are discussed, for example, in Embrechts, Klüppelberg and Mikosch (1997) and are of more theoretical importance. The saddle-point technique is very useful: see Jensen (1995) for an excellent summary, and Embrechts et al. (1985) for an application to compound distributions. Gordy (2002) discusses the importance of saddle-point methods for credit risk modelling, again within the context of CreditRisk+. Wider applications within risk management can be found in Studer (2001) and Glasserman (2003a,b)

Poisson mixture models with insurance applications in mind are summarized in Grandell (1997) (see also Bening and Korolev 2002). In order to enter more deeply into the world of counting processes, one has to study the theory of point processes. Very comprehensive and readable accounts are Daley and Vere-Jones (2003) and Karr (1991). A study of this theory is both mathematically demanding and practically rewarding. Such models are being used increasingly in credit risk. The notion of time change is fundamental to many applications in insurance and finance; for an example of how it can be used to model operational risk, see Embrechts, Kaufmann and Samorodnitsky (2004). For its introduction into finance, see Ané and Geman (2000) and Dacorogna et al. (2001). An excellent survey is to be found in Peeters (2004).

What have we not included in our brief account of the elements of insurance analytics? We have not treated ruin theory and the general stochastic process theory of insurance risk, credibility theory, dynamic financial analysis, also referred to as dynamic solvency testing, and reinsurance, to name but a few omissions.

The stochastic process theory of insurance risk has a long tradition. The first fundamental summary came through the pioneering work of Cramér (1994a,b). Bühlmann (1970) made the field popular to several generations of actuaries. This early work has now been generalized in every way possible. A standard textbook on *ruin theory* is Asmussen (2000). The modelling of large claims and its consequences for ruin estimates can be found in Embrechts, Klüppelberg and Mikosch (1997).

Credibility theory concerns premium calculation for non-homogeneous portfolios and has a very rich history rooted in non-life insurance mathematics. Its basic concepts were first developed by American actuaries in the 1920s; pioneering papers in this early period were Mowbray (1914) and Whitney (1918). Further important work is found in the papers of Bailey (1945), Robbins (1955, 1964) and Bühlmann (1967, 1968, 1971). An excellent review article tracing the historical development of the basic ideas is Norberg (1979); see also Jewell (1990) for a more recent review. Various textbook versions exist: Bühlmann and Gisler (2005) give an authoritative account of its actuarial usage and hint at applications to financial risk management.

Dynamic financial analysis (DFA), also referred to as *dynamic solvency testing* (DST), is a systematic approach, based on large-scale computer simulations, for the integrated financial modelling of non-life insurance and reinsurance companies aimed at assessing the risks and benefits associated with strategic decisions (see Blum 2005; Blum and Dacorogna 2004). An easy introduction can be found in Kaufmann, Gadmer and Klett (2001). The interested reader can consult the website of the Casualty Actuarial Society (www.casact.org/research/drm).

Appendix

A.1 Miscellaneous Definitions and Results

A.1.1 *Type of Distribution*

Definition A.1 (equality in type). Two rvs V and W (or their distributions) are said to be of the same type if there exist constants $a > 0$ and $b \in \mathbb{R}$ such that $V \stackrel{\mathrm{d}}{=} aW + b$.

In other words, distributions of the same type are obtained from one another by location and scale transformations.

A.1.2 *Generalized Inverses and Quantiles*

Let T be an *increasing* function, i.e. a function satisfying $y > x \implies T(y) \geqslant T(x)$, with strict inequality on the right-hand side for some pair $y > x$. Thus an increasing function may have *flat sections*; if we want to rule this out, we stipulate that T is *strictly increasing*, so $y > x \iff T(y) > T(x)$. We first note some useful facts concerning what happens when increasing transformations are applied to rvs.

Lemma A.2.

(i) *If X is an rv and T is increasing, then $\{X \leqslant x\} \subset \{T(X) \leqslant T(x)\}$ and*

$$P(T(X) \leqslant T(x)) = P(X \leqslant x) + P(T(X) = T(x),\ X > x). \tag{A.1}$$

(ii) *If F is the df of the rv X, then $P(F(X) \leqslant F(x)) = P(X \leqslant x)$.*

The second statement follows from (A.1) by noting that, for any x, the event given by $\{F(X) = F(x),\ X > x\}$ corresponds to a flat piece of the df F and thus has zero probability mass.

The generalized inverse of an increasing function T is defined to be $T^{\leftarrow}(y) = \inf\{x : T(x) \geqslant y\}$, where we use the convention $\inf \emptyset = \infty$. Strictly speaking, this generalized inverse is known as the *left-continuous* generalized inverse. The following basic properties may be verified quite easily.

Proposition A.3 (properties of the generalized inverse). *For T increasing, the following hold.*

(i) *$T^{\leftarrow}$ is an increasing, left-continuous function.*

(ii) *T is continuous $\iff$ $T^{\leftarrow}$ is strictly increasing.*

(iii) *T is strictly increasing $\iff$ $T^{\leftarrow}$ is continuous.*

For the remaining properties assume additionally that $T^{\leftarrow}(y) < \infty$.

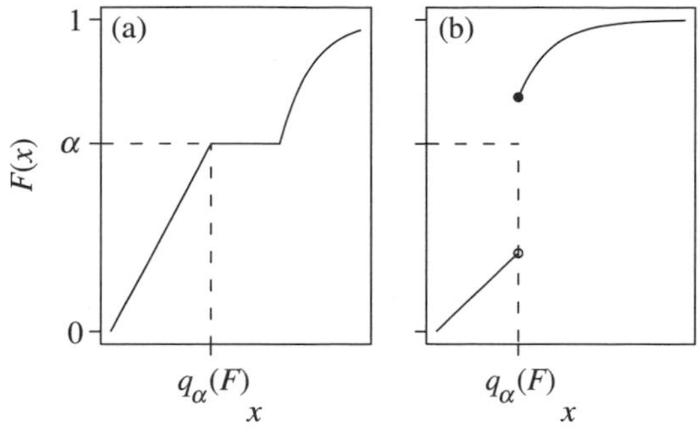

Figure A.1. Calculation of quantiles in tricky cases. The first case (a) is a continuous df, but the flat piece corresponds to an interval with zero probability mass. In the second case (b) there is an atom of probability mass such that, for X with df F, we have $P(X = q_\alpha(F)) > 0$.

(iv) *If* T *is right-continuous,* $T(x) \geqslant y \iff T^{\leftarrow}(y) \leqslant x$.

(v) $T^{\leftarrow} \circ T(x) \leqslant x$.

(vi) $T \circ T^{\leftarrow}(y) \geqslant y$.

(vii) T *is strictly increasing* $\Longrightarrow T^{\leftarrow} \circ T(x) = x$.

(viii) T *is continuous* $\Longrightarrow T \circ T^{\leftarrow}(y) = y$.

We apply the idea of generalized inverses to distribution functions. If F is a df, then the generalized inverse $F^{\leftarrow}$ is known as the quantile function of F. In this case, for $\alpha \in (0, 1)$, we also use the alternative notation $q_\alpha(F) = F^{\leftarrow}(\alpha)$ for the α-quantile of F. Figure A.1 illustrates the calculation of quantiles in two tricky cases.

In general, since a df need not be strictly increasing (part (a) of the figure), we have $F^{\leftarrow} \circ F(x) \leqslant x$, by Proposition A.3(v). But the values x, where $F^{\leftarrow} \circ F(x) \neq x$, correspond to flat pieces and have zero probability mass. That is, we have the following useful fact.

Proposition A.4. *If* X *is an rv with df* F, *then* $P(F^{\leftarrow} \circ F(X) = X) = 1$.

A.1.3 Karamata's Theorem

The following result for regularly varying functions is used in Chapter 7. For more details see Bingham, Goldie and Teugels (1987). Essentially, the result says that the slowly varying function can be taken outside the integral as if it were a constant. Note that the symbol "∼" indicates asymptotic equality here, i.e. if we write $a(x) \sim b(x)$ as $x \to x_0$, we mean $\lim_{x \to x_0} a(x)/b(x) = 1$.

Theorem A.5 (Karamata's Theorem). *Let* L *be a slowly varying function which is locally bounded in* $[x_0, \infty)$ *for some* $x_0 \geqslant 0$. *Then,*

(a) *for* $\kappa > -1$, $\displaystyle\int_{x_0}^{x} t^{\kappa} L(t)\,\mathrm{d}t \sim \frac{1}{\kappa + 1} x^{\kappa+1} L(x),\ x \to \infty,$

(b) *for* $\kappa < -1$, $\displaystyle\int_{x}^{\infty} t^{\kappa} L(t)\,\mathrm{d}t \sim -\frac{1}{\kappa + 1} x^{\kappa+1} L(x),\ x \to \infty.$

A.2 Probability Distributions

The gamma and beta functions appear in the definitions of a number of these distributions. The gamma function is

$$\Gamma(\alpha) = \int_0^\infty x^{\alpha-1} e^{-x}\, dx, \quad \alpha > 0, \tag{A.2}$$

and satisfies the useful recursive relationship $\Gamma(\alpha + 1) = \alpha\Gamma(\alpha)$. The β function is

$$\beta(a, b) = \int_0^1 x^{a-1}(1 - x)^{b-1}\, dx, \quad a, b > 0. \tag{A.3}$$

It is related to the gamma function by $\beta(a, b) = \Gamma(a)\Gamma(b)/\Gamma(a + b)$.

A.2.1 *Beta*

The rv X has a beta distribution, written $X \sim \text{Beta}(a, b)$, if its density is

$$f(x) = \frac{1}{\beta(a, b)} x^{a-1}(1 - x)^{b-1}, \quad 0 < x < 1,\ a, b > 0, \tag{A.4}$$

where $\beta(a, b)$ is the beta function in (A.3). The uniform distribution $X \sim U(0, 1)$ is obtained as a special case when $a = b = 1$. The mean and variance of the distribution are, respectively, $E(X) = \alpha/(\alpha + \beta)$ and $\text{var}(X) = (\alpha\beta)/((\alpha + \beta + 1)(\alpha + \beta)^2)$.

A.2.2 *Exponential*

The rv X has an exponential distribution, written $X \sim \text{Exp}(\lambda)$, if its density is

$$f(x) = \lambda \exp(-\lambda x), \quad x > 0,\ \lambda > 0. \tag{A.5}$$

The mean of this distribution is $E(X) = \lambda^{-1}$ and the variance is $\text{var}(X) = \lambda^{-2}$.

A.2.3 *F*

The rv X has an F distribution, written $X \sim F(\nu_1, \nu_2)$, if its density is

$$f(x) = \frac{1}{\beta(\frac{1}{2}\nu_1, \frac{1}{2}\nu_2)} \left(\frac{\nu_1}{\nu_2}\right)^{\nu_1/2} \frac{x^{(\nu_1-2)/2}}{(1 + \nu_1 x/\nu_2)^{(\nu_1+\nu_2)/2}}, \quad x > 0,\ \nu_1, \nu_2 > 0. \tag{A.6}$$

The mean of this distribution is $E(X) = \nu_2/(\nu_2 - 2)$ provided that $\nu_2 > 2$. Provided that $\nu_2 > 4$, the variance is

$$\text{var}(X) = 2\left(\frac{\nu_2}{\nu_2 - 2}\right)^2 \frac{\nu_1 + \nu_2 - 2}{\nu_1(\nu_1 - 4)}.$$

A.2.4 *Gamma*

The rv X has a gamma distribution, written $X \sim \text{Ga}(\alpha, \beta)$, if its density is

$$f(x) = \frac{\beta^\alpha}{\Gamma(\alpha)} x^{\alpha-1} \exp(-\beta x), \quad x > 0,\ \alpha > 0,\ \beta > 0, \tag{A.7}$$

where $\Gamma(\alpha)$ denotes the gamma function in (A.2). Using the recursive property of the gamma function, the mean and variance of the gamma distribution are easily calculated to be $E(X) = \alpha/\beta$ and $\mathrm{var}(X) = \alpha/\beta^2$. For fitting a multivariate t distribution using the EM approach of Section 3.2.4 it is also useful to know that $E(\ln X) = \psi(\alpha) - \ln(\beta)$, where $\psi(k) = \mathrm{d}\ln(\Gamma(k))/\mathrm{d}k$ is the digamma or psi function.

An exponential distribution is obtained in the special case when $\alpha = 1$. If $X \sim \mathrm{Ga}(\alpha, \beta)$ and $k > 0$, then $kX \sim \mathrm{Ga}(\alpha, \beta/k)$. For two independent gamma variates $X_1 \sim \mathrm{Ga}(\alpha_1, \beta)$ and $X_2 \sim \mathrm{Ga}(\alpha_2, \beta)$ we have that $X_1 + X_2 \sim \mathrm{Ga}(\alpha_1 + \alpha_2, \beta)$. Note also that, if $X \sim \mathrm{Ga}(\frac{1}{2}\nu, \frac{1}{2})$, then X has a chi-squared distribution with ν degrees of freedom, also written $X \sim \chi^2_\nu$.

A.2.5 Generalized Inverse Gaussian

The rv X has a generalized inverse Gaussian (GIG) distribution, written $X \sim N^-(\lambda, \chi, \psi)$, if its density is

$$f(x) = \frac{\chi^{-\lambda}(\sqrt{\chi\psi})^\lambda}{2K_\lambda(\sqrt{\chi\psi})} x^{\lambda-1} \exp(-\tfrac{1}{2}(\chi x^{-1} + \psi x)), \quad x > 0, \tag{A.8}$$

where K_λ denotes a modified Bessel function of the third kind with index λ and the parameters satisfy $\chi > 0$, $\psi \geqslant 0$ if $\lambda < 0$; $\chi > 0$, $\psi > 0$ if $\lambda = 0$; and $\chi \geqslant 0$, $\psi > 0$ if $\lambda > 0$. For more on this Bessel function see Abramowitz and Stegun (1965).

The GIG density actually contains the gamma and inverse gamma densities as special limiting cases, corresponding to $\chi = 0$ and $\psi = 0$, respectively. In these cases (A.8) must be interpreted as a limit, which can be evaluated using the asymptotic relations $K_\lambda(x) \sim \Gamma(\lambda)2^{\lambda-1}x^{-\lambda}$ as $x \to 0+$ for $\lambda > 0$ and $K_\lambda(x) \sim \Gamma(-\lambda)2^{-\lambda-1}x^\lambda$ as $x \to 0+$ for $\lambda < 0$. The fact that $K_\lambda(x) = K_{-\lambda}(x)$ is also useful. In this way it can be verified that, for $\lambda > 0$ and $\chi = 0$, $X \sim \mathrm{Ga}(\lambda, \frac{1}{2}\psi)$. If $\lambda < 0$ and $\psi = 0$, we have $X \sim \mathrm{Ig}(-\lambda, \frac{1}{2}\chi)$. The case $\lambda = -\frac{1}{2}$ is known as the inverse Gaussian distribution. Note that, in general, if $Y \sim N^-(\lambda, \chi, \psi)$, then $1/Y \sim N^-(-\lambda, \psi, \chi)$.

For the non-limiting case when $\chi > 0$ and $\psi > 0$ it may be calculated that

$$E(X^\alpha) = \left(\frac{\chi}{\psi}\right)^{\alpha/2} \frac{K_{\lambda+\alpha}(\sqrt{\chi\psi})}{K_\lambda(\sqrt{\chi\psi})}, \quad \alpha \in \mathbb{R}, \tag{A.9}$$

$$E(\ln X) = \left.\frac{\mathrm{d}E(X^\alpha)}{\mathrm{d}\alpha}\right|_{\alpha=0}. \tag{A.10}$$

A.2.6 Inverse Gamma

The rv X has an inverse gamma distribution, written $X \sim \mathrm{Ig}(\alpha, \beta)$, if its density is

$$f(x) = \frac{\beta^\alpha}{\Gamma(\alpha)} x^{-(\alpha+1)} \exp(-\beta/x), \quad x > 0,\ \alpha > 0,\ \beta > 0. \tag{A.11}$$

Note that if $Y \sim \mathrm{Ga}(\alpha, \beta)$, then $1/Y \sim \mathrm{Ig}(\alpha, \beta)$. Provided that $\alpha > 1$, the mean is $E(X) = \beta/(\alpha - 1)$, and provided that $\alpha > 2$ the variance is $\mathrm{var}(X) = \beta^2/((\alpha - 1)^2(\alpha - 2))$. Moreover, $E(\ln X) = \ln(\beta) - \psi(\alpha)$.

A.2.7 *Negative Binomial*

The rv N has a negative binomial distribution with parameters $\alpha > 0$ and $0 < p < 1$, written $X \sim \text{NB}(\alpha, p)$, if its probability mass function is

$$P(N = k) = \binom{\alpha + k - 1}{k} p^{\alpha}(1-p)^k, \quad k = 0, 1, 2, \dots, \tag{A.12}$$

where $\binom{x}{k}$ for $x \in \mathbb{R}$ and $k \in \mathbb{N}_0$ denotes an extended binomial coefficient defined by $\binom{x}{0} = 1$ and

$$\binom{x}{k} = \frac{x(x-1)\cdots(x-k+1)}{k!}, \quad k > 0.$$

The moments of this distribution are

$$E(N) = \alpha(1-p)/p \quad \text{and} \quad \text{var}(N) = \alpha(1-p)/p^2.$$

For $\alpha = r \in \mathbb{N}$ the rv $N + r$ represents the waiting time until the rth success in independent Bernoulli trials with success probability p, i.e. the total number of trials that are required until we have r successes. For $\alpha = 1$ the rv $N + 1$ is said to have a geometric distribution.

A.2.8 *Pareto*

The rv X has a Pareto distribution, written $X \sim \text{Pa}(\alpha, \kappa)$, if its df is

$$F(x) = 1 - \left(\frac{\kappa}{\kappa + x}\right)^{\alpha}, \quad \alpha, \kappa > 0, \ x \geqslant 0. \tag{A.13}$$

Provided that $\alpha > n$, the moments of this distribution are given by

$$E(X^n) = \frac{\kappa^n n!}{\prod_{i=1}^{n}(\alpha - i)}.$$

A.2.9 *Stable*

The rv X has an α-stable distribution, written $X \sim \text{St}(\alpha, \beta, \gamma, \delta)$, if its characteristic function is

$$\phi(t) = E\exp(\mathrm{i}tX) = \begin{cases} \exp(-\gamma^{\alpha}|t|^{\alpha}(1 - \mathrm{i}\beta\,\text{sign}(t)\tan(\pi/2)\alpha) + \mathrm{i}\delta t), & \alpha \neq 1, \\ \exp(-\gamma|t|(1 + \mathrm{i}\beta\,\text{sign}(t)(2/\pi)\ln|t|) + \mathrm{i}\delta t), & \alpha = 1, \end{cases} \tag{A.14}$$

where $\alpha \in (0, 2]$, $\beta \in [-1, 1]$, $\gamma > 0$ and $\delta \in \mathbb{R}$. Note that there are various alternative parametrizations of the stable distributions and we use a parametrization of Nolan (2005, Definition 1.8). The case $X \sim \text{St}(\alpha, 1, \gamma, 0)$ for $\alpha < 1$ gives a distribution on the positive half-axis, which we refer to as a positive stable distribution.

A simulation algorithm for a standardized variate $Z \sim \text{St}(\alpha, \beta, 1, 0)$ is given in Nolan (2005, Theorem 1.19). In the case where $\alpha \neq 1$, $X = \delta + \gamma Z$ has a $\text{St}(\alpha, \beta, \gamma, \delta)$ distribution; the case $\alpha = 1$ is more complicated.

A.3 Likelihood Inference

This appendix summarizes the mechanics of performing likelihood inference, but omits theoretical details. A good starting reference for the theory is Casella and Berger (2002), which we refer to in this appendix where relevant. Other useful books include Serfling (1980), Lehmann (1983), Schervish (1995) and Stuart, Ord and Arnold (1999), all of which give details concerning the famous *regularity conditions* that are required for the asymptotic statements.

A.3.1 Maximum Likelihood Estimators

Suppose that the random vector $\boldsymbol{X} = (X_1, \dots, X_n)'$ has joint probability density (or mass function) in some parametric family $f_{\boldsymbol{X}}(\boldsymbol{x}; \boldsymbol{\theta})$, indexed by a parameter vector $\boldsymbol{\theta} = (\theta_1, \dots, \theta_p)'$ in a parameter space $\boldsymbol{\Theta}$. We consider our data to be a realization of $\boldsymbol{X}$ for some unknown value of θ.

The *likelihood function* for the parameter vector $\boldsymbol{\theta}$ given the data is $L(\boldsymbol{\theta}; \boldsymbol{X}) = f_{\boldsymbol{X}}(\boldsymbol{X}; \boldsymbol{\theta})$ and the maximum likelihood estimator (MLE) $\hat{\boldsymbol{\theta}}$ is the value of $\boldsymbol{\theta}$ maximizing $L(\boldsymbol{\theta}; \boldsymbol{X})$, or equivalently the value maximizing the *log-likelihood function* $l(\boldsymbol{\theta}; \boldsymbol{X}) = \ln L(\boldsymbol{\theta}; \boldsymbol{X})$. We will also write this estimator as $\hat{\boldsymbol{\theta}}_n$ when we want to emphasize its dependence on the sample size n.

For large n we expect that the estimate $\hat{\theta}_n$ should be *close* to the true value $\boldsymbol{\theta}$, and various well-known asymptotic results give information about the quality of the estimator in large samples. In describing these results we consider the classical situation where $\boldsymbol{X}$ is assumed to be a vector of *iid components* with univariate density f so that

$$\ln L(\boldsymbol{\theta}; \boldsymbol{X}) = \ln \prod_{i=1}^{n} f(X_i; \boldsymbol{\theta}) = \sum_{i=1}^{n} \ln L(\boldsymbol{\theta}; X_i).$$

A.3.2 Asymptotic Results: Scalar Parameter

We consider the case when $p = 1$ and we have a single parameter θ. Under suitable *regularity conditions* (see, for example, Casella and Berger 2002, p. 516), $\hat{\theta}_n$ may be shown to be a *consistent* estimator of θ (i.e. tending to θ in probability as the sample size n is increased). Notable among the regularity conditions are that θ should be an *identifiable* parameter ($\theta \neq \tilde{\theta} \Rightarrow f(x; \theta) \neq f(x; \tilde{\theta})$), the true parameter θ should be an interior point of the parameter space Θ, and that the support of $f(x; \theta)$ should not depend on θ.

Under stronger regularity conditions (see again Casella and Berger 2002, p. 516), $\hat{\theta}_n$ may be shown to be an *asymptotically efficient* estimator of θ, so it satisfies

$$\sqrt{n}(\hat{\theta}_n - \theta) \xrightarrow{\mathrm{d}} N(0, I(\theta)^{-1}), \tag{A.15}$$

where $I(\theta)$ denotes the *Fisher information of an observation*, defined by

$$I(\theta) = E\left(\frac{\partial}{\partial\theta} \ln L(\theta; X)\right)^2. \tag{A.16}$$

Under the regularity conditions, the Fisher information can generally also be calculated as

$$I(\theta) = -E\left(\frac{\partial^2}{\partial\theta^2} \ln L(\theta; X)\right). \tag{A.17}$$

Asymptotic efficiency entails both asymptotic normality and consistency. Moreover, it implies that, in a large enough sample, $\text{var}(\hat{\theta}) \approx 1/(nI(\theta))$, where the right-hand side is the so-called Cramér–Rao lower bound, which is a lower bound for the variance of an unbiased estimator of θ constructed from an iid sample $X_1, \dots, X_n$. The MLE is efficient in the sense that it attains this lowest possible bound asymptotically.

A.3.3 Asymptotic Results: Vector of Parameters

When $p > 1$ and we have a vector of parameters to estimate, similar results apply. The ML estimator $\hat{\boldsymbol{\theta}}_n$ of $\boldsymbol{\theta}$ is asymptotically efficient in the sense that, as $n \to \infty$ and under suitable regularity conditions,

$$\sqrt{n}(\hat{\boldsymbol{\theta}}_n - \boldsymbol{\theta}) \xrightarrow{\text{d}} N_p(\mathbf{0}, I(\boldsymbol{\theta})^{-1}), \tag{A.18}$$

where $I(\boldsymbol{\theta})$ denotes the expected Fisher information *matrix* for a single observation, given, in analogy to (A.16) and (A.17), by

$$I(\boldsymbol{\theta}) = E\left(\frac{\partial}{\partial\boldsymbol{\theta}} \ln L(\boldsymbol{\theta}; X) \frac{\partial}{\partial\boldsymbol{\theta}'} \ln L(\boldsymbol{\theta}; X)\right) = -E\left(\frac{\partial^2}{\partial\boldsymbol{\theta}\partial\boldsymbol{\theta}'} \ln L(\boldsymbol{\theta}; X)\right).$$

The notation employed here should be taken to mean a matrix with components

$$I(\boldsymbol{\theta})_{ij} = E\left(\frac{\partial}{\partial\theta_i} \ln L(\boldsymbol{\theta}; X) \frac{\partial}{\partial\theta_j} \ln L(\boldsymbol{\theta}; X)\right) = -E\left(\frac{\partial^2}{\partial\theta_i\partial\theta_j} \ln L(\boldsymbol{\theta}; X)\right).$$

The convergence result (A.18) implies that, for n sufficiently large, we have

$$\hat{\boldsymbol{\theta}}_n \sim N_p(\boldsymbol{\theta}, n^{-1} I(\boldsymbol{\theta})^{-1}), \tag{A.19}$$

and this can be used to construct asymptotic confidence regions for $\boldsymbol{\theta}$ or intervals for any component θ_j. In practice, it is often easier to approximate $I(\boldsymbol{\theta})$ with the *observed Fisher information matrix*

$$\bar{I}(\boldsymbol{\theta}) = -\frac{1}{n}\sum_{i=1}^{n} \frac{\partial^2}{\partial\boldsymbol{\theta}\partial\boldsymbol{\theta}'} \ln L(\boldsymbol{\theta}; X_i)$$

for whatever realization of $\boldsymbol{X}$ has been obtained. This should converge to the expected information matrix by the law of large numbers and it has been suggested that in some situations this may even lead to more accurate inference (Efron and Hinkley 1978). In either case, the information matrices depend on the unknown parameters of the model and are usually estimated by taking $I(\hat{\boldsymbol{\theta}})$ or $\bar{I}(\hat{\boldsymbol{\theta}})$.

A.3.4 Wald Test and Confidence Intervals

From (A.19) we have that, for n sufficiently large,

$$Z := \frac{\hat{\theta}_j - \theta_j}{\mathrm{se}(\hat{\theta}_j)} \sim N(0, 1), \tag{A.20}$$

where $\mathrm{se}(\hat{\theta}_j)$ denotes an *asymptotic standard error* (estimate of the asymptotic standard deviation) for $\hat{\theta}_j$, given by

$$\mathrm{se}(\hat{\theta}_j) = \sqrt{n^{-1} I(\hat{\boldsymbol{\theta}})^{-1}_{jj}} \text{ or } \sqrt{n^{-1} \bar{I}(\hat{\boldsymbol{\theta}})^{-1}_{jj}}.$$

Equation (A.20) can be used to test the null hypothesis $H_0 : \theta_j = \theta_{j,0}$ for some value of interest $\theta_{j,0}$ against the alternative $H_1 : \theta_j \neq \theta_{j,0}$. For an asymptotic test of size α we would reject H_0 if $|Z| \geqslant \Phi^{-1}(1 - \frac{1}{2}\alpha)$.

An asymptotic $100(1-\alpha)\%$ *confidence interval* for θ_j consists of those values $\theta_{j,0}$ for which the null hypothesis is not rejected and it is given by

$$(\hat{\theta}_j - \mathrm{se}(\hat{\theta}_j)\Phi^{-1}(1 - \tfrac{1}{2}\alpha), \hat{\theta}_j + \mathrm{se}(\hat{\theta}_j)\Phi^{-1}(1 - \tfrac{1}{2}\alpha)). \tag{A.21}$$

A.3.5 Likelihood Ratio Test and Confidence Intervals

Now consider testing the null hypothesis $H_0 : \boldsymbol{\theta} \in \Theta_0$ against the alternative $H_1 : \boldsymbol{\theta} \in \Theta_0^{\mathrm{c}}$, where $\Theta_0 \subset \Theta$. We consider the *likelihood ratio test statistic*

$$\lambda(\boldsymbol{X}) = \frac{\sup_{\boldsymbol{\theta} \in \Theta_0} L(\boldsymbol{\theta}; \boldsymbol{X})}{\sup_{\boldsymbol{\theta} \in \Theta} L(\boldsymbol{\theta}; \boldsymbol{X})}$$

and assume, as before, that $X_1, \dots, X_n$ are iid and that appropriate *regularity conditions* apply. Under the null hypothesis it can be shown that, as $n \to \infty$, $-2 \ln \lambda(\boldsymbol{X}) \sim \chi^2_\nu$, where the degrees-of-freedom parameter ν of the chi-squared distribution is essentially given by the number of free parameters specified by Θ minus the number of free parameters specified by the null hypothesis $\boldsymbol{\theta} \in \Theta_0$.

For example, suppose that we partition $\boldsymbol{\theta}$ so that $\boldsymbol{\theta}' = (\boldsymbol{\theta}_1', \boldsymbol{\theta}_2')$, where $\boldsymbol{\theta}_1$ has dimension q and $\boldsymbol{\theta}_2$ has dimension $p - q$. We wish to test $H_0 : \boldsymbol{\theta}_1 = \boldsymbol{\theta}_{1,0}$ against $H_1 : \boldsymbol{\theta}_1 \neq \boldsymbol{\theta}_{1,0}$. Writing the likelihood as $L(\boldsymbol{\theta}_1, \boldsymbol{\theta}_2)$, the likelihood ratio test statistic satisfies

$$-2 \ln \lambda(\boldsymbol{X}) = -2(\ln L(\boldsymbol{\theta}_{1,0}, \hat{\boldsymbol{\theta}}_{2,0}; \boldsymbol{X}) - \ln L(\hat{\boldsymbol{\theta}}_1, \hat{\boldsymbol{\theta}}_2; \boldsymbol{X})) \sim \chi^2_q,$$

asymptotically, where $\hat{\boldsymbol{\theta}}_1$ and $\hat{\boldsymbol{\theta}}_2$ are the *unconstrained* MLEs of $\boldsymbol{\theta}_1$ and $\boldsymbol{\theta}_2$, and $\hat{\boldsymbol{\theta}}_{2,0}$ is the *constrained* MLE of $\boldsymbol{\theta}_2$ under the null hypothesis. We would reject H_0 if $-2 \ln \lambda(\boldsymbol{X}) > c_{q,1-\alpha}$, where $c_{q,1-\alpha}$ is the $(1-\alpha)$-quantile of the χ^2_q distribution.

An asymptotic $100(1-\alpha)\%$ confidence set for $\boldsymbol{\theta}_1$ consists of the values $\boldsymbol{\theta}_{1,0}$ for which the null hypothesis $H_0 : \boldsymbol{\theta}_1 = \boldsymbol{\theta}_{1,0}$ is not rejected, that is

$$\{\boldsymbol{\theta}_{1,0} : \ln L(\boldsymbol{\theta}_{1,0}, \hat{\boldsymbol{\theta}}_{2,0}; \boldsymbol{x}) \geqslant \ln L(\hat{\boldsymbol{\theta}}_1, \hat{\boldsymbol{\theta}}_2; \boldsymbol{x}) - 0.5 c_{q,1-\alpha}\}.$$

In particular, if $q = 1$, so that we are interested only in θ_1, we get the confidence interval

$$\{\theta_{1,0} : \ln L(\theta_{1,0}, \hat{\boldsymbol{\theta}}_{2,0}; \boldsymbol{x}) \geqslant \ln L(\hat{\theta}_1, \hat{\boldsymbol{\theta}}_2; \boldsymbol{x}) - 0.5 c_{1,1-\alpha}\}. \tag{A.22}$$

Note that such an interval will, in general, be asymmetric about the MLE $\hat{\theta}_1$, in the sense that the distance from the MLE to the upper and lower bounds will be different. This is in contrast to the Wald interval in (A.21), which is rigidly symmetric.

The curve $(\theta_{1,0}, \ln L(\theta_{1,0}, \hat{\boldsymbol{\theta}}_{2,0}; \boldsymbol{x}))$ is sometimes known as the *profile log-likelihood* curve for θ_1 and attains its maximum at $\hat{\theta}_1$.

A.3.6 Akaike Information Criterion

The likelihood ratio test is applicable to the comparison of nested models, i.e. situations where one model forms a special case of a more general model when certain parameter values are constrained. We often encounter situations where we would like to compare non-nested models with possibly quite different numbers of parameters.

Suppose we have m models $M_1, \dots, M_m$ and that model j has k_j parameters denoted by $\boldsymbol{\theta}_j = (\theta_{j1}, \dots, \theta_{jk_j})'$ and a likelihood function $L_j(\boldsymbol{\theta}_j; \boldsymbol{X})$. In Akaike's approach we choose the model minimizing

$$\text{AIC}(M_j) = -2 \ln L_j(\hat{\boldsymbol{\theta}}_j; \boldsymbol{X}) + 2k_j,$$

where $\hat{\boldsymbol{\theta}}_j$ denotes the MLE of $\boldsymbol{\theta}_j$. The AIC number essentially imposes a penalty equal to the number of model parameters k_j on the value of the log-likelihood at the maximum. The model favoured is the one for which the penalized log-likelihood $\ln L_j(\hat{\boldsymbol{\theta}}_j; \boldsymbol{X}) - k_j$ is largest. There are alternatives to the AIC, such as the Bayesian information criterion (BIC) of Schwartz, which impose different penalties for the number of parameters. See Burnham and Anderson (2002) for more about model comparison using these criteria.

References

Abdous, B., K. Ghoudi and A. Khoudraji. 1999. Non parametric estimation of the limit dependence function of multivariate extremes. *Extremes* 2(3):245–268.

Abraham, B. and J. Ledolter. 1983. *Statistical Methods for Forecasting*. Wiley.

Abramowitz, M. and I. A. Stegun (eds). 1965. *Handbook of Mathematical Functions*. New York: Dover.

Acerbi, C. 2002. Spectral measures of risk: a coherent representation of subjective risk aversion. *Journal of Banking and Finance* 26(7):1505–1518.

Acerbi, C. and D. Tasche. 2002. On the coherence of expected shortfall. *Journal of Banking and Finance* 26:1487–1503.

Albanese, C. 1997. Credit exposure, diversification risk and coherent VaR. Preprint, Department of Mathematics, University of Toronto.

Alexander, C. 2001. *Market Models: A Guide to Financial Data Analysis*. Wiley.

Allen, F. and D. Gale. 2000. Financial contagion. *Journal of Political Economy* 108:1–33.

Almgren, R. and N. Chriss. 2001. Optimal execution of portfolio transactions. *Journal of Risk* 3(2):5–39.

Alsina, C., M. J. Frank and B. Schweizer. 2005. *Associative Functions on Intervals: A Primer of Triangular Norms*. Forthcoming.

Altman, E. L. 1993. *Corporate Financial Distress and Bankruptcy*. Wiley.

Altman, E. L. and H. Suggitt. 2000. Default rates in the syndicated loan market: a mortality analysis. *Journal of Banking and Finance* 24:229–253.

Andersen, L. and J. Sidenius. 2004. Extensions to the Gaussian copula: random recovery and random factor loadings. *Journal of Credit Risk* 1:29–70.

Andersen, P. K., Ø. Borgan, R. Gill and N. Keiding. 1993. *Statistical Models Based on Counting Processes*. Springer.

Ané, T. and H. Geman. 2000. Order flow, transaction clock, and normality of asset returns. *Journal of Finance* 55:2259–2284.

Artzner, P. and F. Delbaen. 1995. Default risk insurance and incomplete markets. *Mathematical Finance* 5:187–195.

Artzner, P., F. Delbaen, J. M. Eber and D. Heath. 1997. Thinking coherently. *Risk* 10(11):68–71.

——. 1999. Coherent measures of risk. *Mathematical Finance* 9:203–228.

Artzner, P., F. Delbaen, J.-M. Eber, D. Heath and H. Ku. 2005. Coherent multiperiod risk-adjusted values and Bellman's principle. *Annals of Operations Research*. Forthcoming.

Asmussen, S. 2000. *Ruin Probabilities*. World Scientific.

Asmussen, S., K. Binswanger and B. Højgaard. 2000. Rare events simulation for heavy-tailed distributions. *Bernoulli* 6(2):303–322.

Atkinson, A. C. 1982. The simulation of generalized inverse Gaussian and hyperbolic random variables. *SIAM Journal on Scientific Computing* 3(4):502–515.

Attanasio, O. P. 1991. Risk, time varying second moments and market efficiency. *Review of Economic Studies* 58:479–494.

Aubin, J.-P. 1979. *Mathematical Methods of Game and Economic Theory*. Amsterdam: North-Holland.

Bailey, A. L. 1945. A generalized theory of credibility. *Proceedings of the Casualty Actuarial Society* 32:13–20.

Balkema, A. A. and P. Embrechts. 2004. Multivariate excess distributions. Preprint, ETH Zurich.

Balkema, A. A. and L. de Haan. 1974. Residual life time at great age. *Annals of Probability* 2:792–804.

Balkema, A. A. and S. I. Resnick. 1977. Max-infinite divisibility. *Journal of Applied Probability* 14:309–319.

Bangia, A., F. X. Diebold, A. Kronimus, C. Schlagen and T. Schuermann. 2002. Ratings migration and the business cycle, with application to credit portfolio stress testing. *Journal of Banking and Finance* 26:445–474.

Bank, P. and D. Baum. 2004. Hedging and portfolio optimization in financial markets with a large trader. *Mathematical Finance* 14:1–18.

Baringhaus, L. 1991. Testing for spherical symmetry of a multivariate distribution. *Annals of Statistics* 19(2):899–917.

Barndorff-Nielsen, O. E. 1978. Hyperbolic distributions and distributions on hyperbolae. *Scandinavian Journal of Statistics* 5:151–157.

——. 1997. Normal inverse Gaussian distributions and stochastic volatility modelling. *Scandinavian Journal of Statistics* 24:1–13.

Barndorff-Nielsen, O. E. and P. Blæsild. 1981. Hyperbolic distributions and ramifications: contributions to theory and application. In *Statistical Distributions in Scientific Work* (ed. C. Taillie, G. Patil and B. Baldessari), vol. 4, pp. 19–44. Dordrecht: Reidel.

Barndorff-Nielsen, O. E. and N. Shephard. 2005. *Continuous Time Approach to Financial Volatility*. Cambridge University Press. Forthcoming.

Barone-Adesi, G., F. Bourgoin and K. Giannopoulos. 1998. Don't look back. *Risk* 11(8):100–103.

Basak, S. and A. Shapiro. 2001. Value-at-Risk based risk management: optimal policies and asset prices. *Review of Financial Studies* 14(2):371–405.

Basel Committee on Banking Supervision. 2003. The 2002 loss data collection exercise for operational risk: summary of the data collected. Risk Management Group, Bank of International Settlements. (Available from www.bis.org/bcbs/.)

——. 2004. International convergence of capital measurement and capital standards. A revised framework. Bank of International Settlements. (Available from www.bis.org/bcbs/.)

Bauwens, L., S. Laurent and J. V. K. Rombouts. 2005. Multivariate GARCH models: a survey. *Journal of Applied Economics*. Forthcoming.

Baxter, M. and A. Rennie. 1996. *Financial Calculus*. Cambridge University Press.

Becherer, D. 2004. Utility indifference hedging and valuation via reaction–diffusion systems. *Proceedings of the Royal Society of London, Series A* 460:27–51.

Becherer, D. and M. Schweizer. 2005. Classical solutions to reaction diffusion systems for hedging problems with interacting Itô and point processes. *Annals of Applied Probability* 15(2). Forthcoming.

Bedford, T. and R. Cooke. 2001. *Probabilistic Risk Analysis: Foundations and Methods*. Cambridge University Press.

Beirlant, J., Y. Goegebeur, T. Segers and J. L. Teugels. 2004. *Statistics of Extremes: Theory and Applications*. Wiley.

Bélanger, A., S. Shreve and D. Wong. 2004. A general framework for pricing credit risk. *Mathematical Finance* 14:317–350.

Bening, V. E. and V. Yu. Korolev. 2002. *Generalized Poisson Models and Their Applications in Insurance and Finance*. Utrecht: VSP.

Beran, J. 1979. Testing for ellipsoidal symmetry of a multivariate density. *Annals of Statistics* 7(1):150–162.

Berk, J. B. 1997. Necessary conditions for the CAPM. *Journal of Economic Theory* 73:245–257.

Berkes, I., L. Horváth and P. Kokoszka. 2003. GARCH processes: structure and estimation. *Bernoulli* 9:201–228.

Berkowitz, J. 2001. Testing the accuracy of density forecasts, applications to risk management. *Journal of Business and Economic Statistics* 19:465–474.

——. 2002. Testing distributions. *Risk* 15(6):77–80.

Berkowitz, J. and J. O'Brien. 2002. How accurate are Value-at-Risk models at commercial banks? *Journal of Finance* 57:1093–1112.

Berndt, A., R. Douglas, D. Duffie, F. Ferguson and D. Schranz. 2004. Measuring default risk premia from default swap rates and EDFs. Preprint, Stanford University.

Berndt, E. K., B. H. Hall, R. E. Hall and J. A. Hausman. 1974. Estimation and inference in nonlinear structural models. *Annals of Economic and Social Measurement* 3:653–665.

Bernstein, P. L. 1998. *Against the Gods: The Remarkable Story of Risk*. Wiley.

Bibby, B. M. and M. Sørensen. 2003. Hyperbolic processes in finance. In *Handbook of Heavy Tailed Distributions in Finance* (ed. S. T. Rachev), pp. 211–248. Amsterdam: Elsevier.

Bickel, P. J. and K. A. Doksum. 2001. *Mathematical Statistics: Basic Ideas and Selected Topics*, 2nd edn, vol. 1. Upper Saddle River, NJ: Prentice Hall.

Bielecki, T. and M. Rutkowski. 2002. *Credit Risk: Modeling, Valuation, and Hedging*. Springer.

Bielecki, T., M. Jeanblanc and M. Rutkowski. 2004. Hedging of defaultable claims. In *Paris–Princeton Lectures on Mathematical Finance, 2003* (ed. R. A. Carmona et al.). Springer.

Billingsley, P. 1995. *Probability and Measure*, 3rd edn. Wiley.

Bingham, N. H. and R. Kiesel. 1998. *Risk-Neutral Valuation*. Springer.

——. 2002. Semi-parametric modelling in finance: theoretical foundations. *Quantitative Finance* 2:241–250.

Bingham, N. H., C. M. Goldie and J. L. Teugels. 1987. *Regular Variation*. Cambridge University Press.

Björk, T. 1998. *Arbitrage Theory in Continuous Time*. Oxford University Press.

Black, F. and J. Cox. 1976. Valuing corporate securities: some effects of bond indenture provisions. *Journal of Finance* 31(2):351–367.

Black, F. and M. Scholes. 1973. The pricing of options and corporate liabilities. *Journal of Political Economy* 81(3):637–654.

Blæsild, P. 1981. The two-dimensional hyperbolic distribution and related distributions, with an application to Johannsen's bean data. *Biometrika* 68(1):251–263.

Blæsild, P. and J. L. Jensen. 1981. Multivariate distributions of hyperbolic type. In *Statistical Distributions in Scientific Work* (ed. C. Taillie, G. Patil and B. Baldessari), vol. 4, pp. 45–66. Dordrecht: Reidel.

Bluhm, C., L. Overbeck and C. Wagner. 2002. *An Introduction to Credit Risk Modeling*. London: Chapman & Hall.

Blum, P. 2005. On some mathematical aspects of dynamic financial analysis. PhD thesis, ETH Zurich.

Blum, P. and M. Dacorogna. 2004. DFA—dynamic financial analysis. In *Encyclopedia of Actuarial Science* (ed. J. L. Teugels and B. Sundt), pp. 505–519. Wiley.

Bodnar, G. M., G. Hyat and R. Marston. 1999. Wharton 1998 survey of risk management by US non-financial firms. *Financial Management* 27(4): 70–91.

Bohn, J. R. 2000. An empirical assessment of a simple contingent-claims model for the valuation of risky debt. *Journal of Risk Finance* 1(4):55–77.

Bollerslev, T. 1986. Generalized autoregressive conditional heteroskedasticity. *Journal of Econometrics* 31:307–327.

——. 1990. Modelling the coherence in short-run nominal exchange rates: a multivariate generalized ARCH approach. *Review of Economics and Statistics* 72:498–505.

Bollerslev, T., T. Chou and K. Kroner. 1992. ARCH modelling in finance: a selective review of theory and empirical evidence. *Journal of Econometrics* 52:201–224.

Bollerslev, T., R. F. Engle and D. B. Nelson. 1994. ARCH models. In *Handbook of Econometrics* (ed. R. F. Engle and D. L. McFadden), vol. 4, pp. 2959–3038. Amsterdam: North-Holland.

Bollerslev, T., R. F. Engle and J. M. Wooldridge. 1988. A capital-asset pricing model with time-varying covariances. *Journal of Political Economy* 96:116–131.

Bougerol, P. and N. Picard. 1992. Stationarity of GARCH processes and of some non-negative time series. *Journal of Econometrics* 52:115–127.

Bowers, N. L., H. U. Gerber, J. C. Hickman, D. A. Jones and C. J. Nesbitt. 1986. *Actuarial Mathematics*. Itasca, IL: Society of Actuaries.

Box, G. E. P. and G. M. Jenkins. 1970. *Time Series Analysis: Forecasting and Control*. San Francisco, CA: Holden-Day.

Box, G. E. P. and D. A. Pierce. 1970. Distribution of residual autocorrelations in autoregressive-integrated moving average time series models. *Journal of the American Statistical Association* 65:1509–1526.

Boyle, P. and F. Boyle. 2001. *Derivatives. The Tools that Changed Finance*. London: Risk Waters Group.

Brand, L. and R. Bahr. 2001. Ratings performance 2000: default, transition, recovery, and spreads. New York: Standard & Poor's.

Brandt, A. 1986. The stochastic equation $y_{n+1} = a_n y_n + b_n$ with stationary coefficients. *Advances in Applied Probability* 18:211–220.

Brealey, R. and S. Myers. 2000. *Principles of Corporate Finance*, 6th edn. New York: McGraw-Hill.

Breiman, L. 1965. On some limit theorems similar to the arc-sin law. *Theory of Probability and Its Applications* 10:323–331.

Brémaud, P. 1981. *Point Processes and Queues: Martingale Dynamics*. Springer.

Brennan, M. J. and L. Trigeorgis. 2000. *Project Flexibility, Agency, and Competition*. Oxford University Press.

Breslow, N. and D. G. Clayton. 1993. Approximate inference in generalized linear mixed models. *Journal of the American Statistical Association* 88:9–25.

Breymann, W., A. Dias and P. Embrechts. 2003. Dependence structures for multivariate high-frequency data in finance. *Quantitative Finance* 3:1–14.

Briys, E. and F. de Varenne. 2001. *Insurance. From Underwriting to Derivatives. Asset Liabilitiy Management in Insurance Companies*. Wiley.

Brockwell, P. J. and R. A. Davis. 1991. *Time Series: Theory and Methods*, 2nd edn. Springer.

——. 2002. *Introduction to Time Series and Forecasting*, 2nd edn. Springer.

Brooks, C., S. P. Burke and G. Persand. 2001. Benchmarks and the accuracy of GARCH model estimation. *International Journal of Forecasting* 17:45–56.

Brummelhuis, R. G. M. and R. Kaufmann. 2004. Time scaling for GARCH(1,1) and AR(1)–GARCH(1,1) processes. Preprint, ETH Zurich.

Bühlmann, H. 1967. Experience rating and credibility. *ASTIN Bulletin* 4(3):199–207.

——. 1968. Experience rating and credibility. *ASTIN Bulletin* 5(2):157–165.

——. 1970. *Mathematical Methods in Risk Theory*. Springer.

——. 1971. Credibility procedures. In *Proceedings of the 6th Berkeley Symposium on Probability and Statistics*, vol. 1, pp. 515–525. Berkeley, CA: University of California Press.

Bühlmann, H. 1984. Numerical evaluation of the compound Poisson distribution: recursion or the fast Fourier transform? *Scandinavian Actuarial Journal*, pp. 116–126.

Bühlmann, H. and A. Gisler. 2005. *A Course in Credibility Theory and its Applications*. Springer. Forthcoming.

Bühlmann, P. and A. J. McNeil. 2002. An algorithm for nonparametric GARCH modelling. *Journal of Computational Statistics and Data Analysis* 40:665–683.

Burnham, K. P. and D. R. Anderson. 2002. *Model Selection and Multimodel Inference: A Practical Information-Theoretic Approach*. Springer.

Burtschell, X., J. Gregory and J.-P. Laurent. 2005. A comparative analysis of CDO pricing models. Working paper, BNP Paribas and ISFA, University of Lyon.

Cambanis, S., S. Huang and G. Simons. 1981. On the theory of elliptically contoured distributions. *Journal of Multivariate Analysis* 11:368–385.

Campbell, J. Y., A. W. Lo and A. C. MacKinlay. 1997. *The Econometrics of Financial Markets*. Princeton University Press.

Casella, G. and R. L. Berger. 2002. *Statistical Inference*. Pacific Grove, CA: Duxbury.

Chamberlain, G. 1983. A characterization of the distributions that imply mean-variance utility functions. *Journal of Economic Theory* 29:185–201.

Chatfield, C. 1996. *The Analysis of Time Series: An Introduction*, 5th edn. London: Chapman & Hall.

Chavez-Demoulin, V. and P. Embrechts. 2004. Smooth extremal models in insurance and finance. *Journal of Risk and Insurance* 71(2):183–199.

Chavez-Demoulin, V., A. C. Davison and A. J. McNeil. 2005. A point process approach to Value-at-Risk estimation. *Quantitative Finance*. Forthcoming.

Chavez-Demoulin, V., P. Embrechts and J. Nešlehová. 2005. Quantitative models for operational risk: extremes, dependence and aggregation. Preprint, ETH Zurich.

Chekhlov, H., S. Uryasev and M. Zabarankin. 2005. Drawdown measure in portfolio optimization. *International Journal of Theoretical and Applied Finance* 8(1):13–58.

Chen, X. and Y. Fan. 2005. Estimation of copula-based semiparametric time series models. *Journal of Econometrics*. Forthcoming.

——. 2005. Pseudo-likelihood ratio tests for selecting semiparametric multivariate copula models. *Canadian Journal of Statistics* 33(2). Forthcoming.

Cherubini, U., E. Luciano and W. Vecchiato. 2004. *Copula Methods in Finance*. Wiley.

Christoffersen, P. F., F. X. Diebold and T. Schuermann. 1998. Horizon problems and extreme events in financial risk management. *Federal Reserve Bank of New York, Economic Policy Review* October 1998:109–118.

Clayton, D. G. 1978. A model for association in bivariate life tables and its application in epidemiological studies of familial tendency in chronic disease incidence. *Biometrika* 65:141–151.

——. 1996. Generalized linear mixed models. In *Markov Chain Monte Carlo in Practice* (ed. W. R. Gilks, S. Richardson, and D. J. Spiegelhalter), pp. 275–301. London: Chapman & Hall.

——. 2002. Op risk modelling for extremes. Part 1. Small sample modelling. *Operational Risk* 3(12):8–11.

——. 2003. Op risk modelling for extremes. Part 2. Statistical methods. *Operational Risk* 4(1):6–9.

Coles, S. G. 2001. *An Introduction to Statistical Modeling of Extreme Values*. Springer.

Coles, S. G. and J. A. Tawn. 1991. Modelling extreme multivariate events. *Journal of the Royal Statistical Society: Series B (Statistical Methodology)* 53(2):377–392.

Coles, S. G., J. Heffernan and J. A. Tawn. 1999. Dependence measures for extreme value analyses. *Extremes* 2(4):339–365.

Collin-Dufresne, P., R. Goldstein and J. Helwege. 2003. Is credit event risk priced? Modeling contagion via the updating of beliefs. Preprint, Carnegie Mellon University.

Collin-Dufresne, P., R. Goldstein and J. Hugonnier. 2004. A general formula for valuing defaultable securities. *Econometrica* 72:1377–1407.

Comte, F. and O. Lieberman. 2003. Asymptotic theory for multivariate GARCH processes. *Journal of Multivariate Analysis* 84:61–84.

Connor, G. 1995. The three types of factor models: a comparison of their explanatory power. *Financial Analysts Journal* 51(3):42–46.

Conover, W. J. 1999. *Practical Nonparametric Statistics*. Wiley.

Cont, R. 2005. Model uncertainty and its impact on the pricing of derivative instruments. *Mathematical Finance*. Forthcoming.

Copeland, T. and V. Antikarov. 2001. *Real Options*. New York: Texere.

Cox, D. R. and V. Isham. 1980. *Point Processes*. London: Chapman & Hall.

Cox, J. C. and M. Rubinstein. 1985. *Options markets*. Englewood Cliffs, NJ: Prentice Hall.

Cox, J. C., J. E. Ingersoll and S. A. Ross. 1985. A theory of the term structure of interest rates. *Econometrica* 53(2):385–407.

Cramér, H. 1994a. *Collected Works* (ed. A. Martin-Löf), vol. I. Springer.

——. 1994b. *Collected Works* (ed. A. Martin-Löf), vol. II. Springer.

Credit Suisse Financial Products. 1997. CreditRisk+: a credit risk management framework. Technical Document. (Available from www.csfb.com/creditrisk.)

Crosbie, P. J. and J. R. Bohn. 2002. Modeling default risk. KMV working paper. (Available from www.kmv.com.)

Crouhy, M., D. Galai and R. Mark. 2000. A comparative analysis of current credit risk models. *Journal of Banking and Finance* 24:59–117.

——. 2001. *Risk Management*. New York: McGraw-Hill.

Crowder, M. J. 1976. Maximum likelihood estimation for dependent observations. *Journal of the Royal Statistical Society: Series B (Statistical Methodology)* 38:45–53.

Crowder, M. J., M. Davis and G. Giampieri. 2005. A hidden Markov model of default interaction. *Quantitative Finance*. Forthcoming.

Cruz, M. G. 2002. *Modelling, Measuring and Hedging Operational Risk*. Wiley.

Cruz, M. G. (ed.). 2004. *Operational Risk Modelling and Analysis: Theory and Practice*. London: Risk Waters Group.

Dacorogna, M. M., R. Gençay, U. Müller, R. B. Olsen and O. V. Pictet. 2001. *An Introduction to High-Frequency Finance*. Academic Press.

Daley, D. J. and D. Vere-Jones. 2003. *An Introduction to the Theory of Point Processes*, vol. I: *Elementary Theory and Methods*, 2nd edn. Springer.

Daníelsson, J. and C. G. de Vries. 1997a. Tail index and quantile estimation with very high frequency data. *Journal of Empirical Finance* 4:241–257.

——. 1997b. Beyond the sample: extreme quantile and probability estimation. Preprint, Tinbergen Institute, Rotterdam.

——. 1997c. Value-at-Risk and extreme returns. In *Extremes and Integrated Risk Management* (ed. P. Embrechts), pp. 85–106. London: Risk Waters Group.

Daníelsson, J., L. de Haan, L. Peng and C. G. de Vries. 2001. Using a bootstrap method to choose the sample fraction in the tail index estimation. *Journal of Multivariate Analysis* 76:226–248.

Das, S. R., D. Duffie and N. Kapadia. 2005. Common failings: how corporate defaults are correlated. Preprint, Santa Clara University.

Daul, S., E. De Giorgi, F. Lindskog and A. J. McNeil. 2003. The grouped t-copula with an application to credit risk. *Risk* 16(11):73–76.

David, F. N. 1947. A power function for tests of randomness in a sequence of alternatives. *Biometrika* 34:335–339.

Davis, M. H. A. 1993. *Markov Models and Optimization*. London: Chapman & Hall.

Davis, M. H. A. and V. Lo. 2001. Infectious defaults. *Quantitative Finance* 1(4):382–387.

Davison, A. C. 1984. Modelling excesses over high thresholds, with an application. In *Statistical Extremes and Applications* (ed. J. T. de Oliveira), pp. 461–482. Dordrecht: Reidel.

——. 2003. *Statistical Models*. Cambridge University Press.

Davison, A. C. and R. L. Smith. 1990. Models for exceedances over high thresholds (with discussion). *Journal of the Royal Statistical Society: Series B (Statistical Methodology)* 52:393–442.

deFontnouvelle, P., V. DeJesus-Rueff, J. Jordan and E. Rosengren. 2003. Using loss data to quantify operational risk. Preprint, Federal Reserve Bank of Boston.

de la Vega, J. 1966. Confusión de confusiones. In *Extraordinary Popular Delusions and the Madness of Crowds & Confusión de Confusiones* (ed. M. S. Fridson), pp. 125–211. Wiley.

de Matos, J. A. 2001. *Theoretical Foundations of Corporate Finance*. Princeton University Press.

de Servigny, A. and O. Renault. 2002. Default correlation: empirical evidence. Working paper, Standard & Poor's, Risk Solutions.

De Vylder, F. 1996. *Advanced Risk Theory. A Self-Contained Introduction*. Brussels: Editions de l'Université de Bruxelles.

Deheuvels, P. 1980. The decomposition of infinite order and extreme multivariate distributions. In *Asymptotic Theory of Statistical Tests and Estimation* (ed. I. M. Chakravarti), pp. 259–286. Academic Press.

Dekkers, A. L. M. and L. de Haan. 1989. On the estimation of the extreme-value index and large quantile estimation. *Annals of Statistics* 17(4):1795–1832.

——. 1993. Optimal choice of sample fraction in extreme-value estimation. *Journal of Multivariate Analysis* 47:173–195.

Dekkers, A. L. M., J. H. J. Einmahl and L. de Haan. 1989. A moment estimator for the index of an extreme-value distribution. *Annals of Statistics* 17:1833–1855.

Delbaen, F. 2000. *Coherent Risk Measures*. Pisa: Cattedra Galiliana, Scuola Normale Superiore.

——. 2002. Coherent risk measures on general probability spaces. In *Advances in Finance and Stochastics* (ed. K. Sandmann and P. J. Schönbucher), pp. 1–37. Springer.

Delbaen, F., P. Grandits, T. Rheinländer, D. Sampieri, M. Schweizer and C. Stricker. 2002. Exponential hedging and entropic penalties. *Mathematical Finance* 12:99–123.

Dell'Aquila, R. and E. Ronchetti. 2005. *Robust Statistics and Econometrics with Economic and Financial Applications*. Wiley. Forthcoming.

Demarta, S. and A. J. McNeil. 2005. The *t* copula and related copulas. *International Statistical Review* 73(1):111–129.

Dembo, A., J.-D. Deuschel and D. Duffie. 2004. Large portfolio losses. *Finance Stochastics* 8:3–16.

Denault, M. 2001. Coherent allocation of risk capital. *Journal of Risk* 4(1):7–21.

Denuit, M. and A. Charpentier. 2004. *Mathématiques de l'Assurance Non-Vie*, vol. 1: *Principes Fondamentaux de Théorie de Risque*. Paris: Economica.

Denuit, M., J. Dhaene, M. J. Goovaerts and R. Kaas. 2005. *Actuarial Theory for Dependent Risks*. Wiley. Forthcoming.

Devlin, S. J., R. Gnanadesikan and J. R. Kettenring. 1975. Robust estimation and outlier detection with correlation coefficients. *Biometrika* 62(3):531–545.

——. 1981. Robust estimation of dispersion matrices and principal components. *Journal of the American Statistical Association* 76:354–362.

Diebold, F. X., T. Schuermann, A. Hickmann and A. Inoue. 1998. Scale models. *Risk* 11:104–107.

Dillmann, T. 2002. *Modelle zur Bewertung von Optionen in Lebensversicherungsverträgen*. Ulm: Ifa-Schriftenreihe.

Ding, Z. 1994. Time Series Analysis of Speculative Returns. PhD thesis, University of California, San Diego.

Ding, Z., C. W. Granger and R. F. Engle. 1993. A long memory property of stock market returns and a new model. *Journal of Empirical Finance* 1:83–106.

Döbeli, B., M. Leippold and P. Vanini. 2003. From operational risk to operational excellence. In *Advances in Operational Risk: Firm-Wide Issues for Financial Institutions*, 2nd edn, pp. 213–234. London: Risk Waters Group.

Does, R. J. M. M., K. C. B. Roes and A. Trip. 1999. *Statistical Process Control in Industry: Implementation and Assurance of SPC*. Dordrecht: Kluwer.

Doherty, J. N. A. 2000. *Integrated Risk Management. Techniques and Strategies for Reducing Risk*. New York: McGraw-Hill.

Dowd, K. 1998. *Beyond Value at Risk: The New Science of Risk Management*. Wiley.

Driessen, J. 2005. Is default event risk priced in corporate bonds? *Review of Financial Studies* 18(1):165–195.

Drzik, J., P. Nakada and T. Schuermann. 1998. Risk capital measurement in financial institutions. Part 1: the debt-holder's perspective. *ERisk.com*, 30 July, pp. 1–5.

Duffee, G. 1999. Estimating the price of default risk. *Review of Financial Studies* 12:197–226.

Duffie, D. 2001. *Dynamic Asset Pricing Theory*, 3rd edn. Princeton University Press.

Duffie, D. 2004. Time to adapt copula methods for modelling credit risk correlation. *Risk* 17(4):77.

Duffie, D. and N. Gârleanu. 2001. Risk and valuation of collateralized debt obligations. *Financial Analysts Journal* 57(1):41–59.

Duffie, D. and R. Kan. 1996. A yield-factor model of interest rates. *Mathematical Finance* 6(4):921–950.

Duffie, D. and D. Lando. 2001. Term structure of credit risk with incomplete accounting observations. *Econometrica* 69:633–664.

Duffie, D. and J. Pan. 1997. An overview of Value at Risk. *Journal of Derivatives* 4:7–49.

——. 2001. Analytical Value-at-Risk with jumps and credit risk. *Finance Stochastics* 5:155–180.

Duffie, D. and K. Singleton. 1999a. Modeling term structures of defaultable bonds. *Review of Financial Studies* 12:687–720.

——. 1999b. Simulating correlated defaults. Preprint, Stanford University Graduate School of Business.

——. 2003. *Credit Risk: Pricing, Measurement, and Management*. Princeton University Press.

Duffie, D., D. Filipovic and W. Schachermayer. 2003. Affine processes and applications in finance. *Annals of Applied Probability* 13:984–1053.

Duffie, D., J. Pan and K. Singleton. 2000. Transform analysis and asset pricing for affine jump diffusions. *Econometrica* 68:1343–1376.

Duffie, D., M. Schroder and C. Skiadas. 1996. Recursive valuation of defaultable securities and the resolution of uncertainty. *Annals of Applied Probability* 6:1075–1090.

Dumas, B., J. Fleming and R. E. Whaley. 1998. Implied volatility functions: empirical tests. *Journal of Finance* 53(6):2059–2106.

Dunbar, N. 2000. *Inventing Money*. Wiley.

Eberlein, E. and U. Keller. 1995. Hyperbolic distributions in finance. *Bernoulli* 1:281–299.

Eberlein, E., U. Keller and K. Prause. 1998. New insights into smile, mispricing, and value at risk: the hyperbolic model. *Journal of Business* 38:371–405.

Ebnöther, S., P. Vanini, A. McNeil and P. Antolinez-Fehr. 2003. Operational risk: a practitioner's view. *Journal of Risk* 5(3):1–15.

Efron, B. F. and D. V. Hinkley. 1978. Assessing the accuracy of the maximum likelihood estimator: observed versus expected Fisher information. *Biometrika* 65:457–487.

Efron, B. F. and R. J. Tibshirani. 1994. *An Introduction to the Bootstrap*. New York: Chapman & Hall.

Egloff, D., M. Leippold and P. Vanini. 2004. A simple model of credit contagion. Preprint, University of Zurich, Swiss Banking Institute.

Eisenberg, L. and T. H. Noe. 2001. Systemic risk in financial systems. *Management Science* 47(2):236–249.

El Karoui, N. and M.-C. Quenez. 1995. Dynamic programming and pricing of contingent claims in an incomplete market. *SIAM Journal on Control and Optimization* 33(1):27–66.

Elliot, R. J., M. Jeanblanc and M. Yor. 2000. On models of default risk. *Mathematical Finance* 10:179–195.

Embrechts, P. 2000. Actuarial versus financial pricing of insurance. *Risk Finance* 1(4):17–26.

——. 2002. Insurance analytics. *British Actuarial Journal* 8(IV):639–641.

Embrechts, P. and C. M. Goldie. 1980. On closure and factorization properties of subexponential and related distributions. *Journal of the Australian Mathematical Society, Series A* 29:243–256.

Embrechts, P. and G. Puccetti. 2005. Bounds for functions of dependent risks. *Finance Stochastics*. Forthcoming.

Embrechts, P., R. Frey and H. Furrer. 2001. Stochastic processes in insurance and finance. In *Handbook of Statistics* (ed. D. N. Shanbag and C. R. Rao), vol. 19, pp. 365–412. Amsterdam: North-Holland.

Embrechts, P., H. Furrer and R. Kaufmann. 2003. Quantifying regulatory capital for operational risk. *Derivatives Use, Trading & Regulation* 9(3):217–233.

Embrechts, P., R. Grübel and S. Pitts. 1993. Some applications of the fast Fourier transform algorithm in insurance mathematics. *Statistica Neerlandica* 47:59–75.

Embrechts, P., A. Höing and A. Juri. 2003. Using copulae to bound the Value-at-Risk for functions of dependent risks. *Finance Stochastics* 7(2):145–167.

Embrechts, P., A. Höing and G. Puccetti. 2005. Worst VaR scenarios. *Insurance: Mathematics and Economics*. Forthcoming.

Embrechts, P., R. Kaufmann and P. Patie. 2005. Strategic long-term financial risks: single risk factors. *Computational Optimization and Applications*. Forthcoming.

Embrechts, P., R. Kaufmann and G. Samorodnitsky. 2004. Ruin theory revisited: stochastic models for operational risk. In *Risk Management for Central Bank Foreign Reserves* (ed. C. Bernadell et al.), pp. 243–261. Frankfurt: European Central Bank.

Embrechts, P., C. Klüppelberg and T. Mikosch. 1997. *Modelling Extremal Events for Insurance and Finance*. Springer.

Embrechts, P., A. J. McNeil and D. Straumann. 2002. Correlation and dependency in risk management: properties and pitfalls. In *Risk Management: Value at Risk and Beyond* (ed. M. Dempster), pp. 176–223. Cambridge University Press.

Embrechts, P., J. L. Jensen, M. Maejima and J. L. Teugels. 1985. Approximations for compound Poisson and Pólya processes. *Advances in Applied Probability* 17:623–637.

Emmer, S., C. Klüppelberg and R. Korn. 2001. Optimal portfolios with bounded capital at risk. *Mathematical Finance* 11(4):365–384.

Engle, R. F. 1982. Autoregressive conditional heteroskedasticity with estimates of the variance of UK inflation. *Econometrica* 50:987–1008.

——. 2002. Dynamic conditional correlation—a simple class of multivariate GARCH models. *Journal of Business and Economic Statistics* 20:339–350.

Engle, R. F. and T. Bollerslev. 1986. Modeling the persistence of conditional variances. *Econometric Review* 5:1–50.

Engle, R. F. and K. F. Kroner. 1995. Multivariate simultaneous generalized ARCH. *Econometric Theory* 11:122–150.

Engle, R. F. and K. Sheppard. 2001. Theoretical and empirical properties of dynamic conditional correlation multivariate GARCH. Technical Report 2001-15, University of California at San Diego.

Fahrmeir, L. and G. Tutz. 1994. *Multivariate Statistical Modelling Based on Generalized Linear Models*. Springer.

Falk, M., J. Hüsler and R. D. Reiss. 1994. *Laws of Small Numbers: Extremes and Rare Events*. Basel: Birkhäuser.

Fang, H. B. and K. T. Fang. 2002. The meta-elliptical distributions with given marginals. *Journal of Multivariate Analysis* 82:1–16.

Fang, K.-T., S. Kotz and K.-W. Ng. 1987. *Symmetric Multivariate and Related Distributions*. London: Chapman & Hall.

Federal Reserve System. 2005. Results of the 2004 loss data collection exercise for operational risk. Preprint, Federal Reserve Bank of Boston.

Feilmeier, M. and J. Bertram. 1987. *Anwendung Numerischer Methoden in der Risikotheorie*. Karlsruhe: Versicherungswirtschaft.

Feller, W. 1971. *An Introduction to Probability Theory and Its Applications*, vol. II. Wiley.

Field, P. (ed.). 2003. *Modern Risk Management: A History*. London: Risk Waters Group.

Fischer, T. 2003. Risk capital allocation by coherent risk measures based on one-sided moments. *Insurance: Mathematics and Economics* 32:135–146.

Fisher, R. A. and L. H. C. Tippett. 1928. Limiting forms of the frequency distribution of the largest or smallest member of a sample. *Proceedings of the Cambridge Philosophical Society* 24:180–190.

Focardi, F. J. and S. M. Fabozzi. 2004. A percolation approach to modeling credit loss distribution under contagion. *Journal of Risk* 7:75–94.

Föllmer, H. 1994. Stock price fluctuation as a diffusion in a random environment. *Philosophical Transactions of the Royal Society of London, Series A* 347:471–483.

Föllmer, H. and P. Leukert. 1999. Quantile hedging. *Finance Stochastics* 3:251–273.

——. 2002. Convex measures of risk and trading constraints. *Finance and Stochastics* 6:429–447.

——. 2004. *Stochastic Finance: An Introduction in Discrete Time*, 2nd edn. Berlin: Walter de Gruyter.

Föllmer, H. and M. Schweizer. 1991. Hedging of contingent claims under incomplete information. In *Applied Stochastic Analysis* (ed. M. H. A. Davis and R. J. Elliot), pp. 389–414. London: Gordon and Breach.

Föllmer, H. and D. Sondermann. 1986. Hedging of non-redundant contingent-claims. In *Contributions to Mathematical Economics* (ed. W. Hildenbrand and A. Mas-Colell), pp. 147–160. Amsterdam: North-Holland.

Fons, J. S. 1994. Using default rates to model the term structure of credit risk. *Financial Analysts Journal* 50:25–33.

Fornari, F. and A. Mele. 1997. Signa and volatility switching ARCH models. *Journal of Applied Econometrics* 12:49–65.

Fortin, I. and C. Kuzmics. 2002. Tail-dependence in stock-return pairs. *International Journal of Intelligent Systems in Accounting, Finance & Management* 11:89–107.

Frachot, A. 2004. Operational risk: from theory to practice. Presentation, The Three Way Seminar, Versailles, 4 May 2004.

Frachot, A., P. Georges and T. Roncalli. 2001. Loss distribution approach for operational risk. Working paper, Crédit Lyonnais, Groupe de Recherche Opérationelle.

Frahm, G. 2004. Generalized Elliptical Distributions: Theory and Applications. PhD thesis, Faculty of Economics, Business Administration and Social Sciences, University of Cologne.

Frahm, G., M. Junker and A. Szimayer. 2003. Elliptical copulas: applicability and limitations. *Statistics & Probability Letters* 63:275–286.

Frank, M. 1979. On the simultaneous additivity of $f(x, y)$ and $x + y - f(x, y)$. *Aequationes Mathematicae* 19:194–226.

Frank, M., R. Nelsen and B. Schweizer. 1987. Best-possible bounds on the distribution of a sum—a problem of Kolmogorov. *Probability Theory and Related Fields* 74:199–211.

Fréchet, M. 1951. Sur les tableaux de corrélation dont les marges sont données. *Annales de l'Université de Lyon, Série A* 9:53–77.

Frees, E. W. and E. A. Valdez. 1997. Understanding relationships using copulas. *North American Actuarial Journal* 2(1):1–25.

Frey, R. 1998. Perfect option replication for a large trader. *Finance Stochastics* 2:115–148.

——. 2000. Market illiquidity as a source of model risk in dynamic hedging. In *Model Risk* (ed. R. Gibson), pp. 125–136. London: Risk Waters Group.

Frey, R. and J. Backhaus. 2004. Portfolio credit risk models with interacting default intensities: a Markovian approach. Preprint, University of Leipzig.

Frey, R. and A. J. McNeil. 2001. Modelling dependent defaults. ETH E-Collection, ETH Zurich. (Available from www.e-collection.ethbib.ethz.ch/show?type=bericht&nr=273.)

——. 2002. VaR and expected shortfall in portfolios of dependent credit risks: conceptual and practical insights. *Journal of Banking and Finance* 26:1317–1344.

——. 2003. Dependent defaults in models of portfolio credit risk. *Journal of Risk* 6(1):59–92.

Frey, R., A. J. McNeil and M. Nyfeler. 2001. Copulas and credit models. *Risk* 14(10):111–114.

Frittelli, E., and M. Rosazza. 2002. Putting order in risk measures. *Journal of Banking and Finance* 26:1473–1486.

Froot, K. A. 2005. Risk management, capital budgeting and capital structure policy for insurers and reinsurers. *Journal of Risk and Insurance*. Forthcoming.

Froot, K. A. and J. C. Stein. 1998. Risk management, capital budgeting and capital structure policy for financial institutions: an integrated approach. *Journal of Financial Economics* 47:55–82.

Froot, K. A., D. S. Scharfstein and J. C. Stein. 1993. Risk management: coordinating corporate investment and financing policies. *Journal of Finance* 48:1629–1658.

Frye, J. 2000. Depressing recoveries. Preprint, Federal Reserve Bank of Chicago, 2000. A short version appeared in *Risk* 13(11):106–111.

Gagliardini, P. and C. Gourieroux. 2005. Stochastic migration models with application to corporate risk. *Journal of Financial Econometrics* 3(2):188–226.

Galambos, J. 1975. Order statistics of samples from multivariate distributions. *Journal of the American Statistical Association* 70:674–680.

——. 1987. *The Asymptotic Theory of Extreme Order Statistics*. Melbourne: Krieger.

Gardner Jr, E. S. 1985. Exponential smoothing: the state of the art. *Journal of Forecasting* 2:1–21.

Geffroy, J. 1958. Contributions à la theorie des valeurs extrèmes. *Publications de l'Institut de Statistique de l'Université de Paris* 7–8:37–185.

Geman, H. 2005. *Commodities and Commodity Derivatives: Modelling and Pricing for Agriculturals, Metals and Energy*. Wiley.

Gençay, R. and F. Selçuk. 2004. Extreme value theory and Value-at-Risk: relative performance in emerging markets. *International Journal of Forecasting* 20:287–303.

Gençay, R., F. Selçuk and A. Ulugülyağci. 2003. High volatility, thick tails and extreme value theory in Value-at-Risk estimation. *Insurance: Mathematics and Economics* 33:337–356.

Genest, C. and J. MacKay. 1986. The joy of copulas: bivariate distributions with uniform marginals. *American Statistician* 40:280–285.

Genest, C. and L. Rivest. 1993. Statistical inference procedures for bivariate archimedean copulas. *Journal of the American Statistical Association* 88:1034–1043.

Genest, C., K. Ghoudi and L. Rivest. 1995. A semi-parametric estimation procedure of dependence parameters in multivariate families of distributions. *Biometrika* 82:543–552.

——. 1998. Commentary on "Understanding relationships using copulas" by E. W. Frees and E. A. Valdez. *North American Actuarial Journal* 2:143–149.

Genton, M. G. (ed.). 2004. *Skew-Elliptical Distributions and Their Applications*. Boca Raton, FL: Chapman & Hall/CRC.

Gibson, R. (ed.). 2000. *Model Risk, Concepts, Calibration and Pricing*. London: Risk Waters Group.

Giese, G. 2003. Enhancing CreditRisk+. *Risk* 16(4):73–77.

Giesecke, K. 2004. Credit risk modeling and valuation: an introduction. In *Credit Risk: Models and Management* (ed. D. Shimko), vol. 2. London: Risk Waters Group. (Reprinted in 2004: *Journal of Financial Risk Management* 2(1):1–40.)

——. 2005. Default and information. *Journal of Economic Dynamics and Control*. Forthcoming.

Giesecke, K. and L. R. Goldberg. 2004. Sequential defaults and incomplete information. *Journal of Risk* 7:1–26.

——. 2005. The market price of credit risk. Preprint, Cornell University.

Giesecke, K. and S. Weber. 2004. Cyclical correlation, credit contagion and portfolio losses. *Journal of Banking and Finance* 28:3009–3036.

——. 2005. Credit contagion and aggregate losses. *Journal of Economic Dynamics and Control*. Forthcoming.

Giné, E. M. 1975. Invariant tests for uniformity on compact Riemannian manifolds based on Sobolev norms. *Annals of Statistics* 3(6):1243–1266.

Giri, N. C. 1996. *Multivariate Statistical Analysis*. New York: Marcel Dekker.

Glasserman, P. 2003a. *Monte Carlo Methods in Financial Engineering*. Springer.

——. 2003b. Tail approximations for portfolio credit risk. Preprint, Columbia University, Graduate School of Business.

Glasserman, P. and J. Li. 2003a. Importance sampling for portfolio credit risk. Preprint, Columbia University, Graduate School of Business.

——. 2003b. Importance sampling for a mixed Poisson model of portfolio credit risk. In *Proceedings of the 2003 Winter Simulation Conference* (ed. S. Chick, P. J. Sánchez, D. Ferrin, and D. J. Morrice).

Glasserman, P., P. Heidelberger and P. Shahabuddin. 1999. Importance sampling and stratification for Value at Risk. In *Proceedings of the 6th International Conference on Computational Finance* (ed. Y. S. Abu-Mostafa, B. LeBaron, A. W. Lo and A. S. Weigand). Cambridge, MA: MIT Press.

Glosten, L. R., R. Jagannathan and D. E. Runkle. 1993. On the relation between the expected value and the volatility of the nominal excess return on stocks. *Journal of Finance* 48(5):1779–1801.

Gnanadesikan, R. 1997. *Methods for Statistical Data Analysis of Multivariate Observations*, 2nd edn. Wiley.

Gnanadesikan, R. and J. R. Kettenring. 1972. Robust estimates, residuals, and outlier detection with multiresponse data. *Biometrics* 28:81–124.

Gnedenko, B. V. 1941. Limit theorems for the maximal term of a variational series. *Comptes Rendus (Doklady) de L'Académie des Sciences de l'URSS* 32:7–9.

Gnedenko, B. V. 1943. Sur la distribution limite du terme maximum d'une série aléatoire. *Annals of Mathematics* 44:423–453.

Goovaerts, M. J., F. De Vylder and J. Haezendonck. 1984. *Insurance Premiums*. Amsterdam: North-Holland.

Goovaerts, M. J., J. Dhaene and R. Kaas. 2003. Capital allocation derived from risk measures. *North American Actuarial Journal* 7:44–49.

Goovaerts, M. J., E. van den Boor and R. J. A. Laeven. 2005. Managing economic and virtual economic capital within financial conglomerates. *North American Actuarial Journal*. Forthcoming.

Goovaerts, M. J., R. Kaas, J. Dhaene and Q. Tang. 2003. A unified approach to generate risk measures. *ASTIN Bulletin* 33(2):173–191.

Gordy, M. B. 2000. A comparative anatomy of credit risk models. *Journal of Banking and Finance* 24:119–149.

——. 2001. A risk-factor model foundation for ratings-based capital rules. *Journal of Financial Intermediation* 12:199–232.

Gordy, M. B. 2002. Saddlepoint approximation of CreditRisk+. *Journal of Banking and Finance* 26:1335–1353.

Gordy, M. B. and E. Heitfield. 2002. Estimating default correlations from short panels of credit rating performance data. Technical Report, Federal Reserve Board.

Gourieroux, C. 1997. *ARCH-Models and Financial Applications*. Springer.

Gourieroux, C. and J. Jasak. 2001. *Financial Econometrics: Problems, Models, and Methods*. Princeton University Press.

Gourieroux, C. and O. Scaillet. 2000. Sensitivity analysis of Values at Risk. *Journal of Empirical Finance* 7:225–245.

Gourieroux, C., A. Montfort and A. Trognon. 1984. Pseudo maximum likelihood methods: theory. *Econometrica* 52:681–700.

Graham, J. R. and D. A. Rogers. 2002. Do firms hedge in response to tax incentives? *Journal of Finance* 57(2):815–839.

Grandell, J. 1997. *Mixed Poisson Processes*. London: Chapman & Hall.

Greenspan, A. 2002. Speech before the Council on Foreign Relations. In *International Financial Risk Management, Washington, DC*, 19th November.

Gregory, J. (ed.). 2003. *Credit Derivatives: The Definitive Guide*. London: Risk Waters Group.

Grübel, R. and R. Hermesmeier. 1999. Computation of compound distributions. I. Aliasing errors and exponential tilting. *ASTIN Bulletin* 29(2):197–214.

——. 2000. Computation of compound distributions. II. Discretization errors and Richardson extrapolation. *ASTIN Bulletin* 30(2):309–331.

Gumbel, E. J. 1958. *Statistics of Extremes*. New York: Columbia University Press.

Haaf, H., O. Reiss and J. Schoenmakers. 2004. Numerically stable computation of CreditRisk+. *Journal of Risk* 6(4):1–10.

Haan, L. de. 1985. Extremes in higher dimensions: the model and some statistics. In *Proceedings of the 45th Session International Statistical Institute*, paper 26.3. The Hague: International Statistical Institute.

Haan, L. de and S. I. Resnick. 1977. Limit theory for multivariate sample extremes. *Zeitschrift für Wahrscheinlichkeitstheorie und Verwandte Gebiete* 40:317–337.

Haan, L. de and H. Rootzén. 1993. On the estimation of high quantiles. *Journal of Statistical Planning and Inference* 35:1–13.

Haan, L. de, S. I. Resnick, H. Rootzén and C. G. de Vries. 1989. Extremal behaviour of solutions to a stochastic difference equation with applications to ARCH processes. *Stochastic Processes and Their Applications* 32:213–224.

Hafner, C. M. and P. H. Franses. 2003. A generalized dynamic conditional correlation model for many asset returns. Econometric Institute Report 323, Erasmus University, Rotterdam.

Hall, P. G. 1982. On some simple estimates of an exponent of regular variation. *Journal of the Royal Statistical Society: Series B (Statistical Methodology)* 44:37–42.

——. 1990. Using the bootstrap to estimate mean squared error and select smoothing parameter in nonparametric problems. *Journal of Multivariate Analysis* 32:177–203.

Hamilton, J. 1994. *Time Series Analysis*. Princeton University Press.

Hampel, F. R., E. M. Ronchetti, P. J. Rousseeuw and W. A. Stahel. 1986. *Robust Statistics: The Approach Based on Influence Functions*. Wiley.

Hancock, J., P. Huber and P. Koch. 2001. The economics of insurance: how insurers create value for shareholders. Technical Report, Swiss Re, Zurich.

Hardy, M. 2003. *Investment Guarantees*. Wiley.

Haug, E. G. 1998. *Option Pricing Formulas*. New York: McGraw-Hill.

Hawke Jr, J. D. 2003. Remarks before the Institute of International Bankers, 3 March 2003, Washington, DC. (Available from www.occ.treas.gov/ftp/release/2003-15a.pdf/.)

Hawkes, A. G. 1971. Point spectra of some mutually exciting point processes. *Journal of the Royal Statistical Society: Series B (Statistical Methodology)* 33:438–443.

Heffernan, J. E. and J. A. Tawn. 2004. A conditional approach for multivariate extreme values. *Journal of the Royal Statistical Society: Series B (Statistical Methodology)* 66(3):497–546.

Hesselager, O. 1996. Recursions for certain bivariate counting distributions and their compound distributions. *ASTIN Bulletin* 26(1):35–52.

Hilberink, B. and C. Rogers. 2002. Optimal capital structure and endogenous default. *Finance and Stochastics* 6(2):237–263.

Hill, B. M. 1975. A simple general approach to inference about the tail of a distribution. *Annals of Statistics* 3:1163–1174.

Höffding, W. 1940. Massstabinvariante Korrelationstheorie. *Schriften des Mathematischen Seminars und des Instituts für Angewandte Mathematik der Universität Berlin* 5:181–233.

Hogg, R. V. and S. A. Klugman. 1984. *Loss Distributions*. Wiley.

Horst, U. 2004. Stochastic cascades, credit contagion and large portfolio losses. Preprint, Humboldt Universität, Berlin.

Hosking, J. R. M. 1985. Maximum likelihood estimation of the parameters of the generalized extreme-value distribution. *Applied Statistics* 34:301–310.

Hosking, J. R. M. and J. R. Wallis. 1987. Parameter and quantile estimation for the generalized Pareto distribution. *Technometrics* 29:339–349.

Hosking, J. R. M., J. R. Wallis and E. F. Wood. 1985. Estimation of the generalized extreme-value distribution by the method of probability-weighted moments. *Technometrics* 27:251–261.

Hsing, T. 1991. On tail index estimation using dependent data. *Annals of Statistics* 19:1547–1569.

Hu, Y.-T., R. Kiesel and W. Perraudin. 2002. The estimation of transition matrices for sovereign credit ratings. *Journal of Banking and Finance* 26:1383–1406.

Huang, J. and M. Huang. 2003. How much of the corporate-treasury yield spread is due to credit risk? Results from a new calibration approach. Preprint, Graduate School of Business, Stanford University.

Huber, P. J. 1981. *Robust Statistics*. Wiley.

Hull, J. 1997. *Options, Futures and Other Derivatives*, 3rd edn. Englewood Cliffs, NJ: Prentice Hall.

Hull, J. and A. White. 1998. Incorporating volatility updating into the historical simulation method for VaR. *Journal of Risk* 1(1):5–19.

——. 2001. Valuing credit default swaps. II. Modelling default correlations. *Journal of Derivatives* 8(3):12–22.

——. 2004. Valuation of a CDO and an *n*th to default CDS without Monte Carlo simulation. *Journal of Derivatives* 12:8–23.

Hult, H. and F. Lindskog. 2002. Multivariate extremes, aggregation and dependence in elliptical distributions. *Advances in Applied Probability* 34:587–608.

Hutchinson, T. P. and C. D. Lai. 1990. *Continuous Bivariate Distributions, Emphasizing Applications*. Adelaide: Rumsby Scientific Publishing.

Iman, R. L. and W. J. Conover. 1982. A distribution-free approach to inducing rank correlation among input variables. *Communications in Statistics: Simulation and Computation* 11:311–334.

Jacod, J. 1975. Multivariate point processes: predictable projection, Radon–Nikodym derivatives, representation of martingales. *Zeitschrift für Wahrscheinlichkeitstheorie und Verwandte Gebiete* 31:235–253.

Jacod, J. and A. S. Shiryaev. 1987. *Limit Theorems for Stochastic Processes*. Springer.

Jaeger, L. 2005. *Through the Alpha Smoke Screens: A Guide to Hedge Fund Return Sources*. New York: Institutional Investor Books.

Jarque, C. M. and A. K. Bera. 1987. A test for normality of observations and regression residuals. *International Statistical Review* 55(5):163–172.

Jarrow, R. A. 1994. Derivative securities markets, market manipulation and option pricing theory. *Journal of Financial and Quantitative Analysis* 29:241–261.

Jarrow, R. A. and P. Protter. 2004. Structural versus reduced-form models: a new information based perspective. *Journal of Investment Management* 2:1–10.

Jarrow, R. A. and S. M. Turnbull. 1995. Pricing derivatives on financial securities subject to credit risk. *Journal of Finance* 50(1):53–85.

——. 1999. *Derivative Securities*, 2nd edn. Cincinnatti, OH: South Western Publishing.

Jarrow, R. A. and F. Yu. 2001. Counterparty risk and the pricing of defaultable securities. *Journal of Finance* 53:2225–2243.

Jarrow, R. A., D. Lando and S. M. Turnbull. 1997. A Markov model for the term structure of credit risk spreads. *Review of Financial Studies* 10:481–523.

Jarrow, R. A., D. Lando and F. Yu. 2005. Default risk and diversification: theory and empirical implications. *Mathematical Finance* 15:1–26.

Jeantheau, T. 1998. Strong consistency of estimators of multivariate ARCH models. *Econometric Theory* 14(1):70–86.

Jensen, B. A. and J. A. Nielsen. 1996. Pricing by no-arbitrage. In *Time Series Models in Econometrics, Finance and Other Fields* (ed. D. R. Cox, D. V. Hinkley and O. E. Barndorff-Nielsen). London: Chapman & Hall.

Jensen, J. L. 1995. *Saddlepoint Approximations*. Oxford: Clarendon.

Jewell, W. S. 1990. Credibility prediction of first and second moments in the hierarchical model. In *Festgabe Bühlmann*, pp. 81–110. Bern: Stämpfli.

Joag-Dev, K. 1984. Measures of dependence. In *Handbook of Statistics* (ed. P. R. Krishnaiah), vol. 4, pp. 79–88. New York: North-Holland/Elsevier.

Joe, H. 1993. Parametric family of multivariate distributions with given margins. *Journal of Multivariate Analysis* 46:262–282.

——. 1997. *Multivariate Models and Dependence Concepts*. London: Chapman & Hall.

Joe, H., R. L. Smith and I. Weissman. 1992. Bivariate threshold methods for extremes. *Journal of the Royal Statistical Society: Series B (Statistical Methodology)* 54(1):171–183.

Johnson, N. L. and S. Kotz. 1969. *Distributions in Statistics: Discrete Distributions*. Boston, MA: Houghton Mifflin.

Johnson, R. A. and D. W. Wichern. 2002. *Applied Multivariate Statistical Analysis*, 5th edn. Upper Saddle River, NJ: Prentice Hall.

Jorion, P. 2000. Risk management lessons from Long-Term Capital Management. *European Financial Management* 6:277–300.

——. 2001. *Value at Risk: The New Benchmark for Measuring Financial Risk*, 2nd edn. New York: McGraw-Hill.

——. 2002a. *Financial Risk Manager Handbook 2001–2002*. Wiley.

——. 2002b. Fallacies about the effects of market risk management systems. *Journal of Risk* 5(1):75–96.

JPMorgan. 1996. *RiskMetrics Technical Document*, 3rd edn. New York: JPMorgan.

Juri, A. and M. V. Wüthrich. 2002. Copula convergence theorems for tail events. *Insurance: Mathematics and Economics* 30:411–427.

——. 2003. Tail dependence from a distributional point of view. *Extremes* 6:213–246.

Kaas, R., M. J. Goovaerts, J. Dhaene and M. Denuit. 2001. *Modern Actuarial Risk Theory*. Boston, MA: Kluwer Academic Press.

Kalkbrener, M. 2005. An axiomatic approach to capital allocation. *Mathematical Finance* 15(3):425–437.

Kalkbrener, M., H. Lotter and L. Overbeck. 2004. Sensible and efficient capital allocation for credit portfolios. *Risk* 17(1):S19–S24.

Kallenberg, O. 1983. *Random Measures*, 3rd edn. Academic Press.

Karatzas, I. and S. E. Shreve. 1988. *Brownian Motion and Stochastic Calculus*. Springer.

——. 1998. *Methods of Mathematical Finance*. Springer.

Kariya, T. and M. L. Eaton. 1977. Robust tests for spherical symmetry. *Annals of Statistics* 5(1):206–215.

Karr, A. F. 1991. *Point Processes and Their Statistical Inference*, 2nd edn. New York: Marcel Dekker.

Kaufmann, R. 2004. Long-Term Risk Management. PhD thesis, ETH Zurich.

Kaufmann, R., R. Gadmer and R. Klett. 2001. Introduction to dynamic financial analysis. *ASTIN Bulletin* 31(1):213–249.

Kealhofer, S. and J. R. Bohn. 2001. Portfolio management of default risk. KMV working paper. (Available from www.kmv.com.)

Kelker, D. 1970. Distribution theory of spherical distributions and a location-scale parameter generalization. *Sankhyā A* 32:419–430.

Kesten, H. 1973. Random difference equations and renewal theory for products of random matrices. *Acta Mathematica* 131:207–248.

Khoudraji, A. 1995. Contribution à l'Étude des Copules et à la Modélisation des Copules de Valeurs Extrèmes Bivariées. PhD thesis, Université Laval, Québec.

Kimberling, C. H. 1974. A probabilistic interpretation of complete monotonicity. *Aequationes Mathematicae* 10:152–164.

King, J. L. 2001. *Measurement and Modelling Operational Risk*. Wiley.

Kloman, H. F. 1990. Risk management agonists. *Risk Analysis* 10:201–205.

Klugman, S. A. and R. Parsa. 1999. Fitting bivariate loss distributions with copulas. *Insurance: Mathematics and Economics* 24:139–148.

Klugman, S. A., H. H. Panjer and G. E. Willmot. 1998. *Loss Models: From Data to Decisions*. Wiley.

Koedijk, K., M. Schafgans and C. de Vries. 1990. The tail index of exchange rate returns. *Journal of International Economics* 29:93–108.

Kolmogorov, A. N. 1933. *Grundbegriffe der Wahrscheinlichkeitsrechnung*. Ergebnisse der Mathematik, Springer.

Koryciorz, S. 2004. *Sicherheitskapitalbestimmung und -allokation in der Schadenversicherung*. Karlsruhe: Versicherungswirtschaft.

Kotz, S. and S. Nadarajah. 2000. *Extreme Value Distributions, Theory and Applications*. London: Imperial College Press.

——. 2004. *Multivariate t Distributions and Their Applications*. Cambridge University Press.

Kotz, S., N. L. Johnson and C. B. Read (eds). 1985. *Encyclopedia of Statistical Sciences*. Wiley.

Kotz, S., T. J. Kozubowski and K. Podgórski. 2001. *The Laplace Distribution and Generalizations*. Boston, MA: Birkhäuser.

Koyluoglu, U. and A. Hickman. 1998. Reconciling the differences. *Risk* 11(10):56–62.

Kramkov, D. 1996. Optional decomposition of supermartingales and hedging contingent claims in incomplete security markets. *Probability Theory and Related Fields* 105:459–479.

Krokhmal, P., J. Palmquist and S. Uryasev. 2002. Portfolio optimization with conditional Value-at-Risk. *Journal of Risk* 4(2):11–27.

Kruskal, W. H. 1958. Ordinal measures of association. *Journal of the American Statistical Association* 53:814–861.

Kurth, A. and D. Tasche. 2003. Contributions to credit risk. *Risk* 16(3):84–88.

Kusuoka, S. 1999. A remark on default risk models. *Advances in Mathematical Economics* 1:69–81.

——. 2001. On law invariant coherent risk measures. *Advances in Mathematical Economics* 3:83–95.

Lamberton, D. and B. Lapeyre. 1996. *Introduction to Stochastic Calculus Applied to Finance*. London: Chapman & Hall.

Lando, D. 1998. Cox processes and credit risky securities. *Review of Derivatives Research* 2:99–120.

——. 2004. *Credit Risk Modeling: Theory and Applications*. Princeton University Press.

Lando, D. and T. Skodeberg. 2002. Analyzing rating transitions and rating drift with continuous observations. *Journal of Banking and Finance* 26:423–444.

Landsman, Z. M. and E. A. Valdez. 2003. Tail conditional expectations for elliptical distributions. *North American Actuarial Journal* 7(4):55–71.

Lang, L. and R. Stulz. 1992. Contagion and competitive intra-industry effects of bankruptcy announcements. *Journal of Financial Economics* 32:45–60.

Laurent, J. P. and J. Gregory. 2003. Basket default swaps, CDO's and factor copulas. Preprint, Université de Lyon and BNP Paribas.

Lawrence, C. and G. Robinson. 1995. Liquid measures. *Risk* 8(7):52–55.

Leadbetter, M. R. 1983. Extremes and local dependence of stationary sequences. *Zeitschrift für Wahrscheinlichkeitstheorie und Verwandte Gebiete* 65:291–306.

——. 1991. On a basis for "Peaks over Threshold" modeling. *Statistics & Probability Letters* 12:357–362.

Leadbetter, M. R., G. Lindgren and H. Rootzén. 1983. *Extremes and Related Properties of Random Sequences and Processes*. Springer.

Ledford, A. W. and J. A. Tawn. 1996. Statistics for near independence in multivariate extreme values. *Biometrika* 83(1):169–187.

Lee, S. and B. Hansen. 1994. Asymptotic properties of the maximum likelihood estimator and test of the stability of parameters of GARCH and IGARCH models. *Econometric Theory* 10:29–52.

Lehmann, E. L. 1983. *Theory of Point Estimation*. Wiley.

——. 1986. *Testing Statistical Hypotheses*, 2nd edn. Wiley.

Leland, H. E. 1994. Corporate debt value, bond covenants, and optimal capital structure. *Journal of Finance* 49:157–196.

Leland, H. E. and K. Toft 1996. Optimal capital structure, endogenous bankruptcy and the term structure of credit spreads. *Journal of Finance* 51:987–1019.

Lemaire, J. 1984. An application of game theory: cost allocation. *ASTIN Bulletin* 14(1):61–82.

Li, D. 2001. On default correlation: a copula function approach. *Journal of Fixed Income* 9:43–54.

Li, R.-Z., K.-T. Fang and L.-X. Zhu. 1997. Some Q–Q probability plots to test spherical and elliptical symmetry. *Journal of Computational and Graphical Statistics* 6(4):435–450.

Lindsey, J. K. 1996. *Parametric Statistical Inference*. Oxford University Press.

Lindskog, F. 2000. Linear correlation estimation. RiskLab Report, ETH Zurich.

Lindskog, F. and A. J. McNeil. 2003. Common Poisson shock models: applications to insurance and credit risk modelling. *ASTIN Bulletin* 33(2):209–238.

Lindskog, F., A. J. McNeil and U. Schmock. 2003. Kendall's tau for elliptical distributions. In *Credit Risk: Measurement, Evaluation and Management* (ed. G. Bol, G. Nakhaeizadeh, S. T. Rachev, T. Ridder and K.-H. Vollmer), pp. 149–156. Heidelberg: Physica.

Liu, C. 1997. ML estimation of the multivariate *t* distribution and the EM algorithm. *Journal of Mathematical Economics* 63:296–312.

Liu, C. and D. B. Rubin. 1994. The ECME algorithm: a simple extension of EM and ECM with faster monotone convergence. *Biometrika* 81:633–648.

——. 1995. ML estimation of the *t* distribution using EM and its extensions, ECM and ECME. *Statistica Sinica* 5:19–39.

Ljung, G. M. and G. E. P. Box. 1978. On a measure of lack of fit in time series models. *Biometrika* 65:297–303.

Lo, A. W. and A. C. MacKinlay. 1999. *A Non-Random Walk Down Wall Street.* Princeton University Press.

Longin, F. M. 1996. The asymptotic distribution of extreme stock market returns. *Journal of Business* 69:383–408.

Longstaff, F. E. and E. S. Schwartz. 1995. Valuing risky debt: a new approach. *Journal of Finance* 50:789–821.

Lowenstein, R. 2000. *When Genius Failed. The Rise and Fall of Long-Term Capital Management.* Random House.

Lucas, D. 1995. Default correlation and credit analysis. *Journal of Fixed Income* (March), pp. 76–87.

Lumsdaine, R. 1996. Asymptotic properties of the quasi maximum likelihood estimator in GARCH(1, 1) and IGARCH(1, 1) models. *Econometrica* 64:575–596.

Lütkepohl, H. 1993. *Introduction to Multiple Time Series Analysis*, 2nd edn. Springer.

Lux, T. 1996. The stable Paretian hypothesis and the frequency of large returns: an analysis of major German stocks. *Applied Financial Economics* 6:463–475.

McCullagh, P. and J. A. Nelder. 1989. *Generalized linear models*, 2nd edn. London: Chapman & Hall.

McCullough, B. D. and C. G. Renfro. 1999. Benchmarks and software standards: a case study of GARCH procedures. *Journal of Economic and Social Measurement* 25:59–71.

McGinty, L., R. Beinstein, E. Ahluwalia and M. Watts. 2004. Introducing base correlation. Preprint, JPMorgan.

McLeish, D. L. and C. G. Small. 1988. *The Theory and Applications of Statistical Inference Functions*. Lecture Notes in Statistics, vol. 44. Springer.

McNeil, A. J. 1997. Estimating the tails of loss severity distributions using extreme value theory. *ASTIN Bulletin* 27:117–137.

——. 1998. History repeating. *Risk* 11(1):99.

McNeil, A. J. and R. Frey. 2000. Estimation of tail-related risk measures for heteroscedastic financial time series: an extreme value approach. *Journal of Empirical Finance* 7:271–300.

McNeil, A. J. and T. Saladin. 2000. Developing scenarios for future extreme losses using the POT method. In *Extremes and Integrated Risk Management* (ed. P. Embrechts), pp. 253–267. London: Risk Waters Group.

McNeil, A. J. and J. Wendin. 2003. Generalised linear mixed models in portfolio credit risk modelling. Preprint, ETH Zurich.

Madan, D. B. and E. Seneta. 1990. The variance gamma (v.g.) model for share market returns. *Journal of Business* 63:511–524.

Madan, D. B., P. Carr and E. C. Chang. 1998. The variance gamma process and option pricing. *European Finance Review* 2:74–105.

Makarov, G. 1981. Estimates for the distribution function of a sum of two random variables when the marginal distributions are fixed. *Theory of Probability and Its Applications* 26:803–806.

Marazzi, A. 1993. *Algorithms, Routines and S-Functions for Robust Statistics*. Boca Raton, FL: CRC Press.

Mardia, K. V. 1970. Measures of multivariate skewness and kurtosis with applications. *Biometrika* 57:519–530.

——. 1972. *Statistics of Directional Data*. Academic Press.

——. 1974. Applications of some measures of multivariate skewness and kurtosis in testing normality and robustness studies. *Sankhyā* 36:115–128.

——. 1975. Assessment of multinormality and the robustness of Hotelling's T^2 test. *Journal of the Royal Statistical Society: Series C (Applied Statistics)* 24:163–171.

Mardia, K. V., J. T. Kent and J. M. Bibby. 1979. *Multivariate Analysis*. Academic Press.

Markowitz, H. M. 1952. Portfolio selection. *Journal of Finance* 7:77–91.

——. 1959. *Portfolio Selection: Efficient Diversification of Investments*. Wiley.

Maronna, R. A. 1976. Robust M-estimators of multivariate location and scatter. *Annals of Statistics* 4:51–67.

Marshall, A. W. 1996. Copulas, marginals and joint distributions. In *Distributions with Fixed Marginals and Related Topics* (ed. L. Rüschendorff, B. Schweizer and M. D. Taylor), pp. 213–222. Hayward, CA: Institute of Mathematical Statistics.

Marshall, A. W. and I. Olkin. 1967a. A generalized bivariate exponential distribution. *Journal of Applied Probability* 4:291–302.

——. 1967b. A multivariate exponential distribution. *Journal of the American Statistical Association* 62:30–44.

——. 1988. Families of multivariate distributions. *Journal of the American Statistical Association* 83:834–841.

Martin, R., K. Thompson and C. Browne. 2001. Taking to the saddle. *Risk* 14(6):91–94.

Mas-Colell, A., M. D. Whinston and J. R. Green. 1995. *Microeconomic Theory*. Oxford University Press.

Mashal, R. and A. Zeevi. 2002. Beyond correlation: extreme co-movements between financial assets. Preprint, Columbia University.

Matten, C. 2000. *Managing Bank Capital: Capital Allocation and Performance Measurement*, 2nd edn. Wiley.

Matthys, G. and J. Beirlant. 2000. Adaptive selection in tail index estimation. In *Extremes and Integrated Risk Management* (ed. P. Embrechts), pp. 37–49. London: Risk Waters Group.

Medova, E. A. 2000a. Measuring risk by extreme values. *Risk* 13:S20–S26.

——. 2000b. Extreme values and the measurement of operational risk. I. *Operational Risk* 1(7):13–17.

Meng, X. L. and D. B. Rubin. 1993. Maximum likelihood estimation via the ECM algorithm: a general framework. *Biometrika* 80:267–278.

Meng, X. L. and D. van Dyk. 1997. The EM algorithm—an old folk song sung to a fast new tune (with discussion). *Journal of the Royal Statistical Society: Series B (Statistical Methodology)* 59:511–567.

Merino, S. and M. Nyfeler. 2003. Estimating expected shortfall contributions within the conditional independence framework using importance sampling. Preprint, UBS AG.

Merton, R. C. 1973. The theory of rational option pricing. *Bell Journal of Economics and Management Science* 7:141–183.

——. 1974. On the pricing of corporate debt: the risk structure of interest rates. *Journal of Finance* 29:449–470.

Mikosch, T. 2003. Modeling dependence and tails of financial time series. In *Extreme Values in Finance, Telecommunications, and the Environment* (ed. B. Finkenstaedt and H. Rootzén), pp. 185–286. London: Chapman & Hall.

——. 2004. *Non-Life Insurance Mathematics. An Introduction with Stochastic Processes.* Springer.

Mikosch, T. and C. Stărică. 2000. Limit theory for the sample autocorrelations and extremes of a GARCH(1, 1) process. *Annals of Statistics* 28:1427–1451.

Mikosch, T. and D. Straumann. 2005. Stable limits of martingale transforms with application to the estimation of GARCH parameters. *Annals of Statistics*. Forthcoming.

Mina, J. and J. Y. Xiao. 2001. Return to RiskMetrics: the evolution of a standard. Technical Report, RiskMetrics Group, New York. (Available from www.riskmetrics.com.)

Modigliani, F. and M. H. Miller. 1958. The cost of capital, corporation finance, and the theory of investment. *American Economic Review* 48:261–297.

Moscadelli, M. 2004. The modelling of operational risk: experience with the analysis of the data, collected by the Basel Committee. Banca d'Italia, Temi di discussione del Servizio Studi, no. 517–July 2004.

Mowbray, A. H. 1914. How extensive a payroll exposure is necessary to give a dependable pure premium. *Proceedings of the Casualty Actuarial Society* 1:24–30.

Müller, A. and D. Stoyan. 2002. *Comparison Methods for Stochastic Models and Risks*. Wiley.

Musiela, M. and M. Rutkowski. 1997. *Martingale Methods in Financial Modelling*. Springer.

Nagpal, K. and R. Bahar. 2001. Measuring default correlation. *Risk* 14(3):129–132.

Nelsen, R. B. 1999. *An Introduction to Copulas*. Springer.

Nelson, D. B. 1990. Stationarity and persistence in the GARCH(1, 1) model. *Econometric Theory* 6:318–334.

——. 1991. Conditional heteroskedasticity in asset returns: a new approach. *Econometrica* 59:347–370.

Nickell, P., W. Perraudin and S. Varotto. 2000. Stability of ratings transitions. *Journal of Banking and Finance* 24:203–227.

Nolan, J. P. 2005. *Stable Distributions*. Forthcoming.

Norberg, R. 1979. The credibility approach to experience rating. *Scandinavian Actuarial Journal* 1979:181–221.

Norris, J. R. 1997. *Markov Chains*. Cambridge University Press.

Nyberg, M., M. Sellers and J. Zhang. 2001. Private firm model: introduction to the modeling methodology. Working paper, KMV Corporation.

Ogata, Y. 1988. Statistical models for earthquake occurrences and residual analysis for point processes. *Journal of the American Statistical Association* 83:9–27.

Ong, M. K. (ed). 2004. *The Basel Handbook. A Guide for Financial Practitioners*. London: Risk Waters Group.

Overbeck, L. and W. Schmidt. 2003. Modeling default dependence with threshold models. Preprint, Deutsche Bank AG.

Owen, R. and R. Rabinovitch. 1983. On the class of elliptical distributions and their application to the theory of portfolio choice. *Journal of Finance* 38:745–752.

Palisade. 1997. *Manual for @RISK*. Newfield, NY: Palisade Corporation.

Panjer, H. H. 1981. Recursive evaluation of a family of compound distributions. *ASTIN Bulletin* 12(1):22–26.

Panjer, H. H. et al. (eds). 1998. *Financial Economics With Applications to Investment, Insurance and Pensions*. Schaumburg, IL: The Actuarial Foundation.

Partrat, C. and J.-L. Besson. 2004. *Assurance Non-Vie: Modélisation, Simulation*. Paris: Economica.

Patel, N. 2002. The vanilla explosion. *Risk* 15(2):S24–S26.

Patrik, G., S. Bernegger and M. B. Rüegg. 1999. The use of risk adjusted capital to support business decision-making. *CAS Forum, Spring 1999*, Reinsurance Call Papers. Arlington, VA: Casualty Actuarial Society.

Patton, A. J. 2004. On the out-of-sample importance of skewness and asymmetric dependence for asset allocation. *Journal of Financial Economics* 2(1):130–168.

——. 2005. Modelling asymmetric exchange rate dependence. *International Economic Review*. Forthcoming.

Peeters, R. T. 2004. Financial Time and Volatility. PhD thesis, University of Amsterdam.

Perraudin, W. (ed.). 2004. *Structured Credit Products Pricing, Rating, Risk Management and Basel II*. London: Risk Waters Group.

Pézier, J. 2002a. A constructive review of Basel's proposals on operational risk. Preprint, University of Reading.

——. 2002b. Operational risk management. Preprint, University of Reading.

Pfeifer, D. 2004. VaR oder expected shortfall: welche Risikomasse sind für Solvency II geeignet? Preprint, University of Oldenburg.

Pfeifer, D. and J. Nešlehová. 2004. Modeling and generating dependent risk processes for IRM and DFA. *ASTIN Bulletin* 34(2):333–360.

Pickands, J. 1971. The two-dimensional Poisson process and extremal processes. *Journal of Applied Probability* 8:745–756.

——. 1975. Statistical inference using extreme order statistics. *Annals of Statistics* 3:119–131.

——. 1981. Multivariate extreme value distribution. *Proceedings of the 43rd Session of the International Statistics Institute, Buenos Aires*, vol. 2, pp. 859–878. The Hague: International Statistical Institute.

Prause, K. 1999. The Generalized Hyperbolic Model: Estimation, Financial Derivatives and Risk Measures. PhD thesis, Institut für Mathematische Statistik, Albert-Ludwigs-Universität, Freiburg.

Prentice, M. J. 1978. On invariant tests of uniformity for directions and orientations. *Annals of Statistics* 6(1):169–176.

Press, W. H., S. A. Teukolsky, W. T. Vetterling and B. P. Flannery. 1992. *Numerical Recipes in C*. Cambridge University Press.

Priestley, M. B. 1981. *Spectral Analysis and Time Series*, vols I and II. Academic Press.

Protassov, R. S. 2004. EM-based maximum likelihood parameter estimation of multivariate generalized hyperbolic distributions with fixed λ. *Statistics and Computing* 14:67–77.

Protter, P. 1992. *Stochastic Integration and Differential Equations: A New Approach*. Springer.

Reiss, R.-D. and M. Thomas. 1997. *Statistical Analysis of Extreme Values*. Basel: Birkhäuser.

Resnick, S. I. 1987. *Extreme Values, Regular Variation and Point Processes*. Springer.

——. 1992. *Adventures in Stochastic Processes*. Boston: Birkhäuser.

——1997. Discussion of the Danish data on large fire insurance losses. *ASTIN Bulletin* 27(1):139–151.

Resnick, S. I. and C. Stărică. 1995. Consistency of Hill's estimator for dependent data. *Journal of Applied Probability* 32:239–167.

——. 1996. Tail index estimation for dependent data. Technical Report, School of Operations Research and Industrial Engineering, Cornell University.

——. 1997. Smoothing the Hill estimator. *Advances in Applied Probability* 29:291–293.

Rice, J. A. 1995. *Mathematical Statistics and Data Analysis*, 2nd edn. Belmont, TN: Duxbury.

Riedel, F. 2004. Dynamic coherent risk measures. *Stochastic Processes and Their Applications* 112:185–200.

Ripley, B. D. 1987. *Stochastic Simulation*. Wiley.

Risk Books. 2003. *Advances in Operational Risk: Firm-Wide Issues for Financial Institutions*, 2nd edn. London: Risk Waters Group.

RiskMetrics Group. 1997. CreditMetrics technical document. The benchmark for understanding credit risk. (Available from http://www.riskmetrics.com/research.html.)

Robbins, H. 1955. An empirical Bayes approach to statistics. In *Proceedings of the 3rd Berkeley Symposium on Mathematical Statistics and Probability*, vol. 1, pp. 157–163. Berkeley, CA: University of California Press.

——. 1964. The empirical Bayes approach to statistical problems. *Annals of Mathematical Statistics* 35:1–20.

Robert, C. P. and G. Casella. 1999. *Monte Carlo Statistical Methods*. Springer.

Rockafellar, R. T. 1970. *Convex Analysis*. Princeton University Press.

Rockafellar, R. T. and S. Uryasev. 2000. Optimization of conditional Value-at-Risk. *Journal of Risk* 2:21–42.

——. 2002. Conditional Value-at-Risk for general loss distributions. *Journal of Banking and Finance* 26(7):1443–1471.

Rogers, L. C. G. and D. Williams. 1994. *Diffusions, Markov Processes, and Martingales. Volume One: Foundations*, 2nd edn. Wiley.

Rogge, E. and P. J. Schönbucher. 2003. Modeling dynamic portfolio credit risk. Preprint, Imperial College and ETH Zürich.

Rolski, T., H. Schmidli, V. Schmidt and J. L. Teugels. 1999. *Stochastic Processes for Insurance and Finance*. Wiley.

Rootzén, H. and N. Tajvidi. 1997. Extreme value statistics and wind storm losses: a case study. *Scandinavian Actuarial Journal* 1997:70–94.

Rosenberg, J. and T. Schuermann. 2004. Integrated risk management using copulas. Preprint, Federal Reserve Bank of New York.

Rousseeuw, P. J. and G. Molenberghs. 1993. Transformation of non positive semidefinite correlation matrices. *Communications in Statistics: Theory and Methods* 22(4):965–984.

Rouvinez, C. 1997. Going Greek with VaR. *Risk* 10(2):57–65.

Rüschendorf, L. 1982. Random variables with maximum sums. *Advances in Applied Probability* 14:623–632.

Sandström, A. S. G. 2005. *Solvency: Towards a Standard Approach*. Forthcoming.

Schervish, M. J. 1995. *Theory of Statistics*. Springer.

Schlather, M. and J. A. Tawn. 2002. Inequalities for the extremal coefficients of multivariate extreme value distributions. *Extremes* 5:87–102.

Schmeidler, D. 1986. Integral representation without additivity. *Proceedings of the American Mathematical Society* 97:255–261.

Schmidt, R. 2002. Tail dependence for elliptically contoured distributions. *Mathematical Methods of Operations Research* 55:301–327.

Schmidt, T. and W. Stute. 2004. Credit risk: a survey. *Contemporary Mathematics* 336:75–115.

Schmock, U. 1999. Estimating the value of the wincat coupons of the Winterthur Insurance convertible bond: a study of the model risk. *ASTIN Bulletin* 29(1):101–163.

Schoenberg, I. J. 1938. Metric spaces and completely monotone functions. *Annals of Mathematics* 39:811–841.

Scholes, M. S. 2000. Crisis and risk management. *American Economic Review* 90(2):17–22.

Schönbucher, P. J. 2002. Taken to the limit: simple and not-so-simple loss distributions. Preprint, ETH Zurich and Universität Bonn.

Schönbucher, P. J. 2003. *Credit Derivatives Pricing Models*. Wiley.

——. 2004. Information-driven default contagion. Preprint, Department of Mathematics, ETH Zurich.

Schönbucher, P. J. and D. Schubert. 2001. Copula-dependent default risk in intensity models. Preprint, ETH Zurich and Universität Bonn.

Schönbucher, P. J. and P. Wilmott. 2000. The feedback-effect of hedging in illiquid markets. *SIAM Journal of Applied Mathematics* 61:232–272.

Schuermann, T. 2003. What do we know about loss-given-default. In *Credit Risk Models and Management* (ed. D. Shimko), ch. 9. London: Risk Waters Group.

Schweizer, B. and A. Sklar. 1983. *Probabilistic Metric Spaces*. New York: North-Holland/Elsevier.

Schweizer, B. and E. F. Wolff. 1981. On nonparametric measures of dependence for random variables. *Annals of Statistics* 9:879–885.

Schweizer, M. 2001a. From actuarial to financial valuation principles. *Insurance: Mathematics and Economics* 28:31–47.

——. 2001b. A guided tour through quadratic hedging approaches. In *Option Pricing, Interest Rates and Risk Management* (ed. E. Jouini, J. Cvitanic and M. Musiela), pp. 538–574. Cambridge University Press.

Seal, H. L. 1969. *Stochastic Theory of a Risk Business*. Wiley.

Seber, G. A. F. 1984. *Multivariate Observations*. Wiley.

Serfling, R. J. 1980. *Approximation Theorems of Mathematical Statistics*. Wiley.

Seneta, E. 1976. *Regularly Varying Functions*. Lecture Notes in Mathematics. Springer.

Shea, G. A. 1983. Höffding's lemma. In *Encyclopaedia of Statistical Science* (ed. S. Kotz, N. L. Johnson and C. B. Read), vol. 3, pp. 648–649. Wiley.

Shephard, N. 1996. Statistical aspects of ARCH and stochastic volatility. In *Time Series Models in Econometrics, Finance and Other Fields* (ed. D. R. Cox, D. V. Hinkley and O. E. Barndorff-Nielsen), pp. 1–67. London: Chapman & Hall.

Shiller, R. J. 2003. *The New Financial Order: Risk in the Twenty-First Century*. Princeton University Press.

Shimpi, P. K. (ed.). 1999. *Integrating Corporate Risk Management*. Zurich: Swiss Re New Markets.

Shreve, S. 2004. *Stochastic Calculus for Finance. II. Continuous-Time Models*. Springer.

Sibuya, M. 1960. Bivariate extreme statistics. *Annals of the Institite of Statistical Mathematics* 11:195–210.

Sklar, A. 1959. Fonctions de répartition à n dimensions et leurs marges. *Publications de l'Institut de Statistique de l'Université de Paris* 8:229–231.

Small, N. J. H. 1978. Plotting squared radii. *Biometrika* 65:657–658.

Smith, P. J. 1977. A nonparametric test for bivariate circular symmetry based on the empirical CDF. *Communications in Statistics: Theory and Methods A* 6(3):209–220.

Smith, R. L. 1985. Maximum likelihood estimation in a class of nonregular cases. *Biometrika* 72:67–92.

——. 1987. Estimating tails of probability distributions. *Annals of Statistics* 15:1174–1207.

——. 1989. Extreme value analysis of environmental time series: an application to trend detection in ground-level ozone. *Statistical Science* 4:367–393.

——. 1994. Multivariate threshold methods. In *Extreme Value Theory and Applications* (ed. J. Galambos), pp. 225–248. Boston, MA: Kluwer Academic Press.

Smith, R. L. and D. Goodman. 2000. Bayesian risk analysis. In *Extremes and Integrated Risk Management* (ed. P. Embrechts), pp. 235–267. London: Risk Waters Group.

Smith, R. L. and T. S. Shively. 1995. Point process approach to modeling trends in tropospheric ozone based on exceedances of a high threshold. *Atmospheric Environment* 29:3489–3499.

Smith, R. L. and I. Weissman. 1994. Estimating the extremal index. *Journal of the Royal Statistical Society: Series B (Statistical Methodology)* 56:515–528.

Smith, R. L., J. A. Tawn and S. G. Coles. 1997. Markov chain models for threshold exceedances. *Biometrika* 84:249–268.

Steinherr, A. 1998. *Derivatives. The Wild Beast of Finance*. Wiley.

Stiglitz, J. and L. Weiss. 1981. Credit rationing with imperfect information. *American Economic Review* 71:393–410.

Stoll, H. R. 2000. Friction. *Journal of Finance* 55(4):1479–1514.

Straumann, D. 2003. *Estimation in Conditionally Heteroscedastic Time Series Models*. Lecture Notes in Statistics, vol. 181. Springer.

Stuart, A., J. K. Ord and S. Arnold. 1999. Classical inference and the linear model. In *Kendall's Advanced Theory of Statistics*, 6th edn, vol. 2A. Oxford University Press.

Studer, M. 2001. Stochastic Taylor Expansions and Saddlepoint Approximations for Risk Management. PhD thesis, ETH Zurich.

Stulz, R. M. 1996. Rethinking risk management. *Journal of Applied Corporate Finance* 9(3):8–24.

——. 2002. *Risk Management and Derivatives*. Mason, OH: South-Western.

Sundt, B. 1999. On multivariate Panjer recursions. *ASTIN Bulletin* 29(1):29–45.

——. 2000. On multivariate Vernic recursions. *ASTIN Bulletin* 30(1):111–122.

Sundt, B. and W. S. Jewell. 1982. Further results on recursive evaluation of compound distributions. *ASTIN Bulletin* 12(1):27–39.

Takahashi, R. 1994. Domains of attraction of multivariate extreme value distributions. *Journal of Research of the National Institute of Standards and Technology* 99:551–554.

Tasche, D. 1999. Risk contributions and performance measurement. Preprint, Department of Mathematics, TU-München.

——. 2000. Conditional expectation as a quantile derivative. Preprint, Department of Mathematics, TU-München.

——. 2002. Expected shortfall and beyond. *Journal of Banking and Finance* 26:1519–1533.

Tavakoli, J. M. 2001. *Credit Derivatives and Synthetic Structures: A Guide to Investments and Applications*, 2nd edn. Wiley.

Tawn, J. A. 1988. Bivariate extreme value theory: models and estimation. *Biometrika* 75(3):397–415.

——. 1990. Modelling multivariate extreme value distributions. *Biometrika* 77(2):245–253.

Taylor, S. J. 1986. *Modelling Financial Time Series*. Wiley.

Teugels, J. L. and B. Sundt (eds). 2004. *Encyclopedia of Actuarial Science*. Wiley.

Tiago de Oliveira, J. 1958. Extremal distributions. *Revista da Faculdade de Ciências de Lisboa: Série A* 7:215–227.

Tiit, E. 1996. Mixtures of multivariate quasi-extremal distributions having given marginals. In *Distributions with Fixed Marginals and Related Topics* (ed. L. Rüschendorff, B. Schweizer and M. D. Taylor), pp. 337–357. Hayward, CA: Institute of Mathematical Statistics.

Tsay, R. S. 2002. *Analysis of Financial Time Series*. Wiley.

Tsay, R. S. and G. C. Tiao. 1984. Consistent estimates of autoregressive parameters and extended sample autocorrelation function for stationary and nonstationary ARMA models. *Journal of the American Statistical Association* 79:84–96.

Tse, Y. and A. Tsui. 2002. A multivariate GARCH model with time-varying correlations. *Journal of Business and Economic Statistics* 20:351–362.

Tyler, D. E. 1983. Robustness and efficiency properties of scatter matrices. *Biometrika* 70(2):411–420.

——. 1987. A distribution-free M-estimator of multivariate scatter. *Annals of Statistics* 15(1):234–251.

Vasicek, O. 1997. The loan loss distribution. Preprint, KMV Corporation.

Venter, J. H. and P. J. de Jongh. 2001. Risk estimation using the normal inverse Gaussian distribution. *Journal of Risk* 4(2):1–23.

Vyncke, D. 2004. Comonotonicity. In *Encyclopedia of Actuarial Science* (ed. J. L. Teugels and B. Sundt), vol. 1A–D, pp. 302–305. Wiley.

Wang, S. 1996. Premium calculation by transforming the layer premium density. *ASTIN Bulletin* 26:71–92.

Wang, S. and J. Dhaene. 1998. Comonoticity, correlation order and premium principles. *Insurance: Mathematics and Economics* 22:235–242.

Weber, S. 2004. Distribution-invariant dynamic risk measures, information and dynamic consistency. *Mathematical Finance* Forthcoming.

Wendin, J. and A. J. McNeil. 2004. Dependent credit migrations. Preprint, ETH Zurich.

White, H. 1981. Maximum likelihood estimation of misspecified models. *Econometrica* 50:1–25.

Whitney, A. W. 1918. The theory of experience rating. *Proceedings of the Casualty Actuarial Society* 4:274–292.

Wilcox, R. 1997. *Introduction to Robust Estimation and Hypothesis Testing*. Academic Press.

Williams, D. 1991. *Probability with Martingales*. Cambridge University Press.

Williamson, R. C. and T. Downs. 1990. Probabilistic arithmetic. I. Numerical methods for calculating convolutions and dependency bounds. *International Journal of Approximate Reasoning* 4:89–158.

Wilson, T. 1997a. Portfolio credit risk. I. *Risk* 10(9):111–117.

Wilson, T. 1997b. Portfolio credit risk. II. *Risk* 10(10):56–61.

Yaari, M. E. 1987. The dual theory of choice under risk. *Econometrica* 55:95–115.

Yang, L., W. Härdle and J. P. Nielsen. 1999. Nonparametric autoregression with multiplicative volatility and additive mean. *Journal of Time Series Analysis* 20:579–604.

Yu, F. 2005a. Default correlation in reduced-form models. *Journal of Investment Management*. Forthcoming.

——. 2005b. Correlated defaults and the valuation of defaultable securities. *Mathematical Finance*. Forthcoming.

Zhou, C. 2001. The term structure of credit spreads with jump risk. *Journal of Banking and Finance* 25(11), 2015–2040.

Zivot, E. and J. Wang. 2003. *Modeling Financial Time Series with S-PLUS*. Springer.

Index